The Sporting Life

TRAINERS
REVIEW
Flat Season 1993

Compiled by
John Bigley, Colin Havercroft and Michael Frost

Published 1993 by The Sporting Life
Orbit House, 1 New Fetter Lane, London EC4A 1AR

© 1993 The Sporting Life

ISBN 0 901091 70 7

Editorial and Production by Martin Pickering Bloodstock Services
Cover designed by P. W. Reprosharp Ltd, London EC1
Cover printed by Ark Litho Ltd, London SW19
Text printed by Bath Press Ltd, Bath and London

Cover picture
Collage of Leading Trainers: *Left to right: John Gosden, Mark Prescott, Richard Hannon, Henry Cecil, Jack Berry, Michael Stoute, Mark Johnston, Paul Cole, John Dunlop and Mary Reveley* (Photographs: Phil Smith, The Sporting Life)

CONTENTS

TRAINER SECTION

MRS V ACONLEY (Westow, North Yorks)

	No. of Horses	Races Run	1st	2nd	3rd	Unpl	Per cent	£1 Level Stake
2-y-o	3	9	0	1	1	7	-	- 9.00
3-y-o	2	7	1	0	0	6	14.3	+ 8.00
4-y-o+	10	37	5	3	4	25	13.5	- 14.00
Totals	15	53	6	4	5	38	11.3	- 15.00

Jan	Feb	Mar	Apr	May	Jun	Jul	Aug	Sep	Oct/Nov
0-6	0-5	0-1	0-2	0-7	3-6	1-11	1-8	1-5	0-2

Winning Jockeys	W-R	£1 Level Stake		W-R	£1 Level Stake
L Dettori	2-5	+ 4.00	D Wright	1-2	+ 3.50
J Lowe	2-7	+ 1.50	S Mulvey	1-9	+ 6.00

Winning Courses		£1 Level Stake		W-R	£1 Level Stake
Pontefract	2-9	+ 2.50	Nottingham	1-1	+ 1.00
Chester	1-1	+ 3.00	Catterick	1-6	+ 9.00
Edinburgh	1-1	+ 4.50			

Winning Horses	Age	Races Run	1st	2nd	3rd	Unpl	Win £
Silver Samurai	4	14	4	1	3	6	16,608
Iron Baron	4	4	1	0	1	2	2,927
Mountain Willow	3	5	1	0	0	4	2,758

| Favourites | 3-4 | 75.0% | + 6.50 | Total winning prize-money | £22,293 |

1992 Form	0-51			1990 Form	0-2
1991 Form	1-32	3.1%	- 23.00		

J AKEHURST (Upper Lambourn, Berks)

	No. of Horses	Races Run	1st	2nd	3rd	Unpl	Per cent	£1 Level Stake
2-y-o	3	18	2	1	4	11	11.1	- 8.62
3-y-o	2	10	0	0	0	10	-	- 10.00
4-y-o+	9	45	1	3	4	37	2.2	- 39.50
Totals	14	73	3	4	8	58	4.1	- 58.12

Jan	Feb	Mar	Apr	May	Jun	Jul	Aug	Sep	Oct/Nov
0-5	0-2	0-3	1-9	0-8	1-15	1-13	0-10	0-5	0-3

Winning Jockeys	W-R	£1 Level Stake		W-R	£1 Level Stake
M Roberts	1-3	+ 2.50	J Reid	1-8	- 5.62
D Holland	1-6	+ 1.00			

Winning Courses		£1 Level Stake		W-R	£1 Level Stake
Leicester	1-2	+ 5.00	Folkestone	1-4	- 1.62
Newbury	1-3	+ 2.50			

Winning Horses	Age	Races Run	1st	2nd	3rd	Unpl	Win £
Lord Oberon	5	12	1	1	2	8	5,381
Admiralella	2	8	1	1	1	5	2,713
Thatcherella	2	7	1	0	3	3	2,691

Favourites	1-3	33.3%	- 0.62	Total winning prize-money			£10,785

1992 Form	6-87	6.9%	- 53.50	1990 Form	4-31	12.9%	- 10.62
1991 Form	13-95	13.7%	+ 35.63				

R AKEHURST (Epsom, Surrey)

	No. of Horses	Races Run	1st	2nd	3rd	Unpl	Per cent	£1 Level Stake
2-y-o	8	16	0	0	1	15	-	- 16.00
3-y-o	15	78	7	11	3	57	9.0	- 41.00
4-y-o+	36	194	39	25	13	117	20.1	+ 67.26
Totals	59	288	46	36	17	189	16.0	+ 10.26

BY MONTH

2-y-o	W-R	Per cent	£1 Level Stake	3-y-o	W-R	Per cent	£1 Level Stake
January	0-0	-	0.00	January	0-0	-	0.00
February	0-0	-	0.00	February	0-0	-	0.00
March	0-0	-	0.00	March	0-0	-	0.00
April	0-0	-	0.00	April	0-3	-	- 3.00
May	0-0	-	0.00	May	3-12	25.0	+ 2.00
June	0-2	-	- 2.00	June	3-16	18.8	- 2.00
July	0-5	-	- 5.00	July	0-15	-	- 15.00
August	0-2	-	- 2.00	August	0-14	-	- 14.00
September	0-4	-	- 4.00	September	1-9	11.1	0.00
Oct/Nov	0-3	-	- 3.00	Oct/Nov	0-9	-	- 9.00

4-y-o+	W-R	Per cent	£1 Level Stake	Totals	W-R	Per cent	£1 Level Stake
January	1-4	25.0	+ 0.33	January	1-4	25.0	+ 0.33
February	0-2	-	- 2.00	February	0-2	-	- 2.00
March	2-4	50.0	+ 9.25	March	2-4	50.0	+ 9.25
April	3-20	15.0	- 2.50	April	3-23	13.0	- 5.50
May	8-24	33.3	+ 41.33	May	11-36	30.6	+ 43.33
June	6-37	16.2	- 12.49	June	9-55	16.4	- 16.49
July	6-35	17.1	- 12.99	July	6-55	10.9	- 32.99
August	3-27	11.1	+ 0.50	August	3-43	7.0	- 15.50
September	4-17	23.5	+ 25.83	September	5-30	16.7	+ 21.83
Oct/Nov	6-24	25.0	+ 20.00	Oct/Nov	6-36	16.7	+ 8.00

DISTANCE

2-y-o	W-R	Per cent	£1 Level Stake	3-y-o	W-R	Per cent	£1 Level Stake
5f-6f	0-11	-	- 11.00	5f-6f	1-10	10.0	- 6.50
7f-8f	0-5	-	- 5.00	7f-8f	4-48	8.3	- 25.00
9f-13f	0-0	-	0.00	9f-13f	1-16	6.3	- 9.50
14f+	0-0	-	0.00	14f+	1-4	25.0	0.00

4-y-o+	W-R	Per cent	£1 Level Stake	Totals	W-R	Per cent	£1 Level Stake
5f-6f	4-29	13.8	- 12.17	5f-6f	5-50	10.0	- 29.67
7f-8f	10-41	24.4	+ 32.13	7f-8f	14-94	14.9	+ 2.13
9f-13f	19-79	24.1	+ 51.05	9f-13f	20-95	21.1	+ 41.35
14f+	6-45	13.3	- 3.75	14f+	7-49	14.3	- 3.75

TYPE OF RACE

Non-Handicaps	W-R	Per cent	£1 Level Stake	Handicaps	W-R	Per cent	£1 Level Stake
2-y-o	0-16	-	- 16.00	2-y-o	0-0	-	0.00
3-y-o	4-22	18.2	- 3.00	3-y-o	3-53	5.7	- 35.00
4-y-o+	5-14	35.7	+ 28.25	4-y-o+	30-156	19.2	+ 42.50
Selling	0-4	-	- 4.00	Selling	2-6	33.3	+ 9.00
Apprentice	0-0	-	0.00	Apprentice	2-14	14.3	- 8.49
Amat/Ladies	0-1	-	- 1.00	Amat/Ladies	0-2	-	- 2.00
Totals	9-57	15.8	+ 4.25	Totals	37-231	16.0	+ 6.01

COURSE GRADE

	W-R	Per cent	£1 Level Stake
Group 1	17-149	11.4	- 28.03
Group 2	12-63	19.0	+ 14.33
Group 3	6-38	15.8	+ 9.63
Group 4	11-38	28.9	+ 14.33

FIRST TIME OUT

	W-R	Per cent	£1 Level Stake
2-y-o	0-8	-	- 8.00
3-y-o	1-11	9.1	- 7.00
4-y-o+	5-28	17.9	- 0.92
Totals	6-47	12.8	- 15.92

JOCKEYS RIDING

	W-R	Per cent	£1 Level Stake		W-R	Per cent	£1 Level Stake
T Quinn	23-112	20.5	+ 49.91	L Carter	2-19	10.5	- 9.62
J Reid	7-16	43.8	+ 15.51	D McKeown	1-2	50.0	+ 4.50
A Munro	3-14	21.4	+ 22.00	R Cochrane	1-3	33.3	+ 14.00
D Holland	2-6	33.3	+ 0.50	M Perrett	1-4	25.0	+ 2.00
D Wright	2-11	18.2	- 4.37	D Harrison	1-9	11.1	- 2.50
J Quinn	2-16	12.5	- 8.42	R Perham	1-20	5.0	- 17.25

B Russell	0-14	L Dettori	0-3	W Newnes	0-2
T Ashley	0-7	A Clark	0-2	A Tucker	0-1
A McGlone	0-4	Mr T McCarthy	0-2	D Toole	0-1
G Carter	0-4	N Adams	0-2	Mr P Taiano	0-1
S Dawson	0-4	S Whitworth	0-2	Pat Eddery	0-1
F Norton	0-3	W Carson	0-2	Paul Eddery	0-1

COURSE RECORD

	Total W-R	Non-Handicaps 2-y-o	3-y-o+	Handicaps 2-y-o	3-y-o+	Per cent	£1 Level Stake
Folkestone	7-20	0-1	2-4	0-0	5-15	35.0	+ 8.00
Brighton	6-22	0-0	2-6	0-0	4-16	27.3	+ 19.50
Goodwood	4-18	0-0	2-3	0-0	2-15	22.2	+ 7.63
Bath	3-9	0-2	0-2	0-0	3-5	33.3	+ 6.75
Warwick	3-9	0-0	0-0	0-0	3-9	33.3	+ 11.00
Lingfield	3-25	0-3	0-5	0-0	3-17	12.0	- 10.17
Newmarket	3-27	0-1	1-4	0-0	2-22	11.1	- 3.04
Sandown	3-27	0-0	0-3	0-0	3-24	11.1	- 3.00
Redcar	2-5	0-1	0-1	0-0	2-3	40.0	+ 10.00
Chepstow	2-7	0-0	0-1	0-0	2-6	28.6	- 1.12
Epsom	2-17	0-1	1-2	0-0	1-14	11.8	- 10.62
Newbury	2-21	0-4	0-1	0-0	2-16	9.5	- 10.00
York	1-3	0-0	0-0	0-0	1-3	33.3	+ 12.00
Lingfield (AW)	1-3	0-0	0-0	0-0	1-3	33.3	+ 1.33
Leicester	1-4	0-0	0-0	0-0	1-4	25.0	+ 22.00
Doncaster	1-9	0-0	0-1	0-0	1-8	11.1	0.00
Salisbury	1-9	0-0	0-2	0-0	1-7	11.1	- 3.00
Kempton	1-16	0-0	1-3	0-0	0-13	6.3	- 10.00

Ascot	0-10	Southwell (AW)	0-5	Chester	0-1
Windsor	0-10	Yarmouth	0-2	Haydock	0-1
Nottingham	0-6	Catterick	0-1	Ripon	0-1

WINNING HORSES

	Age	Races Run	1st	2nd	3rd	Unpl	Win £
Sarawat	5	3	1	0	1	1	66,185
Night Clubbing	4	8	4	0	2	2	25,023
Croft Valley	6	8	3	0	0	5	23,262
Mr Tate	4	8	4	1	0	3	14,642
Dancing Sensation	6	9	3	3	1	2	10,324
Final Frontier	3	8	2	1	1	4	9,317
Sarah-Clare	5	7	3	1	0	3	8,939
Green Lane	5	8	2	2	0	4	7,993
Here He Comes	7	6	2	2	1	1	6,419
Face North	5	11	2	3	0	6	5,796
Requested	6	8	1	1	0	6	5,678
Knowth	4	9	1	4	1	3	5,385
Faugeron	4	3	1	0	0	2	4,815
Millsolin	5	6	1	0	0	5	4,709

Jazilah	5	3	1	1	0	1	4,515
Pharamineux	7	7	1	0	1	5	4,455
Domulla	3	7	1	1	0	5	3,623
Amazon Express	4	7	1	1	0	5	3,623
Unification	4	7	1	0	0	6	3,600
Simply Finesse	3	9	1	3	0	5	3,558
Seren Quest	3	4	1	1	0	2	3,494
Quantity Surveyor	4	1	1	0	0	0	3,448
Island Blade	4	7	1	1	1	4	3,210
Fay's Song	5	10	1	0	1	8	3,184
Umbria	4	5	1	1	1	2	2,958
Bransby Road	3	6	1	0	0	5	2,899
Romanian	5	7	1	1	0	5	2,820
Fanfold	3	6	1	2	0	3	2,243
Ragtime Song	4	3	1	0	0	2	2,070
Ibsen	5	3	1	0	0	2	2,070

WINNING OWNERS

	Races Won	Value £		Races Won	Value £
S Aitken	2	70,700	A W Boon	1	3,623
Sheikh Essa Bin Mubarak	4	25,023	Mrs Jill Moss	1	3,623
Miss Vivian Pratt	3	23,262	New House Farm Livery Stables	1	3,600
A D Spence	4	15,663	Food Brokers Ltd	1	3,558
Normandy Developments London	4	15,320	N M Stewart	1	3,494
John Falvey	4	14,642	The Lime St Racing Syndicate	1	3,210
Chelgate Public Relations Ltd	3	10,324	S Harper	1	3,184
Miss Clare Coyne	3	8,939	S Kay	1	2,958
R N C Lynch	2	7,993	Mrs J Sturgis	1	2,820
E Harrington	2	6,419	Miss Judy Smith	1	2,243
G S Beccle	1	5,678	William Alexander	1	2,070
Ruelles Partners	1	5,385	R Akehurst	1	2,070
Nicholas Roteman	1	4,455			

Favourites	22-66	33.3%	+ 19.93	Total winning prize-money		£250,252
Longest winning sequence			3	Average SP of winner		5.5/1
Longest losing sequence			25	Return on stakes invested		3.6%
1992 Form	30-270	11.1%	- 39.79	1990 Form	34-344	9.9%	- 129.61
1991 Form	42-301	14.0%	+ 27.04	1989 Form	33-259	12.7%	- 17.09

R ALLAN (Cornhill-on-Tweed, Northumberland)

	No. of Horses	Races Run	1st	2nd	3rd	Unpl	Per cent	£1 Level Stake
2-y-o	0	0	0	0	0	0	-	0.00
3-y-o	5	11	0	0	1	10	-	- 11.00
4-y-o+	7	46	6	5	7	28	13.0	+ 9.88
Totals	12	57	6	5	8	38	10.5	- 1.12

Jan	Feb	Mar	Apr	May	Jun	Jul	Aug	Sep	Oct/Nov
0-0	0-0	0-0	0-4	1-7	2-7	2-11	0-10	1-11	0-7

Winning Jockeys	W-R	£1 Level Stake		W-R	£1 Level Stake
J Weaver	4-22	+ 8.88	J Fanning	1-6	+ 11.00
S Davies	1-5	+ 3.00			

Winning Courses	W-R	£1 Level Stake		W-R	£1 Level Stake
Edinburgh	3-10	+ 5.88	Newcastle	1-2	+ 15.00
Catterick	1-2	+ 6.00	Hamilton	1-9	+ 6.00

Winning Horses	Age	Races Run	1st	2nd	3rd	Unpl	Win £
Tawafij	4	10	2	1	3	4	15,855
Latvian	6	7	2	1	0	4	5,455
American Hero	5	9	1	1	2	5	4,078
Creselly	6	7	1	1	1	4	2,479

Favourites	0-1		Total winning prize-money		£27,867

1992 Form	2-23	8.7%	- 5.50	1990 Form	1-33	3.0%	- 30.00
1991 Form	1-19	5.3%	- 15.50	1989 Form	1-29	3.4%	- 22.50

C N ALLEN (Newmarket)

	No. of Horses	Races Run	1st	2nd	3rd	Unpl	Per cent	£1 Level Stake
2-y-o	6	27	1	2	3	21	3.7	- 23.50
3-y-o	4	24	2	3	3	16	8.3	+ 6.00
4-y-o+	3	26	1	2	3	20	3.8	- 21.00
Totals	13	77	4	7	9	57	5.2	- 38.50

Jan	Feb	Mar	Apr	May	Jun	Jul	Aug	Sep	Oct/Nov
0-12	1-5	1-5	0-7	0-6	0-10	1-11	1-12	0-4	0-5

Winning Jockeys	W-R	£1 Level Stake		W-R	£1 Level Stake
F Norton	1-4	+ 1.00	N Carlisle	1-7	+ 8.00
D Wright	1-6	+ 9.00	G Forster	1-21	- 17.50

Winning Courses	W-R	£1 Level Stake		W-R	£1 Level Stake
Southwell (AW)	2-18	+ 2.00	Folkestone	1-4	+ 11.00
Salisbury	1-1	+ 2.50			

Winning Horses	Age	Races Run	1st	2nd	3rd	Unpl	Win £
Badawi (Fr)	3	10	1	1	2	6	3,106
Nakita	2	9	1	2	2	4	2,534
Hush Baby	3	10	1	1	1	7	2,427
Digger Doyle	4	7	1	0	2	4	2,406

Favourites	0-4		Total winning prize-money		£10,473

1992 Form	7-118	5.9%	- 58.37	1990 Form	19-269	7.1%	-119.09
1991 Form	15-184	8.2%	- 76.97	1989 Form	8-151	5.3%	- 93.50

E J ALSTON (Preston, Lancs)

	No. of Horses	Races Run	1st	2nd	3rd	Unpl	Per cent	£1 Level Stake
2-y-o	4	20	2	0	0	18	10.0	+ 12.00
3-y-o	8	45	4	3	4	34	8.9	- 3.00
4-y-o+	13	122	14	10	19	79	11.5	- 9.57
Totals	25	187	20	13	23	131	10.7	- 0.57

BY MONTH

2-y-o	W-R	Per cent	£1 Level Stake	3-y-o	W-R	Per cent	£1 Level Stake
January	0-0	-	0.00	January	0-0	-	0.00
February	0-0	-	0.00	February	0-2	-	- 2.00
March	0-1	-	- 1.00	March	0-3	-	- 3.00
April	1-2	50.0	+ 9.00	April	0-3	-	- 3.00
May	0-3	-	- 3.00	May	0-3	-	- 3.00
June	1-3	33.3	+ 18.00	June	1-5	20.0	+ 6.00
July	0-3	-	- 3.00	July	0-4	-	- 4.00
August	0-1	-	- 1.00	August	0-5	-	- 5.00
September	0-6	-	- 6.00	September	0-4	-	- 4.00
Oct/Nov	0-1	-	- 1.00	Oct/Nov	3-16	18.8	+ 15.00

4-y-o+	W-R	Per cent	£1 Level Stake	Totals	W-R	Per cent	£1 Level Stake
January	0-7	-	- 7.00	January	0-7	-	- 7.00
February	2-6	33.3	+ 1.60	February	2-8	25.0	- 0.40
March	1-3	33.3	+ 8.00	March	1-7	14.3	+ 4.00
April	0-8	-	- 8.00	April	1-13	7.7	- 2.00
May	2-19	10.5	- 2.00	May	2-25	8.0	- 8.00
June	3-20	15.0	+ 5.50	June	5-28	17.9	+ 29.50
July	5-16	31.3	+ 25.33	July	5-23	21.7	+ 18.33
August	1-15	6.7	- 5.00	August	1-21	4.8	- 11.00
September	0-10	-	- 10.00	September	0-20	-	- 20.00
Oct/Nov	0-18	-	- 18.00	Oct/Nov	3-35	8.6	- 4.00

DISTANCE

2-y-o	W-R	Per cent	£1 Level Stake	3-y-o	W-R	Per cent	£1 Level Stake
5f-6f	2-17	11.8	+ 15.00	5f-6f	2-14	14.3	+ 6.00
7f-8f	0-3	-	- 3.00	7f-8f	1-15	6.7	- 4.00
9f-13f	0-0	-	0.00	9f-13f	0-13	-	- 13.00
14f+	0-0	-	0.00	14f+	1-3	33.3	+ 8.00

4-y-o+	W-R	Per cent	£1 Level Stake	Totals	W-R	Per cent	£1 Level Stake
5f-6f	8-42	19.0	+ 12.93	5f-6f	12-73	16.4	+ 33.93
7f-8f	4-45	8.9	- 6.50	7f-8f	5-63	7.9	- 13.50
9f-13f	0-28	-	- 28.00	9f-13f	0-41	-	- 41.00
14f+	2-7	28.6	+ 12.00	14f+	3-10	30.0	+ 20.00

TYPE OF RACE

Non-Handicaps	W-R	Per cent	£1 Level Stake	Handicaps	W-R	Per cent	£1 Level Stake
2-y-o	2-17	11.8	+ 15.00	2-y-o	0-3	-	- 3.00
3-y-o	1-25	4.0	- 14.00	3-y-o	3-12	25.0	+ 19.00
4-y-o+	4-12	33.3	+ 20.00	4-y-o+	8-96	8.3	- 33.57
Selling	0-2	-	- 2.00	Selling	0-4	-	- 4.00
Apprentice	1-4	25.0	+ 3.00	Apprentice	1-11	9.1	0.00
Amat/Ladies	0-0	-	0.00	Amat/Ladies	0-1	-	- 1.00
Totals	8-60	13.3	+ 22.00	Totals	12-127	9.4	- 22.57

COURSE GRADE

	W-R	Per cent	£1 Level Stake
Group 1	5-57	8.8	- 17.67
Group 2	5-40	12.5	+ 20.00
Group 3	3-37	8.1	- 7.50
Group 4	7-53	13.2	+ 4.60

FIRST TIME OUT

	W-R	Per cent	£1 Level Stake
2-y-o	1-4	25.0	+ 17.00
3-y-o	0-7	-	- 7.00
4-y-o+	0-13	-	- 13.00
Totals	1-24	4.2	- 3.00

JOCKEYS RIDING

	W-R	Per cent	£1 Level Stake		W-R	Per cent	£1 Level Stake
K Fallon	7-50	14.0	+ 27.00	Claire Balding	1-4	25.0	+ 7.00
S Knott	5-30	16.7	+ 8.33	Julie Bowker	1-4	25.0	+ 11.00
J Weaver	2-8	25.0	+ 11.00	S Webster	1-8	12.5	+ 3.00
S Davies	2-12	16.7	- 2.40	J Quinn	1-21	4.8	- 15.50

D Wright	0-13	T Williams	0-2	N Connorton	0-1
N Adams	0-4	A Garth	0-1	O Pears	0-1
S Maloney	0-4	A Tucker	0-1	P Robinson	0-1
S Wood	0-4	B Raymond	0-1	Paul Eddery	0-1
J Fanning	0-3	D Griffiths	0-1	S O'Gorman	0-1
J Fortune	0-3	D Holland	0-1	W Hawksley	0-1
F Norton	0-2	J Reid	0-1		
N Carlisle	0-2	Miss I D W Jones	0-1		

COURSE RECORD

	Total W-R	Non-Handicaps 2-y-o	Non-Handicaps 3-y-o+	Handicaps 2-y-o	Handicaps 3-y-o+	Per cent	£1 Level Stake
Chester	4-16	1-4	2-3	0-0	1-9	25.0	+ 29.00
Catterick	2-7	0-0	1-4	0-0	1-3	28.6	+ 15.00
Newcastle	2-8	0-0	1-3	0-0	1-5	25.0	+ 10.00
Hamilton	2-16	1-2	0-4	0-0	1-10	12.5	+ 6.00
Southwell (AW)	2-27	0-2	1-9	0-0	1-16	7.4	- 19.40
Edinburgh	1-1	0-0	0-0	0-0	1-1	100.0	+ 10.00
Newmarket	1-3	0-0	1-1	0-0	0-2	33.3	+ 7.00
Warwick	1-4	0-0	0-1	0-0	1-3	25.0	+ 5.00

8

Alston E J

Ayr	1-7	0-0	0-1	0-1	1-5	14.3	-	2.67
Ripon	1-7	0-1	0-2	0-0	1-4	14.3	+	8.00
Carlisle	1-10	0-0	0-2	0-0	1-8	10.0	-	2.00
Pontefract	1-15	0-0	0-2	0-0	1-13	6.7	-	7.50
Haydock	1-23	0-3	0-2	0-1	1-17	4.3	-	16.00

Redcar	0-16	Doncaster	0-6	Newbury	0-1
York	0-8	Southwell (Turf)	0-4	Thirsk	0-1
Beverley	0-6	Ascot	0-1		

WINNING HORSES

	Age	Races Run	1st	2nd	3rd	Unpl	Win £
Stack Rock	6	10	4	1	2	3	33,591
Magic Pearl	3	9	2	2	0	5	8,690
Gondo	6	18	2	0	4	12	6,336
Shannon Express	6	15	2	0	0	13	6,238
Continuity	4	11	2	0	1	8	5,912
Kummel King	5	10	1	2	0	7	3,850
Bettykimvic	2	1	1	0	0	0	3,548
My Abbey	4	8	1	0	1	6	3,436
Moonlight Eclipse	3	7	1	0	1	5	2,742
Vilamar	3	14	1	1	2	10	2,467
Hiltons Travel	2	10	1	0	0	9	2,445
Johnston's Express	5	4	1	2	1	0	2,238
Marowins	4	13	1	1	6	5	2,070

WINNING OWNERS

	Races Won	Value £		Races Won	Value £
Castle Racing	4	33,591	Abbey Racing	1	3,436
G G Sanderson	2	8,690	R Smalley	1	2,742
Mrs Helen O'Brien	2	6,336	Pleasant Racing Club	1	2,467
R Cottam	2	6,238	Mrs Dot Jones	1	2,445
Mrs Stella Barclay	2	5,912	Frank McKevitt	1	2,238
David Hall	1	3,850	Whitehills Racing Syndicate	1	2,070
John Patrick Barry	1	3,548			

Favourites	1-10	10.0%	- 7.90	Total winning prize-money			£83,561
Longest winning sequence			2	Average SP of winner			8.3/1
Longest losing sequence			33	Return on stakes invested			-0.3%
1992 Form	14-190	7.4%	- 78.00	1990 Form	6-82	7.3%	- 15.50
1991 Form	12-111	10.8%	+ 6.50	1989 Form	1-58	1.7%	- 54.50

D W P ARBUTHNOT (Compton, Berks)

	No. of Horses	Races Run	1st	2nd	3rd	Unpl	Per cent	£1 Level Stake
2-y-o	7	25	3	1	1	20	12.0	- 10.50
3-y-o	3	17	2	4	0	11	11.8	+ 5.00
4-y-o+	10	79	12	7	5	55	15.2	+ 32.25
Totals	20	121	17	12	6	86	14.0	+ 26.75

BY MONTH

2-y-o	W-R	Per cent	£1 Level Stake	3-y-o	W-R	Per cent	£1 Level Stake
January	0-0	-	0.00	January	0-0	-	0.00
February	0-0	-	0.00	February	0-1	-	- 1.00
March	0-0	-	0.00	March	0-1	-	- 1.00
April	0-0	-	0.00	April	1-1	100.0	+ 16.00
May	1-2	50.0	+ 2.50	May	1-1	100.0	+ 4.00
June	0-2	-	- 2.00	June	0-2	-	- 2.00
July	0-3	-	- 3.00	July	0-3	-	- 3.00
August	0-6	-	- 6.00	August	0-3	-	- 3.00
September	2-7	28.6	+ 3.00	September	0-2	-	- 2.00
Oct/Nov	0-5	-	- 5.00	Oct/Nov	0-3	-	- 3.00

4-y-o+	W-R	Per cent	£1 Level Stake	Totals	W-R	Per cent	£1 Level Stake
January	1-2	50.0	+ 2.50	January	1-2	50.0	+ 2.50
February	2-7	28.6	+ 5.00	February	2-8	25.0	+ 4.00
March	2-5	40.0	+ 1.75	March	2-6	33.3	+ 0.75
April	0-5	-	- 5.00	April	1-6	16.7	+ 11.00
May	0-8	-	- 8.00	May	2-11	18.2	- 1.50
June	1-5	20.0	+ 6.00	June	1-9	11.1	+ 2.00
July	1-11	9.1	- 3.50	July	1-17	5.9	- 9.50
August	1-14	7.1	- 10.50	August	1-23	4.3	- 19.50
September	2-10	20.0	+ 22.00	September	4-19	21.1	+ 23.00
Oct/Nov	2-12	16.7	+ 22.00	Oct/Nov	2-20	10.0	+ 14.00

DISTANCE

2-y-o	W-R	Per cent	£1 Level Stake	3-y-o	W-R	Per cent	£1 Level Stake
5f-6f	3-12	25.0	+ 2.50	5f-6f	0-8	-	- 8.00
7f-8f	0-13	-	- 13.00	7f-8f	0-3	-	- 3.00
9f-13f	0-0	-	0.00	9f-13f	2-6	33.3	+ 16.00
14f+	0-0	-	0.00	14f+	0-0	-	0.00

4-y-o+	W-R	Per cent	£1 Level Stake	Totals	W-R	Per cent	£1 Level Stake
5f-6f	2-22	9.1	- 5.50	5f-6f	5-42	11.9	- 11.00
7f-8f	2-21	9.5	+ 11.00	7f-8f	2-37	5.4	- 5.00
9f-13f	8-34	23.5	+ 28.75	9f-13f	10-40	25.0	+ 44.75
14f+	0-2	-	- 2.00	14f+	0-2	-	- 2.00

Arbuthnot D W P

TYPE OF RACE

Non-Handicaps	W-R	Per cent	£1 Level Stake	Handicaps	W-R	Per cent	£1 Level Stake
2-y-o	3-20	15.0	- 5.50	2-y-o	0-4	-	- 4.00
3-y-o	2-6	33.3	+ 16.00	3-y-o	0-10	-	- 10.00
4-y-o+	1-5	20.0	0.00	4-y-o+	10-67	14.9	+ 32.25
Selling	0-2	-	- 2.00	Selling	0-0	-	0.00
Apprentice	0-0	-	0.00	Apprentice	0-2	-	- 2.00
Amat/Ladies	0-0	-	0.00	Amat/Ladies	1-5	20.0	+ 2.00
Totals	6-33	18.2	+ 8.50	Totals	11-88	12.5	+ 18.25

COURSE GRADE

	W-R	Per cent	£1 Level Stake
Group 1	4-47	8.5	- 4.50
Group 2	2-20	10.0	- 9.00
Group 3	5-31	16.1	+ 35.50
Group 4	6-23	26.1	+ 4.75

FIRST TIME OUT

	W-R	Per cent	£1 Level Stake
2-y-o	1-7	14.3	- 2.50
3-y-o	0-3	-	- 3.00
4-y-o+	1-10	10.0	- 5.50
Totals	2-20	10.0	- 11.00

JOCKEYS RIDING

	W-R	Per cent	£1 Level Stake		W-R	Per cent	£1 Level Stake
T Quinn	5-31	16.1	+ 1.50	J Williams	1-3	33.3	+ 18.00
R Price	4-32	12.5	+ 15.50	J Weaver	1-3	33.3	+ 0.25
A Munro	2-7	28.6	+ 10.50	Paul Eddery	1-3	33.3	+ 0.50
B Doyle	1-1	100.0	+ 10.00	Mrs D Arbuthnot	1-6	16.7	+ 1.00
J Quinn	1-3	33.3	+ 1.50				

F Norton	0-4	R Cochrane	0-2	K Darley	0-1
A Procter	0-3	S D Williams	0-2	M Birch	0-1
L Dettori	0-3	W R Swinburn	0-2	M Roberts	0-1
N Varley	0-3	D O'Neill	0-1	T G McLaughlin	0-1
B Procter	0-2	J Lowe	0-1	W Carson	0-1
M Hills	0-2	J Reid	0-1	W Ryan	0-1

COURSE RECORD

	Total W-R	Non-Handicaps 2-y-o	Non-Handicaps 3-y-o+	Handicaps 2-y-o	Handicaps 3-y-o+	Per cent	£1 Level Stake
Lingfield (AW)	3-12	0-0	0-1	0-0	3-11	25.0	+ 2.75
Bath	2-7	1-1	1-2	0-0	0-4	28.6	+ 14.50
Southwell (AW)	2-8	0-2	1-2	0-0	1-4	25.0	+ 0.50
Folkestone	1-2	1-2	0-0	0-0	0-0	50.0	+ 2.50
Redcar	1-2	0-0	0-0	0-0	1-2	50.0	+ 1.50
Pontefract	1-3	0-0	0-0	0-1	1-2	33.3	+ 10.00
Doncaster	1-4	0-1	1-1	0-0	0-2	25.0	+ 1.00

11

Arbuthnot D W P

Lingfield	1-4	0-2	0-0	0-0	1-2	25.0	+ 3.50
Sandown	1-5	1-2	0-0	0-0	0-3	20.0	+ 0.50
Windsor	1-5	0-1	0-0	0-0	1-4	20.0	+ 6.00
Chepstow	1-6	0-1	0-2	0-1	1-2	16.7	+ 15.00
Newmarket	1-8	0-0	0-0	0-1	1-7	12.5	+ 13.00
Newbury	1-12	0-2	0-0	0-1	1-9	8.3	- 1.00

Leicester	0-8	Chester	0-3	Salisbury	0-2
York	0-5	Epsom	0-3	Ascot	0-1
Brighton	0-4	Kempton	0-3	Southwell (Turf)	0-1
Goodwood	0-4	Beverley	0-2	Thirsk	0-1
Ripon	0-4	Haydock	0-2		

WINNING HORSES

	Age	Races Run	1st	2nd	3rd	Unpl	Win £
Love Legend	8	18	2	1	1	14	8,542
Strat's Legacy	6	10	3	2	0	5	8,313
May Hills Legacy	4	10	2	2	0	6	7,105
Wassl This Then	4	11	2	0	1	8	6,294
Prenonamoss	5	11	1	1	1	8	6,258
Hoochiecoochieman	3	8	2	2	0	4	5,969
Kimberley Park	5	6	1	0	0	5	5,816
Elevator Shaft	2	9	2	1	0	6	5,001
Robellion	2	2	1	0	1	0	2,833
Mr Poppleton	4	3	1	1	0	1	2,070

WINNING OWNERS

	Races Won	Value £		Races Won	Value £
George S Thompson	3	11,375	Mrs Josephine Carter	2	6,294
Christopher Wright	4	10,970	Mrs W A Oram	1	6,258
Jack Blumenow	3	8,313	G W Mills	1	5,816
Mrs G P Williams	2	7,105	S T A Management Ltd	1	2,070

Favourites	4-14	28.6%	+ 3.25	Total winning prize-money		£58,201

Longest winning sequence	2	Average SP of winner	7.7/1
Longest losing sequence	21	Return on stakes invested	22.1%

1992 Form	12-171	7.0%	- 52.25	1990 Form	20-147	13.6%	+ 59.75
1991 Form	12-155	7.7%	- 56.57	1989 Form	10-136	7.4%	- 50.25

R W ARMSTRONG (Newmarket)

	No. of Horses	Races Run	1st	2nd	3rd	Unpl	Per cent	£1 Level Stake
2-y-o	15	47	12	5	6	24	25.5	+ 46.61
3-y-o	18	78	8	9	8	53	10.3	- 9.84
4-y-o+	3	22	6	2	0	14	27.3	+ 11.73
Totals	36	147	26	16	14	91	17.7	+ 48.50

BY MONTH

2-y-o	W-R	Per cent	£1 Level Stake	3-y-o	W-R	Per cent	£1 Level Stake
January	0-0	-	0.00	January	0-0	-	0.00
February	0-0	-	0.00	February	0-0	-	0.00
March	0-0	-	0.00	March	0-2	-	- 2.00
April	0-1	-	- 1.00	April	2-8	25.0	+ 14.00
May	1-5	20.0	- 1.75	May	1-15	6.7	+ 2.00
June	0-3	-	- 3.00	June	0-12	-	- 12.00
July	0-2	-	- 2.00	July	1-11	9.1	- 9.09
August	4-9	44.4	+ 13.36	August	1-7	14.3	+ 1.00
September	6-17	35.3	+ 30.00	September	2-13	15.4	+ 1.75
Oct/Nov	1-10	10.0	+ 11.00	Oct/Nov	1-10	10.0	- 5.50

4-y-o+	W-R	Per cent	£1 Level Stake	Totals	W-R	Per cent	£1 Level Stake
January	0-0	-	0.00	January	0-0	-	0.00
February	0-1	-	- 1.00	February	0-1	-	- 1.00
March	0-4	-	- 4.00	March	0-6	-	- 6.00
April	0-3	-	- 3.00	April	2-12	16.7	+ 10.00
May	1-2	50.0	+ 3.00	May	3-22	13.6	+ 3.25
June	1-3	33.3	+ 6.00	June	1-18	5.6	- 9.00
July	3-5	60.0	+ 1.73	July	4-18	22.2	- 9.36
August	0-2	-	- 2.00	August	5-18	27.8	+ 12.36
September	0-0	-	0.00	September	8-30	26.7	+ 31.75
Oct/Nov	1-2	50.0	+ 11.00	Oct/Nov	3-22	13.6	+ 16.50

DISTANCE

2-y-o	W-R	Per cent	£1 Level Stake	3-y-o	W-R	Per cent	£1 Level Stake
5f-6f	7-24	29.2	+ 8.61	5f-6f	1-4	25.0	+ 7.00
7f-8f	5-22	22.7	+ 39.00	7f-8f	6-57	10.5	- 11.84
9f-13f	0-1	-	- 1.00	9f-13f	1-16	6.3	- 4.00
14f+	0-0	-	0.00	14f+	0-1	-	- 1.00

4-y-o+	W-R	Per cent	£1 Level Stake	Totals	W-R	Per cent	£1 Level Stake
5f-6f	0-0	-	0.00	5f-6f	8-28	28.6	+ 15.61
7f-8f	1-7	14.3	+ 2.00	7f-8f	12-86	14.0	+ 29.16
9f-13f	3-8	37.5	+ 1.43	9f-13f	4-25	16.0	- 3.57
14f+	2-7	28.6	+ 8.30	14f+	2-8	25.0	+ 7.30

TYPE OF RACE

Non-Handicaps	W-R	Per cent	£1 Level Stake	Handicaps	W-R	Per cent	£1 Level Stake
2-y-o	10-38	26.3	+ 28.61	2-y-o	2-8	25.0	+ 19.00
3-y-o	5-41	12.2	- 9.84	3-y-o	3-37	8.1	0.00
4-y-o+	0-4	-	- 4.00	4-y-o+	6-17	35.3	+ 16.73
Selling	0-1	-	- 1.00	Selling	0-0	-	0.00
Apprentice	0-0	-	0.00	Apprentice	0-0	-	0.00
Amat/Ladies	0-0	-	0.00	Amat/Ladies	0-1	-	- 1.00
Totals	15-84	17.9	+ 13.77	Totals	11-63	17.5	+ 34.73

COURSE GRADE

	W-R	Per cent	£1 Level Stake
Group 1	12-75	16.0	+ 6.29
Group 2	4-20	20.0	+ 12.53
Group 3	5-32	15.6	+ 20.25
Group 4	5-20	25.0	+ 9.43

FIRST TIME OUT

	W-R	Per cent	£1 Level Stake
2-y-o	2-15	13.3	- 7.42
3-y-o	3-18	16.7	+ 6.75
4-y-o+	0-3	-	- 3.00
Totals	5-36	13.9	- 3.67

JOCKEYS RIDING

	W-R	Per cent	£1 Level Stake		W-R	Per cent	£1 Level Stake
R Price	8-58	13.8	+ 8.50	W Woods	1-1	100.0	+ 20.00
R Hills	5-19	26.3	+ 2.61	Pat Eddery	1-2	50.0	+ 7.00
L Dettori	4-8	50.0	+ 11.73	G Carter	1-3	33.3	+ 2.00
W Carson	4-31	12.9	- 10.34	N Carlisle	1-4	25.0	+ 13.00
D Biggs	1-1	100.0	+ 14.00				

L Piggott	0-10	M Roberts	0-3	Mr M Armytage	0-1
M Hills	0-4	J Reid	0-1	Mrs M Haggas	0-1

COURSE RECORD

	Total W-R	Non-Handicaps 2-y-o	Non-Handicaps 3-y-o+	Handicaps 2-y-o	Handicaps 3-y-o+	Per cent	£1 Level Stake
Kempton	3-5	3-4	0-0	0-0	0-1	60.0	+ 6.50
Southwell (AW)	3-14	0-2	0-4	0-0	3-8	21.4	- 4.57
Newmarket	3-22	1-10	2-7	0-2	0-3	13.6	- 2.17
Thirsk	2-4	1-1	0-2	0-0	1-1	50.0	+ 14.53
Doncaster	2-11	1-3	0-4	0-2	1-2	18.2	+ 23.00
Sandown	2-11	0-3	0-3	0-0	2-5	18.2	+ 0.30
Yarmouth	2-12	0-1	0-4	2-3	0-4	16.7	+ 15.00
Southwell (Turf)	1-1	0-0	0-0	0-0	1-1	100.0	+ 11.00
Lingfield (AW)	1-3	0-0	0-1	0-0	1-2	33.3	+ 5.00
Newbury	1-4	0-1	1-3	0-0	0-0	25.0	- 1.25

Brighton	1-5	1-3	0-1	0-1	0-0	20.0	0.00
Pontefract	1-5	1-2	0-2	0-0	0-1	20.0	+ 6.00
Leicester	1-6	1-1	0-2	0-0	0-3	16.7	- 2.75
Nottingham	1-6	0-1	1-2	0-0	0-3	16.7	+ 5.00
Lingfield	1-8	1-2	0-2	0-0	0-4	12.5	+ 1.00
Goodwood	1-9	0-1	1-5	0-0	0-3	11.1	- 7.09

Ascot	0-5	Windsor	0-3	Haydock	0-1
York	0-4	Ripon	0-2	Redcar	0-1
Epsom	0-3	Warwick	0-2		

WINNING HORSES

	Age	Races Run	1st	2nd	3rd	Unpl	Win £
Gabr	3	7	2	1	1	3	17,295
Shujan	4	16	5	2	0	9	16,301
Watani	2	3	2	0	0	1	13,053
Friendly Champ	2	6	3	1	1	1	11,834
Zajira	3	6	2	1	0	3	7,632
Benfleet	2	8	2	1	0	5	7,119
Maroof	3	1	1	0	0	0	5,057
Fawz	4	4	1	0	0	3	4,978
Greatest	2	4	1	0	1	2	4,950
Dance Turn	2	2	1	0	0	1	4,932
Fawaakeh	2	4	1	1	0	2	4,628
Shepherd Market	2	6	1	1	1	3	4,307
Matila	3	7	1	3	0	3	3,655
Ikhtiraa	3	6	1	0	0	5	3,582
Hadeer's Dance	3	7	1	1	1	4	3,407
Ishtiyak	2	1	1	0	0	0	3,260

WINNING OWNERS

	Races Won	Value £		Races Won	Value £
Hamdan Al-Maktoum	11	58,162	Miss Therese Sevremont	1	4,950
M J Polglase	5	16,301	George Ward	1	4,932
Dr Meou Tsen Geoffrey Yeh	3	11,834	Hugh Hart	1	4,307
C G Donovan	2	7,119	Khalifa Dasmal	1	3,407
Jeremy Gompertz	1	4,978			

Favourites	8-16	50.0% + 6.12	Total winning prize-money		£115,989

Longest winning sequence		3	Average SP of winner	6.5/1
Longest losing sequence		14	Return on stakes invested	33.3%

1992 Form	15-152	9.9%	- 5.75	1990 Form	26-155	16.8% - 24.88
1991 Form	10-114	8.8%	- 28.89	1989 Form	21-139	15.1% + 31.20

A BAILEY (Tarporley, Cheshire)

	No. of Horses	Races Run	1st	2nd	3rd	Unpl	Per cent	£1 Level Stake
2-y-o	10	55	4	1	3	47	7.3	- 17.25
3-y-o	11	58	2	5	3	48	3.4	- 44.12
4-y-o+	15	137	16	17	14	90	11.7	- 47.59
Totals	36	250	22	23	20	185	8.8	-108.96

BY MONTH

2-y-o	W-R	Per cent	£1 Level Stake	3-y-o	W-R	Per cent	£1 Level Stake
January	0-0	-	0.00	January	1-3	33.3	- 0.12
February	0-0	-	0.00	February	0-1	-	- 1.00
March	0-1	-	- 1.00	March	0-0	-	0.00
April	1-1	100.0	+ 1.75	April	0-3	-	- 3.00
May	0-2	-	- 2.00	May	0-2	-	- 2.00
June	0-5	-	- 5.00	June	0-5	-	- 5.00
July	0-7	-	- 7.00	July	1-10	10.0	+ 1.00
August	0-9	-	- 9.00	August	0-14	-	- 14.00
September	3-16	18.8	+ 19.00	September	0-14	-	- 14.00
Oct/Nov	0-14	-	- 14.00	Oct/Nov	0-6	-	- 6.00

4-y-o+	W-R	Per cent	£1 Level Stake	Totals	W-R	Per cent	£1 Level Stake
January	0-7	-	- 7.00	January	1-10	10.0	- 7.12
February	1-5	20.0	- 2.00	February	1-6	16.7	- 3.00
March	1-9	11.1	- 4.00	March	1-10	10.0	- 5.00
April	0-13	-	- 13.00	April	1-17	5.9	- 14.25
May	1-25	4.0	- 21.00	May	1-29	3.4	- 25.00
June	3-24	12.5	- 2.00	June	3-34	8.8	- 12.00
July	6-20	30.0	+ 10.41	July	7-37	18.9	+ 4.41
August	1-12	8.3	- 8.00	August	1-35	2.9	- 31.00
September	2-10	20.0	0.00	September	5-40	12.5	+ 5.00
Oct/Nov	1-12	8.3	- 1.00	Oct/Nov	1-32	3.1	- 21.00

DISTANCE

2-y-o	W-R	Per cent	£1 Level Stake	3-y-o	W-R	Per cent	£1 Level Stake
5f-6f	4-43	9.3	- 5.25	5f-6f	0-8	-	- 8.00
7f-8f	0-12	-	- 12.00	7f-8f	2-30	6.7	- 16.12
9f-13f	0-0	-	0.00	9f-13f	0-20	-	- 20.00
14f+	0-0	-	0.00	14f+	0-0	-	0.00

4-y-o+	W-R	Per cent	£1 Level Stake	Totals	W-R	Per cent	£1 Level Stake
5f-6f	0-17	-	- 17.00	5f-6f	4-68	5.9	- 30.25
7f-8f	9-59	15.3	- 9.50	7f-8f	11-101	10.9	- 37.62
9f-13f	2-41	4.9	- 26.00	9f-13f	2-61	3.3	- 46.00
14f+	5-20	25.0	+ 4.91	14f+	5-20	25.0	+ 4.91

TYPE OF RACE

Non-Handicaps	W-R	Per cent	£1 Level Stake	Handicaps	W-R	Per cent	£1 Level Stake
2-y-o	1-34	2.9	- 31.25	2-y-o	3-16	18.8	+ 19.00
3-y-o	1-22	4.5	- 19.12	3-y-o	1-27	3.7	- 16.00
4-y-o+	2-23	8.7	- 15.00	4-y-o+	13-97	13.4	- 19.59
Selling	0-5	-	- 5.00	Selling	0-9	-	- 9.00
Apprentice	0-2	-	- 2.00	Apprentice	1-9	11.1	- 5.00
Amat/Ladies	0-0	-	0.00	Amat/Ladies	0-6	-	- 6.00
Totals	4-86	4.7	- 72.37	Totals	18-164	11.0	- 36.59

COURSE GRADE

	W-R	Per cent	£1 Level Stake
Group 1	11-95	11.6	- 15.75
Group 2	1-54	1.9	- 50.00
Group 3	3-52	5.8	- 31.00
Group 4	7-49	14.3	- 12.21

FIRST TIME OUT

	W-R	Per cent	£1 Level Stake
2-y-o	0-10	-	- 10.00
3-y-o	1-10	10.0	- 7.12
4-y-o+	0-12	-	- 12.00
Totals	1-32	3.1	- 29.12

JOCKEYS RIDING

	W-R	Per cent	£1 Level Stake		W-R	Per cent	£1 Level Stake
A Mackay	14-128	10.9	- 31.75	W Carson	1-2	50.0	+ 4.00
D Wright	3-43	7.0	- 24.00	J Quinn	1-10	10.0	- 7.12
G Duffield	2-2	100.0	+ 3.91	F Norton	1-10	10.0	+ 1.00

A Tucker	0-9	N Connorton	0-2	Miss E Gatehouse	0-1
W Hollick	0-8	A Munro	0-1	Mr W Dixon	0-1
W Hawksley	0-7	F Savage	0-1	Mrs J Crossley	0-1
Angela Gallimore	0-5	G Bardwell	0-1	N Day	0-1
L Charnock	0-3	G Baxter	0-1	O Pears	0-1
L Piggott	0-3	G Carter	0-1	Sarah Chittenden	0-1
J Carroll	0-2	M Fenton	0-1	W Newnes	0-1
Miss D Pomeroy	0-2	Miss D J Jones	0-1		

COURSE RECORD

	Total W-R	Non-Handicaps 2-y-o	Non-Handicaps 3-y-o+	Handicaps 2-y-o	Handicaps 3-y-o+	Per cent	£1 Level Stake
Ayr	5-31	0-7	1-8	1-4	3-12	16.1	+ 1.50
Edinburgh	3-5	0-0	0-1	0-0	3-4	60.0	+ 16.91
Haydock	3-27	0-7	1-7	0-3	2-10	11.1	- 9.00
Southwell (AW)	2-15	0-1	0-2	0-0	2-12	13.3	- 7.00
Kempton	1-2	0-0	0-0	1-1	0-1	50.0	+ 9.00
Newcastle	1-6	1-1	0-0	0-1	0-4	16.7	- 3.25
Folkestone	1-7	0-0	0-3	0-0	1-4	14.3	- 3.00

Bailey A

Nottingham	1-7	0-0	0-3	0-0	1-4	14.3	− 3.00
Leicester	1-9	0-2	0-3	0-0	1-4	11.1	+ 2.00
Lingfield (AW)	1-11	0-0	1-2	0-0	0-9	9.1	− 8.12
Newmarket	1-13	0-1	0-1	1-3	0-8	7.7	+ 2.00
Hamilton	1-19	0-5	0-2	0-0	1-12	5.3	− 13.00
Chester	1-34	0-5	0-3	0-1	1-25	2.9	− 30.00

Doncaster	0-8	Goodwood	0-4	Bath	0-2
Pontefract	0-8	Redcar	0-4	Yarmouth	0-2
Ripon	0-7	Thirsk	0-4	Chepstow	0-1
Beverley	0-4	Warwick	0-4	Lingfield	0-1
Brighton	0-4	Carlisle	0-3	Newbury	0-1
Catterick	0-4	York	0-3		

WINNING HORSES

	Age	Races Run	1st	2nd	3rd	Unpl	Win £
Hunting Ground	5	15	5	0	0	10	15,481
Mentalasanythin	4	26	4	3	3	16	13,820
Veloce	5	24	3	4	2	15	12,558
No Mean City	2	11	2	1	2	6	11,380
Killick	5	10	1	2	1	6	7,148
Lombard Ships	6	19	2	6	4	7	5,080
My Gallery	2	9	1	0	0	8	3,494
Mahaasin	5	5	1	0	1	3	3,079
Diwali Dancer	3	10	1	2	0	7	2,930
Saddam The Log	2	7	1	0	0	6	2,880
Bold Street	3	7	1	0	0	6	2,208

WINNING OWNERS

	Races Won	Value £		Races Won	Value £
Mrs M O'Donnell	7	28,080	Gordon Mytton	1	3,494
Esprit De Corps Racing	6	22,629	Mrs Joan Cosgrove	1	3,079
Maximo Gonzalez	3	12,558	Mrs Ann Case	1	2,930
Mrs D M Mitchell	2	5,080	B E Case	1	2,208

Favourites	8-27	29.6%	+ 0.54	Total winning prize-money			£80,058

Longest winning sequence		2	Average SP of winner	5.4/1
Longest losing sequence		46	Return on stakes invested	−43.6%

1992 Form	16-180	8.9%	− 57.58	1990 Form	10-180	5.6%	− 88.09
1991 Form	11-95	11.6%	− 32.87	1989 Form	12-210	5.7%	−100.67

R J BAKER (Tiverton, Devon)

	No. of Horses	Races Run	1st	2nd	3rd	Unpl	Per cent	£1 Level Stake
2-y-o	0	0	0	0	0	0	-	0.00
3-y-o	2	5	0	0	1	4	-	- 5.00
4-y-o+	11	62	2	7	6	47	3.2	- 51.00
Totals	13	67	2	7	7	51	3.0	- 56.00

Jan	Feb	Mar	Apr	May	Jun	Jul	Aug	Sep	Oct/Nov
0-0	0-0	0-5	0-6	0-14	1-16	1-7	0-6	0-7	0-6

Winning Jockeys	W-R	£1 Level Stake			W-R	£1 Level Stake
W Newnes	1-5	+ 0.50	J Williams		1-9	- 3.50

Winning Courses	W-R	£1 Level Stake			W-R	£1 Level Stake
Warwick	1-9	- 3.50	Bath		1-10	- 4.50

Winning Horses	Age	Races Run	1st	2nd	3rd	Unpl	Win £
Athar	4	7	1	1	1	4	3,290
Fanatical	7	13	1	2	0	10	2,511

Favourites	0-0		Total winning prize-money	£5,801

1992 Form	2-40	5.0%	- 3.00

G B BALDING (Dorchester, Dorset)

	No. of Horses	Races Run	1st	2nd	3rd	Unpl	Per cent	£1 Level Stake
2-y-o	5	17	0	0	0	17	-	- 17.00
3-y-o	5	28	3	0	3	22	10.7	- 1.50
4-y-o+	8	36	4	3	3	26	11.1	+ 5.10
Totals	18	81	7	3	6	65	8.6	- 13.40

Jan	Feb	Mar	Apr	May	Jun	Jul	Aug	Sep	Oct/Nov
0-1	0-0	0-0	0-3	0-15	3-13	2-13	1-9	1-17	0-10

Winning Jockeys	W-R	£1 Level Stake			W-R	£1 Level Stake
J Williams	5-33	+ 19.50	Pat Eddery		1-3	- 0.90
Iona Wands	1-2	+ 11.00				

Winning Courses	W-R	£1 Level Stake			W-R	£1 Level Stake
Sandown	2-6	+ 5.10	Warwick		1-8	- 4.50
Kempton	2-9	+ 21.00	Salisbury		1-17	- 9.00
Newmarket	1-3	+ 12.00				

Balding G B

Winning Horses	Age	Races Run	1st	2nd	3rd	Unpl	Win £
Lady Lacey	6	14	2	2	1	9	6,807
Chili Heights	3	9	1	0	2	6	6,165
War Requiem	3	7	2	0	1	4	5,434
Singers Image	4	8	1	0	0	7	3,582
Gone Savage	5	3	1	0	0	2	2,843

Favourites	1-5	20.0%	- 2.90	Total winning prize-money			£24,831

1992 Form	15-196	7.7%	- 75.79	1990 Form	18-188	9.6%	- 8.59
1991 Form	18-247	7.3%	- 67.47	1989 Form	15-181	8.3%	- 35.36

I A BALDING (Kingsclere, Berks)

	No. of Horses	Races Run	1st	2nd	3rd	Unpl	Per cent	£1 Level Stake
2-y-o	31	93	12	13	10	58	12.9	- 38.03
3-y-o	27	155	20	16	18	101	12.9	- 43.67
4-y-o+	12	91	18	7	10	56	19.8	+ 21.90
Totals	70	339	50	36	38	215	14.7	- 59.80

BY MONTH

2-y-o	W-R	Per cent	£1 Level Stake	3-y-o	W-R	Per cent	£1 Level Stake
January	0-0	-	0.00	January	0-0	-	0.00
February	0-0	-	0.00	February	0-0	-	0.00
March	0-0	-	0.00	March	0-0	-	0.00
April	0-0	-	0.00	April	4-26	15.4	- 6.42
May	1-2	50.0	+ 9.00	May	4-34	11.8	- 17.62
June	3-14	21.4	- 2.90	June	3-25	12.0	+ 0.50
July	0-12	-	- 12.00	July	6-25	24.0	+ 4.62
August	5-16	31.3	- 0.88	August	3-20	15.0	+ 0.25
September	1-29	3.4	- 20.00	September	0-19	-	- 19.00
Oct/Nov	2-20	10.0	- 11.25	Oct/Nov	0-6	-	- 6.00

4-y-o+	W-R	Per cent	£1 Level Stake	Totals	W-R	Per cent	£1 Level Stake
January	0-0	-	0.00	January	0-0	-	0.00
February	0-0	-	0.00	February	0-0	-	0.00
March	0-2	-	- 2.00	March	0-2	-	- 2.00
April	3-18	16.7	+ 7.34	April	7-44	15.9	+ 0.92
May	4-14	28.6	+ 15.00	May	9-50	18.0	+ 6.38
June	0-11	-	- 11.00	June	6-50	12.0	- 13.40
July	6-16	37.5	+ 6.01	July	12-53	22.6	- 1.37
August	2-14	14.3	- 1.20	August	10-50	20.0	- 1.83
September	3-11	27.3	+ 12.75	September	4-59	6.8	- 26.25
Oct/Nov	0-5	-	- 5.00	Oct/Nov	2-31	6.5	- 22.25

DISTANCE

2-y-o	W-R	Per cent	£1 Level Stake	3-y-o	W-R	Per cent	£1 Level Stake
5f-6f	7-45	15.6	- 15.95	5f-6f	0-12	-	- 12.00
7f-8f	5-46	10.9	- 20.08	7f-8f	12-73	16.4	- 4.30
9f-13f	0-2	-	- 2.00	9f-13f	6-61	9.8	- 26.75
14f+	0-0	-	0.00	14f+	2-9	22.2	- 0.62

4-y-o+	W-R	Per cent	£1 Level Stake	Totals	W-R	Per cent	£1 Level Stake
5f-6f	3-7	42.9	+ 9.76	5f-6f	10-64	15.6	- 18.19
7f-8f	6-34	17.6	+ 16.05	7f-8f	23-153	15.0	- 8.33
9f-13f	5-32	15.6	- 0.16	9f-13f	11-95	11.6	- 28.91
14f+	4-18	22.2	- 3.75	14f+	6-27	22.2	- 4.37

TYPE OF RACE

Non-Handicaps	W-R	Per cent	£1 Level Stake	Handicaps	W-R	Per cent	£1 Level Stake
2-y-o	11-86	12.8	- 34.78	2-y-o	1-7	14.3	- 3.25
3-y-o	10-85	11.8	- 31.33	3-y-o	8-63	12.7	- 13.67
4-y-o+	7-25	28.0	+ 2.40	4-y-o+	10-61	16.4	+ 9.50
Selling	0-0	-	0.00	Selling	1-1	100.0	+ 3.00
Apprentice	1-4	25.0	+ 0.33	Apprentice	1-7	14.3	+ 8.00
Amat/Ladies	0-0	-	0.00	Amat/Ladies	0-0	-	0.00
Totals	29-200	14.5	- 63.38	Totals	21-139	15.1	+ 3.58

COURSE GRADE

	W-R	Per cent	£1 Level Stake
Group 1	25-201	12.4	- 15.36
Group 2	12-56	21.4	- 14.00
Group 3	9-62	14.5	- 21.48
Group 4	4-20	20.0	- 8.96

FIRST TIME OUT

	W-R	Per cent	£1 Level Stake
2-y-o	3-31	9.7	- 11.00
3-y-o	2-27	7.4	- 16.17
4-y-o+	2-12	16.7	+ 10.09
Totals	7-70	10.0	- 17.08

JOCKEYS RIDING

	W-R	Per cent	£1 Level Stake		W-R	Per cent	£1 Level Stake
L Dettori	27-146	18.5	+ 3.03	K Darley	1-2	50.0	- 0.71
S O'Gorman	7-56	12.5	- 7.25	Martin Dwyer	1-3	33.3	+ 1.33
R Cochrane	6-36	16.7	- 14.58	W Ryan	1-4	25.0	0.00
M Hills	3-39	7.7	- 23.50	C Scudder	1-4	25.0	+ 11.00
L Piggott	1-2	50.0	+ 11.00	Pat Eddery	1-7	14.3	- 4.62
W Newnes	1-2	50.0	+ 2.50				

Balding I A

D Griffiths	0-8	W Carson	0-2	N Connorton	0-1
J Reid	0-6	A Clark	0-1	T Quinn	0-1
B Raymond	0-5	A Munro	0-1	T Sprake	0-1
G Carter	0-3	D Harrison	0-1	W R Swinburn	0-1
Paul Eddery	0-3	G Duffield	0-1		
S Davies	0-2	Miss C Balding	0-1		

COURSE RECORD

	Total W-R	Non-Handicaps 2-y-o	3-y-o+	Handicaps 2-y-o	3-y-o+	Per cent	£1 Level Stake
Sandown	6-26	2-9	2-5	0-0	2-12	23.1	+ 28.13
Salisbury	4-23	1-7	2-8	0-0	1-8	17.4	- 10.47
Newmarket	4-30	1-6	2-8	0-2	1-14	13.3	- 1.62
Nottingham	3-6	0-1	2-3	0-0	1-2	50.0	+ 10.25
Brighton	3-12	0-2	2-3	0-1	1-6	25.0	- 4.78
York	3-20	0-3	1-4	0-0	2-13	15.0	+ 1.00
Ayr	2-3	0-0	0-1	0-0	2-2	66.7	+ 4.25
Beverley	2-7	0-1	0-2	0-0	2-4	28.6	+ 1.50
Lingfield	2-8	0-2	1-2	0-0	1-4	25.0	+ 1.00
Doncaster	2-9	0-3	1-2	0-0	1-4	22.2	+ 0.75
Windsor	2-10	1-3	0-2	0-0	1-5	20.0	- 2.40
Kempton	2-23	1-6	0-12	0-0	1-5	8.7	- 1.00
Goodwood	2-24	1-9	1-7	0-0	0-8	8.3	- 17.37
Newbury	2-31	0-10	1-10	0-0	1-11	6.5	- 3.50
Edinburgh	1-1	0-0	1-1	0-0	0-0	100.0	+ 0.29
Southwell (Turf)	1-1	1-1	0-0	0-0	0-0	100.0	+ 0.67
Chester	1-3	0-0	0-0	0-0	1-3	33.3	+ 1.50
Newcastle	1-3	0-0	0-0	0-0	1-3	33.3	+ 1.00
Lingfield (AW)	1-3	0-1	0-0	1-1	0-1	33.3	+ 0.75
Ripon	1-4	1-1	0-1	0-0	0-2	25.0	- 0.75
Redcar	1-6	0-0	1-3	0-0	0-3	16.7	- 0.50
Epsom	1-10	1-2	0-4	0-0	0-4	10.0	- 5.00
Pontefract	1-11	1-3	0-5	0-1	0-2	9.1	- 9.33
Warwick	1-12	0-1	1-5	0-1	0-5	8.3	- 7.67
Bath	1-15	0-3	0-9	0-1	1-2	6.7	- 8.50

Ascot	0-15	Haydock	0-7	Folkestone	0-3
Chepstow	0-8	Leicester	0-5		

WINNING HORSES

	Age	Races Run	1st	2nd	3rd	Unpl	Win £
Lochsong	5	7	3	0	2	2	122,649
Pay Homage	5	11	3	0	1	7	39,790
Abbey's Gal	3	7	3	1	2	1	23,302
Brandon Prince	5	9	3	1	1	4	19,012
Tissisat	4	10	1	1	1	7	17,994
Crystal Cross	4	9	2	1	0	6	13,790
Spring To Action	3	6	2	1	0	3	13,249
Moccasin Run	2	1	1	0	0	0	10,430
Knock Knock	8	13	2	1	1	9	9,085

Blaze Away	2	5	2	1	0	2	8,830
Song Of Sixpence	9	12	1	0	1	10	8,415
Blue Siren	2	5	2	2	0	1	7,711
Powerful Edge	4	9	2	2	1	4	7,257
Winged Victory (Ire)	3	8	2	1	1	4	7,136
Palana	2	6	2	1	0	3	7,058
Weigh Anchor	2	2	1	0	1	0	5,936
Susquehanna Days	3	7	2	1	1	3	5,679
Brandonhurst	3	9	1	1	0	7	5,550
Dynamic Deluxe	2	6	1	0	2	3	4,807
Spinning	6	2	1	0	1	0	4,464
East Liberty	3	7	1	0	1	5	4,078
Master Charlie	3	5	1	1	2	1	3,915
Double Down	2	6	1	1	1	3	3,747
Blair Castle	2	5	1	1	0	3	3,590
Clouded Elegance	3	5	1	1	0	3	3,553
Java Queen	3	3	1	0	0	2	3,545
Palace Pageant	3	3	1	0	0	2	3,319
Hill Of Dreams	3	9	1	0	0	8	3,143
Singer On The Roof	3	7	1	0	0	6	2,795
Smart Daisy	3	5	1	0	0	4	2,713
Lt Welsh	3	8	1	2	0	5	2,579
Euphonic	3	5	1	0	1	3	2,511
Sulitelma	2	5	1	1	0	3	2,040

WINNING OWNERS

	Races Won	Value £		Races Won	Value £
J C Smith	9	144,158	G M Smart	2	9,085
Paul Mellon	12	48,608	Robert Hitchins	1	5,936
Miss A V Hill	3	39,790	David R Watson	1	3,915
The Queen	3	31,243	Highflyers	1	3,590
R P B Michaelson	4	24,562	Mrs Michael Wates	1	3,553
Jerrard Williamson	3	23,302	Robert Jenkinson	1	2,713
George Strawbridge	4	20,067	Paul Stamp	1	2,511
Urs E Schwarzenbach	3	18,597	Miss K Rausing	1	2,040

Favourites	19-58	32.8%	- 6.84	Total winning prize-money		£383,671
Longest winning sequence			3	Average SP of winner		4.6/1
Longest losing sequence			44	Return on stakes invested		-17.6%
1992 Form	36-316	11.4%	- 42.11	1990 Form	48-375	12.8%	- 41.74
1991 Form	53-362	14.6%	- 50.22	1989 Form	41-349	11.7%	- 89.91

J BALDING (Bawtry, South Yorks)

	No. of Horses	Races Run	1st	2nd	3rd	Unpl	Per cent	£1 Level Stake
2-y-o	2	9	0	0	0	9	-	- 9.00
3-y-o	6	44	4	2	4	34	9.1	- 22.67
4-y-o+	5	24	2	3	2	17	8.3	- 11.75
Totals	13	77	6	5	6	60	7.8	- 43.42

Jan	Feb	Mar	Apr	May	Jun	Jul	Aug	Sep	Oct/Nov
0-3	0-3	0-1	0-8	0-11	4-14	2-12	0-13	0-7	0-5

Winning Jockeys	W-R	£1 Level Stake				W-R	£1 Level Stake
Claire Balding	4-59	- 37.42	G Hind			1-3	+ 6.00
S Whitworth	1-2	+ 1.00					

Winning Courses							
Hamilton	3-6	+ 17.00	Pontefract			1-5	- 0.67
Edinburgh	2-5	+ 1.25					

Winning Horses	Age	Races Run	1st	2nd	3rd	Unpl	Win £
Miss Siham	4	6	2	1	0	3	4,565
Rain Splash	3	10	1	1	0	8	3,753
Kimbolton Korker	3	7	1	0	2	4	2,726
Magication	3	14	1	1	2	10	2,685
Joellise	3	9	1	0	0	8	2,301

Favourites	2-2	100.0%	+ 5.58	Total winning prize-money			£16,028

1992 Form	0-81			1990 Form	7-120	5.8%	- 53.50
1991 Form	4-125	3.2%	-102.50	1989 Form	5-115	4.3%	- 62.50

J E BANKS (Newmarket)

	No. of Horses	Races Run	1st	2nd	3rd	Unpl	Per cent	£1 Level Stake
2-y-o	5	8	2	1	0	5	25.0	+ 14.00
3-y-o	1	3	2	0	0	1	66.7	+ 6.33
4-y-o+	8	34	3	4	2	25	8.8	- 1.00
Totals	14	45	7	5	2	31	15.6	+ 19.33

Jan	Feb	Mar	Apr	May	Jun	Jul	Aug	Sep	Oct/Nov
0-2	0-0	0-1	1-4	1-5	1-7	1-8	1-8	1-5	1-5

Winning Jockeys	W-R	£1 Level Stake				W-R	£1 Level Stake
J Quinn	5-17	+ 21.33	L Newton			1-11	0.00
L Dettori	1-2	+ 13.00					

Winning Courses	W-R	£1 Level Stake				W-R	£1 Level Stake
Yarmouth	3-7	+ 22.00	Southwell (Turf)			1-2	+ 13.00
Haydock	1-1	+ 3.33	Newmarket			1-7	+ 4.00
Leicester	1-2	+ 3.00					

Winning Horses	Age	Races Run	1st	2nd	3rd	Unpl	Win £
Indhar	2	2	2	0	0	0	13,259
Premier League	3	3	2	0	0	1	7,630
Yaakum	4	4	1	0	0	3	3,002
Jess Rebec	5	8	1	1	1	5	2,950
Mizyan	5	6	1	2	0	3	2,601

Favourites	1-3	33.3%	+ 2.00	Total winning prize-money			£29,443

1992 Form	4-52	7.7%	- 31.75	1991 Form	3-61	4.9%	- 27.00

MRS P A BARKER (Wetherby, West Yorks)

	No. of Horses	Races Run	1st	2nd	3rd	Unpl	Per cent	£1 Level Stake
2-y-o	1	1	0	0	0	1	-	- 1.00
3-y-o	3	7	0	0	0	7	-	- 7.00
4-y-o+	6	22	1	0	3	18	4.5	- 14.50
Totals	10	30	1	0	3	26	3.3	- 22.50

Jan	Feb	Mar	Apr	May	Jun	Jul	Aug	Sep	Oct/Nov
0-0	0-0	0-1	0-6	1-11	0-4	0-1	0-2	0-4	0-1

Winning Jockey	W-R	£1 Level Stake	Winning Course	W-R	£1 Level Stake
D Moffatt	1-7	+ 0.50	Redcar	1-3	+ 4.50

Winning Horse	Age	Races Run	1st	2nd	3rd	Unpl	Win £
Ballad Dancer	8	7	1	0	3	3	2,070

Favourites	0-2		Total winning prize-money	£2,070

1992 Form	0-15			1990 Form	0-30	
1991 Form	1-23	4.3%	+ 3.00			

W L BARKER (Richmond, North Yorks)

	No. of Horses	Races Run	1st	2nd	3rd	Unpl	Per cent	£1 Level Stake
2-y-o	2	9	0	2	2	5	-	- 9.00
3-y-o	3	11	0	0	1	10	-	- 11.00
4-y-o+	6	27	1	1	6	19	3.7	- 14.00
Totals	11	47	1	3	9	34	2.1	- 34.00

Jan	Feb	Mar	Apr	May	Jun	Jul	Aug	Sep	Oct/Nov
0-0	0-0	0-2	0-3	0-10	0-9	1-5	0-5	0-8	0-5

		£1 Level				£1 Level
Winning Jockey	W-R	Stake		Winning Course	W-R	Stake
S Webster	1-31	- 18.00		Catterick	1-13	0.00

		Races					Win
Winning Horse	Age	Run	1st	2nd	3rd	Unpl	£
McA Below The Line	5	13	1	1	5	6	3,377

Favourites	0-0		Total winning prize-money	£3,377

1992 Form	1-35	2.9%	- 23.00	1991 Form	0-7

M F BARRACLOUGH (Claverdon, Warwicks)

	No. of Horses	Races Run	1st	2nd	3rd	Unpl	Per cent	£1 Level Stake
2-y-o	1	2	0	0	0	2	-	- 2.00
3-y-o	0	0	0	0	0	0	-	0.00
4-y-o+	6	28	1	0	0	27	3.6	- 15.00
Totals	7	30	1	0	0	29	3.3	- 17.00

Jan	Feb	Mar	Apr	May	Jun	Jul	Aug	Sep	Oct/Nov
0-0	0-1	0-1	0-6	0-3	0-4	0-4	1-7	0-4	0-0

		£1 Level				£1 Level
Winning Jockey	W-R	Stake		Winning Course	W-R	Stake
N Varley	1-3	+ 10.00		Southwell (Turf)	1-2	+ 11.00

		Races					Win
Winning Horse	Age	Run	1st	2nd	3rd	Unpl	£
Fairy Wisher	4	11	1	0	0	10	3,391

Favourites	0-0		Total winning prize-money	£3,391

1992 Form	2-25	8.0%	- 12.00	1991 Form	0-13

T D BARRON (Thirsk, North Yorks)

	No. of Horses	Races Run	1st	2nd	3rd	Unpl	Per cent	£1 Level Stake
2-y-o	11	33	1	2	2	28	3.0	- 31.27
3-y-o	18	95	13	9	15	58	13.7	- 5.52
4-y-o+	16	121	12	10	17	82	9.9	- 54.13
Totals	45	249	26	21	34	168	10.4	- 90.92

BY MONTH

2-y-o	W-R	Per cent	£1 Level Stake	3-y-o	W-R	Per cent	£1 Level Stake
January	0-0	-	0.00	January	3-13	23.1	+ 5.25
February	0-0	-	0.00	February	2-4	50.0	+ 1.63
March	0-0	-	0.00	March	1-6	16.7	0.00
April	0-1	-	- 1.00	April	2-7	28.6	+ 7.50
May	0-3	-	- 3.00	May	1-7	14.3	+ 4.00
June	0-9	-	- 9.00	June	2-10	20.0	+ 7.00
July	1-5	20.0	- 3.27	July	1-17	5.9	- 14.90
August	0-4	-	- 4.00	August	0-14	-	- 14.00
September	0-4	-	- 4.00	September	0-9	-	- 9.00
Oct/Nov	0-7	-	- 7.00	Oct/Nov	1-8	12.5	+ 7.00

4-y-o+	W-R	Per cent	£1 Level Stake	Totals	W-R	Per cent	£1 Level Stake
January	1-11	9.1	- 9.09	January	4-24	16.7	- 3.84
February	2-6	33.3	+ 6.00	February	4-10	40.0	+ 7.63
March	0-11	-	- 11.00	March	1-17	5.9	- 11.00
April	0-10	-	- 10.00	April	2-18	11.1	- 3.50
May	2-14	14.3	- 4.00	May	3-24	12.5	- 3.00
June	0-11	-	- 11.00	June	2-30	6.7	- 13.00
July	4-17	23.5	- 2.54	July	6-39	15.4	- 20.71
August	0-11	-	- 11.00	August	0-29	-	- 29.00
September	1-9	11.1	- 1.00	September	1-22	4.5	- 14.00
Oct/Nov	2-21	9.5	- 0.50	Oct/Nov	3-36	8.3	- 0.50

DISTANCE

2-y-o	W-R	Per cent	£1 Level Stake	3-y-o	W-R	Per cent	£1 Level Stake
5f-6f	0-20	-	- 20.00	5f-6f	4-40	10.0	- 13.40
7f-8f	1-13	7.7	- 11.27	7f-8f	7-43	16.3	+ 11.25
9f-13f	0-0	-	0.00	9f-13f	2-12	16.7	- 3.37
14f+	0-0	-	0.00	14f+	0-0	-	0.00

4-y-o+	W-R	Per cent	£1 Level Stake	Totals	W-R	Per cent	£1 Level Stake
5f-6f	3-27	11.1	- 9.00	5f-6f	7-87	8.0	- 42.40
7f-8f	5-52	9.6	- 17.59	7f-8f	13-108	12.0	- 17.61
9f-13f	4-38	10.5	- 23.54	9f-13f	6-50	12.0	- 26.91
14f+	0-4	-	- 4.00	14f+	0-4	-	- 4.00

Barron T D

TYPE OF RACE

Non-Handicaps	W-R	Per cent	£1 Level Stake	Handicaps	W-R	Per cent	£1 Level Stake
2-y-o	1-23	4.3	- 21.27	2-y-o	0-7	-	- 7.00
3-y-o	3-24	12.5	+ 3.50	3-y-o	9-61	14.8	- 9.02
4-y-o+	4-17	23.5	+ 2.41	4-y-o+	7-95	7.4	- 49.92
Selling	0-5	-	- 5.00	Selling	0-3	-	- 3.00
Apprentice	0-4	-	- 4.00	Apprentice	1-7	14.3	+ 3.00
Amat/Ladies	0-0	-	0.00	Amat/Ladies	1-3	33.3	- 0.62
Totals	8-73	11.0	- 24.36	Totals	18-176	10.2	- 66.56

COURSE GRADE

	W-R	Per cent	£1 Level Stake
Group 1	4-52	7.7	- 21.50
Group 2	4-55	7.3	- 30.42
Group 3	2-44	4.5	- 33.62
Group 4	16-98	16.3	- 5.38

FIRST TIME OUT

	W-R	Per cent	£1 Level Stake
2-y-o	0-10	-	- 10.00
3-y-o	2-17	11.8	+ 0.50
4-y-o+	0-14	-	- 14.00
Totals	2-41	4.9	- 23.50

JOCKEYS RIDING

	W-R	Per cent	£1 Level Stake		W-R	Per cent	£1 Level Stake
V Halliday	6-44	13.6	+ 7.50	Mrs A Farrell	1-3	33.3	- 0.62
Alex Greaves	6-56	10.7	- 28.46	A Mackay	1-3	33.3	+ 5.00
K Darley	5-46	10.9	- 19.17	B Raymond	1-4	25.0	+ 2.00
W Newnes	2-5	40.0	+ 3.83	R Cochrane	1-6	16.7	- 0.50
W Ryan	2-10	20.0	+ 8.50	J Fanning	1-12	8.3	- 9.00

Kimberley Hart	0-8	J Reid	0-2	L Piggott	0-1
T Williams	0-6	M Birch	0-2	M Wigham	0-1
J Lowe	0-5	O Pears	0-2	Miss F Burke	0-1
J Fortune	0-4	S Maloney	0-2	Miss P Robson	0-1
A McGlone	0-3	A Munro	0-1	N Carlisle	0-1
L Dettori	0-3	D McKeown	0-1	N Connorton	0-1
Paul Eddery	0-3	F Norton	0-1	T Quinn	0-1
D Wright	0-2	G Duffield	0-1	W Carson	0-1
Dale Gibson	0-2	J Tate	0-1		
G Carter	0-2	K Fallon	0-1		

COURSE RECORD

	Total W-R	Non-Handicaps 2-y-o	Non-Handicaps 3-y-o+	Handicaps 2-y-o	Handicaps 3-y-o+	Per cent	£1 Level Stake
Southwell (AW)	8-48	0-1	2-14	0-0	6-33	16.7	+ 9.16
Lingfield (AW)	4-8	0-0	1-2	0-0	3-6	50.0	+ 13.63
Ripon	2-16	0-4	0-1	0-0	2-11	12.5	+ 1.00
Yarmouth	1-2	0-0	0-1	0-0	1-1	50.0	+ 6.00
Haydock	1-3	0-0	1-1	0-0	0-2	33.3	+ 4.50

Southwell (Turf)	1-4	0-0	1-2	0-0	0-2	25.0	+ 0.50
Carlisle	1-7	0-0	1-3	0-0	0-4	14.3	- 1.50
Edinburgh	1-8	1-3	0-2	0-0	0-3	12.5	- 6.27
Newcastle	1-10	0-2	0-2	0-0	1-6	10.0	+ 1.00
Redcar	1-10	0-2	0-2	0-1	1-5	10.0	- 6.75
Doncaster	1-12	0-1	1-1	0-1	0-9	8.3	- 4.50
Ayr	1-17	0-1	0-1	0-1	1-14	5.9	- 12.50
Beverley	1-17	0-1	0-3	0-0	1-13	5.9	- 14.62
Catterick	1-22	0-3	0-2	0-3	1-14	4.5	- 19.90
Thirsk	1-29	0-6	0-2	0-0	1-21	3.4	- 24.67

Pontefract	0-11	York	0-5	Leicester	0-1
Hamilton	0-7	Newmarket	0-3	Sandown	0-1
Nottingham	0-6	Goodwood	0-1	Warwick	0-1

WINNING HORSES

	Age	Races Run	1st	2nd	3rd	Unpl	Win £
Brackenthwaite	3	13	5	1	2	5	13,818
Slades Hill	6	18	3	2	1	12	10,898
Sea Gazer	3	3	1	0	0	2	10,575
Allinson's Mate	5	10	3	0	0	7	9,739
For The Present	3	8	2	1	0	5	8,621
So So	3	5	1	0	0	4	7,440
Dream Carrier	5	16	2	0	3	11	7,411
Super Blues	6	9	2	0	1	6	6,419
Touch Above	7	12	2	3	2	5	5,812
Savings Bank	3	5	1	0	0	4	3,260
Ashover	3	6	1	1	1	3	2,979
Prizefighter	2	6	1	1	0	4	2,933
Gussie Fink-Nottle	3	13	1	3	4	5	2,847
Mark's Club	3	4	1	0	1	2	2,377

WINNING OWNERS

	Races Won	Value £		Races Won	Value £
Mrs J Hazell	4	14,433	Stephen Woodall	2	7,425
P D Savill	2	13,508	David Barron Racing Club	3	7,113
James E Greaves	3	10,898	W H Clarke	2	6,419
Peter Jones	3	9,739	J Baggott	1	3,260
Alex Gorrie	3	9,069	Timothy Cox	1	2,979
Geoffrey Martin	1	7,440	Mrs S Sturman	1	2,847

Favourites	7-27	25.9%	- 9.75	Total winning prize-money		£95,129

Longest winning sequence		3	Average SP of winner	5.1/1
Longest losing sequence		42	Return on stakes invested	-36.5%

1992 Form	41-345	11.9%	- 48.70	1990 Form	58-337	17.2%	- 42.83
1991 Form	39-331	11.8%	- 75.22	1989 Form	24-275	8.7%	-122.25

A BARROW (Bridgwater, Somerset)

	No. of Horses	Races Run	1st	2nd	3rd	Unpl	Per cent	£1 Level Stake
2-y-o	0	0	0	0	0	0	-	0.00
3-y-o	0	0	0	0	0	0	-	0.00
4-y-o+	2	7	1	0	0	6	14.3	+ 27.00
Totals	2	7	1	0	0	6	14.3	+ 27.00

Jan	Feb	Mar	Apr	May	Jun	Jul	Aug	Sep	Oct/Nov
0-0	0-0	0-1	0-0	0-0	0-1	1-4	0-1	0-0	0-0

Winning Jockey	W-R	£1 Level Stake	Winning Course	W-R	£1 Level Stake
N Carlisle	1-4	+ 30.00	Warwick	1-2	+ 32.00

Winning Horse	Age	Races Run	1st	2nd	3rd	Unpl	Win £
Green's Stubbs	6	6	1	0	0	5	2,070

Favourites	0-0		Total winning prize-money	£2,070

1992 Form	0-20	1990 Form	0-12
1991 Form	0-31	1989 Form	0-3

C R BARWELL (Tiverton, Devon)

	No. of Horses	Races Run	1st	2nd	3rd	Unpl	Per cent	£1 Level Stake
2-y-o	3	7	0	0	0	7	-	- 7.00
3-y-o	1	2	0	0	0	2	-	- 2.00
4-y-o+	1	5	1	0	0	4	20.0	+ 29.00
Totals	5	14	1	0	0	13	7.1	+ 20.00

Jan	Feb	Mar	Apr	May	Jun	Jul	Aug	Sep	Oct/Nov
0-0	0-0	0-1	1-2	0-1	0-3	0-2	0-0	0-0	0-5

Winning Jockey	W-R	£1 Level Stake	Winning Course	W-R	£1 Level Stake
T Lang	1-5	+ 29.00	Bath	1-3	+ 31.00

Winning Horse	Age	Races Run	1st	2nd	3rd	Unpl	Win £
Cobblers Hill	4	5	1	0	0	4	3,210

Favourites	0-0		Total winning prize-money	£3,210

1992 Form	0-8	1990 Form	0-15
1991 Form	0-13		

R BASTIMAN (Wetherby, West Yorks)

	No. of Horses	Races Run	1st	2nd	3rd	Unpl	Per cent	£1 Level Stake
2-y-o	3	4	0	0	0	4	-	- 4.00
3-y-o	4	21	1	1	0	19	4.8	+ 46.00
4-y-o+	11	79	7	4	9	59	8.9	- 21.50
Totals	18	104	8	5	9	82	7.7	+ 20.50

Jan	Feb	Mar	Apr	May	Jun	Jul	Aug	Sep	Oct/Nov
1-3	0-3	0-4	1-12	0-17	0-17	3-12	0-13	1-7	2-16

Winning Jockeys	W-R	£1 Level Stake		W-R	£1 Level Stake
H Bastiman	5-65	- 30.00	L Charnock	1-2	+ 65.00
M Hills	1-2	+ 5.50	N Carlisle	1-3	+ 12.00

Winning Courses					
Yarmouth	2-7	+ 17.00	Newcastle	1-7	- 2.00
Ascot	1-1	+ 10.00	Pontefract	1-9	+ 58.00
Brighton	1-1	+ 4.50	Southwell (AW)	1-14	- 6.50
Edinburgh	1-4	+ 0.50			

Winning Horses	Age	Races Run	1st	2nd	3rd	Unpl	Win £
Hillzah	5	14	2	1	3	8	8,193
Beckyhannah	3	7	1	0	0	6	3,003
Meeson Times	5	4	1	1	1	1	2,899
Golden Torque	6	14	1	1	2	10	2,880
Sea Paddy	5	7	1	1	0	5	2,406
Company Cash	5	9	1	0	0	8	2,343
Super Rocky	4	9	1	0	1	7	2,232

Favourites	1-7	14.3%	- 2.00	Total winning prize-money			£23,956

1992 Form	10-127	7.9%	- 37.67	1990 Form	12-119	10.1%	- 8.25
1991 Form	14-127	11.0%	+ 4.25	1989 Form	7-56	12.5%	+ 5.50

B BEASLEY (Thirsk, North Yorks)

	No. of Horses	Races Run	1st	2nd	3rd	Unpl	Per cent	£1 Level Stake
2-y-o	4	13	0	2	0	11	-	- 13.00
3-y-o	9	49	3	4	6	36	6.1	- 28.50
4-y-o+	8	39	3	7	4	25	7.7	- 4.50
Totals	21	101	6	13	10	72	5.9	- 46.00

Jan	Feb	Mar	Apr	May	Jun	Jul	Aug	Sep	Oct/Nov
0-0	0-0	0-3	1-6	2-13	0-12	1-18	2-19	0-14	0-16

Beasley B

		£1 Level				£1 Level
Winning Jockeys	W-R	Stake		W-R		Stake
O Pears	3-18	+ 12.00	J Tate	1-12		- 6.50
L Aspell	1-3	+ 3.50	J Fortune	1-13		0.00

		£1 Level			£1 Level
Winning Courses	W-R	Stake		W-R	Stake
Thirsk	2-14	+ 10.00	Ripon	1-7	- 1.50
Ayr	1-5	+ 1.50	Redcar	1-10	+ 3.00
Pontefract	1-6	0.00			

		Races					Win
Winning Horses	Age	Run	1st	2nd	3rd	Unpl	£
Taufan Blu	4	12	1	2	1	8	15,400
Pine Ridge Lad	3	8	1	0	2	5	3,720
Chickcharnie	3	4	1	0	1	2	3,407
Eightandahalf	4	3	1	0	1	1	3,132
My Godson	3	10	1	1	0	8	3,054
Super Benz	7	11	1	2	1	7	2,596

Favourites	0-6			Total winning prize-money	£31,308
1992 Form	14-152	9.2%	- 32.02		

M BELL (Newmarket)

	No. of Horses	Races Run	1st	2nd	3rd	Unpl	Per cent	£1 Level Stake
2-y-o	35	132	18	15	12	87	13.6	- 26.66
3-y-o	31	199	24	24	22	129	12.1	- 23.48
4-y-o+	7	33	0	3	0	30	-	- 33.00
Totals	73	364	42	42	34	246	11.5	- 83.14

BY MONTH

2-y-o	W-R	Per cent	£1 Level Stake	3-y-o	W-R	Per cent	£1 Level Stake
January	0-0	-	0.00	January	0-4	-	- 4.00
February	0-0	-	0.00	February	1-3	33.3	- 1.56
March	1-4	25.0	- 2.09	March	1-11	9.1	- 8.37
April	0-10	-	- 10.00	April	6-31	19.4	+ 6.25
May	3-11	27.3	+ 3.00	May	4-26	15.4	- 4.00
June	3-12	25.0	- 0.50	June	6-31	19.4	+ 11.95
July	4-27	14.8	- 0.40	July	1-32	3.1	- 28.00
August	4-27	14.8	+ 2.83	August	2-27	7.4	+ 2.00
September	1-18	5.6	- 16.00	September	1-22	4.5	- 19.75
Oct/Nov	2-23	8.7	- 3.50	Oct/Nov	2-12	16.7	+ 22.00

4-y-o+	W-R	Per cent	£1 Level Stake	Totals	W-R	Per cent	£1 Level Stake
January	0-0	-	0.00	January	0-4	-	- 4.00
February	0-0	-	0.00	February	1-3	33.3	- 1.56
March	0-3	-	- 3.00	March	2-18	11.1	- 13.46
April	0-7	-	- 7.00	April	6-48	12.5	- 10.75
May	0-4	-	- 4.00	May	7-41	17.1	- 5.00
June	0-4	-	- 4.00	June	9-47	19.1	+ 7.45
July	0-7	-	- 7.00	July	5-66	7.6	- 35.40
August	0-4	-	- 4.00	August	6-58	10.3	+ 0.83
September	0-3	-	- 3.00	September	2-43	4.7	- 38.75
Oct/Nov	0-1	-	- 1.00	Oct/Nov	4-36	11.1	+ 17.50

DISTANCE

2-y-o	W-R	Per cent	£1 Level Stake	3-y-o	W-R	Per cent	£1 Level Stake
5f-6f	11-78	14.1	- 4.49	5f-6f	1-31	3.2	- 10.00
7f-8f	6-51	11.8	- 21.67	7f-8f	5-61	8.2	- 37.36
9f-13f	1-3	33.3	- 0.50	9f-13f	18-97	18.6	+ 33.88
14f+	0-0	-	0.00	14f+	0-10	-	- 10.00

4-y-o+	W-R	Per cent	£1 Level Stake	Totals	W-R	Per cent	£1 Level Stake
5f-6f	0-3	-	- 3.00	5f-6f	12-112	10.7	- 17.49
7f-8f	0-20	-	- 20.00	7f-8f	11-132	8.3	- 79.03
9f-13f	0-7	-	- 7.00	9f-13f	19-107	17.8	+ 26.38
14f+	0-3	-	- 3.00	14f+	0-13	-	- 13.00

TYPE OF RACE

Non-Handicaps	W-R	Per cent	£1 Level Stake	Handicaps	W-R	Per cent	£1 Level Stake
2-y-o	15-98	15.3	- 34.66	2-y-o	2-27	7.4	+ 1.00
3-y-o	8-56	14.3	- 22.18	3-y-o	14-126	11.1	+ 4.70
4-y-o+	0-4	-	- 4.00	4-y-o+	0-26	-	- 26.00
Selling	1-10	10.0	+ 4.00	Selling	0-6	-	- 6.00
Apprentice	0-1	-	- 1.00	Apprentice	1-8	12.5	- 1.00
Amat/Ladies	1-1	100.0	+ 3.00	Amat/Ladies	0-1	-	- 1.00
Totals	25-170	14.7	- 54.84	Totals	17-194	8.8	- 28.30

COURSE GRADE

	W-R	Per cent	£1 Level Stake
Group 1	10-153	6.5	- 61.75
Group 2	5-52	9.6	- 24.17
Group 3	19-98	19.4	+ 10.73
Group 4	8-61	13.1	- 7.95

FIRST TIME OUT

	W-R	Per cent	£1 Level Stake
2-y-o	1-35	2.9	- 31.00
3-y-o	4-31	12.9	- 13.62
4-y-o+	0-7	-	- 7.00
Totals	5-73	6.8	- 51.62

Bell M

JOCKEYS RIDING

	W-R	Per cent	£1 Level Stake			W-R	Per cent	£1 Level Stake
M Hills	17-120	14.2	- 37.17	Pat Eddery		1-1	100.0	+ 4.50
M Fenton	13-143	9.1	- 38.05	J Fortune		1-1	100.0	+ 1.00
G Duffield	3-11	27.3	- 0.42	Mr G Lewis		1-1	100.0	+ 3.00
D Moffatt	2-2	100.0	+ 32.00	K Fallon		1-3	33.3	+ 12.00
A Munro	2-13	15.4	+ 2.00	J O'Dwyer		1-14	7.1	- 7.00

L Dettori	0-7	N Varley	0-2	Mrs G Bell	0-1
R Hills	0-5	B Doyle	0-1	Mrs L Lawson	0-1
A Mackay	0-4	D Harrison	0-1	N Connorton	0-1
D Biggs	0-4	D Wright	0-1	P Scudamore	0-1
T Quinn	0-4	G Carter	0-1	R Adams	0-1
F Norton	0-2	J Quinn	0-1	R Cochrane	0-1
J Carroll	0-2	J Reid	0-1	S O'Gorman	0 1
J Weaver	0-2	J Tate	0-1	S Whitworth	0-1
K Darley	0-2	L Piggott	0-1	W R Swinburn	0-1
M Roberts	0-2	M Baird	0-1	W Ryan	0-1

COURSE RECORD

	Total W-R	Non-Handicaps 2-y-o	3-y-o+	Handicaps 2-y-o	3-y-o+	Per cent	£1 Level Stake
Hamilton	7-13	4-5	3-4	0-1	0-3	53.8	+ 4.38
Newmarket	4-51	0-16	1-6	1-3	2-26	7.8	+ 0.75
Beverley	3-6	0-2	0-0	0-0	3-4	50.0	+ 16.50
Leicester	3-19	1-3	1-7	0-2	1-7	15.8	+ 21.00
Southwell (AW)	3-22	0-4	2-7	0-0	1-11	13.6	- 4.06
Catterick	2-5	1-2	0-1	1-1	0-1	40.0	+ 13.91
Salisbury	2-11	0-2	1-3	0-0	1-6	18.2	0.00
Windsor	2-14	2-4	0-3	0-1	0-6	14.3	- 9.65
Newbury	2-16	1-5	0-2	0-2	1-7	12.5	- 1.50
Yarmouth	2-21	1-3	0-1	0-4	1-13	9.5	- 3.00
Edinburgh	1-1	0-0	0-0	0-0	1-1	100.0	+ 1.20
Bath	1-5	0-1	1-2	0-1	0-1	20.0	- 1.00
Chester	1-5	1-3	0-1	0-0	0-1	20.0	- 0.67
Epsom	1-7	1-2	0-1	0-1	0-3	14.3	- 1.50
Lingfield	1-8	1-3	0-0	0-1	0-4	12.5	- 4.50
York	1-8	0-1	0-2	0-2	1-3	12.5	- 3.50
Goodwood	1-9	0-2	0-1	0-0	1-6	11.1	- 5.00
Warwick	1-9	1-4	0-1	0-1	0-3	11.1	- 2.00
Southwell (Turf)	1-10	1-3	0-2	0-0	0-5	10.0	- 3.00
Ripon	1-11	0-4	0-1	0-0	1-6	9.1	- 2.00
Haydock	1-16	0-2	0-3	0-1	1-10	6.3	- 5.00
Nottingham	1-16	1-6	0-1	0-1	0-8	6.3	- 13.50

Doncaster	0-14	Newcastle	0-7	Pontefract	0-3
Folkestone	0-9	Ascot	0-6	Thirsk	0-2
Sandown	0-9	Ayr	0-5	Chepstow	0-1
Redcar	0-8	Kempton	0-5		
Brighton	0-7	Lingfield (AW)	0-5		

WINNING HORSES

	Age	Races Run	1st	2nd	3rd	Unpl	Win £
Royal Insignia	2	8	2	1	1	4	18,300
Bay Queen	3	12	4	1	1	6	15,475
Duveen	3	14	5	2	1	6	15,220
Petula	2	4	2	1	1	0	12,748
Persian Brave	3	6	2	0	3	1	11,510
King Curan	2	4	2	0	0	2	8,578
Marros Mill	3	9	2	1	3	3	7,716
Isabella Sharp	2	9	2	1	3	3	7,481
King Paris	3	12	2	2	0	8	7,099
Indian Dreamer	2	8	2	1	1	4	6,933
Yunus Emre	3	10	2	0	1	7	5,819
Princess Oberon	3	10	1	2	1	6	5,428
Orange Place	2	6	2	1	0	3	5,272
Riz Biz	3	8	1	0	1	6	5,020
Persian Affair	2	5	1	0	0	4	3,676
Lord Nitrogen	3	2	1	0	0	1	3,483
Manila Bay	3	5	1	1	1	2	3,465
Pampered Guest	2	3	1	0	0	2	3,377
Puget Dancer	3	8	1	0	1	6	3,236
Home From The Hill	3	6	1	0	1	4	3,132
Titania's Dance	2	3	1	0	0	2	2,669
Captain Starlight	2	5	1	2	0	2	2,601
Siganca	2	4	1	0	0	3	2,512
Admiring	2	6	1	1	0	4	2,259
Green's Fair	3	15	1	4	1	9	2,070

WINNING OWNERS

	Races Won	Value £		Races Won	Value £
Fahd Salman	3	21,765	Archer Van & Truck Hire Ltd	2	5,272
B J Warren	4	15,475	Anthony Rizzo	1	5,020
Mrs D Weatherby	5	15,220	R D A Kelly	1	3,676
M A Khan	2	12,748	John Purcell	1	3,483
Persian Partnership	2	11,510	J L C Pearce	1	3,377
Billy Maguire	2	8,578	W J P Jackson	1	3,236
R P B Michaelson	2	8,029	Capt B W Bell	1	3,132
Alasdair Simpson	2	7,716	Miss Lucille Boden	1	2,669
Christopher Wright	2	7,481	Mrs B Long	1	2,512
Mrs Pauline Karpidas	2	7,099	Friendly Society	1	2,259
R B Holt	2	6,933	Richard Green (Fine Paintings)	1	2,070
Yucel Birol	2	5,819			

Favourites	17-53	32.1%	- 10.14	Total winning prize-money	£165,076
Longest winning sequence			2	Average SP of winner	5.7/1
Longest losing sequence			51	Return on stakes invested	-22.8%
1992 Form	39-327	11.9%	-120.01	1990 Form	21-200	10.5%	- 17.64
1991 Form	43-278	15.5%	+ 9.14	1989 Form	18-142	12.7%	- 36.27

J A BENNETT (Wantage, Oxon)

	No. of Horses	Races Run	1st	2nd	3rd	Unpl	Per cent	£1 Level Stake
2-y-o	2	4	0	0	0	4	-	- 4.00
3-y-o	4	20	0	1	2	17	-	- 20.00
4-y-o+	11	59	3	4	1	51	5.1	- 25.25
Totals	17	83	3	5	3	72	3.6	- 49.25

Jan	Feb	Mar	Apr	May	Jun	Jul	Aug	Sep	Oct/Nov
1-8	0-6	0-7	0-7	1-13	1-13	0-10	0-6	0-8	0-5

Winning Jockeys	W-R	£1 Level Stake			W-R	£1 Level Stake
W Newnes	1-4	+ 5.00	Miss A Purdy		1-11	+ 10.00
J Weaver	1-4	- 0.25				

Winning Course		W-R	£1 Level Stake
Southwell (AW)		3-17	+ 16.75

Winning Horses	Age	Races Run	1st	2nd	3rd	Unpl	Win £
Superlativemaximus	5	6	2	2	1	1	6,325
Ripsnorter	4	12	1	2	0	9	2,511

Favourites	1-3	33.3%	+ 0.75	Total winning prize-money	£8,836

1992 Form	1-61	1.6%	- 55.00	1990 Form	0-24		
1991 Form	2-30	6.7%	- 7.00	1989 Form	0-31		

R A BENNETT (Maidenhead, Berks)

	No. of Horses	Races Run	1st	2nd	3rd	Unpl	Per cent	£1 Level Stake
2-y-o	0	0	0	0	0	0	-	0.00
3-y-o	0	0	0	0	0	0	-	0.00
4-y-o+	3	25	1	1	1	22	4.0	- 17.00
Totals	3	25	1	1	1	22	4.0	- 17.00

Jan	Feb	Mar	Apr	May	Jun	Jul	Aug	Sep	Oct/Nov
0-0	0-0	0-0	0-3	0-5	1-8	0-8	0-1	0-0	0-0

Winning Jockey	W-R	£1 Level Stake	Winning Course	W-R	£1 Level Stake
M Roberts	1-1	+ 7.00	Kempton	1-1	+ 7.00

Winning Horse	Age	Races Run	1st	2nd	3rd	Unpl	Win £
Anatroccolo	6	11	1	1	0	9	3,288

Favourites	0-1		Total winning prize-money	£3,288

1992 Form	1-23	4.3%	- 15.50	1990 Form	4-116	3.4%	- 84.75
1991 Form	1-73	1.4%	- 62.00	1989 Form	1-35	2.9%	- 14.00

C J BENSTEAD (Epsom, Surrey)

	No. of Horses	Races Run	1st	2nd	3rd	Unpl	Per cent	£1 Level Stake
2-y-o	5	14	0	0	3	11	-	- 14.00
3-y-o	6	37	2	2	3	30	5.4	- 32.87
4-y-o+	5	40	7	7	3	23	17.5	- 3.42
Totals	16	91	9	9	9	64	9.9	- 50.29

Jan	Feb	Mar	Apr	May	Jun	Jul	Aug	Sep	Oct/Nov
0-1	0-1	0-3	0-9	3-12	4-15	2-15	0-13	0-15	0-7

Winning Jockeys	W-R	£1 Level Stake		W-R	£1 Level Stake
G Duffield	2-4	+ 9.00	T Quinn	1-8	- 6.17
P Robinson	2-8	+ 1.75	R Hills	1-8	- 5.37
R Cochrane	1-1	+ 5.50	W Carson	1-19	- 17.50
C Rutter	1-2	+ 3.50			

Winning Courses					
Brighton	3-3	+ 9.25	Kempton	1-6	+ 0.50
Doncaster	1-1	+ 0.50	Newmarket	1-9	- 2.00
Epsom	1-3	+ 6.00	Windsor	1-10	- 8.17
Folkestone	1-4	- 1.37			

Winning Horses	Age	Races Run	1st	2nd	3rd	Unpl	Win £
Deevee	4	10	5	1	1	3	17,852
Mahrajan	9	7	2	1	0	4	6,755
Jalib	3	6	1	0	0	5	2,977
Aroom	3	9	1	1	2	5	2,898

Favourites	5-10	50.0%	+ 2.71	Total winning prize-money		£30,481

1992 Form	9-124	7.3%	- 31.25	1990 Form	6-161	3.7%	-124.00
1991 Form	5-99	5.1%	- 62.00	1989 Form	9-111	8.1%	- 24.50

W BENTLEY (Middleham, North Yorks)

	No. of Horses	Races Run	1st	2nd	3rd	Unpl	Per cent	£1 Level Stake
2-y-o	3	6	0	0	0	6	-	- 6.00
3-y-o	1	14	1	1	3	9	7.1	- 10.00
4-y-o+	1	3	0	0	0	3	-	- 3.00
Totals	5	23	1	1	3	18	4.3	- 19.00

Jan	Feb	Mar	Apr	May	Jun	Jul	Aug	Sep	Oct/Nov
0-0	0-0	0-0	1-3	0-6	0-8	0-3	0-0	0-2	0-1

Bentley W

Winning Jockey	W-R	£1 Level Stake	Winning Course	W-R	£1 Level Stake
G Duffield	1-2	+ 2.00	Hamilton	1-5	- 1.00

Winning Horse	Age	Races Run	1st	2nd	3rd	Unpl	Win £
The Premier Expres	3	14	1	1	3	9	2,243

Favourites	1-3	33.3%	+ 1.00	Total winning prize-money		£2,243

1992 Form	0-12		1990 Form	1-53	1.9%	- 44.00
1991 Form	0-22		1989 Form	1-61	1.6%	- 56.50

J BERRY (Cockerham, Lancs)

	No. of Horses	Races Run	1st	2nd	3rd	Unpl	Per cent	£1 Level Stake
2-y-o	63	353	48	48	39	218	13.6	- 84.52
3-y-o	38	279	54	40	42	143	19.4	- 1.86
4-y-o+	21	174	30	28	17	99	17.2	+ 6.19
Totals	122	806	132	116	98	460	16.4	- 80.19

BY MONTH

2-y-o	W-R	Per cent	£1 Level Stake	3-y-o	W-R	Per cent	£1 Level Stake
January	0-0	-	0.00	January	1-8	12.5	+ 1.50
February	0-0	-	0.00	February	2-5	40.0	+ 5.44
March	1-8	12.5	- 1.00	March	7-18	38.9	+ 2.99
April	6-29	20.7	- 6.84	April	8-32	25.0	+ 37.00
May	7-40	17.5	- 12.13	May	10-45	22.2	- 2.32
June	5-54	9.3	- 29.20	June	7-40	17.5	- 6.37
July	7-64	10.9	- 24.50	July	8-54	14.8	- 23.13
August	8-66	12.1	- 35.92	August	7-33	21.2	+ 13.27
September	7-49	14.3	+ 12.25	September	4-32	12.5	- 18.24
Oct/Nov	7-43	16.3	+ 12.82	Oct/Nov	0-12	-	- 12.00

4-y-o+	W-R	Per cent	£1 Level Stake	Totals	W-R	Per cent	£1 Level Stake
January	2-10	20.0	- 2.00	January	3-18	16.7	- 0.50
February	0-5	-	- 5.00	February	2-10	20.0	+ 0.44
March	4-10	40.0	+ 34.50	March	12-36	33.3	+ 36.49
April	4-17	23.5	+ 4.69	April	18-78	23.1	+ 34.85
May	4-33	12.1	- 7.00	May	21-118	17.8	- 21.45
June	2-21	9.5	- 17.73	June	14-115	12.2	- 53.30
July	6-27	22.2	+ 1.50	July	21-145	14.5	- 46.13
August	6-23	26.1	+ 8.48	August	21-122	17.2	- 14.17
September	2-16	12.5	+ 0.75	September	13-97	13.4	- 5.24
Oct/Nov	0-12	-	- 12.00	Oct/Nov	7-67	10.4	- 11.18

38

DISTANCE

2-y-o	W-R	Per cent	£1 Level Stake	3-y-o	W-R	Per cent	£1 Level Stake
5f-6f	48-292	16.4	- 23.52	5f-6f	42-199	21.1	+ 5.84
7f-8f	0-59	-	- 59.00	7f-8f	10-59	16.9	+ 4.67
9f-13f	0-2	-	- 2.00	9f-13f	2-18	11.1	- 9.37
14f+	0-0	-	0.00	14f+	0-3	-	- 3.00

4-y-o+	W-R	Per cent	£1 Level Stake	Totals	W-R	Per cent	£1 Level Stake
5f-6f	23-136	16.9	+ 3.77	5f-6f	113-627	18.0	- 13.91
7f-8f	7-33	21.2	+ 7.42	7f-8f	17-151	11.3	- 46.91
9f-13f	0-4	-	- 4.00	9f-13f	2-24	8.3	- 15.37
14f+	0-1	-	- 1.00	14f+	0-4	-	- 4.00

TYPE OF RACE

Non-Handicaps	W-R	Per cent	£1 Level Stake	Handicaps	W-R	Per cent	£1 Level Stake
2-y-o	33-244	13.5	- 64.24	2-y-o	8-49	16.3	- 0.33
3-y-o	29-111	26.1	+ 22.60	3-y-o	20-134	14.9	- 7.16
4-y-o+	12-45	26.7	- 3.89	4-y-o+	14-106	13.2	+ 14.50
Selling	12-81	14.8	- 36.42	Selling	2-14	14.3	+ 7.50
Apprentice	0-4	-	- 4.00	Apprentice	1-15	6.7	- 11.75
Amat/Ladies	0-0	-	0.00	Amat/Ladies	1-3	33.3	+ 3.00
Totals	86-485	17.7	- 85.95	Totals	46-321	14.3	+ 5.76

COURSE GRADE

	W-R	Per cent	£1 Level Stake
Group 1	36-251	14.3	+ 1.19
Group 2	27-149	18.1	+ 18.07
Group 3	33-168	19.6	- 24.23
Group 4	36-238	15.1	- 75.22

FIRST TIME OUT

	W-R	Per cent	£1 Level Stake
2-y-o	5-62	8.1	- 35.25
3-y-o	10-35	28.6	+ 24.49
4-y-o+	4-18	22.2	+ 15.50
Totals	19-115	16.5	+ 4.74

JOCKEYS RIDING

	W-R	Per cent	£1 Level Stake		W-R	Per cent	£1 Level Stake
J Carroll	72-391	18.4	- 21.98	G Hind	1-1	100.0	+ 12.00
G Carter	15-99	15.2	- 20.92	L Dettori	1-2	50.0	+ 3.00
J Fortune	8-57	14.0	+ 15.32	W R Swinburn	1-2	50.0	+ 4.50
P Roberts	6-51	11.8	- 26.09	O Pears	1-2	50.0	- 0.09
W Carson	4-14	28.6	- 0.83	D Holland	1-4	25.0	+ 9.00
T Quinn	4-15	26.7	- 0.43	J Weaver	1-5	20.0	0.00
Emma O'Gorman	4-21	19.0	+ 0.50	K Darley	1-6	16.7	+ 2.50
N Carlisle	3-13	23.1	+ 15.50	A Munro	1-7	14.3	+ 1.00
L Charnock	3-23	13.0	+ 2.00	L Piggott	1-8	12.5	- 6.09
Pat Eddery	2-18	11.1	- 11.33	G Duffield	1-9	11.1	- 5.75
Miss I D W Jones	1-1	100.0	+ 5.00				

Ruth Coulter	0-9	A Clark	0-1	Mr D Parker	0-1
P Fessey	0-7	A Daly	0-1	Mr J Berry	0-1
Alex Greaves	0-4	Claire Balding	0-1	N Connorton	0-1
N Adams	0-4	D Nicholls	0-1	N Day	0-1
B Crossley	0-3	G Bardwell	0-1	P Robinson	0-1
Dale Gibson	0-3	J Reid	0-1	R Hills	0-1
J Fanning	0-3	J Tate	0-1	S Giles	0-1
D McKeown	0-2	J Williams	0-1	W Ryan	0-1
J Lowe	0-2	M Hills	0-1		
S D Williams	0-2	Miss D J Jones	0-1		

COURSE RECORD

	Total W-R	Non-Handicaps 2-y-o	Non-Handicaps 3 y o	Handicaps 2-y-o	Handicaps 3-y-o+	Per cent	£1 Level Stake
Hamilton	14-65	3-23	8-18	1-3	2-21	21.5	- 17.00
Southwell (AW)	8-62	6-24	1-13	0-0	1-25	12.9	- 18.62
Doncaster	7-28	1-9	1-6	0-1	5-12	25.0	+ 44.50
Haydock	7-37	1-13	2-8	2-4	2-12	18.9	+ 10.08
Lingfield (AW)	6-21	0-1	2-9	0-1	4-10	28.6	+ 4.69
Carlisle	6-23	1-8	3-11	0-0	2-4	26.1	- 2.27
Ripon	6-33	1-17	2-5	0-1	3-10	18.2	+ 11.50
Catterick	6-48	0-17	3-12	1-5	2-14	12.5	- 17.67
Lingfield	5-13	1-5	2-4	0-0	2-4	38.5	+ 9.32
Chester	5-29	2-12	0-2	1-3	2-12	17.2	+ 2.00
Newcastle	5-34	2-15	3-9	0-2	0-8	14.7	- 19.18
Redcar	5-38	3-18	1-6	0-4	1-10	13.2	+ 4.50
Edinburgh	5-43	2-20	2-6	0-2	1-15	11.6	- 12.15
Ayr	5-48	3-15	2-9	0-2	0-22	10.4	- 7.00
Nottingham	4-19	2-12	0-4	2-2	0-1	21.1	+ 10.25
Beverley	4-23	3-15	1-5	0-2	0-1	17.4	- 9.00
Southwell (Turf)	3-15	0-8	2-4	0-1	1-2	20.0	- 7.37
Leicester	3-17	0-6	2-5	1-3	0-3	17.6	- 6.50
Pontefract	3-25	2-10	1-5	0-3	0-7	12.0	- 3.00
Thirsk	3-26	1-11	1-5	0-0	1-10	11.5	- 13.25
Bath	2-3	1-1	1-1	0-0	0-1	66.7	+ 3.79
Kempton	2-6	0-3	1-2	0-0	1-1	33.3	+ 1.38
Brighton	2-8	0-3	0-0	1-2	1-3	25.0	+ 1.67
Epsom	2-8	0-1	1-1	0-0	1-6	25.0	+ 6.91
Yarmouth	2-10	0-5	2-3	0-1	0-1	20.0	- 2.27
Sandown	2-14	0-2	1-6	0-1	1-5	14.3	- 3.00
Goodwood	2-18	0-3	0-3	1-2	1-10	11.1	- 0.50
Salisbury	1-2	0-0	0-1	0-0	1-1	50.0	+ 2.33
Folkestone	1-5	0-2	1-3	0-0	0-0	20.0	- 3.33
Newbury	1-5	0-0	0-2	0-1	1-2	20.0	+ 3.50
Windsor	1-6	1-4	0-0	0-0	0-2	16.7	- 0.50
Ascot	1-12	1-3	0-2	0-0	0-7	8.3	- 8.25
Newmarket	1-20	0-1	1-7	0-4	0-8	5.0	- 10.00
York	1-20	1-3	0-1	0-1	0-15	5.0	- 16.25
Warwick	1-21	0-10	1-6	0-2	0-3	4.8	- 18.50
Uttoxeter	0-1						

WINNING HORSES

	Age	Races Run	1st	2nd	3rd	Unpl	Win £
Paris House	4	5	2	2	1	0	55,557
Cee-Jay-Ay	6	14	2	3	3	6	27,696
Gorinsky	5	13	4	2	1	6	26,842
Amron	6	10	3	0	0	7	26,321
Lucky Parkes	3	10	6	2	2	0	23,602
Selhurstpark Flyer	2	8	4	1	1	2	23,249
Palacegate Jack	2	8	3	2	1	2	21,001
Laurel Queen	5	14	6	2	1	5	18,667
Margaret's Gift	3	11	2	0	4	5	18,635
Jimmy The Skunk	2	11	6	0	2	3	15,901
Mr M-E-N	2	7	3	0	1	3	15,641
Miss Whittingham	3	19	5	6	3	5	14,838
Palacegate Touch	3	14	4	2	0	8	14,163
Sabre Rattler	3	8	2	1	1	4	13,227
Press The Bell	3	12	4	2	2	4	12,130
Heaven-Liegh-Grey	5	7	2	0	0	5	11,512
Bella Parkes	2	8	3	1	1	3	10,075
White Creek	3	14	4	1	1	8	9,969
Palacegate Jo	2	10	3	4	0	3	9,865
Best Kept Secret	2	8	3	2	1	2	9,327
Trentesimo	3	7	4	0	0	3	9,273
Monkey's Wedding	2	13	3	4	0	6	9,034
Anusha	3	8	3	0	2	3	8,792
The Fernhill Flyer	2	11	3	3	1	4	8,568
Palacegate Episode	3	4	1	3	0	0	8,090
Dokkha Oyston	5	14	3	1	1	9	8,017
Garnock Valley	3	8	2	0	1	5	8,015
Daaniera	3	6	3	1	1	1	7,138
Soba Guest	4	12	3	1	2	6	7,038
Murray's Mazda	4	11	3	4	0	4	6,656
Tuscan Dawn	3	8	2	3	2	1	6,638
Killy's Filly	3	14	2	5	2	5	5,678
Fylde Flyer	4	12	1	1	0	10	5,061
Floating Trial	2	15	2	4	1	8	5,046
Raggerty	3	4	2	0	0	2	4,643
Randonneur	2	3	2	0	0	1	4,486
Teetotaller	2	4	1	1	1	1	3,980
Antonias Folly	2	8	1	3	0	4	3,915
Iva's Flyer	2	8	1	1	1	5	3,913
Monkey Music	2	9	1	1	2	5	3,524
Zanzara	2	2	1	0	0	1	3,501
Miss Amy Lou	2	3	1	0	0	2	3,407
Sudden Spin	3	9	1	0	2	6	3,210
Mister Bloy	2	6	1	0	1	4	3,179
First Play	3	4	1	0	0	3	3,173
Two Moves In Front	3	10	1	0	2	7	3,114
Our Mica	3	9	1	2	1	5	3,106
Never In The Red	5	9	1	1	2	5	3,080
Frisky Miss	2	5	1	3	1	0	2,905
Stephensons Rocket	2	6	1	0	2	3	2,851
Laurel Romeo	2	11	1	1	1	8	2,422

Palacegate Sunset	3	9	1	0	4	4	2,243
Charity Express	3	2	1	0	1	0	2,243
Cockerham Ranger	3	2	1	0	0	1	2,070
Bev's Folly	2	1	1	0	0	0	2,070
Daily Star	2	9	1	3	0	5	2,070
Mad About Men	2	7	1	0	1	5	1,903
Drumdonna	3	15	1	5	0	9	1,548

WINNING OWNERS

	Races Won	Value £		Races Won	Value £
P E T Chandler	2	55,557	Manny Bernstein (Racing) Ltd	3	9,327
Palacegate Corporation Ltd	12	55,362	Yahya Nasib	3	8,792
Richard Jinks	5	34,734	P J Evans	3	8,568
Joseph Heler	9	33,677	Miss Antonia Taverner	2	6,638
Chris Deuters	5	27,164	Raymond Kilgour Holdings Ltd	2	5,678
William Robertson	4	26,842	Blackpool Gazette & Herald Ltd	1	5,061
Roy Peebles	3	26,321	David Fish	2	5,046
Laurel (Leisure) Ltd	7	21,089	Mrs M Taylor	1	4,710
Mrs T G Holdcroft	2	18,635	Norman Jackson	2	4,643
H B Hughes	3	16,406	J Nixon	2	4,486
J David Abell	6	15,901	Highflyers	1	3,980
J W Barrett	5	14,838	Mrs Iva Winton	1	3,913
Murray Grubb	6	14,672	Skyline Racing Ltd	1	3,501
Robert Aird	4	14,209	Countess Of Lonsdale	1	3,210
Manchester Evening News Ltd	3	12,834	Keith H Ewbank	1	3,173
B R Allen	5	12,680	Mike Dodds	1	3,106
The Monkey Racing Club Ltd	4	12,558	Mrs Margaret Sinanan	1	2,905
Sydney Mason	4	12,130	John Stephenson & Sons (Nelson)	1	2,851
Peter M Dodd	2	11,512	Mrs Beverley Thompson	1	2,070
J Berry	5	11,451	Express Newspapers Plc	1	2,070
J K Brown	4	9,969	Mrs Norma Peebles	1	1,548

Favourites	62-164	37.8%	+ 9.98	Total winning prize-money	£553,814
Longest winning sequence			4	Average SP of winner	4.5/1
Longest losing sequence			46	Return on stakes invested	-9.9%
1992 Form	107-800	13.4%	-164.48	1990 Form 127-807 15.7%	-158.61
1991 Form	143-837	17.1%	-184.88	1989 Form 92-645 14.3%	-184.22

J D BETHELL (Middleham, North Yorks)

	No. of Horses	Races Run	1st	2nd	3rd	Unpl	Per cent	£1 Level Stake
2-y-o	8	29	0	2	4	23	-	- 29.00
3-y-o	8	52	4	3	6	39	7.7	- 11.00
4-y-o+	6	41	3	2	3	33	7.3	- 8.00
Totals	22	122	7	7	13	95	5.7	- 48.00

Jan	Feb	Mar	Apr	May	Jun	Jul	Aug	Sep	Oct/Nov
0-0	0-0	0-1	1-7	1-21	2-20	1-22	2-15	0-22	0-14

Winning Jockeys	W-R	£1 Level Stake		W-R	£1 Level Stake
W Carson	2-11	+ 5.00	J Carroll	1-10	+ 5.00
A Munro	2-12	+ 8.00	L Charnock	1-11	- 3.00
G Duffield	1-3	+ 12.00			

Winning Courses					
Chepstow	1-1	+ 8.00	Ayr	1-7	+ 8.00
Windsor	1-3	+ 8.00	Newcastle	1-10	+ 5.00
Chester	1-4	+ 3.00	York	1-12	- 3.00
Newmarket	1-6	+ 2.00			

Winning Horses	Age	Races Run	1st	2nd	3rd	Unpl	Win £
True Precision	3	10	2	1	1	6	27,995
Hunters Of Brora	3	6	2	0	2	2	11,503
Double Echo	5	7	1	0	0	6	10,673
Tumbling (USA)	5	8	1	0	1	6	3,276
Coureur	4	8	1	1	0	6	3,262

Favourites	0-7	Total winning prize-money	£56,708

1992 Form	5-112	4.5%	- 70.50	1990 Form	10-120	8.3%	- 48.00
1991 Form	11-156	7.1%	- 21.62	1989 Form	11-120	9.2%	- 12.12

P J BEVAN (Uttoxeter, Staffs)

	No. of Horses	Races Run	1st	2nd	3rd	Unpl	Per cent	£1 Level Stake
2-y-o	1	2	0	0	0	2	-	- 2.00
3-y-o	1	3	1	0	0	2	33.3	+ 5.50
4-y-o+	4	16	2	0	2	12	12.5	- 0.50
Totals	6	21	3	0	2	16	14.3	+ 3.00

Jan	Feb	Mar	Apr	May	Jun	Jul	Aug	Sep	Oct/Nov
0-0	0-0	0-0	0-0	0-1	1-3	1-4	1-5	0-5	0-3

43

Bevan P J

Winning Jockeys	W-R	£1 Level Stake		W-R	£1 Level Stake
C Hawksley	2-14	+ 1.50	D Griffiths	1-1	+ 7.50

Winning Courses					
Newmarket	1-1	+ 7.00	Southwell (AW)	1-3	+ 4.50
Chester	1-3	+ 5.50			

Winning Horses	Age	Races Run	1st	2nd	3rd	Unpl	Win £
Heart Of Spain	3	3	1	0	0	2	2,975
My Rossini	4	6	1	0	1	4	2,794
Smiles Ahead	5	5	1	0	1	3	2,070

Favourites	0-0		Total winning prize-money		£7,839

1992 Form	2-16	12.5%	+ 2.00	1990 Form	0-14		
1991 Form	1-20	5.0%	- 15.50	1989 Form	0-23		

M BLANSHARD (Upper Lambourn, Berks)

	No. of Horses	Races Run	1st	2nd	3rd	Unpl	Per cent	£1 Level Stake
2-y-o	6	28	0	0	3	25	-	- 28.00
3-y-o	4	39	1	4	3	31	2.6	- 35.00
4-y-o+	5	55	5	8	7	35	9.1	- 6.00
Totals	15	122	6	12	13	91	4.9	- 69.00

Jan	Feb	Mar	Apr	May	Jun	Jul	Aug	Sep	Oct/Nov
0-3	0-1	0-1	0-9	0-16	2-8	0-31	2-22	0-19	2-12

Winning Jockeys	W-R	£1 Level Stake		W-R	£1 Level Stake
J Quinn	2-23	- 9.50	R Cochrane	1-18	- 5.00
K Fallon	1-2	+ 5.50	N Adams	1-18	- 14.00
J Williams	1-3	+ 12.00			

Winning Courses					
Chester	2-6	+ 7.50	Chepstow	1-8	+ 7.00
Newcastle	1-1	+ 6.50	Brighton	1-10	- 6.00
Windsor	1-5	+ 8.00			

Winning Horses	Age	Races Run	1st	2nd	3rd	Unpl	Win £
Welshman	7	9	3	0	3	3	17,487
Sunday's Hill	4	12	1	0	1	10	3,405
Kensworth Lady	3	11	1	1	1	8	3,173
Taunting	5	17	1	3	2	11	2,010

Favourites	2-7	28.6%	+ 0.50	Total winning prize-money		£26,074

1992 Form	8-179	4.5%	- 88.25	1990 Form	5-128	3.9%	- 76.50
1991 Form	6-136	4.4%	- 85.00	1989 Form	8-120	6.7%	- 10.50

C B B BOOTH (Flaxton, North Yorks)

	No. of Horses	Races Run	1st	2nd	3rd	Unpl	Per cent	£1 Level Stake
2-y-o	3	8	0	0	0	8	-	- 8.00
3-y-o	8	46	1	1	4	40	2.2	- 40.00
4-y-o+	1	4	1	0	0	3	25.0	+ 7.00
Totals	12	58	2	1	4	51	3.4	- 41.00

Jan	Feb	Mar	Apr	May	Jun	Jul	Aug	Sep	Oct/Nov
1-3	0-3	0-2	0-3	0-7	1-6	0-7	0-7	0-10	0-10

Winning Jockeys	W-R	£1 Level Stake			W-R	£1 Level Stake
L Charnock	1-8	+ 3.00	K Fallon		1-9	- 3.00

Winning Courses						
Redcar	1-7	- 1.00	Southwell (AW)		1-8	+ 3.00

Winning Horses	Age	Races Run	1st	2nd	3rd	Unpl	Win £
Baliana	3	9	1	0	1	7	3,085
Innocent George	4	4	1	0	0	3	2,070

Favourites	0-2			Total winning prize-money			£5,155
1992 Form	3-80	3.8%	- 63.75	1990 Form	4-74	5.4%	- 48.50
1991 Form	5-59	8.5%	- 11.70	1989 Form	4-81	4.9%	- 60.50

J R BOSLEY (Bampton, Oxon)

	No. of Horses	Races Run	1st	2nd	3rd	Unpl	Per cent	£1 Level Stake
2-y-o	2	7	0	0	0	7	-	- 7.00
3-y-o	1	3	0	0	0	3	-	- 3.00
4-y-o+	5	24	3	4	3	14	12.5	+ 11.00
Totals	8	34	3	4	3	24	8.8	+ 1.00

Jan	Feb	Mar	Apr	May	Jun	Jul	Aug	Sep	Oct/Nov
0-0	0-0	0-0	0-0	1-1	0-4	0-8	1-7	1-4	0-10

Winning Jockey	W-R	£1 Level Stake			W-R	£1 Level Stake
Mrs S Bosley	3-14	+ 21.00				

Winning Courses						
Redcar	2-3	+ 19.00	Warwick		1-3	+ 10.00

Winning Horse	Age	Races Run	1st	2nd	3rd	Unpl	Win £
Pusey Street Boy	6	14	3	4	2	5	8,896

Favourites	0-1		Total winning prize-money		£8,896
1992 Form	0-27		1990 Form	0-22	
1991 Form	0-7		1989 Form	0-31	

R BOSS (Newmarket)

	No. of Horses	Races Run	1st	2nd	3rd	Unpl	Per cent	£1 Level Stake
2-y-o	12	40	4	4	4	28	10.0	- 19.50
3-y-o	5	36	3	6	1	26	8.3	- 18.75
4-y-o+	4	30	3	1	1	25	10.0	- 7.00
Totals	21	106	10	11	6	79	9.4	- 45.25

BY MONTH

2-y-o	W-R	Per cent	£1 Level Stake	3-y-o	W-R	Per cent	£1 Level Stake
January	0-0	-	0.00	January	0-0	-	0.00
February	0-0	-	0.00	February	0-1	-	- 1.00
March	1-1	100.0	+ 4.50	March	1-3	33.3	+ 0.75
April	1-6	16.7	- 1.50	April	0-7	-	- 7.00
May	0-2	-	- 2.00	May	0-4	-	- 4.00
June	1-5	20.0	+ 1.00	June	1-5	20.0	+ 0.50
July	0-5	-	- 5.00	July	1-5	20.0	+ 3.00
August	0-5	-	- 5.00	August	0-5	-	- 5.00
September	1-7	14.3	- 2.50	September	0-2	-	- 2.00
Oct/Nov	0-9	-	- 9.00	Oct/Nov	0-4	-	- 4.00

4-y-o+	W-R	Per cent	£1 Level Stake	Totals	W-R	Per cent	£1 Level Stake
January	0-1	-	- 1.00	January	0-1	-	- 1.00
February	0-2	-	- 2.00	February	0-3	-	- 3.00
March	0-1	-	- 1.00	March	2-5	40.0	+ 4.25
April	0-2	-	- 2.00	April	1-15	6.7	- 10.50
May	0-4	-	- 4.00	May	0-10	-	- 10.00
June	0-5	-	- 5.00	June	2-15	13.3	- 3.50
July	1-6	16.7	- 0.50	July	2-16	12.5	- 2.50
August	1-4	25.0	+ 7.00	August	1-14	7.1	- 3.00
September	1-3	33.3	+ 3.50	September	2-12	16.7	- 1.00
Oct/Nov	0-2	-	- 2.00	Oct/Nov	0-15	-	- 15.00

DISTANCE

2-y-o	W-R	Per cent	£1 Level Stake	3-y-o	W-R	Per cent	£1 Level Stake
5f-6f	4-24	16.7	- 3.50	5f-6f	1-12	8.3	- 6.50
7f-8f	0-16	-	- 16.00	7f-8f	0-9	-	- 9.00
9f-13f	0-0	-	0.00	9f-13f	2-14	14.3	- 2.25
14f+	0-0	-	0.00	14f+	0-1	-	- 1.00

4-y-o+	W-R	Per cent	£1 Level Stake	Totals	W-R	Per cent	£1 Level Stake
5f-6f	1-9	11.1	- 3.50	5f-6f	6-45	13.3	- 13.50
7f-8f	2-18	11.1	- 0.50	7f-8f	2-43	4.7	- 25.50
9f-13f	0-2	-	- 2.00	9f-13f	2-16	12.5	- 4.25
14f+	0-1	-	- 1.00	14f+	0-2	-	- 2.00

TYPE OF RACE

Non-Handicaps	W-R	Per cent	£1 Level Stake	Handicaps	W-R	Per cent	£1 Level Stake
2-y-o	4-36	11.1	- 15.50	2-y-o	0-4	-	- 4.00
3-y-o	1-13	7.7	- 9.25	3-y-o	2-21	9.5	- 7.50
4-y-o+	0-2	-	- 2.00	4-y-o+	3-27	11.1	- 4.00
Selling	0-1	-	- 1.00	Selling	0-1	-	- 1.00
Apprentice	0-0	-	0.00	Apprentice	0-0	-	0.00
Amat/Ladies	0-0	-	0.00	Amat/Ladies	0-1	-	- 1.00
Totals	5-52	9.6	- 27.75	Totals	5-54	9.3	- 17.50

COURSE GRADE

	W-R	Per cent	£1 Level Stake
Group 1	2-38	5.3	- 27.00
Group 2	2-20	10.0	- 4.50
Group 3	3-20	15.0	- 0.50
Group 4	3-28	10.7	- 13.25

FIRST TIME OUT

	W-R	Per cent	£1 Level Stake
2-y-o	1-12	8.3	- 6.50
3-y-o	0-5	-	- 5.00
4-y-o+	0-4	-	- 4.00
Totals	1-21	4.8	- 15.50

JOCKEYS RIDING

	W-R	Per cent	£1 Level Stake		W-R	Per cent	£1 Level Stake
W Woods	3-19	15.8	- 2.00	W Ryan	1-9	11.1	- 5.25
W Carson	2-5	40.0	+ 12.50	R Cochrane	1-11	9.1	- 5.50
T Quinn	1-2	50.0	+ 2.50	G Duffield	1-14	7.1	- 6.00
M Roberts	1-7	14.3	- 2.50				

Pat Eddery	0-6	D Holland	0-1	Mrs L Pearce	0-1
M Tebbutt	0-5	D McKeown	0-1	N Kennedy	0-1
L Dettori	0-3	D Wright	0-1	P Robinson	0-1
A Culhane	0-2	G Carter	0-1	R Hills	0-1
A Mackay	0-2	J Quinn	0-1	S Raymont	0-1
J Carroll	0-2	J Reid	0-1	Sandrine Tarrou	0-1
A Clark	0-1	J Weaver	0-1	T Sprake	0-1
A McGlone	0-1	K Fallon	0-1		
B Raymond	0-1	M Fenton	0-1		

COURSE RECORD

	Total W-R	Non-Handicaps 2-y-o	Non-Handicaps 3-y-o+	Handicaps 2-y-o	Handicaps 3-y-o+	Per cent	£1 Level Stake
Yarmouth	2-6	0-1	0-1	0-0	2-4	33.3	+ 7.50
Brighton	2-10	1-2	0-2	0-1	1-5	20.0	+ 5.50
Warwick	1-2	1-1	0-0	0-0	0-1	50.0	+ 3.50
Windsor	1-2	1-2	0-0	0-0	0-0	50.0	+ 4.00
York	1-2	1-1	0-0	0-0	0-1	50.0	+ 2.50
Southwell (Turf)	1-2	0-1	0-0	0-0	1-1	50.0	+ 3.50
Haydock	1-3	0-2	0-0	0-0	1-1	33.3	+ 3.50
Lingfield (AW)	1-7	0-0	1-3	0-1	0-3	14.3	- 3.25

Boss R

Newmarket	0-15	Beverley	0-3	Sandown	0-2
Folkestone	0-6	Newbury	0-3	Chester	0-1
Southwell (AW)	0-6	Pontefract	0-3	Edinburgh	0-1
Catterick	0-4	Redcar	0-3	Goodwood	0-1
Doncaster	0-4	Epsom	0-2	Kempton	0-1
Ripon	0-4	Lingfield	0-2	Leicester	0-1
Ayr	0-3	Newcastle	0-2		
Bath	0-3	Nottingham	0-2		

WINNING HORSES

	Age	Races Run	1st	2nd	3rd	Unpl	Win £
Caleman	4	12	2	0	1	9	13,157
Welsh Mist	2	5	2	0	0	3	6,836
Tutu Sixtysix	2	10	2	1	1	6	6,766
Daring Past	3	13	2	4	0	7	5,054
Prince Songline	3	13	1	2	1	9	3,558
Miss Haggis	4	8	1	1	0	6	3,202

WINNING OWNERS

	Races Won	Value £		Races Won	Value £
M Berger	2	13,157	Keith Sturgis	3	8,612
P Asquith	3	10,038	Mrs Ann Gover	2	6,766

Favourites	0-8		Total winning prize-money	£38,572

Longest winning sequence		1	Average SP of winner	5.1/1
Longest losing sequence		22	Return on stakes invested	-42.7%

1992 Form	9-110	8.2%	- 55.50	1990 Form	36-230	15.7%	- 40.88
1991 Form	18-194	9.3%	- 78.53	1989 Form	23-170	13.5%	+ 5.06

J F BOTTOMLEY (Malton, North Yorks)

	No. of Horses	Races Run	1st	2nd	3rd	Unpl	Per cent	£1 Level Stake
2-y-o	3	12	1	2	0	9	8.3	- 8.00
3-y-o	3	19	1	1	2	15	5.3	- 4.00
4-y-o+	6	19	0	2	2	15	-	- 19.00
Totals	12	50	2	5	4	39	4.0	- 31.00

Jan	Feb	Mar	Apr	May	Jun	Jul	Aug	Sep	Oct/Nov
0-1	0-0	0-0	0-3	0-4	1-12	0-7	0-8	0-5	1-10

Winning Jockeys	W-R	£1 Level Stake		W-R	£1 Level Stake
M Humphries	1-4	+ 11.00	L Charnock	1-29	- 25.00

Winning Courses	W-R	£1 Level Stake		W-R	£1 Level Stake
Ayr	1-1	+ 3.00	York	1-3	+ 12.00

Winning Horses	Age	Races Run	1st	2nd	3rd	Unpl	Win £
Merry Mermaid	3	13	1	1	1	10	7,044
Fort Erie	2	2	1	1	0	0	2,400

Favourites	1-3	33.3%	+ 1.00	Total winning prize-money		£9,444

1992 Form	3-53	5.7%	- 19.50	1990 Form	5-108	4.6%	- 57.25
1991 Form	4-94	4.3%	- 29.00	1989 Form	5-41	12.2%	+ 0.50

S R BOWRING (Edwinstowe, Notts)

	No. of Horses	Races Run	1st	2nd	3rd	Unpl	Per cent	£1 Level Stake
2-y-o	1	1	0	0	0	1	-	- 1.00
3-y-o	4	35	2	4	5	24	5.7	- 30.00
4-y-o+	6	55	6	10	6	33	10.9	- 9.50
Totals	11	91	8	14	11	58	8.8	- 40.50

Jan	Feb	Mar	Apr	May	Jun	Jul	Aug	Sep	Oct/Nov
1-7	2-15	1-6	1-10	1-9	0-5	2-11	0-9	0-10	0-9

Winning Jockeys	W-R	£1 Level Stake		W-R	£1 Level Stake
S Webster	3-23	+ 0.75	O Pears	1-1	+ 1.25
G Strange	3-45	- 27.00	B Russell	1-1	+ 5.50

Winning Courses	W-R	£1 Level Stake		W-R	£1 Level Stake
Southwell (AW)	6-43	- 7.50	Beverley	1-5	+ 6.00
Carlisle	1-3	+ 1.00			

Winning Horses	Age	Races Run	1st	2nd	3rd	Unpl	Win £
Sandmoor Denim	6	12	2	5	0	5	10,990
Strip Cartoon	5	24	3	4	3	14	7,994
Hershebar	3	17	2	4	2	9	4,371
Lincstone Boy	5	5	1	0	0	4	2,343

Favourites	2-7	28.6%	- 2.00	Total winning prize-money		£25,698

1992 Form	9-104	8.7%	+ 24.90	1990 Form	4-78	5.1%	- 6.00
1991 Form	2-56	3.6%	- 19.00	1989 Form	2-75	2.7%	- 53.00

J M BRADLEY (Chepstow, Gwent)

	No. of Horses	Races Run	1st	2nd	3rd	Unpl	Per cent	£1 Level Stake
2-y-o	2	7	0	0	0	7	-	- 7.00
3-y-o	1	2	0	0	0	2	-	- 2.00
4-y-o+	15	74	6	7	5	56	8.1	- 24.25
Totals	18	83	6	7	5	65	7.2	- 33.25

Jan	Feb	Mar	Apr	May	Jun	Jul	Aug	Sep	Oct/Nov
0-3	0-3	0-4	1-7	0-19	1-15	3-16	1-11	0-4	0-1

Winning Jockeys	W-R	£1 Level Stake				W-R	£1 Level Stake
Mark Denaro	3-17	+ 7.50		J Weaver		1-6	- 2.75
Mrs D McHale	1-1	+ 6.00		Michael Bradley		1-14	+ 1.00

Winning Courses							
Ripon	2-4	+ 14.00		Ayr		1-1	+ 2.25
Thirsk	2-4	+ 9.50		Southwell (AW)		1-10	+ 5.00

Winning Horses	Age	Races Run	1st	2nd	3rd	Unpl	Win £
Sooty Tern	6	16	3	5	2	6	11,034
Asterix	5	15	2	1	2	10	6,006
Royal Acclaim	8	8	1	0	0	7	2,070

Favourites	1-3	33.3%	+ 0.25	Total winning prize-money			£19,110
1992 Form	3-85	3.5%	- 46.00	1990 Form	4-73	5.5%	- 30.50
1991 Form	2-58	3.4%	- 26.00	1989 Form	1-86	1.2%	- 77.00

MRS S BRAMALL (Thirsk, North Yorks)

	No. of Horses	Races Run	1st	2nd	3rd	Unpl	Per cent	£1 Level Stake
2-y-o	0	0	0	0	0	0	-	0.00
3-y-o	1	5	1	0	0	4	20.0	+ 21.00
4-y-o+	2	3	0	0	0	3	-	- 3.00
Totals	3	8	1	0	0	7	12.5	+ 18.00

Jan	Feb	Mar	Apr	May	Jun	Jul	Aug	Sep	Oct/Nov
0-0	0-0	0-0	0-2	1-6	0-0	0-0	0-0	0-0	0-0

Winning Jockey	W-R	£1 Level Stake	Winning Course	W-R	£1 Level Stake
J Fortune	1-4	+ 22.00	Hamilton	1-1	+ 25.00

Winning Horse	Age	Races Run	1st	2nd	3rd	Unpl	Win £
Volunteer Point	3	5	1	0	0	4	2,427

Favourites	0-0		Total winning prize-money		£2,427
1992 Form	0-4		1991 Form	0-4	

G C BRAVERY (Newmarket)

	No. of Horses	Races Run	1st	2nd	3rd	Unpl	Per cent	£1 Level Stake
2-y-o	8	34	3	3	4	24	8.8	+ 2.00
3-y-o	6	28	0	4	2	22	-	- 28.00
4-y-o+	1	11	1	1	2	7	9.1	+ 6.00
Totals	15	73	4	8	8	53	5.5	- 20.00

Jan	Feb	Mar	Apr	May	Jun	Jul	Aug	Sep	Oct/Nov
0-0	0-0	1-3	0-9	0-14	1-8	0-10	1-12	1-9	0-8

Winning Jockeys	W-R	£1 Level Stake			W-R	£1 Level Stake
N Day	2-22	+ 0.50		F Norton	1-2	+ 24.00
D McCabe	1-2	+ 2.50				

Winning Courses	W-R	£1 Level Stake			W-R	£1 Level Stake
Ayr	1-1	+ 4.50		Southwell (AW)	1-4	+ 0.50
Warwick	1-4	+ 13.00		Nottingham	1-7	+ 19.00

Winning Horses	Age	Races Run	1st	2nd	3rd	Unpl	Win £
Stradishall	2	9	1	0	0	8	3,758
Martinosky	7	11	1	1	2	7	3,287
Hobart	2	2	1	0	0	1	3,011
Paradise News	2	5	1	1	1	2	1,534

Favourites	0-5		Total winning prize-money	£11,590

1992 Form	5-23	21.7%	+ 20.63

J J BRIDGER (Liphook, Hants)

	No. of Horses	Races Run	1st	2nd	3rd	Unpl	Per cent	£1 Level Stake
2-y-o	3	18	0	0	1	17	-	- 18.00
3-y-o	4	14	2	0	0	12	14.3	+ 27.00
4-y-o+	7	33	0	0	0	33	-	- 33.00
Totals	14	65	2	0	1	62	3.1	- 24.00

Jan	Feb	Mar	Apr	May	Jun	Jul	Aug	Sep	Oct/Nov
0-3	0-1	0-0	1-6	0-12	0-9	1-13	0-14	0-6	0-1

Winning Jockeys	W-R	£1 Level Stake			W-R	£1 Level Stake
Antoinette Armes	1-4	+ 3.00		G Bardwell	1-21	+ 13.00

Winning Courses	W-R	£1 Level Stake			W-R	£1 Level Stake
Newmarket	1-3	+ 4.00		Bath	1-6	+ 28.00

Bridger J J

Winning Horses	Age	Races Run	1st	2nd	3rd	Unpl	Win £
Perfect Passion	3	10	1	0	0	9	2,872
Air Command	3	2	1	0	0	1	2,406

Favourites	0-0			Total winning prize-money			£5,278

1992 Form	2-73	2.7%	- 53.37	1990 Form	2-57	3.5%	- 18.00
1991 Form	0-63			1989 Form	0-43		

W M BRISBOURNE (Great Ness, Salop)

	No. of Horses	Races Run	1st	2nd	3rd	Unpl	Per cent	£1 Level Stake
2-y-o	1	3	0	0	1	2	-	- 3.00
3-y-o	2	5	0	0	0	5	-	- 5.00
4-y-o+	3	24	2	3	1	18	8.3	- 1.00
Totals	6	32	2	3	2	25	6.3	- 9.00

Jan	Feb	Mar	Apr	May	Jun	Jul	Aug	Sep	Oct/Nov
0-0	0-0	0-1	0-1	0-5	1-4	0-9	1-3	0-4	0-5

Winning Jockeys	W-R	£1 Level Stake				W-R	£1 Level Stake
S Maloney	1-4	+ 6.00	A Garth			1-10	+ 3.00

Winning Courses	W-R	£1 Level Stake				W-R	£1 Level Stake
Haydock	1-3	+ 10.00	Nottingham			1-5	+ 5.00

Winning Horses	Age	Races Run	1st	2nd	3rd	Unpl	Win £
Princess Of Orange	4	10	1	2	0	7	2,870
Green's Cassatt	5	9	1	1	1	6	2,724

Favourites	0-1		Total winning prize-money		£5,594

1992 Form	2-27	7.4%	- 7.00	1991 Form	0-15

C E BRITTAIN (Newmarket)

	No. of Horses	Races Run	1st	2nd	3rd	Unpl	Per cent	£1 Level Stake
2-y-o	36	104	4	8	11	81	3.8	- 79.12
3-y-o	39	202	15	14	14	159	7.4	- 78.72
4-y-o+	24	131	15	7	12	97	11.5	+ 17.73
Totals	99	437	34	29	37	337	7.8	-140.11

BY MONTH

2-y-o	W-R	Per cent	£1 Level Stake	3-y-o	W-R	Per cent	£1 Level Stake
January	0-0	-	0.00	January	0-0	-	0.00
February	0-0	-	0.00	February	0-2	-	- 2.00
March	0-0	-	0.00	March	0-7	-	- 7.00
April	0-1	-	- 1.00	April	3-25	12.0	- 14.40
May	0-1	-	- 1.00	May	1-30	3.3	- 25.67
June	0-8	-	- 8.00	June	3-23	13.0	+ 0.75
July	1-19	5.3	- 8.00	July	2-38	5.3	- 9.40
August	0-21	-	- 21.00	August	3-30	10.0	- 0.50
September	1-32	3.1	- 27.50	September	3-30	10.0	- 3.50
Oct/Nov	2-22	9.1	- 12.62	Oct/Nov	0-17	-	- 17.00

4-y-o+	W-R	Per cent	£1 Level Stake	Totals	W-R	Per cent	£1 Level Stake
January	0-0	-	0.00	January	0-0	-	0.00
February	0-1	-	- 1.00	February	0-3	-	- 3.00
March	2-10	20.0	+ 5.63	March	2-17	11.8	- 1.37
April	3-17	17.6	+ 16.00	April	6-43	14.0	+ 0.60
May	2-17	11.8	- 6.90	May	3-48	6.3	- 33.57
June	3-15	20.0	+ 22.50	June	6-46	13.0	+ 15.25
July	1-18	5.6	- 12.00	July	4-75	5.3	- 29.40
August	1-21	4.8	- 15.50	August	4-72	5.6	- 37.00
September	1-15	6.7	- 9.00	September	5-77	6.5	- 40.00
Oct/Nov	2-17	11.8	+ 18.00	Oct/Nov	4-56	7.1	- 11.62

DISTANCE

2-y-o	W-R	Per cent	£1 Level Stake	3-y-o	W-R	Per cent	£1 Level Stake
5f-6f	3-43	7.0	- 29.12	5f-6f	0-18	-	- 18.00
7f-8f	1-60	1.7	- 49.00	7f-8f	7-89	7.9	- 18.57
9f-13f	0-1	-	- 1.00	9f-13f	7-79	8.9	- 29.15
14f+	0-0	-	0.00	14f+	1-16	6.3	- 13.00

4-y-o+	W-R	Per cent	£1 Level Stake	Totals	W-R	Per cent	£1 Level Stake
5f-6f	0-0	-	0.00	5f-6f	3-61	4.9	- 47.12
7f-8f	8-43	18.6	+ 60.00	7f-8f	16-192	8.3	- 7.47
9f-13f	7-75	9.3	- 29.37	9f-13f	14-155	9.0	- 59.52
14f+	0-13	-	- 13.00	14f+	1-29	3.4	- 26.00

TYPE OF RACE

Non-Handicaps	W-R	Per cent	£1 Level Stake	Handicaps	W-R	Per cent	£1 Level Stake
2-y-o	4-96	4.2	- 71.12	2-y-o	0-8	-	- 8.00
3-y-o	10-117	8.5	- 42.22	3-y-o	5-81	6.2	- 32.50
4-y-o+	7-44	15.9	+ 9.23	4-y-o+	7-85	8.2	+ 5.00
Selling	0-2	-	- 2.00	Selling	0-1	-	- 1.00
Apprentice	1-1	100.0	+ 4.50	Apprentice	0-2	-	- 2.00
Amat/Ladies	0-0	-	0.00	Amat/Ladies	0-0	-	0.00
Totals	22-260	8.5	-101.61	Totals	12-177	6.8	- 38.50

COURSE GRADE

	W-R	Per cent	£1 Level Stake
Group 1	21-290	7.2	- 93.16
Group 2	6-55	10.9	- 21.30
Group 3	6-70	8.6	- 16.65
Group 4	1-22	4.5	- 9.00

FIRST TIME OUT

	W-R	Per cent	£1 Level Stake
2-y-o	1-36	2.8	- 25.00
3-y-o	3-39	7.7	- 16.40
4-y-o+	3-24	12.5	+ 2.63
Totals	7-99	7.1	- 38.77

JOCKEYS RIDING

	W-R	Per cent	£1 Level Stake		W-R	Per cent	£1 Level Stake
B Doyle	11-145	7.6	- 8.57	B Marcus	2-26	7.7	- 6.50
M Roberts	7-91	7.7	- 57.39	M J Kinane	1-3	33.3	+ 18.00
W R Swinburn	4-22	18.2	- 1.25	J Weaver	1-5	20.0	- 2.00
A Munro	3-8	37.5	+ 17.00	R Cochrane	1-9	11.1	- 6.90
M Birch	3-19	15.8	- 0.50	L Dettori	1-16	6.3	+ 1.00

W Carson	0-13	M Hills	0-4	R Hills	0-2
J Penza	0-9	W Ryan	0-4	A Clark	0-1
G Duffield	0-6	C Asmussen	0-3	D Biggs	0-1
Pat Eddery	0-6	J Carroll	0-3	D Harrison	0-1
T Quinn	0-6	S Whitworth	0-3	D Wright	0-1
G Bardwell	0-5	D McKeown	0-2	Dale Gibson	0-1
J Quinn	0-5	J Reid	0-2	J Fortune	0-1
W Newnes	0-5	L Piggott	0-2	W Woods	0-1
B Raymond	0-4	Paul Eddery	0-2		

COURSE RECORD

	Total W-R	Non-Handicaps 2-y-o	3-y-o+	Handicaps 2-y-o	3-y-o+	Per cent	£1 Level Stake
Newmarket	5-89	1-32	3-32	0-2	1-23	5.6	- 26.50
Kempton	4-21	0-3	3-11	0-0	1-7	19.0	+ 8.83
York	3-31	2-6	0-9	0-1	1-15	9.7	- 6.62
Ascot	3-34	1-9	1-11	0-0	1-14	8.8	+ 15.00
Yarmouth	3-42	0-10	1-13	0-1	2-18	7.1	- 0.40
Brighton	2-9	0-0	1-2	0-0	1-7	22.2	+ 1.60
Lingfield	2-20	0-7	2-7	0-0	0-6	10.0	- 13.90
Doncaster	2-24	0-3	1-10	0-1	1-10	8.3	- 13.37
Chepstow	1-1	0-0	1-1	0-0	0-0	100.0	+ 2.75
Pontefract	1-4	0-1	1-2	0-0	0-1	25.0	+ 1.00
Nottingham	1-5	0-0	1-2	0-0	0-3	20.0	- 2.00
Redcar	1-7	0-2	0-1	0-0	1-4	14.3	+ 2.00
Epsom	1-8	0-1	1-4	0-0	0-3	12.5	- 2.50
Haydock	1-9	0-3	0-2	0-0	1-4	11.1	- 3.50
Lingfield (AW)	1-10	0-0	0-5	0-0	1-5	10.0	+ 3.00
Chester	1-11	0-1	1-6	0-1	0-3	9.1	- 3.00
Sandown	1-21	0-1	0-4	0-0	1-16	4.8	- 15.00
Newbury	1-28	0-4	1-14	0-1	0-9	3.6	- 24.50

Goodwood	0-21	Salisbury	0-4	Catterick	0-2
Leicester	0-14	Ayr	0-3	Newcastle	0-1
Folkestone	0-6	Ripon	0-3	Southwell (AW)	0-1
Beverley	0-4	Warwick	0-3	Thirsk	0-1

WINNING HORSES

		Races					Win
	Age	Run	1st	2nd	3rd	Unpl	£
Sayyedati	3	4	1	1	1	1	107,064
Alflora	4	6	2	1	0	3	57,819
Shambo	6	8	2	0	1	5	37,983
Spartan Shareef	4	4	2	0	1	1	37,283
Tender Moment	5	7	2	0	0	5	24,116
Sueboog	3	4	1	0	2	1	23,463
Aljazzaf	3	7	2	0	0	5	12,673
Ionio	2	1	1	0	0	0	10,052
Fuchu	3	8	2	0	0	6	7,993
Lobilio	4	12	2	1	1	8	7,759
Braveboy	5	8	1	1	0	6	7,564
Chatham Island	5	10	1	3	1	5	7,440
Karachi	3	5	2	0	0	3	6,374
Luana	2	4	1	0	2	1	5,663
Cool Jazz	2	3	1	0	1	1	5,580
Pinkerton's Pal	2	5	1	2	0	2	5,390
Ertlon	3	13	1	1	1	10	5,254
Boloardo	4	10	1	0	2	7	4,747
Big Blue	4	6	1	0	1	4	3,883
Tudor Island	4	2	1	0	0	1	3,850
Aneesati	3	5	1	0	1	3	3,728
Pearly Mist	3	4	1	1	0	2	3,611
Rani	3	7	1	0	1	5	3,357
Ericolin	3	8	1	0	1	6	3,319
Wahem	3	11	1	1	0	9	3,080
Hoosie	3	9	1	2	1	5	2,847

WINNING OWNERS

	Races Won	Value £		Races Won	Value £
Mohammed Obaida	5	146,928	Saeed Manana	2	11,243
Circlechart Ltd	2	57,819	Sheikh Marwan Al Maktoum	2	6,930
Mrs C E Brittain	2	37,983	Mrs J L Hislop	2	6,374
C T Olley	2	37,283	Mrs E G Macgregor	1	5,390
Dowager Lady Beaverbrook	4	25,375	Mrs Celia Miller	1	3,883
Ray Richards	2	24,116	D Sieff	1	3,850
C E Brittain	4	16,326	Mohammed Obaid Al Maktoum	1	3,357
B H Voak	2	12,187	Sheikh Mohammed	1	2,847

Favourites	4-25	16.0%	- 11.97	Total winning prize-money		£401,890
Longest winning sequence			2	Average SP of winner		7.7/1
Longest losing sequence			55	Return on stakes invested		-32.1%
1992 Form	63-599	10.5%	-157.44	1990 Form	42-507	8.3% - 71.96
1991 Form	53-545	9.7%	-121.61	1989 Form	36-508	7.1% -205.68

M BRITTAIN (Warthill, North Yorks)

	No. of Horses	Races Run	1st	2nd	3rd	Unpl	Per cent	£1 Level Stake
2-y-o	15	73	1	4	2	66	1.4	- 64.00
3-y-o	10	58	2	3	5	48	3.4	- 46.00
4-y-o+	7	72	6	4	11	51	8.3	- 13.00
Totals	32	203	9	11	18	165	4.4	-123.00

Jan	Feb	Mar	Apr	May	Jun	Jul	Aug	Sep	Oct/Nov
0-1	0-7	1-9	1-33	1-37	4-37	0-22	0-15	2-27	0-15

Winning Jockeys	W-R	£1 Level Stake			W-R	£1 Level Stake
J Lowe	4-45	- 9.00		A Mackay	1-16	- 3.00
G Duffield	1-3	+ 5.00		J Marshall	1-17	- 11.00
G Bardwell	1-12	- 3.00		M Wigham	1-52	- 44.00

Winning Courses	W-R	£1 Level Stake			W-R	£1 Level Stake
Edinburgh	2-15	+ 2.00		Leicester	1-6	+ 7.00
Newcastle	2-16	- 3.00		Hamilton	1-13	+ 4.00
Beverley	2-22	- 8.00		Ayr	1-16	- 10.00

Winning Horses	Age	Races Run	1st	2nd	3rd	Unpl	Win £
Eire Leath-Sceal	6	19	3	0	3	13	10,853
Tanoda	7	14	2	1	3	8	6,026
Sharquin	6	15	1	3	2	9	3,366
Desirable Miss	3	14	1	2	0	11	2,560
Gold Desire	3	12	1	0	2	9	2,346
Dockyard Dora	2	11	1	0	2	8	2,180

Favourites	0-3			Total winning prize-money		£27,330
1992 Form	7-224	3.1%	-141.00	1990 Form	27-543	5.0% -260.59
1991 Form	21-420	5.0%	-214.25	1989 Form	26-505	5.1% -173.14

C D BROAD (Westbury-on-Severn, Glos)

	No. of Horses	Races Run	1st	2nd	3rd	Unpl	Per cent	£1 Level Stake
2-y-o	1	1	0	0	0	1	-	- 1.00
3-y-o	1	5	1	0	0	4	20.0	+ 1.50
4-y-o+	6	18	1	2	2	13	5.6	- 3.00
Totals	8	24	2	2	2	18	8.3	- 2.50

Jan	Feb	Mar	Apr	May	Jun	Jul	Aug	Sep	Oct/Nov
0-1	1-1	0-2	0-1	0-3	1-5	0-4	0-2	0-2	0-3

Winning Jockeys	W-R	£1 Level Stake			W-R	£1 Level Stake
T Quinn	1-2	+ 4.50	B Russell		1-4	+ 11.00

Winning Courses	W-R	£1 Level Stake			W-R	£1 Level Stake
Southwell (AW)	1-3	+ 12.00	Warwick		1-6	+ 0.50

Winning Horses	Age	Races Run	1st	2nd	3rd	Unpl	Win £
Farm Street	6	4	1	1	0	2	2,385
Junction Twentytwo	3	5	1	0	0	4	1,917

Favourites	0-1			Total winning prize-money		£4,302

1992 Form	1-34	2.9%	- 19.00	1991 Form	1-20	5.0%	+ 14.00

C P E BROOKS (Lambourn, Berks)

	No. of Horses	Races Run	1st	2nd	3rd	Unpl	Per cent	£1 Level Stake
2-y-o	0	0	0	0	0	0	-	0.00
3-y-o	1	2	0	0	0	2	-	- 2.00
4-y-o+	5	15	1	3	1	10	6.7	- 4.00
Totals	6	17	1	3	1	12	5.9	- 6.00

Jan	Feb	Mar	Apr	May	Jun	Jul	Aug	Sep	Oct/Nov
0-0	0-0	0-0	0-1	0-4	1-8	0-3	0-1	0-0	0-0

Winning Jockey	W-R	£1 Level Stake	Winning Course		W-R	£1 Level Stake
Pat Eddery	1-3	+ 8.00	Epsom		1-1	+ 10.00

Winning Horse	Age	Races Run	1st	2nd	3rd	Unpl	Win £
Fieldridge	4	5	1	1	0	3	12,231

Favourites	0-0			Total winning prize-money		£12,231

1992 Form	0-1			1990 Form	0-1		
1991 Form	1-9	11.1%	- 4.00	1989 Form	1-6	16.7%	- 2.00

R BROTHERTON (Pershore, H'ford & Worcs)

	No. of Horses	Races Run	1st	2nd	3rd	Unpl	Per cent	£1 Level Stake
2-y-o	6	12	0	1	0	11	-	- 12.00
3-y-o	3	10	0	0	1	9	-	- 10.00
4-y-o+	7	19	1	0	0	18	5.3	+ 15.00
Totals	16	41	1	1	1	38	2.4	- 7.00

Jan	Feb	Mar	Apr	May	Jun	Jul	Aug	Sep	Oct/Nov
0-4	0-2	0-2	0-5	0-3	0-3	1-10	0-4	0-2	0-6

Winning Jockey	W-R	£1 Level Stake	Winning Course	W-R	£1 Level Stake
A Mackay	1-14	+ 20.00	Windsor	1-2	+ 32.00

Winning Horse	Age	Races Run	1st	2nd	3rd	Unpl	Win £
Failand	6	5	1	0	0	4	1,954

Favourites	0-0	Total winning prize-money	£1,954

1992 Form	0-25		

D BURCHELL (Ebbw Vale, Gwent)

	No. of Horses	Races Run	1st	2nd	3rd	Unpl	Per cent	£1 Level Stake
2-y-o	1	1	0	0	0	1	-	- 1.00
3-y-o	7	27	4	2	4	17	14.8	+ 11.80
4-y-o+	13	34	6	5	0	23	17.6	+ 14.00
Totals	21	62	10	7	4	41	16.1	+ 24.80

BY MONTH

2-y-o	W-R	Per cent	£1 Level Stake	3-y-o	W-R	Per cent	£1 Level Stake
January	0-0	-	0.00	January	0-1	-	- 1.00
February	0-0	-	0.00	February	0-1	-	- 1.00
March	0-0	-	0.00	March	0-2	-	- 2.00
April	0-0	-	0.00	April	1-1	100.0	+ 8.00
May	0-0	-	0.00	May	1-1	100.0	+ 6.00
June	0-0	-	0.00	June	2-7	28.6	+ 15.80
July	0-0	-	0.00	July	0-5	-	- 5.00
August	0-0	-	0.00	August	0-1	-	- 1.00
September	0-0	-	0.00	September	0-6	-	- 6.00
Oct/Nov	0-1	-	- 1.00	Oct/Nov	0-2	-	- 2.00

4-y-o+	W-R	Per cent	£1 Level Stake		Totals	W-R	Per cent	£1 Level Stake
January	2-7	28.6	+	13.00	January	2-8	25.0	+ 12.00
February	1-5	20.0	-	1.50	February	1-6	16.7	- 2.50
March	0-7	-	-	7.00	March	0-9	-	- 9.00
April	0-1	-	-	1.00	April	1-2	50.0	+ 7.00
May	0-1	-	-	1.00	May	1-2	50.0	+ 5.00
June	0-3	-	-	3.00	June	2-10	20.0	+ 12.80
July	2-4	50.0	+	12.50	July	2-9	22.2	+ 7.50
August	1-1	100.0	+	7.00	August	1-2	50.0	+ 6.00
September	0-2	-	-	2.00	September	0-8	-	- 8.00
Oct/Nov	0-3	-	-	3.00	Oct/Nov	0-6	-	- 6.00

DISTANCE

2-y-o	W-R	Per cent	£1 Level Stake	3-y-o	W-R	Per cent	£1 Level Stake
5f-6f	0-0	-	0.00	5f-6f	0-1	-	- 1.00
7f-8f	0-1	-	- 1.00	7f-8f	3-14	21.4	+ 15.80
9f-13f	0-0	-	0.00	9f-13f	1-12	8.3	- 3.00
14f+	0-0	-	0.00	14f+	0-0	-	0.00

4-y-o+	W-R	Per cent	£1 Level Stake	Totals	W-R	Per cent	£1 Level Stake
5f-6f	2-4	50.0	+ 6.50	5f-6f	2-5	40.0	+ 5.50
7f-8f	3-14	21.4	+ 20.00	7f-8f	6-29	20.7	+ 34.80
9f-13f	1-11	9.1	- 7.50	9f-13f	2-23	8.7	- 10.50
14f+	0-5	-	- 5.00	14f+	0-5	-	- 5.00

TYPE OF RACE

Non-Handicaps	W-R	Per cent	£1 Level Stake	Handicaps	W-R	Per cent	£1 Level Stake
2-y-o	0-1	-	- 1.00	2-y-o	0-0	-	0.00
3-y-o	2-6	33.3	+ 2.80	3-y-o	2-18	11.1	+ 12.00
4-y-o+	3-13	23.1	+ 5.50	4-y-o+	2-14	14.3	+ 2.50
Selling	1-3	33.3	+ 10.00	Selling	0-2	-	- 2.00
Apprentice	0-2	-	- 2.00	Apprentice	0-0	-	0.00
Amat/Ladies	0-0	-	0.00	Amat/Ladies	0-3	-	- 3.00
Totals	6-25	24.0	+ 15.30	Totals	4-37	10.8	+ 9.50

COURSE GRADE

	W-R	Per cent	£1 Level Stake
Group 1	2-10	20.0	- 4.70
Group 2	0-3	-	- 3.00
Group 3	5-22	22.7	+ 36.00
Group 4	3-27	11.1	- 3.50

FIRST TIME OUT

	W-R	Per cent	£1 Level Stake
2-y-o	0-1	-	- 1.00
3-y-o	1-4	25.0	+ 17.00
4-y-o+	1-12	8.3	+ 1.00
Totals	2-17	11.8	+ 17.00

JOCKEYS RIDING

	W-R	Per cent	£1 Level Stake		W-R	Per cent	£1 Level Stake
L Charnock	5-18	27.8	+ 22.00	J Reid	1-1	100.0	+ 0.80
S Davies	3-15	20.0	+ 22.00	M Harris	1-1	100.0	+ 7.00

R Price	0-12	S Mulvey	0-2	N Adams			0-1
S Drowne	0-3	T Wilson	0-2	V Slattery			0-1
A Dicks	0-2	D Wright	0-1				
Mr N Miles	0-2	Mr S Blackwell	0-1				

COURSE RECORD

	Total W-R	Non-Handicaps 2-y-o	3-y-o+	Handicaps 2-y-o	3-y-o+	Per cent	£1 Level Stake
Southwell (AW)	3-18	0-0	1-9	0-0	2-9	16.7	+ 5.50
Epsom	1-2	0-0	1-1	0-0	0-1	50.0	- 0.20
Windsor	1-2	0-0	1-1	0-0	0-1	50.0	+ 5.00
Ayr	1-3	0-0	1-1	0-0	0-2	33.3	+ 0.50
Leicester	1-3	0-0	0-1	0-0	1-2	33.3	+ 6.00
Nottingham	1-3	0-0	1-1	0-0	0-2	33.3	+ 5.00
Hamilton	1-4	0-0	1-1	0-0	0-3	25.0	+ 9.00
Bath	1-5	0-1	0-2	0-0	1-2	20.0	+ 16.00

Lingfield (AW)	0-7	Sandown	0-2	Chester	0-1
Chepstow	0-5	Southwell (Turf)	0-2	Doncaster	0-1
Salisbury	0-2	Ascot	0-1	Kempton	0-1

WINNING HORSES

	Age	Races Run	1st	2nd	3rd	Unpl	Win £
Prime Mover	5	5	3	0	0	2	7,878
Quick Silver Boy	3	8	2	1	1	4	6,340
Missy-S	4	2	2	0	0	0	4,049
Bold Acre	3	7	1	0	2	4	3,623
General Chase	3	5	1	0	1	3	3,522
Desert Power	4	5	1	2	0	2	3,494

WINNING OWNERS

	Races Won	Value £		Races Won	Value £
T R Pearson	3	9,862	Mrs Marion C Morgan	1	3,623
Mrs M E Brooks	3	7,878	Rhys Thomas Williams	1	3,494
B J Llewellyn	2	4,049			

Favourites	1-3	33.3%	- 1.20	Total winning prize-money	£28,905

Longest winning sequence		2	Average SP of winner	7.7/1
Longest losing sequence		15	Return on stakes invested	40.0%

1992 Form	1-48	2.1%	- 45.75	1990 Form	7-75	9.3%	- 27.50
1991 Form	4-63	6.3%	+ 29.00	1989 Form	1-31	3.2%	- 28.25

P BURGOYNE (Upper Lambourn, Berks)

	No. of Horses	Races Run	1st	2nd	3rd	Unpl	Per cent	£1 Level Stake
2-y-o	2	5	0	0	0	5	-	- 5.00
3-y-o	4	13	0	0	1	12	-	- 13.00
4-y-o+	4	20	1	1	1	17	5.0	- 14.00
Totals	10	38	1	1	2	34	2.6	- 32.00

Jan	Feb	Mar	Apr	May	Jun	Jul	Aug	Sep	Oct/Nov
0-0	0-0	0-2	0-3	1-2	0-9	0-4	0-3	0-6	0-9

Winning Jockey	W-R	£1 Level Stake	Winning Course	W-R	£1 Level Stake
C Hodgson	1-3	+ 3.00	Leicester	1-7	- 1.00

Winning Horse	Age	Races Run	1st	2nd	3rd	Unpl	Win £
Rock The Barney	4	11	1	1	0	9	3,036

Favourites	1-2	50.0%	+ 4.00	Total winning prize-money	£3,036

1992 Form	0-16	1990 Form	0-35
1991 Form	0-36	1989 Form	0-33

K R BURKE (Broadway, H'ford & Worcs)

	No. of Horses	Races Run	1st	2nd	3rd	Unpl	Per cent	£1 Level Stake
2-y-o	5	17	1	1	1	14	5.9	- 10.00
3-y-o	5	21	3	1	0	17	14.3	- 2.00
4-y-o+	8	45	3	1	7	34	6.7	- 20.50
Totals	18	83	7	3	8	65	8.4	- 32.50

Jan	Feb	Mar	Apr	May	Jun	Jul	Aug	Sep	Oct/Nov
2-4	1-2	0-7	1-9	1-12	0-13	1-20	0-7	1-7	0-2

Winning Jockeys	W-R	£1 Level Stake		W-R	£1 Level Stake
S Webster	2-12	0.00	P McCabe	1-6	+ 0.50
T Sprake	2-18	- 5.00	D Holland	1-9	- 2.00
G Carter	1-5	+ 7.00			

Winning Courses					
Lingfield (AW)	2-8	+ 4.00	Southwell (Turf)	1-3	+ 3.00
Southwell (AW)	2-11	+ 8.00	Folkestone	1-4	+ 3.00
Ripon	1-3	+ 3.50			

Burke K R

Winning Horses		Age	Races Run	1st	2nd	3rd	Unpl	Win £
The Institute Boy		3	7	2	1	0	4	5,042
Daring Destiny		2	3	1	0	1	1	4,557
Northern Trial		5	9	1	0	2	6	3,465
Tommy Tempest		4	10	1	0	2	7	2,924
Roseate Lodge		7	10	1	0	2	7	2,238
Jake The Pake		3	5	1	0	0	4	1,380

Favourites	0-5			Total winning prize-money	£19,606

1992 Form	1-38	2.6%	- 31.50	1990 Form	0-14
1991 Form	2-42	4.8%	- 17.00		

P BUTLER (Lewes, East Sussex)

	No. of Horses	Races Run	1st	2nd	3rd	Unpl	Per cent	£1 Level Stake
2-y-o	3	24	1	1	1	21	4.2	- 9.00
3-y-o	1	3	0	0	0	3	-	- 3.00
4-y-o+	6	33	2	1	3	27	6.1	- 5.50
Totals	10	60	3	2	4	51	5.0	- 17.50

Jan	Feb	Mar	Apr	May	Jun	Jul	Aug	Sep	Oct/Nov
0-1	0-0	0-3	0-10	0-9	2-11	0-8	1-6	0-4	0-8

Winning Jockeys	W-R	£1 Level Stake			W-R	£1 Level Stake
S Drowne	2-18	+ 18.00	Mrs J Crossley		1-1	+ 5.50

Winning Courses	W-R	£1 Level Stake		W-R	£1 Level Stake
Chepstow	1-2	+ 4.50	Folkestone	1-13	+ 2.00
Goodwood	1-2	+ 19.00			

Winning Horses	Age	Races Run	1st	2nd	3rd	Unpl	Win £
Prince Rooney	5	10	2	0	0	8	5,874
Forever Blushing	2	11	1	1	0	9	2,070

Favourites	1-2	50.0%	+ 4.50	Total winning prize-money	£7,944

1992 Form	3-42	7.1%	- 15.50	1990 Form	0-11
1991 Form	0-28			1989 Form	0-30

N BYCROFT (Brandsby, North Yorks)

	No. of Horses	Races Run	1st	2nd	3rd	Unpl	Per cent	£1 Level Stake
2-y-o	12	52	0	2	1	49	–	– 52.00
3-y-o	5	47	4	2	7	34	8.5	– 11.17
4-y-o+	7	34	1	2	1	30	2.9	– 27.00
Totals	24	133	5	6	9	113	3.8	– 90.17

Jan	Feb	Mar	Apr	May	Jun	Jul	Aug	Sep	Oct/Nov
0-4	0-3	0-5	0-8	1-12	0-14	0-24	3-21	1-22	0-20

Winning Jockeys	W-R	£1 Level Stake			W-R	£1 Level Stake
S Maloney	2-10	+ 14.50	S Copp		1-3	+ 4.00
J Quinn	1-3	+ 1.33	D Wright		1-6	+ 1.00

Winning Courses						
Hamilton	2-4	+ 20.00	Thirsk		1-19	– 11.50
Ayr	2-8	+ 3.33				

Winning Horses	Age	Races Run	1st	2nd	3rd	Unpl	Win £
Craigie Boy	3	15	2	0	1	12	6,212
Plum First	3	15	1	2	3	9	5,117
Doctor Roy	5	11	1	1	1	8	3,290
Shotley Again	3	6	1	0	2	3	2,379

Favourites	1-3	33.3%	+ 1.33	Total winning prize-money	£16,998

1992 Form	4-106	3.8%	– 66.25	1990 Form	2-169	1.2%	–141.00
1991 Form	6-114	5.3%	– 48.25	1989 Form	2-149	1.3%	–118.00

N A CALLAGHAN (Newmarket)

	No. of Horses	Races Run	1st	2nd	3rd	Unpl	Per cent	£1 Level Stake
2-y-o	16	74	7	9	7	51	9.5	– 44.14
3-y-o	4	22	1	2	1	18	4.5	– 19.00
4-y-o+	6	42	2	5	6	29	4.8	– 23.50
Totals	26	138	10	16	14	98	7.2	– 86.64

BY MONTH

2-y-o	W-R	Per cent	£1 Level Stake	3-y-o	W-R	Per cent	£1 Level Stake
January	0-0	-	0.00	January	0-2	-	- 2.00
February	0-0	-	0.00	February	0-0	-	0.00
March	0-0	-	0.00	March	0-0	-	0.00
April	0-1	-	- 1.00	April	0-2	-	- 2.00
May	1-6	16.7	- 3.90	May	1-7	14.3	- 4.00
June	1-9	11.1	- 6.50	June	0-2	-	- 2.00
July	2-20	10.0	- 13.87	July	0-4	-	- 4.00
August	1-15	6.7	- 10.50	August	0-4	-	- 4.00
September	2-14	14.3	+ 0.63	September	0-1	-	- 1.00
Oct/Nov	0-9	-	- 9.00	Oct/Nov	0-0	-	0.00

4-y-o+	W-R	Per cent	£1 Level Stake	Totals	W-R	Per cent	£1 Level Stake
January	1-2	50.0	+ 8.00	January	1-4	25.0	+ 6.00
February	0-1	-	- 1.00	February	0-1	-	- 1.00
March	0-1	-	- 1.00	March	0-1	-	- 1.00
April	0-4	-	- 4.00	April	0-7	-	- 7.00
May	0-7	-	- 7.00	May	2-20	10.0	- 14.90
June	0-8	-	- 8.00	June	1-19	5.3	- 16.50
July	1-14	7.1	- 5.50	July	3-38	7.9	- 23.37
August	0-3	-	- 3.00	August	1-22	4.5	- 17.50
September	0-2	-	- 2.00	September	2-17	11.8	- 2.37
Oct/Nov	0-0	-	0.00	Oct/Nov	0-9	-	- 9.00

DISTANCE

2-y-o	W-R	Per cent	£1 Level Stake	3-y-o	W-R	Per cent	£1 Level Stake
5f-6f	3-38	7.9	- 31.47	5f-6f	0-2	-	- 2.00
7f-8f	4-36	11.1	- 12.67	7f-8f	1-15	6.7	- 12.00
9f-13f	0-0	-	0.00	9f-13f	0-5	-	- 5.00
14f+	0-0	-	0.00	14f+	0-0	-	0.00

4-y-o+	W-R	Per cent	£1 Level Stake	Totals	W-R	Per cent	£1 Level Stake
5f-6f	1-16	6.3	- 7.50	5f-6f	4-56	7.1	- 40.97
7f-8f	0-11	-	- 11.00	7f-8f	5-62	8.1	- 35.67
9f-13f	1-11	9.1	- 1.00	9f-13f	1-16	6.3	- 6.00
14f+	0-4	-	- 4.00	14f+	0-4	-	- 4.00

TYPE OF RACE

Non-Handicaps	W-R	Per cent	£1 Level Stake	Handicaps	W-R	Per cent	£1 Level Stake
2-y-o	6-46	13.0	- 17.94	2-y-o	1-13	7.7	- 11.20
3-y-o	0-6	-	- 6.00	3-y-o	1-12	8.3	- 9.00
4-y-o+	1-15	6.7	- 5.00	4-y-o+	1-20	5.0	- 11.50
Selling	0-15	-	- 15.00	Selling	0-9	-	- 9.00
Apprentice	0-0	-	0.00	Apprentice	0-1	-	- 1.00
Amat/Ladies	0-0	-	0.00	Amat/Ladies	0-1	-	- 1.00
Totals	7-82	8.5	- 43.94	Totals	3-56	5.4	- 42.70

COURSE GRADE					FIRST TIME OUT			
	W-R	Per cent	£1 Level Stake			W-R	Per cent	£1 Level Stake
Group 1	3-58	5.2	- 37.17	2-y-o		0-16	-	- 16.00
Group 2	3-21	14.3	- 12.87	3-y-o		0-4	-	- 4.00
Group 3	1-25	4.0	- 16.50	4-y-o+		1-4	25.0	+ 6.00
Group 4	3-34	8.8	- 20.10					
				Totals		1-24	4.2	- 14.00

JOCKEYS RIDING

	W-R	Per cent	£1 Level Stake			W-R	Per cent	£1 Level Stake
Pat Eddery	4-24	16.7	- 12.37	A Munro		1-3	33.3	+ 1.50
W Carson	2-6	33.3	+ 4.60	T Quinn		1-3	33.3	- 0.37
C Asmussen	1-2	50.0	+ 10.00	T Williams		1-4	25.0	+ 6.00

N Carlisle	0-9	W R Swinburn	0-4	J Lowe		0-1
J Reid	0-7	J Quinn	0-3	J Tate		0-1
A Mackay	0-6	K Darley	0-3	J Weaver		0-1
W Ryan	0-6	D Harrison	0-2	L Piggott		0-1
B Raymond	0-5	M Hills	0-2	M Roberts		0-1
D Wright	0-5	A Procter	0-1	Mr C Appleby		0-1
J Williams	0-5	B Rouse	0-1	N Adams		0-1
M Wigham	0-5	B Russell	0-1	N Kennedy		0-1
W Newnes	0-5	C Hodgson	0-1	N Varley		0-1
G Hind	0-4	G Bardwell	0-1	R Cochrane		0-1
L Dettori	0-4	G Carter	0-1			
S Whitworth	0-4	G Duffield	0-1			

COURSE RECORD

	Total W-R	Non-Handicaps 2-y-o	3-y-o+	Handicaps 2-y-o	3-y-o+	Per cent	£1 Level Stake
Folkestone	2-8	1-2	0-4	1-1	0-1	25.0	- 4.10
Newmarket	2-25	2-15	0-3	0-3	0-4	8.0	- 16.17
Beverley	1-2	0-0	0-0	0-0	1-2	50.0	+ 6.50
Salisbury	1-2	1-1	0-0	0-0	0-1	50.0	+ 0.50
Ascot	1-5	1-2	0-1	0-1	0-1	20.0	+ 7.00
Brighton	1-9	0-2	0-1	0-0	1-6	11.1	- 6.00
Lingfield	1-9	1-3	0-2	0-1	0-3	11.1	- 6.37
Lingfield (AW)	1-10	0-1	1-3	0-0	0-6	10.0	0.00

Yarmouth	0-10	Nottingham	0-4	Windsor	0-2
Southwell (AW)	0-8	Southwell (Turf)	0-4	Bath	0-1
York	0-6	Pontefract	0-3	Chepstow	0-1
Doncaster	0-5	Sandown	0-3	Haydock	0-1
Goodwood	0-5	Catterick	0-2	Thirsk	0-1
Epsom	0-4	Leicester	0-2		
Kempton	0-4	Warwick	0-2		

WINNING HORSES

	Age	Races Run	1st	2nd	3rd	Unpl	Win £
Fairy Heights	2	5	3	1	0	1	106,929
Prince Azzaan	2	8	2	1	0	5	5,979
Aquado	4	13	1	1	3	8	3,582
Fiveofive	3	9	1	0	0	8	3,287
Lugano	2	5	1	0	0	4	3,106
Asking For Aces	2	8	1	2	1	4	2,821
Naseer	4	7	1	1	2	3	2,478

WINNING OWNERS

	Races Won	Value £		Races Won	Value £
Frank W Golding	3	106,929	Yahya Nasib	1	3,106
K Al-Said	2	5,979	Mrs G R Smith	1	2,821
Gallagher Materials Ltd	1	3,582	Mrs J Callaghan	1	2,478
T A Foreman	1	3,287			

Favourites	4-21	19.0%	- 11.97	Total winning prize-money	£128,182
Longest winning sequence			1	Average SP of winner	4.1/1
Longest losing sequence			26	Return on stakes invested	-62.8%
1992 Form	21-178	11.8%	- 65.03	1990 Form	31-197	15.7%	- 17.39
1991 Form	30-265	11.3%	- 30.99	1989 Form	32-237	13.5%	- 27.34

P CALVER (Ripon, North Yorks)

	No. of Horses	Races Run	1st	2nd	3rd	Unpl	Per cent	£1 Level Stake
2-y-o	4	8	0	0	2	6	-	- 8.00
3-y-o	4	21	3	0	1	17	14.3	+ 34.00
4-y-o+	6	70	9	6	9	46	12.9	- 11.17
Totals	14	99	12	6	12	69	12.1	+ 14.83

BY MONTH

2-y-o	W-R	Per cent	£1 Level Stake	3-y-o	W-R	Per cent	£1 Level Stake
January	0-0	-	0.00	January	0-0	-	0.00
February	0-0	-	0.00	February	0-0	-	0.00
March	0-0	-	0.00	March	0-0	-	0.00
April	0-0	-	0.00	April	1-3	33.3	+ 18.00
May	0-0	-	0.00	May	0-2	-	- 2.00
June	0-1	-	- 1.00	June	1-3	33.3	+ 14.00
July	0-2	-	- 2.00	July	0-2	-	- 2.00
August	0-1	-	- 1.00	August	0-4	-	- 4.00
September	0-1	-	- 1.00	September	0-4	-	- 4.00
Oct/Nov	0-3	-	- 3.00	Oct/Nov	1-3	33.3	+ 14.00

4-y-o+	W-R	Per cent	£1 Level Stake		Totals	W-R	Per cent	£1 Level Stake
January	0-2	-	- 2.00		January	0-2	-	- 2.00
February	0-0	-	0.00		February	0-0	-	0.00
March	0-3	-	- 3.00		March	0-3	-	- 3.00
April	0-6	-	- 6.00		April	1-9	11.1	+ 12.00
May	0-10	-	- 10.00		May	0-12	-	- 12.00
June	4-10	40.0	+ 19.50		June	5-14	35.7	+ 32.50
July	3-16	18.8	- 4.17		July	3-20	15.0	- 8.17
August	2-12	16.7	+ 5.50		August	2-17	11.8	+ 0.50
September	0-8	-	- 8.00		September	0-13	-	- 13.00
Oct/Nov	0-3	-	- 3.00		Oct/Nov	1-9	11.1	+ 8.00

DISTANCE

2-y-o	W-R	Per cent	£1 Level Stake		3-y-o	W-R	Per cent	£1 Level Stake
5f-6f	0-4	-	- 4.00		5f-6f	0-2	-	- 2.00
7f-8f	0-4	-	- 4.00		7f-8f	2-9	22.2	+ 29.00
9f-13f	0-0	-	0.00		9f-13f	0-6	-	- 6.00
14f+	0-0	-	0.00		14f+	1-4	25.0	+ 13.00

4-y-o+	W-R	Per cent	£1 Level Stake		Totals	W-R	Per cent	£1 Level Stake
5f-6f	2-18	11.1	- 1.67		5f-6f	2-24	8.3	- 7.67
7f-8f	7-36	19.4	+ 6.50		7f-8f	9-49	18.4	+ 31.50
9f-13f	0-14	-	- 14.00		9f-13f	0-20	-	- 20.00
14f+	0-2	-	- 2.00		14f+	1-6	16.7	+ 11.00

TYPE OF RACE

Non-Handicaps	W-R	Per cent	£1 Level Stake		Handicaps	W-R	Per cent	£1 Level Stake
2-y-o	0-6	-	- 6.00		2-y-o	0-0	-	0.00
3-y-o	2-7	28.6	+ 31.00		3-y-o	1-14	7.1	+ 3.00
4-y-o+	0-4	-	- 4.00		4-y-o+	7-57	12.3	- 6.67
Selling	0-4	-	- 4.00		Selling	1-2	50.0	+ 3.00
Apprentice	0-0	-	0.00		Apprentice	0-4	-	- 4.00
Amat/Ladies	0-0	-	0.00		Amat/Ladies	1-1	100.0	+ 2.50
Totals	2-21	9.5	+ 17.00		Totals	10-78	12.8	- 2.17

COURSE GRADE	W-R	Per cent	£1 Level Stake		FIRST TIME OUT	W-R	Per cent	£1 Level Stake
Group 1	2-22	9.1	+ 3.00		2-y-o	0-4	-	- 4.00
Group 2	6-36	16.7	+ 33.83		3-y-o	0-3	-	- 3.00
Group 3	3-16	18.8	- 1.00		4-y-o+	0-5	-	- 5.00
Group 4	1-25	4.0	- 21.00		Totals	0-12	-	- 12.00

JOCKEYS RIDING

	W–R	Per cent	£1 Level Stake		W–R	Per cent	£1 Level Stake
K Darley	3-8	37.5	+ 11.50	Mrs A Farrell	1-1	100.0	+ 2.50
G Hind	2-8	25.0	+ 30.00	J Carroll	1-2	50.0	+ 9.00
J Tate	2-9	22.2	− 0.50	Dale Gibson	1-28	3.6	− 11.00
M Birch	2-10	20.0	+ 6.33				

W Newnes	0-8	W Ryan	0-2	F Savage	0-1
N Carlisle	0-5	A Garth	0-1	Kim McDonnell	0-1
D Moffatt	0-3	A Tucker	0-1	Paul Eddery	0-1
J Fanning	0-3	D McKeown	0-1	R Cochrane	0-1
J Fortune	0-3	F Norton	0-1	T Williams	0-1

COURSE RECORD

	Total W–R	Non-Handicaps 2-y-o	Non-Handicaps 3-y-o+	Handicaps 2-y-o	Handicaps 3-y-o+	Per cent	£1 Level Stake
Newcastle	2-6	0-1	0-0	0-0	2-5	33.3	+ 19.00
Pontefract	2-6	0-1	0-1	0-0	2-4	33.3	+ 5.50
Thirsk	2-10	0-0	1-4	0-0	1-6	20.0	+ 15.50
Ripon	2-12	0-1	0-4	0-0	2-7	16.7	+ 11.00
Redcar	2-13	0-0	1-1	0-0	1-12	15.4	+ 8.33
Beverley	1-5	0-1	0-0	0-0	1-4	20.0	− 1.50
Edinburgh	1-7	0-1	0-0	0-0	1-6	14.3	− 3.00

Catterick	0-10	Southwell (AW)	0-3	Hamilton	0-1
Haydock	0-8	Newmarket	0-2	Leicester	0-1
Carlisle	0-4	York	0-2	Southwell (Turf)	0-1
Doncaster	0-3	Ayr	0-1		
Nottingham	0-3	Chester	0-1		

WINNING HORSES

	Age	Races Run	1st	2nd	3rd	Unpl	Win £
Pride Of Pendle	4	18	5	4	1	8	15,264
Ballad Dancer	8	22	2	2	2	16	6,694
Leave It To Lib	6	8	2	0	1	5	6,069
Cicerone	3	10	2	0	0	8	5,815
Cara's Pride	3	6	1	0	1	4	3,319

WINNING OWNERS

	Races Won	Value £		Races Won	Value £
W B Imison	7	21,958	Miss S Moore	2	5,815
Mrs C Calver	2	6,069	Greenland Park Ltd	1	3,319

Favourites	3-10	30.0%	+ 6.50	Total winning prize-money	£37,160
Longest winning sequence			2	Average SP of winner	8.5/1
Longest losing sequence			22	Return on stakes invested	15.0%

1992 Form	6-70	8.6%	− 18.75	1990 Form	18-131	13.7%	− 26.90
1991 Form	8-109	7.3%	− 0.25	1989 Form	7-92	7.6%	− 17.00

M J CAMACHO (Malton, North Yorks)

	No. of Horses	Races Run	1st	2nd	3rd	Unpl	Per cent	£1 Level Stake
2-y-o	8	24	0	1	1	22	-	- 24.00
3-y-o	4	18	5	2	2	9	27.8	+ 20.13
4-y-o+	11	58	6	6	7	39	10.3	- 36.71
Totals	23	100	11	9	10	70	11.0	- 40.58

BY MONTH

2-y-o	W-R	Per cent	£1 Level Stake	3-y-o	W-R	Per cent	£1 Level Stake
January	0-0	-	0.00	January	0-1	-	- 1.00
February	0-0	-	0.00	February	0-0	-	0.00
March	0-0	-	0.00	March	0-0	-	0.00
April	0-0	-	0.00	April	0-3	-	- 3.00
May	0-1	-	- 1.00	May	2-2	100.0	+ 7.50
June	0-4	-	- 4.00	June	1-2	50.0	+ 15.00
July	0-4	-	- 4.00	July	0-4	-	- 4.00
August	0-5	-	- 5.00	August	1-2	50.0	+ 7.00
September	0-5	-	- 5.00	September	1-2	50.0	+ 0.63
Oct/Nov	0-5	-	- 5.00	Oct/Nov	0-2	-	- 2.00

4-y-o+	W-R	Per cent	£1 Level Stake	Totals	W-R	Per cent	£1 Level Stake
January	0-2	-	- 2.00	January	0-3	-	- 3.00
February	0-0	-	0.00	February	0-0	-	0.00
March	0-3	-	- 3.00	March	0-3	-	- 3.00
April	1-8	12.5	- 3.50	April	1-11	9.1	- 6.50
May	0-10	-	- 10.00	May	2-13	15.4	- 3.50
June	0-4	-	- 4.00	June	1-10	10.0	+ 7.00
July	0-6	-	- 6.00	July	0-14	-	- 14.00
August	1-4	25.0	+ 1.50	August	2-11	18.2	+ 3.50
September	1-8	12.5	- 4.75	September	2-15	13.3	- 9.12
Oct/Nov	3-13	23.1	- 4.96	Oct/Nov	3-20	15.0	- 11.96

DISTANCE

2-y-o	W-R	Per cent	£1 Level Stake	3-y-o	W-R	Per cent	£1 Level Stake
5f-6f	0-12	-	- 12.00	5f-6f	0-1	-	- 1.00
7f-8f	0-9	-	- 9.00	7f-8f	3-10	30.0	+ 2.13
9f-13f	0-3	-	- 3.00	9f-13f	2-6	33.3	+ 20.00
14f+	0-0	-	0.00	14f+	0-1	-	- 1.00

4-y-o+	W-R	Per cent	£1 Level Stake	Totals	W-R	Per cent	£1 Level Stake
5f-6f	5-27	18.5	- 10.21	5f-6f	5-40	12.5	- 23.21
7f-8f	0-18	-	- 18.00	7f-8f	3-37	8.1	- 24.87
9f-13f	0-10	-	- 10.00	9f-13f	2-19	10.5	+ 7.00
14f+	1-3	33.3	+ 1.50	14f+	1-4	25.0	+ 0.50

TYPE OF RACE

Non-Handicaps	W-R	Per cent	£1 Level Stake	Handicaps	W-R	Per cent	£1 Level Stake
2-y-o	0-17	-	- 17.00	2-y-o	0-1	-	- 1.00
3-y-o	0-5	-	- 5.00	3-y-o	5-12	41.7	+ 26.13
4-y-o+	3-11	27.3	- 2.59	4-y-o+	3-45	6.7	- 32.12
Selling	0-3	-	- 3.00	Selling	0-5	-	- 5.00
Apprentice	0-0	-	0.00	Apprentice	0-0	-	0.00
Amat/Ladies	0-0	-	0.00	Amat/Ladies	0-1	-	- 1.00
Totals	3-36	8.3	- 27.59	Totals	8-64	12.5	- 12.99

COURSE GRADE

	W-R	Per cent	£1 Level Stake
Group 1	3-37	8.1	- 25.12
Group 2	4-23	17.4	+ 2.29
Group 3	3-25	12.0	- 11.75
Group 4	1-15	6.7	- 6.00

FIRST TIME OUT

	W-R	Per cent	£1 Level Stake
2-y-o	0-7	-	- 7.00
3-y-o	0-4	-	- 4.00
4-y-o+	0-11	-	- 11.00
Totals	0-22	-	- 22.00

JOCKEYS RIDING

	W-R	Per cent	£1 Level Stake		W-R	Per cent	£1 Level Stake
N Connorton	7-48	14.6	- 2.62	L Charnock	2-20	10.0	- 11.12
S Webster	2-11	18.2	- 5.84				

S Morris	0-3	J Fanning	0-1	M Roberts	0-1
G Bardwell	0-2	J Fortune	0-1	Miss I D W Jones	0-1
B Raymond	0-1	J Reid	0-1	N Kennedy	0-1
D McKeown	0-1	L Dettori	0-1	Paul Eddery	0-1
E Johnson	0-1	L Piggott	0-1	R Cochrane	0-1
G Duffield	0-1	M Birch	0-1	S Wood	0-1

COURSE RECORD

	Total W-R	Non-Handicaps 2-y-o	Non-Handicaps 3-y-o+	Handicaps 2-y-o	Handicaps 3-y-o+	Per cent	£1 Level Stake
Pontefract	2-5	0-1	0-0	0-0	2-4	40.0	+ 5.00
Redcar	2-13	0-5	1-1	0-0	1-7	15.4	+ 5.91
Ayr	1-1	0-0	0-0	0-0	1-1	100.0	+ 1.63
Chester	1-1	0-0	0-0	0-0	1-1	100.0	+ 1.88
Thirsk	1-5	0-0	0-1	0-0	1-4	20.0	- 1.50
Doncaster	1-7	0-0	1-1	0-0	0-6	14.3	- 3.75
Southwell (AW)	1-8	0-0	0-3	0-0	1-5	12.5	+ 1.00
Nottingham	1-9	0-3	1-2	0-1	0-3	11.1	- 5.75
York	1-13	0-3	0-2	0-0	1-8	7.7	- 7.00

Beverley	0-7	Ripon	0-4	Goodwood	0-1
Newcastle	0-5	Catterick	0-2	Newbury	0-1
Newmarket	0-5	Haydock	0-2	Southwell (Turf)	0-1
Carlisle	0-4	Ascot	0-1	
Hamilton	0-4	Epsom	0-1	

WINNING HORSES

	Age	Races Run	1st	2nd	3rd	Unpl	Win £
Hi Nod	3	7	3	2	0	2	25,885
Blyton Lad	7	7	2	0	2	3	14,099
Nordan Raider	5	7	3	0	1	3	11,559
Silky Heights	3	5	2	0	0	3	6,264
Avro Anson	5	3	1	0	0	2	3,436

WINNING OWNERS

	Races Won	Value £		Races Won	Value £
Brian Nordan	3	25,885	Bernard Bloom	2	6,264
Mrs J Addleshaw	2	14,099	B P Skirton	1	3,436
Miss J A Camacho	3	11,559			

Favourites	9-18	50.0%	+ 15.42	Total winning prize-money	£61,244

Longest winning sequence			2	Average SP of winner		4.4/1
Longest losing sequence			18	Return on stakes invested		-40.6%

1992 Form	20-113	17.7%	+ 31.76	1990 Form	20-140	14.3%	+ 63.18
1991 Form	15-109	13.8%	- 11.21	1989 Form	12-97	12.4%	+ 23.75

B R CAMBIDGE (Bishop's Wood, Staffs)

	No. of Horses	Races Run	1st	2nd	3rd	Unpl	Per cent	£1 Level Stake
2-y-o	0	0	0	0	0	0	-	0.00
3-y-o	1	4	0	0	0	4	-	- 4.00
4-y-o+	6	38	2	0	2	34	5.3	- 24.50
Totals	7	42	2	0	2	38	4.8	- 28.50

Jan	Feb	Mar	Apr	May	Jun	Jul	Aug	Sep	Oct/Nov
0-4	0-3	0-3	0-2	1-5	0-6	1-7	0-6	0-3	0-3

Winning Jockeys	W-R	£1 Level Stake		W-R	£1 Level Stake
D Wright	1-6	+ 1.50	J Lowe	1-9	- 3.00

Winning Courses					
Thirsk	1-1	+ 5.00	Chepstow	1-3	+ 4.50

Winning Horses	Age	Races Run	1st	2nd	3rd	Unpl	Win £
Rimouski	5	5	1	0	0	4	2,469
Desert Splendour	5	6	1	0	0	5	2,427

Favourites	0-0			Total winning prize-money			£4,896
1992 Form	0-26			1990 Form	2-19	10.5%	- 8.00
1991 Form	4-22	18.2%	+ 17.50	1989 Form	1-16	6.3%	- 3.00

I CAMPBELL (Newmarket)

	No. of Horses	Races Run	1st	2nd	3rd	Unpl	Per cent	£1 Level Stake
2-y-o	2	8	0	0	0	8	-	- 8.00
3-y-o	2	4	0	0	0	4	-	- 4.00
4-y-o+	10	26	2	1	4	19	7.7	- 22.62
Totals	14	38	2	1	4	31	5.3	- 34.62

Jan	Feb	Mar	Apr	May	Jun	Jul	Aug	Sep	Oct/Nov
0-0	0-2	0-3	0-5	0-3	1-6	1-8	0-1	0-4	0-6

Winning Jockey	W-R	£1 Level Stake			W-R	£1 Level Stake
Dale Gibson	2-14	- 10.62				

Winning Courses						
Redcar	1-1	+ 1.00	Hamilton		1-2	- 0.62

Winning Horses	Age	Races Run	1st	2nd	3rd	Unpl	Win £
Qualitair Rhythm	5	8	1	1	3	3	2,899
Northern Rainbow	5	5	1	0	0	4	1,051

Favourites	2-4	50.0%	- 0.12	Total winning prize-money	£3,950

1992 Form	5-54	9.3%	- 38.16	1990 Form	7-85	8.2%	- 10.62
1991 Form	1-42	2.4%	- 37.50	1989 Form	3-68	4.4%	- 40.67

MARK CAMPION (Findon, West Sussex)

	No. of Horses	Races Run	1st	2nd	3rd	Unpl	Per cent	£1 Level Stake
2-y-o	10	19	0	2	4	13	-	- 19.00
3-y-o	0	0	0	0	0	0	-	0.00
4-y-o+	1	3	1	0	0	2	33.3	+ 18.00
Totals	11	22	1	2	4	15	4.5	- 1.00

Jan	Feb	Mar	Apr	May	Jun	Jul	Aug	Sep	Oct/Nov
0-0	0-0	0-0	0-0	0-1	1-4	0-5	0-2	0-2	0-8

Winning Jockey	W-R	£1 Level Stake	Winning Course	W-R	£1 Level Stake
B Rouse	1-4	+ 17.00	Salisbury	1-3	+ 18.00

Winning Horse	Age	Races Run	1st	2nd	3rd	Unpl	Win £
Wild Strawberry	4	3	1	0	0	2	2,826

Favourites	0-0	Total winning prize-money	£2,826

H CANDY (Wantage, Oxon)

	No. of Horses	Races Run	1st	2nd	3rd	Unpl	Per cent	£1 Level Stake
2-y-o	12	24	1	1	0	22	4.2	+ 2.00
3-y-o	16	52	1	3	4	44	1.9	- 46.00
4-y-o+	8	51	4	4	6	37	7.8	- 23.17
Totals	36	127	6	8	10	103	4.7	- 67.17

Jan	Feb	Mar	Apr	May	Jun	Jul	Aug	Sep	Oct/Nov
0-0	0-0	0-0	0-12	0-10	0-14	2-22	1-21	2-20	1-28

Winning Jockeys	W-R	£1 Level Stake		W-R	£1 Level Stake
W Newnes	3-43	- 2.00	A Munro	1-16	- 11.67
S Drake	1-3	+ 6.00	C Rutter	1-17	- 11.50

Winning Courses					
Newmarket	2-17	+ 13.33	Haydock	1-2	+ 7.00
Chester	1-1	+ 8.00	Bath	1-3	+ 3.00
Yarmouth	1-1	+ 4.50			

Winning Horses	Age	Races Run	1st	2nd	3rd	Unpl	Win £
Make A Stand	2	4	1	0	0	3	9,325
Always Friendly	5	2	1	0	1	0	4,761
Celia Brady	5	6	1	0	2	3	4,557
Dukrame	3	4	1	0	1	2	4,045
Exclusion	4	8	1	1	0	6	3,079
Will Soon	4	8	1	0	0	7	2,861

Favourites	1-6	16.7%	0.00	Total winning prize-money		£28,628

1992 Form	21-200	10.5%	+ 11.93	1990 Form	23-189	12.2%	+ 23.20
1991 Form	16-220	7.3%	- 55.00	1989 Form	16-201	8.0%	- 37.44

J M CARR (Malton, North Yorks)

	No. of Horses	Races Run	1st	2nd	3rd	Unpl	Per cent	£1 Level Stake
2-y-o	4	16	2	2	3	9	12.5	+ 0.50
3-y-o	3	16	2	4	3	7	12.5	- 9.25
4-y-o+	3	15	1	1	3	10	6.7	- 11.25
Totals	10	47	5	7	9	26	10.6	- 20.00

Jan	Feb	Mar	Apr	May	Jun	Jul	Aug	Sep	Oct/Nov
0-1	0-1	0-1	0-5	1-5	0-8	3-7	0-6	0-5	1-8

Carr J M

Winning Jockeys	W-R	£1 Level Stake		W-R	£1 Level Stake
Julie Bowker	2-3	+ 3.75	A Clark	1-4	- 0.25
S Morris	2-24	- 7.50			

Winning Courses	W-R	£1 Level Stake		W-R	£1 Level Stake
Folkestone	1-2	+ 1.50	Catterick	1-5	- 2.25
Leicester	1-3	+ 0.75	Beverley	1-7	- 3.00
Thirsk	1-3	+ 10.00			

Winning Horses	Age	Races Run	1st	2nd	3rd	Unpl	Win £
Ho-Joe	3	7	2	1	2	2	4,004
Here Comes A Star	5	12	1	1	3	7	3,080
Sporting Warrior	2	3	1	1	1	0	2,781
Kaitak	2	5	1	1	1	2	2,005

Favourites	1-3	33.3%	+ 0.75	Total winning prize-money	£11,869
1992 Form	2-34	5.9%	- 22.00		

W CARTER (Epsom, Surrey)

	No. of Horses	Races Run	1st	2nd	3rd	Unpl	Per cent	£1 Level Stake
2-y-o	0	0	0	0	0	0	-	0.00
3-y-o	2	2	1	0	0	1	50.0	+ 0.75
4-y-o+	0	0	0	0	0	0	-	0.00
Totals	2	2	1	0	0	1	50.0	+ 0.75

Jan	Feb	Mar	Apr	May	Jun	Jul	Aug	Sep	Oct/Nov
1-2	0-0	0-0	0-0	0-0	0-0	0-0	0-0	0-0	0-0

Winning Jockey	W-R	£1 Level Stake	Winning Course	W-R	£1 Level Stake
N Gwilliams	1-2	+ 0.75	Southwell (AW)	1-1	+ 1.75

Winning Horse	Age	Races Run	1st	2nd	3rd	Unpl	Win £
Greenwich Chalenge	3	1	1	0	0	0	2,427

Favourites	1-1	100.0%	+ 1.75	Total winning prize-money	£2,427

1992 Form	19-213	8.9%	- 8.75	1990 Form	20-281	7.1%	-161.74
1991 Form	15-299	5.0%	-130.52	1989 Form	23-182	12.6%	+ 66.83

T CASEY (Upper Lambourn, Berks)

	No. of Horses	Races Run	1st	2nd	3rd	Unpl	Per cent	£1 Level Stake
2-y-o	0	0	0	0	0	0	-	0.00
3-y-o	6	19	1	0	3	15	5.3	- 12.50
4-y-o+	3	29	0	2	1	26	-	- 29.00
Totals	9	48	1	2	4	41	2.1	- 41.50

Jan	Feb	Mar	Apr	May	Jun	Jul	Aug	Sep	Oct/Nov
0-3	0-3	0-3	0-4	0-8	0-4	1-8	0-5	0-5	0-5

Winning Jockey	W-R	£1 Level Stake	Winning Course	W-R	£1 Level Stake
J Reid	1-11	- 4.50	Leicester	1-2	+ 4.50

Winning Horse	Age	Races Run	1st	2nd	3rd	Unpl	Win £
The Ordinary Girl	3	10	1	0	3	6	2,238

Favourites	0-2		Total winning prize-money	£2,238

1992 Form	5-51	9.8%	- 17.50	1990 Form	4-74	5.4%	- 37.50
1991 Form	5-63	7.9%	- 20.67	1989 Form	1-28	3.6%	- 17.00

H R A CECIL (Newmarket)

	No. of Horses	Races Run	1st	2nd	3rd	Unpl	Per cent	£1 Level Stake
2-y-o	34	78	21	9	9	39	26.9	- 0.50
3-y-o	63	272	62	43	43	124	22.8	- 10.82
4-y-o+	11	56	11	11	11	23	19.6	- 3.96
Totals	108	406	94	63	63	186	23.2	- 15.28

BY MONTH

2-y-o	W-R	Per cent	£1 Level Stake	3-y-o	W-R	Per cent	£1 Level Stake
Mar/Apr	0-0	-	0.00	Mar/Apr	5-32	15.6	- 8.07
May	1-2	50.0	+ 1.75	May	15-43	34.9	+ 2.08
June	1-8	12.5	- 6.20	June	19-50	38.0	+ 20.42
July	8-13	61.5	+ 13.76	July	13-52	25.0	+ 23.44
August	0-10	-	- 10.00	August	7-45	15.6	- 9.67
September	6-23	26.1	- 9.04	September	2-24	8.3	- 16.77
Oct/Nov	5-22	22.7	+ 9.23	Oct/Nov	1-26	3.8	- 22.25

75

Cecil H R A

4-y-o+	W-R	Per cent	£1 Level Stake	Totals	W-R	Per cent	£1 Level Stake
Mar/Apr	3-8	37.5	+ 4.86	Mar/Apr	8-40	20.0	- 3.21
May	0-15	-	- 15.00	May	16-60	26.7	- 11.17
June	2-10	20.0	+ 15.50	June	22-68	32.4	+ 29.72
July	3-8	37.5	- 1.62	July	24-73	32.9	+ 35.58
August	1-6	16.7	- 3.00	August	8-61	13.1	- 22.67
September	0-5	-	- 5.00	September	8-52	15.4	- 30.81
Oct/Nov	2-4	50.0	+ 0.30	Oct/Nov	8-52	15.4	- 12.72

DISTANCE

2-y-o	W-R	Per cent	£1 Level Stake	3-y-o	W-R	Per cent	£1 Level Stake
5f-6f	4-15	26.7	+ 1.80	5f-6f	1-2	50.0	+ 1.50
7f-8f	17-63	27.0	- 2.30	7f-8f	7-57	12.3	- 14.50
9f-13f	0-0	-	0.00	9f-13f	47-177	26.6	+ 13.37
14f+	0-0	-	0.00	14f+	7-36	19.4	- 11.19

4-y-o+	W-R	Per cent	£1 Level Stake	Totals	W-R	Per cent	£1 Level Stake
5f-6f	1-11	9.1	- 8.37	5f-6f	6-28	21.4	- 5.07
7f-8f	3-10	30.0	+ 14.40	7f-8f	27-130	20.8	- 2.40
9f-13f	4-17	23.5	+ 2.05	9f-13f	51-194	26.3	+ 15.42
14f+	3-18	16.7	- 12.04	14f+	10-54	18.5	- 23.23

TYPE OF RACE

Non-Handicaps	W-R	Per cent	£1 Level Stake	Handicaps	W-R	Per cent	£1 Level Stake
2-y-o	21-76	27.6	+ 1.50	2-y-o	0-2	-	- 2.00
3-y-o	54-216	25.0	+ 1.73	3-y-o	8-56	14.3	- 12.55
4-y-o+	8-30	26.7	- 13.46	4-y-o+	3-26	11.5	+ 9.50
Selling	0-0	-	0.00	Selling	0-0	-	0.00
Apprentice	0-0	-	0.00	Apprentice	0-0	-	0.00
Amat/Ladies	0-0	-	0.00	Amat/Ladies	0-0	-	0.00
Totals	83-322	25.8	- 10.23	Totals	11-84	13.1	- 5.05

COURSE GRADE

	W-R	Per cent	£1 Level Stake
Group 1	51-249	20.5	- 7.40
Group 2	18-57	31.6	- 5.11
Group 3	23-88	26.1	+ 4.12
Group 4	2-12	16.7	- 6.89

FIRST TIME OUT

	W-R	Per cent	£1 Level Stake
2-y-o	8-34	23.5	- 9.49
3-y-o	13-63	20.6	+ 8.49
4-y-o+	4-11	36.4	+ 3.66
Totals	25-108	23.1	+ 2.66

Cecil H R A

JOCKEYS RIDING

	W-R	Per cent	£1 Level Stake		W-R	Per cent	£1 Level Stake
W Ryan	49-192	25.5	+ 6.79	W Woods	1-1	100.0	+ 5.00
Pat Eddery	25-80	31.3	+ 12.68	L Piggott	1-2	50.0	+ 2.50
A McGlone	9-69	13.0	- 16.08	M J Kinane	1-3	33.3	+ 5.50
M Roberts	7-36	19.4	- 11.42	R Cochrane	1-4	25.0	- 1.25

J Lowe	0-2	D Holland	0-1	S Perks	0-1
K Fallon	0-2	F Norton	0-1	S Whitworth	0-1
W R Swinburn	0-2	J Carroll	0-1	W Carson	0-1
B Raymond	0-1	J Reid	0-1	W Newnes	0-1
C Asmussen	0-1	L Dettori	0-1		
C Rutter	0-1	M Tebbutt	0-1		

COURSE RECORD

	Total W-R	Non-Handicaps 2-y-o	Non-Handicaps 3-y-o+	Handicaps 2-y-o	Handicaps 3-y-o+	Per cent	£1 Level Stake
Newmarket	12-68	1-14	10-43	0-0	1-11	17.6	- 14.44
York	8-31	2-3	5-18	0-1	1-9	25.8	- 6.87
Haydock	7-11	1-1	5-7	0-0	1-3	63.6	+ 11.52
Doncaster	6-26	3-9	3-14	0-0	0-3	23.1	+ 2.65
Salisbury	5-14	0-0	5-13	0-0	0-1	35.7	- 1.70
Ascot	5-20	0-4	3-11	0-0	2-5	25.0	+ 37.50
Goodwood	5-22	3-6	2-10	0-0	0-6	22.7	+ 1.25
Pontefract	4-11	0-0	4-11	0-0	0-0	36.4	+ 8.25
Nottingham	4-16	0-5	3-7	0-0	1-4	25.0	- 6.01
Lingfield	3-7	1-1	2-5	0-0	0-1	42.9	+ 6.32
Beverley	3-8	1-1	1-5	0-0	1-2	37.5	+ 3.23
Chepstow	3-9	1-3	2-5	0-0	0-1	33.3	+ 10.00
Chester	3-9	0-1	3-5	0-0	0-3	33.3	- 2.33
Thirsk	3-10	1-1	2-7	0-0	0-2	30.0	- 1.25
Leicester	3-16	1-5	1-7	0-0	1-4	18.8	+ 1.91
Yarmouth	3-16	2-7	1-7	0-1	0-1	18.8	- 10.17
Epsom	2-4	0-1	1-2	0-0	1-1	50.0	+ 8.83
Ripon	2-8	0-0	2-5	0-0	0-3	25.0	- 1.40
Newcastle	2-9	0-2	0-2	0-0	2-5	22.2	+ 0.12
Windsor	2-9	0-0	2-9	0-0	0-0	22.2	- 2.84
Newbury	2-24	1-4	1-15	0-0	0-5	8.3	- 18.99
Brighton	1-2	1-1	0-1	0-0	0-0	50.0	+ 0.75
Bath	1-3	1-1	0-2	0-0	0-0	33.3	- 0.25
Catterick	1-3	0-1	1-2	0-0	0-0	33.3	+ 0.75
Warwick	1-4	0-1	1-3	0-0	0-0	25.0	- 2.64
Redcar	1-7	0-2	1-3	0-0	0-2	14.3	- 5.50
Kempton	1-15	0-0	1-12	0-0	0-3	6.7	- 11.50
Sandown	1-19	1-1	0-13	0-0	0-5	5.3	- 17.47

Southwell (Turf)	0-2	Lingfield (AW)	0-1
Folkestone	0-1	Southwell (AW)	0-1

WINNING HORSES

	Age	Races Run	1st	2nd	3rd	Unpl	Win £
Commander In Chief	3	5	4	0	1	0	461,311
King's Theatre	2	4	3	0	0	1	97,205
Lyphard's Delta	3	7	4	1	0	2	79,355
Tenby	3	7	2	0	1	4	72,927
Placerville	3	3	2	1	0	0	67,148
Imperial Ballet	4	3	2	0	0	1	46,040
Ardkinglass	3	7	1	1	2	3	40,432
Rainbow Lake	3	6	3	0	0	3	33,713
Armiger	3	3	1	1	0	1	33,526
Edbaysaan	3	8	2	2	2	2	16,693
Licorne	3	8	3	1	2	2	16,637
Queenbird	2	8	3	1	1	3	12,813
Moscow Sea	3	5	2	1	0	2	12,299
Peter Quince	3	5	1	2	1	1	11,053
Wharf	3	6	1	3	0	2	10,116
Bal Harbour	2	2	1	0	0	1	9,190
Alinova	3	6	2	1	1	2	8,628
Kaiser Wilhelm	4	8	2	2	2	2	8,465
Allegan	4	8	2	3	1	2	8,240
Mecklenburg	3	7	2	0	0	5	7,713
Danish Fort	3	4	2	0	1	1	7,338
Kissing Cousin	2	7	2	1	1	3	7,225
Sculler	3	4	1	0	2	1	7,205
Highland Legend	2	2	2	0	0	0	6,901
Dover Patrol	3	5	2	2	0	1	6,802
Averti (USA)	2	3	1	1	0	1	5,390
Electrify	2	3	1	0	1	1	5,163
Tapis Rouge	4	5	1	0	1	3	4,966
Sabrehill	3	3	1	1	0	1	4,893
Khubza	3	3	1	1	0	1	4,581
Ice Pool	3	3	1	1	0	1	4,503
Cicerao	2	2	1	0	0	1	4,503
Coigach	2	3	1	1	1	0	4,485
Florid	2	3	1	1	0	1	4,464
Kerkura	3	3	1	2	0	0	4,403
Big Sky	3	2	1	0	0	1	4,347
Colza	2	1	1	0	0	0	4,305
State Crystal	2	2	1	0	0	1	4,203
Bude	2	2	1	0	1	0	4,085
Winter Forest	3	5	2	1	2	0	4,021
Imaginary	3	3	1	0	2	0	4,013
Vistec Express	3	1	1	0	0	0	3,948
Princess Borghese	3	1	1	0	0	0	3,915
Dreams Are Free	3	6	1	0	0	5	3,883
Trammel	3	3	1	1	0	1	3,816
Vishnu	3	7	1	1	2	3	3,758
Saint Keyne	3	7	1	1	2	3	3,753
Alkhafji	4	3	1	0	1	1	3,728
El Gahar	3	7	1	2	2	2	3,699
Call The Guv'nor	4	8	1	1	1	5	3,655
Graegos	3	4	1	1	0	2	3,641
El Jubail	3	3	1	0	1	1	3,611

Moonshine Lake	3	5	1	0	1	3	3,524
Yeltsin	3	5	1	0	2	2	3,465
Monsignor Pat	3	7	1	0	0	6	3,465
Savoy Truffle	3	6	1	0	1	4	3,436
Cromarty	3	7	1	1	0	5	3,436
Gone Troppo	3	6	1	3	0	2	3,377
Truckhaven Secret	2	2	1	0	0	1	3,377
Garah	4	9	1	2	3	3	3,363
Haunted Wood	3	3	1	0	1	1	3,348
Peto	4	4	1	2	0	1	3,294
Refugio	3	3	1	0	0	2	3,205
Trippiano	3	6	1	0	0	5	3,173
Gingerbird	2	5	1	0	1	3	2,736
Usk The Way	3	7	1	1	1	4	2,489

WINNING OWNERS

	Races Won	Value £		Races Won	Value £
K Abdulla	24	734,061	Prince A A Faisal	4	14,402
Michael Poland	5	104,873	Charles H Wacker III	2	8,465
Sheikh Mohammed	21	83,001	Angus Dundee Ltd	2	6,901
S Khaled	4	79,355	L B Holliday	2	6,802
R E Sangster	3	49,922	Ivan Allan	1	4,503
Sir David Wills	3	48,353	A L R Morton	1	3,948
Lord Howard De Walden	8	44,067	W H Ponsonby	1	3,655
Sheikh Essa Bin Mubarak	2	16,693	Truckhaven Ltd	1	3,377
A S Reid	4	15,549	Mrs Mark Burrell	1	3,173
L Marinopoulos	4	14,801	Cliveden Stud	1	2,489

Favourites	54-138	39.1%	- 14.19	Total winning prize-money		£1,248,388
Longest winning sequence			3	Average SP of winner		3.2/1
Longest losing sequence			24	Return on stakes invested		-2.0%
1992 Form	109-383	28.5%	- 11.43	1990 Form	111-351	31.6%	- 8.67
1991 Form	119-381	31.2%	+ 17.10	1989 Form	116-363	32.0%	+ 48.42

MRS J CECIL (Newmarket)

	No. of Horses	Races Run	1st	2nd	3rd	Unpl	Per cent	£1 Level Stake
2-y-o	20	56	12	8	7	29	21.4	- 5.29
3-y-o	19	89	8	9	13	59	9.0	- 42.45
4-y-o+	13	60	8	5	8	39	13.3	- 31.32
Totals	52	205	28	22	28	127	13.7	- 79.06

Cecil Mrs J

BY MONTH

2-y-o	W-R	Per cent	£1 Level Stake	3-y-o	W-R	Per cent	£1 Level Stake
January	0-0	-	0.00	January	0-0	-	0.00
February	0-0	-	0.00	February	0-0	-	0.00
March	0-0	-	0.00	March	0-0	-	0.00
April	1-1	100.0	+ 1.50	April	2-9	22.2	+ 10.50
May	0-0	-	0.00	May	1-15	6.7	- 11.25
June	1-6	16.7	- 4.27	June	2-19	10.5	- 12.50
July	1-6	16.7	- 3.80	July	2-19	10.5	- 8.20
August	1-14	7.1	- 3.00	August	1-13	7.7	- 7.00
September	3-17	17.6	- 6.72	September	0-10	-	- 10.00
Oct/Nov	5-12	41.7	+ 11.00	Oct/Nov	0-4	-	- 4.00

4-y-o+	W-R	Per cent	£1 Level Stake	Totals	W-R	Per cent	£1 Level Stake
January	0-3	-	- 3.00	January	0-3	-	- 3.00
February	0-2	-	- 2.00	February	0-2	-	- 2.00
March	0-0	-	0.00	March	0-0	-	0.00
April	3-8	37.5	+ 3.13	April	6-18	33.3	+ 15.13
May	3-14	21.4	- 3.20	May	4-29	13.8	- 14.45
June	1-5	20.0	- 1.25	June	4-30	13.3	- 18.02
July	0-6	-	- 6.00	July	3-31	9.7	- 18.00
August	0-7	-	- 7.00	August	2-34	5.9	- 17.00
September	0-9	-	- 9.00	September	3-36	8.3	- 25.72
Oct/Nov	1-6	16.7	- 3.00	Oct/Nov	6-22	27.3	+ 4.00

DISTANCE

2-y-o	W-R	Per cent	£1 Level Stake	3-y-o	W-R	Per cent	£1 Level Stake
5f-6f	7-31	22.6	- 5.49	5f-6f	3-19	15.8	- 3.00
7f-8f	5-25	20.0	+ 0.20	7f-8f	5-37	13.5	- 6.45
9f-13f	0-0	-	0.00	9f-13f	0-30	-	- 30.00
14f+	0-0	-	0.00	14f+	0-3	-	- 3.00

4-y-o+	W-R	Per cent	£1 Level Stake	Totals	W-R	Per cent	£1 Level Stake
5f-6f	0-4	-	- 4.00	5f-6f	10-54	18.5	- 12.49
7f-8f	1-17	5.9	- 14.00	7f-8f	11-79	13.9	- 20.25
9f-13f	6-28	21.4	- 4.12	9f-13f	6-58	10.3	- 34.12
14f+	1-11	9.1	- 9.20	14f+	1-14	7.1	- 12.20

TYPE OF RACE

Non-Handicaps	W-R	Per cent	£1 Level Stake	Handicaps	W-R	Per cent	£1 Level Stake
2-y-o	12-49	24.5	+ 1.71	2-y-o	0-7	-	- 7.00
3-y-o	6-61	9.8	- 29.45	3-y-o	2-26	7.7	- 11.00
4-y-o+	2-9	22.2	- 4.20	4-y-o+	6-50	12.0	- 26.12
Selling	0-1	-	- 1.00	Selling	0-0	-	0.00
Apprentice	0-0	-	0.00	Apprentice	0-1	-	- 1.00
Amat/Ladies	0-1	-	- 1.00	Amat/Ladies	0-0	-	0.00
Totals	20-121	16.5	- 33.94	Totals	8-84	9.5	- 45.12

Cecil Mrs J

	COURSE GRADE				FIRST TIME OUT		
	W-R	Per cent	£1 Level Stake		W-R	Per cent	£1 Level Stake
Group 1	8-107	7.5	- 69.47	2-y-o	1-20	5.0	- 17.50
Group 2	6-43	14.0	- 12.70	3-y-o	1-19	5.3	- 4.00
Group 3	8-42	19.0	- 7.47	4-y-o+	1-13	7.7	- 7.00
Group 4	6-13	46.2	+ 10.58				
				Totals	3-52	5.8	- 28.50

JOCKEYS RIDING

	W-R	Per cent	£1 Level Stake		W-R	Per cent	£1 Level Stake
Paul Eddery	16-77	20.8	- 6.04	R Hills	1-4	25.0	- 1.00
L Piggott	3-13	23.1	- 3.52	D Biggs	1-5	20.0	- 2.50
G Duffield	3-15	20.0	- 3.70	B Raymond	1-12	8.3	- 9.80
P Robinson	2-15	13.3	+ 9.00	L Dettori	1-16	6.3	- 13.50

W Newnes	0-11	M Hills	0-2	J Reid	0-1		
J Quinn	0-6	W R Swinburn	0-2	M Birch	0-1		
J Carroll	0-5	A Clark	0-1	Mrs J Crossley	0-1		
M Roberts	0-5	A Garth	0-1	T Kent	0-1		
W Ryan	0-4	D Holland	0-1	T Quinn	0-1		
C Asmussen	0-3	F Norton	0-1	W Woods	0-1		

COURSE RECORD

	Total W-R	Non-Handicaps 2-y-o	Non-Handicaps 3-y-o+	Handicaps 2-y-o	Handicaps 3-y-o+	Per cent	£1 Level Stake
Kempton	4-12	0-1	3-6	0-0	1-5	33.3	+ 12.55
Nottingham	3-11	2-3	0-5	0-0	1-3	27.3	- 3.97
Catterick	2-2	2-2	0-0	0-0	0-0	100.0	+ 4.20
Folkestone	2-2	0-0	1-1	0-0	1-1	100.0	+ 8.50
Warwick	2-2	1-1	0-0	0-0	1-1	100.0	+ 4.88
Redcar	2-8	1-4	1-1	0-0	0-3	25.0	- 1.50
Lingfield	2-11	2-4	0-5	0-0	0-2	18.2	0.00
Yarmouth	2-14	0-4	1-6	0-1	1-3	14.3	- 1.00
Bath	1-3	0-1	0-1	0-0	1-1	33.3	+ 3.00
Beverley	1-3	1-2	0-1	0-0	0-0	33.3	+ 3.00
Thirsk	1-4	0-0	1-2	0-0	0-2	25.0	- 2.20
Leicester	1-5	1-2	0-3	0-0	0-0	20.0	- 2.50
Ascot	1-6	0-1	0-2	0-0	1-3	16.7	- 2.25
Brighton	1-6	1-2	0-3	0-1	0-0	16.7	+ 5.00
Doncaster	1-10	0-3	1-4	0-0	0-3	10.0	- 7.50
York	1-14	0-3	0-1	0-3	1-7	7.1	- 9.00
Newmarket	1-29	1-10	0-9	0-2	0-8	3.4	- 27.27

Sandown	0-14	Goodwood	0-5	Chester	0-1
Haydock	0-8	Pontefract	0-4	Edinburgh	0-1
Newbury	0-8	Lingfield (AW)	0-3	Hamilton	0-1
Ripon	0-7	Southwell (AW)	0-3	Newcastle	0-1
Salisbury	0-6	Chepstow	0-1		

Cecil Mrs J

WINNING HORSES

	Age	Races Run	1st	2nd	3rd	Unpl	Win £
Alderbrook	4	8	5	1	0	2	21,874
Baby Loves	2	2	1	1	0	0	11,326
Mary Hinge	2	6	3	1	2	0	10,746
Press Gallery	3	10	2	0	0	8	8,127
Saihat	2	5	2	0	2	1	7,101
Ambiguously Regal	4	8	1	2	2	3	5,345
Stoller	2	3	1	1	0	1	4,807
Golden Guest	3	7	1	0	4	2	4,581
Bold Sixteen	2	2	1	0	0	1	4,450
Gneiss	2	3	1	1	0	1	4,226
Laune	2	5	1	1	0	3	4,128
Star Jazz	2	4	1	1	1	1	4,110
Awestrike	3	7	1	1	1	4	3,641
Pixton	3	4	1	0	0	3	3,553
Dramanice	3	4	1	2	1	0	3,524
Hilary Gerrard	3	6	1	0	1	4	3,377
Pater Noster	4	5	1	1	1	2	3,260
Putout	3	7	1	2	0	4	3,231
Nera	2	6	1	1	1	3	3,161
Long Silence	4	3	1	0	1	1	3,143

WINNING OWNERS

	Races Won	Value £		Races Won	Value £
E Pick	5	21,874	Exors of the late –		
Lord Howard De Walden	3	12,255	Mrs V Hue-Williams	1	4,581
S S Niarchos	1	11,326	Miss Donna E Dillard	1	4,450
Mrs J Cecil	3	10,746	Matthew Oram	1	4,226
George L Ohrstrom	2	8,985	Southgate Racing	1	4,110
Prince A A Faisal	2	7,101	Mrs J Yarnold	1	3,553
W S Farish III	2	6,667	Lord Tavistock	1	3,231
Martin Myers	2	6,638	Lady Portman	1	3,161
Dr Howard J Baker	1	4,807			

Favourites	16-40	40.0%	+ 4.19	
Longest winning sequence			2	
Longest losing sequence			33	
1992 Form	30-162	18.5%	+ 75.32	

Total winning prize-money		£117,709
Average SP of winner		3.5/1
Return on stakes invested		-38.6%
1991 Form	19-95	20.0%	- 3.45

N CHAMBERLAIN (West Auckland, Co Durham)

	No. of Horses	Races Run	1st	2nd	3rd	Unpl	Per cent	£1 Level Stake
2-y-o	1	1	0	0	0	1	-	- 1.00
3-y-o	3	27	1	2	3	21	3.7	- 10.00
4-y-o+	1	2	0	0	0	2	-	- 2.00
Totals	5	30	1	2	3	24	3.3	- 13.00

Jan	Feb	Mar	Apr	May	Jun	Jul	Aug	Sep	Oct/Nov
0-0	0-0	0-0	0-3	0-7	0-4	0-4	0-7	0-3	1-2

Winning Jockey	W-R	£1 Level Stake	Winning Course	W-R	£1 Level Stake
M Fenton	1-1	+ 16.00	Newcastle	1-5	+ 12.00

Winning Horse	Age	Races Run	1st	2nd	3rd	Unpl	Win £
Public Way	3	15	1	1	2	11	2,960

Favourites	0-0		Total winning prize-money	£2,960

1992 Form	1-10	10.0%	+ 16.00	1990 Form	0-14
1991 Form	0-18			1989 Form	0-6

M R CHANNON (Upper Lambourn, Berks)

	No. of Horses	Races Run	1st	2nd	3rd	Unpl	Per cent	£1 Level Stake
2-y-o	32	178	17	19	21	121	9.6	- 50.37
3-y-o	20	127	14	18	11	84	11.0	+ 0.63
4-y-o+	14	101	8	11	6	76	7.9	- 17.00
Totals	66	406	39	48	38	281	9.6	- 66.74

BY MONTH

2-y-o	W-R	Per cent	£1 Level Stake	3-y-o	W-R	Per cent	£1 Level Stake
January	0-0	-	0.00	January	0-5	-	- 5.00
February	0-0	-	0.00	February	0-3	-	- 3.00
March	0-0	-	0.00	March	1-4	25.0	0.00
April	3-11	27.3	+ 2.88	April	1-9	11.1	- 0.50
May	1-24	4.2	- 22.33	May	0-14	-	- 14.00
June	3-22	13.6	- 2.67	June	5-17	29.4	+ 29.63
July	0-32	-	- 32.00	July	2-19	10.5	- 7.50
August	6-41	14.6	- 8.25	August	1-22	4.5	- 5.00
September	2-25	8.0	+ 1.00	September	0-14	-	- 14.00
Oct/Nov	2-23	8.7	+ 11.00	Oct/Nov	4-20	20.0	+ 20.00

Channon M R

4-y-o+	W-R	Per cent	£1 Level Stake		Totals	W-R	Per cent	£1 Level Stake
January	0-1	-	-	1.00	January	0-6	-	- 6.00
February	0-5	-	-	5.00	February	0-8	-	- 8.00
March	1-9	11.1	+	1.00	March	2-13	15.4	+ 1.00
April	0-13	-	-	13.00	April	4-33	12.1	- 10.62
May	4-15	26.7	+	21.00	May	5-53	9.4	- 15.33
June	0-12	-	-	12.00	June	8-51	15.7	+ 14.96
July	0-13	-	-	13.00	July	2-64	3.1	- 52.50
August	0-9	-	-	9.00	August	7-72	9.7	- 22.25
September	2-8	25.0	+	15.00	September	4-47	8.5	+ 2.00
Oct/Nov	1-16	6.3	-	1.00	Oct/Nov	7-59	11.9	+ 30.00

DISTANCE

2-y-o	W-R	Per cent	£1 Level Stake	3-y-o	W-R	Per cent	£1 Level Stake
5f-6f	12-126	9.5	- 28.12	5f-6f	4-29	13.8	+ 27.00
7f-8f	5-51	9.8	- 21.25	7f-8f	5-44	11.4	+ 1.50
9f-13f	0-1	-	- 1.00	9f-13f	3-39	7.7	- 22.50
14f+	0-0	-	0.00	14f+	2-15	13.3	- 5.37

4-y-o+	W-R	Per cent	£1 Level Stake	Totals	W-R	Per cent	£1 Level Stake
5f-6f	3-18	16.7	+ 16.00	5f-6f	19-173	11.0	- 14.88
7f-8f	3-58	5.2	- 22.00	7f-8f	13-153	8.5	- 41.75
9f-13f	2-23	8.7	- 9.00	9f-13f	5-63	7.9	- 32.50
14f+	0-2	-	- 2.00	14f+	2-17	11.8	- 7.37

TYPE OF RACE

Non-Handicaps	W-R	Per cent	£1 Level Stake	Handicaps	W-R	Per cent	£1 Level Stake
2-y-o	13-117	11.1	- 11.12	2-y-o	2-28	7.1	- 16.75
3-y-o	2-47	4.3	- 37.50	3-y-o	7-59	11.9	+ 21.50
4-y-o+	2-15	13.3	+ 4.00	4-y-o+	6-77	7.8	- 12.00
Selling	3-33	9.1	- 11.00	Selling	1-10	10.0	- 6.00
Apprentice	1-3	33.3	- 0.37	Apprentice	2-16	12.5	+ 3.50
Amat/Ladies	0-0	-	0.00	Amat/Ladies	0-1	-	- 1.00
Totals	21-215	9.8	- 55.99	Totals	18-191	9.4	- 10.75

COURSE GRADE

	W-R	Per cent	£1 Level Stake
Group 1	14-144	9.7	- 2.58
Group 2	3-72	4.2	- 56.17
Group 3	12-115	10.4	- 3.37
Group 4	10-75	13.3	- 4.62

FIRST TIME OUT

	W-R	Per cent	£1 Level Stake
2-y-o	3-31	9.7	- 2.67
3-y-o	1-17	5.9	- 13.00
4-y-o+	0-13	-	- 13.00
Totals	4-61	6.6	- 28.67

JOCKEYS RIDING

	W-R	Per cent	£1 Level Stake		W-R	Per cent	£1 Level Stake
R Painter	9-47	19.1	+ 24.63	W Woods	1-8	12.5	+ 13.00
T Quinn	8-41	19.5	+ 28.33	J Williams	1-10	10.0	- 1.50
Pat Eddery	5-28	17.9	- 4.33	N Adams	1-10	10.0	+ 11.00
C Rutter	3-41	7.3	- 20.00	P Robinson	1-10	10.0	- 5.50
W Carson	2-11	18.2	+ 8.00	B Doyle	1-12	8.3	- 1.00
S Whitworth	2-18	11.1	+ 3.50	G Duffield	1-12	8.3	- 9.62
M Roberts	1-3	33.3	+ 5.50	Lorna Vincent	1-15	6.7	- 8.00
L Piggott	1-3	33.3	+ 0.25	Paul Eddery	1-28	3.6	- 2.00

J Quinn	0-12	M Hills	0-3	J Carroll	0-1
A Munro	0-8	R Hills	0-3	J Fortune	0-1
F Norton	0-8	B Rouse	0-2	Kim McDonnell	0-1
G Carter	0-8	D McKeown	0-2	M Fenton	0-1
D Holland	0-7	Mark Denaro	0-2	M J Kinane	0-1
K Fallon	0-6	N Varley	0-2	Mr Raymond White	0-1
N Carlisle	0-5	T Williams	0-2	N Day	0-1
L Dettori	0-4	A Culhane	0-1	P McCabe	0-1
W Newnes	0-4	A Mackay	0-1	R Cochrane	0-1
A Tucker	0-3	B Raymond	0-1	S Davies	0-1
Antoinette Armes	0-3	G Bardwell	0-1	S Wood	0-1
D Wright	0-3	G Hind	0-1	W Ryan	0-1
J Reid	0-3	G McCourt	0-1	Wendy Jones	0-1

COURSE RECORD

	Total W-R	Non-Handicaps 2-y-o	3-y-o+	Handicaps 2-y-o	3-y-o+	Per cent	£1 Level Stake
Folkestone	4-22	1-10	1-5	0-1	2-6	18.2	+ 6.00
Pontefract	3-12	2-6	0-3	1-1	0-2	25.0	+ 21.00
Goodwood	3-15	2-4	0-2	0-3	1-6	20.0	+ 18.67
Doncaster	3-18	1-5	0-2	0-1	2-10	16.7	+ 4.00
Southwell (Turf)	2-3	1-1	1-1	0-0	0-1	66.7	+ 12.00
Leicester	2-21	0-12	1-5	0-1	1-3	9.5	- 2.50
Sandown	2-24	1-7	0-5	0-2	1-10	8.3	- 14.50
Bath	2-25	0-9	0-3	0-1	2-12	8.0	0.00
Edinburgh	1-2	1-1	0-0	0-0	0-1	50.0	+ 0.38
Catterick	1-3	0-0	0-0	0-1	1-2	33.3	+ 4.00
Hamilton	1-3	0-1	1-2	0-0	0-0	33.3	+ 1.50
Newcastle	1-4	0-3	0-0	1-1	0-0	25.0	- 0.75
York	1-5	0-2	0-0	0-1	1-2	20.0	+ 21.00
Southwell (AW)	1-7	1-3	0-1	0-0	0-3	14.3	- 4.00
Ascot	1-8	1-5	0-0	0-0	0-3	12.5	+ 3.00
Beverley	1-8	0-3	0-0	0-1	1-4	12.5	- 1.00
Redcar	1-8	0-2	1-2	0-1	0-3	12.5	- 3.00
Yarmouth	1-8	0-3	0-2	1-2	0-1	12.5	- 4.00
Nottingham	1-10	0-2	1-2	0-2	0-4	10.0	- 7.37
Haydock	1-12	0-1	0-3	0-1	1-7	8.3	0.00
Newbury	1-14	0-6	0-1	0-1	1-6	7.1	- 3.00
Warwick	1-15	0-4	1-5	0-2	0-4	6.7	0.00
Brighton	1-20	1-9	0-2	0-1	0-8	5.0	- 13.50
Windsor	1-20	0-14	0-2	0-2	1-2	5.0	- 3.00
Newmarket	1-21	1-9	0-2	0-1	0-9	4.8	- 8.00
Salisbury	1-22	1-9	0-2	0-0	0-11	4.5	- 17.67

Lingfield (AW)	0-23	Lingfield	0-10	Ripon	0-3
Epsom	0-11	Chepstow	0-8	Ayr	0-1
Kempton	0-11	Chester	0-8	Thirsk	0-1

WINNING HORSES

	Age	Races Run	1st	2nd	3rd	Unpl	Win £
Aradanza	3	8	1	0	1	6	28,543
Great Deeds	2	7	2	1	2	2	21,929
Domicksky	5	17	3	2	1	11	14,389
Champagne Grandy	3	15	4	3	1	7	11,939
Dodgy Dancer	3	11	3	1	2	5	8,257
Rohita	2	6	2	1	1	2	7,765
Cyarna Quinn	2	15	2	3	1	9	6,250
Proud Brigadier	5	12	2	1	3	6	6,171
Indefence	2	8	2	3	2	1	6,003
Crazy For You	2	6	1	2	0	3	5,205
Princess Tateum	3	14	2	3	2	7	5,183
Cheveux Mitchell	6	10	1	2	0	7	5,090
Mr Butch	3	3	1	0	0	2	4,752
Piccolo	2	6	1	0	3	2	4,191
Henry's Luck	2	9	2	0	2	5	3,795
Sixpees	2	1	1	0	0	0	3,758
Glowing Jade	3	5	1	0	0	4	3,493
Knobbleeneeze	3	9	1	2	2	4	3,340
Strapped	2	16	1	1	1	13	3,248
Va Utu	5	6	1	1	0	4	3,210
Kingswell Prince	2	6	1	0	1	4	3,054
Waki Gold	6	10	1	2	0	7	2,469
Little Hooligan	2	13	1	1	0	11	2,243
Window Display	2	11	1	3	2	5	2,070
She Knew The Rules	3	5	1	0	0	4	2,070

WINNING OWNERS

	Races Won	Value £		Races Won	Value £
Mrs P Lewis	1	28,543	Chitty Ltd	1	5,090
Dubai Racing Syndicate	2	21,929	G Herridge	1	4,752
M J Watson	4	17,637	T Leigh	1	4,191
T W Langley	5	12,052	Mrs N K Crook	1	3,758
Grandy Girls	4	11,939	Brian T Eastick	1	3,493
M Quinn	3	9,460	Anthony Andrews	1	3,340
B J Taylor	2	7,765	Stephen Crown	1	3,054
M T Lawrance	2	6,171	Mrs Susan Tate	1	2,469
Les Hamilton	2	6,003	A Kinghorn	1	2,243
Club 7 Racing	1	5,205	Sheet & Roll Converters Ltd	1	2,070
J R Good	2	5,183	Peter Jolliffe	1	2,070

Favourites	9-49	18.4%	- 17.74	Total winning prize-money		£168,414
Longest winning sequence			2	Average SP of winner		7.7/1
Longest losing sequence			35	Return on stakes invested		-16.4%
1992 Form	27-303	8.9%	-120.09	1990 Form	16-162	9.9% + 2.66
1991 Form	22-235	9.4%	- 55.25			

D W CHAPMAN (Stillington, North Yorks)

	No. of Horses	Races Run	1st	2nd	3rd	Unpl	Per cent	£1 Level Stake
2-y-o	6	32	1	1	3	27	3.1	- 27.00
3-y-o	8	46	3	2	4	37	6.5	- 38.77
4-y-o+	22	171	18	17	12	124	10.5	- 62.96
Totals	36	249	22	20	19	188	8.8	-128.73

BY MONTH

2-y-o	W-R	Per cent	£1 Level Stake	3-y-o	W-R	Per cent	£1 Level Stake
January	0-0	-	0.00	January	0-4	-	- 4.00
February	0-0	-	0.00	February	0-6	-	- 6.00
March	0-0	-	0.00	March	0-2	-	- 2.00
April	0-1	-	- 1.00	April	1-7	14.3	- 3.75
May	0-3	-	- 3.00	May	1-5	20.0	- 3.27
June	1-4	25.0	+ 1.00	June	1-3	33.3	- 0.75
July	0-9	-	- 9.00	July	0-0	-	0.00
August	0-7	-	- 7.00	August	0-5	-	- 5.00
September	0-3	-	- 3.00	September	0-5	-	- 5.00
Oct/Nov	0-5	-	- 5.00	Oct/Nov	0-9	-	- 9.00

4-y-o+	W-R	Per cent	£1 Level Stake	Totals	W-R	Per cent	£1 Level Stake
January	7-18	38.9	+ 14.26	January	7-22	31.8	+ 10.26
February	2-26	7.7	- 21.60	February	2-32	6.3	- 27.60
March	3-17	17.6	- 10.87	March	3-19	15.8	- 12.87
April	2-13	15.4	+ 10.75	April	3-21	14.3	+ 6.00
May	1-20	5.0	- 13.00	May	2-28	7.1	- 19.27
June	0-15	-	- 15.00	June	2-22	9.1	- 14.75
July	1-24	4.2	- 17.00	July	1-33	3.0	- 26.00
August	2-15	13.3	+ 12.50	August	2-27	7.4	+ 0.50
September	0-16	-	- 16.00	September	0-24	-	- 24.00
Oct/Nov	0-7	-	- 7.00	Oct/Nov	0-21	-	- 21.00

DISTANCE

2-y-o	W-R	Per cent	£1 Level Stake	3-y-o	W-R	Per cent	£1 Level Stake
5f-6f	1-28	3.6	- 23.00	5f-6f	3-26	11.5	- 18.77
7f-8f	0-4	-	- 4.00	7f-8f	0-18	-	- 18.00
9f-13f	0-0	-	0.00	9f-13f	0-2	-	- 2.00
14f+	0-0	-	0.00	14f+	0-0	-	0.00

4-y-o+	W-R	Per cent	£1 Level Stake	Totals	W-R	Per cent	£1 Level Stake
5f-6f	5-84	6.0	- 35.50	5f-6f	9-138	6.5	- 77.27
7f-8f	6-54	11.1	- 7.79	7f-8f	6-76	7.9	- 29.79
9f-13f	6-28	21.4	- 16.34	9f-13f	6-30	20.0	- 18.34
14f+	1-5	20.0	- 3.33	14f+	1-5	20.0	- 3.33

TYPE OF RACE

Non-Handicaps	W-R	Per cent	£1 Level Stake	Handicaps	W-R	Per cent	£1 Level Stake
2-y-o	1-15	6.7	- 10.00	2-y-o	0-8	-	- 8.00
3-y-o	1-11	9.1	- 9.27	3-y-o	2-31	6.5	- 25.50
4-y-o+	10-41	24.4	- 17.37	4-y-o+	6-107	5.6	- 36.59
Selling	1-9	11.1	- 2.00	Selling	0-11	-	- 11.00
Apprentice	0-1	-	- 1.00	Apprentice	1-7	14.3	0.00
Amat/Ladies	0-0	-	0.00	Amat/Ladies	0-8	-	- 8.00
Totals	13-77	16.9	- 39.64	Totals	9-172	5.2	- 89.09

COURSE GRADE

	W-R	Per cent	£1 Level Stake
Group 1	1-35	2.9	- 33.27
Group 2	2-42	4.8	0.00
Group 3	2-32	6.3	- 22.25
Group 4	17-140	12.1	- 73.21

FIRST TIME OUT

	W-R	Per cent	£1 Level Stake
2-y-o	0-5	-	- 5.00
3-y-o	0-7	-	- 7.00
4-y-o+	2-19	10.5	- 0.33
Totals	2-31	6.5	- 12.33

JOCKEYS RIDING

	W-R	Per cent	£1 Level Stake		W-R	Per cent	£1 Level Stake
S Wood	17-132	12.9	- 30.96	Claire Balding	1-6	16.7	+ 1.00
K Darley	3-16	18.8	- 8.77	D Nicholls	1-15	6.7	- 10.00

J Fanning	0-16	K Fallon	0-2	J Quinn	0-1
Miss R Clark	0-8	L Dettori	0-2	Mrs L Pearce	0-1
O Pears	0-8	N Adams	0-2	Mrs M Cowdrey	0-1
Alex Greaves	0-5	S Maloney	0-2	N Carlisle	0-1
N Connorton	0-4	W Carson	0-2	N Kennedy	0-1
A McGlone	0-3	D Harrison	0-1	Paul Eddery	0-1
J Fortune	0-3	D McCabe	0-1	R Hills	0-1
C Teague	0-2	D Wright	0-1	T Lucas	0-1
Carl Llewellyn	0-2	Dale Gibson	0-1	W Newnes	0-1
D Moffatt	0-2	G Bardwell	0-1		
J Williams	0-2	G Duffield	0-1		

COURSE RECORD

	Total W-R	Non-Handicaps 2-y-o	3-y-o+	Handicaps 2-y-o	3-y-o+	Per cent	£1 Level Stake
Southwell (AW)	14-90	0-7	10-36	0-0	4-47	15.6	- 33.46
Edinburgh	2-14	1-3	0-0	0-0	1-11	14.3	- 6.75
Thirsk	2-18	0-1	0-0	0-1	2-16	11.1	+ 24.00
Hamilton	1-5	0-0	0-1	0-0	1-4	20.0	- 1.75
Ayr	1-7	0-0	1-1	0-2	0-4	14.3	- 5.27
Pontefract	1-12	0-0	0-4	0-0	1-8	8.3	- 5.50
Lingfield (AW)	1-15	0-0	1-5	0-0	0-10	6.7	- 12.00

Redcar	0-15	Doncaster	0-6	Goodwood	0-2
Haydock	0-11	Newcastle	0-6	Yarmouth	0-2
Catterick	0-9	Nottingham	0-4	York	0-2
Ripon	0-7	Leicester	0-3	Chester	0-1
Beverley	0-6	Southwell (Turf)	0-3	Lingfield	0-1
Carlisle	0-6	Warwick	0-3	Sandown	0-1

WINNING HORSES

	Age	Races Run	1st	2nd	3rd	Unpl	Win £
Tempering	7	13	7	3	0	3	17,675
No Submission	7	26	6	4	1	15	15,599
Shadow Jury	3	17	3	2	2	10	9,117
Kalar	4	18	2	2	1	13	5,857
Kabcast	8	10	1	2	2	5	3,818
Lucky Fourteen	2	7	1	0	1	5	2,365
Buzbour	5	3	1	0	1	1	2,070
Appealing Times	4	9	1	1	0	7	2,070

WINNING OWNERS

	Races Won	Value £		Races Won	Value £
David W Chapman	8	19,745	Mrs M M Marshall	1	3,818
T S Redman	6	15,599	Ian W Glenton	1	2,365
P D Savill	3	9,117	Miss N F Thesiger	1	2,070
E Stockdale	2	5,857			

Favourites	12-31	38.7%	- 8.48	Total winning prize-money		£58,571

Longest winning sequence	2	Average SP of winner	4.5/1
Longest losing sequence	49	Return on stakes invested	-51.7%

1992 Form	15-282	5.3%	- 79.75	1990 Form	22-415	5.3%	-245.78
1991 Form	24-365	6.6%	-158.10	1989 Form	29-474	6.1%	-253.81

M C CHAPMAN (Market Rasen, Lincs)

	No. of Horses	Races Run	1st	2nd	3rd	Unpl	Per cent	£1 Level Stake
2-y-o	3	12	0	0	1	11	-	- 12.00
3-y-o	4	40	5	6	5	24	12.5	+ 18.50
4-y-o+	14	103	4	10	11	78	3.9	- 72.75
Totals	21	155	9	16	17	113	5.8	- 66.25

Jan	Feb	Mar	Apr	May	Jun	Jul	Aug	Sep	Oct/Nov
4-20	1-26	1-20	0-11	0-16	1-16	0-23	1-8	1-8	0-7

Winning Jockeys	W-R	£1 Level Stake		W-R	£1 Level Stake
D McCabe	7-63	+ 2.50	S Wood	1-14	+ 7.00
S D Williams	1-12	- 9.75			

Winning Courses	W-R	£1 Level Stake		W-R	£1 Level Stake
Southwell (AW)	7-82	- 29.25	Pontefract	1-11	+ 15.00
York	1-6	+ 4.00			

Winning Horses	Age	Races Run	1st	2nd	3rd	Unpl	Win £
Karinska	3	10	2	1	0	7	7,755
Rose Flyer	3	27	3	5	5	14	5,961
Sugemar	7	20	2	5	6	7	4,623
Kronprinz	5	7	1	0	0	6	2,616
Master's Crown	5	6	1	2	1	2	2,511

Favourites	4-10	40.0%	+ 2.25	Total winning prize-money		£23,466

1992 Form	1-79	1.3%	- 72.00	1990 Form	1-62	1.6%	- 28.00
1991 Form	7-111	6.3%	+ 3.50	1989 Form	0-47		

D N CHAPPELL (West Ilsley, Berks)

	No. of Horses	Races Run	1st	2nd	3rd	Unpl	Per cent	£1 Level Stake
2-y-o	2	5	1	0	0	4	20.0	+ 29.00
3-y-o	0	0	0	0	0	0	-	0.00
4-y-o+	1	3	0	0	0	3	-	- 3.00
Totals	3	8	1	0	0	7	12.5	+ 26.00

Jan	Feb	Mar	Apr	May	Jun	Jul	Aug	Sep	Oct/Nov
0-0	0-0	0-0	0-1	0-2	0-0	0-0	0-1	0-0	1-4

Winning Jockey	W-R	£1 Level Stake	Winning Course	W-R	£1 Level Stake
A Tucker	1-6	+ 28.00	Warwick	1-2	+ 32.00

Winning Horse	Age	Races Run	1st	2nd	3rd	Unpl	Win £
White Shoot	2	2	1	0	0	1	3,465

Favourites	0-0	Total winning prize-money	£3,465

P CHAPPLE-HYAM (Marlborough, Wilts)

	No. of Horses	Races Run	1st	2nd	3rd	Unpl	Per cent	£1 Level Stake
2-y-o	33	84	28	17	6	33	33.3	+ 6.48
3-y-o	34	134	23	16	16	79	17.2	- 43.50
4-y-o+	5	20	1	3	1	15	5.0	- 12.50
Totals	72	238	52	36	23	127	21.8	- 49.52

BY MONTH

2-y-o	W-R	Per cent	£1 Level Stake	3-y-o	W-R	Per cent	£1 Level Stake
January	0-0	-	0.00	January	0-0	-	0.00
February	0-0	-	0.00	February	0-2	-	- 2.00
March	0-0	-	0.00	March	0-3	-	- 3.00
April	1-1	100.0	+ 1.63	April	7-26	26.9	+ 4.01
May	2-3	66.7	+ 1.87	May	9-27	33.3	- 1.98
June	3-5	60.0	+ 2.62	June	3-28	10.7	- 20.78
July	4-18	22.2	- 6.86	July	2-19	10.5	- 3.00
August	9-16	56.3	+ 11.48	August	2-14	14.3	- 1.75
September	5-20	25.0	+ 3.03	September	0-11	-	- 11.00
Oct/Nov	4-21	19.0	- 7.29	Oct/Nov	0-4	-	- 4.00

4-y-o+	W-R	Per cent	£1 Level Stake		Totals	W-R	Per cent	£1 Level Stake
January	0-0	-	0.00		January	0-0	-	0.00
February	0-0	-	0.00		February	0-2	-	- 2.00
March	0-0	-	0.00		March	0-3	-	- 3.00
April	1-4	25.0	+ 3.50		April	9-31	29.0	+ 9.14
May	0-2	-	- 2.00		May	11-32	34.4	- 2.11
June	0-2	-	- 2.00		June	6-35	17.1	- 20.16
July	0-5	-	- 5.00		July	6-42	14.3	- 14.86
August	0-3	-	- 3.00		August	11-33	33.3	+ 6.73
September	0-4	-	- 4.00		September	5-35	14.3	- 11.97
Oct/Nov	0-0	-	0.00		Oct/Nov	4-25	16.0	- 11.29

DISTANCE

2-y-o	W-R	Per cent	£1 Level Stake	3-y-o	W-R	Per cent	£1 Level Stake
5f-6f	15-39	38.5	- 1.07	5f-6f	1-11	9.1	- 8.90
7f-8f	13-44	29.5	+ 8.55	7f-8f	8-54	14.8	- 21.61
9f-13f	0-1	-	- 1.00	9f-13f	14-65	21.5	- 8.99
14f+	0-0	-	0.00	14f+	0-4	-	- 4.00

4-y-o+	W-R	Per cent	£1 Level Stake	Totals	W-R	Per cent	£1 Level Stake
5f-6f	0-3	-	- 3.00	5f-6f	16-53	30.2	- 12.97
7f-8f	1-12	8.3	- 4.50	7f-8f	22-110	20.0	- 17.56
9f-13f	0-5	-	- 5.00	9f-13f	14-71	19.7	- 14.99
14f+	0-0	-	0.00	14f+	0-4	-	- 4.00

TYPE OF RACE

	W-R	Per cent	£1 Level Stake		W-R	Per cent	£1 Level Stake
Non-Handicaps				Handicaps			
2-y-o	26-80	32.5	- 8.85	2-y-o	2-4	50.0	+ 15.33
3-y-o	19-98	19.4	- 39.40	3-y-o	4-35	11.4	- 3.10
4-y-o+	1-12	8.3	- 4.50	4-y-o+	0-2	-	- 2.00
Selling	0-0	-	0.00	Selling	0-0	-	0.00
Apprentice	0-0	-	0.00	Apprentice	0-2	-	- 2.00
Amat/Ladies	0-2	-	- 2.00	Amat/Ladies	0-3	-	- 3.00
Totals	46-192	24.0	- 54.75	Totals	6-46	13.0	+ 5.23

COURSE GRADE / FIRST TIME OUT

	W-R	Per cent	£1 Level Stake		W-R	Per cent	£1 Level Stake
Group 1	31-140	22.1	- 17.55	2-y-o	11-32	34.4	+ 2.49
Group 2	10-35	28.6	- 2.71	3-y-o	6-32	18.8	- 0.02
Group 3	5-38	13.2	- 19.19	4-y-o+	1-5	20.0	+ 2.50
Group 4	6-25	24.0	- 10.07	Totals	18-69	26.1	+ 4.97

JOCKEYS RIDING

	W-R	Per cent	£1 Level Stake		W-R	Per cent	£1 Level Stake
J Reid	30-127	23.6	- 5.36	Paul Eddery	2-6	33.3	+ 4.38
S Davies	8-46	17.4	- 16.31	T Quinn	1-1	100.0	+ 1.25
D Holland	6-22	27.3	- 5.72	K Fallon	1-2	50.0	- 0.60
Pat Eddery	3-5	60.0	+ 0.34	W Carson	1-4	25.0	- 2.50

Mrs J Chapple-Hyam	0-6	R Cochrane	0-2	M Birch	0-1
S Whitworth	0-4	A Clark	0-1	M Fenton	0-1
L Dettori	0-3	F Norton	0-1	M Hills	0-1
M Roberts	0-3	Kate Dovey	0-1	W Newnes	0-1

COURSE RECORD

	Total W-R	Non-Handicaps 2-y-o	3-y-o+	Handicaps 2-y-o	3-y-o+	Per cent	£1 Level Stake
Newbury	11-34	7-15	3-13	1-2	0-4	32.4	- 0.71
York	4-12	3-4	0-6	0-0	1-2	33.3	+ 6.37
Ascot	4-15	3-3	1-9	0-0	0-3	26.7	- 6.13
Newmarket	4-31	1-15	1-12	1-1	1-3	12.9	+ 9.75
Ayr	3-7	1-2	1-3	0-0	1-2	42.9	+ 0.19
Beverley	3-7	1-1	2-4	0-0	0-2	42.9	+ 7.08
Warwick	3-9	2-4	1-4	0-0	0-1	33.3	+ 1.04
Chester	3-10	1-2	2-5	0-0	0-3	30.0	+ 3.75
Ripon	2-4	1-1	0-2	0-0	1-1	50.0	+ 1.84
Catterick	2-7	0-1	2-4	0-0	0-2	28.6	- 3.28
Salisbury	2-9	2-5	0-3	0-0	0-1	22.2	- 3.75
Doncaster	2-13	2-5	0-6	0-1	0-1	15.4	- 8.52
Brighton	1-3	0-0	1-3	0-0	0-0	33.3	- 0.12
Edinburgh	1-3	0-0	1-2	0-0	0-1	33.3	- 1.83
Haydock	1-3	1-2	0-1	0-0	0-0	33.3	+ 0.25
Lingfield	1-4	0-1	1-2	0-0	0-1	25.0	- 1.00
Pontefract	1-4	0-1	1-3	0-0	0-0	25.0	- 2.27
Thirsk	1-5	0-1	1-3	0-0	0-1	20.0	- 3.43
Chepstow	1-6	0-3	1-2	0-0	0-1	16.7	- 3.00
Epsom	1-9	0-0	1-8	0-0	0-1	11.1	- 6.75
Goodwood	1-12	1-8	0-1	0-0	0-3	8.3	- 8.00

Bath	0-11	Windsor	0-3	Sandown	0-2
Hamilton	0-5	Folkestone	0-2	Kempton	0-1
Southwell (AW)	0-4	Nottingham	0-2	Newcastle	0-1

WINNING HORSES

	Age	Races Run	1st	2nd	3rd	Unpl	Win £
Turtle Island	2	6	3	0	1	2	84,426
State Performer	2	4	3	1	0	0	37,440
Stonehatch	2	4	2	2	0	0	32,783
Abury	3	4	1	0	0	3	23,815
White Muzzle	3	6	4	1	0	1	20,881
Manhattan Sunset	2	6	1	2	1	2	20,225

Stoney Valley	3	6	2	0	0	4	17,785
Oakmead	3	5	2	1	1	1	13,905
Colonel Collins	2	3	2	1	0	0	13,483
Balanchine	2	2	2	0	0	0	11,983
Toledo Queen	3	5	2	1	0	2	11,675
Brown's	3	5	2	1	0	2	10,452
Charity Crusader	2	2	2	0	0	0	10,372
Newton's Law	3	3	2	0	1	0	9,637
Canaska Dancer	2	3	2	0	0	1	9,547
Escarpment	2	3	2	1	0	0	9,396
Pencader	2	2	1	1	0	0	5,053
Golden Nashwan	2	1	1	0	0	0	4,932
Barossa Valley	2	3	1	1	0	1	4,760
Delta One	2	1	1	0	0	0	4,307
Areciba	2	3	1	1	0	1	4,305
Planetary Aspect	3	7	1	2	1	3	4,175
Shalbourne	2	4	1	0	0	3	4,175
En Cachette	2	3	1	0	0	2	3,913
Shepton Mallet	2	2	1	1	0	0	3,840
Cairo Prince	3	4	1	0	0	3	3,753
Canaska Star	3	1	1	0	0	0	3,590
Lacerta	3	10	1	1	2	6	3,494
Salvezza	2	3	1	1	0	1	3,436
Eaton Row	3	2	1	1	0	0	3,319
Zind	3	4	1	1	0	2	3,266
Knight Of Shalot	3	5	1	1	1	2	3,202
Thousla Rock	4	4	1	1	0	2	3,143
Cherhill	3	4	1	0	1	2	2,718

WINNING OWNERS

	Races Won	Value £		Races Won	Value £
R E Sangster	38	340,708	Express Marie Curie Racing	2	10,372
Luciano Gaucci	4	20,881	Scuderia Golden Horse SRL	1	4,932
F M Kalla	3	13,718	Skyline Racing Ltd	1	3,436
Mrs June M Sifton	3	13,137			

Favourites	33-62	53.2%	+ 2.95	Total winning prize-money			£407,184
Longest winning sequence			3	Average SP of winner			2.6/1
Longest losing sequence			20	Return on stakes invested			-20.8%
1992 Form	41-245	16.7%	- 54.70	1991 Form	27-112	24.1%	+ 20.35

R CHARLTON (Beckhampton, Wilts)

	No. of Horses	Races Run	1st	2nd	3rd	Unpl	Per cent	£1 Level Stake
2-y-o	26	62	16	11	7	28	25.8	+ 29.65
3-y-o	24	101	24	20	7	50	23.8	+ 9.41
4-y-o+	5	22	7	3	1	11	31.8	+ 35.18
Totals	55	185	47	34	15	89	25.4	+ 74.24

BY MONTH

2-y-o	W-R	Per cent	£1 Level Stake	3-y-o	W-R	Per cent	£1 Level Stake
Mar/Apr	0-0	-	0.00	Mar/Apr	2-10	20.0	- 2.50
May	0-0	-	0.00	May	3-14	21.4	- 3.60
June	0-1	-	- 1.00	June	4-12	33.3	+ 6.48
July	5-13	38.5	+ 16.54	July	5-19	26.3	+ 8.13
August	6-13	46.2	+ 13.98	August	4-22	18.2	- 5.45
September	1-18	5.6	- 12.00	September	3-16	18.8	+ 0.25
Oct/Nov	4-17	23.5	+ 12.13	Oct/Nov	3-8	37.5	+ 6.10

4-y-o+	W-R	Per cent	£1 Level Stake	Totals	W-R	Per cent	£1 Level Stake
Mar/Apr	0-2	-	- 1.00	Mar/Apr	2-12	16.7	- 3.50
May	2-3	66.7	+ 31.00	May	5-17	29.4	+ 27.40
June	3-7	42.9	+ 9.18	June	7-20	35.0	+ 14.66
July	1-3	33.3	+ 2.00	July	11-35	31.4	+ 26.67
August	1-3	33.3	- 1.00	August	11-38	28.9	+ 7.53
September	0-3	-	- 3.00	September	4-37	10.8	- 14.75
Oct/Nov	0-1	-	- 1.00	Oct/Nov	7-26	26.9	+ 17.23

DISTANCE

2-y-o	W-R	Per cent	£1 Level Stake	3-y-o	W-R	Per cent	£1 Level Stake
5f-6f	9-31	29.0	+ 18.27	5f-6f	6-15	40.0	+ 11.65
7f-8f	7-31	22.6	+ 11.38	7f-8f	11-44	25.0	+ 4.41
9f-13f	0-0	-	0.00	9f-13f	7-40	17.5	- 4.65
14f+	0-0	-	0.00	14f+	0-2	-	- 2.00

4-y-o+	W-R	Per cent	£1 Level Stake	Totals	W-R	Per cent	£1 Level Stake
5f-6f	3-8	37.5	+ 20.00	5f-6f	18-54	33.3	+ 49.92
7f-8f	2-6	33.3	+ 8.80	7f-8f	20-81	24.7	+ 24.59
9f-13f	2-7	28.6	+ 7.38	9f-13f	9-47	19.1	+ 2.73
14f+	0-1	-	- 1.00	14f+	0-3	-	- 3.00

TYPE OF RACE

Non-Handicaps	W-R	Per cent	£1 Level Stake	Handicaps	W-R	Per cent	£1 Level Stake
2-y-o	15-57	26.3	+ 31.90	2-y-o	1-5	20.0	- 2.25
3-y-o	16-71	22.5	- 16.10	3-y-o	7-28	25.0	+ 24.26
4-y-o+	1-6	16.7	- 4.20	4-y-o+	6-16	37.5	+ 39.38
Selling	0-1	-	- 1.00	Selling	0-0	-	0.00
Apprentice	0-0	-	0.00	Apprentice	0-0	-	0.00
Amat/Ladies	1-1	100.0	+ 2.25	Amat/Ladies	0-0	-	0.00
Totals	33-136	24.3	+ 12.85	Totals	14-49	28.6	+ 61.39

COURSE GRADE

	W-R	Per cent	£1 Level Stake
Group 1	27-106	25.5	+ 79.73
Group 2	10-42	23.8	- 12.52
Group 3	8-31	25.8	+ 7.03
Group 4	2-6	33.3	0.00

FIRST TIME OUT

	W-R	Per cent	£1 Level Stake
2-y-o	9-26	34.6	+ 39.54
3-y-o	4-24	16.7	- 6.93
4-y-o+	3-5	60.0	+ 30.80
Totals	16-55	29.1	+ 63.41

JOCKEYS RIDING

	W-R	Per cent	£1 Level Stake		W-R	Per cent	£1 Level Stake
Pat Eddery	22-73	30.1	+ 31.54	Mrs M Cowdrey	1-1	100.0	+ 2.25
R Cochrane	6-15	40.0	+ 0.90	D Holland	1-3	33.3	0.00
S Raymont	6-37	16.2	+ 5.80	W Carson	1-4	25.0	+ 4.00
Paul Eddery	4-10	40.0	+ 32.25	K Darley	1-4	25.0	+ 2.00
L Dettori	2-5	40.0	+ 2.50	T Quinn	1-5	20.0	+ 3.00
T Sprake	2-10	20.0	+ 8.00				

W R Swinburn	0-9	G Carter	0-1	M Roberts	0-1
C Asmussen	0-2	J Reid	0-1	R Hills	0-1
B Raymond	0-1	M Hills	0-1	S Davies	0-1

COURSE RECORD

	Total W-R	Non-Handicaps 2-y-o	3-y-o+	Handicaps 2-y-o	3-y-o+	Per cent	£1 Level Stake
Newmarket	7-18	5-6	1-8	0-1	1-3	38.9	+ 26.94
Newbury	7-29	1-8	4-13	0-2	2-6	24.1	+ 31.00
York	5-8	2-3	0-0	0-0	3-5	62.5	+ 19.63
Ascot	4-13	0-3	2-3	0-0	2-7	30.8	+ 12.16
Redcar	3-4	1-2	2-2	0-0	0-0	75.0	+ 9.10
Ripon	3-5	1-1	1-2	0-0	1-2	60.0	+ 1.67
Nottingham	3-8	1-2	1-3	0-0	1-3	37.5	+ 10.88
Salisbury	3-21	2-8	0-9	0-0	1-4	14.3	- 12.79
Windsor	2-5	1-1	0-3	0-0	1-1	40.0	+ 9.38
Goodwood	2-13	0-5	1-4	0-0	1-4	15.4	+ 5.25
Catterick	1-1	1-1	0-0	0-0	0-0	100.0	+ 2.00

Pontefract	1-1	0-0	1-1	0-0	0-0	100.0	+ 0.57
Beverley	1-2	0-0	1-2	0-0	0-0	50.0	- 0.20
Warwick	1-2	0-0	1-2	0-0	0-0	50.0	+ 1.00
Brighton	1-3	0-0	1-3	0-0	0-0	33.3	- 1.50
Epsom	1-3	0-1	0-0	1-1	0-1	33.3	- 0.25
Bath	1-5	0-1	1-4	0-0	0-0	20.0	- 3.60
Kempton	1-8	0-0	1-6	0-0	0-2	12.5	- 1.00

Chepstow	0-6	Sandown	0-4	Ayr	0-1
Lingfield	0-6	Chester	0-3	Folkestone	0-1
Doncaster	0-5	Haydock	0-3	Newcastle	0-1
Leicester	0-4	Southwell (Turf)	0-2		

WINNING HORSES

	Age	Races Run	1st	2nd	3rd	Unpl	Win £
Inchinor	3	6	3	0	1	2	68,073
Western Cape	3	6	2	0	0	4	45,021
Baron Ferdinand	3	4	2	2	0	0	37,635
Source Of Light	4	6	2	2	1	1	25,925
Andromaque	3	7	4	2	0	1	25,880
In Case	3	4	2	0	0	2	19,838
Everglades	5	6	3	0	0	3	18,739
Concordial	2	3	2	1	0	0	17,764
Athens Belle	3	2	1	0	0	1	10,690
Forest Gazelle	2	3	2	0	0	1	7,853
Ballet Shoes	3	6	2	1	1	2	6,842
El Duco	3	6	2	1	2	1	6,842
Morocco	4	3	1	0	0	2	6,056
Magnasonic	2	1	1	0	0	0	5,572
Cajun Cadet	2	2	1	1	0	0	5,439
King Of Naples	2	1	1	0	0	0	5,436
Silver Hut	2	3	1	1	0	1	5,254
Monticino	2	4	1	0	1	2	4,986
Harvest Mouse	2	2	1	0	1	0	4,598
Hello Ireland	2	6	1	0	1	4	4,542
Solar Wagon	2	2	1	0	0	1	4,485
Wild Planet	2	4	1	1	1	1	4,464
Tricorne	2	4	1	0	1	2	4,342
Tufa	2	1	1	0	0	0	3,992
Pluck	3	3	1	0	0	2	3,883
Fox Sparrow	3	6	1	1	0	4	3,818
Tremolando	3	4	1	3	0	0	3,611
Number One Spot	3	3	1	1	0	1	3,582
Bagalino	3	4	1	1	0	2	3,493
Common Law	3	5	1	2	0	2	3,377
Underwater	4	5	1	1	0	3	3,363
Strumpet City	2	2	1	1	0	0	2,721

WINNING OWNERS

	Races Won	Value £		Races Won	Value £
K Abdulla	18	147,757	The Lady Vestey	1	4,598
Sir Philip Oppenheimer	3	68,073	Cliveden Stud	1	4,542
Mrs J De Rothschild	2	37,635	S S Niarchos	1	4,464
Dr Carlos E Stelling	5	31,133	S P Tindall	1	4,342
Miss Sophie Oppenheimer	3	18,739	Lord Derby	1	3,883
Lord Weinstock	3	17,532	Miss M Sheriffe	1	3,818
Martin Myers	1	6,056	Helena Springfield Ltd	1	3,582
Michael Pescod	1	5,439	Mrs Nicole Myers	1	3,377
Lord De La Warr and - Mrs M Kerr-Dineen	1	5,436	Mrs M Bryce-Smith	1	2,721
Mrs Rupert Hambro	1	4,986			

Favourites	25-61	41.0%	+ 1.24	Total winning prize-money			£378,112
Longest winning sequence			3	Average SP of winner			4.6/1
Longest losing sequence			14	Return on stakes invested			41.8%
1992 Form	43-170	25.3%	+ 61.61	1990 Form	37-159	23.3%	+ 19.55
1991 Form	26-180	14.4%	- 57.48				

P CHEESBROUGH (Bishop Auckland, Co Durham)

	No. of Horses	Races Run	1st	2nd	3rd	Unpl	Per cent	£1 Level Stake
2-y-o	0	0	0	0	0	0	-	0.00
3-y-o	1	5	1	0	0	4	20.0	+ 21.00
4-y-o+	1	3	0	1	0	2	-	- 3.00
Totals	2	8	1	1	0	6	12.5	+ 18.00

Jan	Feb	Mar	Apr	May	Jun	Jul	Aug	Sep	Oct/Nov
0-0	0-0	0-1	0-0	0-2	1-4	0-0	0-1	0-0	0-0

Winning Jockey	W-R	£1 Level Stake	Winning Course	W-R	£1 Level Stake
J Lowe	1-5	+ 21.00	Doncaster	1-2	+ 24.00

Winning Horse	Age	Races Run	1st	2nd	3rd	Unpl	Win £
Stylish Rose	3	5	1	0	0	4	3,553

Favourites	0-0	Total winning prize-money	£3,553

W CLAY (Stoke-on-Trent, Staffs)

	No. of Horses	Races Run	1st	2nd	3rd	Unpl	Per cent	£1 Level Stake
2-y-o	1	3	0	0	0	3	-	- 3.00
3-y-o	1	2	0	0	0	2	-	- 2.00
4-y-o+	5	10	1	1	1	7	10.0	- 1.00
Totals	7	15	1	1	1	12	6.7	- 6.00

Jan	Feb	Mar	Apr	May	Jun	Jul	Aug	Sep	Oct/Nov
0-0	0-1	0-1	0-1	0-3	1-4	0-3	0-0	0-1	0-1

Winning Jockey	W-R	£1 Level Stake	Winning Course	W-R	£1 Level Stake
D Wright	1-6	+ 3.00	Beverley	1-1	+ 8.00

Winning Horse	Age	Races Run	1st	2nd	3rd	Unpl	Win £
Rising Tempo	5	5	1	1	0	3	1,725

Favourites	0-0	Total winning prize-money	£1,725

1992 Form	0-22	1990 Form	0-1
1991 Form	0-2		

P F I COLE (Whatcombe, Oxon)

	No. of Horses	Races Run	1st	2nd	3rd	Unpl	Per cent	£1 Level Stake
2-y-o	62	181	33	33	30	85	18.2	- 7.00
3-y-o	45	238	25	24	39	150	10.5	-112.45
4-y-o+	12	49	5	5	11	28	10.2	- 17.50
Totals	119	468	63	62	80	263	13.5	-136.95

BY MONTH

2-y-o	W-R	Per cent	£1 Level Stake	3-y-o	W-R	Per cent	£1 Level Stake
January	0-0	-	0.00	January	0-0	-	0.00
February	0-0	-	0.00	February	0-0	-	0.00
March	0-0	-	0.00	March	0-3	-	- 3.00
April	0-11	-	- 11.00	April	7-44	15.9	- 21.94
May	4-16	25.0	- 5.34	May	5-50	10.0	- 23.50
June	3-16	18.8	- 5.27	June	6-40	15.0	- 18.51
July	9-23	39.1	+ 7.42	July	3-35	8.6	- 18.50
August	6-26	23.1	+ 1.93	August	1-21	4.8	- 14.50
September	2-41	4.9	- 27.50	September	2-24	8.3	+ 5.25
Oct/Nov	9-48	18.8	+ 32.76	Oct/Nov	1-21	4.8	- 17.75

Cole P F I

4-y-o+	W-R	Per cent	£1 Level Stake	Totals	W-R	Per cent	£1 Level Stake
January	0-0	-	0.00	January	0-0	-	0.00
February	0-0	-	0.00	February	0-0	-	0.00
March	0-0	-	0.00	March	0-3	-	- 3.00
April	1-8	12.5	- 2.50	April	8-63	12.7	- 35.44
May	0-7	-	- 7.00	May	9-73	12.3	- 35.84
June	1-7	14.3	- 2.00	June	10-63	15.9	- 25.78
July	1-9	11.1	- 5.00	July	13-67	19.4	- 16.08
August	0-3	-	- 3.00	August	7-50	14.0	- 15.57
September	0-4	-	- 4.00	September	4-69	5.8	- 26.25
Oct/Nov	2-11	18.2	+ 6.00	Oct/Nov	12-80	15.0	+ 21.01

DISTANCE

2-y-o	W-R	Per cent	£1 Level Stake	3-y-o	W-R	Per cent	£1 Level Stake
5f-6f	16-76	21.1	- 12.52	5f-6f	2-24	8.3	- 19.57
7f-8f	16-102	15.7	- 0.48	7f-8f	9-100	9.0	- 48.17
9f-13f	1-3	33.3	+ 6.00	9f-13f	12-95	12.6	- 30.25
14f+	0-0	-	0.00	14f+	2-19	10.5	- 14.46

4-y-o+	W-R	Per cent	£1 Level Stake	Totals	W-R	Per cent	£1 Level Stake
5f-6f	0-2	-	- 2.00	5f-6f	18-102	17.6	- 34.09
7f-8f	0-11	-	- 11.00	7f-8f	25-213	11.7	- 59.65
9f-13f	1-17	5.9	- 11.50	9f-13f	14-115	12.2	- 35.75
14f+	4-19	21.1	+ 7.00	14f+	6-38	15.8	- 7.46

TYPE OF RACE

Non-Handicaps	W-R	Per cent	£1 Level Stake	Handicaps	W-R	Per cent	£1 Level Stake
2-y-o	30-155	19.4	+ 9.45	2-y-o	2-22	9.1	- 15.20
3-y-o	17-149	11.4	-100.20	3-y-o	8-73	11.0	+ 3.75
4-y-o+	1-23	4.3	- 17.50	4-y-o+	4-25	16.0	+ 1.00
Selling	0-8	-	- 8.00	Selling	1-3	33.3	- 0.25
Apprentice	0-2	-	- 2.00	Apprentice	0-6	-	- 6.00
Amat/Ladies	0-1	-	- 1.00	Amat/Ladies	0-1	-	- 1.00
Totals	48-338	14.2	-119.25	Totals	15-130	11.5	- 17.70

COURSE GRADE

	W-R	Per cent	£1 Level Stake
Group 1	23-201	11.4	- 67.47
Group 2	10-93	10.8	- 60.32
Group 3	12-113	10.6	- 55.90
Group 4	18-61	29.5	+ 46.74

FIRST TIME OUT

	W-R	Per cent	£1 Level Stake
2-y-o	9-62	14.5	- 0.09
3-y-o	5-45	11.1	- 27.80
4-y-o+	1-12	8.3	- 6.50
Totals	15-119	12.6	- 34.39

JOCKEYS RIDING

	W-R	Per cent	£1 Level Stake		W-R	Per cent	£1 Level Stake
T Quinn	31-195	15.9	- 43.59	C Rutter	3-43	7.0	- 6.50
A Munro	16-118	13.6	- 56.18	M Roberts	2-4	50.0	+ 4.91
T G McLaughlin	5-49	10.2	+ 4.25	S Perks	2-4	50.0	+ 0.66
W Carson	3-10	30.0	+ 2.25	K Darley	1-1	100.0	+ 1.25

A Clark	0-4	Miss M Clark	0-2	J Williams	0-1
A Daly	0-4	R Cochrane	0-2	L Aspell	0-1
Pat Eddery	0-4	B Raymond	0-1	M Tebbutt	0-1
J Reid	0-3	D Meredith	0-1	N Day	0-1
M Hills	0-3	F Norton	0-1	P Robinson	0-1
A McGlone	0-2	J Carroll	0-1	Paul Eddery	0-1
D Goggin	0-2	J Frost	0-1	S Davies	0-1
J D Smith	0-2	J O'Dwyer	0-1		
L Dettori	0-2	J Tate	0-1		

COURSE RECORD

	Total W-R	Non-Handicaps 2-y-o	Non-Handicaps 3-y-o+	Handicaps 2-y-o	Handicaps 3-y-o+	Per cent	£1 Level Stake
Southwell (AW)	6-19	2-5	1-6	0-2	3-6	31.6	+ 7.91
Newmarket	6-46	3-20	2-14	1-4	0-8	13.0	- 26.99
Folkestone	4-9	3-5	1-3	0-0	0-1	44.4	+ 35.30
Warwick	4-17	2-5	1-6	0-1	1-5	23.5	+ 6.50
York	4-17	4-10	0-4	0-1	0-2	23.5	+ 5.45
Brighton	4-28	0-4	2-14	0-1	2-9	14.3	- 11.80
Newbury	4-32	2-12	0-10	0-3	2-7	12.5	+ 6.41
Southwell (Turf)	3-4	2-2	0-1	0-0	1-1	75.0	+ 7.23
Doncaster	3-9	1-3	1-5	0-0	1-1	33.3	+ 16.25
Haydock	3-18	1-5	1-8	0-0	1-5	16.7	+ 0.91
Bath	3-32	2-10	0-9	0-1	1-12	9.4	- 7.50
Pontefract	2-3	1-1	0-0	1-2	0-0	66.7	+ 0.80
Salisbury	2-17	0-4	2-9	0-0	0-4	11.8	- 11.00
Hamilton	1-1	0-0	1-1	0-0	0-0	100.0	+ 1.25
Ripon	1-1	1-1	0-0	0-0	0-0	100.0	+ 4.00
Catterick	1-3	1-1	0-2	0-0	0-0	33.3	- 1.20
Yarmouth	1-4	1-2	0-1	0-1	0-0	25.0	+ 1.50
Beverley	1-5	0-3	1-1	0-0	0-1	20.0	- 1.00
Thirsk	1-5	0-0	1-4	0-0	0-1	20.0	- 2.25
Windsor	1-10	1-3	0-1	0-2	0-4	10.0	- 8.33
Ascot	1-11	0-5	1-4	0-0	0-2	9.1	- 8.25
Chester	1-11	1-1	0-6	0-1	0-3	9.1	- 9.56
Nottingham	1-16	0-4	1-7	0-0	0-5	6.3	- 13.37
Chepstow	1-17	1-9	0-5	0-1	0-2	5.9	- 7.00
Kempton	1-19	1-8	0-7	0-0	0-4	5.3	- 17.75
Lingfield	1-24	0-8	1-10	0-0	0-6	4.2	- 22.71
Leicester	1-25	0-6	0-14	1-2	0-3	4.0	- 22.25
Sandown	1-25	0-6	1-15	0-1	0-3	4.0	- 19.50

Goodwood	0-14	Redcar	0-7	Newcastle	0-1
Epsom	0-8	Edinburgh	0-2		
Lingfield (AW)	0-7	Ayr	0-1		

WINNING HORSES

	Age	Races Run	1st	2nd	3rd	Unpl	Win £
Velvet Moon	2	5	3	0	0	2	46,891
Ruby Tiger	6	2	1	0	0	1	21,519
Moorish	3	7	1	0	1	5	20,388
Tioman Island	3	8	3	2	0	3	17,768
Lindon Lime	3	8	1	0	0	7	15,593
Gold Land	2	6	3	3	0	0	14,216
Runaway Pete	3	9	3	0	2	4	11,673
Monarda	6	10	3	0	3	4	11,296
Carmot	2	2	2	0	0	0	8,623
Footsteps	2	7	2	1	1	3	8,288
Instant Affair	3	7	2	1	1	3	7,656
Darren Boy	2	4	2	1	0	1	6,937
Serious Option	2	5	2	1	0	2	6,639
Gran Senorum	3	13	2	5	2	4	6,433
Crime Ofthecentury	3	5	2	0	0	3	5,958
Bardolph	6	11	1	1	3	6	5,572
Firm Pledge	3	4	1	0	0	3	5,070
Summer Hail	2	2	1	0	1	0	4,986
Dontforget Insight	2	3	1	0	0	2	4,737
Forgotten Lady	2	3	1	0	0	2	4,378
Jacob Bogdani	2	3	1	2	0	0	4,378
Sugar Town	2	4	1	0	0	3	4,342
Girl From Ipanema	2	1	1	0	0	0	4,232
Star Selection	2	4	1	2	0	1	4,204
Blaaziing Joe	2	2	1	0	0	1	4,175
Waiting	2	4	1	1	1	1	4,175
Fayrooz	2	3	1	1	1	0	4,152
Hawker Hunter	2	3	1	0	0	2	3,980
Star Manager	3	5	1	0	2	2	3,850
River Life	3	1	1	0	0	0	3,720
Smart Family	2	4	1	1	1	1	3,699
Conspicuous	3	6	1	2	1	2	3,465
Tasset	3	8	1	0	2	5	3,465
Persian Elite	2	2	1	0	1	0	3,465
West Quest	2	1	1	0	0	0	3,231
Highly Fashionable	2	6	1	1	1	3	3,202
Cyprian Dancer	3	7	1	0	0	6	3,114
Good Fetch	2	4	1	1	0	2	3,080
Alderney Prince	3	5	1	0	0	4	2,977
Mr Cube	3	9	1	1	1	6	2,700
Lord Sky	2	6	1	0	0	5	2,691
Greenson	2	5	1	1	1	2	2,595
Biljan	3	11	1	3	2	5	2,562
Fawlty Towers	2	4	1	0	1	2	2,243
Allegation	3	1	1	0	0	0	2,070
Soviet Express	3	8	1	0	0	7	1,604

Cole P F I

WINNING OWNERS

	Races Won	Value £		Races Won	Value £
Fahd Salman	27	165,735	Richard Green (Fine Paintings)	2	6,973
Mrs Philip Blacker	1	21,519	D F Allport	2	6,937
H R H Sultan Ahmad Shah	3	17,768	Elite Racing Club	2	6,545
Sheikh Mohammed	3	12,088	Stephen Crown	2	5,893
Thomas T S Liang	3	11,673	Sir George Meyrick	1	5,572
Lord Portman	3	10,981	Insight Cartons Ltd	1	4,737
Christopher Wright	3	10,190	Alan C Elliot	1	3,699
Mrs Linda Gardiner	2	8,553	C Shiacolas	1	3,114
M Arbib	2	8,054	Mrs David Anderson	1	2,700
Athos Christodoulou	2	7,656	Brook Land	1	1,604

Favourites	31-91	34.1%	- 17.45	Total winning prize-money £321,990

Longest winning sequence		3	Average SP of winner	4.3/1
Longest losing sequence		36	Return on stakes invested	-29.2%

1992 Form	86-461	18.7%	- 71.61	1990 Form	53-394	13.5%	- 60.48
1991 Form	73-392	18.6%	- 31.18	1989 Form	51-403	12.7%	-116.41

H J COLLINGRIDGE (Newmarket)

	No. of Horses	Races Run	1st	2nd	3rd	Unpl	Per cent	£1 Level Stake
2-y-o	7	12	0	0	0	12	-	- 12.00
3-y-o	5	33	1	1	1	30	3.0	- 30.00
4-y-o+	12	93	6	13	10	64	6.5	- 42.50
Totals	24	138	7	14	11	106	5.1	- 84.50

Jan	Feb	Mar	Apr	May	Jun	Jul	Aug	Sep	Oct/Nov
0-5	0-3	1-7	0-13	1-22	3-24	1-26	0-13	1-13	0-12

Winning Jockeys	W-R	£1 Level Stake		W-R	£1 Level Stake
J Quinn	4-75	- 44.00	Dale Gibson	1-7	- 0.50
M Hills	1-1	+ 12.00	C Dwyer	1-13	- 10.00

Winning Courses					
Edinburgh	1-2	+ 4.50	Leicester	1-7	+ 3.00
Hamilton	1-3	+ 10.00	Warwick	1-7	+ 1.50
Haydock	1-3	+ 3.00	Southwell (AW)	1-8	- 5.00
Doncaster	1-7	- 0.50			

Winning Horses	Age	Races Run	1st	2nd	3rd	Unpl	Win £
Ballyranter	4	13	2	3	2	6	10,607
James Is Special	5	9	1	0	2	6	4,878
Buzzards Bellbuoy	4	10	1	1	1	7	4,794
Westfield Moves	5	17	1	5	2	9	3,348
Bright Paragon	4	16	1	2	1	12	2,979
Moving Image	3	12	1	1	0	10	2,951

Favourites	0-11				Total winning prize-money			£29,556
1992 Form	10-143	7.0%	- 50.12		1990 Form	7-158	4.4%	-100.75
1991 Form	9-139	6.5%	- 6.50		1989 Form	12-175	6.9%	- 12.00

D J S COSGROVE (Newmarket)

	No. of Horses	Races Run	1st	2nd	3rd	Unpl	Per cent	£1 Level Stake
2-y-o	8	22	2	2	2	16	9.1	- 13.27
3-y-o	2	24	3	0	2	19	12.5	- 5.17
4-y-o+	4	10	1	0	1	8	10.0	+ 11.00
Totals	14	56	6	2	5	43	10.7	- 7.44

Jan	Feb	Mar	Apr	May	Jun	Jul	Aug	Sep	Oct/Nov
0-1	0-2	0-0	0-3	0-5	3-8	2-11	1-9	0-3	0-14

Winning Jockeys	W-R	£1 Level Stake				W-R	£1 Level Stake
L Newton	4-21	+ 13.23		D Biggs		1-8	+ 3.20
J Reid	1-1	+ 2.13					

Winning Courses							
Ripon	2-3	+ 19.73		Doncaster		1-4	+ 7.20
Bath	1-2	+ 1.13		Newmarket		1-5	- 0.50
Nottingham	1-2	+ 5.00					

Winning Horses	Age	Races Run	1st	2nd	3rd	Unpl	Win £
Charity Express	3	13	2	0	1	10	5,492
Yo-Cando	2	3	1	0	0	2	3,845
My Bonus	3	11	1	0	1	9	3,655
Heavy Rock	4	5	1	0	1	3	3,052
Twice In Bundoran	2	8	1	2	1	4	2,820

Favourites	1-3	33.3%	- 1.27	Total winning prize-money	£18,864
1992 Form	3-50	6.0%	- 27.00		

L G COTTRELL (Cullompton, Devon)

	No. of Horses	Races Run	1st	2nd	3rd	Unpl	Per cent	£1 Level Stake
2-y-o	2	8	1	2	1	4	12.5	- 4.50
3-y-o	3	19	2	2	2	13	10.5	+ 30.00
4-y-o+	9	60	7	10	7	36	11.7	+ 16.45
Totals	14	87	10	14	10	53	11.5	+ 41.95

BY MONTH

2-y-o	W-R	Per cent	£1 Level Stake	3-y-o	W-R	Per cent	£1 Level Stake
January	0-0	-	0.00	January	0-0	-	0.00
February	0-0	-	0.00	February	0-0	-	0.00
March	0-1	-	- 1.00	March	0-0	-	0.00
April	0-1	-	- 1.00	April	1-2	50.0	+ 32.00
May	0-1	-	- 1.00	May	0-4	-	- 4.00
June	0-3	-	- 3.00	June	0-1	-	- 1.00
July	0-0	-	0.00	July	0-1	-	- 1.00
August	1-1	100.0	+ 2.50	August	0-0	-	0.00
September	0-1	-	- 1.00	September	0-4	-	- 4.00
Oct/Nov	0-0	-	0.00	Oct/Nov	1-7	14.3	+ 8.00

4-y-o+	W-R	Per cent	£1 Level Stake	Totals	W-R	Per cent	£1 Level Stake
January	0-0	-	0.00	January	0-0	-	0.00
February	0-4	-	- 4.00	February	0-4	-	- 4.00
March	1-3	33.3	+ 4.00	March	1-4	25.0	+ 3.00
April	1-6	16.7	+ 4.00	April	2-9	22.2	+ 35.00
May	2-10	20.0	+ 14.00	May	2-15	13.3	+ 9.00
June	1-13	7.7	+ 4.00	June	1-17	5.9	0.00
July	1-6	16.7	- 4.55	July	1-7	14.3	- 5.55
August	0-10	-	- 10.00	August	1-11	9.1	- 7.50
September	1-5	20.0	+ 12.00	September	1-10	10.0	+ 7.00
Oct/Nov	0-3	-	- 3.00	Oct/Nov	1-10	10.0	+ 5.00

DISTANCE

2-y-o	W-R	Per cent	£1 Level Stake	3-y-o	W-R	Per cent	£1 Level Stake
5f-6f	1-8	12.5	- 4.50	5f-6f	0-0	-	0.00
7f-8f	0-0	-	0.00	7f-8f	1-8	12.5	+ 26.00
9f-13f	0-0	-	0.00	9f-13f	1-11	9.1	+ 4.00
14f+	0-0	-	0.00	14f+	0-0	-	0.00

4-y-o+	W-R	Per cent	£1 Level Stake	Totals	W-R	Per cent	£1 Level Stake
5f-6f	0-8	-	- 8.00	5f-6f	1-16	6.3	- 12.50
7f-8f	4-31	12.9	+ 14.45	7f-8f	5-39	12.8	+ 40.45
9f-13f	2-18	11.1	- 4.00	9f-13f	3-29	10.3	0.00
14f+	1-3	33.3	+ 14.00	14f+	1-3	33.3	+ 14.00

TYPE OF RACE

Non-Handicaps	W-R	Per cent	£1 Level Stake	Handicaps	W-R	Per cent	£1 Level Stake
2-y-o	0-4	-	- 4.00	2-y-o	0-0	-	0.00
3-y-o	1-12	8.3	+ 22.00	3-y-o	1-6	16.7	+ 9.00
4-y-o+	2-9	22.2	- 0.55	4-y-o+	3-43	7.0	+ 1.00
Selling	1-5	20.0	- 1.50	Selling	0-0	-	0.00
Apprentice	1-1	100.0	+ 6.00	Apprentice	1-6	16.7	+ 11.00
Amat/Ladies	0-0	-	0.00	Amat/Ladies	0-1	-	- 1.00
Totals	5-31	16.1	+ 21.95	Totals	5-56	8.9	+ 20.00

COURSE GRADE

	W-R	Per cent	£1 Level Stake		W-R	Per cent	£1 Level Stake
Group 1	1-19	5.3	- 2.00				
Group 2	3-24	12.5	+ 4.45				
Group 3	1-19	5.3	- 15.50				
Group 4	5-25	20.0	+ 55.00				

FIRST TIME OUT

	W-R	Per cent	£1 Level Stake
2-y-o	0-2	-	- 2.00
3-y-o	1-3	33.3	+ 31.00
4-y-o+	2-9	22.2	+ 18.00
Totals	3-14	21.4	+ 47.00

JOCKEYS RIDING

	W-R	Per cent	£1 Level Stake		W-R	Per cent	£1 Level Stake
N Carlisle	4-33	12.1	+ 29.50	Mark Denaro	1-11	9.1	+ 6.00
D Holland	3-7	42.9	+ 28.45	A Munro	1-13	7.7	- 6.00
J Weaver	1-3	33.3	+ 4.00				

D McCabe	0-4	J Quinn	0-2	Mrs L Lawson	0-1
G Carter	0-3	D Harrison	0-1	P McCabe	0-1
J Reid	0-3	G Hind	0-1	T Lang	0-1
G Bardwell	0-2	M Fenton	0-1		

COURSE RECORD

	Total W-R	Non-Handicaps 2-y-o	Non-Handicaps 3-y-o+	Handicaps 2-y-o	Handicaps 3-y-o+	Per cent	£1 Level Stake
Warwick	3-9	0-1	1-3	0-0	2-5	33.3	+ 57.00
Lingfield (AW)	2-9	0-0	2-4	0-0	0-5	22.2	+ 5.00
Ascot	1-2	0-0	0-0	0-0	1-2	50.0	+ 15.00
Lingfield	1-5	0-1	0-1	0-0	1-3	20.0	+ 12.00
Bath	1-6	1-1	0-3	0-0	0-2	16.7	- 2.50
Salisbury	1-9	0-0	0-2	0-0	1-7	11.1	+ 1.00
Brighton	1-10	0-1	1-3	0-0	0-6	10.0	- 8.55

Chepstow	0-7	Windsor	0-5	Leicester	0-1
Folkestone	0-6	Epsom	0-3	Southwell (AW)	0-1
Goodwood	0-5	Newbury	0-3		
Kempton	0-5	Haydock	0-1		

WINNING HORSES

	Age	Races Run	1st	2nd	3rd	Unpl	Win £
Pride Of Britain	4	4	1	0	2	1	11,963
Cape Pigeon	8	10	2	2	2	4	5,857
Storm Free	7	10	2	2	2	4	4,765
Wakil	4	6	1	4	0	1	4,208
Knyaz	3	8	1	0	0	7	3,077
Sky Burst	3	9	1	2	2	4	3,015
Rosietoes	5	7	1	0	0	6	2,952
Little Emmeline	2	6	1	2	1	2	2,490

WINNING OWNERS

	Races Won	Value £		Races Won	Value £
E J S Gadsden	5	14,829	Mrs D Jenks	1	3,015
Pride Of Britain Ltd	1	11,963	Mrs Anne Yearley	1	2,952
Terence M Molossi	1	3,077	J K Morrish	1	2,490

Favourites	2-10	20.0%	- 5.05	Total winning prize-money	£38,325

Longest winning sequence	3	Average SP of winner	11.9/1
Longest losing sequence	21	Return on stakes invested	48.2%

1992 Form	8-98	8.2%	- 38.42	1990 Form	4-125	3.2%	- 97.00
1991 Form	10-83	12.0%	+ 4.00	1989 Form	12-219	5.5%	-114.50

T CRAIG (Dunbar, Lothian)

	No. of Horses	Races Run	1st	2nd	3rd	Unpl	Per cent	£1 Level Stake
2-y-o	1	4	0	0	0	4	-	- 4.00
3-y-o	0	0	0	0	0	0	-	0.00
4-y-o+	8	37	2	1	5	29	5.4	- 23.75
Totals	9	41	2	1	5	33	4.9	- 27.75

Jan	Feb	Mar	Apr	May	Jun	Jul	Aug	Sep	Oct/Nov
0-0	0-0	0-1	0-1	0-9	1-18	1-11	0-1	0-0	0-0

Winning Jockeys	W-R	£1 Level Stake		W-R	£1 Level Stake
Miss L Eaton	1-2	+ 8.00	N Varley	1-6	- 2.75

Winning Courses	W-R	£1 Level Stake		W-R	£1 Level Stake
Hamilton	1-12	- 2.00	Edinburgh	1-19	- 15.75

Winning Horses	Age	Races Run	1st	2nd	3rd	Unpl	Win £
Lord Advocate	5	5	1	0	1	3	2,353
Rapid Mover	6	8	1	1	1	5	1,646

Favourites	0-0	Total winning prize-money	£3,999

1992 Form	1-47	2.1%	- 44.62	1990 Form	1-66	1.5%	- 61.67
1991 Form	1-21	4.8%	- 4.00	1989 Form	4-62	6.5%	+ 23.50

L M CUMANI (Newmarket)

	No. of Horses	Races Run	1st	2nd	3rd	Unpl	Per cent	£1 Level Stake
2-y-o	20	48	12	9	3	24	25.0	+ 9.14
3-y-o	41	197	24	34	25	114	12.2	- 98.78
4-y-o+	10	32	3	7	4	18	9.4	- 6.00
Totals	71	277	39	50	32	156	14.1	- 95.64

BY MONTH

2-y-o	W-R	Per cent	£1 Level Stake	3-y-o	W-R	Per cent	£1 Level Stake
Mar/Apr	0-0	-	0.00	Mar/Apr	1-20	5.0	- 18.33
May	0-0	-	0.00	May	2-26	7.7	- 22.01
June	0-1	-	- 1.00	June	6-34	17.6	- 3.75
July	0-2	-	- 2.00	July	1-30	3.3	- 20.00
August	2-9	22.2	- 2.37	August	11-34	32.4	- 2.19
September	7-20	35.0	+ 20.88	September	2-36	5.6	- 20.50
Oct/Nov	3-16	18.8	- 6.37	Oct/Nov	1-17	5.9	- 12.00

4-y-o+	W-R	Per cent	£1 Level Stake	Totals	W-R	Per cent	£1 Level Stake
Mar/Apr	0-3	-	- 3.00	Mar/Apr	1-23	4.3	- 21.33
May	1-3	33.3	+ 8.00	May	3-29	10.3	- 14.01
June	0-7	-	- 7.00	June	6-42	14.3	- 11.75
July	0-8	-	- 8.00	July	1-40	2.5	- 30.00
August	1-3	33.3	+ 8.00	August	14-46	30.4	+ 3.44
September	1-4	25.0	0.00	September	10-60	16.7	+ 0.38
Oct/Nov	0-4	-	- 4.00	Oct/Nov	4-37	10.8	- 22.37

DISTANCE

2-y-o	W-R	Per cent	£1 Level Stake	3-y-o	W-R	Per cent	£1 Level Stake
5f-6f	4-18	22.2	+ 4.26	5f-6f	1-8	12.5	- 5.12
7f-8f	8-30	26.7	+ 4.88	7f-8f	8-68	11.8	- 48.66
9f-13f	0-0	-	0.00	9f-13f	12-106	11.3	- 55.50
14f+	0-0	-	0.00	14f+	3-15	20.0	+ 10.50

4-y-o+	W-R	Per cent	£1 Level Stake	Totals	W-R	Per cent	£1 Level Stake
5f-6f	0-0	-	0.00	5f-6f	5-26	19.2	- 0.86
7f-8f	1-14	7.1	- 3.00	7f-8f	17-112	15.2	- 46.78
9f-13f	2-16	12.5	- 1.00	9f-13f	14-122	11.5	- 56.50
14f+	0-2	-	- 2.00	14f+	3-17	17.6	+ 8.50

TYPE OF RACE

Non-Handicaps	W-R	Per cent	£1 Level Stake	Handicaps	W-R	Per cent	£1 Level Stake
2-y-o	12-47	25.5	+ 10.14	2-y-o	0-1	-	- 1.00
3-y-o	17-128	13.3	- 62.04	3-y-o	6-64	9.4	- 33.74
4-y-o+	1-15	6.7	- 4.00	4-y-o+	2-17	11.8	- 2.00
Selling	0-0	-	0.00	Selling	0-0	-	0.00
Apprentice	1-4	25.0	- 2.00	Apprentice	0-1	-	- 1.00
Amat/Ladies	0-0	-	0.00	Amat/Ladies	0-0	-	0.00
Totals	31-194	16.0	- 57.90	Totals	8-83	9.6	- 37.74

COURSE GRADE

	W-R	Per cent	£1 Level Stake
Group 1	14-164	8.5	- 96.20
Group 2	11-44	25.0	+ 5.39
Group 3	12-58	20.7	- 1.08
Group 4	2-11	18.2	- 3.75

FIRST TIME OUT

	W-R	Per cent	£1 Level Stake
2-y-o	4-20	20.0	+ 4.13
3-y-o	2-41	4.9	- 32.83
4-y-o+	1-9	11.1	+ 2.00
Totals	7-70	10.0	- 26.70

JOCKEYS RIDING

	W-R	Per cent	£1 Level Stake		W-R	Per cent	£1 Level Stake
R Cochrane	22-173	12.7	- 67.72	A Munro	1-1	100.0	+ 0.91
J Weaver	9-47	19.1	+ 1.11	J Reid	1-1	100.0	+ 1.75
M Roberts	5-25	20.0	- 10.69	W R Swinburn	1-1	100.0	+ 8.00

C Hodgson	0-10	D Harrison	0-1	M Marongiu	0-1
Jo Hunnam	0-4	G Carter	0-1	M Simonaggio	0-1
M Denaro	0-4	J Carroll	0-1	Mrs S Cumani	0-1
A McGlone	0-1	J Quinn	0-1	N Gwilliams	0-1
B Doyle	0-1	M Esposito	0-1		

COURSE RECORD

	Total W-R	Non-Handicaps 2-y-o	3-y-o+	Handicaps 2-y-o	3-y-o+	Per cent	£1 Level Stake
Brighton	4-16	1-4	0-9	0-0	3-3	25.0	- 4.99
Newmarket	4-64	1-13	2-32	0-0	1-19	6.3	- 43.95
Nottingham	3-8	2-3	1-4	0-0	0-1	37.5	+ 10.00
Salisbury	3-9	2-2	0-3	0-0	1-4	33.3	+ 10.25
Newbury	3-13	1-3	2-5	0-0	0-5	23.1	- 1.00
Windsor	2-5	0-0	2-5	0-0	0-0	40.0	+ 0.88
Beverley	2-6	1-1	0-2	0-0	1-3	33.3	+ 0.50
Doncaster	2-10	0-1	2-6	0-0	0-3	20.0	- 1.62
Leicester	2-11	1-3	1-7	0-0	0-1	18.2	- 2.25
York	2-15	0-1	2-6	0-0	0-8	13.3	- 1.37
Yarmouth	2-17	2-7	0-7	0-0	0-3	11.8	- 1.12
Thirsk	1-2	0-1	0-0	0-0	1-1	50.0	+ 1.00

Cumani L M

Warwick	1-2	0-0	1-2	0-0	0-0	50.0	+	0.75
Newcastle	1-3	0-0	1-2	0-0	0-1	33.3	-	1.89
Chepstow	1-4	0-0	1-4	0-0	0-0	25.0	-	2.09
Folkestone	1-4	0-0	1-4	0-0	0-0	25.0	+	0.50
Lingfield	1-4	0-0	1-3	0-0	0-1	25.0	+	7.00
Ripon	1-5	0-0	1-4	0-0	0-1	20.0	-	2.62
Redcar	1-8	0-2	1-4	0-0	0-2	12.5	-	5.25
Goodwood	1-13	0-0	0-5	0-0	1-8	7.7	-	3.00
Kempton	1-13	1-2	0-10	0-0	0-1	7.7	-	10.37

Sandown	0-11	Epsom	0-3	Carlisle	0-1
Ascot	0-10	Bath	0-2	Catterick	0-1
Haydock	0-8	Southwell (Turf)	0-2	Edinburgh	0-1
Pontefract	0-5	Ayr	0-1		

WINNING HORSES

	Age	Races Run	1st	2nd	3rd	Unpl	Win £
Only Royale	4	4	1	3	0	0	78,598
Kithanga	3	5	3	2	0	0	39,605
Tatami	2	4	3	0	0	1	35,082
Relatively Special	2	4	2	0	0	2	20,910
Lille Hammer	3	5	1	1	2	1	10,203
Naif	3	6	2	0	2	2	7,076
Stella Mystika	3	5	2	0	0	3	7,071
Tej Singh	3	7	2	1	2	2	6,667
Dress Sense	4	3	1	0	1	1	6,212
Old Provence	3	2	2	0	0	0	6,206
Noble Rose	2	2	1	1	0	0	5,343
Declassified	3	5	1	1	1	2	5,190
Violet Crown	2	1	1	0	0	0	4,485
Glimpse	2	2	1	0	0	1	4,464
Daronne	2	3	1	1	0	1	4,307
Midnight Legend	2	3	1	0	0	2	4,092
Maradonna	4	4	1	0	1	2	4,045
Raneen Alwatar	3	4	1	0	1	2	4,013
Wannabe	3	6	1	1	0	4	3,845
Spin Doctor	3	6	1	1	1	3	3,436
Kamikaze	3	3	1	0	0	2	3,436
Tree Of Life	3	4	1	1	1	1	3,348
Al Battar	2	2	1	0	0	1	3,290
Queen's View	3	4	1	1	1	1	3,231
Time Again	3	5	1	0	1	3	3,173
Dragon's Teeth	3	3	1	1	0	1	3,143
Trapezium	3	8	1	3	2	2	3,114
Suris	2	2	1	1	0	0	3,080
Dancing Tralthee	3	5	1	0	0	4	3,054
Mamara Reef	3	5	1	0	0	4	2,893

WINNING OWNERS

	Races Won	Value £		Races Won	Value £
Sheikh Mohammed	16	85,153	Edward P Evans	1	5,190
G Sainaghi	1	78,598	G Keller	1	4,464
Fittocks Stud Ltd	3	39,605	Gerald Leigh	1	4,045
Helena Springfield Ltd	2	20,910	Michael Davey	1	3,845
Baron Edouard De Rothschild	1	10,203	Princess Nicholas Von Preussen	1	3,436
Umm Qarn Racing	2	7,382	R J Shannon	1	3,173
Sultan Mohammed	2	7,076	Lord Weinstock	1	3,143
Sheikh Ahmed Al Maktoum	2	7,067	Scuderia Rencati SRL	1	3,080
Lord Halifax	2	6,241			

Favourites	19-78	24.4%	- 27.65	
Longest winning sequence			4	
Longest losing sequence			43	

Total winning prize-money			£292,610
Average SP of winner			3.7/1
Return on stakes invested			-34.5%

1992 Form	54-292	18.5%	- 69.25	1990 Form	108-405	26.7%	+ 16.83
1991 Form	72-334	21.6%	- 63.91	1989 Form	88-330	26.7%	- 23.72

P D CUNDELL (Newbury, Berks)

	No. of Horses	Races Run	1st	2nd	3rd	Unpl	Per cent	£1 Level Stake
2-y-o	3	8	0	0	0	8	-	- 8.00
3-y-o	1	3	0	0	0	3	-	- 3.00
4-y-o+	7	49	7	4	3	35	14.3	+ 17.50
Totals	11	60	7	4	3	46	11.7	+ 6.50

Jan	Feb	Mar	Apr	May	Jun	Jul	Aug	Sep	Oct/Nov
0-4	0-1	0-3	0-3	2-8	2-10	0-7	1-9	1-6	1-9

Winning Jockeys	W-R	£1 Level Stake		W-R	£1 Level Stake
D Griffiths	2-6	+ 11.00	A Mackay	1-4	+ 6.00
J Williams	2-11	+ 6.00	G Hind	1-4	+ 11.00
W Newnes	1-1	+ 6.50			

Winning Courses	W-R	£1 Level Stake		W-R	£1 Level Stake
Leicester	2-12	+ 7.00	Newbury	1-2	+ 6.00
Chepstow	1-2	+ 13.00	Lingfield	1-5	+ 4.00
Haydock	1-2	+ 5.50	Windsor	1-5	+ 3.00

Winning Horses	Age	Races Run	1st	2nd	3rd	Unpl	Win £
Great Hall	4	19	4	2	3	10	12,621
Leigh Crofter	4	9	2	1	0	6	7,332
Precious Caroline	5	9	1	0	0	8	2,951

Favourites	0-3	Total winning prize-money	£22,904

1992 Form	1-37	2.7%	- 20.00	1990 Form	0-22		
1991 Form	1-16	6.3%	+ 18.00	1989 Form	1-48	2.1%	- 33.00

K O CUNNINGHAM-BROWN (Stockbridge, Hants)

	No. of Horses	Races Run	1st	2nd	3rd	Unpl	Per cent	£1 Level Stake
2-y-o	5	15	0	0	0	15	-	- 15.00
3-y-o	16	66	1	4	2	59	1.5	- 32.00
4-y-o+	13	75	3	5	3	64	4.0	- 25.50
Totals	34	156	4	9	5	138	2.6	- 72.50

Jan	Feb	Mar	Apr	May	Jun	Jul	Aug	Sep	Oct/Nov
0-20	0-6	0-8	1-20	0-14	1-10	2-27	0-15	0-22	0-14

Winning Jockeys	W-R	£1 Level Stake			W-R	£1 Level Stake
J Williams	1-5	+ 5.00	N Carlisle		1-10	+ 24.00
T Quinn	1-6	- 0.50	B Doyle		1-11	+ 23.00

Winning Courses		£1 Level Stake				£1 Level Stake
Lingfield (AW)	2-40	+ 4.00	Windsor		1-12	- 6.50
Salisbury	1-11	+ 23.00				

Winning Horses	Age	Races Run	1st	2nd	3rd	Unpl	Win £
Modesto	5	11	1	1	0	9	7,310
With Gusto	6	12	2	2	0	8	4,106
Western Valley	3	8	1	0	0	7	2,781

Favourites	0-2	Total winning prize-money	£14,197

1992 Form	18-143	12.6%	+100.33	1990 Form	4-98	4.1%	- 43.00
1991 Form	2-68	2.9%	- 30.00	1989 Form	7-107	6.5%	- 74.50

B J CURLEY (Newmarket)

	No. of Horses	Races Run	1st	2nd	3rd	Unpl	Per cent	£1 Level Stake
2-y-o	1	3	0	0	0	3	-	- 3.00
3-y-o	1	4	0	0	0	4	-	- 4.00
4-y-o+	3	12	2	1	0	9	16.7	+ 0.25
Totals	5	19	2	1	0	16	10.5	- 6.75

Jan	Feb	Mar	Apr	May	Jun	Jul	Aug	Sep	Oct/Nov
0-0	0-0	0-0	0-0	0-1	0-5	1-4	1-7	0-1	0-1

Winning Jockeys	W-R	£1 Level Stake		W-R	£1 Level Stake
L Dettori	1-2	+ 1.25	B Raymond	1-3	+ 6.00

Winning Courses		£1 Level Stake			£1 Level Stake
Yarmouth	1-2	+ 7.00	Folkestone	1-3	+ 0.25

Winning Horses	Age	Races Run	1st	2nd	3rd	Unpl	Win £
Utrillo	4	4	1	0	0	3	2,893
Case For The Crown	6	3	1	1	0	1	2,847

Favourites	1-4	25.0%	- 0.75	Total winning prize-money			£5,740

1992 Form	0-6			1990 Form	3-33	9.1%	- 17.00
1991 Form	3-27	11.1%	- 15.90	1989 Form	0-14		

C A CYZER (Horsham, West Sussex)

	No. of Horses	Races Run	1st	2nd	3rd	Unpl	Per cent	£1 Level Stake
2-y-o	10	22	3	1	2	16	13.6	0.00
3-y-o	24	151	9	16	16	110	6.0	- 61.12
4-y-o+	5	47	8	5	5	29	17.0	- 0.62
Totals	39	220	20	22	23	155	9.1	- 61.74

BY MONTH

2-y-o	W-R	Per cent	£1 Level Stake	3-y-o	W-R	Per cent	£1 Level Stake
January	0-0	-	0.00	January	0-0	-	0.00
February	0-0	-	0.00	February	0-0	-	0.00
March	0-0	-	0.00	March	0-5	-	- 5.00
April	0-0	-	0.00	April	2-21	9.5	+ 17.00
May	0-2	-	- 2.00	May	0-27	-	- 27.00
June	1-4	25.0	+ 8.00	June	1-18	5.6	- 3.00
July	1-5	20.0	+ 2.00	July	3-17	17.6	+ 6.50
August	1-2	50.0	+ 1.00	August	2-36	5.6	- 30.62
September	0-7	-	- 7.00	September	1-19	5.3	- 11.00
Oct/Nov	0-2	-	- 2.00	Oct/Nov	0-8	-	- 8.00

4-y-o+	W-R	Per cent	£1 Level Stake	Totals	W-R	Per cent	£1 Level Stake
January	0-0	-	0.00	January	0-0	-	0.00
February	0-0	-	0.00	February	0-0	-	0.00
March	0-1	-	- 1.00	March	0-6	-	- 6.00
April	2-7	28.6	+ 10.50	April	4-28	14.3	+ 27.50
May	0-6	-	- 6.00	May	0-35	-	- 35.00
June	0-7	-	- 7.00	June	2-29	6.9	- 2.00
July	3-8	37.5	+ 8.00	July	7-30	23.3	+ 16.50
August	2-11	18.2	- 5.12	August	5-49	10.2	- 34.74
September	1-5	20.0	+ 2.00	September	2-31	6.5	- 16.00
Oct/Nov	0-2	-	- 2.00	Oct/Nov	0-12	-	- 12.00

Cyzer C A

DISTANCE

2-y-o	W-R	Per cent	£1 Level Stake	3-y-o	W-R	Per cent	£1 Level Stake
5f-6f	3-13	23.1	+ 9.00	5f-6f	0-8	-	- 8.00
7f-8f	0-8	-	- 8.00	7f-8f	2-47	4.3	- 28.50
9f-13f	0-1	-	- 1.00	9f-13f	7-82	8.5	- 10.62
14f+	0-0	-	0.00	14f+	0-14	-	- 14.00

4-y-o+	W-R	Per cent	£1 Level Stake	Totals	W-R	Per cent	£1 Level Stake
5f-6f	2-11	18.2	+ 0.50	5f-6f	5-32	15.6	+ 1.50
7f-8f	1-5	20.0	+ 6.00	7f-8f	3-60	5.0	- 30.50
9f-13f	2-16	12.5	- 4.00	9f-13f	9-99	9.1	- 15.62
14f+	3-15	20.0	- 3.12	14f+	3-29	10.3	- 17.12

TYPE OF RACE

Non-Handicaps	W-R	Per cent	£1 Level Stake	Handicaps	W-R	Per cent	£1 Level Stake
2-y-o	3-21	14.3	+ 1.00	2-y-o	0-0	-	0.00
3-y-o	5-82	6.1	- 29.75	3-y-o	2-53	3.8	- 30.00
4-y-o+	0-5	-	- 5.00	4-y-o+	7-38	18.4	- 2.62
Selling	1-3	33.3	+ 9.00	Selling	1-8	12.5	- 5.37
Apprentice	0-2	-	- 2.00	Apprentice	1-8	12.5	+ 3.00
Amat/Ladies	0-0	-	0.00	Amat/Ladies	0-0	-	0.00
Totals	9-113	8.0	- 26.75	Totals	11-107	10.3	- 34.99

COURSE GRADE

	W-R	Per cent	£1 Level Stake
Group 1	12-113	10.6	- 4.62
Group 2	6-44	13.6	+ 0.25
Group 3	1-25	4.0	- 22.00
Group 4	1-38	2.6	- 35.37

FIRST TIME OUT

	W-R	Per cent	£1 Level Stake
2-y-o	1-10	10.0	+ 2.00
3-y-o	2-24	8.3	+ 8.00
4-y-o+	1-5	20.0	+ 6.00
Totals	4-39	10.3	+ 16.00

JOCKEYS RIDING

	W-R	Per cent	£1 Level Stake		W-R	Per cent	£1 Level Stake
M Roberts	7-17	41.2	+ 32.63	G Duffield	1-1	100.0	+ 2.00
J D Smith	6-37	16.2	+ 0.63	S James	1-3	33.3	+ 8.00
D Biggs	5-86	5.8	- 29.00				

W Newnes	0-13	K Darley	0-3	J Quinn	0-1
A Clark	0-6	M Wigham	0-3	J Reid	0-1
M Hunt	0-5	R Cochrane	0-3	J Weaver	0-1
Pat Eddery	0-5	A McGlone	0-2	L Dettori	0-1
T Quinn	0-5	G Bardwell	0-2	M Hills	0-1
Dale Gibson	0-4	W Carson	0-2	P D'Arcy	0-1
G Carter	0-4	C Asmussen	0-1	P Robinson	0-1
K Fallon	0-4	D Holland	0-1	T Thomas	0-1
J Williams	0-3	D McKeown	0-1	W Ryan	0-1

COURSE RECORD

	Total W-R	Non-Handicaps 2-y-o	3-y-o+	Handicaps 2-y-o	3-y-o+	Per cent	£1 Level Stake
Brighton	5-14	0-1	3-8	0-0	2-5	35.7	+ 23.25
Goodwood	3-24	1-4	0-9	0-0	2-11	12.5	+ 8.50
Newmarket	3-30	0-4	1-11	0-0	2-15	10.0	- 1.00
Epsom	1-5	0-0	1-4	0-0	0-1	20.0	+ 1.50
York	1-5	0-0	0-1	0-0	1-4	20.0	+ 2.00
Newbury	1-8	0-1	0-4	0-0	1-3	12.5	- 5.62
Yarmouth	1-9	1-1	0-7	0-0	0-1	11.1	- 6.00
Ascot	1-10	0-2	0-2	0-0	1-6	10.0	- 4.00
Kempton	1-12	0-0	1-7	0-0	0-5	8.3	+ 5.00
Lingfield	1-12	1-2	0-4	0-0	0-6	8.3	- 5.00
Sandown	1-12	0-2	0-5	0-0	1-5	8.3	- 4.00
Lingfield (AW)	1-23	0-0	0-6	0-0	1-17	4.3	- 20.37

Folkestone	0-11	Nottingham	0-4	Doncaster	0-2
Salisbury	0-10	Ripon	0-4	Haydock	0-2
Windsor	0-5	Ayr	0-3	Warwick	0-1
Bath	0-4	Chepstow	0-3		
Chester	0-4	Southwell (AW)	0-3		

WINNING HORSES

	Age	Races Run	1st	2nd	3rd	Unpl	Win £
Bold Resolution	5	12	3	1	0	8	22,962
Master Planner	4	15	2	1	3	9	20,099
Magical Retreat	3	10	2	0	3	5	16,468
Day Of History	4	8	2	2	1	3	8,527
Crazy Paving	2	2	1	0	0	1	5,385
Formal Affair	3	11	2	0	2	7	5,193
Contract Court	3	2	1	0	0	1	3,524
Big Squeeze	2	4	1	0	0	3	3,377
Without A Flag	3	15	1	4	2	8	3,087
Molly Splash	6	5	1	0	0	4	2,925
Impeccable Taste	3	8	1	0	0	7	2,243
Noeprob	3	4	1	0	0	3	2,070
Early To Rise	3	13	1	2	2	8	2,011
Pursuit Of Glory	2	3	1	0	1	1	1,830

WINNING OWNERS

	Races Won	Value £		Races Won	Value £
R M Cyzer	19	97,871	Gerald Leigh	1	1,830

Favourites	7-18	38.9%	+ 10.76	Total winning prize-money	£99,701

Longest winning sequence		2	Average SP of winner	6.9/1
Longest losing sequence		40	Return on stakes invested	-28.1%

1992 Form	27-200	13.5%	+ 81.75	1990 Form	9-165	5.5%	- 70.50
1991 Form	20-217	9.2%	- 79.48	1989 Form	14-148	9.5%	- 1.75

MRS J C DAWE (Bridgwater, Somerset)

	No. of Horses	Races Run	1st	2nd	3rd	Unpl	Per cent	£1 Level Stake
2-y-o	2	3	0	0	0	3	-	- 3.00
3-y-o	1	4	0	0	0	4	-	- 4.00
4-y-o+	5	24	1	0	3	20	4.2	+ 10.00
Totals	8	31	1	0	3	27	3.2	+ 3.00

Jan	Feb	Mar	Apr	May	Jun	Jul	Aug	Sep	Oct/Nov
0-3	0-3	0-4	1-3	0-8	0-10	0-0	0-0	0-0	0-0

Winning Jockey	W-R	£1 Level Stake	Winning Course	W-R	£1 Level Stake
S McCarthy	1-3	+ 31.00	Salisbury	1-4	+ 30.00

Winning Horse	Age	Races Run	1st	2nd	3rd	Unpl	Win £
Sareen Express	5	10	1	0	1	8	2,700

Favourites	0-0			Total winning prize-money	£2,700
1992 Form	3-52	5.8%	- 14.00		

R DICKIN (Newent, Glos)

	No. of Horses	Races Run	1st	2nd	3rd	Unpl	Per cent	£1 Level Stake
2-y-o	4	10	0	0	0	10	-	- 10.00
3-y-o	3	19	1	2	0	16	5.3	- 2.00
4-y-o+	6	37	3	4	4	26	8.1	- 2.00
Totals	13	66	4	6	4	52	6.1	- 14.00

Jan	Feb	Mar	Apr	May	Jun	Jul	Aug	Sep	Oct/Nov
0-0	0-0	0-2	0-9	0-9	1-5	1-7	1-7	1-17	0-10

Winning Jockeys	W-R	£1 Level Stake		W-R	£1 Level Stake
D Meredith	3-12	+ 23.00	T Quinn	1-6	+ 11.00

Winning Courses					
Epsom	1-2	+ 3.50	Goodwood	1-6	+ 15.00
Salisbury	1-3	+ 5.50	Nottingham	1-8	+ 9.00

Winning Horses	Age	Races Run	1st	2nd	3rd	Unpl	Win £
Ballasecret	5	16	3	2	3	8	23,540
Kadastrof	3	10	1	2	0	7	3,641

Favourites	0-1			Total winning prize-money		£27,181
1992 Form	3-42	7.1%	+ 23.50	1990 Form	1-28	3.6%	- 2.00
1991 Form	5-46	10.9%	- 2.75	1989 Form	0-33		

M DIXON (Epsom, Surrey)

	No. of Horses	Races Run	1st	2nd	3rd	Unpl	Per cent	£1 Level Stake
2-y-o	4	6	0	0	0	6	-	- 6.00
3-y-o	4	15	0	0	1	14	-	- 15.00
4-y-o+	4	28	5	2	2	19	17.9	+ 19.00
Totals	12	49	5	2	3	39	10.2	- 2.00

Jan	Feb	Mar	Apr	May	Jun	Jul	Aug	Sep	Oct/Nov
0-2	0-2	0-2	0-5	1-10	1-5	0-8	2-8	1-3	0-4

Winning Jockeys	W-R	£1 Level Stake			W-R	£1 Level Stake
B Russell	1-1	+ 14.00		D Wright	1-14	- 9.00
D Gibbs	1-1	+ 1.75		A Clark	1-14	- 10.75
Kim McDonnell	1-2	+ 19.00				

Winning Courses						
Sandown	1-2	+ 0.75		Kempton	1-7	+ 8.00
Warwick	1-3	+ 0.25		Lingfield (AW)	1-10	- 5.00
Brighton	1-5	+ 16.00				

Winning Horses	Age	Races Run	1st	2nd	3rd	Unpl	Win £
Dr Zeva	7	12	2	2	0	8	7,152
Princess Ermyn	4	7	2	0	1	4	5,907
Prosequendo	6	5	1	0	1	3	2,899

Favourites	2-5	40.0%	+ 1.00	Total winning prize-money		£15,958
1992 Form	5-79	6.3%	- 20.50	1991 Form	0-1	

M DODS (Darlington, Co Durham)

	No. of Horses	Races Run	1st	2nd	3rd	Unpl	Per cent	£1 Level Stake
2-y-o	4	26	1	2	4	19	3.8	- 15.00
3-y-o	3	18	0	1	1	16	-	- 18.00
4-y-o+	10	74	4	6	4	60	5.4	- 22.00
Totals	17	118	5	9	9	95	4.2	- 55.00

Jan	Feb	Mar	Apr	May	Jun	Jul	Aug	Sep	Oct/Nov
0-3	0-0	0-2	1-10	2-15	0-18	1-22	0-16	0-16	1-16

Winning Jockeys	W-R	£1 Level Stake			W-R	£1 Level Stake
S Webster	2-26	- 11.00		Pat Eddery	1-2	+ 5.00
J Lowe	2-43	- 2.00				

Winning Courses						
Ayr	1-4	0.00		Pontefract	1-9	+ 17.00
Newmarket	1-4	+ 3.00		Southwell (AW)	1-11	0.00
Thirsk	1-7	+ 8.00				

Dods M

Winning Horses	Age	Races Run	1st	2nd	3rd	Unpl	Win £
So Superb	4	17	2	0	1	14	6,688
Ned's Bonanza	4	9	1	2	0	6	4,464
Blue Grit	7	18	1	3	0	14	3,980
Red Grit	2	12	1	1	1	9	2,925

Favourites	0-6		Total winning prize-money				£18,056

1992 Form	7-69	10.1%	+ 2.55	1990 Form	0-5
1991 Form	3-40	7.5%	- 26.50		

T W DONNELLY (Swadlincote, Leics)

	No. of Horses	Races Run	1st	2nd	3rd	Unpl	Per cent	£1 Level Stake
2-y-o	0	0	0	0	0	0	-	0.00
3-y-o	3	9	1	0	0	8	11.1	+ 6.00
4-y-o+	3	6	0	0	0	6	-	- 6.00
Totals	6	15	1	0	0	14	6.7	0.00

Jan	Feb	Mar	Apr	May	Jun	Jul	Aug	Sep	Oct/Nov
0-0	0-0	0-0	0-0	1-1	0-1	0-2	0-6	0-1	0-4

Winning Jockey	W-R	£1 Level Stake	Winning Course	W-R	£1 Level Stake
S D Williams	1-9	+ 6.00	Beverley	1-2	+ 13.00

Winning Horse	Age	Races Run	1st	2nd	3rd	Unpl	Win £
Cavatina	3	5	1	0	0	4	3,202

Favourites	0-0	Total winning prize-money	£3,202

1992 Form	0-6	1991 Form	0-3

S DOW (Epsom, Surrey)

	No. of Horses	Races Run	1st	2nd	3rd	Unpl	Per cent	£1 Level Stake
2-y-o	9	42	3	2	3	34	7.1	- 8.00
3-y-o	18	119	13	8	11	87	10.9	+ 3.33
4-y-o+	14	92	5	9	8	70	5.4	- 40.00
Totals	41	253	21	19	22	191	8.3	- 44.67

BY MONTH

2-y-o	W-R	Per cent	£1 Level Stake	3-y-o	W-R	Per cent	£1 Level Stake
January	0-0	-	0.00	January	0-5	-	- 5.00
February	0-0	-	0.00	February	0-4	-	- 4.00
March	0-0	-	0.00	March	1-1	100.0	+ 3.00
April	0-0	-	0.00	April	1-13	7.7	- 7.00
May	0-4	-	- 4.00	May	0-25	-	- 25.00
June	1-7	14.3	+ 6.00	June	3-15	20.0	+ 16.00
July	0-10	-	- 10.00	July	2-16	12.5	+ 8.00
August	2-9	22.2	+ 12.00	August	3-24	12.5	- 4.17
September	0-11	-	- 11.00	September	1-12	8.3	+ 14.00
Oct/Nov	0-1	-	- 1.00	Oct/Nov	2-4	50.0	+ 7.50

4-y-o+	W-R	Per cent	£1 Level Stake	Totals	W-R	Per cent	£1 Level Stake
January	0-1	-	- 1.00	January	0-6	-	- 6.00
February	1-1	100.0	+ 16.00	February	1-5	20.0	+ 12.00
March	0-7	-	- 7.00	March	1-8	12.5	- 4.00
April	0-11	-	- 11.00	April	1-24	4.2	- 18.00
May	0-10	-	- 10.00	May	0-39	-	- 39.00
June	1-16	6.3	+ 5.00	June	5-38	13.2	+ 27.00
July	2-17	11.8	- 9.50	July	4-43	9.3	- 11.50
August	1-11	9.1	- 4.50	August	6-44	13.6	+ 3.33
September	0-11	-	- 11.00	September	1-34	2.9	- 8.00
Oct/Nov	0-7	-	- 7.00	Oct/Nov	2-12	16.7	- 0.50

DISTANCE

2-y-o	W-R	Per cent	£1 Level Stake	3-y-o	W-R	Per cent	£1 Level Stake
5f-6f	2-21	9.5	+ 7.00	5f-6f	0-30	-	- 30.00
7f-8f	1-21	4.8	- 15.00	7f-8f	5-55	9.1	0.00
9f-13f	0-0	-	0.00	9f-13f	6-30	20.0	+ 28.50
14f+	0-0	-	0.00	14f+	2-4	50.0	+ 4.83

4-y-o+	W-R	Per cent	£1 Level Stake	Totals	W-R	Per cent	£1 Level Stake
5f-6f	1-15	6.7	+ 6.00	5f-6f	3-66	4.5	- 17.00
7f-8f	2-36	5.6	- 26.50	7f-8f	8-112	7.1	- 41.50
9f-13f	1-24	4.2	- 7.00	9f-13f	7-54	13.0	+ 21.50
14f+	1-17	5.9	- 12.50	14f+	3-21	14.3	- 7.67

TYPE OF RACE

Non-Handicaps	W-R	Per cent	£1 Level Stake	Handicaps	W-R	Per cent	£1 Level Stake
2-y-o	2-22	9.1	- 3.00	2-y-o	0-9	-	- 9.00
3-y-o	2-41	4.9	- 25.50	3-y-o	7-60	11.7	+ 6.83
4-y-o+	1-16	6.3	- 13.00	4-y-o+	2-59	3.4	- 33.50
Selling	2-17	11.8	+ 4.00	Selling	0-1	-	- 1.00
Apprentice	0-1	-	- 1.00	Apprentice	0-8	-	- 8.00
Amat/Ladies	0-4	-	- 4.00	Amat/Ladies	5-15	33.3	+ 42.50
Totals	7-101	6.9	- 42.50	Totals	14-152	9.2	- 2.17

	COURSE GRADE					FIRST TIME OUT		
	W-R	Per cent	£1 Level Stake			W-R	Per cent	£1 Level Stake
Group 1	5-83	6.0	- 10.00	2-y-o		1-9	11.1	+ 4.00
Group 2	4-67	6.0	- 29.50	3-y-o		0-16	-	- 16.00
Group 3	3-24	12.5	- 7.00	4-y-o+		1-12	8.3	+ 9.00
Group 4	9-79	11.4	+ 1.83					
				Totals		2-37	5.4	- 3.00

JOCKEYS RIDING

	W-R	Per cent	£1 Level Stake		W-R	Per cent	£1 Level Stake
Mr T Cuff	5-19	26.3	+ 38.50	B Raymond	1-3	33.3	+ 8.00
T Quinn	5-37	13.5	- 2.67	D McKeown	1-3	33.3	+ 3.00
G Duffield	3-10	30.0	+ 13.50	W Ryan	1-8	12.5	+ 18.00
A Munro	2-9	22.2	+ 1.00	J Weaver	1-9	11.1	+ 4.00
M Roberts	2-15	13.3	+ 12.00				

C Rutter	0-34	N Adams	0-4	K Darley	0-1
A Martinez	0-17	B Russell	0-3	M Denaro	0-1
G Hind	0-8	L Dettori	0-3	M Hills	0-1
A McGlone	0-7	L Piggott	0-3	M Perrett	0-1
D Harrison	0-7	N Kennedy	0-3	Miss J Winter	0-1
F Norton	0-7	B Rouse	0-2	Mrs D Arbuthnot	0-1
G Carter	0-6	J Quinn	0-2	N Carlisle	0-1
D Wright	0-5	Paul Eddery	0-2	P Robinson	0-1
D Biggs	0-4	R Cochrane	0-2	S O'Gorman	0-1
J Reid	0-4	T Williams	0-2	W R Swinburn	0-1
J Williams	0-4	A Tucker	0-1		

COURSE RECORD

	Total W-R	Non-Handicaps		Handicaps		Per cent	£1 Level Stake
		2-y-o	3-y-o+	2-y-o	3-y-o+		
Lingfield (AW)	6-34	0-2	0-11	0-1	6-20	17.6	+ 31.33
Goodwood	3-17	1-3	1-2	0-0	1-12	17.6	+ 9.00
Brighton	3-28	1-4	1-10	0-3	1-11	10.7	+ 3.50
Beverley	2-6	0-0	0-0	0-0	2-6	33.3	+ 5.00
Catterick	1-1	0-0	0-0	0-0	1-1	100.0	+ 6.00
Thirsk	1-1	1-1	0-0	0-0	0-0	100.0	+ 5.00
Pontefract	1-3	0-0	1-1	0-1	0-1	33.3	+ 3.00
Edinburgh	1-4	0-1	1-1	0-0	0-2	25.0	- 1.00
Ascot	1-8	0-0	0-0	0-0	1-8	12.5	+ 18.00
Epsom	1-17	0-1	0-3	0-0	1-13	5.9	+ 4.00
Folkestone	1-21	0-5	0-6	0-0	1-10	4.8	- 15.50

Lingfield	0-28	Warwick	0-7	Nottingham	0-3
Kempton	0-13	Windsor	0-5	Southwell (Turf)	0-3
Newmarket	0-9	Doncaster	0-4	York	0-2
Salisbury	0-9	Newbury	0-4	Ayr	0-1
Southwell (AW)	0-9	Bath	0-3	Chepstow	0-1
Sandown	0-8	Leicester	0-3	Redcar	0-1

WINNING HORSES

	Age	Races Run	1st	2nd	3rd	Unpl	Win £
Young Ern	3	12	2	2	1	7	57,480
Sir Thomas Beecham	3	12	3	1	0	8	7,353
Desert Nomad	3	13	2	0	2	9	5,634
Born To Be	4	10	1	1	3	5	5,436
Pondering	3	7	2	0	1	4	5,320
Night Edition	3	7	2	0	0	5	4,707
Beautete	2	4	1	0	0	3	3,582
Syabas	2	3	1	0	1	1	3,184
Persian Gusher	3	11	1	3	0	7	3,143
Chakalak	5	12	1	1	3	7	3,114
Native Chieftain	4	9	1	0	0	8	3,054
Dancing Beau	4	15	1	4	2	8	2,821
Hillsdown Boy	3	8	1	0	0	7	2,574
Across The Bay	6	6	1	1	0	4	2,549
Charisma Girl	2	13	1	2	0	10	2,070

WINNING OWNERS

	Races Won	Value £		Races Won	Value £
M F Kentish	2	57,480	D G Churston	1	3,582
J A Redmond	2	7,985	S T Oon	1	3,184
Mrs Heather Chakko	3	7,353	Gravy Boys Racing	1	3,143
Eurostrait Ltd	2	5,634	P F Chakko	1	3,114
Mrs S R Crowe	2	5,628	Lennard Lazarus	1	2,821
Paul Deakin	2	5,320	Clear Height Racing	1	2,070
Ray Hawthorn	2	4,707			

Favourites	0-11		Total winning prize-money		£112,021
Longest winning sequence		2	Average SP of winner		8.9/1
Longest losing sequence		46	Return on stakes invested		-17.7%

1992 Form	17-205	8.3%	- 73.62	1990 Form	5-188	2.7%	-163.54
1991 Form	17-213	8.0%	- 31.92	1989 Form	7-116	6.0%	- 64.00

MISS J S DOYLE (Newbury, Berks)

	No. of Horses	Races Run	1st	2nd	3rd	Unpl	Per cent	£1 Level Stake
2-y-o	2	10	1	1	0	8	10.0	- 2.50
3-y-o	1	10	1	0	2	7	10.0	- 6.00
4-y-o+	5	11	0	0	0	11	-	- 11.00
Totals	8	31	2	1	2	26	6.5	- 19.50

Jan	Feb	Mar	Apr	May	Jun	Jul	Aug	Sep	Oct/Nov
0-0	0-0	0-0	0-3	0-3	1-7	0-4	0-5	0-4	1-5

Doyle Miss J S

Winning Jockeys	W-R	£1 Level Stake			W-R	£1 Level Stake
J Quinn	1-2	+ 5.50	J Reid		1-10	- 6.00

Winning Courses						
Pontefract	1-1	+ 6.50	Lingfield		1-3	+ 1.00

Winning Horses	Age	Races Run	1st	2nd	3rd	Unpl	Win £
Petersford Girl	3	10	1	0	2	7	3,699
Rafter-J	2	4	1	1	0	2	2,905

Favourites	1-2	50.0%	+ 2.00	Total winning prize-money	£6,604

1992 Form	0-5

J L DUNLOP (Arundel, West Sussex)

	No. of Horses	Races Run	1st	2nd	3rd	Unpl	Per cent	£1 Level Stake
2-y-o	54	182	21	30	24	107	11.5	- 41.32
3-y-o	43	254	56	35	30	133	22.0	+ 34.86
4-y-o+	18	100	16	8	15	61	16.0	- 11.33
Totals	115	536	93	73	69	301	17.4	- 17.79

BY MONTH

2-y-o	W-R	Per cent	£1 Level Stake	3-y-o	W-R	Per cent	£1 Level Stake
Mar/Apr	0-3	-	- 3.00	Mar/Apr	13-46	28.3	+ 31.01
May	0-9	-	- 9.00	May	13-42	31.0	+ 13.17
June	1-20	5.0	- 3.00	June	5-44	11.4	- 25.61
July	0-26	-	- 26.00	July	10-38	26.3	+ 24.41
August	5-38	13.2	- 19.56	August	7-26	26.9	+ 10.83
September	6-47	12.8	- 1.77	September	5-35	14.3	- 11.20
Oct/Nov	9-39	23.1	+ 21.01	Oct/Nov	3-23	13.0	- 7.75

4-y-o+	W-R	Per cent	£1 Level Stake	Totals	W-R	Per cent	£1 Level Stake
Mar/Apr	6-20	30.0	+ 9.37	Mar/Apr	19-69	27.5	+ 37.38
May	3-19	15.8	- 11.70	May	16-70	22.9	- 7.53
June	2-13	15.4	- 3.50	June	8-77	10.4	- 32.11
July	1-7	14.3	+ 4.00	July	11-71	15.5	+ 2.41
August	2-14	14.3	+ 1.00	August	14-78	17.9	- 7.73
September	0-15	-	- 15.00	September	11-97	11.3	- 27.97
Oct/Nov	2-12	16.7	+ 4.50	Oct/Nov	14-74	18.9	+ 17.76

DISTANCE

2-y-o	W-R	Per cent	£1 Level Stake	3-y-o	W-R	Per cent	£1 Level Stake
5f-6f	2-60	3.3	- 40.00	5f-6f	0-2	-	- 2.00
7f-8f	18-119	15.1	- 2.82	7f-8f	18-85	21.2	+ 15.21
9f-13f	1-3	33.3	+ 1.50	9f-13f	23-121	19.0	+ 5.55
14f+	0-0	-	0.00	14f+	15-46	32.6	+ 16.10

4-y-o+	W-R	Per cent	£1 Level Stake	Totals	W-R	Per cent	£1 Level Stake
5f-6f	0-6	-	- 6.00	5f-6f	2-68	2.9	- 48.00
7f-8f	4-15	26.7	+ 12.00	7f-8f	40-219	18.3	+ 24.39
9f-13f	11-59	18.6	- 5.33	9f-13f	35-183	19.1	+ 1.72
14f+	1-20	5.0	- 12.00	14f+	16-66	24.2	+ 4.10

TYPE OF RACE

Non-Handicaps	W-R	Per cent	£1 Level Stake	Handicaps	W-R	Per cent	£1 Level Stake
2-y-o	17-156	10.9	- 55.65	2-y-o	3-25	12.0	+ 11.33
3-y-o	29-122	23.8	+ 22.16	3-y-o	27-130	20.8	+ 14.70
4-y-o+	8-36	22.2	- 0.13	4-y-o+	9-63	14.3	- 6.20
Selling	0-0	-	0.00	Selling	0-0	-	0.00
Apprentice	0-0	-	0.00	Apprentice	0-3	-	- 3.00
Amat/Ladies	0-0	-	0.00	Amat/Ladies	0-1	-	- 1.00
Totals	54-314	17.2	- 33.62	Totals	39-222	17.6	+ 15.83

COURSE GRADE

	W-R	Per cent	£1 Level Stake
Group 1	50-300	16.7	- 14.50
Group 2	15-91	16.5	- 8.26
Group 3	17-108	15.7	- 15.78
Group 4	11-37	29.7	+ 20.75

FIRST TIME OUT

	W-R	Per cent	£1 Level Stake
2-y-o	2-54	3.7	- 30.00
3-y-o	8-43	18.6	+ 8.38
4-y-o+	5-18	27.8	+ 6.37
Totals	15-115	13.0	- 15.25

JOCKEYS RIDING

	W-R	Per cent	£1 Level Stake		W-R	Per cent	£1 Level Stake
W Carson	31-182	17.0	- 45.99	R Hills	3-22	13.6	- 9.00
Pat Eddery	14-34	41.2	+ 28.25	W Ryan	3-24	12.5	- 12.12
G Carter	11-21	52.4	+ 32.35	Paul Eddery	2-9	22.2	- 0.09
W Newnes	4-16	25.0	+ 11.25	A McGlone	2-16	12.5	- 5.00
B Raymond	4-21	19.0	+ 23.00	T Quinn	2-24	8.3	- 15.27
L Piggott	4-21	19.0	+ 28.50	K Darley	1-4	25.0	+ 1.00
J Reid	4-27	14.8	+ 3.00	N Carlisle	1-4	25.0	+ 11.00
R Cochrane	3-12	25.0	+ 1.25	T Williams	1-6	16.7	+ 11.00
L Dettori	3-15	20.0	- 2.92				

M Hills	0-12	J Carroll	0-2	G Bardwell	0-1
G Duffield	0-11	N Adams	0-2	G Starkey	0-1
A Munro	0-9	S Davies	0-2	J D Smith	0-1
B Rouse	0-6	S Raymont	0-2	J Lowe	0-1
J Williams	0-6	W R Swinburn	0-2	M J Kinane	0-1
S Whitworth	0-4	A Clark	0-1	Miss E Houghton	0-1
D Holland	0-3	C Asmussen	0-1	S Dawson	0-1
P Robinson	0-3	D Biggs	0-1	T G McLaughlin	0-1
G Hind	0-2	D Harrison	0-1		

COURSE RECORD

	Total W-R	Non-Handicaps 2-y-o	Non-Handicaps 3-y-o+	Handicaps 2-y-o	Handicaps 3-y-o+	Per cent	£1 Level Stake
Newmarket	9-62	2-19	3-15	0-5	4-23	14.5	- 1.25
Doncaster	7-29	2-14	2-7	1-2	2-6	24.1	+ 19.93
Folkestone	6-14	0-5	2-2	0-0	4-7	42.9	+ 19.00
York	6-24	2-7	2-8	0-1	2-8	25.0	+ 9.88
Sandown	5-17	1-6	2-5	0-0	2-6	29.4	+ 18.38
Leicester	5-29	2-11	1-10	0-0	2-8	17.2	+ 3.53
Newbury	5-40	0-10	2-9	1-5	2-16	12.5	- 8.17
Newcastle	4-7	2-2	1-1	0-0	1-4	57.1	+ 9.13
Ripon	4-9	0-1	2-4	0-0	2-4	44.4	+ 16.13
Thirsk	4-9	1-2	2-4	0-0	1-3	44.4	+ 20.00
Haydock	4-16	1-5	2-4	0-0	1-7	25.0	- 3.25
Nottingham	4-21	0-7	2-3	0-0	2-11	19.0	- 10.72
Kempton	4-30	1-6	3-14	0-1	0-9	13.3	- 9.27
Pontefract	3-8	1-3	1-2	1-1	0-2	37.5	+ 16.25
Warwick	3-9	0-2	1-3	0-0	2-4	33.3	+ 5.25
Salisbury	3-26	0-7	2-9	0-0	1-10	11.5	- 15.27
Ayr	2-6	1-1	1-2	0-1	0-2	33.3	- 2.13
Beverley	2-13	0-2	1-3	0-0	1-8	15.4	- 1.00
Bath	2-18	0-4	0-5	0-0	2-9	11.1	- 6.75
Brighton	2-20	0-3	1-7	0-3	1-7	10.0	- 8.00
Lingfield	2-21	1-8	1-9	0-0	0-4	9.5	- 15.12
Ascot	2-24	0-3	1-12	0-0	1-9	8.3	- 9.50
Carlisle	1-2	0-1	0-0	0-0	1-1	50.0	+ 1.50
Yarmouth	1-7	0-1	0-1	0-1	1-4	14.3	- 5.09
Epsom	1-8	0-2	1-3	0-0	0-3	12.5	- 5.25
Southwell (Turf)	1-9	0-4	0-1	0-1	1-3	11.1	- 2.00
Goodwood	1-37	0-15	1-9	0-2	0-11	2.7	- 33.00

Chepstow	0-7	Windsor	0-5	Chester	0-1
Redcar	0-5	Catterick	0-2	Southwell (AW)	0-1

WINNING HORSES

	Age	Races Run	1st	2nd	3rd	Unpl	Win £
Smarginato	3	5	4	1	0	0	61,068
Thawakib	3	4	1	0	0	3	59,407
Azzilfi	3	6	2	0	1	3	43,382
Talented	3	5	2	2	1	0	39,069
Alhijaz	4	5	1	0	0	4	35,325

Eurolink Thunder	3	7	3	0	1	3	34,865
Dawning Street	5	5	2	0	1	2	33,181
My Patriarch	3	11	5	0	2	4	29,744
Beauchamp Hero	3	7	2	2	0	3	26,932
Fumo Di Londra	2	2	1	0	1	0	26,797
Captain Horatius	4	3	2	0	1	0	19,761
Gisarne	3	5	2	0	0	3	17,755
Acanthus	3	6	3	0	0	3	13,129
Lucky Guest	6	6	1	1	1	3	12,792
Midnight Heights	3	8	3	2	0	3	11,884
Kassab	3	6	3	1	1	1	11,868
Duty Time	2	8	2	1	0	5	10,584
Sun Grebe	3	8	3	0	0	5	10,449
Bobbysoxer	3	11	3	2	1	5	10,329
Circus Colours	3	8	2	0	0	6	9,915
Blackpatch Hill	4	11	3	1	1	6	9,302
Ultimo Imperatore	2	1	1	0	0	0	8,358
Bulaxie	2	2	1	0	1	0	7,995
Bold Stroke	4	8	1	1	1	5	7,985
He's A King	3	10	2	3	1	4	7,733
Erhaab	2	6	2	1	1	2	7,495
Harlestone Brook	3	10	2	4	0	4	6,824
Prince Hannibal	6	8	2	0	3	3	6,727
Dumaani	2	2	1	0	0	1	6,570
Casteddu	4	3	1	0	0	2	6,505
Armenian Coffee	3	8	2	2	1	3	5,509
Pembridge Place	2	2	1	0	0	1	5,254
Muwafik	2	4	1	1	0	2	4,698
Sheridan	2	4	1	1	0	2	4,593
Clyde Goddess	2	3	1	0	2	0	4,542
Jazeel	2	5	1	2	2	0	4,397
Delve	4	1	1	0	0	0	4,247
Mehthaaf	2	3	1	0	1	1	4,111
Luhuk	2	2	1	0	0	1	4,111
Mashair	3	4	1	1	1	1	3,883
Be Exciting	2	7	1	2	0	4	3,782
Eurolink Chieftain	2	2	1	0	0	1	3,624
Riviere Actor	3	9	1	2	1	5	3,525
Tabkir	3	3	1	0	0	2	3,524
Katiba	3	9	1	2	1	5	3,513
Dagny Juel	3	3	1	1	0	1	3,465
Alaflak	2	4	1	2	1	0	3,420
Son Of Sharp Shot	3	7	1	0	1	5	3,379
Sawlajan	2	4	1	0	1	2	3,377
Cazzuto	2	3	1	1	0	1	3,290
Carelaman	3	8	1	1	3	3	3,260
Spectacular Dawn	4	8	1	1	0	6	3,202
Badie	4	8	1	0	4	3	3,202
Jadirah	3	6	1	0	0	5	3,132
Safir	3	8	1	1	3	3	3,114
Special Dawn	3	7	1	0	1	5	3,106
Play With Me	3	8	1	2	0	5	2,793
Imposing Groom	2	5	1	0	0	4	2,783
Guestwick	3	11	1	0	1	9	2,243

WINNING OWNERS

	Races Won	Value £		Races Won	Value £
Hamdan Al-Maktoum	19	129,819	Cuadra Africa	3	13,129
Prince A A Faisal	3	78,707	Aubrey Ison	2	10,584
Gerecon Italia	4	61,068	Sir John Pilkington	3	10,449
P G Goulandris	7	60,652	Cyril Humphris	2	9,135
Windflower O'seas Holdings Inc	5	52,458	Tom Wilson	1	7,985
Eurolink Group Plc	4	38,489	Lady Swaythling	2	7,733
Gerecon Italia	2	35,154	Az Agr Associate Srl	2	5,509
Peter S Winfield	6	32,946	Lady Cohen	1	5,254
E Penser	2	26,932	Stonethorn Stud Farms Ltd	1	3,782
D R Hunnisett	4	26,488	S Khaled	1	3,525
J L Dunlop	6	19,415	Miss K Rausing	1	3,465
Ettore Landi	4	18,389	Miss Katherine Gearon	1	2,793
Racing Welfare	2	17,755	Ian Cameron	1	2,783
Executors of the late – Sir Robin McAlpine	3	14,162	Sir Gordon Reece	1	2,243

Favourites	37-110	33.6%	- 6.25	Total winning prize-money		£700,801
Longest winning sequence			3	Average SP of winner		4.6/1
Longest losing sequence			31	Return on stakes invested		-3.3%
1992 Form	75-505	14.9%	- 167.24	1990 Form	78-444	17.6%	- 50.88
1991 Form	58-366	15.8%	- 64.77	1989 Form	66-456	14.5%	- 89.29

T DYER (Invergowrie, Dundee)

	No. of Horses	Races Run	1st	2nd	3rd	Unpl	Per cent	£1 Level Stake
2-y-o	0	0	0	0	0	0	-	0.00
3-y-o	0	0	0	0	0	0	-	0.00
4-y-o+	4	11	2	1	0	8	18.2	- 1.75
Totals	4	11	2	1	0	8	18.2	- 1.75

Jan	Feb	Mar	Apr	May	Jun	Jul	Aug	Sep	Oct/Nov
0-0	0-0	0-0	0-0	0-0	0-5	1-4	1-1	0-1	0-0

Winning Jockeys	W-R	£1 Level Stake			W-R	£1 Level Stake
K Darley	1-1	+ 1.25	J Weaver		1-1	+ 6.00

Winning Course		
Ayr	2-2	+ 7.25

Winning Horses	Age	Races Run	1st	2nd	3rd	Unpl	Win £
Bay Tern	7	4	1	1	0	2	2,913
Blackdown	6	5	1	0	0	4	1,814

Favourites	1-2	50.0%	+ 0.25	Total winning prize-money	£4,727

M H EASTERBY (Malton, North Yorks)

	No. of Horses	Races Run	1st	2nd	3rd	Unpl	Per cent	£1 Level Stake
2-y-o	31	142	16	22	21	83	11.3	- 43.67
3-y-o	16	129	18	17	13	81	14.0	- 10.08
4-y-o+	19	122	7	12	19	84	5.7	- 82.42
Totals	66	393	41	51	53	248	10.4	-136.17

BY MONTH

2-y-o	W-R	Per cent	£1 Level Stake	3-y-o	W-R	Per cent	£1 Level Stake
January	0-0	-	0.00	January	0-0	-	0.00
February	0-0	-	0.00	February	0-0	-	0.00
March	0-0	-	0.00	March	0-1	-	- 1.00
April	1-9	11.1	+ 1.00	April	0-11	-	- 11.00
May	1-17	5.9	- 14.75	May	4-17	23.5	+ 15.75
June	2-26	7.7	- 13.33	June	3-19	15.8	+ 5.45
July	4-21	19.0	- 10.09	July	3-18	16.7	- 10.63
August	3-21	14.3	- 6.50	August	6-26	23.1	+ 7.35
September	1-28	3.6	- 24.00	September	1-17	5.9	- 2.00
Oct/Nov	4-20	20.0	+ 24.00	Oct/Nov	1-20	5.0	- 14.00

4-y-o+	W-R	Per cent	£1 Level Stake	Totals	W-R	Per cent	£1 Level Stake
January	0-3	-	- 3.00	January	0-3	-	- 3.00
February	0-1	-	- 1.00	February	0-1	-	- 1.00
March	0-1	-	- 1.00	March	0-2	-	- 2.00
April	0-12	-	- 12.00	April	1-32	3.1	- 22.00
May	1-16	6.3	- 7.00	May	6-50	12.0	- 6.00
June	1-24	4.2	- 20.00	June	6-69	8.7	- 27.88
July	4-28	14.3	- 3.67	July	11-67	16.4	- 24.39
August	1-19	5.3	- 16.75	August	10-66	15.2	- 15.90
September	0-12	-	- 12.00	September	2-57	3.5	- 38.00
Oct/Nov	0-6	-	- 6.00	Oct/Nov	5-46	10.9	+ 4.00

DISTANCE

2-y-o	W-R	Per cent	£1 Level Stake	3-y-o	W-R	Per cent	£1 Level Stake
5f-6f	6-79	7.6	- 48.58	5f-6f	4-31	12.9	- 5.25
7f-8f	10-59	16.9	+ 8.91	7f-8f	8-54	14.8	- 21.83
9f-13f	0-4	-	- 4.00	9f-13f	5-37	13.5	+ 11.00
14f+	0-0	-	0.00	14f+	1-7	14.3	+ 6.00

4-y-o+	W-R	Per cent	£1 Level Stake	Totals	W-R	Per cent	£1 Level Stake
5f-6f	1-28	3.6	- 25.75	5f-6f	11-138	8.0	- 79.58
7f-8f	5-73	6.8	- 39.67	7f-8f	23-186	12.4	- 52.59
9f-13f	1-21	4.8	- 17.00	9f-13f	6-62	9.7	- 10.00
14f+	0-0	-	0.00	14f+	1-7	14.3	+ 6.00

TYPE OF RACE

Non-Handicaps	W-R	Per cent	£1 Level Stake	Handicaps	W-R	Per cent	£1 Level Stake
2-y-o	7-91	7.7	- 59.67	2-y-o	4-29	13.8	+ 16.00
3-y-o	6-23	26.1	+ 25.37	3-y-o	11-96	11.5	- 28.70
4-y-o+	2-16	12.5	- 7.50	4-y-o+	4-97	4.1	- 68.17
Selling	6-27	22.2	- 2.75	Selling	0-4	-	- 4.00
Apprentice	0-3	-	- 3.00	Apprentice	1-4	25.0	- 0.75
Amat/Ladies	0-0	-	0.00	Amat/Ladies	0-3	-	- 3.00
Totals	21-160	13.1	- 47.55	Totals	20-233	8.6	- 88.62

COURSE GRADE

	W-R	Per cent	£1 Level Stake
Group 1	13-115	11.3	- 28.40
Group 2	12-126	9.5	- 48.00
Group 3	7-82	8.5	- 42.63
Group 4	9-70	12.9	- 17.14

FIRST TIME OUT

	W-R	Per cent	£1 Level Stake
2-y-o	1-31	3.2	- 20.00
3-y-o	2-16	12.5	+ 9.00
4-y-o+	1-19	5.3	- 15.00
Totals	4-66	6.1	- 26.00

JOCKEYS RIDING

	W-R	Per cent	£1 Level Stake		W-R	Per cent	£1 Level Stake
M Birch	13-183	7.1	-105.34	W Carson	1-1	100.0	+ 3.00
S Maloney	12-105	11.4	- 10.92	Julie Bowker	1-2	50.0	+ 19.00
K Darley	8-53	15.1	- 33.03	W Ryan	1-3	33.3	- 1.38
K Fallon	3-4	75.0	+ 19.00	J Carroll	1-4	25.0	+ 6.00
D Holland	1-1	100.0	+ 4.50				

J Quinn	0-6	T Lucas	0-2	M Roberts	0-1
J Lowe	0-5	D Moffatt	0-1	Mark Denaro	0-1
G Duffield	0-3	F Norton	0-1	Mrs G Rees	0-1
D Biggs	0-2	G Bardwell	0-1	N Connorton	0-1
L Charnock	0-2	G Hind	0-1	O Pears	0-1
Mrs Sarah Easterby	0-2	J Williams	0-1	P Johnson	0-1
Pat Eddery	0-2	L Dettori	0-1	S Wood	0-1

COURSE RECORD

	Total W-R	Non-Handicaps 2-y-o	3-y-o+	Handicaps 2-y-o	3-y-o+	Per cent	£1 Level Stake
Thirsk	6-31	4-14	1-4	0-0	1-13	19.4	+ 21.50
Ayr	5-13	1-2	0-0	0-1	4-10	38.5	+ 2.75
Redcar	5-46	2-22	0-1	1-5	2-18	10.9	- 25.00
Southwell (Turf)	3-7	1-3	1-1	0-0	1-3	42.9	+ 26.25
Edinburgh	3-11	1-3	0-1	0-1	2-6	27.3	- 1.05
Doncaster	3-22	1-1	0-1	2-7	0-13	13.6	+ 12.25
Newcastle	2-18	0-3	0-3	0-0	2-12	11.1	- 9.90
Catterick	2-25	1-7	1-9	0-2	0-7	8.0	- 20.84

Pontefract	2-28	0-9	1-4	0-3	1-12	7.1	- 10.00
York	2-28	0-2	0-0	1-4	1-22	7.1	- 12.50
Beverley	2-29	0-10	1-3	0-3	1-13	6.9	- 16.75
Warwick	1-2	0-0	1-1	0-0	0-1	50.0	+ 3.50
Windsor	1-3	0-0	1-2	0-0	0-1	33.3	- 1.38
Chester	1-6	0-1	1-2	0-0	0-3	16.7	- 1.50
Hamilton	1-7	1-5	0-0	0-0	0-2	14.3	- 3.50
Nottingham	1-7	0-1	1-3	0-1	0-2	14.3	- 3.00
Haydock	1-18	0-4	0-0	0-0	1-14	5.6	- 5.00

Ripon	0-42	Newmarket	0-5	Kempton	0-1
Carlisle	0-14	Ascot	0-4	Lingfield	0-1
Southwell (AW)	0-11	Sandown	0-3	Newbury	0-1
Leicester	0-7	Goodwood	0-2	Yarmouth	0-1

WINNING HORSES

	Age	Races Run	1st	2nd	3rd	Unpl	Win £
Forever Diamonds	6	11	2	2	0	7	19,842
Cumbrian Rhapsody	3	12	4	1	2	5	16,379
Call To Mind	2	6	2	2	1	1	15,912
Dancing Domino	3	13	5	3	2	3	13,123
Beneficiary	2	11	4	1	2	4	11,170
Thornton Gate	4	13	2	1	1	9	6,311
Northern Chief	3	13	2	1	1	9	6,205
First Option	3	12	2	3	2	5	5,590
Milbank Challenger	3	16	2	3	1	10	5,488
Bold Angel	6	9	1	0	3	5	4,500
Non Vintage	2	8	1	1	3	3	4,435
Harpoon Louie	3	10	1	1	0	8	4,013
Sandmoor Chambray	2	6	1	0	2	3	3,948
Sinners Reprieve	2	7	1	4	1	1	3,436
Mheanmetoo	2	3	1	0	0	2	3,297
St Ninian	7	5	1	0	1	3	3,173
Winning Line	2	6	1	0	1	4	3,036
Parkside Lady	2	3	1	1	0	1	2,601
Celestial Rumour	2	6	1	2	1	2	2,549
Duplicate	3	12	1	2	2	7	2,534
Sense Of Priority	4	12	1	1	2	8	2,490
Two D's	2	6	1	0	0	5	2,448
Madam Gymcrak	3	2	1	1	0	0	2,243
Passion Sunday	2	10	1	4	1	4	2,164
Carapelle	2	8	1	2	0	5	2,070

WINNING OWNERS

	Races Won	Value £		Races Won	Value £
P D Savill	11	29,928	Sandmoor Textiles Co Ltd	1	3,948
Mrs J B Russell	2	19,842	Mrs J B Mountfield	1	3,436
Cumbrian Industrials Ltd	4	16,379	C H Stevens	1	3,340
G Graham	2	15,912	Ken Dyke	1	3,297
Reg Griffin	4	11,170	The Winning Line	1	3,036
T H Bennett	2	6,311	Mrs Margaret Liles	1	2,601
T C Chiang	2	6,205	G H Leatham	1	2,534
M H Easterby	2	5,621	Gymcrak Th'bred Racing Club	1	2,243
A M Wragg	1	4,500	Milbank Foods Ltd	1	2,148
H R Leetham	1	4,435	C A Webster	1	2,070

Favourites	21-69	30.4%	- 4.75	Total winning prize-money	£148,955

Longest winning sequence	2	Average SP of winner	5.3/1
Longest losing sequence	30	Return on stakes invested	-34.6%

1992 Form	38-386	9.8%	-144.69	1990 Form	61-562	10.9%	-230.30
1991 Form	58-531	10.9%	-187.51	1989 Form	57-494	11.5%	-202.88

M W EASTERBY (Sherriff Hutton, North Yorks)

	No. of Horses	Races Run	1st	2nd	3rd	Unpl	Per cent	£1 Level Stake
2-y-o	22	99	5	8	6	80	5.1	- 68.00
3-y-o	10	72	6	7	5	54	8.3	- 26.12
4-y-o+	3	38	5	2	2	29	13.2	- 4.83
Totals	35	209	16	17	13	163	7.7	- 98.95

BY MONTH

2-y-o	W-R	Per cent	£1 Level Stake	3-y-o	W-R	Per cent	£1 Level Stake
Mar/Apr	0-3	-	- 3.00	Mar/Apr	0-7	-	- 6.00
May	1-16	6.3	- 11.50	May	2-10	20.0	- 2.87
June	2-22	9.1	- 13.50	June	2-19	10.5	+ 3.00
July	1-24	4.2	- 12.00	July	1-16	6.3	- 12.25
August	1-24	4.2	- 18.00	August	0-11	-	- 11.00
September	0-8	-	- 8.00	September	0-6	-	- 6.00
Oct/Nov	0-2	-	- 2.00	Oct/Nov	1-3	33.3	+ 10.00

4-y-o+	W-R	Per cent	£1 Level Stake	Totals	W-R	Per cent	£1 Level Stake
Mar/Apr	2-5	40.0	- 2.33	Mar/Apr	2-15	13.3	- 11.33
May	0-8	-	- 8.00	May	3-34	8.8	- 22.37
June	2-9	22.2	+ 7.00	June	6-50	12.0	- 3.50
July	1-8	12.5	- 1.50	July	3-48	6.3	- 25.75
August	0-4	-	- 4.00	August	1-39	2.6	- 33.00
September	0-4	-	- 4.00	September	0-18	-	- 18.00
Oct/Nov	0-0	-	0.00	Oct/Nov	1-5	20.0	+ 8.00

DISTANCE

2-y-o	W-R	Per cent	£1 Level Stake	3-y-o	W-R	Per cent	£1 Level Stake
5f-6f	5-73	6.8	- 42.00	5f-6f	4-42	9.5	- 8.87
7f-8f	0-26	-	- 26.00	7f-8f	0-12	-	- 12.00
9f-13f	0-0	-	0.00	9f-13f	2-16	12.5	- 3.25
14f+	0-0	-	0.00	14f+	0-2	-	- 2.00

4-y-o+	W-R	Per cent	£1 Level Stake	Totals	W-R	Per cent	£1 Level Stake
5f-6f	5-38	13.2	- 4.83	5f-6f	14-153	9.2	- 55.70
7f-8f	0-0	-	0.00	7f-8f	0-38	-	- 38.00
9f-13f	0-0	-	0.00	9f-13f	2-16	12.5	- 3.25
14f+	0-0	-	0.00	14f+	0-2	-	- 2.00

TYPE OF RACE

Non-Handicaps	W-R	Per cent	£1 Level Stake	Handicaps	W-R	Per cent	£1 Level Stake
2-y-o	4-53	7.5	- 25.00	2-y-o	0-11	-	- 11.00
3-y-o	0-20	-	- 20.00	3-y-o	6-46	13.0	- 0.12
4-y-o+	1-2	50.0	- 0.33	4-y-o+	4-34	11.8	- 2.50
Selling	1-34	2.9	- 31.00	Selling	0-2	-	- 2.00
Apprentice	0-1	-	- 1.00	Apprentice	0-5	-	- 5.00
Amat/Ladies	0-0	-	0.00	Amat/Ladies	0-1	-	- 1.00
Totals	6-110	5.5	- 77.33	Totals	10-99	10.1	- 21.62

COURSE GRADE

	W-R	Per cent	£1 Level Stake
Group 1	4-47	8.5	- 12.00
Group 2	1-65	1.5	- 58.50
Group 3	6-48	12.5	- 5.33
Group 4	5-49	10.2	- 23.12

FIRST TIME OUT

	W-R	Per cent	£1 Level Stake
2-y-o	1-22	4.5	- 10.00
3-y-o	0-10	-	- 10.00
4-y-o+	1-3	33.3	+ 6.00
Totals	2-35	5.7	- 14.00

JOCKEYS RIDING

	W-R	Per cent	£1 Level Stake		W-R	Per cent	£1 Level Stake
T Lucas	9-108	8.3	- 41.20	L Charnock	3-28	10.7	- 10.75
K Darley	3-12	25.0	+ 6.50	P Johnson	1-13	7.7	- 5.50

C Munday	0-10	D Moffatt	0-1	N Carlisle	0-1
C Dwyer	0-6	G Hind	0-1	N Connorton	0-1
S Maloney	0-5	G Parkin	0-1	Paul Eddery	0-1
L Newton	0-3	J Carroll	0-1	R Cochrane	0-1
M Birch	0-3	K Fallon	0-1	R Hills	0-1
B Raymond	0-2	L Dettori	0-1	R P Elliott	0-1
S Wood	0-2	Mrs A Farrell	0-1	T Quinn	0-1
D McKeown	0-1	N Adams	0-1	W Carson	0-1

COURSE RECORD

	Total W–R	Non-Handicaps 2-y-o	3-y-o+	Handicaps 2-y-o	3-y-o+	Per cent	£1 Level Stake
Beverley	4–27	3–14	0–5	0–2	1–6	14.8	+ 9.50
Newcastle	2–9	0–2	0–0	0–1	2–6	22.2	+ 4.50
York	2–10	0–4	0–0	0–0	2–6	20.0	+ 11.50
Carlisle	2–11	0–2	0–2	0–0	2–7	18.2	– 0.87
Catterick	2–11	1–4	0–3	0–1	1–3	18.2	+ 1.00
Hamilton	1–1	1–1	0–0	0–0	0–0	100.0	+ 3.50
Pontefract	1–9	0–1	1–2	0–0	0–6	11.1	– 7.33
Southwell (AW)	1–24	0–16	0–0	0–0	1–8	4.2	– 20.25
Thirsk	1–32	0–15	0–2	0–1	1–14	3.1	– 25.50

Redcar	0–18	Ayr	0–4	Goodwood	0–1
Ripon	0–14	Leicester	0–4	Southwell (Turf)	0–1
Doncaster	0–12	Edinburgh	0–2	Windsor	0–1
Haydock	0–9	Newmarket	0–2		
Nottingham	0–6	Chester	0–1		

WINNING HORSES

	Age	Races Run	1st	2nd	3rd	Unpl	Win £
Benzoe	3	10	1	1	0	8	13,500
Catherines Well	10	14	2	1	1	10	9,664
Pete Afrique	2	4	2	0	0	2	9,136
Penny Hasset	5	13	2	1	0	10	7,292
Covent Garden Girl	3	13	2	4	1	6	5,918
Hasta La Vista	3	9	2	1	0	6	5,849
Lady Sheriff	2	10	2	3	0	5	5,554
Knayton Lass	2	5	1	3	1	0	3,377
Master Pokey	9	11	1	0	1	9	3,261
Lida's Delight	3	13	1	1	2	9	3,106

WINNING OWNERS

	Races Won	Value £		Races Won	Value £
K Hodgson	4	15,513	E J Mangan	2	5,554
Tony Fawcett	1	13,500	Mrs J M Davenport	1	3,377
P D Savill	2	9,136	Lady Manton	1	3,261
Mrs Anne Henson	2	7,292	Patrington Haven Leisure Park	1	3,106
New Covent Garden Flower Sales	2	5,918			

Favourites	3–14	21.4%	– 6.70	Total winning prize-money			£66,657

Longest winning sequence		1	Average SP of winner		5.9/1
Longest losing sequence		40	Return on stakes invested		–47.3%

1992 Form	12–150	8.0%	– 45.50	1990 Form	25–286	8.7%	– 94.71
1991 Form	14–258	5.4%	–182.09	1989 Form	19–271	7.0%	–145.29

G H EDEN (Newmarket)

	No. of Horses	Races Run	1st	2nd	3rd	Unpl	Per cent	£1 Level Stake
2-y-o	4	14	0	0	0	14	-	- 14.00
3-y-o	3	19	0	0	2	17	-	- 19.00
4-y-o+	4	33	2	3	2	26	6.1	- 27.42
Totals	11	66	2	3	4	57	3.0	- 60.42

Jan	Feb	Mar	Apr	May	Jun	Jul	Aug	Sep	Oct/Nov
0-5	0-0	0-0	0-5	0-8	0-10	0-12	1-9	1-11	0-6

Winning Jockey	W-R	£1 Level Stake				W-R	£1 Level Stake
W Carson	2-3	+ 2.58					

Winning Courses							
Leicester	1-1	+ 0.83		Lingfield		1-5	- 1.25

Winning Horse		Age	Races Run	1st	2nd	3rd	Unpl	Win £
Artistic Reef		4	9	2	0	1	6	8,028

Favourites	1-3	33.3%	- 1.17	Total winning prize-money			£8,028

1992 Form	5-68	7.4%	- 42.00	1990 Form	2-78	2.6%	- 65.50
1991 Form	4-70	5.7%	- 10.75				

C R EGERTON (Newbury, Berks)

	No. of Horses	Races Run	1st	2nd	3rd	Unpl	Per cent	£1 Level Stake
2-y-o	4	11	1	1	1	8	9.1	- 7.50
3-y-o	1	1	0	0	0	1	-	- 1.00
4-y-o+	0	0	0	0	0	0	-	0.00
Totals	5	12	1	1	1	9	8.3	- 8.50

Jan	Feb	Mar	Apr	May	Jun	Jul	Aug	Sep	Oct/Nov
0-0	0-0	0-0	0-0	0-0	0-0	0-0	1-2	0-6	0-4

Winning Jockey	W-R	£1 Level Stake		Winning Course	W-R	£1 Level Stake
C Asmussen	1-1	+ 2.50		Goodwood	1-2	+ 1.50

Winning Horse	Age	Races Run	1st	2nd	3rd	Unpl	Win £
Arndilly	2	4	1	1	0	2	3,392

Favourites	1-2	50.0%	+ 1.50	Total winning prize-money	£3,392

B ELLISON (Malton, North Yorks)

	No. of Horses	Races Run	1st	2nd	3rd	Unpl	Per cent	£1 Level Stake
2-y-o	4	6	1	0	0	5	16.7	+ 2.50
3-y-o	2	11	0	1	0	10	-	- 11.00
4-y-o+	7	36	0	0	1	35	-	- 36.00
Totals	13	53	1	1	1	50	1.9	- 44.50

Jan	Feb	Mar	Apr	May	Jun	Jul	Aug	Sep	Oct/Nov
0-14	0-3	0-5	1-8	0-5	0-7	0-5	0-1	0-2	0-3

Winning Jockey	W-R	£1 Level Stake	Winning Course	W-R	£1 Level Stake
J Lowe	1-7	+ 1.50	Hamilton	1-7	+ 1.50

Winning Horse	Age	Races Run	1st	2nd	3rd	Unpl	Win £
Dundeelin	2	2	1	0	0	1	2,070

Favourites	0-1		Total winning prize-money	£2,070

1992 Form	4-87	4.6%	- 60.50	1990 Form	0-6
1991 Form	3-51	5.9%	- 1.50		

C C ELSEY (Lambourn, Berks)

	No. of Horses	Races Run	1st	2nd	3rd	Unpl	Per cent	£1 Level Stake
2-y-o	3	15	0	0	0	15	-	- 15.00
3-y-o	4	22	2	0	3	17	9.1	- 1.50
4-y-o+	7	80	8	4	6	62	10.0	- 13.67
Totals	14	117	10	4	9	94	8.5	- 30.17

BY MONTH

2-y-o	W-R	Per cent	£1 Level Stake	3-y-o	W-R	Per cent	£1 Level Stake
January	0-0	-	0.00	January	1-1	100.0	+ 2.50
February	0-0	-	0.00	February	1-4	25.0	+ 13.00
March	0-0	-	0.00	March	0-2	-	- 2.00
April	0-2	-	- 2.00	April	0-3	-	- 3.00
May	0-1	-	- 1.00	May	0-3	-	- 3.00
June	0-1	-	- 1.00	June	0-2	-	- 2.00
July	0-1	-	- 1.00	July	0-1	-	- 1.00
August	0-2	-	- 2.00	August	0-3	-	- 3.00
September	0-4	-	- 4.00	September	0-3	-	- 3.00
Oct/Nov	0-4	-	- 4.00	Oct/Nov	0-0	-	0.00

4-y-o+	W-R	Per cent	£1 Level Stake	Totals	W-R	Per cent	£1 Level Stake
January	2-6	33.3	+ 30.00	January	3-7	42.9	+ 32.50
February	1-5	20.0	- 0.50	February	2-9	22.2	+ 12.50
March	2-6	33.3	+ 1.00	March	2-8	25.0	- 1.00
April	0-8	-	- 8.00	April	0-13	-	- 13.00
May	1-11	9.1	- 2.00	May	1-15	6.7	- 6.00
June	0-13	-	- 13.00	June	0-16	-	- 16.00
July	0-8	-	- 8.00	July	0-10	-	- 10.00
August	1-11	9.1	- 5.50	August	1-16	6.3	- 10.50
September	1-6	16.7	- 1.67	September	1-13	7.7	- 8.67
Oct/Nov	0-6	-	- 6.00	Oct/Nov	0-10	-	- 10.00

DISTANCE

2-y-o	W-R	Per cent	£1 Level Stake	3-y-o	W-R	Per cent	£1 Level Stake
5f-6f	0-13	-	- 13.00	5f-6f	0-0	-	0.00
7f-8f	0-2	-	- 2.00	7f-8f	0-8	-	- 8.00
9f-13f	0-0	-	0.00	9f-13f	2-13	15.4	+ 7.50
14f+	0-0	-	0.00	14f+	0-1	-	- 1.00

4-y-o+	W-R	Per cent	£1 Level Stake	Totals	W-R	Per cent	£1 Level Stake
5f-6f	3-23	13.0	- 6.25	5f-6f	3-36	8.3	- 19.25
7f-8f	1-20	5.0	- 10.00	7f-8f	1-30	3.3	- 20.00
9f-13f	4-25	16.0	+ 14.58	9f-13f	6-38	15.8	+ 22.08
14f+	0-12	-	- 12.00	14f+	0-13	-	- 13.00

TYPE OF RACE

Non-Handicaps	W-R	Per cent	£1 Level Stake	Handicaps	W-R	Per cent	£1 Level Stake
2-y-o	0-13	-	- 13.00	2-y-o	0-1	-	- 1.00
3-y-o	1-10	10.0	+ 7.00	3-y-o	1-8	12.5	- 4.50
4-y-o+	1-10	10.0	- 6.25	4-y-o+	6-56	10.7	+ 2.25
Selling	0-6	-	- 6.00	Selling	0-3	-	- 3.00
Apprentice	0-0	-	0.00	Apprentice	0-7	-	- 7.00
Amat/Ladies	1-1	100.0	+ 3.33	Amat/Ladies	0-2	-	- 2.00
Totals	3-40	7.5	- 14.92	Totals	7-77	9.1	- 15.25

COURSE GRADE

	W-R	Per cent	£1 Level Stake
Group 1	0-32	-	- 32.00
Group 2	3-22	13.6	- 3.17
Group 3	0-22	-	- 22.00
Group 4	7-41	17.1	+ 27.00

FIRST TIME OUT

	W-R	Per cent	£1 Level Stake
2-y-o	0-3	-	- 3.00
3-y-o	1-4	25.0	- 0.50
4-y-o+	2-7	28.6	+ 29.00
Totals	3-14	21.4	+ 25.50

Elsey C C

JOCKEYS RIDING

	W-R	Per cent	£1 Level Stake		W-R	Per cent	£1 Level Stake
T Quinn	3-13	23.1	+ 3.75	B Doyle	1-4	25.0	+ 6.00
W Newnes	3-33	9.1	- 6.75	Miss A Elsey	1-5	20.0	- 0.67
J Williams	2-7	28.6	+ 22.50				

Kim McDonnell	0-7	L Dettori	0-2	G Bardwell	0-1
F Norton	0-6	M Roberts	0-2	J Lowe	0-1
J Quinn	0-5	N Adams	0-2	K Fallon	0-1
J Reid	0-4	A Clark	0-1	N Connorton	0-1
A Munro	0-3	A Procter	0-1	R Hills	0-1
Antoinette Armes	0-3	B Russell	0-1	S Davies	0-1
D Holland	0-3	D Biggs	0-1	W Carson	0-1
B Rouse	0-2	D Harrison	0-1	Wendy Jones	0-1
G Duffield	0-2	D McKeown	0-1		

COURSE RECORD

	Total W-R	Non-Handicaps 2-y-o	3-y-o+	Handicaps 2-y-o	3-y-o+	Per cent	£1 Level Stake
Lingfield (AW)	7-28	0-1	2-6	0-0	5-21	25.0	+ 40.00
Lingfield	3-12	0-2	1-2	0-0	2-8	25.0	+ 6.83

Newbury	0-9	Sandown	0-5	Ascot	0-1
Southwell (AW)	0-7	Bath	0-4	Doncaster	0-1
Windsor	0-7	Chepstow	0-4	Redcar	0-1
Goodwood	0-6	Leicester	0-4	Southwell (Turf)	0-1
Kempton	0-6	Brighton	0-3	Yarmouth	0-1
Salisbury	0-6	Newmarket	0-3	York	0-1
Folkestone	0-5	Nottingham	0-2		

WINNING HORSES

	Age	Races Run	1st	2nd	3rd	Unpl	Win £
Rapporteur	7	16	4	2	1	9	14,065
Serious Hurry	5	17	3	1	1	12	8,864
Kissavos	7	14	1	1	1	11	3,106
Absolutely Fact	3	8	1	0	2	5	2,872
Nedaarah	3	3	1	0	0	2	2,208

WINNING OWNERS

			Races Won	Value £				Races Won	Value £
Richard Berenson			9	28,906	T C Marshall			1	2,208
Favourites	1-6	16.7%	- 2.75		Total winning prize-money				£31,114
Longest winning sequence			2		Average SP of winner				7.7/1
Longest losing sequence			43		Return on stakes invested				-25.8%
1992 Form	9-110	8.2%	- 63.19		1990 Form	8-98	8.2%	- 36.27
1991 Form	7-121	5.8%	- 70.00		1989 Form	3-60	5.0%	- 32.00

C W C ELSEY (Malton, North Yorks)

	No. of Horses	Races Run	1st	2nd	3rd	Unpl	Per cent	£1 Level Stake
2-y-o	5	18	0	1	0	17	-	- 18.00
3-y-o	6	39	0	2	2	35	-	- 39.00
4-y-o+	6	35	4	3	4	24	11.4	+ 35.00
Totals	17	92	4	6	6	76	4.3	- 22.00

Jan	Feb	Mar	Apr	May	Jun	Jul	Aug	Sep	Oct/Nov
0-0	0-1	0-4	2-10	1-15	0-15	0-10	0-14	0-8	1-15

Winning Jockeys	W-R	£1 Level Stake				W-R	£1 Level Stake
L Dettori	1-3	+ 23.00		N Kennedy		1-5	+ 8.00
T Williams	1-3	+ 18.00		S Maloney		1-17	- 7.00

Winning Courses							
Redcar	1-4	+ 17.00		Hamilton		1-6	+ 4.00
Newbury	1-5	+ 21.00		Haydock		1-6	+ 7.00

Winning Horses	Age	Races Run	1st	2nd	3rd	Unpl	Win £
Linpac West	7	4	1	0	2	1	20,439
Philgun	4	16	2	3	1	10	6,305
Bilberry	4	7	1	0	1	5	3,236

Favourites	0-3		Total winning prize-money	£29,979

1992 Form	9-100	9.0%	- 25.57	1990 Form	9-140	6.4%	- 77.04
1991 Form	4-88	4.5%	- 61.00	1989 Form	10-114	8.8%	- 35.25

D R C ELSWORTH (Whitsbury, Hants)

	No. of Horses	Races Run	1st	2nd	3rd	Unpl	Per cent	£1 Level Stake
2-y-o	17	56	10	3	5	38	17.9	+ 5.33
3-y-o	20	119	14	17	12	76	11.8	- 30.00
4-y-o+	19	96	8	7	9	72	8.3	- 32.12
Totals	56	271	32	27	26	186	11.8	- 56.79

Elsworth D R C

BY MONTH

2-y-o	W-R	Per cent	£1 Level Stake	3-y-o	W-R	Per cent	£1 Level Stake
January	0-0	-	0.00	January	0-1	-	- 1.00
February	0-0	-	0.00	February	0-3	-	- 3.00
March	0-0	-	0.00	March	0-2	-	- 2.00
April	0-1	-	- 1.00	April	1-14	7.1	- 10.25
May	0-3	-	- 3.00	May	0-16	-	- 16.00
June	0-6	-	- 6.00	June	5-21	23.8	+ 7.25
July	2-6	33.3	+ 6.00	July	7-24	29.2	+ 21.00
August	2-12	16.7	+ 5.75	August	1-17	5.9	- 5.00
September	5-15	33.3	+ 10.08	September	0-15	-	- 15.00
Oct/Nov	1-13	7.7	- 6.50	Oct/Nov	0-6	-	- 6.00

4-y-o+	W-R	Per cent	£1 Level Stake	Totals	W-R	Per cent	£1 Level Stake
January	0-0	-	0.00	January	0-1	-	- 1.00
February	0-2	-	- 2.00	February	0-5	-	- 5.00
March	1-5	20.0	- 0.50	March	1-7	14.3	- 2.50
April	3-17	17.6	+ 16.00	April	4-32	12.5	+ 4.75
May	0-22	-	- 22.00	May	0-41	-	- 41.00
June	2-15	13.3	+ 3.00	June	7-42	16.7	+ 4.25
July	2-18	11.1	- 9.62	July	11-48	22.9	+ 17.38
August	0-10	-	- 10.00	August	3-39	7.7	- 9.25
September	0-4	-	- 4.00	September	5-34	14.7	- 8.92
Oct/Nov	0-3	-	- 3.00	Oct/Nov	1-22	4.5	- 15.50

DISTANCE

2-y-o	W-R	Per cent	£1 Level Stake	3-y-o	W-R	Per cent	£1 Level Stake
5f-6f	6-33	18.2	- 0.42	5f-6f	0-7	-	- 7.00
7f-8f	4-23	17.4	+ 5.75	7f-8f	5-46	10.9	- 4.75
9f-13f	0-0	-	0.00	9f-13f	6-56	10.7	- 30.25
14f+	0-0	-	0.00	14f+	3-10	30.0	+ 12.00

4-y-o+	W-R	Per cent	£1 Level Stake	Totals	W-R	Per cent	£1 Level Stake
5f-6f	1-15	6.7	- 9.50	5f-6f	7-55	12.7	- 16.92
7f-8f	1-16	6.3	- 7.00	7f-8f	10-85	11.8	- 6.00
9f-13f	4-53	7.5	- 19.50	9f-13f	10-109	9.2	- 49.75
14f+	2-12	16.7	+ 3.88	14f+	5-22	22.7	+ 15.88

TYPE OF RACE

Non-Handicaps	W-R	Per cent	£1 Level Stake	Handicaps	W-R	Per cent	£1 Level Stake
2-y-o	10-52	19.2	+ 9.33	2-y-o	0-1	-	- 1.00
3-y-o	8-75	10.7	- 35.75	3-y-o	5-41	12.2	+ 1.75
4-y-o+	2-23	8.7	- 1.00	4-y-o+	6-67	9.0	- 25.12
Selling	0-4	-	- 4.00	Selling	0-0	-	0.00
Apprentice	0-0	-	0.00	Apprentice	1-5	20.0	+ 2.00
Amat/Ladies	0-2	-	- 2.00	Amat/Ladies	0-1	-	- 1.00
Totals	20-156	12.8	- 33.42	Totals	12-115	10.4	- 23.37

Elsworth D R C

<table>
<tr><td colspan="5">COURSE GRADE</td><td colspan="5">FIRST TIME OUT</td></tr>
<tr><td></td><td>W-R</td><td>Per cent</td><td colspan="2">£1 Level Stake</td><td></td><td>W-R</td><td>Per cent</td><td colspan="2">£1 Level Stake</td></tr>
<tr><td>Group 1</td><td>20-174</td><td>11.5</td><td>-</td><td>27.37</td><td>2-y-o</td><td>2-17</td><td>11.8</td><td>-</td><td>3.50</td></tr>
<tr><td>Group 2</td><td>6-42</td><td>14.3</td><td>+</td><td>2.50</td><td>3-y-o</td><td>2-20</td><td>10.0</td><td>+</td><td>2.00</td></tr>
<tr><td>Group 3</td><td>3-31</td><td>9.7</td><td>-</td><td>18.42</td><td>4-y-o+</td><td>1-19</td><td>5.3</td><td>-</td><td>6.00</td></tr>
<tr><td>Group 4</td><td>3-24</td><td>12.5</td><td>-</td><td>13.50</td><td></td><td></td><td></td><td></td><td></td></tr>
<tr><td></td><td></td><td></td><td></td><td></td><td>Totals</td><td>5-56</td><td>8.9</td><td>-</td><td>7.50</td></tr>
</table>

JOCKEYS RIDING

<table>
<tr><td></td><td>W-R</td><td>Per cent</td><td colspan="2">£1 Level Stake</td><td></td><td>W-R</td><td>Per cent</td><td colspan="2">£1 Level Stake</td></tr>
<tr><td>J Williams</td><td>9-120</td><td>7.5</td><td>-</td><td>60.62</td><td>M Roberts</td><td>1-3</td><td>33.3</td><td>+</td><td>2.00</td></tr>
<tr><td>R Cochrane</td><td>7-18</td><td>38.9</td><td>+</td><td>21.33</td><td>W Newnes</td><td>1-3</td><td>33.3</td><td>+</td><td>3.50</td></tr>
<tr><td>B Doyle</td><td>6-14</td><td>42.9</td><td>+</td><td>20.25</td><td>B Rouse</td><td>1-5</td><td>20.0</td><td>+</td><td>8.00</td></tr>
<tr><td>A Procter</td><td>4-25</td><td>16.0</td><td>+</td><td>11.50</td><td>D Harrison</td><td>1-10</td><td>10.0</td><td>-</td><td>2.00</td></tr>
<tr><td>Pat Eddery</td><td>2-13</td><td>15.4</td><td>-</td><td>0.75</td><td></td><td></td><td></td><td></td><td></td></tr>
</table>

<table>
<tr><td>T Quinn</td><td>0-9</td><td>L Piggott</td><td>0-3</td><td>G Duffield</td><td>0-1</td></tr>
<tr><td>W Carson</td><td>0-9</td><td>D Wright</td><td>0-2</td><td>J Reid</td><td>0-1</td></tr>
<tr><td>Tracey Purseglove</td><td>0-7</td><td>R Price</td><td>0-2</td><td>Mr S Swiers</td><td>0-1</td></tr>
<tr><td>A Mackay</td><td>0-6</td><td>Antoinette Armes</td><td>0-1</td><td>Mrs D Arbuthnot</td><td>0-1</td></tr>
<tr><td>C Asmussen</td><td>0-4</td><td>B Raymond</td><td>0-1</td><td>Mrs P Nash</td><td>0-1</td></tr>
<tr><td>G Bardwell</td><td>0-4</td><td>D Holland</td><td>0-1</td><td>Paul Eddery</td><td>0-1</td></tr>
<tr><td>L Dettori</td><td>0-3</td><td>Dale Gibson</td><td>0-1</td><td>R Hills</td><td>0-1</td></tr>
</table>

COURSE RECORD

<table>
<tr><td></td><td>Total W-R</td><td colspan="2">Non-Handicaps
2-y-o   3-y-o+</td><td colspan="2">Handicaps
2-y-o   3-y-o+</td><td>Per cent</td><td colspan="2">£1 Level Stake</td></tr>
<tr><td>Epsom</td><td>4-12</td><td>1-2</td><td>3-6</td><td>0-0</td><td>0-4</td><td>33.3</td><td>+</td><td>17.25</td></tr>
<tr><td>Sandown</td><td>4-24</td><td>1-1</td><td>2-8</td><td>0-0</td><td>1-15</td><td>16.7</td><td>+</td><td>6.00</td></tr>
<tr><td>Lingfield</td><td>3-9</td><td>2-3</td><td>0-4</td><td>0-0</td><td>1-2</td><td>33.3</td><td>+</td><td>5.75</td></tr>
<tr><td>Lingfield (AW)</td><td>3-14</td><td>0-0</td><td>1-6</td><td>0-0</td><td>2-8</td><td>21.4</td><td>-</td><td>3.50</td></tr>
<tr><td>Ascot</td><td>3-18</td><td>0-2</td><td>1-7</td><td>0-0</td><td>2-9</td><td>16.7</td><td>+</td><td>11.00</td></tr>
<tr><td>Goodwood</td><td>3-19</td><td>1-5</td><td>1-3</td><td>0-0</td><td>1-11</td><td>15.8</td><td>+</td><td>2.00</td></tr>
<tr><td>Salisbury</td><td>3-30</td><td>1-5</td><td>0-12</td><td>0-0</td><td>2-13</td><td>10.0</td><td>-</td><td>0.25</td></tr>
<tr><td>Newbury</td><td>3-37</td><td>2-11</td><td>0-11</td><td>0-0</td><td>1-15</td><td>8.1</td><td>-</td><td>18.50</td></tr>
<tr><td>Bath</td><td>2-8</td><td>2-3</td><td>0-3</td><td>0-0</td><td>0-2</td><td>25.0</td><td>+</td><td>0.83</td></tr>
<tr><td>Haydock</td><td>1-4</td><td>0-0</td><td>1-1</td><td>0-0</td><td>0-3</td><td>25.0</td><td>+</td><td>3.00</td></tr>
<tr><td>Windsor</td><td>1-14</td><td>0-2</td><td>1-7</td><td>0-0</td><td>0-5</td><td>7.1</td><td>-</td><td>10.25</td></tr>
<tr><td>Kempton</td><td>1-23</td><td>0-2</td><td>0-12</td><td>0-0</td><td>1-9</td><td>4.3</td><td>-</td><td>14.00</td></tr>
<tr><td>Newmarket</td><td>1-27</td><td>0-11</td><td>0-8</td><td>0-0</td><td>1-8</td><td>3.7</td><td>-</td><td>24.12</td></tr>
</table>

<table>
<tr><td>York</td><td>0-6</td><td>Brighton</td><td>0-3</td><td>Hamilton</td><td>0-1</td></tr>
<tr><td>Chepstow</td><td>0-5</td><td>Doncaster</td><td>0-3</td><td>Leicester</td><td>0-1</td></tr>
<tr><td>Folkestone</td><td>0-5</td><td>Nottingham</td><td>0-2</td><td>Southwell (AW)</td><td>0-1</td></tr>
<tr><td>Warwick</td><td>0-4</td><td>Ayr</td><td>0-1</td><td></td><td></td></tr>
</table>

Elsworth D R C

WINNING HORSES

	Age	Races Run	1st	2nd	3rd	Unpl	Win £
Roll A Dollar	7	4	1	0	1	2	26,892
Barboukh	3	7	2	2	0	3	16,155
Summer Wind	3	9	4	0	0	5	13,003
Star Talent	2	4	2	1	0	1	11,156
Bookcase	6	13	2	1	1	9	8,178
Reason To Dance	2	4	2	0	1	1	8,079
Camden's Ransom	6	11	2	2	3	4	8,042
Oh So Risky	6	5	1	1	0	3	7,015
Halham Tarn	3	12	2	1	4	5	5,685
Aberdeen Heather	3	12	1	0	1	10	5,061
Rapid Success	3	5	1	0	0	4	4,542
Poyle George	8	6	1	0	2	3	4,533
Southern Ridge	2	5	1	0	0	4	4,500
Fragrant Belle	2	2	1	0	0	1	4,280
Tochar Ban	3	7	1	2	2	2	4,079
Darkwood Bay	2	1	1	0	0	0	4,021
First Veil	3	4	1	0	1	2	3,708
Fabulous Mtoto	3	5	1	1	0	3	3,590
Spot Prize	2	5	1	0	1	3	3,498
French Gift	2	4	1	1	0	2	3,377
Stay With Me Baby	3	4	1	2	0	1	3,366
Mougins	4	6	1	0	0	5	3,363
Mighty Forum	2	3	1	0	0	2	3,184

WINNING OWNERS

	Races Won	Value £		Races Won	Value £
K Higson	1	26,892	Lady Dundas	2	5,685
R J McCreery	2	16,155	Major H S Cayzer	1	5,061
J C Smith	3	14,654	Yoshiki Akazawa	1	4,542
Raymond Tooth	4	14,468	Cecil Wiggins	1	4,533
Ray Richards	4	13,003	Bill Brown	1	4,500
Adept (80) Ltd	3	11,544	W H O'Gorman	1	4,280
Mrs D Joly	2	8,079	D R C Elsworth	1	4,079
Bob Cullen	2	8,042	Sheikh Ahmed Al Maktoum	1	3,590
The Oh So Risky Syndicate	1	7,015	R J Tory	1	3,184

Favourites	7-26	26.9%	- 0.67	Total winning prize-money	£159,304
Longest winning sequence			2	Average SP of winner	5.7/1
Longest losing sequence			48	Return on stakes invested	-21.0%
1992 Form	32-325	9.8%	- 55.51	1990 Form	44-335	13.1%	+ 11.79
1991 Form	40-354	11.3%	- 93.91	1989 Form	35-202	17.3%	+ 34.24

J ETHERINGTON (Malton, North Yorks)

	No. of Horses	Races Run	1st	2nd	3rd	Unpl	Per cent	£1 Level Stake
2-y-o	12	61	3	5	14	39	4.9	- 46.00
3-y-o	5	28	1	3	2	22	3.6	- 15.00
4-y-o+	4	39	6	7	2	24	15.4	+ 9.75
Totals	21	128	10	15	18	85	7.8	- 51.25

BY MONTH

2-y-o	W-R	Per cent	£1 Level Stake	3-y-o	W-R	Per cent	£1 Level Stake
Mar/Apr	0-1	-	- 1.00	Mar/Apr	0-0	-	0.00
May	1-4	25.0	+ 4.00	May	0-6	-	- 6.00
June	0-5	-	- 5.00	June	0-1	-	- 1.00
July	1-11	9.1	- 6.50	July	0-2	-	- 2.00
August	0-7	-	- 7.00	August	0-6	-	- 6.00
September	1-20	5.0	- 17.50	September	0-7	-	- 7.00
Oct/Nov	0-13	-	- 13.00	Oct/Nov	1-6	16.7	+ 7.00

4-y-o+	W-R	Per cent	£1 Level Stake	Totals	W-R	Per cent	£1 Level Stake
Mar/Apr	0-5	-	- 5.00	Mar/Apr	0-6	-	- 6.00
May	1-7	14.3	- 3.00	May	2-17	11.8	- 5.00
June	0-6	-	- 6.00	June	0-12	-	- 12.00
July	2-5	40.0	+ 1.75	July	3-18	16.7	- 6.75
August	1-4	25.0	+ 4.00	August	1-17	5.9	- 9.00
September	0-5	-	- 5.00	September	1-32	3.1	- 29.50
Oct/Nov	2-7	28.6	+ 23.00	Oct/Nov	3-26	11.5	+ 17.00

DISTANCE

2-y-o	W-R	Per cent	£1 Level Stake	3-y-o	W-R	Per cent	£1 Level Stake
5f-6f	2-36	5.6	- 25.50	5f-6f	0-10	-	- 10.00
7f-8f	1-24	4.2	- 19.50	7f-8f	0-15	-	- 15.00
9f-13f	0-1	-	- 1.00	9f-13f	1-3	33.3	+ 10.00
14f+	0-0	-	0.00	14f+	0-0	-	0.00

4-y-o+	W-R	Per cent	£1 Level Stake	Totals	W-R	Per cent	£1 Level Stake
5f-6f	0-0	-	0.00	5f-6f	2-46	4.3	- 35.50
7f-8f	0-2	-	- 2.00	7f-8f	1-41	2.4	- 36.50
9f-13f	4-26	15.4	+ 5.75	9f-13f	5-30	16.7	+ 14.75
14f+	2-11	18.2	+ 6.00	14f+	2-11	18.2	+ 6.00

TYPE OF RACE

Non-Handicaps	W-R	Per cent	£1 Level Stake	Handicaps	W-R	Per cent	£1 Level Stake
2-y-o	3-42	7.1	- 27.00	2-y-o	0-15	-	- 15.00
3-y-o	0-17	-	- 17.00	3-y-o	1-11	9.1	+ 2.00
4-y-o+	3-12	25.0	+ 4.00	4-y-o+	3-26	11.5	+ 6.75
Selling	0-4	-	- 4.00	Selling	0-1	-	- 1.00
Apprentice	0-0	-	0.00	Apprentice	0-0	-	0.00
Amat/Ladies	0-0	-	0.00	Amat/Ladies	0-0	-	0.00
Totals	6-75	8.0	- 44.00	Totals	4-53	7.5	- 7.25

COURSE GRADE

	W-R	Per cent	£1 Level Stake
Group 1	0-33	-	- 33.00
Group 2	2-34	5.9	- 13.00
Group 3	5-44	11.4	- 5.50
Group 4	3-17	17.6	+ 0.25

FIRST TIME OUT

	W-R	Per cent	£1 Level Stake
2-y-o	1-12	8.3	- 4.00
3-y-o	0-4	-	- 4.00
4-y-o+	0-4	-	- 4.00
Totals	1-20	5.0	- 12.00

JOCKEYS RIDING

	W-R	Per cent	£1 Level Stake		W-R	Per cent	£1 Level Stake
J Carroll	3-18	16.7	+ 3.00	A Culhane	1-9	11.1	+ 4.00
J Weaver	2-7	28.6	+ 17.00	K Darley	1-12	8.3	- 4.00
J Reid	1-1	100.0	+ 1.50	G Duffield	1-15	6.7	- 11.25
S Webster	1-6	16.7	- 1.50				

M Birch	0-15	Dale Gibson	0-2	W Carson	0-2
J Lowe	0-12	F Norton	0-2	B Rouse	0-1
L Charnock	0-4	K Fallon	0-2	C Rutter	0-1
W Newnes	0-4	R Cochrane	0-2	J Williams	0-1
G Hind	0-3	T Lucas	0-2	N Kennedy	0-1
W Ryan	0-3	T Quinn	0-2	S Maloney	0-1

COURSE RECORD

	Total W-R	Non-Handicaps 2-y-o	Non-Handicaps 3-y-o+	Handicaps 2-y-o	Handicaps 3-y-o+	Per cent	£1 Level Stake
Edinburgh	2-6	1-3	0-1	0-1	1-1	33.3	+ 2.25
Hamilton	2-10	0-1	2-5	0-1	0-3	20.0	- 3.00
Leicester	1-1	0-0	0-0	0-0	1-1	100.0	+ 20.00
Chester	1-3	0-1	0-0	0-1	1-1	33.3	+ 10.00
Catterick	1-4	0-2	1-2	0-0	0-0	25.0	+ 5.00
Thirsk	1-7	0-2	0-2	0-0	1-3	14.3	+ 1.00
Pontefract	1-12	1-5	0-1	0-1	0-5	8.3	- 9.50
Beverley	1-14	1-8	0-2	0-1	0-3	7.1	- 6.00

Redcar	0-16	Doncaster	0-4	Carlisle	0-1
Newcastle	0-12	Southwell (AW)	0-4	Folkestone	0-1
Haydock	0-9	York	0-4	Newmarket	0-1
Nottingham	0-6	Ayr	0-3	Warwick	0-1
Ripon	0-6	Lingfield	0-2	Yarmouth	0-1

WINNING HORSES

	Age	Races Run	1st	2nd	3rd	Unpl	Win £
Salu	4	17	3	2	2	10	9,672
Aegaen Lady	4	14	3	3	0	8	8,057
Soba Up	3	7	1	0	1	5	4,630
Legatee	2	10	1	0	2	7	3,054
Lucky Message	2	7	1	2	2	2	2,898
Just Bill	2	6	1	0	2	3	2,201

WINNING OWNERS

	Races Won	Value £		Races Won	Value £
W N Lumley	3	9,672	W L Armitage	1	2,898
D H Blackwood	2	5,657	Ron Watkins	1	2,400
Mrs M Hills	1	4,630	W H Turner	1	2,201
Mrs J E Young	1	3,054			

Favourites	2-11	18.2%	- 5.50	Total winning prize-money			£30,511
Longest winning sequence			2	Average SP of winner			6.7/1
Longest losing sequence			24	Return on stakes invested			-40.0%
1992 Form	15-147	10.2%	- 45.08	1990 Form	17-201	8.5%	- 98.77
1991 Form	9-193	4.7%	- 87.71	1989 Form	18-180	10.0%	- 30.00

J M P EUSTACE (Newmarket)

	No. of Horses	Races Run	1st	2nd	3rd	Unpl	Per cent	£1 Level Stake
2-y-o	8	23	2	1	6	14	8.7	- 11.50
3-y-o	3	23	2	0	1	20	8.7	- 4.50
4-y-o+	4	32	2	4	3	23	6.3	- 13.50
Totals	15	78	6	5	10	57	7.7	- 29.50

Jan	Feb	Mar	Apr	May	Jun	Jul	Aug	Sep	Oct/Nov
0-0	0-0	1-2	0-6	0-12	1-13	2-18	0-12	1-7	1-8

Winning Jockeys	W-R	£1 Level Stake			W-R	£1 Level Stake
M Tebbutt	2-29	- 10.00	R Cochrane		1-14	- 10.50
B Raymond	1-1	+ 11.00	N Kennedy		1-14	- 6.50
J Tate	1-5	+ 1.50				

Winning Courses						
Nottingham	1-1	+ 10.00	Goodwood		1-4	+ 3.50
Haydock	1-3	+ 3.50	Newbury		1-4	+ 8.00
Redcar	1-3	+ 5.00	Folkestone		1-6	- 2.50

Winning Horses	Age	Races Run	1st	2nd	3rd	Unpl	Win £
Philidor	4	7	1	2	1	3	65,423
Midyan Blue	3	9	2	0	0	7	10,067
Briggsmaid	5	14	1	2	1	10	3,495
Election Special	2	3	1	0	1	1	3,465
Madame Gregoire	2	7	1	1	2	3	2,925

Favourites	0-7			Total winning prize-money			£85,373

1992 Form	7-91	7.7%	- 59.00	1990 Form	6-78	7.7%	- 3.00
1991 Form	10-118	8.5%	- 59.82				

P D EVANS (Welshpool, Powys)

	No. of Horses	Races Run	1st	2nd	3rd	Unpl	Per cent	£1 Level Stake
2-y-o	6	27	6	3	1	17	22.2	+ 5.88
3-y-o	2	10	1	3	3	3	10.0	0.00
4-y-o+	15	57	6	2	5	44	10.5	+ 9.30
Totals	23	94	13	8	9	64	13.8	+ 15.18

BY MONTH

2-y-o	W-R	Per cent	£1 Level Stake	3-y-o	W-R	Per cent	£1 Level Stake
January	0-0	-	0.00	January	0-0	-	0.00
February	0-0	-	0.00	February	0-0	-	0.00
March	0-3	-	- 3.00	March	0-0	-	0.00
April	0-2	-	- 2.00	April	0-0	-	0.00
May	2-3	66.7	+ 17.00	May	0-0	-	0.00
June	3-5	60.0	+ 5.25	June	0-1	-	- 1.00
July	0-7	-	- 7.00	July	0-3	-	- 3.00
August	1-4	25.0	- 1.37	August	0-2	-	- 2.00
September	0-1	-	- 1.00	September	0-1	-	- 1.00
Oct/Nov	0-2	-	- 2.00	Oct/Nov	1-3	33.3	+ 7.00

4-y-o+	W-R	Per cent	£1 Level Stake	Totals	W-R	Per cent	£1 Level Stake
January	0-2	-	- 2.00	January	0-2	-	- 2.00
February	0-1	-	- 1.00	February	0-1	-	- 1.00
March	0-1	-	- 1.00	March	0-4	-	- 4.00
April	4-8	50.0	+ 29.30	April	4-10	40.0	+ 27.30
May	0-9	-	- 9.00	May	2-12	16.7	+ 8.00
June	0-7	-	- 7.00	June	3-13	23.1	- 2.75
July	0-11	-	- 11.00	July	0-21	-	- 21.00
August	1-12	8.3	- 4.00	August	2-18	11.1	- 7.37
September	0-2	-	- 2.00	September	0-4	-	- 4.00
Oct/Nov	1-4	25.0	+ 17.00	Oct/Nov	2-9	22.2	+ 22.00

DISTANCE

2-y-o	W-R	Per cent	£1 Level Stake	3-y-o	W-R	Per cent	£1 Level Stake
5f-6f	6-23	26.1	+ 9.88	5f-6f	0-0	-	0.00
7f-8f	0-4	-	- 4.00	7f-8f	0-3	-	- 3.00
9f-13f	0-0	-	0.00	9f-13f	1-6	16.7	+ 4.00
14f+	0-0	-	0.00	14f+	0-1	-	- 1.00

4-y-o+	W-R	Per cent	£1 Level Stake	Totals	W-R	Per cent	£1 Level Stake
5f-6f	1-5	20.0	+ 16.00	5f-6f	7-28	25.0	+ 25.88
7f-8f	1-7	14.3	+ 10.00	7f-8f	1-14	7.1	+ 3.00
9f-13f	2-30	6.7	- 20.70	9f-13f	3-36	8.3	- 16.70
14f+	2-15	13.3	+ 4.00	14f+	2-16	12.5	+ 3.00

TYPE OF RACE

Non-Handicaps	W-R	Per cent	£1 Level Stake	Handicaps	W-R	Per cent	£1 Level Stake
2-y-o	2-13	15.4	- 6.75	2-y-o	0-5	-	- 5.00
3-y-o	0-1	-	- 1.00	3-y-o	0-5	-	- 5.00
4-y-o+	1-8	12.5	- 6.20	4-y-o+	4-35	11.4	+ 12.50
Selling	5-11	45.5	+ 32.63	Selling	0-5	-	- 5.00
Apprentice	0-1	-	- 1.00	Apprentice	1-6	16.7	+ 4.00
Amat/Ladies	0-0	-	0.00	Amat/Ladies	0-4	-	- 4.00
Totals	8-34	23.5	+ 17.68	Totals	5-60	8.3	- 2.50

COURSE GRADE

	W-R	Per cent	£1 Level Stake
Group 1	3-21	14.3	+ 14.00
Group 2	0-6	-	- 6.00
Group 3	7-32	21.9	+ 22.55
Group 4	3-35	8.6	- 15.37

FIRST TIME OUT

	W-R	Per cent	£1 Level Stake
2-y-o	0-5	-	- 5.00
3-y-o	0-1	-	- 1.00
4-y-o+	2-13	15.4	+ 15.00
Totals	2-19	10.5	+ 9.00

JOCKEYS RIDING

	W–R	Per cent	£1 Level Stake		W–R	Per cent	£1 Level Stake
D Holland	4-18	22.2	+ 21.50	S Maloney	1-3	33.3	- 0.75
S Sanders	2-7	28.6	+ 24.00	L Charnock	1-3	33.3	+ 5.00
G Duffield	1-1	100.0	+ 8.00	J Williams	1-5	20.0	- 1.00
K Darley	1-2	50.0	- 0.20	L Dettori	1-9	11.1	- 6.37
W Carson	1-3	33.3	+ 8.00				

Mr W McLaughlin	0-4	M Hills	0-2	J Weaver	0-1
Paul Eddery	0-4	N Connorton	0-2	M Wigham	0-1
Dale Gibson	0-3	A Clark	0-1	Miss I D W Jones	0-1
A Mackay	0-2	A Garth	0-1	N Day	0-1
B Raymond	0-2	A Munro	0-1	R Cochrane	0-1
Claire Balding	0-2	A Tucker	0-1	R Havlin	0-1
D McKeown	0-2	C Hodgson	0-1	S Davies	0-1
D Wright	0-2	G Milligan	0-1	W R Swinburn	0-1
L Piggott	0-2	J Quinn	0-1	W Woods	0-1

COURSE RECORD

	Total W–R	Non-Handicaps 2-y-o	3-y-o+	Handicaps 2-y-o	3-y-o+	Per cent	£1 Level Stake
Carlisle	2-6	1-2	0-2	0-0	1-2	33.3	+ 11.00
Doncaster	2-7	1-3	0-0	0-0	1-4	28.6	+ 18.00
Beverley	2-8	1-2	0-0	0-0	1-6	25.0	+ 10.50
Nottingham	2-11	1-3	0-1	0-0	1-7	18.2	+ 4.00
Chepstow	1-3	1-1	0-0	0-0	0-2	33.3	- 0.75
Hamilton	1-3	0-1	1-2	0-0	0-0	33.3	- 1.20
Newmarket	1-3	0-0	0-0	0-1	1-2	33.3	+ 7.00
Pontefract	1-3	0-1	1-1	0-0	0-1	33.3	+ 14.00
Edinburgh	1-4	1-2	0-1	0-0	0-1	25.0	- 1.37

Haydock	0-8	Folkestone	0-2	Newbury	0-1
Southwell (AW)	0-8	Redcar	0-2	Salisbury	0-1
Catterick	0-5	Windsor	0-2	Yarmouth	0-1
Southwell (Turf)	0-5	Kempton	0-1	York	0-1
Warwick	0-5	Leicester	0-1		
Chester	0-2	Lingfield	0-1		

WINNING HORSES

	Age	Races Run	1st	2nd	3rd	Unpl	Win £
Romola Nijinsky	5	11	3	1	0	7	8,646
Brookhead Lady	2	7	3	1	0	3	7,338
Alllegsnobrain	2	8	2	1	0	5	4,922
Master Beveled	3	3	1	0	2	0	4,500
Educated Pet	4	1	1	0	0	0	3,845
Enfant Du Paradis	5	7	1	0	1	5	3,339
Scalp 'Em	5	4	1	1	1	1	2,669
Hill Farm Katie	2	6	1	1	1	3	2,448

WINNING OWNERS

	Races Won	Value £		Races Won	Value £
Mrs L A Windsor	4	11,315	M Woodall	2	4,922
Mrs E J Williams	2	8,345	P A Taylor	1	3,339
J E Abbey	3	7,338	Dennis Newton	1	2,448

Favourites	5-10	50.0%	+ 8.18	Total winning prize-money		£37,706
Longest winning sequence			2	Average SP of winner		7.4/1
Longest losing sequence			32	Return on stakes invested		16.1%
1992 Form	6-87	6.9%	- 11.50	1990 Form	0-33	
1991 Form	3-55	5.5%	- 22.50	1989 Form	0-17	

J L EYRE (Dewsbury, West Yorks)

	No. of Horses	Races Run	1st	2nd	3rd	Unpl	Per cent	£1 Level Stake
2-y-o	3	13	0	1	1	11	-	- 13.00
3-y-o	1	6	0	0	1	5	-	- 6.00
4-y-o+	11	64	5	4	11	44	7.8	- 15.50
Totals	15	83	5	5	13	60	6.0	- 34.50

Jan	Feb	Mar	Apr	May	Jun	Jul	Aug	Sep	Oct/Nov
0-0	0-0	0-1	0-4	1-13	2-13	1-22	0-10	1-9	0-11

Winning Jockeys	W-R	£1 Level Stake		W-R	£1 Level Stake
N Adams	2-19	- 6.00	W Ryan	1-2	+ 24.00
D Wright	1-1	+ 4.00	M Humphries	1-7	- 2.50

Winning Courses	W-R	£1 Level Stake		W-R	£1 Level Stake
Carlisle	2-4	+ 5.50	Ayr	1-5	+ 21.00
Pontefract	2-17	- 4.00			

Winning Horses	Age	Races Run	1st	2nd	3rd	Unpl	Win £
Sobering Thoughts	7	16	4	3	5	4	24,787
Bidweaya	6	8	1	0	1	6	3,080

Favourites	2-4	50.0%	+ 4.50	Total winning prize-money	£27,867
1992 Form	1-22	4.5%	- 17.50		

R A FAHEY (Malton, North Yorks)

	No. of Horses	Races Run	1st	2nd	3rd	Unpl	Per cent	£1 Level Stake
2-y-o	2	5	0	0	0	5	-	- 5.00
3-y-o	1	4	1	0	1	2	25.0	+ 9.00
4-y-o+	0	0	0	0	0	0	-	0.00
Totals	3	9	1	0	1	7	11.1	+ 4.00

Jan	Feb	Mar	Apr	May	Jun	Jul	Aug	Sep	Oct/Nov
0-0	0-0	0-0	0-0	0-0	0-0	0-1	0-5	1-3	0-0

Winning Jockey	W-R	£1 Level Stake	Winning Course	W-R	£1 Level Stake
S Maloney	1-1	+ 12.00	Haydock	1-1	+ 12.00

Winning Horse	Age	Races Run	1st	2nd	3rd	Unpl	Win £
OK Bertie	3	4	1	0	1	2	5,901

Favourites	0-0	Total winning prize-money	£5,901

T FAIRHURST (Middleham, North Yorks)

	No. of Horses	Races Run	1st	2nd	3rd	Unpl	Per cent	£1 Level Stake
2-y-o	6	35	2	0	4	29	5.7	+ 20.50
3-y-o	8	77	6	3	8	60	7.8	- 35.45
4-y-o+	2	26	1	3	4	18	3.8	- 19.00
Totals	16	138	9	6	16	107	6.5	- 33.95

Jan	Feb	Mar	Apr	May	Jun	Jul	Aug	Sep	Oct/Nov
1-8	0-5	1-3	1-13	2-23	1-14	2-31	0-15	1-19	0-7

Winning Jockeys	W-R	£1 Level Stake		W-R	£1 Level Stake
J Fanning	7-107	- 17.95	O Pears	1-3	+ 4.00
D Nicholls	1-2	+ 6.00			

Winning Courses					
Southwell (AW)	3-20	+ 3.50	Hamilton	1-8	- 2.50
Catterick	2-8	+ 6.00	Beverley	1-12	- 3.00
Pontefract	1-5	- 3.95	Redcar	1-14	+ 37.00

Winning Horses	Age	Races Run	1st	2nd	3rd	Unpl	Win £
Larn Fort	3	16	2	1	2	11	5,672
Barley Cake	3	17	2	2	2	11	4,061
Celestine	4	12	1	2	2	7	3,444
Persian Traveller	3	3	1	0	0	2	2,364
En-Cee-Tee	2	3	1	0	1	1	2,070
Highfield Lad	2	4	1	0	0	3	1,553
Cracker Jack	3	10	1	0	0	9	1,520

Favourites	1-4	25.0%	- 2.45	Total winning prize-money			£20,684

1992 Form	9-209	4.3%	-119.37	1990 Form	12-259	4.6%	- 162.25
1991 Form	15-236	6.4%	- 31.50	1989 Form	11-201	5.5%	- 90.25

J R FANSHAWE (Newmarket)

	No. of Horses	Races Run	1st	2nd	3rd	Unpl	Per cent	£1 Level Stake
2-y-o	14	33	4	4	2	23	12.1	- 20.50
3-y-o	36	188	25	33	22	108	13.3	- 39.67
4-y-o+	9	47	5	5	8	29	10.6	+ 4.00
Totals	59	268	34	42	32	160	12.7	- 56.17

BY MONTH

2-y-o	W-R	Per cent	£1 Level Stake	3-y-o	W-R	Per cent	£1 Level Stake
Mar/Apr	0-0	-	0.00	Mar/Apr	3-25	12.0	- 4.00
May	0-1	-	- 1.00	May	8-37	21.6	+ 19.10
June	1-1	100.0	+ 1.75	June	4-35	11.4	- 16.87
July	1-5	20.0	- 2.50	July	3-29	10.3	- 9.00
August	0-7	-	- 7.00	August	3-25	12.0	- 16.50
September	1-12	8.3	- 8.00	September	4-21	19.0	+ 0.10
Oct/Nov	1-7	14.3	- 3.75	Oct/Nov	0-16	-	- 16.00

4-y-o+	W-R	Per cent	£1 Level Stake	Totals	W-R	Per cent	£1 Level Stake
Mar/Apr	2-7	28.6	+ 6.00	Mar/Apr	5-32	15.6	+ 2.00
May	1-7	14.3	+ 1.00	May	9-45	20.0	+ 19.10
June	1-6	16.7	- 1.00	June	6-42	14.3	- 16.12
July	1-8	12.5	+ 18.00	July	5-42	11.9	+ 6.50
August	0-5	-	- 5.00	August	3-37	8.1	- 28.50
September	0-7	-	- 7.00	September	5-40	12.5	- 14.90
Oct/Nov	0-7	-	- 7.00	Oct/Nov	1-30	3.3	- 26.75

Fanshawe J R

DISTANCE

	W-R	Per cent	£1 Level Stake		W-R	Per cent	£1 Level Stake
2-y-o				3-y-o			
5f-6f	3-16	18.8	- 7.50	5f-6f	2-25	8.0	- 9.90
7f-8f	1-16	6.3	- 12.00	7f-8f	5-58	8.6	- 28.90
9f-13f	0-1	-	- 1.00	9f-13f	15-83	18.1	+ 9.00
14f+	0-0	-	0.00	14f+	3-22	13.6	- 9.87
4-y-o+	W-R	Per cent	£1 Level Stake	Totals	W-R	Per cent	£1 Level Stake
5f-6f	2-7	28.6	+ 5.00	5f-6f	7-48	14.6	- 12.40
7f-8f	0-2	-	- 2.00	7f-8f	6-76	7.9	- 42.90
9f-13f	3-34	8.8	+ 5.00	9f-13f	18-118	15.3	+ 13.00
14f+	0-4	-	- 4.00	14f+	3-26	11.5	- 13.87

TYPE OF RACE

Non-Handicaps	W-R	Per cent	£1 Level Stake	Handicaps	W-R	Per cent	£1 Level Stake
2-y-o	4-31	12.9	- 18.50	2-y-o	0-2	-	- 2.00
3-y-o	11-90	12.2	- 25.67	3-y-o	12-88	13.6	- 23.25
4-y-o+	1-21	4.8	- 14.00	4-y-o+	4-26	15.4	+ 18.00
Selling	1-2	50.0	+ 0.25	Selling	1-2	50.0	+ 15.00
Apprentice	0-3	-	- 3.00	Apprentice	0-3	-	- 3.00
Amat/Ladies	0-0	-	0.00	Amat/Ladies	0-0	-	0.00
Totals	17-147	11.6	- 60.92	Totals	17-121	14.0	+ 4.75

COURSE GRADE

	W-R	Per cent	£1 Level Stake
Group 1	14-131	10.7	- 24.40
Group 2	7-37	18.9	- 0.25
Group 3	9-78	11.5	- 27.77
Group 4	4-22	18.2	- 3.75

FIRST TIME OUT

	W-R	Per cent	£1 Level Stake
2-y-o	0-14	-	- 14.00
3-y-o	4-36	11.1	+ 1.50
4-y-o+	1-8	12.5	- 1.00
Totals	5-58	8.6	- 13.50

JOCKEYS RIDING

	W-R	Per cent	£1 Level Stake		W-R	Per cent	£1 Level Stake
G Duffield	9-41	22.0	+ 27.35	A Munro	2-11	18.2	+ 3.50
W R Swinburn	7-57	12.3	- 18.90	G Carter	2-19	10.5	- 11.50
B Raymond	3-15	20.0	+ 10.50	N Varley	2-20	10.0	- 0.75
P Robinson	3-23	13.0	- 12.37	K Fallon	1-4	25.0	- 0.75
W Ryan	2-6	33.3	+ 0.25	M Roberts	1-5	20.0	0.00
T Quinn	2-9	22.2	+ 4.50				

L Dettori	0-7	D Biggs	0-3	J Lowe	0-2
R Hills	0-7	M Hills	0-3	R Cochrane	0-2
Pat Eddery	0-6	Paul Eddery	0-3	A Mackay	0-1
W Carson	0-6	A Cairns	0-2	D McKeown	0-1
J Reid	0-5	G Bardwell	0-2	N Day	0-1
K Darley	0-4	J Carroll	0-2	S Whitworth	0-1

COURSE RECORD

	Total	Non-Handicaps		Handicaps		Per	£1 Level
	W-R	2-y-o	3-y-o+	2-y-o	3-y-o+	cent	Stake
Newmarket	5-55	0-6	2-26	0-1	3-22	9.1	- 10.00
Beverley	3-11	0-1	1-3	0-0	2-7	27.3	+ 8.50
Yarmouth	3-21	0-1	2-8	0-0	1-12	14.3	- 12.27
Chester	2-3	0-0	0-0	0-0	2-3	66.7	+ 7.50
Folkestone	2-4	0-0	1-3	0-0	1-1	50.0	+ 7.50
Salisbury	2-5	0-0	1-4	0-0	1-1	40.0	+ 8.00
Doncaster	2-8	2-3	0-4	0-0	0-1	25.0	- 1.50
Goodwood	2-12	0-1	0-3	0-0	2-8	16.7	+ 19.50
Sandown	2-12	0-0	1-4	0-0	1-8	16.7	- 4.90
Kempton	2-13	0-1	1-5	0-0	1-7	15.4	- 1.50
Nottingham	2-15	1-3	0-5	0-1	1-6	13.3	+ 4.75
Edinburgh	1-2	0-0	1-2	0-0	0-0	50.0	+ 1.50
Thirsk	1-3	0-1	0-0	0-0	1-2	33.3	+ 3.50
Brighton	1-5	0-0	1-4	0-0	0-1	20.0	- 2.00
Catterick	1-6	1-2	0-2	0-0	0-2	16.7	- 2.75
Ascot	1-9	0-1	1-3	0-0	0-5	11.1	- 4.00
Lingfield	1-9	0-2	0-3	0-0	1-4	11.1	- 5.25
Windsor	1-9	0-1	1-6	0-0	0-2	11.1	- 6.75

Leicester	0-12	Pontefract	0-4	Epsom	0-3
Ripon	0-8	Redcar	0-4	Lingfield (AW)	0-1
Warwick	0-8	York	0-4	Newcastle	0-1
Haydock	0-7	Bath	0-3	Southwell (Turf)	0-1
Newbury	0-7	Chepstow	0-3		

WINNING HORSES

		Races					Win
	Age	Run	1st	2nd	3rd	Unpl	£
Rose Alto	5	9	2	1	2	4	47,877
Unblest	2	5	3	1	0	1	46,394
Polka Dancer	3	2	2	0	0	0	20,476
Splice	4	8	2	1	0	5	19,379
Nassma	3	6	2	3	0	1	17,516
Misbelief	3	7	3	1	1	2	10,987
Summer Pageant	3	8	3	1	0	4	10,510
Moidart	3	9	2	2	1	4	7,583
Seek The Pearl	3	9	2	1	1	5	6,607
Jura Forest	3	7	1	1	2	3	5,301
Kiawah	3	9	2	2	0	5	5,064
Major Yaasi	3	3	1	0	0	2	4,836

Beaming	2	3	1	1	0	1	4,342
Jetbeeah	3	8	1	1	1	5	4,273
Solartica	3	9	1	4	1	3	4,269
Waffle On	3	8	1	0	0	7	3,493
Remany	4	3	1	0	0	2	3,266
Nemea	3	10	1	1	2	6	3,049
Ela Billante	3	8	1	0	2	5	2,846
Breakfast Boogie	3	8	1	4	1	2	2,794
Spring Sixpence	3	2	1	0	0	1	2,243

WINNING OWNERS

	Races Won	Value £		Races Won	Value £
T & J Vestey	5	58,864	Mohamed Suhail	1	4,836
Lord Vestey	4	51,695	Mrs Dare Wigan	1	4,342
Cheveley Park Stud	7	36,496	Butti Mussabah	1	4,273
S J Richmond-Watson	2	20,476	T D Holland-Martin	1	3,493
Sheikh Ahmed Bin Saeed - Al Maktoum	2	17,516	A C Hall	1	3,266
			Mrs James McAllister	1	2,846
Sir David Wills	2	7,583	Mrs Mary Watt	1	2,794
B E Nielson	2	7,318	C I T Racing Ltd	1	2,243
R S Field	2	5,064			

Favourites	17-49	34.7%	+ 14.58	Total winning prize-money		£233,104
Longest winning sequence			2	Average SP of winner		5.2/1
Longest losing sequence			34	Return on stakes invested		-21.0%
1992 Form	28-248	11.3%	- 48.70	1990 Form	18-113	15.9% + 58.96
1991 Form	22-152	14.5%	+ 7.14			

P S FELGATE (Melton Mowbray, Leics)

	No. of Horses	Races Run	1st	2nd	3rd	Unpl	Per cent	£1 Level Stake
2-y-o	2	5	0	0	0	5	-	- 5.00
3-y-o	4	16	1	0	2	13	6.3	- 11.00
4-y-o+	8	68	7	6	8	47	10.3	- 36.80
Totals	14	89	8	6	10	65	9.0	- 52.80

Jan	Feb	Mar	Apr	May	Jun	Jul	Aug	Sep	Oct/Nov
0-2	0-2	0-0	0-14	1-16	4-13	1-11	1-8	1-12	0-11

		£1 Level				£1 Level
Winning Jockeys	W-R	Stake			W-R	Stake
G Hind	7-29	+ 2.20	J Edmunds		1-2	+ 3.00

		£1 Level			
Winning Courses					
Southwell (AW)	5-30	- 8.55	Redcar	1-1	+ 5.50
Southwell (Turf)	2-4	+ 4.25			

Winning Horses	Age	Races Run	1st	2nd	3rd	Unpl	Win £
Highborn	4	12	4	2	2	4	10,832
Macs Maharanee	6	12	2	2	1	7	8,376
Glenfield Greta	5	12	1	0	4	7	3,365
Melodic Drive	3	9	1	0	2	6	2,070

Favourites	5-14	35.7%	+ 1.70	Total winning prize-money			£24,642

1992 Form	10-83	12.0%	- 24.04	1990 Form	10-156	6.4%	- 79.25
1991 Form	6-97	6.2%	- 46.37	1989 Form	12-152	7.9%	- 20.00

M J FETHERSTON-GODLEY (East Ilsley, Berks)

	No. of Horses	Races Run	1st	2nd	3rd	Unpl	Per cent	£1 Level Stake
2-y-o	8	36	4	0	3	29	11.1	- 18.00
3-y-o	1	2	0	0	0	2	-	- 2.00
4-y-o+	3	37	3	4	3	27	8.1	- 10.00
Totals	12	75	7	4	6	58	9.3	- 30.00

Jan	Feb	Mar	Apr	May	Jun	Jul	Aug	Sep	Oct/Nov
0-0	0-0	0-1	0-6	1-11	2-11	0-9	1-13	1-11	2-13

Winning Jockeys	W-R	£1 Level Stake			W-R	£1 Level Stake
W R Swinburn	2-6	+ 5.50	D Holland		1-4	0.00
F Norton	2-16	+ 8.00	M Roberts		1-4	- 1.00
J Reid	1-1	+ 1.50				

Winning Courses						
York	2-5	+ 15.00	Warwick		1-5	- 1.00
Yarmouth	1-2	+ 3.00	Doncaster		1-8	- 5.50
Chester	1-4	+ 3.00	Newbury		1-11	- 4.50

Winning Horses	Age	Races Run	1st	2nd	3rd	Unpl	Win £
Macfarlane	5	14	2	3	3	6	19,049
Royal Figurine	2	9	3	0	2	4	13,518
Highland Magic	5	11	1	1	0	9	6,264
Miriam	2	7	1	0	0	6	3,377

Favourites	3-7	42.9%	+ 2.50	Total winning prize-money			£42,208

1992 Form	7-98	7.1%	- 26.00	1990 Form	7-123	5.7%	- 72.59
1991 Form	13-151	8.6%	- 74.79	1989 Form	2-115	1.7%	- 91.00

R F FISHER (Ulverston, Cumbria)

	No. of Horses	Races Run	1st	2nd	3rd	Unpl	Per cent	£1 Level Stake
2-y-o	6	14	1	1	1	11	7.1	+ 3.00
3-y-o	3	16	2	1	2	11	12.5	- 9.00
4-y-o+	1	19	2	1	2	14	10.5	- 6.50
Totals	10	49	5	3	5	36	10.2	- 12.50

Jan	Feb	Mar	Apr	May	Jun	Jul	Aug	Sep	Oct/Nov
0-3	0-2	0-1	1-12	2-11	0-6	1-6	0-2	0-1	1-5

Winning Jockeys	W-R	£1 Level Stake		W-R	£1 Level Stake
D Nicholls	2-18	+ 3.50	L Aspell	1-3	- 0.50
J Quinn	1-1	+ 4.50	K Fallon	1-8	- 1.00

Winning Courses	W-R	£1 Level Stake		W-R	£1 Level Stake
Catterick	1-2	+ 5.00	Edinburgh	1-8	- 2.50
Carlisle	1-5	- 0.50	Hamilton	1-11	- 8.50
Ripon	1-5	+ 12.00			

Winning Horses	Age	Races Run	1st	2nd	3rd	Unpl	Win £
Mingus	6	19	2	1	2	14	6,377
Prime Painter	3	9	2	1	1	5	4,844
Kierchem	2	3	1	1	0	1	3,173

Favourites	1-1	100.0%	+ 1.50	Total winning prize-money	£14,393

1992 Form	0-12			1990 Form	0-6		
1991 Form	0-3			1989 Form	1-15	6.7%	- 11.00

J G FITZGERALD (Malton, North Yorks)

	No. of Horses	Races Run	1st	2nd	3rd	Unpl	Per cent	£1 Level Stake
2-y-o	7	41	4	8	7	22	9.8	- 27.92
3-y-o	14	84	9	11	7	57	10.7	- 17.57
4-y-o+	13	39	3	4	1	31	7.7	- 15.75
Totals	34	164	16	23	15	110	9.8	- 61.24

BY MONTH

2-y-o	W-R	Per cent	£1 Level Stake	3-y-o	W-R	Per cent	£1 Level Stake
January	0-0	-	0.00	January	0-0	-	0.00
February	0-0	-	0.00	February	0-0	-	0.00
March	0-0	-	0.00	March	0-0	-	0.00
April	0-0	-	0.00	April	0-2	-	- 2.00
May	0-4	-	- 4.00	May	1-20	5.0	+ 1.00
June	0-5	-	- 5.00	June	2-16	12.5	- 10.12
July	2-13	15.4	- 8.25	July	3-20	15.0	+ 5.80
August	1-7	14.3	- 2.67	August	2-11	18.2	- 1.75
September	0-7	-	- 7.00	September	0-5	-	- 5.00
Oct/Nov	1-5	20.0	- 1.00	Oct/Nov	1-10	10.0	- 5.50

4-y-o+	W-R	Per cent	£1 Level Stake	Totals	W-R	Per cent	£1 Level Stake
January	0-0	-	0.00	January	0-0	-	0.00
February	0-3	-	- 3.00	February	0-3	-	- 3.00
March	0-2	-	- 2.00	March	0-2	-	- 2.00
April	0-6	-	- 6.00	April	0-8	-	- 8.00
May	2-9	22.2	- 0.75	May	3-33	9.1	- 3.75
June	0-5	-	- 5.00	June	2-26	7.7	- 20.12
July	0-4	-	- 4.00	July	5-37	13.5	- 6.45
August	1-8	12.5	+ 7.00	August	4-26	15.4	+ 2.58
September	0-1	-	- 1.00	September	0-13	-	- 13.00
Oct/Nov	0-1	-	- 1.00	Oct/Nov	2-16	12.5	- 7.50

DISTANCE

2-y-o	W-R	Per cent	£1 Level Stake	3-y-o	W-R	Per cent	£1 Level Stake
5f-6f	1-22	4.5	- 20.00	5f-6f	2-20	10.0	+ 2.80
7f-8f	3-18	16.7	- 6.92	7f-8f	4-38	10.5	- 10.50
9f-13f	0-1	-	- 1.00	9f-13f	3-23	13.0	- 6.87
14f+	0-0	-	0.00	14f+	0-3	-	- 3.00

4-y-o+	W-R	Per cent	£1 Level Stake	Totals	W-R	Per cent	£1 Level Stake
5f-6f	0-0	-	0.00	5f-6f	3-42	7.1	- 17.20
7f-8f	3-9	33.3	+ 14.25	7f-8f	10-65	15.4	- 3.17
9f-13f	0-21	-	- 21.00	9f-13f	3-45	6.7	- 28.87
14f+	0-9	-	- 9.00	14f+	0-12	-	- 12.00

TYPE OF RACE

Non-Handicaps	W-R	Per cent	£1 Level Stake	Handicaps	W-R	Per cent	£1 Level Stake
2-y-o	3-26	11.5	- 17.25	2-y-o	1-8	12.5	- 3.67
3-y-o	5-30	16.7	+ 14.18	3-y-o	4-47	8.5	- 24.75
4-y-o+	1-15	6.7	- 9.00	4-y-o+	0-17	-	- 17.00
Selling	1-9	11.1	- 6.75	Selling	1-8	12.5	+ 7.00
Apprentice	0-0	-	0.00	Apprentice	0-3	-	- 3.00
Amat/Ladies	0-0	-	0.00	Amat/Ladies	0-1	-	- 1.00
Totals	10-80	12.5	- 18.82	Totals	6-84	7.1	- 42.42

		COURSE GRADE					FIRST TIME OUT		
	W-R	Per cent	£1 Level Stake				W-R	Per cent	£1 Level Stake
Group 1	2-34	5.9	- 25.17		2-y-o		0-7	-	- 7.00
Group 2	1-42	2.4	- 27.00		3-y-o		1-14	7.1	+ 7.00
Group 3	5-37	13.5	+ 5.63		4-y-o+		0-13	-	- 13.00
Group 4	8-51	15.7	- 14.70						
					Totals		1-34	2.9	- 13.00

JOCKEYS RIDING

	W-R	Per cent	£1 Level Stake			W-R	Per cent	£1 Level Stake
K Fallon	10-75	13.3	- 4.70		W Ryan	2-3	66.7	+ 16.50
W R Swinburn	3-10	30.0	+ 0.96		L Charnock	1-13	7.7	- 11.00

M Birch	0-9	J Quinn	0-2	Mr R Hale	0-1
S Maloney	0-6	K Darley	0-2	N Carlisle	0-1
Paul Eddery	0-5	S Morris	0-2	O Pears	0-1
T Lucas	0-4	W Carson	0-2	P Robinson	0-1
D McCabe	0-3	A Culhane	0-1	Pat Eddery	0-1
D McKeown	0-3	D Holland	0-1	R Cochrane	0-1
F Norton	0-3	F Savage	0-1	S D Williams	0-1
J Fanning	0-3	J Lowe	0-1	S Perks	0-1
B Raymond	0-2	L Piggott	0-1	S Wood	0-1
G Duffield	0-2	M Wigham	0-1		

COURSE RECORD

	Total W-R	Non-Handicaps 2-y-o	3-y-o+	Handicaps 2-y-o	3-y-o+	Per cent	£1 Level Stake
Southwell (AW)	6-24	2-7	3-6	0-0	1-11	25.0	+ 4.55
Pontefract	2-7	1-3	1-3	0-1	0-0	28.6	+ 3.00
Edinburgh	1-4	0-2	1-1	0-0	0-1	25.0	- 1.75
Hamilton	1-4	0-1	0-0	0-0	1-3	25.0	+ 5.00
Southwell (Turf)	1-4	0-1	0-0	0-0	1-3	25.0	+ 1.50
Nottingham	1-6	0-0	1-3	0-0	0-3	16.7	- 3.37
Newmarket	1-7	0-4	0-0	1-1	0-2	14.3	- 2.67
Newcastle	1-8	0-0	0-0	0-0	1-8	12.5	- 3.50
Thirsk	1-10	0-1	0-4	0-1	1-4	10.0	+ 5.00
Beverley	1-16	0-2	1-5	0-2	0-7	6.3	+ 5.00

Redcar	0-16	York	0-8	Ayr	0-3
Ripon	0-12	Chester	0-4	Doncaster	0-3
Carlisle	0-10	Haydock	0-4	Sandown	0-1
Catterick	0-8	Leicester	0-4	Warwick	0-1

WINNING HORSES

	Age	Races Run	1st	2nd	3rd	Unpl	Win £
Barbaroja	2	8	3	3	1	1	20,434
Best Appearance	3	9	2	2	1	4	5,997
Corona Gold	3	12	2	1	1	8	5,306

Mohican Brave	3	9	2	0	2	5	4,955
Delpiombo	7	7	2	1	1	3	4,607
Jade City	3	10	1	2	0	7	3,720
Biloela	3	9	1	2	1	5	3,348
Slumber Thyme	4	7	1	0	0	6	2,763
Mister Beat	2	9	1	2	2	4	2,534
Heart Broken	3	8	1	2	0	5	2,217

WINNING OWNERS

	Races Won	Value £		Races Won	Value £
Marquesa De Moratalla	3	20,434	Norman Jackson	1	3,720
Bezwell Fixings Ltd	2	5,997	R Brewis	1	3,348
T J FitzGerald	2	5,306	J W Searle	1	2,763
J Dick	2	4,955	P Asquith	1	2,534
Paul Coulter	2	4,607	J G FitzGerald	1	2,217

Favourites	6-17	35.3%	- 1.24	Total winning prize-money	£55,880

Longest winning sequence		2	Average SP of winner	5.4/1
Longest losing sequence		21	Return on stakes invested	-37.3%

1992 Form	8-151	5.3%	- 79.67	1990 Form	21-206	10.2%	- 24.70
1991 Form	12-176	6.8%	- 98.25	1989 Form	22-162	13.6%	- 4.97

R M FLOWER (Jevington, East Sussex)

	No. of Horses	Races Run	1st	2nd	3rd	Unpl	Per cent	£1 Level Stake
2-y-o	0	0	0	0	0	0	-	0.00
3-y-o	2	5	0	0	0	5	-	- 5.00
4-y-o+	3	16	3	2	1	10	18.8	+ 5.00
Totals	5	21	3	2	1	15	14.3	0.00

Jan	Feb	Mar	Apr	May	Jun	Jul	Aug	Sep	Oct/Nov
0-0	0-0	0-0	0-1	0-1	0-0	1-5	0-3	1-5	1-6

Winning Jockeys	W-R	£1 Level Stake		W-R	£1 Level Stake
M Denaro	2-2	+ 15.00	D Wright	1-3	+ 1.00

Winning Courses					
Goodwood	1-1	+ 3.00	Yarmouth	1-5	+ 4.00
Newbury	1-2	+ 6.00			

Winning Horse	Age	Races Run	1st	2nd	3rd	Unpl	Win £
Duckey Fuzz	5	10	3	1	1	5	12,074

Favourites	0-1	Total winning prize-money	£12,074

A G FOSTER (Lambourn, Berks)

	No. of Horses	Races Run	1st	2nd	3rd	Unpl	Per cent	£1 Level Stake
2-y-o	2	3	1	0	0	2	33.3	+ 48.00
3-y-o	0	0	0	0	0	0	-	0.00
4-y-o+	1	2	0	0	0	2	-	- 2.00
Totals	3	5	1	0	0	4	20.0	+ 46.00

Jan	Feb	Mar	Apr	May	Jun	Jul	Aug	Sep	Oct/Nov
0-0	0-0	0-0	0-0	0-0	0-0	0-0	0-0	0-0	1-5

Winning Jockey	W-R	£1 Level Stake	Winning Course	W-R	£1 Level Stake
J Fortune	1-2	+ 49.00	Doncaster	1-1	+ 50.00

Winning Horse	Age	Races Run	1st	2nd	3rd	Unpl	Win £
Oggi	2	1	1	0	0	0	4,092

Favourites	0-0	Total winning prize-money	£4,092

J A GLOVER (Worksop, Notts)

	No. of Horses	Races Run	1st	2nd	3rd	Unpl	Per cent	£1 Level Stake
2-y-o	7	19	1	2	3	13	5.3	- 16.00
3-y-o	2	16	1	0	3	12	6.3	- 9.00
4-y-o+	18	86	7	5	10	64	8.1	- 31.75
Totals	27	121	9	7	16	89	7.4	- 56.75

Jan	Feb	Mar	Apr	May	Jun	Jul	Aug	Sep	Oct/Nov
0-3	0-3	0-5	1-9	1-19	2-15	0-12	4-25	1-13	0-17

Winning Jockeys	W-R	£1 Level Stake		W-R	£1 Level Stake
D McKeown	3-9	- 1.75	P Robinson	1-4	+ 2.50
M Birch	2-6	+ 5.50	N Carlisle	1-4	+ 7.00
D Moffatt	1-2	+ 9.00	J Fortune	1-18	- 1.00

Winning Courses					
Pontefract	2-18	+ 2.00	Newcastle	1-4	+ 3.00
Goodwood	1-1	+ 0.50	Ripon	1-4	+ 7.00
Ascot	1-2	+ 4.50	Doncaster	1-10	+ 1.00
Catterick	1-3	- 0.25	Southwell (AW)	1-19	- 14.50

Winning Horses	Age	Races Run	1st	2nd	3rd	Unpl	Win £
Rambo's Hall	8	9	2	1	2	4	12,388
Fighter Squadron	4	13	1	0	0	12	4,794
Samain	6	5	1	0	0	4	4,175
Atherton Green	3	9	1	0	3	5	3,915
Sweet Revivial	5	8	1	1	1	5	3,262
Secret Serenade	2	5	1	1	1	2	3,028
Arc Lamp	7	18	1	1	5	11	3,002
Gipsy Fiddler	5	5	1	1	1	2	2,301

Favourites	4-7	57.1%	+ 4.75	Total winning prize-money			£36,865
1992 Form	25-194	12.9%	+ 2.25	1990 Form	5-84	6.0%	- 16.50
1991 Form	4-103	3.9%	- 51.00	1989 Form	3-103	2.9%	- 65.50

J H M GOSDEN (Newmarket)

	No. of Horses	Races Run	1st	2nd	3rd	Unpl	Per cent	£1 Level Stake
2-y-o	32	62	18	12	5	27	29.0	+ 34.67
3-y-o	75	292	62	43	27	160	21.2	- 7.14
4-y-o+	22	99	30	13	14	42	30.3	+ 54.38
Totals	129	453	110	68	46	229	24.3	+ 81.91

BY MONTH

2-y-o	W-R	Per cent	£1 Level Stake	3-y-o	W-R	Per cent	£1 Level Stake
January	0-0	-	0.00	January	0-1	-	- 1.00
February	0-0	-	0.00	February	0-0	-	0.00
March	0-0	-	0.00	March	0-7	-	- 7.00
April	0-0	-	0.00	April	5-28	17.9	+ 8.50
May	0-0	-	0.00	May	7-34	20.6	- 4.05
June	0-0	-	0.00	June	9-35	25.7	+ 2.66
July	2-6	33.3	+ 3.00	July	9-47	19.1	- 16.80
August	1-6	16.7	- 3.25	August	12-52	23.1	+ 16.42
September	9-22	40.9	+ 29.01	September	10-51	19.6	- 13.30
Oct/Nov	6-28	21.4	+ 5.91	Oct/Nov	10-37	27.0	+ 7.43

4-y-o+	W-R	Per cent	£1 Level Stake	Totals	W-R	Per cent	£1 Level Stake
January	1-2	50.0	+ 3.50	January	1-3	33.3	+ 2.50
February	0-1	-	- 1.00	February	0-1	-	- 1.00
March	0-0	-	0.00	March	0-7	-	- 7.00
April	2-10	20.0	- 2.93	April	7-38	18.4	+ 5.57
May	5-15	33.3	+ 11.78	May	12-49	24.5	+ 7.73
June	5-14	35.7	+ 11.38	June	14-49	28.6	+ 14.04
July	2-16	12.5	+ 6.00	July	13-69	18.8	- 7.80
August	2-12	16.7	- 6.15	August	15-70	21.4	+ 7.02
September	9-13	69.2	+ 28.17	September	28-86	32.6	+ 43.88
Oct/Nov	4-16	25.0	+ 3.63	Oct/Nov	20-81	24.7	+ 16.97

DISTANCE

2-y-o	W-R	Per cent	£1 Level Stake	3-y-o	W-R	Per cent	£1 Level Stake
5f-6f	6-21	28.6	+ 11.94	5f-6f	9-23	39.1	- 0.54
7f-8f	12-41	29.3	+ 22.73	7f-8f	29-147	19.7	- 20.99
9f-13f	0-0	-	0.00	9f-13f	23-106	21.7	+ 21.39
14f+	0-0	-	0.00	14f+	1-16	6.3	- 7.00

4-y-o+	W-R	Per cent	£1 Level Stake	Totals	W-R	Per cent	£1 Level Stake
5f-6f	4-11	36.4	+ 27.00	5f-6f	19-55	34.5	+ 38.40
7f-8f	5-19	26.3	+ 9.00	7f-8f	46-207	22.2	+ 10.74
9f-13f	16-53	30.2	+ 9.75	9f-13f	39-159	24.5	+ 31.14
14f+	5-16	31.3	+ 8.63	14f+	6-32	18.8	+ 1.63

TYPE OF RACE

Non-Handicaps	W-R	Per cent	£1 Level Stake	Handicaps	W-R	Per cent	£1 Level Stake
2-y-o	16-58	27.6	+ 22.17	2-y-o	2-4	50.0	+ 12.50
3-y-o	57-227	25.1	+ 24.55	3-y-o	5-63	7.9	- 29.69
4-y-o+	22-62	35.5	+ 25.83	4-y-o+	6-35	17.1	+ 26.00
Selling	0-1	-	- 1.00	Selling	0-0	-	0.00
Apprentice	1-1	100.0	+ 2.25	Apprentice	0-1	-	- 1.00
Amat/Ladies	1-1	100.0	+ 0.30	Amat/Ladies	0-0	-	0.00
Totals	97-350	27.7	+ 74.10	Totals	13-103	12.6	+ 7.81

COURSE GRADE

	W-R	Per cent	£1 Level Stake
Group 1	72-310	23.2	+ 72.26
Group 2	16-61	26.2	- 6.52
Group 3	19-63	30.2	+ 23.55
Group 4	3-19	15.8	- 7.38

FIRST TIME OUT

	W-R	Per cent	£1 Level Stake
2-y-o	8-31	25.8	+ 12.25
3-y-o	11-74	14.9	- 1.93
4-y-o+	10-22	45.5	+ 33.45
Totals	29-127	22.8	+ 43.77

JOCKEYS RIDING

	W-R	Per cent	£1 Level Stake		W-R	Per cent	£1 Level Stake
M Roberts	28-117	23.9	- 21.76	J Reid	2-9	22.2	- 6.34
L Dettori	14-61	23.0	+ 25.04	B Raymond	2-9	22.2	- 4.82
Pat Eddery	12-35	34.3	+ 34.88	B Crossley	2-9	22.2	+ 6.00
J Carroll	10-30	33.3	+ 17.23	D Holland	2-12	16.7	- 5.06
G Hind	10-59	16.9	- 5.69	P McCabe	1-1	100.0	+ 2.25
W Carson	8-28	28.6	+ 7.44	Mrs L Pearce	1-2	50.0	- 0.70
W R Swinburn	5-12	41.7	+ 12.00	N Day	1-2	50.0	+ 13.00
R Cochrane	5-28	17.9	+ 8.15	M Hills	1-4	25.0	+ 5.00
G Duffield	2-4	50.0	+ 1.38	L Piggott	1-5	20.0	+ 10.00
Paul Eddery	2-7	28.6	+ 1.00	R Hills	1-5	20.0	- 3.09

J Weaver	0-2	D Harrison	0-1	Robin Gray	0-1
J Williams	0-2	Dale Gibson	0-1	S Raymont	0-1
W Ryan	0-2	J Quinn	0-1	T Quinn	0-1
C Nutter	0-1	P Robinson	0-1		

COURSE RECORD

| | Total | Non-Handicaps | | Handicaps | | Per | £1 Level |
	W-R	2-y-o	3-y-o+	2-y-o	3-y-o+	cent	Stake
Newmarket	14-81	4-19	9-44	0-1	1-17	17.3	+ 13.43
Sandown	9-22	0-0	9-18	0-0	0-4	40.9	+ 24.29
Goodwood	8-28	1-2	4-16	1-1	2-9	28.6	+ 27.25
Doncaster	8-39	2-7	5-23	1-1	0-8	20.5	- 0.55
Yarmouth	7-23	2-4	5-15	0-0	0-4	30.4	+ 2.81
York	7-33	1-5	6-18	0-1	0-9	21.2	- 6.34
Haydock	6-19	1-2	4-10	0-0	1-7	31.6	- 2.08
Newbury	6-32	0-1	5-26	0-0	1-5	18.8	+ 5.58
Newcastle	5-6	0-0	3-4	0-0	2-2	83.3	+ 18.40
Nottingham	5-8	0-0	5-8	0-0	0-0	62.5	+ 19.88
Ripon	4-12	0-0	3-11	0-0	1-1	33.3	- 1.05
Ascot	4-27	1-4	2-15	0-0	1-8	14.8	- 5.27
Lingfield	3-6	1-1	2-4	0-0	0-1	50.0	+ 3.47
Salisbury	3-9	1-2	2-5	0-0	0-2	33.3	+ 6.70
Leicester	3-12	1-3	2-9	0-0	0-0	25.0	- 1.18
Ayr	2-4	0-0	1-3	0-0	1-1	50.0	+ 3.80
Brighton	2-4	1-1	1-3	0-0	0-0	50.0	+ 5.00
Chester	2-13	0-1	2-7	0-0	0-5	15.4	- 8.12
Redcar	2-13	0-4	2-7	0-0	0-2	15.4	- 8.52
Kempton	2-15	0-1	2-12	0-0	0-2	13.3	- 4.25
Beverley	1-3	0-0	1-1	0-0	0-2	33.3	- 1.87
Chepstow	1-3	0-0	1-2	0-0	0-1	33.3	- 1.09
Catterick	1-4	0-0	1-3	0-0	0-1	25.0	- 2.38
Epsom	1-4	0-0	1-3	0-0	0-1	25.0	- 2.00
Lingfield (AW)	1-4	0-0	0-1	0-0	1-3	25.0	+ 1.50
Pontefract	1-5	0-0	1-4	0-0	0-1	20.0	- 3.00
Warwick	1-6	0-0	1-5	0-0	0-1	16.7	- 1.50
Windsor	1-9	0-0	1-8	0-0	0-1	11.1	+ 8.00

| Thirsk | 0-4 | Southwell (Turf) | 0-3 | Folkestone | 0-2 |

WINNING HORSES

| | | Races | | | | | Win |
	Age	Run	1st	2nd	3rd	Unpl	£
Catrail	3	7	5	1	0	1	98,342
Prophecy	2	5	3	0	0	2	83,980
Wolfhound	4	4	1	3	0	0	81,701
King's Signet	4	4	3	0	1	0	73,975
Brier Creek	4	3	3	0	0	0	46,627
Knifebox	5	3	2	0	0	1	42,487
Sonus	4	5	2	1	2	0	36,794
Anna Of Saxony	4	8	3	2	0	3	31,711

Red Bishop	5	6	2	1	2	1	30,057
True Hero	3	2	1	1	0	0	29,376
Meadow Pipit	4	4	4	0	0	0	25,136
Marillette	3	3	1	0	0	2	25,003
Tinners Way	3	4	2	0	1	1	23,295
Emperor Jones	3	5	1	1	2	1	23,136
Learmont	3	6	2	0	0	4	23,120
Wainwright	4	11	2	1	0	8	18,603
Darmstadt	3	10	3	0	0	7	18,130
Arjuzah	3	4	2	1	0	1	17,905
Muhtarram	4	3	2	0	0	1	15,459
Storm Canyon	3	5	3	1	0	1	13,040
Specified	3	3	2	0	0	1	12,441
Diesan	2	7	3	2	1	1	12,375
Mutakddim	2	3	1	1	0	1	10,464
Winged Victory (USA)	3	6	1	2	0	3	10,309
Teshami	3	6	2	1	1	2	10,212
Wafayt	2	4	2	0	1	1	9,576
Half Term	3	5	2	1	0	2	9,225
Del Deya	3	4	2	0	0	2	7,595
Campana	3	3	2	0	0	1	7,367
Lower Egypt	3	4	2	0	0	2	7,296
Mashaallah	5	4	1	0	0	3	7,270
Arid	3	8	2	0	1	5	6,901
Icy South	3	6	2	1	1	2	6,521
Fluvial	3	2	1	0	1	0	6,316
Reflecting	4	4	2	0	1	1	6,260
Darnay	2	1	1	0	0	0	5,595
Zama	2	1	1	0	0	0	5,127
Witness Box	6	3	1	0	0	2	5,078
Rameau	2	1	1	0	0	0	4,776
Silver Maple	3	2	1	0	1	0	4,503
Fawran	2	4	1	1	0	2	4,378
Linney Head	2	1	1	0	0	0	4,372
Lacotte	3	6	1	3	0	2	4,305
Link River	3	3	1	0	0	2	4,128
Felawnah	3	3	1	0	1	1	4,085
Mytilene	2	2	1	0	0	1	4,050
Silverdale	3	8	1	4	1	2	3,948
Minatina	3	1	1	0	0	0	3,818
Mujaazafah	3	5	1	1	0	3	3,728
Elatis	3	5	1	1	1	2	3,728
Labudd	3	3	1	0	0	2	3,582
Xylem	2	2	1	0	0	1	3,532
Astern	3	6	1	0	1	4	3,524
Ghost Tree	3	7	1	2	0	4	3,524
Cascassi	3	3	1	0	0	2	3,524
Collier Bay	3	10	1	2	3	4	3,494
Arvola	3	4	1	0	1	2	3,494
Quaver	3	4	1	2	0	1	3,493
Realize	2	4	1	0	1	2	3,465
Simaat	3	4	1	0	1	2	3,436
Nimphidia	2	1	1	0	0	0	3,407
Full Feather	3	5	1	1	0	3	3,348
Colin Muset	3	5	1	0	0	4	3,290
Pembroke	3	6	1	1	0	4	3,262

La Spezia	3	6	1	1	0	4	3,260
Smuggler's Point	3	4	1	0	0	3	3,231
Livonian	3	6	1	0	0	5	3,210
Flowing Ocean	3	3	1	1	0	1	3,202
Daru	4	7	1	0	0	6	3,173
Ivory Palm	3	4	1	1	0	2	3,143
Vratislav	4	5	1	1	2	1	2,814

WINNING OWNERS

	Races Won	Value £		Races Won	Value £
Sheikh Mohammed	69	715,698	P A Leonard	2	6,260
K Abdulla	11	137,769	P G Goulandris	1	4,050
Hamdan Al-Maktoum	7	50,846	Lord Derby	1	3,494
Sheikh Ahmed Al Maktoum	11	49,007	Lord Hartington	1	3,465
Ali Saeed	2	30,057	Anthony Speelman	1	3,348
Pin Oak Stable	1	10,309	Herbert Allen	1	3,202
Saeed Manana	2	6,521			

Favourites	51-130	39.2%	- 13.97	Total winning prize-money	£1,024,025
Longest winning sequence			3	Average SP of winner	3.9/1
Longest losing sequence			15	Return on stakes invested	18.3%
1992 Form	113-519	21.8%	+ 7.73	1990 Form	87-354	24.6%	+ 12.87
1991 Form	86-384	22.4%	- 7.12	1989 Form	28-144	19.4%	- 14.66

N A GRAHAM (Newmarket)

	No. of Horses	Races Run	1st	2nd	3rd	Unpl	Per cent	£1 Level Stake
2-y-o	9	17	0	0	0	17	-	- 17.00
3-y-o	5	20	2	0	0	18	10.0	+ 3.00
4-y-o+	6	41	5	5	9	22	12.2	+ 6.30
Totals	20	78	7	5	9	57	9.0	- 7.70

Jan	Feb	Mar	Apr	May	Jun	Jul	Aug	Sep	Oct/Nov
0-2	2-3	1-3	0-7	0-8	0-11	3-15	0-9	1-10	0-10

Winning Jockeys	W-R	£1 Level Stake		W-R	£1 Level Stake
W Ryan	2-4	+ 33.00	B Raymond	1-7	+ 8.00
T Quinn	2-6	- 1.70	A McGlone	1-10	- 2.00
W Carson	1-7	- 1.00			

Winning Courses	W-R			W-R	
Warwick	2-5	+ 18.00	Southwell (AW)	1-7	- 4.37
Lingfield (AW)	2-8	- 3.33	Leicester	1-10	+ 24.00
Sandown	1-3	+ 3.00			

Winning Horses	Age	Races Run	1st	2nd	3rd	Unpl	Win £
Gold Blade	4	12	3	3	1	5	9,030
Legal Artist	3	8	2	0	0	6	5,222
Free Mover	4	8	1	0	3	4	4,713
Karamoja	4	7	1	2	1	3	2,217

Favourites	3-8	37.5%	- 0.70	Total winning prize-money			£21,182

1992 Form	6-90	6.7%	- 48.21	1990 Form	6-73	8.2%	- 38.50
1991 Form	7-81	8.6%	- 24.56				

B GUBBY (Bagshot, Surrey)

	No. of Horses	Races Run	1st	2nd	3rd	Unpl	Per cent	£1 Level Stake
2-y-o	2	5	1	0	0	4	20.0	- 1.25
3-y-o	2	6	0	0	1	5	-	- 6.00
4-y-o+	3	18	0	4	1	13	-	- 18.00
Totals	7	29	1	4	2	22	3.4	- 25.25

Jan	Feb	Mar	Apr	May	Jun	Jul	Aug	Sep	Oct/Nov
0-0	0-1	0-2	0-0	0-7	1-9	0-5	0-2	0-2	0-1

Winning Jockey	W-R	£1 Level Stake	Winning Course	W-R	£1 Level Stake
W Woods	1-1	+ 2.75	Leicester	1-3	+ 0.75

Winning Horse	Age	Races Run	1st	2nd	3rd	Unpl	Win £
Left Stranded	2	1	1	0	0	0	2,553

Favourites	0-1	Total winning prize-money		£2,553

1992 Form	2-70	2.9%	- 36.00	1990 Form	7-49	14.3%	+ 74.50
1991 Form	0-52			1989 Form	0-39		

R GUEST (Newmarket)

	No. of Horses	Races Run	1st	2nd	3rd	Unpl	Per cent	£1 Level Stake
2-y-o	6	21	3	0	4	14	14.3	+ 1.75
3-y-o	7	25	3	1	1	20	12.0	- 12.00
4-y-o+	6	26	3	5	5	13	11.5	- 10.67
Totals	19	72	9	6	10	47	12.5	- 20.92

Jan	Feb	Mar	Apr	May	Jun	Jul	Aug	Sep	Oct/Nov
0-1	0-0	0-1	1-7	2-14	2-7	1-8	1-13	2-8	0-13

Winning Jockeys	W-R	£1 Level Stake		W-R	£1 Level Stake
L Dettori	2-4	+ 8.83	W Carson	1-3	- 0.75
C Hawksley	2-7	+ 4.75	K Fallon	1-3	+ 8.00
J Fanning	1-2	+ 4.00	S Eiffert	1-10	- 5.00
K Darley	1-2	+ 0.25			

Winning Courses	W-R	£1 Level Stake		W-R	£1 Level Stake
Edinburgh	2-2	+ 9.00	Chepstow	1-2	+ 0.25
Beverley	1-1	+ 10.00	Folkestone	1-5	- 1.75
Hamilton	1-1	+ 1.25	Brighton	1-8	+ 0.50
Windsor	1-1	+ 7.50	Newmarket	1-13	- 8.67

Winning Horses	Age	Races Run	1st	2nd	3rd	Unpl	Win £
Indian Flash	3	10	3	1	0	6	9,020
Indian Slave	5	8	1	1	1	5	4,110
Gipsy Kid	2	3	2	0	0	1	4,038
Gloriette	2	8	1	0	1	6	3,049
Princess Evita	4	7	1	3	2	1	2,579
Gallery Artist	5	6	1	1	1	3	1,679

Favourites	4-9	44.4%	+ 3.08	Total winning prize-money		£24,475

1992 Form	15-86	17.4%	+ 23.50	1990 Form	7-151	4.6%	-110.95
1991 Form	5-92	5.4%	- 60.87	1989 Form	7-99	7.1%	- 24.50

W J HAGGAS (Newmarket)

	No. of Horses	Races Run	1st	2nd	3rd	Unpl	Per cent	£1 Level Stake
2-y-o	13	32	3	3	4	22	9.4	- 19.95
3-y-o	11	49	6	5	7	31	12.2	- 12.17
4-y-o+	7	44	4	10	3	27	9.1	- 6.00
Totals	31	125	13	18	14	80	10.4	- 38.12

BY MONTH

2-y-o	W-R	Per cent	£1 Level Stake	3-y-o	W-R	Per cent	£1 Level Stake
January	0-0	-	0.00	January	0-0	-	0.00
February	0-0	-	0.00	February	0-0	-	0.00
March	0-0	-	0.00	March	0-0	-	0.00
April	0-0	-	0.00	April	0-7	-	- 7.00
May	0-1	-	- 1.00	May	3-13	23.1	+ 4.33
June	0-2	-	- 2.00	June	1-8	12.5	0.00
July	0-9	-	- 9.00	July	1-8	12.5	- 2.50
August	2-9	22.2	- 4.95	August	1-7	14.3	- 1.00
September	0-4	-	- 4.00	September	0-5	-	- 5.00
Oct/Nov	1-7	14.3	+ 1.00	Oct/Nov	0-1	-	- 1.00

Haggas W J

4-y-o+	W-R	Per cent	£1 Level Stake	Totals	W-R	Per cent	£1 Level Stake
January	0-0	-	0.00	January	0-0	-	0.00
February	1-1	100.0	+ 6.00	February	1-1	100.0	+ 6.00
March	0-0	-	0.00	March	0-0	-	0.00
April	0-1	-	- 1.00	April	0-8	-	- 8.00
May	0-7	-	- 7.00	May	3-21	14.3	- 3.67
June	1-2	50.0	+ 9.00	June	2-12	16.7	+ 7.00
July	0-9	-	- 9.00	July	1-26	3.8	- 20.50
August	1-9	11.1	0.00	August	4-25	16.0	- 5.95
September	1-8	12.5	+ 3.00	September	1-17	5.9	- 6.00
Oct/Nov	0-7	-	- 7.00	Oct/Nov	1-15	6.7	- 7.00

DISTANCE

2-y-o	W-R	Per cent	£1 Level Stake	3-y-o	W-R	Per cent	£1 Level Stake
5f-6f	2-19	10.5	- 14.95	5f-6f	1-13	7.7	- 7.50
7f-8f	1-13	7.7	- 5.00	7f-8f	3-27	11.1	- 5.67
9f-13f	0-0	-	0.00	9f-13f	2-9	22.2	+ 1.00
14f+	0-0	-	0.00	14f+	0-0	-	0.00

4-y-o+	W-R	Per cent	£1 Level Stake	Totals	W-R	Per cent	£1 Level Stake
5f-6f	2-12	16.7	+ 8.00	5f-6f	5-44	11.4	- 14.45
7f-8f	2-20	10.0	- 2.00	7f-8f	6-60	10.0	- 12.67
9f-13f	0-12	-	- 12.00	9f-13f	2-21	9.5	- 11.00
14f+	0-0	-	0.00	14f+	0-0	-	0.00

TYPE OF RACE

Non-Handicaps	W-R	Per cent	£1 Level Stake	Handicaps	W-R	Per cent	£1 Level Stake
2-y-o	1-25	4.0	- 22.62	2-y-o	1-4	25.0	- 2.33
3-y-o	2-20	10.0	- 6.67	3-y-o	2-23	8.7	- 11.50
4-y-o+	0-6	-	- 6.00	4-y-o+	1-30	3.3	- 19.00
Selling	2-6	33.3	+ 10.00	Selling	0-2	-	- 2.00
Apprentice	2-2	100.0	+ 9.00	Apprentice	1-5	20.0	+ 4.00
Amat/Ladies	0-0	-	0.00	Amat/Ladies	1-2	50.0	+ 9.00
Totals	7-59	11.9	- 16.29	Totals	6-66	9.1	- 21.83

COURSE GRADE

	W-R	Per cent	£1 Level Stake
Group 1	3-48	6.3	- 25.00
Group 2	2-22	9.1	- 7.00
Group 3	5-37	13.5	- 8.45
Group 4	3-18	16.7	+ 2.33

FIRST TIME OUT

	W-R	Per cent	£1 Level Stake
2-y-o	0-13	-	- 13.00
3-y-o	1-11	9.1	- 2.00
4-y-o+	2-7	28.6	+ 11.00
Totals	3-31	9.7	- 4.00

Haggas W J

JOCKEYS RIDING

	W-R	Per cent	£1 Level Stake		W-R	Per cent	£1 Level Stake
M Hills	4-17	23.5	+ 4.05	G Duffield	1-7	14.3	- 2.67
Sally Radford-Howes	3-9	33.3	+ 11.00	M Roberts	1-7	14.3	+ 1.00
Mrs M Haggas	1-2	50.0	+ 9.00	C Rutter	1-9	11.1	+ 2.00
W Woods	1-5	20.0	+ 0.50	N Day	1-24	4.2	- 18.00

R Hills	0-7	P Robinson	0-2	J Reid	0-1
S Giles	0-4	Pat Eddery	0-2	J Williams	0-1
J Quinn	0-3	Paul Eddery	0-2	L Dettori	0-1
L Piggott	0-3	R Cochrane	0-2	M Tebbutt	0-1
A Munro	0-2	W R Swinburn	0-2	T Quinn	0-1
D Harrison	0-2	D Holland	0-1	W Carson	0-1
G Milligan	0-2	J Carroll	0-1	W Ryan	0-1
K Fallon	0-2	J Fanning	0-1		

COURSE RECORD

	Total W-R	Non-Handicaps 2-y-o	Non-Handicaps 3-y-o+	Handicaps 2-y-o	Handicaps 3-y-o+	Per cent	£1 Level Stake
Southwell (AW)	2-8	0-0	2-5	0-0	0-3	25.0	+ 3.33
Yarmouth	2-13	0-4	0-0	1-3	1-6	15.4	- 5.83
Warwick	1-2	0-0	1-1	0-0	0-1	50.0	+ 7.00
Chepstow	1-3	0-1	1-1	0-0	0-1	33.3	+ 5.00
Ayr	1-4	0-2	0-0	0-0	1-2	25.0	+ 2.00
Nottingham	1-4	1-2	0-1	0-0	0-1	25.0	- 1.62
Leicester	1-5	0-0	0-2	0-0	1-3	20.0	+ 6.00
Redcar	1-5	0-1	0-1	0-0	1-3	20.0	+ 6.00
Goodwood	1-6	0-1	0-1	0-0	1-4	16.7	+ 3.00
Lingfield	1-7	0-2	1-4	0-0	0-1	14.3	- 3.00
Newmarket	1-12	1-3	0-3	0-0	0-6	8.3	- 4.00

Kempton	0-7	York	0-3	Chester	0-1
Sandown	0-6	Bath	0-2	Edinburgh	0-1
Ascot	0-4	Beverley	0-2	Lingfield (AW)	0-1
Hamilton	0-4	Catterick	0-2	Pontefract	0-1
Ripon	0-4	Doncaster	0-2	Southwell (Turf)	0-1
Folkestone	0-3	Haydock	0-2	Thirsk	0-1
Salisbury	0-3	Newbury	0-2		
Windsor	0-3	Brighton	0-1		

WINNING HORSES

	Age	Races Run	1st	2nd	3rd	Unpl	Win £
Choir Practice	6	16	2	3	1	10	8,253
Sharaar	3	8	2	1	1	4	5,673
One On One	2	5	2	1	0	2	5,664
Slmaat	2	3	1	1	0	1	4,955
Absolute Magic	3	6	1	0	2	3	3,641
Jobie	3	10	1	0	0	9	3,395
Awestruck	3	7	1	2	1	3	3,173
Let's Get Lost	4	8	1	1	1	5	3,028
Maastricht	3	5	1	1	1	2	2,385
Fiaba	5	1	1	0	0	0	2,322

WINNING OWNERS

	Races Won	Value £		Races Won	Value £
Ali K Al Jafleh	3	10,628	Mrs M M Haggas	1	3,173
Stephen Chapman	2	8,253	A D Shead	1	3,028
Cheveley Park Stud	2	5,664	P A Deal	1	2,385
Mrs Barbara Bassett	1	3,641	William Haggas	1	2,322
J A Redmond	1	3,395			

Favourites	2-14	14.3%	- 9.95	Total winning prize-money	£42,487
Longest winning sequence			2	Average SP of winner	5.7/1
Longest losing sequence			25	Return on stakes invested	-30.5%
1992 Form	13-132	9.8%	- 58.49	1990 Form	21-141	14.9%	- 20.68
1991 Form	27-136	19.9%	+ 37.00	1989 Form	16-153	10.5%	- 66.04

W W HAIGH (Malton, North Yorks)

	No. of Horses	Races Run	1st	2nd	3rd	Unpl	Per cent	£1 Level Stake
2-y-o	7	23	0	0	0	23	-	- 23.00
3-y-o	4	22	4	3	5	10	18.2	+ 2.25
4-y-o+	8	55	7	9	6	33	12.7	- 9.25
Totals	19	100	11	12	11	66	11.0	- 30.00

BY MONTH

2-y-o	W-R	Per cent	£1 Level Stake	3-y-o	W-R	Per cent	£1 Level Stake
January	0-0	-	0.00	January	0-1	-	- 1.00
February	0-0	-	0.00	February	0-1	-	- 1.00
March	0-0	-	0.00	March	0-1	-	- 1.00
April	0-2	-	- 2.00	April	0-3	-	- 3.00
May	0-0	-	0.00	May	1-3	33.3	+ 6.00
June	0-6	-	- 6.00	June	2-3	66.7	+ 8.50
July	0-4	-	- 4.00	July	1-3	33.3	+ 0.75
August	0-1	-	- 1.00	August	0-5	-	- 5.00
September	0-3	-	- 3.00	September	0-2	-	- 2.00
Oct/Nov	0-7	-	- 7.00	Oct/Nov	0-0	-	0.00

Haigh W W

4-y-o+	W-R	Per cent	£1 Level Stake	Totals	W-R	Per cent	£1 Level Stake
January	0-3	-	- 3.00	January	0-4	-	- 4.00
February	1-6	16.7	0.00	February	1-7	14.3	- 1.00
March	2-6	33.3	+ 9.00	March	2-7	28.6	+ 8.00
April	2-8	25.0	+ 4.25	April	2-13	15.4	- 0.75
May	1-7	14.3	- 1.50	May	2-10	20.0	+ 4.50
June	1-6	16.7	+ 1.00	June	3-15	20.0	+ 3.50
July	0-6	-	- 6.00	July	1-13	7.7	- 9.25
August	0-5	-	- 5.00	August	0-11	-	- 11.00
September	0-4	-	- 4.00	September	0-9	-	- 9.00
Oct/Nov	0-4	-	- 4.00	Oct/Nov	0-11	-	- 11.00

DISTANCE

2-y-o	W-R	Per cent	£1 Level Stake	3-y-o	W-R	Per cent	£1 Level Stake
5f-6f	0-13	-	- 13.00	5f-6f	0-1	-	- 1.00
7f-8f	0-9	-	- 9.00	7f-8f	1-10	10.0	- 2.50
9f-13f	0-1	-	- 1.00	9f-13f	3-11	27.3	+ 5.75
14f+	0-0	-	0.00	14f+	0-0	-	0.00

4-y-o+	W-R	Per cent	£1 Level Stake	Totals	W-R	Per cent	£1 Level Stake
5f-6f	0-3	-	- 3.00	5f-6f	0-17	-	- 17.00
7f-8f	4-29	13.8	- 1.50	7f-8f	5-48	10.4	- 13.00
9f-13f	2-20	10.0	- 9.75	9f-13f	5-32	15.6	- 5.00
14f+	1-3	33.3	+ 5.00	14f+	1-3	33.3	+ 5.00

TYPE OF RACE

Non-Handicaps	W-R	Per cent	£1 Level Stake	Handicaps	W-R	Per cent	£1 Level Stake
2-y-o	0-12	-	- 12.00	2-y-o	0-2	-	- 2.00
3-y-o	3-12	25.0	+ 3.25	3-y-o	1-9	11.1	0.00
4-y-o+	5-17	29.4	+ 17.50	4-y-o+	2-34	5.9	- 22.75
Selling	0-11	-	- 11.00	Selling	0-2	-	- 2.00
Apprentice	0-1	-	- 1.00	Apprentice	0-0	-	0.00
Amat/Ladies	0-0	-	0.00	Amat/Ladies	0-0	-	0.00
Totals	8-53	15.1	- 3.25	Totals	3-47	6.4	- 26.75

COURSE GRADE

	W-R	Per cent	£1 Level Stake
Group 1	0-16	-	- 16.00
Group 2	3-27	11.1	- 10.25
Group 3	2-21	9.5	- 10.25
Group 4	6-36	16.7	+ 6.50

FIRST TIME OUT

	W-R	Per cent	£1 Level Stake
2-y-o	0-7	-	- 7.00
3-y-o	0-4	-	- 4.00
4-y-o+	0-8	-	- 8.00
Totals	0-19	-	- 19.00

Haigh W W

JOCKEYS RIDING

	W-R	Per cent	£1 Level Stake		W-R	Per cent	£1 Level Stake
D McKeown	9-38	23.7	+ 21.75	S Webster	1-15	6.7	- 8.00
J Fanning	1-4	25.0	- 0.75				

Dale Gibson	0-26	A Culhane	0-1	N Kennedy	0-1
S D Williams	0-7	D Biggs	0-1	P Robinson	0-1
F Norton	0-2	J Lowe	0-1		
W Newnes	0-2	L Charnock	0-1		

COURSE RECORD

	Total W-R	Non-Handicaps 2-y-o	3-y-o	Handicaps 2-y-o	3-y-o+	Per cent	£1 Level Stake
Southwell (AW)	4-30	0-3	3-13	0-1	1-13	13.3	- 2.00
Redcar	3-15	0-4	2-5	0-0	1-6	20.0	+ 1.75
Carlisle	2-4	0-1	2-2	0-0	0-1	50.0	+ 10.50
Beverley	2-13	0-4	1-1	0-0	1-8	15.4	- 2.25

Doncaster	0-9	Ripon	0-4	Nottingham	0-2
Thirsk	0-8	Catterick	0-2	York	0-1
Haydock	0-4	Hamilton	0-2		
Pontefract	0-4	Newcastle	0-2		

WINNING HORSES

	Age	Races Run	1st	2nd	3rd	Unpl	Win £
Claudia Miss	6	14	3	2	1	8	7,598
Solomon's Dancer	3	5	2	0	2	1	6,636
I'm A Dreamer	3	12	2	2	2	6	5,660
Red Indian	7	11	1	3	1	6	2,951
Pharly Dancer	4	10	1	4	1	4	2,769
Steppey Lane	8	3	1	0	0	2	2,427
Round By The River	4	5	1	0	0	4	2,280

WINNING OWNERS

	Races Won	Value £		Races Won	Value £
Dave Marshall	3	8,610	A Marucci	1	2,769
G Whorton	3	7,598	Dr C I Emmerson	1	2,427
D D Hart	2	6,636	W W Haigh	1	2,280

Favourites	2-7	28.6%	+ 0.25	Total winning prize-money		£30,320

Longest winning sequence			1	Average SP of winner		5.4/1
Longest losing sequence			33	Return on stakes invested		-30.0%

1992 Form	9-100	9.0%	- 27.37	1990 Form	5-87	5.7%	- 19.00
1991 Form	7-80	8.8%	- 48.29	1989 Form	3-65	4.6%	- 16.00

MISS S E HALL (Middleham, North Yorks)

	No. of Horses	Races Run	1st	2nd	3rd	Unpl	Per cent	£1 Level Stake
2-y-o	8	25	4	4	2	15	16.0	- 4.50
3-y-o	8	42	4	3	4	31	9.5	- 27.47
4-y-o+	3	26	6	0	1	19	23.1	+ 10.50
Totals	19	93	14	7	7	65	15.1	- 21.47

BY MONTH

2-y-o	W-R	Per cent	£1 Level Stake	3-y-o	W-R	Per cent	£1 Level Stake
Mar/Apr	0-0	-	0.00	Mar/Apr	0-6	-	- 6.00
May	0-1	-	- 1.00	May	1-7	14.3	- 2.67
June	2-4	50.0	+ 11.00	June	0-5	-	- 5.00
July	0-3	-	- 3.00	July	2-7	28.6	- 2.80
August	1-5	20.0	- 1.00	August	1-8	12.5	- 2.00
September	0-6	-	- 6.00	September	0-4	-	- 4.00
Oct/Nov	1-6	16.7	- 4.50	Oct/Nov	0-5	-	- 5.00

4-y-o+	W-R	Per cent	£1 Level Stake	Totals	W-R	Per cent	£1 Level Stake
Mar/Apr	3-6	50.0	+ 6.50	Mar/Apr	3-12	25.0	+ 0.50
May	0-3	-	- 3.00	May	1-11	9.1	- 6.67
June	1-5	20.0	+ 4.00	June	3-14	21.4	+ 10.00
July	1-4	25.0	+ 0.50	July	3-14	21.4	- 5.30
August	1-3	33.3	+ 4.00	August	3-16	18.8	+ 1.00
September	0-4	-	- 4.00	September	0-14	-	- 14.00
Oct/Nov	0-1	-	- 1.00	Oct/Nov	1-12	8.3	- 10.50

DISTANCE

2-y-o	W-R	Per cent	£1 Level Stake	3-y-o	W-R	Per cent	£1 Level Stake
5f-6f	3-11	27.3	+ 8.00	5f-6f	0-4	-	- 4.00
7f-8f	1-13	7.7	- 11.50	7f-8f	2-22	9.1	- 17.80
9f-13f	0-1	-	- 1.00	9f-13f	2-15	13.3	- 4.67
14f+	0-0	-	0.00	14f+	0-1	-	- 1.00

4-y-o+	W-R	Per cent	£1 Level Stake	Totals	W-R	Per cent	£1 Level Stake
5f-6f	0-2	-	- 2.00	5f-6f	3-17	17.6	+ 2.00
7f-8f	6-20	30.0	+ 16.50	7f-8f	9-55	16.4	- 12.80
9f-13f	0-4	-	- 4.00	9f-13f	2-20	10.0	- 9.67
14f+	0-0	-	0.00	14f+	0-1	-	- 1.00

TYPE OF RACE

Non-Handicaps	W-R	Per cent	£1 Level Stake	Handicaps	W-R	Per cent	£1 Level Stake
2-y-o	3-18	16.7	- 1.50	2-y-o	1-6	16.7	- 2.00
3-y-o	3-16	18.8	- 7.47	3-y-o	1-20	5.0	- 14.00
4-y-o+	0-4	-	- 4.00	4-y-o+	5-19	26.3	+ 12.00
Selling	1-6	16.7	- 0.50	Selling	0-2	-	- 2.00
Apprentice	0-0	-	0.00	Apprentice	0-1	-	- 1.00
Amat/Ladies	0-1	-	- 1.00	Amat/Ladies	0-0	-	0.00
Totals	7-45	15.6	- 14.47	Totals	7-48	14.6	- 7.00

COURSE GRADE

	W-R	Per cent	£1 Level Stake
Group 1	6-35	17.1	+ 1.50
Group 2	3-32	9.4	- 18.87
Group 3	2-15	13.3	- 6.93
Group 4	3-11	27.3	+ 2.83

FIRST TIME OUT

	W-R	Per cent	£1 Level Stake
2-y-o	1-8	12.5	+ 2.00
3-y-o	0-7	-	- 7.00
4-y-o+	1-3	33.3	+ 2.50
Totals	2-18	11.1	- 2.50

JOCKEYS RIDING

	W-R	Per cent	£1 Level Stake
N Connorton	14-63	22.2	+ 8.53

J Lowe	0-5	A McGlone	0-1	M Fenton	0-1
S Webster	0-4	D Harrison	0-1	M Roberts	0-1
J Tate	0-3	D McKeown	0-1	Mrs A Farrell	0-1
S Maloney	0-3	J Quinn	0-1	O Pears	0-1
J Fortune	0-2	J Williams	0-1	T G McLaughlin	0-1
Paul Eddery	0-2	M Birch	0-1		

COURSE RECORD

	Total W-R	Non-Handicaps 2-y-o	Non-Handicaps 3-y-o+	Handicaps 2-y-o	Handicaps 3-y-o+	Per cent	£1 Level Stake
Newcastle	4-11	2-4	0-1	1-1	1-5	36.4	+ 11.50
Catterick	2-7	0-1	2-4	0-0	0-2	28.6	+ 2.83
Ripon	2-17	0-3	1-6	0-0	1-8	11.8	- 8.37
Carlisle	1-2	0-0	0-0	0-0	1-2	50.0	+ 2.00
Pontefract	1-2	0-0	0-1	0-0	1-1	50.0	+ 4.50
Haydock	1-4	1-2	0-1	0-0	0-1	25.0	+ 1.00
Doncaster	1-8	0-3	0-0	0-1	1-4	12.5	+ 1.00
Beverley	1-9	0-1	1-2	0-1	0-5	11.1	- 7.43
Redcar	1-9	0-2	0-4	0-0	1-3	11.1	- 4.50

Thirsk	0-5	Hamilton	0-4	Chester	0-1
York	0-5	Ascot	0-2	Newmarket	0-1
Ayr	0-4	Southwell (AW)	0-2		

WINNING HORSES

	Age	Races Run	1st	2nd	3rd	Unpl	Win £
Royal Girl	6	9	4	0	1	4	12,397
Silverlocks	3	10	3	0	1	6	11,383
Smart Pet	2	6	2	1	0	3	10,965
Leif The Lucky	4	11	2	0	0	9	10,743
Mosaic Gold	2	7	1	0	1	5	3,524
Moving Arrow	2	4	1	2	0	1	3,290
Young Tess	3	6	1	0	0	5	2,781

WINNING OWNERS

	Races Won	Value £		Races Won	Value £
Miss Betty Duxbury	7	28,429	Mrs George Ward	2	10,965
Miss S E Hall	4	12,397	W G Barker	1	3,290

Favourites	6-10	60.0%	+ 11.90	Total winning prize-money		£55,080

Longest winning sequence		2	Average SP of winner		4.1/1
Longest losing sequence		20	Return on stakes invested		-23.1%

1992 Form	9-84	10.7%	- 9.52	1990 Form	12-133	9.0%	- 46.35
1991 Form	6-88	6.8%	- 39.17	1989 Form	6-81	7.4%	- 32.75

A A HAMBLY (Abbots Bromley, Staffs)

	No. of Horses	Races Run	1st	2nd	3rd	Unpl	Per cent	£1 Level Stake
2-y-o	3	18	0	0	0	18	-	- 18.00
3-y-o	5	19	1	3	2	13	5.3	- 6.00
4-y-o+	5	18	0	1	1	16	-	- 18.00
Totals	13	55	1	4	3	47	1.8	- 42.00

Jan	Feb	Mar	Apr	May	Jun	Jul	Aug	Sep	Oct/Nov
0-0	0-0	0-3	1-8	0-9	0-6	0-9	0-4	0-9	0-7

Winning Jockey	W-R	£1 Level Stake	Winning Course	W-R	£1 Level Stake
J O'Reilly	1-22	- 9.00	Southwell (AW)	1-10	+ 3.00

Winning Horse	Age	Races Run	1st	2nd	3rd	Unpl	Win £
Girl Next Door	3	8	1	1	1	5	2,951

Favourites	0-0		Total winning prize-money	£2,951

M D HAMMOND (Middleham, North Yorks)

	No. of Horses	Races Run	1st	2nd	3rd	Unpl	Per cent	£1 Level Stake
2-y-o	3	16	3	4	0	9	18.8	+ 6.50
3-y-o	9	40	3	6	3	28	7.5	- 6.00
4-y-o+	22	99	5	9	12	73	5.1	- 46.50
Totals	34	155	11	19	15	110	7.1	- 46.00

BY MONTH

2-y-o	W-R	Per cent	£1 Level Stake	3-y-o	W-R	Per cent	£1 Level Stake
January	0-0	-	0.00	January	0-0	-	0.00
February	0-0	-	0.00	February	0-0	-	0.00
March	0-0	-	0.00	March	0-0	-	0.00
April	0-0	-	0.00	April	0-0	-	0.00
May	0-3	-	- 3.00	May	0-7	-	- 7.00
June	1-3	33.3	+ 12.00	June	1-8	12.5	- 2.00
July	2-6	33.3	+ 1.50	July	2-17	11.8	+ 11.00
August	0-3	-	- 3.00	August	0-7	-	- 7.00
September	0-1	-	- 1.00	September	0-1	-	- 1.00
Oct/Nov	0-0	-	0.00	Oct/Nov	0-0	-	0.00

4-y-o+	W-R	Per cent	£1 Level Stake	Totals	W-R	Per cent	£1 Level Stake
January	0-1	-	- 1.00	January	0-1	-	- 1.00
February	0-0	-	0.00	February	0-0	-	0.00
March	0-5	-	- 5.00	March	0-5	-	- 5.00
April	0-10	-	- 10.00	April	0-10	-	- 10.00
May	1-19	5.3	- 10.00	May	1-29	3.4	- 20.00
June	1-19	5.3	- 10.00	June	3-30	10.0	0.00
July	2-21	9.5	- 7.50	July	6-44	13.6	+ 5.00
August	0-12	-	- 12.00	August	0-22	-	- 22.00
September	0-3	-	- 3.00	September	0-5	-	- 5.00
Oct/Nov	1-9	11.1	+ 12.00	Oct/Nov	1-9	11.1	+ 12.00

DISTANCE

2-y-o	W-R	Per cent	£1 Level Stake	3-y-o	W-R	Per cent	£1 Level Stake
5f-6f	1-10	10.0	- 5.50	5f-6f	2-9	22.2	+ 8.00
7f-8f	2-6	33.3	+ 12.00	7f-8f	1-20	5.0	- 3.00
9f-13f	0-0	-	0.00	9f-13f	0-11	-	- 11.00
14f+	0-0	-	0.00	14f+	0-0	-	0.00

4-y-o+	W-R	Per cent	£1 Level Stake	Totals	W-R	Per cent	£1 Level Stake
5f-6f	1-12	8.3	- 3.00	5f-6f	4-31	12.9	- 0.50
7f-8f	2-35	5.7	- 9.00	7f-8f	5-61	8.2	0.00
9f-13f	2-33	6.1	- 15.50	9f-13f	2-44	4.5	- 26.50
14f+	0-19	-	- 19.00	14f+	0-19	-	- 19.00

TYPE OF RACE

Non-Handicaps	W-R	Per cent	£1 Level Stake	Handicaps	W-R	Per cent	£1 Level Stake
2-y-o	1-9	11.1	+ 6.00	2-y-o	0-2	-	- 2.00
3-y-o	1-17	5.9	0.00	3-y-o	2-15	13.3	+ 2.00
4-y-o+	1-8	12.5	+ 1.00	4-y-o+	3-72	4.2	- 37.00
Selling	2-11	18.2	- 3.50	Selling	0-5	-	- 5.00
Apprentice	0-0	-	0.00	Apprentice	1-9	11.1	- 0.50
Amat/Ladies	0-0	-	0.00	Amat/Ladies	0-7	-	- 7.00
Totals	5-45	11.1	+ 3.50	Totals	6-110	5.5	- 49.50

COURSE GRADE

	W-R	Per cent	£1 Level Stake
Group 1	1-29	3.4	- 24.50
Group 2	4-44	9.1	+ 1.00
Group 3	2-29	6.9	- 1.00
Group 4	4-53	7.5	- 21.50

FIRST TIME OUT

	W-R	Per cent	£1 Level Stake
2-y-o	0-2	-	- 2.00
3-y-o	0-6	-	- 6.00
4-y-o+	0-20	-	- 20.00
Totals	0-28	-	- 28.00

JOCKEYS RIDING

	W-R	Per cent	£1 Level Stake		W-R	Per cent	£1 Level Stake
J Marshall	8-56	14.3	+ 27.00	D McKeown	1-12	8.3	- 3.00
J Lowe	1-4	25.0	+ 2.00	G Duffield	1-31	3.2	- 20.00

J Carroll	0-7	K Fallon	0-2	L Charnock	0-1
M Birch	0-5	Miss K Milligan	0-2	L Dettori	0-1
S Wood	0-4	Mr C Bonner	0-2	M Tebbutt	0-1
J Fanning	0-3	Mrs L Pearce	0-2	Mrs A Farrell	0-1
S Maloney	0-3	N Kennedy	0-2	N Varley	0-1
S Perks	0-3	A Mackay	0-1	R Cochrane	0-1
C N Adamson	0-2	B Raymond	0-1	W Newnes	0-1
J Quinn	0-2	Dale Gibson	0-1		
K Darley	0-2	F Norton	0-1		

COURSE RECORD

	Total W-R	Non-Handicaps 2-y-o	3-y-o+	Handicaps 2-y-o	3-y-o+	Per cent	£1 Level Stake
Edinburgh	3-14	1-4	0-0	0-0	2-10	21.4	+ 2.50
Thirsk	2-13	0-0	0-4	0-0	2-9	15.4	+ 2.00
Redcar	2-15	0-1	1-3	0-0	1-11	13.3	+ 15.00
Hamilton	1-6	0-0	1-2	0-1	0-3	16.7	+ 11.00
Haydock	1-9	1-2	0-0	0-0	0-7	11.1	- 4.50
Pontefract	1-9	0-0	0-4	0-0	1-5	11.1	+ 2.00
Catterick	1-14	1-1	0-3	0-0	0-10	7.1	+ 1.00

Carlisle	0-16	Southwell (AW)	0-8	York	0-3
Ripon	0-15	Doncaster	0-3	Chester	0-1
Ayr	0-11	Newcastle	0-3	Leicester	0-1
Beverley	0-10	Nottingham	0-3	Southwell (Turf)	0-1

WINNING HORSES

	Age	Races Run	1st	2nd	3rd	Unpl	Win £
Sartigila	4	15	2	1	2	10	7,721
Formidable Liz	3	11	2	2	1	6	7,570
Mokaite	2	9	2	3	0	4	4,630
Common Council	4	9	2	0	2	5	4,475
Routing	5	12	1	2	2	7	3,063
Olicana	3	5	1	0	0	4	2,579
Springhead	2	5	1	1	0	3	2,451

WINNING OWNERS

	Races Won	Value £		Races Won	Value £
John Lishman	2	7,721	Mrs E E Newbould	2	4,475
J Johnson	2	7,570	Mrs M A Doohan	1	3,063
The Bridge Club	3	7,081	Ecudawn	1	2,579

Favourites	2-13	15.4%	- 4.00	Total winning prize-money		£32,488
Longest winning sequence			2	Average SP of winner		8.9/1
Longest losing sequence			35	Return on stakes invested		-29.7%
1992 Form	9-58	15.5%	- 3.49	1990 Form	5-25	20.0% + 15.50
1991 Form	1-42	2.4%	- 31.00			

B HANBURY (Newmarket)

	No. of Horses	Races Run	1st	2nd	3rd	Unpl	Per cent	£1 Level Stake
2-y-o	15	44	4	9	5	26	9.1	- 23.47
3-y-o	20	103	18	12	12	61	17.5	- 29.68
4-y-o+	8	75	13	7	18	37	17.3	+ 11.28
Totals	43	222	35	28	35	124	15.8	- 41.87

BY MONTH

2-y-o	W-R	Per cent	£1 Level Stake	3-y-o	W-R	Per cent	£1 Level Stake
January	0-0	-	0.00	January	0-0	-	0.00
February	0-0	-	0.00	February	0-0	-	0.00
March	0-0	-	0.00	March	0-0	-	0.00
April	0-0	-	0.00	April	0-7	-	- 7.00
May	2-4	50.0	+ 8.53	May	3-19	15.8	- 1.00
June	0-4	-	- 4.00	June	7-24	29.2	- 1.80
July	1-10	10.0	- 7.00	July	6-28	21.4	- 11.88
August	0-6	-	- 6.00	August	0-14	-	- 14.00
September	1-13	7.7	- 8.00	September	2-8	25.0	+ 9.00
Oct/Nov	0-7	-	- 7.00	Oct/Nov	0-3	-	- 3.00

Hanbury B

4-y-o+	W-R	Per cent	£1 Level Stake	Totals	W-R	Per cent	£1 Level Stake
January	0-0	-	0.00	January	0-0	-	0.00
February	0-1	-	- 1.00	February	0-1	-	- 1.00
March	0-0	-	0.00	March	0-0	-	0.00
April	1-12	8.3	- 10.56	April	1-19	5.3	- 17.56
May	0-11	-	- 11.00	May	5-34	14.7	- 3.47
June	6-16	37.5	+ 16.84	June	13-44	29.5	+ 11.04
July	3-15	20.0	+ 12.00	July	10-53	18.9	- 6.88
August	3-10	30.0	+ 15.00	August	3-30	10.0	- 5.00
September	0-6	-	- 6.00	September	3-27	11.1	- 5.00
Oct/Nov	0-4	-	- 4.00	Oct/Nov	0-14	-	- 14.00

DISTANCE

2-y-o	W-R	Per cent	£1 Level Stake	3-y-o	W-R	Per cent	£1 Level Stake
5f-6f	3-16	18.8	+ 1.53	5f-6f	1-8	12.5	- 5.50
7f-8f	1-28	3.6	- 25.00	7f-8f	8-48	16.7	- 10.09
9f-13f	0-0	-	0.00	9f-13f	5-36	13.9	- 13.71
14f+	0-0	-	0.00	14f+	4-11	36.4	- 0.38

4-y-o+	W-R	Per cent	£1 Level Stake	Totals	W-R	Per cent	£1 Level Stake
5f-6f	0-1	-	- 1.00	5f-6f	4-25	16.0	- 4.97
7f-8f	6-33	18.2	+ 14.44	7f-8f	15-109	13.8	- 20.65
9f-13f	7-38	18.4	+ 0.84	9f-13f	12-74	16.2	- 12.87
14f+	0-3	-	- 3.00	14f+	4-14	28.6	- 3.38

TYPE OF RACE

Non-Handicaps	W-R	Per cent	£1 Level Stake	Handicaps	W-R	Per cent	£1 Level Stake
2-y-o	4-39	10.3	- 18.47	2-y-o	0-1	-	- 1.00
3-y-o	7-60	11.7	- 29.97	3-y-o	11-40	27.5	+ 3.29
4-y-o+	4-18	22.2	- 6.89	4-y-o+	9-55	16.4	+ 20.17
Selling	0-6	-	- 6.00	Selling	0-0	-	0.00
Apprentice	0-1	-	- 1.00	Apprentice	0-1	-	- 1.00
Amat/Ladies	0-0	-	0.00	Amat/Ladies	0-1	-	- 1.00
Totals	15-124	12.1	- 62.33	Totals	20-98	20.4	+ 20.46

COURSE GRADE

	W-R	Per cent	£1 Level Stake
Group 1	18-127	14.2	- 16.34
Group 2	6-26	23.1	- 5.63
Group 3	9-57	15.8	- 21.40
Group 4	2-12	16.7	+ 1.50

FIRST TIME OUT

	W-R	Per cent	£1 Level Stake
2-y-o	1-15	6.7	- 4.00
3-y-o	2-20	10.0	- 6.50
4-y-o+	0-8	-	- 8.00
Totals	3-43	7.0	- 18.50

JOCKEYS RIDING

	W-R	Per cent	£1 Level Stake		W-R	Per cent	£1 Level Stake
W R Swinburn	9-42	21.4	− 8.18	W Ryan	2-16	12.5	+ 2.00
B Raymond	5-55	9.1	− 38.48	J Reid	1-1	100.0	+ 4.00
L Dettori	4-8	50.0	+ 19.50	D McKeown	1-2	50.0	+ 9.00
J Tate	4-10	40.0	− 0.08	J Quinn	1-2	50.0	− 0.47
M Hills	2-7	28.6	+ 8.50	O Pears	1-2	50.0	+ 6.00
L Piggott	2-9	22.2	+ 14.00	D Harrison	1-4	25.0	+ 0.50
M Roberts	2-11	18.2	− 5.16				

M Tebbutt	0-6	K Fallon	0-2	J Marshall		0-1
R Hills	0-5	N Carlisle	0-2	M Fenton		0-1
W Carson	0-5	A McGlone	0-1	Mr F Grasso-Caprioli		0-1
D Holland	0-4	A Munro	0-1	N Day		0-1
G Duffield	0-3	B Rouse	0-1	P Robinson		0-1
M Birch	0-3	E Johnson	0-1	Pat Eddery		0-1
R Cochrane	0-3	G Baxter	0-1	S Maloney		0-1
Antoinette Armes	0-2	J Carroll	0-1	T Quinn		0-1
J Weaver	0-2	J Fortune	0-1	W Newnes		0-1

COURSE RECORD

	Total W-R	Non-Handicaps 2-y-o	Non-Handicaps 3-y-o+	Handicaps 2-y-o	Handicaps 3-y-o+	Per cent	£1 Level Stake
Goodwood	4-12	0-1	2-3	0-0	2-8	33.3	+ 2.91
Pontefract	3-5	0-0	2-3	0-0	1-2	60.0	+ 1.57
Newbury	3-9	2-3	0-2	0-0	1-4	33.3	+ 0.91
Yarmouth	3-21	0-6	2-9	0-0	1-6	14.3	− 10.47
Newmarket	3-41	0-13	0-16	0-0	3-12	7.3	− 6.00
Ripon	2-7	0-0	1-3	0-0	1-4	28.6	− 3.66
Haydock	2-9	0-0	1-4	0-0	1-5	22.2	+ 0.50
Kempton	2-11	0-1	0-3	0-0	2-7	18.2	+ 12.00
Sandown	2-12	0-3	0-3	0-0	2-6	16.7	− 7.41
Folkestone	1-1	0-0	0-0	0-0	1-1	100.0	+ 4.50
Thirsk	1-1	0-0	0-0	0-0	1-1	100.0	+ 3.00
Chepstow	1-2	0-0	0-1	0-0	1-1	50.0	+ 2.50
Chester	1-3	0-1	0-0	0-0	1-2	33.3	+ 6.00
Hamilton	1-3	0-0	1-2	0-0	0-1	33.3	+ 8.00
Lingfield	1-3	0-1	1-1	0-0	0-1	33.3	− 0.50
Ayr	1-4	0-0	1-3	0-0	0-1	25.0	− 1.25
Carlisle	1-4	0-0	0-2	0-0	1-2	25.0	+ 4.00
Doncaster	1-4	1-2	0-0	0-0	0-2	25.0	+ 7.00
Brighton	1-7	1-2	0-2	0-1	0-2	14.3	− 5.47
Nottingham	1-7	0-2	0-2	0-0	1-3	14.3	− 4.00

Beverley	0-12	Epsom	0-3	Edinburgh	0-1
York	0-12	Redcar	0-3	Lingfield (AW)	0-1
Leicester	0-7	Catterick	0-2	Warwick	0-1
Ascot	0-6	Salisbury	0-2		
Newcastle	0-4	Southwell (AW)	0-2		

WINNING HORSES

	Age	Races Run	1st	2nd	3rd	Unpl	Win £
En Attendant	5	12	3	1	5	3	53,954
Polish Laughter	2	4	2	1	0	1	32,671
Dusty Point	3	9	5	0	0	4	18,394
Persiansky	3	11	4	1	1	5	13,293
Moonlight Quest	5	12	3	0	1	8	11,297
Classic Sky	2	7	2	1	1	3	10,930
Haddaaj	3	6	3	0	0	3	9,690
Sovereign Page	4	11	3	1	3	4	9,679
Tik Fa	4	7	2	1	0	4	9,088
Dixieland Melody	3	5	1	1	1	2	6,709
Wisham	3	9	1	2	2	4	3,436
Midhish	3	4	1	2	0	1	3,348
Abbraak	3	4	1	0	1	2	3,231
Jahangir	4	16	1	3	2	10	3,184
Rasayel	3	7	1	0	2	4	2,742
Surrey Dancer	5	12	1	1	3	7	2,710
Blue Blazer	3	11	1	2	0	8	2,269

WINNING OWNERS

	Races Won	Value £		Races Won	Value £
Mrs B Newton	3	53,954	Sheikh Ahmed Al Maktoum	3	9,690
Juma Humaid	2	32,671	P G Goulandris	1	3,436
Abdullah Ali	7	27,482	Nasser Abdullah	1	3,231
Saeed Suhail	5	23,730	S W Macfarlane	1	3,184
Mrs J M Beeby	7	22,971	Cronk Th'bred Racing Ltd	1	2,710
Mrs John Lamb	3	11,297	McHalapar Syndicate	1	2,269

Favourites	13-34	38.2%	- 3.20	Total winning prize-money	£196,624
Longest winning sequence			3	Average SP of winner	4.2/1
Longest losing sequence			26	Return on stakes invested	-18.2%
1992 Form	39-308	12.7%	- 64.98	1990 Form	36-274	13.1%	- 51.86
1991 Form	36-302	11.9%	- 45.68	1989 Form	42-225	18.7%	+ 32.78

R HANNON (East Everleigh, Wilts)

	No. of Horses	Races Run	1st	2nd	3rd	Unpl	Per cent	£1 Level Stake
2-y-o	115	553	98	85	75	295	17.7	- 75.87
3-y-o	65	442	65	62	51	264	14.7	- 8.19
4-y-o+	27	197	19	28	22	128	9.6	- 52.87
Totals	207	1192	182	175	148	687	15.3	-136.93

BY MONTH

2-y-o	W-R	Per cent	£1 Level Stake		3-y-o	W-R	Per cent	£1 Level Stake
January	0-0	-		0.00	January	0-2	-	- 2.00
February	0-0	-		0.00	February	0-0	-	0.00
March	0-4	-	-	4.00	March	2-10	20.0	+ 3.50
April	7-26	26.9	+	4.96	April	11-56	19.6	+ 16.75
May	7-49	14.3	-	24.96	May	17-83	20.5	+ 52.91
June	14-74	18.9	-	8.20	June	8-75	10.7	- 37.83
July	17-81	21.0	-	2.46	July	10-65	15.4	- 1.87
August	16-88	18.2	-	10.26	August	6-52	11.5	- 16.54
September	14-111	12.6	-	19.92	September	9-60	15.0	+ 6.14
Oct/Nov	23-120	19.2	-	11.03	Oct/Nov	2-39	5.1	- 29.25

4-y-o+	W-R	Per cent	£1 Level Stake		Totals	W-R	Per cent	£1 Level Stake
January	2-6	33.3	+	9.00	January	2-8	25.0	+ 7.00
February	0-2	-	-	2.00	February	0-2	-	- 2.00
March	0-9	-	-	9.00	March	2-23	8.7	- 9.50
April	2-26	7.7	+	2.00	April	20-108	18.5	+ 23.71
May	2-28	7.1	-	5.00	May	26-160	16.3	+ 22.95
June	1-32	3.1	-	23.50	June	23-181	12.7	- 69.53
July	5-29	17.2	-	1.00	July	32-175	18.3	- 5.33
August	3-20	15.0	+	3.00	August	25-160	15.6	- 23.80
September	3-22	13.6	-	6.25	September	26-193	13.5	- 20.03
Oct/Nov	1-23	4.3	-	20.12	Oct/Nov	26-182	14.3	- 60.40

DISTANCE

2-y-o	W-R	Per cent	£1 Level Stake	3-y-o	W-R	Per cent	£1 Level Stake
5f-6f	60-333	18.0	- 45.17	5f-6f	11-77	14.3	+ 31.46
7f-8f	38-216	17.6	- 26.70	7f-8f	33-201	16.4	- 0.95
9f-13f	0-4	-	- 4.00	9f-13f	19-145	13.1	- 23.75
14f+	0-0	-	0.00	14f+	2-19	10.5	- 14.95

4-y-o+	W-R	Per cent	£1 Level Stake	Totals	W-R	Per cent	£1 Level Stake
5f-6f	3-54	5.6	- 29.12	5f-6f	74-464	15.9	- 42.83
7f-8f	10-76	13.2	+ 4.50	7f-8f	81-493	16.4	- 23.15
9f-13f	3-47	6.4	- 29.50	9f-13f	22-196	11.2	- 57.25
14f+	3-20	15.0	+ 1.25	14f+	5-39	12.8	- 13.70

TYPE OF RACE

Non-Handicaps	W-R	Per cent	£1 Level Stake	Handicaps	W-R	Per cent	£1 Level Stake
2-y-o	79-450	17.6	- 85.80	2-y-o	14-84	16.7	+ 5.18
3-y-o	37-204	18.1	+ 13.93	3-y-o	23-201	11.4	- 7.25
4-y-o+	9-53	17.0	+ 14.75	4-y-o+	9-126	7.1	- 53.62
Selling	5-21	23.8	+ 2.75	Selling	0-4	-	- 4.00
Apprentice	2-7	28.6	- 1.25	Apprentice	4-26	15.4	- 5.62
Amat/Ladies	0-4	-	- 4.00	Amat/Ladies	0-12	-	- 12.00
Totals	132-739	17.9	- 59.62	Totals	50-453	11.0	- 77.31

COURSE GRADE					FIRST TIME OUT			
	W-R	Per cent	£1 Level Stake			W-R	Per cent	£1 Level Stake
Group 1	89-690	12.9	- 115.73	2-y-o		11-114	9.6	- 59.01
Group 2	35-200	17.5	- 20.19	3-y-o		13-65	20.0	+ 63.00
Group 3	41-208	19.7	+ 9.58	4-y-o+		3-26	11.5	+ 6.00
Group 4	17-94	18.1	- 10.59					
				Totals		27-205	13.2	+ 9.99

JOCKEYS RIDING

	W-R	Per cent	£1 Level Stake		W-R	Per cent	£1 Level Stake
Pat Eddery	37-167	22.2	- 7.89	D Gibbs	3-25	12.0	- 5.00
J Reid	25-164	15.2	- 26.26	R Perham	3-28	10.7	- 11.87
L Dettori	18-87	20.7	+ 11.36	M Roberts	3-42	7.1	- 27.50
L Piggott	14-49	28.6	+ 29.13	W Newnes	2-10	20.0	0.00
K Darley	13-76	17.1	+ 3.19	D O'Neill	2-11	18.2	- 4.62
B Raymond	7-47	14.9	- 13.67	A Whelan	2-12	16.7	+ 24.25
T Quinn	7-56	12.5	- 24.97	J Williams	1-2	50.0	+ 10.00
A McGlone	6-62	9.7	- 1.00	D Holland	1-3	33.3	- 0.50
W R Swinburn	5-25	20.0	+ 0.17	J Comber	1-4	25.0	+ 3.50
B Rouse	5-31	16.1	+ 27.33	Wendy Jones	1-6	16.7	+ 4.00
S Raymont	5-44	11.4	- 11.02	R Cochrane	1-8	12.5	+ 7.00
Mark Denaro	5-51	9.8	- 19.00	M J Kinane	1-9	11.1	+ 2.00
W Ryan	4-12	33.3	+ 17.50	R Hills	1-12	8.3	- 9.50
A Munro	4-17	23.5	+ 0.94	M Hills	1-16	6.3	- 13.50
G Duffield	3-12	25.0	- 0.50	W Carson	1-29	3.4	- 25.50

Mrs J Boggis	0-16	A Cruz	0-3	Miss K Hannon	0-1
D Biggs	0-7	B Marcus	0-3	Mrs D McHale	0-1
G Bardwell	0-6	C Asmussen	0-2	Rhona Gent	0-1
Paul Eddery	0-6	E Greehy	0-2	S Whitworth	0-1
W Woods	0-6	P Robinson	0-2	T Sprake	0-1
G Hind	0-5	G Carter	0-1	W O'Connor	0-1
N Adams	0-5	J Lowe	0-1		
A Clark	0-3	M Tebbutt	0-1		

COURSE RECORD

	Total W-R	Non-Handicaps 2-y-o	Non-Handicaps 3-y-o+	Handicaps 2-y-o	Handicaps 3-y-o+	Per cent	£1 Level Stake
Newmarket	13-139	7-50	4-31	0-12	2-46	9.4	- 74.38
Sandown	12-59	5-27	3-11	1-1	3-20	20.3	- 1.15
Kempton	12-69	5-22	2-19	0-3	5-25	17.4	+ 41.88
Newbury	12-104	5-38	4-23	1-10	2-33	11.5	- 27.52
Goodwood	11-76	2-24	5-18	1-6	3-28	14.5	+ 5.44
Windsor	10-47	3-22	3-11	0-2	4-12	21.3	- 6.75
Salisbury	9-61	5-25	2-16	0-0	2-20	14.8	+ 17.75
Leicester	8-40	3-19	4-10	0-1	1-10	20.0	+ 13.50
Nottingham	8-41	4-24	3-5	0-4	1-8	19.5	- 3.40
Folkestone	7-37	4-19	1-12	0-2	2-4	18.9	- 13.44
Brighton	7-40	4-12	3-14	0-2	0-12	17.5	- 6.17

Lingfield	7-53	4-27	2-13	0-3	1-10	13.2	- 26.00
York	7-54	4-21	1-12	2-5	0-16	13.0	- 7.12
Redcar	6-16	4-7	1-3	1-2	0-4	37.5	+ 2.69
Haydock	6-27	5-8	0-8	0-1	1-10	22.2	+ 1.68
Doncaster	6-63	1-22	3-11	1-10	1-20	9.5	- 6.80
Chester	5-21	3-9	1-2	1-2	0-8	23.8	- 3.21
Chepstow	5-24	3-11	0-0	1-2	1-11	20.8	+ 3.60
Ascot	4-52	3-15	0-16	0-1	1-20	7.7	- 23.12
Edinburgh	3-3	3-3	0-0	0-0	0-0	100.0	+ 6.35
Hamilton	3-4	1-2	1-1	1-1	0-0	75.0	+ 10.38
Yarmouth	3-19	1-7	0-2	1-3	1-7	15.8	- 7.00
Warwick	3-26	0-12	0-2	1-5	2-7	11.5	+ 1.00
Bath	3-28	1-14	1-5	0-1	1-8	10.7	+ 0.25
Epsom	3-31	1-8	1-11	0-1	1-11	9.7	- 16.50
Newcastle	2-9	1-6	1-3	0-0	0-0	22.2	- 2.50
Lingfield (AW)	2-17	0-1	1-6	0-0	1-10	11.8	- 2.00
Beverley	1-1	0-0	0-0	1-1	0-0	100.0	+ 3.00
Southwell (AW)	1-2	0-1	0-0	1-1	0-0	50.0	+ 4.00
Catterick	1-4	1-2	0-2	0-0	0-0	25.0	- 1.50
Thirsk	1-6	0-2	1-3	0-0	0-1	16.7	- 2.25
Ayr	1-7	1-3	0-0	0-0	0-4	14.3	- 5.64

Pontefract	0-4	Southwell (Turf)	0-3
Ripon	0-3	Carlisle	0-2

WINNING HORSES

	Age	Races Run	1st	2nd	3rd	Unpl	Win £
Risky	2	9	5	4	0	0	114,172
Swing Low	4	9	4	0	1	4	107,671
Assessor	4	8	2	4	1	1	69,849
Niche	3	3	2	1	0	0	60,445
Dana Springs	3	7	4	0	2	1	49,776
Right Win	3	5	2	1	0	2	34,197
Fourforfun	3	10	5	0	0	5	28,140
Show Faith	3	9	2	1	1	5	26,285
A Smooth One	2	4	2	0	1	1	26,249
Lemon Souffle	2	4	3	0	1	0	24,990
Geisway	3	7	1	1	0	5	21,540
Flight Lieutenant	4	8	1	1	2	4	21,500
Eastern Memories	3	4	3	0	0	1	21,267
Rajmapata	2	8	1	2	1	4	17,730
Bearall	2	8	3	1	1	3	16,574
Innishowen	2	5	2	1	0	2	15,530
In Like Flynn	2	7	3	3	1	0	15,175
Pips Pride	3	3	1	0	0	2	15,140
Governor George	2	7	2	0	4	1	14,945
Bid For Blue	2	10	2	2	3	3	13,991
Supreme Master	3	11	3	2	1	5	13,977

Redoubtable	2	5	2	0	2	1	13,244
Night Melody	3	10	3	3	1	3	12,337
Pistols At Dawn	3	9	4	1	1	3	11,868
Darecliff	3	6	2	1	1	2	10,808
Lyric Fantasy	3	4	1	0	0	3	10,029
Wajiba Riva	2	5	2	0	1	2	10,019
Bluegrass Prince	2	7	2	2	2	1	9,645
Tony's Mist	3	11	3	3	1	4	9,334
Lime Street Blues	2	6	2	1	0	3	9,316
Moscow Road	2	8	3	1	1	3	9,137
Embankment	3	12	2	2	2	6	9,133
Perusal	2	6	2	1	0	3	9,121
Link Miles	2	5	2	2	1	0	8,945
Circle Of Friends	2	4	1	1	1	1	8,610
Balandra Bay	2	5	2	1	0	2	8,310
Scottish Bambi	5	9	2	2	1	4	8,285
Lomas	2	3	2	0	1	0	7,929
Mazentre Forward	2	7	2	1	2	2	7,821
Crystal Magic	2	6	2	0	2	2	7,573
Brigante Di Cielo	3	9	1	1	2	5	7,570
Blue Bomber	2	6	2	1	0	3	7,472
Make A Note	2	6	2	2	1	1	7,405
Efra	4	6	2	0	0	4	7,273
Ham N'Eggs	2	5	2	0	1	2	7,163
Jade Pet	2	7	2	1	2	2	7,019
Dollar Gamble	2	11	2	4	1	4	6,918
Princely Favour	3	14	2	2	0	10	6,808
Tilty	3	11	2	0	4	5	6,802
Exhibit Air	3	8	2	0	0	6	6,736
Art Tatum	2	6	2	0	1	3	6,640
Surprise Offer	3	5	1	0	1	3	6,509
Down D Islands	2	8	2	0	0	6	6,409
Daily Sport Don	3	14	2	1	2	9	6,055
Wishing	2	5	1	1	2	1	5,936
Danny Boy	3	12	2	1	0	9	5,875
Echo-Logical	4	9	1	1	0	7	5,775
Easy Access	3	5	1	0	0	4	5,692
Alpine Skier	2	7	1	0	0	6	5,663
Prairie Grove	3	12	2	0	3	7	5,535
Grand Vitesse	4	10	1	1	1	7	5,527
Silver Slipper	2	6	2	0	0	4	5,491
Blurred Image	2	9	2	2	0	5	5,245
Jafeica	2	4	1	1	0	2	4,807
Heavenly Risk	3	8	1	1	0	6	4,760
Pistol River	3	8	1	3	1	3	4,752
Sister Susan	2	8	2	0	1	5	4,734
Port Lucaya	3	8	1	4	1	2	4,658
Primo Stampari	2	6	1	0	1	4	4,557
Tickerty's Gift	3	7	1	0	0	6	4,542
Uncle Oswald	2	3	1	0	0	2	4,435
Rooftop Flyer	2	6	1	1	2	2	4,378
Twin Falls	2	3	1	1	0	1	4,307

Brave Edge	2	9	1	3	2	3	4,241
Hopeful Bid	4	13	1	2	1	9	4,235
Bitter's End	3	5	1	0	3	1	4,230
Southern Power	2	6	1	2	1	2	4,199
Jasari	2	8	1	0	1	6	4,143
Southern Memories	3	9	1	0	1	7	4,110
Reprehend	2	4	1	1	1	1	4,078
Wayfarers Way	2	4	1	0	0	3	4,055
Petonellajill	3	6	1	2	0	3	3,980
Million Lights	2	8	1	2	1	4	3,933
Stash The Cash	2	6	1	3	0	2	3,810
Majestic Heights	2	4	1	1	0	2	3,699
Slasher Jack	2	4	1	0	0	3	3,626
Pommes Frites	2	5	1	2	0	2	3,623
Danger Point	2	8	1	2	4	1	3,509
Holly Golightly	3	4	1	0	0	3	3,465
Peter Rowley	2	9	1	2	2	4	3,444
Battling Blue	2	5	1	0	2	2	3,415
Gallant Spirit	2	5	1	0	0	4	3,340
Rose Ciel	2	9	1	1	2	5	3,321
Brockton Dancer	3	5	1	0	1	3	3,231
Dancing Spirit	3	8	1	1	0	6	3,202
Alcove	2	7	1	1	2	3	3,176
Prince Rodney	4	12	1	2	1	8	3,154
Mr Devious	2	5	1	0	0	4	3,128
Absonal	6	3	1	1	0	1	3,080
Make The Break	2	9	1	2	0	6	3,046
Eighteen Twelve	2	3	1	0	0	2	2,967
Port Sunlight	5	13	1	1	2	9	2,851
Western Fleet	2	7	1	3	1	2	2,668
Comeonup	2	5	1	1	0	3	2,579
Forgotten Dancer	2	5	1	1	1	2	2,495
Don't Forget Marie	3	7	1	3	0	3	2,406
Sweet Whisper	2	11	1	1	2	7	2,243
The Little Ferret	3	10	1	2	1	6	2,243
Sirmoor	4	6	1	2	0	3	2,174
Grecian Garden	2	3	1	1	0	1	2,070
Merlins Wish	4	8	1	1	1	5	1,828

WINNING OWNERS

	Races Won	Value £		Races Won	Value £
Roldvale Limited	12	232,658	J A Leek	2	6,918
Lord Carnarvon	8	97,636	C M Hamer	2	6,808
B E Nielson	4	83,093	K Higson	2	6,785
G Howard-Spink	8	61,644	Archie Hornall	2	6,736
Conal Kavanagh	4	49,727	David Thompson	2	6,734
The Winning Team	10	43,673	R Cohen & Mr A F Merritt	2	6,640
P D Savill	8	33,423	R J Shannon	2	6,409
Bob Lalemant	3	30,479	M W Grant	1	5,936
Mrs R F Knipe	5	28,140	Ivan Twigden	2	5,875
Paul Green	2	26,292	G A Bosley	2	5,649
I A N Wright	2	26,285	Giles Gleadell	2	5,535
Jim Horgan	4	25,377	Robert Whitworth	1	5,527
P & S Lever Partners	1	21,500	S M Threadwell	2	5,491
Lucayan Stud Limited	3	19,144	N T C (Racing) Ltd	1	4,807
Cheveley Park Stud	3	18,144	T A Johnsey	2	4,734
Peter Green	1	17,730	Edward St George	1	4,658
Mr And Mrs M Winterford	3	16,574	Nimrod Company	1	4,435
Lady Tennant	4	16,509	Exors of the late D F Cock	1	4,290
Fahd Salman	4	15,745	C J Petyt	1	4,241
M M Matalon	3	15,175	N Capon	1	4,235
Mrs V S Grant	1	15,140	Mrs J Cash	1	3,980
Harry W Hopgood	3	13,977	Million In Mind Partnership (2)	1	3,933
N Ahamad	3	10,937	J G Davis	1	3,810
A D Latter	2	10,808	Mrs C A Hawkings	1	3,699
Mrs P Jubert	3	10,717	Victor Behrens	1	3,465
J A Lazzari	3	10,138	P B Adams	1	3,340
Mrs John Magnier	1	10,029	Mrs D A La Trobe	1	3,231
Bezwell Fixings Ltd	2	9,645	L H J Ward	1	3,202
Mrs Chris Harrington	3	9,334	Highclere Th'bred Racing Ltd	1	3,176
D B Gallop	2	9,316	Theobalds Stud	1	3,128
G C Sampson	3	9,137	Capt R W Hornall	1	3,080
Miss L J Vickers	2	8,935	Mrs J Reglar	1	3,046
Mrs S H Spencer-Phillips	1	8,610	Mrs L M Davies	1	2,967
William J Kelly	2	8,285	Dr Susan Barnes	1	2,668
D Sieff	2	7,573	David Roberts	1	2,579
P J Christey	1	7,570	Mrs P R Cock	1	2,512
Peter Hammond	2	7,163	Norman Harper	1	2,406
Geoffrey C Greenwood	2	7,019	Christopher Wilson	1	2,174
Mrs C J Powell	2	6,929			

Favourites	86-230	37.4%	+ 33.37	
Longest winning sequence			3	
Longest losing sequence			25	
1992 Form	154-113	13.5%	-261.59	
1991 Form	126-958	13.2%	-149.42	

Total winning prize-money			£1,229,046
Average SP of winner			4.8/1
Return on stakes invested			-11.4%
1990 Form	73-796	9.2%	-192.68
1989 Form	55-603	9.1%	-198.78

J HANSON (Wetherby, West Yorks)

	No. of Horses	Races Run	1st	2nd	3rd	Unpl	Per cent	£1 Level Stake
2-y-o	4	14	2	4	1	7	14.3	+ 9.25
3-y-o	5	15	0	0	1	14	-	- 15.00
4-y-o+	0	0	0	0	0	0	-	0.00
Totals	9	29	2	4	2	21	6.9	- 5.75

Jan	Feb	Mar	Apr	May	Jun	Jul	Aug	Sep	Oct/Nov
0-0	0-0	0-0	0-0	0-1	0-9	0-6	1-2	0-4	1-7

Winning Jockeys	W-R	£1 Level Stake			W-R	£1 Level Stake
W Carson	1-6	- 3.75	E Johnson		1-9	+ 12.00

Winning Courses	W-R	£1 Level Stake			W-R	£1 Level Stake
Chester	1-2	+ 0.25	Redcar		1-4	+ 17.00

Winning Horses	Age	Races Run	1st	2nd	3rd	Unpl	Win £
Amber Valley	2	7	1	4	0	2	3,647
Askern	2	3	1	0	0	2	3,290

Favourites	1-2	50.0%	+ 0.25	Total winning prize-money	£6,937

1992 Form	1-13	7.7%	- 10.50	1990 Form	0-0		
1991 Form	0-0			1989 Form	2-19	10.5%	- 13.93

J L HARRIS (Melton Mowbray, Leics)

	No. of Horses	Races Run	1st	2nd	3rd	Unpl	Per cent	£1 Level Stake
2-y-o	5	18	0	1	0	17	-	- 18.00
3-y-o	3	8	0	1	0	7	-	- 8.00
4-y-o+	23	121	9	7	8	97	7.4	- 41.37
Totals	31	147	9	9	8	121	6.1	- 67.37

Jan	Feb	Mar	Apr	May	Jun	Jul	Aug	Sep	Oct/Nov
1-6	0-6	0-8	1-12	1-19	2-18	2-25	1-13	0-20	1-20

Winning Jockeys	W-R	£1 Level Stake		W-R	£1 Level Stake
L Dettori	2-10	+ 0.50	D Moffatt	1-11	- 1.00
G Strange	1-2	+ 15.00	R Cochrane	1-13	- 2.00
K Darley	1-5	- 2.37	J Quinn	1-15	- 11.50
Paul Eddery	1-6	+ 6.00	P Robinson	1-15	- 2.00

Winning Courses	W-R	£1 Level Stake		W-R	£1 Level Stake
Beverley	3-11	+ 18.63	Doncaster	2-14	+ 2.50
Southwell (AW)	3-26	- 3.50	Lingfield	1-4	+ 7.00

Winning Horses		Age	Races Run	1st	2nd	3rd	Unpl	Win £
Nordoora		4	13	2	1	0	10	6,072
Post Impressionist		4	7	2	2	0	3	5,709
Legend Dulac		4	11	1	1	1	8	3,377
Merryhill Maid		5	9	1	1	2	5	3,150
Sir Tasker		5	26	1	2	2	21	2,977
Clifton Chase		4	5	1	0	1	3	2,951
Merryhill Madam		4	7	1	0	0	6	2,070

Favourites	0-6				Total winning prize-money			£26,305

1992 Form	9-132	6.8%	- 54.75	1990 Form	6-51	11.8%	+ 26.50
1991 Form	8-128	6.3%	- 35.75	1989 Form	0-25		

P W HARRIS (Berkhamsted, Herts)

	No. of Horses	Races Run	1st	2nd	3rd	Unpl	Per cent	£1 Level Stake
2-y-o	8	21	1	1	4	15	4.8	- 16.00
3-y-o	18	98	11	13	7	67	11.2	+ 47.50
4-y-o+	11	60	9	11	12	28	15.0	+ 10.75
Totals	37	179	21	25	23	110	11.7	+ 42.25

BY MONTH

2-y-o	W-R	Per cent	£1 Level Stake	3-y-o	W-R	Per cent	£1 Level Stake
January	0-0	-	0.00	January	0-0	-	0.00
February	0-0	-	0.00	February	0-0	-	0.00
March	0-0	-	0.00	March	0-0	-	0.00
April	0-2	-	- 2.00	April	2-8	25.0	+ 37.00
May	0-2	-	- 2.00	May	2-20	10.0	+ 4.00
June	0-1	-	- 1.00	June	2-11	18.2	+ 5.50
July	1-6	16.7	- 1.00	July	2-20	10.0	+ 4.00
August	0-2	-	- 2.00	August	0-11	-	- 11.00
September	0-5	-	- 5.00	September	2-17	11.8	- 2.00
Oct/Nov	0-3	-	- 3.00	Oct/Nov	1-11	9.1	+ 10.00

4-y-o+	W-R	Per cent	£1 Level Stake	Totals	W-R	Per cent	£1 Level Stake
January	0-1	-	- 1.00	January	0-1	-	- 1.00
February	1-3	33.3	+ 14.00	February	1-3	33.3	+ 14.00
March	1-3	33.3	+ 0.50	March	1-3	33.3	+ 0.50
April	1-8	12.5	+ 5.00	April	3-18	16.7	+ 40.00
May	1-7	14.3	+ 1.50	May	3-29	10.3	+ 3.50
June	2-9	22.2	- 2.75	June	4-21	19.0	+ 1.75
July	1-8	12.5	- 0.50	July	4-34	11.8	+ 2.50
August	0-10	-	- 10.00	August	0-23	-	- 23.00
September	2-8	25.0	+ 7.00	September	4-30	13.3	0.00
Oct/Nov	0-3	-	- 3.00	Oct/Nov	1-17	5.9	+ 4.00

DISTANCE

2-y-o	W-R	Per cent	£1 Level Stake	3-y-o	W-R	Per cent	£1 Level Stake
5f-6f	1-11	9.1	- 6.00	5f-6f	2-8	25.0	+ 16.00
7f-8f	0-10	-	- 10.00	7f-8f	6-46	13.0	+ 56.00
9f-13f	0-0	-	0.00	9f-13f	3-40	7.5	- 20.50
14f+	0-0	-	0.00	14f+	0-4	-	- 4.00

4-y-o+	W-R	Per cent	£1 Level Stake	Totals	W-R	Per cent	£1 Level Stake
5f-6f	4-16	25.0	+ 17.00	5f-6f	7-35	20.0	+ 27.00
7f-8f	0-10	-	- 10.00	7f-8f	6-66	9.1	+ 36.00
9f-13f	3-24	12.5	+ 1.00	9f-13f	6-64	9.4	- 19.50
14f+	2-10	20.0	+ 2.75	14f+	2-14	14.3	- 1.25

TYPE OF RACE

Non-Handicaps	W-R	Per cent	£1 Level Stake	Handicaps	W-R	Per cent	£1 Level Stake
2-y-o	1-21	4.8	- 16.00	2-y-o	0-0	-	0.00
3-y-o	4-50	8.0	+ 11.50	3-y-o	7-48	14.6	+ 36.00
4-y-o+	0-4	-	- 4.00	4-y-o+	9-56	16.1	+ 14.75
Selling	0-0	-	0.00	Selling	0-0	-	0.00
Apprentice	0-0	-	0.00	Apprentice	0-0	-	0.00
Amat/Ladies	0-0	-	0.00	Amat/Ladies	0-0	-	0.00
Totals	5-75	6.7	- 8.50	Totals	16-104	15.4	+ 50.75

COURSE GRADE

	W-R	Per cent	£1 Level Stake
Group 1	3-82	3.7	- 39.00
Group 2	5-42	11.9	+ 16.50
Group 3	10-43	23.3	+ 43.25
Group 4	3-12	25.0	+ 21.50

FIRST TIME OUT

	W-R	Per cent	£1 Level Stake
2-y-o	0-8	-	- 8.00
3-y-o	1-18	5.6	- 7.00
4-y-o+	2-11	18.2	+ 19.00
Totals	3-37	8.1	+ 4.00

JOCKEYS RIDING

	W-R	Per cent	£1 Level Stake		W-R	Per cent	£1 Level Stake
Paul Eddery	6-40	15.0	+ 20.00	M Birch	2-19	10.5	- 2.50
F Norton	3-17	17.6	+ 17.00	P Robinson	1-2	50.0	+ 3.00
N Adams	3-27	11.1	+ 27.50	G Duffield	1-6	16.7	+ 7.00
G Hind	2-11	18.2	- 0.75	W Ryan	1-6	16.7	+ 4.00
W R Swinburn	2-17	11.8	+ 1.00				

W Newnes	0-5	A Tucker	0-1	J Reid	0-1
S Whitworth	0-4	B Rouse	0-1	L Piggott	0-1
A McGlone	0-3	B Russell	0-1	M Hills	0-1
J Tate	0-3	C Rutter	0-1	M Roberts	0-1
Pat Eddery	0-3	D Harrison	0-1	R Cochrane	0-1
J Quinn	0-2	J Fanning	0-1	W Carson	0-1
A Clark	0-1	J Fortune	0-1		

COURSE RECORD

	Total W-R	Non-Handicaps 2-y-o	3-y-o+	Handicaps 2-y-o	3-y-o+	Per cent	£1 Level Stake
Beverley	4-9	0-2	0-0	0-0	4-7	44.4	+ 36.50
Yarmouth	3-4	0-0	0-1	0-0	3-3	75.0	+ 16.00
Redcar	2-6	0-0	0-0	0-0	2-6	33.3	+ 7.50
Lingfield (AW)	2-7	0-0	0-1	0-0	2-6	28.6	+ 13.50
Catterick	1-2	0-0	1-1	0-0	0-1	50.0	+ 11.00
Bath	1-3	0-0	0-1	0-0	1-2	33.3	- 0.25
Thirsk	1-6	0-0	0-2	0-0	1-4	16.7	+ 1.50
Leicester	1-7	0-0	0-4	0-0	1-3	14.3	+ 6.00
Ripon	1-9	0-0	1-4	0-0	0-5	11.1	- 5.50
Nottingham	1-10	1-4	0-2	0-0	0-4	10.0	- 5.00
Salisbury	1-10	0-2	1-3	0-0	0-5	10.0	+ 24.00
Doncaster	1-13	0-3	0-4	0-0	1-6	7.7	+ 8.00
Kempton	1-14	0-1	0-5	0-0	1-8	7.1	- 3.00
Newmarket	1-14	0-3	1-3	0-0	0-8	7.1	- 3.00

Sandown	0-11	Pontefract	0-6	Folkestone	0-2
Haydock	0-10	Brighton	0-3	Chepstow	0-1
York	0-9	Goodwood	0-3	Warwick	0-1
Lingfield	0-8	Windsor	0-3		
Newbury	0-6	Ascot	0-2		

WINNING HORSES

	Age	Races Run	1st	2nd	3rd	Unpl	Win £
My Best Valentine	3	12	3	2	1	6	13,248
American Swinger	3	7	2	3	0	2	9,182
Provence	6	8	2	2	1	3	8,831
Supertop	5	9	2	1	2	4	8,206
Spender	4	3	2	0	1	0	6,137
Vallance	5	7	1	0	1	5	4,709
Ever So Lyrical	3	4	1	0	0	3	3,933
So Intrepid	3	6	1	0	1	4	3,688
George Dillingham	3	5	1	2	1	1	3,641
Top Cees	3	6	1	3	0	2	3,524
Smart Teacher	3	7	1	1	0	5	3,377
Face The Future	4	9	1	3	2	3	3,366
Absolutely Fayre	2	6	1	0	2	3	3,348
Sharp Prospect	3	7	1	0	0	6	3,202
Supreme Boy	4	9	1	2	1	5	2,977

WINNING OWNERS

	Races Won	Value £		Races Won	Value £
Mrs P W Harris	7	27,757	The Pendley Punters	1	3,933
The Valentines	3	13,248	Triple Crowners III	1	3,377
Triple Crowners I	2	9,182	The Bloodstock Brothers	1	3,348
Mrs G A Godfrey	2	8,206	The Pendley Associates	1	3,202
The Entrepreneurs	2	6,137	The Superlatives	1	2,977

Favourites	3-22	13.6%	- 5.75	Total winning prize-money			£81,366
Longest winning sequence			2	Average SP of winner			9.5/1
Longest losing sequence			35	Return on stakes invested			23.6%
1992 Form	13-154	8.4%	- 2.00	1990 Form	8-69	11.6%	+ 3.25
1991 Form	3-74	4.1%	- 50.50	1989 Form	2-37	5.4%	- 16.75

R HARRIS (Newmarket)

	No. of Horses	Races Run	1st	2nd	3rd	Unpl	Per cent	£1 Level Stake
2-y-o	2	4	0	0	0	4	-	- 4.00
3-y-o	2	13	0	0	3	10	-	- 13.00
4-y-o+	3	12	1	0	0	11	8.3	+ 3.00
Totals	7	29	1	0	3	25	3.4	- 14.00

Jan	Feb	Mar	Apr	May	Jun	Jul	Aug	Sep	Oct/Nov
0-0	0-2	0-2	0-3	0-4	0-5	1-6	0-4	0-2	0-1

Winning Jockey	W-R	£1 Level Stake	Winning Course	W-R	£1 Level Stake
J Quinn	1-5	+ 10.00	Folkestone	1-3	+ 12.00

Winning Horse	Age	Races Run	1st	2nd	3rd	Unpl	Win £
Nigel's Lucky Girl	5	10	1	0	0	9	3,106

Favourites	0-0		Total winning prize-money	£3,106

A HARRISON (Middleham, North Yorks)

	No. of Horses	Races Run	1st	2nd	3rd	Unpl	Per cent	£1 Level Stake
2-y-o	2	15	0	0	2	13	-	- 15.00
3-y-o	2	8	0	0	0	8	-	- 8.00
4-y-o+	5	24	1	1	1	21	4.2	- 15.00
Totals	9	47	1	1	3	42	2.1	- 38.00

Jan	Feb	Mar	Apr	May	Jun	Jul	Aug	Sep	Oct/Nov
0-1	0-0	0-1	0-1	0-2	0-5	0-12	0-8	1-7	0-10

Winning Jockey	W-R	£1 Level Stake	Winning Course	W-R	£1 Level Stake
J Lowe	1-5	+ 4.00	Edinburgh	1-11	- 2.00

Winning Horse	Age	Races Run	1st	2nd	3rd	Unpl	Win £
Thisonesforalice	5	7	1	0	0	6	2,243

Favourites	0-0			Total winning prize-money			£2,243

1992 Form	3-68	4.4%	- 55.75	1990 Form	7-50	14.0%	- 12.12
1991 Form	4-103	3.9%	- 78.50				

G HARWOOD (Pulborough, West Sussex)

	No. of Horses	Races Run	1st	2nd	3rd	Unpl	Per cent	£1 Level Stake
2-y-o	15	33	2	3	6	22	6.1	- 24.17
3-y-o	26	115	13	14	16	72	11.3	- 13.59
4-y-o+	7	66	6	12	9	39	9.1	- 36.25
Totals	48	214	21	29	31	133	9.8	- 74.01

BY MONTH

2-y-o	W-R	Per cent	£1 Level Stake	3-y-o	W-R	Per cent	£1 Level Stake
January	0-0	-	0.00	January	0-1	-	- 1.00
February	0-0	-	0.00	February	0-1	-	- 1.00
March	0-0	-	0.00	March	1-1	100.0	+ 2.50
April	0-0	-	0.00	April	1-13	7.7	- 4.00
May	0-0	-	0.00	May	3-26	11.5	- 4.57
June	0-1	-	- 1.00	June	1-22	4.5	- 5.00
July	1-4	25.0	+ 0.50	July	1-17	5.9	- 13.50
August	1-6	16.7	- 1.67	August	6-23	26.1	+ 23.98
September	0-14	-	- 14.00	September	0-5	-	- 5.00
Oct/Nov	0-8	-	- 8.00	Oct/Nov	0-6	-	- 6.00

4-y-o+	W-R	Per cent	£1 Level Stake	Totals	W-R	Per cent	£1 Level Stake
January	1-4	25.0	- 0.50	January	1-5	20.0	- 1.50
February	1-3	33.3	+ 4.00	February	1-4	25.0	+ 3.00
March	0-4	-	- 4.00	March	1-5	20.0	- 1.50
April	0-7	-	- 7.00	April	1-20	5.0	- 11.00
May	0-12	-	- 12.00	May	3-38	7.9	- 16.57
June	0-7	-	- 7.00	June	1-30	3.3	- 13.00
July	2-10	20.0	- 2.25	July	4-31	12.9	- 15.25
August	2-7	28.6	+ 4.50	August	9-36	25.0	+ 26.81
September	0-4	-	- 4.00	September	0-23	-	- 23.00
Oct/Nov	0-8	-	- 8.00	Oct/Nov	0-22	-	- 22.00

DISTANCE

2-y-o	W-R	Per cent	£1 Level Stake	3-y-o	W-R	Per cent	£1 Level Stake
5f-6f	1-8	12.5	- 3.67	5f-6f	0-5	-	- 5.00
7f-8f	1-25	4.0	- 20.50	7f-8f	8-44	18.2	+ 41.55
9f-13f	0-0	-	0.00	9f-13f	4-58	6.9	- 43.50
14f+	0-0	-	0.00	14f+	1-8	12.5	- 6.64

4-y-o+	W-R	Per cent	£1 Level Stake	Totals	W-R	Per cent	£1 Level Stake
5f-6f	0-2	-	- 2.00	5f-6f	1-15	6.7	- 10.67
7f-8f	3-32	9.4	- 18.25	7f-8f	12-101	11.9	+ 2.80
9f-13f	3-31	9.7	- 15.00	9f-13f	7-89	7.9	- 58.50
14f+	0-1	-	- 1.00	14f+	1-9	11.1	- 7.64

TYPE OF RACE

Non-Handicaps	W-R	Per cent	£1 Level Stake	Handicaps	W-R	Per cent	£1 Level Stake
2-y-o	1-28	3.6	- 23.67	2-y-o	0-4	-	- 4.00
3-y-o	9-62	14.5	- 7.46	3-y-o	1-45	2.2	- 36.00
4-y-o+	2-17	11.8	- 9.25	4-y-o+	2-38	5.3	- 27.50
Selling	1-2	50.0	+ 2.50	Selling	1-1	100.0	+ 33.00
Apprentice	1-1	100.0	+ 1.20	Apprentice	1-3	33.3	+ 3.00
Amat/Ladies	1-1	100.0	+ 0.67	Amat/Ladies	1-12	8.3	- 6.50
Totals	15-111	13.5	- 36.01	Totals	6-103	5.8	- 38.00

COURSE GRADE

	W-R	Per cent	£1 Level Stake
Group 1	9-113	8.0	- 34.33
Group 2	3-44	6.8	- 31.47
Group 3	5-33	15.2	- 0.57
Group 4	4-24	16.7	- 7.64

FIRST TIME OUT

	W-R	Per cent	£1 Level Stake
2-y-o	0-15	-	- 15.00
3-y-o	3-25	12.0	- 9.00
4-y-o+	1-7	14.3	- 3.50
Totals	4-47	8.5	- 27.50

JOCKEYS RIDING

	W-R	Per cent	£1 Level Stake		W-R	Per cent	£1 Level Stake
R Hills	4-12	33.3	+ 16.58	K Darley	1-6	16.7	- 4.64
Pat Eddery	4-18	22.2	+ 3.83	J Reid	1-9	11.1	- 5.50
P Houghton	2-5	40.0	+ 3.20	W R Swinburn	1-9	11.1	- 4.50
Miss A Harwood	2-11	18.2	- 3.83	M Hills	1-16	6.3	- 9.00
Gaye Harwood	2-12	16.7	+ 37.00	W Carson	1-19	5.3	- 15.75
W Woods	1-5	20.0	- 1.50	M Perrett	1-28	3.6	- 25.90

T Quinn	0-14	G Duffield	0-4	Mr J Durkan	0-2
Paul Eddery	0-7	L Piggott	0-3	E Johnson	0-1
A Clark	0-6	W Ryan	0-3	K Fallon	0-1
M Roberts	0-6	A McGlone	0-2	L Dettori	0-1
R Cochrane	0-5	A Munro	0-2	N Day	0-1
C Rutter	0-4	B Raymond	0-2		

COURSE RECORD

	Total W-R	Non-Handicaps 2-y-o	3-y-o+	Handicaps 2-y-o	3-y-o+	Per cent	£1 Level Stake
Newmarket	3-37	0-6	1-11	0-2	2-18	8.1	+ 8.75
Bath	2-8	0-2	2-3	0-0	0-3	25.0	+ 13.33
Lingfield	2-11	1-2	0-4	0-0	1-5	18.2	- 0.67
Lingfield (AW)	2-13	0-0	0-3	0-0	2-10	15.4	- 2.50
Thirsk	1-1	0-0	1-1	0-0	0-0	100.0	+ 1.20
Southwell (Turf)	1-1	1-1	0-0	0-0	0-0	100.0	+ 3.50
York	1-2	0-0	1-2	0-0	0-0	50.0	+ 1.25
Chepstow	1-5	0-1	1-2	0-0	0-2	20.0	- 2.90
Leicester	1-5	0-1	1-4	0-0	0-0	20.0	- 1.50
Pontefract	1-5	0-1	0-1	0-0	1-3	20.0	+ 0.50
Doncaster	1-6	0-1	1-3	0-0	0-2	16.7	- 2.50
Epsom	1-6	0-0	1-4	0-0	0-2	16.7	- 1.00
Folkestone	1-6	0-0	1-2	0-0	0-4	16.7	- 4.64
Newbury	1-8	0-0	1-4	0-0	0-4	12.5	- 3.50
Kempton	1-12	0-3	1-5	0-0	0-4	8.3	+ 3.00
Sandown	1-14	0-0	1-6	0-0	0-8	7.1	- 12.33

Goodwood	0-15	Beverley	0-3	Ripon	0-2
Salisbury	0-15	Yarmouth	0-3	Windsor	0-2
Brighton	0-13	Newcastle	0-2	Haydock	0-1
Ascot	0-10	Nottingham	0-2		
Warwick	0-4	Redcar	0-2		

WINNING HORSES

	Age	Races Run	1st	2nd	3rd	Unpl	Win £
So Factual	3	3	1	0	0	2	18,035
Thourios	4	8	2	2	0	4	14,068
Mulciber	5	10	3	2	2	3	11,130
Rue Rembrandt	3	6	2	2	0	2	6,773
River Boyne	3	4	2	1	0	1	6,632
Blowing	3	8	1	0	0	7	4,016
Glen Echo	3	5	1	0	0	4	3,641
Captain's Guest	3	5	1	2	0	2	3,524
Robleu	3	4	1	0	1	2	3,407
Bag Of Tricks	3	3	1	1	0	1	3,054
Lucky Noire	5	11	1	0	0	10	2,954
Marastani	3	7	1	2	0	4	2,880
Ferryman	2	4	1	0	0	3	2,624
Clever Minstrel	3	6	1	0	2	3	2,534
Elburg	3	3	1	0	1	1	2,243
Love Of The North	2	2	1	0	0	1	2,070

WINNING OWNERS

	Races Won	Value £		Races Won	Value £
K Abdulla	7	37,116	K J Buchanan	1	3,524
Athos Christodoulou	2	14,068	Mrs Carol Harrison	1	2,954
Mrs Penny Treadwell	3	11,130	Cecil J Hedigan	1	2,880
G Harwood	2	7,423	Sheikh Mohammed	1	2,243
Seymour Cohn	2	6,175	J H Richmond-Watson	1	2,070

Harwood G

Favourites	11-30	36.7%	+ 6.41	Total winning prize-money			£89,582
Longest winning sequence			3	Average SP of winner			5.7/1
Longest losing sequence			45	Return on stakes invested			-34.6%
1992 Form	29-236	12.3%	- 81.96	1990 Form	69-396	17.4%	- 46.87
1991 Form	55-326	16.9%	- 47.76	1989 Form	109-410	26.6%	+ 26.79

P C HASLAM (Middleham, North Yorks)

	No. of Horses	Races Run	1st	2nd	3rd	Unpl	Per cent	£1 Level Stake
2-y-o	18	81	7	5	12	57	8.6	- 21.18
3-y-o	12	58	1	7	1	49	1.7	- 37.00
4-y-o+	11	80	9	3	8	60	11.3	+ 2.00
Totals	41	219	17	15	21	166	7.8	- 56.18

BY MONTH

2-y-o	W-R	Per cent	£1 Level Stake	3-y-o	W-R	Per cent	£1 Level Stake
January	0-0	-	0.00	January	0-1	-	- 1.00
February	0-0	-	0.00	February	0-2	-	- 2.00
March	0-0	-	0.00	March	0-1	-	- 1.00
April	1-11	9.1	+ 6.00	April	1-3	33.3	+ 18.00
May	1-6	16.7	- 4.43	May	0-8	-	- 8.00
June	0-5	-	- 5.00	June	0-7	-	- 7.00
July	2-12	16.7	+ 10.50	July	0-14	-	- 14.00
August	1-15	6.7	- 5.50	August	0-14	-	- 14.00
September	2-18	11.1	- 8.75	September	0-7	-	- 7.00
Oct/Nov	0-14	-	- 14.00	Oct/Nov	0-1	-	- 1.00

4-y-o+	W-R	Per cent	£1 Level Stake	Totals	W-R	Per cent	£1 Level Stake
January	0-2	-	- 2.00	January	0-3	-	- 3.00
February	0-1	-	- 1.00	February	0-3	-	- 3.00
March	0-0	-	0.00	March	0-1	-	- 1.00
April	0-13	-	- 13.00	April	2-27	7.4	+ 11.00
May	0-10	-	- 10.00	May	1-24	4.2	- 22.43
June	0-11	-	- 11.00	June	0-23	-	- 23.00
July	5-16	31.3	+ 19.75	July	7-42	16.7	+ 16.25
August	4-18	22.2	+ 28.25	August	5-47	10.6	+ 8.75
September	0-6	-	- 6.00	September	2-31	6.5	- 21.75
Oct/Nov	0-3	-	- 3.00	Oct/Nov	0-18	-	- 18.00

DISTANCE

2-y-o	W-R	Per cent	£1 Level Stake	3-y-o	W-R	Per cent	£1 Level Stake
5f-6f	5-50	10.0	+ 0.57	5f-6f	0-14	-	- 14.00
7f-8f	2-26	7.7	- 16.75	7f-8f	0-24	-	- 24.00
9f-13f	0-5	-	- 5.00	9f-13f	1-18	5.6	+ 3.00
14f+	0-0	-	0.00	14f+	0-2	-	- 2.00

4-y-o+	W-R	Per cent	£1 Level Stake	Totals	W-R	Per cent	£1 Level Stake
5f-6f	2-25	8.0	+ 14.50	5f-6f	7-89	7.9	+ 1.07
7f-8f	2-22	9.1	- 10.75	7f-8f	4-72	5.6	- 51.50
9f-13f	3-23	13.0	- 2.50	9f-13f	4-46	8.7	- 4.50
14f+	2-10	20.0	+ 0.75	14f+	2-12	16.7	- 1.25

TYPE OF RACE

Non-Handicaps	W-R	Per cent	£1 Level Stake	Handicaps	W-R	Per cent	£1 Level Stake
2-y-o	6-44	13.6	+ 12.57	2-y-o	1-14	7.1	- 10.75
3-y-o	0-21	-	- 21.00	3-y-o	0-20	-	- 20.00
4-y-o+	0-7	-	- 7.00	4-y-o+	4-49	8.2	- 20.25
Selling	2-23	8.7	+ 1.00	Selling	2-25	8.0	- 14.25
Apprentice	0-0	-	0.00	Apprentice	2-14	14.3	+ 25.50
Amat/Ladies	0-0	-	0.00	Amat/Ladies	0-2	-	- 2.00
Totals	8-95	8.4	- 14.43	Totals	9-124	7.3	- 41.75

COURSE GRADE

	W-R	Per cent	£1 Level Stake
Group 1	2-43	4.7	- 5.75
Group 2	5-51	9.8	+ 5.57
Group 3	8-76	10.5	- 28.00
Group 4	2-49	4.1	- 28.00

FIRST TIME OUT

	W-R	Per cent	£1 Level Stake
2-y-o	2-16	12.5	+ 18.00
3-y-o	1-11	9.1	+ 10.00
4-y-o+	0-11	-	- 11.00
Totals	3-38	7.9	+ 17.00

JOCKEYS RIDING

	W-R	Per cent	£1 Level Stake		W-R	Per cent	£1 Level Stake
J Weaver	4-20	20.0	+ 1.25	C N Adamson	2-19	10.5	+ 20.50
K Darley	3-13	23.1	- 5.00	E Johnson	1-5	20.0	+ 16.00
D McKeown	3-17	17.6	+ 18.57	R Cochrane	1-16	6.3	- 8.50
G Duffield	2-4	50.0	+ 11.00	Dale Gibson	1-64	1.6	- 49.00

Haslam P C

J Gracey	0-9	A Clark	0-1	Mrs L Pearce	0-1
N Carlisle	0-8	A McGlone	0-1	N Day	0-1
C Hodgson	0-5	D Biggs	0-1	N Kennedy	0-1
J Marshall	0-4	D Harrison	0-1	S Davies	0-1
L Piggott	0-4	D Holland	0-1	S Maloney	0-1
W Ryan	0-4	D McCabe	0-1	T Quinn	0-1
T Williams	0-3	G Forster	0-1	W R Swinburn	0-1
M Roberts	0-2	J Carroll	0-1	W Woods	0-1
Nicola Howarth	0-2	Miss A Armitage	0-1		
S Webster	0-2	Mrs J Crossley	0-1		

COURSE RECORD

	Total W-R	Non-Handicaps 2-y-o	Non-Handicaps 3-y-o+	Handicaps 2-y-o	Handicaps 3-y-o+	Per cent	£1 Level Stake
Hamilton	5-34	1-9	1-6	0-1	3-18	14.7	- 8.75
Ripon	3-22	2-7	1-4	0-1	0-10	13.6	+ 25.50
Ayr	1-3	0-0	0-2	0-0	1-1	33.3	+ 0.25
Edinburgh	1-10	1-4	0-0	0-0	0-6	10.0	- 4.00
Beverley	1-11	1-4	0-1	0-1	0-5	9.1	+ 6.00
Redcar	1-11	0-6	0-1	0-2	1-2	9.1	- 3.50
Yarmouth	1-11	0-1	0-2	1-2	0-6	9.1	- 7.75
Catterick	1-12	0-2	0-3	0-1	1-6	8.3	+ 3.00
Nottingham	1-12	0-3	0-0	0-3	1-6	8.3	- 9.50
Thirsk	1-15	1-4	0-2	0-2	0-7	6.7	- 13.43
Newmarket	1-17	0-5	0-2	0-2	1-8	5.9	+ 17.00

Southwell (AW)	0-11	Southwell (Turf)	0-4	Folkestone	0-1
Carlisle	0-10	Kempton	0-3	Goodwood	0-1
York	0-7	Brighton	0-2	Haydock	0-1
Doncaster	0-6	Leicester	0-2	Warwick	0-1
Pontefract	0-5	Ascot	0-1	Windsor	0-1
Newcastle	0-4	Chester	0-1		

WINNING HORSES

	Age	Races Run	1st	2nd	3rd	Unpl	Win £
Talented Ting	4	11	3	0	4	4	9,142
Hannah's Music	2	4	2	0	0	2	7,764
Dance Of The Swans	2	2	2	0	0	0	6,057
Amoret	2	2	1	0	0	1	4,981
Carrolls Marc	5	9	2	0	0	7	4,968
General John	4	8	1	0	0	7	4,893
Velvet Heart	3	7	1	1	0	5	2,637
Reel Of Tulloch	4	9	1	2	2	4	2,623
Pageboy	4	13	1	1	0	11	1,970
Claret Bumble	2	6	1	1	1	3	1,953
Shuttlecock	2	10	1	2	1	6	1,606
Bold Melody	4	9	1	0	0	8	1,051

WINNING OWNERS

	Races Won	Value £		Races Won	Value £
Martin Wickens	3	9,142	P I P Electrics Ltd	2	4,968
Lord Scarsdale	3	8,469	Gordon Milne	1	2,637
S A B Dinsmore	3	8,010	Darren Croft	1	2,623
Pat Fitzgerald	2	7,764	W J Whitaker	1	1,051
W J Whitaker	1	4,981			

Favourites	5-16	31.3%	- 3.18	Total winning prize-money			£49,644
Longest winning sequence			2	Average SP of winner			8.6/1
Longest losing sequence			44	Return on stakes invested			-25.4%
1992 Form	29-227	12.8%	- 90.30	1991 Form	14-145	9.7%	- 56.76

M J HAYNES (Epsom, Surrey)

	No. of Horses	Races Run	1st	2nd	3rd	Unpl	Per cent	£1 Level Stake
2-y-o	5	24	1	3	4	16	4.2	- 18.00
3-y-o	2	6	0	0	0	6	-	- 6.00
4-y-o+	6	36	3	4	3	26	8.3	+ 3.50
Totals	13	66	4	7	7	48	6.1	- 20.50

Jan	Feb	Mar	Apr	May	Jun	Jul	Aug	Sep	Oct/Nov
0-0	0-1	0-0	1-12	1-11	0-12	0-7	1-8	1-7	0-8

Winning Jockeys	W-R	£1 Level Stake			W-R	£1 Level Stake
R Cochrane	2-13	+ 0.50	D Toole		1-8	+ 18.00
B Raymond	1-6	0.00				

Winning Courses						
Kempton	3-5	+ 34.50	Epsom		1-4	+ 2.00

Winning Horses	Age	Races Run	1st	2nd	3rd	Unpl	Win £
Bold Lez	6	11	2	0	2	7	8,713
Popsi's Legacy	6	6	1	1	0	4	3,933
Kerrie-Jo	2	11	1	2	3	5	2,820

Favourites	0-1			Total winning prize-money			£15,466
1992 Form	4-101	4.0%	- 51.00	1990 Form	9-134	6.7%	- 52.00
1991 Form	9-122	7.4%	+ 6.83	1989 Form	6-111	5.4%	- 64.50

M J B HEATON-ELLIS (Wroughton, Wilts)

	No. of Horses	Races Run	1st	2nd	3rd	Unpl	Per cent	£1 Level Stake
2-y-o	14	43	6	4	2	31	14.0	+ 22.90
3-y-o	16	102	4	10	8	80	3.9	- 60.50
4-y-o+	11	71	9	6	5	51	12.7	+ 19.50
Totals	41	216	19	20	15	162	8.8	- 18.10

BY MONTH

2-y-o	W-R	Per cent	£1 Level Stake	3-y-o	W-R	Per cent	£1 Level Stake
January	0-0	-	0.00	January	0-1	-	- 1.00
February	0-0	-	0.00	February	0-2	-	- 2.00
March	0-0	-	0.00	March	1-4	25.0	+ 7.00
April	0-3	-	- 3.00	April	0-15	-	- 15.00
May	0-3	-	- 3.00	May	0-15	-	- 15.00
June	1-6	16.7	+ 1.00	June	0-15	-	- 15.00
July	3-8	37.5	+ 32.50	July	1-17	5.9	- 2.00
August	0-6	-	- 6.00	August	1-16	6.3	- 12.50
September	1-6	16.7	+ 3.00	September	0-8	-	- 8.00
Oct/Nov	1-11	9.1	- 1.60	Oct/Nov	1-9	11.1	+ 3.00

4-y-o+	W-R	Per cent	£1 Level Stake	Totals	W-R	Per cent	£1 Level Stake
January	1-2	50.0	+ 4.50	January	1-3	33.3	+ 3.50
February	0-0	-	0.00	February	0-2	-	- 2.00
March	0-1	-	- 1.00	March	1-5	20.0	+ 6.00
April	3-7	42.9	+ 22.50	April	3-25	12.0	+ 4.50
May	3-9	33.3	+ 19.50	May	3-27	11.1	+ 1.50
June	0-12	-	- 12.00	June	1-33	3.0	- 26.00
July	0-9	-	- 9.00	July	4-34	11.8	+ 21.50
August	1-8	12.5	- 3.00	August	2-30	6.7	- 21.50
September	0-8	-	- 8.00	September	1-22	4.5	- 13.00
Oct/Nov	1-15	6.7	+ 6.00	Oct/Nov	3-35	8.6	+ 7.40

DISTANCE

2-y-o	W-R	Per cent	£1 Level Stake	3-y-o	W-R	Per cent	£1 Level Stake
5f-6f	5-33	15.2	+ 23.50	5f-6f	0-27	-	- 27.00
7f-8f	1-10	10.0	- 0.60	7f-8f	3-54	5.6	- 16.00
9f-13f	0-0	-	0.00	9f-13f	1-20	5.0	- 16.50
14f+	0-0	-	0.00	14f+	0-1	-	- 1.00

4-y-o+	W-R	Per cent	£1 Level Stake	Totals	W-R	Per cent	£1 Level Stake
5f-6f	5-32	15.6	+ 28.50	5f-6f	10-92	10.9	+ 25.00
7f-8f	0-7	-	- 7.00	7f-8f	4-71	5.6	- 23.60
9f-13f	4-29	13.8	+ 1.00	9f-13f	5-49	10.2	- 15.50
14f+	0-3	-	- 3.00	14f+	0-4	-	- 4.00

Heaton-Ellis M J B

TYPE OF RACE

Non-Handicaps	W-R	Per cent	£1 Level Stake	Handicaps	W-R	Per cent	£1 Level Stake
2-y-o	3-37	8.1	- 10.60	2-y-o	3-5	60.0	+ 34.50
3-y-o	2-32	6.3	- 6.00	3-y-o	1-51	2.0	- 39.00
4-y-o+	0-6	-	- 6.00	4-y-o+	7-56	12.5	+ 24.00
Selling	0-8	-	- 8.00	Selling	0-7	-	- 7.00
Apprentice	0-0	-	0.00	Apprentice	3-13	23.1	+ 1.00
Amat/Ladies	0-0	-	0.00	Amat/Ladies	0-1	-	- 1.00
Totals	5-83	6.0	- 30.60	Totals	14-133	10.5	+ 12.50

COURSE GRADE

	W-R	Per cent	£1 Level Stake
Group 1	9-85	10.6	+ 28.50
Group 2	2-42	4.8	- 29.50
Group 3	6-55	10.9	- 2.60
Group 4	2-34	5.9	- 14.50

FIRST TIME OUT

	W-R	Per cent	£1 Level Stake
2-y-o	2-13	15.4	+ 3.40
3-y-o	2-14	14.3	+ 12.00
4-y-o+	1-11	9.1	- 4.50
Totals	5-38	13.2	+ 10.90

JOCKEYS RIDING

	W-R	Per cent	£1 Level Stake		W-R	Per cent	£1 Level Stake
D McCabe	3-14	21.4	+ 17.50	T Quinn	1-10	10.0	+ 1.00
D Holland	3-24	12.5	+ 8.00	R Perham	1-10	10.0	+ 11.00
M Roberts	2-10	20.0	+ 10.00	A Munro	1-10	10.0	- 1.00
J Reid	2-11	18.2	+ 5.00	J Carroll	1-10	10.0	- 0.60
P McCabe	1-2	50.0	+ 1.50	W Ryan	1-14	7.1	+ 7.00
Ruth Coulter	1-5	20.0	0.00	D Wright	1-19	5.3	- 12.50
W R Swinburn	1-6	16.7	+ 6.00				

Paul Eddery	0-7	P Robinson	0-3	J Lowe	0-1
W Newnes	0-6	S Davies	0-3	J O'Dwyer	0-1
W Woods	0-6	G Carter	0-2	J Tate	0-1
B Raymond	0-5	Pat Eddery	0-2	J Williams	0-1
L Dettori	0-5	A Clark	0-1	K Darley	0-1
S Raymont	0-5	A McGlone	0-1	L Piggott	0-1
D Harrison	0-3	A Whelan	0-1	Miss F Haynes	0-1
G Duffield	0-3	D Gibbs	0-1	N Adams	0-1
M Hills	0-3	Dale Gibson	0-1	R Cochrane	0-1
M J Kinane	0-3	E Johnson	0-1		

COURSE RECORD

	Total W-R	Non-Handicaps 2-y-o	3-y-o+	Handicaps 2-y-o	3-y-o+	Per cent	£1 Level Stake
Doncaster	2-14	0-3	1-4	0-0	1-7	14.3	+ 18.00
Windsor	2-21	1-2	0-5	0-0	1-14	9.5	- 6.00
Haydock	1-1	0-0	0-0	0-0	1-1	100.0	+ 8.00
Redcar	1-4	0-2	0-1	1-1	0-0	25.0	+ 5.00

199

Chepstow	1-5	0-2	0-0	0-0	1-3	20.0	+	7.00
Epsom	1-5	1-1	0-1	0-0	0-3	20.0	+	2.00
Brighton	1-7	0-1	0-0	0-1	1-5	14.3	-	3.50
Nottingham	1-7	1-1	0-1	0-0	0-5	14.3	+	2.40
York	1-7	0-2	0-0	1-1	0-4	14.3	+	14.00
Lingfield (AW)	1-7	0-0	0-3	0-0	1-4	14.3	-	0.50
Ascot	1-8	0-2	0-0	0-0	1-6	12.5	-	2.50
Bath	1-8	0-0	0-4	0-0	1-4	12.5	-	1.50
Sandown	1-8	0-1	0-0	0-0	1-7	12.5	+	3.00
Kempton	1-11	0-1	0-2	0-0	1-8	9.1	+	2.00
Leicester	1-11	0-2	0-2	1-1	0-6	9.1	-	1.50
Newmarket	1-12	0-0	1-3	0-0	0-9	8.3	+	3.00
Warwick	1-12	0-2	0-3	0-0	1-7	8.3	+	1.00

Salisbury	0-16	Catterick	0-4	Pontefract	0-1
Lingfield	0-14	Southwell (Turf)	0-4	Southwell (AW)	0-1
Newbury	0-9	Newcastle	0-3	Yarmouth	0-1
Goodwood	0-7	Beverley	0-1		
Folkestone	0-6	Chester	0-1		

WINNING HORSES

	Age	Races Run	1st	2nd	3rd	Unpl	Win £
Lord High Admiral	5	8	3	0	0	5	14,688
Roxanian	2	8	3	1	0	4	11,588
Broughton's Tango	4	7	2	1	2	2	7,958
Golden Memories	2	1	1	0	0	0	5,673
Nightitude	2	6	1	1	1	3	5,254
Massiba	4	8	1	1	0	6	5,132
Elaine Tully	5	7	1	1	0	5	3,260
Santana Lady	4	11	1	2	2	6	3,132
Water Gypsy	3	3	1	0	0	2	3,080
Thunder River	3	5	1	0	1	3	2,880
Speedy Classic	4	3	1	0	1	1	2,783
Marjorie's Memory	2	7	1	1	0	5	2,406
Waterlord	3	13	1	3	1	8	2,286
Queens Contractor	3	8	1	0	3	4	2,070

WINNING OWNERS

	Races Won	Value £		Races Won	Value £
F J Sainsbury	5	19,603	John B Sunley	1	3,080
E J G Young	3	14,688	Tam Wong	1	2,783
Mrs Elaine Mitchell	4	14,468	Mrs Francoise Jansen	1	2,286
S P Lansdown	2	7,958	P G Lowe	1	2,070
Miss Gloria Abbey	1	5,254			

Favourites	0-14		Total winning prize-money	£72,189
Longest winning sequence		2	Average SP of winner	9.4/1
Longest losing sequence		31	Return on stakes invested	-8.4%

| 1992 Form | 8-138 | 5.8% | - 71.00 | 1991 Form | 0-6 |

P R HEDGER (Chichester, West Sussex)

	No. of Horses	Races Run	1st	2nd	3rd	Unpl	Per cent	£1 Level Stake
2-y-o	2	5	0	0	1	4	-	- 5.00
3-y-o	2	7	0	0	0	7	-	- 7.00
4-y-o+	5	25	2	2	3	18	8.0	- 15.75
Totals	9	37	2	2	4	29	5.4	- 27.75

Jan	Feb	Mar	Apr	May	Jun	Jul	Aug	Sep	Oct/Nov
0-3	1-2	0-1	0-4	0-4	1-6	0-3	0-4	0-6	0-4

Winning Jockeys	W-R	£1 Level Stake			W-R	£1 Level Stake
A Tucker	1-5	+ 1.00	M Perrett		1-9	- 5.75

Winning Courses	W-R	£1 Level Stake			W-R	£1 Level Stake
Newbury	1-4	- 0.75	Lingfield (AW)		1-6	0.00

Winning Horses	Age	Races Run	1st	2nd	3rd	Unpl	Win £
Wave Hill	4	12	1	0	2	9	3,641
Lyph	7	7	1	2	1	3	2,557

Favourites	1-4	25.0%	- 0.75	Total winning prize-money	£6,197

1992 Form 0-17

N J HENDERSON (Newbury, Berks)

	No. of Horses	Races Run	1st	2nd	3rd	Unpl	Per cent	£1 Level Stake
2-y-o	0	0	0	0	0	0	-	0.00
3-y-o	0	0	0	0	0	0	-	0.00
4-y-o+	2	3	1	0	0	2	33.3	+ 6.00
Totals	2	3	1	0	0	2	33.3	+ 6.00

Jan	Feb	Mar	Apr	May	Jun	Jul	Aug	Sep	Oct/Nov
0-0	0-0	0-0	1-1	0-1	0-0	0-0	0-0	0-0	0-1

Winning Jockey	W-R	£1 Level Stake	Winning Course	W-R	£1 Level Stake
W Carson	1-2	+ 7.00	Newmarket	1-1	+ 8.00

Winning Horse	Age	Races Run	1st	2nd	3rd	Unpl	Win £
Thinking Twice	4	2	1	0	0	1	5,299

Favourites	0-0		Total winning prize-money	£5,299

1992 Form	0-3	1990 Form	0-0
1991 Form	0-0	1989 Form	0-3

W R HERN (Lambourn, Berks)

	No. of Horses	Races Run	1st	2nd	3rd	Unpl	Per cent	£1 Level Stake
2-y-o	15	22	0	1	2	19	-	- 22.00
3-y-o	26	115	7	21	18	69	6.1	- 74.96
4-y-o+	3	20	6	2	2	10	30.0	+ 4.80
Totals	44	157	13	24	22	98	8.3	- 92.16

BY MONTH

2-y-o	W-R	Per cent	£1 Level Stake	3-y-o	W-R	Per cent	£1 Level Stake
January	0-0	-	0.00	January	0-0	-	0.00
February	0-0	-	0.00	February	0-0	-	0.00
March	0-0	-	0.00	March	0-1	-	- 1.00
April	0-0	-	0.00	April	0-7	-	- 7.00
May	0-0	-	0.00	May	0-16	-	- 16.00
June	0-0	-	0.00	June	3-19	15.8	- 8.87
July	0-1	-	- 1.00	July	1-18	5.6	+ 10.00
August	0-1	-	- 1.00	August	1-20	5.0	- 5.00
September	0-4	-	- 4.00	September	1-18	5.6	- 16.09
Oct/Nov	0-16	-	- 16.00	Oct/Nov	1-16	6.3	- 11.00

4-y-o+	W-R	Per cent	£1 Level Stake	Totals	W-R	Per cent	£1 Level Stake
January	0-2	-	- 2.00	January	0-2	-	- 2.00
February	0-0	-	0.00	February	0-0	-	0.00
March	0-2	-	- 2.00	March	0-3	-	- 3.00
April	0-0	-	0.00	April	0-7	-	- 7.00
May	0-2	-	- 2.00	May	0-18	-	- 18.00
June	2-2	100.0	+ 8.25	June	5-21	23.8	- 0.62
July	3-5	60.0	+ 5.55	July	4-24	16.7	- 5.45
August	1-4	25.0	0.00	August	2-25	8.0	- 6.00
September	0-3	-	- 3.00	September	1-25	4.0	- 23.09
Oct/Nov	0-0	-	0.00	Oct/Nov	1-32	3.1	- 27.00

DISTANCE

2-y-o	W-R	Per cent	£1 Level Stake	3-y-o	W-R	Per cent	£1 Level Stake
5f-6f	0-6	-	- 6.00	5f-6f	1-5	20.0	+ 10.00
7f-8f	0-16	-	- 16.00	7f-8f	2-33	6.1	- 23.50
9f-13f	0-0	-	0.00	9f-13f	3-70	4.3	- 57.09
14f+	0-0	-	0.00	14f+	1-7	14.3	- 4.37

4-y-o+	W-R	Per cent	£1 Level Stake	Totals	W-R	Per cent	£1 Level Stake
5f-6f	0-0	-	0.00	5f-6f	1-11	9.1	+ 4.00
7f-8f	3-8	37.5	+ 9.00	7f-8f	5-57	8.8	- 30.50
9f-13f	3-12	25.0	- 4.20	9f-13f	6-82	7.3	- 61.29
14f+	0-0	-	0.00	14f+	1-7	14.3	- 4.37

TYPE OF RACE

Non-Handicaps	W-R	Per cent	£1 Level Stake	Handicaps	W-R	Per cent	£1 Level Stake
2-y-o	0-22	-	- 22.00	2-y-o	0-0	-	0.00
3-y-o	7-93	7.5	- 52.96	3-y-o	0-21	-	- 21.00
4-y-o+	2-5	40.0	- 0.95	4-y-o+	4-15	26.7	+ 5.75
Selling	0-0	-	0.00	Selling	0-0	-	0.00
Apprentice	0-0	-	0.00	Apprentice	0-1	-	- 1.00
Amat/Ladies	0-0	-	0.00	Amat/Ladies	0-0	-	0.00
Totals	9-120	7.5	- 75.91	Totals	4-37	10.8	- 16.25

COURSE GRADE

	W-R	Per cent	£1 Level Stake
Group 1	3-67	4.5	- 55.59
Group 2	3-37	8.1	- 15.62
Group 3	5-43	11.6	- 16.33
Group 4	2-10	20.0	- 4.62

FIRST TIME OUT

	W-R	Per cent	£1 Level Stake
2-y-o	0-15	-	- 15.00
3-y-o	1-26	3.8	- 18.00
4-y-o+	1-3	33.3	- 1.33
Totals	2-44	4.5	- 34.33

JOCKEYS RIDING

	W-R	Per cent	£1 Level Stake		W-R	Per cent	£1 Level Stake
Paul Eddery	3-11	27.3	+ 6.00	W Ryan	1-6	16.7	- 4.09
R Hills	3-20	15.0	+ 1.38	L Piggott	1-9	11.1	- 7.33
W R Swinburn	2-4	50.0	+ 1.38	A Clark	1-13	7.7	- 5.00
W Carson	2-47	4.3	- 37.50				

J Reid	0-12	M Birch	0-5	B Rouse	0-1
B Procter	0-9	A McGlone	0-2	Brough Scott	0-1
M Roberts	0-7	M Hills	0-2	L Dettori	0-1
J Williams	0-5	A Munro	0-1	P D'Arcy	0-1

COURSE RECORD

	Total W-R	Non-Handicaps 2-y-o	Non-Handicaps 3-y-o+	Handicaps 2-y-o	Handicaps 3-y-o+	Per cent	£1 Level Stake
York	2-4	0-0	2-4	0-0	0-0	50.0	+ 5.50
Warwick	2-5	0-1	2-3	0-0	0-1	40.0	+ 0.38
Chepstow	2-6	0-0	1-4	0-0	1-2	33.3	+ 2.17
Redcar	2-8	0-1	1-5	0-0	1-2	25.0	- 1.62
Bath	2-12	0-2	1-6	0-0	1-4	16.7	+ 2.50
Haydock	1-3	0-0	1-3	0-0	0-0	33.3	- 1.09
Lingfield	1-6	0-0	1-6	0-0	0-0	16.7	+ 9.00
Windsor	1-7	0-0	0-6	0-0	1-1	14.3	- 3.00

Hern W R

Newmarket	0-16	Brighton	0-5	Pontefract	0-3
Salisbury	0-11	Chester	0-5	Folkestone	0-2
Doncaster	0-9	Sandown	0-5	Lingfield (AW)	0-2
Goodwood	0-8	Nottingham	0-4	Epsom	0-1
Newbury	0-8	Yarmouth	0-4	Ripon	0-1
Kempton	0-7	Ascot	0-3	Southwell (Turf)	0-1
Leicester	0-7	Ayr	0-3	Thirsk	0-1

WINNING HORSES

	Age	Races Run	1st	2nd	3rd	Unpl	Win £
Moon Spin	4	12	4	1	1	6	14,499
Mack The Knife	4	5	2	1	1	1	12,598
Frogmarch	3	6	1	0	0	5	5,380
Bashayer	3	10	1	1	1	7	5,346
Wajih	3	3	1	1	1	0	3,844
Northern Bound	3	4	1	1	0	2	3,611
Hatta River	3	7	1	2	0	4	2,951
Jaazim	3	9	1	1	2	5	2,595
Barraak	3	5	1	1	2	1	2,243

WINNING OWNERS

	Races Won	Value £		Races Won	Value £
Mrs W R Hern	4	14,499	Sheikh Ahmed Al Maktoum	2	6,562
Hamdan Al-Maktoum	4	14,028	Lord Chelsea	1	5,380
Sir John Astor	2	12,598			

Favourites	6-25	24.0%	- 8.04	Total winning prize-money		£53,067
Longest winning sequence			2	Average SP of winner		4.0/1
Longest losing sequence			30	Return on stakes invested		-58.7%
1992 Form	17-126	13.5%	- 26.91	1990 Form	30-152	19.7%	- 45.58
1991 Form	23-138	16.7%	- 27.87	1989 Form	45-228	19.7%	- 72.98

LADY HERRIES (Littlehampton, West Sussex)

	No. of Horses	Races Run	1st	2nd	3rd	Unpl	Per cent	£1 Level Stake
2-y-o	4	11	0	1	2	8	-	- 11.00
3-y-o	8	42	13	6	5	18	31.0	+ 24.18
4-y-o+	6	34	4	4	5	21	11.8	- 7.50
Totals	18	87	17	11	12	47	19.5	+ 5.68

BY MONTH

2-y-o	W-R	Per cent	£1 Level Stake	3-y-o	W-R	Per cent	£1 Level Stake
Mar/Apr	0-0	-	0.00	Mar/Apr	2-8	25.0	+ 1.50
May	0-0	-	0.00	May	3-5	60.0	+ 11.38
June	0-0	-	0.00	June	1-4	25.0	- 1.90
July	0-1	-	- 1.00	July	1-3	33.3	+ 1.33
August	0-4	-	- 4.00	August	2-5	40.0	+ 18.00
September	0-3	-	- 3.00	September	2-7	28.6	+ 2.50
Oct/Nov	0-3	-	- 3.00	Oct/Nov	2-10	20.0	- 5.63

4-y-o+	W-R	Per cent	£1 Level Stake	Totals	W-R	Per cent	£1 Level Stake
Mar/Apr	0-9	-	- 8.00	Mar/Apr	2-17	11.8	- 6.50
May	3-4	75.0	+ 18.00	May	6-9	66.7	+ 29.38
June	0-6	-	- 6.00	June	1-10	10.0	- 7.90
July	0-4	-	- 4.00	July	1-8	12.5	- 3.67
August	0-4	-	- 4.00	August	2-13	15.4	+ 10.00
September	1-4	25.0	+ 0.50	September	3-14	21.4	0.00
Oct/Nov	0-3	-	- 3.00	Oct/Nov	2-16	12.5	- 11.63

DISTANCE

2-y-o	W-R	Per cent	£1 Level Stake	3-y-o	W-R	Per cent	£1 Level Stake
5f-6f	0-0	-	0.00	5f-6f	0-2	-	- 2.00
7f-8f	0-11	-	- 11.00	7f-8f	2-9	22.2	+ 8.00
9f-13f	0-0	-	0.00	9f-13f	6-22	27.3	+ 0.31
14f+	0-0	-	0.00	14f+	5-9	55.6	+ 17.87

4-y-o+	W-R	Per cent	£1 Level Stake	Totals	W-R	Per cent	£1 Level Stake
5f-6f	0-0	-	0.00	5f-6f	0-2	-	- 2.00
7f-8f	2-16	12.5	+ 2.00	7f-8f	4-36	11.1	- 1.00
9f-13f	0-8	-	- 8.00	9f-13f	6-30	20.0	- 7.69
14f+	2-10	20.0	- 1.50	14f+	7-19	36.8	+ 16.37

TYPE OF RACE

Non-Handicaps	W-R	Per cent	£1 Level Stake	Handicaps	W-R	Per cent	£1 Level Stake
2-y-o	0-10	-	- 10.00	2-y-o	0-1	-	- 1.00
3-y-o	2-14	14.3	- 6.92	3-y-o	11-27	40.7	+ 32.10
4-y-o+	0-2	-	- 2.00	4-y-o+	3-26	11.5	- 7.50
Selling	0-0	-	0.00	Selling	0-0	-	0.00
Apprentice	0-0	-	0.00	Apprentice	0-1	-	- 1.00
Amat/Ladies	0-1	-	- 1.00	Amat/Ladies	1-5	20.0	+ 3.00
Totals	2-27	7.4	- 19.92	Totals	15-60	25.0	+ 25.60

Herries Lady

<table>
<tr><th colspan="4">COURSE GRADE</th><th colspan="4">FIRST TIME OUT</th></tr>
<tr><th></th><th>W-R</th><th>Per cent</th><th>£1 Level Stake</th><th></th><th>W-R</th><th>Per cent</th><th>£1 Level Stake</th></tr>
<tr><td>Group 1</td><td>6-46</td><td>13.0</td><td>- 8.07</td><td>2-y-o</td><td>0-4</td><td>-</td><td>- 4.00</td></tr>
<tr><td>Group 2</td><td>9-21</td><td>42.9</td><td>+ 24.50</td><td>3-y-o</td><td>0-6</td><td>-</td><td>- 6.00</td></tr>
<tr><td>Group 3</td><td>1-15</td><td>6.7</td><td>- 8.50</td><td>4-y-o+</td><td>0-6</td><td>-</td><td>- 6.00</td></tr>
<tr><td>Group 4</td><td>1-5</td><td>20.0</td><td>- 2.25</td><td></td><td></td><td></td><td></td></tr>
<tr><td></td><td></td><td></td><td></td><td>Totals</td><td>0-16</td><td>-</td><td>- 16.00</td></tr>
</table>

JOCKEYS RIDING

<table>
<tr><th></th><th>W-R</th><th>Per cent</th><th>£1 Level Stake</th><th></th><th>W-R</th><th>Per cent</th><th>£1 Level Stake</th></tr>
<tr><td>K Darley</td><td>6-14</td><td>42.9</td><td>+ 13.56</td><td>J Williams</td><td>2-10</td><td>20.0</td><td>+ 13.00</td></tr>
<tr><td>J Quinn</td><td>4-8</td><td>50.0</td><td>+ 5.87</td><td>J Reid</td><td>2-12</td><td>16.7</td><td>- 1.00</td></tr>
<tr><td>A Clark</td><td>2-10</td><td>20.0</td><td>- 0.75</td><td>Mrs M Cowdrey</td><td>1-6</td><td>16.7</td><td>+ 2.00</td></tr>
</table>

<table>
<tr><td>L Dettori</td><td>0-5</td><td>Paul Eddery</td><td>0-2</td><td>Miss J Winter</td><td>0-1</td></tr>
<tr><td>C Dwyer</td><td>0-4</td><td>A McGlone</td><td>0-1</td><td>R Price</td><td>0-1</td></tr>
<tr><td>W Ryan</td><td>0-4</td><td>J Tate</td><td>0-1</td><td>T Williams</td><td>0-1</td></tr>
<tr><td>T Quinn</td><td>0-3</td><td>K Fallon</td><td>0-1</td><td></td><td></td></tr>
<tr><td>D Harrison</td><td>0-2</td><td>M Wigham</td><td>0-1</td><td></td><td></td></tr>
</table>

COURSE RECORD

<table>
<tr><th></th><th>Total W-R</th><th colspan="2">Non-Handicaps</th><th colspan="2">Handicaps</th><th>Per cent</th><th>£1 Level Stake</th></tr>
<tr><th></th><th></th><th>2-y-o</th><th>3-y-o+</th><th>2-y-o</th><th>3-y-o+</th><th></th><th></th></tr>
<tr><td>Redcar</td><td>4-5</td><td>0-1</td><td>0-0</td><td>0-0</td><td>4-4</td><td>80.0</td><td>+ 6.75</td></tr>
<tr><td>Lingfield</td><td>2-3</td><td>0-1</td><td>0-0</td><td>0-0</td><td>2-2</td><td>66.7</td><td>+ 10.00</td></tr>
<tr><td>Salisbury</td><td>2-7</td><td>0-1</td><td>0-2</td><td>0-0</td><td>2-4</td><td>28.6</td><td>+ 10.00</td></tr>
<tr><td>Ayr</td><td>1-1</td><td>0-0</td><td>1-1</td><td>0-0</td><td>0-0</td><td>100.0</td><td>+ 3.33</td></tr>
<tr><td>Ascot</td><td>1-2</td><td>0-0</td><td>0-1</td><td>0-0</td><td>1-1</td><td>50.0</td><td>+ 2.50</td></tr>
<tr><td>Ripon</td><td>1-2</td><td>0-0</td><td>0-0</td><td>0-0</td><td>1-2</td><td>50.0</td><td>+ 1.75</td></tr>
<tr><td>Warwick</td><td>1-2</td><td>0-0</td><td>1-1</td><td>0-0</td><td>0-1</td><td>50.0</td><td>+ 0.75</td></tr>
<tr><td>Goodwood</td><td>1-3</td><td>0-0</td><td>0-1</td><td>0-0</td><td>1-2</td><td>33.3</td><td>+ 1.00</td></tr>
<tr><td>York</td><td>1-3</td><td>0-0</td><td>0-0</td><td>0-0</td><td>1-3</td><td>33.3</td><td>- 0.90</td></tr>
<tr><td>Haydock</td><td>1-4</td><td>0-0</td><td>0-0</td><td>0-0</td><td>1-4</td><td>25.0</td><td>+ 6.00</td></tr>
<tr><td>Sandown</td><td>1-4</td><td>0-0</td><td>0-0</td><td>0-0</td><td>1-4</td><td>25.0</td><td>+ 9.00</td></tr>
<tr><td>Windsor</td><td>1-5</td><td>0-0</td><td>0-1</td><td>0-0</td><td>1-4</td><td>20.0</td><td>+ 1.50</td></tr>
</table>

<table>
<tr><td>Doncaster</td><td>0-10</td><td>Chepstow</td><td>0-3</td><td>Southwell (AW)</td><td>0-2</td></tr>
<tr><td>Newmarket</td><td>0-8</td><td>Beverley</td><td>0-2</td><td>Chester</td><td>0-1</td></tr>
<tr><td>Kempton</td><td>0-5</td><td>Leicester</td><td>0-2</td><td>Folkestone</td><td>0-1</td></tr>
<tr><td>Newbury</td><td>0-4</td><td>Newcastle</td><td>0-2</td><td>Pontefract</td><td>0-1</td></tr>
<tr><td>Brighton</td><td>0-3</td><td>Nottingham</td><td>0-2</td><td></td><td></td></tr>
</table>

WINNING HORSES

<table>
<tr><th></th><th>Age</th><th>Races Run</th><th>1st</th><th>2nd</th><th>3rd</th><th>Unpl</th><th>Win £</th></tr>
<tr><td>River North</td><td>3</td><td>8</td><td>4</td><td>2</td><td>1</td><td>1</td><td>52,396</td></tr>
<tr><td>Safety In Numbers</td><td>3</td><td>6</td><td>4</td><td>1</td><td>0</td><td>1</td><td>27,672</td></tr>
<tr><td>Castle Courageous</td><td>6</td><td>7</td><td>2</td><td>2</td><td>0</td><td>3</td><td>12,618</td></tr>
<tr><td>Polar Storm</td><td>3</td><td>9</td><td>2</td><td>0</td><td>1</td><td>6</td><td>11,120</td></tr>
</table>

Moon Carnival	3	5	2	0	2	1	5,581
Amaze	4	7	1	0	1	5	4,963
Wings Cove	3	6	1	1	0	4	3,870
Aitch N'Bee	10	11	1	2	1	7	3,028

WINNING OWNERS

	Races Won	Value £		Races Won	Value £
P D Savill	4	52,396	Lavinia Duchess Of Norfolk	2	5,581
Edwin N Cohen	5	31,542	Lady Katharine Phillips	1	4,963
Lady Mary Mumford	2	12,618	Lady Herries	1	3,028
Dexam International Ltd	2	11,120			

Favourites	10-18	55.6%	+ 18.35	Total winning prize-money		£121,248
Longest winning sequence			4	Average SP of winner		4.5/1
Longest losing sequence			11	Return on stakes invested		6.5%
1992 Form	6-77	7.8%	- 19.00	1990 Form	4-60	6.7%	- 30.70
1991 Form	14-99	14.1%	- 6.18	1989 Form	9-76	11.8%	- 30.46

J HETHERTON (Malton, North Yorks)

	No. of Horses	Races Run	1st	2nd	3rd	Unpl	Per cent	£1 Level Stake
2-y-o	5	23	0	3	2	18	-	- 23.00
3-y-o	6	44	1	6	5	32	2.3	- 10.00
4-y-o+	3	11	1	0	0	10	9.1	+ 4.00
Totals	14	78	2	9	7	60	2.6	- 29.00

Jan	Feb	Mar	Apr	May	Jun	Jul	Aug	Sep	Oct/Nov
0-0	0-2	0-3	0-8	0-11	0-12	0-13	0-6	1-10	1-13

Winning Jockeys	W-R	£1 Level Stake		W-R	£1 Level Stake
L Charnock	1-2	+ 32.00	B Raymond	1-4	+ 11.00

Winning Courses	W-R	£1 Level Stake		W-R	£1 Level Stake
Southwell (Turf)	1-1	+ 14.00	Catterick	1-5	+ 29.00

Winning Horses	Age	Races Run	1st	2nd	3rd	Unpl	Win £
Absalom's Pillar	3	10	1	3	1	5	4,050
Eternal Flame	5	4	1	0	0	3	3,005

Favourites	0-0			Total winning prize-money		£7,055
1992 Form	1-8	12.5%	- 5.25	1990 Form	4-49	8.2%	- 27.37
1991 Form	10-91	11.0%	- 20.42	1989 Form	2-38	5.3%	- 25.50

A HIDE (Newmarket)

	No. of Horses	Races Run	1st	2nd	3rd	Unpl	Per cent	£1 Level Stake
2-y-o	7	18	1	1	4	12	5.6	- 5.00
3-y-o	8	46	2	3	5	36	4.3	- 28.50
4-y-o+	4	25	3	2	4	16	12.0	+ 9.00
Totals	19	89	6	6	13	64	6.7	- 24.50

Jan	Feb	Mar	Apr	May	Jun	Jul	Aug	Sep	Oct/Nov
0-1	0-1	0-0	2-8	0-10	2-17	1-16	0-12	0-9	1-15

Winning Jockeys	W-R	£1 Level Stake		W-R	£1 Level Stake
N Varley	2-6	+ 18.00	J Tate	1-10	- 7.50
K Darley	1-3	+ 12.00	W Woods	1-19	- 6.00
Miss L Hide	1-6	+ 4.00			

Winning Courses					
Edinburgh	1-1	+ 1.50	Warwick	1-3	+ 10.00
Ripon	1-1	+ 9.00	Redcar	1-4	+ 11.00
Sandown	1-3	+ 4.00	Nottingham	1-5	+ 12.00

Winning Horses	Age	Races Run	1st	2nd	3rd	Unpl	Win £
Asian Punter	4	4	2	0	1	1	9,191
Nitouche	3	11	1	1	1	8	3,779
Scenic Dancer	5	11	1	2	1	7	3,236
Carrie Kool	2	4	1	1	1	1	3,054
Francia	3	9	1	0	2	6	2,739

Favourites	1-3	33.3%	- 0.50	Total winning prize-money	£21,999

1992 Form	5-77	6.5%	- 36.00	1990 Form	10-94	10.6%	+ 1.00
1991 Form	15-163	9.2%	- 7.92	1989 Form	11-126	8.7%	- 22.75

C J HILL (Barnstaple, Devon)

	No. of Horses	Races Run	1st	2nd	3rd	Unpl	Per cent	£1 Level Stake
2-y-o	1	5	0	0	0	5	-	- 5.00
3-y-o	8	50	13	5	2	30	26.0	+ 26.17
4-y-o+	22	109	14	10	11	74	12.8	- 17.73
Totals	31	164	27	15	13	109	16.5	+ 3.44

BY MONTH

2-y-o	W-R	Per cent	£1 Level Stake	3-y-o	W-R	Per cent	£1 Level Stake
January	0-0	-	0.00	January	4-10	40.0	+ 2.51
February	0-0	-	0.00	February	2-6	33.3	- 2.09
March	0-0	-	0.00	March	2-5	40.0	+ 5.25
April	0-0	-	0.00	April	0-4	-	- 4.00
May	0-1	-	- 1.00	May	0-5	-	- 5.00
June	0-1	-	- 1.00	June	0-4	-	- 4.00
July	0-1	-	- 1.00	July	1-3	33.3	+ 3.50
August	0-1	-	- 1.00	August	2-7	28.6	+ 14.50
September	0-1	-	- 1.00	September	2-5	40.0	+ 16.50
Oct/Nov	0-0	-	0.00	Oct/Nov	0-1	-	- 1.00

4-y-o+	W-R	Per cent	£1 Level Stake	Totals	W-R	Per cent	£1 Level Stake
January	4-21	19.0	- 9.67	January	8-31	25.8	- 7.16
February	2-19	10.5	- 10.56	February	4-25	16.0	- 12.65
March	1-9	11.1	- 2.50	March	3-14	21.4	+ 2.75
April	2-6	33.3	+ 17.50	April	2-10	20.0	+ 13.50
May	3-13	23.1	+ 15.50	May	3-19	15.8	+ 9.50
June	1-6	16.7	+ 2.00	June	1-11	9.1	- 3.00
July	0-12	-	- 12.00	July	1-16	6.3	- 9.50
August	1-10	10.0	- 5.00	August	3-18	16.7	+ 8.50
September	0-8	-	- 8.00	September	2-14	14.3	+ 7.50
Oct/Nov	0-5	-	- 5.00	Oct/Nov	0-6	-	- 6.00

DISTANCE

2-y-o	W-R	Per cent	£1 Level Stake	3-y-o	W-R	Per cent	£1 Level Stake
5f-6f	0-3	-	- 3.00	5f-6f	1-3	33.3	+ 1.33
7f-8f	0-2	-	- 2.00	7f-8f	10-35	28.6	+ 6.84
9f-13f	0-0	-	0.00	9f-13f	2-12	16.7	+ 18.00
14f+	0-0	-	0.00	14f+	0-0	-	0.00

4-y-o+	W-R	Per cent	£1 Level Stake	Totals	W-R	Per cent	£1 Level Stake
5f-6f	4-23	17.4	+ 19.00	5f-6f	5-29	17.2	+ 17.33
7f-8f	2-33	6.1	- 29.56	7f-8f	12-70	17.1	- 24.72
9f-13f	6-45	13.3	- 6.67	9f-13f	8-57	14.0	+ 11.33
14f+	2-8	25.0	- 0.50	14f+	2-8	25.0	- 0.50

TYPE OF RACE

Non-Handicaps	W-R	Per cent	£1 Level Stake	Handicaps	W-R	Per cent	£1 Level Stake
2-y-o	0-3	-	- 3.00	2-y-o	0-0	-	0.00
3-y-o	5-21	23.8	- 1.79	3-y-o	7-24	29.2	+ 26.46
4-y-o+	4-25	16.0	- 2.23	4-y-o+	10-69	14.5	- 0.50
Selling	1-4	25.0	+ 2.50	Selling	0-9	-	- 9.00
Apprentice	0-2	-	- 2.00	Apprentice	0-7	-	- 7.00
Amat/Ladies	0-0	-	0.00	Amat/Ladies	0-0	-	0.00
Totals	10-55	18.2	- 6.52	Totals	17-109	15.6	+ 9.96

COURSE GRADE

	W–R	Per cent	£1 Level Stake
Group 1	4–24	16.7	+ 19.00
Group 2	1–12	8.3	– 5.50
Group 3	5–40	12.5	– 5.00
Group 4	17–88	19.3	– 5.06

FIRST TIME OUT

	W–R	Per cent	£1 Level Stake
2-y-o	0–1	–	– 1.00
3-y-o	3–8	37.5	+ 2.13
4-y-o+	3–18	16.7	+ 3.50
Totals	6–27	22.2	+ 4.63

JOCKEYS RIDING

	W–R	Per cent	£1 Level Stake		W–R	Per cent	£1 Level Stake
G Bardwell	8–41	19.5	+ 16.33	J Weaver	1–3	33.3	+ 3.50
J Quinn	8–41	19.5	– 17.30	G Duffield	1–3	33.3	+ 2.00
M Roberts	3–5	60.0	+ 16.00	D Wright	1–4	25.0	+ 2.50
D Holland	2–7	28.6	+ 14.50	P McCabe	1–5	20.0	+ 10.00
P Robinson	1–1	100.0	+ 8.00	D Biggs	1–7	14.3	– 5.09

N Adams	0–10	A Munro	0–1	L Dettori	0–1
B Russell	0–6	A Tucker	0–1	M Baird	0–1
S Wood	0–4	D Harrison	0–1	N Varley	0–1
R Cochrane	0–3	E Johnson	0–1	R Painter	0–1
D McCabe	0–2	F Norton	0–1	S Davies	0–1
M Hills	0–2	J Lowe	0–1	S Dawson	0–1
N Carlisle	0–2	J Tate	0–1	S Whitworth	0–1
N Kennedy	0–2	Kim McDonnell	0–1	T Williams	0–1

COURSE RECORD

	Total W–R	Non-Handicaps 2-y-o	Non-Handicaps 3-y-o+	Handicaps 2-y-o	Handicaps 3-y-o+	Per cent	£1 Level Stake
Southwell (AW)	15–77	0–1	7–39	0–0	8–37	19.5	– 24.06
Pontefract	3–6	0–1	1–1	0–0	2–4	50.0	+ 16.00
Haydock	3–7	0–0	1–1	0–0	2–6	42.9	+ 29.50
Warwick	2–8	0–0	1–2	0–0	1–6	25.0	+ 22.00
Sandown	1–1	0–0	0–0	0–0	1–1	100.0	+ 5.50
Yarmouth	1–3	0–0	0–1	0–0	1–2	33.3	+ 2.00
Brighton	1–7	0–0	0–0	0–0	1–7	14.3	– 0.50
Chepstow	1–10	0–0	0–1	0–0	1–9	10.0	– 2.00

Bath	0–12	Nottingham	0–4	Lingfield (AW)	0–1
Kempton	0–6	Folkestone	0–2	Windsor	0–1
Newbury	0–5	Newmarket	0–2	York	0–1
Salisbury	0–5	Ascot	0–1		
Leicester	0–4	Epsom	0–1		

WINNING HORSES

	Age	Races Run	1st	2nd	3rd	Unpl	Win £
Dorazine	3	14	6	0	0	8	20,277
Atlantic Way	5	18	5	2	1	10	13,608
Nikki Noo Noo	3	8	3	2	2	1	7,029

Tendresse	5	9	2	0	1	6	6,716
Golden Klair	3	6	2	1	0	3	6,690
Glowing Path	3	9	2	2	0	5	5,081
Goody Four Shoes	5	4	1	0	0	3	3,236
Beatle Song	5	7	1	0	0	6	3,210
Quatre Femme	6	4	1	0	1	2	2,364
Juvenara	7	6	1	2	1	2	2,322
Lock Keeper	7	7	1	2	0	4	2,301
Top One	8	9	1	0	0	8	2,243
Annacurragh	4	2	1	0	1	0	2,238

WINNING OWNERS

	Races Won	Value £		Races Won	Value £
C John Hill	26	74,078	A G Newcombe	1	3,236

Favourites	10-28	35.7%	- 1.89	Total winning prize-money	£77,314

Longest winning sequence		3	Average SP of winner	5.2/1
Longest losing sequence		20	Return on stakes invested	2.1%

1992 Form	19-204	9.3%	- 66.04	1990 Form	11-125	8.8%	- 56.33
1991 Form	16-221	7.2%	-106.00	1989 Form	3-111	2.7%	- 88.50

B W HILLS (Lambourn, Berks)

	No. of Horses	Races Run	1st	2nd	3rd	Unpl	Per cent	£1 Level Stake
2-y-o	38	98	13	8	12	65	13.3	- 19.39
3-y-o	49	203	20	21	27	135	9.9	-113.07
4-y-o+	9	52	6	8	3	35	11.5	- 15.75
Totals	96	353	39	37	42	235	11.0	-148.21

BY MONTH

2-y-o	W-R	Per cent	£1 Level Stake	3-y-o	W-R	Per cent	£1 Level Stake
January	0-0	-	0.00	January	1-2	50.0	- 0.67
February	0-0	-	0.00	February	1-6	16.7	- 4.67
March	0-0	-	0.00	March	1-7	14.3	- 4.90
April	0-6	-	- 6.00	April	3-32	9.4	- 11.00
May	0-11	-	- 11.00	May	2-29	6.9	- 20.50
June	2-10	20.0	- 1.50	June	5-31	16.1	- 8.71
July	2-13	15.4	+ 2.00	July	2-25	8.0	- 19.62
August	3-15	20.0	+ 2.38	August	0-24	-	- 24.00
September	5-25	20.0	+ 3.73	September	2-27	7.4	- 17.50
Oct/Nov	1-18	5.6	- 9.00	Oct/Nov	3-20	15.0	- 1.50

Hills B W

4-y-o+	W-R	Per cent	£1 Level Stake		Totals	W-R	Per cent	£1 Level Stake
January	0-0	-	0.00		January	1-2	50.0	- 0.67
February	0-0	-	0.00		February	1-6	16.7	- 4.67
March	1-1	100.0	+ 1.75		March	2-8	25.0	- 3.15
April	1-7	14.3	- 3.00		April	4-45	8.9	- 20.00
May	0-12	-	- 12.00		May	2-52	3.8	- 43.50
June	0-6	-	- 6.00		June	7-47	14.9	- 16.21
July	0-8	-	- 8.00		July	4-46	8.7	- 25.62
August	2-6	33.3	+ 14.00		August	5-45	11.1	- 7.62
September	1-9	11.1	- 2.50		September	8-61	13.1	- 16.27
Oct/Nov	1-3	33.3	0.00		Oct/Nov	5-41	12.2	- 10.50

DISTANCE

2-y-o	W-R	Per cent	£1 Level Stake		3-y-o	W-R	Per cent	£1 Level Stake
5f-6f	8-64	12.5	- 19.12		5f-6f	0-8	-	- 8.00
7f-8f	5-34	14.7	- 0.27		7f-8f	8-81	9.9	- 39.17
9f-13f	0-0	-	0.00		9f-13f	9-93	9.7	- 57.40
14f+	0-0	-	0.00		14f+	3-21	14.3	- 8.50

4-y-o+	W-R	Per cent	£1 Level Stake		Totals	W-R	Per cent	£1 Level Stake
5f-6f	0-3	-	- 3.00		5f-6f	8-75	10.7	- 30.12
7f-8f	1-14	7.1	- 7.50		7f-8f	14-129	10.9	- 46.94
9f-13f	1-16	6.3	- 3.00		9f-13f	10-109	9.2	- 60.40
14f+	4-19	21.1	- 2.25		14f+	7-40	17.5	- 10.75

TYPE OF RACE

Non-Handicaps	W-R	Per cent	£1 Level Stake		Handicaps	W-R	Per cent	£1 Level Stake
2-y-o	8-89	9.0	- 42.77		2-y-o	3-6	50.0	+ 11.38
3-y-o	14-122	11.5	- 57.32		3-y-o	5-71	7.0	- 48.75
4-y-o+	2-11	18.2	- 1.00		4-y-o+	4-39	10.3	- 12.75
Selling	2-5	40.0	+ 10.00		Selling	0-3	-	- 3.00
Apprentice	1-2	50.0	+ 1.00		Apprentice	0-4	-	- 4.00
Amat/Ladies	0-0	-	0.00		Amat/Ladies	0-1	-	- 1.00
Totals	27-229	11.8	- 90.09		Totals	12-124	9.7	- 58.12

COURSE GRADE

	W-R	Per cent	£1 Level Stake
Group 1	22-189	11.6	- 58.61
Group 2	7-53	13.2	- 21.64
Group 3	6-69	8.7	- 37.62
Group 4	4-42	9.5	- 30.34

FIRST TIME OUT

	W-R	Per cent	£1 Level Stake
2-y-o	3-38	7.9	- 17.00
3-y-o	7-48	14.6	- 18.61
4-y-o+	2-8	25.0	- 1.25
Totals	12-94	12.8	- 36.86

JOCKEYS RIDING

	W-R	Per cent	£1 Level Stake		W-R	Per cent	£1 Level Stake
D Holland	16-151	10.6	- 47.83	Pat Eddery	2-35	5.7	- 25.50
M Hills	5-19	26.3	+ 0.56	D McKeown	1-2	50.0	- 0.67
W Carson	5-28	17.9	- 1.75	S McCarthy	1-3	33.3	0.00
M Roberts	3-15	20.0	- 0.90	S Maloney	1-3	33.3	+ 3.00
K Darley	2-5	40.0	+ 1.38	G Duffield	1-4	25.0	0.00
D Harrison	2-9	22.2	+ 2.50				

R Hills	0-9	J Williams	0-2	L Dettori	0-1
J Reid	0-8	M J Kinane	0-2	L Piggott	0-1
R Street	0-8	S Dawson	0-2	M Baird	0-1
W Ryan	0-7	S Raymont	0-2	M Birch	0-1
R Cochrane	0-4	A McGlone	0-1	M Denaro	0-1
T Quinn	0-4	B Raymond	0-1	Miss E Houghton	0-1
W R Swinburn	0-4	Dale Gibson	0-1	N Varley	0-1
A Munro	0-3	G Hind	0-1	P Robinson	0-1
D Biggs	0-3	J Fortune	0-1	W Woods	0-1
Paul Eddery	0-3	J Lowe	0-1		
C Rutter	0-2	J Quinn	0-1		

COURSE RECORD

	Total W-R	Non-Handicaps 2-y-o	Non-Handicaps 3-y-o+	Handicaps 2-y-o	Handicaps 3-y-o+	Per cent	£1 Level Stake
Newmarket	6-46	2-12	1-12	0-0	3-22	13.0	- 12.75
Doncaster	4-14	1-3	2-7	0-0	1-4	28.6	+ 8.85
Ayr	3-6	1-2	1-1	0-0	1-3	50.0	+ 1.54
Brighton	3-9	0-1	2-7	1-1	0-0	33.3	+ 0.13
York	3-22	1-5	1-7	0-0	1-10	13.6	+ 1.25
Lingfield	2-4	2-3	0-1	0-0	0-0	50.0	+ 10.73
Yarmouth	2-5	1-2	0-0	0-0	1-3	40.0	+ 4.50
Catterick	2-7	0-1	2-4	0-1	0-1	28.6	+ 2.00
Lingfield (AW)	2-10	0-0	2-6	0-1	0-3	20.0	- 7.34
Windsor	2-11	0-5	0-4	2-2	0-0	18.2	+ 4.00
Kempton	2-12	0-2	1-8	0-0	1-2	16.7	+ 9.50
Newcastle	1-2	0-0	1-2	0-0	0-0	50.0	+ 2.00
Nottingham	1-5	1-2	0-2	0-0	0-1	20.0	- 1.00
Epsom	1-8	0-0	0-4	0-0	1-4	12.5	- 2.00
Salisbury	1-11	0-1	1-8	0-0	0-2	9.1	- 8.00
Chester	1-18	0-3	1-9	0-0	0-6	5.6	- 13.50
Bath	1-21	0-7	1-7	0-1	0-6	4.8	- 18.12
Sandown	1-21	0-8	1-7	0-0	0-6	4.8	- 13.50
Newbury	1-26	1-9	0-7	0-0	0-10	3.8	- 21.50

Ascot	0-12	Warwick	0-8	Southwell (Turf)	0-4
Goodwood	0-12	Beverley	0-6	Redcar	0-3
Leicester	0-11	Pontefract	0-6	Chepstow	0-2
Folkestone	0-9	Ripon	0-6	Hamilton	0-2
Haydock	0-8	Southwell (AW)	0-4	Thirsk	0-2

WINNING HORSES

	Age	Races Run	1st	2nd	3rd	Unpl	Win £
Further Flight	7	6	2	1	0	3	31,690
Braari	2	6	3	0	1	2	26,315
Major Success	2	9	4	0	2	3	13,255
Yildiz	4	10	1	2	1	6	12,818
Dee Raft	3	12	3	2	2	5	9,778
Nicer	3	3	1	0	0	2	9,663
Marco Magnifico	3	5	2	0	0	3	7,689
Lake Poopo	3	8	2	3	1	2	7,619
Dime Bag	4	5	1	0	1	3	7,327
Northern Bird	3	7	1	0	0	6	7,245
Snow Board	4	6	1	2	0	3	6,400
Tychonic	3	7	1	1	3	2	5,481
The Deep	2	2	1	1	0	0	5,127
Heathcliff	2	3	1	0	0	2	4,776
Factual	3	4	1	0	0	3	4,013
Arzina	2	3	1	0	0	2	3,845
Monsieur Dupont	3	5	1	1	1	2	3,818
Casting Shadows	4	7	1	2	1	3	3,787
Black Dragon	3	5	1	1	1	2	3,747
Rainbow Heights	2	2	1	0	0	1	3,582
Woodwardia	3	3	1	0	0	2	3,553
Majority	3	6	1	0	1	4	3,494
Ritto	3	7	1	3	2	1	3,436
Suntara	3	6	1	0	1	4	3,436
Kosata	3	4	1	0	0	3	3,436
Rawya	2	1	1	0	0	0	3,436
Torch Rouge	2	5	1	2	1	1	3,319
Urgent Request	3	4	1	0	1	2	3,319
Chummy's Pal	3	7	1	0	1	5	2,511

WINNING OWNERS

	Races Won	Value £		Races Won	Value £
S Wingfield Digby	2	31,690	J Hanson	2	9,719
Hamdan Al-Maktoum	3	26,315	K Al-Said	2	8,563
Sheikh Mohammed	5	17,958	Mrs Leonard Simpson	2	7,689
K Abdulla	4	16,365	R J McAlpine	1	7,327
Mrs J M Corbett	2	14,439	John E Bradley	1	7,245
W J Gredley	4	13,255	Wafic Said	1	3,818
S Mino	1	12,818	S Skelding	1	3,787
R E Sangster	3	11,055	Broughton Homes Ltd	1	3,582
D O Pickering	3	9,778	B W Hills	1	2,511

Favourites	17-69	24.6%	- 20.09	Total winning prize-money	£207,911
Longest winning sequence			2	Average SP of winner	4.3/1
Longest losing sequence			49	Return on stakes invested	-42.0%
1992 Form	63-424	14.9%	-101.91	1990 Form	113-579	19.5%	- 52.11
1991 Form	99-491	20.2%	+ 7.81	1989 Form	73-463	15.8%	-156.28

J W HILLS (Lambourn, Berks)

	No. of Horses	Races Run	1st	2nd	3rd	Unpl	Per cent	£1 Level Stake
2-y-o	17	54	5	8	5	36	9.3	- 25.68
3-y-o	14	87	9	13	9	56	10.3	- 22.00
4-y-o+	15	98	10	16	7	65	10.2	- 18.12
Totals	46	239	24	37	21	157	10.0	- 65.80

BY MONTH

2-y-o	W-R	Per cent	£1 Level Stake	3-y-o	W-R	Per cent	£1 Level Stake
January	0-0	-	0.00	January	0-0	-	0.00
February	0-0	-	0.00	February	0-0	-	0.00
March	0-0	-	0.00	March	0-1	-	- 1.00
April	0-4	-	- 4.00	April	0-8	-	- 8.00
May	0-3	-	- 3.00	May	0-19	-	- 19.00
June	1-3	33.3	- 1.00	June	4-13	30.8	+ 13.50
July	1-8	12.5	- 5.25	July	2-19	10.5	+ 0.50
August	2-12	16.7	+ 6.57	August	1-11	9.1	- 6.00
September	0-7	-	- 7.00	September	2-8	25.0	+ 6.00
Oct/Nov	1-17	5.9	- 12.00	Oct/Nov	0-8	-	- 8.00

4-y-o+	W-R	Per cent	£1 Level Stake	Totals	W-R	Per cent	£1 Level Stake
January	0-3	-	- 3.00	January	0-3	-	- 3.00
February	0-2	-	- 2.00	February	0-2	-	- 2.00
March	0-5	-	- 5.00	March	0-6	-	- 6.00
April	0-9	-	- 9.00	April	0-21	-	- 21.00
May	3-22	13.6	- 2.00	May	3-44	6.8	- 24.00
June	1-18	5.6	- 3.00	June	6-34	17.6	+ 9.50
July	2-12	16.7	+ 12.00	July	5-39	12.8	+ 7.25
August	2-13	15.4	- 6.12	August	5-36	13.9	- 5.55
September	2-5	40.0	+ 9.00	September	4-20	20.0	+ 8.00
Oct/Nov	0-9	-	- 9.00	Oct/Nov	1-34	2.9	- 29.00

DISTANCE

2-y-o	W-R	Per cent	£1 Level Stake	3-y-o	W-R	Per cent	£1 Level Stake
5f-6f	3-27	11.1	- 20.68	5f-6f	0-5	-	- 5.00
7f-8f	2-27	7.4	- 5.00	7f-8f	4-41	9.8	- 22.00
9f-13f	0-0	-	0.00	9f-13f	5-37	13.5	+ 9.00
14f+	0-0	-	0.00	14f+	0-4	-	- 4.00

4-y-o+	W-R	Per cent	£1 Level Stake	Totals	W-R	Per cent	£1 Level Stake
5f-6f	0-5	-	- 5.00	5f-6f	3-37	8.1	- 30.68
7f-8f	2-27	7.4	- 16.00	7f-8f	8-95	8.4	- 43.00
9f-13f	6-55	10.9	0.00	9f-13f	11-92	12.0	+ 9.00
14f+	2-11	18.2	+ 2.88	14f+	2-15	13.3	- 1.12

TYPE OF RACE

Non-Handicaps	W-R	Per cent	£1 Level Stake	Handicaps	W-R	Per cent	£1 Level Stake
2-y-o	4-48	8.3	- 36.68	2-y-o	0-3	-	- 3.00
3-y-o	5-46	10.9	- 11.00	3-y-o	3-32	9.4	- 7.00
4-y-o+	3-17	17.6	- 7.12	4-y-o+	7-70	10.0	0.00
Selling	1-5	20.0	0.00	Selling	1-3	33.3	+ 14.00
Apprentice	0-3	-	- 3.00	Apprentice	0-7	-	- 7.00
Amat/Ladies	0-2	-	- 2.00	Amat/Ladies	0-3	-	- 3.00
Totals	13-121	10.7	- 59.80	Totals	11-118	9.3	- 6.00

COURSE GRADE

	W-R	Per cent	£1 Level Stake
Group 1	8-112	7.1	- 21.50
Group 2	5-37	13.5	- 15.43
Group 3	10-65	15.4	- 18.87
Group 4	1-25	4.0	- 10.00

FIRST TIME OUT

	W-R	Per cent	£1 Level Stake
2-y-o	0-17	-	- 17.00
3-y-o	0-14	-	- 14.00
4-y-o+	0-15	-	- 15.00
Totals	0-46	-	- 46.00

JOCKEYS RIDING

	W-R	Per cent	£1 Level Stake		W-R	Per cent	£1 Level Stake
M Hills	7-80	8.8	- 44.18	D Holland	2-26	7.7	- 16.00
D Harrison	5-25	20.0	+ 4.50	Paul Eddery	1-1	100.0	+ 4.00
R Hills	5-32	15.6	+ 23.00	G Duffield	1-2	50.0	+ 0.88
J Williams	2-9	22.2	+ 11.00	T Quinn	1-3	33.3	+ 12.00

B Doyle	0-6	Miss S Francome	0-2	Mark Denaro	0-1
W Ryan	0-6	W Carson	0-2	Mrs S Wray	0-1
M Henry	0-5	B Rouse	0-1	N Carlisle	0-1
Mr C Vigors	0-4	C Asmussen	0-1	Pat Eddery	0-1
R Perham	0-4	D Biggs	0-1	R Cochrane	0-1
S Dawson	0-4	D Gibbs	0-1	R Street	0-1
A Munro	0-3	G Carter	0-1	S O'Gorman	0-1
B Raymond	0-3	J Carroll	0-1	S Raymont	0-1
F Norton	0-2	J Marshall	0-1	S Whitworth	0-1
L Dettori	0-2	M Fenton	0-1	T G McLaughlin	0-1

COURSE RECORD

	Total W-R	Non-Handicaps 2-y-o	Non-Handicaps 3-y-o+	Handicaps 2-y-o	Handicaps 3-y-o+	Per cent	£1 Level Stake
Bath	4-17	2-6	1-5	0-0	1-6	23.5	+ 5.00
Windsor	3-12	1-1	2-8	0-0	0-3	25.0	+ 0.25
Brighton	2-6	0-0	1-3	0-0	1-3	33.3	+ 7.00
Salisbury	2-7	1-2	1-3	0-0	0-2	28.6	- 0.93
Yarmouth	2-9	0-2	2-5	0-0	0-2	22.2	- 1.12
Newbury	2-15	0-3	0-5	0-0	2-7	13.3	+ 3.00

Haydock	1-2	0-0	0-0	0-0	1-2	50.0	+ 19.00
Chester	1-3	0-0	0-1	0-0	1-2	33.3	- 0.50
Chepstow	1-5	0-2	1-2	0-0	0-1	20.0	- 1.00
Warwick	1-5	0-1	0-1	0-0	1-3	20.0	+ 10.00
York	1-5	0-0	1-1	0-0	0-4	20.0	- 2.00
Epsom	1-6	0-0	0-2	0-0	1-4	16.7	+ 1.50
Sandown	1-12	0-3	0-3	1-1	0-5	8.3	+ 5.00
Goodwood	1-20	0-3	0-5	0-0	1-12	5.0	- 11.00
Newmarket	1-23	0-8	0-2	0-3	1-10	4.3	- 8.00

Leicester	0-13	Nottingham	0-6	Southwell (Turf)	0-2
Lingfield (AW)	0-13	Lingfield	0-5	Thirsk	0-2
Redcar	0-11	Folkestone	0-4	Beverley	0-1
Ascot	0-9	Ripon	0-3	Catterick	0-1
Doncaster	0-9	Newcastle	0-2		
Kempton	0-9	Pontefract	0-2		

WINNING HORSES

	Age	Races Run	1st	2nd	3rd	Unpl	Win £
Glide Path	4	11	3	1	0	7	26,647
Forthwith	3	7	2	3	0	2	17,814
Castoret	7	8	1	0	0	7	15,963
Jade Vale	4	8	3	2	0	3	14,388
Fairy Story	3	7	2	1	0	4	12,465
Scorched Air	3	7	2	1	3	1	6,512
Majestic Eagle	2	4	1	2	0	1	4,464
Kissininthebackrow	2	5	1	0	0	4	3,728
Broadway Flyer	2	2	1	0	0	1	3,535
Gilderdale	11	11	1	3	4	3	3,290
Cragganmore	2	7	1	2	2	2	3,003
Sheriff	2	8	1	2	0	5	2,900
Perdition	3	10	1	2	2	5	2,489
Patong Beach	3	5	1	1	0	3	2,406
Sparky's Song	3	12	1	2	0	9	2,385
Ice Strike	4	6	1	0	0	5	2,070
Edge Of Darkness	4	9	1	2	1	5	2,070

WINNING OWNERS

	Races Won	Value £		Races Won	Value £
The Jampot Partnership	3	26,647	Abbott Racing Partners	1	3,290
Mrs S Bosher	4	17,923	A Stoddard	1	3,003
L H J Ward	2	17,814	Christopher P J Brown	1	2,900
Lady D'Avigdor-Goldsmid	1	15,963	The Losers Owners Group	1	2,489
The Fairy Story Partnership	2	12,465	Tim Newsome	1	2,406
Michael Wauchope	2	6,512	Mrs Annette Barwick	1	2,385
Garrett J Freyne	1	4,464	C R Nelson	1	2,070
Christopher Wright	1	3,728	Mrs Marie Tinkler	1	2,070

Favourites	7-33	21.2%	- 14.05	Total winning prize-money			£126,128
Longest winning sequence			5	Average SP of winner			6.2/1
Longest losing sequence			51	Return on stakes invested			-27.5%
1992 Form	25-225	11.1%	- 70.33	1990 Form	28-202	13.9%	+ 20.72
1991 Form	20-191	10.5%	- 24.75	1989 Form	16-183	8.7%	- 72.07

R J HODGES (Charlton Adam, Somerset)

	No. of Horses	Races Run	1st	2nd	3rd	Unpl	Per cent	£1 Level Stake
2-y-o	8	17	0	0	0	17	-	- 17.00
3-y-o	12	57	1	4	3	49	1.8	- 51.00
4-y-o+	35	241	19	20	25	177	7.9	- 47.75
Totals	55	315	20	24	28	243	6.3	-115.75

BY MONTH

2-y-o	W-R	Per cent	£1 Level Stake	3-y-o	W-R	Per cent	£1 Level Stake
January	0-0	-	0.00	January	0-0	-	0.00
February	0-0	-	0.00	February	0-1	-	- 1.00
March	0-0	-	0.00	March	0-1	-	- 1.00
April	0-0	-	0.00	April	0-4	-	- 4.00
May	0-5	-	- 5.00	May	0-15	-	- 15.00
June	0-2	-	- 2.00	June	0-8	-	- 8.00
July	0-3	-	- 3.00	July	0-11	-	- 11.00
August	0-2	-	- 2.00	August	0-7	-	- 7.00
September	0-2	-	- 2.00	September	1-6	16.7	0.00
Oct/Nov	0-3	-	- 3.00	Oct/Nov	0-4	-	- 4.00

4-y-o+	W-R	Per cent	£1 Level Stake	Totals	W-R	Per cent	£1 Level Stake
January	1-6	16.7	+ 5.00	January	1-6	16.7	+ 5.00
February	0-9	-	- 9.00	February	0-10	-	- 10.00
March	0-14	-	- 14.00	March	0-15	-	- 15.00
April	4-26	15.4	- 12.00	April	4-30	13.3	- 16.00
May	1-37	2.7	- 11.00	May	1-57	1.8	- 31.00
June	7-41	17.1	+ 28.25	June	7-51	13.7	+ 18.25
July	1-36	2.8	- 28.00	July	1-50	2.0	- 42.00
August	3-28	10.7	+ 3.00	August	3-37	8.1	- 6.00
September	2-22	9.1	+ 12.00	September	3-30	10.0	+ 10.00
Oct/Nov	0-22	-	- 22.00	Oct/Nov	0-29	-	- 29.00

DISTANCE

2-y-o	W-R	Per cent	£1 Level Stake	3-y-o	W-R	Per cent	£1 Level Stake
5f-6f	0-14	-	- 14.00	5f-6f	0-20	-	- 20.00
7f-8f	0-3	-	- 3.00	7f-8f	1-25	4.0	- 19.00
9f-13f	0-0	-	0.00	9f-13f	0-11	-	- 11.00
14f+	0-0	-	0.00	14f+	0-1	-	- 1.00

4-y-o+	W-R	Per cent	£1 Level Stake	Totals	W-R	Per cent	£1 Level Stake
5f-6f	14-133	10.5	- 18.75	5f-6f	14-167	8.4	- 52.75
7f-8f	3-64	4.7	- 7.00	7f-8f	4-92	4.3	- 29.00
9f-13f	2-37	5.4	- 15.00	9f-13f	2-48	4.2	- 26.00
14f+	0-7	-	- 7.00	14f+	0-8	-	- 8.00

TYPE OF RACE

Non-Handicaps	W-R	Per cent	£1 Level Stake	Handicaps	W-R	Per cent	£1 Level Stake
2-y-o	0-9	-	- 9.00	2-y-o	0-0	-	0.00
3-y-o	0-25	-	- 25.00	3-y-o	0-22	-	- 22.00
4-y-o+	3-29	10.3	- 21.00	4-y-o+	13-173	7.5	- 35.75
Selling	1-21	4.8	- 10.00	Selling	1-11	9.1	0.00
Apprentice	0-2	-	- 2.00	Apprentice	1-18	5.6	- 12.00
Amat/Ladies	0-0	-	0.00	Amat/Ladies	1-5	20.0	+ 21.00
Totals	4-86	4.7	- 67.00	Totals	16-229	7.0	- 48.75

COURSE GRADE

	W-R	Per cent	£1 Level Stake
Group 1	4-67	6.0	- 33.50
Group 2	6-68	8.8	+ 24.00
Group 3	6-117	5.1	- 70.25
Group 4	4-63	6.3	- 36.00

FIRST TIME OUT

	W-R	Per cent	£1 Level Stake
2-y-o	0-7	-	- 7.00
3-y-o	0-9	-	- 9.00
4-y-o+	2-34	5.9	+ 3.00
Totals	2-50	4.0	- 13.00

JOCKEYS RIDING

	W-R	Per cent	£1 Level Stake		W-R	Per cent	£1 Level Stake
S Drowne	5-107	4.7	- 47.00	R Cochrane	1-7	14.3	+ 6.00
A Munro	4-25	16.0	+ 3.50	L Dettori	1-7	14.3	+ 19.00
W Carson	4-31	12.9	- 17.00	J Williams	1-8	12.5	- 4.25
Miss J Southcombe	1-2	50.0	+ 24.00	A McGlone	1-10	10.0	+ 1.00
J Lowe	1-5	20.0	+ 5.00	M Hills	1-11	9.1	- 4.00

Hodges R J

J Quinn	0-15	M Wigham	0-2	L Aspell	0-1
T Sprake	0-12	N Adams	0-2	M Humphries	0-1
Paul Eddery	0-7	N Carlisle	0-2	M Perrett	0-1
Pat Eddery	0-6	R Waterfield	0-2	Miss S Mitchell	0-1
R Perham	0-5	S Mulvey	0-2	N Gwilliams	0-1
F Norton	0-4	T G McLaughlin	0-2	N Kennedy	0-1
D Biggs	0-3	A Tucker	0-1	P McCabe	0-1
Dale Gibson	0-3	B Doyle	0-1	R Price	0-1
M Roberts	0-3	D Gibbs	0-1	Ruth Coulter	0-1
Miss A Sanders	0-3	Debbie Biggs	0-1	S Davies	0-1
W Ryan	0-3	G Bardwell	0-1	S Dawson	0-1
A Dicks	0-2	G Milligan	0-1	T Quinn	0-1
C Rutter	0-2	J Carroll	0-1		
L Piggott	0-2	J O'Dwyer	0-1		

COURSE RECORD

	Total W-R	Non-Handicaps 2-y-o	3-y-o+	Handicaps 2-y-o	3-y-o+	Per cent	£1 Level Stake
Brighton	3-21	0-1	1-4	0-0	2-16	14.3	+ 8.00
Bath	3-43	0-4	1-14	0-0	2-25	7.0	- 22.25
Folkestone	2-12	0-1	2-4	0-0	0-7	16.7	- 6.00
Goodwood	2-18	0-0	0-4	0-0	2-14	11.1	- 6.50
Ripon	1-1	0-0	0-0	0-0	1-1	100.0	+ 10.00
Ayr	1-2	0-0	0-0	0-0	1-2	50.0	+ 11.00
Yarmouth	1-2	0-0	0-0	0-0	1-2	50.0	+ 6.00
York	1-10	0-0	0-1	0-0	1-9	10.0	- 1.00
Windsor	1-14	0-1	0-1	0-0	1-12	7.1	- 7.00
Lingfield	1-17	0-3	0-4	0-0	1-10	5.9	+ 9.00
Lingfield (AW)	1-18	0-0	0-3	0-0	1-15	5.6	- 7.00
Nottingham	1-19	0-1	0-8	0-0	1-10	5.3	- 8.00
Warwick	1-26	0-2	0-8	0-0	1-16	3.8	- 16.00
Salisbury	1-29	0-1	0-3	0-0	1-25	3.4	- 3.00

Chepstow	0-23	Newbury	0-6	Sandown	0-4
Leicester	0-13	Ascot	0-5	Doncaster	0-3
Kempton	0-7	Newmarket	0-5	Haydock	0-3
Southwell (AW)	0-7	Epsom	0-4	Pontefract	0-3

WINNING HORSES

	Age	Races Run	1st	2nd	3rd	Unpl	Win £
Hard To Figure	7	15	2	2	1	10	66,593
How's Yer Father	7	14	2	1	1	10	16,278
Mister Jolson	4	16	3	2	1	10	10,441
Palacegate Gold	4	16	2	1	4	9	5,834
Unveiled	5	17	2	1	0	14	5,504
Baligay	8	5	1	0	1	3	5,288
Harry's Coming	9	15	2	1	1	11	4,775

220

Mustahil	4	8	1	1	0	6	3,290
Sir Oliver	4	9	1	0	1	7	3,002
Tiger Claw	7	8	1	1	1	5	2,889
My Minnie	3	9	1	0	2	6	2,847
Sinclair Lad	5	12	1	1	1	9	2,658
Navaresque	8	12	1	1	2	8	2,560

WINNING OWNERS

	Races Won	Value £		Races Won	Value £
J W Mursell	5	77,033	Mrs D A Wetherall	2	4,775
Unity Farm Holiday Centre Ltd	4	22,456	Ms S A Joyner	1	3,002
R J Hodges	2	5,834	Mrs W Protheroe-Beynon	1	2,847
Mrs K M Burge	2	5,504	Miss R Dobson	1	2,658
H G Carnell & Son Ltd	1	5,288	Mrs D Pickford	1	2,560

Favourites	5-27	18.5%	- 3.25	Total winning prize-money	£131,957
Longest winning sequence			2	Average SP of winner	9.0/1
Longest losing sequence			62	Return on stakes invested	-36.7%

1992 Form	21-371	5.7%	-167.96	1990 Form	25-245	10.2%	- 76.57
1991 Form	27-287	9.4%	- 93.74	1989 Form	12-123	9.8%	- 13.87

K W HOGG (Isle of Man)

	No. of Horses	Races Run	1st	2nd	3rd	Unpl	Per cent	£1 Level Stake
2-y-o	4	26	2	0	0	24	7.7	- 12.50
3-y-o	3	28	0	6	1	21	-	- 28.00
4-y-o+	3	15	2	1	2	10	13.3	- 1.12
Totals	10	69	4	7	3	55	5.8	- 41.62

Jan	Feb	Mar	Apr	May	Jun	Jul	Aug	Sep	Oct/Nov
0-0	0-0	1-6	1-9	0-3	1-19	0-18	0-8	1-2	0-4

		£1 Level			£1 Level
Winning Jockeys	W-R	Stake		W-R	Stake
K Darley	3-11	+ 7.38	J Weaver	1-6	+ 3.00

		£1 Level			£1 Level
Winning Courses					
Newcastle	1-1	+ 3.50	Nottingham	1-3	+ 8.00
Haydock	1-2	+ 7.00	Catterick	1-14	- 11.12

		Races					Win
Winning Horses	Age	Run	1st	2nd	3rd	Unpl	£
Kinoko	5	13	2	1	2	8	6,667
Top Show	2	11	2	0	0	9	6,205

Favourites	0-3		Total winning prize-money	£12,872

1992 Form	4-45	8.9%	+ 6.00

R HOLLINSHEAD (Upper Longdon, Staffs)

	No. of Horses	Races Run	1st	2nd	3rd	Unpl	Per cent	£1 Level Stake
2-y-o	29	166	11	21	14	120	6.6	- 99.70
3-y-o	27	203	9	24	21	149	4.4	-163.71
4-y-o+	28	211	22	16	26	147	10.4	- 46.94
Totals	84	580	42	61	61	416	7.2	-310.35

BY MONTH

2-y-o	W-R	Per cent	£1 Level Stake	3-y-o	W-R	Per cent	£1 Level Stake
January	0-0	-	0.00	January	1-8	12.5	- 5.25
February	0-0	-	0.00	February	0-3	-	- 3.00
March	0-3	-	- 3.00	March	0-10	-	- 10.00
April	3-12	25.0	+ 10.25	April	0-25	-	- 25.00
May	1-9	11.1	- 6.00	May	1-29	3.4	- 24.00
June	0-16	-	- 16.00	June	1-33	3.0	- 30.50
July	4-24	16.7	- 2.45	July	4-33	12.1	- 11.71
August	2-29	6.9	- 15.50	August	2-25	8.0	- 17.25
September	0-28	-	- 28.00	September	0-20	-	- 20.00
Oct/Nov	1-45	2.2	- 39.00	Oct/Nov	0-17	-	- 17.00

4-y-o+	W-R	Per cent	£1 Level Stake	Totals	W-R	Per cent	£1 Level Stake
January	6-22	27.3	+ 1.68	January	7-30	23.3	- 3.57
February	1-14	7.1	- 7.00	February	1-17	5.9	- 10.00
March	0-14	-	- 14.00	March	0-27	-	- 27.00
April	1-18	5.6	- 10.00	April	4-55	7.3	- 24.75
May	2-27	7.4	- 8.00	May	4-65	6.2	- 38.00
June	6-30	20.0	+ 22.50	June	7-79	8.9	- 24.00
July	1-30	3.3	- 27.12	July	9-87	10.3	- 41.28
August	3-19	15.8	0.00	August	7-73	9.6	- 32.75
September	0-17	-	- 17.00	September	0-65	-	- 65.00
Oct/Nov	2-20	10.0	+ 12.00	Oct/Nov	3-82	3.7	- 44.00

DISTANCE

2-y-o	W-R	Per cent	£1 Level Stake	3-y-o	W-R	Per cent	£1 Level Stake
5f-6f	11-122	9.0	- 55.70	5f-6f	2-46	4.3	- 35.00
7f-8f	0-42	-	- 42.00	7f-8f	0-58	-	- 58.00
9f-13f	0-2	-	- 2.00	9f-13f	7-74	9.5	- 45.71
14f+	0-0	-	0.00	14f+	0-25	-	- 25.00

4-y-o+	W-R	Per cent	£1 Level Stake	Totals	W-R	Per cent	£1 Level Stake
5f-6f	7-64	10.9	+ 8.00	5f-6f	20-232	8.6	- 82.70
7f-8f	5-37	13.5	- 18.82	7f-8f	5-137	3.6	-118.82
9f-13f	8-83	9.6	- 21.00	9f-13f	15-159	9.4	- 68.71
14f+	2-27	7.4	- 15.12	14f+	2-52	3.8	- 40.12

TYPE OF RACE

Non-Handicaps	W-R	Per cent	£1 Level Stake	Handicaps	W-R	Per cent	£1 Level Stake
2-y-o	10-134	7.5	- 74.70	2-y-o	1-31	3.2	- 24.00
3-y-o	5-89	5.6	- 74.21	3-y-o	2-86	2.3	- 69.00
4-y-o+	5-51	9.8	- 34.82	4-y-o+	12-124	9.7	- 12.50
Selling	3-18	16.7	+ 1.88	Selling	3-18	16.7	0.00
Apprentice	1-5	20.0	+ 1.00	Apprentice	0-20	-	- 20.00
Amat/Ladies	0-0	-	0.00	Amat/Ladies	0-4	-	- 4.00
Totals	24-297	8.1	-180.85	Totals	18-283	6.4	-129.50

COURSE GRADE

	W-R	Per cent	£1 Level Stake
Group 1	8-155	5.2	- 68.12
Group 2	9-103	8.7	- 49.12
Group 3	6-151	4.0	-111.00
Group 4	19-171	11.1	- 82.11

FIRST TIME OUT

	W-R	Per cent	£1 Level Stake
2-y-o	0-29	-	- 29.00
3-y-o	0-27	-	- 27.00
4-y-o+	1-28	3.6	- 26.86
Totals	1-84	1.2	- 82.86

JOCKEYS RIDING

	W-R	Per cent	£1 Level Stake		W-R	Per cent	£1 Level Stake
S Perks	11-163	6.7	-101.29	M Hills	1-1	100.0	+ 2.25
W Ryan	10-123	8.1	- 55.57	J Quinn	1-5	20.0	+ 6.00
K Darley	5-45	11.1	- 5.62	W R Swinburn	1-7	14.3	- 3.00
D Carson	3-6	50.0	+ 9.75	L Dettori	1-10	10.0	- 7.62
A Garth	3-70	4.3	- 44.00	L Aspell	1-15	6.7	- 3.00
M Tebbutt	2-3	66.7	+ 12.50	M Humphries	1-39	2.6	- 36.25
S Wynne	2-17	11.8	- 8.50				

J Dennis	0-18	G Duffield	0-2	J Reid	0-1
Paul Eddery	0-7	Miss J Southall	0-2	J Williams	0-1
R Cochrane	0-7	Mrs G Rees	0-2	L Charnock	0-1
W Carson	0-7	N Carlisle	0-2	L Harvey	0-1
A Munro	0-3	Pat Eddery	0-2	M Roberts	0-1
L Piggott	0-3	A Culhane	0-1	Miss C Carden	0-1
A Eddery	0-2	A Mackay	0-1	Miss L Perratt	0-1
B Raymond	0-2	A McGlone	0-1	Miss S Boston	0-1
D Denby	0-2	G Carter	0-1		
F Savage	0-2	J Fanning	0-1		

COURSE RECORD

	Total W-R	Non-Handicaps 2-y-o	3-y-o+	Handicaps 2-y-o	3-y-o+	Per cent	£1 Level Stake
Lingfield (AW)	8-33	0-1	5-17	0-0	3-15	24.2	+ 0.43
Warwick	4-22	1-5	2-8	0-0	1-9	18.2	- 4.25
Redcar	4-24	1-6	1-3	0-3	2-12	16.7	- 2.50
Pontefract	4-33	2-12	1-7	0-4	1-10	12.1	- 4.75

Hollinshead R

Haydock	3-41	0-12	1-10	1-2	1-17	7.3	- 10.62
Southwell (AW)	3-69	2-10	0-25	0-1	1-33	4.3	- 50.00
Southwell (Turf)	2-8	1-2	1-3	0-0	0-3	25.0	- 4.29
Thirsk	2-21	1-6	1-4	0-1	0-10	9.5	- 6.50
Ripon	2-22	0-6	1-5	0-1	1-10	9.1	- 8.12
Goodwood	1-5	0-1	0-0	0-1	1-3	20.0	+ 3.00
Newcastle	1-14	0-4	0-1	0-1	1-8	7.1	- 8.50
Carlisle	1-16	0-1	1-8	0-0	0-7	6.3	- 4.00
York	1-16	0-5	0-1	0-1	1-9	6.3	+ 1.00
Catterick	1-19	1-4	0-6	0-3	0-6	5.3	- 16.00
Newmarket	1-19	0-4	0-5	0-2	1-8	5.3	- 8.00
Beverley	1-25	1-8	0-8	0-0	0-9	4.0	- 22.25
Nottingham	1-27	0-7	0-8	0-1	1-11	3.7	- 18.00
Chester	1-33	0-10	0-8	0-2	1-13	3.0	- 29.00
Doncaster	1-45	0-10	0-11	0-5	1-19	2.2	- 30.00

Leicester	0-29	Ascot	0-3	Newbury	0-2
Chepstow	0-15	Kempton	0-3	Sandown	0-1
Bath	0-14	Lingfield	0-3	Yarmouth	0-1
Hamilton	0-7	Edinburgh	0-2		
Ayr	0-6	Folkestone	0-2		

WINNING HORSES

	Age	Races Run	1st	2nd	3rd	Unpl	Win £
Castlerea Lad	4	10	3	1	0	6	28,453
In The Money	4	10	2	0	2	6	14,455
Eastleigh	4	8	3	1	0	4	8,014
Eager Deva	6	12	2	3	0	7	7,850
Civil Law	3	14	3	1	2	8	7,599
Ann Hill	3	17	3	3	4	7	6,931
Simmie's Special	5	15	1	1	1	12	6,255
Indiahra	2	11	2	4	0	5	5,899
Jalore	4	7	3	0	1	3	5,770
My Lifetime Lady	2	8	2	2	1	3	5,490
Mad Militant	4	12	1	1	2	8	5,374
Ferdia	4	6	2	1	1	2	5,043
Respectable Jones	7	13	2	2	3	6	4,703
Culsyth Flyer	2	13	2	3	1	7	4,644
Nordico Princess	2	11	1	2	0	8	4,092
The Auction Bidder	6	11	1	0	0	10	3,611
Raven's Return	2	7	1	0	0	6	3,436
Rousitto	5	21	1	2	4	14	3,236
Rankaidade	2	8	1	3	2	2	3,002
Heathyards Gem	3	13	1	0	0	12	2,951
Desert Laughter	3	5	1	0	1	3	2,924
Birchwood Sun	3	5	1	0	0	4	2,601
Bold Aristocrat	2	10	1	1	2	6	2,445
Famous Beauty	6	18	1	2	4	11	2,364
Heathyards Crusade	2	9	1	0	0	8	2,243

WINNING OWNERS

	Races Won	Value £		Races Won	Value £
Mrs Tess Graham	3	28,453	Heathavon Stables Ltd	1	3,611
J E Bigg	6	24,833	J Pattison	1	3,236
Mrs B Facchino	4	12,973	S B Bell	1	3,002
A S Hill	4	10,367	Mrs B L Morgan	1	2,951
Mrs E G Faulkner	2	7,850	H S Yates	1	2,924
D Coppenhall	1	6,255	P D Savill	1	2,601
P J Lawton	2	5,899	Mrs J Hughes	1	2,445
Lifetime U K Ltd	2	5,490	Mrs J Coathup	1	2,280
Noel Sweeney	2	5,043	L A Morgan	1	2,243
Mrs B Ramsden	2	4,703	R Hollinshead	1	2,110
W Cully	2	4,644	Miss Jane Southall	1	1,380
J D Graham	1	4,092			

Favourites	12-44	27.3%	- 14.61	Total winning prize-money		£149,385
Longest winning sequence			3	Average SP of winner		5.4/1
Longest losing sequence			79	Return on stakes invested		-53.5%
1992 Form	60-611	9.8%	-118.14	1990 Form	41-549	7.5%	-221.15
1991 Form	31-549	5.6%	-264.91	1989 Form	30-518	5.8%	-260.62

L J HOLT (Basingstoke, Hants)

	No. of Horses	Races Run	1st	2nd	3rd	Unpl	Per cent	£1 Level Stake
2-y-o	6	15	0	0	1	14	-	- 15.00
3-y-o	8	65	5	9	2	49	7.7	- 9.50
4-y-o+	8	72	4	7	4	57	5.6	- 42.67
Totals	22	152	9	16	7	120	5.9	- 67.17

Jan	Feb	Mar	Apr	May	Jun	Jul	Aug	Sep	Oct/Nov
0-0	0-0	0-1	0-19	3-27	2-29	2-34	2-22	0-12	0-8

Winning Jockeys	W-R	£1 Level Stake		W-R	£1 Level Stake
A Munro	3-25	- 7.67	A McGlone	2-16	+ 7.50
J Reid	3-39	- 2.00	W Newnes	1-5	+ 2.00

Winning Courses	W-R	£1 Level Stake		W-R	£1 Level Stake
Lingfield	2-15	+ 21.00	Bath	1-8	- 1.00
Ascot	1-3	+ 5.50	Brighton	1-8	- 4.00
Epsom	1-5	+ 2.00	Newbury	1-11	- 2.00
Kempton	1-7	- 2.67	Salisbury	1-15	- 6.00

Winning Horses	Age	Races Run	1st	2nd	3rd	Unpl	Win £
Loch Patrick	3	7	2	1	0	4	20,632
Aragrove	3	10	2	2	0	6	7,978
Sea-Deer	4	10	2	2	0	6	7,798
Alltruthenight	4	11	1	0	2	8	4,625
Court Minstrel	4	11	1	0	0	10	3,758
Walnut Burl	3	15	1	1	2	11	3,348

Favourites	2-12	16.7%	- 3.67	Total winning prize-money			£48,138

1992 Form	11-146	7.5%	- 59.75	1990 Form	6-178	3.4%	- 102.75
1991 Form	4-160	2.5%	-131.12	1989 Form	13-140	9.3%	- 19.75

C A HORGAN (Billingbear, Berks)

	No. of Horses	Races Run	1st	2nd	3rd	Unpl	Per cent	£1 Level Stake
2-y-o	2	9	0	0	0	9	-	- 9.00
3-y-o	4	30	3	3	4	20	10.0	- 13.37
4-y-o+	8	48	2	4	5	37	4.2	- 23.50
Totals	14	87	5	7	9	66	5.7	- 45.87

Jan	Feb	Mar	Apr	May	Jun	Jul	Aug	Sep	Oct/Nov
0-0	0-0	0-2	0-11	2-13	0-16	2-16	0-14	1-9	0-6

Winning Jockeys	W-R	£1 Level Stake		W-R	£1 Level Stake
R Hills	2-15	+ 4.63	D Holland	1-8	- 3.00
D Wright	1-7	+ 0.50	E Johnson	1-10	- 1.00

Winning Courses					
York	1-1	+ 16.00	Lingfield	1-3	+ 2.00
Haydock	1-2	+ 0.63	Windsor	1-9	- 1.50
Yarmouth	1-2	+ 7.00			

Winning Horses	Age	Races Run	1st	2nd	3rd	Unpl	Win £
Risk Master	4	10	1	1	1	7	13,047
Belfry Green	3	8	1	1	1	5	3,407
Starlight Rose	3	10	1	1	1	7	3,158
Trinity Hall	3	9	1	1	2	5	2,685
Brown Carpet	6	6	1	0	0	5	2,233

Favourites	1-2	50.0%	+ 0.63	Total winning prize-money			£24,529

1992 Form	5-85	5.9%	- 17.00	1990 Form	3-69	4.3%	- 26.50
1991 Form	4-105	3.8%	- 57.62	1989 Form	9-97	9.3%	- 37.80

R F JOHNSON HOUGHTON (Didcot, Oxon)

	No. of Horses	Races Run	1st	2nd	3rd	Unpl	Per cent	£1 Level Stake
2-y-o	9	41	1	5	9	26	2.4	- 34.00
3-y-o	9	63	5	6	12	40	7.9	- 24.18
4-y-o+	7	23	1	2	2	18	4.3	- 10.00
Totals	25	127	7	13	23	84	5.5	- 68.18

Jan	Feb	Mar	Apr	May	Jun	Jul	Aug	Sep	Oct/Nov
0-4	0-2	0-3	0-8	2-25	2-19	0-11	2-23	1-24	0-8

Winning Jockeys	W-R	£1 Level Stake			W-R	£1 Level Stake
J Reid	3-14	+ 7.82		S Whitworth	1-5	+ 8.00
W Newnes	1-1	+ 5.00		J Carroll	1-6	+ 9.00
T Sprake	1-3	0.00				

Winning Courses						
Epsom	2-3	+ 8.82		Haydock	1-6	+ 4.00
Ripon	1-3	+ 12.00		Leicester	1-9	- 6.00
Kempton	1-4	+ 2.00		Bath	1-10	+ 3.00

Winning Horses	Age	Races Run	1st	2nd	3rd	Unpl	Win £
The Executor	3	5	2	1	0	2	6,319
No Reservations	3	9	1	0	1	7	5,898
Hard Task	3	10	1	0	2	7	3,840
Baskerville	2	7	1	0	3	3	3,558
Mr Geneaology	3	5	1	0	2	2	3,443
Mogwai	4	10	1	2	0	7	2,742

Favourites	1-7	14.3%	- 4.00	Total winning prize-money		£25,799

1992 Form	10-132	7.6%	- 67.57	1990 Form	25-191	13.1%	- 31.02
1991 Form	13-171	7.6%	- 57.07	1989 Form	24-211	11.4%	- 82.46

P HOWLING (Guildford, Surrey)

	No. of Horses	Races Run	1st	2nd	3rd	Unpl	Per cent	£1 Level Stake
2-y-o	8	23	0	0	0	23	-	- 23.00
3-y-o	14	95	2	3	5	85	2.1	- 78.50
4-y-o+	10	58	6	2	3	47	10.3	- 13.92
Totals	32	176	8	5	8	155	4.5	-115.42

Jan	Feb	Mar	Apr	May	Jun	Jul	Aug	Sep	Oct/Nov
0-8	2-8	0-4	1-17	1-25	0-27	3-26	1-28	0-15	0-18

Winning Jockeys	W-R	£1 Level Stake		W-R	£1 Level Stake
K Darley	4-6	+ 24.75	D McKeown	1-2	+ 1.50
J Quinn	3-46	- 19.67			

Winning Courses					
Lingfield (AW)	2-19	- 2.50	Bath	1-11	- 6.67
Doncaster	1-5	- 1.75	Lingfield	1-15	- 2.00
Newmarket	1-6	+ 1.50	Yarmouth	1-21	- 14.00
Brighton	1-10	- 1.00			

Winning Horses	Age	Races Run	1st	2nd	3rd	Unpl	Win £
Samsolom	5	18	6	2	1	9	20,776
Purbeck Centenary	3	15	2	1	3	9	5,297

Favourites	1-3	33.3%	+ 0.25	Total winning prize-money		£26,072

1992 Form	3-180	1.7%	-119.37	1990 Form	6-185	3.2%	-102.50
1991 Form	6-185	3.2%	-110.50	1989 Form	5-165	3.0%	-121.00

LORD HUNTINGDON (West Ilsley, Berks)

	No. of Horses	Races Run	1st	2nd	3rd	Unpl	Per cent	£1 Level Stake
2-y-o	19	42	3	4	1	34	7.1	- 26.62
3-y-o	22	101	11	17	18	55	10.9	- 52.50
4-y-o+	26	126	25	19	12	70	19.8	+ 10.89
Totals	67	269	39	40	31	159	14.5	- 68.23

BY MONTH

2-y-o	W-R	Per cent	£1 Level Stake	3-y-o	W-R	Per cent	£1 Level Stake
January	0-0	-	0.00	January	3-7	42.9	+ 6.50
February	0-0	-	0.00	February	0-5	-	- 5.00
March	0-0	-	0.00	March	0-5	-	- 5.00
April	0-0	-	0.00	April	0-11	-	- 11.00
May	2-5	40.0	+ 1.38	May	1-4	25.0	- 1.75
June	0-3	-	- 3.00	June	0-9	-	- 9.00
July	0-7	-	- 7.00	July	3-17	17.6	- 1.00
August	0-5	-	- 5.00	August	1-24	4.2	- 23.00
September	1-12	8.3	- 3.00	September	2-13	15.4	- 5.25
Oct/Nov	0-10	-	- 10.00	Oct/Nov	1-6	16.7	+ 2.00

4-y-o+	W-R	Per cent	£1 Level Stake	Totals	W-R	Per cent	£1 Level Stake
January	1-5	20.0	- 0.50	January	4-12	33.3	+ 6.00
February	4-11	36.4	+ 5.25	February	4-16	25.0	+ 0.25
March	2-11	18.2	- 2.75	March	2-16	12.5	- 7.75
April	0-12	-	- 12.00	April	0-23	-	- 23.00
May	0-11	-	- 11.00	May	3-20	15.0	- 11.37
June	5-20	25.0	+ 22.00	June	5-32	15.6	+ 10.00
July	5-15	33.3	+ 8.35	July	8-39	20.5	+ 0.35
August	2-11	18.2	- 2.09	August	3-40	7.5	- 30.09
September	4-11	36.4	+ 11.38	September	7-36	19.4	+ 3.13
Oct/Nov	2-19	10.5	- 7.75	Oct/Nov	3-35	8.6	- 15.75

DISTANCE

2-y-o	W-R	Per cent	£1 Level Stake	3-y-o	W-R	Per cent	£1 Level Stake
5f-6f	3-32	9.4	- 16.62	5f-6f	1-7	14.3	- 1.00
7f-8f	0-10	-	- 10.00	7f-8f	1-34	2.9	- 28.50
9f-13f	0-0	-	0.00	9f-13f	6-50	12.0	- 26.50
14f+	0-0	-	0.00	14f+	3-10	30.0	+ 3.50

4-y-o+	W-R	Per cent	£1 Level Stake	Totals	W-R	Per cent	£1 Level Stake
5f-6f	1-3	33.3	+ 3.00	5f-6f	5-42	11.9	- 14.62
7f-8f	12-56	21.4	+ 1.89	7f-8f	13-100	13.0	- 36.61
9f-13f	8-45	17.8	+ 3.75	9f-13f	14-95	14.7	- 22.75
14f+	4-22	18.2	+ 2.25	14f+	7-32	21.9	+ 5.75

TYPE OF RACE

Non-Handicaps	W-R	Per cent	£1 Level Stake	Handicaps	W-R	Per cent	£1 Level Stake
2-y-o	2-36	5.6	- 29.62	2-y-o	0-5	-	- 5.00
3-y-o	8-46	17.4	- 8.50	3-y-o	2-47	4.3	- 40.50
4-y-o+	5-21	23.8	+ 13.75	4-y-o+	15-94	16.0	- 14.40
Selling	2-3	66.7	+ 13.00	Selling	0-2	-	- 2.00
Apprentice	0-3	-	- 3.00	Apprentice	2-9	22.2	- 3.34
Amat/Ladies	2-2	100.0	+ 5.38	Amat/Ladies	1-1	100.0	+ 6.00
Totals	19-111	17.1	- 8.99	Totals	20-158	12.7	- 59.24

COURSE GRADE

	W-R	Per cent	£1 Level Stake
Group 1	15-130	11.5	- 25.87
Group 2	5-31	16.1	- 8.37
Group 3	3-39	7.7	- 25.09
Group 4	16-69	23.2	- 8.90

FIRST TIME OUT

	W-R	Per cent	£1 Level Stake
2-y-o	1-18	5.6	- 14.00
3-y-o	2-22	9.1	- 10.50
4-y-o+	2-26	7.7	- 14.00
Totals	5-66	7.6	- 38.50

JOCKEYS RIDING

	W-R	Per cent	£1 Level Stake		W-R	Per cent	£1 Level Stake
D Harrison	9-82	11.0	- 32.49	Mrs M Cowdrey	1-1	100.0	+ 1.88
D McKeown	7-29	24.1	+ 1.00	D Holland	1-2	50.0	+ 1.25
A Munro	6-55	10.9	- 26.62	J Williams	1-4	25.0	+ 2.00
L Dettori	4-15	26.7	+ 10.25	L Piggott	1-5	20.0	- 1.00
T Quinn	2-4	50.0	+ 5.75	J Wilkinson	1-6	16.7	- 2.25
W R Swinburn	2-18	11.1	- 5.50	M Roberts	1-6	16.7	0.00
Miss I D W Jones	1-1	100.0	+ 3.50	Pat Eddery	1-6	16.7	+ 2.00
Mr L A Urbano	1-1	100.0	+ 6.00				

B Raymond	0-6	B Rouse	0-1	K Darley	0-1
M Hills	0-6	C Asmussen	0-1	M Birch	0-1
D Salt	0-3	C Rutter	0-1	N Adams	0-1
J Carroll	0-3	D Wright	0-1	P Robinson	0-1
K Fallon	0-2	G Duffield	0-1	R Cochrane	0-1
W Newnes	0-2	J Reid	0-1	R P Elliott	0-1

COURSE RECORD

	Total W-R	Non-Handicaps 2-y-o	Non-Handicaps 3-y-o+	Handicaps 2-y-o	Handicaps 3-y-o+	Per cent	£1 Level Stake
Lingfield (AW)	9-33	0-0	2-12	0-0	7-21	27.3	+ 0.50
Southwell (AW)	5-24	0-2	3-9	0-0	2-13	20.8	- 2.90
Kempton	3-13	0-1	2-3	0-1	1-8	23.1	+ 8.00
Folkestone	2-4	0-1	2-3	0-0	0-0	50.0	+ 1.50
Bath	2-5	1-2	0-0	0-0	1-3	40.0	+ 0.91
Goodwood	2-5	0-2	1-1	0-0	1-2	40.0	+ 4.88
Epsom	2-6	0-0	1-2	0-0	1-4	33.3	+ 18.00
Haydock	2-7	0-0	1-3	0-0	1-4	28.6	+ 3.25
Brighton	2-9	0-1	1-5	0-0	1-3	22.2	- 2.25
Ascot	2-18	0-1	1-4	0-0	1-13	11.1	- 6.00
Newbury	2-24	0-6	0-3	0-1	2-14	8.3	- 12.00
Newmarket	2-24	0-2	0-3	0-3	2-16	8.3	- 9.00
Lingfield	1-4	1-3	0-1	0-0	0-0	25.0	- 1.62
Redcar	1-4	1-1	0-1	0-0	0-2	25.0	+ 5.00
Leicester	1-6	0-1	1-2	0-0	0-3	16.7	+ 2.00
Salisbury	1-8	0-2	1-4	0-0	0-2	12.5	- 3.50

Sandown	0-15	York	0-5	Yarmouth	0-2
Windsor	0-10	Newcastle	0-4	Beverley	0-1
Doncaster	0-9	Chepstow	0-3	Ripon	0-1
Nottingham	0-7	Chester	0-3	Southwell (Turf)	0-1
Pontefract	0-5	Carlisle	0-2		
Warwick	0-5	Thirsk	0-2		

WINNING HORSES

	Age	Races Run	1st	2nd	3rd	Unpl	Win £
Drum Taps	7	2	1	0	0	1	107,465
Penny Drops	4	7	3	2	2	0	74,235
Enharmonic	6	3	1	0	0	2	21,843
Set The Fashion	4	15	5	4	3	3	17,775

Welsh Mill	4	2	1	0	0	1	11,999
Discord	7	4	2	0	0	2	11,161
Heniu	4	5	2	1	0	2	10,312
Spencer's Revenge	4	4	2	1	0	1	9,347
High Summer	3	9	3	4	0	2	8,377
Coltrane	5	8	3	0	1	4	7,906
Whitechapel	5	5	1	2	0	2	7,505
Record Lover	3	8	2	1	4	1	5,953
Rosina Mae	4	7	1	1	1	4	5,436
Scottish Peak	3	5	1	0	1	3	4,449
Desert Lore	2	1	1	0	0	0	3,699
Talent	5	9	1	2	1	5	3,688
Straight Arrow	2	5	1	1	1	2	3,524
Majhola	3	2	1	0	1	0	3,494
Hierarch	4	10	1	1	1	7	3,377
Empire Pool	3	4	1	1	0	2	3,218
Scarlet Tunic	3	4	1	0	0	3	2,742
King Parrot	5	6	1	0	0	5	2,536
Kryptos	3	6	1	0	3	2	2,208
Criminal Record	3	6	1	0	2	3	2,070
Mockingbird	2	8	1	0	0	7	2,070

WINNING OWNERS

	Races Won	Value £		Races Won	Value £
Yoshio Asakawa	3	118,626	Lord Crawshaw	2	9,347
Stanley J Sharp	3	74,235	Greenland Park Ltd	1	5,436
The Queen	15	72,223	J R Bailey	1	3,524
Lord Weinstock	2	16,447	Sultan Mohammed	1	3,494
M L Oberstein	6	15,928	Lord Huntingdon	1	2,536
Henryk De Kwiatowski	3	12,520	Lord Carnarvon	1	2,070

Favourites	16-55	29.1%	+ 6.52	Total winning prize-money	£336,386
Longest winning sequence			2	Average SP of winner	4.2/1
Longest losing sequence			38	Return on stakes invested	-24.3%

1992 Form	60-331	18.1%	+ 12.32	1990 Form	20-197	10.2%	- 53.59
1991 Form	36-254	14.2%	+ 91.26	1989 Form	26-171	15.2%	- 42.55

R INGRAM (Epsom, Surrey)

	No. of Horses	Races Run	1st	2nd	3rd	Unpl	Per cent	£1 Level Stake
2-y-o	1	6	0	0	1	5	-	- 6.00
3-y-o	3	22	2	0	6	14	9.1	- 6.00
4-y-o+	5	21	3	1	1	16	14.3	+ 11.00
Totals	9	49	5	1	8	35	10.2	- 1.00

Jan	Feb	Mar	Apr	May	Jun	Jul	Aug	Sep	Oct/Nov
0-2	0-2	0-0	0-1	0-3	1-6	1-12	2-10	1-7	0-6

Winning Jockeys	W-R	£1 Level Stake				W-R	£1 Level Stake
B Russell	1-1	+ 4.50	A Tucker			1-11	- 0.50
N Gwilliams	1-4	+ 9.00	A McGlone			1-14	- 1.00
J Weaver	1-9	- 3.00					

Winning Courses							
Redcar	1-1	+ 12.00	Goodwood			1-3	+ 7.50
Bath	1-2	+ 11.00	Lingfield			1-6	- 0.50
Sandown	1-2	+ 4.00					

Winning Horses	Age	Races Run	1st	2nd	3rd	Unpl	Win £
Lyndon's Linnet	5	7	1	1	0	5	3,583
Kinnegad Kid	4	7	1	0	1	5	3,184
Coalisland	3	11	1	0	3	7	2,977
Dam Certain	4	2	1	0	0	1	2,686
Lochore	3	10	1	0	3	6	2,269

Favourites	0-1			Total winning prize-money			£14,698

1992 Form	1-37	2.7%	- 3.00	1991 Form	2-27	7.4%	- 4.00

K T IVORY (Radlett, Herts)

	No. of Horses	Races Run	1st	2nd	3rd	Unpl	Per cent	£1 Level Stake
2-y-o	4	20	0	2	2	16	-	- 20.00
3-y-o	6	35	2	0	6	27	5.7	- 12.50
4-y-o+	4	36	0	4	4	28	-	- 36.00
Totals	14	91	2	6	12	71	2.2	- 68.50

Jan	Feb	Mar	Apr	May	Jun	Jul	Aug	Sep	Oct/Nov
0-0	0-0	0-7	0-7	0-8	0-14	1-14	1-16	0-18	0-7

Winning Jockeys	W-R	£1 Level Stake		W-R	£1 Level Stake
W Newnes	1-10	- 2.50	M Wigham	1-32	- 17.00

Winning Courses					
Windsor	1-1	+ 14.00	Folkestone	1-8	- 0.50

Winning Horses	Age	Races Run	1st	2nd	3rd	Unpl	Win £
Our Shadee	3	14	1	0	4	9	2,490
Double Bounce	3	7	1	0	1	5	2,243

Favourites	0-1		Total winning prize-money		£4,733

1992 Form	9-91	9.9%	+ 13.23	1990 Form	7-128	5.5%	- 46.00
1991 Form	5-148	3.4%	- 97.00	1989 Form	7-145	4.8%	- 54.37

C JAMES (Newbury, Berks)

	No. of Horses	Races Run	1st	2nd	3rd	Unpl	Per cent	£1 Level Stake
2-y-o	6	26	0	2	1	23	-	- 26.00
3-y-o	3	14	2	1	0	11	14.3	+ 41.00
4-y-o+	4	26	2	1	0	23	7.7	- 1.00
Totals	13	66	4	4	1	57	6.1	+ 14.00

Jan	Feb	Mar	Apr	May	Jun	Jul	Aug	Sep	Oct/Nov
0-2	0-2	0-0	1-2	1-10	1-10	1-14	0-9	0-11	0-6

Winning Jockeys	W-R	£1 Level Stake		W-R	£1 Level Stake
J Reid	2-5	+ 50.00	W Newnes	2-26	- 1.00

Winning Courses					
Goodwood	1-3	+ 31.00	Lingfield	1-8	+ 13.00
Salisbury	1-5	+ 12.00	Windsor	1-10	- 2.00

Winning Horses	Age	Races Run	1st	2nd	3rd	Unpl	Win £
Moon Over Miami	3	7	2	1	0	4	20,331
Grey Charmer	4	11	2	1	0	8	8,168

Favourites	0-1		Total winning prize-money		£28,499

1992 Form	4-55	7.3%	+ 1.75	1990 Form	1-45	2.2%	- 40.00
1991 Form	3-56	5.4%	- 37.25	1989 Form	1-37	2.7%	- 33.00

A P JARVIS (Aston Upthorpe, Oxon)

	No. of Horses	Races Run	1st	2nd	3rd	Unpl	Per cent	£1 Level Stake
2-y-o	9	40	0	0	2	38	-	- 40.00
3-y-o	8	75	7	12	6	50	9.3	- 27.25
4-y-o+	2	17	0	0	1	16	-	- 17.00
Totals	19	132	7	12	9	104	5.3	- 84.25

Jan	Feb	Mar	Apr	May	Jun	Jul	Aug	Sep	Oct/Nov
0-0	0-3	0-4	2-10	1-24	1-24	1-23	1-12	1-10	0-22

Winning Jockeys	W-R	£1 Level Stake		W-R	£1 Level Stake
S Whitworth	3-32	- 18.50	D McCabe	1-2	+ 11.00
G McGrath	2-6	+ 2.25	T Quinn	1-5	+ 8.00

Winning Courses					
Brighton	1-1	+ 3.00	Sandown	1-6	+ 7.00
Haydock	1-1	+ 3.50	Chepstow	1-9	- 4.00
Kempton	1-5	+ 8.00	Nottingham	1-13	- 9.25
Pontefract	1-5	- 0.50			

Jarvis A P

Winning Horses	Age	Races Run	1st	2nd	3rd	Unpl	Win £
Another Jade	3	18	3	3	1	11	9,640
Who's The Best	3	11	2	0	0	9	6,045
Silver Groom	3	16	2	3	3	8	5,461

Favourites	2-11	18.2%	- 2.75	Total winning prize-money	£21,146
1992 Form	2-73	2.7%	- 41.00	1991 Form 1-11 9.1%	- 2.00

M A JARVIS (Newmarket)

	No. of Horses	Races Run	1st	2nd	3rd	Unpl	Per cent	£1 Level Stake
2-y-o	11	37	5	6	4	22	13.5	- 12.25
3-y-o	14	65	5	8	8	44	7.7	- 47.70
4-y-o+	7	45	11	7	5	22	24.4	+ 10.13
Totals	32	147	21	21	17	88	14.3	- 49.82

BY MONTH

2-y-o	W-R	Per cent	£1 Level Stake	3-y-o	W-R	Per cent	£1 Level Stake
January	0-0	-	0.00	January	0-0	-	0.00
February	0-0	-	0.00	February	0-0	-	0.00
March	0-0	-	0.00	March	0-0	-	0.00
April	0-1	-	- 1.00	April	1-7	14.3	- 4.50
May	0-4	-	- 4.00	May	1-10	10.0	- 9.00
June	1-4	25.0	- 0.50	June	1-12	8.3	- 10.20
July	0-3	-	- 3.00	July	0-11	-	- 11.00
August	0-6	-	- 6.00	August	2-11	18.2	+ 1.00
September	3-7	42.9	+ 12.15	September	0-8	-	- 8.00
Oct/Nov	1-12	8.3	- 9.90	Oct/Nov	0-6	-	- 6.00

4-y-o+	W-R	Per cent	£1 Level Stake	Totals	W-R	Per cent	£1 Level Stake
January	1-2	50.0	+ 1.75	January	1-2	50.0	+ 1.75
February	0-0	-	0.00	February	0-0	-	0.00
March	0-1	-	- 1.00	March	0-1	-	- 1.00
April	0-2	-	- 2.00	April	1-10	10.0	- 7.50
May	2-5	40.0	+ 15.25	May	3-19	15.8	+ 2.25
June	0-9	-	- 9.00	June	2-25	8.0	- 19.70
July	6-11	54.5	+ 12.25	July	6-25	24.0	- 1.75
August	2-6	33.3	+ 1.88	August	4-23	17.4	- 3.12
September	0-4	-	- 4.00	September	3-19	15.8	+ 0.15
Oct/Nov	0-5	-	- 5.00	Oct/Nov	1-23	4.3	- 20.90

DISTANCE

2-y-o	W-R	Per cent	£1 Level Stake	3-y-o	W-R	Per cent	£1 Level Stake
5f-6f	2-19	10.5	- 13.40	5f-6f	0-10	-	- 10.00
7f-8f	3-18	16.7	+ 1.15	7f-8f	2-27	7.4	- 18.20
9f-13f	0-0	-	0.00	9f-13f	3-25	12.0	- 16.50
14f+	0-0	-	0.00	14f+	0-3	-	- 3.00

4-y-o+	W-R	Per cent	£1 Level Stake	Totals	W-R	Per cent	£1 Level Stake
5f-6f	4-5	80.0	+ 19.63	5f-6f	6-34	17.6	- 3.77
7f-8f	0-8	-	- 8.00	7f-8f	5-53	9.4	- 25.05
9f-13f	7-32	21.9	- 1.50	9f-13f	10-57	17.5	- 18.00
14f+	0-0	-	0.00	14f+	0-3	-	- 3.00

TYPE OF RACE

Non-Handicaps	W-R	Per cent	£1 Level Stake	Handicaps	W-R	Per cent	£1 Level Stake
2-y-o	4-31	12.9	- 21.25	2-y-o	1-3	33.3	+ 12.00
3-y-o	3-31	9.7	- 25.70	3-y-o	2-30	6.7	- 18.00
4-y-o+	0-6	-	- 6.00	4-y-o+	11-36	30.6	+ 19.13
Selling	0-2	-	- 2.00	Selling	0-2	-	- 2.00
Apprentice	0-0	-	0.00	Apprentice	0-5	-	- 5.00
Amat/Ladies	0-1	-	- 1.00	Amat/Ladies	0-0	-	0.00
Totals	7-71	9.9	- 55.95	Totals	14-76	18.4	+ 6.13

COURSE GRADE

	W-R	Per cent	£1 Level Stake
Group 1	4-61	6.6	- 45.10
Group 2	5-21	23.8	+ 16.65
Group 3	6-48	12.5	- 26.75
Group 4	6-17	35.3	+ 5.38

FIRST TIME OUT

	W-R	Per cent	£1 Level Stake
2-y-o	0-11	-	- 11.00
3-y-o	2-14	14.3	- 10.28
4-y-o+	2-7	28.6	+ 13.75
Totals	4-32	12.5	- 7.53

JOCKEYS RIDING

	W-R	Per cent	£1 Level Stake		W-R	Per cent	£1 Level Stake
P Robinson	7-39	17.9	- 4.47	G Duffield	1-5	20.0	- 4.00
Pat Eddery	4-9	44.4	+ 1.55	A Munro	1-5	20.0	- 2.90
K Rutter	3-25	12.0	+ 2.50	J Carroll	1-6	16.7	- 3.50
W Woods	2-7	28.6	+ 2.75	N Day	1-9	11.1	- 3.50
D McKeown	1-1	100.0	+ 2.75				

W Ryan	0-8	M Hills	0-2	G Bardwell	0-1
B Raymond	0-3	M Roberts	0-2	Mrs G Jarvis	0-1
J Quinn	0-3	M Tebbutt	0-2	N Carlisle	0-1
R Cochrane	0-3	Paul Eddery	0-2	P McCabe	0-1
G Carter	0-2	W Carson	0-2	W Newnes	0-1
J Reid	0-2	C Asmussen	0-1	W R Swinburn	0-1
L Dettori	0-2	D Biggs	0-1		

COURSE RECORD

	Total	Non-Handicaps		Handicaps		Per	£1 Level
	W-R	2-y-o	3-y-o+	2-y-o	3-y-o+	cent	Stake
Southwell (Turf)	3-3	1-1	0-0	0-0	2-2	100.0	+ 11.25
Southwell (AW)	3-5	0-1	0-0	0-0	3-4	60.0	+ 3.13
Windsor	3-7	0-0	0-2	0-0	3-5	42.9	+ 1.75
Brighton	3-9	0-1	1-4	0-0	2-4	33.3	+ 12.25
Nottingham	2-8	1-1	0-4	0-0	1-3	25.0	+ 2.00
Thirsk	1-1	1-1	0-0	0-0	0-0	100.0	+ 0.40
Epsom	1-3	0-1	0-0	0-0	1-2	33.3	+ 4.00
Hamilton	1-4	0-0	1-2	0-0	0-2	25.0	- 1.50
Lingfield	1-5	0-1	0-1	1-1	0-2	20.0	+ 10.00
Sandown	1-8	0-0	1-4	0-0	0-4	12.5	- 6.20
Doncaster	1-10	1-4	0-1	0-0	0-5	10.0	- 7.90
Newmarket	1-22	0-5	0-5	0-2	1-10	4.5	- 17.00

Yarmouth	0-11	Folkestone	0-3	Chepstow	0-1
Pontefract	0-9	Ascot	0-2	Haydock	0-1
Leicester	0-6	Bath	0-2	Lingfield (AW)	0-1
Goodwood	0-5	Carlisle	0-2	Ripon	0-1
Kempton	0-4	Catterick	0-2	Warwick	0-1
Newbury	0-4	Redcar	0-2		
Chester	0-3	York	0-2		

WINNING HORSES

	Age	Races Run	1st	2nd	3rd	Unpl	Win £
Sakharov	4	5	4	1	0	0	10,701
Sharjah	3	8	1	0	2	5	9,472
Bentico	4	12	3	1	1	7	9,327
Miss Fascination	3	9	2	3	0	4	6,980
Misty Goddess	5	9	2	2	0	5	5,744
New Capricorn	3	8	1	1	1	5	5,360
Green Golightly	2	2	1	0	0	1	3,758
Northern Celadon	2	9	1	3	3	2	3,676
Co Pilot	2	3	1	1	0	1	3,626
Ragsat Al Omor	2	4	1	1	0	2	3,494
Rival Bid	5	9	1	2	1	5	3,348
Chiappucci	3	6	1	2	2	1	2,692
Clifton Chase	4	2	1	0	0	1	2,490
Sparkling Lyric	2	4	1	0	1	2	2,243

WINNING OWNERS

	Races Won	Value £		Races Won	Value £
J R Good	6	16,445	R P Marchant	1	3,676
Sheikh Ahmed Al Maktoum	2	12,966	Denis J Larke	1	3,626
Mark Christofi	3	9,327	David Altham	1	3,348
N S Yong	3	9,223	M A Jarvis	1	2,692
Kamal Bhatia	1	5,360	A K Smeaton	1	2,490
Raymond Anderson Green	1	3,758			

Favourites	12-27	44.4%	+ 6.18	Total winning prize-money			£72,910
Longest winning sequence			2	Average SP of winner			3.6/1
Longest losing sequence			22	Return on stakes invested			-33.7%
1992 Form	28-192	14.6%	- 28.31	1990 Form	28-258	10.9%	- 70.12
1991 Form	24-249	9.6%	- 55.22	1989 Form	28-270	10.4%	-119.08

W JARVIS (Newmarket)

	No. of Horses	Races Run	1st	2nd	3rd	Unpl	Per cent	£1 Level Stake
2-y-o	21	45	4	1	3	37	8.9	- 30.50
3-y-o	22	111	11	18	10	72	9.9	- 47.86
4-y-o+	4	27	5	2	0	20	18.5	+ 27.00
Totals	47	183	20	21	13	129	10.9	- 51.36

BY MONTH

2-y-o	W-R	Per cent	£1 Level Stake	3-y-o	W-R	Per cent	£1 Level Stake
January	0-0	-	0.00	January	0-1	-	- 1.00
February	0-0	-	0.00	February	0-0	-	0.00
March	0-0	-	0.00	March	1-1	100.0	+ 6.00
April	0-3	-	- 3.00	April	0-8	-	- 8.00
May	1-3	33.3	0.00	May	0-17	-	- 17.00
June	0-1	-	- 1.00	June	0-12	-	- 12.00
July	1-3	33.3	+ 0.75	July	2-19	10.5	- 2.50
August	0-9	-	- 9.00	August	4-20	20.0	- 3.37
September	0-9	-	- 9.00	September	2-19	10.5	- 5.37
Oct/Nov	2-17	11.8	- 9.25	Oct/Nov	2-14	14.3	- 4.62

4-y-o+	W-R	Per cent	£1 Level Stake	Totals	W-R	Per cent	£1 Level Stake
January	0-0	-	0.00	January	0-1	-	- 1.00
February	0-0	-	0.00	February	0-0	-	0.00
March	0-0	-	0.00	March	1-1	100.0	+ 6.00
April	0-2	-	- 2.00	April	0-13	-	- 13.00
May	0-4	-	- 4.00	May	1-24	4.2	- 21.00
June	0-1	-	- 1.00	June	0-14	-	- 14.00
July	1-5	20.0	+ 6.00	July	4-27	14.8	+ 4.25
August	4-8	50.0	+ 35.00	August	8-37	21.6	+ 22.63
September	0-5	-	- 5.00	September	2-33	6.1	- 19.37
Oct/Nov	0-2	-	- 2.00	Oct/Nov	4-33	12.1	- 15.87

DISTANCE

2-y-o	W-R	Per cent	£1 Level Stake	3-y-o	W-R	Per cent	£1 Level Stake
5f-6f	2-22	9.1	- 15.25	5f-6f	3-20	15.0	- 1.37
7f-8f	2-23	8.7	- 15.25	7f-8f	0-36	-	- 36.00
9f-13f	0-0	-	0.00	9f-13f	7-46	15.2	- 12.49
14f+	0-0	-	0.00	14f+	1-9	11.1	+ 2.00

4-y-o+	W-R	Per cent	£1 Level Stake	Totals	W-R	Per cent	£1 Level Stake
5f-6f	2-11	18.2	+ 4.50	5f-6f	7-53	13.2	- 12.12
7f-8f	3-15	20.0	+ 23.50	7f-8f	5-74	6.8	- 27.75
9f-13f	0-1	-	- 1.00	9f-13f	7-47	14.9	- 13.49
14f+	0-0	-	0.00	14f+	1-9	11.1	+ 2.00

TYPE OF RACE

Non-Handicaps	W-R	Per cent	£1 Level Stake	Handicaps	W-R	Per cent	£1 Level Stake
2-y-o	4-39	10.3	- 24.50	2-y-o	0-3	-	- 3.00
3-y-o	4-63	6.3	- 42.62	3-y-o	5-39	12.8	- 1.50
4-y-o+	1-9	11.1	+ 12.00	4-y-o+	4-16	25.0	+ 17.00
Selling	0-5	-	- 5.00	Selling	0-1	-	- 1.00
Apprentice	1-1	100.0	+ 1.88	Apprentice	1-6	16.7	- 3.62
Amat/Ladies	0-1	-	- 1.00	Amat/Ladies	0-0	-	0.00
Totals	10-118	8.5	- 59.24	Totals	10-65	15.4	+ 7.88

COURSE GRADE

	W-R	Per cent	£1 Level Stake
Group 1	8-87	9.2	- 20.87
Group 2	4-21	19.0	+ 4.88
Group 3	5-55	9.1	- 25.25
Group 4	3-20	15.0	- 10.12

FIRST TIME OUT

	W-R	Per cent	£1 Level Stake
2-y-o	1-21	4.8	- 17.25
3-y-o	1-21	4.8	- 14.00
4-y-o+	0-4	-	- 4.00
Totals	2-46	4.3	- 35.25

JOCKEYS RIDING

	W-R	Per cent	£1 Level Stake		W-R	Per cent	£1 Level Stake
M Tebbutt	8-56	14.3	+ 4.25	R Hills	1-4	25.0	+ 3.00
L Dettori	3-12	25.0	+ 3.38	G Duffield	1-5	20.0	+ 2.50
Pat Eddery	2-4	50.0	+ 3.75	N Kennedy	1-5	20.0	+ 6.00
M Baird	1-1	100.0	+ 1.88	J Williams	1-5	20.0	+ 7.00
D Gibbs	1-3	33.3	- 0.62	N Day	1-9	11.1	- 3.50

J Reid	0-13	A McGlone	0-2	K Darley	0-1
P Robinson	0-7	Miss I Foustok	0-2	M Fenton	0-1
A Munro	0-6	W Woods	0-2	M Humphries	0-1
W Carson	0-6	A Garth	0-1	O Pears	0-1
D Harrison	0-5	B Raymond	0-1	R Cochrane	0-1
J Carroll	0-5	B Rouse	0-1	R Price	0-1
K Rutter	0-4	D Wright	0-1	S Davies	0-1
S Jones	0-4	F Norton	0-1	S Maloney	0-1
W Ryan	0-4	J Quinn	0-1	S Sherwood	0-1
T Quinn	0-3	J Weaver	0-1		

COURSE RECORD

	Total W-R	Non-Handicaps 2-y-o	Non-Handicaps 3-y-o+	Handicaps 2-y-o	Handicaps 3-y-o+	Per cent	£1 Level Stake
Pontefract	3-4	0-0	2-2	0-0	1-2	75.0	+ 12.25
Redcar	2-4	0-1	0-1	0-0	2-2	50.0	+ 2.88
Folkestone	2-5	0-0	1-3	0-0	1-2	40.0	+ 1.88
Haydock	2-8	0-1	1-3	0-0	1-4	25.0	+ 5.63
Newmarket	2-30	2-12	0-10	0-1	0-7	6.7	- 22.25
Salisbury	1-2	0-1	0-0	0-0	1-1	50.0	+ 10.00
Ascot	1-3	1-1	0-1	0-0	0-1	33.3	+ 0.75
Carlisle	1-3	1-1	0-1	0-0	0-1	33.3	0.00
Newcastle	1-3	0-1	0-0	0-0	1-2	33.3	+ 8.00
Ripon	1-3	0-0	0-1	0-0	1-2	33.3	+ 4.00
Sandown	1-6	0-0	1-3	0-0	0-3	16.7	+ 15.00
Leicester	1-7	0-3	1-3	0-0	0-1	14.3	0.00
Doncaster	1-12	0-3	0-2	0-1	1-6	8.3	- 3.00
Yarmouth	1-16	0-2	0-9	0-1	1-4	6.3	- 9.50

Beverley	0-9	York	0-5	Warwick	0-3
Windsor	0-8	Kempton	0-4	Ayr	0-2
Brighton	0-6	Bath	0-3	Southwell (Turf)	0-2
Epsom	0-6	Goodwood	0-3	Catterick	0-1
Hamilton	0-5	Lingfield	0-3	Edinburgh	0-1
Newbury	0-5	Nottingham	0-3		
Southwell (AW)	0-5	Thirsk	0-3		

WINNING HORSES

	Age	Races Run	1st	2nd	3rd	Unpl	Win £
Grand Lodge	2	4	3	0	1	0	138,708
Lap Of Luxury	4	5	2	0	0	3	15,770
Love Returned	6	10	2	0	0	8	10,765
Alasib	3	7	2	1	2	2	8,094
Tinsashe	3	9	2	1	0	6	6,548
Keylock	3	9	1	2	1	5	3,597
Lord Olivier	3	9	1	1	1	6	3,202
Jokist	10	9	1	2	0	6	3,015

Meavy	3	6	1	0	1	4	2,954
Storm Venture	3	10	1	3	0	6	2,950
Rose Noble	3	8	1	1	1	5	2,925
Private Fixture	2	4	1	0	0	3	2,803
Serotina	3	7	1	2	1	3	2,557
Diplomatist	3	10	1	5	1	3	1,548

WINNING OWNERS

	Races Won	Value £		Races Won	Value £
Lord Howard De Walden	4	142,305	William Jarvis	1	3,015
I C Hill-Wood	2	15,770	Venture Racing Ltd	1	2,950
A Foustok	4	14,642	Lady Howard De Walden	1	2,925
J M Ratcliffe	2	10,765	H J W Steckmest	1	2,803
Lord & Lady Roborough	2	5,511	Mrs S Page	1	1,548
Miss V R Jarvis	1	3,202			

Favourites	7-18	38.9%	+ 3.89	Total winning prize-money			£205,435
Longest winning sequence			2	Average SP of winner			5.6/1
Longest losing sequence			28	Return on stakes invested			-28.1%
1992 Form	22-183	12.0%	- 64.45	1990 Form	31-239	13.0%	- 69.91
1991 Form	29-208	13.9%	- 43.94	1989 Form	32-218	14.7%	- 18.25

J R JENKINS (Royston, Herts)

	No. of Horses	Races Run	1st	2nd	3rd	Unpl	Per cent	£1 Level Stake
2-y-o	6	29	0	1	3	25	-	- 29.00
3-y-o	7	39	1	1	5	32	2.6	- 26.00
4-y-o+	18	72	3	4	5	60	4.2	- 50.50
Totals	31	140	4	6	13	117	2.9	-105.50

Jan	Feb	Mar	Apr	May	Jun	Jul	Aug	Sep	Oct/Nov
0-3	0-7	0-1	0-18	0-23	0-21	2-28	1-20	0-10	1-9

Winning Jockeys	W-R	£1 Level Stake		W-R	£1 Level Stake
L Dettori	2-12	- 1.50	S Whitworth	1-29	- 18.00
M Roberts	1-6	+ 7.00			

Winning Courses	W-R	£1 Level Stake		W-R	£1 Level Stake
Pontefract	1-1	+ 2.00	Folkestone	1-9	+ 2.00
Newbury	1-3	+ 4.50	Sandown	1-9	+ 4.00

Winning Horses	Age	Races Run	1st	2nd	3rd	Unpl	Win £
Star Quest	6	9	1	0	0	8	4,890
Stormy Heights	3	10	1	0	1	8	3,610
Vanroy	9	9	1	1	1	6	2,364
Go South	9	5	1	0	0	4	2,243

Favourites	1-3	33.3%	0.00	Total winning prize-money			£13,107

1992 Form	12-156	7.7%	- 42.00	1990 Form	13-239	5.4%	-137.84
1991 Form	12-152	7.9%	- 27.87	1989 Form	10-209	4.8%	- 94.50

M S JOHNSTON (Middleham, North Yorks)

	No. of Horses	Races Run	1st	2nd	3rd	Unpl	Per cent	£1 Level Stake
2-y-o	27	119	21	18	13	67	17.6	- 9.40
3-y-o	23	222	36	41	28	117	16.2	- 45.52
4-y-o+	18	165	16	31	19	99	9.7	- 51.75
Totals	68	506	73	90	60	283	14.4	-106.67

BY MONTH

2-y-o	W-R	Per cent	£1 Level Stake	3-y-o	W-R	Per cent	£1 Level Stake
January	0-0	-	0.00	January	1-7	14.3	+ 6.00
February	0-0	-	0.00	February	8-12	66.7	+ 16.06
March	0-1	-	- 1.00	March	0-7	-	- 7.00
April	0-4	-	- 4.00	April	3-23	13.0	- 6.50
May	2-17	11.8	- 9.27	May	3-31	9.7	- 14.59
June	6-17	35.3	+ 13.75	June	3-28	10.7	- 13.25
July	4-24	16.7	- 6.39	July	11-49	22.4	+ 6.68
August	1-20	5.0	- 14.50	August	3-24	12.5	- 16.42
September	5-20	25.0	+ 5.51	September	3-21	14.3	- 4.50
Oct/Nov	3-16	18.8	+ 6.50	Oct/Nov	1-20	5.0	- 12.00

4-y-o+	W-R	Per cent	£1 Level Stake	Totals	W-R	Per cent	£1 Level Stake
January	3-9	33.3	+ 1.75	January	4-16	25.0	+ 7.75
February	1-9	11.1	- 4.50	February	9-21	42.9	+ 11.56
March	0-10	-	- 10.00	March	0-18	-	- 18.00
April	2-15	13.3	+ 0.50	April	5-42	11.9	- 10.00
May	2-26	7.7	- 4.50	May	7-74	9.5	- 28.36
June	2-21	9.5	- 7.50	June	11-66	16.7	- 7.00
July	0-23	-	- 23.00	July	15-96	15.6	- 22.71
August	3-23	13.0	+ 3.00	August	7-67	10.4	- 27.92
September	0-15	-	- 15.00	September	8-56	14.3	- 13.99
Oct/Nov	3-14	21.4	+ 7.50	Oct/Nov	7-50	14.0	+ 2.00

DISTANCE

2-y-o	W-R	Per cent	£1 Level Stake	3-y-o	W-R	Per cent	£1 Level Stake
5f-6f	13-88	14.8	- 15.77	5f-6f	6-65	9.2	- 43.32
7f-8f	6-27	22.2	- 8.63	7f-8f	19-94	20.2	+ 13.63
9f-13f	2-4	50.0	+ 15.00	9f-13f	9-56	16.1	- 15.58
14f+	0-0	-	0.00	14f+	2-7	28.6	- 0.25

4-y-o+	W-R	Per cent	£1 Level Stake	Totals	W-R	Per cent	£1 Level Stake
5f-6f	11-76	14.5	- 2.25	5f-6f	30-229	13.1	- 61.34
7f-8f	0-31	-	- 31.00	7f-8f	25-152	16.4	- 26.00
9f-13f	3-39	7.7	- 17.00	9f-13f	14-99	14.1	- 17.58
14f+	2-19	10.5	- 1.50	14f+	4-26	15.4	- 1.75

TYPE OF RACE

Non-Handicaps	W-R	Per cent	£1 Level Stake	Handicaps	W-R	Per cent	£1 Level Stake
2-y-o	15-78	19.2	+ 1.55	2-y-o	3-21	14.3	+ 1.30
3-y-o	11-60	18.3	- 25.26	3-y-o	22-142	15.5	- 13.50
4-y-o+	2-26	7.7	- 19.00	4-y-o+	14-133	10.5	- 26.75
Selling	5-27	18.5	- 10.34	Selling	1-12	8.3	- 7.67
Apprentice	0-1	-	- 1.00	Apprentice	0-6	-	- 6.00
Amat/Ladies	0-0	-	0.00	Amat/Ladies	0-0	-	0.00
Totals	33-192	17.2	- 54.05	Totals	40-314	12.7	- 52.62

COURSE GRADE

	W-R	Per cent	£1 Level Stake
Group 1	17-159	10.7	- 60.93
Group 2	16-100	16.0	+ 14.00
Group 3	12-105	11.4	- 38.84
Group 4	28-142	19.7	- 20.90

FIRST TIME OUT

	W-R	Per cent	£1 Level Stake
2-y-o	6-27	22.2	+ 16.38
3-y-o	3-23	13.0	+ 3.38
4-y-o+	3-17	17.6	+ 3.00
Totals	12-67	17.9	+ 22.76

JOCKEYS RIDING

	W-R	Per cent	£1 Level Stake		W-R	Per cent	£1 Level Stake
D McKeown	30-177	16.9	- 43.40	B Doyle	3-11	27.3	+ 16.50
T Williams	14-102	13.7	- 20.86	G Duffield	3-17	17.6	- 2.00
M Roberts	8-24	33.3	+ 15.71	A Garth	1-5	20.0	+ 5.00
J Weaver	8-33	24.2	+ 28.30	J Fanning	1-17	5.9	- 9.00
L Dettori	4-14	28.6	+ 4.08	R P Elliott	1-34	2.9	- 29.00

J Lowe	0-12	Dale Gibson	0-2	J Fortune	0-1
M Baird	0-8	K Darley	0-2	J Quinn	0-1
Paul Eddery	0-6	A McGlone	0-1	N Adams	0-1
T Quinn	0-6	A Munro	0-1	N Varley	0-1
J Carroll	0-4	D Biggs	0-1	O Pears	0-1
J Reid	0-4	D McCabe	0-1	Pat Eddery	0-1
E Johnson	0-3	D Moffatt	0-1	R Cochrane	0-1
F Norton	0-3	D Wright	0-1	W Carson	0-1
M Hills	0-3	G Bardwell	0-1		
R Hills	0-3	J Dennis	0-1		

COURSE RECORD

	Total W-R	Non-Handicaps 2-y-o	3-y-o+	Handicaps 2-y-o	3-y-o+	Per cent	£1 Level Stake
Southwell (AW)	10-45	0-2	5-11	0-0	5-32	22.2	- 12.82
Lingfield (AW)	8-30	0-0	2-6	0-0	6-24	26.7	+ 11.29
Edinburgh	5-26	2-5	1-4	2-2	0-15	19.2	- 8.87
Redcar	5-44	3-13	1-8	0-2	1-21	11.4	- 16.00
Thirsk	4-23	1-4	1-4	0-1	2-14	17.4	+ 18.00
Yarmouth	3-6	1-2	0-0	0-1	2-3	50.0	+ 8.50
Lingfield	3-10	0-1	1-3	0-1	2-5	30.0	+ 15.00
Catterick	3-20	0-4	0-4	1-3	2-9	15.0	+ 4.00
Ripon	3-20	1-6	0-1	0-0	2-13	15.0	- 2.00
York	3-20	1-4	0-1	0-1	2-14	15.0	- 4.62
Newcastle	3-23	1-5	0-2	0-1	2-15	13.0	- 3.50
Doncaster	3-30	0-8	1-6	0-2	2-14	10.0	- 14.00
Hamilton	3-36	2-10	0-6	0-1	1-19	8.3	- 18.00
Windsor	2-4	0-0	1-1	0-0	1-3	50.0	+ 0.33
Sandown	2-8	0-2	0-3	0-0	2-3	25.0	+ 12.00
Nottingham	2-10	0-1	1-5	0-0	1-4	20.0	+ 6.00
Newmarket	2-26	1-4	0-5	0-2	1-15	7.7	- 15.00
Brighton	1-2	1-1	0-1	0-0	0-0	50.0	0.00
Folkestone	1-5	0-0	0-3	0-0	1-2	20.0	- 2.00
Newbury	1-5	0-1	0-0	0-0	1-4	20.0	+ 2.50
Ascot	1-8	1-1	0-1	0-0	0-6	12.5	- 3.67
Carlisle	1-8	0-0	1-5	0-0	0-3	12.5	- 4.50
Goodwood	1-11	1-3	0-1	0-0	0-7	9.1	- 8.37
Ayr	1-13	1-4	0-3	0-0	0-6	7.7	- 11.27
Pontefract	1-18	1-6	0-3	0-2	0-7	5.6	- 9.00
Beverley	1-21	0-3	0-4	0-1	1-13	4.8	- 16.67

Haydock	0-10	Warwick	0-4	Chester	0-1
Leicester	0-10	Kempton	0-3		
Southwell (Turf)	0-4	Epsom	0-2		

WINNING HORSES

	Age	Races Run	1st	2nd	3rd	Unpl	Win £
Mister Baileys	2	5	3	0	1	1	85,541
Quick Ransom	5	8	2	1	2	3	31,082
Branston Abby	4	13	4	3	0	6	29,309
Shirley Rose	3	13	6	2	4	1	18,466

Penny Banger	3	16	5	6	0	5	14,236
Field Of Vision	3	15	3	5	1	6	14,207
Double Trigger	2	2	2	0	0	0	12,268
Ewald	5	20	3	4	3	10	11,698
Arctic Guest	3	12	4	6	0	2	11,573
North Ardar	3	15	3	3	4	5	9,100
Miss Mah-Jong	2	11	3	2	3	3	7,526
Marina Park	3	6	1	2	0	3	6,750
Pine Ridge Lad	3	10	3	2	1	4	6,735
Milngavie	3	17	2	3	3	9	6,189
Ashgore	3	14	2	1	2	9	6,035
Pretonic	5	8	2	1	1	4	5,929
Take Your Partner	3	10	2	0	2	6	5,641
Braille	2	9	2	4	0	3	5,524
Certificate-X	2	10	2	3	2	3	5,318
Stardust Express	3	17	2	4	2	9	4,845
Encore Une Fois	4	10	1	1	1	7	4,836
King Rat	2	9	2	4	0	3	4,497
Potsclose	2	4	1	0	0	3	4,450
Pearl Kite	2	1	1	0	0	0	4,308
Jubran	7	10	1	4	1	4	4,305
Educated Pet	4	12	1	1	0	10	3,761
Fair Flyer	4	13	1	5	1	6	3,558
Can Can Charlie	3	6	1	0	1	4	3,496
Indian Crystal	2	8	1	0	2	5	3,028
Sweet Romeo	3	10	1	2	1	6	3,026
Cut The Red Tape	2	6	1	2	0	3	3,021
Don't Be Koi	2	4	1	0	0	3	2,448
Hinari Video	8	13	1	1	1	10	2,322
Roche Abbey	2	5	1	0	0	4	2,322
Caspian Gold	2	4	1	0	0	3	2,259
Always Baileys	3	4	1	0	1	2	2,070

WINNING OWNERS

	Races Won	Value £		Races Won	Value £
G R Bailey Ltd (Horse Feed)	4	87,611	Mrs R A Johnson	2	4,845
R W Huggins	10	40,711	S & G Gutters	1	4,836
J S Morrison	2	31,082	Duke Of Roxburghe	1	4,450
J David Abell	4	29,309	Saeed Manana	1	4,308
Greenland Park Ltd	7	25,216	Mrs Elke Scullion	1	4,305
The Fairyhouse 1992 Partnership	7	20,240	Billy Morgan	1	3,761
The 2nd Kingsley House P'ship	5	12,263	William Provan Hunter	1	3,558
L Webster	3	9,100	A W Robinson	1	3,496
Mark Johnston Racing Ltd	2	8,525	Daniel Scullion	1	3,173
R Robinson (Wigan)	3	7,526	Mrs B A Matthews	1	3,028
R Jenkinson	3	6,735	Julian Clopit & Partners	1	3,021
A S Robertson	2	6,189	L G McMullan	1	2,322
Harvey Ashworth	2	6,035	Stephen Philip Sage	1	2,322
Brian Yeardley Continental Ltd	2	5,929	P Navabi	1	2,259
Kingsley Partnership	2	5,524			

Favourites	34-88	38.6%	+ 19.00	Total winning prize-money		£351,678

Longest winning sequence		3	Average SP of winner		4.5/1
Longest losing sequence		40	Return on stakes invested		-21.0%

1992 Form	53-400	13.3%	+ 2.87	1990 Form	28-261	10.7%	- 4.63
1991 Form	31-287	10.8%	-116.01	1989 Form	15-122	12.3%	+ 27.58

A P JONES (Eastbury, Berks)

	No. of Horses	Races Run	1st	2nd	3rd	Unpl	Per cent	£1 Level Stake
2-y-o	0	0	0	0	0	0	-	0.00
3-y-o	3	30	1	4	2	23	3.3	- 15.00
4-y-o+	3	16	2	3	2	9	12.5	+ 8.00
Totals	6	46	3	7	4	32	6.5	- 7.00

Jan	Feb	Mar	Apr	May	Jun	Jul	Aug	Sep	Oct/Nov
0-0	0-0	1-2	0-5	0-7	0-10	1-10	0-9	1-3	0-0

Winning Jockeys	W-R	£1 Level Stake				W-R	£1 Level Stake
R Painter	1-2	+ 1.00		N Adams		1-20	+ 1.00
Dale Gibson	1-2	+ 13.00					

Winning Courses							
Bath	2-9	+ 9.00		Warwick		1-3	+ 18.00

Winning Horses	Age	Races Run	1st	2nd	3rd	Unpl	Win £
Trioming	7	14	2	3	2	7	5,683
Kildee Lad	3	13	1	3	2	7	4,175

Favourites	1-1	100.0%	+ 2.00	Total winning prize-money		£9,858

1992 Form	0-29		1991 Form	0-4

A W JONES (Oswestry, Salop)

	No. of Horses	Races Run	1st	2nd	3rd	Unpl	Per cent	£1 Level Stake
2-y-o	0	0	0	0	0	0	-	0.00
3-y-o	0	0	0	0	0	0	-	0.00
4-y-o+	6	32	3	2	5	22	9.4	- 6.50
Totals	6	32	3	2	5	22	9.4	- 6.50

Jan	Feb	Mar	Apr	May	Jun	Jul	Aug	Sep	Oct/Nov
0-2	2-6	0-2	0-2	0-4	1-6	0-6	0-1	0-2	0-1

	W–R	£1 Level Stake		W–R	£1 Level Stake
Winning Jockeys					
Claire Balding	2–12	+ 2.50	Miss I D W Jones	1–9	+ 2.00
Winning Courses					
Southwell (AW)	2–8	+ 6.50	Nottingham	1–4	+ 7.00

Winning Horses	Age	Races Run	1st	2nd	3rd	Unpl	Win £
Last Straw	5	12	2	1	3	6	4,917
Thundering	8	7	1	1	1	4	2,624

Favourites	0–0			Total winning prize-money			£7,541
1992 Form	1–46	2.2%	– 37.00	1990 Form	1–31	3.2%	+ 3.00
1991 Form	0–10			1989 Form	1–44	2.3%	– 27.00

BOB JONES (Newmarket)

	No. of Horses	Races Run	1st	2nd	3rd	Unpl	Per cent	£1 Level Stake
2-y-o	7	28	2	1	2	23	7.1	– 12.50
3-y-o	5	22	1	2	1	18	4.5	– 7.00
4-y-o+	7	70	9	12	13	36	12.9	– 26.47
Totals	19	120	12	15	16	77	10.0	– 45.97

BY MONTH

2-y-o	W–R	Per cent	£1 Level Stake	3-y-o	W–R	Per cent	£1 Level Stake
January	0–0	–	0.00	January	0–0	–	0.00
February	0–0	–	0.00	February	0–0	–	0.00
March	0–0	–	0.00	March	0–2	–	– 2.00
April	0–3	–	– 3.00	April	0–3	–	– 3.00
May	0–2	–	– 2.00	May	0–4	–	– 4.00
June	0–4	–	– 4.00	June	0–2	–	– 2.00
July	0–6	–	– 6.00	July	1–5	20.0	+ 10.00
August	2–7	28.6	+ 8.50	August	0–3	–	– 3.00
September	0–5	–	– 5.00	September	0–3	–	– 3.00
Oct/Nov	0–1	–	– 1.00	Oct/Nov	0–0	–	0.00

4-y-o+	W–R	Per cent	£1 Level Stake	Totals	W–R	Per cent	£1 Level Stake
January	1–4	25.0	+ 1.50	January	1–4	25.0	+ 1.50
February	2–6	33.3	+ 3.00	February	2–6	33.3	+ 3.00
March	0–5	–	– 5.00	March	0–7	–	– 7.00
April	2–7	28.6	+ 0.91	April	2–13	15.4	– 5.09
May	1–10	10.0	– 8.38	May	1–16	6.3	– 14.38
June	0–7	–	– 7.00	June	0–13	–	– 13.00
July	1–5	20.0	+ 1.50	July	2–16	12.5	+ 5.50
August	0–8	–	– 8.00	August	2–18	11.1	– 2.50
September	0–5	–	– 5.00	September	0–13	–	– 13.00
Oct/Nov	2–13	15.4	0.00	Oct/Nov	2–14	14.3	– 1.00

DISTANCE

2-y-o	W-R	Per cent	£1 Level Stake	3-y-o	W-R	Per cent	£1 Level Stake
5f-6f	1-16	6.3	- 6.00	5f-6f	0-10	-	- 10.00
7f-8f	1-12	8.3	- 6.50	7f-8f	0-6	-	- 6.00
9f-13f	0-0	-	0.00	9f-13f	0-3	-	- 3.00
14f+	0-0	-	0.00	14f+	1-3	33.3	+ 12.00

4-y-o+	W-R	Per cent	£1 Level Stake	Totals	W-R	Per cent	£1 Level Stake
5f-6f	0-0	-	0.00	5f-6f	1-26	3.8	- 16.00
7f-8f	0-6	-	- 6.00	7f-8f	1-24	4.2	- 18.50
9f-13f	5-30	16.7	- 3.00	9f-13f	5-33	15.2	- 6.00
14f+	4-34	11.8	- 17.47	14f+	5-37	13.5	- 5.47

TYPE OF RACE

Non-Handicaps	W-R	Per cent	£1 Level Stake	Handicaps	W-R	Per cent	£1 Level Stake
2-y-o	1-18	5.6	- 8.00	2-y-o	0-7	-	- 7.00
3-y-o	1-12	8.3	+ 3.00	3-y-o	0-6	-	- 6.00
4-y-o+	2-9	22.2	- 5.47	4-y-o+	7-54	13.0	- 14.00
Selling	1-2	50.0	+ 3.50	Selling	0-4	-	- 4.00
Apprentice	0-0	-	0.00	Apprentice	0-4	-	- 4.00
Amat/Ladies	0-1	-	- 1.00	Amat/Ladies	0-3	-	- 3.00
Totals	5-42	11.9	- 7.97	Totals	7-78	9.0	- 38.00

COURSE GRADE

	W-R	Per cent	£1 Level Stake
Group 1	3-41	7.3	- 31.97
Group 2	2-25	8.0	- 8.50
Group 3	3-25	12.0	+ 3.50
Group 4	4-29	13.8	- 9.00

FIRST TIME OUT

	W-R	Per cent	£1 Level Stake
2-y-o	0-7	-	- 7.00
3-y-o	0-5	-	- 5.00
4-y-o+	1-7	14.3	- 1.50
Totals	1-19	5.3	- 13.50

JOCKEYS RIDING

	W-R	Per cent	£1 Level Stake		W-R	Per cent	£1 Level Stake
N Day	7-45	15.6	- 14.47	G Duffield	1-6	16.7	+ 9.00
M Wigham	2-8	25.0	+ 5.00	N Connorton	1-12	8.3	- 6.50
R Hills	1-2	50.0	+ 8.00				

N Carlisle	0-9	M Tebbutt	0-2	L Piggott	0-1
Miss D J Jones	0-5	Sally Radford-Howes	0-2	M Hills	0-1
G Bardwell	0-4	E Johnson	0-1	N Kennedy	0-1
J Quinn	0-3	G Carter	0-1	P Robinson	0-1
W R Swinburn	0-3	J Dennis	0-1	R Perham	0-1
A Mackay	0-2	J Lowe	0-1	V Smith	0-1
B Raymond	0-2	L Charnock	0-1	W Carson	0-1
D Wright	0-2	L Dettori	0-1		

COURSE RECORD

	Total W-R	Non-Handicaps 2-y-o	3-y-o+	Handicaps 2-y-o	3-y-o+	Per cent	£1 Level Stake
Bath	2-5	0-1	0-0	0-0	2-4	40.0	+ 8.50
Haydock	2-5	0-1	2-3	0-0	0-1	40.0	- 1.47
Lingfield (AW)	2-6	0-0	0-0	0-0	2-6	33.3	+ 3.00
Salisbury	1-1	1-1	0-0	0-0	0-0	100.0	+ 9.00
Catterick	1-4	1-1	0-1	0-2	0-0	25.0	+ 1.50
Brighton	1-5	0-1	0-0	0-1	1-3	20.0	+ 1.50
Yarmouth	1-7	0-0	1-3	0-1	0-3	14.3	+ 8.00
Southwell (AW)	1-10	0-1	0-0	0-0	1-9	10.0	- 4.50
Doncaster	1-12	0-1	0-3	0-1	1-7	8.3	- 6.50

Newmarket	0-9	Ascot	0-3	Ayr	0-1
Thirsk	0-8	Goodwood	0-3	Beverley	0-1
Nottingham	0-6	Kempton	0-3	Chester	0-1
Folkestone	0-5	Leicester	0-3	Hamilton	0-1
Redcar	0-4	Lingfield	0-2	Pontefract	0-1
Ripon	0-4	Newbury	0-2	Sandown	0-1
Warwick	0-4	York	0-2	Windsor	0-1

WINNING HORSES

	Age	Races Run	1st	2nd	3rd	Unpl	Win £
Sword Master	4	20	4	2	5	9	12,499
Jack Button	4	15	2	5	4	4	10,689
Lookingforarainbow	5	23	3	5	3	12	8,901
Lady-Bo-K	2	5	1	1	0	3	3,391
Danger Baby	3	5	1	1	1	2	2,400
Komplicity	2	10	1	0	1	8	2,058

WINNING OWNERS

	Races Won	Value £		Races Won	Value £
Ian A Vogt	4	12,499	David S Blake	1	2,400
A and B Racing	2	10,689	Hole In The Wall -		
B M Saumtally	3	8,901	Breeding-Racing	1	2,058
Ms Theresa McEvoy	1	3,391			

Favourites	3-13	23.1%	- 5.97	Total winning prize-money		£39,937
Longest winning sequence			2	Average SP of winner		5.2/1
Longest losing sequence			36	Return on stakes invested		-38.3%
1992 Form	11-100	11.0%	- 18.75	1991 Form	4-52	7.7% - 4.00

D HAYDN JONES (Pontypridd, Mid-Glamorgan)

	No. of Horses	Races Run	1st	2nd	3rd	Unpl	Per cent	£1 Level Stake
2-y-o	6	27	0	2	4	21	-	- 27.00
3-y-o	7	46	2	3	2	39	4.3	- 28.00
4-y-o+	8	62	7	5	8	42	11.3	- 5.75
Totals	21	135	9	10	14	102	6.7	- 60.75

Jan	Feb	Mar	Apr	May	Jun	Jul	Aug	Sep	Oct/Nov
1-9	2-7	0-5	0-11	0-22	2-20	1-25	3-19	0-12	0-5

Winning Jockeys	W-R	£1 Level Stake			W-R	£1 Level Stake
J Williams	5-32	+ 2.25	D Wright		1-7	- 1.50
A Mackay	3-52	- 17.50				

Winning Courses						
Southwell (AW)	4-38	- 6.25	Bath		1-14	- 3.00
Chepstow	2-8	+ 4.50	Lingfield (AW)		1-17	- 10.00
Doncaster	1-1	+ 11.00				

Winning Horses	Age	Races Run	1st	2nd	3rd	Unpl	Win £
Quinzii Martin	5	12	3	0	2	7	7,181
White River	7	9	1	1	1	6	3,366
Johns Act	3	3	1	1	1	0	3,173
Gallant Jack	4	5	1	0	0	4	3,054
Rocky Bay	4	8	1	0	1	6	2,679
Galejade	3	8	1	0	0	7	2,434
Premier Dance	6	14	1	4	3	6	1,770

Favourites	1-2	50.0%	+ 1.75	Total winning prize-money		£23,657

1992 Form	5-153	3.3%	- 83.50	1990 Form	7-159	4.4%	-114.62
1991 Form	2-131	1.5%	-109.50	1989 Form	3-97	3.1%	- 67.75

H THOMSON JONES (Newmarket)

	No. of Horses	Races Run	1st	2nd	3rd	Unpl	Per cent	£1 Level Stake
2-y-o	20	53	10	14	7	22	18.9	- 12.68
3-y-o	23	121	18	16	13	74	14.9	- 10.71
4-y-o+	2	7	0	0	2	5	-	- 7.00
Totals	45	181	28	30	22	101	15.5	- 30.39

BY MONTH

2-y-o	W-R	Per cent	£1 Level Stake	3-y-o	W-R	Per cent	£1 Level Stake
Mar/Apr	0-0	-	0.00	Mar/Apr	5-19	26.3	+ 7.85
May	1-2	50.0	0.00	May	0-16	-	- 16.00
June	0-6	-	- 6.00	June	3-18	16.7	+ 7.63
July	3-11	27.3	- 4.43	July	4-23	17.4	- 6.15
August	3-13	23.1	+ 5.50	August	3-19	15.8	+ 0.63
September	2-11	18.2	- 3.25	September	3-21	14.3	+ 0.33
Oct/Nov	1-10	10.0	- 4.50	Oct/Nov	0-5	-	- 5.00

4-y-o+	W-R	Per cent	£1 Level Stake	Totals	W-R	Per cent	£1 Level Stake
Mar/Apr	0-3	-	- 3.00	Mar/Apr	5-22	22.7	+ 4.85
May	0-1	-	- 1.00	May	1-19	5.3	- 17.00
June	0-1	-	- 1.00	June	3-25	12.0	+ 0.63
July	0-0	-	0.00	July	7-34	20.6	- 10.58
August	0-1	-	- 1.00	August	6-33	18.2	+ 5.13
September	0-1	-	- 1.00	September	5-33	15.2	- 3.92
Oct/Nov	0-0	-	0.00	Oct/Nov	1-15	6.7	- 9.50

DISTANCE

2-y-o	W-R	Per cent	£1 Level Stake	3-y-o	W-R	Per cent	£1 Level Stake
5f-6f	6-30	20.0	- 10.75	5f-6f	1-20	5.0	- 12.00
7f-8f	4-22	18.2	- 0.93	7f-8f	12-68	17.6	+ 8.11
9f-13f	0-1	-	- 1.00	9f-13f	5-27	18.5	- 0.82
14f+	0-0	-	0.00	14f+	0-6	-	- 6.00

4-y-o+	W-R	Per cent	£1 Level Stake	Totals	W-R	Per cent	£1 Level Stake
5f-6f	0-2	-	- 2.00	5f-6f	7-52	13.5	- 24.75
7f-8f	0-4	-	- 4.00	7f-8f	16-94	17.0	+ 3.18
9f-13f	0-1	-	- 1.00	9f-13f	5-29	17.2	- 2.82
14f+	0-0	-	0.00	14f+	0-6	-	- 6.00

TYPE OF RACE

Non-Handicaps	W-R	Per cent	£1 Level Stake	Handicaps	W-R	Per cent	£1 Level Stake
2-y-o	9-47	19.1	- 12.18	2-y-o	1-6	16.7	- 0.50
3-y-o	11-59	18.6	- 9.14	3-y-o	7-61	11.5	- 0.57
4-y-o+	0-6	-	- 6.00	4-y-o+	0-1	-	- 1.00
Selling	0-0	-	0.00	Selling	0-0	-	0.00
Apprentice	0-0	-	0.00	Apprentice	0-1	-	- 1.00
Amat/Ladies	0-0	-	0.00	Amat/Ladies	0-0	-	0.00
Totals	20-112	17.9	- 27.32	Totals	8-69	11.6	- 3.07

COURSE GRADE

	W-R	Per cent	£1 Level Stake
Group 1	8-82	9.8	- 29.79
Group 2	5-31	16.1	- 0.70
Group 3	13-56	23.2	+ 7.68
Group 4	2-12	16.7	- 7.58

FIRST TIME OUT

	W-R	Per cent	£1 Level Stake
2-y-o	2-20	10.0	- 13.00
3-y-o	4-23	17.4	+ 2.68
4-y-o+	0-2	-	- 2.00
Totals	6-45	13.3	- 12.32

JOCKEYS RIDING

	W-R	Per cent	£1 Level Stake		W-R	Per cent	£1 Level Stake
R Hills	25-135	18.5	- 5.82	W Carson	1-8	12.5	- 5.90
Bill Smith	1-1	100.0	+ 3.33	N Carlisle	1-26	3.8	- 11.00

B Crossley	0-2	G Duffield	0-1	M Hills	0-1
Lisa Jacobs	0-2	H Ballantine	0-1	S Maloney	0-1
A Garth	0-1	L Piggott	0-1	Wally Swinburn	0-1

COURSE RECORD

	Total W-R	Non-Handicaps 2-y-o	Non-Handicaps 3-y-o+	Handicaps 2-y-o	Handicaps 3-y-o+	Per cent	£1 Level Stake
Yarmouth	4-21	1-7	1-5	0-1	2-8	19.0	+ 7.07
Pontefract	3-7	1-1	1-1	1-2	0-3	42.9	+ 8.75
Edinburgh	2-3	0-1	2-2	0-0	0-0	66.7	+ 1.42
Nottingham	2-5	1-3	1-2	0-0	0-0	40.0	+ 3.13
Leicester	2-6	1-2	0-2	0-0	1-2	33.3	- 1.90
Lingfield	2-6	0-2	2-3	0-0	0-1	33.3	+ 16.00
Kempton	2-10	1-2	1-5	0-0	0-3	20.0	+ 1.38
Ripon	1-2	1-1	0-1	0-0	0-0	50.0	+ 3.00
Bath	1-4	1-1	0-0	0-0	0-3	25.0	+ 1.00
Newbury	1-4	0-0	0-2	0-0	1-2	25.0	+ 4.00
Sandown	1-4	1-1	0-2	0-0	0-1	25.0	- 0.50
Brighton	1-6	0-1	1-3	0-0	0-2	16.7	- 4.20
Doncaster	1-6	0-1	1-3	0-1	0-1	16.7	- 4.00
Newcastle	1-6	0-1	0-2	0-0	1-3	16.7	+ 2.00
Redcar	1-6	1-3	0-0	0-0	0-3	16.7	- 4.50
Beverley	1-8	0-2	1-2	0-0	0-4	12.5	- 5.37
Haydock	1-8	0-1	0-4	0-0	1-3	12.5	+ 7.00
Ascot	1-11	0-4	0-2	0-0	1-5	9.1	- 6.67

Newmarket	0-17	Goodwood	0-3	Warwick	0-2
York	0-7	Windsor	0-3	Chepstow	0-1
Thirsk	0-5	Catterick	0-2	Hamilton	0-1
Salisbury	0-4	Chester	0-2	Southwell (AW)	0-1
Ayr	0-3	Folkestone	0-2		
Epsom	0-3	Southwell (Turf)	0-2		

WINNING HORSES

	Age	Races Run	1st	2nd	3rd	Unpl	Win £
Ihtiraz	3	8	3	0	0	5	22,830
Elrafa Ah	2	3	2	0	1	0	13,696
Ehtfaal	2	4	2	0	1	1	12,726
Yaqthan	3	8	2	0	0	6	8,248
Ajfan	3	5	2	1	1	1	7,799
Rahil	3	6	3	0	0	3	7,597
Mujawab	3	7	2	1	0	4	7,473
Sherman	2	4	1	1	0	2	4,988
Arz	2	6	1	2	1	2	4,815
Bumaan	2	5	1	2	0	2	4,414
Suaad	2	4	1	2	1	0	4,308
Nizaal	2	3	1	1	0	1	4,271
Alyukkh	3	5	1	2	0	2	3,377
Taalif	3	3	1	0	0	2	3,348
Taghareed	2	3	1	2	0	0	3,200
Tajdid	3	6	1	0	0	5	3,106
Mutakallam	3	7	1	1	1	4	2,950
Lakab	3	7	1	0	2	4	2,144
Qamoos	3	6	1	1	1	3	1,630

WINNING OWNERS

	Races Won	Value £		Races Won	Value £
Hamdan Al-Maktoum	27	117,931	Mrs H T Jones	1	4,988

Favourites	12-33	36.4%	- 6.97	Total winning prize-money		£122,918
Longest winning sequence			3	Average SP of winner		4.4/1
Longest losing sequence			27	Return on stakes invested		-16.8%
1992 Form	27-188	14.4%	- 33.53	1990 Form	34-209	16.3%	- 13.92
1991 Form	37-190	19.5%	+ 25.39	1989 Form	37-189	19.6%	- 25.69

T M JONES (Guildford, Surrey)

	No. of Horses	Races Run	1st	2nd	3rd	Unpl	Per cent	£1 Level Stake
2-y-o	3	12	2	1	0	9	16.7	+ 6.00
3-y-o	3	14	1	1	0	12	7.1	+ 20.00
4-y-o+	0	0	0	0	0	0	-	0.00
Totals	6	26	3	2	0	21	11.5	+ 26.00

Jan	Feb	Mar	Apr	May	Jun	Jul	Aug	Sep	Oct/Nov
0-2	0-1	0-1	1-2	0-5	1-4	1-4	0-0	0-3	0-4

Winning Jockeys	W-R	£1 Level Stake		W-R	£1 Level Stake
D Toole	1-4	+ 30.00	R Perham	1-10	- 3.00
T Williams	1-4	+ 7.00			

Winning Courses					
Lingfield	1-1	+ 10.00	Folkestone	1-2	+ 32.00
Chepstow	1-2	+ 5.00			

Winning Horses	Age	Races Run	1st	2nd	3rd	Unpl	Win £
Rambold	2	8	2	1	0	5	9,271
Buckski Echo	3	11	1	1	0	9	2,427

Favourites	0-0		Total winning prize-money		£11,698

1992 Form	0-12		1990 Form	2-30	6.7%	- 4.00
1991 Form	0-14		1989 Form	0-35		

T THOMSON JONES (Upper Lambourn, Berks)

	No. of Horses	Races Run	1st	2nd	3rd	Unpl	Per cent	£1 Level Stake
2-y-o	4	11	1	0	4	6	9.1	- 5.00
3-y-o	4	17	0	0	2	15	-	- 17.00
4-y-o+	12	59	10	2	2	45	16.9	+ 4.59
Totals	20	87	11	2	8	66	12.6	- 17.41

BY MONTH

2-y-o	W-R	Per cent	£1 Level Stake	3-y-o	W-R	Per cent	£1 Level Stake
January	0-0	-	0.00	January	0-0	-	0.00
February	0-0	-	0.00	February	0-0	-	0.00
March	0-0	-	0.00	March	0-0	-	0.00
April	0-0	-	0.00	April	0-5	-	- 5.00
May	0-0	-	0.00	May	0-4	-	- 4.00
June	0-1	-	- 1.00	June	0-4	-	- 4.00
July	0-2	-	- 2.00	July	0-2	-	- 2.00
August	1-2	50.0	+ 4.00	August	0-0	-	0.00
September	0-3	-	- 3.00	September	0-0	-	0.00
Oct/Nov	0-3	-	- 3.00	Oct/Nov	0-2	-	- 2.00

Jones T Thomson

4-y-o+	W-R	Per cent	£1 Level Stake		Totals	W-R	Per cent	£1 Level Stake
January	0-1	-	- 1.00		January	0-1	-	- 1.00
February	5-6	83.3	+ 7.59		February	5-6	83.3	+ 7.59
March	1-3	33.3	+ 1.00		March	1-3	33.3	+ 1.00
April	1-6	16.7	+ 6.00		April	1-11	9.1	+ 1.00
May	1-12	8.3	- 3.00		May	1-16	6.3	- 7.00
June	0-8	-	- 8.00		June	0-13	-	- 13.00
July	1-10	10.0	+ 3.00		July	1-14	7.1	- 1.00
August	0-8	-	- 8.00		August	1-10	10.0	- 4.00
September	0-2	-	- 2.00		September	0-5	-	- 5.00
Oct/Nov	1-3	33.3	+ 9.00		Oct/Nov	1-8	12.5	+ 4.00

DISTANCE

2-y-o	W-R	Per cent	£1 Level Stake		3-y-o	W-R	Per cent	£1 Level Stake
5f-6f	1-10	10.0	- 4.00		5f-6f	0-1	-	- 1.00
7f-8f	0-1	-	- 1.00		7f-8f	0-9	-	- 9.00
9f-13f	0-0	-	0.00		9f-13f	0-6	-	- 6.00
14f+	0-0	-	0.00		14f+	0-1	-	- 1.00

4-y-o+	W-R	Per cent	£1 Level Stake		Totals	W-R	Per cent	£1 Level Stake
5f-6f	1-8	12.5	+ 4.00		5f-6f	2-19	10.5	- 1.00
7f-8f	3-16	18.8	+ 6.62		7f-8f	3-26	11.5	- 3.38
9f-13f	3-24	12.5	- 4.88		9f-13f	3-30	10.0	- 10.88
14f+	3-11	27.3	- 1.15		14f+	3-12	25.0	- 2.15

TYPE OF RACE

Non-Handicaps	W-R	Per cent	£1 Level Stake		Handicaps	W-R	Per cent	£1 Level Stake
2-y-o	1-10	10.0	- 4.00		2-y-o	0-1	-	- 1.00
3-y-o	0-3	-	- 3.00		3-y-o	0-11	-	- 11.00
4-y-o+	1-8	12.5	- 6.38		4-y-o+	9-48	18.8	+ 13.97
Selling	0-0	-	0.00		Selling	0-1	-	- 1.00
Apprentice	0-0	-	0.00		Apprentice	0-3	-	- 3.00
Amat/Ladies	0-0	-	0.00		Amat/Ladies	0-2	-	- 2.00
Totals	2-21	9.5	- 13.38		Totals	9-66	13.6	- 4.03

COURSE GRADE

	W-R	Per cent	£1 Level Stake
Group 1	0-19	-	- 19.00
Group 2	2-15	13.3	+ 4.00
Group 3	2-32	6.3	- 8.00
Group 4	7-21	33.3	+ 5.59

FIRST TIME OUT

	W-R	Per cent	£1 Level Stake
2-y-o	0-4	-	- 4.00
3-y-o	0-4	-	- 4.00
4-y-o+	2-12	16.7	+ 4.50
Totals	2-20	10.0	- 3.50

JOCKEYS RIDING

	W-R	Per cent	£1 Level Stake		W-R	Per cent	£1 Level Stake
D Biggs	7-11	63.6	+ 25.97	K Darley	1-9	11.1	+ 3.00
D McKeown	1-5	20.0	- 3.38	S Whitworth	1-21	4.8	- 8.00
W Carson	1-6	16.7	0.00				

A Tucker	0-6	J Lowe	0-1	N Adams	0-1
N Carlisle	0-3	J O'Dwyer	0-1	N Day	0-1
R Hills	0-3	L Dettori	0-1	Paul Eddery	0-1
J Quinn	0-2	M Hills	0-1	S Copp	0-1
Pat Eddery	0-2	Mark Denaro	0-1	S Maloney	0-1
W Newnes	0-2	Miss A Harwood	0-1	S Wood	0-1
A McGlone	0-1	Mr F Grasso-Caprioli	0-1	W Ryan	0-1
G Duffield	0-1	Mrs M Cowdrey	0-1		

COURSE RECORD

	Total W-R	Non-Handicaps 2-y-o	3-y-o+	Handicaps 2-y-o	3-y-o+	Per cent	£1 Level Stake
Southwell (AW)	7-12	0-0	1-2	0-0	6-10	58.3	+ 14.59
Nottingham	2-11	0-2	0-0	0-0	2-9	18.2	+ 13.00
Brighton	1-2	1-2	0-0	0-0	0-0	50.0	+ 4.00
Salisbury	1-5	0-0	0-2	0-0	1-3	20.0	+ 8.00

Windsor	0-8	Newbury	0-3	Pontefract	0-2
Warwick	0-6	Redcar	0-3	Thirsk	0-2
Goodwood	0-4	Yarmouth	0-3	Carlisle	0-1
Newmarket	0-4	Chester	0-2	Epsom	0-1
Bath	0-3	Kempton	0-2	Haydock	0-1
Chepstow	0-3	Leicester	0-2	Lingfield	0-1
Doncaster	0-3	Lingfield (AW)	0-2	Sandown	0-1

WINNING HORSES

	Age	Races Run	1st	2nd	3rd	Unpl	Win £
Horizon	5	10	5	0	1	4	13,516
Themaam	4	12	2	1	1	8	5,202
Monis	2	4	1	0	2	1	3,949
Affa	4	6	1	0	0	5	3,754
Blazon Of Troy	4	7	1	0	0	6	3,558
Honey Seeker	4	9	1	1	0	7	3,339

WINNING OWNERS

	Races Won	Value £		Races Won	Value £
Mrs Solna Thomson Jones	5	13,516	G Oliver	1	3,754
Wetherby Racing Bureau Plc	2	5,202	David F Wilson	1	3,558
Hamdan Al-Maktoum	1	3,949	P D Savill	1	3,339

Jones T Thomson

Favourites	5-9	55.6%	+ 9.09	Total winning prize-money		£33,317
Longest winning sequence			4	Average SP of winner		5.3/1
Longest losing sequence			31	Return on stakes invested		-20.0%
1992 Form	5-86	5.8%	- 42.00	1990 Form	8-131	6.1%	- 84.11
1991 Form	7-106	6.6%	- 38.50	1989 Form	7-50	14.0%	+ 20.00

F JORDAN (Leominster, H'ford & Worcs)

	No. of Horses	Races Run	1st	2nd	3rd	Unpl	Per cent	£1 Level Stake
2-y-o	0	0	0	0	0	0	-	0.00
3-y-o	0	0	0	0	0	0	-	0.00
4-y-o+	4	16	1	1	1	13	6.3	- 7.00
Totals	4	16	1	1	1	13	6.3	- 7.00

Jan	Feb	Mar	Apr	May	Jun	Jul	Aug	Sep	Oct/Nov
0-1	0-0	0-1	0-3	0-2	1-3	0-2	0-2	0-1	0-1

Winning Jockey	W-R	£1 Level Stake	Winning Course	W-R	£1 Level Stake
Mr M Buckley	1-1	+ 8.00	Haydock	1-2	+ 7.00

Winning Horse	Age	Races Run	1st	2nd	3rd	Unpl	Win £
Saint Ciel	5	12	1	1	1	9	2,679

Favourites	0-0		Total winning prize-money		£2,679

1992 Form	0-20		1990 Form	1-19	5.3%	- 9.00
1991 Form	0-4		1989 Form	3-36	8.3%	- 10.50

MISS GAY KELLEWAY (Newmarket)

	No. of Horses	Races Run	1st	2nd	3rd	Unpl	Per cent	£1 Level Stake
2-y-o	6	25	1	4	3	17	4.0	- 14.00
3-y-o	9	39	5	3	5	26	12.8	- 10.70
4-y-o+	5	29	4	5	4	16	13.8	+ 2.50
Totals	20	93	10	12	12	59	10.8	- 22.20

BY MONTH

2-y-o	W-R	Per cent	£1 Level Stake		3-y-o	W-R	Per cent	£1 Level Stake
January	0-0	-		0.00	January	0-2	-	- 2.00
February	0-0	-		0.00	February	0-0	-	0.00
March	0-0	-		0.00	March	0-1	-	- 1.00
April	0-2	-	-	2.00	April	1-2	50.0	+ 6.00
May	1-2	50.0	+	9.00	May	2-9	22.2	+ 4.00
June	0-2	-	-	2.00	June	1-5	20.0	- 3.20
July	0-5	-	-	5.00	July	1-10	10.0	- 4.50
August	0-6	-	-	6.00	August	0-6	-	- 6.00
September	0-5	-	-	5.00	September	0-2	-	- 2.00
Oct/Nov	0-3	-	-	3.00	Oct/Nov	0-2	-	- 2.00

4-y-o+	W-R	Per cent	£1 Level Stake		Totals	W-R	Per cent	£1 Level Stake
January	0-1	-	-	1.00	January	0-3	-	- 3.00
February	0-0	-		0.00	February	0-0	-	0.00
March	1-3	33.3	+	5.00	March	1-4	25.0	+ 4.00
April	0-2	-	-	2.00	April	1-6	16.7	+ 2.00
May	0-2	-	-	2.00	May	3-13	23.1	+ 11.00
June	0-5	-	-	5.00	June	1-12	8.3	- 10.20
July	1-9	11.1	-	2.00	July	2-24	8.3	- 11.50
August	1-6	16.7	+	1.50	August	1-18	5.6	- 10.50
September	1-1	100.0	+	8.00	September	1-8	12.5	+ 1.00
Oct/Nov	0-0	-		0.00	Oct/Nov	0-5	-	- 5.00

DISTANCE

2-y-o	W-R	Per cent	£1 Level Stake		3-y-o	W-R	Per cent	£1 Level Stake
5f-6f	1-15	6.7	-	4.00	5f-6f	3-10	30.0	+ 9.50
7f-8f	0-10	-	-	10.00	7f-8f	2-23	8.7	- 14.20
9f-13f	0-0	-		0.00	9f-13f	0-5	-	- 5.00
14f+	0-0	-		0.00	14f+	0-1	-	- 1.00

4-y-o+	W-R	Per cent	£1 Level Stake		Totals	W-R	Per cent	£1 Level Stake
5f-6f	0-5	-	-	5.00	5f-6f	4-30	13.3	+ 0.50
7f-8f	2-9	22.2	+	8.00	7f-8f	4-42	9.5	- 16.20
9f-13f	1-9	11.1	-	1.50	9f-13f	1-14	7.1	- 6.50
14f+	1-6	16.7	+	1.00	14f+	1-7	14.3	0.00

TYPE OF RACE

Non-Handicaps	W-R	Per cent	£1 Level Stake		Handicaps	W-R	Per cent	£1 Level Stake
2-y-o	1-15	6.7	-	4.00	2-y-o	0-5	-	- 5.00
3-y-o	3-21	14.3	-	6.70	3-y-o	1-16	6.3	- 10.00
4-y-o+	0-5	-	-	5.00	4-y-o+	3-19	15.8	+ 5.00
Selling	1-8	12.5		0.00	Selling	0-0	-	0.00
Apprentice	0-0	-		0.00	Apprentice	1-4	25.0	+ 3.50
Amat/Ladies	0-0	-		0.00	Amat/Ladies	0-0	-	0.00
Totals	5-49	10.2	-	15.70	Totals	5-44	11.4	- 6.50

Kelleway Miss Gay

	COURSE GRADE						FIRST TIME OUT		
	W–R	Per cent	£1 Level Stake				W–R	Per cent	£1 Level Stake
Group 1	1-20	5.0	- 14.00	2-y-o			1-3	33.3	+ 8.00
Group 2	0-14	-	- 14.00	3-y-o			2-7	28.6	+ 6.50
Group 3	4-18	22.2	+ 15.50	4-y-o+			0-5	-	- 5.00
Group 4	5-41	12.2	- 9.70						
				Totals			3-15	20.0	+ 9.50

JOCKEYS RIDING

	W–R	Per cent	£1 Level Stake		W–R	Per cent	£1 Level Stake
N Carlisle	2-5	40.0	+ 11.00	T Quinn	1-6	16.7	+ 5.00
J Weaver	2-7	28.6	+ 0.30	D McCabe	1-9	11.1	- 2.00
S Davies	2-8	25.0	+ 8.50	A Munro	1-11	9.1	- 4.00
K Darley	1-3	33.3	+ 3.00				

Gay Kelleway	0-7	A Mackay	0-1	J Dennis	0-1
J Lowe	0-5	B Raymond	0-1	M Tebbutt	0-1
S O'Gorman	0-4	D Biggs	0-1	N Day	0-1
W Newnes	0-4	D Harrison	0-1	P McCabe	0-1
D Holland	0-3	G Duffield	0-1	P Robinson	0-1
K Fallon	0-3	G Hind	0-1	S Mulvey	0-1
A Garth	0-2	G Milligan	0-1		
Pat Eddery	0-2	Irmtraud Weiner	0-1		

COURSE RECORD

	Total W–R	Non-Handicaps 2-y-o	3-y-o+	Handicaps 2-y-o	3-y-o+	Per cent	£1 Level Stake
Southwell (AW)	3-23	0-5	2-8	0-0	1-10	13.0	- 6.70
Bath	2-4	0-0	0-1	0-0	2-3	50.0	+ 10.50
Leicester	1-2	1-1	0-0	0-1	0-0	50.0	+ 9.00
Nottingham	1-2	0-0	1-2	0-0	0-0	50.0	+ 6.00
Catterick	1-4	0-0	0-2	0-0	1-2	25.0	+ 4.00
Newcastle	1-6	0-2	0-0	0-0	1-4	16.7	0.00
Folkestone	1-7	0-2	1-2	0-0	0-3	14.3	0.00

Newmarket	0-11	Beverley	0-3	Haydock	0-1
Brighton	0-6	Chester	0-2	Pontefract	0-1
Lingfield	0-4	Goodwood	0-2	Redcar	0-1
Lingfield (AW)	0-4	Warwick	0-2	Southwell (Turf)	0-1
Yarmouth	0-4	Windsor	0-2	Thirsk	0-1

WINNING HORSES

	Age	Races Run	1st	2nd	3rd	Unpl	Win £
Dailysportdutch	3	4	2	0	0	2	3,688
Tyrone Flyer	4	5	1	1	0	3	3,407
Aljaz	3	3	1	0	1	1	3,348
Forest Star	4	6	1	1	1	3	3,301

Nsx	2	5	1	1	0	3	3,231
Charlie Bigtime	3	10	1	2	2	5	3,085
Miliyel	4	6	1	0	1	4	2,884
Inderaputeri	3	8	1	0	1	6	2,243
Family Rose	4	8	1	1	2	4	2,243

WINNING OWNERS

	Races Won	Value £		Races Won	Value £
Ron Dawson	3	9,317	H R H Sultan Ahmad Shah	2	5,474
J Naughton	3	8,950	Brian T Eastick	2	3,688

Favourites	1-4	25.0%	– 2.20	Total winning prize-money	£27,429
Longest winning sequence			2	Average SP of winner	6.1/1
Longest losing sequence			19	Return on stakes invested	-23.9%
1992 Form	0-75				

P A KELLEWAY (Newmarket)

	No. of Horses	Races Run	1st	2nd	3rd	Unpl	Per cent	£1 Level Stake
2-y-o	14	40	4	4	3	29	10.0	+ 6.00
3-y-o	9	37	2	3	4	28	5.4	- 13.00
4-y-o+	3	9	1	1	0	7	11.1	- 5.00
Totals	26	86	7	8	7	64	8.1	- 12.00

Jan	Feb	Mar	Apr	May	Jun	Jul	Aug	Sep	Oct/Nov
1-6	0-2	0-4	0-10	0-8	3-14	1-14	0-9	1-8	1-11

Winning Jockeys	W-R	£1 Level Stake		W-R	£1 Level Stake
D Harrison	2-8	+ 16.00	M Wigham	1-5	+ 6.00
W R Swinburn	1-2	+ 11.00	R Cochrane	1-10	- 5.00
L Dettori	1-5	+ 12.00	G Bardwell	1-12	- 8.00

Winning Courses					
Sandown	2-7	+ 23.00	Nottingham	1-5	+ 16.00
Ayr	1-2	+ 9.00	Lingfield (AW)	1-10	- 6.00
York	1-3	0.00	Newmarket	1-14	- 9.00

Kelleway P A

Winning Horses	Age	Races Run	1st	2nd	3rd	Unpl	Win £
Devils Den	3	4	2	1	0	1	8,202
News And Echo	2	4	1	1	1	1	7,701
Venta De Possa	2	3	1	0	0	2	3,747
Mr Eubanks	2	4	1	0	0	3	3,720
Kezio Rufo	2	2	1	0	0	1	3,285
Slight Risk	4	6	1	1	0	4	2,905

Favourites	1-3	33.3%	0.00	Total winning prize-money			£29,559

1992 Form	16-179	8.9%	- 58.72	1990 Form	8-170	4.7%	-123.20
1991 Form	13-156	8.3%	- 56.92	1989 Form	13-138	9.4%	- 50.38

T KERSEY (Rotherham, Lancs)

	No. of Horses	Races Run	1st	2nd	3rd	Unpl	Per cent	£1 Level Stake
2-y-o	1	2	0	0	0	2	-	- 2.00
3-y-o	0	0	0	0	0	0	-	0.00
4-y-o+	6	27	1	2	0	24	3.7	- 20.50
Totals	7	29	1	2	0	26	3.4	- 22.50

Jan	Feb	Mar	Apr	May	Jun	Jul	Aug	Sep	Oct/Nov
0-0	0-0	0-1	0-2	0-4	0-8	1-3	0-5	0-1	0-5

Winning Jockey	W-R	£1 Level Stake	Winning Course	W-R	£1 Level Stake
J Lowe	1-8	- 1.50	Catterick	1-6	+ 0.50

Winning Horse	Age	Races Run	1st	2nd	3rd	Unpl	Win £
Bold Ambition	6	8	1	2	0	5	3,704

Favourites	0-0			Total winning prize-money			£3,704
1992 Form	0-56			1990 Form	0-43		
1991 Form	2-44	4.5%	0.00	1989 Form	1-38	2.6%	- 4.00

S E KETTLEWELL (Middleham, North Yorks)

	No. of Horses	Races Run	1st	2nd	3rd	Unpl	Per cent	£1 Level Stake
2-y-o	0	0	0	0	0	0	-	0.00
3-y-o	5	11	0	0	0	11	-	- 11.00
4-y-o+	7	57	5	3	6	43	8.8	- 16.25
Totals	12	68	5	3	6	54	7.4	- 27.25

Jan	Feb	Mar	Apr	May	Jun	Jul	Aug	Sep	Oct/Nov
0-6	0-6	0-2	1-5	3-11	1-14	0-10	0-5	0-7	0-2

Winning Jockeys	W-R	£1 Level Stake		W-R	£1 Level Stake
J Fortune	3-28	+ 4.50	J Tate	1-5	- 0.50
Mrs D Kettlewell	1-5	- 1.25			

Winning Courses					
Hamilton	2-7	+ 2.25	Edinburgh	1-3	+ 3.00
Thirsk	1-2	+ 19.00	Ayr	1-8	- 3.50

Winning Horses	Age	Races Run	1st	2nd	3rd	Unpl	Win £
Just Bob	4	17	4	2	2	9	10,579
Gold Surprise	4	14	1	1	1	11	1,702

Favourites	2-6	33.3%	+ 2.25	Total winning prize-money			£12,281

1992 Form	5-36	13.9%	+ 9.00	1990 Form	1-17	5.9%	+ 4.00
1991 Form	2-17	11.8%	+ 3.00	1989 Form	0-20		

MRS A L M KING (Stratford-upon-Avon, Warwicks)

	No. of Horses	Races Run	1st	2nd	3rd	Unpl	Per cent	£1 Level Stake
2-y-o	1	2	0	0	0	2	-	- 2.00
3-y-o	0	0	0	0	0	0	-	0.00
4-y-o+	4	29	1	3	1	24	3.4	- 3.00
Totals	5	31	1	3	1	26	3.2	- 5.00

Jan	Feb	Mar	Apr	May	Jun	Jul	Aug	Sep	Oct/Nov
0-1	0-1	0-2	1-3	0-5	0-4	0-1	0-8	0-4	0-2

Winning Jockey	W-R	£1 Level Stake	Winning Course	W-R	£1 Level Stake
A Garth	1-9	+ 17.00	Nottingham	1-4	+ 22.00

Winning Horse	Age	Races Run	1st	2nd	3rd	Unpl	Win £
Followmegirls	4	13	1	3	0	9	2,669

Favourites	0-3			Total winning prize-money		£2,669

1992 Form	2-32	6.3%	+ 73.50	1990 Form	1-12	8.3%	+ 1.00
1991 Form	3-22	13.6%	+ 32.00				

J S KING (Swindon, Wilts)

	No. of Horses	Races Run	1st	2nd	3rd	Unpl	Per cent	£1 Level Stake
2-y-o	1	3	0	0	1	2	-	- 3.00
3-y-o	1	3	0	0	0	3	-	- 3.00
4-y-o+	6	30	2	5	3	20	6.7	- 20.00
Totals	8	36	2	5	4	25	5.6	- 26.00

Jan	Feb	Mar	Apr	May	Jun	Jul	Aug	Sep	Oct/Nov
0-0	0-1	0-0	0-2	0-4	1-6	1-6	0-6	0-5	0-6

Winning Jockeys	W-R	£1 Level Stake				W-R	£1 Level Stake
T Quinn	1-6	- 0.50		Paul Eddery		1-7	- 2.50

Winning Courses	W-R	£1 Level Stake				W-R	£1 Level Stake
Chepstow	1-3	+ 1.50		Bath		1-6	- 0.50

Winning Horses	Age	Races Run	1st	2nd	3rd	Unpl	Win £
Marchman	8	7	1	1	1	4	3,377
Chucklestone	10	10	1	2	0	7	3,080

Favourites	0-2		Total winning prize-money	£6,457

1992 Form	5-21	23.8%	+ 6.75	1990 Form	2-25	8.0%	- 11.50
1991 Form	0-19			1989 Form	4-36	11.1%	+ 4.00

MRS A KNIGHT (Cullompton, Devon)

	No. of Horses	Races Run	1st	2nd	3rd	Unpl	Per cent	£1 Level Stake
2-y-o	1	3	0	0	0	3	-	- 3.00
3-y-o	2	5	0	0	0	5	-	- 5.00
4-y-o+	17	75	6	4	6	59	8.0	+ 8.33
Totals	20	83	6	4	6	67	7.2	+ 0.33

Jan	Feb	Mar	Apr	May	Jun	Jul	Aug	Sep	Oct/Nov
1-9	0-18	2-12	0-8	0-8	0-2	0-9	0-4	2-7	1-6

Winning Jockeys	W-R	£1 Level Stake				W-R	£1 Level Stake
Marie Plowright	2-11	+ 31.00		Alex Greaves		1-1	+ 3.33
F Norton	2-27	- 11.00		J Quinn		1-9	+ 12.00

Winning Courses	W-R	£1 Level Stake				W-R	£1 Level Stake
Lingfield (AW)	3-14	+ 23.00		Salisbury		1-5	+ 16.00
Chepstow	1-5	+ 16.00		Southwell (AW)		1-31	- 26.67

Winning Horses	Age	Races Run	1st	2nd	3rd	Unpl	Win £
La Reine Rouge	5	12	2	1	1	8	5,667
Courting Newmarket	5	15	2	2	2	9	5,527
Caspian Beluga	5	5	1	0	0	4	3,652
Predictable	7	2	1	0	0	1	2,301

Favourites	1-1	100.0%	+ 2.00	Total winning prize-money		£17,146

1992 Form	12-131	9.2%	+ 14.75	1990 Form	0-9
1991 Form	4-50	8.0%	- 12.00	1989 Form	0-13

D R LAING (Lambourn, Berks)

	No. of Horses	Races Run	1st	2nd	3rd	Unpl	Per cent	£1 Level Stake
2-y-o	3	11	1	0	0	10	9.1	+ 2.00
3-y-o	6	37	2	2	2	31	5.4	- 30.50
4-y-o+	9	69	6	3	7	53	8.7	- 18.25
Totals	18	117	9	5	9	94	7.7	- 46.75

Jan	Feb	Mar	Apr	May	Jun	Jul	Aug	Sep	Oct/Nov
0-3	0-0	0-2	0-8	1-21	1-22	4-19	2-16	1-11	0-15

Winning Jockeys	W-R	£1 Level Stake		W-R	£1 Level Stake
T Williams	6-47	+ 2.50	R Price	1-5	+ 8.00
S Whitworth	1-3	+ 1.50	S Davies	1-8	- 4.75

Winning Courses	W-R	£1 Level Stake		W-R	£1 Level Stake
Lingfield	2-13	+ 0.50	Leicester	1-8	+ 5.00
Salisbury	2-14	- 1.75	Chepstow	1-9	+ 4.00
Sandown	1-1	+ 11.00	Brighton	1-12	- 8.75
Folkestone	1-7	- 3.75			

Winning Horses	Age	Races Run	1st	2nd	3rd	Unpl	Win £
My Ruby Ring	6	16	3	1	3	9	9,185
Charmed Knave	8	12	2	1	0	9	6,029
Bellsabanging	3	15	2	2	2	9	5,755
Bells Of Longwick	4	12	1	0	2	9	4,622
Fromage	2	5	1	0	0	4	3,120

Favourites	4-7	57.1%	+ 7.25	Total winning prize-money		£28,711

1992 Form	8-126	6.3%	- 31.50	1991 Form	4-100	4.0%	- 73.50

P LEACH (Taunton, Somerset)

	No. of Horses	Races Run	1st	2nd	3rd	Unpl	Per cent	£1 Level Stake
2-y-o	0	0	0	0	0	0	-	0.00
3-y-o	1	3	0	0	1	2	-	- 3.00
4-y-o+	5	14	3	1	0	10	21.4	- 1.25
Totals	6	17	3	1	1	12	17.6	- 4.25

Jan	Feb	Mar	Apr	May	Jun	Jul	Aug	Sep	Oct/Nov
0-0	0-1	0-0	0-0	1-1	2-4	0-4	0-3	0-2	0-2

Winning Jockeys	W-R	£1 Level Stake		W-R	£1 Level Stake
S Wood	2-5	+ 5.00	J Williams	1-1	+ 1.75

Winning Courses					
Catterick	1-1	+ 3.50	Pontefract	1-2	+ 3.50
Chepstow	1-2	+ 0.75			

Winning Horse	Age	Races Run	1st	2nd	3rd	Unpl	Win £
Mardood	8	6	3	1	0	2	8,891

Favourites	3-4	75.0%	+ 8.75	Total winning prize-money			£8,891
1992 Form	0-6			1990 Form	1-14	7.1%	- 5.00
1991 Form	0-4			1989 Form	0-1		

F H LEE (Wilmslow, Cheshire)

	No. of Horses	Races Run	1st	2nd	3rd	Unpl	Per cent	£1 Level Stake
2-y-o	8	24	2	2	3	17	8.3	- 14.00
3-y-o	16	130	7	10	13	100	5.4	- 75.50
4-y-o+	11	79	2	6	4	67	2.5	- 61.00
Totals	35	233	11	18	20	184	4.7	-150.50

BY MONTH

2-y-o	W-R	Per cent	£1 Level Stake	3-y-o	W-R	Per cent	£1 Level Stake
January	0-0	-	0.00	January	0-0	-	0.00
February	0-0	-	0.00	February	0-0	-	0.00
March	0-0	-	0.00	March	0-8	-	- 8.00
April	0-0	-	0.00	April	0-14	-	- 14.00
May	0-1	-	- 1.00	May	1-17	5.9	- 14.50
June	1-7	14.3	- 2.00	June	1-20	5.0	- 14.00
July	0-3	-	- 3.00	July	5-26	19.2	+ 20.00
August	0-3	-	- 3.00	August	0-19	-	- 19.00
September	1-3	33.3	+ 2.00	September	0-8	-	- 8.00
Oct/Nov	0-7	-	- 7.00	Oct/Nov	0-18	-	- 18.00

4-y-o+	W-R	Per cent	£1 Level Stake	Totals	W-R	Per cent	£1 Level Stake
January	0-0	-	0.00	January	0-0	-	0.00
February	0-0	-	0.00	February	0-0	-	0.00
March	0-5	-	- 5.00	March	0-13	-	- 13.00
April	1-8	12.5	- 3.00	April	1-22	4.5	- 17.00
May	0-13	-	- 13.00	May	1-31	3.2	- 28.50
June	0-11	-	- 11.00	June	2-38	5.3	- 27.00
July	1-12	8.3	+ 1.00	July	6-41	14.6	+ 18.00
August	0-15	-	- 15.00	August	0-37	-	- 37.00
September	0-11	-	- 11.00	September	1-22	4.5	- 17.00
Oct/Nov	0-4	-	- 4.00	Oct/Nov	0-29	-	- 29.00

DISTANCE

2-y-o	W-R	Per cent	£1 Level Stake	3-y-o	W-R	Per cent	£1 Level Stake
5f-6f	2-18	11.1	- 8.00	5f-6f	3-36	8.3	- 5.50
7f-8f	0-6	-	- 6.00	7f-8f	1-51	2.0	- 45.00
9f-13f	0-0	-	0.00	9f-13f	3-41	7.3	- 23.00
14f+	0-0	-	0.00	14f+	0-2	-	- 2.00

4-y-o+	W-R	Per cent	£1 Level Stake	Totals	W-R	Per cent	£1 Level Stake
5f-6f	1-43	2.3	- 38.00	5f-6f	6-97	6.2	- 51.50
7f-8f	1-26	3.8	- 13.00	7f-8f	2-83	2.4	- 64.00
9f-13f	0-10	-	- 10.00	9f-13f	3-51	5.9	- 33.00
14f+	0-0	-	0.00	14f+	0-2	-	- 2.00

TYPE OF RACE

Non-Handicaps	W-R	Per cent	£1 Level Stake	Handicaps	W-R	Per cent	£1 Level Stake
2-y-o	1-19	5.3	- 14.00	2-y-o	1-5	20.0	- 1.00
3-y-o	2-40	5.0	- 27.50	3-y-o	5-73	6.8	- 31.00
4-y-o+	1-9	11.1	- 4.00	4-y-o+	0-53	-	- 53.00
Selling	0-5	-	- 5.00	Selling	0-11	-	- 11.00
Apprentice	0-3	-	- 3.00	Apprentice	1-13	7.7	0.00
Amat/Ladies	0-0	-	0.00	Amat/Ladies	0-2	-	- 2.00
Totals	4-76	5.3	- 53.50	Totals	7-157	4.5	- 97.00

COURSE GRADE

	W-R	Per cent	£1 Level Stake
Group 1	3-102	2.9	- 85.50
Group 2	2-49	4.1	- 31.00
Group 3	4-47	8.5	- 7.50
Group 4	2-35	5.7	- 26.50

FIRST TIME OUT

	W-R	Per cent	£1 Level Stake
2-y-o	0-8	-	- 8.00
3-y-o	0-16	-	- 16.00
4-y-o+	2-11	18.2	+ 7.00
Totals	2-35	5.7	- 17.00

JOCKEYS RIDING

	W-R	Per cent	£1 Level Stake		W-R	Per cent	£1 Level Stake
S Perks	6-63	9.5	- 17.00	B Raymond	1-8	12.5	- 3.00
J Dennis	1-4	25.0	+ 9.00	Paul Eddery	1-13	7.7	- 8.00
J Carroll	1-5	20.0	- 2.50	R Lappin	1-40	2.5	- 29.00

N Kennedy	0-38	A Culhane	0-1	M Humphries	0-1
G Carter	0-7	A Mackay	0-1	M Roberts	0-1
N Carlisle	0-5	A Munro	0-1	Miss J Winter	0-1
W Carson	0-5	D Griffiths	0-1	Mrs G Rees	0-1
G Bardwell	0-3	D Holland	0-1	O Pears	0-1
K Darley	0-3	D Moffatt	0-1	P Robinson	0-1
L Charnock	0-3	D Wright	0-1	Pat Eddery	0-1
R Cochrane	0-3	F Savage	0-1	S Wood	0-1
A Whelan	0-2	G Milligan	0-1	T G McLaughlin	0-1
D McKeown	0-2	J Fanning	0-1	T Quinn	0-1
H Bastiman	0-2	J Weaver	0-1	W Ryan	0-1
J Fortune	0-2	K Fallon	0-1		
A Clark	0-1	M Hills	0-1		

COURSE RECORD

	Total W-R	Non-Handicaps 2-y-o	Non-Handicaps 3-y-o+	Handicaps 2-y-o	Handicaps 3-y-o+	Per cent	£1 Level Stake
Hamilton	2-10	0-0	0-2	0-0	2-8	20.0	+ 10.00
Pontefract	2-16	0-1	0-4	0-0	2-11	12.5	+ 3.50
Haydock	2-23	1-4	1-8	0-0	0-11	8.7	- 13.00
Warwick	1-3	0-1	1-1	0-0	0-1	33.3	+ 3.00
Edinburgh	1-7	0-0	0-1	0-0	1-6	14.3	- 4.50
Thirsk	1-13	0-2	0-2	0-0	1-9	7.7	0.00
Redcar	1-14	0-0	0-5	1-2	0-7	7.1	- 9.00
Ayr	1-20	0-2	1-6	0-0	0-12	5.0	- 13.50

Doncaster	0-25	Newcastle	0-7	Southwell (Turf)	0-3
Ripon	0-14	Chester	0-6	Ascot	0-2
York	0-11	Lingfield (AW)	0-6	Lingfield	0-2
Newmarket	0-9	Carlisle	0-5	Goodwood	0-1
Nottingham	0-9	Leicester	0-5	Sandown	0-1
Catterick	0-8	Epsom	0-3		
Beverley	0-7	Southwell (AW)	0-3		

WINNING HORSES

	Age	Races Run	1st	2nd	3rd	Unpl	Win £
Allwight Then	2	6	2	0	1	3	6,820
Sir Harry Hardman	5	10	1	2	0	7	6,292
Argyle Cavalier	3	9	1	0	2	6	3,825
Sir Edward Henry	3	11	1	0	0	10	3,005
Dayjuz	3	11	1	0	2	8	3,002
Young Jason	10	8	1	1	1	5	2,925

Ttyfran	3	10	1	4	1	4	2,679
Bold Seven	3	9	1	0	0	8	2,489
Peacefull Reply	3	7	1	0	2	4	2,385
Umbubuzi	3	11	1	2	1	7	2,243

WINNING OWNERS

	Races Won	Value £		Races Won	Value £
P J Cosgrove	2	6,820	E H Jones (Paints) Ltd	1	3,825
P D Hobbs	1	6,292	P Asquith	1	3,002
Peter Barr	2	5,390	Mrs Gillian Lee	1	2,925
F H Lee	2	4,732	Mrs C E Collinson	1	2,679

Favourites	3-11	27.3%	+ 1.00	Total winning prize-money		£35,664
Longest winning sequence			1	Average SP of winner		6.5/1
Longest losing sequence			59	Return on stakes invested		-64.6%
1992 Form	27-302	8.9%	- 77.25	1990 Form	25-256	9.8%	- 49.25
1991 Form	30-285	10.5%	- 11.12	1989 Form	27-221	12.2%	- 30.46

R LEE (Presteigne, Powys)

	No. of Horses	Races Run	1st	2nd	3rd	Unpl	Per cent	£1 Level Stake
2-y-o	3	8	0	0	0	8	-	- 8.00
3-y-o	0	0	0	0	0	0	-	0.00
4-y-o+	10	41	2	2	5	32	4.9	- 12.50
Totals	13	49	2	2	5	40	4.1	- 20.50

Jan	Feb	Mar	Apr	May	Jun	Jul	Aug	Sep	Oct/Nov
0-0	0-0	0-1	0-4	1-10	0-6	0-8	1-5	0-10	0-5

Winning Jockeys	W-R	£1 Level Stake		W-R	£1 Level Stake
A Munro	1-2	+ 5.50	O Pears	1-6	+ 15.00

Winning Courses					
Catterick	1-3	+ 18.00	Chepstow	1-5	+ 2.50

Winning Horses	Age	Races Run	1st	2nd	3rd	Unpl	Win £
Decided	10	3	1	0	0	2	2,448
Pickles	5	6	1	0	1	4	1,770

Favourites	0-3	Total winning prize-money	£4,218

1992 Form	3-63	4.8%	- 40.50	1990 Form	0-5
1991 Form	2-13	15.4%	+ 6.00	1989 Form	0-1

J P LEIGH (Gainsborough, Lincs)

	No. of Horses	Races Run	1st	2nd	3rd	Unpl	Per cent	£1 Level Stake
2-y-o	3	9	1	1	0	7	11.1	+ 4.00
3-y-o	4	15	0	1	1	13	-	- 15.00
4-y-o+	5	17	0	1	0	16	-	- 17.00
Totals	12	41	1	3	1	36	2.4	- 28.00

Jan	Feb	Mar	Apr	May	Jun	Jul	Aug	Sep	Oct/Nov
0-6	0-5	0-4	0-9	0-10	0-1	0-0	1-5	0-1	0-0

Winning Jockey	W-R	£1 Level Stake	Winning Course	W-R	£1 Level Stake
J Weaver	1-1	+ 12.00	Thirsk	1-2	+ 11.00

Winning Horse	Age	Races Run	1st	2nd	3rd	Unpl	Win £
Johnnie The Joker	2	7	1	1	0	5	3,158

Favourites	0-1		Total winning prize-money		£3,158

1992 Form	1-83	1.2%	- 74.00	1990 Form	4-57	7.0%	- 17.50
1991 Form	5-54	9.3%	- 12.00	1989 Form	1-48	2.1%	- 22.00

G LEWIS (Epsom, Surrey)

	No. of Horses	Races Run	1st	2nd	3rd	Unpl	Per cent	£1 Level Stake
2-y-o	25	125	19	9	13	84	15.2	- 11.57
3-y-o	15	77	7	2	3	65	9.1	- 13.37
4-y-o+	7	45	4	2	5	34	8.9	- 27.75
Totals	47	247	30	13	21	183	12.1	- 52.69

BY MONTH

2-y-o	W-R	Per cent	£1 Level Stake	3-y-o	W-R	Per cent	£1 Level Stake
Mar/Apr	0-9	-	- 9.00	Mar/Apr	2-19	10.5	- 7.50
May	1-8	12.5	+ 13.00	May	3-17	17.6	+ 28.50
June	4-20	20.0	- 10.08	June	1-18	5.6	- 14.25
July	7-23	30.4	+ 11.76	July	0-9	-	- 9.00
August	4-24	16.7	- 6.75	August	0-3	-	- 3.00
September	3-23	13.0	+ 7.50	September	0-6	-	- 6.00
Oct/Nov	0-18	-	- 18.00	Oct/Nov	1-5	20.0	0.00

4-y-o+	W-R	Per cent	£1 Level Stake	Totals	W-R	Per cent	£1 Level Stake
Mar/Apr	1-8	12.5	- 2.00	Mar/Apr	3-36	8.3	- 18.50
May	0-7	-	- 7.00	May	4-32	12.5	+ 34.50
June	0-14	-	- 14.00	June	5-52	9.6	- 38.33
July	1-6	16.7	- 4.38	July	8-38	21.1	- 1.62
August	2-7	28.6	+ 2.63	August	6-34	17.6	- 7.12
September	0-1	-	- 1.00	September	3-30	10.0	+ 0.50
Oct/Nov	0-2	-	- 2.00	Oct/Nov	1-25	4.0	- 20.00

DISTANCE

2-y-o	W-R	Per cent	£1 Level Stake	3-y-o	W-R	Per cent	£1 Level Stake
5f-6f	15-91	16.5	- 0.84	5f-6f	1-6	16.7	- 3.12
7f-8f	4-33	12.1	- 9.73	7f-8f	4-44	9.1	- 22.25
9f-13f	0-1	-	- 1.00	9f-13f	2-26	7.7	+ 13.00
14f+	0-0	-	0.00	14f+	0-1	-	- 1.00

4-y-o+	W-R	Per cent	£1 Level Stake	Totals	W-R	Per cent	£1 Level Stake
5f-6f	3-23	13.0	- 11.75	5f-6f	19-120	15.8	- 15.71
7f-8f	0-4	-	- 4.00	7f-8f	8-81	9.9	- 35.98
9f-13f	1-17	5.9	- 11.00	9f-13f	3-44	6.8	+ 1.00
14f+	0-1	-	- 1.00	14f+	0-2	-	- 2.00

TYPE OF RACE

Non-Handicaps	W-R	Per cent	£1 Level Stake	Handicaps	W-R	Per cent	£1 Level Stake
2-y-o	8-83	9.6	- 23.25	2-y-o	6-30	20.0	+ 4.75
3-y-o	4-35	11.4	- 18.87	3-y-o	3-34	8.8	+ 13.50
4-y-o+	2-11	18.2	- 2.38	4-y-o+	1-29	3.4	- 23.00
Selling	5-12	41.7	+ 6.93	Selling	1-4	25.0	- 1.37
Apprentice	0-1	-	- 1.00	Apprentice	0-3	-	- 3.00
Amat/Ladies	0-4	-	- 4.00	Amat/Ladies	0-1	-	- 1.00
Totals	19-146	13.0	- 42.57	Totals	11-101	10.9	- 10.12

COURSE GRADE

	W-R	Per cent	£1 Level Stake
Group 1	10-115	8.7	- 16.98
Group 2	8-48	16.7	- 1.01
Group 3	5-44	11.4	- 23.95
Group 4	7-40	17.5	- 10.75

FIRST TIME OUT

	W-R	Per cent	£1 Level Stake
2-y-o	0-24	-	- 24.00
3-y-o	1-13	7.7	- 10.12
4-y-o+	1-6	16.7	0.00
Totals	2-43	4.7	- 34.12

JOCKEYS RIDING

	W-R	Per cent	£1 Level Stake		W-R	Per cent	£1 Level Stake
Paul Eddery	9-60	15.0	+ 3.09	J Weaver	1-2	50.0	+ 32.00
K Darley	5-12	41.7	+ 14.75	C Hawksley	1-5	20.0	- 0.50
D Harrison	4-46	8.7	- 26.12	B Rouse	1-6	16.7	- 1.50
Pat Eddery	3-15	20.0	- 5.29	B Raymond	1-12	8.3	+ 1.00
G Hind	2-5	40.0	+ 0.38	D Wright	1-14	7.1	- 9.50
B Russell	2-27	7.4	- 18.00				

J Reid	0-5	L Dettori	0-2	Miss A Dare	0-1	
A Munro	0-4	L Piggott	0-2	Mrs C Dunwoody	0-1	
J Lowe	0-3	M Hills	0-2	N Carlisle	0-1	
M Payne	0-3	S Whitworth	0-2	R Cochrane	0-1	
Mr K Santana	0-3	B Marcus	0-1	T Sprake	0-1	
N Adams	0-3	D Moffatt	0-1	W Woods	0-1	
Dale Gibson	0-2	G Duffield	0-1			
F Norton	0-2	J Williams	0-1			

COURSE RECORD

	Total W-R	Non-Handicaps 2-y-o	Non-Handicaps 3-y-o+	Handicaps 2-y-o	Handicaps 3-y-o+	Per cent	£1 Level Stake
Lingfield (AW)	4-6	1-1	2-4	0-0	1-1	66.7	+ 14.25
Goodwood	3-13	1-7	0-1	2-4	0-1	23.1	+ 15.25
Ripon	2-2	1-1	0-0	0-0	1-1	100.0	+ 2.36
Lingfield	2-15	2-9	0-1	0-1	0-4	13.3	- 6.37
Newbury	2-16	0-5	0-2	1-4	1-5	12.5	+ 31.00
Folkestone	2-22	0-9	1-7	1-2	0-4	9.1	- 14.62
Beverley	1-1	0-0	0-0	1-1	0-0	100.0	+ 3.50
Redcar	1-1	0-0	0-0	1-1	0-0	100.0	+ 4.50
Newcastle	1-2	1-2	0-0	0-0	0-0	50.0	+ 2.50
Yarmouth	1-2	1-1	0-1	0-0	0-0	50.0	- 0.20
Southwell (Turf)	1-2	0-0	1-1	0-1	0-0	50.0	- 0.38
Chester	1-4	1-4	0-0	0-0	0-0	25.0	+ 7.00
Doncaster	1-5	1-2	0-1	0-2	0-0	20.0	- 3.56
Nottingham	1-7	1-3	0-2	0-2	0-0	14.3	- 4.25
Bath	1-8	0-2	1-1	0-1	0-4	12.5	- 1.00
Brighton	1-11	1-4	0-3	0-0	0-4	9.1	+ 2.00
Salisbury	1-14	0-5	1-3	0-0	0-6	7.1	- 9.50
Windsor	1-15	1-6	0-3	0-0	0-6	6.7	- 11.00
Newmarket	1-16	0-4	0-4	0-4	1-4	6.3	- 10.00
Sandown	1-16	1-7	0-3	0-1	0-5	6.3	- 11.67
Kempton	1-19	0-8	0-3	0-2	1-6	5.3	- 12.50

Epsom	0-21	York	0-3	Haydock	0-1
Warwick	0-8	Chepstow	0-2	Southwell (AW)	0-1
Leicester	0-7	Pontefract	0-2	Thirsk	0-1
Ascot	0-3	Catterick	0-1		

WINNING HORSES

		Races					Win
	Age	Run	1st	2nd	3rd	Unpl	£
Left Stranded	2	6	3	0	1	2	10,374
Vercingetorix	2	5	2	1	0	2	9,754
Dances With Risk	2	10	3	1	1	5	9,119
Loki	5	4	1	0	2	1	7,310
Zuno Star	2	5	2	1	0	2	7,029
Star Speeder	2	11	2	2	1	6	6,039
Noriski'Maringer	2	6	2	0	0	4	5,952
Ballah Shack	2	6	2	0	3	1	5,908
Mr Vincent	3	7	2	1	1	3	5,854
Raging Thunder	3	8	2	1	2	3	5,820
Martina	5	13	2	1	0	10	5,491
Devilry	3	9	1	0	0	8	5,470
Plunder Bay	2	6	1	0	0	5	5,309
Silver Wedge	2	8	1	3	0	4	4,182
Just Jamie	3	6	1	0	0	5	3,028
Bet A Plan	2	9	1	1	2	5	2,259
Lady Sabo	4	6	1	0	0	5	2,243
Dancing Diamond	3	3	1	0	0	2	1,553

WINNING OWNERS

	Races Won	Value £		Races Won	Value £
P D Savill	5	16,194	Abdulla Al Khalifa	2	5,908
Mrs Shirley Robins	4	15,345	Laurel (Leisure) Ltd	2	5,491
Roldvale Limited	5	15,071	Lady McIndoe	1	5,470
Lord Hartington	2	9,754	A R Perry	1	3,028
Michael H Watt	1	7,310	Planflow (Leasing) Ltd	1	2,259
Vic Fatah	2	7,029	Cronk Th'bred Racing Ltd	1	2,243
Giles W Pritchard-Gordon	2	6,039	Geoff Lewis	1	1,553

Favourites	13-35	37.1% + 2.73	Total winning prize-money		£102,692
Longest winning sequence		2	Average SP of winner		5.5/1
Longest losing sequence		32	Return on stakes invested		-21.3%
1992 Form	54-355	15.2% + 53.64	1990 Form	26-285	9.1% -118.86
1991 Form	41-355	11.5% - 42.89	1989 Form	23-304	7.6% -132.25

C V LINES (Exning, Suffolk)

	No. of Horses	Races Run	1st	2nd	3rd	Unpl	Per cent	£1 Level Stake
2-y-o	0	0	0	0	0	0	-	0.00
3-y-o	2	10	1	0	3	6	10.0	+ 1.00
4-y-o+	4	24	1	6	2	15	4.2	- 19.50
Totals	6	34	2	6	5	21	5.9	- 18.50

Jan	Feb	Mar	Apr	May	Jun	Jul	Aug	Sep	Oct/Nov
0-0	0-1	0-0	0-4	1-8	0-8	0-2	0-3	1-5	0-3

Winning Jockeys	W-R	£1 Level Stake				W-R	£1 Level Stake
L Newton	1-1	+ 10.00	J Lowe			1-14	- 9.50

Winning Courses							
Yarmouth	1-6	+ 5.00	Southwell (AW)			1-6	- 1.50

Winning Horses	Age	Races Run	1st	2nd	3rd	Unpl	Win £
Ball Gown	3	9	1	0	2	6	2,490
Tiger Shoot	6	11	1	4	0	6	2,243

Favourites	0-1			Total winning prize-money			£4,733

D R LODER (Newmarket)

	No. of Horses	Races Run	1st	2nd	3rd	Unpl	Per cent	£1 Level Stake
2-y-o	20	81	20	16	12	33	24.7	- 14.00
3-y-o	11	64	17	11	8	28	26.6	- 2.03
4-y-o+	9	48	8	5	8	27	16.7	- 5.84
Totals	40	193	45	32	28	88	23.3	- 21.87

BY MONTH

2-y-o	W-R	Per cent	£1 Level Stake	3-y-o	W-R	Per cent	£1 Level Stake
January	0-0	-	0.00	January	0-2	-	- 2.00
February	0-0	-	0.00	February	2-4	50.0	+ 2.75
March	0-0	-	0.00	March	0-2	-	- 2.00
April	1-1	100.0	+ 5.00	April	1-6	16.7	- 3.50
May	1-8	12.5	- 5.50	May	0-9	-	- 9.00
June	5-10	50.0	+ 8.35	June	1-10	10.0	- 5.00
July	9-20	45.0	+ 8.74	July	7-15	46.7	+ 10.77
August	2-15	13.3	- 7.70	August	4-8	50.0	+ 4.95
September	2-16	12.5	- 11.89	September	2-4	50.0	+ 5.00
Oct/Nov	0-11	-	- 11.00	Oct/Nov	0-4	-	- 4.00

4-y-o+	W-R	Per cent	£1 Level Stake	Totals	W-R	Per cent	£1 Level Stake
January	0-0	-	0.00	January	0-2	-	- 2.00
February	0-0	-	0.00	February	2-4	50.0	+ 2.75
March	0-2	-	- 2.00	March	0-4	-	- 4.00
April	1-7	14.3	+ 1.00	April	3-14	21.4	+ 2.50
May	1-10	10.0	- 4.50	May	2-27	7.4	- 19.00
June	1-10	10.0	- 6.00	June	7-30	23.3	- 2.65
July	4-11	36.4	+ 7.66	July	20-46	43.5	+ 27.17
August	0-2	-	- 2.00	August	6-25	24.0	- 4.75
September	1-4	25.0	+ 2.00	September	5-24	20.8	- 4.89
Oct/Nov	0-2	-	- 2.00	Oct/Nov	0-17	-	- 17.00

DISTANCE

2-y-o	W-R	Per cent	£1 Level Stake	3-y-o	W-R	Per cent	£1 Level Stake
5f-6f	10-32	31.3	- 3.15	5f-6f	2-8	25.0	- 0.50
7f-8f	10-48	20.8	- 9.85	7f-8f	9-30	30.0	- 2.16
9f-13f	0-1	-	- 1.00	9f-13f	6-20	30.0	+ 6.63
14f+	0-0	-	0.00	14f+	0-6	-	- 6.00

4-y-o+	W-R	Per cent	£1 Level Stake	Totals	W-R	Per cent	£1 Level Stake
5f-6f	0-1	-	- 1.00	5f-6f	12-41	29.3	- 4.65
7f-8f	5-24	20.8	+ 4.83	7f-8f	24-102	23.5	- 7.18
9f-13f	2-14	14.3	- 6.17	9f-13f	8-35	22.9	- 0.54
14f+	1-9	11.1	- 3.50	14f+	1-15	6.7	- 9.50

TYPE OF RACE

Non-Handicaps	W-R	Per cent	£1 Level Stake	Handicaps	W-R	Per cent	£1 Level Stake
2-y-o	16-66	24.2	- 16.20	2-y-o	0-10	-	- 10.00
3-y-o	12-36	33.3	+ 11.09	3-y-o	2-22	9.1	- 15.75
4-y-o+	4-19	21.1	- 1.67	4-y-o+	4-28	14.3	- 3.17
Selling	7-9	77.8	+ 16.83	Selling	0-2	-	- 2.00
Apprentice	0-0	-	0.00	Apprentice	0-1	-	- 1.00
Amat/Ladies	0-0	-	0.00	Amat/Ladies	0-0	-	0.00
Totals	39-130	30.0	+ 10.05	Totals	6-63	9.5	- 31.92

COURSE GRADE

	W-R	Per cent	£1 Level Stake
Group 1	12-76	15.8	- 29.59
Group 2	7-26	26.9	+ 8.51
Group 3	11-49	22.4	- 8.86
Group 4	15-42	35.7	+ 8.07

FIRST TIME OUT

	W-R	Per cent	£1 Level Stake
2-y-o	4-19	21.1	- 0.37
3-y-o	1-10	10.0	- 7.50
4-y-o+	2-8	25.0	+ 6.00
Totals	7-37	18.9	- 1.87

JOCKEYS RIDING

	W-R	Per cent	£1 Level Stake		W-R	Per cent	£1 Level Stake
L Dettori	22-94	23.4	- 12.75	M Roberts	2-5	40.0	- 0.89
M Hills	5-6	83.3	+ 8.85	M Tebbutt	2-19	10.5	- 4.00
K Darley	5-14	35.7	+ 2.76	W R Swinburn	1-2	50.0	+ 1.00
G Carter	4-11	36.4	+ 7.41	J Carroll	1-2	50.0	+ 3.50
W Carson	2-3	66.7	+ 3.75	B Raymond	1-3	33.3	+ 2.50

F Norton	0-8	L Piggott	0-2	I Hughes	0-1
J Weaver	0-6	R Cochrane	0-2	K Rutter	0-1
T Quinn	0-3	W Ryan	0-2	M Birch	0-1
G Duffield	0-2	A McGlone	0-1	Miss J Allison	0-1
J Quinn	0-2	G Bardwell	0-1	P Robinson	0-1

COURSE RECORD

	Total W-R	Non-Handicaps 2-y-o	3-y-o+	Handicaps 2-y-o	3-y-o+	Per cent	£1 Level Stake
Southwell (AW)	8-21	3-6	3-5	0-1	2-9	38.1	+ 5.06
Beverley	5-9	4-4	0-1	0-0	1-4	55.6	+ 5.38
Redcar	3-8	1-4	2-3	0-0	0-1	37.5	+ 1.68
Southwell (Turf)	2-2	1-1	1-1	0-0	0-0	100.0	+ 4.88
Chester	2-3	0-1	1-1	0-0	1-1	66.7	+ 4.33
Warwick	2-3	2-2	0-1	0-0	0-0	66.7	+ 7.00
Sandown	2-7	1-5	0-0	0-0	1-2	28.6	− 1.31
Leicester	2-8	1-5	1-2	0-0	0-1	25.0	− 2.74
Lingfield (AW)	2-8	0-0	2-3	0-1	0-4	25.0	− 3.50
Doncaster	2-10	1-4	1-3	0-1	0-2	20.0	− 3.28
Yarmouth	2-12	0-2	2-6	0-2	0-2	16.7	0.00
Newmarket	2-21	2-11	0-4	0-3	0-3	9.5	− 12.50
Epsom	1-1	0-0	1-1	0-0	0-0	100.0	+ 3.00
Salisbury	1-1	0-0	1-1	0-0	0-0	100.0	+ 9.00
Windsor	1-1	1-1	0-0	0-0	0-0	100.0	+ 2.00
Chepstow	1-2	1-1	0-1	0-0	0-0	50.0	+ 3.50
Edinburgh	1-2	0-0	1-2	0-0	0-0	50.0	+ 0.63
Ayr	1-3	0-0	1-2	0-0	0-1	33.3	+ 3.00
Haydock	1-4	1-1	0-2	0-0	0-1	25.0	− 1.25
York	1-4	0-1	0-2	0-0	1-1	25.0	+ 3.00
Brighton	1-5	1-2	0-1	0-0	0-2	20.0	+ 2.50
Ascot	1-6	0-3	1-2	0-0	0-1	16.7	− 3.00
Newbury	1-6	0-1	1-1	0-0	0-4	16.7	− 3.25

Nottingham	0-10	Pontefract	0-4	Folkestone	0-2
Newcastle	0-8	Thirsk	0-4	Kempton	0-2
Catterick	0-4	Lingfield	0-3	Ripon	0-2
Goodwood	0-4	Bath	0-2	Hamilton	0-1

WINNING HORSES

	Age	Races Run	1st	2nd	3rd	Unpl	Win £
Prince Of Andros	3	6	5	1	0	0	49,938
Peter Davies	5	4	2	1	0	1	17,381
Mild Rebuke	2	7	3	1	1	2	10,773
Overbury	2	5	2	1	1	1	10,628
Lucayan Treasure	3	8	3	2	1	2	9,670
Dune River	4	8	2	0	1	5	9,443
John Balliol	5	2	1	0	0	1	9,354
Miss Plum	4	8	1	0	3	4	7,096
Demi-Plie	2	9	3	0	0	6	6,978
Overact	2	5	2	1	0	2	6,521
Kingston Brown	3	12	3	3	2	4	6,334
Essex Girl	3	6	2	0	0	4	6,101
Wandering Angel	2	3	2	0	0	1	5,301
Azola	3	7	2	0	2	3	5,245
Bonny Bride	2	3	1	1	0	1	4,435
Privy Council	2	2	1	0	0	1	4,199
Stelloso	2	4	1	0	3	0	4,092
Fast Eddy	2	6	1	2	2	1	3,915

Truben	4	7	1	1	1	4	3,460
Brigade	4	11	1	1	2	7	3,401
Roveredo	3	2	1	0	0	1	3,085
Leap Of Faith	2	8	2	2	0	4	3,082
Eleuthera	2	5	1	2	1	1	2,873
Ocara	3	6	1	1	0	4	2,794
Pavaka	2	5	1	1	1	2	2,070

WINNING OWNERS

	Races Won	Value £		Races Won	Value £
Lucayan Stud Limited	13	89,642	Lady Hayward	2	6,521
Sheikh Mohammed	3	19,982	E R W Stanley	1	6,212
H E Lhendup Dorji	6	16,004	Mrs P T Fenwick	2	5,301
P D Player	3	10,773	Mrs Jenny Harris	1	3,915
E J Loder	3	9,680	Edward St George	1	3,085
Davie Wong	2	8,291	R M Stevenson	2	3,082
Mrs C A B St George	3	6,978	Michael Worth	1	2,070
D R Loder	2	6,632			

Favourites	26-55	47.3%	+ 13.13	Total winning prize-money	£198,168
Longest winning sequence			2	Average SP of winner	2.9/1
Longest losing sequence			23	Return on stakes invested	-9.6%
1992 Form	2-13	15.4%	+ 18.00		

MRS N MACAULEY (Melton Mowbray, Leics)

	No. of Horses	Races Run	1st	2nd	3rd	Unpl	Per cent	£1 Level Stake
2-y-o	5	21	1	1	2	17	4.8	- 18.25
3-y-o	5	25	2	1	1	21	8.0	- 15.50
4-y-o+	9	76	7	7	13	49	9.2	- 22.75
Totals	19	122	10	9	16	87	8.2	- 56.50

BY MONTH

2-y-o	W-R	Per cent	£1 Level Stake	3-y-o	W-R	Per cent	£1 Level Stake
January	0-0	-	0.00	January	0-2	-	- 2.00
February	0-0	-	0.00	February	0-3	-	- 3.00
March	0-0	-	0.00	March	0-2	-	- 2.00
April	0-1	-	- 1.00	April	0-5	-	- 5.00
May	0-1	-	- 1.00	May	0-2	-	- 2.00
June	1-2	50.0	+ 0.75	June	0-1	-	- 1.00
July	0-1	-	- 1.00	July	0-1	-	- 1.00
August	0-5	-	- 5.00	August	0-2	-	- 2.00
September	0-6	-	- 6.00	September	0-2	-	- 2.00
Oct/Nov	0-5	-	- 5.00	Oct/Nov	2-5	40.0	+ 4.50

Macauley Mrs N

4-y-o+	W-R	Per cent	£1 Level Stake	Totals	W-R	Per cent	£1 Level Stake
January	0-7	-	- 7.00	January	0-9	-	- 9.00
February	2-8	25.0	+ 15.25	February	2-11	18.2	+ 12.25
March	1-6	16.7	+ 6.00	March	1-8	12.5	+ 4.00
April	0-4	-	- 4.00	April	0-10	-	- 10.00
May	0-5	-	- 5.00	May	0-8	-	- 8.00
June	1-12	8.3	- 7.50	June	2-15	13.3	- 7.75
July	2-12	16.7	- 2.00	July	2-14	14.3	- 4.00
August	1-9	11.1	- 5.50	August	1-16	6.3	- 12.50
September	0-7	-	- 7.00	September	0-15	-	- 15.00
Oct/Nov	0-6	-	- 6.00	Oct/Nov	2-16	12.5	- 6.50

DISTANCE

2-y-o	W-R	Per cent	£1 Level Stake	3-y-o	W-R	Per cent	£1 Level Stake
5f-6f	1-17	5.9	- 14.25	5f-6f	0-8	-	- 8.00
7f-8f	0-4	-	- 4.00	7f-8f	2-9	22.2	+ 0.50
9f-13f	0-0	-	0.00	9f-13f	0-7	-	- 7.00
14f+	0-0	-	0.00	14f+	0-1	-	- 1.00

4-y-o+	W-R	Per cent	£1 Level Stake	Totals	W-R	Per cent	£1 Level Stake
5f-6f	6-53	11.3	- 3.25	5f-6f	7-78	9.0	- 25.50
7f-8f	1-21	4.8	- 17.50	7f-8f	3-34	8.8	- 21.00
9f-13f	0-1	-	- 1.00	9f-13f	0-8	-	- 8.00
14f+	0-1	-	- 1.00	14f+	0-2	-	- 2.00

TYPE OF RACE

Non-Handicaps	W-R	Per cent	£1 Level Stake	Handicaps	W-R	Per cent	£1 Level Stake
2-y-o	1-12	8.3	- 9.25	2-y-o	0-8	-	- 8.00
3-y-o	2-14	14.3	- 4.50	3-y-o	0-8	-	- 8.00
4-y-o+	2-15	13.3	- 9.25	4-y-o+	5-57	8.8	- 9.50
Selling	0-3	-	- 3.00	Selling	0-2	-	- 2.00
Apprentice	0-0	-	0.00	Apprentice	0-1	-	- 1.00
Amat/Ladies	0-2	-	- 2.00	Amat/Ladies	0-0	-	0.00
Totals	5-46	10.9	- 28.00	Totals	5-76	6.6	- 28.50

COURSE GRADE

	W-R	Per cent	£1 Level Stake
Group 1	1-16	6.3	- 11.50
Group 2	1-10	10.0	- 4.50
Group 3	3-45	6.7	- 31.00
Group 4	5-51	9.8	- 9.50

FIRST TIME OUT

	W-R	Per cent	£1 Level Stake
2-y-o	0-4	-	- 4.00
3-y-o	0-4	-	- 4.00
4-y-o+	0-8	-	- 8.00
Totals	0-16	-	- 16.00

JOCKEYS RIDING

	W-R	Per cent	£1 Level Stake		W-R	Per cent	£1 Level Stake
E Husband	3-11	27.3	+ 25.50	M Humphries	1-7	14.3	- 4.75
J Quinn	2-7	28.6	+ 2.50	D McKeown	1-8	12.5	- 3.50
G Duffield	1-3	33.3	- 0.25	L Dettori	1-11	9.1	- 6.50
J Reid	1-3	33.3	+ 2.50				

N Adams	0-10	Paul Eddery	0-2	J Lowe	0-1
Madeleine Smith	0-9	A Mackay	0-1	J Marshall	0-1
F Norton	0-7	A Tucker	0-1	Kim McDonnell	0-1
M Roberts	0-6	B Raymond	0-1	R Cochrane	0-1
Dale Gibson	0-5	C Rutter	0-1	R Price	0-1
A Clark	0-4	Claire Balding	0-1	S D Williams	0-1
Alex Greaves	0-3	D Biggs	0-1	S Drowne	0-1
N Day	0-3	D Carson	0-1	T Sprake	0-1
A Munro	0-2	D Holland	0-1	W Carson	0-1
Miss A Sanders	0-2	D McCabe	0-1	W Newnes	0-1

COURSE RECORD

	Total W-R	Non-Handicaps 2-y-o	Non-Handicaps 3-y-o+	Handicaps 2-y-o	Handicaps 3-y-o+	Per cent	£1 Level Stake
Southwell (AW)	3-33	1-4	1-6	0-0	1-23	9.1	- 14.75
Lingfield (AW)	2-12	0-0	1-8	0-0	1-4	16.7	+ 11.25
Leicester	2-16	0-2	1-6	0-1	1-7	12.5	- 5.00
Doncaster	1-3	0-1	0-0	0-0	1-2	33.3	+ 1.50
Brighton	1-5	0-0	0-0	0-0	1-5	20.0	+ 0.50
Yarmouth	1-10	0-0	1-2	0-1	0-7	10.0	- 7.00

Nottingham	0-9	Epsom	0-2	Haydock	0-1
Bath	0-7	Folkestone	0-2	Redcar	0-1
Goodwood	0-3	Kempton	0-2	Thirsk	0-1
Newmarket	0-3	Lingfield	0-2	Warwick	0-1
Southwell (Turf)	0-3	Sandown	0-2	Windsor	0-1
Beverley	0-2	Chester	0-1		

WINNING HORSES

	Age	Races Run	1st	2nd	3rd	Unpl	Win £
Creche	4	14	4	0	4	6	10,420
Always Risky	3	2	2	0	0	0	6,245
Join The Clan	4	6	2	1	2	1	6,056
Farmer Jock	11	13	1	2	2	8	2,899
Hali	2	7	1	0	2	4	2,400

WINNING OWNERS

	Races Won	Value £		Races Won	Value £
Brian Pollins	4	10,420	S Thompson	1	2,899
J Redden	2	6,056	Stephen Roots	1	2,899
Donald Cooper	2	5,746			

Favourites	2-9	22.2%	- 1.50	Total winning prize-money	£28,019

Longest winning sequence		2	Average SP of winner	5.6/1
Longest losing sequence		31	Return on stakes invested	-45.9%

1992 Form	12-227	5.3%	-125.64	1990 Form	24-271	8.9%	- 66.10
1991 Form	21-307	6.8%	-105.60	1989 Form	14-241	5.8%	-123.17

J MACKIE (Church Broughton, Derbys)

	No. of Horses	Races Run	1st	2nd	3rd	Unpl	Per cent	£1 Level Stake
2-y-o	1	9	0	1	2	6	-	- 9.00
3-y-o	3	11	0	0	0	11	-	- 11.00
4-y-o+	8	35	4	2	4	25	11.4	+ 7.00
Totals	12	55	4	3	6	42	7.3	- 13.00

Jan	Feb	Mar	Apr	May	Jun	Jul	Aug	Sep	Oct/Nov
1-3	0-1	0-1	0-2	0-10	0-7	2-10	0-9	1-3	0-9

Winning Jockeys	W-R	£1 Level Stake			W-R	£1 Level Stake
L Dettori	1-1	+ 12.00		W Newnes	1-3	+ 18.00
J Quinn	1-3	- 1.00		G Carter	1-6	0.00

Winning Courses					
Southwell (AW)	3-18	+ 18.00	Southwell (Turf)	1-2	+ 4.00

Winning Horses	Age	Races Run	1st	2nd	3rd	Unpl	Win £
Abalene	4	6	1	0	1	4	2,574
Lock Keeper	7	3	1	0	2	0	2,364
Must Be Magical	5	7	1	2	1	3	2,243
Izitallworthit	4	7	1	0	0	6	1,725

Favourites	1-2	50.0%	0.00	Total winning prize-money	£8,906

1992 Form	4-58	6.9%	- 32.62	1990 Form	8-73	11.0%	+ 16.00
1991 Form	3-61	4.9%	- 30.00	1989 Form	6-120	5.0%	- 64.75

P J MAKIN (Marlborough, Wilts)

	No. of Horses	Races Run	1st	2nd	3rd	Unpl	Per cent	£1 Level Stake
2-y-o	10	28	3	1	3	21	10.7	- 15.70
3-y-o	10	54	5	6	7	36	9.3	- 21.09
4-y-o+	9	57	5	7	3	42	8.8	+ 6.57
Totals	29	139	13	14	13	99	9.4	- 30.22

BY MONTH

2-y-o	W-R	Per cent	£1 Level Stake		3-y-o	W-R	Per cent	£1 Level Stake	
January	0-0	-		0.00	January	0-2	-	-	2.00
February	0-0	-		0.00	February	0-0	-		0.00
March	0-0	-		0.00	March	1-2	50.0	+	3.00
April	0-0	-		0.00	April	0-2	-	-	2.00
May	0-0	-		0.00	May	1-7	14.3	-	5.09
June	1-3	33.3	+	6.00	June	1-8	12.5	+	9.00
July	1-4	25.0	-	2.43	July	1-9	11.1	-	5.00
August	1-4	25.0	-	2.27	August	0-5	-	-	5.00
September	0-8	-	-	8.00	September	0-8	-	-	8.00
Oct/Nov	0-9	-	-	9.00	Oct/Nov	1-11	9.1	-	6.00

4-y-o+	W-R	Per cent	£1 Level Stake		Totals	W-R	Per cent	£1 Level Stake	
January	0-3	-	-	3.00	January	0-5	-	-	5.00
February	2-2	100.0	+	1.57	February	2-2	100.0	+	1.57
March	0-2	-	-	2.00	March	1-4	25.0	+	1.00
April	0-2	-	-	2.00	April	0-4	-	-	4.00
May	0-5	-	-	5.00	May	1-12	8.3	-	10.09
June	2-9	22.2	+	17.00	June	4-20	20.0	+	32.00
July	0-9	-	-	9.00	July	2-22	9.1	-	16.43
August	0-6	-	-	6.00	August	1-15	6.7	-	13.27
September	0-10	-	-	10.00	September	0-26	-	-	26.00
Oct/Nov	1-9	11.1	+	25.00	Oct/Nov	2-29	6.9	+	10.00

DISTANCE

2-y-o	W-R	Per cent	£1 Level Stake		3-y-o	W-R	Per cent	£1 Level Stake	
5f-6f	3-21	14.3	-	8.70	5f-6f	0-6	-	-	6.00
7f-8f	0-7	-	-	7.00	7f-8f	2-20	10.0	-	11.00
9f-13f	0-0	-		0.00	9f-13f	2-26	7.7	-	7.09
14f+	0-0	-		0.00	14f+	1-2	50.0	+	3.00

4-y-o+	W-R	Per cent	£1 Level Stake		Totals	W-R	Per cent	£1 Level Stake	
5f-6f	4-20	20.0	+	9.57	5f-6f	7-47	14.9	-	5.13
7f-8f	0-8	-	-	8.00	7f-8f	2-35	5.7	-	26.00
9f-13f	0-24	-	-	24.00	9f-13f	2-50	4.0	-	31.09
14f+	1-5	20.0	+	29.00	14f+	2-7	28.6	+	32.00

TYPE OF RACE

Non-Handicaps	W-R	Per cent	£1 Level Stake		Handicaps	W-R	Per cent	£1 Level Stake	
2-y-o	3-24	12.5	-	11.70	2-y-o	0-4	-	-	4.00
3-y-o	5-29	17.2	+	3.91	3-y-o	0-19	-	-	19.00
4-y-o+	3-13	23.1	+	3.57	4-y-o+	2-37	5.4	+	10.00
Selling	0-5	-	-	5.00	Selling	0-3	-	-	3.00
Apprentice	0-0	-		0.00	Apprentice	0-5	-	-	5.00
Amat/Ladies	0-0	-		0.00	Amat/Ladies	0-0	-		0.00
Totals	11-71	15.5	-	9.22	Totals	2-68	2.9	-	21.00

COURSE GRADE					FIRST TIME OUT		
	W-R	Per cent	£1 Level Stake			W-R	Per cent	£1 Level Stake
Group 1	4-69	5.8	+ 8.00	2-y-o	1-9	11.1	0.00
Group 2	4-22	18.2	- 2.27	3-y-o	0-10	-	- 10.00
Group 3	2-24	8.3	- 20.52	4-y-o+	1-9	11.1	+ 4.00
Group 4	3-24	12.5	- 15.43				
				Totals	2-28	7.1	- 6.00

JOCKEYS RIDING

	W-R	Per cent	£1 Level Stake		W-R	Per cent	£1 Level Stake
W Ryan	3-14	21.4	- 5.43	B Raymond	1-7	14.3	- 3.00
T Sprake	3-34	8.8	+ 10.57	Pat Eddery	1-11	9.1	- 9.09
L Dettori	1-3	33.3	+ 2.00	A Munro	1-12	8.3	+ 1.00
W Newnes	1-4	25.0	+ 13.00	W R Swinburn	1-15	6.7	- 2.00
K Darley	1-4	25.0	- 2.27				

T Quinn	0-7	J Carroll	0-2	J Reid	0-1
D Holland	0-4	M Hills	0-2	N Adams	0-1
C Asmussen	0-3	S Dawson	0-2	Paul Eddery	0-1
L Piggott	0-3	C Rutter	0-1	R Cochrane	0-1
S Mulvey	0-3	D Harrison	0-1		
C Webb	0-2	Dale Gibson	0-1		

COURSE RECORD

	Total W-R	Non-Handicaps 2-y-o	3-y-o+	Handicaps 2-y-o	3-y-o+	Per cent	£1 Level Stake
Lingfield (AW)	3-8	0-0	3-4	0-0	0-4	37.5	+ 0.57
Lingfield	2-7	1-4	1-1	0-0	0-2	28.6	+ 7.00
Redcar	1-1	1-1	0-0	0-0	0-0	100.0	+ 0.73
Thirsk	1-1	0-0	1-1	0-0	0-0	100.0	+ 3.00
Nottingham	1-4	1-2	0-2	0-0	0-0	25.0	- 2.43
Ascot	1-6	0-0	1-1	0-0	0-5	16.7	+ 7.00
Sandown	1-8	0-1	1-4	0-0	0-3	12.5	+ 9.00
Windsor	1-8	0-1	1-4	0-0	0-3	12.5	- 6.09
Goodwood	1-12	0-2	0-5	0-0	1-5	8.3	+ 1.00
Newmarket	1-12	0-2	0-3	0-1	1-6	8.3	+ 22.00

Newbury	0-11	Brighton	0-4	Epsom	0-2
Salisbury	0-8	Folkestone	0-4	Chepstow	0-1
Bath	0-7	Warwick	0-4	Chester	0-1
Southwell (AW)	0-7	York	0-4	Southwell (Turf)	0-1
Doncaster	0-6	Haydock	0-3	Yarmouth	0-1
Kempton	0-5	Leicester	0-3		

WINNING HORSES

	Age	Races Run	1st	2nd	3rd	Unpl	Win £
Elbio	6	3	1	0	0	2	60,361
Little Saboteur	4	11	3	2	0	6	6,944
Addicted To Love	4	9	1	2	1	5	5,754
Heart Of Spain	3	8	2	1	0	5	5,043
Purple Splash	3	6	1	3	0	2	3,524
Champagne Girl	2	5	1	0	0	4	3,407
City Rocket	3	7	1	0	0	6	3,200
Ann's Pearl	2	4	1	0	1	2	2,243
Claret Bumble	2	3	1	1	0	1	2,087
Gone For A Burton	3	8	1	1	4	2	2,061

WINNING OWNERS

	Races Won	Value £		Races Won	Value £
Brian Brackpool	1	60,361	Avon Industries Ltd	1	2,835
Mrs P J Makin	5	12,438	Mrs Paul Levinson	1	2,243
Mascalls Stud	1	5,754	J S Hobhouse	1	2,208
Christopher Walford	1	3,524	H P Carrington	1	2,061
Mrs C R Walford	1	3,200			

Favourites	5-20	25.0%	- 10.72	Total winning prize-money		£94,623
Longest winning sequence			3	Average SP of winner		7.4/1
Longest losing sequence			40	Return on stakes invested		-21.4%
1992 Form	12-162	7.4%	- 50.09	1990 Form	27-146	18.5%	- 28.65
1991 Form	23-200	11.5%	- 44.46	1989 Form	29-186	15.6%	+ 23.75

D MARKS (Upper Lambourn, Berks)

	No. of Horses	Races Run	1st	2nd	3rd	Unpl	Per cent	£1 Level Stake
2-y-o	1	4	0	0	0	4	-	- 4.00
3-y-o	2	14	0	1	0	13	-	- 14.00
4-y-o+	5	34	2	1	4	27	5.9	- 12.50
Totals	8	52	2	2	4	44	3.8	- 30.50

Jan	Feb	Mar	Apr	May	Jun	Jul	Aug	Sep	Oct/Nov
0-5	0-6	0-3	1-5	0-5	0-5	0-5	0-8	1-5	0-5

Winning Jockeys	W-R	£1 Level Stake		W-R	£1 Level Stake
Miss K Marks	1-3	+ 3.50	S Dawson	1-19	- 4.00

Winning Courses					
Newbury	1-3	+ 3.50	Warwick	1-5	+ 10.00

Marks D

Winning Horses	Age	Races Run	1st	2nd	3rd	Unpl	Win £
Crackling	4	9	1	0	0	8	6,255
Tenayestelign	5	7	1	1	2	3	3,417

Favourites	1-3	33.3%	+ 3.50	Total winning prize-money			£9,672

1992 Form	8-77	10.4%	- 14.25	1990 Form	1-32	3.1%	+ 19.00
1991 Form	0-41			1989 Form	2-26	7.7%	+ 4.00

P J MCBRIDE (Newmarket)

	No. of Horses	Races Run	1st	2nd	3rd	Unpl	Per cent	£1 Level Stake
2-y-o	3	5	0	0	0	5	-	- 5.00
3-y-o	4	10	1	1	0	8	10.0	- 4.00
4-y-o+	3	6	0	0	0	6	-	- 6.00
Totals	10	21	1	1	0	19	4.8	- 15.00

Jan	Feb	Mar	Apr	May	Jun	Jul	Aug	Sep	Oct/Nov
0-0	0-0	0-0	0-0	0-0	0-7	1-5	0-3	0-2	0-4

Winning Jockey	W-R	£1 Level Stake	Winning Course	W-R	£1 Level Stake
G Forster	1-5	+ 1.00	Thirsk	1-1	+ 5.00

Winning Horse	Age	Races Run	1st	2nd	3rd	Unpl	Win £
Royal Roller	3	5	1	0	0	4	2,601

Favourites	0-1		Total winning prize-money	£2,601

M MCCORMACK (Wantage, Oxon)

	No. of Horses	Races Run	1st	2nd	3rd	Unpl	Per cent	£1 Level Stake
2-y-o	9	40	5	2	5	28	12.5	+ 1.62
3-y-o	12	37	3	1	2	31	8.1	- 22.50
4-y-o+	9	59	7	7	10	35	11.9	+ 8.00
Totals	30	136	15	10	17	94	11.0	- 12.88

BY MONTH

2-y-o	W-R	Per cent	£1 Level Stake	3-y-o	W-R	Per cent	£1 Level Stake
Mar/Apr	0-1	-	- 1.00	Mar/Apr	0-9	-	- 7.00
May	3-3	100.0	+ 21.12	May	1-9	11.1	- 5.00
June	0-7	-	- 7.00	June	0-7	-	- 7.00
July	0-2	-	- 2.00	July	1-6	16.7	- 1.00
August	0-12	-	- 12.00	August	0-3	-	- 3.00
September	1-11	9.1	+ 2.00	September	1-2	50.0	+ 3.50
Oct/Nov	1-4	25.0	+ 0.50	Oct/Nov	0-1	-	- 1.00

4-y-o+	W-R	Per cent	£1 Level Stake	Totals	W-R	Per cent	£1 Level Stake
Mar/Apr	1-9	11.1	+ 5.00	Mar/Apr	1-19	5.3	- 3.00
May	1-13	7.7	- 3.00	May	5-25	20.0	+ 13.12
June	0-10	-	- 10.00	June	0-24	-	- 24.00
July	1-5	20.0	+ 3.50	July	2-13	15.4	+ 0.50
August	1-8	12.5	- 3.50	August	1-23	4.3	- 18.50
September	0-5	-	- 5.00	September	2-18	11.1	+ 0.50
Oct/Nov	3-9	33.3	+ 22.00	Oct/Nov	4-14	28.6	+ 21.50

DISTANCE

2-y-o	W-R	Per cent	£1 Level Stake	3-y-o	W-R	Per cent	£1 Level Stake
5f-6f	4-35	11.4	+ 2.12	5f-6f	1-13	7.7	- 8.00
7f-8f	1-5	20.0	- 0.50	7f-8f	2-15	13.3	- 5.50
9f-13f	0-0	-	0.00	9f-13f	0-9	-	- 9.00
14f+	0-0	-	0.00	14f+	0-0	-	0.00

4-y-o+	W-R	Per cent	£1 Level Stake	Totals	W-R	Per cent	£1 Level Stake
5f-6f	6-46	13.0	+ 11.00	5f-6f	11-94	11.7	+ 5.12
7f-8f	1-13	7.7	- 3.00	7f-8f	4-33	12.1	- 9.00
9f-13f	0-0	-	0.00	9f-13f	0-9	-	- 9.00
14f+	0-0	-	0.00	14f+	0-0	-	0.00

TYPE OF RACE

Non-Handicaps	W-R	Per cent	£1 Level Stake	Handicaps	W-R	Per cent	£1 Level Stake
2-y-o	5-38	13.2	+ 3.62	2-y-o	0-2	-	- 2.00
3-y-o	3-20	15.0	- 5.50	3-y-o	0-11	-	- 11.00
4-y-o+	1-19	5.3	- 2.00	4-y-o+	5-35	14.3	+ 5.00
Selling	0-4	-	- 4.00	Selling	0-1	-	- 1.00
Apprentice	0-0	-	0.00	Apprentice	1-5	20.0	+ 5.00
Amat/Ladies	0-0	-	0.00	Amat/Ladies	0-1	-	- 1.00
Totals	9-81	11.1	- 7.88	Totals	6-55	10.9	- 5.00

COURSE GRADE

	W-R	Per cent	£1 Level Stake
Group 1	5-49	10.2	- 14.00
Group 2	4-35	11.4	+ 2.12
Group 3	3-32	9.4	- 14.00
Group 4	3-20	15.0	+ 13.00

FIRST TIME OUT

	W-R	Per cent	£1 Level Stake
2-y-o	2-9	22.2	+ 13.50
3-y-o	0-11	-	- 11.00
4-y-o+	2-8	25.0	+ 15.00
Totals	4-28	14.3	+ 17.50

JOCKEYS RIDING

	W-R	Per cent	£1 Level Stake		W-R	Per cent	£1 Level Stake
J Reid	4-37	10.8	- 7.38	W Newnes	1-3	33.3	+ 1.00
A Clark	4-40	10.0	- 1.00	Pat Eddery	1-3	33.3	+ 1.00
G Duffield	2-4	50.0	+ 9.50	D Gibbs	1-3	33.3	+ 7.00
G Carter	1-2	50.0	+ 8.00	Gina Faulkner	1-7	14.3	+ 6.00

W Carson	0-9	B Raymond	0-1	L Dettori	0-1
C Rutter	0-4	C Hodgson	0-1	M Perrett	0-1
A Munro	0-2	D Holland	0-1	Miss S Farrant	0-1
A Tucker	0-2	G Bardwell	0-1	P V Gilson	0-1
M Birch	0-2	J Carroll	0-1	R Perham	0-1
M Roberts	0-2	J D Smith	0-1	S Raymont	0-1
N Adams	0-2	K Fallon	0-1	W Ryan	0-1

COURSE RECORD

	Total W-R	Non-Handicaps 2-y-o	3-y-o+	Handicaps 2-y-o	3-y-o+	Per cent	£1 Level Stake
Lingfield	3-11	2-4	0-2	0-0	1-5	27.3	+ 24.50
Yarmouth	1-1	0-0	1-1	0-0	0-0	100.0	+ 4.00
Carlisle	1-3	0-0	0-1	0-0	1-2	33.3	+ 7.00
Haydock	1-3	0-2	1-1	0-0	0-0	33.3	+ 1.00
Southwell (AW)	1-3	0-1	0-0	0-0	1-2	33.3	+ 7.00
Doncaster	1-4	0-0	0-2	0-0	1-2	25.0	0.00
Folkestone	1-4	1-2	0-1	0-1	0-0	25.0	+ 9.00
Newmarket	1-6	0-0	1-4	0-0	0-2	16.7	+ 11.00
York	1-7	1-5	0-1	0-0	0-1	14.3	- 2.50
Bath	1-10	0-0	0-3	0-0	1-7	10.0	- 5.50
Newbury	1-10	0-4	1-2	0-0	0-4	10.0	- 4.50
Windsor	1-10	0-3	0-2	0-0	1-5	10.0	- 1.50
Salisbury	1-11	1-5	0-2	0-0	0-4	9.1	- 9.38

Warwick	0-7	Beverley	0-3	Chepstow	0-2
Goodwood	0-6	Leicester	0-3	Nottingham	0-2
Kempton	0-5	Redcar	0-3	Ayr	0-1
Sandown	0-4	Ripon	0-3	Chester	0-1
Thirsk	0-4	Brighton	0-2	Lingfield (AW)	0-1
Ascot	0-3	Catterick	0-2	Pontefract	0-1

WINNING HORSES

	Age	Races Run	1st	2nd	3rd	Unpl	Win £
Montendre	6	9	1	1	2	5	10,464
Tamar's Brigade	2	6	2	0	1	3	8,776
High Domain	2	7	2	0	1	4	8,521
Inherent Magic	4	8	1	2	1	4	6,640
The Noble Oak	5	10	2	1	1	6	6,190
Good For The Roses	7	3	1	0	0	2	3,915
Windrush Lady	3	3	1	0	0	2	3,720
Feather Face	3	4	1	0	1	2	3,590
Newbury Coat	3	7	1	0	1	5	3,525
Call To The Bar	4	11	1	3	2	5	3,436
Pharaoh's Dancer	6	4	1	0	1	2	3,339
Lightning Belle	2	5	1	0	0	4	2,951

WINNING OWNERS

	Races Won	Value £		Races Won	Value £
Mrs S J Stovold	3	15,161	M A Wilkins	1	3,720
David Mort	1	10,464	J A Mountain	1	3,590
P R Cruden	2	8,776	John R Goddard	1	3,525
Trow Lane Farm	2	7,351	Pharaohs Computers Ltd	1	3,339
M McCormack	2	6,190	Mrs Satu Marks	1	2,951

Favourites	3-14	21.4%	- 3.88	Total winning prize-money	£65,066
Longest winning sequence			2	Average SP of winner	7.2/1
Longest losing sequence			33	Return on stakes invested	-9.5%
1992 Form	16-175	9.1%	- 69.97	1990 Form	5-152	3.3%	-116.25
1991 Form	16-145	11.0%	- 22.50	1989 Form	12-106	11.3%	- 12.75

P M MCENTEE (Windsor, Berks)

	No. of Horses	Races Run	1st	2nd	3rd	Unpl	Per cent	£1 Level Stake
2-y-o	3	11	0	0	0	11	-	- 11.00
3-y-o	5	18	1	1	0	16	5.6	- 15.00
4-y-o+	7	27	0	1	0	26	-	- 27.00
Totals	15	56	1	2	0	53	1.8	- 53.00

Jan	Feb	Mar	Apr	May	Jun	Jul	Aug	Sep	Oct/Nov
0-0	0-3	1-3	0-8	0-8	0-9	0-8	0-6	0-6	0-5

Winning Jockey	W-R	£1 Level Stake	Winning Course	W-R	£1 Level Stake
J Weaver	1-11	- 8.00	Southwell (AW)	1-5	- 2.00

Winning Horse	Age	Races Run	1st	2nd	3rd	Unpl	Win £
Belle Soiree	3	2	1	0	0	1	2,070

Favourites	1-2	50.0%	+ 1.00	Total winning prize-money	£2,070
1992 Form	1-18	5.6%	- 13.00		

T P MCGOVERN (Bolney, West Sussex)

	No. of Horses	Races Run	1st	2nd	3rd	Unpl	Per cent	£1 Level Stake
2-y-o	0	0	0	0	0	0	-	0.00
3-y-o	2	11	0	0	1	10	-	- 11.00
4-y-o+	4	17	1	2	0	14	5.9	- 8.00
Totals	6	28	1	2	1	24	3.6	- 19.00

Jan	Feb	Mar	Apr	May	Jun	Jul	Aug	Sep	Oct/Nov
0-0	0-0	0-0	0-5	0-8	0-4	1-4	0-2	0-4	0-1

Winning Jockey		W-R	£1 Level Stake	Winning Course		W-R	£1 Level Stake
S Mulvey		1-13	- 4.00	Southwell (Turf)		1-2	+ 7.00

Winning Horse	Age	Races Run	1st	2nd	3rd	Unpl	Win £
Quick Steel	5	11	1	2	0	8	2,448

Favourites	0-2	Total winning prize-money	£2,448

1992 Form	0-13			1990 Form	0-5
1991 Form	2-35	5.7%	+ 12.00		

B A MCMAHON (Tamworth, Staffs)

	No. of Horses	Races Run	1st	2nd	3rd	Unpl	Per cent	£1 Level Stake
2-y-o	15	47	2	3	4	38	4.3	- 4.00
3-y-o	12	71	4	3	6	58	5.6	- 37.50
4-y-o+	25	153	14	17	15	107	9.2	- 5.20
Totals	52	271	20	23	25	203	7.4	- 46.70

BY MONTH

2-y-o	W-R	Per cent	£1 Level Stake	3-y-o	W-R	Per cent	£1 Level Stake
January	0-0	-	0.00	January	0-0	-	0.00
February	0-0	-	0.00	February	0-0	-	0.00
March	0-0	-	0.00	March	0-1	-	- 1.00
April	0-6	-	- 6.00	April	0-4	-	- 4.00
May	0-3	-	- 3.00	May	1-14	7.1	- 9.00
June	0-6	-	- 6.00	June	1-9	11.1	+ 4.00
July	0-5	-	- 5.00	July	1-15	6.7	- 8.00
August	1-4	25.0	+ 5.00	August	0-14	-	- 14.00
September	1-9	11.1	+ 25.00	September	1-8	12.5	+ 0.50
Oct/Nov	0-14	-	- 14.00	Oct/Nov	0-6	-	- 6.00

4-y-o+	W-R	Per cent	£1 Level Stake	Totals	W-R	Per cent	£1 Level Stake
January	2-19	10.5	- 11.25	January	2-19	10.5	- 11.25
February	0-8	-	- 8.00	February	0-8	-	- 8.00
March	3-7	42.9	+ 55.80	March	3-8	37.5	+ 54.80
April	0-8	-	- 8.00	April	0-18	-	- 18.00
May	1-20	5.0	+ 6.00	May	2-37	5.4	- 6.00
June	1-18	5.6	- 12.00	June	2-33	6.1	- 14.00
July	2-30	6.7	- 18.33	July	3-50	6.0	- 31.33
August	4-19	21.1	+ 10.08	August	5-37	13.5	+ 1.08
September	0-14	-	- 14.00	September	2-31	6.5	+ 11.50
Oct/Nov	1-10	10.0	- 5.50	Oct/Nov	1-30	3.3	- 25.50

DISTANCE

2-y-o	W-R	Per cent	£1 Level Stake	3-y-o	W-R	Per cent	£1 Level Stake
5f-6f	2-40	5.0	+ 3.00	5f-6f	3-34	8.8	- 9.00
7f-8f	0-7	-	- 7.00	7f-8f	1-24	4.2	- 15.50
9f-13f	0-0	-	0.00	9f-13f	0-13	-	- 13.00
14f+	0-0	-	0.00	14f+	0-0	-	0.00

4-y-o+	W-R	Per cent	£1 Level Stake	Totals	W-R	Per cent	£1 Level Stake
5f-6f	10-72	13.9	+ 52.72	5f-6f	15-146	10.3	+ 46.72
7f-8f	3-51	5.9	- 30.67	7f-8f	4-82	4.9	- 53.17
9f-13f	1-24	4.2	- 21.25	9f-13f	1-37	2.7	- 34.25
14f+	0-6	-	- 6.00	14f+	0-6	-	- 6.00

TYPE OF RACE

Non-Handicaps	W-R	Per cent	£1 Level Stake	Handicaps	W-R	Per cent	£1 Level Stake
2-y-o	2-39	5.1	+ 4.00	2-y-o	0-4	-	- 4.00
3-y-o	0-31	-	- 31.00	3-y-o	4-33	12.1	+ 0.50
4-y-o+	7-50	14.0	+ 45.88	4-y-o+	6-81	7.4	- 30.75
Selling	1-13	7.7	- 11.33	Selling	0-7	-	- 7.00
Apprentice	0-4	-	- 4.00	Apprentice	0-7	-	- 7.00
Amat/Ladies	0-0	-	0.00	Amat/Ladies	0-2	-	- 2.00
Totals	10-137	7.3	+ 3.55	Totals	10-134	7.5	- 50.25

COURSE GRADE

	W-R	Per cent	£1 Level Stake
Group 1	5-89	5.6	- 7.50
Group 2	2-27	7.4	- 19.42
Group 3	5-73	6.8	- 2.50
Group 4	8-82	9.8	- 17.28

FIRST TIME OUT

	W-R	Per cent	£1 Level Stake
2-y-o	1-15	6.7	+ 19.00
3-y-o	0-12	-	- 12.00
4-y-o+	1-25	4.0	+ 26.00
Totals	2-52	3.8	+ 33.00

McMahon B A

JOCKEYS RIDING

	W–R	Per cent	£1 Level Stake		W–R	Per cent	£1 Level Stake
T Quinn	5-45	11.1	+ 8.55	G Duffield	1-3	33.3	+ 2.00
A Mackay	3-41	7.3	- 6.50	A Clark	1-3	33.3	+ 1.50
J Fortune	2-27	7.4	- 12.33	B Raymond	1-4	25.0	+ 2.00
S Sanders	2-50	4.0	- 17.00	D Biggs	1-10	10.0	- 7.25
W Carson	1-1	100.0	+ 3.33	L Dettori	1-13	7.7	- 3.00
M Hills	1-2	50.0	+ 3.00	A Munro	1-15	6.7	+ 36.00

J Bramhill	0-12	Mr E McMahon	0-2	J Fanning	0-1
M Birch	0-10	P Robinson	0-2	K Darley	0-1
D McKeown	0-5	R Hills	0-2	K Rutter	0-1
T Wall	0-3	S Dawson	0-2	Paul Eddery	0-1
T Williams	0-3	A Garth	0-1	S Maloney	0-1
C Asmussen	0-2	C N Adamson	0-1	S Saunders	0-1
J Lowe	0-2	D Wright	0-1		
J Quinn	0-2	G Carter	0-1		

COURSE RECORD

	Total W–R	Non-Handicaps 2-y-o	Non-Handicaps 3-y-o+	Handicaps 2-y-o	Handicaps 3-y-o+	Per cent	£1 Level Stake
Haydock	3-23	0-4	0-5	0-0	3-14	13.0	- 2.50
Southwell (AW)	3-42	0-1	1-16	0-0	2-25	7.1	- 27.45
Bath	2-4	1-2	1-2	0-0	0-0	50.0	+ 34.50
Lingfield (AW)	2-4	0-0	1-2	0-0	1-2	50.0	+ 5.50
Beverley	2-13	0-2	0-3	0-0	2-8	15.4	+ 10.00
Salisbury	1-2	0-0	1-2	0-0	0-0	50.0	+ 1.25
Catterick	1-4	0-1	1-1	0-1	0-1	25.0	- 2.33
Ripon	1-7	0-1	1-4	0-0	0-2	14.3	- 2.67
Ascot	1-8	0-0	0-2	0-0	1-6	12.5	+ 2.00
Carlisle	1-11	0-2	1-6	0-0	0-3	9.1	+ 15.00
Warwick	1-11	0-1	0-4	0-0	1-6	9.1	+ 2.00
Doncaster	1-15	0-3	1-4	0-0	0-8	6.7	+ 36.00
Nottingham	1-22	1-8	0-7	0-1	0-6	4.5	- 13.00

Leicester	0-17	Newmarket	0-6	Epsom	0-2
Pontefract	0-17	Thirsk	0-6	Lingfield	0-2
York	0-17	Sandown	0-4	Newcastle	0-2
Chester	0-8	Goodwood	0-3	Redcar	0-2
Southwell (Turf)	0-8	Ayr	0-2		
Newbury	0-7	Edinburgh	0-2		

WINNING HORSES

	Age	Races Run	1st	2nd	3rd	Unpl	Win £
Regal Chimes	4	10	2	0	1	7	20,537
Look Who's Here	3	8	2	0	0	6	14,659
Appledorn	6	10	3	1	1	5	9,210
Samson-Agonistes	7	8	3	2	0	3	7,118
Causley	8	14	2	3	2	7	7,093

Beauman	3	10	1	0	1	8	6,158
Admirals Realm	4	8	1	0	0	7	3,878
Bunty Boo	4	9	1	1	1	6	3,720
Dominion King	2	1	1	0	0	0	3,379
Manor Adventure	3	8	1	1	0	6	3,126
Obsidian Grey	6	5	1	2	0	2	2,758
Well And Truly	6	8	1	2	3	2	2,406
Rocky Two	2	11	1	1	1	8	2,219

WINNING OWNERS

	Races Won	Value £		Races Won	Value £
Michael Sturgess	2	20,537	Mrs R C Mayall	1	3,720
Mrs B Facchino	4	15,367	Mrs D E Kaine	1	3,379
S L Edwards	2	14,659	Mrs Julie Martin	1	3,126
J B Wilcox	3	7,118	D J Allen	1	2,758
Henry Pearce	2	7,093	Peter G Freeman	1	2,406
P W Leslie	1	3,878	R Thornhill	1	2,219

Favourites	4-21	19.0%	- 10.28	Total winning prize-money	£86,259
Longest winning sequence			2	Average SP of winner	10.2/1
Longest losing sequence			28	Return on stakes invested	-17.2%

1992 Form	31-316	9.8%	- 95.02	1990 Form	22-275	8.0%	- 55.74
1991 Form	14-277	5.1%	-150.37	1989 Form	21-195	10.8%	+ 16.56

B J MCMATH (Newmarket)

	No. of Horses	Races Run	1st	2nd	3rd	Unpl	Per cent	£1 Level Stake
2-y-o	4	7	0	0	0	7	-	- 7.00
3-y-o	4	14	1	2	0	11	7.1	- 9.00
4-y-o+	6	21	0	2	1	18	-	- 21.00
Totals	14	42	1	4	1	36	2.4	- 37.00

Jan	Feb	Mar	Apr	May	Jun	Jul	Aug	Sep	Oct/Nov
0-2	0-2	0-0	0-4	0-6	0-5	1-7	0-8	0-5	0-3

		£1 Level				£1 Level
Winning Jockey	W-R	Stake	Winning Course	W-R		Stake
E Johnson	1-22	- 17.00	Southwell (Turf)	1-2		+ 3.00

		Races					Win
Winning Horse	Age	Run	1st	2nd	3rd	Unpl	£
Bronze Maquette	3	8	1	2	0	5	2,070

Favourites	1-2	50.0%	+ 3.00	Total winning prize-money		£2,070

1992 Form	1-35	2.9%	- 29.50	1990 Form	0-14
1991 Form	0-32				

B J MEEHAN (Lambourn, Berks)

	No. of Horses	Races Run	1st	2nd	3rd	Unpl	Per cent	£1 Level Stake
2-y-o	16	91	7	9	10	65	7.7	- 40.78
3-y-o	11	57	4	3	4	46	7.0	- 38.00
4-y-o+	5	34	2	2	4	26	5.9	- 8.00
Totals	32	182	13	14	18	137	7.1	- 86.78

BY MONTH

2-y-o	W-R	Per cent	£1 Level Stake	3-y-o	W-R	Per cent	£1 Level Stake
January	0-0	-	0.00	January	0-1	-	- 1.00
February	0-0	-	0.00	February	0-0	-	0.00
March	0-0	-	0.00	March	0-0	-	0.00
April	0-8	-	- 8.00	April	0-6	-	- 6.00
May	1-7	14.3	- 3.50	May	1-15	6.7	- 10.50
June	0-9	-	- 9.00	June	1-6	16.7	- 1.50
July	2-21	9.5	- 8.78	July	1-11	9.1	- 7.00
August	2-19	10.5	- 2.50	August	1-3	33.3	+ 3.00
September	1-14	7.1	- 3.00	September	0-10	-	- 10.00
Oct/Nov	1-13	7.7	- 6.00	Oct/Nov	0-5	-	- 5.00

4-y-o+	W-R	Per cent	£1 Level Stake	Totals	W-R	Per cent	£1 Level Stake
January	0-0	-	0.00	January	0-1	-	- 1.00
February	0-0	-	0.00	February	0-0	-	0.00
March	0-0	-	0.00	March	0-0	-	0.00
April	0-1	-	- 1.00	April	0-15	-	- 15.00
May	0-7	-	- 7.00	May	2-29	6.9	- 21.00
June	1-9	11.1	+ 6.00	June	2-24	8.3	- 4.50
July	0-9	-	- 9.00	July	3-41	7.3	- 24.78
August	1-4	25.0	+ 7.00	August	4-26	15.4	+ 7.50
September	0-2	-	- 2.00	September	1-26	3.8	- 15.00
Oct/Nov	0-2	-	- 2.00	Oct/Nov	1-20	5.0	- 13.00

DISTANCE

2-y-o	W-R	Per cent	£1 Level Stake	3-y-o	W-R	Per cent	£1 Level Stake
5f-6f	4-55	7.3	- 24.50	5f-6f	0-10	-	- 10.00
7f-8f	3-36	8.3	- 16.28	7f-8f	0-10	-	- 10.00
9f-13f	0-0	-	0.00	9f-13f	3-30	10.0	- 17.00
14f+	0-0	-	0.00	14f+	1-7	14.3	- 1.00

4-y-o+	W-R	Per cent	£1 Level Stake	Totals	W-R	Per cent	£1 Level Stake
5f-6f	0-11	-	- 11.00	5f-6f	4-76	5.3	- 45.50
7f-8f	2-16	12.5	+ 10.00	7f-8f	5-62	8.1	- 16.28
9f-13f	0-7	-	- 7.00	9f-13f	3-37	8.1	- 24.00
14f+	0-0	-	0.00	14f+	1-7	14.3	- 1.00

TYPE OF RACE

Non-Handicaps	W-R	Per cent	£1 Level Stake	Handicaps	W-R	Per cent	£1 Level Stake
2-y-o	4-52	7.7	- 29.28	2-y-o	3-28	10.7	- 0.50
3-y-o	0-18	-	- 18.00	3-y-o	3-26	11.5	- 13.00
4-y-o+	0-2	-	- 2.00	4-y-o+	2-29	6.9	- 3.00
Selling	0-12	-	- 12.00	Selling	0-8	-	- 8.00
Apprentice	0-0	-	0.00	Apprentice	1-7	14.3	- 1.00
Amat/Ladies	0-0	-	0.00	Amat/Ladies	0-0	-	0.00
Totals	4-84	4.8	- 61.28	Totals	9-98	9.2	- 25.50

COURSE GRADE

	W-R	Per cent	£1 Level Stake
Group 1	1-64	1.6	- 55.00
Group 2	6-38	15.8	- 6.28
Group 3	5-56	8.9	- 8.50
Group 4	1-24	4.2	- 17.00

FIRST TIME OUT

	W-R	Per cent	£1 Level Stake
2-y-o	0-16	-	- 16.00
3-y-o	0-8	-	- 8.00
4-y-o+	0-4	-	- 4.00
Totals	0-28	-	- 28.00

JOCKEYS RIDING

	W-R	Per cent	£1 Level Stake		W-R	Per cent	£1 Level Stake
B Doyle	5-36	13.9	+ 2.00	K Fallon	1-4	25.0	0.00
B Rouse	2-22	9.1	- 11.50	N Carlisle	1-7	14.3	+ 4.00
A Tucker	1-2	50.0	+ 2.50	S Whitworth	1-13	7.7	+ 2.00
A Munro	1-3	33.3	+ 8.00	W Newnes	1-19	5.3	- 17.78

R Perham	0-16	D Holland	0-2	M Hills	0-1
A McGlone	0-7	J Reid	0-2	Mark Denaro	0-1
A Lakeman	0-5	M Roberts	0-2	Paul Eddery	0-1
J Quinn	0-5	Pat Eddery	0-2	R Hills	0-1
B Raymond	0-4	T Sprake	0-2	S Davies	0-1
L Dettori	0-4	A Clark	0-1	T Quinn	0-1
W Ryan	0-4	F Norton	0-1	W Carson	0-1
D O'Neill	0-3	G Bardwell	0-1	W Woods	0-1
W R Swinburn	0-3	G Duffield	0-1		
D Gibbs	0-2	L Piggott	0-1		

COURSE RECORD

	Total W-R	Non-Handicaps 2-y-o	3-y-o+	Handicaps 2-y-o	3-y-o+	Per cent	£1 Level Stake
Brighton	3-15	2-5	0-2	1-2	0-6	20.0	- 2.78
Bath	2-12	0-3	0-4	1-1	1-4	16.7	+ 5.00
Redcar	1-2	0-0	0-0	0-0	1-2	50.0	+ 2.00
Lingfield (AW)	1-2	1-1	0-0	0-0	0-1	50.0	+ 5.00
Chepstow	1-4	0-0	0-0	0-0	1-4	25.0	+ 11.00

Meehan B J

Kempton	1-9	0-3	0-1	1-1	0-4	11.1		0.00
Lingfield	1-9	0-3	0-0	0-2	1-4	11.1	-	4.50
Salisbury	1-10	0-2	0-1	0-0	1-7	10.0	+	1.00
Nottingham	1-14	0-6	0-2	0-1	1-5	7.1	-	9.50
Windsor	1-17	1-6	0-4	0-3	0-4	5.9	-	6.00

Newmarket	0-19	Sandown	0-6	Haydock	0-2
Folkestone	0-9	Newbury	0-5	Thirsk	0-2
Warwick	0-8	Southwell (AW)	0-4	Newcastle	0-1
Epsom	0-7	Doncaster	0-3	Pontefract	0-1
Goodwood	0-7	York	0-3	Southwell (Turf)	0-1
Leicester	0-7	Ascot	0-2	Yarmouth	0-1

WINNING HORSES

	Age	Races Run	1st	2nd	3rd	Unpl	Win £
So Saucy	3	13	3	1	1	8	8,362
Lord Alfie	4	13	2	1	2	8	7,476
Nonios	2	11	2	3	2	4	6,764
Captain Scarlet	2	6	1	1	0	4	5,047
Lady Phyl	2	7	1	0	0	6	3,720
Kismetim	3	12	1	1	2	8	3,670
Connect	2	9	1	0	0	8	2,873
Dancing Lawyer	2	9	1	0	3	5	2,826
Phoneaholic	2	7	1	2	1	3	1,907

WINNING OWNERS

	Races Won	Value £		Races Won	Value £
L H J Ward	3	8,362	The Kismetim Partnership	1	3,670
K C Gomm	2	7,476	Mrs J A Hannon	1	2,873
J P Fleming	2	6,764	Vintage Services Ltd	1	2,826
Patrick G O'Sullivan	1	5,047	K Higson	1	1,907
Network Builders Ltd	1	3,720			

Favourites	2-10	20.0% - 4.78	Total winning prize-money		£42,644

Longest winning sequence	2	Average SP of winner	6.3/1
Longest losing sequence	39	Return on stakes invested	-47.7%

1992 Form   0-2

S MELLOR (Swindon, Wilts)

	No. of Horses	Races Run	1st	2nd	3rd	Unpl	Per cent	£1 Level Stake
2-y-o	0	0	0	0	0	0	–	0.00
3-y-o	3	19	0	0	3	16	–	– 19.00
4-y-o+	7	36	4	4	6	22	11.1	+ 11.63
Totals	10	55	4	4	9	38	7.3	– 7.37

Jan	Feb	Mar	Apr	May	Jun	Jul	Aug	Sep	Oct/Nov
0-0	0-1	0-1	0-0	0-10	0-10	4-13	0-13	0-4	0-3

Winning Jockeys	W-R	£1 Level Stake				W-R	£1 Level Stake
T Sprake	2-8	+ 20.00		C Rutter		2-14	+ 5.63

Winning Courses							
Nottingham	1-3	+ 12.00		Chepstow		1-7	+ 10.00
Folkestone	1-4	– 1.37		Windsor		1-9	+ 4.00

Winning Horses	Age	Races Run	1st	2nd	3rd	Unpl	Win £
Batchworth Bound	4	13	2	4	4	3	5,960
Bronze Runner	9	8	2	0	1	5	4,570

Favourites	1-2	50.0%	+ 0.63	Total winning prize-money			£10,530

1992 Form	0-55			1990 Form	0-15		
1991 Form	0-47			1989 Form	2-21	9.5%	– 3.00

B R MILLMAN (Cullompton, Devon)

	No. of Horses	Races Run	1st	2nd	3rd	Unpl	Per cent	£1 Level Stake
2-y-o	5	28	4	2	2	20	14.3	+ 7.00
3-y-o	4	28	1	1	1	25	3.6	– 21.00
4-y-o+	10	64	1	6	6	51	1.6	– 55.00
Totals	19	120	6	9	9	96	5.0	– 69.00

Jan	Feb	Mar	Apr	May	Jun	Jul	Aug	Sep	Oct/Nov
0-0	0-0	0-2	0-8	1-14	0-19	2-16	0-21	1-23	2-17

Winning Jockeys	W-R	£1 Level Stake				W-R	£1 Level Stake
S Whitworth	5-45	– 1.00		J Williams		1-11	– 4.00

Winning Courses							
Folkestone	3-7	+ 12.50		Warwick		1-7	+ 14.00
Chepstow	2-12	– 1.50					

Millman B R

Winning Horses	Age	Races Run	1st	2nd	3rd	Unpl	Win £
Folly Finnesse	2	8	2	0	1	5	5,714
Chickawicka	2	9	1	1	1	6	2,982
Karukera	3	8	1	0	0	7	2,762
Dulford Lad	2	6	1	1	0	4	2,070
Swift Romance	5	9	1	0	1	7	1,957

Favourites	2-7	28.6%	+ 1.00	Total winning prize-money			£15,485

1992 Form	7-107	6.5%	+ 15.00	1990 Form	12-153	7.8%	- 37.25
1991 Form	9-178	5.1%	- 84.92				

T G MILLS (Epsom, Surrey)

	No. of Horses	Races Run	1st	2nd	3rd	Unpl	Per cent	£1 Level Stake
2-y-o	6	24	0	3	3	18	–	- 24.00
3-y-o	11	67	1	9	11	46	1.5	- 60.50
4-y-o+	6	32	8	6	0	18	25.0	+ 25.83
Totals	23	123	9	18	14	82	7.3	- 58.67

Jan	Feb	Mar	Apr	May	Jun	Jul	Aug	Sep	Oct/Nov
0-0	1-1	0-4	0-18	1-14	3-24	3-19	1-21	0-12	0-10

Winning Jockeys	W-R	£1 Level Stake		W-R	£1 Level Stake
J Reid	7-28	+ 14.83	T Quinn	1-4	+ 11.00
J Quinn	1-3	+ 3.50			

Winning Courses					
Newmarket	3-13	+ 0.33	Newbury	1-4	+ 11.00
Windsor	2-8	+ 7.50	Sandown	1-4	+ 2.00
Lingfield (AW)	1-2	+ 4.50	Goodwood	1-8	0.00

Winning Horses	Age	Races Run	1st	2nd	3rd	Unpl	Win £
USAidit	4	7	5	1	0	1	53,039
Bobzao	4	8	2	3	0	3	20,755
Akkazao	5	10	1	2	0	7	4,045
Stevie's Wonder	3	12	1	1	3	7	3,322

Favourites	2-7	28.6%	+ 1.33	Total winning prize-money			£81,160

P MITCHELL (Epsom, Surrey)

	No. of Horses	Races Run	1st	2nd	3rd	Unpl	Per cent	£1 Level Stake
2-y-o	4	14	0	0	1	13	-	- 14.00
3-y-o	6	40	2	2	3	33	5.0	- 20.50
4-y-o+	5	38	7	4	3	24	18.4	+ 7.25
Totals	15	92	9	6	7	70	9.8	- 27.25

Jan	Feb	Mar	Apr	May	Jun	Jul	Aug	Sep	Oct/Nov
3-7	0-4	0-1	0-11	1-12	1-13	3-14	0-15	0-10	1-5

Winning Jockeys	W-R	£1 Level Stake			W-R	£1 Level Stake
W Newnes	6-33	+ 16.00	Mr R Teal		1-6	- 2.25
M Hills	1-2	+ 7.00	S O'Gorman		1-14	- 11.00

Winning Courses						
Lingfield (AW)	6-20	+ 18.25	Folkestone		1-8	- 1.00
Warwick	1-1	+ 14.00	Lingfield		1-10	- 5.50

Winning Horses	Age	Races Run	1st	2nd	3rd	Unpl	Win £
Sylvan Sabre	4	14	3	0	2	9	9,342
Second Chance	3	16	2	2	2	10	7,076
Master Hyde	4	10	2	2	1	5	5,643
Sylvan Breeze	5	7	1	2	0	4	3,054
Beam Me Up Scotty	4	6	1	0	0	5	2,208

Favourites	2-5	40.0%	+ 1.75	Total winning prize-money		£27,323

1992 Form	5-107	4.7%	- 62.75	1990 Form	13-210	6.2%	-118.42
1991 Form	8-149	5.4%	- 63.00	1989 Form	15-169	8.9%	- 62.35

PAT MITCHELL (Newmarket)

	No. of Horses	Races Run	1st	2nd	3rd	Unpl	Per cent	£1 Level Stake
2-y-o	3	14	0	0	0	14	-	- 14.00
3-y-o	7	50	4	5	4	37	8.0	- 18.00
4-y-o+	11	62	3	4	4	51	4.8	- 37.50
Totals	21	126	7	9	8	102	5.6	- 69.50

Jan	Feb	Mar	Apr	May	Jun	Jul	Aug	Sep	Oct/Nov
1-15	1-9	1-8	0-9	3-11	0-16	1-19	0-18	0-11	0-10

Mitchell Pat

Winning Jockeys	W-R	£1 Level Stake		W-R	£1 Level Stake
J Quinn	2-21	- 5.00	R Cochrane	1-8	+ 1.00
Kim McDonnell	2-25	- 9.00	G Forster	1-12	- 6.50
D Biggs	1-8	+ 2.00			

Winning Courses					
Southwell (AW)	5-29	+ 8.50	Newmarket	1-23	- 13.00
Kempton	1-6	+ 3.00			

Winning Horses	Age	Races Run	1st	2nd	3rd	Unpl	Win £
Miss Pin Up	4	12	2	1	1	8	8,415
Comet Whirlpool	3	19	2	3	4	10	5,202
Hotsocks	3	11	2	1	0	8	4,539
Peerage Prince	4	18	1	2	1	14	3,260

Favourites	0-6			Total winning prize-money			£21,416
1992 Form	10-146	6.8%	- 41.50	1990 Form	11-215	5.1%	- 62.17
1991 Form	5-130	3.8%	- 86.00	1989 Form	6-104	5.8%	- 24.00

D MOFFATT (Cartmel, Cumbria)

	No. of Horses	Races Run	1st	2nd	3rd	Unpl	Per cent	£1 Level Stake
2-y-o	6	25	0	1	1	23	-	- 25.00
3-y-o	4	22	2	3	5	12	9.1	- 9.50
4-y-o+	9	34	1	0	3	30	2.9	- 23.00
Totals	19	81	3	4	9	65	3.7	- 57.50

Jan	Feb	Mar	Apr	May	Jun	Jul	Aug	Sep	Oct/Nov
0-0	0-0	1-7	1-11	0-6	0-7	1-14	0-10	0-14	0-12

Winning Jockeys	W-R	£1 Level Stake		W-R	£1 Level Stake
J Quinn	1-3	+ 8.00	D Moffatt	1-47	- 43.00
K Fallon	1-9	- 0.50			

Winning Courses					
York	1-4	+ 4.50	Hamilton	1-12	- 8.00
Catterick	1-9	+ 2.00			

Winning Horses	Age	Races Run	1st	2nd	3rd	Unpl	Win £
Key To My Heart	3	8	1	3	3	1	6,374
Deb's Ball	7	7	1	0	1	5	3,106
High Romance	3	8	1	0	2	5	2,243

Favourites	0-2			Total winning prize-money			£11,723
1992 Form	5-69	7.2%	- 15.50	1990 Form	1-34	2.9%	- 27.50
1991 Form	7-94	7.4%	- 26.50	1989 Form	2-36	5.6%	- 2.00

P MONTEITH (Rosewell, Midlothian)

	No. of Horses	Races Run	1st	2nd	3rd	Unpl	Per cent	£1 Level Stake
2-y-o	1	5	0	0	0	5	-	- 5.00
3-y-o	7	26	4	1	1	20	15.4	+ 1.91
4-y-o+	7	30	0	1	2	27	-	- 30.00
Totals	15	61	4	2	3	52	6.6	- 33.09

Jan	Feb	Mar	Apr	May	Jun	Jul	Aug	Sep	Oct/Nov
0-0	0-0	0-0	0-4	1-16	2-17	1-12	0-10	0-2	0-0

Winning Jockeys	W-R	£1 Level Stake			W-R	£1 Level Stake
S D Williams	2-12	- 4.09	O Pears		1-7	0.00
F Norton	1-2	+ 11.00				

Winning Courses						
Ayr	3-15	+ 5.91	Carlisle		1-7	0.00

Winning Horses	Age	Races Run	1st	2nd	3rd	Unpl	Win £
Funny Choice	3	3	3	0	0	0	7,558
Principal Player	3	10	1	1	1	7	3,095

Favourites	1-1	100.0%	+ 0.91	Total winning prize-money	£10,653

1992 Form	0-59			1990 Form	2-61	3.3%	- 44.00
1991 Form	2-43	4.7%	- 19.50	1989 Form	1-31	3.2%	- 27.25

A MOORE (Brighton, East Sussex)

	No. of Horses	Races Run	1st	2nd	3rd	Unpl	Per cent	£1 Level Stake
2-y-o	1	7	0	0	0	7	-	- 7.00
3-y-o	4	31	5	1	4	21	16.1	- 0.50
4-y-o+	22	76	4	9	7	56	5.3	- 47.50
Totals	27	114	9	10	11	84	7.9	- 55.00

Jan	Feb	Mar	Apr	May	Jun	Jul	Aug	Sep	Oct/Nov
1-10	2-12	0-7	0-12	1-11	2-14	2-15	1-14	0-7	0-12

Winning Jockeys	W-R	£1 Level Stake			W-R	£1 Level Stake
B Rouse	4-28	- 5.00	N Adams		2-29	- 13.50
B Russell	2-21	- 8.00	L Carter		1-3	+ 4.50

Winning Course			
Lingfield (AW)	9-53	+ 6.00	

Moore A

Winning Horses	Age	Races Run	1st	2nd	3rd	Unpl	Win £
One Off The Rail	3	10	4	0	2	4	11,778
Carlowitz	5	5	2	1	0	2	5,535
Invocation	6	17	1	2	3	11	4,092
Juliasdarkinvader	3	15	1	1	2	11	2,660
Ragtime Song	4	8	1	1	0	6	2,259

Favourites	0-4			Total winning prize-money			£26,324
1992 Form	6-128	4.7%	- 40.00	1990 Form	3-80	3.8%	- 52.25
1991 Form	1-92	1.1%	- 79.00	1989 Form	4-51	7.8%	+ 3.88

G L MOORE (Epsom, Surrey)

	No. of Horses	Races Run	1st	2nd	3rd	Unpl	Per cent	£1 Level Stake
2-y-o	12	48	0	0	2	46	-	- 48.00
3-y-o	10	64	7	8	5	44	10.9	+ 3.23
4-y-o+	10	64	6	2	10	46	9.4	- 29.00
Totals	32	176	13	10	17	136	7.4	- 73.77

BY MONTH

2-y-o	W-R	Per cent	£1 Level Stake	3-y-o	W-R	Per cent	£1 Level Stake
Mar/Apr	0-4	-	- 3.00	Mar/Apr	1-8	12.5	- 7.00
May	0-3	-	- 3.00	May	1-16	6.3	- 1.00
June	0-10	-	- 10.00	June	1-11	9.1	+ 4.00
July	0-10	-	- 10.00	July	3-11	27.3	+ 8.23
August	0-4	-	- 4.00	August	0-8	-	- 8.00
September	0-9	-	- 9.00	September	0-5	-	- 5.00
Oct/Nov	0-8	-	- 8.00	Oct/Nov	1-5	20.0	+ 6.00

4-y-o+	W-R	Per cent	£1 Level Stake	Totals	W-R	Per cent	£1 Level Stake
Mar/Apr	0-9	-	- 8.00	Mar/Apr	1-21	4.8	- 18.00
May	0-7	-	- 7.00	May	1-26	3.8	- 11.00
June	0-10	-	- 10.00	June	1-31	3.2	- 16.00
July	3-11	27.3	+ 8.25	July	6-32	18.8	+ 6.48
August	1-11	9.1	- 7.75	August	1-23	4.3	- 19.75
September	2-10	20.0	+ 2.50	September	2-24	8.3	- 11.50
Oct/Nov	0-6	-	- 6.00	Oct/Nov	1-19	5.3	- 8.00

DISTANCE

2-y-o	W-R	Per cent	£1 Level Stake	3-y-o	W-R	Per cent	£1 Level Stake
5f-6f	0-34	-	- 34.00	5f-6f	3-16	18.8	+ 8.23
7f-8f	0-14	-	- 14.00	7f-8f	4-35	11.4	+ 8.00
9f-13f	0-0	-	0.00	9f-13f	0-13	-	- 13.00
14f+	0-0	-	0.00	14f+	0-0	-	0.00

4-y-o+	W-R	Per cent	£1 Level Stake	Totals	W-R	Per cent	£1 Level Stake
5f-6f	0-11	-	- 11.00	5f-6f	3-61	4.9	- 36.77
7f-8f	6-49	12.2	- 14.00	7f-8f	10-98	10.2	- 20.00
9f-13f	0-4	-	- 4.00	9f-13f	0-17	-	- 17.00
14f+	0-0	-	0.00	14f+	0-0	-	0.00

TYPE OF RACE

Non-Handicaps	W-R	Per cent	£1 Level Stake	Handicaps	W-R	Per cent	£1 Level Stake
2-y-o	0-33	-	- 33.00	2-y-o	0-9	-	- 9.00
3-y-o	3-21	14.3	+ 6.73	3-y-o	4-34	11.8	+ 5.50
4-y-o+	0-9	-	- 9.00	4-y-o+	6-52	11.5	- 17.00
Selling	0-8	-	- 8.00	Selling	0-6	-	- 6.00
Apprentice	0-0	-	0.00	Apprentice	0-0	-	0.00
Amat/Ladies	0-2	-	- 2.00	Amat/Ladies	0-2	-	- 2.00
Totals	3-73	4.1	- 45.27	Totals	10-103	9.7	- 28.50

COURSE GRADE

FIRST TIME OUT

	W-R	Per cent	£1 Level Stake		W-R	Per cent	£1 Level Stake
Group 1	6-64	9.4	- 21.27	2-y-o	0-12	-	- 12.00
Group 2	2-49	4.1	- 19.00	3-y-o	2-7	28.6	+ 15.00
Group 3	0-22	-	- 22.00	4-y-o+	0-9	-	- 9.00
Group 4	5-41	12.2	- 11.50	Totals	2-28	7.1	- 6.00

JOCKEYS RIDING

	W-R	Per cent	£1 Level Stake
B Rouse	13-153	8.5	- 50.77

A Morris	0-10	Kim McDonnell	0-2	M Fenton	0-1
Candy Morris	0-4	A Tucker	0-1	Mrs J Moore	0-1
Mr J Keller	0-3	D Harrison	0-1		

COURSE RECORD

	Total W-R	Non-Handicaps 2-y-o	3-y-o+	Handicaps 2-y-o	3-y-o+	Per cent	£1 Level Stake
Sandown	3-9	0-1	1-2	0-1	2-5	33.3	+ 4.73
Folkestone	3-17	0-4	1-4	0-2	2-7	17.6	+ 4.25
Lingfield	2-20	0-5	1-6	0-1	1-8	10.0	+ 10.00
Southwell (AW)	1-4	0-2	0-0	0-0	1-2	25.0	+ 1.00
Epsom	1-6	0-2	0-0	0-0	1-4	16.7	+ 4.00
Goodwood	1-14	0-5	0-2	0-0	1-7	7.1	- 6.00
Lingfield (AW)	1-14	0-1	0-4	0-1	1-8	7.1	- 10.75
Kempton	1-17	0-3	0-2	0-0	1-12	5.9	- 6.00

Moore G L

Brighton	0-18	Newbury	0-5	Edinburgh	0-1
Newmarket	0-12	Chepstow	0-4	Nottingham	0-1
Salisbury	0-11	Warwick	0-4	Southwell (Tur	0-1
Windsor	0-8	Bath	0-2		
Leicester	0-7	Doncaster	0-1		

WINNING HORSES

	Age	Races Run	1st	2nd	3rd	Unpl	Win £
No Extras	3	14	3	4	2	5	11,105
Panchellita	4	8	3	0	4	1	9,309
Daswaki	5	12	2	0	1	9	8,686
Mr Nevermind	3	10	2	1	1	6	7,739
Star Goddess	4	7	1	1	1	4	3,202
Soaking	3	4	1	0	1	2	3,132
Bichette	3	8	1	1	0	6	2,243

WINNING OWNERS

	Races Won	Value £		Races Won	Value £
K Higson	7	25,178	David Allen	2	8,686
C J Pennick	3	9,309	Peter L Higson	1	2,243

Favourites	4-15	26.7%	- 2.27	Total winning prize-money	£45,415
Longest winning sequence			1	Average SP of winner	6.9/1
Longest losing sequence			47	Return on stakes invested	-41.9%

G M MOORE (Middleham, North Yorks)

	No. of Horses	Races Run	1st	2nd	3rd	Unpl	Per cent	£1 Level Stake
2-y-o	4	17	0	0	2	15	-	- 17.00
3-y-o	4	21	3	1	2	15	14.3	+ 11.00
4-y-o+	10	43	3	7	2	31	7.0	- 26.93
Totals	18	81	6	8	6	61	7.4	- 32.93

Jan	Feb	Mar	Apr	May	Jun	Jul	Aug	Sep	Oct/Nov
0-0	0-0	0-1	1-8	2-18	3-18	0-9	0-9	0-12	0-6

Winning Jockeys	W-R	£1 Level Stake		W-R	£1 Level Stake
J Fanning	3-27	+ 2.00	W Newnes	1-12	- 1.00
J Tate	2-10	- 1.93			

Winning Courses	W-R	£1 Level Stake		W-R	£1 Level Stake
Newcastle	3-8	+ 17.00	Catterick	1-8	+ 7.00
York	1-3	+ 3.50	Ripon	1-11	- 9.43

Winning Horses	Age	Races Run	1st	2nd	3rd	Unpl	Win £
Highflying	7	7	3	2	0	2	65,915
Queen Of The Quorn	3	8	2	0	1	5	4,822
Coconut Johnny	3	9	1	1	1	6	3,348

Favourites	1-6	16.7%	- 4.43	Total winning prize-money			£74,085

1992 Form	10-108	9.3%	- 42.77	1990 Form	10-154	6.5%	- 95.17
1991 Form	7-126	5.6%	- 36.50	1989 Form	18-183	9.8%	+ 4.25

J S MOORE (Andover, Hants)

	No. of Horses	Races Run	1st	2nd	3rd	Unpl	Per cent	£1 Level Stake
2-y-o	9	49	1	3	3	42	2.0	- 32.00
3-y-o	1	6	0	0	0	6	-	- 6.00
4-y-o+	7	23	1	2	0	20	4.3	- 19.75
Totals	17	78	2	5	3	68	2.6	- 57.75

Jan	Feb	Mar	Apr	May	Jun	Jul	Aug	Sep	Oct/Nov
0-3	0-2	0-3	0-12	1-5	0-9	1-12	0-17	0-5	0-10

Winning Jockeys	W-R	£1 Level Stake			W-R	£1 Level Stake
Mark Denaro	1-13	+ 4.00	A McGlone		1-14	- 10.75

Winning Courses						
Southwell (Turf)	1-2	+ 1.25	Lingfield		1-3	+ 14.00

Winning Horses	Age	Races Run	1st	2nd	3rd	Unpl	Win £
Riskie Things	2	11	1	3	1	6	3,641
Ima Red Neck	4	6	1	0	0	5	2,322

Favourites	0-2			Total winning prize-money		£5,963

1992 Form	2-67	3.0%	- 47.00	1990 Form	0-8
1991 Form	1-33	3.0%	- 20.00		

D MORLEY (Newmarket)

	No. of Horses	Races Run	1st	2nd	3rd	Unpl	Per cent	£1 Level Stake
2-y-o	11	26	3	3	4	16	11.5	- 12.25
3-y-o	12	80	7	12	9	52	8.8	- 30.25
4-y-o+	4	20	6	0	2	12	30.0	+ 22.50
Totals	27	126	16	15	15	80	12.7	- 20.00

Morley D

BY MONTH

2-y-o	W-R	Per cent	£1 Level Stake	3-y-o	W-R	Per cent	£1 Level Stake
Mar/Apr	0-0	-	0.00	Mar/Apr	1-11	9.1	- 7.00
May	0-0	-	0.00	May	0-13	-	- 13.00
June	1-1	100.0	+ 5.00	June	2-15	13.3	+ 2.00
July	0-2	-	- 2.00	July	1-12	8.3	- 6.00
August	1-4	25.0	0.00	August	1-11	9.1	- 8.25
September	0-10	-	- 10.00	September	2-10	20.0	+ 10.00
Oct/Nov	1-9	11.1	- 5.25	Oct/Nov	0-8	-	- 8.00

4-y-o+	W-R	Per cent	£1 Level Stake	Totals	W-R	Per cent	£1 Level Stake
Mar/Apr	1-6	16.7	- 0.50	Mar/Apr	2-17	11.8	- 7.50
May	1-4	25.0	+ 1.00	May	1-17	5.9	- 12.00
June	0-1	-	- 1.00	June	3-17	17.6	+ 6.00
July	3-4	75.0	+ 22.50	July	4-18	22.2	+ 14.50
August	0-2	-	- 2.00	August	2-17	11.8	- 10.25
September	1-1	100.0	+ 4.50	September	3-21	14.3	+ 4.50
Oct/Nov	0-2	-	- 2.00	Oct/Nov	1-19	5.3	- 15.25

DISTANCE

2-y-o	W-R	Per cent	£1 Level Stake	3-y-o	W-R	Per cent	£1 Level Stake
5f-6f	1-5	20.0	+ 1.00	5f-6f	0-0	-	0.00
7f-8f	1-19	5.3	- 15.00	7f-8f	4-28	14.3	- 1.00
9f-13f	1-2	50.0	+ 1.75	9f-13f	3-39	7.7	- 16.25
14f+	0-0	-	0.00	14f+	0-13	-	- 13.00

4-y-o+	W-R	Per cent	£1 Level Stake	Totals	W-R	Per cent	£1 Level Stake
5f-6f	0-0	-	0.00	5f-6f	1-5	20.0	+ 1.00
7f-8f	0-0	-	0.00	7f-8f	5-47	10.6	- 16.00
9f-13f	4-12	33.3	+ 10.00	9f-13f	8-53	15.1	- 4.50
14f+	2-8	25.0	+ 12.50	14f+	2-21	9.5	- 0.50

TYPE OF RACE

Non-Handicaps	W-R	Per cent	£1 Level Stake	Handicaps	W-R	Per cent	£1 Level Stake
2-y-o	3-25	12.0	- 11.25	2-y-o	0-1	-	- 1.00
3-y-o	2-27	7.4	- 15.25	3-y-o	4-46	8.7	- 14.00
4-y-o+	1-5	20.0	+ 10.00	4-y-o+	5-15	33.3	+ 12.50
Selling	0-2	-	- 2.00	Selling	1-2	50.0	+ 4.00
Apprentice	0-1	-	- 1.00	Apprentice	0-2	-	- 2.00
Amat/Ladies	0-0	-	0.00	Amat/Ladies	0-0	-	0.00
Totals	6-60	10.0	- 19.50	Totals	10-66	15.2	- 0.50

COURSE GRADE

	W-R	Per cent	£1 Level Stake
Group 1	4-40	10.0	- 14.50
Group 2	3-24	12.5	+ 0.75
Group 3	7-49	14.3	- 4.75
Group 4	2-13	15.4	- 1.50

FIRST TIME OUT

	W-R	Per cent	£1 Level Stake
2-y-o	2-11	18.2	- 1.00
3-y-o	1-12	8.3	- 8.00
4-y-o+	0-4	-	- 4.00
Totals	3-27	11.1	- 13.00

JOCKEYS RIDING

	W-R	Per cent	£1 Level Stake		W-R	Per cent	£1 Level Stake
W Carson	5-29	17.2	- 2.25	M Hills	1-4	25.0	+ 7.00
G Duffield	3-13	23.1	+ 3.50	M Roberts	1-5	20.0	+ 0.50
B Raymond	2-5	40.0	+ 3.75	R Hills	1-13	7.7	+ 2.00
L Dettori	1-1	100.0	+ 4.50	M Tebbutt	1-18	5.6	- 14.00
D Holland	1-4	25.0	+ 9.00				

S Whitworth	0-7	A Clark	0-1	J Tate	0-1
D McKeown	0-5	A McGlone	0-1	J Weaver	0-1
K Darley	0-4	A Munro	0-1	L Piggott	0-1
Paul Eddery	0-2	F Norton	0-1	M Birch	0-1
W R Swinburn	0-2	J Dennis	0-1	M Wigham	0-1
W Ryan	0-2	J Lowe	0-1	S Maloney	0-1

COURSE RECORD

	Total W-R	Non-Handicaps 2-y-o	Non-Handicaps 3-y-o+	Handicaps 2-y-o	Handicaps 3-y-o+	Per cent	£1 Level Stake
Yarmouth	3-17	2-6	1-5	0-0	0-6	17.6	+ 8.00
Leicester	2-9	0-2	0-3	0-0	2-4	22.2	+ 2.50
Epsom	1-1	0-0	0-0	0-0	1-1	100.0	+ 3.00
Catterick	1-3	0-0	0-2	0-0	1-1	33.3	+ 3.00
Haydock	1-3	0-0	0-0	0-0	1-3	33.3	+ 2.50
Lingfield	1-3	0-1	0-0	0-0	1-2	33.3	+ 10.00
Brighton	1-4	0-1	1-3	0-0	0-0	25.0	+ 5.00
Doncaster	1-5	0-2	0-0	0-1	1-2	20.0	+ 6.00
Newcastle	1-5	0-0	0-1	0-0	1-4	20.0	0.00
Folkestone	1-6	0-1	0-1	0-0	1-4	16.7	- 0.50
Nottingham	1-6	1-2	0-1	0-0	0-3	16.7	- 2.25
Thirsk	1-6	0-0	1-5	0-0	0-1	16.7	- 3.25
Beverley	1-9	0-1	0-3	0-0	1-5	11.1	- 5.00

Newmarket	0-8	Ripon	0-4	Windsor	0-2
Ascot	0-6	Kempton	0-3	Ayr	0-1
Redcar	0-6	Hamilton	0-2	Carlisle	0-1
York	0-6	Newbury	0-2	Chester	0-1
Pontefract	0-4	Warwick	0-2	Lingfield (AW)	0-1

Morley D

WINNING HORSES

	Age	Races Run	1st	2nd	3rd	Unpl	Win £
Ribhi	3	9	3	1	0	5	30,607
Much Sought After	4	11	4	0	2	5	16,166
Crackling Sike	2	3	1	1	0	1	4,664
Kutbeya	2	5	1	1	3	0	4,464
Tajdif	3	9	1	3	0	5	4,013
Tomos	3	6	1	1	2	2	3,553
Shoofe	5	3	1	0	0	2	3,365
Wakt	3	8	1	2	1	4	3,287
Mistress Bee	4	5	1	0	0	4	2,660
Khatir	2	4	1	0	0	3	2,601
Cubist	3	7	1	0	0	6	2,574

WINNING OWNERS

	Races Won	Value £		Races Won	Value £
Hamdan Al-Maktoum	7	44,972	Saif Ali	1	3,553
The MSA Partnership	4	16,166	Ali K Al Jafleh	1	3,365
Lord Hartington	2	7,238	D R Stoddart	1	2,660

Favourites	3-13	23.1%	- 1.25	Total winning prize-money £77,954
Longest winning sequence		3		Average SP of winner 5.6/1
Longest losing sequence		14		Return on stakes invested -15.9%
1992 Form	19-150	12.7%	- 17.07	1990 Form 24-238 10.1% -102.01
1991 Form	20-181	11.0%	- 45.07	1989 Form 26-193 13.5% - 6.59

D MORRIS (Newmarket)

	No. of Horses	Races Run	1st	2nd	3rd	Unpl	Per cent	£1 Level Stake
2-y-o	4	21	4	2	4	11	19.0	- 0.25
3-y-o	6	35	5	5	5	20	14.3	+ 17.30
4-y-o+	11	71	9	7	7	48	12.7	+ 20.00
Totals	21	127	18	14	16	79	14.2	+ 37.05

BY MONTH

2-y-o	W-R	Per cent	£1 Level Stake	3-y-o	W-R	Per cent	£1 Level Stake
January	0-0	-	0.00	January	0-2	-	- 2.00
February	0-0	-	0.00	February	0-3	-	- 3.00
March	0-0	-	0.00	March	0-2	-	- 2.00
April	0-2	-	- 2.00	April	0-1	-	- 1.00
May	0-1	-	- 1.00	May	1-7	14.3	+ 19.00
June	2-2	100.0	+ 2.75	June	2-7	28.6	- 1.45
July	0-4	-	- 4.00	July	1-5	20.0	- 1.25
August	1-5	20.0	+ 3.00	August	0-3	-	- 3.00
September	1-2	50.0	+ 6.00	September	1-4	25.0	+ 13.00
Oct/Nov	0-5	-	- 5.00	Oct/Nov	0-1	-	- 1.00

4-y-o+	W-R	Per cent	£1 Level Stake	Totals	W-R	Per cent	£1 Level Stake
January	0-0	-	0.00	January	0-2	-	- 2.00
February	1-3	33.3	+ 6.00	February	1-6	16.7	+ 3.00
March	0-2	-	- 2.00	March	0-4	-	- 4.00
April	0-5	-	- 5.00	April	0-8	-	- 8.00
May	0-11	-	- 11.00	May	1-19	5.3	+ 7.00
June	1-16	6.3	- 11.50	June	5-25	20.0	- 10.20
July	2-9	22.2	+ 20.50	July	3-18	16.7	+ 15.25
August	4-11	36.4	+ 24.00	August	5-19	26.3	+ 24.00
September	0-10	-	- 10.00	September	2-16	12.5	+ 9.00
Oct/Nov	1-4	25.0	+ 9.00	Oct/Nov	1-10	10.0	+ 3.00

DISTANCE

2-y-o	W-R	Per cent	£1 Level Stake	3-y-o	W-R	Per cent	£1 Level Stake
5f-6f	2-7	28.6	- 2.25	5f-6f	0-1	-	- 1.00
7f-8f	2-14	14.3	+ 2.00	7f-8f	4-26	15.4	+ 0.30
9f-13f	0-0	-	0.00	9f-13f	1-7	14.3	+ 19.00
14f+	0-0	-	0.00	14f+	0-1	-	- 1.00

4-y-o+	W-R	Per cent	£1 Level Stake	Totals	W-R	Per cent	£1 Level Stake
5f-6f	0-0	-	0.00	5f-6f	2-8	25.0	- 3.25
7f-8f	4-36	11.1	+ 29.00	7f-8f	10-76	13.2	+ 31.30
9f-13f	5-27	18.5	- 1.00	9f-13f	6-34	17.6	+ 18.00
14f+	0-8	-	- 8.00	14f+	0-9	-	- 9.00

TYPE OF RACE

Non-Handicaps	W-R	Per cent	£1 Level Stake	Handicaps	W-R	Per cent	£1 Level Stake
2-y-o	2-7	28.6	+ 3.75	2-y-o	0-8	-	- 8.00
3-y-o	4-13	30.8	+ 22.30	3-y-o	1-12	8.3	+ 5.00
4-y-o+	3-13	23.1	+ 4.00	4-y-o+	6-46	13.0	+ 28.00
Selling	1-9	11.1	- 7.00	Selling	1-12	8.3	- 4.00
Apprentice	0-0	-	0.00	Apprentice	0-2	-	- 2.00
Amat/Ladies	0-1	-	- 1.00	Amat/Ladies	0-4	-	- 4.00
Totals	10-43	23.3	+ 22.05	Totals	8-84	9.5	+ 15.00

Morris D

COURSE GRADE

	W-R	Per cent	£1 Level Stake
Group 1	7-47	14.9	+ 28.75
Group 2	1-14	7.1	+ 3.00
Group 3	6-41	14.6	- 13.70
Group 4	4-25	16.0	+ 19.00

FIRST TIME OUT

	W-R	Per cent	£1 Level Stake
2-y-o	1-4	25.0	- 2.00
3-y-o	0-5	-	- 5.00
4-y-o+	1-11	9.1	- 2.00
Totals	2-20	10.0	- 9.00

JOCKEYS RIDING

	W-R	Per cent	£1 Level Stake		W-R	Per cent	£1 Level Stake
C Hodgson	14-69	20.3	+ 41.05	J Carroll	1-2	50.0	+ 15.00
M Tebbutt	2-23	8.7	+ 5.00	S Davies	1-12	8.3	- 3.00

Mrs L Morris	0-7	C Hawksley	0-1	K Rutter	0-1
J Quinn	0-3	D Biggs	0-1	P Robinson	0-1
A Clark	0-1	G Bardwell	0-1	R Cochrane	0-1
A McGlone	0-1	G Duffield	0-1		
B Crossley	0-1	J Weaver	0-1		

COURSE RECORD

	Total W-R	Non-Handicaps 2-y-o	3-y-o+	Handicaps 2-y-o	3-y-o+	Per cent	£1 Level Stake
Newmarket	4-18	0-3	2-4	0-2	2-9	22.2	+ 28.25
Yarmouth	3-21	1-2	1-6	0-4	1-9	14.3	- 6.50
Haydock	2-5	0-0	0-1	0-0	2-4	40.0	+ 20.00
Lingfield (AW)	2-12	0-0	1-3	0-0	1-9	16.7	- 2.00
Chepstow	1-2	0-0	1-1	0-0	0-1	50.0	+ 0.05
Folkestone	1-3	1-1	0-1	0-0	0-1	33.3	+ 5.00
Doncaster	1-4	0-0	1-2	0-1	0-1	25.0	+ 0.50
Edinburgh	1-4	0-1	1-1	0-0	0-2	25.0	+ 22.00
Pontefract	1-4	1-1	0-0	0-1	0-2	25.0	- 1.25
Salisbury	1-4	0-0	0-0	0-0	1-4	25.0	+ 13.00
Leicester	1-8	0-2	0-2	1-1	0-3	12.5	0.00

Sandown	0-7	Redcar	0-4	Southwell (Turf)	0-1
Kempton	0-5	Brighton	0-2	Windsor	0-1
Newbury	0-5	Goodwood	0-2	York	0-1
Nottingham	0-5	Lingfield	0-2		
Southwell (AW)	0-5	Thirsk	0-2		

WINNING HORSES

	Age	Races Run	1st	2nd	3rd	Unpl	Win £
Saifan	4	8	3	1	2	2	40,925
Silent Expression	3	8	3	2	1	2	15,185
Lowawatha	5	13	3	2	4	4	12,727
Sawtid	2	7	2	0	0	5	5,884

Baladiya	6	9	2	0	1	6	5,359
Norman Warrior	4	7	1	0	0	6	2,965
Ok Bertie	3	5	1	0	0	4	2,924
Mr Rough	2	10	1	2	3	4	2,721
Rosie's Gold	3	6	1	1	1	3	2,460
Pat's Splendour	2	3	1	0	1	1	2,243

WINNING OWNERS

	Races Won	Value £		Races Won	Value £
Mrs Rosalie Hawes	9	63,930	Mrs Patricia Lunn	2	5,208
N Lunn	3	12,727	Peter Newman	1	2,924
J B R Leisure Ltd	2	5,884	Robin Akehurst	1	2,721

Favourites	3-12	25.0%	- 5.20	Total winning prize-money		£93,393
Longest winning sequence			2	Average SP of winner		8.3/1
Longest losing sequence			21	Return on stakes invested		31.3%
1992 Form	8-98	8.2%	- 21.75	1990 Form	2-54	3.7%	- 23.00
1991 Form	6-88	6.8%	- 37.50			

M P MUGGERIDGE (Marlborough, Wilts)

	No. of Horses	Races Run	1st	2nd	3rd	Unpl	Per cent	£1 Level Stake
2-y-o	7	36	0	0	2	34	-	- 36.00
3-y-o	3	18	1	3	1	13	5.6	- 3.00
4-y-o+	5	17	0	2	0	15	-	- 17.00
Totals	15	71	1	5	3	62	1.4	- 56.00

Jan	Feb	Mar	Apr	May	Jun	Jul	Aug	Sep	Oct/Nov
0-1	0-1	0-4	0-7	0-10	0-15	0-6	0-7	1-9	0-11

		£1 Level				£1 Level
Winning Jockey	W-R	Stake	Winning Course	W-R		Stake
Mark Denaro	1-18	- 3.00	Nottingham	1-3		+ 12.00

		Races				Win
Winning Horse	Age	Run	1st	2nd	3rd	Unpl	£
Patsy Grimes	3	10	1	2	1	6	3,598

Favourites	0-0		Total winning prize-money		£3,598
1992 Form	2-46	4.3%	- 16.00	1990 Form	1-42	2.4%	- 25.00
1991 Form	3-55	5.5%	+ 48.88			

W R MUIR (Lambourn, Berks)

	No. of Horses	Races Run	1st	2nd	3rd	Unpl	Per cent	£1 Level Stake
2-y-o	10	35	2	3	1	29	5.7	- 32.00
3-y-o	11	59	3	3	10	43	5.1	- 40.25
4-y-o+	12	76	7	9	8	52	9.2	- 33.47
Totals	33	170	12	15	19	124	7.1	-105.72

BY MONTH

2-y-o	W-R	Per cent	£1 Level Stake	3-y-o	W-R	Per cent	£1 Level Stake
January	0-0	-	0.00	January	0-0	-	0.00
February	0-0	-	0.00	February	0-0	-	0.00
March	0-0	-	0.00	March	0-0	-	0.00
April	0-1	-	- 1.00	April	0-5	-	- 5.00
May	0-3	-	- 3.00	May	1-12	8.3	- 9.25
June	0-6	-	- 6.00	June	1-13	7.7	- 3.00
July	0-7	-	- 7.00	July	0-12	-	- 12.00
August	2-8	25.0	- 5.00	August	1-4	25.0	+ 2.00
September	0-5	-	- 5.00	September	0-8	-	- 8.00
Oct/Nov	0-5	-	- 5.00	Oct/Nov	0-5	-	- 5.00

4-y-o+	W-R	Per cent	£1 Level Stake	Totals	W-R	Per cent	£1 Level Stake
January	2-4	50.0	+ 0.03	January	2-4	50.0	+ 0.03
February	2-6	33.3	+ 2.50	February	2-6	33.3	+ 2.50
March	0-1	-	- 1.00	March	0-1	-	- 1.00
April	1-7	14.3	+ 1.00	April	1-13	7.7	- 5.00
May	0-10	-	- 10.00	May	1-25	4.0	- 22.25
June	1-17	5.9	- 4.00	June	2-36	5.6	- 13.00
July	0-11	-	- 11.00	July	0-30	-	- 30.00
August	0-10	-	- 10.00	August	3-22	13.6	- 13.00
September	1-5	20.0	+ 4.00	September	1-18	5.6	- 9.00
Oct/Nov	0-5	-	- 5.00	Oct/Nov	0-15	-	- 15.00

DISTANCE

2-y-o	W-R	Per cent	£1 Level Stake	3-y-o	W-R	Per cent	£1 Level Stake
5f-6f	2-22	9.1	- 19.00	5f-6f	0-6	-	- 6.00
7f-8f	0-13	-	- 13.00	7f-8f	1-23	4.3	- 17.00
9f-13f	0-0	-	0.00	9f-13f	2-26	7.7	- 13.25
14f+	0-0	-	0.00	14f+	0-4	-	- 4.00

4-y-o+	W-R	Per cent	£1 Level Stake	Totals	W-R	Per cent	£1 Level Stake
5f-6f	1-25	4.0	- 12.00	5f-6f	3-53	5.7	- 37.00
7f-8f	1-12	8.3	- 4.00	7f-8f	2-48	4.2	- 34.00
9f-13f	5-30	16.7	- 8.47	9f-13f	7-56	12.5	- 21.72
14f+	0-9	-	- 9.00	14f+	0-13	-	- 13.00

TYPE OF RACE

Non-Handicaps	W-R	Per cent	£1 Level Stake	Handicaps	W-R	Per cent	£1 Level Stake
2-y-o	2-21	9.5	- 18.00	2-y-o	0-7	-	- 7.00
3-y-o	3-26	11.5	- 7.25	3-y-o	0-25	-	- 25.00
4-y-o+	3-16	18.8	- 7.47	4-y-o+	3-49	6.1	- 24.00
Selling	0-9	-	- 9.00	Selling	1-6	16.7	+ 3.00
Apprentice	0-1	-	- 1.00	Apprentice	0-7	-	- 7.00
Amat/Ladies	0-0	-	0.00	Amat/Ladies	0-3	-	- 3.00
Totals	8-73	11.0	- 42.72	Totals	4-97	4.1	- 63.00

COURSE GRADE

	W-R	Per cent	£1 Level Stake
Group 1	3-57	5.3	- 36.25
Group 2	3-35	8.6	- 15.00
Group 3	1-41	2.4	- 39.00
Group 4	5-37	13.5	- 15.47

FIRST TIME OUT

	W-R	Per cent	£1 Level Stake
2-y-o	1-10	10.0	- 7.62
3-y-o	0-8	-	- 8.00
4-y-o+	2-12	16.7	- 1.37
Totals	3-30	10.0	- 16.99

JOCKEYS RIDING

	W-R	Per cent	£1 Level Stake		W-R	Per cent	£1 Level Stake
T Quinn	4-22	18.2	- 11.87	J Penza	1-2	50.0	+ 6.00
W Ryan	2-5	40.0	+ 1.75	W Carson	1-6	16.7	+ 7.00
Kim McDonnell	2-41	4.9	- 26.00	A Munro	1-14	7.1	- 4.00
J Williams	1-2	50.0	- 0.60				

A Clark	0-11	Miss J Russell	0-3	J Lowe	0-1
W Newnes	0-11	P Robinson	0-3	J Reid	0-1
W Woods	0-10	L Dettori	0-2	K Darley	0-1
R Cochrane	0-5	M Roberts	0-2	M Hills	0-1
D Holland	0-4	N Day	0-2	Pat Eddery	0-1
J Carroll	0-4	A McGlone	0-1	Paul Eddery	0-1
C Rutter	0-3	A Tucker	0-1	S McCarthy	0-1
D Harrison	0-3	D McKeown	0-1	T Williams	0-1
G Duffield	0-3	F Norton	0-1		

COURSE RECORD

	Total W-R	Non-Handicaps 2-y-o	3-y-o+	Handicaps 2-y-o	3-y-o+	Per cent	£1 Level Stake
Lingfield (AW)	5-18	0-0	3-8	0-0	2-10	27.8	+ 3.53
Goodwood	2-3	0-0	2-2	0-0	0-1	66.7	+ 9.75
Windsor	1-5	1-4	0-1	0-0	0-0	20.0	- 3.00
Salisbury	1-7	0-2	0-2	0-0	1-3	14.3	+ 6.00
Lingfield	1-10	1-5	0-3	0-0	0-2	10.0	- 9.00
Kempton	1-11	0-1	0-3	0-1	1-6	9.1	- 3.00
Brighton	1-16	0-3	1-5	0-0	0-8	6.3	- 10.00

Muir W R

Bath	0-10	Leicester	0-6	York	0-3
Newbury	0-9	Sandown	0-6	Ayr	0-2
Newmarket	0-8	Ascot	0-5	Doncaster	0-2
Folkestone	0-7	Chepstow	0-5	Haydock	0-2
Nottingham	0-7	Southwell (AW)	0-5	Chester	0-1
Warwick	0-7	Epsom	0-3	Pontefract	0-1
Yarmouth	0-7	Newcastle	0-3	Ripon	0-1

WINNING HORSES

	Age	Races Run	1st	2nd	3rd	Unpl	Win £
Breakdancer	4	7	4	1	0	2	10,235
Averti	2	2	2	0	0	0	9,966
Lunar Risk	3	10	2	0	2	6	7,283
Sure Lord	4	9	1	1	1	6	5,090
Little Rousillon	5	9	1	0	0	8	4,878
Cretoes Dancer	4	7	1	1	0	5	2,553
Superensis	3	11	1	0	3	7	2,070

WINNING OWNERS

	Races Won	Value £		Races Won	Value £
J Jannaway	4	10,235	Fayzad Thoroughbred Ltd	1	4,878
D J Deer	2	9,966	Mrs W K Ong	1	2,553
R Haim	2	7,283	A J De V Patrick	1	2,070
The Sussex Stud Ltd	1	5,090			

Favourites	3-15	20.0%	- 8.97	Total winning prize-money	£42,074
Longest winning sequence			2	Average SP of winner	4.6/1
Longest losing sequence			53	Return on stakes invested	-60.6%
1992 Form	9-174	5.2%	- 90.25	1991 Form 13-97 13.4%	- 9.08

P G MURPHY (Bristol, Avon)

	No. of Horses	Races Run	1st	2nd	3rd	Unpl	Per cent	£1 Level Stake
2-y-o	12	56	2	1	2	51	3.6	- 50.05
3-y-o	10	48	4	0	3	41	8.3	- 12.00
4-y-o+	11	65	6	6	9	44	9.2	- 4.87
Totals	33	169	12	7	14	136	7.1	- 66.92

BY MONTH

2-y-o	W-R	Per cent	£1 Level Stake	3-y-o	W-R	Per cent	£1 Level Stake
Mar/Apr	0-1	-	- 1.00	Mar/Apr	2-10	20.0	+ 6.00
May	1-6	16.7	- 2.25	May	1-12	8.3	- 1.00
June	1-8	12.5	- 5.80	June	0-10	-	- 10.00
July	0-9	-	- 9.00	July	1-10	10.0	- 3.50
August	0-4	-	- 4.00	August	0-2	-	- 2.00
September	0-13	-	- 13.00	September	0-3	-	- 3.00
Oct/Nov	0-15	-	- 15.00	Oct/Nov	0-1	-	- 1.00

4-y-o+	W-R	Per cent	£1 Level Stake	Totals	W-R	Per cent	£1 Level Stake
Mar/Apr	2-9	22.2	+ 13.00	Mar/Apr	4-20	20.0	+ 18.00
May	2-13	15.4	- 5.87	May	4-31	12.9	- 9.12
June	0-12	-	- 12.00	June	1-30	3.3	- 27.80
July	0-6	-	- 6.00	July	1-25	4.0	- 18.50
August	1-7	14.3	+ 1.00	August	1-13	7.7	- 5.00
September	1-9	11.1	+ 17.00	September	1-25	4.0	+ 1.00
Oct/Nov	0-9	-	- 9.00	Oct/Nov	0-25	-	- 25.00

DISTANCE

2-y-o	W-R	Per cent	£1 Level Stake	3-y-o	W-R	Per cent	£1 Level Stake
5f-6f	2-38	5.3	- 32.05	5f-6f	0-0	-	0.00
7f-8f	0-17	-	- 17.00	7f-8f	1-18	5.6	- 3.00
9f-13f	0-1	-	- 1.00	9f-13f	2-26	7.7	- 16.00
14f+	0-0	-	0.00	14f+	1-4	25.0	+ 7.00

4-y-o+	W-R	Per cent	£1 Level Stake	Totals	W-R	Per cent	£1 Level Stake
5f-6f	4-38	10.5	+ 3.13	5f-6f	6-76	7.9	- 28.92
7f-8f	2-20	10.0	- 1.00	7f-8f	3-55	5.5	- 21.00
9f-13f	0-5	-	- 5.00	9f-13f	2-32	6.3	- 22.00
14f+	0-2	-	- 2.00	14f+	1-6	16.7	+ 5.00

TYPE OF RACE

Non-Handicaps	W-R	Per cent	£1 Level Stake	Handicaps	W-R	Per cent	£1 Level Stake
2-y-o	2-39	5.1	- 33.05	2-y-o	0-13	-	- 13.00
3-y-o	1-21	4.8	- 17.50	3-y-o	2-21	9.5	+ 5.00
4-y-o+	2-10	20.0	+ 9.00	4-y-o+	4-51	7.8	- 9.87
Selling	0-2	-	- 2.00	Selling	1-6	16.7	+ 0.50
Apprentice	0-0	-	0.00	Apprentice	0-5	-	- 5.00
Amat/Ladies	0-0	-	0.00	Amat/Ladies	0-1	-	- 1.00
Totals	5-72	6.9	- 43.55	Totals	7-97	7.2	- 23.37

Murphy P G

<table>
<tr><td colspan="4">**COURSE GRADE**</td><td colspan="4">**FIRST TIME OUT**</td></tr>
<tr><td></td><td>W-R</td><td>Per cent</td><td>£1 Level Stake</td><td></td><td>W-R</td><td>Per cent</td><td>£1 Level Stake</td></tr>
<tr><td>Group 1</td><td>3-49</td><td>6.1</td><td>- 12.80</td><td>2-y-o</td><td>0-12</td><td>-</td><td>- 12.00</td></tr>
<tr><td>Group 2</td><td>2-24</td><td>8.3</td><td>- 11.50</td><td>3-y-o</td><td>2-10</td><td>20.0</td><td>+ 8.50</td></tr>
<tr><td>Group 3</td><td>4-72</td><td>5.6</td><td>- 43.87</td><td>4-y-o+</td><td>1-11</td><td>9.1</td><td>- 3.00</td></tr>
<tr><td>Group 4</td><td>3-24</td><td>12.5</td><td>+ 1.25</td><td></td><td></td><td></td><td></td></tr>
<tr><td></td><td></td><td></td><td></td><td>Totals</td><td>3-33</td><td>9.1</td><td>- 6.50</td></tr>
</table>

JOCKEYS RIDING

	W-R	Per cent	£1 Level Stake		W-R	Per cent	£1 Level Stake
J Williams	3-49	6.1	- 34.87	J Reid	1-2	50.0	+ 2.50
S Drowne	2-29	6.9	+ 8.00	Pat Eddery	1-3	33.3	- 0.80
N Adams	2-33	6.1	- 18.25	M Hills	1-4	25.0	+ 2.50
C Rutter	1-2	50.0	+ 13.00	L Dettori	1-8	12.5	0.00

D Harrison	0-6	A Clark	0-1	M Roberts		0-1
W Ryan	0-4	A Mackay	0-1	Mrs P Nash		0-1
A Dicks	0-3	A McGlone	0-1	P Robinson		0-1
R Waterfield	0-3	D Wright	0-1	R Price		0-1
G Carter	0-2	F Norton	0-1	T Sprake		0-1
J Lowe	0-2	G Duffield	0-1	T Wilson		0-1
J Quinn	0-2	L Piggott	0-1	W R Swinburn		0-1
Paul Eddery	0-2	M Birch	0-1			

COURSE RECORD

	Total W-R	Non-Handicaps 2-y-o	3-y-o+	Handicaps 2-y-o	3-y-o+	Per cent	£1 Level Stake
Warwick	3-24	1-3	0-7	0-2	2-12	12.5	+ 1.25
Lingfield	1-1	0-0	0-0	0-0	1-1	100.0	+ 3.50
Nottingham	1-3	0-1	0-0	0-1	1-1	33.3	+ 8.00
Kempton	1-5	0-1	0-0	0-1	1-3	20.0	+ 3.00
Sandown	1-5	1-4	0-1	0-0	0-0	20.0	- 2.80
Ayr	1-6	0-0	0-1	0-1	1-4	16.7	+ 20.00
Leicester	1-10	0-2	1-2	0-2	0-4	10.0	- 6.50
Windsor	1-18	0-4	1-5	0-2	0-7	5.6	- 7.00
Chepstow	1-20	0-7	0-3	0-2	1-8	5.0	- 17.37
Salisbury	1-22	0-4	1-5	0-0	0-13	4.5	- 14.00

Bath	0-21	Newmarket	0-4	Haydock	0-3
Newbury	0-14	York	0-4	Ascot	0-1
Goodwood	0-4	Doncaster	0-3	Chester	0-1

WINNING HORSES

	Age	Races Run	1st	2nd	3rd	Unpl	Win £
Sir Joey	4	13	3	0	4	6	11,418
Homemaker	3	10	1	0	2	7	3,676
Winsome Wooster	2	5	1	0	0	4	3,454
Paper Days	3	7	1	0	1	5	3,261

Teanarco	5	10	1	3	1	5	3,236
Mount Leinster	2	8	1	0	0	7	3,126
Blue Topaze	5	1	1	0	0	0	3,005
General Chase	3	1	1	0	0	0	2,489
Mexican Dancer	4	7	1	1	0	5	1,912
Shalholme	3	9	1	0	0	8	1,380

WINNING OWNERS

	Races Won	Value £		Races Won	Value £
Mrs A G Sims	3	11,418	M & N Plant Ltd	1	3,126
Racecourse Farm Racing	1	3,676	M S Saunders	1	3,005
Miss Amanda J Rawding	1	3,454	John Astbury	1	2,489
M Dallimore	1	3,261	Mrs Y Moffatt	1	1,912
B K Symonds	1	3,236	Mrs M Palmer	1	1,380

Favourites	4-15	26.7%	- 2.17	Total winning prize-money	£36,956
Longest winning sequence			2	Average SP of winner	7.5/1
Longest losing sequence			38	Return on stakes invested	-39.6%
1992 Form	3-10	30.0%	+ 20.00		

B W MURRAY (Malton, North Yorks)

	No. of Horses	Races Run	1st	2nd	3rd	Unpl	Per cent	£1 Level Stake
2-y-o	3	14	0	2	1	11	-	- 14.00
3-y-o	4	15	0	1	0	14	-	- 15.00
4-y-o+	3	15	1	0	1	13	6.7	- 5.00
Totals	10	44	1	3	2	38	2.3	- 34.00

Jan	Feb	Mar	Apr	May	Jun	Jul	Aug	Sep	Oct/Nov
0-0	0-0	0-0	0-4	0-8	0-5	0-6	1-8	0-7	0-6

Winning Jockey	W-R	£1 Level Stake	Winning Course	W-R	£1 Level Stake
O Pears	1-1	+ 9.00	Catterick	1-6	+ 4.00

Winning Horse	Age	Races Run	1st	2nd	3rd	Unpl	Win £
Royal Comedian	4	8	1	0	0	7	2,709

Favourites	0-0	Total winning prize-money	£2,709
1992 Form	0-44	1990 Form	0-29
1991 Form	1-54	1.9% - 50.00	

W J MUSSON (Newmarket)

	No. of Horses	Races Run	1st	2nd	3rd	Unpl	Per cent	£1 Level Stake
2-y-o	5	23	1	2	0	20	4.3	- 6.00
3-y-o	9	59	4	5	3	47	6.8	- 27.00
4-y-o+	15	90	6	12	4	68	6.7	- 18.00
Totals	29	172	11	19	7	135	6.4	- 51.00

BY MONTH

2-y-o	W-R	Per cent	£1 Level Stake	3-y-o	W-R	Per cent	£1 Level Stake
January	0-0	-	0.00	January	2-3	66.7	+ 10.25
February	0-0	-	0.00	February	1-3	33.3	+ 0.75
March	0-0	-	0.00	March	0-2	-	- 2.00
April	0-0	-	0.00	April	0-5	-	- 5.00
May	0-2	-	- 2.00	May	0-10	-	- 10.00
June	0-1	-	- 1.00	June	0-9	-	- 9.00
July	0-0	-	0.00	July	0-9	-	- 9.00
August	1-6	16.7	+ 11.00	August	1-8	12.5	+ 7.00
September	0-4	-	- 4.00	September	0-3	-	- 3.00
Oct/Nov	0-10	-	- 10.00	Oct/Nov	0-7	-	- 7.00

4-y-o+	W-R	Per cent	£1 Level Stake	Totals	W-R	Per cent	£1 Level Stake
January	0-6	-	- 6.00	January	2-9	22.2	+ 4.25
February	0-3	-	- 3.00	February	1-6	16.7	- 2.25
March	1-2	50.0	+ 24.00	March	1-4	25.0	+ 22.00
April	2-12	16.7	+ 10.00	April	2-17	11.8	+ 5.00
May	1-12	8.3	+ 1.00	May	1-24	4.2	- 11.00
June	0-14	-	- 14.00	June	0-24	-	- 24.00
July	0-14	-	- 14.00	July	0-23	-	- 23.00
August	0-5	-	- 5.00	August	2-19	10.5	+ 13.00
September	0-8	-	- 8.00	September	0-15	-	- 15.00
Oct/Nov	2-14	14.3	- 3.00	Oct/Nov	2-31	6.5	- 20.00

DISTANCE

2-y-o	W-R	Per cent	£1 Level Stake	3-y-o	W-R	Per cent	£1 Level Stake
5f-6f	1-14	7.1	+ 3.00	5f-6f	0-0	-	0.00
7f-8f	0-9	-	- 9.00	7f-8f	2-28	7.1	- 14.75
9f-13f	0-0	-	0.00	9f-13f	2-31	6.5	- 12.25
14f+	0-0	-	0.00	14f+	0-0	-	0.00

4-y-o+	W-R	Per cent	£1 Level Stake	Totals	W-R	Per cent	£1 Level Stake
5f-6f	0-6	-	- 6.00	5f-6f	1-20	5.0	- 3.00
7f-8f	2-35	5.7	- 19.00	7f-8f	4-72	5.6	- 42.75
9f-13f	2-40	5.0	- 21.00	9f-13f	4-71	5.6	- 33.25
14f+	2-9	22.2	+ 28.00	14f+	2-9	22.2	+ 28.00

TYPE OF RACE

Non-Handicaps	W-R	Per cent	£1 Level Stake	Handicaps	W-R	Per cent	£1 Level Stake
2-y-o	1-11	9.1	+ 6.00	2-y-o	0-7	-	- 7.00
3-y-o	0-15	-	- 15.00	3-y-o	4-31	12.9	+ 1.00
4-y-o+	0-4	-	- 4.00	4-y-o+	5-63	7.9	- 17.00
Selling	0-2	-	- 2.00	Selling	0-17	-	- 17.00
Apprentice	0-0	-	0.00	Apprentice	1-16	6.3	+ 10.00
Amat/Ladies	0-0	-	0.00	Amat/Ladies	0-6	-	- 6.00
Totals	1-32	3.1	- 15.00	Totals	10-140	7.1	- 36.00

COURSE GRADE

	W-R	Per cent	£1 Level Stake
Group 1	5-76	6.6	- 28.00
Group 2	1-15	6.7	+ 2.00
Group 3	0-44	-	- 44.00
Group 4	5-37	13.5	+ 19.00

FIRST TIME OUT

	W-R	Per cent	£1 Level Stake
2-y-o	1-4	25.0	+ 13.00
3-y-o	0-9	-	- 9.00
4-y-o+	0-14	-	- 14.00
Totals	1-27	3.7	- 10.00

JOCKEYS RIDING

	W-R	Per cent	£1 Level Stake		W-R	Per cent	£1 Level Stake
D McCabe	5-63	7.9	+ 5.25	Mrs J Musson	1-7	14.3	+ 4.00
Pat Eddery	2-5	40.0	+ 6.00	A McGlone	1-7	14.3	+ 10.00
J Quinn	2-19	10.5	- 5.25				

J Reid	0-11	J Williams	0-2	M Baird	0-1
A Mackay	0-9	N Adams	0-2	M Roberts	0-1
G Faulkner	0-6	N Day	0-2	M Wigham	0-1
D Biggs	0-5	W Newnes	0-2	N Carlisle	0-1
R Cochrane	0-5	C Rutter	0-1	Paul Eddery	0-1
Dale Gibson	0-3	G Hind	0-1	S O'Gorman	0-1
W Carson	0-3	J Lowe	0-1	S Wood	0-1
W R Swinburn	0-3	John Francome	0-1	Sally Radford-Howes	0-1
B Doyle	0-2	L Dettori	0-1		
G Bardwell	0-2	L Newton	0-1		

COURSE RECORD

	Total W-R	Non-Handicaps 2-y-o	Non-Handicaps 3-y-o+	Handicaps 2-y-o	Handicaps 3-y-o+	Per cent	£1 Level Stake
Southwell (AW)	3-9	0-0	0-1	0-0	3-8	33.3	+ 30.25
Newmarket	2-29	0-1	0-4	0-3	2-21	6.9	- 13.00
York	1-2	0-0	0-0	0-0	1-2	50.0	+ 4.00
Newbury	1-3	0-0	0-0	0-0	1-3	33.3	+ 8.00
Goodwood	1-5	0-0	0-1	0-0	1-4	20.0	+ 10.00
Ripon	1-8	1-1	0-0	0-0	0-7	12.5	+ 9.00
Warwick	1-9	0-1	0-2	0-1	1-5	11.1	+ 4.00
Lingfield (AW)	1-15	0-1	0-2	0-0	1-12	6.7	- 11.25

Leicester	0-13	Pontefract	0-5	Ascot	0-2
Windsor	0-13	Haydock	0-4	Ayr	0-2
Sandown	0-11	Nottingham	0-4	Brighton	0-2
Kempton	0-9	Beverley	0-3	Thirsk	0-2
Doncaster	0-8	Folkestone	0-3	Newcastle	0-1
Yarmouth	0-6	Lingfield	0-3	Southwell (Turf)	0-1

WINNING HORSES

	Age	Races Run	1st	2nd	3rd	Unpl	Win £
Broughtons Formula	3	21	4	4	1	12	11,413
Bit On The Side	4	8	2	2	0	4	9,742
Rise Up Singing	5	14	2	2	1	9	9,660
Master Foodbroker	5	6	2	0	0	4	7,305
Mr B Reasonable	2	5	1	0	0	4	3,436

WINNING OWNERS

	Races Won	Value £		Races Won	Value £
Broughton Thermal Insulation	7	22,154	Mrs Rita Brown	2	9,660
Mike Hawkett	2	9,742			

Favourites	3-17	17.6% - 2.75	Total winning prize-money		£41,556
Longest winning sequence		1	Average SP of winner		10.0/1
Longest losing sequence		63	Return on stakes invested		-29.7%
1992 Form	6-130	4.6% - 86.75	1990 Form	4-154	2.6% -134.00
1991 Form	9-114	7.9% - 51.25	1989 Form	6-131	4.6% -103.37

M P NAUGHTON (Richmond, North Yorks)

	No. of Horses	Races Run	1st	2nd	3rd	Unpl	Per cent	£1 Level Stake
2-y-o	0	0	0	0	0	0	-	0.00
3-y-o	0	0	0	0	0	0	-	0.00
4-y-o+	17	117	4	6	5	102	3.4	- 71.00
Totals	17	117	4	6	5	102	3.4	- 71.00

Jan	Feb	Mar	Apr	May	Jun	Jul	Aug	Sep	Oct/Nov
0-2	0-3	0-3	0-5	1-15	1-17	1-22	1-18	0-17	0-15

Winning Jockeys	W-R	£1 Level Stake		W-R	£1 Level Stake
V Halliday	2-15	+ 10.00	J Weaver	1-12	- 4.00
A Culhane	1-7	+ 6.00			

Winning Courses	W-R	£1 Level Stake		W-R	£1 Level Stake
Edinburgh	2-11	+ 12.00	Haydock	1-6	+ 4.00
Carlisle	1-5	+ 8.00			

Winning Horses	Age	Races Run	1st	2nd	3rd	Unpl	Win £
Legion Of Honour	5	13	1	1	1	10	4,844
Pallium	5	15	1	1	0	13	4,175
Absolution	9	14	1	1	1	11	2,787
Lord Advocate	5	7	1	1	0	5	2,377

Favourites	0-3		Total winning prize-money		£14,183

1992 Form	32-356	9.0%	- 121.41	1990 Form	12-219	5.5%	- 102.17
1991 Form	21-201	10.4%	- 42.52	1989 Form	19-164	11.6%	- 7.75

T J NAUGHTON (Epsom, Surrey)

	No. of Horses	Races Run	1st	2nd	3rd	Unpl	Per cent	£1 Level Stake
2-y-o	4	8	2	1	0	5	25.0	+ 5.00
3-y-o	10	63	10	3	5	45	15.9	- 2.06
4-y-o+	10	60	7	4	3	46	11.7	- 3.25
Totals	24	131	19	8	8	96	14.5	- 0.31

BY MONTH

2-y-o	W-R	Per cent	£1 Level Stake	3-y-o	W-R	Per cent	£1 Level Stake
January	0-0	-	0.00	January	4-8	50.0	+ 5.19
February	0-0	-	0.00	February	0-4	-	- 4.00
March	0-0	-	0.00	March	0-0	-	0.00
April	0-0	-	0.00	April	1-5	20.0	0.00
May	0-1	-	- 1.00	May	2-5	40.0	+ 13.25
June	0-0	-	0.00	June	0-7	-	- 7.00
July	2-3	66.7	+ 10.00	July	2-11	18.2	+ 0.50
August	0-0	-	0.00	August	1-7	14.3	+ 6.00
September	0-2	-	- 2.00	September	0-6	-	- 6.00
Oct/Nov	0-2	-	- 2.00	Oct/Nov	0-10	-	- 10.00

4-y-o+	W-R	Per cent	£1 Level Stake		Totals	W-R	Per cent	£1 Level Stake
January	0-4	-	- 4.00		January	4-12	33.3	+ 1.19
February	0-5	-	- 5.00		February	0-9	-	- 9.00
March	0-1	-	- 1.00		March	0-1	-	- 1.00
April	1-5	20.0	+ 2.50		April	2-10	20.0	+ 2.50
May	1-6	16.7	- 2.75		May	3-12	25.0	+ 9.50
June	1-5	20.0	+ 8.00		June	1-12	8.3	+ 1.00
July	2-14	14.3	- 0.50		July	6-28	21.4	+ 10.00
August	1-9	11.1	- 2.50		August	2-16	12.5	+ 3.50
September	1-6	16.7	+ 7.00		September	1-14	7.1	- 1.00
Oct/Nov	0-5	-	- 5.00		Oct/Nov	0-17	-	- 17.00

DISTANCE

2-y-o	W-R	Per cent	£1 Level Stake		3-y-o	W-R	Per cent	£1 Level Stake
5f-6f	1-5	20.0	+ 4.00		5f-6f	6-20	30.0	+ 11.44
7f-8f	1-3	33.3	+ 1.00		7f-8f	4-23	17.4	+ 6.50
9f-13f	0-0	-	0.00		9f-13f	0-16	-	- 16.00
14f+	0-0	-	0.00		14f+	0-4	-	- 4.00

4-y-o+	W-R	Per cent	£1 Level Stake		Totals	W-R	Per cent	£1 Level Stake
5f-6f	1-16	6.3	- 3.00		5f-6f	8-41	19.5	+ 12.44
7f-8f	2-25	8.0	- 5.50		7f-8f	7-51	13.7	+ 2.00
9f-13f	4-12	33.3	+ 12.25		9f-13f	4-28	14.3	- 3.75
14f+	0-7	-	- 7.00		14f+	0-11	-	- 11.00

TYPE OF RACE

Non-Handicaps	W-R	Per cent	£1 Level Stake		Handicaps	W-R	Per cent	£1 Level Stake
2-y-o	1-7	14.3	- 3.00		2-y-o	1-1	100.0	+ 8.00
3-y-o	3-23	13.0	- 14.14		3-y-o	6-33	18.2	+ 13.58
4-y-o+	1-8	12.5	- 0.50		4-y-o+	4-40	10.0	- 11.25
Selling	0-2	-	- 2.00		Selling	1-4	25.0	+ 9.00
Apprentice	0-1	-	- 1.00		Apprentice	1-6	16.7	- 0.50
Amat/Ladies	0-0	-	0.00		Amat/Ladies	1-6	16.7	+ 1.50
Totals	5-41	12.2	- 20.64		Totals	14-90	15.6	+ 20.33

COURSE GRADE

	W-R	Per cent	£1 Level Stake
Group 1	6-44	13.6	+ 6.50
Group 2	2-21	9.5	- 2.75
Group 3	4-25	16.0	+ 6.50
Group 4	7-41	17.1	- 10.56

FIRST TIME OUT

	W-R	Per cent	£1 Level Stake
2-y-o	0-4	-	- 4.00
3-y-o	2-10	20.0	- 2.50
4-y-o+	0-10	-	- 10.00
Totals	2-24	8.3	- 16.50

JOCKEYS RIDING

	W-R	Per cent	£1 Level Stake		W-R	Per cent	£1 Level Stake
D Holland	8-40	20.0	+ 21.61	W Ryan	1-2	50.0	+ 3.00
D Harrison	2-6	33.3	+ 13.50	B Doyle	1-3	33.3	+ 0.25
A Garth	2-10	20.0	+ 1.50	A Munro	1-4	25.0	+ 1.00
Paul Eddery	2-18	11.1	- 5.00	Mrs J Naughton	1-6	16.7	+ 1.50
M Hills	1-2	50.0	+ 2.33				

G Carter	0-7	A Mackay	0-1	P McCabe		0-1
J Quinn	0-4	A McGlone	0-1	R Cochrane		0-1
M Jermy	0-4	C Asmussen	0-1	S Davies		0-1
G Bardwell	0-3	D Gibbs	0-1	S McCarthy		0-1
B Rouse	0-2	F Norton	0-1	T Ashley		0-1
D Wright	0-2	M Humphries	0-1	Wally Swinburn		0-1
Pat Eddery	0-2	Mr R Teal	0-1			
T Quinn	0-2	N Gwilliams	0-1			

COURSE RECORD

	Total W-R	Non-Handicaps 2-y-o	Non-Handicaps 3-y-o+	Handicaps 2-y-o	Handicaps 3-y-o+	Per cent	£1 Level Stake
Southwell (AW)	3-6	0-0	0-1	0-0	3-5	50.0	+ 9.83
Lingfield (AW)	3-25	0-0	2-8	0-0	1-17	12.0	- 17.89
Beverley	1-2	0-0	0-0	0-0	1-2	50.0	+ 4.00
Chepstow	1-3	0-1	0-0	0-0	1-2	33.3	+ 4.50
Kempton	1-4	0-0	0-1	0-0	1-3	25.0	+ 9.00
Pontefract	1-4	0-1	0-1	0-0	1-2	25.0	+ 9.00
Doncaster	1-5	1-2	0-0	0-0	0-3	20.0	- 1.00
Epsom	1-5	0-0	0-0	0-0	1-5	20.0	+ 8.00
Goodwood	1-5	0-1	0-1	0-0	1-3	20.0	+ 1.00
Brighton	1-6	0-0	0-2	0-0	1-4	16.7	- 2.75
Chester	1-6	0-0	0-2	0-0	1-4	16.7	+ 9.00
Sandown	1-6	0-0	0-2	0-0	1-4	16.7	- 0.50
Windsor	1-6	0-0	1-3	0-0	0-3	16.7	- 1.00
Folkestone	1-7	0-0	1-3	0-0	0-4	14.3	+ 0.50
Newmarket	1-10	0-0	0-1	1-1	0-8	10.0	- 1.00

Ascot	0-6	Lingfield	0-3	Redcar	0-1
Bath	0-6	Southwell (Turf)	0-2	Warwick	0-1
Salisbury	0-5	Ayr	0-1	Yarmouth	0-1
Leicester	0-3	Haydock	0-1	York	0-1

WINNING HORSES

	Age	Races Run	1st	2nd	3rd	Unpl	Win £
Play Hever Golf	3	10	6	0	0	4	23,671
Hever Golf Rose	2	4	2	1	0	1	23,602
Comanche Companion	3	9	3	1	0	5	13,854
El Yasaf	5	9	1	1	0	7	12,277
Northern Conqueror	5	14	3	1	0	10	7,884
Allmosa	4	11	2	1	2	6	5,420
Tyrian Purple	5	12	1	1	1	9	2,406
Splash Of Salt	3	12	1	2	1	8	2,304

WINNING OWNERS

	Races Won	Value £		Races Won	Value £
R A Popely	8	47,273	The Durdans Four (II) Two	2	5,420
J Naughton	1	12,277	T O'Flaherty	1	2,406
Drofmor Racing	2	11,499	S J Simmons	1	2,355
Mrs J T Naughton	3	7,884	G Wiltshire	1	2,304

Favourites	7-17	41.2%	+ 9.86	Total winning prize-money	£91,418

Longest winning sequence		2	Average SP of winner	5.9/1
Longest losing sequence		21	Return on stakes invested	-0.2%

1992 Form	9-121	7.4%	+ 6.75	1991 Form	6-88	6.8%	- 39.25

S G NORTON (Barnsley, South Yorks)

	No. of Horses	Races Run	1st	2nd	3rd	Unpl	Per cent	£1 Level Stake
2-y-o	17	76	7	8	11	50	9.2	- 45.49
3-y-o	14	117	17	13	14	73	14.5	- 23.82
4-y-o+	15	100	17	6	9	68	17.0	+ 12.87
Totals	46	293	41	27	34	191	14.0	- 56.44

BY MONTH

2-y-o	W-R	Per cent	£1 Level Stake	3-y-o	W-R	Per cent	£1 Level Stake
January	0-0	-	0.00	January	0-0	-	0.00
February	0-0	-	0.00	February	0-2	-	- 2.00
March	0-2	-	- 2.00	March	3-14	21.4	+ 8.00
April	0-8	-	- 8.00	April	2-11	18.2	+ 3.00
May	0-4	-	- 4.00	May	2-14	14.3	- 2.00
June	0-12	-	- 12.00	June	5-13	38.5	+ 7.63
July	3-13	23.1	+ 3.66	July	2-17	11.8	- 10.20
August	0-6	-	- 6.00	August	1-13	7.7	- 8.00
September	2-12	16.7	- 5.40	September	0-12	-	- 12.00
Oct/Nov	2-19	10.5	- 11.75	Oct/Nov	2-21	9.5	- 8.25

4-y-o+	W-R	Per cent	£1 Level Stake	Totals	W-R	Per cent	£1 Level Stake
January	0-0	-	0.00	January	0-0	-	0.00
February	0-1	-	- 1.00	February	0-3	-	- 3.00
March	1-6	16.7	- 2.00	March	4-22	18.2	+ 4.00
April	3-13	23.1	+ 10.00	April	5-32	15.6	+ 5.00
May	4-15	26.7	+ 1.51	May	6-33	18.2	- 4.49
June	4-18	22.2	+ 1.68	June	9-43	20.9	- 2.69
July	0-14	-	- 14.00	July	5-44	11.4	- 20.54
August	1-15	6.7	- 9.00	August	2-34	5.9	- 23.00
September	1-8	12.5	+ 2.00	September	3-32	9.4	- 15.40
Oct/Nov	3-10	30.0	+ 23.68	Oct/Nov	7-50	14.0	+ 3.68

Norton S G

DISTANCE

2-y-o	W-R	Per cent	£1 Level Stake	3-y-o	W-R	Per cent	£1 Level Stake
5f-6f	7-60	11.7	- 29.49	5f-6f	4-30	13.3	- 1.00
7f-8f	0-15	-	- 15.00	7f-8f	3-32	9.4	- 16.00
9f-13f	0-1	-	- 1.00	9f-13f	3-34	8.8	- 24.95
14f+	0-0	-	0.00	14f+	7-21	33.3	+ 18.13

4-y-o+	W-R	Per cent	£1 Level Stake	Totals	W-R	Per cent	£1 Level Stake
5f-6f	2-6	33.3	+ 13.88	5f-6f	13-96	13.5	- 16.61
7f-8f	6-37	16.2	+ 4.00	7f-8f	9-84	10.7	- 27.00
9f-13f	4-34	11.8	- 12.87	9f-13f	7-69	10.1	- 38.82
14f+	5-23	21.7	+ 7.86	14f+	12-44	27.3	+ 25.99

TYPE OF RACE

Non-Handicaps	W-R	Per cent	£1 Level Stake	Handicaps	W-R	Per cent	£1 Level Stake
2-y-o	7-55	12.7	- 24.49	2-y-o	0-8	-	- 8.00
3-y-o	9-52	17.3	- 10.57	3-y-o	5-44	11.4	- 12.25
4-y-o+	2-14	14.3	- 2.12	4-y-o+	15-74	20.3	+ 26.99
Selling	1-24	4.2	- 19.00	Selling	1-7	14.3	- 2.00
Apprentice	0-1	-	- 1.00	Apprentice	1-10	10.0	0.00
Amat/Ladies	0-0	-	0.00	Amat/Ladies	0-4	-	- 4.00
Totals	19-146	13.0	- 57.18	Totals	22-147	15.0	+ 0.74

COURSE GRADE

	W-R	Per cent	£1 Level Stake
Group 1	1-50	2.0	- 46.25
Group 2	2-44	4.5	- 32.67
Group 3	11-80	13.8	- 16.31
Group 4	27-119	22.7	+ 38.79

FIRST TIME OUT

	W-R	Per cent	£1 Level Stake
2-y-o	0-16	-	- 16.00
3-y-o	1-14	7.1	- 7.00
4-y-o+	3-14	21.4	+ 13.00
Totals	4-44	9.1	- 10.00

JOCKEYS RIDING

	W-R	Per cent	£1 Level Stake		W-R	Per cent	£1 Level Stake
O Pears	19-135	14.1	- 34.68	D Harrison	1-1	100.0	+ 9.00
D Moffatt	5-12	41.7	+ 23.38	M Roberts	1-2	50.0	+ 5.00
S Maloney	4-12	33.3	+ 12.25	R Cochrane	1-2	50.0	+ 2.33
N Connorton	3-18	16.7	- 2.90	W Ryan	1-2	50.0	+ 2.50
G Duffield	2-4	50.0	+ 3.25	J Fortune	1-3	33.3	+ 5.00
J Quinn	2-5	40.0	+ 11.68	K Fallon	1-10	10.0	- 6.25

321

Norton S G

K Darley	0-17	D Holland	0-2	H Bastiman	0-1
C Teague	0-5	G Hind	0-2	J Weaver	0-1
S Davies	0-5	J Carroll	0-2	L Aspell	0-1
D Gibbs	0-4	L Charnock	0-2	L Piggott	0-1
Dale Gibson	0-4	Mrs J Crossley	0-2	Miss I D W Jones	0-1
F Norton	0-4	Pat Eddery	0-2	Mrs M Cowdrey	0-1
B Raymond	0-3	Paul Eddery	0-2	N Varley	0-1
Claire Balding	0-3	T Williams	0-2	S Sanders	0-1
J Tate	0-3	W R Swinburn	0-2	T Marsden	0-1
M Wood	0-3	C Hawksley	0-1	W Carson	0-1
N Kennedy	0-3	D Wright	0-1		
A Munro	0-2	F Savage	0-1		

COURSE RECORD

	Total W-R	Non-Handicaps 2-y-o	Non-Handicaps 3-y-o+	Handicaps 2-y-o	Handicaps 3-y-o+	Per cent	£1 Level Stake
Southwell (AW)	12-48	3-13	5-11	0-0	4-24	25.0	+ 31.38
Hamilton	5-17	0-3	0-5	0-1	5-8	29.4	+ 9.88
Catterick	5-19	2-4	1-8	0-1	2-6	26.3	+ 1.23
Carlisle	4-15	0-2	2-5	0-0	2-8	26.7	+ 12.88
Edinburgh	4-20	0-4	2-5	0-1	2-10	20.0	- 1.95
Nottingham	2-14	0-6	0-1	0-0	2-7	14.3	- 1.62
Pontefract	2-32	0-6	0-10	0-2	2-14	6.3	- 15.32
Yarmouth	1-1	1-1	0-0	0-0	0-0	100.0	+ 3.50
Thirsk	1-6	1-2	0-2	0-0	0-2	16.7	- 1.67
Warwick	1-7	0-2	0-1	0-0	1-4	14.3	+ 3.00
Southwell (Turf)	1-8	0-3	1-1	0-1	0-3	12.5	- 5.75
Beverley	1-13	0-2	0-6	0-0	1-5	7.7	- 9.75
Chester	1-15	0-3	0-3	0-0	1-9	6.7	- 8.00
Haydock	1-16	0-2	1-3	0-1	0-10	6.3	- 12.25

Redcar	0-14	Newcastle	0-6	Folkestone	0-2
Doncaster	0-11	Leicester	0-3	Ascot	0-1
York	0-10	Newmarket	0-3	Goodwood	0-1
Ripon	0-8	Ayr	0-2	Lingfield	0-1

WINNING HORSES

	Age	Races Run	1st	2nd	3rd	Unpl	Win £
Celestial Key	3	12	3	3	1	5	18,460
Debsy Do	4	12	4	1	1	6	12,988
Follingworth Girl	3	11	4	0	3	4	11,427
Goodbye Millie	3	14	5	1	1	7	11,323
Five To Seven	4	10	3	0	1	6	9,638
Shamshom Al Arab	5	9	3	1	0	5	8,724
Promise Fulfilled	2	4	2	1	0	1	7,498
Elle Shaped	3	8	1	0	0	7	7,492
World Without End	4	5	2	0	0	3	6,446
Stoproveritate	4	11	2	0	1	8	5,271
Bold Alex	2	7	1	1	1	4	4,021

Champagne Ateaster	2	3	1	0	0	2	3,260
In A Moment	2	4	1	0	1	2	3,231
Tanagome	3	4	1	1	1	1	3,202
Affordable	5	7	1	1	0	5	3,158
Scottish Wedding	3	9	1	1	0	7	2,821
Susanna's Secret	6	6	1	0	1	4	2,788
Our Aisling	5	9	1	2	2	4	2,779
Nutty Brown	3	12	1	4	1	6	2,413
Turtle Rock	2	7	1	3	2	1	2,377
Formaestre	3	15	1	2	3	9	2,243
Trendy Dancer	2	7	1	0	2	4	2,070

WINNING OWNERS

	Races Won	Value £		Races Won	Value £
Lintscan Ltd	8	21,946	G Charlesworth	1	4,021
M J Brodrick	3	18,460	Jem Racing	1	3,260
Miss Maha Kalaji	4	11,512	David Scott	1	3,231
John L Holdroyd	4	11,427	Q Irshid	1	3,158
The Five To Seven Partnership	3	9,638	J Asquith	1	2,821
S G Norton	3	7,809	A K Smeaton	1	2,779
G G Ashton	2	7,498	John Lawson-Brown	1	2,413
J E Marsden	1	7,492	P D Savill	1	2,377
Mrs Angela Norton	2	6,446	P G Manning	1	2,070
John D Clark	2	5,271			

Favourites	12-25	48.0%	+ 5.97	Total winning prize-money		£133,629
Longest winning sequence			2	Average SP of winner		4.8/1
Longest losing sequence			23	Return on stakes invested		-19.3%
1992 Form	27-193	14.0%	- 21.43	1990 Form	20-199	10.1%	- 39.25
1991 Form	19-153	12.4%	- 7.27	1989 Form	11-254	4.3%	-196.52

J O'DONOGHUE (Reigate, Surrey)

	No. of Horses	Races Run	1st	2nd	3rd	Unpl	Per cent	£1 Level Stake
2-y-o	1	9	1	0	3	5	11.1	0.00
3-y-o	2	5	0	0	0	5	-	- 5.00
4-y-o+	2	14	1	0	1	12	7.1	- 1.00
Totals	5	28	2	0	4	22	7.1	- 6.00

Jan	Feb	Mar	Apr	May	Jun	Jul	Aug	Sep	Oct/Nov
0-0	0-0	0-0	0-0	0-2	0-3	1-5	0-8	1-8	0-2

O'Donoghue J

Winning Jockeys	W-R	£1 Level Stake		W-R	£1 Level Stake
P McCabe	1-3	+ 6.00	N Adams	1-7	+ 6.00

Winning Courses	W-R	£1 Level Stake		W-R	£1 Level Stake
Windsor	1-4	+ 9.00	Sandown	1-5	+ 4.00

Winning Horses	Age	Races Run	1st	2nd	3rd	Unpl	Win £
Hello Mister	2	9	1	0	3	5	4,241
Spectacle Jim	4	8	1	0	1	6	2,532

Favourites	0-0			Total winning prize-money		£6,773
1992 Form	0-11			1990 Form	0-16	
1991 Form	1-15	6.7%	- 6.00	1989 Form	0-7	

W A O'GORMAN (Newmarket)

	No. of Horses	Races Run	1st	2nd	3rd	Unpl	Per cent	£1 Level Stake
2-y-o	6	20	4	4	2	10	20.0	- 8.17
3-y-o	9	52	11	10	5	26	21.2	+ 10.77
4-y-o+	6	55	7	14	7	27	12.7	+ 4.17
Totals	21	127	22	28	14	63	17.3	+ 6.77

BY MONTH

2-y-o	W-R	Per cent	£1 Level Stake	3-y-o	W-R	Per cent	£1 Level Stake
January	0-0	-	0.00	January	3-9	33.3	+ 7.75
February	0-0	-	0.00	February	1-5	20.0	- 3.43
March	0-0	-	0.00	March	1-5	20.0	- 0.50
April	0-3	-	- 3.00	April	2-5	40.0	+ 4.25
May	3-5	60.0	+ 5.10	May	0-5	-	- 5.00
June	0-1	-	- 1.00	June	0-4	-	- 4.00
July	1-6	16.7	- 4.27	July	2-9	22.2	- 2.30
August	0-1	-	- 1.00	August	0-6	-	- 6.00
September	0-1	-	- 1.00	September	1-1	100.0	+ 14.00
Oct/Nov	0-3	-	- 3.00	Oct/Nov	1-3	33.3	+ 6.00

4-y-o+	W-R	Per cent	£1 Level Stake	Totals	W-R	Per cent	£1 Level Stake
January	3-8	37.5	+ 18.00	January	6-17	35.3	+ 25.75
February	2-12	16.7	- 2.83	February	3-17	17.6	- 6.26
March	1-9	11.1	- 2.00	March	2-14	14.3	- 2.50
April	0-6	-	- 6.00	April	2-14	14.3	- 4.75
May	0-8	-	- 8.00	May	3-18	16.7	- 7.90
June	1-2	50.0	+ 15.00	June	1-7	14.3	+ 10.00
July	0-7	-	- 7.00	July	3-22	13.6	- 13.57
August	0-2	-	- 2.00	August	0-9	-	- 9.00
September	0-0	-	0.00	September	1-2	50.0	+ 13.00
Oct/Nov	0-1	-	- 1.00	Oct/Nov	1-7	14.3	+ 2.00

DISTANCE

2-y-o	W-R	Per cent	£1 Level Stake	3-y-o	W-R	Per cent	£1 Level Stake
5f-6f	4-18	22.2	- 6.17	5f-6f	3-9	33.3	+ 15.25
7f-8f	0-2	-	- 2.00	7f-8f	7-37	18.9	- 9.48
9f-13f	0-0	-	0.00	9f-13f	1-6	16.7	+ 5.00
14f+	0-0	-	0.00	14f+	0-0	-	0.00

4-y-o+	W-R	Per cent	£1 Level Stake	Totals	W-R	Per cent	£1 Level Stake
5f-6f	1-18	5.6	- 10.50	5f-6f	8-45	17.8	- 1.42
7f-8f	6-36	16.7	+ 15.67	7f-8f	13-75	17.3	+ 4.19
9f-13f	0-1	-	- 1.00	9f-13f	1-7	14.3	+ 4.00
14f+	0-0	-	0.00	14f+	0-0	-	0.00

TYPE OF RACE

Non-Handicaps	W-R	Per cent	£1 Level Stake	Handicaps	W-R	Per cent	£1 Level Stake
2-y-o	4-17	23.5	- 5.17	2-y-o	0-3	-	- 3.00
3-y-o	6-19	31.6	+ 12.52	3-y-o	5-33	15.2	- 1.75
4-y-o+	3-18	16.7	- 1.83	4-y-o+	3-33	9.1	- 5.00
Selling	0-1	-	- 1.00	Selling	0-0	-	0.00
Apprentice	0-0	-	0.00	Apprentice	1-3	33.3	+ 12.00
Amat/Ladies	0-0	-	0.00	Amat/Ladies	0-0	-	0.00
Totals	13-55	23.6	+ 4.52	Totals	9-72	12.5	+ 2.25

COURSE GRADE

	W-R	Per cent	£1 Level Stake
Group 1	3-13	23.1	+ 12.50
Group 2	0-4	-	- 4.00
Group 3	4-21	19.0	- 8.02
Group 4	15-89	16.9	+ 6.29

FIRST TIME OUT

	W-R	Per cent	£1 Level Stake
2-y-o	0-5	-	- 5.00
3-y-o	3-9	33.3	+ 14.75
4-y-o+	3-6	50.0	+ 34.00
Totals	6-20	30.0	+ 43.75

JOCKEYS RIDING

	W-R	Per cent	£1 Level Stake		W-R	Per cent	£1 Level Stake
Emma O'Gorman	15-109	13.8	- 18.41	D Holland	1-2	50.0	+ 6.00
F Norton	2-4	50.0	+ 5.20	J Williams	1-2	50.0	+ 13.00
D Nicholls	1-1	100.0	+ 2.25	A Munro	1-4	25.0	+ 2.00
Pat Eddery	1-1	100.0	+ 0.73				

T Ives	0-2		B Raymond	0-1	R Cochrane	0-1	

COURSE RECORD

	Total W-R	Non-Handicaps 2-y-o	3-y-o+	Handicaps 2-y-o	3-y-o+	Per cent	£1 Level Stake
Southwell (AW)	8-49	1-1	3-17	0-0	4-31	16.3	+ 6.35
Lingfield (AW)	5-26	0-1	4-10	0-1	1-14	19.2	- 5.26
Newmarket	2-11	0-4	0-2	0-1	2-4	18.2	+ 10.00
Yarmouth	2-11	1-1	0-2	0-1	1-7	18.2	- 4.77
Beverley	1-1	0-0	1-1	0-0	0-0	100.0	+ 2.25
Carlisle	1-1	0-0	1-1	0-0	0-0	100.0	+ 1.20
Goodwood	1-1	1-1	0-0	0-0	0-0	100.0	+ 3.50
Pontefract	1-5	1-2	0-0	0-0	0-3	20.0	- 1.50
Southwell (Turf)	1-10	0-2	0-2	0-0	1-6	10.0	+ 7.00

Warwick	0-3	Leicester		0-1	Salisbury		0-1
Bath	0-2	Lingfield		0-1	Sandown		0-1
Brighton	0-1	Redcar		0-1	Windsor		0-1

WINNING HORSES

	Age	Races Run	1st	2nd	3rd	Unpl	Win £
Miss Gorgeous	3	14	4	3	2	5	12,378
Moon Strike	3	5	2	1	0	2	10,528
Mazeeka	2	3	2	0	0	1	5,931
Tacit Mac	4	2	2	0	0	0	4,896
Sally's Son	7	11	2	0	1	8	4,812
Mister Blake	3	18	2	4	2	10	4,748
Dance Focus	2	6	1	2	1	2	4,191
Saseedo	3	4	1	1	1	1	3,883
Midnight Jazz	3	1	1	0	0	0	3,290
Mindomica	4	7	1	4	0	2	3,287
International Star	2	4	1	2	0	1	3,231
Lord Naskra	4	17	1	4	4	8	2,406
Diamond Lucy	3	4	1	0	0	3	2,208
Express Service	4	12	1	5	2	4	2,208

WINNING OWNERS

	Races Won	Value £		Races Won	Value £
S Fustok	7	25,839	T Mohan	2	4,896
Thomas R Capehart	4	12,378	Red Seven Stable	2	4,748
N S Yong	3	10,709	Curley O'Gorman	1	2,406
W A O'Gorman	3	7,020			

Favourites	6-27	22.2%	- 14.93	Total winning prize-money			£67,996
Longest winning sequence			2	Average SP of winner			5.1/1
Longest losing sequence			15	Return on stakes invested			5.3%
1992 Form	27-197	13.7%	- 93.76	1990 Form	51-209	24.4%	+ 25.24
1991 Form	29-232	12.5%	- 95.24	1989 Form	10-78	12.8%	- 26.58

F O'MAHONY (Lingfield, Surrey)

	No. of Horses	Races Run	1st	2nd	3rd	Unpl	Per cent	£1 Level Stake
2-y-o	0	0	0	0	0	0	-	0.00
3-y-o	1	2	0	0	0	2	-	- 2.00
4-y-o+	4	25	1	2	3	19	4.0	- 15.00
Totals	5	27	1	2	3	21	3.7	- 17.00

Jan	Feb	Mar	Apr	May	Jun	Jul	Aug	Sep	Oct/Nov
0-0	0-0	0-0	0-4	0-4	1-8	0-3	0-4	0-1	0-3

Winning Jockey	W-R	£1 Level Stake	Winning Course	W-R	£1 Level Stake
W R Swinburn	1-4	+ 6.00	Sandown	1-4	+ 6.00

Winning Horse	Age	Races Run	1st	2nd	3rd	Unpl	Win £
Mull House	6	10	1	2	2	5	4,221

Favourites	0-2		Total winning prize-money	£4,221

1992 Form	3-20	15.0%	- 10.17	1990 Form	0-8
1991 Form	0-3				

J J O'NEILL (Penrith, Cumbria)

	No. of Horses	Races Run	1st	2nd	3rd	Unpl	Per cent	£1 Level Stake
2-y-o	3	17	2	1	0	14	11.8	- 1.50
3-y-o	3	12	0	2	3	7	-	- 12.00
4-y-o+	3	5	0	1	0	4	-	- 5.00
Totals	9	34	2	4	3	25	5.9	- 18.50

Jan	Feb	Mar	Apr	May	Jun	Jul	Aug	Sep	Oct/Nov
0-0	0-0	1-2	0-3	0-7	0-1	0-10	0-3	1-3	0-5

Winning Jockeys	W-R	£1 Level Stake		W-R	£1 Level Stake
W Carson	1-1	+ 3.50	K Darley	1-9	+ 2.00

Winning Courses					
Nottingham	1-1	+ 3.50	Hamilton	1-7	+ 4.00

Winning Horse	Age	Races Run	1st	2nd	3rd	Unpl	Win £
Steadfast Elite	2	8	2	1	0	5	5,841

Favourites	0-4		Total winning prize-money	£5,841

1992 Form	1-62	1.6%	- 52.50	1990 Form	8-37	21.6%	+ 2.00
1991 Form	2-68	2.9%	- 56.00	1989 Form	0-51		

O O'NEILL (Cheltenham, Glos)

	No. of Horses	Races Run	1st	2nd	3rd	Unpl	Per cent	£1 Level Stake
2-y-o	0	0	0	0	0	0	-	0.00
3-y-o	1	6	0	1	2	3	-	- 6.00
4-y-o+	7	18	2	1	0	15	11.1	+100.00
Totals	8	24	2	2	2	18	8.3	+ 94.00

Jan	Feb	Mar	Apr	May	Jun	Jul	Aug	Sep	Oct/Nov
0-2	0-0	0-0	0-1	0-3	0-2	0-1	2-5	0-4	0-6

Winning Jockeys	W-R	£1 Level Stake				W-R	£1 Level Stake
A Clark	1-2	+ 65.00		N Adams		1-2	+ 49.00

Winning Course		
Bath	2-2	+116.00

Winning Horses	Age	Races Run	1st	2nd	3rd	Unpl	Win £
Miss Crusty	5	3	1	0	0	2	2,959
Harvest Rose	4	4	1	0	0	3	2,553

Favourites	0-1			Total winning prize-money		£5,512
1992 Form	0-20			1990 Form	2-50	4.0% - 38.75
1991 Form	1-35	2.9%	- 26.00	1989 Form	0-28	

R J O'SULLIVAN (Bognor Regis, West Sussex)

	No. of Horses	Races Run	1st	2nd	3rd	Unpl	Per cent	£1 Level Stake
2-y-o	0	0	0	0	0	0	-	0.00
3-y-o	4	21	1	1	1	18	4.8	- 15.00
4-y-o+	20	110	17	7	7	79	15.5	- 12.75
Totals	24	131	18	8	8	97	13.7	- 27.75

BY MONTH

2-y-o	W-R	Per cent	£1 Level Stake	3-y-o	W-R	Per cent	£1 Level Stake
January	0-0	-	0.00	January	0-0	-	0.00
February	0-0	-	0.00	February	1-2	50.0	+ 4.00
March	0-0	-	0.00	March	0-1	-	- 1.00
April	0-0	-	0.00	April	0-2	-	- 2.00
May	0-0	-	0.00	May	0-2	-	- 2.00
June	0-0	-	0.00	June	0-3	-	- 3.00
July	0-0	-	0.00	July	0-2	-	- 2.00
August	0-0	-	0.00	August	0-4	-	- 4.00
September	0-0	-	0.00	September	0-4	-	- 4.00
Oct/Nov	0-0	-	0.00	Oct/Nov	0-1	-	- 1.00

4-y-o+	W-R	Per cent	£1 Level Stake	Totals	W-R	Per cent	£1 Level Stake
January	3-13	23.1	- 0.25	January	3-13	23.1	- 0.25
February	2-11	18.2	+ 4.50	February	3-13	23.1	+ 8.50
March	4-11	36.4	+ 9.50	March	4-12	33.3	+ 8.50
April	1-10	10.0	- 2.00	April	1-12	8.3	- 4.00
May	1-8	12.5	+ 1.00	May	1-10	10.0	- 1.00
June	3-12	25.0	+ 1.50	June	3-15	20.0	- 1.50
July	1-12	8.3	- 5.00	July	1-14	7.1	- 7.00
August	2-17	11.8	- 6.00	August	2-21	9.5	- 10.00
September	0-10	-	- 10.00	September	0-14	-	- 14.00
Oct/Nov	0-6	-	- 6.00	Oct/Nov	0-7	-	- 7.00

DISTANCE

2-y-o	W-R	Per cent	£1 Level Stake	3-y-o	W-R	Per cent	£1 Level Stake
5f-6f	0-0	-	0.00	5f-6f	0-5	-	- 5.00
7f-8f	0-0	-	0.00	7f-8f	1-14	7.1	- 8.00
9f-13f	0-0	-	0.00	9f-13f	0-1	-	- 1.00
14f+	0-0	-	0.00	14f+	0-1	-	- 1.00

4-y-o+	W-R	Per cent	£1 Level Stake	Totals	W-R	Per cent	£1 Level Stake
5f-6f	3-24	12.5	- 8.00	5f-6f	3-29	10.3	- 13.00
7f-8f	8-40	20.0	+ 6.50	7f-8f	9-54	16.7	- 1.50
9f-13f	6-37	16.2	- 2.25	9f-13f	6-38	15.8	- 3.25
14f+	0-9	-	- 9.00	14f+	0-10	-	- 10.00

TYPE OF RACE

Non-Handicaps	W-R	Per cent	£1 Level Stake	Handicaps	W-R	Per cent	£1 Level Stake
2-y-o	0-0	-	0.00	2-y-o	0-0	-	0.00
3-y-o	1-11	9.1	- 5.00	3-y-o	0-8	-	- 8.00
4-y-o+	1-13	7.7	- 9.50	4-y-o+	12-85	14.1	- 10.75
Selling	3-4	75.0	+ 11.50	Selling	0-1	-	- 1.00
Apprentice	0-0	-	0.00	Apprentice	1-9	11.1	- 5.00
Amat/Ladies	0-0	-	0.00	Amat/Ladies	0-0	-	0.00
Totals	5-28	17.9	- 3.00	Totals	13-103	12.6	- 24.75

COURSE GRADE

	W-R	Per cent	£1 Level Stake
Group 1	1-30	3.3	- 24.50
Group 2	4-33	12.1	- 5.50
Group 3	1-12	8.3	- 7.50
Group 4	12-56	21.4	+ 9.75

FIRST TIME OUT

	W-R	Per cent	£1 Level Stake
2-y-o	0-0	-	0.00
3-y-o	0-3	-	- 3.00
4-y-o+	3-18	16.7	- 1.25
Totals	3-21	14.3	- 4.25

JOCKEYS RIDING

	W-R	Per cent	£1 Level Stake		W-R	Per cent	£1 Level Stake
F Norton	3-6	50.0	+ 9.00	J Quinn	2-8	25.0	+ 2.00
J Weaver	3-11	27.3	+ 6.50	A Clark	2-15	13.3	- 4.00
B Russell	3-17	17.6	- 1.25	L Piggott	1-1	100.0	+ 3.50
D Biggs	3-52	5.8	- 31.50	J Reid	1-4	25.0	+ 5.00

D McCabe	0-4	A Procter	0-1	L Dettori		0-1
W Ryan	0-3	G Carter	0-1	W Newnes		0-1
D Gibbs	0-2	J Lowe	0-1			
M Perrett	0-2	K Rutter	0-1			

COURSE RECORD

	Total W-R	Non-Handicaps 2-y-o	3-y-o+	Handicaps 2-y-o	3-y-o+	Per cent	£1 Level Stake
Lingfield (AW)	11-44	0-0	3-9	0-0	8-35	25.0	+ 17.75
Brighton	3-18	0-0	0-8	0-0	3-10	16.7	+ 4.00
Epsom	1-1	0-0	0-0	0-0	1-1	100.0	+ 4.50
Warwick	1-2	0-0	1-1	0-0	0-1	50.0	+ 2.00
Windsor	1-7	0-0	1-2	0-0	0-5	14.3	- 2.50
Salisbury	1-9	0-0	0-1	0-0	1-8	11.1	- 3.50

Goodwood	0-11	Bath	0-4	Haydock	0-1
Folkestone	0-9	Doncaster	0-2	Leicester	0-1
Lingfield	0-6	Newbury	0-2	Newmarket	0-1
Sandown	0-6	Ascot	0-1		
Kempton	0-5	Catterick	0-1		

WINNING HORSES

	Age	Races Run	1st	2nd	3rd	Unpl	Win £
Belmoredean	8	6	3	0	0	3	9,121
Scots Law	6	14	3	1	2	8	8,984
Agwa	4	4	2	0	0	2	7,137
Pigalle Wonder	5	11	2	2	0	7	7,099
El Volador	6	8	2	1	1	4	6,575
Barahin	4	6	3	1	0	2	5,641
Munday Dean	5	3	1	0	0	2	3,054
Mac's Fighter	8	11	1	0	0	10	2,489
Mark's Club	3	11	1	1	1	8	2,377

WINNING OWNERS

	Races Won	Value £		Races Won	Value £
I A Baker	4	13,713	Martin Hickey	3	5,641
Fred Honour	3	9,121	I Kerman	1	3,054
Mrs R J Doorgachurn	3	8,984	Christopher Lane	1	2,489
Miss Nicola M Pfann	2	7,099	Mrs Barbara Marchant	1	2,377

Favourites	4-15	26.7%	+ 1.25	Total winning prize-money			£52,478
Longest winning sequence			3	Average SP of winner			4.7/1
Longest losing sequence			21	Return on stakes invested			-21.2%
1992 Form	9-75	12.0%	+ 18.63	1990 Form	6-68	8.8%	- 6.50
1991 Form	11-103	10.7%	+ 22.00	1989 Form	7-49	14.3%	- 9.00

G R OLDROYD (York, North Yorks)

	No. of Horses	Races Run	1st	2nd	3rd	Unpl	Per cent	£1 Level Stake
2-y-o	1	2	0	0	0	2	-	- 2.00
3-y-o	3	12	1	0	0	11	8.3	- 8.50
4-y-o+	6	17	1	1	4	11	5.9	- 8.00
Totals	10	31	2	1	4	24	6.5	- 18.50

Jan	Feb	Mar	Apr	May	Jun	Jul	Aug	Sep	Oct/Nov
0-0	0-0	0-0	0-0	0-3	0-6	1-7	1-3	0-5	0-7

Winning Jockeys	W-R	£1 Level Stake			W-R	£1 Level Stake
G Duffield	1-1	+ 2.50	D Wright		1-3	+ 6.00

Winning Courses						
Ripon	1-3	+ 0.50	Pontefract		1-7	+ 2.00

Winning Horses	Age	Races Run	1st	2nd	3rd	Unpl	Win £
Eightandahalf	4	2	1	0	0	1	2,562
Infantry Glen	3	6	1	0	0	5	2,511

Favourites	1-1	100.0%	+ 2.50	Total winning prize-money			£5,073
1992 Form	0-0			1990 Form	1-21	4.8%	- 15.50
1991 Form	5-59	8.5%	- 19.75	1989 Form	0-7		

B PALLING (Cowbridge, South Glamorgan)

	No. of Horses	Races Run	1st	2nd	3rd	Unpl	Per cent	£1 Level Stake
2-y-o	14	51	3	6	5	37	5.9	- 28.67
3-y-o	7	33	3	3	3	24	9.1	- 4.50
4-y-o+	7	27	3	1	3	20	11.1	+ 22.00
Totals	28	111	9	10	11	81	8.1	- 11.17

Jan	Feb	Mar	Apr	May	Jun	Jul	Aug	Sep	Oct/Nov
0-1	0-1	0-4	0-11	1-17	2-10	1-16	2-21	1-11	2-19

Palling B

Winning Jockeys	W-R	£1 Level Stake		W-R	£1 Level Stake
D Holland	2-10	+ 3.33	Wendy Jones	1-3	+ 14.00
M Roberts	1-2	+ 1.50	J Weaver	1-4	+ 5.00
C Avery	1-2	+ 24.00	W Ryan	1-5	+ 16.00
P McCabe	1-2	+ 4.00	S Davies	1-39	- 35.00

Winning Courses	W-R	£1 Level Stake		W-R	£1 Level Stake
Leicester	3-5	+ 16.50	Folkestone	1-6	- 1.67
Chepstow	2-13	+ 30.00	Nottingham	1-14	- 8.00
Newmarket	1-3	+ 1.00	Southwell (AW)	1-14	+ 7.00

Winning Horses	Age	Races Run	1st	2nd	3rd	Unpl	Win £
Carranita	3	10	2	1	2	5	7,018
Mr Bergerac	2	10	2	2	1	5	6,700
Eiras Mood	4	6	1	0	0	5	3,668
Haroldon	4	10	1	1	2	6	3,054
Electrolyte	3	6	1	1	0	4	2,997
Beveled Edge	4	3	1	0	0	2	2,812
Kathanna	2	2	1	0	0	1	2,742

Favourites	0-2		Total winning prize-money		£28,990

1992 Form	8-96	8.3%	- 14.75	1990 Form	4-101	4.0%	- 47.62
1991 Form	1-79	1.3%	- 72.00	1989 Form	4-69	5.8%	- 1.00

C PARKER (Lockerbie, Dumfries)

	No. of Horses	Races Run	1st	2nd	3rd	Unpl	Per cent	£1 Level Stake
2-y-o	0	0	0	0	0	0	-	0.00
3-y-o	0	0	0	0	0	0	-	0.00
4-y-o+	2	8	1	1	0	6	12.5	- 2.50
Totals	2	8	1	1	0	6	12.5	- 2.50

Jan	Feb	Mar	Apr	May	Jun	Jul	Aug	Sep	Oct/Nov
0-0	0-0	0-0	0-1	0-3	1-2	0-1	0-1	0-0	0-0

Winning Jockey	W-R	£1 Level Stake	Winning Course	W-R	£1 Level Stake
Miss L Perratt	1-1	+ 4.50	Carlisle	1-5	+ 0.50

Winning Horse	Age	Races Run	1st	2nd	3rd	Unpl	Win £
Shalabia	4	7	1	1	0	5	2,322

Favourites	0-0		Total winning prize-money		£2,322

1992 Form	1-5	20.0%	- 1.25	1990 Form	0-15
1991 Form	0-6			1989 Form	0-4

J PARKES (Malton, North Yorks)

	No. of Horses	Races Run	1st	2nd	3rd	Unpl	Per cent	£1 Level Stake
2-y-o	0	0	0	0	0	0	-	0.00
3-y-o	4	21	0	3	2	16	-	- 21.00
4-y-o+	5	36	5	7	2	22	13.9	+ 3.33
Totals	9	57	5	10	4	38	8.8	- 17.67

Jan	Feb	Mar	Apr	May	Jun	Jul	Aug	Sep	Oct/Nov
0-3	0-1	0-5	0-4	2-8	1-8	1-8	0-6	1-5	0-9

Winning Jockeys	W-R	£1 Level Stake			W-R	£1 Level Stake
D Moffatt	1-2	+ 2.33	D Harrison		1-6	+ 5.00
D McKeown	1-2	+ 2.00	J Weaver		1-8	+ 3.00
J Tate	1-3	+ 6.00				

Winning Courses						
Edinburgh	1-1	+ 3.00	Catterick		1-7	+ 4.00
Doncaster	1-4	+ 0.33	Southwell (AW)		1-8	+ 1.00
Leicester	1-4	+ 7.00				

Winning Horses	Age	Races Run	1st	2nd	3rd	Unpl	Win £
The Right Time	8	7	2	2	0	3	5,502
Dancing Days	7	6	2	0	2	2	3,654
Ricky's Tornado	4	3	1	0	0	2	3,371

Favourites	2-3	66.7%	+ 5.33	Total winning prize-money		£12,527
1992 Form	4-92	4.3%	- 70.00	1990 Form	2-90	2.2%	- 35.00
1991 Form	3-95	3.2%	- 45.00	1989 Form	6-69	8.7%	+ 24.75

J W PAYNE (Newmarket)

	No. of Horses	Races Run	1st	2nd	3rd	Unpl	Per cent	£1 Level Stake
2-y-o	4	23	3	4	3	13	13.0	- 15.20
3-y-o	8	58	8	1	2	47	13.8	- 18.54
4-y-o+	1	10	0	0	1	9	-	- 10.00
Totals	13	91	11	5	6	69	12.1	- 43.74

BY MONTH

2-y-o	W-R	Per cent	£1 Level Stake	3-y-o	W-R	Per cent	£1 Level Stake
Mar/Apr	0-2	-	- 2.00	Mar/Apr	0-7	-	- 7.00
May	1-3	33.3	- 1.27	May	3-9	33.3	+ 2.08
June	0-2	-	- 2.00	June	1-11	9.1	- 8.62
July	0-5	-	- 5.00	July	3-15	20.0	+ 7.00
August	0-3	-	- 3.00	August	1-4	25.0	0.00
September	1-6	16.7	- 1.50	September	0-5	-	- 5.00
Oct/Nov	1-2	50.0	- 0.43	Oct/Nov	0-7	-	- 7.00

Payne J W

4-y-o+	W-R	Per cent	£1 Level Stake	Totals	W-R	Per cent	£1 Level Stake
Mar/Apr	0-1	-	- 1.00	Mar/Apr	0-10	-	- 10.00
May	0-2	-	- 2.00	May	4-14	28.6	- 1.19
June	0-1	-	- 1.00	June	1-14	7.1	- 11.62
July	0-1	-	- 1.00	July	3-21	14.3	+ 1.00
August	0-0	-	0.00	August	1-7	14.3	- 3.00
September	0-3	-	- 3.00	September	1-14	7.1	- 9.50
Oct/Nov	0-2	-	- 2.00	Oct/Nov	1-11	9.1	- 9.43

DISTANCE

2-y-o	W-R	Per cent	£1 Level Stake	3-y-o	W-R	Per cent	£1 Level Stake
5f-6f	3-20	15.0	- 12.20	5f-6f	1-10	10.0	- 4.00
7f-8f	0-3	-	- 3.00	7f-8f	7-35	20.0	- 1.54
9f-13f	0-0	-	0.00	9f-13f	0-13	-	- 13.00
14f+	0-0	-	0.00	14f+	0-0	-	0.00

4-y-o+	W-R	Per cent	£1 Level Stake	Totals	W-R	Per cent	£1 Level Stake
5f-6f	0-10	-	- 10.00	5f-6f	4-40	10.0	- 26.20
7f-8f	0-0	-	0.00	7f-8f	7-38	18.4	- 4.54
9f-13f	0-0	-	0.00	9f-13f	0-13	-	- 13.00
14f+	0-0	-	0.00	14f+	0-0	-	0.00

TYPE OF RACE

Non-Handicaps	W-R	Per cent	£1 Level Stake	Handicaps	W-R	Per cent	£1 Level Stake
2-y-o	3-17	17.6	- 9.20	2-y-o	0-6	-	- 6.00
3-y-o	3-26	11.5	- 14.17	3-y-o	5-30	16.7	- 2.37
4-y-o+	0-7	-	- 7.00	4-y-o+	0-3	-	- 3.00
Selling	0-0	-	0.00	Selling	0-1	-	- 1.00
Apprentice	0-1	-	- 1.00	Apprentice	0-0	-	0.00
Amat/Ladies	0-0	-	0.00	Amat/Ladies	0-0	-	0.00
Totals	6-51	11.8	- 31.37	Totals	5-40	12.5	- 12.37

COURSE GRADE

	W-R	Per cent	£1 Level Stake
Group 1	2-30	6.7	- 15.50
Group 2	2-22	9.1	- 14.27
Group 3	3-23	13.0	- 10.62
Group 4	4-16	25.0	- 3.35

FIRST TIME OUT

	W-R	Per cent	£1 Level Stake
2-y-o	0-4	-	- 4.00
3-y-o	0-8	-	- 8.00
4-y-o+	0-1	-	- 1.00
Totals	0-13	-	- 13.00

Payne J W

JOCKEYS RIDING

	W-R	Per cent	£1 Level Stake		W-R	Per cent	£1 Level Stake
R Cochrane	5-25	20.0	- 3.32	L Dettori	1-5	20.0	- 1.00
W Hood	3-14	21.4	- 2.92	A Munro	1-10	10.0	- 5.50
D McKeown	1-2	50.0	+ 4.00				

G Duffield	0-4	A Mackay	0-1	M Denaro	0-1
J Quinn	0-4	A McGlone	0-1	M Fenton	0-1
N Carlisle	0-3	C Dwyer	0-1	M Roberts	0-1
B Raymond	0-2	D Biggs	0-1	M Tebbutt	0-1
E Johnson	0-2	G Bardwell	0-1	N Day	0-1
G Carter	0-2	J Reid	0-1	T Quinn	0-1
G Forster	0-2	J Williams	0-1		
J Lowe	0-2	K Fallon	0-1		

COURSE RECORD

	Total W-R	Non-Handicaps 2-y-o	3-y-o+	Handicaps 2-y-o	3-y-o+	Per cent	£1 Level Stake
Edinburgh	2-2	0-0	0-0	0-0	2-2	100.0	+ 7.25
Leicester	2-5	0-0	1-4	0-0	1-1	40.0	+ 1.38
Catterick	1-1	0-0	1-1	0-0	0-0	100.0	+ 0.83
Goodwood	1-1	0-0	0-0	0-0	1-1	100.0	+ 9.00
Beverley	1-3	0-0	1-3	0-0	0-0	33.3	+ 3.00
Ripon	1-4	1-2	0-0	0-0	0-2	25.0	- 2.27
Sandown	1-5	1-2	0-2	0-0	0-1	20.0	- 0.50
Warwick	1-5	1-1	0-2	0-0	0-2	20.0	- 3.43
Redcar	1-6	0-0	0-3	0-0	1-3	16.7	0.00

Newmarket	0-9	Nottingham	0-3	Carlisle	0-1
Yarmouth	0-7	Windsor	0-3	Epsom	0-1
Folkestone	0-5	Salisbury	0-2	Newbury	0-1
Kempton	0-5	Thirsk	0-2	Newcastle	0-1
Lingfield	0-5	York	0-2	Pontefract	0-1
Doncaster	0-4	Ascot	0-1	Southwell (AW)	0-1
Brighton	0-3	Bath	0-1	Southwell (Turf)	0-1

WINNING HORSES

	Age	Races Run	1st	2nd	3rd	Unpl	Win £
Al Moulouki	3	16	5	1	0	10	18,383
Ya Malak	2	6	2	1	1	2	7,438
Glen Miller	3	10	2	0	1	7	5,265
El Arz	3	4	1	0	0	3	3,850
Domino Queen	2	7	1	1	1	4	3,285

WINNING OWNERS

	Races Won	Value £		Races Won	Value £
G Jabre	7	25,821	Nagy Azar	1	3,850
Mrs John Etherton	2	5,265	J G K Borrett	1	3,285

335

Favourites	4-9	44.4%	- 1.49	Total winning prize-money	£38,221

Longest winning sequence			3	Average SP of winner	3.3/1
Longest losing sequence			12	Return on stakes invested	-48.1%

1992 Form	9-103	8.7%	- 45.40	1990 Form	4-88	4.5%	- 67.50
1991 Form	12-82	14.6%	+ 26.83	1989 Form	5-113	4.4%	- 84.75

J PEARCE (Newmarket)

	No. of Horses	Races Run	1st	2nd	3rd	Unpl	Per cent	£1 Level Stake
2-y-o	4	13	0	0	0	13	-	- 13.00
3-y-o	6	27	1	0	1	25	3.7	- 23.75
4-y-o+	19	131	13	13	14	91	9.9	- 44.74
Totals	29	171	14	13	15	129	8.2	- 81.49

BY MONTH

2-y-o	W-R	Per cent	£1 Level Stake	3-y-o	W-R	Per cent	£1 Level Stake
January	0-0	-	0.00	January	0-0	-	0.00
February	0-0	-	0.00	February	0-0	-	0.00
March	0-0	-	0.00	March	0-1	-	- 1.00
April	0-0	-	0.00	April	0-1	-	- 1.00
May	0-0	-	0.00	May	0-5	-	- 5.00
June	0-1	-	- 1.00	June	1-5	20.0	- 1.75
July	0-2	-	- 2.00	July	0-9	-	- 9.00
August	0-2	-	- 2.00	August	0-1	-	- 1.00
September	0-4	-	- 4.00	September	0-2	-	- 2.00
Oct/Nov	0-4	-	- 4.00	Oct/Nov	0-3	-	- 3.00

4-y-o+	W-R	Per cent	£1 Level Stake	Totals	W-R	Per cent	£1 Level Stake
January	0-5	-	- 5.00	January	0-5	-	- 5.00
February	0-5	-	- 5.00	February	0-5	-	- 5.00
March	0-9	-	- 9.00	March	0-10	-	- 10.00
April	0-11	-	- 11.00	April	0-12	-	- 12.00
May	1-12	8.3	- 1.00	May	1-17	5.9	- 6.00
June	3-18	16.7	+ 1.63	June	4-24	16.7	- 1.12
July	0-22	-	- 22.00	July	0-33	-	- 33.00
August	5-20	25.0	+ 8.38	August	5-23	21.7	+ 5.38
September	3-13	23.1	+ 5.25	September	3-19	15.8	- 0.75
Oct/Nov	1-16	6.3	- 7.00	Oct/Nov	1-23	4.3	- 14.00

DISTANCE

2-y-o	W-R	Per cent	£1 Level Stake	3-y-o	W-R	Per cent	£1 Level Stake
5f-6f	0-3	-	- 3.00	5f-6f	0-7	-	- 7.00
7f-8f	0-9	-	- 9.00	7f-8f	0-10	-	- 10.00
9f-13f	0-1	-	- 1.00	9f-13f	1-10	10.0	- 6.75
14f+	0-0	-	0.00	14f+	0-0	-	0.00

4-y-o+	W-R	Per cent	£1 Level Stake	Totals	W-R	Per cent	£1 Level Stake
5f-6f	0-11	-	- 11.00	5f-6f	0-21	-	- 21.00
7f-8f	3-48	6.3	- 24.00	7f-8f	3-67	4.5	- 43.00
9f-13f	9-53	17.0	+ 1.26	9f-13f	10-64	15.6	- 6.49
14f+	1-19	5.3	- 11.00	14f+	1-19	5.3	- 11.00

TYPE OF RACE

Non-Handicaps	W-R	Per cent	£1 Level Stake	Handicaps	W-R	Per cent	£1 Level Stake
2-y-o	0-11	-	- 11.00	2-y-o	0-2	-	- 2.00
3-y-o	1-10	10.0	- 6.75	3-y-o	0-13	-	- 13.00
4-y-o+	2-29	6.9	- 21.87	4-y-o+	7-63	11.1	- 15.87
Selling	0-6	-	- 6.00	Selling	0-9	-	- 9.00
Apprentice	0-0	-	0.00	Apprentice	1-5	20.0	+ 6.00
Amat/Ladies	1-4	25.0	+ 4.00	Amat/Ladies	2-19	10.5	- 6.00
Totals	4-60	6.7	- 41.62	Totals	10-111	9.0	- 39.87

COURSE GRADE

	W-R	Per cent	£1 Level Stake
Group 1	2-43	4.7	- 26.00
Group 2	2-31	6.5	- 22.37
Group 3	4-58	6.9	- 31.25
Group 4	6-39	15.4	- 1.87

FIRST TIME OUT

	W-R	Per cent	£1 Level Stake
2-y-o	0-4	-	- 4.00
3-y-o	0-5	-	- 5.00
4-y-o+	2-18	11.1	0.00
Totals	2-27	7.4	- 9.00

JOCKEYS RIDING

	W-R	Per cent	£1 Level Stake		W-R	Per cent	£1 Level Stake
Mrs L Pearce	4-24	16.7	+ 5.00	M Wigham	2-49	4.1	- 43.12
G Bardwell	4-44	9.1	- 17.75	L Dettori	1-6	16.7	+ 4.00
J Tate	2-5	40.0	+ 2.38	Elizabeth Turner	1-7	14.3	+ 4.00

J McLaughlin	0-4	W Carson	0-2	P Robinson	0-1
F Norton	0-3	A McGlone	0-1	Pat Eddery	0-1
K Darley	0-3	B Raymond	0-1	S Davies	0-1
R Cochrane	0-3	D Nicholls	0-1	S Raymont	0-1
Alex Greaves	0-2	Dale Gibson	0-1	S Webster	0-1
G Duffield	0-2	M Hills	0-1	T G McLaughlin	0-1
J Lowe	0-2	M Tebbutt	0-1		
T Quinn	0-2	Mrs C Wilkinson	0-1		

COURSE RECORD

	Total W–R	Non-Handicaps 2-y-o	3-y-o+	Handicaps 2-y-o	3-y-o+	Per cent	£1 Level Stake
Edinburgh	3-7	0-0	0-2	0-1	3-4	42.9	+ 12.25
Folkestone	3-9	0-1	1-2	0-0	2-6	33.3	+ 8.88
Yarmouth	2-19	0-2	1-5	0-0	1-12	10.5	- 6.50
Epsom	1-1	0-0	0-0	0-0	1-1	100.0	+ 6.00
Brighton	1-2	0-0	0-1	0-0	1-1	50.0	+ 4.00
Ripon	1-5	0-0	1-1	0-0	0-4	20.0	- 2.37
Nottingham	1-9	0-3	1-3	0-0	0-3	11.1	- 5.75
Leicester	1-11	0-1	0-3	0-0	1-7	9.1	0.00
Newmarket	1-20	0-1	0-4	0-0	1-15	5.0	- 10.00

Southwell (AW)	0-13	Warwick	0-4	Ascot	0-1
Beverley	0-9	Chepstow	0-3	Carlisle	0-1
Lingfield	0-8	Lingfield (AW)	0-3	Catterick	0-1
Doncaster	0-7	Sandown	0-3	Chester	0-1
Thirsk	0-7	York	0-3	Hamilton	0-1
Redcar	0-6	Newcastle	0-2	Haydock	0-1
Kempton	0-5	Salisbury	0-2	Southwell (Turf)	0-1
Pontefract	0-4	Windsor	0-2		

WINNING HORSES

	Age	Races Run	1st	2nd	3rd	Unpl	Win £
Big Pat	4	11	5	0	3	3	15,634
Kelimutu	4	9	4	1	0	4	10,533
Guesstimation	4	13	2	1	1	9	5,148
Mysterious Maid	6	9	1	2	1	5	2,385
Beaumont	3	9	1	0	0	8	2,163
Chief Of Staff	4	7	1	0	1	5	1,730

WINNING OWNERS

	Races Won	Value £		Races Won	Value £
Burton Park Country Club	5	15,634	D J Maden	1	2,385
James Furlong	4	10,533	Garth Th'breds Ltd	1	2,163
Quintet Partnership	2	5,148	The Exclusive Partnership	1	1,730

Favourites	3-16	18.8%	- 7.24	Total winning prize-money			£37,592

Longest winning sequence		3	Average SP of winner		5.4/1
Longest losing sequence		47	Return on stakes invested		-47.7%

1992 Form	21-166	12.7%	- 37.81	1990 Form	13-119	10.9%	- 32.00
1991 Form	11-152	7.2%	- 92.25	1989 Form	5-72	6.9%	+ 24.00

MISS L A PERRATT (Ayr, Strathclyde)

	No. of Horses	Races Run	1st	2nd	3rd	Unpl	Per cent	£1 Level Stake
2-y-o	11	51	1	6	4	40	2.0	- 44.00
3-y-o	9	43	0	4	6	33	-	- 43.00
4-y-o+	10	63	6	6	7	44	9.5	- 28.00
Totals	30	157	7	16	17	117	4.5	-115.00

Jan	Feb	Mar	Apr	May	Jun	Jul	Aug	Sep	Oct/Nov
0-0	0-0	0-3	0-10	3-20	2-36	1-30	1-19	0-26	0-13

Winning Jockeys	W-R	£1 Level Stake		W-R	£1 Level Stake
R Havlin	3-23	- 2.25	J Marshall	1-6	0.00
Dale Gibson	2-10	- 1.75	J Fanning	1-49	- 42.00

Winning Courses	W-R	£1 Level Stake		W-R	£1 Level Stake
Hamilton	4-35	- 11.00	Haydock	1-7	- 2.00
Ripon	1-5	+ 2.00	Ayr	1-37	- 31.00

Winning Horses	Age	Races Run	1st	2nd	3rd	Unpl	Win £
Persuasive	6	9	2	2	1	4	10,114
Diet	7	19	3	1	0	15	8,030
Mister Piste	2	5	1	1	0	3	3,236
Francis Ann	5	7	1	1	1	4	2,899

Favourites	1-8	12.5%	- 4.75	Total winning prize-money		£24,279
1992 Form	10-160	6.3%	- 68.95	1991 Form	6-73 8.2%	+ 8.50

R T PHILLIPS (Wantage, Oxon)

	No. of Horses	Races Run	1st	2nd	3rd	Unpl	Per cent	£1 Level Stake
2-y-o	6	14	1	0	0	13	7.1	- 7.60
3-y-o	1	6	0	0	0	6	-	- 6.00
4-y-o+	4	16	0	1	0	15	-	- 16.00
Totals	11	36	1	1	0	34	2.8	- 29.60

Jan	Feb	Mar	Apr	May	Jun	Jul	Aug	Sep	Oct/Nov
0-0	0-0	0-0	0-4	0-4	0-8	0-6	0-4	1-5	0-5

Winning Jockey	W-R	£1 Level Stake	Winning Course	W-R	£1 Level Stake
A Clark	1-3	+ 3.40	Catterick	1-3	+ 3.40

Winning Horse	Age	Races Run	1st	2nd	3rd	Unpl	Win £
Queens Cottage	2	3	1	0	0	2	3,985

Favourites	0-0		Total winning prize-money	£3,985

MRS L PIGGOTT (Newmarket)

	No. of Horses	Races Run	1st	2nd	3rd	Unpl	Per cent	£1 Level Stake
2-y-o	4	17	1	0	2	14	5.9	+ 4.00
3-y-o	7	23	1	1	1	20	4.3	- 14.50
4-y-o+	5	34	8	5	2	19	23.5	+ 12.11
Totals	16	74	10	6	5	53	13.5	+ 1.61

BY MONTH

2-y-o	W-R	Per cent	£1 Level Stake	3-y-o	W-R	Per cent	£1 Level Stake
January	0-0	-	0.00	January	0-1	-	- 1.00
February	0-0	-	0.00	February	0-2	-	- 2.00
March	0-0	-	0.00	March	1-2	50.0	+ 6.50
April	0-0	-	0.00	April	0-6	-	- 6.00
May	0-0	-	0.00	May	0-5	-	- 5.00
June	0-1	-	- 1.00	June	0-1	-	- 1.00
July	0-2	-	- 2.00	July	0-2	-	- 2.00
August	0-6	-	- 6.00	August	0-2	-	- 2.00
September	0-4	-	- 4.00	September	0-1	-	- 1.00
Oct/Nov	1-4	25.0	+ 17.00	Oct/Nov	0-1	-	- 1.00

4-y-o+	W-R	Per cent	£1 Level Stake	Totals	W-R	Per cent	£1 Level Stake
January	0-2	-	- 2.00	January	0-3	-	- 3.00
February	0-1	-	- 1.00	February	0-3	-	- 3.00
March	0-0	-	0.00	March	1-2	50.0	+ 6.50
April	0-2	-	- 2.00	April	0-8	-	- 8.00
May	0-2	-	- 2.00	May	0-7	-	- 7.00
June	0-4	-	- 4.00	June	0-6	-	- 6.00
July	1-3	33.3	- 1.00	July	1-7	14.3	- 5.00
August	5-8	62.5	+ 28.70	August	5-16	31.3	+ 20.70
September	1-7	14.3	- 5.09	September	1-12	8.3	- 10.09
Oct/Nov	1-5	20.0	+ 0.50	Oct/Nov	2-10	20.0	+ 16.50

DISTANCE

2-y-o	W-R	Per cent	£1 Level Stake	3-y-o	W-R	Per cent	£1 Level Stake
5f-6f	0-6	-	- 6.00	5f-6f	0-9	-	- 9.00
7f-8f	1-10	10.0	+ 11.00	7f-8f	1-9	11.1	- 0.50
9f-13f	0-1	-	- 1.00	9f-13f	0-5	-	- 5.00
14f+	0-0	-	0.00	14f+	0-0	-	0.00

4-y-o+	W-R	Per cent	£1 Level Stake	Totals	W-R	Per cent	£1 Level Stake
5f-6f	0-0	-	0.00	5f-6f	0-15	-	- 15.00
7f-8f	4-19	21.1	+ 6.41	7f-8f	6-38	15.8	+ 16.91
9f-13f	3-9	33.3	+ 6.70	9f-13f	3-15	20.0	+ 0.70
14f+	1-6	16.7	- 1.00	14f+	1-6	16.7	- 1.00

TYPE OF RACE

Non-Handicaps	W-R	Per cent	£1 Level Stake	Handicaps	W-R	Per cent	£1 Level Stake
2-y-o	0-10	-	- 10.00	2-y-o	1-3	33.3	+ 18.00
3-y-o	1-10	10.0	- 1.50	3-y-o	0-13	-	- 13.00
4-y-o+	2-5	40.0	- 1.09	4-y-o+	6-24	25.0	+ 18.20
Selling	0-3	-	- 3.00	Selling	0-1	-	- 1.00
Apprentice	0-0	-	0.00	Apprentice	0-3	-	- 3.00
Amat/Ladies	0-0	-	0.00	Amat/Ladies	0-2	-	- 2.00
Totals	3-28	10.7	- 15.59	Totals	7-46	15.2	+ 17.20

COURSE GRADE

	W-R	Per cent	£1 Level Stake
Group 1	1-23	4.3	- 16.50
Group 2	1-8	12.5	0.00
Group 3	3-25	12.0	- 12.59
Group 4	5-18	27.8	+ 30.70

FIRST TIME OUT

	W-R	Per cent	£1 Level Stake
2-y-o	0-4	-	- 4.00
3-y-o	1-7	14.3	+ 1.50
4-y-o+	0-3	-	- 3.00
Totals	1-14	7.1	- 5.50

JOCKEYS RIDING

	W-R	Per cent	£1 Level Stake		W-R	Per cent	£1 Level Stake
J Quinn	4-8	50.0	+ 22.70	Renee Kierans	1-1	100.0	+ 5.50
L Piggott	4-30	13.3	+ 3.41	A Mackay	1-3	33.3	+ 2.00

G Milligan	0-14	W Ryan	0-2	Mr C Appleby	0-1
J Williams	0-5	G Duffield	0-1	Mrs J Crossley	0-1
A McGlone	0-2	L Dettori	0-1	Mrs M Haggas	0-1
A Munro	0-2	M Roberts	0-1	Sally Radford-Howes	0-1

COURSE RECORD

	Total W-R	Non-Handicaps 2-y-o	3-y-o+	Handicaps 2-y-o	3-y-o+	Per cent	£1 Level Stake
Warwick	2-3	0-1	0-0	1-1	1-1	66.7	+ 23.00
Lingfield (AW)	2-9	0-0	0-2	0-0	2-7	22.2	- 1.30
Yarmouth	2-13	0-5	2-2	0-0	0-6	15.4	- 9.09
Ripon	1-1	0-0	0-0	0-0	1-1	100.0	+ 7.00
Southwell (AW)	1-5	0-0	0-2	0-0	1-3	20.0	+ 10.00
Leicester	1-8	0-0	1-5	0-1	0-2	12.5	+ 0.50
Newmarket	1-13	0-3	0-1	0-0	1-9	7.7	- 6.50

Chester	0-3	Nottingham	0-2	Folkestone	0-1
Brighton	0-2	Sandown	0-2	Goodwood	0-1
Kempton	0-2	York	0-2	Pontefract	0-1
Lingfield	0-2	Ascot	0-1		
Newbury	0-2	Bath	0-1		

WINNING HORSES

	Age	Races Run	1st	2nd	3rd	Unpl	Win £
Dashing Fellow	5	9	4	1	1	3	13,886
Shining Jewel	6	14	3	2	1	8	8,218
Shoofk	2	6	1	0	0	5	3,754
Aude La Belle	5	6	1	2	0	3	3,582
Sehailah	3	4	1	0	0	3	3,290

WINNING OWNERS

	Races Won	Value £		Races Won	Value £
Mrs Val Rapkins	5	17,468	Ali K Al Jafleh	2	7,043
D W Rolt	3	8,218			

Favourites	4-7	57.1%	+ 4.11	Total winning prize-money	£32,729

Longest winning sequence	2	Average SP of winner	6.6/1
Longest losing sequence	21	Return on stakes invested	2.2%

1992 Form	10-118	8.5%	- 68.50	1990 Form	13-193	6.7%	- 122.70
1991 Form	15-179	8.4%	- 86.87	1989 Form	34-209	16.3%	- 32.64

M C PIPE (Wellington, Somerset)

	No. of Horses	Races Run	1st	2nd	3rd	Unpl	Per cent	£1 Level Stake
2-y-o	4	14	4	2	2	6	28.6	+ 27.88
3-y-o	9	27	7	5	3	12	25.9	+ 18.50
4-y-o+	15	58	8	8	8	34	13.8	- 8.50
Totals	28	99	19	15	13	52	19.2	+ 37.88

BY MONTH

2-y-o	W-R	Per cent	£1 Level Stake	3-y-o	W-R	Per cent	£1 Level Stake
January	0-0	-	0.00	January	0-0	-	0.00
February	0-0	-	0.00	February	0-0	-	0.00
March	0-0	-	0.00	March	0-0	-	0.00
April	0-0	-	0.00	April	0-2	-	- 2.00
May	0-0	-	0.00	May	0-2	-	- 2.00
June	1-2	50.0	+ 6.00	June	2-9	22.2	+ 2.50
July	0-0	-	0.00	July	1-6	16.7	+ 1.00
August	0-4	-	- 4.00	August	3-4	75.0	+ 14.00
September	2-6	33.3	+ 25.50	September	0-2	-	- 2.00
Oct/Nov	1-2	50.0	+ 0.38	Oct/Nov	1-2	50.0	+ 7.00

4-y-o+	W-R	Per cent	£1 Level Stake	Totals	W-R	Per cent	£1 Level Stake
January	0-0	-	0.00	January	0-0	-	0.00
February	1-1	100.0	+ 5.00	February	1-1	100.0	+ 5.00
March	1-2	50.0	+ 1.50	March	1-2	50.0	+ 1.50
April	1-5	20.0	- 2.00	April	1-7	14.3	- 4.00
May	2-16	12.5	- 5.50	May	2-18	11.1	- 7.50
June	3-15	20.0	+ 11.50	June	6-26	23.1	+ 20.00
July	0-8	-	- 8.00	July	1-14	7.1	- 7.00
August	0-1	-	- 1.00	August	3-9	33.3	+ 9.00
September	0-3	-	- 3.00	September	2-11	18.2	+ 20.50
Oct/Nov	0-7	-	- 7.00	Oct/Nov	2-11	18.2	+ 0.38

DISTANCE

2-y-o	W-R	Per cent	£1 Level Stake	3-y-o	W-R	Per cent	£1 Level Stake
5f-6f	1-7	14.3	+ 1.00	5f-6f	0-1	-	- 1.00
7f-8f	3-6	50.0	+ 27.88	7f-8f	0-3	-	- 3.00
9f-13f	0-1	-	- 1.00	9f-13f	6-19	31.6	+ 19.50
14f+	0-0	-	0.00	14f+	1-4	25.0	+ 3.00

4-y-o+	W-R	Per cent	£1 Level Stake	Totals	W-R	Per cent	£1 Level Stake
5f-6f	0-1	-	- 1.00	5f-6f	1-9	11.1	- 1.00
7f-8f	4-24	16.7	+ 3.00	7f-8f	7-33	21.2	+ 27.88
9f-13f	0-16	-	- 16.00	9f-13f	6-36	16.7	+ 2.50
14f+	4-17	23.5	+ 5.50	14f+	5-21	23.8	+ 8.50

TYPE OF RACE

Non-Handicaps	W-R	Per cent	£1 Level Stake	Handicaps	W-R	Per cent	£1 Level Stake
2-y-o	4-12	33.3	+ 29.88	2-y-o	0-1	-	- 1.00
3-y-o	2-8	25.0	+ 2.00	3-y-o	4-16	25.0	+ 10.50
4-y-o+	2-11	18.2	- 1.50	4-y-o+	5-38	13.2	- 2.50
Selling	0-3	-	- 3.00	Selling	0-3	-	- 3.00
Apprentice	0-0	-	0.00	Apprentice	1-4	25.0	+ 0.50
Amat/Ladies	0-2	-	- 2.00	Amat/Ladies	1-1	100.0	+ 8.00
Totals	8-36	22.2	+ 25.38	Totals	11-63	17.5	+ 12.50

COURSE GRADE

	W-R	Per cent	£1 Level Stake
Group 1	8-38	21.1	+ 20.50
Group 2	3-15	20.0	- 4.12
Group 3	2-27	7.4	+ 6.00
Group 4	6-19	31.6	+ 15.50

FIRST TIME OUT

	W-R	Per cent	£1 Level Stake
2-y-o	1-4	25.0	+ 4.00
3-y-o	0-2	-	- 2.00
4-y-o+	1-15	6.7	- 9.00
Totals	2-21	9.5	- 7.00

343

Pipe M C

JOCKEYS RIDING

	W–R	Per cent	£1 Level Stake		W–R	Per cent	£1 Level Stake
M Perrett	3–16	18.8	+ 3.00	L Dettori	1–3	33.3	+ 1.00
A Munro	2–5	40.0	+ 5.00	R Painter	1–3	33.3	+ 1.50
D Harrison	2–8	25.0	+ 10.50	J Reid	1–3	33.3	+ 3.00
A McGlone	2–9	22.2	+ 5.00	M Roberts	1–4	25.0	+ 4.00
C Asmussen	1–1	100.0	+ 5.00	J Quinn	1–5	20.0	+ 1.00
J Weaver	1–1	100.0	+ 25.00	Paul Eddery	1–5	20.0	– 1.50
Mr N Moore	1–1	100.0	+ 8.00	Pat Eddery	1–6	16.7	– 3.62

J Williams	0–4	D Holland	0–1	O Pears	0–1
W Carson	0–3	L Carter	0–1	R Cochrane	0–1
G Duffield	0–2	L Piggott	0–1	R Hills	0–1
S Davies	0–2	M Hills	0–1	S Drowne	0–1
S Whitworth	0–2	Mrs L Pearce	0–1	S Mulvey	0–1
A Clark	0–1	Mrs M Cowdrey	0–1	W R Swinburn	0–1
B Rouse	0–1	N Adams	0–1	W Ryan	0–1

COURSE RECORD

	Total W–R	Non-Handicaps 2-y-o	Non-Handicaps 3-y-o+	Handicaps 2-y-o	Handicaps 3-y-o+	Per cent	£1 Level Stake
Brighton	2–3	0–0	1–1	0–0	1–2	66.7	+ 5.50
Sandown	2–3	0–0	1–1	0–0	1–2	66.7	+ 6.00
Southwell (Turf)	2–4	2–2	0–0	0–0	0–2	50.0	+ 9.50
Warwick	2–9	0–0	1–3	0–0	1–6	22.2	– 3.00
Folkestone	1–2	0–0	0–1	0–0	1–1	50.0	+ 7.00
Haydock	1–3	0–1	0–0	0–0	1–2	33.3	+ 4.50
Southwell (AW)	1–3	0–0	1–3	0–0	0–0	33.3	+ 3.00
Ascot	1–4	0–0	0–1	0–0	1–3	25.0	+ 5.00
Epsom	1–4	0–0	0–0	0–0	1–4	25.0	+ 9.00
Leicester	1–4	1–1	0–1	0–0	0–2	25.0	+ 22.00
Goodwood	1–5	0–0	0–1	0–0	1–4	20.0	+ 1.00
Kempton	1–5	0–1	0–0	0–0	1–4	20.0	+ 3.00
Newbury	1–5	0–1	0–0	0–0	1–4	20.0	+ 1.00
Chester	1–6	1–1	0–0	0–0	0–5	16.7	– 3.62
Chepstow	1–9	0–1	0–1	0–0	1–7	11.1	– 2.00

Bath	0–5	Nottingham	0–3	York	0–2
Newmarket	0–4	Lingfield	0–2	Doncaster	0–1
Salisbury	0–4	Newcastle	0–2	Lingfield (AW)	0–1
Windsor	0–4	Yarmouth	0–2		

WINNING HORSES

	Age	Races Run	1st	2nd	3rd	Unpl	Win £
Balasani	7	5	2	1	0	2	23,847
General Mouktar	3	8	3	3	1	1	19,085
Robingo	4	4	2	1	0	1	17,120
Silky Siren	4	14	4	3	3	4	12,518

Cotteir Chief	2	5	3	0	2	0	9,957
Pondering	3	4	2	0	1	1	5,418
Tandia	2	4	1	0	0	3	4,271
Top Rank	3	6	1	0	1	4	3,260
Regalsett	3	1	1	0	0	0	2,749

WINNING OWNERS

	Races Won	Value £		Races Won	Value £
M & N Plant Ltd	5	27,077	M C Pipe	2	5,418
M D Smith	2	23,847	Trevor Painting	1	4,271
A S Helaissi	3	19,085	A McPharland	1	3,260
S Nixon	4	12,518	David S Lewis	1	2,749

Favourites	5-29	17.2%	- 11.62	Total winning prize-money		£98,225
Longest winning sequence			2	Average SP of winner		6.2/1
Longest losing sequence			14	Return on stakes invested		38.3%
1992 Form	15-95	15.8%	- 18.42	1990 Form	10-50	20.0% + 2.28
1991 Form	17-97	17.5%	- 2.15	1989 Form	2-23	8.7% - 6.00

SIR MARK PRESCOTT (Newmarket)

	No. of Horses	Races Run	1st	2nd	3rd	Unpl	Per cent	£1 Level Stake
2-y-o	25	70	11	13	6	40	15.7	- 15.52
3-y-o	23	142	35	28	23	56	24.6	- 16.83
4-y-o+	9	48	7	6	6	29	14.6	- 5.50
Totals	57	260	53	47	35	125	20.4	- 37.85

BY MONTH

2-y-o	W-R	Per cent	£1 Level Stake	3-y-o	W-R	Per cent	£1 Level Stake
January	0-0	-	0.00	January	1-5	20.0	- 2.75
February	0-0	-	0.00	February	0-1	-	- 1.00
March	0-0	-	0.00	March	4-10	40.0	+ 4.61
April	0-0	-	0.00	April	5-16	31.3	+ 3.78
May	0-0	-	0.00	May	7-21	33.3	- 3.51
June	1-10	10.0	- 4.00	June	8-27	29.6	- 0.22
July	0-12	-	- 12.00	July	1-13	7.7	- 10.62
August	3-5	60.0	+ 6.62	August	5-18	27.8	- 0.25
September	4-19	21.1	+ 9.20	September	4-20	20.0	+ 4.13
Oct/Nov	3-24	12.5	- 15.34	Oct/Nov	0-11	-	- 11.00

4-y-o+	W-R	Per cent	£1 Level Stake	Totals	W-R	Per cent	£1 Level Stake
January	0-1	–	- 1.00	January	1-6	16.7	- 3.75
February	1-3	33.3	+ 7.00	February	1-4	25.0	+ 6.00
March	0-1	–	- 1.00	March	4-11	36.4	+ 3.61
April	1-4	25.0	- 2.00	April	6-20	30.0	+ 1.78
May	0-5	–	- 5.00	May	7-26	26.9	- 8.51
June	1-7	14.3	+ 1.00	June	10-44	22.7	- 3.22
July	0-6	–	- 6.00	July	1-31	3.2	- 28.62
August	3-11	27.3	+ 7.50	August	11-34	32.4	+ 13.87
September	1-6	16.7	- 2.00	September	9-45	20.0	+ 11.33
Oct/Nov	0-4	–	- 4.00	Oct/Nov	3-39	7.7	- 30.34

DISTANCE

2-y-o	W-R	Per cent	£1 Level Stake	3-y-o	W-R	Per cent	£1 Level Stake
5f-6f	8-39	20.5	- 5.27	5f-6f	8-32	25.0	+ 1.34
7f-8f	3-30	10.0	- 9.25	7f-8f	15-65	23.1	- 8.32
9f-13f	0-1	–	- 1.00	9f-13f	10-36	27.8	- 9.60
14f+	0-0	–	0.00	14f+	2-9	22.2	- 0.25

4-y-o+	W-R	Per cent	£1 Level Stake	Totals	W-R	Per cent	£1 Level Stake
5f-6f	1-3	33.3	- 1.00	5f-6f	17-74	23.0	- 4.93
7f-8f	4-20	20.0	+ 7.00	7f-8f	22-115	19.1	- 10.57
9f-13f	1-20	5.0	- 16.50	9f-13f	11-57	19.3	- 27.10
14f+	1-5	20.0	+ 5.00	14f+	3-14	21.4	+ 4.75

TYPE OF RACE

Non-Handicaps	W-R	Per cent	£1 Level Stake	Handicaps	W-R	Per cent	£1 Level Stake
2-y-o	8-56	14.3	- 26.72	2-y-o	1-12	8.3	+ 3.00
3-y-o	18-63	28.6	- 3.77	3-y-o	15-67	22.4	- 11.61
4-y-o+	3-12	25.0	- 2.00	4-y-o+	2-25	8.0	- 6.00
Selling	2-7	28.6	+ 3.20	Selling	3-8	37.5	+ 6.05
Apprentice	0-0	–	0.00	Apprentice	1-4	25.0	+ 6.00
Amat/Ladies	0-4	–	- 4.00	Amat/Ladies	0-2	–	- 2.00
Totals	31-142	21.8	- 33.29	Totals	22-118	18.6	- 4.56

COURSE GRADE

	W-R	Per cent	£1 Level Stake
Group 1	9-53	17.0	- 25.18
Group 2	10-46	21.7	+ 15.48
Group 3	15-70	21.4	+ 2.78
Group 4	19-91	20.9	- 30.93

FIRST TIME OUT

	W-R	Per cent	£1 Level Stake
2-y-o	3-25	12.0	- 8.00
3-y-o	9-23	39.1	+ 5.41
4-y-o+	1-9	11.1	- 7.00
Totals	13-57	22.8	- 9.59

JOCKEYS RIDING

	W-R	Per cent	£1 Level Stake		W-R	Per cent	£1 Level Stake
G Duffield	40-177	22.6	- 19.58	K Darley	1-3	33.3	+ 1.00
A Munro	2-5	40.0	- 0.52	G Bardwell	1-4	25.0	+ 11.00
M Roberts	2-6	33.3	+ 3.00	Miss I D W Jones	1-4	25.0	- 1.62
M Birch	2-8	25.0	0.00	K Rutter	1-5	20.0	+ 5.00
M Hills	1-1	100.0	+ 0.62	C Nutter	1-22	4.5	- 19.75
R Cochrane	1-1	100.0	+ 7.00				

T Quinn	0-4	Dale Gibson	0-1	Mr T Jenks	0-1
G Carter	0-2	Emma O'Gorman	0-1	N Carlisle	0-1
G Hind	0-2	J Quinn	0-1	R Hills	0-1
Pat Eddery	0-2	K Fallon	0-1	S Davies	0-1
W Ryan	0-2	Miss E Bronson	0-1	T G McLaughlin	0-1
D Biggs	0-1	Mr S Swiers	0-1		

COURSE RECORD

	Total W-R	Non-Handicaps 2-y-o	3-y-o+	Handicaps 2-y-o	3-y-o+	Per cent	£1 Level Stake
Southwell (AW)	7-30	0-3	6-13	0-0	1-14	23.3	- 9.02
Brighton	6-12	1-2	3-5	1-1	1-4	50.0	+ 23.60
Hamilton	4-10	1-1	0-1	0-1	3-7	40.0	- 0.13
Yarmouth	4-16	1-5	0-2	0-0	3-9	25.0	+ 11.62
Carlisle	3-4	0-0	1-1	0-0	2-3	75.0	+ 2.89
Newcastle	3-10	0-3	1-3	0-0	2-4	30.0	- 3.23
Lingfield (AW)	3-12	0-0	2-6	0-0	1-6	25.0	+ 1.47
Folkestone	3-16	1-5	1-6	0-2	1-3	18.8	- 4.75
Kempton	2-5	0-0	1-2	0-0	1-3	40.0	+ 2.10
Ayr	2-6	1-1	1-2	0-0	0-3	33.3	+ 0.20
Bath	2-8	1-2	1-3	0-1	0-2	25.0	- 4.09
Ripon	2-8	1-1	0-2	0-0	1-5	25.0	+ 2.88
Catterick	2-12	1-5	1-4	0-1	0-2	16.7	- 6.62
Nottingham	2-13	0-3	0-3	0-0	2-7	15.4	+ 6.00
Beverley	1-4	0-1	1-2	0-0	0-1	25.0	0.00
Haydock	1-4	0-1	0-0	0-0	1-3	25.0	0.00
York	1-4	0-1	0-1	0-0	1-2	25.0	- 0.25
Chepstow	1-6	1-4	0-2	0-0	0-0	16.7	0.00
Edinburgh	1-7	0-0	0-2	0-0	1-5	14.3	- 4.90
Leicester	1-8	0-0	1-5	0-0	0-3	12.5	- 5.62
Lingfield	1-9	1-3	0-3	0-0	0-3	11.1	0.00
Redcar	1-10	0-4	1-5	0-1	0-0	10.0	- 4.00

Doncaster	0-7	Southwell (Turf)	0-4	Epsom	0-1
Goodwood	0-7	Windsor	0-3	Newbury	0-1
Warwick	0-6	Ascot	0-2	Salisbury	0-1
Newmarket	0-5	Pontefract	0-2	Sandown	0-1
Thirsk	0-5	Chester	0-1		

WINNING HORSES

	Age	Races Run	1st	2nd	3rd	Unpl	Win £
Just You Dare	3	10	4	4	0	2	16,562
The Where Withal	3	8	5	0	0	3	14,140
Quinsigimond	3	9	4	3	0	2	11,593
Hasten To Add	3	6	2	2	1	1	9,141
Quantity Surveyor	4	11	2	1	2	6	7,213
Resonant	2	7	2	2	1	2	6,983
Velasco	3	6	2	1	1	2	6,627
Keyway	3	11	2	1	2	6	6,404
Battle Colours	4	8	2	1	0	5	6,128
Sylvan Starlight	3	8	2	1	1	4	5,504
Nichodoula	3	10	2	3	5	0	5,453
Seama	3	8	2	3	1	2	5,069
Sabo The Hero	3	5	2	0	0	3	4,810
North Reef	2	2	1	0	0	1	4,342
Amnesia	2	2	1	1	0	0	3,609
Time Honored	3	5	1	0	0	4	3,391
Wizard King	2	6	1	1	0	4	3,340
Second Sight	2	6	1	0	0	5	3,325
Case Law	6	3	1	0	0	2	3,145
Purple Fling	2	3	1	1	0	1	3,007
One Voice	3	2	1	0	0	1	2,925
Amoret	2	3	1	0	0	2	2,868
Serious Action	4	4	1	0	2	1	2,832
Sloe Brandy	3	6	1	0	1	4	2,721
Karinska	3	3	1	1	0	1	2,658
Rispoto	3	9	1	2	3	3	2,445
Chilly Breeze	3	10	1	3	2	4	2,355
Diamond Point	3	2	1	0	1	0	2,322
Land O'Lakes	3	3	1	0	0	2	2,243
Post Mistress	2	5	1	1	1	2	2,243
Sharpening	2	1	1	0	0	0	2,243
Pie Hatch	4	8	1	2	2	3	2,070
Segala	2	2	1	0	0	1	2,005

WINNING OWNERS

	Races Won	Value £		Races Won	Value £
Mrs David Thompson	7	24,517	Hesmonds Stud	2	5,453
W E Sturt	7	20,725	Fahd Salman	2	5,069
Cheveley Park Stud	4	12,233	P G Goulandris	2	4,800
A E T Mines	4	11,593	Sheikh Ahmed Bin Saeed –		
Lady Fairhaven	3	9,934	Al Maktoum	1	3,340
Pin Oak Stable	2	9,141	Neil Greig	1	3,325
G E Shouler	2	6,627	Faisal Salman	1	2,868
B Haggas	2	6,404	G Moore	1	2,832
Pinnacle Racing Stable	2	6,316	Saeed Manana	1	2,658
Garth Insoll	2	6,128	Lord Derby	1	2,322
G D Waters	2	5,852	Miss Elizabeth Aldous	1	2,070
Mrs R A Johnson	2	5,504	Mrs Michael Ennever	1	2,005

Favourites	35-79	44.3%	+ 5.65	Total winning prize-money		£161,714

Longest winning sequence		3	Average SP of winner		3.2/1
Longest losing sequence		38	Return on stakes invested		-14.6%

1992 Form	50-281	17.8%	- 42.77	1990 Form	48-265	18.1%	- 35.55
1991 Form	48-238	20.2%	+ 14.32	1989 Form	40-247	16.2%	- 54.45

R J PRICE (Leominster, H'ford & Worcs)

	No. of Horses	Races Run	1st	2nd	3rd	Unpl	Per cent	£1 Level Stake
2-y-o	0	0	0	0	0	0	-	0.00
3-y-o	3	9	0	0	0	9	-	- 9.00
4-y-o+	5	20	2	2	1	15	10.0	- 5.80
Totals	8	29	2	2	1	24	6.9	- 14.80

Jan	Feb	Mar	Apr	May	Jun	Jul	Aug	Sep	Oct/Nov
0-0	0-0	0-2	0-5	0-4	0-3	1-4	0-4	0-3	1-4

Winning Jockey	W-R	£1 Level Stake			W-R	£1 Level Stake
T Sprake	2-4	+ 10.20				

Winning Courses						
Lingfield	1-3	+ 3.00	Nottingham		1-12	- 3.80

Winning Horses	Age	Races Run	1st	2nd	3rd	Unpl	Win £
Flakey Dove	7	3	1	0	0	2	3,816
Singing Reply	5	9	1	2	1	5	3,132

Favourites	1-2	50.0%	+ 4.00	Total winning prize-money	£6,948

1992 Form	2-16	12.5%	+ 6.00

G A PRITCHARD-GORDON (Newmarket)

	No. of Horses	Races Run	1st	2nd	3rd	Unpl	Per cent	£1 Level Stake
2-y-o	13	54	6	5	6	37	11.1	+ 4.75
3-y-o	12	53	4	1	3	45	7.5	- 20.00
4-y-o+	7	23	3	0	0	20	13.0	+ 1.50
Totals	32	130	13	6	9	102	10.0	- 13.75

Pritchard-Gordon G A

BY MONTH

2-y-o	W-R	Per cent	£1 Level Stake	3-y-o	W-R	Per cent	£1 Level Stake
January	0-0	-	0.00	January	0-0	-	0.00
February	0-0	-	0.00	February	0-0	-	0.00
March	0-1	-	- 1.00	March	0-1	-	- 1.00
April	1-5	20.0	+ 1.50	April	2-7	28.6	+ 9.50
May	1-4	25.0	+ 17.00	May	0-9	-	- 9.00
June	0-8	-	- 8.00	June	0-8	-	- 8.00
July	2-11	18.2	- 4.25	July	1-8	12.5	+ 1.00
August	0-7	-	- 7.00	August	1-7	14.3	+ 0.50
September	2-9	22.2	+ 15.50	September	0-9	-	- 9.00
Oct/Nov	0-9	-	- 9.00	Oct/Nov	0-4	-	- 4.00

4-y-o+	W-R	Per cent	£1 Level Stake	Totals	W-R	Per cent	£1 Level Stake
January	0-0	-	0.00	January	0-0	-	0.00
February	0-1	-	- 1.00	February	0-1	-	- 1.00
March	0-0	-	0.00	March	0-2	-	- 2.00
April	0-4	-	- 4.00	April	3-16	18.8	+ 7.00
May	0-6	-	- 6.00	May	1-19	5.3	+ 2.00
June	1-1	100.0	+ 9.00	June	1-17	5.9	- 7.00
July	1-3	33.3	+ 4.00	July	4-22	18.2	+ 0.75
August	1-3	33.3	+ 4.50	August	2-17	11.8	- 2.00
September	0-2	-	- 2.00	September	2-20	10.0	+ 4.50
Oct/Nov	0-3	-	- 3.00	Oct/Nov	0-16	-	- 16.00

DISTANCE

2-y-o	W-R	Per cent	£1 Level Stake	3-y-o	W-R	Per cent	£1 Level Stake
5f-6f	4-41	9.8	- 3.75	5f-6f	1-11	9.1	- 3.00
7f-8f	2-12	16.7	+ 9.50	7f-8f	3-28	10.7	- 3.00
9f-13f	0-1	-	- 1.00	9f-13f	0-14	-	- 14.00
14f+	0-0	-	0.00	14f+	0-0	-	0.00

4-y-o+	W-R	Per cent	£1 Level Stake	Totals	W-R	Per cent	£1 Level Stake
5f-6f	0-0	-	0.00	5f-6f	5-52	9.6	- 6.75
7f-8f	0-9	-	- 9.00	7f-8f	5-49	10.2	- 2.50
9f-13f	0-6	-	- 6.00	9f-13f	0-21	-	- 21.00
14f+	3-8	37.5	+ 16.50	14f+	3-8	37.5	+ 16.50

TYPE OF RACE

Non-Handicaps	W-R	Per cent	£1 Level Stake	Handicaps	W-R	Per cent	£1 Level Stake
2-y-o	5-40	12.5	+ 11.25	2-y-o	1-8	12.5	- 0.50
3-y-o	1-21	4.8	- 12.50	3-y-o	2-17	11.8	- 1.50
4-y-o+	0-0	-	0.00	4-y-o+	2-17	11.8	+ 0.50
Selling	0-11	-	- 11.00	Selling	1-5	20.0	+ 4.00
Apprentice	0-2	-	- 2.00	Apprentice	0-4	-	- 4.00
Amat/Ladies	0-1	-	- 1.00	Amat/Ladies	1-4	25.0	+ 3.00
Totals	6-75	8.0	- 15.25	Totals	7-55	12.7	+ 1.50

350

COURSE GRADE

	W-R	Per cent	£1 Level Stake
Group 1	6-52	11.5	+ 3.50
Group 2	2-17	11.8	+ 2.25
Group 3	3-33	9.1	- 10.00
Group 4	2-28	7.1	- 9.50

FIRST TIME OUT

	W-R	Per cent	£1 Level Stake
2-y-o	2-13	15.4	- 2.00
3-y-o	1-12	8.3	- 3.50
4-y-o+	0-6	-	- 6.00
Totals	3-31	9.7	- 11.50

JOCKEYS RIDING

	W-R	Per cent	£1 Level Stake		W-R	Per cent	£1 Level Stake
G Carter	2-3	66.7	+ 11.50	L Dettori	1-6	16.7	+ 1.50
D Harrison	2-34	5.9	- 10.50	D Wright	1-8	12.5	0.00
T Williams	1-2	50.0	+ 7.00	G Duffield	1-8	12.5	- 5.75
W R Swinburn	1-3	33.3	+ 4.50	N Day	1-9	11.1	+ 12.00
Mr P P-Gordon	1-5	20.0	+ 2.00	W Hood	1-17	5.9	- 8.50
P Robinson	1-5	20.0	+ 2.50				

N Carlisle	0-6	A Martinez	0-1	J Weaver	0-1
Antoinette Armes	0-4	C Hawksley	0-1	M Fenton	0-1
B Doyle	0-3	D Moffatt	0-1	Miss L Hide	0-1
Paul Eddery	0-3	F Norton	0-1	P Tulk	0-1
A McGlone	0-2	J Fanning	0-1		
W Carson	0-2	J O'Dwyer	0-1		

COURSE RECORD

	Total W-R	Non-Handicaps 2-y-o	3-y-o+	Handicaps 2-y-o	3-y-o+	Per cent	£1 Level Stake
Yarmouth	2-16	0-3	0-4	0-0	2-9	12.5	- 1.00
Ascot	1-1	0-0	0-0	1-1	0-0	100.0	+ 6.50
Hamilton	1-1	0-0	0-0	0-0	1-1	100.0	+ 7.00
Ayr	1-2	0-1	0-0	0-0	1-1	50.0	+ 7.00
Ripon	1-3	1-1	0-0	0-1	0-1	33.3	- 0.75
Warwick	1-3	0-0	0-1	0-1	1-1	33.3	+ 7.00
Doncaster	1-5	0-0	0-1	0-0	1-4	20.0	+ 2.00
Newbury	1-5	1-3	0-1	0-1	0-0	20.0	+ 16.00
Brighton	1-6	1-3	0-1	0-0	0-2	16.7	+ 11.00
Kempton	1-6	1-4	0-1	0-0	0-1	16.7	+ 0.50
Sandown	1-7	1-3	0-2	0-1	0-1	14.3	- 2.50
Southwell (AW)	1-7	0-3	1-3	0-0	0-1	14.3	+ 1.50

Newmarket	0-15	Nottingham	0-3	Catterick	0-1
Folkestone	0-14	Salisbury	0-3	Haydock	0-1
Goodwood	0-6	Bath	0-2	Newcastle	0-1
Leicester	0-6	Epsom	0-2	Thirsk	0-1
Windsor	0-5	Lingfield	0-2	York	0-1
Lingfield (AW)	0-3	Redcar	0-2		

WINNING HORSES

	Age	Races Run	1st	2nd	3rd	Unpl	Win £
Alzianah	2	10	2	1	2	5	13,290
Farmer's Pet	4	8	3	0	0	5	9,479
Adamparis	3	8	2	1	0	5	5,679
Prince Babar	2	5	1	2	1	1	4,175
Nijo	2	2	1	1	0	0	3,649
Million At Dawn	2	2	1	0	0	1	3,377
Candi Das	2	9	1	1	2	5	3,261
Burishki	3	4	1	0	0	3	2,768
Trianglepoint	3	6	1	0	0	5	2,243

WINNING OWNERS

	Races Won	Value £		Races Won	Value £
Sheikh Amin Dahlawi	2	13,290	Sheikh Ahmed Bin Saeed -		
Giles W Pritchard-Gordon	3	10,204	Al Maktoum	1	3,649
D R Midwood	3	9,479	Million In Mind Partnership (2)	1	3,377
Invoshire Ltd	2	5,679	S A Meacock	1	2,243

Favourites	3-11	27.3%	+ 2.75	Total winning prize-money £47,922
Longest winning sequence			2	Average SP of winner 7.9/1
Longest losing sequence			27	Return on stakes invested -10.6%
1992 Form	17-183	9.3%	- 63.92	1990 Form 18-201 9.0% - 74.95
1991 Form	14-223	6.3%	- 94.26	1989 Form 16-223 7.2% -108.95

MRS J RAMSDEN (Thirsk, North Yorks)

	No. of Horses	Races Run	1st	2nd	3rd	Unpl	Per cent	£1 Level Stake
2-y-o	17	85	11	12	8	54	12.9	- 25.34
3-y-o	11	68	8	14	6	40	11.8	- 24.62
4-y-o+	17	121	11	7	8	95	9.1	- 1.67
Totals	45	274	30	33	22	189	10.9	- 51.63

BY MONTH

2-y-o	W-R	Per cent	£1 Level Stake	3-y-o	W-R	Per cent	£1 Level Stake
January	0-0	-	0.00	January	0-0	-	0.00
February	0-0	-	0.00	February	0-0	-	0.00
March	0-1	-	- 1.00	March	1-4	25.0	+ 1.00
April	0-3	-	- 3.00	April	1-12	8.3	- 7.00
May	0-2	-	- 2.00	May	2-11	18.2	+ 3.00
June	1-8	12.5	- 4.25	June	1-11	9.1	- 8.25
July	4-25	16.0	+ 5.41	July	0-8	-	- 8.00
August	1-18	5.6	- 15.00	August	1-5	20.0	- 2.37
September	3-15	20.0	0.00	September	2-10	20.0	+ 4.00
Oct/Nov	2-13	15.4	- 5.50	Oct/Nov	0-7	-	- 7.00

4-y-o+	W-R	Per cent	£1 Level Stake	Totals	W-R	Per cent	£1 Level Stake
January	0-4	-	- 4.00	January	0-4	-	- 4.00
February	0-1	-	- 1.00	February	0-1	-	- 1.00
March	1-8	12.5	+ 9.00	March	2-13	15.4	+ 9.00
April	1-19	5.3	- 11.50	April	2-34	5.9	- 21.50
May	1-20	5.0	- 7.00	May	3-33	9.1	- 6.00
June	2-16	12.5	- 0.50	June	4-35	11.4	- 13.00
July	3-17	17.6	+ 24.00	July	7-50	14.0	+ 21.41
August	1-8	12.5	0.00	August	3-31	9.7	- 17.37
September	1-9	11.1	+ 4.00	September	6-34	17.6	+ 8.00
Oct/Nov	1-19	5.3	- 14.67	Oct/Nov	3-39	7.7	- 27.17

DISTANCE

2-y-o	W-R	Per cent	£1 Level Stake	3-y-o	W-R	Per cent	£1 Level Stake
5f-6f	8-60	13.3	- 11.84	5f-6f	3-12	25.0	+ 4.00
7f-8f	3-25	12.0	- 13.50	7f-8f	1-21	4.8	- 14.00
9f-13f	0-0	-	0.00	9f-13f	4-32	12.5	- 11.62
14f+	0-0	-	0.00	14f+	0-3	-	- 3.00

4-y-o+	W-R	Per cent	£1 Level Stake	Totals	W-R	Per cent	£1 Level Stake
5f-6f	1-7	14.3	+ 0.50	5f-6f	12-79	15.2	- 7.34
7f-8f	6-62	9.7	+ 22.50	7f-8f	10-108	9.3	- 5.00
9f-13f	2-31	6.5	- 15.50	9f-13f	6-63	9.5	- 27.12
14f+	2-21	9.5	- 9.17	14f+	2-24	8.3	- 12.17

TYPE OF RACE

Non-Handicaps	W-R	Per cent	£1 Level Stake	Handicaps	W-R	Per cent	£1 Level Stake
2-y-o	5-46	10.9	- 16.09	2-y-o	5-35	14.3	- 9.00
3-y-o	1-10	10.0	- 5.00	3-y-o	6-51	11.8	- 15.25
4-y-o+	1-8	12.5	- 0.50	4-y-o+	9-98	9.2	+ 6.33
Selling	2-6	33.3	+ 0.38	Selling	1-9	11.1	- 1.50
Apprentice	0-1	-	- 1.00	Apprentice	0-9	-	- 9.00
Amat/Ladies	0-0	-	0.00	Amat/Ladies	0-1	-	- 1.00
Totals	9-71	12.7	- 22.21	Totals	21-203	10.3	- 29.42

Ramsden Mrs J

COURSE GRADE

	W-R	Per cent	£1 Level Stake
Group 1	12-123	9.8	- 20.59
Group 2	3-38	7.9	- 14.50
Group 3	9-72	12.5	- 17.92
Group 4	6-41	14.6	+ 1.38

FIRST TIME OUT

	W-R	Per cent	£1 Level Stake
2-y-o	2-16	12.5	+ 2.50
3-y-o	1-10	10.0	- 5.00
4-y-o+	1-15	6.7	+ 2.00
Totals	4-41	9.8	- 0.50

JOCKEYS RIDING

	W-R	Per cent	£1 Level Stake		W-R	Per cent	£1 Level Stake
K Fallon	20-142	14.1	- 27.63	M Roberts	1-3	33.3	+ 4.00
D Thomas	3-21	14.3	+ 9.00	V Halliday	1-3	33.3	+ 3.50
J Weaver	2-6	33.3	+ 12.50	A Mackay	1-5	20.0	+ 8.00
M Hills	1-3	33.3	+ 23.00	J Lowe	1-9	11.1	- 2.00

Raymond Berry	0-8	J Quinn	0-3	G Hind	0-1
S Maloney	0-7	K Darley	0-3	J Reid	0-1
D Moffatt	0-5	B Doyle	0-2	L Dettori	0-1
B Russell	0-4	C Teague	0-2	M Birch	0-1
D Biggs	0-4	D Holland	0-2	Mrs S Cumani	0-1
J Carroll	0-4	D McKeown	0-2	R Cochrane	0-1
M Wigham	0-4	Dale Gibson	0-2	S Drowne	0-1
P Robinson	0-4	N Carlisle	0-2	T Williams	0-1
S Davies	0-4	O Pears	0-2	W Carson	0-1
A Munro	0-3	D Harrison	0-1	W Ryan	0-1
J Fanning	0-3	G Carter	0-1		

COURSE RECORD

	Total W-R	Non-Handicaps 2-y-o	3-y-o+	Handicaps 2-y-o	3-y-o+	Per cent	£1 Level Stake
Doncaster	5-38	0-3	0-2	1-4	4-29	13.2	+ 29.50
Carlisle	3-11	2-5	0-1	0-0	1-5	27.3	+ 18.75
Beverley	3-15	1-3	0-0	0-2	2-10	20.0	+ 6.50
Ayr	2-9	0-0	0-0	1-2	1-7	22.2	+ 2.50
Thirsk	2-12	1-4	0-0	1-3	0-5	16.7	+ 3.50
Nottingham	2-13	0-3	0-1	0-1	2-8	15.4	- 1.17
Catterick	2-18	0-4	1-2	0-6	1-6	11.1	- 8.00
Newmarket	2-21	0-1	1-1	1-2	0-17	9.5	- 10.50
Pontefract	2-28	0-4	0-5	0-3	2-16	7.1	- 14.50
Sandown	1-2	1-1	0-0	0-1	0-0	50.0	+ 1.00
Southwell (Turf)	1-2	0-0	1-2	0-0	0-0	50.0	+ 0.63
Hamilton	1-8	0-3	0-1	0-1	1-3	12.5	- 5.25
Leicester	1-8	0-1	0-1	1-3	0-3	12.5	- 3.50
Redcar	1-10	0-1	0-1	0-2	1-6	10.0	- 2.00
Newcastle	1-19	1-6	0-1	0-2	0-10	5.3	- 17.09
Haydock	1-21	0-3	0-0	0-2	1-16	4.8	- 13.00

Ripon	0-14	Edinburgh	0-3	Goodwood	0-1
Ascot	0-5	Chester	0-2	Warwick	0-1
York	0-5	Lingfield (AW)	0-2		
Southwell (AW)	0-4	Newbury	0-2		

WINNING HORSES

	Age	Races Run	1st	2nd	3rd	Unpl	Win £
High Premium	5	6	1	1	0	4	48,413
Island Magic	2	3	2	1	0	0	26,688
Self Expression	5	18	3	0	1	14	20,121
Rafferty's Rules	2	8	2	2	1	3	12,827
Hob Green	4	11	1	1	0	9	11,453
Primula Bairn	3	11	3	2	0	6	10,361
Hazard A Guess	3	10	3	1	1	5	10,058
Beats Working	2	6	2	0	1	3	7,967
Will Of Steel	4	9	1	0	1	7	7,439
Multi National	2	3	1	2	0	0	4,338
Wordsmith	3	10	1	3	2	4	4,110
Close To Reality	2	10	1	3	1	5	3,641
Sillars Stalker	5	6	1	0	0	5	3,611
Arctic Diamond	2	7	1	0	0	6	3,522
Cool Enough	12	16	1	2	1	12	3,287
Browned Off	4	5	1	0	0	4	3,236
Tahitian	4	7	1	0	0	6	3,080
Harpo's Special	2	8	1	1	1	5	2,553
Midnight Magpie	2	4	1	0	1	2	2,406
Balzino	4	9	1	0	1	7	2,163
Wonderful Years	3	5	1	0	1	3	2,070

WINNING OWNERS

	Races Won	Value £		Races Won	Value £
P A Leonard	2	59,865	O Soberg-Olsen	3	9,891
M R Charlton	4	34,655	Mrs B D Southam	2	7,163
Jonathan Ramsden	3	20,121	L Mann	1	4,338
K E Wheldon	3	12,681	Sir Timothy Kitson	1	4,110
J E Swiers	2	11,131	Sillars Civil Engineering	1	3,611
Kavli	3	10,361	Mrs J R Ramsden	1	3,287
Mrs D Ridley	3	10,058	Milton Wong	1	2,070

Favourites	6-49	12.2%	- 30.96	Total winning prize-money	£193,341
Longest winning sequence			2	Average SP of winner	6.4/1
Longest losing sequence			23	Return on stakes invested	-18.8%
1992 Form	23-249	9.2%	- 87.12	1990 Form	26-239	10.9%	- 104.32
1991 Form	38-294	12.9%	-123.50	1989 Form	32-249	12.9%	- 53.95

MRS M REVELEY (Lingdale, Co Cleveland)

	No. of Horses	Races Run	1st	2nd	3rd	Unpl	Per cent	£1 Level Stake
2-y-o	20	94	10	9	16	59	10.6	- 35.76
3-y-o	23	116	15	15	14	72	12.9	- 24.33
4-y-o+	50	305	57	45	36	167	18.7	- 42.12
Totals	93	515	82	69	66	298	15.9	-102.21

BY MONTH

2-y-o	W-R	Per cent	£1 Level Stake	3-y-o	W-R	Per cent	£1 Level Stake
Mar/Apr	0-0	-	0.00	Mar/Apr	2-7	28.6	+ 2.50
May	2-11	18.2	- 5.05	May	0-18	-	- 18.00
June	0-8	-	- 8.00	June	1-17	5.9	- 13.00
July	3-17	17.6	+ 2.58	July	5-24	20.8	+ 7.79
August	0-14	-	- 14.00	August	5-22	22.7	+ 6.38
September	2-22	9.1	- 5.67	September	0-16	-	- 16.00
Oct/Nov	3-22	13.6	- 5.62	Oct/Nov	2-12	16.7	+ 9.00

4-y-o+	W-R	Per cent	£1 Level Stake	Totals	W-R	Per cent	£1 Level Stake
Mar/Apr	11-30	36.7	+ 7.86	Mar/Apr	13-37	35.1	+ 10.36
May	7-41	17.1	- 6.62	May	9-70	12.9	- 29.67
June	5-51	9.8	- 35.83	June	6-76	7.9	- 56.83
July	18-60	30.0	+ 22.42	July	26-101	25.7	+ 32.79
August	7-48	14.6	- 22.54	August	12-84	14.3	- 30.16
September	2-32	6.3	- 12.50	September	4-70	5.7	- 34.17
Oct/Nov	7-43	16.3	- 13.60	Oct/Nov	12-77	15.6	- 10.22

DISTANCE

2-y-o	W-R	Per cent	£1 Level Stake	3-y-o	W-R	Per cent	£1 Level Stake
5f-6f	8-64	12.5	- 17.09	5f-6f	4-21	19.0	- 3.12
7f-8f	2-29	6.9	- 17.67	7f-8f	2-30	6.7	- 5.00
9f-13f	0-1	-	- 1.00	9f-13f	7-51	13.7	- 15.21
14f+	0-0	-	0.00	14f+	2-14	14.3	- 1.00

4-y-o+	W-R	Per cent	£1 Level Stake	Totals	W-R	Per cent	£1 Level Stake
5f-6f	0-9	-	- 9.00	5f-6f	12-94	12.8	- 29.21
7f-8f	12-77	15.6	- 19.87	7f-8f	16-136	11.8	- 42.54
9f-13f	33-135	24.4	+ 17.50	9f-13f	40-187	21.4	+ 1.29
14f+	12-84	14.3	- 31.94	14f+	14-98	14.3	- 32.94

TYPE OF RACE

Non-Handicaps	W-R	Per cent	£1 Level Stake	Handicaps	W-R	Per cent	£1 Level Stake
2-y-o	6-55	10.9	- 28.14	2-y-o	3-32	9.4	- 10.62
3-y-o	7-35	20.0	+ 14.50	3-y-o	5-59	8.5	- 31.21
4-y-o+	7-41	17.1	- 22.15	4-y-o+	39-216	18.1	- 29.67
Selling	1-19	5.3	- 17.60	Selling	3-13	23.1	+ 5.88
Apprentice	1-4	25.0	0.00	Apprentice	7-23	30.4	+ 15.63
Amat/Ladies	1-1	100.0	+ 0.67	Amat/Ladies	2-17	11.8	+ 0.50
Totals	23-155	14.8	- 52.72	Totals	59-360	16.4	- 49.49

COURSE GRADE

	W-R	Per cent	£1 Level Stake
Group 1	25-184	13.6	- 56.82
Group 2	19-128	14.8	- 18.72
Group 3	26-123	21.1	- 27.84
Group 4	12-80	15.0	+ 1.17

FIRST TIME OUT

	W-R	Per cent	£1 Level Stake
2-y-o	1-17	5.9	- 14.80
3-y-o	2-21	9.5	- 14.50
4-y-o+	9-49	18.4	+ 14.60
Totals	12-87	13.8	- 14.70

JOCKEYS RIDING

	W-R	Per cent	£1 Level Stake		W-R	Per cent	£1 Level Stake
K Darley	42-197	21.3	- 17.30	F Norton	2-10	20.0	- 2.12
D Moffatt	8-71	11.3	- 27.16	Gaye Harwood	1-1	100.0	+ 2.25
J Lowe	6-34	17.6	- 7.25	Mr S Swiers	1-2	50.0	- 0.33
S Copp	5-20	25.0	+ 10.25	J Williams	1-2	50.0	+ 11.00
K Fallon	3-10	30.0	+ 9.52	Wendy Jones	1-3	33.3	+ 3.00
J Fanning	3-34	8.8	- 6.25	G Duffield	1-4	25.0	- 0.25
R Cochrane	2-6	33.3	+ 3.10	T Quinn	1-6	16.7	- 1.67
S Maloney	2-8	25.0	+ 6.00	W Ryan	1-10	10.0	- 5.50
Mr M Buckley	2-9	22.2	+ 8.50				

M Birch	0-15	Mrs M Cowdrey	0-2	M Baird	0-1
Dale Gibson	0-10	N Day	0-2	M Perrett	0-1
D McKeown	0-7	B Raymond	0-1	M Roberts	0-1
W Newnes	0-5	C Rutter	0-1	Mr L Donnelly	0-1
A Munro	0-4	C Teague	0-1	N Connorton	0-1
J Carroll	0-4	D Denby	0-1	N Varley	0-1
L Dettori	0-4	D Griffiths	0-1	P Robinson	0-1
D Wright	0-3	D Harrison	0-1	Pat Eddery	0-1
A Procter	0-2	J Fortune	0-1	Paul Eddery	0-1
G Carter	0-2	J Quinn	0-1	W Carson	0-1
M Hills	0-2	J Reid	0-1	W Hawksley	0-1
Miss A Yardley	0-2	L Charnock	0-1		
Miss J Winter	0-2	L Piggott	0-1		

COURSE RECORD

	Total W-R	Non-Handicaps 2-y-o	3-y-o+	Handicaps 2-y-o	3-y-o+	Per cent	£1 Level Stake
Redcar	14-87	0-10	4-17	0-6	10-54	16.1	+ 2.78
Hamilton	9-30	2-4	2-6	0-1	5-19	30.0	+ 0.52
Newcastle	9-45	2-8	1-8	1-1	5-28	20.0	- 1.13
Beverley	8-31	0-2	1-3	0-1	7-25	25.8	- 9.84
Catterick	6-32	0-2	2-9	0-5	4-16	18.8	+ 9.00
Pontefract	5-28	0-6	1-8	0-2	4-12	17.9	- 4.52
Doncaster	5-43	0-4	1-3	0-5	4-31	11.6	- 18.50
Carlisle	4-16	0-1	1-4	0-0	3-11	25.0	+ 1.17
Newmarket	4-21	0-1	2-4	1-3	1-13	19.0	+ 1.75
Ayr	4-26	2-5	1-7	0-1	1-13	15.4	- 10.02
Thirsk	2-15	0-2	0-4	0-1	2-8	13.3	- 5.75
Nottingham	2-17	0-3	0-1	0-2	2-11	11.8	- 6.50
Haydock	2-19	0-2	0-2	0-1	2-14	10.5	- 1.67
Ripon	2-24	0-1	1-6	0-1	1-16	8.3	16.00
Chepstow	1-2	0-0	0-1	1-1	0-0	50.0	+ 2.00
Chester	1-2	0-0	0-0	0-0	1-2	50.0	+ 0.25
Leicester	1-8	0-1	0-2	0-1	1-4	12.5	- 2.50
Southwell (Turf)	1-8	0-2	0-3	1-1	0-2	12.5	+ 7.00
Edinburgh	1-18	0-0	0-3	0-0	1-15	5.6	- 10.00
York	1-21	0-4	0-1	0-1	1-15	4.8	- 18.25

Yarmouth	0-6	Warwick		0-3	Bath		0-1
Ascot	0-3	Kempton		0-2	Goodwood		0-1
Southwell (AW)	0-3	Newbury		0-2	Sandown		0-1

WINNING HORSES

	Age	Races Run	1st	2nd	3rd	Unpl	Win £
Northern Graduate	4	10	5	3	0	2	22,123
Mellottie	8	6	2	0	0	4	20,831
Efizia	3	10	5	1	1	3	15,852
Sweet Mignonette	5	12	5	0	1	6	14,906
Majed	5	5	2	1	0	2	14,006
Grey Power	6	11	4	1	0	6	12,844
Taroudant	6	9	4	1	0	4	12,816
Amazing Feat	4	9	2	2	1	4	11,848
Azureus	5	12	3	2	0	7	9,599
Express Gift	4	11	2	3	1	5	9,223
Dangerous Shadow	2	13	3	1	3	6	8,833
Sunderland Echo	4	6	3	1	0	2	8,704
White Willow	4	13	2	3	2	6	8,215
Persian Soldier	6	8	2	1	1	4	7,646
My Desire	5	8	2	2	1	3	7,182
Trevorsninepoints	3	11	3	2	2	4	6,943
Merry Nutkin	7	5	2	0	1	2	6,164
Batabanoo	4	5	2	0	1	2	5,951
Kagram Queen	5	5	2	0	1	2	5,562
Mondragon	3	11	2	3	2	4	5,540
Once More For Luck	2	8	2	0	1	5	5,518
Broctune Gold	2	11	2	1	3	5	5,185

Essayeffsee	4	11	2	1	2	6	4,661
Bold Timing	2	2	1	0	0	1	4,125
Mill Force	2	4	1	1	1	1	3,718
Avishayes	6	5	1	0	0	4	3,688
Surrey Dancer	5	4	1	2	0	1	3,678
Roberty Lea	5	7	1	2	0	4	3,630
Jazilah	5	7	1	2	3	1	3,465
Spring Loaded	2	7	1	0	1	5	3,417
Eurythmic	3	4	1	0	1	2	3,273
Kayartis	4	6	1	2	2	1	3,184
Grace Card	7	2	1	0	1	0	3,106
Viardot	4	4	1	0	0	3	3,106
Fletcher's Bounty	4	11	1	1	4	5	3,072
Second Colours	3	10	1	0	1	8	2,951
Lady Donoghue	4	9	1	0	2	6	2,889
Duke Of Dreams	3	8	1	0	1	6	2,821
Try N' Fly	3	6	1	1	1	3	2,660
Jalcanto	3	6	1	0	0	5	2,512
Mr Woodcock	8	8	1	2	1	4	2,469
Mystic Memory	4	7	1	2	1	3	2,385

WINNING OWNERS

	Races Won	Value £		Races Won	Value £
P D Savill	11	46,289	Mrs E A Kettlewell	2	5,562
Mrs J G Fulton	2	20,831	Skeltools Ltd	2	5,540
Laurel (Leisure) Ltd	3	17,684	D Playforth	2	5,185
G A Farndon	5	15,922	Mrs S D Murray	2	4,661
Mrs H I S Calzini	5	15,852	Clearview Partnership	1	4,125
Ron Whitehead	5	14,906	R Meredith	1	3,718
Mrs H North	3	11,321	P Davidson-Brown	1	3,688
J C Murdoch	3	9,599	Wentdale Const Ltd	1	3,630
M Horner, H Young & D Arnold	2	9,223	S Aitken	1	3,465
Prime Maintenance	3	8,833	J Shack	1	3,273
Northeast Press Ltd	3	8,704	Mrs J M Allen	1	3,184
C C Buckley	3	8,407	P Willis	1	3,072
Norman Firth	2	7,646	Miss E Shepherd	1	2,821
Miss Jane Spensley	2	7,182	P Caplan	1	2,660
T S Child	3	6,943	William A Davies	1	2,512
A Frame	2	6,787	P A Tylor	1	2,469
Robert F S Newall	2	6,164	Carnoustie Racing Club Ltd	1	2,385
J P S Racing	2	6,057			

Favourites	42-128	32.8%	- 7.83	Total winning prize-money			£290,295
Longest winning sequence			5	Average SP of winner			4.0/1
Longest losing sequence			50	Return on stakes invested			-19.8%
1992 Form	68-326	20.9%	- 2.87	1990 Form	15-146	10.3%	+ 1.42
1991 Form	34-226	15.0%	- 56.47	1989 Form	15-131	11.5%	- 39.37

B RICHMOND (Wellingore, Lincs)

	No. of Horses	Races Run	1st	2nd	3rd	Unpl	Per cent	£1 Level Stake
2-y-o	0	0	0	0	0	0	-	0.00
3-y-o	2	10	0	0	1	9	-	- 10.00
4-y-o+	7	38	3	3	6	26	7.9	+ 22.00
Totals	9	48	3	3	7	35	6.3	+ 12.00

Jan	Feb	Mar	Apr	May	Jun	Jul	Aug	Sep	Oct/Nov
2-7	0-8	0-5	0-1	0-7	0-5	1-5	0-4	0-2	0-4

Winning Jockeys	W-R	£1 Level Stake		W-R	£1 Level Stake
Mrs M Morris	1-1	+ 33.00	Alex Greaves	1-10	+ 7.00
T Williams	1-7	+ 2.00			

Winning Courses	W-R	£1 Level Stake		W-R	£1 Level Stake
Southwell (AW)	2-27	+ 16.00	Pontefract	1-2	+ 15.00

Winning Horses	Age	Races Run	1st	2nd	3rd	Unpl	Win £
Bedouin Prince	6	13	2	2	4	5	4,896
Modest Hope	6	10	1	0	1	8	3,688

Favourites	0-1	Total winning prize-money	£8,584

1992 Form	0-20	1990 Form	0-17
1991 Form	0-7	1989 Form	0-8

B S ROTHWELL (Catwick, North Humberside)

	No. of Horses	Races Run	1st	2nd	3rd	Unpl	Per cent	£1 Level Stake
2-y-o	13	62	3	2	5	52	4.8	- 32.00
3-y-o	9	54	1	5	5	43	1.9	- 20.00
4-y-o+	3	7	0	0	0	7	-	- 7.00
Totals	25	123	4	7	10	102	3.3	- 59.00

Jan	Feb	Mar	Apr	May	Jun	Jul	Aug	Sep	Oct/Nov
0-0	0-0	1-1	1-9	1-14	0-28	0-10	1-17	0-20	0-24

Winning Jockeys	W-R	£1 Level Stake		W-R	£1 Level Stake
D Harrison	2-41	- 22.00	S Wood	1-27	+ 7.00
J Quinn	1-12	- 1.00			

Winning Courses	W-R	£1 Level Stake		W-R	£1 Level Stake
Doncaster	2-9	+ 13.00	Beverley	1-25	- 17.00
Southwell (AW)	1-10	+ 24.00			

Winning Horses	Age	Races Run	1st	2nd	3rd	Unpl	Win £
Ochos Rios	2	11	2	2	2	5	5,503
Bandon Castle	2	6	1	0	0	5	3,688
Colfax Classic	3	8	1	0	1	6	3,494

Favourites	0-2			Total winning prize-money			£12,685

1992 Form   3-60   5.0%   - 31.00   1991 Form   0-5

R ROWE (Pulborough, West Sussex)

	No. of Horses	Races Run	1st	2nd	3rd	Unpl	Per cent	£1 Level Stake
2-y-o	0	0	0	0	0	0	-	0.00
3-y-o	5	11	0	0	0	11	-	- 11.00
4-y-o+	8	25	1	0	1	23	4.0	- 8.00
Totals	13	36	1	0	1	34	2.8	- 19.00

Jan	Feb	Mar	Apr	May	Jun	Jul	Aug	Sep	Oct/Nov
0-0	0-2	0-0	0-2	0-2	1-3	0-9	0-7	0-6	0-5

Winning Jockey	W-R	£1 Level Stake	Winning Course	W-R	£1 Level Stake
B Raymond	1-1	+ 16.00	Goodwood	1-6	+ 11.00

Winning Horse	Age	Races Run	1st	2nd	3rd	Unpl	Win £
Touching Times	5	5	1	0	0	4	2,415

Favourites	0-2		Total winning prize-money	£2,415

1992 Form   1-12   8.3%   - 5.50

M J RYAN (Newmarket)

	No. of Horses	Races Run	1st	2nd	3rd	Unpl	Per cent	£1 Level Stake
2-y-o	8	38	3	3	3	29	7.9	- 22.50
3-y-o	8	57	8	5	2	42	14.0	+ 9.00
4-y-o+	9	84	12	15	7	50	14.3	- 0.46
Totals	25	179	23	23	12	121	12.8	- 13.96

BY MONTH

2-y-o	W–R	Per cent	£1 Level Stake	3-y-o	W–R	Per cent	£1 Level Stake
January	0-0	-	0.00	January	0-0	-	0.00
February	0-0	-	0.00	February	0-0	-	0.00
March	0-0	-	0.00	March	0-0	-	0.00
April	0-5	-	- 5.00	April	0-3	-	- 3.00
May	0-2	-	- 2.00	May	1-6	16.7	+ 1.00
June	0-6	-	- 6.00	June	0-7	-	- 7.00
July	1-4	25.0	- 1.50	July	2-14	14.3	- 3.50
August	1-7	14.3	- 2.00	August	2-8	25.0	+ 10.50
September	0-6	-	- 6.00	September	0-7	-	- 7.00
Oct/Nov	1-8	12.5	0.00	Oct/Nov	3-12	25.0	+ 18.00

4-y-o+	W–R	Per cent	£1 Level Stake	Totals	W–R	Per cent	£1 Level Stake
January	0-2	-	- 2.00	January	0-2	-	- 2.00
February	0-0	-	0.00	February	0-0	-	0.00
March	0-0	-	0.00	March	0-0	-	0.00
April	0-8	-	- 8.00	April	0-16	-	- 16.00
May	3-13	23.1	+ 29.00	May	4-21	19.0	+ 28.00
June	1-13	7.7	- 8.50	June	1-26	3.8	- 21.50
July	6-20	30.0	+ 6.71	July	9-38	23.7	+ 1.71
August	0-10	-	- 10.00	August	3-25	12.0	- 1.50
September	1-9	11.1	- 3.00	September	1-22	4.5	- 16.00
Oct/Nov	1-9	11.1	- 4.67	Oct/Nov	5-29	17.2	+ 13.33

DISTANCE

2-y-o	W–R	Per cent	£1 Level Stake	3-y-o	W–R	Per cent	£1 Level Stake
5f-6f	3-30	10.0	- 14.50	5f-6f	0-0	-	0.00
7f-8f	0-8	-	- 8.00	7f-8f	5-27	18.5	+ 16.50
9f-13f	0-0	-	0.00	9f-13f	2-20	10.0	- 9.50
14f+	0-0	-	0.00	14f+	1-10	10.0	+ 2.00

4-y-o+	W–R	Per cent	£1 Level Stake	Totals	W–R	Per cent	£1 Level Stake
5f-6f	4-31	12.9	- 12.20	5f-6f	7-61	11.5	- 26.70
7f-8f	6-30	20.0	+ 9.24	7f-8f	11-65	16.9	+ 17.74
9f-13f	0-11	-	- 11.00	9f-13f	2-31	6.5	- 20.50
14f+	2-12	16.7	+ 13.50	14f+	3-22	13.6	+ 15.50

TYPE OF RACE

Non-Handicaps	W–R	Per cent	£1 Level Stake	Handicaps	W–R	Per cent	£1 Level Stake
2-y-o	1-25	4.0	- 22.50	2-y-o	2-10	20.0	+ 3.00
3-y-o	0-13	-	- 13.00	3-y-o	5-34	14.7	+ 6.00
4-y-o+	1-10	10.0	- 8.09	4-y-o+	10-68	14.7	+ 9.13
Selling	0-6	-	- 6.00	Selling	2-5	40.0	+ 12.00
Apprentice	0-0	-	0.00	Apprentice	2-8	25.0	+ 5.50
Amat/Ladies	0-0	-	0.00	Amat/Ladies	0-0	-	0.00
Totals	2-54	3.7	- 49.59	Totals	21-125	16.8	+ 35.63

Ryan M J

COURSE GRADE

	W-R	Per cent	£1 Level Stake
Group 1	3-53	5.7	- 8.00
Group 2	2-36	5.6	- 25.50
Group 3	13-67	19.4	+ 27.50
Group 4	5-23	21.7	- 7.96

FIRST TIME OUT

	W-R	Per cent	£1 Level Stake
2-y-o	0-8	-	- 8.00
3-y-o	0-8	-	- 8.00
4-y-o+	0-9	-	- 9.00
Totals	0-25	-	- 25.00

JOCKEYS RIDING

	W-R	Per cent	£1 Level Stake		W-R	Per cent	£1 Level Stake
D Biggs	8-69	11.6	- 9.20	W Carson	1-3	33.3	+ 3.00
P McCabe	7-40	17.5	+ 10.50	M Baird	1-5	20.0	+ 4.00
P Robinson	3-16	18.8	+ 1.91	G Bardwell	1-9	11.1	- 3.50
A Tucker	2-4	50.0	+ 12.33				

C Hodgson	0-5	M Hills	0-2	G Duffield	0-1
L Piggott	0-4	R Cochrane	0-2	G Hind	0-1
M Tebbutt	0-3	A Procter	0-1	J Weaver	0-1
T Beaver	0-3	D Wright	0-1	K Rutter	0-1
A Clark	0-2	F Norton	0-1	S Davies	0-1
L Dettori	0-2	G Carter	0-1	S Raymont	0-1

COURSE RECORD

	Total W-R	Non-Handicaps 2-y-o	3-y-o+	Handicaps 2-y-o	3-y-o+	Per cent	£1 Level Stake
Leicester	3-18	0-5	0-2	0-1	3-10	16.7	+ 4.00
Yarmouth	3-24	0-4	0-6	0-1	3-13	12.5	- 7.00
Bath	2-3	1-1	0-1	0-0	1-1	66.7	+ 5.50
Pontefract	2-3	0-0	0-0	1-1	1-2	66.7	+ 20.00
Lingfield (AW)	2-4	0-0	0-0	0-0	2-4	50.0	+ 2.13
Nottingham	2-10	0-2	0-3	0-0	2-5	20.0	+ 8.50
Catterick	1-2	0-1	0-0	0-0	1-1	50.0	0.00
Warwick	1-2	0-0	0-0	1-1	0-1	50.0	+ 3.00
Newbury	1-4	0-0	0-0	0-0	1-4	25.0	+ 17.00
Southwell (AW)	1-4	0-0	1-2	0-0	0-2	25.0	- 2.09
Goodwood	1-5	0-0	0-0	0-0	1-5	20.0	+ 10.00
Beverley	1-6	0-0	0-1	0-0	1-5	16.7	- 0.50
Lingfield	1-8	0-2	0-3	0-0	1-3	12.5	- 3.50
Brighton	1-10	0-0	0-2	0-0	1-8	10.0	- 4.00
Newmarket	1-14	0-6	0-0	0-1	1-7	7.1	- 5.00

Kempton	0-13	Haydock	0-3	Ayr	0-1
Folkestone	0-9	Sandown	0-3	Epsom	0-1
Redcar	0-8	Ascot	0-2	Hamilton	0-1
Salisbury	0-7	Southwell (Turf)	0-2	Newcastle	0-1
Doncaster	0-4	Windsor	0-2		
Chester	0-3	York	0-2		

Ryan M J

WINNING HORSES

	Age	Races Run	1st	2nd	3rd	Unpl	Win £
Misty Silks	3	11	4	2	0	5	17,625
Kingchip Boy	4	13	3	2	1	7	11,573
Roca Murada	4	11	3	2	0	6	10,637
Truthful Image	4	16	3	3	0	10	9,233
Western Dynasty	7	15	2	2	2	9	6,233
Prima Silk	2	10	2	1	2	5	5,985
Just Flamenco	2	7	1	0	0	6	3,262
Island Knight	4	15	1	3	2	9	2,821
Tocco Jewel	3	7	1	0	0	6	2,679
Jolis Absent	3	9	1	3	1	4	2,512
Billyback	3	7	1	0	0	6	2,448
Side Bar	3	7	1	0	1	5	2,058

WINNING OWNERS

	Races Won	Value £		Races Won	Value £
P E Axon	7	26,858	Knight Group	1	2,821
Four Jays Racing Partnership	3	11,573	Mrs M J Ryan	1	2,679
Tim Corby	3	10,637	Peter Hart	1	2,512
M F Kentish	2	6,233	M J Ryan	1	2,448
Three Ply Racing	2	5,985	P J Flavin	1	2,058
Mrs S M Martin	1	3,262			

Favourites	5-16	31.3%	- 3.46	Total winning prize-money			£77,066
Longest winning sequence			2	Average SP of winner			6.2/1
Longest losing sequence			29	Return on stakes invested			-7.8%
1992 Form	22-182	12.1%	- 38.74	1990 Form	32-233	13.7%	- 0.16
1991 Form	23-234	9.8%	- 63.50	1989 Form	13-200	6.5%	- 30.49

MISS B SANDERS (Epsom, Surrey)

	No. of Horses	Races Run	1st	2nd	3rd	Unpl	Per cent	£1 Level Stake
2-y-o	1	4	0	0	1	3	-	- 4.00
3-y-o	6	31	3	3	4	21	9.7	+ 34.00
4-y-o+	5	29	4	2	2	21	13.8	+ 28.00
Totals	12	64	7	5	7	45	10.9	+ 58.00

Jan	Feb	Mar	Apr	May	Jun	Jul	Aug	Sep	Oct/Nov
1-4	0-2	0-0	0-4	0-6	4-15	1-14	1-13	0-5	0-1

Winning Jockeys	W-R	£1 Level Stake		W-R	£1 Level Stake
N Adams	1-1	+ 3.00	A Martinez	1-7	+ 8.00
Antoinette Armes	1-4	+ 47.00	A Clark	1-7	+ 19.00
M Roberts	1-5	+ 1.00	W Newnes	1-21	- 11.00
B Rouse	1-6	+ 4.00			

Winning Courses					
Lingfield (AW)	2-10	+ 31.00	Windsor	1-6	+ 4.00
Epsom	2-11	- 1.00	Sandown	1-8	+ 43.00
Brighton	1-5	+ 5.00			

Winning Horses	Age	Races Run	1st	2nd	3rd	Unpl	Win £
Mr Copyforce	3	10	2	2	3	3	9,592
Running Glimpse	5	13	2	1	1	9	8,623
Fact Or Fiction	7	5	1	0	1	3	3,085
Wild Strawberry	4	4	1	1	0	2	2,658
Ice Rebel	3	7	1	1	0	5	2,243

Favourites	2-6	33.3%	+ 4.00	Total winning prize-money		£26,200

1992 Form	4-77	5.2%	- 39.00	1990 Form	4-71	5.6%	- 35.50
1991 Form	7-84	8.3%	- 21.00	1989 Form	7-76	9.2%	- 29.70

M S SAUNDERS (Wells, Somerset)

	No. of Horses	Races Run	1st	2nd	3rd	Unpl	Per cent	£1 Level Stake
2-y-o	1	4	0	0	0	4	-	- 4.00
3-y-o	0	0	0	0	0	0	-	0.00
4-y-o+	3	22	1	2	2	17	4.5	- 14.50
Totals	4	26	1	2	2	21	3.8	- 18.50

Jan	Feb	Mar	Apr	May	Jun	Jul	Aug	Sep	Oct/Nov
0-0	0-0	0-0	0-0	0-3	1-4	0-5	0-7	0-1	0-6

Winning Jockey	W-R	£1 Level Stake	Winning Course	W-R	£1 Level Stake
J Williams	1-13	- 5.50	Leicester	1-3	+ 4.50

Winning Horse	Age	Races Run	1st	2nd	3rd	Unpl	Win £
Blue Topaze	5	12	1	2	2	7	2,553

Favourites	0-2	Total winning prize-money	£2,553

DR J D SCARGILL (Newmarket)

	No. of Horses	Races Run	1st	2nd	3rd	Unpl	Per cent	£1 Level Stake
2-y-o	10	30	2	2	2	24	6.7	+ 6.00
3-y-o	6	31	3	4	6	18	9.7	- 8.12
4-y-o+	9	52	4	7	7	34	7.7	- 23.75
Totals	25	113	9	13	15	76	8.0	- 25.87

Jan	Feb	Mar	Apr	May	Jun	Jul	Aug	Sep	Oct/Nov
0-8	0-7	0-2	0-8	1-13	1-10	2-19	0-13	1-14	4-19

Winning Jockeys	W-R	£1 Level Stake		W-R	£1 Level Stake
G Hind	3-29	- 2.50	J Tate	1-2	+ 0.38
D Holland	2-5	+ 3.25	G Bardwell	1-4	+ 9.00
K Rutter	2-12	+ 25.00			

Winning Courses					
Southwell (AW)	2-13	+ 3.50	Leicester	1-5	+ 8.00
Newcastle	1-1	+ 9.00	Folkestone	1-6	- 3.25
Redcar	1-2	+ 0.38	Nottingham	1-7	+ 4.00
York	1-3	+ 2.50	Lingfield (AW)	1-18	+ 8.00

Winning Horses	Age	Races Run	1st	2nd	3rd	Unpl	Win £
Our Rita	4	10	2	2	1	5	9,615
Dreams End	5	11	1	2	2	6	3,670
Backstabber	3	6	1	2	0	3	3,054
Response	2	3	1	0	2	0	3,054
Mrs Dawson	3	6	1	2	0	3	2,803
Herr Trigger	2	6	1	0	0	5	2,532
First Fling	4	10	1	1	2	6	2,070
Westray	3	9	1	0	4	4	1,993

Favourites	2-9	22.2%	- 1.12	Total winning prize-money		£28,790

1992 Form	9-116	7.8%	- 32.34	1990 Form	18-185	9.7%	- 37.56
1991 Form	7-172	4.1%	-141.87	1989 Form	8-107	7.5%	- 69.95

A A SCOTT (Newmarket)

	No. of Horses	Races Run	1st	2nd	3rd	Unpl	Per cent	£1 Level Stake
2-y-o	19	50	4	11	4	31	8.0	- 35.33
3-y-o	25	109	9	8	8	84	8.3	- 67.30
4-y-o+	6	38	7	6	4	21	18.4	+ 49.75
Totals	50	197	20	25	16	136	10.2	- 52.88

BY MONTH

2-y-o	W-R	Per cent	£1 Level Stake	3-y-o	W-R	Per cent	£1 Level Stake
January	0-0	-	0.00	January	0-0	-	0.00
February	0-0	-	0.00	February	0-0	-	0.00
March	0-0	-	0.00	March	0-1	-	- 1.00
April	0-2	-	- 2.00	April	1-21	4.8	- 19.43
May	0-1	-	- 1.00	May	3-19	15.8	- 7.12
June	0-0	-	0.00	June	0-11	-	- 11.00
July	0-5	-	- 5.00	July	3-13	23.1	+ 1.50
August	0-7	-	- 7.00	August	2-19	10.5	- 5.25
September	3-16	18.8	- 3.43	September	0-16	-	- 16.00
Oct/Nov	1-19	5.3	- 16.90	Oct/Nov	0-9	-	- 9.00

4-y-o+	W-R	Per cent	£1 Level Stake	Totals	W-R	Per cent	£1 Level Stake
January	0-2	-	- 2.00	January	0-2	-	- 2.00
February	0-0	-	0.00	February	0-0	-	0.00
March	0-0	-	0.00	March	0-1	-	- 1.00
April	0-5	-	- 5.00	April	1-28	3.6	- 26.43
May	2-4	50.0	+ 20.00	May	5-24	20.8	+ 11.88
June	0-0	-	0.00	June	0-11	-	- 11.00
July	2-7	28.6	+ 8.00	July	5-25	20.0	+ 4.50
August	0-6	-	- 6.00	August	2-32	6.3	- 18.25
September	2-9	22.2	+ 28.75	September	5-41	12.2	+ 9.32
Oct/Nov	1-5	20.0	+ 6.00	Oct/Nov	2-33	6.1	- 19.90

DISTANCE

2-y-o	W-R	Per cent	£1 Level Stake	3-y-o	W-R	Per cent	£1 Level Stake
5f-6f	3-30	10.0	- 23.33	5f-6f	2-24	8.3	- 14.00
7f-8f	1-20	5.0	- 12.00	7f-8f	6-43	14.0	- 12.87
9f-13f	0-0	-	0.00	9f-13f	1-40	2.5	- 38.43
14f+	0-0	-	0.00	14f+	0-2	-	- 2.00

4-y-o+	W-R	Per cent	£1 Level Stake	Totals	W-R	Per cent	£1 Level Stake
5f-6f	1-12	8.3	- 5.00	5f-6f	6-66	9.1	- 42.33
7f-8f	2-15	13.3	+ 30.00	7f-8f	9-78	11.5	+ 5.13
9f-13f	4-11	36.4	+ 24.75	9f-13f	5-51	9.8	- 13.68
14f+	0-0	-	0.00	14f+	0-2	-	- 2.00

TYPE OF RACE

Non-Handicaps	W-R	Per cent	£1 Level Stake	Handicaps	W-R	Per cent	£1 Level Stake
2-y-o	4-42	9.5	- 27.33	2-y-o	0-8	-	- 8.00
3-y-o	5-61	8.2	- 41.68	3-y-o	4-45	8.9	- 22.62
4-y-o+	1-12	8.3	- 8.25	4-y-o+	6-24	25.0	+ 60.00
Selling	0-0	-	0.00	Selling	0-0	-	0.00
Apprentice	0-2	-	- 2.00	Apprentice	0-2	-	- 2.00
Amat/Ladies	0-0	-	0.00	Amat/Ladies	0-1	-	- 1.00
Totals	10-117	8.5	- 79.26	Totals	10-80	12.5	+ 26.38

Scott A A

<table>
<tr><th colspan="4">COURSE GRADE</th><th colspan="4">FIRST TIME OUT</th></tr>
<tr><th></th><th>W-R</th><th>Per cent</th><th>£1 Level Stake</th><th></th><th>W-R</th><th>Per cent</th><th>£1 Level Stake</th></tr>
<tr><td>Group 1</td><td>14-103</td><td>13.6</td><td>+ 20.35</td><td>2-y-o</td><td>1-19</td><td>5.3</td><td>- 16.90</td></tr>
<tr><td>Group 2</td><td>0-28</td><td>-</td><td>- 28.00</td><td>3-y-o</td><td>0-25</td><td>-</td><td>- 25.00</td></tr>
<tr><td>Group 3</td><td>4-50</td><td>8.0</td><td>- 34.80</td><td>4-y-o+</td><td>1-6</td><td>16.7</td><td>+ 11.00</td></tr>
<tr><td>Group 4</td><td>2-16</td><td>12.5</td><td>- 10.43</td><td></td><td></td><td></td><td></td></tr>
<tr><td></td><td></td><td></td><td></td><td>Totals</td><td>2-50</td><td>4.0</td><td>- 30.90</td></tr>
</table>

JOCKEYS RIDING

<table>
<tr><th></th><th>W-R</th><th>Per cent</th><th>£1 Level Stake</th><th></th><th></th><th>W-R</th><th>Per cent</th><th>£1 Level Stake</th></tr>
<tr><td>W R Swinburn</td><td>14-63</td><td>22.2</td><td>+ 59.60</td><td>J Tate</td><td></td><td>2-27</td><td>7.4</td><td>- 20.12</td></tr>
<tr><td>B Raymond</td><td>3-56</td><td>5.4</td><td>- 48.36</td><td>Paul Eddery</td><td></td><td>1-1</td><td>100.0</td><td>+ 6.00</td></tr>
</table>

<table>
<tr><td>J Fortune</td><td>0-12</td><td>C Asmussen</td><td>0-1</td><td>M Roberts</td><td>0-1</td></tr>
<tr><td>R Hills</td><td>0-8</td><td>D Gibbs</td><td>0-1</td><td>N Kennedy</td><td>0-1</td></tr>
<tr><td>J Quinn</td><td>0-5</td><td>D Harrison</td><td>0-1</td><td>Pat Eddery</td><td>0-1</td></tr>
<tr><td>R Price</td><td>0-3</td><td>G Duffield</td><td>0-1</td><td>W Carson</td><td>0-1</td></tr>
<tr><td>G Carter</td><td>0-2</td><td>G Hind</td><td>0-1</td><td>W Newnes</td><td>0-1</td></tr>
<tr><td>M Hills</td><td>0-2</td><td>J Fanning</td><td>0-1</td><td>W Ryan</td><td>0-1</td></tr>
<tr><td>Miss T Bracegirdle</td><td>0-2</td><td>J Reid</td><td>0-1</td><td>W Woods</td><td>0-1</td></tr>
<tr><td>A Munro</td><td>0-1</td><td>L Dettori</td><td>0-1</td><td></td><td></td></tr>
</table>

COURSE RECORD

<table>
<tr><th></th><th>Total W-R</th><th colspan="2">Non-Handicaps</th><th colspan="2">Handicaps</th><th>Per cent</th><th>£1 Level Stake</th></tr>
<tr><th></th><th></th><th>2-y-o</th><th>3-y-o+</th><th>2-y-o</th><th>3-y-o+</th><th></th><th></th></tr>
<tr><td>Newmarket</td><td>5-37</td><td>0-10</td><td>2-9</td><td>0-3</td><td>3-15</td><td>13.5</td><td>+ 2.25</td></tr>
<tr><td>Newcastle</td><td>3-5</td><td>3-3</td><td>0-2</td><td>0-0</td><td>0-0</td><td>60.0</td><td>+ 8.10</td></tr>
<tr><td>Carlisle</td><td>2-2</td><td>0-0</td><td>2-2</td><td>0-0</td><td>0-0</td><td>100.0</td><td>+ 3.57</td></tr>
<tr><td>Sandown</td><td>2-6</td><td>0-0</td><td>0-3</td><td>0-0</td><td>2-3</td><td>33.3</td><td>+ 9.00</td></tr>
<tr><td>Doncaster</td><td>2-9</td><td>0-5</td><td>1-1</td><td>0-0</td><td>1-3</td><td>22.2</td><td>+ 32.00</td></tr>
<tr><td>Hamilton</td><td>1-2</td><td>1-2</td><td>0-0</td><td>0-0</td><td>0-0</td><td>50.0</td><td>- 0.43</td></tr>
<tr><td>Chepstow</td><td>1-3</td><td>0-0</td><td>0-2</td><td>0-0</td><td>1-1</td><td>33.3</td><td>- 0.12</td></tr>
<tr><td>Windsor</td><td>1-4</td><td>0-0</td><td>1-4</td><td>0-0</td><td>0-0</td><td>25.0</td><td>- 0.25</td></tr>
<tr><td>York</td><td>1-6</td><td>0-1</td><td>0-2</td><td>0-0</td><td>1-3</td><td>16.7</td><td>+ 1.00</td></tr>
<tr><td>Ascot</td><td>1-12</td><td>0-0</td><td>0-4</td><td>0-1</td><td>1-7</td><td>8.3</td><td>- 4.00</td></tr>
<tr><td>Yarmouth</td><td>1-12</td><td>0-2</td><td>0-4</td><td>0-0</td><td>1-6</td><td>8.3</td><td>- 5.00</td></tr>
</table>

<table>
<tr><td>Redcar</td><td>0-10</td><td>Haydock</td><td>0-6</td><td>Southwell (AW)</td><td>0-2</td></tr>
<tr><td>Kempton</td><td>0-8</td><td>Ripon</td><td>0-6</td><td>Warwick</td><td>0-2</td></tr>
<tr><td>Nottingham</td><td>0-8</td><td>Southwell (Turf)</td><td>0-5</td><td>Beverley</td><td>0-1</td></tr>
<tr><td>Leicester</td><td>0-7</td><td>Thirsk</td><td>0-4</td><td>Epsom</td><td>0-1</td></tr>
<tr><td>Newbury</td><td>0-7</td><td>Catterick</td><td>0-3</td><td>Folkestone</td><td>0-1</td></tr>
<tr><td>Pontefract</td><td>0-7</td><td>Salisbury</td><td>0-3</td><td>Lingfield</td><td>0-1</td></tr>
<tr><td>Bath</td><td>0-6</td><td>Brighton</td><td>0-2</td><td>Lingfield (AW)</td><td>0-1</td></tr>
<tr><td>Goodwood</td><td>0-6</td><td>Chester</td><td>0-2</td><td></td><td></td></tr>
</table>

WINNING HORSES

	Age	Races Run	1st	2nd	3rd	Unpl	Win £
Muhayaa	4	9	4	1	2	2	36,025
Fraam	4	6	2	1	0	3	28,703
Kassbaan	3	13	3	1	0	9	14,294
Siwaayib	3	5	2	0	0	3	8,027
Cameo Kirby	3	6	2	0	1	3	5,253
Recaptured Days	2	4	1	1	0	2	4,378
Storm Ship	2	6	1	2	0	3	4,143
Reine De Neige	3	7	1	1	1	4	3,933
Desert Invader	2	1	1	0	0	0	3,688
Lijaam	3	6	1	1	2	2	3,407
Elton Ledger	4	11	1	0	0	10	2,769
Nawafell	2	7	1	1	1	4	2,624

WINNING OWNERS

	Races Won	Value £		Races Won	Value £
Maktoum Al Maktoum	17	105,952	Jimmy Strauss	1	4,143
K Khurbash	1	4,378	A A Scott	1	2,769

Favourites	9-25	36.0%	+ 1.87	Total winning prize-money		£117,241
Longest winning sequence			3	Average SP of winner		6.2/1
Longest losing sequence			27	Return on stakes invested		-26.8%
1992 Form	38-322	11.8%	-124.45	1990 Form	29-194	14.9%	- 78.07
1991 Form	23-225	10.2%	-104.93	1989 Form	24-132	18.2%	- 15.56

D SHAW (Ashington, West Sussex)

	No. of Horses	Races Run	1st	2nd	3rd	Unpl	Per cent	£1 Level Stake
2-y-o	0	0	0	0	0	0	-	0.00
3-y-o	3	13	0	0	0	13	-	- 13.00
4-y-o+	7	30	4	1	1	24	13.3	- 2.00
Totals	10	43	4	1	1	37	9.3	- 15.00

Jan	Feb	Mar	Apr	May	Jun	Jul	Aug	Sep	Oct/Nov
1-2	2-4	0-2	0-10	0-4	0-2	1-7	0-3	0-9	0-0

Winning Jockeys	W-R	£1 Level Stake		W-R	£1 Level Stake
K Rutter	3-11	+ 10.50	G Carter	1-3	+ 3.50

Winning Courses					
Southwell (AW)	2-5	+ 5.50	Windsor	1-4	+ 2.50
Lingfield (AW)	1-2	+ 9.00			

Shaw D

Winning Horses	Age	Races Run	1st	2nd	3rd	Unpl	Win £
Coleridge	5	5	3	1	0	1	7,279
Fascination Waltz	6	12	1	0	1	10	3,785

Favourites	1-1	100.0%	+ 2.50	Total winning prize-money	£11,064

1992 Form	2-53	3.8%	+ 13.00

S SHERWOOD (East Ilsley, Berks)

	No. of Horses	Races Run	1st	2nd	3rd	Unpl	Per cent	£1 Level Stake
2-y-o	0	0	0	0	0	0	-	0.00
3-y-o	0	0	0	0	0	0	-	0.00
4-y-o+	2	5	1	1	0	3	20.0	+ 46.00
Totals	2	5	1	1	0	3	20.0	+ 46.00

Jan	Feb	Mar	Apr	May	Jun	Jul	Aug	Sep	Oct/Nov
0-0	0-0	0-0	0-0	0-1	0-1	0-0	0-0	0-1	1-2

Winning Jockey	W-R	£1 Level Stake	Winning Course	W-R	£1 Level Stake
B Rouse	1-2	+ 49.00	Newmarket	1-2	+ 49.00

Winning Horse	Age	Races Run	1st	2nd	3rd	Unpl	Win £
Derab	7	4	1	1	0	2	8,900

Favourites	0-0	Total winning prize-money	£8,900

1992 Form	0-1	1991 Form	0-4

MISS L C SIDDALL (Tadcaster, North Yorks)

	No. of Horses	Races Run	1st	2nd	3rd	Unpl	Per cent	£1 Level Stake
2-y-o	3	18	2	3	1	12	11.1	+ 19.00
3-y-o	3	14	0	0	1	13	-	- 14.00
4-y-o+	9	77	7	6	13	51	9.1	+ 1.50
Totals	15	109	9	9	15	76	8.3	+ 6.50

Jan	Feb	Mar	Apr	May	Jun	Jul	Aug	Sep	Oct/Nov
0-0	0-0	0-1	0-5	2-9	1-21	0-21	3-18	2-13	1-21

Winning Jockeys	W-R	£1 Level Stake		W-R	£1 Level Stake
D McCabe	3-8	+ 29.00	P McCabe	1-4	+ 2.50
P Robinson	2-5	+ 15.00	O Pears	1-12	+ 1.00
W Newnes	1-3	+ 23.00	D Harrison	1-28	- 15.00

Winning Courses					
Newcastle	2-2	+ 31.00	Sandown	1-7	- 0.50
Redcar	2-16	+ 8.00	Newmarket	1-10	+ 3.00
Carlisle	1-4	+ 5.00	Doncaster	1-15	- 2.00
Haydock	1-4	+ 13.00			

Winning Horses	Age	Races Run	1st	2nd	3rd	Unpl	Win £
Metal Boys	6	10	2	2	1	5	8,419
Miss Aragon	5	15	2	1	2	10	6,139
Obsidian Grey	6	11	2	0	2	7	4,476
Euro Festival	4	19	1	1	4	13	3,728
Takadou	2	6	1	2	0	3	3,319
Featherstone Lane	2	9	1	1	1	6	2,490

Favourites	0-4			Total winning prize-money		£28,571

1992 Form	4-107	3.7%	- 62.00	1990 Form	4-98	4.1%	- 61.25
1991 Form	2-64	3.1%	- 54.67	1989 Form	8-103	7.8%	- 25.25

R SIMPSON (Lambourn, Berks)

	No. of Horses	Races Run	1st	2nd	3rd	Unpl	Per cent	£1 Level Stake
2-y-o	5	12	0	2	0	10	-	- 12.00
3-y-o	7	33	4	5	2	22	12.1	- 3.00
4-y-o+	7	37	1	4	2	30	2.7	- 20.00
Totals	19	82	5	11	4	62	6.1	- 35.00

Jan	Feb	Mar	Apr	May	Jun	Jul	Aug	Sep	Oct/Nov
0-3	0-0	0-1	1-9	1-14	1-13	0-10	0-6	0-12	2-14

Winning Jockeys	W-R	£1 Level Stake		W-R	£1 Level Stake
B Rouse	3-12	+ 10.00	A Tucker	1-20	- 12.00
G Carter	1-4	+ 13.00			

Winning Courses					
Folkestone	1-3	+ 3.50	Goodwood	1-7	+ 1.00
Chepstow	1-4	+ 7.00	Newbury	1-8	+ 9.00
Windsor	1-6	- 1.50			

Winning Horses	Age	Races Run	1st	2nd	3rd	Unpl	Win £
Warm Spell	3	12	3	3	1	5	9,381
Olifantsfontein	5	6	1	0	0	5	6,164
Walk The Beat	3	6	1	0	1	4	3,080

Favourites	0-5			Total winning prize-money			£18,625
1992 Form	11-121	9.1%	- 48.32	1990 Form	6-96	6.3%	- 23.50
1991 Form	5-104	4.8%	- 44.67	1989 Form	7-117	6.0%	- 33.87

B SMART (Lambourn, Berks)

	No. of Horses	Races Run	1st	2nd	3rd	Unpl	Per cent	£1 Level Stake
2-y-o	5	17	1	1	1	14	5.9	- 9.00
3-y-o	4	22	2	0	1	19	9.1	+ 18.00
4-y-o+	3	10	0	1	0	9	-	- 10.00
Totals	12	49	3	2	2	42	6.1	- 1.00

Jan	Feb	Mar	Apr	May	Jun	Jul	Aug	Sep	Oct/Nov
0-1	0-3	0-1	0-1	0-3	0-4	0-6	3-12	0-5	0-13

Winning Jockeys	W-R	£1 Level Stake		W-R	£1 Level Stake
S Davies	2-8	+ 32.00	R Perham	1-5	+ 3.00

Winning Courses	W-R	£1 Level Stake		W-R	£1 Level Stake
Brighton	2-7	+ 33.00	Lingfield	1-5	+ 3.00

Winning Horses	Age	Races Run	1st	2nd	3rd	Unpl	Win £
Sharp Gazelle	3	9	2	0	0	7	4,995
Brierley	2	6	1	1	0	4	2,700

Favourites	0-0			Total winning prize-money		£7,695
1992 Form	2-23	8.7%	- 9.67	1990 Form	0-5	
1991 Form	0-5			1989 Form	0-13	

A SMITH (Beverley, North Humberside)

	No. of Horses	Races Run	1st	2nd	3rd	Unpl	Per cent	£1 Level Stake
2-y-o	2	7	2	1	0	4	28.6	+ 61.00
3-y-o	2	10	1	0	2	7	10.0	- 3.50
4-y-o+	3	18	0	2	0	16	-	- 18.00
Totals	7	35	3	3	2	27	8.6	+ 39.50

Jan	Feb	Mar	Apr	May	Jun	Jul	Aug	Sep	Oct/Nov
0-0	0-1	1-2	0-2	0-4	0-7	0-7	0-4	0-5	2-3

Winning Jockeys	W-R	£1 Level Stake				W-R	£1 Level Stake
J Lowe	1-3	+ 31.00	S Webster			1-18	- 11.50
M Birch	1-5	+ 29.00					

Winning Courses							
Nottingham	1-2	+ 4.50	Doncaster			1-5	+ 29.00
Redcar	1-3	+ 31.00					

Winning Horses	Age	Races Run	1st	2nd	3rd	Unpl	Win £
Cape Merino	2	4	2	1	0	1	92,190
Calamanco	3	7	1	0	2	4	3,094

Favourites	1-1	100.0%	+ 5.50	Total winning prize-money			£95,284

1992 Form	3-63	4.8%	- 35.50	1990 Form	1-28	3.6%	- 20.00
1991 Form	1-113	0.9%	-101.00	1989 Form	1-41	2.4%	- 26.00

C SMITH (Wellingore, Lincs)

	No. of Horses	Races Run	1st	2nd	3rd	Unpl	Per cent	£1 Level Stake
2-y-o	3	12	1	1	1	9	8.3	- 5.50
3-y-o	3	13	1	1	2	9	7.7	- 12.00
4-y-o+	5	8	0	0	0	8	-	- 8.00
Totals	11	33	2	2	3	26	6.1	- 25.50

Jan	Feb	Mar	Apr	May	Jun	Jul	Aug	Sep	Oct/Nov
0-2	0-1	0-1	0-1	0-4	0-9	1-5	1-5	0-2	0-3

Winning Jockey	W-R	£1 Level Stake		W-R	£1 Level Stake
K Rutter	2-12	- 4.50			

Winning Courses					
Lingfield	1-2	- 1.00	Southwell (Turf)	1-3	+ 3.50

Winning Horses	Age	Races Run	1st	2nd	3rd	Unpl	Win £
Moshaajir	3	3	1	0	0	2	4,935
Up The Mariners	2	4	1	1	1	1	1,380

Favourites	0-0	Total winning prize-money	£6,315

1992 Form	0-2

C A SMITH (Hanley Swan, H'ford & Worcs)

	No. of Horses	Races Run	1st	2nd	3rd	Unpl	Per cent	£1 Level Stake
2-y-o	4	10	0	0	0	10	-	- 10.00
3-y-o	7	32	1	2	3	26	3.1	- 23.00
4-y-o+	5	15	0	0	0	15	-	- 15.00
Totals	16	57	1	2	3	51	1.8	- 48.00

Jan	Feb	Mar	Apr	May	Jun	Jul	Aug	Sep	Oct/Nov
0-4	0-2	0-3	0-2	0-10	0-13	1-8	0-5	0-5	0-5

Winning Jockey	W-R	£1 Level Stake	Winning Course	W-R	£1 Level Stake
J Lowe	1-12	- 3.00	Southwell (Turf)	1-4	+ 5.00

Winning Horse	Age	Races Run	1st	2nd	3rd	Unpl	Win £
Workingforpeanuts	3	8	1	0	1	6	2,364

Favourites	0-2		Total winning prize-money		£2,364
1992 Form	0-63		1991 Form	2-33	6.1%	+ 14.00

D J G MURRAY SMITH (Upper Lambourn, Berks)

	No. of Horses	Races Run	1st	2nd	3rd	Unpl	Per cent	£1 Level Stake
2-y-o	4	22	1	3	2	16	4.5	+ 29.00
3-y-o	3	19	2	0	3	14	10.5	+ 13.00
4-y-o+	1	1	0	0	0	1	-	- 1.00
Totals	8	42	3	3	5	31	7.1	+ 41.00

Jan	Feb	Mar	Apr	May	Jun	Jul	Aug	Sep	Oct/Nov
1-2	0-0	0-1	0-2	0-5	0-5	0-5	0-7	1-8	1-7

Winning Jockeys	W-R	£1 Level Stake		W-R	£1 Level Stake
D Wright	1-2	+ 13.00	C Rutter	1-15	+ 36.00
Pat Eddery	1-2	+ 15.00			

Winning Courses	W-R	£1 Level Stake		W-R	£1 Level Stake
Lingfield (AW)	1-3	+ 12.00	Newmarket	1-4	+ 13.00
Lingfield	1-4	+ 47.00			

Winning Horses	Age	Races Run	1st	2nd	3rd	Unpl	Win £
Norfolk Hero	3	10	1	0	1	8	6,664
Alaskan Heir	2	3	1	0	0	2	3,553
Honorary Guest	3	3	1	0	0	2	2,391

Favourites	0-2			Total winning prize-money		£12,608
1992 Form	2-36	5.6%	- 27.50	1990 Form	9-100	9.0%	- 40.69
1991 Form	7-76	9.2%	- 12.00	1989 Form	8-76	10.5%	- 19.50

DENYS SMITH (Bishop Auckland, Co Durham)

	No. of Horses	Races Run	1st	2nd	3rd	Unpl	Per cent	£1 Level Stake
2-y-o	6	34	4	2	5	23	11.8	+ 8.00
3-y-o	3	22	1	2	1	18	4.5	- 11.00
4-y-o+	11	102	7	8	9	78	6.9	- 59.50
Totals	20	158	12	12	15	119	7.6	- 62.50

BY MONTH

2-y-o	W-R	Per cent	£1 Level Stake	3-y-o	W-R	Per cent	£1 Level Stake
January	0-0	-	0.00	January	0-0	-	0.00
February	0-0	-	0.00	February	0-0	-	0.00
March	0-0	-	0.00	March	0-0	-	0.00
April	0-0	-	0.00	April	1-2	50.0	+ 9.00
May	0-3	-	- 3.00	May	0-4	-	- 4.00
June	1-9	11.1	- 1.00	June	0-5	-	- 5.00
July	0-5	-	- 5.00	July	0-3	-	- 3.00
August	2-8	25.0	+ 20.00	August	0-5	-	- 5.00
September	1-4	25.0	+ 2.00	September	0-3	-	- 3.00
Oct/Nov	0-5	-	- 5.00	Oct/Nov	0-0	-	0.00

4-y-o+	W-R	Per cent	£1 Level Stake	Totals	W-R	Per cent	£1 Level Stake
January	0-2	-	- 2.00	January	0-2	-	- 2.00
February	0-2	-	- 2.00	February	0-2	-	- 2.00
March	0-9	-	- 9.00	March	0-9	-	- 9.00
April	0-6	-	- 6.00	April	1-8	12.5	+ 3.00
May	1-10	10.0	- 1.00	May	1-17	5.9	- 8.00
June	1-18	5.6	- 12.50	June	2-32	6.3	- 18.50
July	3-15	20.0	+ 3.00	July	3-23	13.0	- 5.00
August	1-12	8.3	- 6.00	August	3-25	12.0	+ 9.00
September	1-15	6.7	- 11.00	September	2-22	9.1	- 12.00
Oct/Nov	0-13	-	- 13.00	Oct/Nov	0-18	-	- 18.00

DISTANCE

2-y-o	W-R	Per cent	£1 Level Stake	3-y-o	W-R	Per cent	£1 Level Stake
5f-6f	3-27	11.1	+ 9.00	5f-6f	0-4	-	- 4.00
7f-8f	1-7	14.3	- 1.00	7f-8f	1-10	10.0	+ 1.00
9f-13f	0-0	-	0.00	9f-13f	0-7	-	- 7.00
14f+	0-0	-	0.00	14f+	0-1	-	- 1.00

4-y-o+	W-R	Per cent	£1 Level Stake	Totals	W-R	Per cent	£1 Level Stake
5f-6f	1-24	4.2	- 20.00	5f-6f	4-55	7.3	- 15.00
7f-8f	2-55	3.6	- 41.00	7f-8f	4-72	5.6	- 41.00
9f-13f	4-18	22.2	+ 6.50	9f-13f	4-25	16.0	- 0.50
14f+	0-5	-	- 5.00	14f+	0-6	-	- 6.00

TYPE OF RACE

Non-Handicaps	W-R	Per cent	£1 Level Stake	Handicaps	W-R	Per cent	£1 Level Stake
2-y-o	1-26	3.8	- 18.00	2-y-o	3-8	37.5	+ 26.00
3-y-o	1-7	14.3	+ 4.00	3-y-o	0-14	-	- 14.00
4-y-o+	4-15	26.7	+ 9.50	4-y-o+	2-66	3.0	- 54.00
Selling	0-0	-	0.00	Selling	0-5	-	- 5.00
Apprentice	0-2	-	- 2.00	Apprentice	1-7	14.3	- 1.00
Amat/Ladies	0-0	-	0.00	Amat/Ladies	0-8	-	- 8.00
Totals	6-50	12.0	- 6.50	Totals	6-108	5.6	- 56.00

COURSE GRADE

	W-R	Per cent	£1 Level Stake
Group 1	3-43	7.0	- 18.00
Group 2	2-41	4.9	- 22.00
Group 3	4-39	10.3	- 12.50
Group 4	3-35	8.6	- 10.00

FIRST TIME OUT

	W-R	Per cent	£1 Level Stake
2-y-o	1-6	16.7	+ 2.00
3-y-o	1-3	33.3	+ 8.00
4-y-o+	1-11	9.1	- 2.00
Totals	3-20	15.0	+ 8.00

JOCKEYS RIDING

	W-R	Per cent	£1 Level Stake		W-R	Per cent	£1 Level Stake
K Fallon	5-44	11.4	- 10.00	D McKeown	1-2	50.0	+ 3.50
C Teague	3-36	8.3	- 2.00	D Moffatt	1-3	33.3	+ 3.00
N Connorton	2-14	14.3	+ 2.00				

L Charnock	0-13	D Holland	0-2	J Carroll	0-1
Miss M Carson	0-9	J Fortune	0-2	J Quinn	0-1
D Nicholls	0-6	L Piggott	0-2	L Dettori	0-1
J Lowe	0-4	A Mackay	0-1	M Roberts	0-1
M Birch	0-4	B Raymond	0-1	P Robinson	0-1
W Carson	0-4	F Norton	0-1	R Hills	0-1
A Clark	0-2	G Duffield	0-1	S Perks	0-1

COURSE RECORD

	Total W-R	Non-Handicaps 2-y-o	3-y-o+	Handicaps 2-y-o	3-y-o+	Per cent	£1 Level Stake
Hamilton	3-23	0-5	3-5	0-1	0-12	13.0	- 4.50
Catterick	2-4	0-0	1-2	1-1	0-1	50.0	+ 13.00
Ripon	2-7	0-0	1-1	1-1	0-5	28.6	+ 12.00
Ayr	2-17	0-3	0-3	1-2	1-9	11.8	+ 2.00
Pontefract	1-9	0-1	0-0	0-1	1-7	11.1	- 1.00
Newcastle	1-12	0-2	0-2	0-0	1-8	8.3	- 6.00
Edinburgh	1-16	1-3	0-3	0-1	0-9	6.3	- 8.00

Redcar	0-20	Beverley	0-5	Haydock	0-2
Thirsk	0-12	Southwell (AW)	0-5	Nottingham	0-2
Carlisle	0-10	York	0-4	Ascot	0-1
Doncaster	0-6	Chester	0-2	Newmarket	0-1

WINNING HORSES

	Age	Races Run	1st	2nd	3rd	Unpl	Win £
Imperial Bid	5	14	3	1	2	8	8,056
Grey Toppa	2	9	2	0	2	5	5,977
Spanish Verdict	6	18	2	1	2	13	5,525
Densben	9	18	1	1	1	15	3,469
Willshe Gan	3	8	1	0	0	7	3,420
The Happy Loon	2	8	1	1	1	5	3,158
Media Messenger	4	11	1	2	0	8	2,557
Plainsong	2	6	1	1	2	2	2,540

WINNING OWNERS

	Races Won	Value £		Races Won	Value £
Lord Durham	3	8,056	H Hewitson	1	3,420
D Ford	2	5,977	Jim Blair	1	3,158
Cox & Allen (Kendal) Ltd	2	5,525	Lord Lambton	1	2,557
Mrs Janet M Pike	1	3,469	Peter Innes	1	2,540

Favourites	1-5	20.0%	- 1.00	Total winning prize-money	£34,701
Longest winning sequence			2	Average SP of winner	7.0/1
Longest losing sequence			20	Return on stakes invested	-39.6%

1992 Form	15-149	10.1%	- 39.59	1990 Form	8-215	3.7%	-172.13
1991 Form	9-207	4.3%	-144.25	1989 Form	16-214	7.5%	-104.15

N A SMITH (Redditch, Staffs)

	No. of Horses	Races Run	1st	2nd	3rd	Unpl	Per cent	£1 Level Stake
2-y-o	0	0	0	0	0	0	-	0.00
3-y-o	1	2	0	0	0	2	-	- 2.00
4-y-o+	3	15	1	1	1	12	6.7	- 9.50
Totals	4	17	1	1	1	14	5.9	- 11.50

Jan	Feb	Mar	Apr	May	Jun	Jul	Aug	Sep	Oct/Nov
0-3	0-0	0-0	0-0	0-0	0-0	1-5	0-2	0-2	0-5

		£1 Level				£1 Level
	W-R	Stake			W-R	Stake
Winning Jockey			Winning Course			
S D Williams	1-8	- 2.50	Warwick		1-2	+ 3.50

	Age	Races Run	1st	2nd	3rd	Unpl	Win £
Winning Horse							
Petraco	5	10	1	0	1	8	2,832

Favourites	0-0	Total winning prize-money	£2,832
1992 Form	0-4	1990 Form 0-4	
1991 Form	0-6		

J P SMITH (Gentleshaw, Staffs)

	No. of Horses	Races Run	1st	2nd	3rd	Unpl	Per cent	£1 Level Stake
2-y-o	0	0	0	0	0	0	-	0.00
3-y-o	0	0	0	0	0	0	-	0.00
4-y-o+	4	20	1	0	0	19	5.0	+ 1.00
Totals	4	20	1	0	0	19	5.0	+ 1.00

Jan	Feb	Mar	Apr	May	Jun	Jul	Aug	Sep	Oct/Nov
0-2	0-1	0-2	0-3	0-2	0-1	0-3	0-3	0-2	1-1

Winning Jockey	W-R	£1 Level Stake	Winning Course	W-R	£1 Level Stake
Peter Smith	1-1	+ 20.00	Uttoxeter	1-1	+ 20.00

Winning Horse	Age	Races Run	1st	2nd	3rd	Unpl	Win £
My Swan Song	8	2	1	0	0	1	1,551

Favourites	0-0		Total winning prize-money		£1,551

1992 Form	2-28	7.1%	+ 32.00	1990 Form	0-71		
1991 Form	0-28			1989 Form	1-36	2.8%	- 28.00

J L SPEARING (Alcester, Warwicks)

	No. of Horses	Races Run	1st	2nd	3rd	Unpl	Per cent	£1 Level Stake
2-y-o	7	28	3	3	3	19	10.7	+ 7.50
3-y-o	10	35	4	0	3	28	11.4	+ 9.00
4-y-o+	18	109	10	13	6	80	9.2	- 35.85
Totals	35	172	17	16	12	127	9.9	- 19.35

BY MONTH

2-y-o	W-R	Per cent	£1 Level Stake	3-y-o	W-R	Per cent	£1 Level Stake
January	0-0	-	0.00	January	0-1	-	- 1.00
February	0-0	-	0.00	February	1-1	100.0	+ 8.00
March	0-0	-	0.00	March	0-1	-	- 1.00
April	0-0	-	0.00	April	2-6	33.3	+ 12.00
May	0-0	-	0.00	May	0-4	-	- 4.00
June	1-6	16.7	+ 11.00	June	0-6	-	- 6.00
July	2-7	28.6	+ 11.50	July	1-6	16.7	+ 11.00
August	0-5	-	- 5.00	August	0-1	-	- 1.00
September	0-4	-	- 4.00	September	0-3	-	- 3.00
Oct/Nov	0-6	-	- 6.00	Oct/Nov	0-6	-	- 6.00

4-y-o+	W-R	Per cent	£1 Level Stake	Totals	W-R	Per cent	£1 Level Stake
January	0-6	-	- 6.00	January	0-7	-	- 7.00
February	0-3	-	- 3.00	February	1-4	25.0	+ 5.00
March	0-1	-	- 1.00	March	0-2	-	- 2.00
April	0-12	-	- 12.00	April	2-18	11.1	0.00
May	1-13	7.7	- 7.50	May	1-17	5.9	- 11.50
June	4-12	33.3	+ 9.50	June	5-24	20.8	+ 14.50
July	3-23	13.0	- 1.85	July	6-36	16.7	+ 20.65
August	1-15	6.7	- 5.00	August	1-21	4.8	- 11.00
September	1-15	6.7	0.00	September	1-22	4.5	- 7.00
Oct/Nov	0-9	-	- 9.00	Oct/Nov	0-21	-	- 21.00

DISTANCE

2-y-o	W-R	Per cent	£1 Level Stake	3-y-o	W-R	Per cent	£1 Level Stake
5f-6f	3-24	12.5	+ 11.50	5f-6f	4-25	16.0	+ 19.00
7f-8f	0-1	-	- 1.00	7f-8f	0-7	-	- 7.00
9f-13f	0-3	-	- 3.00	9f-13f	0-3	-	- 3.00
14f+	0-0	-	0.00	14f+	0-0	-	0.00

4-y-o+	W-R	Per cent	£1 Level Stake	Totals	W-R	Per cent	£1 Level Stake
5f-6f	6-68	8.8	- 24.35	5f-6f	13-117	11.1	+ 6.15
7f-8f	3-24	12.5	0.00	7f-8f	3-32	9.4	- 8.00
9f-13f	0-9	-	- 9.00	9f-13f	0-15	-	- 15.00
14f+	1-8	12.5	- 2.50	14f+	1-8	12.5	- 2.50

TYPE OF RACE

Non-Handicaps	W-R	Per cent	£1 Level Stake	Handicaps	W-R	Per cent	£1 Level Stake
2-y-o	3-21	14.3	+ 14.50	2-y-o	0-2	-	- 2.00
3-y-o	1-11	9.1	- 2.00	3-y-o	3-21	14.3	+ 14.00
4-y-o+	0-18	-	- 18.00	4-y-o+	9-73	12.3	- 9.85
Selling	0-3	-	- 3.00	Selling	0-7	-	- 7.00
Apprentice	0-3	-	- 3.00	Apprentice	1-8	12.5	+ 2.00
Amat/Ladies	0-0	-	0.00	Amat/Ladies	0-5	-	- 5.00
Totals	4-56	7.1	- 11.50	Totals	13-116	11.2	- 7.85

COURSE GRADE

	W-R	Per cent	£1 Level Stake
Group 1	5-49	10.2	- 1.50
Group 2	2-27	7.4	- 7.00
Group 3	5-48	10.4	- 2.00
Group 4	5-48	10.4	- 8.85

FIRST TIME OUT

	W-R	Per cent	£1 Level Stake
2-y-o	1-7	14.3	+ 10.00
3-y-o	2-9	22.2	+ 12.00
4-y-o+	0-17	-	- 17.00
Totals	3-33	9.1	+ 5.00

Spearing J L

JOCKEYS RIDING

	W–R	Per cent	£1 Level Stake		W–R	Per cent	£1 Level Stake
K Darley	4-17	23.5	+ 12.50	R Painter	1-2	50.0	+ 8.00
A Mackay	4-21	19.0	+ 18.15	T Quinn	1-3	33.3	+ 6.00
M Humphries	3-16	18.8	+ 6.00	Alex Greaves	1-5	20.0	+ 0.50
G Hind	2-15	13.3	+ 15.00	J Lowe	1-18	5.6	- 10.50

Paul Eddery	0-8	C Hawksley	0-2	J Dennis		0-1
L Suthern	0-6	D McCabe	0-2	J Reid		0-1
W Newnes	0-5	F Savage	0-2	J Tate		0-1
D McKeown	0-4	L Dettori	0-2	Kim McDonnell		0-1
J Williams	0-4	M Roberts	0-2	L Aspell		0-1
Miss C Spearing	0-4	Miss T Spearing	0-2	M Birch		0-1
A Tucker	0-3	Antoinette Armes	0-1	M Tebbutt		0-1
D Wright	0-3	C Rutter	0-1	Mrs S Bosley		0-1
V Slattery	0-3	D Denby	0-1	T Williams		0-1
W Carson	0-3	Dale Gibson	0-1	W R Swinburn		0-1
A Garth	0-2	G Bardwell	0-1			
B Raymond	0-2	G Duffield	0-1			

COURSE RECORD

	Total W–R	Non-Handicaps 2-y-o	3-y-o+	Handicaps 2-y-o	3-y-o+	Per cent	£1 Level Stake
Sandown	2-5	0-0	0-0	0-0	2-5	40.0	+ 18.00
Beverley	2-7	1-1	0-0	0-0	1-6	28.6	+ 2.00
York	2-7	0-0	0-0	0-0	2-7	28.6	+ 11.50
Edinburgh	2-9	0-1	0-0	0-1	2-7	22.2	0.00
Catterick	1-3	1-1	0-0	0-0	0-2	33.3	+ 14.00
Lingfield	1-4	0-0	0-0	0-0	1-4	25.0	+ 1.00
Newmarket	1-4	0-0	0-0	0-0	1-4	25.0	+ 2.00
Salisbury	1-4	0-1	0-1	0-0	1-2	25.0	+ 11.00
Yarmouth	1-4	1-2	0-1	0-0	0-1	25.0	+ 11.00
Windsor	1-5	0-0	0-1	0-0	1-4	20.0	+ 5.00
Leicester	1-6	0-1	0-1	0-0	1-4	16.7	+ 6.00
Warwick	1-11	0-1	0-6	0-0	1-4	9.1	- 6.85
Lingfield (AW)	1-14	0-0	1-6	0-0	0-8	7.1	- 5.00

Haydock	0-12	Chepstow	0-4	Hamilton	0-2
Bath	0-10	Folkestone	0-4	Newbury	0-2
Doncaster	0-10	Ripon	0-4	Newcastle	0-2
Nottingham	0-8	Southwell (Turf)	0-3	Pontefract	0-2
Thirsk	0-8	Ascot	0-2	Redcar	0-2
Brighton	0-5	Ayr	0-2	Kempton	0-1
Carlisle	0-4	Epsom	0-2		

WINNING HORSES

	Age	Races Run	1st	2nd	3rd	Unpl	Win £
Miss Vaxette	4	14	3	2	1	8	16,999
Magic Orb	3	9	3	0	2	4	15,145
Dominuet	8	12	1	2	1	8	14,114
Lawnswood Junior	6	15	3	3	0	9	10,154

Evening Falls	2	5	2	1	0	2	7,578
King William	8	7	1	2	1	3	3,340
Ashkernazy	2	6	1	2	2	1	3,319
Rhythmic Dancer	5	8	1	1	1	5	3,260
Jucea	4	7	1	2	0	4	2,301
Squire York	3	4	1	0	0	3	2,208

WINNING OWNERS

	Races Won	Value £		Races Won	Value £
Mrs Robert Heathcote	2	17,375	Group 1 Racing (1989) Ltd	1	3,340
Vax Appliances Ltd	3	16,999	Paul Sharkey	1	3,319
M Olden	3	15,145	A A Campbell	1	2,301
Graham Treglown	3	10,154	J Powell-Tuck	1	2,208
Mrs Carol J Welch	2	7,578			

Favourites	4-18	22.2%	+ 5.50	Total winning prize-money		£78,417
Longest winning sequence			1	Average SP of winner		8.0/1
Longest losing sequence			32	Return on stakes invested		-11.3%
1992 Form	15-204	7.4%	- 84.29	1990 Form	13-176	7.4%	-103.37
1991 Form	12-177	6.8%	- 64.75	1989 Form	8-145	5.5%	-100.87

R C SPICER (Spalding, Lincs)

	No. of Horses	Races Run	1st	2nd	3rd	Unpl	Per cent	£1 Level Stake
2-y-o	4	13	0	0	1	12	-	- 13.00
3-y-o	6	23	0	2	0	21	-	- 23.00
4-y-o+	11	77	12	3	6	56	15.6	+ 31.25
Totals	21	113	12	5	7	89	10.6	- 4.75

BY MONTH

2-y-o	W-R	Per cent	£1 Level Stake	3-y-o	W-R	Per cent	£1 Level Stake
January	0-0	-	0.00	January	0-3	-	- 3.00
February	0-0	-	0.00	February	0-1	-	- 1.00
March	0-0	-	0.00	March	0-4	-	- 4.00
April	0-0	-	0.00	April	0-2	-	- 2.00
May	0-0	-	0.00	May	0-2	-	- 2.00
June	0-1	-	- 1.00	June	0-2	-	- 2.00
July	0-2	-	- 2.00	July	0-2	-	- 2.00
August	0-4	-	- 4.00	August	0-3	-	- 3.00
September	0-2	-	- 2.00	September	0-3	-	- 3.00
Oct/Nov	0-4	-	- 4.00	Oct/Nov	0-1	-	- 1.00

Spicer R C

4-y-o+	W-R	Per cent	£1 Level Stake	Totals	W-R	Per cent	£1 Level Stake
January	2-14	14.3	- 3.75	January	2-17	11.8	- 6.75
February	4-12	33.3	+ 20.50	February	4-13	30.8	+ 19.50
March	2-9	22.2	- 0.50	March	2-13	15.4	- 4.50
April	0-9	-	- 9.00	April	0-11	-	- 11.00
May	1-3	33.3	+ 4.00	May	1-5	20.0	+ 2.00
June	0-6	-	- 6.00	June	0-9	-	- 9.00
July	1-3	33.3	+ 5.00	July	1-7	14.3	+ 1.00
August	0-6	-	- 6.00	August	0-13	-	- 13.00
September	0-3	-	- 3.00	September	0-8	-	- 8.00
Oct/Nov	2-12	16.7	+ 30.00	Oct/Nov	2-17	11.8	+ 25.00

DISTANCE

2-y-o	W-R	Per cent	£1 Level Stake	3-y-o	W-R	Per cent	£1 Level Stake
5f-6f	0-6	-	- 6.00	5f-6f	0-9	-	- 9.00
7f-8f	0-7	-	- 7.00	7f-8f	0-13	-	- 13.00
9f-13f	0-0	-	0.00	9f-13f	0-0	-	0.00
14f+	0-0	-	0.00	14f+	0-1	-	- 1.00

4-y-o+	W-R	Per cent	£1 Level Stake	Totals	W-R	Per cent	£1 Level Stake
5f-6f	0-2	-	- 2.00	5f-6f	0-17	-	- 17.00
7f-8f	8-49	16.3	+ 17.25	7f-8f	8-69	11.6	- 2.75
9f-13f	3-17	17.6	+ 4.00	9f-13f	3-17	17.6	+ 4.00
14f+	1-9	11.1	+ 12.00	14f+	1-10	10.0	+ 11.00

TYPE OF RACE

Non-Handicaps	W-R	Per cent	£1 Level Stake	Handicaps	W-R	Per cent	£1 Level Stake
2-y-o	0-5	-	- 5.00	2-y-o	0-5	-	- 5.00
3-y-o	0-1	-	- 1.00	3-y-o	0-18	-	- 18.00
4-y-o+	1-7	14.3	- 3.75	4-y-o+	11-65	16.9	+ 40.00
Selling	0-4	-	- 4.00	Selling	0-4	-	- 4.00
Apprentice	0-0	-	0.00	Apprentice	0-3	-	- 3.00
Amat/Ladies	0-0	-	0.00	Amat/Ladies	0-1	-	- 1.00
Totals	1-17	5.9	- 13.75	Totals	11-96	11.5	+ 9.00

COURSE GRADE

	W-R	Per cent	£1 Level Stake
Group 1	0-18	-	- 18.00
Group 2	0-8	-	- 8.00
Group 3	1-20	5.0	- 13.00
Group 4	11-67	16.4	+ 34.25

FIRST TIME OUT

	W-R	Per cent	£1 Level Stake
2-y-o	0-2	-	- 2.00
3-y-o	0-2	-	- 2.00
4-y-o+	0-7	-	- 7.00
Totals	0-11	-	- 11.00

JOCKEYS RIDING

	W-R	Per cent	£1 Level Stake		W-R	Per cent	£1 Level Stake
J McLaughlin	7-23	30.4	+ 24.75	G Duffield	1-3	33.3	+ 5.00
A Clark	1-1	100.0	+ 20.00	A Munro	1-3	33.3	+ 18.00
D Holland	1-3	33.3	+ 4.00	A Mackay	1-16	6.3	- 12.50

A Garth	0-15	W Woods	0-2	M Roberts	0-1
D Moffatt	0-10	B Doyle	0-1	Miss S Kelleway	0-1
D Harrison	0-4	Claire Balding	0-1	Mrs L Lawson	0-1
L Dettori	0-4	Dale Gibson	0-1	Pat Eddery	0-1
D Wright	0-3	E Johnson	0-1	S Maloney	0-1
J Quinn	0-3	J Lowe	0-1	S Wynne	0-1
L Charnock	0-3	M Baird	0-1	W Newnes	0-1
G Bardwell	0-2	M Hills	0-1	W R Swinburn	0-1
M Fenton	0-2	M Humphries	0-1		

COURSE RECORD

	Total W-R	Non-Handicaps 2-y-o	Non-Handicaps 3-y-o+	Handicaps 2-y-o	Handicaps 3-y-o+	Per cent	£1 Level Stake
Southwell (AW)	10-40	0-3	1-2	0-0	9-35	25.0	+ 52.25
Beverley	1-4	0-0	0-0	0-0	1-4	25.0	+ 3.00
Lingfield (AW)	1-19	0-0	0-1	0-0	1-18	5.3	- 10.00

Nottingham	0-9	York	0-3	Folkestone	0-1
Newmarket	0-6	Catterick	0-2	Haydock	0-1
Thirsk	0-6	Kempton	0-2	Lingfield	0-1
Leicester	0-4	Pontefract	0-2	Redcar	0-1
Southwell (Turf)	0-4	Sandown	0-2	Warwick	0-1
Doncaster	0-3	Epsom	0-1	Yarmouth	0-1

WINNING HORSES

	Age	Races Run	1st	2nd	3rd	Unpl	Win £
Rural Lad	4	18	3	2	0	13	10,869
Sirtelimar	4	13	4	0	0	9	10,472
Modest Hope	6	8	3	0	3	2	7,684
Malenoir	5	9	1	0	0	8	3,106
Music Dancer	4	6	1	0	0	5	2,847

WINNING OWNERS

	Races Won	Value £		Races Won	Value £
John Purcell	4	11,933	J McManamon	3	7,684
D W Price	4	10,472	Vintage Racing	1	4,890

Favourites	1-7	14.3%	- 3.75	Total winning prize-money	£34,978
Longest winning sequence			2	Average SP of winner	8.0/1
Longest losing sequence			39	Return on stakes invested	-4.2%

1992 Form	5-38	13.2%	+ 38.75

383

A C STEWART (Newmarket)

	No. of Horses	Races Run	1st	2nd	3rd	Unpl	Per cent	£1 Level Stake
2-y-o	10	14	0	0	0	14	-	- 14.00
3-y-o	24	98	11	18	17	52	11.2	- 21.27
4-y-o+	2	8	0	1	1	6	-	- 8.00
Totals	36	120	11	19	18	72	9.2	- 43.27

BY MONTH

2-y-o	W-R	Per cent	£1 Level Stake	3-y-o	W-R	Per cent	£1 Level Stake
Mar/Apr	0-1	-	- 1.00	Mar/Apr	2-10	20.0	+ 17.73
May	0-0	-	0.00	May	1-9	11.1	- 2.00
June	0-0	-	0.00	June	4-20	20.0	- 5.50
July	0-2	-	- 2.00	July	2-18	11.1	- 5.50
August	0-4	-	- 4.00	August	0-12	-	- 12.00
September	0-1	-	- 1.00	September	0-10	-	- 10.00
Oct/Nov	0-6	-	- 6.00	Oct/Nov	2-19	10.5	- 4.00

4-y-o+	W-R	Per cent	£1 Level Stake	Totals	W-R	Per cent	£1 Level Stake
Mar/Apr	0-3	-	- 3.00	Mar/Apr	2-14	14.3	+ 13.73
May	0-2	-	- 2.00	May	1-11	9.1	- 4.00
June	0-1	-	- 1.00	June	4-21	19.0	- 6.50
July	0-2	-	- 2.00	July	2-22	9.1	- 9.50
August	0-0	-	0.00	August	0-16	-	- 16.00
September	0-0	-	0.00	September	0-11	-	- 11.00
Oct/Nov	0-0	-	0.00	Oct/Nov	2-25	8.0	- 10.00

DISTANCE

2-y-o	W-R	Per cent	£1 Level Stake	3-y-o	W-R	Per cent	£1 Level Stake
5f-6f	0-5	-	- 5.00	5f-6f	0-3	-	- 3.00
7f-8f	0-9	-	- 9.00	7f-8f	6-36	16.7	+ 6.98
9f-13f	0-0	-	0.00	9f-13f	4-52	7.7	- 24.25
14f+	0-0	-	0.00	14f+	1-7	14.3	- 1.00

4-y-o+	W-R	Per cent	£1 Level Stake	Totals	W-R	Per cent	£1 Level Stake
5f-6f	0-0	-	0.00	5f-6f	0-8	-	- 8.00
7f-8f	0-1	-	- 1.00	7f-8f	6-46	13.0	- 3.02
9f-13f	0-6	-	- 6.00	9f-13f	4-58	6.9	- 30.25
14f+	0-1	-	- 1.00	14f+	1-8	12.5	- 2.00

TYPE OF RACE

Non-Handicaps	W-R	Per cent	£1 Level Stake	Handicaps	W-R	Per cent	£1 Level Stake
2-y-o	0-14	-	- 14.00	2-y-o	0-0	-	0.00
3-y-o	7-65	10.8	- 2.75	3-y-o	4-30	13.3	- 15.52
4-y-o+	0-6	-	- 6.00	4-y-o+	0-2	-	- 2.00
Selling	0-0	-	0.00	Selling	0-0	-	0.00
Apprentice	0-1	-	- 1.00	Apprentice	0-2	-	- 2.00
Amat/Ladies	0-0	-	0.00	Amat/Ladies	0-0	-	0.00
Totals	7-86	8.1	- 23.75	Totals	4-34	11.8	- 19.52

COURSE GRADE

	W-R	Per cent	£1 Level Stake
Group 1	5-45	11.1	+ 8.00
Group 2	1-17	5.9	- 12.50
Group 3	4-47	8.5	- 34.77
Group 4	1-11	9.1	- 4.00

FIRST TIME OUT

	W-R	Per cent	£1 Level Stake
2-y-o	0-10	-	- 10.00
3-y-o	2-24	8.3	+ 3.73
4-y-o+	0-2	-	- 2.00
Totals	2-36	5.6	- 8.27

JOCKEYS RIDING

	W-R	Per cent	£1 Level Stake		W-R	Per cent	£1 Level Stake
W Carson	4-22	18.2	- 2.27	R Hills	2-15	13.3	+ 14.75
S Whitworth	4-25	16.0	- 4.75	A McGlone	1-27	3.7	- 20.00

M Roberts	0-10	J Reid	0-2	L Piggott	0-1
J Weaver	0-4	L Dettori	0-2	Pat Eddery	0-1
C Dykes	0-3	A Clark	0-1	R Cochrane	0-1
J Carroll	0-2	B Raymond	0-1		
J Quinn	0-2	D McKeown	0-1		

COURSE RECORD

	Total W-R	Non-Handicaps 2-y-o	Non-Handicaps 3-y-o+	Handicaps 2-y-o	Handicaps 3-y-o+	Per cent	£1 Level Stake
Hamilton	2-2	0-0	1-1	0-0	1-1	100.0	+ 4.00
Doncaster	2-7	0-2	2-5	0-0	0-0	28.6	+ 8.00
Southwell (AW)	1-1	0-0	1-1	0-0	0-0	100.0	+ 6.00
Sandown	1-4	0-0	1-3	0-0	0-1	25.0	+ 4.00
Newbury	1-5	0-0	1-5	0-0	0-0	20.0	- 1.00
Salisbury	1-5	0-0	0-2	0-0	1-3	20.0	- 0.50
Nottingham	1-9	0-3	0-4	0-0	1-2	11.1	- 7.27
Yarmouth	1-15	0-5	0-5	0-0	1-5	6.7	- 10.50
Newmarket	1-16	0-1	1-11	0-0	0-4	6.3	+ 10.00

Stewart A C

Leicester	0-6	Ascot	0-2	Carlisle	0-1
Bath	0-5	Catterick	0-2	Chepstow	0-1
Brighton	0-5	Goodwood	0-2	Epsom	0-1
Windsor	0-5	Kempton	0-2	Lingfield	0-1
Folkestone	0-4	Southwell (Turf)	0-2	Lingfield (AW)	0-1
Ripon	0-4	Thirsk	0-2	Newcastle	0-1
Haydock	0-3	Ayr	0-1	York	0-1
Pontefract	0-3	Beverley	0-1		

WINNING HORSES

	Age	Races Run	1st	2nd	3rd	Unpl	Win £
Ajdayt	3	8	3	1	0	4	11,506
Wagon Master	3	5	2	2	0	1	9,732
Barik	3	6	1	0	1	4	4,045
Fair Shirley	3	2	1	0	1	0	3,436
Rafif	3	7	1	1	0	5	3,435
Nawahil	3	8	1	3	3	1	3,056
Bayrak	3	4	1	0	1	2	2,364
Cast The Line	3	8	1	3	0	4	1,380

WINNING OWNERS

	Races Won	Value £		Races Won	Value £
Hamdan Al-Maktoum	6	22,631	D P Barrie	1	1,380
Sheikh Ahmed Al Maktoum	4	14,942			

Favourites	4-20	20.0%	- 7.02	Total winning prize-money	£38,953
Longest winning sequence			2	Average SP of winner	6.0/1
Longest losing sequence			54	Return on stakes invested	-36.1%
1992 Form	22-129	17.1%	- 28.70	1990 Form 40-234 17.1%	- 81.52
1991 Form	29-194	14.9%	- 2.19	1989 Form 30-200 15.0%	- 75.03

M R STOUTE (Newmarket)

	No. of Horses	Races Run	1st	2nd	3rd	Unpl	Per cent	£1 Level Stake
2-y-o	42	83	16	7	12	48	19.3	- 14.28
3-y-o	63	282	40	36	35	171	14.2	- 66.89
4-y-o+	13	54	9	8	6	31	16.7	+ 11.67
Totals	118	419	65	51	53	250	15.5	- 69.50

BY MONTH

2-y-o	W-R	Per cent	£1 Level Stake	3-y-o	W-R	Per cent	£1 Level Stake
Mar/Apr	0-0	-	0.00	Mar/Apr	4-36	11.1	- 2.08
May	1-2	50.0	+ 1.00	May	8-54	14.8	- 16.50
June	0-1	-	- 1.00	June	5-41	12.2	- 11.04
July	0-8	-	- 8.00	July	2-35	5.7	- 27.75
August	7-20	35.0	+ 10.52	August	6-51	11.8	- 19.62
September	5-30	16.7	- 13.13	September	13-44	29.5	+ 10.47
Oct/Nov	3-22	13.6	- 3.67	Oct/Nov	2-21	9.5	0.00

4-y-o+	W-R	Per cent	£1 Level Stake	Totals	W-R	Per cent	£1 Level Stake
Mar/Apr	2-9	22.2	+ 2.00	Mar/Apr	6-45	13.3	- 0.08
May	1-9	11.1	- 6.25	May	10-65	15.4	- 21.75
June	1-11	9.1	- 7.75	June	6-53	11.3	- 19.79
July	2-7	28.6	+ 7.50	July	4-50	8.0	- 28.25
August	1-7	14.3	+ 22.00	August	14-78	17.9	+ 12.90
September	2-7	28.6	- 0.83	September	20-81	24.7	- 3.49
Oct/Nov	0-4	-	- 4.00	Oct/Nov	5-47	10.6	- 7.67

DISTANCE

2-y-o	W-R	Per cent	£1 Level Stake	3-y-o	W-R	Per cent	£1 Level Stake
5f-6f	8-27	29.6	+ 1.68	5f-6f	1-9	11.1	- 5.50
7f-8f	8-56	14.3	- 15.96	7f-8f	9-94	9.6	- 25.00
9f-13f	0-0	-	0.00	9f-13f	28-156	17.9	- 26.39
14f+	0-0	-	0.00	14f+	2-23	8.7	- 10.00

4-y-o+	W-R	Per cent	£1 Level Stake	Totals	W-R	Per cent	£1 Level Stake
5f-6f	1-1	100.0	+ 0.67	5f-6f	10-37	27.0	- 3.15
7f-8f	0-16	-	- 16.00	7f-8f	17-166	10.2	- 56.96
9f-13f	8-33	24.2	+ 31.00	9f-13f	36-189	19.0	+ 4.61
14f+	0-4	-	- 4.00	14f+	2-27	7.4	- 14.00

TYPE OF RACE

Non-Handicaps	W-R	Per cent	£1 Level Stake	Handicaps	W-R	Per cent	£1 Level Stake
2-y-o	15-78	19.2	- 14.78	2-y-o	1-5	20.0	+ 0.50
3-y-o	24-176	13.6	- 64.78	3-y-o	15-101	14.9	+ 0.26
4-y-o+	9-33	27.3	+ 32.67	4-y-o+	0-19	-	- 19.00
Selling	0-0	-	0.00	Selling	0-0	-	0.00
Apprentice	0-2	-	- 2.00	Apprentice	0-2	-	- 2.00
Amat/Ladies	1-2	50.0	+ 0.63	Amat/Ladies	0-1	-	- 1.00
Totals	49-291	16.8	- 48.26	Totals	16-128	12.5	- 21.24

COURSE GRADE

	W-R	Per cent	£1 Level Stake
Group 1	34-243	14.0	- 53.67
Group 2	10-64	15.6	- 16.83
Group 3	18-88	20.5	+ 12.25
Group 4	3-24	12.5	- 11.25

FIRST TIME OUT

	W-R	Per cent	£1 Level Stake
2-y-o	6-42	14.3	- 11.57
3-y-o	7-63	11.1	- 10.20
4-y-o+	4-13	30.8	+ 3.00
Totals	17-118	14.4	- 18.77

JOCKEYS RIDING

	W-R	Per cent	£1 Level Stake		W-R	Per cent	£1 Level Stake
W R Swinburn	20-116	17.2	+ 0.35	W Ryan	2-8	25.0	- 1.12
M Roberts	9-50	18.0	+ 12.25	B Rouse	1-1	100.0	+ 3.33
Paul Eddery	7-47	14.9	- 25.11	M J Kinane	1-1	100.0	+ 4.50
B Raymond	6-32	18.8	- 6.58	M Hills	1-3	33.3	+ 2.00
P D'Arcy	5-27	18.5	+ 11.00	A Munro	1-4	25.0	- 1.25
K Darley	3-14	21.4	- 3.50	Mrs M Cowdrey	1-4	25.0	- 1.37
Pat Eddery	3-19	15.8	- 6.25	L Dettori	1-8	12.5	- 2.00
R Cochrane	3-20	15.0	- 1.75	W Carson	1-10	10.0	+ 1.00

D Holland	0-10	C Dwyer	0-2	K Rutter	0-1
J Tate	0-6	D Harrison	0-2	L Piggott	0-1
K Fallon	0-6	G Duffield	0-2	N Kennedy	0-1
M Birch	0-4	T Quinn	0-2	P Robinson	0-1
D McKeown	0-3	A McGlone	0-1	T Williams	0-1
K Pattinson	0-3	F Norton	0-1	W Woods	0-1
R Hills	0-3	G Carter	0-1		
C Asmussen	0-2	J Reid	0-1		

COURSE RECORD

	Total W-R	Non-Handicaps 2-y-o	Non-Handicaps 3-y-o+	Handicaps 2-y-o	Handicaps 3-y-o+	Per cent	£1 Level Stake
Newmarket	6-56	2-16	2-28	0-0	2-12	10.7	- 13.67
Goodwood	5-16	0-0	5-10	0-0	0-6	31.3	+ 6.34
Kempton	5-18	1-4	2-8	1-1	1-5	27.8	- 1.75
Yarmouth	5-29	3-10	1-10	0-1	1-8	17.2	+ 3.25
Bath	4-5	0-0	4-5	0-0	0-0	80.0	+ 9.00
Leicester	4-14	1-5	3-9	0-0	0-0	28.6	+ 22.67
Pontefract	3-12	1-2	2-8	0-0	0-2	25.0	- 1.75
Ripon	3-14	0-1	1-5	0-0	2-8	21.4	+ 2.00
Ascot	3-18	0-2	1-10	0-1	2-5	16.7	+ 8.00
Doncaster	3-23	2-7	0-8	0-2	1-6	13.0	- 11.00
York	3-26	0-2	2-10	0-0	1-14	11.5	+ 8.51
Salisbury	2-5	0-1	1-3	0-0	1-1	40.0	+ 7.25
Southwell (AW)	2-5	1-1	1-1	0-0	0-3	40.0	+ 1.75
Epsom	2-6	0-0	1-4	0-0	1-2	33.3	+ 4.25
Newcastle	2-12	1-2	1-5	0-0	0-5	16.7	- 7.70
Haydock	2-13	2-2	0-5	0-0	0-6	15.4	- 8.65
Chester	2-14	0-1	1-6	0-0	1-7	14.3	- 3.50
Sandown	2-30	0-3	1-20	0-0	1-7	6.7	- 18.00

Hamilton	1-2	1-1	0-1	0-0	0-0	50.0	+ 0.75
Chepstow	1-3	0-0	1-3	0-0	0-0	33.3	+ 1.33
Thirsk	1-5	0-0	1-4	0-0	0-1	20.0	- 3.33
Ayr	1-6	0-2	0-2	0-0	1-2	16.7	- 1.00
Warwick	1-6	0-1	1-3	0-0	0-2	16.7	0.00
Brighton	1-8	0-1	1-7	0-0	0-0	12.5	- 4.25
Lingfield	1-14	0-2	1-8	0-0	0-4	7.1	- 11.00

Newbury	0-19	Windsor	0-5	Carlisle	0-1
Nottingham	0-13	Redcar	0-4	Lingfield (AW)	0-1
Beverley	0-5	Folkestone	0-3		
Catterick	0-5	Southwell (Turf)	0-3		

WINNING HORSES

		Races				Win
	Age	Run	1st	2nd	3rd	Unpl	£
Opera House	5	3	3	0	0	0	502,097
Ezzoud	4	4	2	1	0	1	178,740
League Leader	3	10	3	2	1	4	68,499
Cambara	3	7	3	0	2	2	34,940
Zinaad	4	6	1	0	2	3	33,794
Azhar	3	9	4	1	2	2	27,290
Hawajiss	2	4	2	1	0	1	22,053
Sun Of Spring	3	8	4	1	0	3	19,415
Tap On Air	3	6	2	1	0	3	18,485
Shaiba	3	5	1	0	1	3	9,894
Dance To The Top	2	3	2	1	0	0	8,654
Darrery	3	4	2	1	0	1	8,486
Amidst	2	5	2	0	3	0	8,093
Ballet Prince	3	3	2	0	0	1	7,928
Cezanne	4	4	1	1	0	2	7,510
Soviet Line	3	6	2	0	2	2	7,252
Miss Shagra	3	7	2	1	0	4	7,211
Um Algowain	3	3	2	0	0	1	6,316
Arkaan	3	6	1	0	1	4	4,794
Finger Of Light	2	1	1	0	0	0	4,737
Green Green Desert	2	1	1	0	0	0	4,581
Green Crusader	2	2	1	0	0	1	4,521
Desert Shot	3	2	1	0	0	1	4,502
Monaassabaat	2	5	1	0	2	2	4,378
Convoy Point	2	3	1	0	0	2	4,271
Knave's Ash	2	3	1	0	0	2	4,164
Ballerina	2	1	1	0	0	0	4,110
Shareek	3	6	1	1	1	3	4,078
Count Of Flanders	3	3	1	0	0	2	3,670
Mithi Al Gamar	3	5	1	0	0	4	3,641
Bella Ballerina	3	3	1	0	0	2	3,582
Princess Kris	3	7	1	1	2	3	3,582
Princess Haifa	3	3	1	0	0	2	3,553
Just Happy	2	2	1	1	0	0	3,552
Tajannab	2	2	1	0	0	1	3,552
Desert Green	4	3	1	1	0	1	3,524

Scorpius	3	4	1	0	0	3	3,465
Ajalan	3	6	1	0	1	4	3,465
Highland Dress	4	5	1	1	1	2	3,348
Clarinda	2	1	1	0	0	0	3,202
Moussahim	3	6	1	0	2	3	3,158
Red Cotton	3	11	1	5	1	4	3,132
Zarani Sidi Anna	3	7	1	1	2	3	3,056

WINNING OWNERS

	Races Won	Value £		Races Won	Value £
Sheikh Mohammed	20	608,781	The Snailwell Stud Co Ltd	1	4,737
Maktoum Al Maktoum	18	283,757	Mana Al Maktoum	1	4,581
Lord Weinstock	7	83,668	Executors of the late -		
Sheikh Ahmed Al Maktoum	8	47,052	Mrs V Hue-Williams	1	3,582
Cheveley Park Stud	3	13,175	Helena Springfield Ltd	1	3,582
Sir Evelyn De Rothschild	2	8,093	Mana Al Maktoum	1	3,524
Sultan Mohammed	2	7,736			

Favourites	25-74	33.8%	+ 1.25	Total winning prize-money			£1,072,267
Longest winning sequence			3	Average SP of winner			4.4/1
Longest losing sequence			15	Return on stakes invested			-16.6%
1992 Form	74-449	16.5%	- 129.10	1990 Form	78-428	18.2%	- 116.07
1991 Form	83-413	20.1%	- 57.70	1989 Form	117-498	23.5%	- 67.47

A P STRINGER (Thirsk, North Yorks)

	No. of Horses	Races Run	1st	2nd	3rd	Unpl	Per cent	£1 Level Stake
2-y-o	0	0	0	0	0	0	-	0.00
3-y-o	3	22	2	0	5	15	9.1	- 8.12
4-y-o+	6	31	4	2	1	24	12.9	- 10.00
Totals	9	53	6	2	6	39	11.3	- 18.12

Jan	Feb	Mar	Apr	May	Jun	Jul	Aug	Sep	Oct/Nov
0-1	1-2	0-4	2-7	1-7	0-11	1-6	1-8	0-5	0-2

Winning Jockeys	W-R	£1 Level Stake		W-R	£1 Level Stake
J Fortune	1-1	+ 3.00	T Williams	1-7	- 4.12
G Duffield	1-2	+ 4.00	S Maloney	1-9	+ 2.00
F Norton	1-4	+ 3.00	K Darley	1-9	- 5.00

Winning Courses					
Southwell (AW)	4-12	+ 12.88	Beverley	1-3	+ 1.00
Ripon	1-2	+ 4.00			

Winning Horses	Age	Races Run	1st	2nd	3rd	Unpl	Win £
Golden Chip	5	13	3	2	1	7	10,429
Nellie's Gamble	3	14	2	0	5	7	5,220
Heir Of Excitement	8	7	1	0	0	6	2,658

Favourites	2-7	28.6%	- 0.12	Total winning prize-money			£18,307

1992 Form	6-72	8.3%	+ 35.50	1990 Form	5-77	6.5%	- 10.50
1991 Form	4-84	4.8%	- 39.00	1989 Form	2-51	3.9%	- 12.00

J SUTCLIFFE (Epsom, Surrey)

	No. of Horses	Races Run	1st	2nd	3rd	Unpl	Per cent	£1 Level Stake
2-y-o	7	24	1	1	3	19	4.2	- 13.00
3-y-o	5	15	0	0	0	15	-	- 15.00
4-y-o+	8	43	3	3	3	34	7.0	- 21.50
Totals	20	82	4	4	6	68	4.9	- 49.50

Jan	Feb	Mar	Apr	May	Jun	Jul	Aug	Sep	Oct/Nov
0-0	0-0	0-0	0-12	0-9	0-13	1-11	2-19	0-8	1-10

Winning Jockeys	W-R	£1 Level Stake		W-R	£1 Level Stake
Pat Eddery	2-6	+ 8.00	M Roberts	1-2	+ 9.00
Mr L A Urbano	1-1	+ 6.50			

Winning Courses					
Leicester	1-2	+ 4.00	Sandown	1-7	+ 1.00
Epsom	1-4	+ 3.50	Newmarket	1-9	+ 2.00

Winning Horses	Age	Races Run	1st	2nd	3rd	Unpl	Win £
Gadge	2	5	1	0	1	3	11,648
Bo Knows Best	4	4	1	0	0	3	8,238
Saafend	5	5	1	0	0	4	4,475
Superoo	7	9	1	0	0	8	3,553

Favourites	0-3		Total winning prize-money	£27,912

1992 Form	14-131	10.7%	- 61.99	1990 Form	17-153	11.1%	- 46.91
1991 Form	3-103	2.9%	- 82.00	1989 Form	18-127	14.2%	- 19.92

D T THOM (Exning, Suffolk)

	No. of Horses	Races Run	1st	2nd	3rd	Unpl	Per cent	£1 Level Stake
2-y-o	3	20	1	3	0	16	5.0	- 14.50
3-y-o	2	10	0	1	0	9	-	- 10.00
4-y-o+	5	38	3	4	6	25	7.9	- 14.67
Totals	10	68	4	8	6	50	5.9	- 39.17

Jan	Feb	Mar	Apr	May	Jun	Jul	Aug	Sep	Oct/Nov
0-0	0-0	1-1	0-11	0-7	2-12	0-11	0-15	0-4	1-7

Winning Jockeys	W-R	£1 Level Stake		W-R	£1 Level Stake
M Roberts	1-2	+ 3.50	K Rutter	1-5	+ 10.00
Pat Eddery	1-3	+ 1.33	S Eiffert	1-8	- 4.00

Winning Courses	W-R	£1 Level Stake		W-R	£1 Level Stake
Kempton	1-2	+ 2.33	Yarmouth	1-13	- 9.00
Southwell (AW)	1-7	+ 8.00	Newmarket	1-15	- 9.50

Winning Horses	Age	Races Run	1st	2nd	3rd	Unpl	Win £
High Holme	2	7	1	2	0	4	3,883
Ballerina Bay	5	12	1	0	2	9	3,319
Yes	5	5	1	0	0	4	2,259
Captain Marmalade	4	14	1	3	2	8	2,070

Favourites	1-5	20.0%	- 0.67	Total winning prize-money		£11,530

1992 Form	7-146	4.8%	- 83.75	1990 Form	11-130	8.5%	- 21.63
1991 Form	3-104	2.9%	- 55.00	1989 Form	6-133	4.5%	- 28.00

R THOMPSON (Grantham, Lincs)

	No. of Horses	Races Run	1st	2nd	3rd	Unpl	Per cent	£1 Level Stake
2-y-o	0	0	0	0	0	0	-	0.00
3-y-o	0	0	0	0	0	0	-	0.00
4-y-o+	5	16	1	0	2	13	6.3	- 3.00
Totals	5	16	1	0	2	13	6.3	- 3.00

Jan	Feb	Mar	Apr	May	Jun	Jul	Aug	Sep	Oct/Nov
0-2	1-2	0-3	0-5	0-1	0-2	0-1	0-0	0-0	0-0

Winning Jockey	W-R	£1 Level Stake	Winning Course	W-R	£1 Level Stake
Nicola Howarth	1-6	+ 7.00	Southwell (AW)	1-6	+ 7.00

Winning Horse	Age	Races Run	1st	2nd	3rd	Unpl	Win £
Sol Rouge	4	7	1	0	1	5	2,343

Favourites	0-0			Total winning prize-money			£2,343

1992 Form	0-42			1990 Form	1-75	1.3%	- 60.00
1991 Form	0-54			1989 Form	4-78	5.1%	- 25.00

RONALD THOMPSON (Doncaster, South Yorks)

	No. of Horses	Races Run	1st	2nd	3rd	Unpl	Per cent	£1 Level Stake
2-y-o	1	7	0	0	1	6	-	- 7.00
3-y-o	4	22	1	2	0	19	4.5	- 12.00
4-y-o+	1	1	0	0	1	0	-	- 1.00
Totals	6	30	1	2	2	25	3.3	- 20.00

Jan	Feb	Mar	Apr	May	Jun	Jul	Aug	Sep	Oct/Nov
0-1	1-4	0-6	0-2	0-2	0-6	0-4	0-0	0-2	0-3

Winning Jockey	W-R	£1 Level Stake	Winning Course	W-R	£1 Level Stake
O Pears	1-6	+ 4.00	Southwell (AW)	1-17	- 7.00

Winning Horse	Age	Races Run	1st	2nd	3rd	Unpl	Win £
Don't Be Saki	3	13	1	2	0	10	2,070

Favourites	0-1			Total winning prize-money			£2,070

1992 Form	3-50	6.0%	- 21.12	1990 Form	7-123	5.7%	- 46.00
1991 Form	4-75	5.3%	- 23.00	1989 Form	5-121	4.1%	- 72.00

C W THORNTON (Middleham, North Yorks)

	No. of Horses	Races Run	1st	2nd	3rd	Unpl	Per cent	£1 Level Stake
2-y-o	6	24	0	0	2	22	-	- 24.00
3-y-o	7	52	1	9	8	34	1.9	- 35.00
4-y-o+	4	21	1	4	5	11	4.8	- 10.00
Totals	17	97	2	13	15	67	2.1	- 69.00

Jan	Feb	Mar	Apr	May	Jun	Jul	Aug	Sep	Oct/Nov
0-0	0-0	0-3	0-13	1-15	1-19	0-20	0-9	0-8	0-10

Winning Jockeys	W-R	£1 Level Stake		W-R	£1 Level Stake
N Carlisle	1-5	+ 6.00	A Mackay	1-9	+ 8.00

Winning Courses					
Newcastle	1-6	+ 11.00	Carlisle	1-9	+ 2.00

Winning Horses	Age	Races Run	1st	2nd	3rd	Unpl	Win £
Contract Elite	3	11	1	3	1	6	7,570
Chantry Bellini	4	13	1	1	3	8	3,184

Favourites	0-7		Total winning prize-money		£10,754

1992 Form	2-94	2.1%	- 84.00	1990 Form	12-146	8.2%	- 47.06
1991 Form	9-102	8.8%	- 54.17	1989 Form	12-172	7.0%	- 35.17

C TINKLER (Malton, North Yorks)

	No. of Horses	Races Run	1st	2nd	3rd	Unpl	Per cent	£1 Level Stake
2-y-o	6	17	0	0	1	16	-	- 17.00
3-y-o	8	54	3	6	6	39	5.6	- 40.04
4-y-o+	10	49	0	5	4	40	-	- 49.00
Totals	24	120	3	11	11	95	2.5	-106.04

Jan	Feb	Mar	Apr	May	Jun	Jul	Aug	Sep	Oct/Nov
0-9	0-4	0-7	3-19	0-27	0-14	0-8	0-12	0-12	0-8

Winning Jockeys	W-R	£1 Level Stake		W-R	£1 Level Stake
M Birch	2-25	- 15.37	L Dettori	1-2	+ 2.33

Winning Courses					
Southwell (AW)	2-31	- 21.37	Nottingham	1-8	- 3.67

Winning Horses	Age	Races Run	1st	2nd	3rd	Unpl	Win £
Certain Way	3	7	2	3	0	2	5,746
Dead Calm	3	19	1	2	3	13	2,243

Favourites	2-5	40.0%	+ 1.96	Total winning prize-money		£7,989

1992 Form	5-139	3.6%	- 51.50	1990 Form	28-284	9.9%	-135.39
1991 Form	15-188	8.0%	- 69.09	1989 Form	35-322	10.9%	-120.83

N TINKLER (Malton, North Yorks)

	No. of Horses	Races Run	1st	2nd	3rd	Unpl	Per cent	£1 Level Stake
2-y-o	3	15	0	0	1	14	-	- 15.00
3-y-o	10	62	10	6	11	35	16.1	- 11.40
4-y-o+	23	65	5	5	5	50	7.7	- 21.50
Totals	36	142	15	11	17	99	10.6	- 47.90

BY MONTH

2-y-o	W-R	Per cent	£1 Level Stake	3-y-o	W-R	Per cent	£1 Level Stake
January	0-0	-	0.00	January	0-4	-	- 4.00
February	0-0	-	0.00	February	0-1	-	- 1.00
March	0-1	-	- 1.00	March	0-2	-	- 2.00
April	0-1	-	- 1.00	April	0-7	-	- 7.00
May	0-0	-	0.00	May	0-7	-	- 7.00
June	0-4	-	- 4.00	June	4-9	44.4	+ 6.35
July	0-4	-	- 4.00	July	5-15	33.3	+ 14.25
August	0-3	-	- 3.00	August	0-7	-	- 7.00
September	0-2	-	- 2.00	September	1-7	14.3	- 1.00
Oct/Nov	0-0	-	0.00	Oct/Nov	0-3	-	- 3.00

4-y-o+	W-R	Per cent	£1 Level Stake	Totals	W-R	Per cent	£1 Level Stake
January	1-7	14.3	- 0.50	January	1-11	9.1	- 4.50
February	0-4	-	- 4.00	February	0-5	-	- 5.00
March	0-3	-	- 3.00	March	0-6	-	- 6.00
April	1-6	16.7	+ 7.00	April	1-14	7.1	- 1.00
May	2-9	22.2	+ 9.50	May	2-16	12.5	+ 2.50
June	0-12	-	- 12.00	June	4-25	16.0	- 9.65
July	0-5	-	- 5.00	July	5-24	20.8	+ 5.25
August	1-4	25.0	+ 1.50	August	1-14	7.1	- 8.50
September	0-3	-	- 3.00	September	1-12	8.3	- 6.00
Oct/Nov	0-12	-	- 12.00	Oct/Nov	0-15	-	- 15.00

DISTANCE

2-y-o	W-R	Per cent	£1 Level Stake	3-y-o	W-R	Per cent	£1 Level Stake
5f-6f	0-6	-	- 6.00	5f-6f	7-19	36.8	+ 14.10
7f-8f	0-9	-	- 9.00	7f-8f	1-29	3.4	- 20.00
9f-13f	0-0	-	0.00	9f-13f	2-11	18.2	- 2.50
14f+	0-0	-	0.00	14f+	0-3	-	- 3.00

4-y-o+	W-R	Per cent	£1 Level Stake	Totals	W-R	Per cent	£1 Level Stake
5f-6f	1-10	10.0	- 1.50	5f-6f	8-35	22.9	+ 6.60
7f-8f	1-10	10.0	- 3.50	7f-8f	2-48	4.2	- 32.50
9f-13f	1-25	4.0	- 19.50	9f-13f	3-36	8.3	- 22.00
14f+	2-20	10.0	+ 3.00	14f+	2-23	8.7	0.00

Tinkler N

TYPE OF RACE

Non-Handicaps	W-R	Per cent	£1 Level Stake	Handicaps	W-R	Per cent	£1 Level Stake
2-y-o	0-7	-	- 7.00	2-y-o	0-1	-	- 1.00
3-y-o	0-22	-	- 22.00	3-y-o	6-33	18.2	- 4.65
4-y-o+	0-17	-	- 17.00	4-y-o+	4-40	10.0	- 2.00
Selling	3-12	25.0	+ 7.00	Selling	1-7	14.3	- 3.75
Apprentice	0-0	-	0.00	Apprentice	1-3	33.3	+ 2.50
Amat/Ladies	0-0	-	0.00	Amat/Ladies	0-0	-	0.00
Totals	3-58	5.2	- 39.00	Totals	12-84	14.3	- 8.90

COURSE GRADE

	W-R	Per cent	£1 Level Stake
Group 1	5-44	11.4	- 10.75
Group 2	4-29	13.8	+ 4.00
Group 3	2-30	6.7	- 20.00
Group 4	4-39	10.3	- 21.15

FIRST TIME OUT

	W-R	Per cent	£1 Level Stake
2-y-o	0-3	-	- 3.00
3-y-o	0-10	-	- 10.00
4-y-o+	1-19	5.3	- 6.00
Totals	1-32	3.1	- 19.00

JOCKEYS RIDING

	W-R	Per cent	£1 Level Stake		W-R	Per cent	£1 Level Stake
Kim Tinkler	4-60	6.7	- 34.50	O Pears	1-2	50.0	+ 0.10
L Piggott	3-13	23.1	+ 3.25	J Fortune	1-3	33.3	+ 1.00
N Carlisle	2-10	20.0	+ 8.50	M Birch	1-6	16.7	0.00
B Doyle	1-1	100.0	+ 12.00	L Charnock	1-26	3.8	- 22.75
P Rose	1-1	100.0	+ 4.50				

G Duffield	0-4	C Munday	0-1	N Tinkler	0-1
W Newnes	0-4	D Nicholls	0-1	Pat Eddery	0-1
E Husband	0-2	M Wood	0-1	S Maloney	0-1
J Quinn	0-2	N Connorton	0-1	S Morris	0-1

COURSE RECORD

	Total W-R	Non-Handicaps 2-y-o	3-y-o+	Handicaps 2-y-o	3-y-o+	Per cent	£1 Level Stake
Ascot	1-1	0-0	0-0	0-0	1-1	100.0	+ 5.00
Windsor	1-1	0-0	0-0	0-0	1-1	100.0	+ 4.50
Goodwood	1-2	0-0	0-0	0-0	1-2	50.0	+ 5.00
Kempton	1-2	0-0	0-0	0-0	1-2	50.0	+ 11.00
Ayr	1-3	0-0	0-1	0-0	1-2	33.3	+ 1.00
Chester	1-3	0-0	0-1	0-0	1-2	33.3	+ 7.00
Carlisle	1-4	0-0	0-2	0-0	1-2	25.0	- 0.75
Catterick	1-4	0-0	0-1	0-0	1-3	25.0	+ 2.00

Tinkler N

Edinburgh	1-4	0-1	0-1	0-0	1-2	25.0	- 1.90
Newmarket	1-5	0-0	0-1	0-1	1-3	20.0	- 1.75
Thirsk	1-6	0-0	0-4	0-0	1-2	16.7	+ 2.50
Ripon	1-7	0-0	1-3	0-0	0-4	14.3	+ 2.00
Pontefract	1-8	0-1	1-2	0-0	0-5	12.5	- 3.50
Redcar	1-13	0-1	1-5	0-0	0-7	7.7	- 7.50
Southwell (AW)	1-23	0-1	0-8	0-0	1-14	4.3	- 16.50

Nottingham	0-10	Beverley	0-5	Sandown	0-1
Newcastle	0-8	Hamilton	0-3	Southwell (Turf)	0-1
York	0-8	Warwick	0-3	Uttoxeter	0-1
Doncaster	0-7	Bath	0-1	Yarmouth	0-1
Haydock	0-6	Leicester	0-1		

WINNING HORSES

	Age	Races Run	1st	2nd	3rd	Unpl	Win £
Rodeo Star	7	6	2	0	1	3	35,075
Call Me I'm Blue	3	12	5	2	2	3	29,754
Norling	3	12	2	1	2	7	4,143
Scoffera	3	15	2	1	3	9	3,985
Sonderise	4	10	1	0	1	8	3,816
Hyde's Happy Hour	3	5	1	1	1	2	2,736
Mentalasanythin	4	1	1	0	0	0	2,490
Le Temeraire	7	11	1	4	1	5	2,243

WINNING OWNERS

	Races Won	Value £		Races Won	Value £
J C Bradbury	2	35,075	Mrs D Wright	1	3,816
Harsh (Tipping Gears)	5	29,754	Travellers T Time Club	1	2,736
S Pedersen	2	4,143	Mrs M O'Donnell	1	2,490
Mrs Christine Cawley	2	3,985	Dave Douglas	1	2,243

Favourites	4-13	30.8%	+ 1.10	Total winning prize-money		£84,241
Longest winning sequence			2	Average SP of winner		5.3/1
Longest losing sequence			20	Return on stakes invested		-33.4%
1992 Form	9-150	6.0%	- 90.92	1990 Form	17-300	5.7% -231.34
1991 Form	13-197	6.6%	-110.64	1989 Form	24-291	8.2% -146.14

J A R TOLLER (Newmarket)

	No. of Horses	Races Run	1st	2nd	3rd	Unpl	Per cent	£1 Level Stake
2-y-o	2	4	1	1	0	2	25.0	- 2.56
3-y-o	6	18	1	0	0	17	5.6	- 8.00
4-y-o+	5	22	1	0	5	16	4.5	- 10.00
Totals	13	44	3	1	5	35	6.8	- 20.56

Jan	Feb	Mar	Apr	May	Jun	Jul	Aug	Sep	Oct/Nov
0-1	0-1	0-1	0-2	1-9	1-3	0-6	1-11	0-5	0-5

Winning Jockeys	W-R	£1 Level Stake			W-R	£1 Level Stake
J Weaver	2-10	+ 12.00	G Duffield		1-5	- 3.56

Winning Courses						
Ascot	1-1	+ 11.00	Nottingham		1-2	- 0.56
Redcar	1-1	+ 9.00				

Winning Horses	Age	Races Run	1st	2nd	3rd	Unpl	Win £
Nagida	4	7	1	0	2	4	39,640
Grotto Pool	2	3	1	1	0	1	3,875
Awesome Venture	3	4	1	0	0	3	3,494

Favourites	1-4	25.0%	- 2.56	Total winning prize-money		£47,009

1992 Form	9-60	15.0%	- 15.44	1990 Form	7-84	8.3%	- 46.75
1991 Form	4-66	6.1%	- 42.12	1989 Form	7-65	10.8%	+ 49.25

M H TOMPKINS (Newmarket)

	No. of Horses	Races Run	1st	2nd	3rd	Unpl	Per cent	£1 Level Stake
2-y-o	31	127	5	14	18	90	3.9	-108.25
3-y-o	17	93	18	9	8	58	19.4	+ 37.31
4-y-o+	15	70	4	9	11	46	5.7	- 53.80
Totals	63	290	27	32	37	194	9.3	-124.74

398

BY MONTH

2-y-o	W-R	Per cent	£1 Level Stake	3-y-o	W-R	Per cent	£1 Level Stake
January	0-0	-	0.00	January	0-3	-	- 3.00
February	0-0	-	0.00	February	0-0	-	0.00
March	0-0	-	0.00	March	0-1	-	- 1.00
April	0-4	-	- 4.00	April	2-9	22.2	+ 6.63
May	1-14	7.1	- 7.00	May	5-13	38.5	+ 21.63
June	2-21	9.5	- 16.50	June	1-20	5.0	- 17.25
July	2-17	11.8	- 9.75	July	0-12	-	- 12.00
August	0-16	-	- 16.00	August	4-11	36.4	+ 29.80
September	0-24	-	- 24.00	September	3-15	20.0	+ 3.50
Oct/Nov	0-31	-	- 31.00	Oct/Nov	3-9	33.3	+ 9.00

4-y-o+	W-R	Per cent	£1 Level Stake	Totals	W-R	Per cent	£1 Level Stake
January	0-1	-	- 1.00	January	0-4	-	- 4.00
February	0-0	-	0.00	February	0-0	-	0.00
March	0-0	-	0.00	March	0-1	-	- 1.00
April	0-6	-	- 6.00	April	2-19	10.5	- 3.37
May	0-8	-	- 8.00	May	6-35	17.1	+ 6.63
June	0-9	-	- 9.00	June	3-50	6.0	- 42.75
July	2-13	15.4	- 6.93	July	4-42	9.5	- 28.68
August	1-12	8.3	- 9.37	August	5-39	12.8	+ 4.43
September	1-7	14.3	+ 0.50	September	4-46	8.7	- 20.00
Oct/Nov	0-14	-	- 14.00	Oct/Nov	3-54	5.6	- 36.00

DISTANCE

2-y-o	W-R	Per cent	£1 Level Stake	3-y-o	W-R	Per cent	£1 Level Stake
5f-6f	2-77	2.6	- 67.75	5f-6f	0-11	-	- 11.00
7f-8f	3-47	6.4	- 37.50	7f-8f	5-32	15.6	+ 0.13
9f-13f	0-3	-	- 3.00	9f-13f	9-37	24.3	+ 39.93
14f+	0-0	-	0.00	14f+	4-13	30.8	+ 8.25

4-y-o+	W-R	Per cent	£1 Level Stake	Totals	W-R	Per cent	£1 Level Stake
5f-6f	0-8	-	- 8.00	5f-6f	2-96	2.1	- 86.75
7f-8f	0-15	-	- 15.00	7f-8f	8-94	8.5	- 52.37
9f-13f	4-44	9.1	- 27.80	9f-13f	13-84	15.5	+ 9.13
14f+	0-3	-	- 3.00	14f+	4-16	25.0	+ 5.25

TYPE OF RACE

Non-Handicaps	W-R	Per cent	£1 Level Stake	Handicaps	W-R	Per cent	£1 Level Stake
2-y-o	3-81	3.7	- 69.50	2-y-o	1-27	3.7	- 23.50
3-y-o	12-45	26.7	+ 52.30	3-y-o	3-36	8.3	- 24.62
4-y-o+	0-10	-	- 10.00	4-y-o+	1-44	2.3	- 36.50
Selling	4-28	14.3	- 12.99	Selling	1-8	12.5	+ 5.00
Apprentice	1-1	100.0	+ 0.57	Apprentice	0-9	-	- 9.00
Amat/Ladies	0-0	-	0.00	Amat/Ladies	1-1	100.0	+ 3.50
Totals	20-165	12.1	- 39.62	Totals	7-125	5.6	- 85.12

COURSE GRADE					FIRST TIME OUT		
	W–R	Per cent	£1 Level Stake			W–R	Per cent	£1 Level Stake
Group 1	7-113	6.2	- 63.25	2-y-o	1-31	3.2	- 24.00
Group 2	2-21	9.5	- 3.37	3-y-o	1-16	6.3	- 1.00
Group 3	10-96	10.4	- 40.87	4-y-o+	0-14	-	- 14.00
Group 4	8-60	13.3	- 17.25				
				Totals	2-61	3.3	- 39.00

JOCKEYS RIDING

	W–R	Per cent	£1 Level Stake			W–R	Per cent	£1 Level Stake
P Robinson	18-178	10.1	- 69.44	Mr M Jenkins	1-1	100.0	+ 3.50
S Mulvey	6-84	7.1	- 46.37	J Gotobed	1-3	33.3	1.43
W Woods	1-1	100.0	+ 12.00				

Dale Gibson	0-7	D Biggs	0-1	R Cochrane	0-1
K Darley	0-4	E Johnson	0-1	S Allen	0-1
A Clark	0-1	G Duffield	0-1	T Quinn	0-1
A Mackay	0-1	J Weaver	0-1	W Ryan	0-1
B Rouse	0-1	M Tebbutt	0-1		

COURSE RECORD

	Total W–R	Non-Handicaps 2-y-o	Non-Handicaps 3-y-o+	Handicaps 2-y-o	Handicaps 3-y-o+	Per cent	£1 Level Stake
Yarmouth	7-33	1-11	3-8	1-6	2-8	21.2	+ 13.25
Ayr	3-4	0-0	1-2	0-0	2-2	75.0	+ 18.50
Southwell (AW)	3-15	1-6	2-6	0-0	0-3	20.0	- 3.95
Carlisle	2-8	1-2	0-1	0-0	1-5	25.0	+ 1.63
Bath	1-2	1-1	0-1	0-0	0-0	50.0	+ 0.25
Southwell (Turf)	1-4	0-1	1-3	0-0	0-0	25.0	- 2.43
Brighton	1-5	0-3	1-1	0-1	0-0	20.0	- 2.37
Catterick	1-5	0-0	1-4	0-0	0-1	20.0	+ 2.50
Lingfield	1-7	0-4	1-1	0-2	0-0	14.3	+ 8.00
Hamilton	1-11	0-5	1-4	0-1	0-1	9.1	- 9.87
Haydock	1-11	0-2	0-2	0-1	1-6	9.1	- 8.25
Warwick	1-11	0-4	1-3	0-1	0-3	9.1	+ 2.00
Doncaster	1-12	0-2	1-3	0-3	0-4	8.3	- 8.00
Nottingham	1-13	0-6	1-1	0-2	0-4	7.7	- 7.50
York	1-14	0-1	1-2	0-1	0-10	7.1	+ 3.00
Newmarket	1-47	0-14	1-12	0-3	0-18	2.1	- 43.50

Pontefract	0-17	Kempton	0-4	Newcastle	0-2
Folkestone	0-12	Beverley	0-3	Redcar	0-2
Leicester	0-9	Edinburgh	0-3	Salisbury	0-2
Sandown	0-7	Epsom	0-3	Chester	0-1
Windsor	0-6	Ripon	0-3	Newbury	0-1
Ascot	0-4	Chepstow	0-2	Thirsk	0-1
Goodwood	0-4	Lingfield (AW)	0-2		

WINNING HORSES

	Age	Races Run	1st	2nd	3rd	Unpl	Win £
Bob's Return	3	4	3	0	0	1	275,271
Shynon	3	6	3	2	0	1	10,641
Cliburnel News	3	10	3	1	1	5	7,580
Don't Jump	3	8	2	0	2	4	6,453
Overpower	9	13	3	2	3	5	6,138
Guv'Nors Gift	3	7	2	1	1	3	5,600
Strephon	3	6	2	0	1	3	5,108
Eden's Close	4	6	1	1	2	2	5,016
The Flying Phantom	2	8	1	2	1	4	4,113
The Multiyorker	2	8	1	1	2	4	3,524
Wixi	2	10	1	2	1	6	3,436
Gweek	3	10	1	4	2	3	3,002
Cabcharge Princess	2	8	1	0	1	6	2,860
O So Neet	3	4	1	0	0	3	2,637
Super Symphonic	2	7	1	0	1	5	2,448
Mrs Snuggs	3	6	1	0	1	4	2,243

WINNING OWNERS

	Races Won	Value £		Races Won	Value £
Mrs G A E Smith	3	275,271	Multiyork Ltd	1	3,524
M P Bowring	6	16,779	Mrs K Dooley	1	3,436
East Lancs Newspapers Readers	3	7,580	Henry B H Chan	1	3,002
Mark Tompkins Racing	2	6,453	Computer Cab Racing Club	1	2,860
The Tompkins Team	2	5,600	Roalco Ltd	1	2,637
Mark Tompkins Elite	2	5,108	Jack Maxwell	1	2,448
Mrs M Barwell	1	5,016	Shane T Ryan	1	2,243
P H Betts (Holdings) Ltd	1	4,113			

Favourites	10-34	29.4%	- 6.62	Total winning prize-money	£346,068

Longest winning sequence	2	Average SP of winner	5.1/1
Longest losing sequence	44	Return on stakes invested	-43.0%

1992 Form	42-372	11.3%	- 88.35	1990 Form	46-435	10.6%	-161.69
1991 Form	42-411	10.2%	-115.54	1989 Form	44-366	12.0%	-104.18

J M TROY (Newmarket)

	No. of Horses	Races Run	1st	2nd	3rd	Unpl	Per cent	£1 Level Stake
2-y-o	8	16	1	1	1	13	6.3	- 10.00
3-y-o	1	5	0	1	0	4	-	- 5.00
4-y-o+	0	0	0	0	0	0	-	0.00
Totals	9	21	1	2	1	17	4.8	- 15.00

Jan	Feb	Mar	Apr	May	Jun	Jul	Aug	Sep	Oct/Nov
0-0	0-0	0-0	1-3	0-6	0-4	0-3	0-3	0-1	0-1

Winning Jockey	W-R	£1 Level Stake	Winning Course		W-R	£1 Level Stake
A Geran	1-7	- 1.00	Sandown		1-3	+ 3.00

Winning Horse	Age	Races Run	1st	2nd	3rd	Unpl	Win £
Montaya	2	4	1	1	0	2	3,630

Favourites	0-2		Total winning prize-money	£3,630

D R TUCKER (Cullompton, Devon)

	No. of Horses	Races Run	1st	2nd	3rd	Unpl	Per cent	£1 Level Stake
2-y-o	1	1	0	0	0	1	-	- 1.00
3-y-o	2	10	0	0	2	8	-	- 10.00
4-y-o+	2	7	1	0	0	6	14.3	+ 2.50
Totals	5	18	1	0	2	15	5.6	- 8.50

Jan	Feb	Mar	Apr	May	Jun	Jul	Aug	Sep	Oct/Nov
0-0	0-0	0-0	0-3	0-2	1-3	0-4	0-4	0-1	0-1

Winning Jockey	W-R	£1 Level Stake	Winning Course		W-R	£1 Level Stake
R Perham	1-7	+ 2.50	Chepstow		1-3	+ 6.50

Winning Horse	Age	Races Run	1st	2nd	3rd	Unpl	Win £
Rich Pickings	4	5	1	0	0	4	2,623

Favourites	0-0		Total winning prize-money	£2,623

1992 Form	1-66	1.5%	- 49.00	1990 Form	0-15
1991 Form	0-26			1989 Form	0-15

W G M TURNER (Sherborne, Dorset)

	No. of Horses	Races Run	1st	2nd	3rd	Unpl	Per cent	£1 Level Stake
2-y-o	11	48	3	3	9	33	6.3	0.00
3-y-o	13	57	5	5	8	39	8.8	- 25.50
4-y-o+	8	20	2	1	1	16	10.0	+ 6.00
Totals	32	125	10	9	18	88	8.0	- 19.50

BY MONTH

2-y-o	W-R	Per cent	£1 Level Stake	3-y-o	W-R	Per cent	£1 Level Stake
January	0-0	-	0.00	January	0-0	-	0.00
February	0-0	-	0.00	February	0-0	-	0.00
March	0-4	-	- 4.00	March	0-2	-	- 2.00
April	1-5	20.0	+ 3.00	April	0-10	-	- 10.00
May	0-7	-	- 7.00	May	2-11	18.2	- 1.00
June	0-9	-	- 9.00	June	2-6	33.3	+ 7.50
July	1-7	14.3	- 1.00	July	1-11	9.1	- 3.00
August	1-6	16.7	+ 28.00	August	0-7	-	- 7.00
September	0-8	-	- 8.00	September	0-3	-	- 3.00
Oct/Nov	0-2	-	- 2.00	Oct/Nov	0-7	-	- 7.00

4-y-o+	W-R	Per cent	£1 Level Stake	Totals	W-R	Per cent	£1 Level Stake
January	0-3	-	- 3.00	January	0-3	-	- 3.00
February	0-0	-	0.00	February	0-0	-	0.00
March	0-2	-	- 2.00	March	0-8	-	- 8.00
April	1-3	33.3	+ 8.00	April	2-18	11.1	+ 1.00
May	1-3	33.3	+ 12.00	May	3-21	14.3	+ 4.00
June	0-1	-	- 1.00	June	2-16	12.5	- 2.50
July	0-1	-	- 1.00	July	2-19	10.5	- 5.00
August	0-4	-	- 4.00	August	1-17	5.9	+ 17.00
September	0-3	-	- 3.00	September	0-14	-	- 14.00
Oct/Nov	0-0	-	0.00	Oct/Nov	0-9	-	- 9.00

DISTANCE

2-y-o	W-R	Per cent	£1 Level Stake	3-y-o	W-R	Per cent	£1 Level Stake
5f-6f	3-36	8.3	+ 12.00	5f-6f	0-19	-	- 19.00
7f-8f	0-10	-	- 10.00	7f-8f	5-30	16.7	+ 1.50
9f-13f	0-2	-	- 2.00	9f-13f	0-8	-	- 8.00
14f+	0-0	-	0.00	14f+	0-0	-	0.00

4-y-o+	W-R	Per cent	£1 Level Stake	Totals	W-R	Per cent	£1 Level Stake
5f-6f	0-5	-	- 5.00	5f-6f	3-60	5.0	- 12.00
7f-8f	1-4	25.0	+ 7.00	7f-8f	6-44	13.6	- 1.50
9f-13f	1-9	11.1	+ 6.00	9f-13f	1-19	5.3	- 4.00
14f+	0-2	-	- 2.00	14f+	0-2	-	- 2.00

TYPE OF RACE

Non-Handicaps	W-R	Per cent	£1 Level Stake	Handicaps	W-R	Per cent	£1 Level Stake
2-y-o	1-22	4.5	- 14.00	2-y-o	0-1	-	- 1.00
3-y-o	3-33	9.1	- 15.50	3-y-o	1-15	6.7	- 7.00
4-y-o+	1-5	20.0	+ 10.00	4-y-o+	1-11	9.1	0.00
Selling	3-28	10.7	+ 18.00	Selling	0-4	-	- 4.00
Apprentice	0-2	-	- 2.00	Apprentice	0-1	-	- 1.00
Amat/Ladies	0-1	-	- 1.00	Amat/Ladies	0-2	-	- 2.00
Totals	8-91	8.8	- 4.50	Totals	2-34	5.9	- 15.00

Turner W G M

COURSE GRADE

	W-R	Per cent	£1 Level Stake
Group 1	0-11	-	- 11.00
Group 2	3-28	10.7	- 1.00
Group 3	2-44	4.5	- 28.00
Group 4	5-42	11.9	+ 20.50

FIRST TIME OUT

	W-R	Per cent	£1 Level Stake
2-y-o	0-11	-	- 11.00
3-y-o	0-13	-	- 13.00
4-y-o+	1-8	12.5	+ 3.00
Totals	1-32	3.1	- 21.00

JOCKEYS RIDING

	W-R	Per cent	£1 Level Stake		W-R	Per cent	£1 Level Stake
T Sprake	5-53	9.4	+ 3.00	D McCabe	2-15	13.3	+ 0.50
G Duffield	2-5	40.0	+ 21.00	P McCabe	1-17	5.9	- 9.00

Paul Eddery	0-5	S Lanigan	0-2	Mrs J Gault	0-1
D Wright	0-3	G Carter	0-1	N Carlisle	0-1
A Tucker	0-2	J Williams	0-1	R Hills	0-1
J Weaver	0-2	L Dettori	0-1	T G McLaughlin	0-1
Mrs C Price	0-2	L Piggott	0-1	T Quinn	0-1
R Cochrane	0-2	L Suthern	0-1	T Williams	0-1
S Davies	0-2	M Baird	0-1		
S Drowne	0-2	M Tebbutt	0-1		

COURSE RECORD

	Total W-R	Non-Handicaps 2-y-o	Non-Handicaps 3-y-o+	Handicaps 2-y-o	Handicaps 3-y-o+	Per cent	£1 Level Stake
Thirsk	2-2	0-0	2-2	0-0	0-0	100.0	+ 19.00
Folkestone	2-14	2-5	0-5	0-0	0-4	14.3	+ 26.00
Catterick	1-2	0-1	0-0	0-0	1-1	50.0	+ 9.00
Lingfield (AW)	1-4	0-0	1-3	0-0	0-1	25.0	+ 3.50
Carlisle	1-6	0-1	1-3	0-0	0-2	16.7	- 2.00
Hamilton	1-6	1-3	0-2	0-0	0-1	16.7	+ 2.00
Beverley	1-7	0-3	0-2	0-1	1-1	14.3	+ 1.00
Brighton	1-18	0-7	1-7	0-1	0-3	5.6	- 12.00

Leicester	0-9	Doncaster	0-3	Lingfield	0-1
Bath	0-8	Pontefract	0-3	Newbury	0-1
Warwick	0-8	Sandown	0-3	Newmarket	0-1
Salisbury	0-7	Edinburgh	0-1	Windsor	0-1
Southwell (AW)	0-7	Epsom	0-1	Yarmouth	0-1
Nottingham	0-6	Goodwood	0-1		
Chepstow	0-3	Kempton	0-1		

WINNING HORSES

	Age	Races Run	1st	2nd	3rd	Unpl	Win £
Royal Interval	3	8	2	2	1	3	7,836
Calisar	3	9	2	0	4	3	4,730
Quinta Royale	6	3	1	0	1	1	3,236

Almost A Princess	5	4	1	0	0	3	3,028
Lying Eyes	2	7	1	2	1	3	2,692
Devious Dancer	3	6	1	1	1	3	2,534
Flair Lady	2	9	1	0	3	5	2,070
Threepenny-Bridge	2	4	1	0	0	3	2,070

WINNING OWNERS

	Races Won	Value £		Races Won	Value £
G L Barker	2	7,836	G J Bush	1	2,534
Laurie Snook	2	6,263	Mrs M S Teversham	1	2,070
A Poole	2	4,730	E Goody	1	2,070
A K Holbrook	1	2,692			

Favourites	1-6	16.7%	- 2.00	Total winning prize-money		£28,194
Longest winning sequence			2	Average SP of winner		9.6/1
Longest losing sequence			34	Return on stakes invested		-15.6%
1992 Form	11-111	9.9%	- 4.12	1990 Form	2-88	2.3% - 62.50
1991 Form	2-61	3.3%	- 38.50	1989 Form	6-59	10.2% - 19.67

N A TWISTON-DAVIES (Cheltenham, Glos)

	No. of Horses	Races Run	1st	2nd	3rd	Unpl	Per cent	£1 Level Stake
2-y-o	2	4	0	0	0	4	-	- 4.00
3-y-o	0	0	0	0	0	0	-	0.00
4-y-o+	3	7	1	0	1	5	14.3	- 3.25
Totals	5	11	1	0	1	9	9.1	- 7.25

Jan	Feb	Mar	Apr	May	Jun	Jul	Aug	Sep	Oct/Nov
0-0	0-0	1-2	0-0	0-4	0-1	0-0	0-3	0-1	0-0

		£1 Level			£1 Level
Winning Jockey	W-R	Stake	Winning Course	W-R	Stake
W Carson	1-1	+ 2.75	Warwick	1-2	+ 1.75

		Races				Win
Winning Horse	Age	Run	1st	2nd	3rd	Unpl	£
Pharoah's Guest	6	3	1	0	0	2	3,417

Favourites	1-2	50.0%	+ 1.75	Total winning prize-money		£3,417

1992 Form	0-7		1991 Form	0-6

M D I USHER (East Garston, Berks)

	No. of Horses	Races Run	1st	2nd	3rd	Unpl	Per cent	£1 Level Stake
2-y-o	12	66	5	7	3	51	7.6	- 23.12
3-y-o	8	37	2	0	3	32	5.4	- 30.87
4-y-o+	11	69	4	0	4	61	5.8	- 39.00
Totals	31	172	11	7	10	144	6.4	- 92.99

BY MONTH

2-y-o	W-R	Per cent	£1 Level Stake	3-y-o	W-R	Per cent	£1 Level Stake
January	0-0	-	0.00	January	0-2	-	- 2.00
February	0-0	-	0.00	February	0-1	-	- 1.00
March	0-0	-	0.00	March	0-1	-	- 1.00
April	0-6	-	- 6.00	April	0-8	-	- 8.00
May	2-5	40.0	+ 7.88	May	1-10	10.0	- 7.62
June	0-11	-	- 11.00	June	1-8	12.5	- 4.25
July	1-12	8.3	- 5.00	July	0-2	-	- 2.00
August	1-13	7.7	- 3.00	August	0-0	-	0.00
September	1-12	8.3	+ 1.00	September	0-1	-	- 1.00
Oct/Nov	0-7	-	- 7.00	Oct/Nov	0-4	-	- 4.00

4-y-o+	W-R	Per cent	£1 Level Stake	Totals	W-R	Per cent	£1 Level Stake
January	0-9	-	- 9.00	January	0-11	-	- 11.00
February	0-3	-	- 3.00	February	0-4	-	- 4.00
March	0-3	-	- 3.00	March	0-4	-	- 4.00
April	0-5	-	- 5.00	April	0-19	-	- 19.00
May	0-10	-	- 10.00	May	3-25	12.0	- 9.74
June	1-16	6.3	- 11.00	June	2-35	5.7	- 26.25
July	0-8	-	- 8.00	July	1-22	4.5	- 15.00
August	0-5	-	- 5.00	August	1-18	5.6	- 8.00
September	2-5	40.0	+ 9.00	September	3-18	16.7	+ 9.00
Oct/Nov	1-5	20.0	+ 6.00	Oct/Nov	1-16	6.3	- 5.00

DISTANCE

2-y-o	W-R	Per cent	£1 Level Stake	3-y-o	W-R	Per cent	£1 Level Stake
5f-6f	4-43	9.3	- 10.12	5f-6f	0-10	-	- 10.00
7f-8f	1-23	4.3	- 13.00	7f-8f	0-12	-	- 12.00
9f-13f	0-0	-	0.00	9f-13f	2-14	14.3	- 7.87
14f+	0-0	-	0.00	14f+	0-1	-	- 1.00

4-y-o+	W-R	Per cent	£1 Level Stake	Totals	W-R	Per cent	£1 Level Stake
5f-6f	4-24	16.7	+ 6.00	5f-6f	8-77	10.4	- 14.12
7f-8f	0-27	-	- 27.00	7f-8f	1-62	1.6	- 52.00
9f-13f	0-12	-	- 12.00	9f-13f	2-26	7.7	- 19.87
14f+	0-6	-	- 6.00	14f+	0-7	-	- 7.00

TYPE OF RACE

Non-Handicaps	W-R	Per cent	£1 Level Stake	Handicaps	W-R	Per cent	£1 Level Stake
2-y-o	3-40	7.5	- 14.12	2-y-o	0-7	-	- 7.00
3-y-o	2-24	8.3	- 17.87	3-y-o	0-7	-	- 7.00
4-y-o+	0-7	-	- 7.00	4-y-o+	4-47	8.5	- 17.00
Selling	2-21	9.5	- 4.00	Selling	0-6	-	- 6.00
Apprentice	0-4	-	- 4.00	Apprentice	0-6	-	- 6.00
Amat/Ladies	0-0	-	0.00	Amat/Ladies	0-3	-	- 3.00
Totals	7-96	7.3	- 46.99	Totals	4-76	5.3	- 46.00

COURSE GRADE

	W-R	Per cent	£1 Level Stake
Group 1	2-55	3.6	- 37.00
Group 2	3-26	11.5	- 9.12
Group 3	3-39	7.7	- 21.87
Group 4	3-52	5.8	- 25.00

FIRST TIME OUT

	W-R	Per cent	£1 Level Stake
2-y-o	0-12	-	- 12.00
3-y-o	0-8	-	- 8.00
4-y-o+	0-11	-	- 11.00
Totals	0-31	-	- 31.00

JOCKEYS RIDING

	W-R	Per cent	£1 Level Stake		W-R	Per cent	£1 Level Stake
N Adams	5-57	8.8	- 32.99	M Wigham	2-10	20.0	+ 7.00
R Street	3-10	30.0	+ 15.00	J Williams	1-6	16.7	+ 7.00

	W-R			W-R			W-R
R Price	0-13	A Tucker	0-2	Dale Gibson	0-1
R Perham	0-10	C N Adamson	0-2	G Bardwell	0-1
B Rouse	0-7	D Holland	0-2	G Duffield	0-1
A Clark	0-5	Mrs A Usher	0-2	G Milligan	0-1
D Harrison	0-5	R Cochrane	0-2	L Dettori	0-1
D Wright	0-5	A Lakeman	0-1	M Baird	0-1
Kim McDonnell	0-4	A Mackay	0-1	Mr G Shenkin	0-1
W R Swinburn	0-4	A McGlone	0-1	Paul Eddery	0-1
C Hawksley	0-3	Antoinette Armes	0-1	T Quinn	0-1
J Quinn	0-3	B Crossley	0-1	T Williams	0-1
M Roberts	0-3	D Moffatt	0-1	W Woods	0-1

COURSE RECORD

	Total W-R	Non-Handicaps 2-y-o	Non-Handicaps 3-y-o+	Handicaps 2-y-o	Handicaps 3-y-o+	Per cent	£1 Level Stake
Southwell (AW)	2-17	2-6	0-4	0-0	0-7	11.8	0.00
Redcar	1-1	0-0	0-0	0-0	1-1	100.0	+ 7.00
Thirsk	1-1	0-0	0-0	0-0	1-1	100.0	+ 5.00
Doncaster	1-4	1-1	0-1	0-0	0-2	25.0	+ 9.00
Bath	1-7	0-2	1-1	0-1	0-3	14.3	- 3.25
Chepstow	1-7	0-0	1-4	0-0	0-3	14.3	- 4.62

Leicester	1-7	0-3	0-1	0-0	1-3	14.3	+	4.00
Goodwood	1-9	0-2	0-2	0-0	1-5	11.1	-	4.00
Brighton	1-10	1-8	0-0	0-0	0-2	10.0	-	7.12
Warwick	1-12	1-3	0-5	0-0	0-4	8.3	-	2.00

Windsor	0-13	Folkestone	0-8	Southwell (Turf)	0-2
Lingfield (AW)	0-12	Salisbury	0-5	Beverley	0-1
Newbury	0-12	Ascot	0-3	Catterick	0-1
Sandown	0-10	Kempton	0-3	Epsom	0-1
Lingfield	0-9	Nottingham	0-3	Haydock	0-1
Newmarket	0-9	York	0-3	Pontefract	0-1

WINNING HORSES

		Races					Win
	Age	Run	1st	2nd	3rd	Unpl	£
Imperial Bailiwick	2	10	3	1	2	4	31,269
Bayin	4	15	3	0	1	11	10,525
Allesca	3	9	2	0	1	6	5,225
Caromish	6	7	1	0	0	6	2,930
Sporting Heir	2	11	1	1	1	8	2,070
Northern Bailiwick	2	14	1	4	0	9	1,725

WINNING OWNERS

	Races Won	Value £		Races Won	Value £
Dr Ian R Shenkin	4	32,994	M D I Usher	1	2,930
Trevor Barker	3	10,525	Sporting Partners	1	2,070
Miss D G Kerr	2	5,225			

Favourites	2-7	28.6%	+ 3.38	Total winning prize-money	£53,744

Longest winning sequence		1	Average SP of winner	6.2/1
Longest losing sequence		40	Return on stakes invested	-54.1%

1992 Form	3-136	2.2%	- 93.00	1990 Form	12-289	4.2%	-101.62
1991 Form	4-166	2.4%	-141.68	1989 Form	14-212	6.6%	-108.59

J S WAINWRIGHT (Malton, North Yorks)

	No. of Horses	Races Run	1st	2nd	3rd	Unpl	Per cent	£1 Level Stake
2-y-o	8	43	1	4	4	34	2.3	- 35.50
3-y-o	3	8	0	0	0	8	-	- 8.00
4-y-o+	6	38	2	2	4	30	5.3	- 18.00
Totals	17	89	3	6	8	72	3.4	- 61.50

Jan	Feb	Mar	Apr	May	Jun	Jul	Aug	Sep	Oct/Nov
0-8	0-6	0-2	0-9	0-10	1-12	1-9	0-13	1-11	0-9

Winning Jockeys	W-R	£1 Level Stake		W-R	£1 Level Stake
Miss A Deniel	1-2	+ 8.00	J Fanning	1-12	- 4.50
D McKeown	1-2	+ 8.00			

Winning Courses					
Nottingham	1-5	+ 5.00	York	1-6	+ 1.50
Redcar	1-6	+ 4.00			

Winning Horses	Age	Races Run	1st	2nd	3rd	Unpl	Win £
Ballard Ring	2	11	1	3	1	6	5,952
Inferring	5	6	1	0	0	5	2,825
Mu-Arrik	5	9	1	0	2	6	2,532

Favourites	0-0		Total winning prize-money	£11,309

1992 Form	1-77	1.3%	- 56.00	1990 Form	3-141	2.1%	-105.00
1991 Form	5-137	3.6%	- 61.50	1989 Form	4-131	3.1%	- 75.17

C F WALL (Newmarket)

	No. of Horses	Races Run	1st	2nd	3rd	Unpl	Per cent	£1 Level Stake
2-y-o	7	24	3	3	0	18	12.5	- 1.00
3-y-o	7	40	7	0	6	27	17.5	+ 2.38
4-y-o+	8	43	3	4	2	34	7.0	- 19.00
Totals	22	107	13	7	8	79	12.1	- 17.62

BY MONTH

2-y-o	W-R	Per cent	£1 Level Stake	3-y-o	W-R	Per cent	£1 Level Stake
January	0-0	-	0.00	January	0-1	-	- 1.00
February	0-0	-	0.00	February	0-1	-	- 1.00
March	0-0	-	0.00	March	0-0	-	0.00
April	0-0	-	0.00	April	0-2	-	- 2.00
May	0-1	-	- 1.00	May	0-4	-	- 4.00
June	0-1	-	- 1.00	June	1-6	16.7	- 3.12
July	3-6	50.0	+ 17.00	July	1-5	20.0	- 0.50
August	0-3	-	- 3.00	August	0-7	-	- 7.00
September	0-6	-	- 6.00	September	3-9	33.3	+ 17.50
Oct/Nov	0-7	-	- 7.00	Oct/Nov	2-5	40.0	+ 3.50

Wall C F

4-y-o+	W-R	Per cent	£1 Level Stake	Totals	W-R	Per cent	£1 Level Stake
January	0-3	-	- 3.00	January	0-4	-	- 4.00
February	0-1	-	- 1.00	February	0-2	-	- 2.00
March	0-0	-	0.00	March	0-0	-	0.00
April	0-3	-	- 3.00	April	0-5	-	- 5.00
May	0-6	-	- 6.00	May	0-11	-	- 11.00
June	0-7	-	- 7.00	June	1-14	7.1	- 11.12
July	1-9	11.1	- 4.00	July	5-20	25.0	+ 12.50
August	1-7	14.3	+ 4.00	August	1-17	5.9	- 6.00
September	1-3	33.3	+ 5.00	September	4-18	22.2	+ 16.50
Oct/Nov	0-4	-	- 4.00	Oct/Nov	2-16	12.5	- 7.50

DISTANCE

2-y-o	W-R	Per cent	£1 Level Stake	3-y-o	W-R	Per cent	£1 Level Stake
5f-6f	1-15	6.7	- 10.00	5f-6f	0-1	-	- 1.00
7f-8f	2-9	22.2	+ 9.00	7f-8f	4-26	15.4	- 10.12
9f-13f	0-0	-	0.00	9f-13f	3-13	23.1	+ 13.50
14f+	0-0	-	0.00	14f+	0-0	-	0.00

4-y-o+	W-R	Per cent	£1 Level Stake	Totals	W-R	Per cent	£1 Level Stake
5f-6f	0-8	-	- 8.00	5f-6f	1-24	4.2	- 19.00
7f-8f	3-26	11.5	- 2.00	7f-8f	9-61	14.8	- 3.12
9f-13f	0-9	-	- 9.00	9f-13f	3-22	13.6	+ 4.50
14f+	0-0	-	0.00	14f+	0-0	-	0.00

TYPE OF RACE

Non-Handicaps	W-R	Per cent	£1 Level Stake	Handicaps	W-R	Per cent	£1 Level Stake
2-y-o	2-19	10.5	- 6.00	2-y-o	1-5	20.0	+ 5.00
3-y-o	3-15	20.0	- 0.12	3-y-o	3-21	14.3	- 2.50
4-y-o+	1-8	12.5	- 3.00	4-y-o+	2-32	6.3	- 13.00
Selling	1-1	100.0	+ 8.00	Selling	0-2	-	- 2.00
Apprentice	0-0	-	0.00	Apprentice	0-4	-	- 4.00
Amat/Ladies	0-0	-	0.00	Amat/Ladies	0-0	-	0.00
Totals	7-43	16.3	- 1.12	Totals	6-64	9.4	- 16.50

COURSE GRADE	W-R	Per cent	£1 Level Stake	FIRST TIME OUT	W-R	Per cent	£1 Level Stake
Group 1	2-42	4.8	- 29.00	2-y-o	1-7	14.3	- 2.00
Group 2	3-18	16.7	+ 0.50	3-y-o	0-7	-	- 7.00
Group 3	5-26	19.2	+ 7.38	4-y-o+	0-8	-	- 8.00
Group 4	3-21	14.3	+ 3.50	Totals	1-22	4.5	- 17.00

JOCKEYS RIDING

	W-R	Per cent	£1 Level Stake		W-R	Per cent	£1 Level Stake
W Woods	4-28	14.3	+ 2.50	P Robinson	2-10	20.0	- 1.62
G Duffield	3-8	37.5	+ 8.50	W Carson	1-2	50.0	+ 9.00
J Weaver	2-3	66.7	+ 15.00	N Day	1-6	16.7	- 1.00

N Carlisle	0-7	Jaki Houston	0-2	F Norton	0-1
S Mulvey	0-5	R Cochrane	0-2	J Fanning	0-1
S Webster	0-4	S Davies	0-2	J McLaughlin	0-1
B Raymond	0-3	Sally Radford-Howes	0-2	L Dettori	0-1
K Rutter	0-3	W R Swinburn	0-2	M Roberts	0-1
M Tebbutt	0-3	W Ryan	0-2	Mrs C Wall	0-1
A McGlone	0-2	A Munro	0-1	T Williams	0-1
J Reid	0-2	Dale Gibson	0-1		

COURSE RECORD

	Total W-R	Non-Handicaps 2-y-o	Non-Handicaps 3-y-o+	Handicaps 2-y-o	Handicaps 3-y-o+	Per cent	£1 Level Stake
Nottingham	2-7	0-0	1-5	0-0	1-2	28.6	+ 6.88
Ayr	1-1	0-0	1-1	0-0	0-0	100.0	+ 4.00
Thirsk	1-1	0-0	0-0	0-0	1-1	100.0	+ 3.50
Catterick	1-2	0-0	0-1	1-1	0-0	50.0	+ 8.00
Chester	1-2	0-0	0-1	0-0	1-1	50.0	+ 9.00
Folkestone	1-4	0-0	1-1	0-0	0-3	25.0	+ 2.50
Redcar	1-4	0-1	0-1	0-1	1-1	25.0	- 1.00
Yarmouth	1-4	1-1	0-1	0-0	0-2	25.0	+ 1.00
Pontefract	1-5	0-0	1-1	0-0	0-4	20.0	+ 0.50
Goodwood	1-6	0-0	0-0	0-1	1-5	16.7	+ 2.00
Leicester	1-6	0-1	1-1	0-0	0-4	16.7	+ 3.00
Southwell (AW)	1-6	1-1	0-1	0-0	0-4	16.7	+ 2.00

Newmarket	0-13	Kempton	0-3	Southwell (Turf)	0-2
Sandown	0-7	Newbury	0-3	Warwick	0-2
Doncaster	0-5	Beverley	0-2	Bath	0-1
Lingfield	0-5	Brighton	0-2	Edinburgh	0-1
Lingfield (AW)	0-4	Ripon	0-2	Newcastle	0-1
Haydock	0-3	Salisbury	0-2	Windsor	0-1

WINNING HORSES

	Age	Races Run	1st	2nd	3rd	Unpl	Win £
Corals Dream	4	11	3	2	0	6	17,939
Missed Flight	3	4	2	0	1	1	10,441
Mysilv	3	11	2	0	4	5	6,723
Mulled Ale	3	7	2	0	0	5	5,442
Extra Bonus	2	5	2	1	0	2	5,427
Polish Admiral	2	3	1	1	0	1	3,158
Dancing Diamond	3	6	1	0	1	4	1,941

411

WINNING OWNERS

	Races Won	Value £		Races Won	Value £
Mrs C Hamson	3	17,939	W J Bridge	2	5,442
Walter Grubmuller	3	13,599	Induna Racing Partners	2	5,427
Jack Fisher	2	6,723	The Equema Partnership	1	1,941

Favourites	2-11	18.2%	- 5.12	Total winning prize-money	£51,071

Longest winning sequence		3	Average SP of winner	5.9/1
Longest losing sequence		26	Return on stakes invested	-16.5%

1992 Form	7-152	4.6%	- 88.80	1990 Form	15-159	9.4%	- 70.56
1991 Form	7-135	5.2%	- 83.77	1989 Form	9-117	7.7%	- 33.27

P T WALWYN (Lambourn, Berks)

	No. of Horses	Races Run	1st	2nd	3rd	Unpl	Per cent	£1 Level Stake
2-y-o	18	52	2	7	8	35	3.8	- 34.62
3-y-o	15	101	8	10	14	69	7.9	- 75.33
4-y-o+	4	32	7	3	2	20	21.9	+ 61.08
Totals	37	185	17	20	24	124	9.2	- 48.87

BY MONTH

2-y-o	W-R	Per cent	£1 Level Stake	3-y-o	W-R	Per cent	£1 Level Stake
January	0-0	-	0.00	January	0-1	-	- 1.00
February	0-0	-	0.00	February	0-0	-	0.00
March	0-0	-	0.00	March	0-0	-	0.00
April	0-0	-	0.00	April	1-11	9.1	- 3.00
May	0-2	-	- 2.00	May	1-20	5.0	- 17.50
June	0-4	-	- 4.00	June	3-20	15.0	- 10.03
July	0-4	-	- 4.00	July	1-17	5.9	- 14.90
August	0-12	-	- 12.00	August	1-12	8.3	- 11.00
September	1-16	6.3	- 1.00	September	0-12	-	- 12.00
Oct/Nov	1-14	7.1	- 11.62	Oct/Nov	1-8	12.5	- 5.90

4-y-o+	W-R	Per cent	£1 Level Stake	Totals	W-R	Per cent	£1 Level Stake
January	0-0	-	0.00	January	0-1	-	- 1.00
February	0-0	-	0.00	February	0-0	-	0.00
March	0-1	-	- 1.00	March	0-1	-	- 1.00
April	1-3	33.3	+ 23.00	April	2-14	14.3	+ 20.00
May	1-4	25.0	+ 11.00	May	2-26	7.7	- 8.50
June	3-6	50.0	+ 8.83	June	6-30	20.0	- 5.20
July	2-7	28.6	+ 30.25	July	3-28	10.7	+ 11.35
August	0-3	-	- 3.00	August	1-27	3.7	- 26.00
September	0-6	-	- 6.00	September	1-34	2.9	- 19.00
Oct/Nov	0-2	-	- 2.00	Oct/Nov	2-24	8.3	- 19.52

DISTANCE

2-y-o	W-R	Per cent	£1 Level Stake	3-y-o	W-R	Per cent	£1 Level Stake
5f-6f	1-27	3.7	- 12.00	5f-6f	0-6	-	- 6.00
7f-8f	1-25	4.0	- 22.62	7f-8f	7-50	14.0	- 26.43
9f-13f	0-0	-	0.00	9f-13f	1-42	2.4	- 39.90
14f+	0-0	-	0.00	14f+	0-3	-	- 3.00

4-y-o+	W-R	Per cent	£1 Level Stake	Totals	W-R	Per cent	£1 Level Stake
5f-6f	2-7	28.6	+ 42.00	5f-6f	3-40	7.5	+ 24.00
7f-8f	4-14	28.6	+ 28.25	7f-8f	12-89	13.5	- 20.80
9f-13f	1-11	9.1	- 9.17	9f-13f	2-53	3.8	- 49.07
14f+	0-0	-	0.00	14f+	0-3	-	- 3.00

TYPE OF RACE

Non-Handicaps	W-R	Per cent	£1 Level Stake	Handicaps	W-R	Per cent	£1 Level Stake
2-y-o	2-48	4.2	- 30.62	2-y-o	0-4	-	- 4.00
3-y-o	5-38	13.2	- 23.43	3-y-o	3-58	5.2	- 46.90
4-y-o+	3-12	25.0	+ 38.83	4-y-o+	4-17	23.5	+ 25.25
Selling	0-0	-	0.00	Selling	0-0	-	0.00
Apprentice	0-0	-	0.00	Apprentice	0-5	-	- 5.00
Amat/Ladies	0-1	-	- 1.00	Amat/Ladies	0-2	-	- 2.00
Totals	10-99	10.1	- 16.22	Totals	7-86	8.1	- 32.65

COURSE GRADE

	W-R	Per cent	£1 Level Stake
Group 1	7-90	7.8	- 11.29
Group 2	1-33	3.0	- 32.00
Group 3	7-36	19.4	+ 12.82
Group 4	2-26	7.7	- 18.40

FIRST TIME OUT

	W-R	Per cent	£1 Level Stake
2-y-o	1-18	5.6	- 3.00
3-y-o	0-15	-	- 15.00
4-y-o+	0-4	-	- 4.00
Totals	1-37	2.7	- 22.00

JOCKEYS RIDING

	W-R	Per cent	£1 Level Stake		W-R	Per cent	£1 Level Stake
W Carson	8-59	13.6	+ 19.87	D Wright	1-7	14.3	- 1.50
Pat Eddery	3-9	33.3	+ 4.13	Paul Eddery	1-11	9.1	- 7.20
P Robinson	2-10	20.0	+ 17.83	R Hills	1-14	7.1	- 11.50
D Holland	1-6	16.7	- 1.50				

Walwyn P T

M Hills	0-10	Mr P Macewan	0-2	J Carroll	0-1
R Cochrane	0-8	T Quinn	0-2	J Weaver	0-1
G Duffield	0-6	W Ryan	0-2	Kim McDonnell	0-1
J Quinn	0-4	A Clark	0-1	M Baird	0-1
N Carlisle	0-4	A McGlone	0-1	M Birch	0-1
L Dettori	0-3	A Munro	0-1	Mrs A Turner	0-1
W R Swinburn	0-3	A Tucker	0-1	Mrs M Cowdrey	0-1
A Mackay	0-2	B Raymond	0-1	P McCabe	0-1
D Biggs	0-2	D Harrison	0-1	T Rogers	0-1
J Williams	0-2	G Carter	0-1		
L Charnock	0-2	G Mitchell	0-1		

COURSE RECORD

	Total W-R	Non-Handicaps 2-y-o	3-y-o+	Handicaps 2-y-o	3-y-o+	Per cent	£1 Level Stake
Newmarket	3-14	1-2	1-5	0-0	1-7	21.4	+ 30.38
Beverley	2-4	0-0	1-1	0-0	1-3	50.0	+ 2.60
Windsor	2-7	0-0	0-2	0-0	2-5	28.6	+ 3.75
Newcastle	1-1	0-0	1-1	0-0	0-0	100.0	+ 0.83
Carlisle	1-2	0-0	0-0	0-0	1-2	50.0	+ 3.50
Warwick	1-3	0-2	1-1	0-0	0-0	33.3	- 0.90
Leicester	1-4	0-2	0-1	0-0	1-1	25.0	+ 22.00
York	1-4	0-1	1-1	0-0	0-2	25.0	+ 11.00
Chepstow	1-5	0-2	1-2	0-1	0-0	20.0	- 1.20
Ascot	1-9	1-3	0-2	0-0	0-4	11.1	+ 6.00
Lingfield	1-9	0-4	0-2	0-0	1-3	11.1	- 8.00
Haydock	1-10	0-3	1-4	0-0	0-3	10.0	- 7.50
Nottingham	1-10	0-2	1-3	0-1	0-4	10.0	- 8.33

Salisbury	0-16	Lingfield (AW)	0-5	Yarmouth	0-3
Newbury	0-14	Brighton	0-4	Pontefract	0-2
Goodwood	0-10	Catterick	0-4	Bath	0-1
Doncaster	0-9	Sandown	0-4	Redcar	0-1
Folkestone	0-7	Southwell (Turf)	0-4	Southwell (AW)	0-1
Epsom	0-6	Ayr	0-3		
Kempton	0-6	Chester	0-3		

WINNING HORSES

	Age	Races Run	1st	2nd	3rd	Unpl	Win £
Hamas	4	7	2	0	0	5	128,344
Tahdid	3	9	3	1	1	4	14,365
Queen Warrior	4	8	3	0	2	3	11,008
Tablah	2	2	1	0	0	1	10,234
Walking The Plank	4	12	2	2	0	8	7,715
Shamam	3	7	1	2	1	3	6,160
Salatin	3	10	1	2	4	3	4,690
Oare Sparrow	3	7	1	0	3	3	3,611
Wali	3	6	1	1	1	3	3,493
Nafuth	3	10	1	1	2	6	3,173
Tom Morgan	2	6	1	2	2	1	000

WINNING OWNERS

	Races Won	Value £		Races Won	Value £
Hamdan Al-Maktoum	10	170,458	Mrs Henry Keswick	1	3,611
Christopher Spence	3	11,008	P T Walwyn	1	000
Michael White	2	7,715			

Favourites	5-22	22.7%	- 10.65	Total winning prize-money		£192,792
Longest winning sequence			2	Average SP of winner		7.2/1
Longest losing sequence			49	Return on stakes invested		-24.9%
1992 Form	22-229	9.6%	- 65.60	1990 Form	48-312	15.4% + 36.45
1991 Form	24-262	9.2%	-101.99	1989 Form	36-327	11.0% - 96.72

MARTYN WANE (Richmond, North Yorks)

	No. of Horses	Races Run	1st	2nd	3rd	Unpl	Per cent	£1 Level Stake
2-y-o	0	0	0	0	0	0	-	0.00
3-y-o	0	0	0	0	0	0	-	0.00
4-y-o+	11	66	5	0	11	50	7.6	+ 6.33
Totals	11	66	5	0	11	50	7.6	+ 6.33

Jan	Feb	Mar	Apr	May	Jun	Jul	Aug	Sep	Oct/Nov
0-0	0-0	0-0	1-3	1-11	1-14	1-14	0-15	0-4	1-5

Winning Jockeys	W-R	£1 Level Stake		W-R	£1 Level Stake
K Fallon	2-9	+ 8.00	J Weaver	1-6	+ 11.00
J Dennis	1-2	+ 2.33	L Charnock	1-15	+ 19.00

Winning Courses					
Warwick	1-1	+ 3.33	Hamilton	1-6	0.00
Leicester	1-2	+ 32.00	Redcar	1-11	0.00
Thirsk	1-5	+ 12.00			

Winning Horses	Age	Races Run	1st	2nd	3rd	Unpl	Win £
Arabat	6	15	2	0	2	11	6,684
Finjan	6	12	2	0	1	9	6,247
Languedoc	6	15	1	0	6	8	5,428

Favourites	1-3	33.3%	+ 1.33	Total winning prize-money	£18,359

MRS B WARING (Chippenham, Wilts)

	No. of Horses	Races Run	1st	2nd	3rd	Unpl	Per cent	£1 Level Stake
2-y-o	1	3	0	0	0	3	-	- 3.00
3-y-o	2	5	0	0	0	5	-	- 5.00
4-y-o+	10	36	2	3	2	29	5.6	- 17.00
Totals	13	44	2	3	2	37	4.5	- 25.00

Jan	Feb	Mar	Apr	May	Jun	Jul	Aug	Sep	Oct/Nov
0-6	0-1	0-1	0-6	1-9	1-5	0-6	0-2	0-5	0-3

Winning Jockeys	W-R	£1 Level Stake					W-R	£1 Level Stake
D Wright	1-15	- 8.00		G Bardwell			1-18	- 6.00

Winning Courses								
Nottingham	1-3	+ 4.00		Bath			1-5	+ 7.00

Winning Horses	Age	Races Run	1st	2nd	3rd	Unpl	Win £
Smilingatstrangers	5	2	1	0	0	1	3,521
Full Quiver	8	9	1	1	1	6	2,512

Favourites	0-1		Total winning prize-money	£6,033

1992 Form	3-106	2.8%	- 75.75	1990 Form	5-83	6.0%	+ 20.25
1991 Form	6-111	5.4%	- 35.00	1989 Form	1-34	2.9%	0.00

J W WATTS (Richmond, North Yorks)

	No. of Horses	Races Run	1st	2nd	3rd	Unpl	Per cent	£1 Level Stake
2-y-o	8	30	3	6	6	15	10.0	- 13.59
3-y-o	15	81	9	11	15	46	11.1	- 6.92
4-y-o+	5	50	5	5	2	38	10.0	- 9.00
Totals	28	161	17	22	23	99	10.6	- 29.51

BY MONTH

2-y-o	W-R	Per cent	£1 Level Stake	3-y-o	W-R	Per cent	£1 Level Stake
Mar/Apr	0-2	-	- 2.00	Mar/Apr	4-14	28.6	+ 23.58
May	1-3	33.3	+ 6.00	May	1-18	5.6	- 14.50
June	1-2	50.0	- 0.09	June	1-15	6.7	- 7.00
July	1-6	16.7	- 0.50	July	1-12	8.3	- 4.00
August	0-8	-	- 8.00	August	1-10	10.0	+ 2.00
September	0-7	-	- 7.00	September	1-9	11.1	- 3.00
Oct/Nov	0-2	-	- 2.00	Oct/Nov	0-3	-	- 3.00

Watts J W

4-y-o+	W-R	Per cent	£1 Level Stake	Totals	W-R	Per cent	£1 Level Stake
Mar/Apr	2-8	25.0	+ 10.50	Mar/Apr	6-24	25.0	+ 32.08
May	2-10	20.0	+ 6.00	May	4-31	12.9	- 2.50
June	0-6	-	- 6.00	June	2-23	8.7	- 13.09
July	0-7	-	- 7.00	July	2-25	8.0	- 11.50
August	0-8	-	- 8.00	August	1-26	3.8	- 14.00
September	0-4	-	- 4.00	September	1-20	5.0	- 14.00
Oct/Nov	1-7	14.3	+ 0.50	Oct/Nov	1-12	8.3	- 4.50

DISTANCE

2-y-o	W-R	Per cent	£1 Level Stake	3-y-o	W-R	Per cent	£1 Level Stake
5f-6f	2-17	11.8	- 2.50	5f-6f	4-17	23.5	+ 4.75
7f-8f	1-13	7.7	- 11.09	7f-8f	3-26	11.5	+ 8.33
9f-13f	0-0	-	0.00	9f-13f	2-33	6.1	- 15.00
14f+	0-0	-	0.00	14f+	0-5	-	- 5.00

4-y-o+	W-R	Per cent	£1 Level Stake	Totals	W-R	Per cent	£1 Level Stake
5f-6f	1-7	14.3	- 4.50	5f-6f	7-41	17.1	- 2.25
7f-8f	2-20	10.0	- 4.50	7f-8f	6-59	10.2	- 7.26
9f-13f	0-8	-	- 8.00	9f-13f	2-41	4.9	- 23.00
14f+	2-15	13.3	+ 8.00	14f+	2-20	10.0	+ 3.00

TYPE OF RACE

Non-Handicaps	W-R	Per cent	£1 Level Stake	Handicaps	W-R	Per cent	£1 Level Stake
2-y-o	3-22	13.6	- 5.59	2-y-o	0-7	-	- 7.00
3-y-o	3-29	10.3	+ 3.25	3-y-o	6-52	11.5	- 10.17
4-y-o+	1-2	50.0	+ 0.50	4-y-o+	4-47	8.5	- 8.50
Selling	0-1	-	- 1.00	Selling	0-0	-	0.00
Apprentice	0-0	-	0.00	Apprentice	0-1	-	- 1.00
Amat/Ladies	0-0	-	0.00	Amat/Ladies	0-0	-	0.00
Totals	7-54	13.0	- 2.84	Totals	10-107	9.3	- 26.67

COURSE GRADE

	W-R	Per cent	£1 Level Stake
Group 1	6-74	8.1	- 34.00
Group 2	7-45	15.6	+ 18.91
Group 3	2-25	8.0	- 9.75
Group 4	2-17	11.8	- 4.67

FIRST TIME OUT

	W-R	Per cent	£1 Level Stake
2-y-o	0-8	-	- 8.00
3-y-o	4-15	26.7	+ 21.58
4-y-o+	1-5	20.0	+ 10.00
Totals	5-28	17.9	+ 23.58

417

JOCKEYS RIDING

	W-R	Per cent	£1 Level Stake		W-R	Per cent	£1 Level Stake
W R Swinburn	5-11	45.5	+ 27.50	J Lowe	2-18	11.1	- 8.09
G Duffield	5-44	11.4	+ 0.08	T Quinn	1-2	50.0	+ 3.50
N Connorton	3-30	10.0	+ 1.00	M Birch	1-8	12.5	- 5.50

M Roberts	0-8	J Reid	0-2	D Holland		0-1
B Raymond	0-5	K Fallon	0-2	J Carroll		0-1
M Hills	0-4	N Kennedy	0-2	J Quinn		0-1
Pat Eddery	0-4	S Davies	0-2	J Tate		0-1
L Charnock	0-3	W Ryan	0-2	R Hills		0-1
P Robinson	0-3	A Mackay	0-1	S Perks		0-1
G Bardwell	0-2	A Munro	0-1	W Carson		0-1

COURSE RECORD

	Total W-R	Non-Handicaps 2-y-o	Non-Handicaps 3-y-o+	Handicaps 2-y-o	Handicaps 3-y-o+	Per cent	£1 Level Stake
Chester	3-9	2-2	0-1	0-0	1-6	33.3	+ 13.00
Thirsk	2-9	1-3	1-4	0-0	0-2	22.2	+ 9.91
Doncaster	2-11	0-1	0-2	0-0	2-8	18.2	+ 0.50
Beverley	2-12	0-3	2-3	0-1	0-5	16.7	+ 3.25
Newmarket	2-12	0-1	0-1	0-0	2-10	16.7	+ 2.00
Ripon	2-14	0-2	0-4	0-0	2-8	14.3	+ 9.00
Newbury	1-2	0-1	0-0	0-0	1-1	50.0	+ 10.00
Edinburgh	1-4	0-0	0-0	0-0	1-4	25.0	+ 0.33
Southwell (AW)	1-4	0-1	0-0	0-0	1-3	25.0	+ 4.00
Newcastle	1-11	0-2	1-1	0-0	0-8	9.1	- 8.50

Redcar	0-12	Ascot	0-5	Hamilton	0-1
Ayr	0-11	Catterick	0-5	Leicester	0-1
Haydock	0-10	Carlisle	0-3	Lingfield	0-1
York	0-10	Nottingham	0-3	Southwell (Turf)	0-1
Pontefract	0-8	Kempton	0-2		

WINNING HORSES

	Age	Races Run	1st	2nd	3rd	Unpl	Win £
Chatoyant	3	5	3	1	0	1	20,211
Good Hand	7	11	2	1	1	7	14,196
Storiths	3	5	2	0	0	3	13,071
Stimulant	2	6	2	2	1	1	9,985
Colway Rock	3	4	1	1	1	1	9,594
Sagebrush Roller	5	14	2	2	0	10	8,548
Habeta	7	14	1	1	0	12	3,850
Cynic	3	4	1	1	0	2	3,143
Ovideo	2	8	1	1	1	5	2,807
Silver Standard	3	8	1	1	0	6	1,826
Red Fan	3	7	1	0	2	4	1,576

WINNING OWNERS

	Races Won	Value £		Races Won	Value £
Lord Derby	6	33,338	R D Bickenson	1	3,850
Mrs M M Haggas	2	14,196	Mrs S Cunliffe-Lister	1	2,807
Mrs M Irwin	2	13,071	Lord Swaythling	1	1,826
R Coleman	1	9,594	Joe L Allbritton	1	1,576
A K Collins	2	8,548			

Favourites	7-21	33.3%	+ 8.16	Total winning prize-money		£88,806

Longest winning sequence		2	Average SP of winner		6.7/1
Longest losing sequence		34	Return on stakes invested		-18.3%

1992 Form	17-162	10.5%	- 7.75	1990 Form	27-228	11.8%	- 74.77
1991 Form	14-192	7.3%	-136.44	1989 Form	25-221	11.3%	- 25.83

C WEEDON (Chiddingfold, Surrey)

	No. of Horses	Races Run	1st	2nd	3rd	Unpl	Per cent	£1 Level Stake
2-y-o	0	0	0	0	0	0	-	0.00
3-y-o	5	24	1	0	2	21	4.2	- 17.00
4-y-o+	5	17	2	0	3	12	11.8	- 6.50
Totals	10	41	3	0	5	33	7.3	- 23.50

Jan	Feb	Mar	Apr	May	Jun	Jul	Aug	Sep	Oct/Nov
0-0	0-1	1-2	1-8	0-8	0-7	0-5	1-4	0-4	0-2

Winning Jockeys	W-R	£1 Level Stake		W-R	£1 Level Stake
J Weaver	1-1	+ 6.00	K Rutter	1-6	+ 1.00
G Duffield	1-3	+ 0.50			

Winning Courses					
Southwell (AW)	1-2	+ 5.00	Folkestone	1-6	- 2.50
Lingfield (AW)	1-5	+ 2.00			

Winning Horses	Age	Races Run	1st	2nd	3rd	Unpl	Win £
Poetic Form	3	8	1	0	0	7	2,925
Saahi	4	9	1	0	1	7	2,512
Natural Lad	8	5	1	0	2	2	2,070

Favourites	1-1	100.0%	+ 2.50	Total winning prize-money		£7,507

1992 Form	0-10			1990 Form	0-7
1991 Form	1-10	10.0%	+ 5.00		

E WEYMES (Middleham, North Yorks)

	No. of Horses	Races Run	1st	2nd	3rd	Unpl	Per cent	£1 Level Stake
2-y-o	8	51	7	8	6	30	13.7	+ 33.50
3-y-o	5	20	1	2	0	17	5.0	- 9.00
4-y-o+	4	24	2	3	2	17	8.3	- 8.25
Totals	17	95	10	13	8	64	10.5	+ 16.25

BY MONTH

2-y-o	W-R	Per cent	£1 Level Stake	3-y-o	W-R	Per cent	£1 Level Stake
Mar/Apr	1-5	20.0	+ 17.00	Mar/Apr	0-2	-	- 2.00
May	1-4	25.0	+ 1.50	May	0-3	-	- 3.00
June	1-5	20.0	+ 16.00	June	1-1	100.0	+ 10.00
July	1-15	6.7	- 9.00	July	0-4	-	- 4.00
August	2-8	25.0	+ 15.00	August	0-3	-	- 3.00
September	0-4	-	- 4.00	September	0-2	-	- 2.00
Oct/Nov	1-10	10.0	- 2.00	Oct/Nov	0-5	-	- 5.00

4-y-o+	W-R	Per cent	£1 Level Stake	Totals	W-R	Per cent	£1 Level Stake
Mar/Apr	0-2	-	- 2.00	Mar/Apr	1-9	11.1	+ 13.00
May	0-4	-	- 4.00	May	1-11	9.1	- 5.50
June	1-4	25.0	- 1.25	June	3-10	30.0	+ 24.75
July	0-7	-	- 7.00	July	1-26	3.8	- 20.00
August	0-4	-	- 4.00	August	2-15	13.3	+ 8.00
September	0-1	-	- 1.00	September	0-7	-	- 7.00
Oct/Nov	1-2	50.0	+ 11.00	Oct/Nov	2-17	11.8	+ 4.00

DISTANCE

2-y-o	W-R	Per cent	£1 Level Stake	3-y-o	W-R	Per cent	£1 Level Stake
5f-6f	4-31	12.9	+ 18.50	5f-6f	1-4	25.0	+ 7.00
7f-8f	3-20	15.0	+ 15.00	7f-8f	0-12	-	- 12.00
9f-13f	0-0	-	0.00	9f-13f	0-3	-	- 3.00
14f+	0-0	-	0.00	14f+	0-1	-	- 1.00

4-y-o+	W-R	Per cent	£1 Level Stake	Totals	W-R	Per cent	£1 Level Stake
5f-6f	0-0	-	0.00	5f-6f	5-35	14.3	+ 25.50
7f-8f	0-3	-	- 3.00	7f-8f	3-35	8.6	0.00
9f-13f	2-20	10.0	- 4.25	9f-13f	2-23	8.7	- 7.25
14f+	0-1	-	- 1.00	14f+	0-2	-	- 2.00

TYPE OF RACE

Non-Handicaps	W-R	Per cent	£1 Level Stake	Handicaps	W-R	Per cent	£1 Level Stake
2-y-o	6-33	18.2	+ 45.50	2-y-o	0-16	-	- 16.00
3-y-o	0-8	-	- 8.00	3-y-o	1-11	9.1	0.00
4-y-o+	0-2	-	- 2.00	4-y-o+	2-14	14.3	+ 1.75
Selling	1-3	33.3	+ 3.00	Selling	0-3	-	- 3.00
Apprentice	0-0	-	0.00	Apprentice	0-3	-	- 3.00
Amat/Ladies	0-1	-	- 1.00	Amat/Ladies	0-1	-	- 1.00
Totals	7-47	14.9	+ 37.50	Totals	3-48	6.3	- 21.25

COURSE GRADE

	W-R	Per cent	£1 Level Stake
Group 1	5-33	15.2	+ 17.25
Group 2	3-29	10.3	+ 18.00
Group 3	1-14	7.1	- 6.00
Group 4	1-19	5.3	- 13.00

FIRST TIME OUT

	W-R	Per cent	£1 Level Stake
2-y-o	2-7	28.6	+ 35.00
3-y-o	1-5	20.0	+ 6.00
4-y-o+	0-4	-	- 4.00
Totals	3-16	18.8	+ 37.00

JOCKEYS RIDING

	W-R	Per cent	£1 Level Stake		W-R	Per cent	£1 Level Stake
G Hind	2-8	25.0	+ 15.00	L Dettori	1-4	25.0	+ 9.00
W Newnes	2-17	11.8	+ 9.50	J Quinn	1-6	16.7	+ 2.00
R Cochrane	1-2	50.0	+ 19.00	D McKeown	1-7	14.3	- 4.25
W R Swinburn	1-2	50.0	+ 4.00	Dale Gibson	1-8	12.5	+ 3.00

J Fanning	0-6	K Darley	0-2	G Duffield	0-1
M Tebbutt	0-5	M Birch	0-2	J Weaver	0-1
A Culhane	0-2	M Humphries	0-2	N Carlisle	0-1
A Garth	0-2	Mr J Weymes	0-2	N Connorton	0-1
A Munro	0-2	Pat Eddery	0-2	P Robinson	0-1
C Hodgson	0-2	W Ryan	0-2	R Lappin	0-1
D Holland	0-2	B Raymond	0-1	S Wynne	0-1

COURSE RECORD

	Total W-R	Non-Handicaps 2-y-o	3-y-o+	Handicaps 2-y-o	3-y-o+	Per cent	£1 Level Stake
Ripon	3-12	2-4	0-2	0-0	1-6	25.0	+ 35.00
Ayr	2-5	2-3	0-0	0-2	0-0	40.0	+ 8.50
Doncaster	2-8	1-2	0-1	0-1	1-4	25.0	+ 15.75
Yarmouth	1-2	1-2	0-0	0-0	0-0	50.0	+ 6.00
York	1-7	0-1	0-0	0-2	1-4	14.3	+ 6.00
Catterick	1-11	1-6	0-2	0-0	0-3	9.1	- 5.00

Redcar	0-11	Chester	0-3	Nottingham	0-2
Newcastle	0-7	Haydock	0-3	Sandown	0-1
Beverley	0-6	Thirsk	0-3	Southwell (AW)	0-1
Edinburgh	0-4	Carlisle	0-2	Southwell (Turf)	0-1
Pontefract	0-4	Newmarket	0-2		

WINNING HORSES

	Age	Races Run	1st	2nd	3rd	Unpl	Win £
Drummer Hicks	4	10	2	2	0	6	14,445
Randonneur	2	7	2	1	2	2	8,602
Lambent	2	6	2	2	1	1	6,372
Oubeck Blue	2	5	1	0	0	4	3,623
Oubeck	3	5	1	1	0	3	3,407
Distinctive Air	2	11	1	3	1	6	2,933
New Inn	2	7	1	1	1	4	2,406

WINNING OWNERS

	Races Won	Value £		Races Won	Value £
Mrs N Napier	2	14,445	R L Heaton	2	6,372
T A Scothern	3	11,534	Mrs Christine Sharratt	1	2,406
Mrs A Birkett	2	7,029			

Favourites	0-4		Total winning prize-money	£41,786
Longest winning sequence		1	Average SP of winner	10.1/1
Longest losing sequence		18	Return on stakes invested	17.1%
1992 Form	12-78	15.4%	- 22.71	1990 Form	5-122	4.1%	- 85.00
1991 Form	2-68	2.9%	- 56.00	1989 Form	6-118	5.1%	- 85.75

J WHARTON (Melton Mowbray, Leics)

	No. of Horses	Races Run	1st	2nd	3rd	Unpl	Per cent	£1 Level Stake
2-y-o	8	31	6	4	3	18	19.4	+ 20.38
3-y-o	9	46	1	7	5	33	2.2	- 42.00
4-y-o+	17	84	7	6	10	61	8.3	- 37.49
Totals	34	161	14	17	18	112	8.7	- 59.11

BY MONTH

2-y-o	W-R	Per cent	£1 Level Stake	3-y-o	W-R	Per cent	£1 Level Stake
January	0-0	-	0.00	January	0-1	-	- 1.00
February	0-0	-	0.00	February	0-0	-	0.00
March	0-1	-	- 1.00	March	0-0	-	0.00
April	2-5	40.0	+ 29.00	April	0-2	-	- 2.00
May	2-3	66.7	+ 8.50	May	0-7	-	- 7.00
June	2-5	40.0	+ 0.88	June	0-9	-	- 9.00
July	0-3	-	- 3.00	July	0-11	-	- 11.00
August	0-6	-	- 6.00	August	0-6	-	- 6.00
September	0-4	-	- 4.00	September	1-4	25.0	0.00
Oct/Nov	0-4	-	- 4.00	Oct/Nov	0-6	-	- 6.00

4-y-o+	W-R	Per cent	£1 Level Stake	Totals	W-R	Per cent	£1 Level Stake
January	0-7	–	– 7.00	January	0-8	–	– 8.00
February	0-0	–	0.00	February	0-0	–	0.00
March	0-8	–	– 8.00	March	0-9	–	– 9.00
April	1-7	14.3	– 2.00	April	3-14	21.4	+ 25.00
May	1-11	9.1	– 3.00	May	3-21	14.3	– 1.50
June	0-10	–	– 10.00	June	2-24	8.3	– 18.12
July	4-13	30.8	+ 3.51	July	4-27	14.8	– 10.49
August	1-18	5.6	– 1.00	August	1-30	3.3	– 13.00
September	0-7	–	– 7.00	September	1-15	6.7	– 11.00
Oct/Nov	0-3	–	– 3.00	Oct/Nov	0-13	–	– 13.00

DISTANCE

2-y-o	W-R	Per cent	£1 Level Stake	3-y-o	W-R	Per cent	£1 Level Stake
5f-6f	6-23	26.1	+ 28.38	5f-6f	0-7	–	– 7.00
7f-8f	0-8	–	– 8.00	7f-8f	1-28	3.6	– 24.00
9f-13f	0-0	–	0.00	9f-13f	0-11	–	– 11.00
14f+	0-0	–	0.00	14f+	0-0	–	0.00

4-y-o+	W-R	Per cent	£1 Level Stake	Totals	W-R	Per cent	£1 Level Stake
5f-6f	4-41	9.8	0.00	5f-6f	10-71	14.1	+ 21.38
7f-8f	2-12	16.7	– 8.87	7f-8f	3-48	6.3	– 40.87
9f-13f	0-10	–	– 10.00	9f-13f	0-21	–	– 21.00
14f+	1-21	4.8	– 18.62	14f+	1-21	4.8	– 18.62

TYPE OF RACE

Non-Handicaps	W-R	Per cent	£1 Level Stake	Handicaps	W-R	Per cent	£1 Level Stake
2-y-o	6-26	23.1	+ 25.38	2-y-o	0-4	–	– 4.00
3-y-o	0-18	–	– 18.00	3-y-o	1-22	4.5	– 18.00
4-y-o+	6-19	31.6	+ 10.51	4-y-o+	1-54	1.9	– 37.00
Selling	0-8	–	– 8.00	Selling	0-3	–	– 3.00
Apprentice	0-1	–	– 1.00	Apprentice	0-5	–	– 5.00
Amat/Ladies	0-0	–	0.00	Amat/Ladies	0-1	–	– 1.00
Totals	12-72	16.7	+ 8.89	Totals	2-89	2.2	– 68.00

COURSE GRADE

	W-R	Per cent	£1 Level Stake
Group 1	3-42	7.1	– 9.50
Group 2	3-24	12.5	– 10.62
Group 3	6-52	11.5	+ 0.88
Group 4	2-43	4.7	– 39.87

FIRST TIME OUT

	W-R	Per cent	£1 Level Stake
2-y-o	1-8	12.5	+ 5.00
3-y-o	0-9	–	– 9.00
4-y-o+	0-17	–	– 17.00
Totals	1-34	2.9	– 21.00

JOCKEYS RIDING

	W-R	Per cent	£1 Level Stake		W-R	Per cent	£1 Level Stake
P Robinson	5-15	33.3	+ 13.38	R Cochrane	1-3	33.3	- 1.27
J Williams	3-25	12.0	+ 18.00	J Fanning	1-7	14.3	+ 1.00
D McKeown	1-3	33.3	+ 3.00	M Birch	1-11	9.1	0.00
K Darley	1-3	33.3	- 1.60	J Quinn	1-25	4.0	- 22.62

S D Williams	0-15	D Moffatt	0-2	Dale Gibson	0-1
N Adams	0-4	F Norton	0-2	J Penza	0-1
N Carlisle	0-4	S Wynne	0-2	L Dettori	0-1
J Reid	0-3	W Carson	0-2	Mrs A Farrell	0-1
K Fallon	0-3	A Clark	0-1	N Kennedy	0-1
M Roberts	0-3	B Doyle	0-1	P McCabe	0-1
S Maloney	0-3	B Raymond	0-1	R Painter	0-1
W Newnes	0-3	C Asmussen	0-1	R Price	0-1
A Mackay	0-2	D Biggs	0-1	S Whitworth	0 1
A Munro	0-2	D Holland	0-1	T Wilson	0-1
B Russell	0-2	D Wright	0-1		

COURSE RECORD

	Total W-R	Non-Handicaps 2-y-o	3-y-o+	Handicaps 2-y-o	3-y-o+	Per cent	£1 Level Stake
Beverley	2-12	1-3	1-5	0-0	0-4	16.7	+ 1.38
Nottingham	2-14	1-2	0-4	0-0	1-8	14.3	+ 16.00
Windsor	1-1	1-1	0-0	0-0	0-0	100.0	+ 4.50
Catterick	1-2	0-0	1-2	0-0	0-0	50.0	- 0.60
Kempton	1-3	1-1	0-1	0-0	0-1	33.3	+ 18.00
Thirsk	1-3	1-1	0-0	0-0	0-2	33.3	+ 3.00
Yarmouth	1-3	0-0	0-1	0-0	1-2	33.3	+ 1.00
Southwell (Turf)	1-8	0-2	1-2	0-0	0-4	12.5	- 6.27
Ripon	1-9	0-1	1-2	0-1	0-5	11.1	- 4.00
Newmarket	1-10	1-2	0-5	0-0	0-3	10.0	- 6.50
Redcar	1-10	0-1	1-3	0-1	0-5	10.0	- 7.62
Doncaster	1-12	0-1	1-1	0-0	0-10	8.3	- 4.00

Southwell (AW)	0-21	Ascot	0-3	Chepstow	0-1
Pontefract	0-12	Haydock	0-3	Chester	0-1
Leicester	0-9	Newcastle	0-3	Folkestone	0-1
Warwick	0-4	Sandown	0-3	Lingfield	0-1
York	0-4	Lingfield (AW)	0-2	Newbury	0-1

WINNING HORSES

	Age	Races Run	1st	2nd	3rd	Unpl	Win £
Snipe Hall	2	8	4	1	0	3	24,314
Martina	5	7	2	0	1	4	5,590
Sizzling Saga	5	8	2	0	3	3	4,779
Kangra Valley	2	6	1	1	0	4	3,699
Clairification	3	10	1	3	0	6	3,652
Valiant Man	2	4	1	0	1	2	3,290
Another Lane	6	10	1	1	1	7	2,624
Food Of Love	5	9	1	0	0	8	2,238
Angelica Park	7	6	1	2	3	0	2,070

WINNING OWNERS

	Races Won	Value £		Races Won	Value £
Mrs R T Watson	5	28,013	J Rose	1	3,290
J David Abell	3	7,017	Mrs E Harris	1	2,624
M J Yarrow	2	5,590	Parkers of Peterborough Plc	1	2,070
Mrs S Hallam	1	3,652			

Favourites	6-14	42.9%	+ 3.89	Total winning prize-money	£52,255

Longest winning sequence	2	Average SP of winner	6.3/1
Longest losing sequence	36	Return on stakes invested	-36.7%

1992 Form	18-156	11.5%	+ 31.95	1990 Form	15-198	7.6%	- 38.00
1991 Form	11-119	9.2%	- 30.17	1989 Form	13-176	7.4%	- 33.00

R M WHITAKER (Wetherby, West Yorks)

	No. of Horses	Races Run	1st	2nd	3rd	Unpl	Per cent	£1 Level Stake
2-y-o	16	68	3	6	5	54	4.4	- 39.50
3-y-o	15	116	10	12	12	82	8.6	- 10.75
4-y-o+	19	136	9	15	12	100	6.6	- 44.17
Totals	50	320	22	33	29	236	6.9	- 94.42

BY MONTH

2-y-o	W-R	Per cent	£1 Level Stake	3-y-o	W-R	Per cent	£1 Level Stake
January	0-0	-	0.00	January	0-0	-	0.00
February	0-0	-	0.00	February	0-0	-	0.00
March	0-1	-	- 1.00	March	0-2	-	- 2.00
April	0-2	-	- 2.00	April	2-17	11.8	+ 2.50
May	1-9	11.1	+ 2.00	May	1-22	4.5	- 15.50
June	1-7	14.3	+ 6.00	June	4-23	17.4	+ 10.75
July	1-10	10.0	- 5.50	July	1-16	6.3	- 8.50
August	0-15	-	- 15.00	August	1-15	6.7	+ 6.00
September	0-13	-	- 13.00	September	1-13	7.7	+ 4.00
Oct/Nov	0-11	-	- 11.00	Oct/Nov	0-8	-	- 8.00

4-y-o+	W-R	Per cent	£1 Level Stake	Totals	W-R	Per cent	£1 Level Stake
January	0-1	-	- 1.00	January	0-1	-	- 1.00
February	0-2	-	- 2.00	February	0-2	-	- 2.00
March	0-4	-	- 4.00	March	0-7	-	- 7.00
April	1-12	8.3	- 3.00	April	3-31	9.7	- 2.50
May	1-25	4.0	- 4.00	May	3-56	5.4	- 17.50
June	1-25	4.0	- 4.00	June	6-55	10.9	+ 12.75
July	1-23	4.3	- 17.00	July	3-49	6.1	- 31.00
August	2-16	12.5	+ 5.00	August	3-46	6.5	- 4.00
September	3-13	23.1	+ 0.83	September	4-39	10.3	- 8.17
Oct/Nov	0-15	-	- 15.00	Oct/Nov	0-34	-	- 34.00

DISTANCE

2-y-o	W-R	Per cent	£1 Level Stake	3-y-o	W-R	Per cent	£1 Level Stake
5f-6f	1-47	2.1	- 36.00	5f-6f	6-69	8.7	- 12.25
7f-8f	2-20	10.0	- 2.50	7f-8f	3-30	10.0	+ 3.50
9f-13f	0-1	-	- 1.00	9f-13f	1-16	6.3	- 1.00
14f+	0-0	-	0.00	14f+	0-1	-	- 1.00

4-y-o+	W-R	Per cent	£1 Level Stake	Totals	W-R	Per cent	£1 Level Stake
5f-6f	0-25	-	- 25.00	5f-6f	7-141	5.0	- 73.25
7f-8f	6-65	9.2	+ 0.83	7f-8f	11-115	9.6	+ 1.83
9f-13f	2-39	5.1	- 24.00	9f-13f	3-56	5.4	- 26.00
14f+	1-7	14.3	+ 4.00	14f+	1-8	12.5	+ 3.00

TYPE OF RACE

Non-Handicaps	W-R	Per cent	£1 Level Stake	Handicaps	W-R	Per cent	£1 Level Stake
2-y-o	2-47	4.3	- 31.50	2-y-o	0-11	-	- 11.00
3-y-o	4-37	10.8	+ 18.75	3-y-o	3-59	5.1	- 30.00
4-y-o+	1-13	7.7	+ 8.00	4-y-o+	5-93	5.4	- 41.00
Selling	5-25	20.0	+ 13.33	Selling	2-14	14.3	0.00
Apprentice	0-3	-	- 3.00	Apprentice	0-13	-	- 13.00
Amat/Ladies	0-0	-	0.00	Amat/Ladies	0-5	-	- 5.00
Totals	12-125	9.6	+ 5.58	Totals	10-195	5.1	-100.00

COURSE GRADE

	W-R	Per cent	£1 Level Stake
Group 1	4-100	4.0	- 42.00
Group 2	7-79	8.9	- 12.17
Group 3	9-80	11.3	- 2.25
Group 4	2-61	3.3	- 38.00

FIRST TIME OUT

	W-R	Per cent	£1 Level Stake
2-y-o	2-16	12.5	+ 8.00
3-y-o	2-15	13.3	+ 4.50
4-y-o+	1-19	5.3	+ 2.00
Totals	5-50	10.0	+ 14.50

JOCKEYS RIDING

	W-R	Per cent	£1 Level Stake		W-R	Per cent	£1 Level Stake
A Culhane	15-173	8.7	- 32.17	B Raymond	1-5	20.0	+ 16.00
A Clark	1-1	100.0	+ 1.75	Alex Greaves	1-5	20.0	+ 16.00
S Maloney	1-2	50.0	+ 13.00	A Munro	1-6	16.7	0.00
J Reid	1-4	25.0	+ 4.00	N Carlisle	1-13	7.7	- 2.00

G Parkin	0-26	J O'Reilly	0-2	L Piggott	0-1
Dale Gibson	0-12	K Fallon	0-2	M Birch	0-1
J Fanning	0-11	Mrs A Farrell	0-2	P McCabe	0-1
W Carson	0-7	N Kennedy	0-2	Paul Eddery	0-1
D Wright	0-6	S Perks	0-2	S Davies	0-1
J Penza	0-5	A Garth	0-1	T Lucas	0-1
A Mackay	0-4	Antoinette Armes	0-1	T Williams	0-1
G Carter	0-3	Claire Balding	0-1	W R Swinburn	0-1
M Baird	0-3	D Biggs	0-1	W Ryan	0-1
Mr S Whitaker	0-3	G Bardwell	0-1	W Woods	0-1
D McKeown	0-2	G Duffield	0-1		
J Lowe	0-2	J Marshall	0-1		

COURSE RECORD

	Total W-R	Non-Handicaps 2-y-o	3-y-o+	Handicaps 2-y-o	3-y-o+	Per cent	£1 Level Stake
Beverley	5-28	1-5	2-8	0-2	2-13	17.9	+ 15.50
Thirsk	4-22	1-5	2-5	0-0	1-12	18.2	+ 14.33
Ayr	3-13	0-1	2-3	0-1	1-8	23.1	+ 40.00
Nottingham	2-12	0-2	0-3	0-0	2-7	16.7	+ 2.50
Chepstow	1-1	0-0	1-1	0-0	0-0	100.0	+ 1.75
Chester	1-2	0-0	0-0	0-0	1-2	50.0	+ 5.50
Carlisle	1-10	0-0	1-2	0-0	0-8	10.0	- 2.00
Leicester	1-12	0-0	1-7	0-1	0-4	8.3	+ 5.00
Doncaster	1-16	0-1	0-4	0-0	1-11	6.3	- 11.00
Catterick	1-21	0-6	0-4	0-2	1-9	4.8	- 6.00
Ripon	1-22	0-7	0-4	0-1	1-10	4.5	- 12.00
Redcar	1-30	1-9	0-9	0-1	0-11	3.3	- 17.00

Newcastle	0-22	Newmarket	0-9	Epsom	0-3
York	0-21	Southwell (Turf)	0-7	Bath	0-2
Pontefract	0-13	Warwick	0-6	Yarmouth	0-2
Edinburgh	0-11	Goodwood	0-5	Kempton	0-1
Hamilton	0-10	Southwell (AW)	0-5	Lingfield (AW)	0-1
Haydock	0-10	Brighton	0-3		

WINNING HORSES

	Age	Races Run	1st	2nd	3rd	Unpl	Win £
First Bid	6	14	2	5	2	5	8,688
Fortis Pavior	3	12	2	3	0	7	6,032
Parfait Amour	4	14	2	2	3	7	5,470
Saint Express	3	12	1	0	3	8	5,452
Hot Off The Press	3	9	2	1	2	4	4,812
Ooh Ah Cantona	2	5	2	0	0	3	4,671
Redstella	4	6	1	0	0	5	3,816
Hotaria	3	9	1	0	3	5	3,670
Gant Bleu	6	11	1	0	0	10	3,210
The Fed	3	12	1	1	1	9	3,085
Young Valentine	4	11	1	0	1	9	2,941

Salda	4	11	1	2	0	8	2,880
Lamsonetti	3	13	1	2	0	10	2,739
Scored Again	3	4	1	0	1	2	2,434
Reach For Glory	4	11	1	1	2	7	2,377
Lock Tight	3	4	1	0	0	3	2,243
Surprise Breeze	2	6	1	1	0	4	2,243

WINNING OWNERS

	Races Won	Value £		Races Won	Value £
R M Whitaker	4	9,917	Mrs Julia Richmond	1	3,670
E R Thomas	3	8,939	E C Alton	1	3,210
Thomlinson's	2	8,688	F E Downes	1	3,085
D Gill	2	6,032	Mrs Kate Hall	1	2,739
M G St Quinton	1	5,452	E Wilkinson	1	2,601
The Pbt Group	2	5,375	D R Brotherton	1	2,243
Harry Whitton	2	4,812			

Favourites	3-19	15.8%	- 9.42	Total winning prize-money	£66,762
Longest winning sequence			1	Average SP of winner	9.3/1
Longest losing sequence			58	Return on stakes invested	-29.5%
1992 Form	23-295	7.8%	-107.49	1990 Form 36-380 9.5%	- 82.40
1991 Form	24-286	8.4%	- 87.80	1989 Form 29-428 6.8%	-219.50

J WHITE (Wendover, Bucks)

	No. of Horses	Races Run	1st	2nd	3rd	Unpl	Per cent	£1 Level Stake
2-y-o	9	13	0	0	0	13	-	- 13.00
3-y-o	5	27	3	5	3	16	11.1	- 20.38
4-y-o+	20	59	8	5	5	41	13.6	+ 14.00
Totals	34	99	11	10	8	70	11.1	- 19.38

BY MONTH

2-y-o	W-R	Per cent	£1 Level Stake	3-y-o	W-R	Per cent	£1 Level Stake
January	0-0	-	0.00	January	1-3	33.3	- 0.80
February	0-0	-	0.00	February	0-1	-	- 1.00
March	0-0	-	0.00	March	0-2	-	- 2.00
April	0-0	-	0.00	April	0-1	-	- 1.00
May	0-0	-	0.00	May	0-6	-	- 6.00
June	0-2	-	- 2.00	June	0-8	-	- 8.00
July	0-1	-	- 1.00	July	2-6	33.3	- 1.58
August	0-4	-	- 4.00	August	0-0	-	0.00
September	0-5	-	- 5.00	September	0-0	-	0.00
Oct/Nov	0-1	-	- 1.00	Oct/Nov	0-0	-	0.00

4-y-o+	W-R	Per cent	£1 Level Stake		Totals	W-R	Per cent	£1 Level Stake
January	0-4	-	- 4.00		January	1-7	14.3	- 4.80
February	0-0	-	0.00		February	0-1	-	- 1.00
March	0-0	-	0.00		March	0-2	-	- 2.00
April	1-3	33.3	+ 1.50		April	1-4	25.0	+ 0.50
May	0-5	-	- 5.00		May	0-11	-	- 11.00
June	2-13	15.4	+ 6.00		June	2-23	8.7	- 4.00
July	4-17	23.5	+ 19.50		July	6-24	25.0	+ 16.92
August	0-7	-	- 7.00		August	0-11	-	- 11.00
September	0-6	-	- 6.00		September	0-11	-	- 11.00
Oct/Nov	1-4	25.0	+ 9.00		Oct/Nov	1-5	20.0	+ 8.00

DISTANCE

2-y-o	W-R	Per cent	£1 Level Stake		3-y-o	W-R	Per cent	£1 Level Stake
5f-6f	0-8	-	- 8.00		5f-6f	1-4	25.0	- 1.80
7f-8f	0-5	-	- 5.00		7f-8f	0-7	-	- 7.00
9f-13f	0-0	-	0.00		9f-13f	1-12	8.3	- 9.25
14f+	0-0	-	0.00		14f+	1-4	25.0	- 2.33

4-y-o+	W-R	Per cent	£1 Level Stake		Totals	W-R	Per cent	£1 Level Stake
5f-6f	1-16	6.3	- 8.00		5f-6f	2-28	7.1	- 17.80
7f-8f	1-14	7.1	- 9.50		7f-8f	1-26	3.8	- 21.50
9f-13f	2-18	11.1	+ 2.50		9f-13f	3-30	10.0	- 6.75
14f+	4-11	36.4	+ 29.00		14f+	5-15	33.3	+ 26.67

TYPE OF RACE

Non-Handicaps	W-R	Per cent	£1 Level Stake		Handicaps	W-R	Per cent	£1 Level Stake
2-y-o	0-11	-	- 11.00		2-y-o	0-0	-	0.00
3-y-o	2-22	9.1	- 17.05		3-y-o	0-2	-	- 2.00
4-y-o+	3-14	21.4	+ 14.50		4-y-o+	2-31	6.5	- 13.00
Selling	0-5	-	- 5.00		Selling	2-8	25.0	+ 10.50
Apprentice	2-2	100.0	+ 7.67		Apprentice	0-3	-	- 3.00
Amat/Ladies	0-1	-	- 1.00		Amat/Ladies	0-0	-	0.00
Totals	7-55	12.7	- 11.88		Totals	4-44	9.1	- 7.50

COURSE GRADE

	W-R	Per cent	£1 Level Stake
Group 1	2-27	7.4	- 9.00
Group 2	1-18	5.6	- 13.50
Group 3	4-29	13.8	+ 5.75
Group 4	4-25	16.0	- 2.63

FIRST TIME OUT

	W-R	Per cent	£1 Level Stake
2-y-o	0-9	-	- 9.00
3-y-o	0-4	-	- 4.00
4-y-o+	2-20	10.0	+ 2.00
Totals	2-33	6.1	- 11.00

White J

JOCKEYS RIDING

	W–R	Per cent	£1 Level Stake		W–R	Per cent	£1 Level Stake
R Price	3–13	23.1	+ 16.50	T Quinn	1–6	16.7	– 1.50
K Rutter	3–13	23.1	+ 9.67	W Newnes	1–10	10.0	– 7.25
J Williams	2–3	66.7	+ 15.00	Dale Gibson	1–13	7.7	– 10.80

D Wright	0–10	W Ryan	0–2	L Piggott		0–1
C Avery	0–9	A Clark	0–1	M Wigham		0–1
G Duffield	0–4	A Munro	0–1	Miss S Davies		0–1
P Robinson	0–4	G Forster	0–1	R Cochrane		0–1
T Fuggle	0–4	J Reid	0–1			

COURSE RECORD

	Total W–R	Non-Handicaps 2-y-o	Non-Handicaps 3-y-o+	Handicaps 2-y-o	Handicaps 3-y-o+	Per cent	£1 Level Stake
Bath	2–4	0–1	1–1	0–0	1–2	50.0	+ 9.75
Lingfield (AW)	2–10	0–0	2–8	0–0	0–2	20.0	+ 3.20
Catterick	1–1	0–0	1–1	0–0	0–0	100.0	+ 0.67
Leicester	1–1	0–0	1–1	0–0	0–0	100.0	+ 12.00
Newmarket	1–4	0–0	0–0	0–0	1–4	25.0	+ 9.00
Yarmouth	1–5	0–0	1–3	0–0	0–2	20.0	+ 3.00
Folkestone	1–6	0–1	0–2	0–0	1–3	16.7	+ 1.50
Goodwood	1–6	0–1	0–1	0–0	1–4	16.7	– 1.00
Brighton	1–9	0–1	1–4	0–0	0–4	11.1	– 4.50

Windsor	0–13	Salisbury	0–3	Sandown	0–2
Southwell (AW)	0–7	Ascot	0–2	Chepstow	0–1
Epsom	0–6	Ayr	0–2	Chester	0–1
Hamilton	0–3	Newbury	0–2	Warwick	0–1
Kempton	0–3	Pontefract	0–2		
Lingfield	0–3	Ripon	0–2		

WINNING HORSES

	Age	Races Run	1st	2nd	3rd	Unpl	Win £
Aahsaylad	7	4	2	1	1	0	61,588
Mr Geneaology	3	4	2	1	0	1	4,811
Shikari's Son	6	13	1	3	1	8	3,996
Misty View	4	5	1	0	0	4	3,077
Norstock	6	2	1	0	0	1	2,611
Bondaid	9	3	1	0	1	1	2,595
Quiet Riot	11	3	1	0	1	1	2,343
Treasure Time	4	10	1	1	1	7	2,301
Pirates Gold	3	9	1	4	2	2	2,208

WINNING OWNERS

	Races Won	Value £		Races Won	Value £
Ms M Horan	3	63,931	Nick Quesnel	1	2,611
Mrs P A White	2	4,811	A J Allright	1	2,595
Alan Spargo	1	3,996	Chiltern Hills Racing Club	1	2,301
M R Pascall	1	3,077	E C Nott	1	2,208

Favourites	4-11	36.4%	+ 0.62	Total winning prize-money	£85,529
Longest winning sequence			2	Average SP of winner	6.2/1
Longest losing sequence			23	Return on stakes invested	-19.6%

1992 Form	9-98	9.2%	- 62.75	1990 Form	2-88	2.3%	- 72.00
1991 Form	5-106	4.7%	- 36.00	1989 Form	5-77	6.5%	- 45.67

P WIGHAM (Malton, North Yorks)

	No. of Horses	Races Run	1st	2nd	3rd	Unpl	Per cent	£1 Level Stake
2-y-o	0	0	0	0	0	0	-	0.00
3-y-o	0	0	0	0	0	0	-	0.00
4-y-o+	3	13	1	0	0	12	7.7	- 8.50
Totals	3	13	1	0	0	12	7.7	- 8.50

Jan	Feb	Mar	Apr	May	Jun	Jul	Aug	Sep	Oct/Nov
0-0	0-0	0-0	0-0	0-0	0-1	0-3	0-3	0-2	1-4

Winning Jockey	W-R	£1 Level Stake	Winning Course	W-R	£1 Level Stake
L Charnock	1-2	+ 2.50	Redcar	1-2	+ 2.50

Winning Horse	Age	Races Run	1st	2nd	3rd	Unpl	Win £
Bold Elect	5	7	1	0	0	6	3,236

Favourites	0-1		Total winning prize-money	£3,236

1992 Form	4-20	20.0%	+ 7.00	1990 Form	1-12	8.3%	+ 5.00
1991 Form	1-15	6.7%	- 11.75	1989 Form	0-12		

W G R WIGHTMAN (Upham, Hants)

	No. of Horses	Races Run	1st	2nd	3rd	Unpl	Per cent	£1 Level Stake
2-y-o	0	0	0	0	0	0	-	0.00
3-y-o	4	28	2	1	1	24	7.1	- 15.00
4-y-o+	4	23	2	3	1	17	8.7	- 9.00
Totals	8	51	4	4	2	41	7.8	- 24.00

Jan	Feb	Mar	Apr	May	Jun	Jul	Aug	Sep	Oct/Nov
0-2	0-2	0-0	0-4	2-11	0-8	1-8	0-5	0-7	1-4

Winning Jockeys	W-R	£1 Level Stake		W-R	£1 Level Stake
J Reid	2-2	+ 12.00	G Bardwell	2-28	- 15.00

Winning Courses	W-R	£1 Level Stake		W-R	£1 Level Stake
Bath	2-2	+ 11.00	Goodwood	1-7	- 3.00
Newbury	1-6	+ 4.00			

Winning Horses	Age	Races Run	1st	2nd	3rd	Unpl	Win £
Googly	4	13	2	3	1	7	11,736
Hallorina	3	11	2	0	1	8	5,784

Favourites	2-7	28.6%	0.00	Total winning prize-money	£17,519

1992 Form	14-113	12.4%	+ 60.50	1990 Form	3-136	2.2%	-122.00
1991 Form	5-108	4.6%	- 78.00	1989 Form	8-100	8.0%	- 49.50

C P WILDMAN (Salisbury, Wilts)

	No. of Horses	Races Run	1st	2nd	3rd	Unpl	Per cent	£1 Level Stake
2-y-o	0	0	0	0	0	0	-	0.00
3-y-o	2	4	0	0	0	4	-	- 4.00
4-y-o+	4	32	2	5	6	19	6.3	- 13.00
Totals	6	36	2	5	6	23	5.6	- 17.00

Jan	Feb	Mar	Apr	May	Jun	Jul	Aug	Sep	Oct/Nov
0-6	0-2	0-4	0-2	0-2	0-5	0-4	0-1	2-3	0-7

Winning Jockeys	W-R	£1 Level Stake		W-R	£1 Level Stake
B Doyle	1-1	+ 10.00	Paul Eddery	1-2	+ 6.00

Winning Courses	W-R	£1 Level Stake		W-R	£1 Level Stake
Salisbury	1-2	+ 6.00	Bath	1-3	+ 8.00

Winning Horse	Age	Races Run	1st	2nd	3rd	Unpl	Win £
Head Turner	5	7	2	0	1	4	6,843

Favourites	0-7		Total winning prize-money	£6,843

1992 Form	3-34	8.8%	- 22.25	1990 Form	3-45	6.7%	+ 6.00
1991 Form	3-31	9.7%	- 8.00	1989 Form	3-56	5.4%	- 15.50

C N WILLIAMS (Newmarket)

	No. of Horses	Races Run	1st	2nd	3rd	Unpl	Per cent	£1 Level Stake
2-y-o	1	6	2	0	0	4	33.3	+ 0.25
3-y-o	2	17	0	3	1	13	-	- 17.00
4-y-o+	3	17	1	0	2	14	5.9	- 10.00
Totals	6	40	3	3	3	31	7.5	- 26.75

Jan	Feb	Mar	Apr	May	Jun	Jul	Aug	Sep	Oct/Nov
0-1	0-1	0-0	0-1	0-2	2-9	1-13	0-6	0-5	0-2

Winning Jockeys	W-R	£1 Level Stake			W-R	£1 Level Stake
J Curant	2-9	- 2.75		D Harrison	1-10	- 3.00

Winning Courses						
Doncaster	1-1	+ 1.75		Yarmouth	1-13	- 6.00
Nottingham	1-2	+ 1.50				

Winning Horses		Age	Races Run	1st	2nd	3rd	Unpl	Win £
Tinker Osmaston		2	6	2	0	0	4	5,601
Yonge Tender		6	7	1	0	1	5	2,826

Favourites	2-6	33.3%	+ 4.50	Total winning prize-money		£8,427

1992 Form	3-34	8.8%	- 25.00	1990 Form	4-60	6.7%	- 15.50
1991 Form	2-36	5.6%	- 26.09	1989 Form	2-68	2.9%	- 39.50

M WILLIAMS (Wellington, Somerset)

	No. of Horses	Races Run	1st	2nd	3rd	Unpl	Per cent	£1 Level Stake
2-y-o	4	27	2	4	2	19	7.4	- 21.60
3-y-o	0	0	0	0	0	0	-	0.00
4-y-o+	5	21	4	0	4	13	19.0	+ 32.85
Totals	9	48	6	4	6	32	12.5	+ 11.25

Jan	Feb	Mar	Apr	May	Jun	Jul	Aug	Sep	Oct/Nov
0-0	0-4	1-3	0-4	1-4	2-9	2-8	0-5	0-8	0-3

Winning Jockey	W-R	£1 Level Stake			W-R	£1 Level Stake
J Williams	6-27	+ 32.25				

Winning Courses						
Leicester	3-6	+ 33.40		Kempton	1-1	+ 3.60
Lingfield (AW)	2-3	+ 12.25				

Winning Horses		Races					Win
	Age	Run	1st	2nd	3rd	Unpl	£
Knock To Enter	5	10	3	0	2	5	8,206
Fathom Five	4	6	1	0	0	5	2,658
Sweet Decision	2	8	1	2	0	5	2,595
Primost	2	9	1	1	1	6	2,469

Favourites	3-6	50.0%	+ 1.65	Total winning prize-money			£15,928

1992 Form   0-6

R J R WILLIAMS (Newmarket)

	No. of Horses	Races Run	1st	2nd	3rd	Unpl	Per cent	£1 Level Stake
2-y-o	11	53	5	6	4	38	9.4	- 1.67
3-y-o	14	93	6	10	6	71	6.5	- 61.67
4-y-o+	6	69	5	13	15	36	7.2	- 39.00
Totals	31	215	16	29	25	145	7.4	-102.34

BY MONTH

2-y-o	W-R	Per cent	£1 Level Stake	3-y-o	W-R	Per cent	£1 Level Stake
January	0-0	-	0.00	January	0-0	-	0.00
February	0-0	-	0.00	February	0-2	-	- 2.00
March	0-0	-	0.00	March	1-2	50.0	+ 9.00
April	0-2	-	- 2.00	April	2-9	22.2	- 0.75
May	1-6	16.7	+ 28.00	May	0-11	-	- 11.00
June	2-8	25.0	- 1.67	June	1-19	5.3	- 14.50
July	0-8	-	- 8.00	July	2-14	14.3	- 6.42
August	0-10	-	- 10.00	August	0-16	-	- 16.00
September	2-8	25.0	+ 3.00	September	0-14	-	- 14.00
Oct/Nov	0-11	-	- 11.00	Oct/Nov	0-6	-	- 6.00

4-y-o+	W-R	Per cent	£1 Level Stake	Totals	W-R	Per cent	£1 Level Stake
January	1-3	33.3	+ 4.00	January	1-3	33.3	+ 4.00
February	0-6	-	- 6.00	February	0-8	-	- 8.00
March	0-1	-	- 1.00	March	1-3	33.3	+ 8.00
April	0-8	-	- 8.00	April	2-19	10.5	- 10.75
May	2-9	22.2	+ 2.00	May	3-26	11.5	+ 19.00
June	2-12	16.7	0.00	June	5-39	12.8	- 16.17
July	0-8	-	- 8.00	July	2-30	6.7	- 22.42
August	0-7	-	- 7.00	August	0-33	-	- 33.00
September	0-5	-	- 5.00	September	2-27	7.4	- 16.00
Oct/Nov	0-10	-	- 10.00	Oct/Nov	0-27	-	- 27.00

DISTANCE

2-y-o	W-R	Per cent	£1 Level Stake	3-y-o	W-R	Per cent	£1 Level Stake
5f-6f	3-28	10.7	+ 12.33	5f-6f	0-6	-	- 6.00
7f-8f	2-24	8.3	- 13.00	7f-8f	0-24	-	- 24.00
9f-13f	0-1	-	- 1.00	9f-13f	6-50	12.0	- 18.67
14f+	0-0	-	0.00	14f+	0-13	-	- 13.00

4-y-o+	W-R	Per cent	£1 Level Stake	Totals	W-R	Per cent	£1 Level Stake
5f-6f	0-7	-	- 7.00	5f-6f	3-41	7.3	- 0.67
7f-8f	4-34	11.8	- 8.00	7f-8f	6-82	7.3	- 45.00
9f-13f	1-15	6.7	- 11.00	9f-13f	7-66	10.6	- 30.67
14f+	0-13	-	- 13.00	14f+	0-26	-	- 26.00

TYPE OF RACE

Non-Handicaps	W-R	Per cent	£1 Level Stake	Handicaps	W-R	Per cent	£1 Level Stake
2-y-o	4-34	11.8	+ 11.83	2-y-o	0-12	-	- 12.00
3-y-o	1-36	2.8	- 32.75	3-y-o	5-42	11.9	- 13.92
4-y-o+	1-10	10.0	- 7.00	4-y-o+	2-50	4.0	- 35.00
Selling	1-10	10.0	- 4.50	Selling	0-6	-	- 6.00
Apprentice	0-3	-	- 3.00	Apprentice	2-12	16.7	0.00
Amat/Ladies	0-0	-	0.00	Amat/Ladies	0-0	-	0.00
Totals	7-93	7.5	- 35.42	Totals	9-122	7.4	- 66.92

COURSE GRADE

	W-R	Per cent	£1 Level Stake
Group 1	6-85	7.1	- 17.84
Group 2	2-28	7.1	- 18.50
Group 3	1-47	2.1	- 43.00
Group 4	7-55	12.7	- 23.00

FIRST TIME OUT

	W-R	Per cent	£1 Level Stake
2-y-o	1-11	9.1	+ 23.00
3-y-o	2-14	14.3	+ 0.25
4-y-o+	1-6	16.7	+ 1.00
Totals	4-31	12.9	+ 24.25

JOCKEYS RIDING

	W-R	Per cent	£1 Level Stake		W-R	Per cent	£1 Level Stake
D Biggs	5-33	15.2	- 14.75	E Hide	1-1	100.0	+ 7.00
W Carson	3-18	16.7	+ 2.33	M Hills	1-7	14.3	0.00
R Cochrane	3-37	8.1	- 23.92	G Bardwell	1-15	6.7	+ 19.00
Sarah Thompson	2-29	6.9	- 17.00				

A Clark	0-11	G Mitchell	0-2	L Dettori	0-1
J Quinn	0-7	J Williams	0-2	M Fenton	0-1
A Munro	0-6	L Newton	0-2	Mrs M Cowdrey	0-1
N Adams	0-5	Pat Eddery	0-2	N Connorton	0-1
M Roberts	0-4	Paul Eddery	0-2	N Kennedy	0-1
N Varley	0-4	B Rouse	0-1	R Barry	0-1
D Harrison	0-3	Bob Davies	0-1	T Quinn	0-1
D Holland	0-3	J Fanning	0-1	W Newnes	0-1
R Hills	0-3	J Lowe	0-1	W Woods	0-1
C Hodgson	0-2	J Reid	0-1		
G Duffield	0-2	J Weaver	0-1		

COURSE RECORD

	Total W-R	Non-Handicaps 2-y-o	3-y-o+	Handicaps 2-y-o	3-y-o+	Per cent	£1 Level Stake
Southwell (AW)	3-17	2-4	1-4	0-0	0-9	17.6	- 6.50
Newmarket	2-28	1-9	0-5	0-2	1-12	7.1	+ 14.00
Ripon	1-5	0-1	0-0	0-0	1-4	20.0	0.00
Southwell (Turf)	1-6	0-1	0-2	0-0	1-3	16.7	- 2.75
Doncaster	1-7	0-0	0-1	0-1	1-5	14.3	+ 4.00
Haydock	1-7	1-1	0-0	0-0	0-6	14.3	- 1.50
Lingfield	1-7	0-3	0-1	0-1	1-2	14.3	- 2.50
Warwick	1-7	0-0	0-2	0-1	1-4	14.3	+ 1.00
Ascot	1-8	1-2	0-0	0-0	0-6	12.5	- 3.67
Newbury	1-9	0-1	0-0	0-1	1-7	11.1	- 4.67
Lingfield (AW)	1-9	0-1	0-4	0-0	1-4	11.1	- 2.00
Folkestone	1-13	0-3	1-4	0-0	0-6	7.7	- 9.75
Yarmouth	1-19	0-3	0-5	0-4	1-7	5.3	- 15.00

Salisbury	0-11	Chepstow	0-3	Ayr	0-1
Leicester	0-10	Windsor	0-3	Hamilton	0-1
Kempton	0-8	Bath	0-2	Pontefract	0-1
Nottingham	0-8	Brighton	0-2	Thirsk	0-1
Sandown	0-7	Epsom	0-2	Uttoxeter	0-1
Goodwood	0-4	Newcastle	0-2	York	0-1
Catterick	0-3	Redcar	0-2		

WINNING HORSES

	Age	Races Run	1st	2nd	3rd	Unpl	Win £
Threatening	2	8	2	1	0	5	10,085
Preston Guild	3	13	3	4	1	5	9,348
Dutosky	3	12	2	1	1	8	8,758
Maragon	2	3	1	1	0	1	8,041
On Y Va	6	20	2	6	4	8	5,001
Lexus	5	14	2	1	3	8	4,749
Golden Grand	2	7	2	1	0	4	4,313
Buddy's Friend	5	12	1	3	2	6	2,544
Forever Shineing	3	10	1	0	0	9	2,243

WINNING OWNERS

	Races Won	Value £		Races Won	Value £
Lord Matthews	5	21,086	The Hon I V Matthews	1	8,041
Marriott Stables Limited	4	9,750	D A Johnson	2	4,313
Lady Matthews	3	9,348	Colin G R Booth	1	2,544

Favourites	4-22	18.2%	- 9.42	Total winning prize-money	£55,082

Longest winning sequence		2	Average SP of winner	6.0/1
Longest losing sequence		55	Return on stakes invested	-47.6%

1992 Form	14-137	10.2%	- 34.97	1990 Form	15-171	8.8%	- 47.67
1991 Form	20-186	10.8%	- 7.96	1989 Form	17-235	7.2%	- 25.95

CAPT J WILSON (Preston, Lancs)

	No. of Horses	Races Run	1st	2nd	3rd	Unpl	Per cent	£1 Level Stake
2-y-o	3	17	2	0	2	13	11.8	- 3.00
3-y-o	3	23	0	6	3	14	-	- 23.00
4-y-o+	7	54	2	3	5	44	3.7	- 12.00
Totals	13	94	4	9	10	71	4.3	- 38.00

Jan	Feb	Mar	Apr	May	Jun	Jul	Aug	Sep	Oct/Nov
0-5	0-2	0-2	0-9	1-14	0-14	1-10	1-7	1-19	0-12

		£1 Level			£1 Level
Winning Jockey	W-R	Stake		W-R	Stake
J Fortune	4-42	+ 14.00			

Winning Courses					
Lingfield (AW)	1-2	+ 3.00	Edinburgh	1-7	+ 14.00
Warwick	1-6	+ 3.00	Southwell (AW)	1-20	+ 1.00

Winning Horses	Age	Races Run	1st	2nd	3rd	Unpl	Win £
Times Zando	2	9	2	0	2	5	5,021
Sie Amato	4	12	1	0	1	10	3,210
Malcesine	4	15	1	2	2	10	2,474

Favourites	1-3	33.3%	+ 2.00	Total winning prize-money	£10,704

1992 Form	5-122	4.1%	- 41.50	1990 Form	7-96	7.3%	- 22.67
1991 Form	12-108	11.1%	+ 15.88	1989 Form	8-132	6.1%	- 57.50

D A WILSON (Epsom, Surrey)

	No. of Horses	Races Run	1st	2nd	3rd	Unpl	Per cent	£1 Level Stake
2-y-o	1	3	0	0	0	3	-	- 3.00
3-y-o	5	33	2	2	2	27	6.1	- 15.50
4-y-o+	15	161	21	9	13	118	13.0	- 13.25
Totals	21	197	23	11	15	148	11.7	- 31.75

BY MONTH

2-y-o	W-R	Per cent	£1 Level Stake	3-y-o	W-R	Per cent	£1 Level Stake
January	0-0	-	0.00	January	0-0	-	0.00
February	0-0	-	0.00	February	0-0	-	0.00
March	0-0	-	0.00	March	0-0	-	0.00
April	0-0	-	0.00	April	0-0	-	0.00
May	0-0	-	0.00	May	0-2	-	- 2.00
June	0-0	-	0.00	June	0-4	-	- 4.00
July	0-1	-	- 1.00	July	0-8	-	- 8.00
August	0-2	-	- 2.00	August	2-12	16.7	+ 5.50
September	0-0	-	0.00	September	0-4	-	- 4.00
Oct/Nov	0-0	-	0.00	Oct/Nov	0-3	-	- 3.00

4-y-o+	W-R	Per cent	£1 Level Stake	Totals	W-R	Per cent	£1 Level Stake
January	2-10	20.0	+ 3.00	January	2-10	20.0	+ 3.00
February	3-8	37.5	+ 9.25	February	3-8	37.5	+ 9.25
March	1-9	11.1	0.00	March	1-9	11.1	0.00
April	2-15	13.3	+ 2.50	April	2-15	13.3	+ 2.50
May	4-22	18.2	+ 12.50	May	4-24	16.7	+ 10.50
June	5-30	16.7	- 2.25	June	5-34	14.7	- 6.25
July	3-25	12.0	- 7.25	July	3-34	8.8	- 16.25
August	0-19	-	- 19.00	August	2-33	6.1	- 15.50
September	1-10	10.0	+ 1.00	September	1-14	7.1	- 3.00
Oct/Nov	0-13	-	- 13.00	Oct/Nov	0-16	-	- 16.00

DISTANCE

2-y-o	W-R	Per cent	£1 Level Stake	3-y-o	W-R	Per cent	£1 Level Stake
5f-6f	0-2	-	- 2.00	5f-6f	0-11	-	- 11.00
7f-8f	0-1	-	- 1.00	7f-8f	2-15	13.3	+ 2.50
9f-13f	0-0	-	0.00	9f-13f	0-7	-	- 7.00
14f+	0-0	-	0.00	14f+	0-0	-	0.00

4-y-o+	W-R	Per cent	£1 Level Stake	Totals	W-R	Per cent	£1 Level Stake
5f-6f	7-42	16.7	+ 10.25	5f-6f	7-55	12.7	- 2.75
7f-8f	6-53	11.3	+ 1.00	7f-8f	8-69	11.6	+ 2.50
9f-13f	6-48	12.5	- 18.50	9f-13f	6-55	10.9	- 25.50
14f+	2-18	11.1	- 6.00	14f+	2-18	11.1	- 6.00

TYPE OF RACE

Non-Handicaps	W-R	Per cent	£1 Level Stake	Handicaps	W-R	Per cent	£1 Level Stake
2-y-o	0-3	-	- 3.00	2-y-o	0-0	-	0.00
3-y-o	0-2	-	- 2.00	3-y-o	2-20	10.0	- 2.50
4-y-o+	0-1	-	- 1.00	4-y-o+	15-126	11.9	- 27.00
Selling	0-0	-	0.00	Selling	0-2	-	- 2.00
Apprentice	0-0	-	0.00	Apprentice	3-26	11.5	+ 2.50
Amat/Ladies	0-0	-	0.00	Amat/Ladies	3-17	17.6	+ 3.25
Totals	0-6	-	- 6.00	Totals	23-191	12.0	- 25.75

COURSE GRADE

	W-R	Per cent	£1 Level Stake
Group 1	8-85	9.4	- 28.50
Group 2	7-42	16.7	+ 13.00
Group 3	0-23	-	- 23.00
Group 4	8-47	17.0	+ 6.75

FIRST TIME OUT

	W-R	Per cent	£1 Level Stake
2-y-o	0-1	-	- 1.00
3-y-o	0-2	-	- 2.00
4-y-o+	0-13	-	- 13.00
Totals	0-16	-	- 16.00

JOCKEYS RIDING

	W-R	Per cent	£1 Level Stake		W-R	Per cent	£1 Level Stake
G Carter	4-15	26.7	+ 13.00	T G McLaughlin	1-4	25.0	+ 11.00
J Quinn	3-13	23.1	+ 4.75	M Roberts	1-4	25.0	+ 1.50
Mrs D Arbuthnot	2-5	40.0	+ 7.75	D Holland	1-4	25.0	- 0.25
J Williams	2-8	25.0	+ 14.00	Miss E Bronson	1-5	20.0	+ 2.50
D Harrison	2-11	18.2	+ 6.50	M Wigham	1-9	11.1	- 4.50
G Bardwell	2-13	15.4	- 1.00	Sharon Millard	1-22	4.5	- 17.50
D McCabe	2-19	10.5	- 4.50				

G Duffield	0-5	Mrs P Nash	0-2	K Rutter	0-1
Miss I D W Jones	0-5	T Williams	0-2	L Carter	0-1
W Newnes	0-5	W Carson	0-2	L Piggott	0-1
A Munro	0-4	A Tucker	0-1	M Dwyer	0-1
M Tebbutt	0-4	B Crossley	0-1	Miss L Hide	0-1
B Rouse	0-3	B Doyle	0-1	N Varley	0-1
F Norton	0-3	C Hodgson	0-1	Olga Hulinska	0-1
A Mackay	0-2	E Johnson	0-1	P Robinson	0-1
A McGlone	0-2	J Lowe	0-1	Pat Eddery	0-1
C Rutter	0-2	J Sandford-Johnson	0-1	R Cochrane	0-1
J D Smith	0-2	J Tate	0-1	S D Williams	0-1
Mrs E Mellor	0-2	K Darley	0-1		

COURSE RECORD

	Total W-R	Non-Handicaps 2-y-o	Non-Handicaps 3-y-o+	Handicaps 2-y-o	Handicaps 3-y-o+	Per cent	£1 Level Stake
Lingfield (AW)	5-18	0-0	0-0	0-0	5-18	27.8	+ 18.25
Salisbury	4-12	0-0	0-0	0-0	4-12	33.3	+ 20.00
Goodwood	4-22	0-2	0-0	0-0	4-20	18.2	- 1.00

Wilson D A

Brighton	3-13	0-0	0-0	0-0	3-13	23.1	+	10.00
Kempton	2-9	0-0	0-1	0-0	2-8	22.2	+	10.50
Southwell (AW)	2-14	0-0	0-0	0-0	2-14	14.3	-	2.00
Doncaster	1-5	0-0	0-0	0-0	1-5	20.0	+	4.00
Folkestone	1-11	0-0	0-0	0-0	1-11	9.1	-	5.50
Sandown	1-14	0-0	0-1	0-0	1-13	7.1	-	7.00

Newmarket	0-15	Pontefract	0-3	Chester	0-1
Lingfield	0-12	Ayr	0-2	Haydock	0-1
Epsom	0-9	Chepstow	0-2	Ripon	0-1
Leicester	0-7	Redcar	0-2	Thirsk	0-1
Newbury	0-6	Windsor	0-2	Warwick	0-1
Bath	0-3	Yarmouth	0-2	York	0-1
Carlisle	0-3	Ascot	0-1		
Nottingham	0-3	Beverley	0-1		

WINNING HORSES

		Races					Win
	Age	Run	1st	2nd	3rd	Unpl	£
Albert	6	20	5	1	1	13	14,572
Nobby Barnes	4	23	4	2	2	15	13,986
Neither Nor	4	13	3	1	1	8	11,757
North Esk	4	20	2	2	0	16	8,948
Bodari	4	19	2	1	2	14	8,579
Barbezieux	6	13	2	0	0	11	6,109
Kovalevskia	8	12	2	1	3	6	5,428
Ahjay	3	11	1	1	1	8	3,231
Corinthian God	4	9	1	0	0	8	2,821
Medland	3	9	1	1	1	6	2,758

WINNING OWNERS

	Races Won	Value £		Races Won	Value £
T S M S Riley-Smith	15	49,245	D A Wilson	2	5,428
R J Thomas	3	11,810	G A Jackman	1	2,758
Alan J Speyer	2	8,948			

Favourites	6-24	25.0%	+ 2.50	Total winning prize-money	£78,188
Longest winning sequence			3	Average SP of winner	6.2/1
Longest losing sequence			30	Return on stakes invested	-16.1%
1992 Form	10-156	6.4%	- 79.25	1990 Form	19-197	9.6%	- 83.54
1991 Form	11-177	6.2%	- 90.00	1989 Form	15-137	10.9%	+ 3.46

S P C WOODS (Newmarket)

	No. of Horses	Races Run	1st	2nd	3rd	Unpl	Per cent	£1 Level Stake
2-y-o	7	36	2	1	3	30	5.6	- 27.25
3-y-o	13	80	5	7	13	55	6.3	- 38.50
4-y-o+	3	15	0	1	2	12	-	- 15.00
Totals	23	131	7	9	18	97	5.3	- 80.75

Jan	Feb	Mar	Apr	May	Jun	Jul	Aug	Sep	Oct/Nov
0-3	0-0	0-5	0-12	2-17	2-23	2-25	0-20	1-15	0-11

Winning Jockeys	W-R	£1 Level Stake			W-R	£1 Level Stake
W Woods	6-118	- 78.75	W Ryan		1-1	+ 10.00

Winning Courses						
Yarmouth	2-22	- 1.00	Epsom		1-3	+ 0.75
Haydock	1-1	+ 6.00	Kempton		1-4	+ 2.50
Ayr	1-2	+ 3.00	Newbury		1-5	+ 2.00

Winning Horses	Age	Races Run	1st	2nd	3rd	Unpl	Win £
Mistle Cat	3	7	2	3	1	1	18,390
Little Beaut	2	3	1	0	1	1	3,590
Storm Regent	2	10	1	0	1	8	3,566
Pondicherry	3	6	1	0	0	5	3,202
Stapleford Lass	3	9	1	1	2	5	2,534
Cosmic Star	3	9	1	0	1	7	2,070

Favourites	0-5		Total winning prize-money	£33,352

1992 Form	10-83	12.0%	+ 15.50

G WRAGG (Newmarket)

	No. of Horses	Races Run	1st	2nd	3rd	Unpl	Per cent	£1 Level Stake
2-y-o	18	45	13	7	7	18	28.9	+ 1.83
3-y-o	22	110	16	17	17	60	14.5	- 18.45
4-y-o+	9	46	6	7	9	24	13.0	- 8.02
Totals	49	201	35	31	33	102	17.4	- 24.64

BY MONTH

2-y-o	W-R	Per cent	£1 Level Stake		3-y-o	W-R	Per cent	£1 Level Stake	
January	0-0	-		0.00	January	0-2	-	-	2.00
February	0-0	-		0.00	February	0-0	-		0.00
March	0-0	-		0.00	March	0-1	-	-	1.00
April	0-0	-		0.00	April	3-19	15.8	+	4.41
May	0-0	-		0.00	May	3-19	15.8	-	6.50
June	2-2	100.0	+	2.88	June	5-19	26.3	+	13.38
July	3-8	37.5	+	3.74	July	2-18	11.1	-	13.24
August	4-10	40.0	-	2.20	August	0-11	-	-	11.00
September	2-12	16.7	-	3.09	September	2-7	28.6	+	7.00
Oct/Nov	2-13	15.4	+	0.50	Oct/Nov	1-14	7.1	-	9.50

4-y-o+	W-R	Per cent	£1 Level Stake		Totals	W-R	Per cent	£1 Level Stake	
January	0-0	-		0.00	January	0-2	-	-	2.00
February	0-0	-		0.00	February	0-0	-		0.00
March	0-2	-	-	2.00	March	0-3	-	-	3.00
April	1-7	14.3	-	5.27	April	4-26	15.4	-	0.86
May	2-7	28.6	+	7.25	May	5-26	19.2	+	0.75
June	1-6	16.7	-	1.50	June	8-27	29.6	+	14.76
July	0-10	-	-	10.00	July	5-36	13.9	-	19.50
August	1-6	16.7	+	5.00	August	5-27	18.5	-	8.20
September	1-2	50.0	+	4.50	September	5-21	23.8	+	8.41
Oct/Nov	0-6	-	-	6.00	Oct/Nov	3-33	9.1	-	15.00

DISTANCE

2-y-o	W-R	Per cent	£1 Level Stake		3-y-o	W-R	Per cent	£1 Level Stake	
5f-6f	9-26	34.6	+	13.37	5f-6f	0-3	-	-	3.00
7f-8f	4-19	21.1	-	11.54	7f-8f	9-57	15.8	-	11.58
9f-13f	0-0	-		0.00	9f-13f	7-50	14.0	-	3.87
14f+	0-0	-		0.00	14f+	0-0	-		0.00

4-y-o+	W-R	Per cent	£1 Level Stake		Totals	W-R	Per cent	£1 Level Stake	
5f-6f	0-0	-		0.00	5f-6f	9-29	31.0	+	10.37
7f-8f	2-10	20.0	+	4.25	7f-8f	15-86	17.4	-	18.87
9f-13f	4-26	15.4	-	2.27	9f-13f	11-76	14.5	-	6.14
14f+	0-10	-	-	10.00	14f+	0-10	-	-	10.00

TYPE OF RACE

Non-Handicaps	W-R	Per cent	£1 Level Stake		Handicaps	W-R	Per cent	£1 Level Stake	
2-y-o	13-45	28.9	+	1.83	2-y-o	0-0	-		0.00
3-y-o	14-81	17.3	+	2.64	3-y-o	1-28	3.6	-	22.00
4-y-o+	4-30	13.3	-	6.27	4-y-o+	2-16	12.5	-	1.75
Selling	0-0	-		0.00	Selling	0-0	-		0.00
Apprentice	1-1	100.0	+	0.91	Apprentice	0-0	-		0.00
Amat/Ladies	0-0	-		0.00	Amat/Ladies	0-0	-		0.00
Totals	32-157	20.4	-	0.89	Totals	3-44	6.8	-	23.75

COURSE GRADE					FIRST TIME OUT			
	W-R	Per cent	£1 Level Stake			W-R	Per cent	£1 Level Stake
Group 1	16-108	14.8	- 40.80	2-y-o		2-18	11.1	- 13.84
Group 2	7-28	25.0	+ 15.76	3-y-o		5-22	22.7	+ 22.13
Group 3	9-49	18.4	+ 5.49	4-y-o+		1-9	11.1	+ 2.00
Group 4	3-16	18.8	- 5.09					
				Totals		8-49	16.3	+ 10.29

JOCKEYS RIDING

	W-R	Per cent	£1 Level Stake			W-R	Per cent	£1 Level Stake
M Hills	23-107	21.5	- 2.44	Pat Eddery		1-5	20.0	+ 1.50
F Norton	5-21	23.8	+ 11.79	R Cochrane		1-8	12.5	- 3.50
Paul Eddery	3-25	12.0	- 8.37	M Roberts		1-10	10.0	- 7.62
A Munro	1-1	100.0	+ 8.00					

R Hills	0-6	G Duffield	0-2	M Wigham		0-1
W R Swinburn	0-4	K Fallon	0-1	S Whitworth		0-1
L Dettori	0-3	L Piggott	0-1	W Newnes		0-1
P Robinson	0-3	M Fenton	0-1			

COURSE RECORD

	Total W-R	Non-Handicaps 2-y-o	3-y-o+	Handicaps 2-y-o	3-y-o+	Per cent	£1 Level Stake
Ascot	4-13	1-2	3-9	0-0	0-2	30.8	+ 1.16
Pontefract	3-8	0-0	2-6	0-0	1-2	37.5	+ 14.73
Redcar	3-8	2-2	0-3	0-0	1-3	37.5	+ 13.38
Yarmouth	3-18	1-7	2-8	0-0	0-3	16.7	- 2.12
Newmarket	3-38	3-12	0-16	0-0	0-10	7.9	- 20.00
Catterick	2-2	0-0	2-2	0-0	0-0	100.0	+ 5.41
Chester	2-6	0-0	2-4	0-0	0-2	33.3	- 0.12
Windsor	2-6	0-0	2-5	0-0	0-1	33.3	+ 5.38
Goodwood	2-8	2-2	0-6	0-0	0-0	25.0	- 2.17
Doncaster	2-10	1-2	1-6	0-0	0-2	20.0	- 1.59
Newbury	2-10	1-3	1-4	0-0	0-3	20.0	+ 3.63
Carlisle	1-1	0-0	1-1	0-0	0-0	100.0	+ 2.50
Haydock	1-1	0-0	0-0	0-0	1-1	100.0	+ 2.25
Leicester	1-3	0-1	1-1	0-0	0-1	33.3	+ 1.50
Lingfield	1-4	0-0	1-2	0-0	0-2	25.0	+ 6.00
Ripon	1-5	0-0	1-3	0-0	0-2	20.0	+ 1.50
Kempton	1-8	1-3	0-4	0-0	0-1	12.5	- 6.33
York	1-9	1-2	0-4	0-0	0-3	11.1	- 6.75

Nottingham	0-9	Lingfield (AW)	0-3	Bath		0-1
Sandown	0-7	Newcastle	0-3	Chepstow		0-1
Southwell (AW)	0-5	Salisbury	0-3	Folkestone		0-1
Warwick	0-4	Thirsk	0-2			
Beverley	0-3	Ayr	0-1			

WINNING HORSES

	Age	Races Run	1st	2nd	3rd	Unpl	Win £
First Trump	2	6	5	0	1	0	145,396
Beneficial	3	6	3	2	1	0	86,542
Jeune	4	5	1	0	2	2	56,700
Glatisant	2	2	2	0	0	0	27,261
Young Buster	5	11	2	3	2	4	11,870
Little Bean	4	6	1	2	0	3	9,229
Nicolotte	2	5	2	1	2	0	9,103
Petardia	3	4	1	0	0	3	8,020
Blue Lion	3	7	2	2	3	0	7,993
Nessun Dorma	3	9	2	2	0	5	7,878
Owington	2	3	1	1	1	0	7,505
Etosha	3	7	2	3	0	2	6,980
Tzu'Mu	2	2	1	1	0	0	5,709
Crossillion	5	3	1	0	0	2	5,340
Croire	3	9	1	3	2	3	4,435
Young Senor	4	7	1	1	1	4	4,396
Miss Rinjani	2	3	1	1	0	1	4,307
Tansy	2	2	1	0	0	1	4,271
Balnaha	3	4	1	1	2	0	3,611
Sumoto	3	5	1	0	0	4	3,407
Castel Rosselo	3	3	1	1	1	0	3,319
Lavender Cottage	3	5	1	0	0	4	3,260
Teen Jay	3	3	1	0	0	2	1,953

WINNING OWNERS

	Races Won	Value £		Races Won	Value £
Mollers Racing	11	178,784	H H Morriss	2	7,878
Executors of the late - Sir Robin McAlpine	5	147,677	Baron G Von Ullmann	1	7,505
			A E Oppenheimer	2	6,980
Sir Philip Oppenheimer	7	52,535	G Wragg	1	5,340
Sheikh Mohammed	3	9,484	J L C Pearce	1	4,307
Sheikh Ahmed Bin Saeed - Al Maktoum	2	7,993			

Favourites	16-44	36.4%	- 4.60	Total winning prize-money	£428,482

Longest winning sequence			3	Average SP of winner	4.0/1
Longest losing sequence			13	Return on stakes invested	-12.3%

1992 Form	45-214	21.0%	- 33.35	1990 Form	32-224	14.3%	+ 0.57
1991 Form	51-220	23.2%	+ 27.73	1989 Form	25-199	12.6%	- 28.49

444

TRAINERS WITH NO WINNERS 1993

	No. of Horses	Races Run	2nd	3rd	Unpl
Mrs S M Austin	3	10	0	0	10
M Avison	3	10	0	0	10
R E Barr	3	10	0	0	10
L J Barratt	5	16	0	0	16
P Beaumont	3	3	0	0	3
Mrs M J Bennett	3	6	0	1	5
T T Bill	3	7	0	0	7
K Bishop	2	9	0	2	7
G Blum	1	1	0	0	1
M J Bolton	5	23	1	2	20
J R Bostock	5	12	0	0	12
Mrs S C Bradburne	8	27	2	2	23
M Bradstock	2	11	0	1	10
K S Bridgwater	9	15	0	0	15
T H Caldwell	7	23	2	2	19
A Chamberlain	6	13	0	0	13
R Champion	1	4	0	0	4
M J Charles	4	12	0	0	12
G F H Charles-Jones	1	3	0	0	3
J I A Charlton	1	2	0	0	2
L J Codd	3	10	0	0	10
R Curtis	16	45	0	1	44
T A K Cuthbert	2	2	0	0	2
P T Dalton	2	5	0	0	5
A W Denson	3	11	1	1	9
M W Dickinson	1	1	0	0	1
J Dooler	7	17	0	0	17
R Earnshaw	2	4	0	0	4
M W Eckley	1	2	0	0	2
M W Ellerby	7	23	1	0	22
G P Enright	1	2	0	0	2
P J Feilden	5	33	5	4	24
J Ffitch-Heyes	12	43	0	4	39
G Fleming	4	5	0	1	4
A L Forbes	7	20	0	0	20
B Forsey	4	12	0	3	9
A M Forte	2	3	0	0	3
R G Frost	3	7	0	0	7
Miss S L Gallie	2	2	0	0	2
D R Gandolfo	2	5	0	1	4
N A Gaselee	1	2	0	0	2
J S Haldane	4	17	3	1	13
T B Hallett	1	6	0	0	6
G A Ham	4	7	0	0	7
P Hayward	4	10	0	1	9
R P C Hoad	7	20	4	2	14
P J Hobbs	6	11	0	0	11
G Holmes	5	12	0	0	12
H S Howe	4	8	0	0	8
D E Incisa	10	59	0	3	56
A P James	3	3	0	0	3
M B James	1	1	0	0	1
J M Jefferson	4	17	0	2	15

	No. of Horses	Races Run	2nd	3rd	Unpl
D C Jermy	3	9	0	0	9
J H Johnson	5	13	1	1	11
G H Jones	3	6	0	0	6
P J Jones	3	8	0	0	8
Mrs J Jordan	2	5	0	0	5
R T Juckes	7	10	0	0	10
G P Kelly	3	9	0	0	9
W T Kemp	1	2	0	0	2
Miss H C Knight	1	1	0	0	1
R Lamb	5	20	0	1	19
M R Leach	5	6	0	0	6
S J Leadbetter	1	2	0	0	2
A N Lee	2	4	0	0	4
K A Linton	1	1	0	0	1
B J Llewellyn	1	1	0	1	0
J E Long	13	57	0	1	56
L Lungo	4	10	1	1	8
M J Madgwick	7	26	1	1	24
R Manning	3	9	0	0	9
R F Marvin	5	12	1	0	11
D McCain	4	9	0	0	9
J C McConnochie	5	13	1	3	9
M McCourt	1	1	0	0	1
Mrs M McCourt	4	17	0	1	16
Martyn Meade	1	2	0	0	2
M G Meagher	4	9	0	0	9
N R Mitchell	4	8	0	0	8
J Mooney	4	9	2	0	7
B C Morgan	12	39	1	1	37
K A Morgan	2	5	0	0	5
C T Nash	7	12	0	0	12
P F Nicholls	1	2	0	0	2
D Nicholson	2	5	0	1	4
D A Nolan	5	8	0	0	8
J Norton	4	19	0	2	17
R O'Leary	8	27	1	1	25
J G M O'Shea	1	2	0	0	2
J A B Old	5	6	0	3	3
E H Owen	1	6	0	0	6
Mrs H Parrott	1	4	1	0	3
S G Payne	2	2	0	0	2
J Peacock	3	5	0	0	5
R E Peacock	8	46	6	0	40
J A Pickering	4	18	0	1	17
Mrs J Pitman	2	4	0	0	4
C L Popham	3	4	0	0	4
A W Potts	7	26	0	0	26
B Preece	2	4	0	1	3
P A Pritchard	2	8	0	0	8
Miss J L Rae	1	1	0	0	1
A S Reid	7	19	1	1	17
Mrs J G Retter	1	1	0	0	1
G Richards	3	3	0	0	3
Mrs S J Smith	1	2	0	0	2
B Stevens	1	5	1	0	4
W Storey	8	21	0	0	21

	No. of Horses	Races Run	2nd	3rd	Unpl
Mrs A Swinbank	15	45	3	3	39
M Tate	2	5	0	0	5
T P Tate	1	4	0	0	4
V Thompson	1	1	0	0	1
G Thorner	1	1	0	0	1
A Turnell	3	13	1	2	10
W G Turner	1	1	0	0	1
John R Upson	1	6	0	0	6
R Voorspuy	14	87	5	1	81
F Watson	2	14	1	1	12
R J Weaver	4	12	1	0	11
J Webber	1	2	1	0	1
E A Wheeler	8	12	0	0	12
K White	8	32	0	1	31
Miss A J Whitfield	6	30	1	1	28
B E Wilkinson	1	6	1	1	4
M J Wilkinson	1	1	0	0	1
D L Williams	3	14	1	0	13
Mrs S D Williams	7	23	2	1	20
Miss S J Wilton	10	14	0	0	14
K G Wingrove	8	30	1	2	27
D J Wintle	8	24	5	0	19
R D E Woodhouse	4	12	0	2	10
S Woodman	3	11	0	3	8
N C Wright	15	48	2	2	44
F J Yardley	1	6	0	0	6
G H Yardley	3	6	0	0	6

WINNING OVERSEAS TRAINERS 1993

J S BOLGER (Ireland)

	No. of Horses	Races Run	1st	2nd	3rd	Unpl	Per cent	£1 Level Stake
2-y-o	3	3	0	0	0	3	-	- 3.00
3-y-o	9	18	1	5	2	10	5.6	- 7.00
4-y-o+	3	4	1	0	0	3	25.0	+ 1.50
Totals	15	25	2	5	2	16	8.0	- 8.50

Jan	Feb	Mar	Apr	May	Jun	Jul	Aug	Sep	Oct/Nov
0-0	0-0	0-0	0-6	0-2	1-7	1-4	0-2	0-4	0-0

Winning Jockeys	W-R	£1 Level Stake				W-R	£1 Level Stake
W Carson	1-2	+ 9.00	C Roche			1-19	- 13.50

Winning Courses							
Ascot	1-8	- 2.50	Newmarket			1-10	+ 1.00

Winning Horses	Age	Races Run	1st	2nd	3rd	Unpl	Win £
Desert Team	3	5	1	1	1	2	38,046
Riszard	4	2	1	0	0	1	16,570

Favourites	0-2			Total winning prize-money			£54,616
1992 Form	2-23	8.7%	- 18.20	1990 Form	1-5	20.0%	+ 1.00
1991 Form	2-20	10.0%	+ 40.00	1989 Form	0-2		

F BOUTIN (France)

	No. of Horses	Races Run	1st	2nd	3rd	Unpl	Per cent	£1 Level Stake
2-y-o	1	1	0	0	0	1	-	- 1.00
3-y-o	2	3	1	0	1	1	33.3	- 1.60
4-y-o+	1	1	0	1	0	0	-	- 1.00
Totals	4	5	1	1	1	2	20.0	- 3.60

Jan	Feb	Mar	Apr	May	Jun	Jul	Aug	Sep	Oct/Nov
0-0	0-0	0-0	0-1	0-0	1-1	0-0	0-0	0-1	0-2

Winning Jockey	W-R	£1 Level Stake	Winning Course	W-R	£1 Level Stake
C Asmussen	1-5	- 3.60	Ascot	1-2	- 0.60

Winning Horse	Age	Races Run	1st	2nd	3rd	Unpl	Win £
Kingmambo	3	2	1	0	1	0	116,335

Favourites	1-2	50.0%	- 0.60	Total winning prize-money		£116,335
1992 Form	0-5			1990 Form	0-5	
1991 Form	0-6			1989 Form	0-1	

A FABRE (France)

	No. of Horses	Races Run	1st	2nd	3rd	Unpl	Per cent	£1 Level Stake
2-y-o	0	0	0	0	0	0	-	0.00
3-y-o	8	10	3	2	2	3	30.0	+ 1.83
4-y-o+	4	5	0	2	1	2	-	- 5.00
Totals	12	15	3	4	3	5	20.0	- 3.17

Jan	Feb	Mar	Apr	May	Jun	Jul	Aug	Sep	Oct/Nov
0-0	0-0	0-0	0-2	1-2	2-7	0-3	0-0	0-0	0-1

Winning Jockeys	W-R	£1 Level Stake			W-R	£1 Level Stake
Pat Eddery	2-4	+ 1.83		M Roberts	1-3	+ 3.00

Winning Courses						
Epsom	1-3	+ 3.00		Newmarket	1-6	- 4.17
Ascot	1-4	0.00				

Winning Horses	Age	Races Run	1st	2nd	3rd	Unpl	Win £
Intrepidity	3	1	1	0	0	0	147,500
Zafonic	3	2	1	0	0	1	110,871
Infrasonic	3	1	1	0	0	0	34,640

Favourites	2-4	50.0%	+ 1.83	Total winning prize-money		£293,011

1992 Form	4-20	20.0%	- 3.54	1990 Form	2-7	28.6%	- 1.49
1991 Form	5-12	41.7%	+ 15.94	1989 Form	1-6	16.7%	- 1.50

MRS C HEAD (France)

	No. of Horses	Races Run	1st	2nd	3rd	Unpl	Per cent	£1 Level Stake
2-y-o	0	0	0	0	0	0	-	0.00
3-y-o	1	1	1	0	0	0	100.0	+ 3.33
4-y-o+	1	1	1	0	0	0	100.0	+ 2.50
Totals	2	2	2	0	0	0	100.0	+ 5.83

Jan	Feb	Mar	Apr	May	Jun	Jul	Aug	Sep	Oct/Nov
0-0	0-0	0-0	0-0	0-0	1-1	0-0	0-0	0-0	1-1

Winning Jockeys	W-R	£1 Level Stake			W-R	£1 Level Stake
G Mosse	1-1	+ 3.33		W R Swinburn	1-1	+ 2.50

Winning Courses						
Ascot	1-1	+ 3.33		Newmarket	1-1	+ 2.50

Head Mrs C (Fra)

Winning Horses	Age	Races Run	1st	2nd	3rd	Unpl	Win £
Hatoof	4	1	1	0	0	0	205,707
Gold Splash	3	1	1	0	0	0	109,538

Favourites	1-1	100.0%	+ 2.50	Total winning prize-money		£315,245

1992 Form	1-1	100.0%	+ 5.00	1990 Form	0-2
1991 Form	0-1				

E LELLOUCHE (France)

	No. of Horses	Races Run	1st	2nd	3rd	Unpl	Per cent	£1 Level Stake
2-y-o	0	0	0	0	0	0	-	0.00
3-y-o	1	2	2	0	0	0	100.0	+ 17.33
4-y-o+	0	0	0	0	0	0	-	0.00
Totals	1	2	2	0	0	0	100.0	+ 17.33

Jan	Feb	Mar	Apr	May	Jun	Jul	Aug	Sep	Oct/Nov
0-0	0-0	0-0	0-0	0-0	0-0	1-1	0-0	1-1	0-0

Winning Jockeys	W-R	£1 Level Stake		W-R	£1 Level Stake
D Boeuf	1-1	+ 14.00	Pat Eddery	1-1	+ 3.33

Winning Courses					
Ascot	1-1	+ 3.33	Goodwood	1-1	+ 14.00

Winning Horse	Age	Races Run	1st	2nd	3rd	Unpl	Win £
Bigstone	3	2	2	0	0	0	273,980

Favourites	0-0	Total winning prize-money	£273,980

1992 Form	0-1	1991 Form	0-1

M V O'BRIEN (Ireland)

	No. of Horses	Races Run	1st	2nd	3rd	Unpl	Per cent	£1 Level Stake
2-y-o	0	0	0	0	0	0	-	0.00
3-y-o	2	5	1	1	1	2	20.0	- 0.50
4-y-o+	0	0	0	0	0	0	-	0.00
Totals	2	5	1	1	1	2	20.0	- 0.50

Jan	Feb	Mar	Apr	May	Jun	Jul	Aug	Sep	Oct/Nov
0-0	0-0	0-0	0-0	0-0	1-2	0-1	0-1	0-1	0-0

Winning Jockey	W-R	£1 Level Stake	Winning Course	W-R	£1 Level Stake
L Piggott	1-5	- 0.50	Ascot	1-1	+ 3.50

Winning Horse	Age	Races Run	1st	2nd	3rd	Unpl	Win £
College Chapel	3	4	1	1	1	1	40,645

Favourites	1-4	25.0%	+ 0.50	Total winning prize-money		£40,645

1992 Form	0-3			1990 Form	2-3	66.7%	+ 13.00
1991 Form	0-3			1989 Form	0-3		

SEEMAR SATISH (UAE)

	No. of Horses	Races Run	1st	2nd	3rd	Unpl	Per cent	£1 Level Stake
2-y-o	0	0	0	0	0	0	-	0.00
3-y-o	1	2	1	0	0	1	50.0	0.00
4-y-o+	0	0	0	0	0	0	-	0.00
Totals	1	2	1	0	0	1	50.0	0.00

Jan	Feb	Mar	Apr	May	Jun	Jul	Aug	Sep	Oct/Nov
0-0	0-0	0-0	0-1	1-1	0-0	0-0	0-0	0-0	0-0

Winning Jockey	W-R	£1 Level Stake	Winning Course	W-R	£1 Level Stake
W R Swinburn	1-1	+ 1.00	York	1-1	+ 1.00

Winning Horse	Age	Races Run	1st	2nd	3rd	Unpl	Win £
Dayflower	3	2	1	0	0	1	5,024

Favourites	1-1	100.0%	+ 1.00	Total winning prize-money		£5,024

A SMITH (Belgium)

	No. of Horses	Races Run	1st	2nd	3rd	Unpl	Per cent	£1 Level Stake
2-y-o	2	7	1	0	0	6	14.3	+ 14.00
3-y-o	1	6	0	0	1	5	-	- 6.00
4-y-o+	0	0	0	0	0	0	-	0.00
Totals	3	13	1	0	1	11	7.7	+ 8.00

Jan	Feb	Mar	Apr	May	Jun	Jul	Aug	Sep	Oct/Nov
0-0	0-0	0-1	0-2	0-2	1-1	0-1	0-1	0-5	0-0

	W-R	£1 Level Stake		W-R	£1 Level Stake
Winning Jockey			Winning Course		
B Doyle	1-3	+ 18.00	Folkestone	1-3	+ 18.00

		Races Run	1st	2nd	3rd	Unpl	Win £
Winning Horse	Age						
Old Hook	2	5	1	0	0	4	2,070

Favourites	0-0	Total winning prize-money	£2,070

1992 Form	0-0	1990 Form	0-5
1991 Form	0-0	1989 Form	0-3

T STACK (Ireland)

	No. of Horses	Races Run	1st	2nd	3rd	Unpl	Per cent	£1 Level Stake
2-y-o	0	0	0	0	0	0	-	0.00
3-y-o	1	1	1	0	0	0	100.0	+ 11.00
4-y-o+	0	0	0	0	0	0	-	0.00
Totals	1	1	1	0	0	0	100.0	+ 11.00

Jan	Feb	Mar	Apr	May	Jun	Jul	Aug	Sep	Oct/Nov
0-0	0-0	0-0	0-0	0-0	0-0	0-0	0-0	1-1	0-0

	W-R	£1 Level Stake		W-R	£1 Level Stake
Winning Jockey			Winning Course		
M Roberts	1-1	+ 11.00	Newmarket	1-1	+ 11.00

		Races Run	1st	2nd	3rd	Unpl	Win £
Winning Horse	Age						
My-O-My	3	1	1	0	0	0	9,681

Favourites	0-0	Total winning prize-money	£9,681

1992 Form	0-6			1990 Form	0-4		
1991 Form	1-5	20.0%	+ 4.00	1989 Form	1-3	33.3%	- 0.90

OVERSEAS TRAINERS WITH NO WINNERS 1993

	No. of Horses	Races Run	2nd	3rd	Unpl
L Browne (Ire)	2	2	0	0	2
J Burns (Ire)	1	1	0	0	1
V Caruso (Ity)	1	1	1	0	0
R Conway (UAE)	3	3	0	0	3
J G Coogan (Ire)	1	2	1	0	1
Ms D England (Can)	1	1	0	0	1
P J Flynn (Ire)	2	2	0	0	2
M Grassick (Ire)	1	1	0	0	1
J E Hammond (Fra)	2	2	0	1	1
M Kauntze (Ire)	4	5	2	0	3
P Lautner (Ger)	1	1	0	0	1
J Lesbordes (Fra)	1	1	1	0	0
N Meade (Ire)	1	1	0	0	1
J E Mulhern (Ire)	1	2	0	0	2
A P O'Brien (Ire)	1	1	0	0	1
C O'Brien (Ire)	2	2	0	0	2
P O'Leary (Ire)	1	1	0	0	1
John Oxx (Ire)	2	3	1	0	2
J Pease (Fra)	1	1	0	1	0
K Prendergast (Ire)	1	1	0	0	1
A Renzoni (Ita)	1	1	0	0	1
B Schutz (Ger)	1	1	0	0	1
D K Weld (Ire)	5	5	0	0	5

COURSE SECTION

ASCOT (Group 1)

Leading Trainers 1989-93

	Total W-R	Non-handicaps 2-y-o	3-y-o+	Handicaps 2-y-o	3-y-o+	Per cent	£1 Level Stake
H R A Cecil	27-105	4-23	17-63	0-0	6-19	25.7	+ 93.12
M R Stoute	24-153	4-29	14-76	0-3	6-45	15.7	- 11.92
J H M Gosden	19-97	3-15	10-39	0-0	6-43	19.6	- 0.24
L M Cumani	18-110	8-24	8-43	0-0	2-43	16.4	- 23.09
G Harwood	18-131	2-18	10-46	0-5	6-62	13.7	+ 3.29
R Hannon	18-204	9-59	3-41	2-15	4-89	8.8	+ 65.00
D R C Elsworth	17-115	7-25	2-37	0-2	8-51	14.8	+ 88.58
Lord Huntingdon	15-75	0-2	6-19	1-2	8-52	20.0	+ 67.17
C E Brittain	14-242	3-56	4-82	1-3	6-101	5.8	- 73.50
G Wragg	13-68	4-12	7-36	0-0	2-20	19.1	+ 2.80
P F I Cole	13-79	7-32	4-22	0-3	2-22	16.5	- 25.12
J L Dunlop	13-102	4-24	5-40	0-2	4-36	12.7	+ 12.07
H Thomson Jones	8-62	4-26	1-17	1-1	2-18	12.9	- 3.54
R Charlton	7-38	2-8	2-6	0-1	3-23	18.4	+ 7.91
I A Balding	7-99	0-19	1-29	0-1	6-50	7.1	+ 1.50
M S Johnston	6-31	2-5	1-6	0-0	3-20	19.4	+ 22.17
P T Walwyn	6-90	2-19	0-33	0-2	4-36	6.7	- 53.13
B W Hills	6-98	4-23	2-39	0-2	0-34	6.1	- 45.79
G Lewis	5-49	0-10	0-10	1-6	4-23	10.2	+ 5.00
A A Scott	5-56	2-18	2-21	0-1	1-16	8.9	- 26.50
C A Cyzer	4-22	0-5	0-3	0-0	4-14	18.2	+ 4.75
W R Hern	4-25	0-6	2-9	0-0	2-10	16.0	- 5.28

Leading Jockeys

	Total W-R	Per cent	£1 Level Stake	Best Trainer	W-R	Per cent	£1 Level Stake
Pat Eddery	51-247	20.6	+ 80.05	G Harwood	8-21	38.1	+ 16.73
W Carson	32-248	12.9	- 50.94	J L Dunlop	8-45	17.8	- 5.42
L Dettori	30-200	15.0	+ 56.10	L M Cumani	16-77	20.8	+ 5.27
M Roberts	26-251	10.4	- 58.46	C E Brittain	8-113	7.1	- 42.50
W R Swinburn	23-177	13.0	- 18.12	M R Stoute	8-65	12.3	- 32.26
R Cochrane	14-158	8.9	+ 26.50	I A Balding	3-25	12.0	+ 18.00
A Munro	13-116	11.2	- 32.14	P F I Cole	7-32	21.9	- 10.97
T Quinn	11-124	8.9	- 35.50	P F I Cole	4-30	13.3	- 12.25
J Reid	11-162	6.8	- 62.63	P Chapple-Hyam	4-15	26.7	- 6.13
R Hills	8-84	9.5	- 21.87	H Thomson Jones	7-48	14.6	+ 6.13
M Hills	6-129	4.7	- 76.34	G Wragg	4-15	26.7	+ 0.66
W Ryan	5-23	21.7	+ 50.00	H R A Cecil	3-12	25.0	+ 31.00

How the Favourites Fared

Non-handicaps	W-R	Per cent	£1 Level Stake	Handicaps	W-R	Per cent	£1 Level Stake
2-y-o	40-101	39.6	- 2.11	2-y-o	0-10	-	- 10.00
3-y-o	27-57	47.4	+ 10.92	3-y-o	6-29	20.7	- 3.25
Weight-for-age	37-82	45.1	+ 7.82	All-aged	21-121	17.4	- 29.10
Totals	104-240	43.3	+ 16.63	Totals	27-160	16.9	- 42.35
All favs	131-400	32.8	- 25.72				

Leading Trainers by Month at Ascot

March/Apr	Total W-R	Non-handicaps 2-y-o	3-y-o+	Handicaps 2-y-o	3-y-o+	Per cent	£1 Level Stake
Lord Huntingdon	3-6	0-0	2-3	0-0	1-3	50.0	+ 4.83
H R A Cecil	2-4	0-0	2-4	0-0	0-0	50.0	+ 24.38
R Hannon	2-7	2-3	0-1	0-0	0-3	28.6	- 1.63
B A McMahon	1-1	0-0	0-0	0-0	1-1	100.0	+ 16.00
J A B Old	1-1	0-0	1-1	0-0	0-0	100.0	+ 33.00

May	Total W-R	Non-handicaps 2-y-o	3-y-o+	Handicaps 2-y-o	3-y-o+	Per cent	£1 Level Stake
P F I Cole	3-6	1-1	1-3	0-0	1-2	50.0	+ 7.60
M R Stoute	2-5	0-0	2-5	0-0	0-0	40.0	+ 5.50
J Berry	1-1	1-1	0-0	0-0	0-0	100.0	+ 2.00
B Hanbury	1-1	0-0	1-1	0-0	0-0	100.0	+ 1.00
M S Johnston	1-1	0-0	1-1	0-0	0-0	100.0	+ 10.00

June	Total W-R	Non-handicaps 2-y-o	3-y-o+	Handicaps 2-y-o	3-y-o+	Per cent	£1 Level Stake
H R A Cecil	15-51	1-3	10-36	0-0	4-12	29.4	+ 68.90
R Hannon	10-100	4-28	2-27	0-0	4-45	10.0	+ 91.88
G Wragg	9-35	3-5	5-22	0-0	1-8	25.7	+ 20.64
J L Dunlop	8-40	1-2	4-23	0-0	3-15	20.0	+ 36.71
M R Stoute	8-60	0-5	7-44	0-0	1-11	13.3	- 21.72

July	Total W-R	Non-handicaps 2-y-o	3-y-o+	Handicaps 2-y-o	3-y-o+	Per cent	£1 Level Stake
H R A Cecil	5-16	2-5	2-9	0-0	1-2	31.3	+ 17.63
D R C Elsworth	4-17	2-5	0-3	0-0	2-9	23.5	+ 19.50
M R Stoute	4-24	1-4	2-10	0-0	1-10	16.7	+ 2.63
Lord Huntingdon	3-13	0-0	0-2	0-0	3-11	23.1	- 0.25
J H M Gosden	3-13	0-1	2-6	0-0	1-6	23.1	- 1.04

September	Total W-R	Non-handicaps 2-y-o	3-y-o+	Handicaps 2-y-o	3-y-o+	Per cent	£1 Level Stake
L M Cumani	11-49	7-18	2-9	0-0	2-22	22.4	+ 12.54
M R Stoute	9-42	3-14	3-9	0-2	3-17	21.4	+ 15.68
J H M Gosden	6-28	1-6	5-8	0-0	0-14	21.4	- 7.52
G Harwood	5-27	1-5	2-5	0-1	2-16	18.5	+ 9.00
A C Stewart	3-13	0-1	0-1	0-1	3-10	23.1	+ 9.50

Oct/Nov	Total W-R	Non-handicaps 2-y-o	3-y-o+	Handicaps 2-y-o	3-y-o+	Per cent	£1 Level Stake
L M Cumani	5-15	1-4	4-9	0-0	0-2	33.3	- 1.38
J H M Gosden	5-16	1-5	1-5	0-0	3-6	31.3	+ 3.41
D R C Elsworth	5-20	2-7	0-5	0-2	3-6	25.0	+ 34.33
G Harwood	3-22	1-7	1-2	0-4	1-9	13.6	- 9.17
C E Brittain	3-27	0-7	0-4	1-2	2-14	11.1	+ 24.00

AYR (Group 1)

Leading Trainers 1989-93

	Total W-R	Non-handicaps 2-y-o	3-y-o+	Handicaps 2-y-o	3-y-o+	Per cent	£1 Level Stake
J Berry	32-231	14-76	11-41	1-25	6-89	13.9	- 20.23
B W Hills	18-46	3-11	10-20	0-0	5-15	39.1	+ 9.94
M H Easterby	17-106	3-17	2-13	1-11	11-65	16.0	- 37.27
Mrs J Ramsden	16-66	2-5	3-6	3-7	8-48	24.2	+ 16.21
P Chapple-Hyam	15-34	8-16	3-7	1-1	3-10	44.1	+ 27.77
F H Lee	12-109	1-17	1-16	1-4	9-72	11.0	- 27.38
Mrs M Reveley	11-61	2-9	5-19	0-2	4-31	18.0	- 10.43
A Bailey	10-76	0-18	2-16	2-11	6-31	13.2	- 24.22
M H Tompkins	10-77	0-12	4-13	0-8	6-44	13.0	- 10.50
M Brittain	10-108	0-16	1-9	0-9	9-74	9.3	+ 39.25
J L Dunlop	9-24	4-7	3-7	0-1	2-9	37.5	- 2.88
M P Naughton	9-88	0-2	0-24	0-0	9-62	10.2	- 31.25
T D Barron	8-54	0-5	0-4	3-8	5-37	14.8	- 16.92
R M Whitaker	8-109	1-18	3-21	0-6	4-64	7.3	+ 14.25
M S Johnston	7-60	2-10	1-11	0-5	4-34	11.7	- 11.52
I A Balding	6-19	0-1	2-8	0-0	4-10	31.6	+ 18.50
M W Easterby	6-45	2-7	0-6	0-6	4-26	13.3	- 10.92
J W Watts	6-77	2-14	1-10	0-8	3-45	7.8	- 45.77
N Tinkler	6-93	0-15	2-27	1-7	3-44	6.5	- 52.56
P C Haslam	5-15	0-1	0-4	0-0	5-10	33.3	- 0.90
H Thomson Jones	5-24	2-10	2-5	0-0	1-9	20.8	+ 2.54
Sir M Prescott	5-26	2-6	2-7	0-2	1-11	19.2	- 13.20

Leading Jockeys

	Total W-R	Per cent	£1 Level Stake	Best Trainer	W-R	Per cent	£1 Level Stake
K Darley	43-216	19.9	- 43.19	M H Easterby	7-22	31.8	- 3.05
J Carroll	20-167	12.0	- 55.93	J Berry	17-114	14.9	- 31.43
M Birch	16-118	13.6	- 29.81	M H Easterby	5-47	10.6	- 27.31
K Fallon	16-135	11.9	- 48.73	M P Naughton	5-29	17.2	- 2.25
M Hills	15-63	23.8	+ 5.45	B W Hills	8-20	40.0	+ 3.29
D Holland	11-38	28.9	+ 4.28	P Chapple-Hyam	5-7	71.4	+ 7.99
M Roberts	10-42	23.8	+ 19.38	Mrs J Ramsden	1-1	100.0	+ 2.50
W Carson	10-53	18.9	- 14.22	J L Dunlop	3-10	30.0	- 2.30
J Fortune	9-71	12.7	+ 65.25	M O'Neill	2-14	14.3	+ 42.00
A Mackay	9-96	9.4	33.59	A Bailey	6-42	14.3	- 8.09
L Charnock	9-119	7.6	- 54.54	G M Moore	2-4	50.0	+ 27.50
A Munro	8-40	20.0	+ 44.61	M Brittain	3-10	30.0	+ 53.00

How the Favourites Fared

Non-handicaps	W-R	Per cent	£1 Level Stake	Handicaps	W-R	Per cent	£1 Level Stake
2-y-o	45-92	48.9	- 3.05	2-y-o	7-25	28.0	- 6.71
3-y-o	16-43	37.2	- 6.73	3-y-o	16-48	33.3	+ 0.55
Weight-for-age	29-73	39.7	- 9.91	All-aged	54-155	34.8	+ 22.62
Totals	90-208	43.3	- 19.69	Totals	77-228	33.8	+ 16.46
All favs	167-436	38.3	- 3.23				

Leading Trainers by Month at Ayr

March/Apr

	Total W-R	Non-handicaps 2-y-o	3-y-o+	Handicaps 2-y-o	3-y-o+	Per cent	£1 Level Stake
J Berry	5-16	1-1	2-7	0-0	2-8	31.3	+ 9.80
Mrs J Ramsden	3-7	0-0	1-1	0-0	2-6	42.9	+ 6.75
M H Easterby	3-13	0-2	1-3	0-0	2-8	23.1	- 5.05
B W Hills	2-2	0-0	2-2	0-0	0-0	100.0	+ 4.12
M S Johnston	2-4	0-0	1-1	0-0	1-3	50.0	+ 14.00

May

	Total W-R	Non-handicaps 2-y-o	3-y-o+	Handicaps 2-y-o	3-y-o+	Per cent	£1 Level Stake
M H Tompkins	2-2	0-0	1-1	0-0	1-1	100.0	+ 13.00
P Chapple-Hyam	2-3	0-0	1-2	0-0	1-1	66.7	+ 2.79
J Berry	2-9	1-3	1-2	0-0	0-4	22.2	- 1.00
D W Chapman	1-1	0-0	1-1	0-0	0-0	100.0	+ 0.73
E Weymes	1-1	1-1	0-0	0-0	0-0	100.0	+ 4.50

June

	Total W-R	Non-handicaps 2-y-o	3-y-o+	Handicaps 2-y-o	3-y-o+	Per cent	£1 Level Stake
F H Lee	4-14	1-4	0-0	0-0	3-10	28.6	+ 14.00
J Berry	4-29	2-15	1-3	0-0	1-11	13.8	- 5.50
P Chapple-Hyam	3-7	0-1	1-2	0-0	2-4	42.9	+ 11.70
C Tinkler	3-8	0-1	1-2	0-0	2-5	37.5	+ 2.75
M S Johnston	2-7	1-2	0-3	0-0	1-2	28.6	- 0.25

July

	Total W-R	Non-handicaps 2-y-o	3-y-o+	Handicaps 2-y-o	3-y-o+	Per cent	£1 Level Stake
J Berry	10-54	4-18	4-15	0-3	2-18	18.5	- 19.05
A Bailey	7-30	0-4	1-7	1-3	5-16	23.3	+ 1.78
Mrs M Reveley	7-31	1-4	4-10	0-0	2-17	22.6	+ 4.90
F H Lee	7-43	0-5	1-6	1-3	5-29	16.3	- 2.38
M H Easterby	6-37	1-7	1-5	0-2	4-23	16.2	- 19.58

August

	Total W-R	Non-handicaps 2-y-o	3-y-o+	Handicaps 2-y-o	3-y-o+	Per cent	£1 Level Stake
J Berry	4-19	1-5	3-6	0-3	0-5	21.1	+ 23.08
Lord Huntingdon	2-3	1-1	0-0	1-1	0-1	66.7	+ 1.50
P Chapple-Hyam	2-3	2-3	0-0	0-0	0-0	66.7	+ 1.65
M H Easterby	2-5	0-0	0-2	1-1	1-2	40.0	+ 3.25
N Bycroft	2-7	0-1	0-1	0-0	2-5	28.6	+ 4.33

September

	Total W-R	Non-handicaps 2-y-o	3-y-o+	Handicaps 2-y-o	3-y-o+	Per cent	£1 Level Stake
B W Hills	10-26	3-8	5-10	0-0	2-8	38.5	+ 5.04
M H Tompkins	8-52	0-9	3-8	0-6	5-29	15.4	- 0.50
P Chapple-Hyam	6-10	4-5	1-2	1-1	0-2	60.0	+ 19.70
J L Dunlop	6-17	3-5	2-5	0-1	1-6	35.3	- 2.42
Mrs J Ramsden	6-28	1-4	1-1	2-6	2-17	21.4	+ 5.25

Oct/Nov

	Total W-R	Non-handicaps 2-y-o	3-y-o+	Handicaps 2-y-o	3-y-o+	Per cent	£1 Level Stake
T D Barron	2-5	0-2	0-0	1-1	1-2	40.0	+ 6.50
M Brittain	2-14	0-2	1-4	0-2	1-6	14.3	+ 23.00
N Tinkler	2-16	0-3	1-6	1-2	0-5	12.5	+ 11.00
J Berry	2-20	2-10	0-4	0-2	0-4	10.0	- 16.18
H J Collingridge	1-1	0-0	0-0	0-0	1-1	100.0	+ 16.00

BATH (Group 3)

Leading Trainers 1989-93

	Total W-R	Non-handicaps 2-y-o	3-y-o+	Handicaps 2-y-o	3-y-o+	Per cent	£1 Level Stake
B W Hills	19-89	2-16	10-38	1-2	6-33	21.3	- 19.92
R Hannon	19-125	6-47	6-30	1-5	6-43	15.2	- 16.49
G Harwood	16-52	1-8	11-22	0-0	4-22	30.8	+ 19.15
R J Hodges	16-152	1-12	1-35	0-1	14-104	10.5	- 31.67
I A Balding	14-110	2-23	3-38	0-3	9-46	12.7	- 20.07
P F I Cole	14-125	4-28	3-38	0-4	7-55	11.2	- 52.50
G Lewis	13-55	1-15	4-13	1-5	7-22	23.6	+ 19.13
J Berry	11-55	8-23	3-10	0-4	0-18	20.0	+ 4.91
C J Hill	10-98	0-14	1-20	1-1	8-63	10.2	- 38.42
R Akehurst	9-41	0-6	2-6	0-0	7-29	22.0	+ 41.08
W R Hern	9-43	1-5	3-20	1-1	4-17	20.9	+ 5.00
D R C Elsworth	8-46	3-13	2-15	0-1	3-17	17.4	+ 1.33
J S King	7-21	0-1	0-1	0-0	7-19	33.3	+ 27.00
D W P Arbuthnot	7-38	4-10	1-9	0-1	2-18	18.4	+ 28.10
J W Hills	7-46	2-9	1-16	0-1	4-20	15.2	- 5.50
J L Dunlop	7-63	1-11	1-19	0-1	5-32	11.1	- 32.51
R Charlton	6-17	3-6	3-11	0-0	0-0	35.3	+ 0.80
R F J Houghton	6-38	0-8	4-12	0-1	2-17	15.8	+ 9.45
M R Channon	6-56	2-21	1-11	0-3	3-21	10.7	- 6.52
H Thomson Jones	5-15	4-5	1-3	0-0	0-7	33.3	+ 13.50
M Bell	5-20	0-3	1-4	1-2	3-11	25.0	+ 6.83
L G Cottrell	5-53	1-13	0-12	0-1	4-27	9.4	- 13.50

Leading Jockeys

	Total W-R	Per cent	£1 Level Stake	Best Trainer	W-R	Per cent	£1 Level Stake
J Reid	26-135	19.3	+ 6.84	I A Balding	4-19	21.1	+ 8.10
Pat Eddery	25-87	28.7	- 11.25	B W Hills	8-16	50.0	+ 4.73
T Quinn	25-144	17.4	+ 49.61	P F I Cole	9-67	13.4	- 13.66
J Williams	23-213	10.8	- 27.24	D R C Elsworth	5-18	27.8	+ 16.00
W Carson	17-79	21.5	- 2.80	W R Hern	5-12	41.7	+ 16.25
G Duffield	12-62	19.4	+ 13.79	Sir M Prescott	3-14	21.4	- 8.09
Paul Eddery	12-75	16.0	- 26.22	G Lewis	3-15	20.0	- 2.25
A Munro	12-81	14.8	- 18.65	P F I Cole	3-16	18.8	- 7.33
R Cochrane	11-73	15.1	- 31.31	D R C Elsworth	2-3	66.7	+ 5.83
A Clark	11-85	12.9	+ 40.45	G Harwood	4-20	20.0	- 4.80
W Newnes	8-71	11.3	- 28.02	Dr J D Scargill	2-2	100.0	+ 15.50
D Holland	8-105	7.6	- 52.98	B W Hills	4-35	11.4	- 13.58

How the Favourites Fared

Non-handicaps	W-R	Per cent	£1 Level Stake	Handicaps	W-R	Per cent	£1 Level Stake
2-y-o	31-82	37.8	- 9.68	2-y-o	6-11	54.5	+ 9.75
3-y-o	42-84	50.0	+ 6.84	3-y-o	19-50	38.0	+ 5.42
Weight-for-age	7-21	33.3	- 3.93	All-aged	34-132	25.8	- 20.64
Totals	80-187	42.8	- 6.77	Totals	59-193	30.6	- 5.47
All favs	139-380	36.6	- 12.24				

Leading Trainers by Month at Bath

March/Apr	Total W-R	Non-handicaps 2-y-o	Non-handicaps 3-y-o+	Handicaps 2-y-o	Handicaps 3-y-o+	Per cent	£1 Level Stake
Dr J D Scargill	2-4	1-2	1-1	0-0	0-1	50.0	+ 13.50
J L Dunlop	2-8	0-1	1-3	0-0	1-4	25.0	- 2.55
Sir M Prescott	1-1	0-0	1-1	0-0	0-0	100.0	+ 1.00
P Hayward	1-1	0-0	0-0	0-0	1-1	100.0	+ 14.00
C R Barwell	1-1	0-0	0-0	0-0	1-1	100.0	+ 33.00

May	Total W-R	Non-handicaps 2-y-o	Non-handicaps 3-y-o+	Handicaps 2-y-o	Handicaps 3-y-o+	Per cent	£1 Level Stake
G Harwood	8-14	1-1	6-11	0-0	1-2	57.1	+ 15.37
B W Hills	6-20	0-1	2-11	0-0	4-8	30.0	- 2.40
R Hannon	5-33	2-10	2-11	0-0	1-12	15.2	+ 0.25
R Charlton	3-7	0-0	3-7	0-0	0-0	42.9	+ 0.65
M Bell	3-10	0-3	1-2	0-0	2-5	30.0	+ 9.50

June	Total W-R	Non-handicaps 2-y-o	Non-handicaps 3-y-o+	Handicaps 2-y-o	Handicaps 3-y-o+	Per cent	£1 Level Stake
R J Hodges	6-24	0-1	1-7	0-0	5-16	25.0	+ 9.38
R Akehurst	4-8	0-1	2-2	0-0	2-5	50.0	+ 40.08
J W Hills	3-5	1-1	1-2	0-0	1-2	60.0	+ 14.00
P F I Cole	3-13	0-4	1-3	0-0	2-6	23.1	- 0.10
C R Nelson	2-4	0-0	2-3	0-0	0-1	50.0	+ 4.50

July	Total W-R	Non-handicaps 2-y-o	Non-handicaps 3-y-o+	Handicaps 2-y-o	Handicaps 3-y-o+	Per cent	£1 Level Stake
B W Hills	7-14	1-1	5-10	0-0	1-3	50.0	+ 2.85
J Berry	6-21	4-10	2-2	0-0	0-9	28.6	+ 15.54
G Harwood	5-15	0-1	3-5	0-0	2-9	33.3	+ 1.17
I A Balding	5-25	1-6	1-6	0-0	3-13	20.0	+ 7.33
R J Hodges	5-33	0-1	0-4	0-0	5-28	15.2	- 11.04

August	Total W-R	Non-handicaps 2-y-o	Non-handicaps 3-y-o+	Handicaps 2-y-o	Handicaps 3-y-o+	Per cent	£1 Level Stake
G Lewis	4-5	0-1	2-2	1-1	1-1	80.0	+ 14.25
R Hannon	4-11	1-3	2-3	0-1	1-4	36.4	+ 2.82
H Thomson Jones	2-3	1-1	1-1	0-0	0-1	66.7	+ 10.00
O O'Neill	2-3	0-0	1-1	0-0	1-2	66.7	+115.00
Lord Huntingdon	2-5	0-1	0-1	0-0	2-3	40.0	+ 2.91

September	Total W-R	Non-handicaps 2-y-o	Non-handicaps 3-y-o+	Handicaps 2-y-o	Handicaps 3-y-o+	Per cent	£1 Level Stake
H Candy	4-14	0-2	4-5	0-1	0-6	28.6	+ 7.87
C J Hill	4-20	0-3	0-2	0-0	4-15	20.0	+ 5.33
P F I Cole	4-22	2-6	1-4	0-3	1-9	18.2	+ 3.50
D R C Elsworth	3-7	2-4	1-2	0-0	0-1	42.9	+ 6.33
I A Balding	3-18	1-8	0-4	0-2	2-4	16.7	+ 1.10

Oct/Nov	Total W-R	Non-handicaps 2-y-o	Non-handicaps 3-y-o+	Handicaps 2-y-o	Handicaps 3-y-o+	Per cent	£1 Level Stake
H Thomson Jones	2-2	2-2	0-0	0-0	0-0	100.0	+ 8.00
W Jarvis	2-3	0-1	1-1	0-0	1-1	66.7	+ 7.00
Bob Jones	2-3	1-2	0-0	0-0	1-1	66.7	+ 19.50
C J Hill	2-6	0-0	0-3	1-1	1-2	33.3	+ 4.25
W R Hern	2-8	1-4	0-0	0-0	1-4	25.0	- 2.00

BEVERLEY (Group 3)

Leading Trainers 1989-93

	Total W-R	Non-handicaps 2-y-o	3-y-o+	Handicaps 2-y-o	3-y-o+	Per cent	£1 Level Stake
J Berry	22-158	16-97	2-32	1-8	3-21	13.9	- 53.13
M H Easterby	22-190	9-71	3-27	1-12	9-80	11.6	- 72.14
Mrs M Reveley	19-84	4-14	1-5	0-4	14-61	22.6	+ 6.57
H R A Cecil	16-41	1-4	12-30	0-0	3-7	39.0	+ 0.58
I A Balding	16-47	3-7	2-14	0-0	11-26	34.0	+ 10.69
T D Barron	15-123	1-20	1-15	2-9	11-79	12.2	- 31.28
R Hollinshead	15-136	4-31	3-38	0-0	8-67	11.0	- 44.95
R M Whitaker	15-147	4-27	4-33	0-6	7-81	10.2	- 24.38
M Brittain	15-159	5-54	2-23	1-4	7-78	9.4	- 6.38
M R Stoute	12-48	1-6	11-31	0-0	0-11	25.0	- 19.63
L M Cumani	10-22	1-1	8-17	0-0	1-4	45.5	+ 3.11
S G Norton	10-69	1-11	2-15	0-1	7-42	14.5	+ 7.73
D Morley	9-54	1-5	2-13	0-0	6-36	16.7	- 2.42
Mrs J Ramsden	9-56	3-12	0-8	0-3	6-33	16.1	+ 0.92
J L Spearing	9-64	1-6	0-8	0-1	8-49	14.1	- 7.75
M H Tompkins	8-58	0-19	4-13	0-3	4-23	13.8	- 12.02
F H Lee	8-63	1-9	1-8	1-2	5-44	12.7	- 7.75
P F I Cole	7-20	1-6	5-10	0-0	1-4	35.0	+ 2.57
J R Fanshawe	7-25	0-1	3-10	0-0	4-14	28.0	+ 19.00
M R Channon	7-26	2-7	1-3	0-2	4-14	26.9	+ 23.00
J L Dunlop	7-28	2-5	2-7	0-1	3-15	25.0	- 3.60
C E Brittain	7-38	1-5	4-19	0-0	2-14	18.4	+ 7.58

Leading Jockeys

	Total W-R	Per cent	£1 Level Stake	Best Trainer	W-R	Per cent	£1 Level Stake
K Darley	40-227	17.6	- 32.19	Mrs M Reveley	7-21	33.3	- 6.22
J Lowe	21-219	9.6	- 61.37	Mrs M Reveley	7-23	30.4	+ 31.33
M Birch	19-212	9.0	-105.19	M H Easterby	9-84	10.7	- 39.69
W R Swinburn	16-74	21.6	- 6.79	M R Stoute	7-24	29.2	- 8.29
M Roberts	16-75	21.3	+ 10.49	C E Brittain	4-12	33.3	+ 9.83
G Duffield	16-107	15.0	- 15.41	J R Fanshawe	3-4	75.0	+ 20.00
W Ryan	15-92	16.3	- 25.66	H R A Cecil	9-22	40.9	+ 0.49
J Carroll	14-113	12.4	- 55.78	J Berry	12-80	15.0	- 38.78
A Culhane	14-118	11.9	- 20.87	R M Whitaker	5-68	7.4	- 30.87
W Carson	12-56	21.4	- 15.11	D R Loder	2-2	100.0	+ 4.75
D Holland	12-61	19.7	+ 4.50	B W Hills	4-17	23.5	+ 0.25
B Raymond	12-81	14.8	- 20.63	A A Scott	2-5	40.0	+ 2.91

How the Favourites Fared

Non-handicaps	W-R	Per cent	£1 Level Stake	Handicaps	W-R	Per cent	£1 Level Stake
2-y-o	55-131	42.0	- 12.31	2-y-o	6-15	40.0	+ 5.13
3-y-o	29-65	44.6	+ 0.96	3-y-o	15-59	25.4	- 21.20
Weight-for-age	42-90	46.7	- 10.97	All-aged	66-205	32.2	+ 5.21
Totals	126-286	44.1	- 22.32	Totals	87-279	31.2	- 10.86
All favs	213-565	37.7	- 33.18				

462

Leading Trainers by Month at Beverley

March/April	Total W-R	Non-handicaps 2-y-o	3-y-o+	Handicaps 2-y-o	3-y-o+	Per cent	£1 Level Stake
R Hollinshead	4-22	1-5	0-8	0-0	3-9	18.2	- 1.80
J Berry	4-24	3-14	1-3	0-0	0-7	16.7	- 9.60
M R Channon	3-5	0-0	1-2	0-0	2-3	60.0	+ 18.50
Mrs M Reveley	3-6	1-2	0-1	0-0	2-3	50.0	- 0.43
H R A Cecil	3-7	0-0	3-7	0-0	0-0	42.9	- 1.10

May	Total W-R	Non-handicaps 2-y-o	3-y-o+	Handicaps 2-y-o	3-y-o+	Per cent	£1 Level Stake
S G Norton	6-15	1-2	1-4	0-0	4-9	40.0	+ 25.73
M R Stoute	5-13	0-0	5-12	0-0	0-1	38.5	- 0.03
J Berry	5-32	4-25	1-7	0-0	0-0	15.6	- 13.00
M Brittain	5-41	2-19	1-7	0-0	2-15	12.2	+ 3.50
M H Easterby	5-44	2-19	0-9	0-0	3-16	11.4	- 10.00

June	Total W-R	Non-handicaps 2-y-o	3-y-o+	Handicaps 2-y-o	3-y-o+	Per cent	£1 Level Stake
M H Easterby	6-29	5-12	0-0	0-0	1-17	20.7	- 8.53
L M Cumani	4-6	0-0	4-6	0-0	0-0	66.7	+ 3.46
P F I Cole	4-10	0-1	3-6	0-0	1-3	40.0	+ 1.16
J Berry	4-26	3-19	0-4	0-0	1-3	15.4	- 8.00
M Brittain	4-30	1-8	0-0	0-0	3-22	13.3	+ 34.00

July	Total W-R	Non-handicaps 2-y-o	3-y-o+	Handicaps 2-y-o	3-y-o+	Per cent	£1 Level Stake
Mrs M Reveley	8-24	1-1	1-1	0-1	6-21	33.3	+ 16.42
J Berry	6-30	5-20	0-4	0-0	1-6	20.0	- 3.03
D R Loder	5-5	4-4	0-0	0-0	1-1	100.0	+ 9.38
I A Balding	5-14	0-1	0-1	0-0	5-12	35.7	+ 7.25
T D Barron	5-30	0-4	0-2	1-4	4-20	16.7	- 3.03

August	Total W-R	Non-handicaps 2-y-o	3-y-o+	Handicaps 2-y-o	3-y-o+	Per cent	£1 Level Stake
I A Balding	4-5	1-2	0-0	0-0	3-3	80.0	+ 6.75
H R A Cecil	3-6	0-0	3-5	0-0	0-1	50.0	+ 2.94
Mrs M Reveley	3-17	0-2	0-1	0-1	3-13	17.6	- 6.88
R Hollinshead	3-22	1-5	1-6	0-0	1-11	13.6	+ 6.00
M H Easterby	3-24	1-6	2-5	0-4	0-9	12.5	- 13.65

September	Total W-R	Non-handicaps 2-y-o	3-y-o+	Handicaps 2-y-o	3-y-o+	Per cent	£1 Level Stake
R M Whitaker	4-18	0-4	1-3	0-4	3-7	22.2	+ 13.00
L M Cumani	3-5	1-1	1-2	0-0	1-2	60.0	+ 4.75
J L Dunlop	3-5	1-3	1-1	0-0	1-1	60.0	+ 8.10
B W Hills	3-7	1-1	2-5	0-0	0-1	42.9	+ 4.75
I A Balding	2-3	2-3	0-0	0-0	0-0	66.7	+ 1.62

BRIGHTON (Group 2)

Leading Trainers 1989-93

	Total W-R	Non-handicaps 2-y-o	3-y-o+	Handicaps 2-y-o	3-y-o+	Per cent	£1 Level Stake
R Hannon	38-218	18-60	13-63	1-10	6-85	17.4	- 38.92
L M Cumani	26-59	9-14	12-32	1-2	4-11	44.1	+ 8.79
Sir M Prescott	23-80	2-14	6-16	1-4	14-46	28.8	+ 31.45
R Akehurst	21-107	0-3	9-28	1-2	11-74	19.6	+ 25.25
P F I Cole	19-123	4-27	10-46	1-4	4-46	15.4	- 52.65
G Harwood	18-67	1-8	15-43	1-2	1-14	26.9	+ 1.07
R J Hodges	17-135	0-1	1-20	0-0	16-114	12.6	- 30.40
J L Dunlop	16-82	4-21	6-30	0-7	6-24	19.5	- 2.01
M J Ryan	13-60	3-6	0-8	0-0	10-46	21.7	+ 18.38
J H M Gosden	11-36	2-3	8-29	0-0	1-4	30.6	- 6.19
M A Jarvis	11-46	0-6	5-18	0-2	6-20	23.9	+ 19.25
C A Cyzer	11-84	2-10	4-30	0-0	5-44	13.1	+ 18.25
R Boss	10-34	2-6	1-6	0-2	7-20	29.4	+ 35.53
J Berry	9-31	4-14	0-1	2-6	3-10	29.0	+ 4.58
W Carter	9-64	2-8	0-14	0-1	7-41	14.1	- 16.25
G Lewis	8-77	2-19	1-19	2-3	3-36	10.4	- 3.83
S Dow	8-88	2-13	2-20	0-4	4-51	9.1	- 24.00
J White	7-35	0-5	1-9	0-0	6-21	20.0	- 6.25
B W Hills	7-37	0-4	4-21	1-1	2-11	18.9	- 10.28
I A Balding	7-48	1-8	3-15	0-3	3-22	14.6	- 13.78
M Bell	6-27	2-8	0-5	2-7	2-7	22.2	+ 5.75
C E Brittain	6-33	1-3	4-13	0-2	1-15	18.2	+ 6.13

Leading Jockeys

	Total W-R	Per cent	£1 Level Stake	Best Trainer	W-R	Per cent	£1 Level Stake
W Carson	50-205	24.4	+ 33.34	J L Dunlop	10-32	31.3	+ 17.83
T Quinn	38-225	16.9	+ 25.04	P F I Cole	11-71	15.5	- 25.11
J Reid	32-226	14.2	- 36.31	R Hannon	6-26	23.1	+ 20.93
M Roberts	29-121	24.0	+ 8.14	R Boss	5-9	55.6	+ 26.13
L Dettori	26-102	25.5	- 10.06	L M Cumani	17-31	54.8	+ 26.57
G Duffield	25-126	19.8	- 2.92	Sir M Prescott	18-66	27.3	+ 15.08
R Cochrane	24-145	16.6	- 47.62	G Harwood	6-22	27.3	- 8.53
Pat Eddery	21-100	21.0	- 7.86	J H M Gosden	3-6	50.0	+ 0.38
A Munro	19-116	16.4	- 25.10	P F I Cole	4-16	25.0	- 6.42
B Rouse	18-190	9.5	- 82.75	R Hannon	5-67	7.5	- 48.30
T Williams	12-152	7.9	- 52.42	P Howling	3-17	17.6	+ 8.50
J Williams	11-163	6.7	- 77.62	G B Balding	4-13	30.8	+ 13.63

How the Favourites Fared

Non-handicaps	W-R	Per cent	£1 Level Stake	Handicaps	W-R	Per cent	£1 Level Stake
2-y-o	49-102	48.0	+ 1.41	2-y-o	5-16	31.3	+ 0.80
3-y-o	36-83	43.4	- 4.51	3-y-o	14-60	23.3	- 26.94
Weight-for-age	40-92	43.5	- 15.87	All-aged	54-202	26.7	- 36.95
Totals	125-277	45.1	- 18.97	Totals	73-278	26.3	- 63.09
All favs	198-555	35.7	- 82.06				

Leading Trainers by Month at Brighton

March/April

	Total W-R	Non-handicaps 2-y-o	3-y-o+	Handicaps 2-y-o	3-y-o+	Per cent	£1 Level Stake
R J Hodges	7-25	0-0	1-6	0-0	6-19	28.0	+ 15.50
R Hannon	7-43	2-5	4-22	0-0	1-16	16.3	- 1.00
G Harwood	5-9	0-0	5-7	0-0	0-2	55.6	+ 15.17
Sir M Prescott	5-11	0-0	3-5	0-0	2-6	45.5	+ 9.88
P F I Cole	5-21	0-1	5-15	0-0	0-5	23.8	- 3.59

May

	Total W-R	Non-handicaps 2-y-o	3-y-o+	Handicaps 2-y-o	3-y-o+	Per cent	£1 Level Stake
R Hannon	9-41	5-11	3-11	0-0	1-19	22.0	- 6.90
M A Jarvis	6-15	0-0	4-11	0-0	2-4	40.0	+ 21.25
R Akehurst	5-20	0-1	2-6	0-0	3-13	25.0	+ 9.50
N A Callaghan	4-12	0-2	0-1	0-0	4-9	33.3	+ 5.00
S Dow	4-12	1-3	1-2	0-0	2-7	33.3	+ 9.50

June

	Total W-R	Non-handicaps 2-y-o	3-y-o+	Handicaps 2-y-o	3-y-o+	Per cent	£1 Level Stake
P F I Cole	5-24	2-4	2-10	0-0	1-10	20.8	- 5.43
R Hannon	5-37	2-12	2-11	0-0	1-14	13.5	- 12.48
G B Balding	3-5	0-0	1-2	0-0	2-3	60.0	+ 18.38
M C Pipe	3-5	0-0	2-3	0-0	1-2	60.0	+ 10.50
J L Dunlop	3-7	0-1	2-3	0-0	1-3	42.9	+ 14.58

July

	Total W-R	Non-handicaps 2-y-o	3-y-o+	Handicaps 2-y-o	3-y-o+	Per cent	£1 Level Stake
R Boss	3-5	1-1	0-0	0-0	2-4	60.0	+ 20.91
J White	3-6	0-1	0-1	0-0	3-4	50.0	+ 7.00
R Hannon	3-13	0-3	1-3	0-0	2-7	23.1	+ 14.00
A C Stewart	2-2	0-0	2-2	0-0	0-0	100.0	+ 2.61
L G Cottrell	2-3	0-0	1-2	0-0	1-1	66.7	+ 2.95

August

	Total W-R	Non-handicaps 2-y-o	3-y-o+	Handicaps 2-y-o	3-y-o+	Per cent	£1 Level Stake
Sir M Prescott	11-25	2-6	1-4	0-1	8-14	44.0	+ 19.55
L M Cumani	9-12	3-3	2-3	0-0	4-6	75.0	+ 13.73
R Akehurst	7-23	0-0	3-7	1-1	3-15	30.4	+ 23.50
R Hannon	7-45	3-11	3-13	1-4	0-17	15.6	- 17.33
J Berry	6-18	2-5	0-1	2-6	2-6	33.3	+ 5.50

September

	Total W-R	Non-handicaps 2-y-o	3-y-o+	Handicaps 2-y-o	3-y-o+	Per cent	£1 Level Stake
R Hannon	6-25	5-13	0-3	0-3	1-6	24.0	- 3.43
Sir M Prescott	5-15	0-4	1-1	1-2	3-8	33.3	+ 24.00
L M Cumani	5-18	2-6	3-9	0-1	0-2	27.8	- 3.97
R W Armstrong	4-7	2-3	1-1	0-1	1-2	57.1	+ 44.50
M J Ryan	3-4	1-1	0-0	0-0	2-3	75.0	+ 14.50

Oct/Nov

	Total W-R	Non-handicaps 2-y-o	3-y-o+	Handicaps 2-y-o	3-y-o+	Per cent	£1 Level Stake
L M Cumani	7-8	4-4	2-3	1-1	0-0	87.5	+ 7.61
G Harwood	2-3	0-0	0-1	1-1	1-1	66.7	+ 8.33
G Wragg	2-4	1-1	1-3	0-0	0-0	50.0	+ 2.50
W Carter	1-2	0-0	0-0	0-0	1-2	50.0	+ 5.00
G Lewis	1-3	0-0	0-0	1-1	0-2	33.3	+ 2.00

CARLISLE (Group 4)

Leading Trainers 1989-93

	Total W-R	Non-handicaps 2-y-o	3-y-o+	Handicaps 2-y-o	3-y-o+	Per cent	£1 Level Stake
J Berry	28-124	12-57	9-40	0-1	7-26	22.6	+ 35.23
Sir M Prescott	12-43	3-7	4-15	0-0	5-21	27.9	+ 10.09
M H Tompkins	12-44	4-7	4-12	0-2	4-23	27.3	+ 7.58
Mrs M Reveley	10-54	0-4	2-17	0-0	8-33	18.5	- 0.67
M S Johnston	9-43	1-5	3-15	0-0	5-23	20.9	+ 54.19
S G Norton	9-54	1-12	5-21	0-0	3-21	16.7	+ 3.88
M H Easterby	9-76	4-26	2-20	0-0	3-30	11.8	- 43.55
Denys Smith	8-55	1-8	3-13	0-1	4-33	14.5	+ 6.00
R Hollinshead	8-103	2-16	2-34	0-1	4-52	7.8	- 18.13
N Tinkler	7-33	2-12	2-10	0-0	3-11	21.2	+ 10.28
J W Watts	7-35	0-4	2-12	0-0	5-19	20.0	+ 31.33
R M Whitaker	7-42	2-4	4-13	0-1	1-24	16.7	+ 20.00
J L Dunlop	5-8	1-3	2-2	0-0	2-3	62.5	+ 13.12
E J Alston	5-35	0-9	0-6	0-0	5-20	14.3	+ 14.50
T D Barron	5-41	0-8	3-10	0-2	2-21	12.2	- 6.00
Mrs J Ramsden	5-42	2-9	0-6	0-1	3-26	11.9	- 3.00
W Jarvis	4-13	1-2	3-7	0-0	0-4	30.8	+ 6.50
W W Haigh	4-24	0-3	4-7	0-0	0-14	16.7	+ 13.60
M W Easterby	4-34	0-11	0-9	0-0	4-14	11.8	- 13.38
J Etherington	4-43	2-16	1-12	0-0	1-15	9.3	- 8.65
A A Scott	3-9	0-1	3-7	0-0	0-1	33.3	- 1.70
H Thomson Jones	3-12	1-3	1-6	0-0	1-3	25.0	- 6.82

Leading Jockeys

	Total W-R	Per cent	£1 Level Stake	Best Trainer	W-R	Per cent	£1 Level Stake
G Duffield	22-112	19.6	+ 0.47	Sir M Prescott	12-39	30.8	+ 15.19
K Darley	20-125	16.0	- 19.26	J Berry	4-6	66.7	+ 12.75
J Carroll	17-130	13.1	- 50.93	J Berry	17-90	18.9	- 10.93
M Birch	11-108	10.2	- 49.27	M H Easterby	6-45	13.3	- 19.00
A Culhane	10-59	16.9	+ 34.50	R M Whitaker	6-27	22.2	+ 27.50
P Robinson	8-20	40.0	+ 24.08	M H Tompkins	4-13	30.8	+ 7.00
K Fallon	8-83	9.6	- 16.75	R Bastiman	2-4	50.0	+ 16.00
O Pears	7-32	21.9	+ 10.29	S G Norton	3-10	30.0	+ 8.88
L Charnock	7-85	8.2	- 24.75	Denys Smith	2-9	22.2	+ 13.00
R Cochrane	6-23	26.1	- 0.77	M H Tompkins	4-12	33.3	+ 1.23
B Raymond	6-39	15.4	- 9.71	B A McMahon	2-6	33.3	+ 10.00
Kim Tinkler	5-58	8.6	- 18.00	N Tinkler	4-26	15.4	+ 7.50

How the Favourites Fared

Non-handicaps	W-R	Per cent	£1 Level Stake	Handicaps	W-R	Per cent	£1 Level Stake
2-y-o	15-54	27.8	- 18.54	2-y-o	0-1	-	- 1.00
3-y-o	28-57	49.1	+ 0.89	3-y-o	14-39	35.9	- 0.22
Weight-for-age	17-46	37.0	- 0.91	All-aged	22-92	23.9	- 18.36
Totals	60-157	38.2	- 18.56	Totals	36-132	27.3	- 19.58
All favs	96-289	33.2	- 38.14				

Leading Trainers by Month at Carlisle

March/April

	Total W-R	Non-handicaps 2-y-o	3-y-o+	Handicaps 2-y-o	3-y-o+	Per cent	£1 Level Stake
J Berry	6-21	4-6	2-11	0-0	0-4	28.6	+ 1.00
M R Stoute	3-4	0-0	3-4	0-0	0-0	75.0	+ 1.83
J W Watts	3-12	0-0	2-7	0-0	1-5	25.0	+ 17.33
M H Tompkins	2-6	0-0	1-2	0-0	1-4	33.3	+ 4.63
J Etherington	2-7	1-2	0-2	0-0	1-3	28.6	+ 4.25

May

	Total W-R	Non-handicaps 2-y-o	3-y-o+	Handicaps 2-y-o	3-y-o+	Per cent	£1 Level Stake
M H Tompkins	6-20	2-4	1-7	0-0	3-9	30.0	+ 9.35
J Berry	6-36	2-18	3-13	0-0	1-5	16.7	+ 15.85
Sir M Prescott	5-17	1-2	1-6	0-0	3-9	29.4	+ 7.91
M S Johnston	4-16	1-2	1-7	0-0	2-7	25.0	+ 15.50
F H Lee	3-9	0-0	0-0	0-0	3-9	33.3	+ 4.38

June

	Total W-R	Non-handicaps 2-y-o	3-y-o+	Handicaps 2-y-o	3-y-o+	Per cent	£1 Level Stake
J Berry	9-40	2-17	2-12	0-0	5-11	22.5	+ 8.47
Denys Smith	6-18	1-2	2-5	0-0	3-11	33.3	+ 29.00
Mrs M Reveley	5-18	0-2	2-5	0-0	3-11	27.8	+ 2.58
M H Tompkins	4-14	2-3	2-3	0-0	0-8	28.6	- 2.40
Sir M Prescott	4-15	1-2	1-5	0-0	2-8	26.7	- 5.32

July

	Total W-R	Non-handicaps 2-y-o	3-y-o+	Handicaps 2-y-o	3-y-o+	Per cent	£1 Level Stake
J Berry	4-10	1-4	2-3	0-0	1-3	40.0	+ 9.00
J L Dunlop	2-2	1-1	0-0	0-0	1-1	100.0	+ 3.00
Mrs M Reveley	2-7	0-0	0-2	0-0	2-5	28.6	+ 0.25
O Brennan	1-1	0-0	0-0	0-0	1-1	100.0	+ 3.50
C R Nelson	1-1	0-0	1-1	0-0	0-0	100.0	+ 1.75

August

	Total W-R	Non-handicaps 2-y-o	3-y-o+	Handicaps 2-y-o	3-y-o+	Per cent	£1 Level Stake
B Hanbury	1-1	0-0	0-0	0-0	1-1	100.0	+ 7.00
M P Naughton	1-2	0-0	0-0	0-0	1-2	50.0	+ 11.00
S G Norton	1-2	0-0	0-1	0-0	1-1	50.0	+ 4.00
J Berry	1-3	1-2	0-0	0-0	0-1	33.3	- 1.09
R Hollinshead	1-3	0-1	1-1	0-0	0-1	33.3	+ 9.00

September

	Total W-R	Non-handicaps 2-y-o	3-y-o+	Handicaps 2-y-o	3-y-o+	Per cent	£1 Level Stake
J G FitzGerald	2-2	2-2	0-0	0-0	0-0	100.0	+ 8.50
J Berry	2-13	2-10	0-1	0-0	0-2	15.4	+ 3.00
B R Cambidge	1-1	0-0	0-0	0-0	1-1	100.0	+ 3.50
D Morley	1-1	0-0	1-1	0-0	0-0	100.0	+ 1.10
A Smith	1-1	0-0	0-0	0-0	1-1	100.0	+ 11.00

Oct/Nov

	Total W-R	Non-handicaps 2-y-o	3-y-o+	Handicaps 2-y-o	3-y-o+	Per cent	£1 Level Stake
H Thomson Jones	2-3	1-1	1-1	0-0	0-1	66.7	- 0.19
S R Bowring	1-1	0-0	0-0	0-0	1-1	100.0	+ 8.00
J G FitzGerald	1-2	0-0	0-0	0-0	1-2	50.0	+ 9.00
B W Hills	1-2	1-1	0-0	0-0	0-1	50.0	+ 3.50
R O'Leary	1-3	0-2	0-0	1-1	0-0	33.3	+ 7.00

CATTERICK (Group 4)

Leading Trainers 1989-93

	Total W-R	Non-handicaps 2-y-o	Non-handicaps 3-y-o+	Handicaps 2-y-o	Handicaps 3-y-o+	Per cent	£1 Level Stake
J Berry	32-203	19-106	8-34	2-17	3-46	15.8	- 32.25
T D Barron	22-132	6-29	3-18	1-11	12-74	16.7	+ 3.46
B W Hills	15-46	1-6	13-32	0-1	1-7	32.6	+ 19.78
M H Easterby	15-151	6-54	3-33	2-7	4-57	9.9	- 94.06
Mrs M Reveley	14-68	0-10	6-19	0-6	8-33	20.6	+ 7.90
Sir M Prescott	13-56	6-23	5-16	0-1	2-16	23.2	- 11.33
H R A Cecil	12-23	1-2	11-21	0-0	0-0	52.2	+ 13.33
S G Norton	11-57	2-14	3-23	0-3	6-17	19.3	- 5.15
M W Easterby	10-80	4-31	0-13	0-5	6-31	12.5	- 11.77
R M Whitaker	10-103	1-26	1-25	0-4	8-48	9.7	- 28.30
J H M Gosden	9-25	1-2	7-18	0-1	1-4	36.0	+ 10.92
G Wragg	9-26	1-2	7-22	0-0	1-2	34.6	+ 26.41
M H Tompkins	8-28	5-12	2-8	0-2	1-6	28.6	+ 16.98
M R Stoute	8-32	1-4	7-26	0-1	0-1	25.0	- 5.67
Mrs J Ramsden	8-97	2-24	1-9	0-8	5-56	8.2	- 57.63
N A Callaghan	7-15	4-5	2-6	1-2	0-2	46.7	+ 25.25
L M Cumani	7-19	0-3	7-15	0-0	0-1	36.8	- 7.75
P F I Cole	7-29	4-12	2-13	0-0	1-4	24.1	- 12.24
M P Naughton	7-59	0-2	0-15	0-0	7-42	11.9	- 12.96
M Bell	6-23	1-9	3-6	1-1	1-7	26.1	+ 14.73
Miss S E Hall	6-30	1-5	3-11	0-0	2-14	20.0	- 0.63
D Morley	6-44	0-3	2-17	0-0	4-23	13.6	- 17.58

Leading Jockeys

	Total W-R	Per cent	£1 Level Stake	Best Trainer	W-R	Per cent	£1 Level Stake
K Darley	35-191	18.3	- 15.18	Mrs M Reveley	7-14	50.0	+ 29.20
J Carroll	31-174	17.8	- 19.29	J Berry	23-123	18.7	- 18.66
M Birch	23-169	13.6	- 40.62	M H Easterby	9-76	11.8	- 45.21
G Duffield	21-139	15.1	- 33.12	Sir M Prescott	10-44	22.7	- 8.32
J Lowe	14-155	9.0	- 36.37	Mrs M Reveley	3-17	17.6	+ 5.00
N Connorton	12-77	15.6	- 30.93	R M Whitaker	3-4	75.0	+ 11.10
J Fortune	12-94	12.8	+ 1.97	L M Cumani	3-6	50.0	- 0.95
J Fanning	12-123	9.8	- 7.26	T D Barron	3-9	33.3	+ 8.00
W Ryan	10-55	18.2	- 13.20	H R A Cecil	8-14	57.1	+ 12.92
O Pears	10-58	17.2	+ 13.76	S G Norton	6-23	26.1	+ 7.01
Alex Greaves	10-67	14.9	+ 6.88	T D Barron	10-56	17.9	+ 17.88
L Charnock	10-126	7.9	+ 11.00	Lady Herries	1-1	100.0	+ 9.00

How the Favourites Fared

Non-handicaps	W-R	Per cent	£1 Level Stake	Handicaps	W-R	Per cent	£1 Level Stake
2-y-o	48-115	41.7	- 12.38	2-y-o	5-15	33.3	- 0.62
3-y-o	42-89	47.2	- 8.65	3-y-o	14-46	30.4	- 1.68
Weight-for-age	30-60	50.0	+ 0.33	All-aged	36-131	27.5	- 24.47
Totals	120-264	45.5	- 20.70	Totals	55-192	28.6	- 26.77
All favs	175-456	38.4	- 47.47				

Leading Trainers by Month at Catterick

March/April	Total W-R	Non-handicaps 2-y-o	3-y-o+	Handicaps 2-y-o	3-y-o+	Per cent	£1 Level Stake
J Berry	10-37	6-15	3-8	0-0	1-14	27.0	+ 5.57
T D Barron	6-27	0-5	0-5	0-0	6-17	22.2	- 0.59
Mrs J Ramsden	4-22	0-1	1-5	0-0	3-16	18.2	- 5.29
G Wragg	3-4	0-0	3-4	0-0	0-0	75.0	+ 5.41
M Bell	3-7	1-3	2-4	0-0	0-0	42.9	+ 9.16

May	Total W-R	Non-handicaps 2-y-o	3-y-o+	Handicaps 2-y-o	3-y-o+	Per cent	£1 Level Stake
N A Callaghan	2-2	1-1	1-1	0-0	0-0	100.0	+ 19.50
M R Stoute	2-2	0-0	2-2	0-0	0-0	100.0	+ 4.33
G Wragg	2-2	0-0	2-2	0-0	0-0	100.0	+ 10.50
R Hollinshead	2-10	1-2	0-4	0-0	1-4	20.0	- 2.00
T D Barron	2-11	1-2	0-1	0-0	1-8	18.2	- 2.80

June	Total W-R	Non-handicaps 2-y-o	3-y-o+	Handicaps 2-y-o	3-y-o+	Per cent	£1 Level Stake
J Berry	6-27	3-14	2-6	0-0	1-7	22.2	+ 0.53
P F I Cole	5-14	2-4	2-7	0-0	1-3	35.7	- 0.04
S G Norton	4-8	0-1	2-4	0-0	2-3	50.0	+ 8.50
L M Cumani	3-3	0-0	3-3	0-0	0-0	100.0	+ 1.69
B W Hills	3-7	0-0	3-6	0-0	0-1	42.9	+ 3.60

July	Total W-R	Non-handicaps 2-y-o	3-y-o+	Handicaps 2-y-o	3-y-o+	Per cent	£1 Level Stake
M H Easterby	10-55	4-19	2-11	0-0	4-25	18.2	- 19.23
J Berry	8-49	4-30	3-11	0-0	1-8	16.3	- 17.60
B W Hills	5-10	0-0	5-10	0-0	0-0	50.0	+ 14.19
Mrs M Reveley	5-21	0-4	2-7	0-0	3-10	23.8	+ 1.82
L M Cumani	4-7	0-0	4-7	0-0	0-0	57.1	- 0.44

August	Total W-R	Non-handicaps 2-y-o	3-y-o+	Handicaps 2-y-o	3-y-o+	Per cent	£1 Level Stake
Sir M Prescott	3-8	2-5	1-1	0-0	0-2	37.5	+ 1.85
R M Whitaker	3-14	0-5	0-2	0-1	3-6	21.4	+ 17.10
N Tinkler	2-2	0-0	2-2	0-0	0-0	100.0	+ 0.62
N A Callaghan	2-3	1-1	0-1	1-1	0-0	66.7	+ 3.00
Mrs M Reveley	2-7	0-1	1-1	0-1	1-4	28.6	- 0.80

September	Total W-R	Non-handicaps 2-y-o	3-y-o+	Handicaps 2-y-o	3-y-o+	Per cent	£1 Level Stake
R J R Williams	2-4	0-0	2-4	0-0	0-0	50.0	+ 12.00
Mrs M Reveley	2-4	0-0	0-0	0-1	2-3	50.0	+ 2.38
J H M Gosden	2-4	0-0	2-3	0-1	0-0	50.0	+ 4.25
T D Barron	2-12	1-2	0-1	1-5	0-4	16.7	+ 3.38
J L Dunlop	1-1	1-1	0-0	0-0	0-0	100.0	+ 0.80

Oct/Nov	Total W-R	Non-handicaps 2-y-o	3-y-o+	Handicaps 2-y-o	3-y-o+	Per cent	£1 Level Stake
H R A Cecil	5-8	1-1	4-7	0-0	0-0	62.5	+ 8.50
T D Barron	5-23	2-6	1-2	0-4	2-11	21.7	+ 17.88
B W Hills	4-18	1-5	2-8	0-1	1-4	22.2	+ 1.62
J Berry	4-41	4-26	0-1	0-6	0-8	9.8	- 15.25
M H Tompkins	3-10	3-5	0-3	0-1	0-1	30.0	+ 12.50

CHEPSTOW (Group 3)

Leading Trainers 1989-93

	Total W-R	Non-handicaps 2-y-o	3-y-o+	Handicaps 2-y-o	3-y-o+	Per cent	£1 Level Stake
R Hannon	19-140	8-52	3-25	2-10	6-53	13.6	- 37.99
R J Hodges	13-120	0-5	1-20	0-1	12-94	10.8	- 27.04
L M Cumani	11-22	0-0	10-18	1-1	0-3	50.0	+ 1.38
H R A Cecil	11-25	2-5	6-15	0-0	3-5	44.0	+ 22.73
P F I Cole	10-76	6-34	1-23	0-1	3-18	13.2	- 12.25
B W Hills	8-40	1-5	6-18	0-1	1-16	20.0	+ 20.05
H Candy	7-42	1-5	2-11	0-1	4-25	16.7	+ 31.00
H Thomson Jones	6-15	1-3	2-8	0-0	3-4	40.0	+ 21.90
J Berry	6-27	2-10	3-9	0-2	1-6	22.2	+ 0.83
I A Balding	6-46	2-19	2-11	0-1	2-15	13.0	- 1.52
J L Dunlop	6-48	1-18	3-11	0-0	2-19	12.5	- 15.58
J H M Gosden	5-16	1-5	3-7	0-0	1-4	31.3	+ 2.89
M C Pipe	5-27	0-1	0-8	0-0	5-18	18.5	+ 6.13
P T Walwyn	5-31	0-9	3-13	0-2	2-7	16.1	- 4.47
G Lewis	5-37	0-4	2-10	1-6	2-17	13.5	- 21.13
R Hollinshead	5-51	1-7	0-14	0-3	4-27	9.8	+ 6.00
B R Millman	5-52	2-7	1-11	0-2	2-32	9.6	+ 54.50
M R Stoute	4-18	2-7	2-9	0-0	0-2	22.2	+ 0.39
W R Hern	4-20	0-3	3-12	0-0	1-5	20.0	- 4.61
Lord Huntingdon	4-21	0-4	3-8	0-0	1-9	19.0	+ 11.00
Sir M Prescott	4-22	1-9	3-10	0-1	0-2	18.2	- 8.03
R F J Houghton	4-23	1-6	2-9	0-1	1-7	17.4	+ 5.50

Leading Jockeys

	Total W-R	Per cent	£1 Level Stake	Best Trainer	W-R	Per cent	£1 Level Stake
J Williams	17-162	10.5	+ 51.71	B R Millman	3-11	27.3	+ 80.00
J Reid	14-98	14.3	- 22.69	J L Dunlop	2-4	50.0	+ 0.18
M Roberts	13-40	32.5	+ 27.02	M C Pipe	3-3	100.0	+ 8.13
L Dettori	12-46	26.1	- 6.05	L M Cumani	7-11	63.6	+ 6.10
T Quinn	11-90	12.2	- 14.59	P F I Cole	5-35	14.3	- 4.75
W Carson	10-64	15.6	- 25.81	M R Stoute	2-2	100.0	+ 1.06
Pat Eddery	8-43	18.6	- 10.92	R Lee	1-1	100.0	+ 7.00
A Munro	8-47	17.0	+ 12.31	L M Cumani	1-1	100.0	+ 0.91
T Sprake	8-57	14.0	- 5.12	R J Hodges	7-30	23.3	+ 19.13
R Perham	8-65	12.3	- 9.75	R Hannon	6-39	15.4	- 0.25
A Clark	8-74	10.8	- 28.84	J L Dunlop	2-3	66.7	+ 11.00
R Hills	7-26	26.9	+ 25.16	H Thomson Jones	4-6	66.7	+ 27.00

How the Favourites Fared

Non-handicaps	W-R	Per cent	£1 Level Stake	Handicaps	W-R	Per cent	£1 Level Stake
2-y-o	14-54	25.9	- 19.34	2-y-o	5-12	41.7	+ 3.10
3-y-o	29-54	53.7	+ 3.92	3-y-o	8-22	36.4	+ 2.34
Weight-for-age	30-52	57.7	+ 6.67	All-aged	36-118	30.5	+ 9.29
Totals	73-160	45.6	- 8.75	Totals	49-152	32.2	+ 14.73
All favs	122-312	39.1	+ 5.98				

Leading Trainers by Month at Chepstow

May

	Total W-R	Non-handicaps 2-y-o	3-y-o+	Handicaps 2-y-o	3-y-o+	Per cent	£1 Level Stake
R J Hodges	4-17	0-0	0-0	0-0	4-17	23.5	- 2.88
H Thomson Jones	2-3	0-0	2-3	0-0	0-0	66.7	+ 0.90
R F J Houghton	2-4	1-2	1-2	0-0	0-0	50.0	+ 6.00
J L Dunlop	2-6	0-0	2-4	0-0	0-2	33.3	- 1.83
R Hannon	2-15	0-5	0-2	0-0	2-8	13.3	- 2.50

June

	Total W-R	Non-handicaps 2-y-o	3-y-o+	Handicaps 2-y-o	3-y-o+	Per cent	£1 Level Stake
J Berry	4-8	1-4	3-4	0-0	0-0	50.0	+ 0.92
P T Walwyn	3-7	0-1	1-2	0-0	2-4	42.9	+ 16.30
D A Wilson	3-7	0-0	0-0	0-0	3-7	42.9	+ 19.50
P F I Cole	3-13	2-4	0-4	0-0	1-5	23.1	- 0.50
R Hollinshead	3-18	1-3	0-4	0-0	2-11	16.7	+ 18.50

July

	Total W-R	Non-handicaps 2-y-o	3-y-o+	Handicaps 2-y-o	3-y-o+	Per cent	£1 Level Stake
R Hannon	7-29	2-6	2-9	1-2	2-12	24.1	+ 0.41
R J Hodges	5-27	0-1	0-7	0-0	5-19	18.5	+ 15.33
L M Cumani	4-6	0-0	4-6	0-0	0-0	66.7	+ 4.03
H R A Cecil	4-7	0-0	4-7	0-0	0-0	57.1	- 1.52
M C Pipe	3-8	0-0	0-2	0-0	3-6	37.5	+ 7.13

August

	Total W-R	Non-handicaps 2-y-o	3-y-o+	Handicaps 2-y-o	3-y-o+	Per cent	£1 Level Stake
L M Cumani	5-6	0-0	4-4	1-1	0-1	83.3	+ 4.90
I A Balding	3-13	2-7	0-1	0-0	1-5	23.1	+ 19.73
R Hannon	3-21	2-10	0-0	1-5	0-6	14.3	- 10.40
M R Stoute	2-4	2-3	0-0	0-0	0-1	50.0	+ 8.62
H Candy	2-7	0-1	0-0	0-1	2-5	28.6	+ 3.00

September

	Total W-R	Non-handicaps 2-y-o	3-y-o+	Handicaps 2-y-o	3-y-o+	Per cent	£1 Level Stake
L M Cumani	2-5	0-0	2-5	0-0	0-0	40.0	- 2.55
R Hannon	2-10	1-3	1-4	0-0	0-3	20.0	+ 2.00
P Butler	1-1	0-0	1-1	0-0	0-0	100.0	+ 8.00
B W Hills	1-1	0-0	1-1	0-0	0-0	100.0	+ 0.57
R F J Houghton	1-1	0-0	0-0	0-0	1-1	100.0	+ 10.00

Oct/Nov

	Total W-R	Non-handicaps 2-y-o	3-y-o+	Handicaps 2-y-o	3-y-o+	Per cent	£1 Level Stake
H R A Cecil	3-9	2-3	0-3	0-0	1-3	33.3	+ 10.50
B W Hills	3-10	1-3	1-2	0-0	1-5	30.0	+ 31.75
J H M Gosden	3-10	1-5	1-1	0-0	1-4	30.0	+ 5.25
P F I Cole	3-22	2-11	1-6	0-1	0-4	13.6	- 1.75
R Hannon	3-46	2-22	0-9	0-3	1-12	6.5	- 18.00

CHESTER (Group 2)

Leading Trainers 1989-93

	Total W-R	Non-handicaps 2-y-o	3-y-o+	Handicaps 2-y-o	3-y-o+	Per cent	£1 Level Stake
B W Hills	21-80	4-13	12-41	1-1	4-25	26.3	+ 19.04
M R Stoute	14-57	5-8	6-23	0-1	3-25	24.6	- 13.37
J H M Gosden	13-51	3-6	5-21	0-0	5-24	25.5	+ 4.60
J Berry	13-117	8-45	1-8	1-10	3-54	11.1	- 34.13
H R A Cecil	12-38	3-7	8-21	0-0	1-10	31.6	- 6.68
R Hannon	12-54	6-21	2-7	3-8	1-18	22.2	- 9.52
C E Brittain	11-76	5-18	4-24	0-3	2-31	14.5	+ 5.62
A Bailey	10-80	1-15	4-13	0-3	5-49	12.5	- 2.33
R Hollinshead	9-141	4-44	2-27	0-7	3-63	6.4	- 60.75
F H Lee	8-48	2-11	0-6	0-2	6-29	16.7	+ 12.50
S G Norton	8-59	2-18	0-10	1-2	5-29	13.6	+ 2.25
B A McMahon	8-61	0-10	0-9	0-4	8-38	13.1	+ 25.96
B Hanbury	7-28	3-8	3-5	0-2	1-13	25.0	+ 1.83
G Wragg	6-30	0-3	6-17	0-1	0-9	20.0	- 6.13
P F I Cole	6-46	6-13	0-18	0-2	0-13	13.0	- 31.02
M H Easterby	6-61	2-19	1-6	0-6	3-30	9.8	- 17.75
G Lewis	5-15	4-8	0-0	0-1	1-6	33.3	+ 9.41
R M Whitaker	5-29	0-3	0-0	0-1	5-25	17.2	+ 21.00
J W Watts	5-31	2-3	0-1	1-2	2-25	16.1	+ 3.50
E J Alston	5-45	1-11	2-5	1-1	1-28	11.1	+ 11.00
J D Bethell	4-15	0-0	0-0	0-2	4-13	26.7	+ 12.38
P Chapple-Hyam	4-17	2-4	2-9	0-0	0-4	23.5	- 1.15

Leading Jockeys

	Total W-R	Per cent	£1 Level Stake	Best Trainer	W-R	Per cent	£1 Level Stake
Pat Eddery	27-92	29.3	- 2.10	B W Hills	6-13	46.2	+ 4.58
M Roberts	17-89	19.1	+ 14.01	C E Brittain	6-34	17.6	+ 24.75
W R Swinburn	14-80	17.5	- 14.06	M R Stoute	7-32	21.9	- 10.56
A Munro	14-94	14.9	- 30.95	C E Brittain	2-5	40.0	- 0.80
W Carson	12-84	14.3	- 27.82	W R Hern	3-17	17.6	- 7.82
D Holland	11-61	18.0	+ 15.50	B W Hills	6-22	27.3	+ 19.00
J Carroll	10-96	10.4	- 53.12	J Berry	8-74	10.8	- 42.62
W Ryan	9-54	16.7	- 15.51	H R A Cecil	5-15	33.3	+ 1.49
Paul Eddery	9-60	15.0	- 6.11	G Lewis	4-7	57.1	+ 14.66
J Lowe	9-61	14.8	+ 6.13	S G Norton	3-7	42.9	+ 13.00
G Duffield	8-33	24.2	+ 37.83	J W Watts	3-4	75.0	+ 16.00
T Quinn	8-42	19.0	- 8.17	P F I Cole	3-22	13.6	- 13.25

How the Favourites Fared

Non-handicaps	W-R	Per cent	£1 Level Stake	Handicaps	W-R	Per cent	£1 Level Stake
2-y-o	35-77	45.5	- 3.13	2-y-o	3-13	23.1	- 5.37
3-y-o	25-47	53.2	+ 7.62	3-y-o	9-34	26.5	- 2.75
Weight-for-age	10-25	40.0	- 4.49	All-aged	23-95	24.2	- 15.78
Totals	70-149	47.0	+ 0.00	Totals	35-142	24.6	- 23.90
All favs	105-291	36.1	- 23.90				

Leading Trainers by Month at Chester

May	Total W-R	Non-handicaps 2-y-o	3-y-o+	Handicaps 2-y-o	3-y-o+	Per cent	£1 Level Stake
B W Hills	9-42	0-3	7-26	0-0	2-13	21.4	- 3.15
H R A Cecil	6-14	0-0	6-13	0-0	0-1	42.9	+ 1.51
J H M Gosden	6-17	0-0	2-9	0-0	4-8	35.3	+ 14.25
R Hannon	5-16	4-6	1-4	0-0	0-6	31.3	+ 4.44
M R Stoute	5-23	0-0	3-15	0-0	2-8	21.7	- 7.96

June	Total W-R	Non-handicaps 2-y-o	3-y-o+	Handicaps 2-y-o	3-y-o+	Per cent	£1 Level Stake
P F I Cole	3-4	3-3	0-0	0-0	0-1	75.0	+ 4.66
B A McMahon	3-8	0-4	0-0	0-0	3-4	37.5	+ 6.63
S G Norton	3-12	2-5	0-4	0-0	1-3	25.0	+ 3.25
B W Hills	2-3	0-0	2-2	0-0	0-1	66.7	+ 2.94
E J Alston	2-4	1-1	0-1	0-0	1-2	50.0	+ 24.50

July	Total W-R	Non-handicaps 2-y-o	3-y-o+	Handicaps 2-y-o	3-y-o+	Per cent	£1 Level Stake
G Lewis	5-6	4-4	0-0	0-0	1-2	83.3	+ 18.41
J H M Gosden	4-9	2-2	2-4	0-0	0-3	44.4	+ 4.13
A Bailey	4-17	1-5	1-2	0-0	2-10	23.5	+ 22.50
R M Whitaker	3-5	0-0	0-0	0-0	3-5	60.0	+ 13.00
F H Lee	3-14	1-6	0-1	0-0	2-7	21.4	+ 2.50

August	Total W-R	Non-handicaps 2-y-o	3-y-o+	Handicaps 2-y-o	3-y-o+	Per cent	£1 Level Stake
R Hannon	4-9	1-3	0-1	3-4	0-1	44.4	+ 7.71
B W Hills	3-11	1-4	1-5	0-0	1-2	27.3	- 1.26
J Berry	3-23	2-9	0-1	0-6	1-7	13.0	+ 3.00
R Hollinshead	3-25	1-6	1-4	0-2	1-13	12.0	+ 15.00
G Wragg	2-5	0-0	2-2	0-1	0-2	40.0	+ 3.50

September	Total W-R	Non-handicaps 2-y-o	3-y-o+	Handicaps 2-y-o	3-y-o+	Per cent	£1 Level Stake
M R Stoute	3-7	2-2	1-3	0-0	0-2	42.9	+ 5.23
B Hanbury	2-4	2-2	0-0	0-1	0-1	50.0	+ 4.00
W R Hern	2-5	0-1	1-2	1-1	0-1	40.0	+ 2.08
G Wragg	1-1	0-0	1-1	0-0	0-0	100.0	+ 1.00
Mrs L Piggott	1-1	0-0	1-1	0-0	0-0	100.0	+ 7.50

Oct/Nov	Total W-R	Non-handicaps 2-y-o	3-y-o+	Handicaps 2-y-o	3-y-o+	Per cent	£1 Level Stake
B W Hills	6-15	3-5	1-2	1-1	1-7	40.0	+ 27.00
M R Stoute	3-7	2-3	1-1	0-1	0-2	42.9	+ 2.17
J W Watts	3-7	0-1	0-0	1-1	2-5	42.9	+ 13.00
M J Camacho	3-9	1-1	0-1	0-1	2-6	33.3	+ 3.50
C E Brittain	3-16	3-6	0-1	0-3	0-6	18.8	- 5.80

DONCASTER (Group 1)

Leading Trainers 1989-93

	Total W-R	Non-handicaps 2-y-o	3-y-o+	Handicaps 2-y-o	3-y-o+	Per cent	£1 Level Stake
H R A Cecil	32-100	14-29	17-57	0-0	1-14	32.0	+ 20.18
J H M Gosden	30-117	11-31	11-47	1-2	7-37	25.6	+ 33.10
B W Hills	26-109	5-29	17-51	0-2	4-27	23.9	+ 1.82
R Hannon	26-212	10-62	7-46	4-29	5-75	12.3	- 36.80
J Berry	19-116	9-57	3-16	0-8	7-35	16.4	+ 43.89
Mrs J Ramsden	19-158	2-22	3-18	4-12	10-106	12.0	- 3.31
M R Stoute	16-94	6-32	5-33	2-7	3-22	17.0	- 3.78
L M Cumani	13-67	0-10	9-33	0-1	4-23	19.4	- 24.37
J L Dunlop	11-81	2-22	3-25	1-4	5-30	13.6	+ 2.93
Mrs M Reveley	11-88	0-12	1-6	0-8	10-62	12.5	- 25.75
M S Johnston	11-108	2-23	2-16	0-9	7-58	10.2	- 9.00
M H Easterby	11-145	3-36	1-11	4-14	3-84	7.6	- 42.25
R W Armstrong	9-40	5-10	1-9	0-5	3-16	22.5	+ 35.11
A C Stewart	9-44	1-10	4-14	0-1	4-19	20.5	+ 11.50
I A Balding	9-59	1-11	3-16	0-2	5-30	15.3	+ 11.78
C E Brittain	9-136	0-25	4-47	1-7	4-57	6.6	- 60.67
R Hollinshead	9-204	1-49	2-47	0-15	6-93	4.4	-104.04
G Wragg	8-48	3-7	2-24	0-0	3-17	16.7	- 13.92
M A Jarvis	8-49	2-11	2-11	0-3	4-24	16.3	- 20.20
F H Lee	8-99	1-11	0-14	0-14	7-60	8.1	- 22.38
A A Scott	7-52	2-28	2-9	0-3	3-12	13.5	+ 15.83
J G FitzGerald	6-45	0-5	3-8	0-2	3-30	13.3	+ 28.50

Leading Jockeys

	Total W-R	Per cent	£1 Level Stake	Best Trainer	W-R	Per cent	£1 Level Stake
Pat Eddery	43-206	20.9	- 7.04	J H M Gosden	6-12	50.0	+ 8.43
W Carson	29-223	13.0	- 87.04	J H M Gosden	4-12	33.3	+ 6.00
M Roberts	25-201	12.4	- 56.44	A C Stewart	6-27	22.2	+ 8.50
K Darley	22-176	12.5	- 15.48	R Hannon	4-11	36.4	+ 12.02
B Raymond	21-147	14.3	+ 12.27	B Hanbury	3-15	20.0	+ 21.50
W Ryan	20-131	15.3	- 18.61	H R A Cecil	10-34	29.4	+ 9.25
R Cochrane	19-167	11.4	- 42.70	L M Cumani	4-10	40.0	+ 3.58
M Hills	18-121	14.9	+ 24.54	B W Hills	7-41	17.1	- 11.59
L Dettori	18-161	11.2	- 53.44	L M Cumani	4-39	10.3	- 29.14
A Munro	17-163	10.4	+ 45.80	Mrs J Ramsden	3-24	12.5	+ 2.00
J Reid	16-138	11.6	- 45.89	R Hannon	5-37	13.5	- 2.00
W R Swinburn	16-147	10.9	- 34.32	A A Scott	4-10	40.0	+ 37.01

How the Favourites Fared

Non-handicaps	W-R	Per cent	£1 Level Stake	Handicaps	W-R	Per cent	£1 Level Stake
2-y-o	54-143	37.8	- 24.78	2-y-o	7-27	25.9	+ 3.50
3-y-o	25-65	38.5	- 5.36	3-y-o	15-59	25.4	- 4.61
Weight-for-age	44-95	46.3	+ 8.90	All-aged	59-197	29.9	+ 14.88
Totals	123-303	40.6	- 21.24	Totals	81-283	28.6	+ 13.77
All favs	204-586	34.8	- 7.47				

Leading Trainers by Month at Doncaster

March/April

	Total W-R	Non-handicaps 2-y-o	Non-handicaps 3-y-o+	Handicaps 2-y-o	Handicaps 3-y-o+	Per cent	£1 Level Stake
J Berry	12-35	4-16	3-5	0-0	5-14	34.3	+ 83.73
B W Hills	8-23	1-3	6-15	0-0	1-5	34.8	+ 7.88
C E Brittain	4-37	0-0	3-20	0-0	1-17	10.8	- 12.42
Mrs J Ramsden	4-39	0-1	1-7	0-0	3-31	10.3	+ 1.50
W A O'Gorman	3-9	2-4	1-5	0-0	0-0	33.3	+ 5.00

May

	Total W-R	Non-handicaps 2-y-o	Non-handicaps 3-y-o+	Handicaps 2-y-o	Handicaps 3-y-o+	Per cent	£1 Level Stake
H R A Cecil	8-16	1-1	7-14	0-0	0-1	50.0	+ 10.06
M R Stoute	5-12	1-1	1-5	0-0	3-6	41.7	+ 16.00
B W Hills	5-14	1-3	4-6	0-0	0-5	35.7	+ 4.54
F H Lee	4-21	1-2	0-2	0-0	3-17	19.0	+ 15.00
J W Watts	4-27	0-1	0-3	0-0	4-23	14.8	- 4.25

June

	Total W-R	Non-handicaps 2-y-o	Non-handicaps 3-y-o+	Handicaps 2-y-o	Handicaps 3-y-o+	Per cent	£1 Level Stake
Mrs L Piggott	4-13	2-3	0-6	0-0	2-4	30.8	+ 0.10
G Wragg	3-5	0-0	0-1	0-0	3-4	60.0	+ 11.50
J H M Gosden	3-5	0-1	2-3	0-0	1-1	60.0	+ 1.80
A C Stewart	3-6	0-0	1-2	0-0	2-4	50.0	+ 6.50
M H Easterby	3-19	2-9	1-3	0-0	0-7	15.8	0.00

July

	Total W-R	Non-handicaps 2-y-o	Non-handicaps 3-y-o+	Handicaps 2-y-o	Handicaps 3-y-o+	Per cent	£1 Level Stake
L M Cumani	4-6	0-0	2-3	0-0	2-3	66.7	+ 4.61
R Hannon	4-15	3-7	0-2	0-0	1-6	26.7	- 4.75
R Hollinshead	4-27	1-9	1-4	0-0	2-14	14.8	- 6.67
H R A Cecil	3-6	1-1	1-4	0-0	1-1	50.0	- 0.25
I A Balding	3-8	0-2	1-1	0-0	2-5	37.5	+ 4.63

September

	Total W-R	Non-handicaps 2-y-o	Non-handicaps 3-y-o+	Handicaps 2-y-o	Handicaps 3-y-o+	Per cent	£1 Level Stake
R Hannon	14-74	1-18	6-13	3-16	4-27	18.9	+ 45.20
J H M Gosden	10-40	3-6	5-22	0-0	2-12	25.0	+ 13.08
H R A Cecil	9-34	4-10	5-18	0-0	0-6	26.5	- 1.13
M R Stoute	7-41	3-11	2-14	2-6	0-10	17.1	- 3.88
Mrs J Ramsden	6-25	0-3	0-2	3-5	3-15	24.0	+ 16.00

Oct/Nov

	Total W-R	Non-handicaps 2-y-o	Non-handicaps 3-y-o+	Handicaps 2-y-o	Handicaps 3-y-o+	Per cent	£1 Level Stake
J H M Gosden	14-53	7-21	3-12	1-2	3-18	26.4	+ 31.52
H R A Cecil	11-32	8-16	3-11	0-0	0-5	34.4	+ 21.39
B W Hills	5-18	2-9	2-5	0-0	1-4	27.8	+ 16.00
M H Easterby	5-26	0-2	0-1	4-9	1-14	19.2	+ 44.00
J L Dunlop	5-33	2-14	1-5	0-3	2-11	15.2	+ 10.88

EDINBURGH (Group 4)

Leading Trainers 1989-93

	Total W-R	Non-handicaps 2-y-o	3-y-o+	Handicaps 2-y-o	3-y-o+	Per cent	£1 Level Stake
J Berry	36-176	20-85	10-33	1-6	5-52	20.5	- 26.75
M P Naughton	17-105	0-2	2-29	0-0	15-74	16.2	+ 52.98
Sir M Prescott	14-58	4-15	4-20	0-0	6-23	24.1	+ 7.60
M H Tompkins	9-24	3-7	2-7	0-2	4-8	37.5	+ 13.65
M H Easterby	9-49	3-15	2-9	0-1	4-24	18.4	- 21.80
M S Johnston	9-55	4-17	2-7	2-2	1-29	16.4	- 17.12
Mrs M Reveley	9-65	3-10	0-10	0-0	6-45	13.8	- 14.75
J L Spearing	8-52	1-10	0-7	0-1	7-34	15.4	- 16.63
S G Norton	8-63	1-20	5-21	0-2	2-20	12.7	- 9.95
D W Chapman	8-114	2-8	0-17	1-2	5-87	7.0	- 23.75
J H M Gosden	7-21	2-7	4-11	0-0	1-3	33.3	- 1.73
J G FitzGerald	7-33	1-9	3-12	0-1	3-11	21.2	+ 2.21
C Tinkler	7-35	2-9	1-3	0-1	4-22	20.0	+ 9.17
R M Whitaker	7-53	1-8	0-11	1-2	5-32	13.2	- 11.33
M D Hammond	6-24	1-4	0-0	0-0	5-20	25.0	+ 14.88
P C Haslam	6-26	1-5	1-3	0-0	4-18	23.1	+ 1.32
F H Lee	6-44	1-7	0-3	0-2	5-32	13.6	- 17.59
T D Barron	6-70	1-17	0-11	1-2	4-40	8.6	- 36.44
B W Hills	5-14	0-2	4-9	0-0	1-3	35.7	+ 0.10
B Hanbury	5-17	1-3	4-11	0-0	0-3	29.4	+ 16.91
M J Camacho	5-20	0-4	2-6	0-2	3-8	25.0	- 0.53
J Etherington	5-22	2-6	2-5	0-1	1-10	22.7	+ 15.25

Leading Jockeys

	Total W-R	Per cent	£1 Level Stake	Best Trainer	W-R	Per cent	£1 Level Stake
J Carroll	32-154	20.8	- 13.11	J Berry	24-96	25.0	- 22.61
G Duffield	30-153	19.6	- 12.97	Sir M Prescott	11-49	22.4	+ 8.85
K Darley	25-145	17.2	+ 19.43	J L Spearing	5-12	41.7	+ 10.50
K Fallon	18-150	12.0	- 18.61	J G FitzGerald	5-18	27.8	+ 1.58
J Weaver	13-49	26.5	+ 17.22	R Allan	4-10	40.0	+ 8.38
N Connorton	11-83	13.3	+ 21.48	M J Camacho	5-15	33.3	+ 4.48
J Fanning	11-136	8.1	+ 8.05	Miss L A Perrat	3-31	9.7	+ 0.05
A Munro	9-43	20.9	+ 8.75	N A Callaghan	2-2	100.0	+ 7.00
S Webster	9-102	8.8	- 4.00	F H Lee	2-6	33.3	+ 10.50
J Lowe	9-175	5.1	-126.95	Mrs M Reveley	4-21	19.0	+ 2.30
G Hind	8-55	14.5	- 31.59	J H M Gosden	4-8	50.0	+ 1.78
P Burke	7-52	13.5	+ 24.83	C Tinkler	3-8	37.5	+ 14.83

How the Favourites Fared

Non-handicaps	W-R	Per cent	£1 Level Stake	Handicaps	W-R	Per cent	£1 Level Stake
2-y-o	41-92	44.6	- 7.03	2-y-o	4-6	66.7	+ 6.25
3-y-o	23-41	56.1	+ 8.17	3-y-o	11-25	44.0	- 0.35
Weight-for-age	26-61	42.6	- 5.11	All-aged	46-154	29.9	- 2.71
Totals	90-194	46.4	- 3.97	Totals	61-185	33.0	+ 3.19
All favs	151-379	39.8	- 0.78				

Leading Trainers by Month at Edinburgh

March/April

	Total W-R	Non-handicaps 2-y-o	3-y-o+	Handicaps 2-y-o	3-y-o+	Per cent	£1 Level Stake
J Berry	5-15	3-5	2-6	0-0	0-4	33.3	+ 13.49
Sir M Prescott	4-7	0-0	2-3	0-0	2-4	57.1	+ 6.85
J H M Gosden	2-2	0-0	2-2	0-0	0-0	100.0	+ 1.87
J W Watts	2-4	0-0	1-2	0-0	1-2	50.0	+ 5.83
M J Camacho	1-1	0-0	0-0	0-0	1-1	100.0	+ 1.38

May

	Total W-R	Non-handicaps 2-y-o	3-y-o+	Handicaps 2-y-o	3-y-o+	Per cent	£1 Level Stake
J Berry	5-22	2-7	1-6	0-0	2-9	22.7	+ 9.50
J G FitzGerald	3-8	0-0	2-4	0-0	1-4	37.5	+ 4.75
M S Johnston	3-10	2-3	1-3	0-0	0-4	30.0	- 0.02
J W Payne	2-2	0-0	0-0	0-0	2-2	100.0	+ 7.25
S G Norton	2-4	0-1	1-2	0-0	1-1	50.0	+ 11.00

June

	Total W-R	Non-handicaps 2-y-o	3-y-o+	Handicaps 2-y-o	3-y-o+	Per cent	£1 Level Stake
J Berry	13-45	7-21	5-10	0-0	1-14	28.9	- 6.64
B W Hills	4-9	0-0	3-7	0-0	1-2	44.4	+ 2.60
R M Whitaker	4-16	1-1	0-3	0-0	3-12	25.0	+ 13.60
M P Naughton	4-28	0-0	1-9	0-0	3-19	14.3	+ 23.50
W Jarvis	3-4	0-0	2-3	0-0	1-1	75.0	+ 5.20

July

	Total W-R	Non-handicaps 2-y-o	3-y-o+	Handicaps 2-y-o	3-y-o+	Per cent	£1 Level Stake
J Berry	8-41	5-22	1-5	1-1	1-13	19.5	- 13.91
M P Naughton	7-23	0-0	1-7	0-0	6-16	30.4	+ 6.88
M D Hammond	4-12	1-3	0-0	0-0	3-9	33.3	+ 6.88
Sir M Prescott	4-16	0-2	1-7	0-0	3-7	25.0	+ 4.50
F H Lee	3-7	1-2	0-0	0-0	2-5	42.9	+ 3.66

August

	Total W-R	Non-handicaps 2-y-o	3-y-o+	Handicaps 2-y-o	3-y-o+	Per cent	£1 Level Stake
M H Easterby	3-6	1-2	0-0	0-1	2-3	50.0	+ 5.83
Mrs M Reveley	2-5	0-1	0-1	0-0	2-3	40.0	+ 4.80
J Berry	2-12	2-7	0-0	0-1	0-4	16.7	- 7.94
J Etherington	1-1	0-0	1-1	0-0	0-0	100.0	+ 0.40
A N Lee	1-1	0-0	0-0	0-0	1-1	100.0	+ 1.25

September

	Total W-R	Non-handicaps 2-y-o	3-y-o+	Handicaps 2-y-o	3-y-o+	Per cent	£1 Level Stake
J Pearce	2-3	0-0	0-0	0-1	2-2	66.7	+ 7.25
A Harrison	2-4	1-1	0-0	0-1	1-2	50.0	+ 12.00
M P Naughton	2-8	0-0	0-1	0-0	2-7	25.0	+ 11.50
Mrs M Reveley	2-8	1-2	0-0	0-0	1-6	25.0	+ 4.67
N A Callaghan	1-1	1-1	0-0	0-0	0-0	100.0	+ 2.50

Oct/Nov

	Total W-R	Non-handicaps 2-y-o	3-y-o+	Handicaps 2-y-o	3-y-o+	Per cent	£1 Level Stake
R Hannon	3-3	3-3	0-0	0-0	0-0	100.0	+ 6.35
C Tinkler	3-10	0-4	1-1	0-1	2-4	30.0	+ 17.50
Sir M Prescott	3-12	3-10	0-1	0-0	0-1	25.0	+ 2.25
M S Johnston	3-15	2-8	0-0	0-0	1-7	20.0	+ 3.50
D W Chapman	3-21	0-1	0-2	1-2	2-16	14.3	+ 16.00

EPSOM (Group 1)

Leading Trainers 1989-93

	Total W-R	Non-handicaps 2-y-o	3-y-o+	Handicaps 2-y-o	3-y-o+	Per cent	£1 Level Stake
R Hannon	14-120	4-30	3-36	1-4	6-50	11.7	- 39.38
J Berry	11-42	5-17	2-4	0-0	4-21	26.2	+ 10.94
D R C Elsworth	10-52	1-4	5-26	0-0	4-22	19.2	+ 26.98
R Akehurst	10-66	1-6	1-7	0-0	8-53	15.2	- 4.88
M R Stoute	9-45	1-2	4-29	0-0	4-14	20.0	- 12.96
H R A Cecil	7-24	0-2	5-19	0-0	2-3	29.2	+ 12.17
P F I Cole	7-52	2-12	1-21	0-0	4-19	13.5	- 6.25
C E Brittain	7-59	2-5	3-28	0-1	2-25	11.9	+ 9.50
G Lewis	7-92	2-26	2-21	0-2	3-43	7.6	- 50.42
Lord Huntingdon	5-16	1-2	2-4	0-1	2-9	31.3	+ 31.38
A C Stewart	5-21	0-0	4-12	0-0	1-9	23.8	- 4.04
J L Dunlop	5-26	1-4	3-10	1-1	0-11	19.2	- 7.88
M McCormack	4-11	0-0	1-2	0-0	3-9	36.4	+ 32.50
L M Cumani	4-22	0-0	1-10	0-0	3-12	18.2	- 5.75
P T Walwyn	4-30	0-0	1-10	0-0	3-20	13.3	+ 20.00
L G Cottrell	4-35	0-1	0-4	0-0	4-30	11.4	- 3.00
H Thomson Jones	3-19	0-1	1-5	0-0	2-13	15.8	+ 2.33
J W Hills	3-19	0-0	1-7	0-0	2-12	15.8	0.00
B Hanbury	3-22	0-0	1-9	0-0	2-13	13.6	+ 7.00
B R Millman	3-26	0-3	0-4	0-0	3-19	11.5	- 5.00
Miss B Sanders	3-34	0-3	0-13	0-0	3-18	8.8	- 19.00
R Charlton	2-5	0-1	1-2	1-1	0-1	40.0	+ 5.75

Leading Jockeys

	Total W-R	Per cent	£1 Level Stake	Best Trainer	W-R	Per cent	£1 Level Stake
M Roberts	24-131	18.3	+ 25.34	A C Stewart	5-18	27.8	- 1.04
Pat Eddery	22-135	16.3	- 21.38	J Berry	5-18	27.8	- 2.96
W Carson	17-97	17.5	+ 8.86	J L Dunlop	3-11	27.3	- 1.12
J Reid	14-89	15.7	+ 17.20	M McCormack	2-6	33.3	+ 12.50
R Cochrane	12-69	17.4	+ 1.13	L M Cumani	2-6	33.3	+ 3.00
T Quinn	8-87	9.2	- 44.75	P F I Cole	4-34	11.8	- 5.75
L Dettori	7-57	12.3	+ 3.25	L M Cumani	2-13	15.4	- 5.75
A Munro	6-51	11.8	+ 27.00	Lord Huntingdon	2-6	33.3	+ 22.00
M Hills	5-46	10.9	- 6.25	M Bell	2-8	25.0	+ 1.25
B Rouse	5-59	8.5	- 22.38	R Hannon	3-21	14.3	- 6.38
C Asmussen	4-15	26.7	+ 23.88	J Berry	1-1	100.0	+ 7.00
D Holland	4-32	12.5	+ 1.50	M J Heaton-Elli	1-2	50.0	+ 5.00

How the Favourites Fared

Non-handicaps	W-R	Per cent	£1 Level Stake	Handicaps	W-R	Per cent	£1 Level Stake
2-y-o	9-32	28.1	- 10.14	2-y-o	2-3	66.7	+ 5.25
3-y-o	21-52	40.4	- 0.53	3-y-o	10-39	25.6	+ 0.21
Weight-for-age	10-19	52.6	+ 4.42	All-aged	10-67	14.9	- 31.52
Totals	40-103	38.8	- 6.25	Totals	22-109	20.2	- 26.06
All favs	62-212	29.2	- 32.31				

Leading Trainers by Month at Epsom

March/April

	Total W-R	Non-handicaps 2-y-o	3-y-o+	Handicaps 2-y-o	3-y-o+	Per cent	£1 Level Stake
H R A Cecil	3-4	0-0	3-4	0-0	0-0	75.0	+ 4.83
J Berry	3-6	2-3	0-0	0-0	1-3	50.0	+ 4.13
M McCormack	2-4	0-0	0-0	0-0	2-4	50.0	+ 15.50
P F I Cole	2-12	0-0	0-5	0-0	2-7	16.7	+ 7.00
R J Hodges	1-1	0-0	0-0	0-0	1-1	100.0	+ 6.00

June

	Total W-R	Non-handicaps 2-y-o	3-y-o+	Handicaps 2-y-o	3-y-o+	Per cent	£1 Level Stake
R Hannon	9-81	4-21	2-25	0-0	3-35	11.1	- 39.88
M R Stoute	8-41	0-1	4-26	0-0	4-14	19.5	- 10.40
D R C Elsworth	6-42	0-2	4-22	0-0	2-18	14.3	+ 6.75
C E Brittain	6-48	2-4	2-23	0-0	2-21	12.5	+ 15.00
J Berry	5-26	3-13	0-1	0-0	2-12	19.2	+ 0.41

July

	Total W-R	Non-handicaps 2-y-o	3-y-o+	Handicaps 2-y-o	3-y-o+	Per cent	£1 Level Stake
R Akehurst	2-8	0-0	0-2	0-0	2-6	25.0	- 2.38
G Lewis	2-8	0-2	0-3	0-0	2-3	25.0	+ 11.50
J L Dunlop	1-1	0-0	1-1	0-0	0-0	100.0	+ 1.75
D R C Elsworth	1-1	0-0	1-1	0-0	0-0	100.0	+ 0.73
C A Cyzer	1-1	0-0	1-1	0-0	0-0	100.0	+ 5.50

August

	Total W-R	Non-handicaps 2-y-o	3-y-o+	Handicaps 2-y-o	3-y-o+	Per cent	£1 Level Stake
A C Stewart	2-4	0-0	2-2	0-0	0-2	50.0	- 0.95
J Berry	2-7	0-1	1-2	0-0	1-4	28.6	+ 7.91
D R C Elsworth	2-8	1-2	0-3	0-0	1-3	25.0	+ 13.00
R Akehurst	2-9	1-3	0-0	0-0	1-6	22.2	+ 0.50
P F I Cole	2-9	1-5	0-1	0-0	1-3	22.2	- 1.50

September

	Total W-R	Non-handicaps 2-y-o	3-y-o+	Handicaps 2-y-o	3-y-o+	Per cent	£1 Level Stake
H Candy	1-1	0-0	0-0	0-0	1-1	100.0	+ 5.00
J L Dunlop	1-1	0-0	0-0	1-1	0-0	100.0	+ 4.50
D R C Elsworth	1-1	0-0	0-0	0-0	1-1	100.0	+ 6.50
J Berry	1-2	0-0	1-1	0-0	0-1	50.0	- 0.50
Lord Huntingdon	1-2	0-0	1-1	0-1	0-0	50.0	+ 15.00

FOLKESTONE (Group 4)

Leading Trainers 1989-93

	Total W-R	Non-handicaps 2-y-o	3-y-o+	Handicaps 2-y-o	3-y-o+	Per cent	£1 Level Stake
G Harwood	23-68	5-12	14-36	0-0	4-20	33.8	+ 29.80
R Hannon	21-146	7-53	7-34	1-9	6-50	14.4	- 40.54
P F I Cole	17-69	7-14	4-23	1-4	5-28	24.6	+ 34.93
R Akehurst	15-86	2-11	4-22	0-2	9-51	17.4	+ 23.88
J L Dunlop	10-54	1-15	4-15	1-1	4-23	18.5	- 12.96
Mrs L Piggott	9-41	0-5	7-17	0-1	2-18	22.0	+ 4.63
N A Callaghan	9-42	2-7	2-13	3-7	2-15	21.4	- 1.88
L M Cumani	7-22	1-5	6-15	0-0	0-2	31.8	+ 5.18
J Berry	7-36	3-19	4-10	0-5	0-2	19.4	- 17.72
D A Wilson	7-66	0-4	0-8	0-0	7-54	10.6	- 20.67
W Carter	7-66	3-17	2-17	0-4	2-28	10.6	- 12.88
S Dow	7-77	1-15	1-19	0-2	5-41	9.1	+ 47.88
G Lewis	7-110	0-28	2-29	1-6	4-47	6.4	- 61.63
J Pearce	6-30	0-4	3-11	0-1	3-14	20.0	+ 0.50
M R Channon	6-39	2-14	1-12	0-1	3-12	15.4	- 0.50
P T Walwyn	6-40	1-15	4-13	0-1	1-11	15.0	- 5.20
C A Cyzer	6-44	0-3	1-18	0-0	5-23	13.6	+ 26.00
Mrs J Cecil	5-7	2-3	1-2	0-0	2-2	71.4	+ 16.83
A Turnell	5-15	1-3	0-1	0-0	4-11	33.3	+ 11.75
J H M Gosden	5-24	0-3	5-18	0-0	0-3	20.8	+ 2.11
J Akehurst	5-28	3-7	1-7	0-0	1-14	17.9	+ 28.00
G B Balding	5-30	1-3	1-3	0-1	3-23	16.7	- 6.02

Leading Jockeys

	Total W-R	Per cent	£1 Level Stake	Best Trainer	W-R	Per cent	£1 Level Stake
Pat Eddery	33-106	31.1	- 12.70	G Harwood	6-7	85.7	+ 3.13
R Cochrane	32-152	21.1	- 20.96	G Harwood	9-18	50.0	+ 17.63
T Quinn	24-149	16.1	+ 57.31	P F I Cole	11-41	26.8	+ 12.43
Paul Eddery	16-112	14.3	+ 20.05	Mrs J Cecil	3-3	100.0	+ 12.00
B Rouse	15-192	7.8	- 97.23	R Hannon	4-48	8.3	- 37.56
G Duffield	14-105	13.3	- 25.67	Sir M Prescott	4-30	13.3	- 14.25
W Newnes	14-142	9.9	- 33.37	Miss B Sanders	2-13	15.4	+ 3.00
S Whitworth	13-154	8.4	- 46.33	B R Millman	3-5	60.0	+ 14.50
W Carson	11-41	26.8	+ 3.46	J L Dunlop	3-6	50.0	+ 8.50
M Roberts	11-65	16.9	+ 3.46	A C Stewart	3-7	42.9	+ 10.38
J Reid	11-108	10.2	- 65.37	R Akehurst	2-10	20.0	- 3.25
L Piggott	9-34	26.5	+ 6.75	Mrs L Piggott	3-11	27.3	+ 1.25

How the Favourites Fared

Non-handicaps	W-R	Per cent	£1 Level Stake	Handicaps	W-R	Per cent	£1 Level Stake
2-y-o	36-102	35.3	- 14.03	2-y-o	8-18	44.4	+ 6.55
3-y-o	35-77	45.5	- 6.05	3-y-o	13-36	36.1	- 1.08
Weight-for-age	37-70	52.9	+ 22.30	All-aged	43-150	28.7	- 11.15
Totals	108-249	43.4	+ 2.22	Totals	64-204	31.4	- 5.68
All favs	172-453	38.0	- 3.46				

Leading Trainers by Month at Folkestone

March/April	Total W-R	Non-handicaps 2-y-o	Non-handicaps 3-y-o+	Handicaps 2-y-o	Handicaps 3-y-o+	Per cent	£1 Level Stake
Mrs L Piggott	5-9	0-0	3-5	0-0	2-4	55.6	+ 23.00
R Hannon	5-29	1-4	4-13	0-0	0-12	17.2	- 13.81
P F I Cole	4-14	0-0	2-8	0-0	2-6	28.6	- 1.58
P T Walwyn	3-5	0-0	3-5	0-0	0-0	60.0	+ 2.70
J Berry	3-11	1-4	2-5	0-0	0-2	27.3	- 4.08

May	Total W-R	Non-handicaps 2-y-o	Non-handicaps 3-y-o+	Handicaps 2-y-o	Handicaps 3-y-o+	Per cent	£1 Level Stake
G Harwood	4-4	0-0	3-3	0-0	1-1	100.0	+ 7.18
J Berry	2-2	1-1	1-1	0-0	0-0	100.0	+ 2.12
W A O'Gorman	2-3	2-2	0-1	0-0	0-0	66.7	+ 1.41
N A Callaghan	2-7	1-2	1-4	0-0	0-1	28.6	- 0.40
H Candy	1-1	0-0	0-0	0-0	1-1	100.0	+ 2.75

June	Total W-R	Non-handicaps 2-y-o	Non-handicaps 3-y-o+	Handicaps 2-y-o	Handicaps 3-y-o+	Per cent	£1 Level Stake
G Harwood	3-6	1-1	2-4	0-0	0-1	50.0	+ 0.24
S Dow	3-9	1-2	0-1	0-0	2-6	33.3	+ 10.38
J Pearce	2-3	0-0	0-0	0-0	2-3	66.7	+ 6.63
W G M Turner	2-4	0-2	1-1	0-0	1-1	50.0	+ 17.00
P S Felgate	1-1	0-0	0-0	0-0	1-1	100.0	+ 10.00

July	Total W-R	Non-handicaps 2-y-o	Non-handicaps 3-y-o+	Handicaps 2-y-o	Handicaps 3-y-o+	Per cent	£1 Level Stake
P F I Cole	6-16	1-2	2-4	0-0	3-10	37.5	+ 15.00
W Carter	4-11	3-6	0-0	0-0	1-5	36.4	+ 24.50
N A Callaghan	4-13	1-2	0-1	2-4	1-6	30.8	- 0.08
R Hannon	4-18	1-5	1-5	1-3	1-5	22.2	+ 3.89
B W Hills	3-4	0-0	2-2	0-0	1-2	75.0	+ 3.76

August	Total W-R	Non-handicaps 2-y-o	Non-handicaps 3-y-o+	Handicaps 2-y-o	Handicaps 3-y-o+	Per cent	£1 Level Stake
J Pearce	3-3	0-0	2-2	0-0	1-1	100.0	+ 9.88
W Carter	3-11	0-2	2-4	0-0	1-5	27.3	+ 6.63
G Harwood	3-12	0-0	2-7	0-0	1-5	25.0	+ 13.86
W Jarvis	2-3	0-0	0-0	0-0	2-3	66.7	+ 3.20
L G Cottrell	2-4	0-0	0-0	0-0	2-4	50.0	+ 5.75

September	Total W-R	Non-handicaps 2-y-o	Non-handicaps 3-y-o+	Handicaps 2-y-o	Handicaps 3-y-o+	Per cent	£1 Level Stake
G Harwood	4-14	0-3	3-8	0-0	1-3	28.6	+ 13.50
L M Cumani	3-6	1-2	2-4	0-0	0-0	50.0	+ 5.00
J L Dunlop	3-8	0-1	2-2	0-0	1-5	37.5	+ 2.30
R Akehurst	3-19	2-4	1-4	0-0	0-11	15.8	+ 30.88
Mrs J Cecil	2-3	2-2	0-1	0-0	0-0	66.7	+ 5.83

Oct/Nov	Total W-R	Non-handicaps 2-y-o	Non-handicaps 3-y-o+	Handicaps 2-y-o	Handicaps 3-y-o+	Per cent	£1 Level Stake
R Hannon	7-47	5-23	0-7	0-6	2-11	14.9	- 13.00
G Harwood	6-19	4-8	1-4	0-0	1-7	31.6	+ 3.17
P F I Cole	4-15	3-5	0-5	1-4	0-1	26.7	+ 28.75
R Akehurst	4-27	0-5	1-6	0-2	3-14	14.8	- 7.00
B Hanbury	3-5	0-1	3-3	0-0	0-1	60.0	+ 10.00

GOODWOOD (Group 1)

Leading Trainers 1989-93

	Total W-R	Non-handicaps 2-y-o	Non-handicaps 3-y-o+	Handicaps 2-y-o	Handicaps 3-y-o+	Per cent	£1 Level Stake
R Hannon	36-319	9-113	12-71	2-25	13-110	11.3	- 46.49
H R A Cecil	27-86	11-17	14-49	0-1	2-19	31.4	+ 20.34
I A Balding	23-136	5-37	8-43	2-5	8-51	16.9	+ 33.93
D R C Elsworth	23-159	8-38	4-46	0-1	11-74	14.5	- 32.81
J L Dunlop	23-181	7-72	8-42	3-11	5-56	12.7	- 66.24
M R Stoute	20-92	4-17	13-39	0-4	3-32	21.7	- 7.82
J H M Gosden	19-87	4-14	7-39	2-3	6-31	21.8	+ 33.75
L M Cumani	16-81	2-8	10-46	0-0	4-27	19.8	- 2.36
P F I Cole	14-86	4-30	5-29	0-0	5-27	16.3	- 12.10
G Lewis	14-94	3-37	4-15	2-13	5-29	14.9	+ 24.07
R Akehurst	13-93	0-7	3-14	1-5	9-67	14.0	- 4.04
B W Hills	13-95	4-23	9-39	0-4	0-29	13.7	- 29.33
G Harwood	12-148	4-27	4-53	0-6	4-62	8.1	- 84.84
Lord Huntingdon	11-45	1-7	6-17	0-2	4-19	24.4	+ 47.38
D A Wilson	11-54	0-3	0-0	0-0	11-51	20.4	+ 9.21
J Berry	11-86	5-29	0-12	4-15	2-30	12.8	- 24.91
B Hanbury	9-47	0-6	2-19	1-2	6-20	19.1	+ 3.92
J W Hills	9-71	0-11	3-18	0-0	6-42	12.7	- 10.13
R Charlton	8-36	0-9	3-8	0-1	5-18	22.2	+ 13.88
P J Makin	8-63	0-8	3-23	0-0	5-32	12.7	+ 2.18
P T Walwyn	7-76	1-15	3-27	0-2	3-32	9.2	- 11.75
G Wragg	6-31	2-3	2-21	0-0	2-7	19.4	- 0.57

Leading Jockeys

	Total W-R	Per cent	£1 Level Stake	Best Trainer	W-R	Per cent	£1 Level Stake
Pat Eddery	52-248	21.0	- 16.73	J H M Gosden	7-15	46.7	+ 15.83
W Carson	49-278	17.6	- 54.87	J L Dunlop	13-75	17.3	- 37.97
J Reid	35-206	17.0	+ 27.15	R Hannon	7-26	26.9	+ 23.73
R Cochrane	27-213	12.7	+ 1.55	I A Balding	10-29	34.5	+ 55.30
M Roberts	26-187	13.9	- 16.93	R Hannon	4-21	19.0	+ 20.79
A Munro	24-133	18.0	+ 27.56	Lord Huntingdon	4-10	40.0	+ 42.25
L Dettori	22-153	14.4	- 54.91	L M Cumani	14-45	31.1	+ 11.64
M Hills	21-110	19.1	+ 53.91	B W Hills	8-33	24.2	+ 8.08
T Quinn	19-178	10.7	- 39.12	P F I Cole	7-46	15.2	+ 5.25
D Holland	16-77	20.8	+113.38	D A Wilson	2-2	100.0	+ 7.25
B Raymond	15-93	16.1	+ 37.83	R Hannon	4-23	17.4	+ 10.50
W R Swinburn	14-125	11.2	- 65.48	M R Stoute	9-36	25.0	- 2.17

How the Favourites Fared

Non-handicaps	W-R	Per cent	£1 Level Stake	Handicaps	W-R	Per cent	£1 Level Stake
2-y-o	70-129	54.3	+ 32.04	2-y-o	8-29	27.6	+ 0.50
3-y-o	34-95	35.8	- 7.71	3-y-o	17-70	24.3	- 17.57
Weight-for-age	24-80	30.0	- 20.97	All-aged	41-170	24.1	- 23.23
Totals	128-304	42.1	+ 3.36	Totals	66-269	24.5	- 40.30
All favs	194-573	33.9	- 36.94				

Leading Trainers by Month at Goodwood

May

	Total W-R	Non-handicaps 2-y-o	Non-handicaps 3-y-o+	Handicaps 2-y-o	Handicaps 3-y-o+	Per cent	£1 Level Stake
R Hannon	11-62	1-19	5-22	0-0	5-21	17.7	+ 7.04
J H M Gosden	6-15	0-1	2-10	0-0	4-4	40.0	+ 15.50
I A Balding	5-22	1-1	3-17	0-0	1-4	22.7	+ 35.50
H R A Cecil	4-10	0-0	4-9	0-0	0-1	40.0	+ 3.00
M R Stoute	4-14	0-0	3-9	0-0	1-5	28.6	+ 9.25

June

	Total W-R	Non-handicaps 2-y-o	Non-handicaps 3-y-o+	Handicaps 2-y-o	Handicaps 3-y-o+	Per cent	£1 Level Stake
D A Wilson	7-16	0-1	0-0	0-0	7-15	43.8	+ 20.46
J L Dunlop	7-40	3-13	2-9	0-0	2-18	17.5	- 18.06
D R C Elsworth	5-25	0-3	2-7	0-0	3-15	20.0	+ 3.25
R Hannon	5-66	3-26	1-19	0-0	1-21	7.6	- 48.95
J Berry	4-10	4-7	0-0	0-0	0-3	40.0	+ 1.59

July

	Total W-R	Non-handicaps 2-y-o	Non-handicaps 3-y-o+	Handicaps 2-y-o	Handicaps 3-y-o+	Per cent	£1 Level Stake
R Hannon	10-75	2-23	2-8	2-8	4-36	13.3	+ 21.94
H R A Cecil	8-31	5-6	2-14	0-0	1-11	25.8	- 0.75
M R Stoute	6-30	1-6	4-11	0-0	1-13	20.0	- 10.25
D R C Elsworth	5-24	2-6	0-2	0-0	3-16	20.8	+ 17.91
L M Cumani	5-30	0-1	3-15	0-0	2-14	16.7	+ 9.33

August

	Total W-R	Non-handicaps 2-y-o	Non-handicaps 3-y-o+	Handicaps 2-y-o	Handicaps 3-y-o+	Per cent	£1 Level Stake
I A Balding	7-27	0-5	2-8	2-2	3-12	25.9	+ 4.00
H R A Cecil	7-27	3-6	4-17	0-0	0-4	25.9	- 9.11
J L Dunlop	6-34	2-16	2-6	1-1	1-11	17.6	- 7.93
P F I Cole	5-18	0-6	4-9	0-0	1-3	27.8	+ 11.63
D R C Elsworth	5-36	2-10	1-10	0-0	2-16	13.9	- 19.38

September

	Total W-R	Non-handicaps 2-y-o	Non-handicaps 3-y-o+	Handicaps 2-y-o	Handicaps 3-y-o+	Per cent	£1 Level Stake
R Akehurst	4-9	0-0	0-2	1-1	3-6	44.4	+ 18.33
J H M Gosden	4-15	1-4	2-6	1-1	0-4	26.7	+ 23.25
B W Hills	3-4	1-1	2-2	0-0	0-1	75.0	+ 7.83
R Charlton	3-7	0-2	2-3	0-0	1-2	42.9	+ 4.38
L M Cumani	3-9	2-3	1-4	0-0	0-2	33.3	- 3.01

Oct/Nov

	Total W-R	Non-handicaps 2-y-o	Non-handicaps 3-y-o+	Handicaps 2-y-o	Handicaps 3-y-o+	Per cent	£1 Level Stake
J L Dunlop	4-23	0-8	2-7	2-5	0-3	17.4	+ 16.50
R Hannon	4-33	2-14	1-6	0-5	1-8	12.1	+ 11.25
H R A Cecil	3-5	0-0	2-3	0-1	1-1	60.0	+ 22.50
H Thomson Jones	3-8	1-2	1-3	0-0	1-3	37.5	+ 20.17
Lord Huntingdon	3-12	0-1	2-4	0-1	1-6	25.0	+ 15.25

HAMILTON (Group 3)

Leading Trainers 1989-93

	Total W-R	Non-handicaps 2-y-o	3-y-o+	Handicaps 2-y-o	3-y-o+	Per cent	£1 Level Stake
J Berry	56-287	24-105	16-73	5-22	11-87	19.5	- 55.72
Mrs M Reveley	25-104	4-18	8-31	0-2	13-53	24.0	- 11.85
M S Johnston	21-143	5-30	5-36	0-4	11-73	14.7	- 1.65
Mrs J Ramsden	13-61	1-10	2-13	0-2	10-36	21.3	+ 22.28
S G Norton	13-73	3-16	5-21	0-2	5-34	17.8	+ 8.88
M Bell	12-32	6-10	4-8	0-3	2-11	37.5	+ 1.21
B Hanbury	12-35	2-4	6-17	1-1	3-13	34.3	+ 22.68
M H Tompkins	12-63	4-16	6-13	0-7	2-27	19.0	- 2.24
M H Easterby	12-69	6-17	2-12	1-10	3-30	17.4	+ 11.59
P C Haslam	12-78	1-12	5-16	0-4	6-46	15.4	+ 3.00
C Tinkler	12-90	3-28	3-21	1-8	5-33	13.3	- 37.05
Miss L A Perratt	12-100	0-20	3-18	1-7	8-55	12.0	+ 23.50
Sir M Prescott	11-54	3-9	3-16	0-4	5-25	20.4	- 23.85
M P Naughton	9-90	0-1	2-32	0-0	7-57	10.0	- 18.00
D Moffatt	7-64	2-11	2-12	0-2	3-39	10.9	+ 23.50
Denys Smith	7-81	0-10	6-26	0-2	1-43	8.6	- 41.75
J Etherington	6-28	2-7	3-10	0-4	1-7	21.4	+ 0.15
M A Jarvis	6-31	0-3	5-13	0-2	1-13	19.4	+ 4.62
F H Lee	6-49	0-4	1-5	0-0	5-40	12.2	+ 3.50
T D Barron	6-66	2-11	0-11	2-5	2-39	9.1	- 37.19
P J Makin	5-11	0-2	4-6	0-0	1-3	45.5	+ 9.08
R Hannon	5-13	1-2	2-5	1-3	1-3	38.5	+ 8.18

Leading Jockeys

	Total W-R	Per cent	£1 Level Stake	Best Trainer	W-R	Per cent	£1 Level Stake
K Darley	49-270	18.1	- 80.47	Mrs M Reveley	13-35	37.1	+ 10.94
J Carroll	47-239	19.7	- 61.05	J Berry	39-163	23.9	- 20.53
G Duffield	22-183	12.0	-108.57	Sir M Prescott	8-41	19.5	- 19.28
K Fallon	22-205	10.7	- 47.00	M P Naughton	5-35	14.3	- 7.50
J Lowe	20-228	8.8	- 51.75	M J Bolton	4-12	33.3	+ 12.50
J Fanning	17-139	12.2	- 15.07	Miss L A Perrat	3-30	10.0	+ 11.00
J Fortune	16-135	11.9	+ 14.48	Capt J Wilson	3-6	50.0	+ 22.00
B Raymond	14-64	21.9	+ 11.88	B Hanbury	8-19	42.1	+ 12.81
M Birch	14-148	9.5	- 78.42	C Tinkler	8-48	16.7	- 11.25
N Connorton	11-104	10.6	+ 0.15	M J Camacho	5-23	21.7	+ 40.50
L Charnock	10-165	6.1	- 53.24	J Berry	3-10	30.0	+ 24.88
M Hills	9-23	39.1	+ 22.21	M Bell	6-14	42.9	+ 0.71

How the Favourites Fared

Non-handicaps	W-R	Per cent	£1 Level Stake	Handicaps	W-R	Per cent	£1 Level Stake
2-y-o	42-105	40.0	- 18.69	2-y-o	6-21	28.6	+ 0.46
3-y-o	42-89	47.2	- 4.58	3-y-o	21-54	38.9	+ 4.22
Weight-for-age	30-70	42.9	- 0.30	All-aged	56-191	29.3	- 10.66
Totals	114-264	43.2	- 23.57	Totals	83-266	31.2	- 5.98
All favs	197-530	37.2	- 29.55				

Leading Trainers by Month at Hamilton

March/April

	Total W-R	Non-handicaps 2-y-o	3-y-o+	Handicaps 2-y-o	3-y-o+	Per cent	£1 Level Stake
J Berry	12-45	3-13	5-12	0-0	4-20	26.7	+ 21.52
E J Alston	4-10	1-2	0-3	0-0	3-5	40.0	+ 26.50
D Moffatt	4-16	2-5	2-3	0-0	0-8	25.0	+ 33.00
S G Norton	4-18	0-2	1-7	0-0	3-9	22.2	+ 18.00
Mrs J Ramsden	4-18	0-0	0-5	0-0	4-13	22.2	- 2.38

May

	Total W-R	Non-handicaps 2-y-o	3-y-o+	Handicaps 2-y-o	3-y-o+	Per cent	£1 Level Stake
J Berry	13-54	9-23	2-14	0-0	2-17	24.1	- 1.61
Miss L A Perratt	5-17	0-2	1-1	0-0	4-14	29.4	+ 25.00
M H Tompkins	5-20	1-6	4-6	0-0	0-8	25.0	+ 13.13
M S Johnston	4-32	0-6	3-13	0-0	1-13	12.5	- 6.00
P J Makin	3-3	0-0	3-3	0-0	0-0	100.0	+ 6.35

June

	Total W-R	Non-handicaps 2-y-o	3-y-o+	Handicaps 2-y-o	3-y-o+	Per cent	£1 Level Stake
M S Johnston	7-26	3-6	1-5	0-0	3-15	26.9	+ 3.13
J Berry	7-47	3-18	3-13	0-0	1-16	14.9	- 21.43
S G Norton	5-14	1-4	3-3	0-0	1-7	35.7	+ 14.25
Sir M Prescott	3-10	0-1	1-2	0-0	2-7	30.0	- 4.23
M H Easterby	3-11	2-5	0-3	0-0	1-3	27.3	- 3.07

July

	Total W-R	Non-handicaps 2-y-o	3-y-o+	Handicaps 2-y-o	3-y-o+	Per cent	£1 Level Stake
J Berry	16-66	7-32	2-13	3-7	4-14	24.2	- 15.55
Mrs M Reveley	15-41	2-6	6-15	0-1	7-19	36.6	+ 10.15
P C Haslam	7-13	1-1	2-4	0-0	4-8	53.8	+ 20.75
C Tinkler	7-21	2-8	2-5	0-1	3-7	33.3	+ 6.70
M H Easterby	4-16	2-4	0-2	0-3	2-7	25.0	+ 2.75

August

	Total W-R	Non-handicaps 2-y-o	3-y-o+	Handicaps 2-y-o	3-y-o+	Per cent	£1 Level Stake
J Berry	4-17	1-3	3-7	0-0	0-7	23.5	- 9.91
Mrs M Reveley	3-12	1-4	0-2	0-0	2-6	25.0	+ 3.00
N Tinkler	2-4	0-0	2-2	0-0	0-2	50.0	+ 0.65
P C Haslam	2-8	0-0	1-1	0-0	1-7	25.0	+ 0.25
M S Johnston	2-8	0-2	0-0	0-0	2-6	25.0	+ 20.00

September

	Total W-R	Non-handicaps 2-y-o	3-y-o+	Handicaps 2-y-o	3-y-o+	Per cent	£1 Level Stake
B Hanbury	8-16	2-4	4-7	1-1	1-4	50.0	+ 19.21
R Hannon	3-4	1-2	1-1	1-1	0-0	75.0	+ 10.38
Sir M Prescott	3-12	2-2	1-4	0-2	0-4	25.0	- 2.75
C Tinkler	3-19	0-5	1-2	1-5	1-7	15.8	- 0.50
M Bell	2-4	1-1	1-1	0-1	0-1	50.0	+ 0.25

Oct/Nov

	Total W-R	Non-handicaps 2-y-o	3-y-o+	Handicaps 2-y-o	3-y-o+	Per cent	£1 Level Stake
R Akehurst	2-4	0-0	0-0	0-0	2-4	50.0	+ 11.00
R Earnshaw	2-5	1-2	0-0	1-1	0-2	40.0	+ 29.00
M J Camacho	2-6	0-1	0-0	0-1	2-4	33.3	+ 6.50
Mrs J Ramsden	2-6	0-1	1-1	0-1	1-3	33.3	+ 6.50
J Berry	2-17	1-6	1-3	0-4	0-4	11.8	- 7.75

HAYDOCK (Group 1)

Leading Trainers 1989-93

	Total W-R	Non-handicaps 2-y-o	3-y-o+	Handicaps 2-y-o	3-y-o+	Per cent	£1 Level Stake
J H M Gosden	24-76	4-10	14-45	0-0	6-21	31.6	+ 52.49
H R A Cecil	21-58	5-9	12-34	0-0	4-15	36.2	+ 21.05
J L Dunlop	18-88	5-26	6-22	0-0	7-40	20.5	+ 9.96
J Berry	18-216	6-82	5-52	3-30	4-52	8.3	-109.27
R Hollinshead	16-199	3-54	4-44	2-12	7-89	8.0	- 19.53
L M Cumani	14-76	3-10	6-32	0-0	5-34	18.4	+ 3.26
M R Stoute	14-82	2-10	9-42	0-2	3-28	17.1	- 36.64
H Thomson Jones	13-61	6-16	3-21	0-1	4-23	21.3	+ 28.74
R Hannon	13-75	8-22	1-20	1-4	3-29	17.3	+ 1.68
B W Hills	13-82	4-18	8-31	0-1	1-32	15.9	- 33.55
F H Lee	13-141	3-29	2-23	1-5	7-84	9.2	- 38.50
M H Easterby	13-147	7-38	1-14	0-11	5-84	8.8	- 68.75
R Boss	12-37	2-14	3-11	1-1	6-11	32.4	+ 30.25
M H Tompkins	12-87	2-11	2-26	2-11	6-39	13.8	- 10.15
J W Watts	11-78	1-9	1-15	0-1	9-53	14.1	- 12.18
Mrs J Ramsden	10-104	2-17	2-7	1-7	5-73	9.6	- 53.75
B A McMahon	10-138	2-24	1-40	1-1	6-73	7.2	- 37.17
R Charlton	8-34	2-4	3-13	0-0	3-17	23.5	- 5.24
P F I Cole	8-49	2-14	4-18	1-1	1-16	16.3	+ 5.91
B Hanbury	8-65	2-16	4-27	0-0	2-22	12.3	- 4.00
G Wragg	7-18	1-1	4-14	0-0	2-3	38.9	+ 18.05
M J Camacho	7-36	0-1	2-10	1-3	4-22	19.4	+ 48.50

Leading Jockeys

	Total W-R	Per cent	£1 Level Stake	Best Trainer	W-R	Per cent	£1 Level Stake
Pat Eddery	35-132	26.5	+ 7.44	B W Hills	5-14	35.7	+ 5.54
W Ryan	25-143	17.5	+ 5.10	H R A Cecil	12-30	40.0	+ 16.84
L Dettori	22-110	20.0	+ 6.76	L M Cumani	6-29	20.7	+ 3.32
M Roberts	21-116	18.1	- 10.51	A C Stewart	4-17	23.5	- 4.90
J Carroll	19-188	10.1	- 31.34	J Berry	11-126	8.7	- 67.25
J Reid	18-79	22.8	+ 18.42	J L Dunlop	4-7	57.1	+ 13.75
M Hills	15-97	15.5	- 11.14	B W Hills	6-28	21.4	- 11.92
W Carson	15-109	13.8	- 49.24	J L Dunlop	3-23	13.0	- 12.50
R Hills	15-119	12.6	- 28.56	H Thomson Jones	9-48	18.8	- 10.26
B Raymond	15-130	11.5	- 51.13	B Hanbury	3-19	15.8	- 6.00
M Birch	15-139	10.8	- 38.27	M H Easterby	10-71	14.1	- 20.25
Paul Eddery	11-95	11.6	- 44.42	G Lewis	2-5	40.0	+ 6.00

How the Favourites Fared

Non-handicaps	W-R	Per cent	£1 Level Stake	Handicaps	W-R	Per cent	£1 Level Stake
2-y-o	48-115	41.7	- 7.33	2-y-o	2-23	8.7	- 16.75
3-y-o	40-98	40.8	- 9.38	3-y-o	10-55	18.2	- 22.74
Weight-for-age	27-73	37.0	- 10.29	All-aged	46-195	23.6	- 45.26
Totals	115-286	40.2	- 27.00	Totals	58-273	21.2	- 84.75
All favs	173-559	30.9	-111.75				

Leading Trainers by Month at Haydock

March/April

	Total W-R	Non-handicaps 2-y-o	Non-handicaps 3-y-o+	Handicaps 2-y-o	Handicaps 3-y-o+	Per cent	£1 Level Stake
M H Easterby	3-12	3-4	0-3	0-0	0-5	25.0	+ 2.25
R Charlton	2-2	0-0	2-2	0-0	0-0	100.0	+ 1.91
T D Barron	2-3	0-0	2-3	0-0	0-0	66.7	+ 11.50
R Hannon	2-6	1-1	0-3	0-0	1-2	33.3	+ 5.00
J Berry	2-16	0-5	1-9	0-0	1-2	12.5	- 2.00

May

	Total W-R	Non-handicaps 2-y-o	Non-handicaps 3-y-o+	Handicaps 2-y-o	Handicaps 3-y-o+	Per cent	£1 Level Stake
M R Stoute	8-20	0-0	6-13	0-0	2-7	40.0	+ 4.16
P F I Cole	5-12	2-2	2-7	0-0	1-3	41.7	+ 15.91
B W Hills	4-11	1-1	3-7	0-0	0-3	36.4	+ 3.48
H Thomson Jones	4-13	3-4	1-6	0-0	0-3	30.8	- 0.26
G Wragg	3-5	0-0	2-4	0-0	1-1	60.0	+ 3.75

June

	Total W-R	Non-handicaps 2-y-o	Non-handicaps 3-y-o+	Handicaps 2-y-o	Handicaps 3-y-o+	Per cent	£1 Level Stake
B W Hills	4-10	0-1	3-4	0-0	1-5	40.0	+ 4.25
R Hollinshead	4-20	0-2	1-4	0-0	3-14	20.0	+ 29.00
B Hanbury	3-7	0-1	2-3	0-0	1-3	42.9	+ 34.00
F Jordan	2-2	0-0	0-0	0-0	2-2	100.0	+ 17.00
M Bell	2-3	1-1	0-0	0-0	1-2	66.7	+ 35.00

July

	Total W-R	Non-handicaps 2-y-o	Non-handicaps 3-y-o+	Handicaps 2-y-o	Handicaps 3-y-o+	Per cent	£1 Level Stake
H R A Cecil	6-12	1-1	3-8	0-0	2-3	50.0	+ 20.79
J H M Gosden	5-12	0-0	5-10	0-0	0-2	41.7	+ 7.91
J L Dunlop	4-10	0-0	2-5	0-0	2-5	40.0	+ 8.00
M H Easterby	4-18	3-9	0-2	0-0	1-7	22.2	- 3.50
M P Naughton	3-9	0-0	0-1	0-0	3-8	33.3	+ 7.50

August

	Total W-R	Non-handicaps 2-y-o	Non-handicaps 3-y-o+	Handicaps 2-y-o	Handicaps 3-y-o+	Per cent	£1 Level Stake
F H Lee	6-32	1-8	0-2	1-2	4-20	18.8	+ 10.00
J H M Gosden	5-16	2-2	2-10	0-0	1-4	31.3	+ 2.26
J Berry	5-34	2-13	2-7	0-6	1-8	14.7	- 17.58
H R A Cecil	4-7	1-1	3-5	0-0	0-1	57.1	- 0.91
J W Watts	4-9	0-0	1-3	0-0	3-6	44.4	+ 18.19

September

	Total W-R	Non-handicaps 2-y-o	Non-handicaps 3-y-o+	Handicaps 2-y-o	Handicaps 3-y-o+	Per cent	£1 Level Stake
J H M Gosden	10-29	2-4	5-18	0-0	3-7	34.5	+ 42.00
H R A Cecil	6-17	2-5	3-6	0-0	1-6	35.3	+ 11.30
H Thomson Jones	5-13	1-2	1-3	0-1	3-7	38.5	+ 48.00
R Charlton	5-15	2-3	1-7	0-0	2-5	33.3	+ 6.10
L M Cumani	5-22	1-3	2-8	0-0	2-11	22.7	- 0.81

Oct/Nov

	Total W-R	Non-handicaps 2-y-o	Non-handicaps 3-y-o+	Handicaps 2-y-o	Handicaps 3-y-o+	Per cent	£1 Level Stake
L M Cumani	3-9	1-3	0-1	0-0	2-5	33.3	+ 9.90
C E Brittain	3-12	1-5	0-3	0-2	2-2	25.0	+ 22.00
J L Dunlop	3-15	2-10	1-1	0-0	0-4	20.0	+ 5.25
H R A Cecil	2-3	1-1	0-0	0-0	1-2	66.7	+ 1.75
B Hanbury	2-7	2-4	0-1	0-0	0-2	28.6	- 1.00

KEMPTON (Group 1)

Leading Trainers 1989-93

	Total W-R	Non-handicaps 2-y-o	3-y-o+	Handicaps 2-y-o	3-y-o+	Per cent	£1 Level Stake
R Hannon	28-267	13-80	4-63	1-13	10-111	10.5	- 46.53
M R Stoute	16-84	4-19	6-46	2-2	4-17	19.0	- 17.63
J H M Gosden	15-92	1-5	11-66	0-1	3-20	16.3	- 23.63
J L Dunlop	14-120	4-30	8-50	0-1	2-39	11.7	- 17.27
P T Walwyn	13-80	1-13	6-34	0-0	6-33	16.3	+ 22.24
C E Brittain	13-122	0-15	5-51	1-4	7-52	10.7	- 11.29
D R C Elsworth	13-124	3-21	7-59	0-0	3-44	10.5	- 15.76
B W Hills	11-77	2-23	4-37	0-0	5-17	14.3	+ 23.03
I A Balding	11-112	2-21	5-46	0-2	4-43	9.8	- 7.00
R Charlton	10-50	3-8	7-26	0-0	0-16	20.0	+ 15.65
G Harwood	10-83	2-11	5-33	1-3	2-36	12.0	- 30.16
B Hanbury	9-47	1-6	6-20	0-1	2-20	19.1	+ 24.72
A A Scott	9-48	1-6	2-18	0-2	6-22	18.8	+ 9.08
M J Ryan	9-62	0-2	4-13	0-0	5-47	14.5	+ 31.00
Lord Huntingdon	9-71	1-8	4-27	0-2	4-34	12.7	- 5.38
G Lewis	9-95	3-26	1-17	0-5	5-47	9.5	- 30.63
H R A Cecil	8-42	0-2	8-32	0-0	0-8	19.0	- 4.01
L M Cumani	8-56	1-6	5-35	0-0	2-15	14.3	- 16.38
H Candy	8-68	0-4	2-30	0-1	6-33	11.8	+ 88.00
G B Balding	8-72	1-7	0-14	0-2	7-49	11.1	+ 43.00
J R Fanshawe	7-42	1-8	4-20	0-2	2-12	16.7	+ 3.33
R F J Houghton	7-50	1-12	5-20	0-3	1-15	14.0	+ 25.50

Leading Jockeys

	Total W-R	Per cent	£1 Level Stake	Best Trainer	W-R	Per cent	£1 Level Stake
Pat Eddery	45-225	20.0	- 0.28	R Charlton	7-30	23.3	+ 9.15
W Carson	29-217	13.4	- 43.01	R Hannon	4-20	20.0	- 0.25
R Cochrane	24-209	11.5	- 42.20	L M Cumani	5-15	33.3	+ 14.63
M Roberts	22-187	11.8	- 18.29	C E Brittain	5-54	9.3	- 3.00
A Munro	21-133	15.8	+ 44.51	C E Brittain	2-2	100.0	+ 15.00
W R Swinburn	18-167	10.8	- 48.24	M R Stoute	7-48	14.6	- 12.20
J Reid	16-184	8.7	- 38.45	R Hannon	4-13	30.8	+ 9.30
T Quinn	15-160	9.4	- 74.74	P F I Cole	4-57	7.0	- 43.80
L Dettori	15-171	8.8	- 43.00	L M Cumani	3-30	10.0	- 20.00
J Williams	14-172	8.1	- 27.40	D R C Elsworth	7-45	15.6	+ 19.50
Paul Eddery	12-122	9.8	+ 16.80	G Lewis	3-34	8.8	+ 3.50
B Raymond	11-114	9.6	- 55.29	R Hannon	3-11	27.3	+ 1.58

How the Favourites Fared

Non-handicaps	W-R	Per cent	£1 Level Stake	Handicaps	W-R	Per cent	£1 Level Stake
2-y-o	28-73	38.4	- 7.26	2-y-o	5-12	41.7	+ 10.75
3-y-o	37-98	37.8	- 6.71	3-y-o	14-53	26.4	- 2.19
Weight-for-age	16-50	32.0	- 6.85	All-aged	33-160	20.6	- 36.95
Totals	81-221	36.7	- 20.82	Totals	52-225	23.1	- 28.39
All favs	133-446	29.8	- 49.21				

Leading Trainers by Month at Kempton

March/April

	Total W-R	Non-handicaps 2-y-o	3-y-o+	Handicaps 2-y-o	3-y-o+	Per cent	£1 Level Stake
R Hannon	9-75	5-21	3-19	0-0	1-35	12.0	- 22.58
M J Ryan	5-17	0-1	2-5	0-0	3-11	29.4	+ 36.50
P T Walwyn	5-20	0-0	2-5	0-0	3-15	25.0	+ 30.36
J L Dunlop	5-31	0-0	5-20	0-0	0-11	16.1	+ 16.00
G Lewis	5-38	1-11	0-6	0-0	4-21	13.2	- 5.50

May

	Total W-R	Non-handicaps 2-y-o	3-y-o+	Handicaps 2-y-o	3-y-o+	Per cent	£1 Level Stake
Mrs J Cecil	4-8	0-0	3-7	0-0	1-1	50.0	+ 8.55
M R Stoute	4-23	0-0	3-18	0-0	1-5	17.4	- 1.06
I A Balding	4-25	0-0	3-14	0-0	1-11	16.0	+ 9.00
P F I Cole	4-26	2-3	0-13	0-0	2-10	15.4	- 10.05
M A Jarvis	3-11	1-3	1-5	0-0	1-3	27.3	+ 10.13

June

	Total W-R	Non-handicaps 2-y-o	3-y-o+	Handicaps 2-y-o	3-y-o+	Per cent	£1 Level Stake
R Hannon	4-23	2-6	0-8	0-0	2-9	17.4	+ 6.50
D R C Elsworth	4-25	0-1	3-15	0-0	1-9	16.0	+ 8.83
Lord Huntingdon	3-9	0-0	1-6	0-0	2-3	33.3	+ 6.25
A A Scott	3-10	1-1	1-7	0-0	1-2	30.0	+ 3.75
P T Walwyn	3-13	0-0	3-10	0-0	0-3	23.1	+ 7.88

July

	Total W-R	Non-handicaps 2-y-o	3-y-o+	Handicaps 2-y-o	3-y-o+	Per cent	£1 Level Stake
M R Stoute	3-10	0-1	1-6	0-0	2-3	30.0	+ 1.00
P T Walwyn	3-10	1-2	0-5	0-0	2-3	30.0	+ 8.00
G Harwood	3-11	0-1	2-4	0-0	1-6	27.3	+ 3.24
J H M Gosden	3-13	0-1	1-8	0-0	2-4	23.1	+ 4.12
I A Balding	3-15	1-5	0-3	0-0	2-7	20.0	+ 4.50

August

	Total W-R	Non-handicaps 2-y-o	3-y-o+	Handicaps 2-y-o	3-y-o+	Per cent	£1 Level Stake
R Hannon	4-25	2-11	0-1	1-6	1-7	16.0	- 2.00
C E Brittain	3-7	0-0	1-1	1-2	1-4	42.9	+ 16.00
H Thomson Jones	2-4	2-3	0-0	0-0	0-1	50.0	+ 6.75
W R Hern	2-5	0-3	0-0	0-0	2-2	40.0	+ 15.00
B W Hills	2-10	1-7	1-1	0-0	0-2	20.0	- 4.30

September

	Total W-R	Non-handicaps 2-y-o	3-y-o+	Handicaps 2-y-o	3-y-o+	Per cent	£1 Level Stake
M R Stoute	7-26	4-15	1-7	2-2	0-2	26.9	- 0.95
G Wragg	5-13	0-2	3-5	0-0	2-6	38.5	+ 17.50
L M Cumani	5-25	1-6	3-11	0-0	1-8	20.0	+ 2.13
R Hannon	5-61	2-26	0-8	0-7	3-20	8.2	+ 16.00
G Harwood	4-20	1-4	1-5	1-1	1-10	20.0	- 1.97

LEICESTER (Group 3)

Leading Trainers 1989-93

	Total W-R	Non-handicaps 2-y-o	Non-handicaps 3-y-o+	Handicaps 2-y-o	Handicaps 3-y-o+	Per cent	£1 Level Stake
H R A Cecil	23-98	9-36	13-53	0-0	1-9	23.5	- 29.58
M R Stoute	22-92	11-49	10-34	0-1	1-8	23.9	- 6.35
J H M Gosden	20-74	9-30	8-32	0-1	3-11	27.0	- 7.26
R Hannon	19-160	8-80	6-28	2-13	3-39	11.9	- 43.25
J L Dunlop	15-101	6-37	5-35	1-4	3-25	14.9	- 29.77
G Wragg	12-57	3-19	8-25	0-1	1-12	21.1	+ 17.17
J Berry	11-75	5-42	4-13	2-12	0-8	14.7	- 21.89
P F I Cole	10-94	4-30	4-42	1-6	1-16	10.6	- 39.13
G Harwood	9-50	2-16	4-22	0-1	3-11	18.0	+ 2.48
B Hanbury	9-66	4-28	3-26	0-0	2-12	13.6	- 16.01
M J Ryan	9-88	0-21	1-15	0-2	8-50	10.2	- 15.25
M A Jarvis	8-57	0-14	5-23	1-3	2-17	14.0	- 4.38
M Bell	8-66	4-26	2-14	0-4	2-22	12.1	- 0.25
C E Brittain	8-78	2-28	5-31	1-3	0-16	10.3	- 29.71
L M Cumani	7-43	4-10	3-29	0-0	0-4	16.3	- 20.34
R F J Houghton	7-46	1-15	6-17	0-3	0-11	15.2	- 24.33
G Lewis	7-47	4-17	2-8	0-6	1-16	14.9	+ 10.48
P T Walwyn	7-48	1-18	4-18	0-1	2-11	14.6	+ 35.25
W R Hern	7-51	1-14	4-22	0-0	2-15	13.7	- 23.20
H Thomson Jones	6-21	4-6	1-6	0-0	1-9	28.6	+ 2.76
Sir M Prescott	6-43	3-17	1-13	1-1	1-12	14.0	- 0.83
B W Hills	6-73	4-42	0-17	0-0	2-14	8.2	- 42.76

Leading Jockeys

	Total W-R	Per cent	£1 Level Stake	Best Trainer	W-R	Per cent	£1 Level Stake
W Carson	32-179	17.9	- 42.04	J H M Gosden	5-10	50.0	- 0.97
L Dettori	27-163	16.6	+ 9.57	L M Cumani	3-22	13.6	- 11.37
W R Swinburn	24-132	18.2	- 42.92	M R Stoute	13-40	32.5	- 8.47
Pat Eddery	23-133	17.3	- 27.88	J H M Gosden	3-6	50.0	+ 7.33
M Roberts	23-182	12.6	- 65.11	C E Brittain	6-38	15.8	- 3.21
W Ryan	21-174	12.1	- 39.75	H R A Cecil	10-45	22.2	- 11.96
T Quinn	20-152	13.2	- 3.21	P F I Cole	9-53	17.0	+ 0.38
R Cochrane	19-154	12.3	- 53.72	G Harwood	5-20	25.0	+ 2.48
Paul Eddery	18-131	13.7	+ 3.05	Mrs J Cecil	3-11	27.3	+ 3.13
B Raymond	15-135	11.1	- 25.87	B Hanbury	4-28	14.3	- 6.00
A Munro	13-136	9.6	- 49.79	Mrs J Ramsden	2-4	50.0	+ 7.00
R Hills	12-89	13.5	- 21.24	H Thomson Jones	5-16	31.3	+ 5.66

How the Favourites Fared

Non-handicaps	W-R	Per cent	£1 Level Stake	Handicaps	W-R	Per cent	£1 Level Stake
2-y-o	68-152	44.7	+ 13.04	2-y-o	8-26	30.8	- 1.58
3-y-o	60-145	41.4	- 13.51	3-y-o	13-51	25.5	- 4.57
Weight-for-age	13-38	34.2	- 7.60	All-aged	19-109	17.4	- 32.67
Totals	141-335	42.1	- 8.07	Totals	40-186	21.5	- 38.82
All favs	181-521	34.7	- 46.89				

Leading Trainers by Month at Leicester

March/April

	Total W-R	Non-handicaps 2-y-o	3-y-o+	Handicaps 2-y-o	3-y-o+	Per cent	£1 Level Stake
M R Stoute	6-17	0-0	6-17	0-0	0-0	35.3	+ 20.03
H R A Cecil	4-15	0-0	3-13	0-0	1-2	26.7	+ 0.81
J Berry	4-18	3-13	1-3	0-0	0-2	22.2	- 5.10
B Hanbury	3-9	0-0	2-5	0-0	1-4	33.3	- 0.88
M Bell	3-19	2-7	0-7	0-0	1-5	15.8	- 2.50

May

	Total W-R	Non-handicaps 2-y-o	3-y-o+	Handicaps 2-y-o	3-y-o+	Per cent	£1 Level Stake
M R Stoute	6-15	2-4	3-8	0-0	1-3	40.0	+ 3.69
J Berry	4-13	2-8	2-5	0-0	0-0	30.8	+ 16.30
H Thomson Jones	3-7	2-2	1-3	0-0	0-2	42.9	- 1.09
P D Cundell	2-3	0-0	0-0	0-0	2-3	66.7	+ 16.00
C E Brittain	2-4	1-1	1-3	0-0	0-0	50.0	+ 5.83

June

	Total W-R	Non-handicaps 2-y-o	3-y-o+	Handicaps 2-y-o	3-y-o+	Per cent	£1 Level Stake
J H M Gosden	6-13	2-4	4-7	0-0	0-2	46.2	+ 1.17
L M Cumani	2-4	1-2	1-2	0-0	0-0	50.0	+ 4.30
N A Callaghan	2-5	1-2	1-2	0-0	0-1	40.0	+ 0.35
R Charlton	2-5	0-2	1-1	0-0	1-2	40.0	+ 1.00
Mrs L Piggott	2-7	0-1	0-1	0-0	2-5	28.6	+ 9.50

July

	Total W-R	Non-handicaps 2-y-o	3-y-o+	Handicaps 2-y-o	3-y-o+	Per cent	£1 Level Stake
H R A Cecil	7-13	1-2	6-10	0-0	0-1	53.8	- 0.14
M J Ryan	4-21	0-8	1-3	0-0	3-10	19.0	+ 6.25
G Wragg	3-4	1-1	2-3	0-0	0-0	75.0	+ 30.00
B A McMahon	3-16	2-3	1-6	0-2	0-5	18.8	+ 5.50
G Lewis	2-4	1-1	1-1	0-0	0-2	50.0	+ 4.08

August

	Total W-R	Non-handicaps 2-y-o	3-y-o+	Handicaps 2-y-o	3-y-o+	Per cent	£1 Level Stake
R Hannon	5-11	1-3	1-2	1-2	2-4	45.5	+ 12.25
W R Hern	3-4	0-1	2-2	0-0	1-1	75.0	+ 8.50
M H Tompkins	2-4	1-2	1-1	0-0	0-1	50.0	- 0.10
Mrs L Piggott	2-4	0-0	2-3	0-1	0-0	50.0	+ 20.00
M J Ryan	2-6	0-0	0-0	0-1	2-5	33.3	+ 17.50

September

	Total W-R	Non-handicaps 2-y-o	3-y-o+	Handicaps 2-y-o	3-y-o+	Per cent	£1 Level Stake
J H M Gosden	5-13	3-6	0-3	0-0	2-4	38.5	+ 8.70
J L Dunlop	5-19	4-15	0-1	0-1	1-2	26.3	- 5.83
A Hide	3-8	1-3	1-2	0-0	1-3	37.5	+ 26.50
H R A Cecil	3-11	2-7	1-3	0-0	0-1	27.3	+ 2.25
R M Whitaker	2-7	0-0	2-6	0-1	0-0	28.6	+ 17.00

Oct/Nov

	Total W-R	Non-handicaps 2-y-o	3-y-o+	Handicaps 2-y-o	3-y-o+	Per cent	£1 Level Stake
M R Stoute	7-36	7-35	0-1	0-0	0-0	19.4	- 22.57
H R A Cecil	7-41	6-26	1-13	0-0	0-2	17.1	- 21.80
R Hannon	7-46	4-31	1-2	1-6	1-7	15.2	- 2.75
G Wragg	5-22	2-13	2-4	0-0	1-5	22.7	+ 1.80
G Harwood	5-23	2-13	1-6	0-1	2-3	21.7	+ 11.60

LINGFIELD (Group 2)

Leading Trainers 1989-93

	Total W-R	Non-handicaps 2-y-o	3-y-o+	Handicaps 2-y-o	3-y-o+	Per cent	£1 Level Stake
R Hannon	22-194	9-66	9-45	0-16	4-67	11.3	- 107.80
P F I Cole	19-96	4-27	9-39	1-4	5-26	19.8	+ 1.28
G Harwood	16-73	5-15	6-29	0-3	5-26	21.9	- 4.88
J L Dunlop	16-98	3-39	7-29	0-3	6-27	16.3	- 10.78
R Akehurst	16-149	0-21	0-31	0-3	16-94	10.7	- 42.42
H R A Cecil	14-43	5-12	8-26	0-0	1-5	32.6	- 8.74
L M Cumani	13-32	1-3	12-26	0-0	0-3	40.6	+ 13.21
B W Hills	13-40	5-13	2-11	1-1	5-15	32.5	+ 27.85
M R Stoute	11-58	4-18	7-25	0-1	0-14	19.0	- 22.15
Sir M Prescott	10-45	1-15	4-13	0-2	5-15	22.2	- 6.63
J H M Gosden	10-49	4-17	6-24	0-0	0-8	20.4	- 20.74
C E Brittain	10-81	1-18	4-25	0-1	5-37	12.3	- 19.65
P Mitchell	9-80	0-14	4-21	1-4	4-41	11.3	- 5.50
G Lewis	9-101	4-38	2-17	0-6	3-40	8.9	- 43.63
N A Callaghan	8-38	2-10	1-8	1-3	4-17	21.1	+ 4.96
P J Makin	8-42	1-10	3-12	0-0	4-20	19.0	+ 11.25
J Berry	8-55	4-30	2-7	0-6	2-12	14.5	- 21.56
Pat Mitchell	8-76	1-18	0-11	0-5	7-42	10.5	- 12.92
A C Stewart	7-15	0-3	2-7	0-0	5-5	46.7	+ 13.74
I A Balding	7-49	0-9	6-16	0-0	1-24	14.3	- 21.47
B Hanbury	6-29	2-6	1-8	0-1	3-14	20.7	+ 30.13
C C Elsey	6-40	0-6	1-7	0-0	5-27	15.0	+ 2.83

Leading Jockeys

	Total W-R	Per cent	£1 Level Stake	Best Trainer	W-R	Per cent	£1 Level Stake
T Quinn	32-205	15.6	- 1.38	P F I Cole	14-62	22.6	- 2.22
J Reid	31-152	20.4	+ 4.98	P J Makin	3-8	37.5	+ 10.25
W Carson	27-118	22.9	- 14.78	J L Dunlop	8-25	32.0	- 3.42
R Cochrane	27-151	17.9	+ 23.69	G Harwood	5-12	41.7	+ 13.42
M Roberts	21-146	14.4	- 0.79	A C Stewart	7-11	63.6	+ 17.75
L Dettori	18-88	20.5	- 5.94	L M Cumani	5-11	45.5	+ 1.50
Pat Eddery	17-89	19.1	- 23.87	G Harwood	3-8	37.5	+ 0.77
M Hills	16-81	19.8	+ 0.65	J W Hills	3-7	42.9	+ 11.75
B Raymond	14-86	16.3	- 5.62	B Hanbury	3-13	23.1	+ 3.63
R Hills	13-69	18.8	+ 22.75	M R Channon	4-5	80.0	+ 24.25
W Newnes	13-123	10.6	- 40.00	C C Elsey	4-12	33.3	+ 17.50
D Holland	12-64	18.8	+ 37.27	B W Hills	4-11	36.4	+ 16.00

How the Favourites Fared

Non-handicaps	W-R	Per cent	£1 Level Stake	Handicaps	W-R	Per cent	£1 Level Stake
2-y-o	37-117	31.6	- 42.29	2-y-o	6-16	37.5	+ 5.83
3-y-o	35-86	40.7	- 8.49	3-y-o	17-49	34.7	+ 0.38
Weight-for-age	36-69	52.2	+ 6.55	All-aged	49-190	25.8	- 28.48
Totals	108-272	39.7	- 44.23	Totals	72-255	28.2	- 22.27
All favs	180-527	34.2	- 66.50				

Leading Trainers by Month at Lingfield

March/April

	Total W-R	Non-handicaps 2-y-o	Non-handicaps 3-y-o+	Handicaps 2-y-o	Handicaps 3-y-o+	Per cent	£1 Level Stake
L J Holt	2-3	1-1	0-0	0-0	1-2	66.7	+ 18.50
R Boss	1-1	0-0	0-0	0-0	1-1	100.0	+ 6.00
H Thomson Jones	1-1	0-0	1-1	0-0	0-0	100.0	+ 12.00
Lord Huntingdon	1-1	0-0	1-1	0-0	0-0	100.0	+ 3.33
K R Burke	1-1	0-0	0-0	0-0	1-1	100.0	+ 5.50

May

	Total W-R	Non-handicaps 2-y-o	Non-handicaps 3-y-o+	Handicaps 2-y-o	Handicaps 3-y-o+	Per cent	£1 Level Stake
R Hannon	8-46	1-12	6-15	0-0	1-19	17.4	- 18.88
M R Stoute	6-20	0-1	6-16	0-0	0-3	30.0	- 1.51
H R A Cecil	5-15	2-3	3-10	0-0	0-2	33.3	- 5.88
J H M Gosden	4-11	0-1	4-9	0-0	0-1	36.4	+ 2.03
N A Callaghan	4-19	1-5	1-3	0-0	2-11	21.1	+ 4.50

June

	Total W-R	Non-handicaps 2-y-o	Non-handicaps 3-y-o+	Handicaps 2-y-o	Handicaps 3-y-o+	Per cent	£1 Level Stake
P F I Cole	7-15	2-4	3-6	0-0	2-5	46.7	+ 21.69
R Hannon	7-31	3-6	2-9	0-0	2-16	22.6	- 5.17
J L Dunlop	5-13	1-2	2-5	0-0	2-6	38.5	- 0.25
G Harwood	5-15	1-2	3-10	0-0	1-3	33.3	+ 13.82
R Charlton	4-5	0-0	3-4	0-0	1-1	80.0	+ 14.43

July

	Total W-R	Non-handicaps 2-y-o	Non-handicaps 3-y-o+	Handicaps 2-y-o	Handicaps 3-y-o+	Per cent	£1 Level Stake
R Akehurst	5-24	0-2	0-3	0-1	5-18	20.8	- 1.50
L M Cumani	4-6	0-0	4-6	0-0	0-0	66.7	+ 2.67
G Harwood	4-11	1-1	1-2	0-0	2-8	36.4	+ 5.25
G Lewis	4-13	3-5	0-1	0-3	1-4	30.8	+ 4.13
P F I Cole	4-14	1-3	2-3	0-1	1-7	28.6	- 2.25

August

	Total W-R	Non-handicaps 2-y-o	Non-handicaps 3-y-o+	Handicaps 2-y-o	Handicaps 3-y-o+	Per cent	£1 Level Stake
G Harwood	5-11	3-4	0-0	0-1	2-6	45.5	+ 7.27
P F I Cole	4-9	0-2	3-3	1-2	0-2	44.4	+ 6.83
H R A Cecil	3-4	1-2	2-2	0-0	0-0	75.0	+ 9.04
P J Makin	3-10	0-0	1-3	0-0	2-7	30.0	+ 8.25
M D I Usher	3-10	2-4	0-2	1-3	0-1	30.0	+ 14.00

September

	Total W-R	Non-handicaps 2-y-o	Non-handicaps 3-y-o+	Handicaps 2-y-o	Handicaps 3-y-o+	Per cent	£1 Level Stake
B W Hills	6-8	4-6	1-1	0-0	1-1	75.0	+ 28.73
J H M Gosden	3-9	2-6	1-2	0-0	0-1	33.3	- 1.56
G Wragg	2-2	1-1	1-1	0-0	0-0	100.0	+ 19.00
R Bastiman	2-2	0-0	0-0	0-0	2-2	100.0	+ 11.00
N A Callaghan	2-3	1-2	0-0	0-0	1-1	66.7	+ 6.63

Oct/Nov

	Total W-R	Non-handicaps 2-y-o	Non-handicaps 3-y-o+	Handicaps 2-y-o	Handicaps 3-y-o+	Per cent	£1 Level Stake
J L Dunlop	4-16	0-6	4-6	0-2	0-2	25.0	+ 8.65
M R Stoute	3-12	3-9	0-1	0-1	0-1	25.0	- 6.55
R Hannon	3-20	2-5	0-4	0-3	1-8	15.0	0.00
Mrs J Cecil	2-4	2-2	0-0	0-0	0-2	50.0	+ 7.00
D W P Arbuthnot	2-5	1-1	0-1	1-1	0-2	40.0	+ 20.00

LINGFIELD (AW)

Leading Trainers 1989-93

	Total W-R	Non-handicaps 2-y-o	Non-handicaps 3-y-o+	Handicaps 2-y-o	Handicaps 3-y-o+	Per cent	£1 Level Stake
W A O'Gorman	32-146	2-12	17-51	2-4	11-79	21.9	+ 7.89
R J O'Sullivan	28-139	0-0	5-19	0-0	23-120	20.1	+ 25.13
B W Hills	21-66	1-7	11-23	0-2	9-34	31.8	- 13.60
C C Elsey	20-118	1-11	3-21	0-1	16-85	16.9	+ 17.06
P F I Cole	19-104	4-26	9-30	1-5	5-43	18.3	- 39.04
P Mitchell	19-121	0-7	3-22	0-4	16-88	15.7	+ 19.83
M S Johnston	18-87	2-5	3-17	0-1	13-64	20.7	+ 13.53
Sir M Prescott	17-76	4-21	6-21	0-2	7-32	22.4	- 14.37
S Dow	17-157	3-15	3-48	1-5	10-89	10.8	- 15.67
Lord Huntingdon	16-69	0-4	6-29	0-3	10-33	23.2	+ 8.46
C A Cyzer	16-106	0-8	6-37	0-0	10-61	15.1	- 21.18
J Berry	15-47	5-15	4-14	0-1	6-17	31.9	+ 8.42
R Hannon	14-118	5-36	4-31	1-10	4-41	11.9	+ 6.25
A Moore	13-140	0-13	3-56	0-0	10-71	9.3	- 14.00
N A Callaghan	12-64	5-10	3-17	3-9	1-28	18.8	+ 11.62
K O C-Brown	12-127	0-8	1-31	0-1	11-87	9.4	+ 14.00
R Hollinshead	11-41	0-1	8-22	0-0	3-18	26.8	+ 0.93
D R C Elsworth	11-57	5-14	2-20	2-2	2-21	19.3	- 15.95
D Murray Smith	11-73	1-7	3-21	0-3	7-42	15.1	+ 6.31
T D Barron	10-44	0-3	3-13	0-0	7-28	22.7	+ 0.63
D W P Arbuthnot	10-57	0-2	0-6	0-0	10-49	17.5	+ 4.25
Mrs L Piggott	10-65	2-11	3-20	0-3	5-31	15.4	- 1.80

Leading Jockeys

	Total W-R	Per cent	£1 Level Stake	Best Trainer	W-R	Per cent	£1 Level Stake
T Quinn	56-290	19.3	- 7.12	P F I Cole	8-58	13.8	- 36.26
J Williams	49-341	14.4	- 15.77	D R C Elsworth	9-35	25.7	- 1.20
Emma O'Gorman	33-139	23.7	+ 35.09	W A O'Gorman	26-112	23.2	+ 20.46
G Duffield	30-154	19.5	- 19.90	Sir M Prescott	14-47	29.8	- 6.03
D Biggs	29-253	11.5	- 61.40	R J O'Sullivan	13-66	19.7	+ 31.25
M Hills	26-176	14.8	- 68.52	B W Hills	7-27	25.9	- 11.19
W Ryan	24-162	14.8	- 59.50	R Hollinshead	6-18	33.3	- 0.07
N Adams	23-292	7.9	- 31.75	A Moore	5-26	19.2	+ 50.50
J Quinn	23-308	7.5	-114.72	D A Wilson	2-2	100.0	+ 4.75
W Newnes	20-165	12.1	- 42.32	C C Elsey	7-31	22.6	+ 11.68
N Day	17-93	18.3	+ 20.81	R Boss	4-10	40.0	+ 3.05
A Munro	17-108	15.7	- 27.91	W A O'Gorman	2-6	33.3	+ 1.83

How the Favourites Fared

Non-handicaps	W-R	Per cent	£1 Level Stake	Handicaps	W-R	Per cent	£1 Level Stake
2-y-o	30-80	37.5	- 7.71	2-y-o	7-15	46.7	+ 10.00
3-y-o	52-111	46.8	- 5.91	3-y-o	22-58	37.9	- 8.44
Weight-for-age	61-152	40.1	- 4.01	All-aged	115-392	29.3	- 40.16
Totals	143-343	41.7	- 17.63	Totals	144-465	31.0	- 38.60
All favs	287-808	35.5	- 56.23				

Leading Trainers by Month at Lingfield (AW)

January

	Total W-R	Non-handicaps 2-y-o	3-y-o+	Handicaps 2-y-o	3-y-o+	Per cent	£1 Level Stake
W A O'Gorman	9-26	0-0	4-13	0-0	5-13	34.6	+ 14.75
R Hollinshead	7-14	0-0	5-8	0-0	2-6	50.0	+ 12.43

February

	Total W-R	Non-handicaps 2-y-o	3-y-o+	Handicaps 2-y-o	3-y-o+	Per cent	£1 Level Stake
M S Johnston	6-24	0-0	1-3	0-0	5-21	25.0	+ 3.13
Dr J D Scargill	6-24	0-0	1-7	0-0	5-17	25.0	+ 10.73

March

	Total W-R	Non-handicaps 2-y-o	3-y-o+	Handicaps 2-y-o	3-y-o+	Per cent	£1 Level Stake
W A O'Gorman	6-24	0-0	3-10	0-0	3-14	25.0	+ 5.33
R J O'Sullivan	6-30	0-0	1-6	0-0	5-24	20.0	+ 0.50

April

	Total W-R	Non-handicaps 2-y-o	3-y-o+	Handicaps 2-y-o	3-y-o+	Per cent	£1 Level Stake
Sir M Prescott	5-8	0-0	3-3	0-0	2-5	62.5	+ 3.40
N A Callaghan	2-2	1-1	1-1	0-0	0-0	100.0	+ 10.25

May

	Total W-R	Non-handicaps 2-y-o	3-y-o+	Handicaps 2-y-o	3-y-o+	Per cent	£1 Level Stake
G Lewis	2-4	0-0	0-1	0-0	2-3	50.0	+ 8.50
M Dixon	2-4	0-0	1-1	0-0	1-3	50.0	+ 4.50

June

	Total W-R	Non-handicaps 2-y-o	3-y-o+	Handicaps 2-y-o	3-y-o+	Per cent	£1 Level Stake
J Berry	2-2	1-1	0-0	0-0	1-1	100.0	+ 5.50
P A Kelleway	2-3	0-0	1-2	0-0	1-1	66.7	+ 11.50

July

	Total W-R	Non-handicaps 2-y-o	3-y-o+	Handicaps 2-y-o	3-y-o+	Per cent	£1 Level Stake
P F I Cole	3-4	0-0	2-3	0-0	1-1	75.0	+ 0.83
B W Hills	2-2	0-0	2-2	0-0	0-0	100.0	+ 3.79

August

	Total W-R	Non-handicaps 2-y-o	3-y-o+	Handicaps 2-y-o	3-y-o+	Per cent	£1 Level Stake
C A Cyzer	5-17	0-3	0-0	0-0	5-14	29.4	+ 12.13
Mrs L Piggott	3-4	0-0	1-1	0-0	2-3	75.0	+ 16.20

September

	Total W-R	Non-handicaps 2-y-o	3-y-o+	Handicaps 2-y-o	3-y-o+	Per cent	£1 Level Stake
B W Hills	2-3	0-0	1-2	0-0	1-1	66.7	+ 7.50
G Lewis	1-1	0-0	1-1	0-0	0-0	100.0	+ 14.00

October

	Total W-R	Non-handicaps 2-y-o	3-y-o+	Handicaps 2-y-o	3-y-o+	Per cent	£1 Level Stake
D W Chapman	1-1	0-0	1-1	0-0	0-0	100.0	+ 2.00
G Wragg	1-1	0-0	1-1	0-0	0-0	100.0	+ 4.50

November

	Total W-R	Non-handicaps 2-y-o	3-y-o+	Handicaps 2-y-o	3-y-o+	Per cent	£1 Level Stake
B W Hills	7-26	1-3	2-3	0-2	4-18	26.9	- 7.27
R Boss	6-15	4-8	1-1	1-3	0-3	40.0	+ 18.88

December

	Total W-R	Non-handicaps 2-y-o	3-y-o+	Handicaps 2-y-o	3-y-o+	Per cent	£1 Level Stake
R J O'Sullivan	9-23	0-0	1-2	0-0	8-21	39.1	+ 30.88
J D Bethell	6-22	2-4	2-5	0-1	2-12	27.3	+ 61.38

NEWBURY (Group 1)

Leading Trainers 1989-93

	Total W-R	Non-handicaps 2-y-o	3-y-o+	Handicaps 2-y-o	3-y-o+	Per cent	£1 Level Stake
R Hannon	38-402	16-176	8-67	4-31	10-128	9.5	- 125.81
H R A Cecil	29-107	5-14	20-73	0-0	4-20	27.1	+ 14.04
J H M Gosden	22-111	4-19	11-58	0-0	7-34	19.8	+ 19.22
M R Stoute	22-122	5-26	11-55	1-3	5-38	18.0	+ 10.42
I A Balding	20-203	7-71	3-46	0-2	10-84	9.9	- 45.85
P Chapple-Hyam	19-60	12-34	5-18	1-2	1-6	31.7	+ 24.33
B W Hills	18-165	7-59	6-58	0-0	5-48	10.9	- 36.53
P F I Cole	16-147	8-53	4-41	1-7	3-46	10.9	- 9.61
R Charlton	15-91	2-27	7-32	0-4	6-28	16.5	+ 24.25
C E Brittain	13-157	2-36	6-59	1-8	4-54	8.3	- 61.17
J L Dunlop	13-169	3-43	4-65	1-6	5-55	7.7	- 88.44
L M Cumani	12-73	4-10	5-30	0-2	3-31	16.4	- 27.89
P T Walwyn	12-124	3-28	0-42	1-3	8-51	9.7	- 37.00
Lord Huntingdon	12-125	0-25	3-27	1-4	8-69	9.6	- 40.25
D R C Elsworth	11-150	3-44	0-46	1-5	7-55	7.3	- 45.50
R W Armstrong	8-32	2-8	3-13	0-0	3-11	25.0	+ 23.25
B Hanbury	8-68	3-24	4-25	0-0	1-19	11.8	- 31.34
W R Hern	8-69	4-17	3-39	0-0	1-13	11.6	- 26.52
J Berry	7-45	5-17	1-11	0-6	1-11	15.6	+ 2.67
A C Stewart	7-48	0-4	2-25	0-1	5-18	14.6	- 9.05
G B Balding	6-93	0-24	0-9	2-7	4-53	6.5	- 12.00
H Thomson Jones	5-26	1-2	2-5	0-0	2-19	19.2	+ 9.63

Leading Jockeys

	Total W-R	Per cent	£1 Level Stake	Best Trainer	W-R	Per cent	£1 Level Stake
Pat Eddery	51-282	18.1	- 13.30	H R A Cecil	7-21	33.3	+ 7.66
M Roberts	42-276	15.2	- 10.90	C E Brittain	9-71	12.7	+ 3.83
W Carson	40-267	15.0	- 34.68	W R Hern	7-42	16.7	- 7.53
L Dettori	27-177	15.3	+ 57.75	L M Cumani	7-33	21.2	- 5.50
W R Swinburn	27-193	14.0	- 48.66	M R Stoute	11-57	19.3	+ 10.25
J Reid	25-195	12.8	- 39.96	P Chapple-Hyam	8-23	34.8	+ 3.70
R Cochrane	22-200	11.0	- 51.97	I A Balding	8-31	25.8	+ 19.95
T Quinn	20-192	10.4	- 59.64	P F I Cole	10-84	11.9	- 37.02
B Raymond	10-174	5.7	- 61.50	R Hannon	5-43	11.6	+ 19.50
D Harrison	9-54	16.7	+ 24.50	J W Hills	3-7	42.9	+ 20.00
A Munro	9-111	8.1	- 40.37	W A O'Gorman	2-2	100.0	+ 4.03
M Hills	9-124	7.3	- 57.49	B W Hills	5-50	10.0	- 15.12

How the Favourites Fared

Non-handicaps	W-R	Per cent	£1 Level Stake	Handicaps	W-R	Per cent	£1 Level Stake
2-y-o	58-128	45.3	+ 4.10	2-y-o	7-19	36.8	+ 9.41
3-y-o	28-83	33.7	- 12.47	3-y-o	17-69	24.6	- 17.69
Weight-for-age	20-58	34.5	- 0.73	All-aged	32-122	26.2	+ 6.15
Totals	106-269	39.4	- 9.10	Totals	56-210	26.7	- 2.13
All favs	162-479	33.8	- 11.23				

Leading Trainers by Month at Newbury

March/April

	Total W-R	Non-handicaps 2-y-o	3-y-o+	Handicaps 2-y-o	3-y-o+	Per cent	£1 Level Stake
H R A Cecil	9-25	0-0	8-23	0-0	1-2	36.0	+ 16.53
P Chapple-Hyam	6-12	1-1	4-8	0-0	1-3	50.0	+ 26.03
I A Balding	5-32	1-3	1-20	0-0	3-9	15.6	+ 21.00
R Hannon	5-50	2-12	2-20	0-0	1-18	10.0	+ 12.00
B W Hills	3-28	0-0	2-23	0-0	1-5	10.7	+ 1.00

May

	Total W-R	Non-handicaps 2-y-o	3-y-o+	Handicaps 2-y-o	3-y-o+	Per cent	£1 Level Stake
R Hannon	7-57	3-27	4-16	0-0	0-14	12.3	- 18.58
I A Balding	6-21	1-6	2-7	0-0	3-8	28.6	+ 36.00
M R Stoute	6-24	0-0	4-18	0-0	2-6	25.0	+ 5.50
H R A Cecil	4-23	0-1	3-18	0-0	1-4	17.4	- 0.05
P F I Cole	4-30	3-10	1-11	0-0	0-9	13.3	- 15.77

June

	Total W-R	Non-handicaps 2-y-o	3-y-o+	Handicaps 2-y-o	3-y-o+	Per cent	£1 Level Stake
R Hannon	7-63	5-35	0-8	0-0	2-20	11.1	+ 4.65
H R A Cecil	6-16	1-2	5-12	0-0	0-2	37.5	+ 4.03
A C Stewart	4-6	0-0	2-2	0-0	2-4	66.7	+ 7.95
Lord Huntingdon	4-16	0-3	2-6	0-0	2-7	25.0	+ 20.50
A A Scott	3-9	3-6	0-1	0-0	0-2	33.3	+ 10.75

July

	Total W-R	Non-handicaps 2-y-o	3-y-o+	Handicaps 2-y-o	3-y-o+	Per cent	£1 Level Stake
L M Cumani	5-9	0-0	3-4	0-0	2-5	55.6	+ 14.13
H R A Cecil	5-12	0-1	4-8	0-0	1-3	41.7	+ 3.59
J H M Gosden	3-5	0-0	2-3	0-0	1-2	60.0	+ 14.83
P Chapple-Hyam	3-9	3-7	0-2	0-0	0-0	33.3	- 2.11
W R Hern	3-13	2-4	1-8	0-0	0-1	23.1	+ 3.50

August

	Total W-R	Non-handicaps 2-y-o	3-y-o+	Handicaps 2-y-o	3-y-o+	Per cent	£1 Level Stake
B W Hills	5-21	2-9	2-7	0-0	1-5	23.8	+ 8.88
P Chapple-Hyam	4-10	4-8	0-1	0-0	0-1	40.0	- 1.15
J L Dunlop	4-13	1-6	1-3	1-1	1-3	30.8	+ 13.33
R Hannon	4-64	0-29	1-8	1-5	2-22	6.3	- 42.50
J Berry	3-8	2-5	0-0	0-0	1-3	37.5	+ 8.83

September

	Total W-R	Non-handicaps 2-y-o	3-y-o+	Handicaps 2-y-o	3-y-o+	Per cent	£1 Level Stake
R Hannon	7-56	1-23	1-5	2-12	3-16	12.5	- 17.75
J H M Gosden	5-20	1-7	2-5	0-0	2-8	25.0	- 1.25
M R Stoute	4-19	2-7	1-3	1-1	0-8	21.1	+ 2.25
B W Hills	3-20	1-13	0-0	0-0	2-7	15.0	+ 1.10
J L Dunlop	3-24	2-12	0-3	0-2	1-7	12.5	+ 0.50

Oct/Nov

	Total W-R	Non-handicaps 2-y-o	3-y-o+	Handicaps 2-y-o	3-y-o+	Per cent	£1 Level Stake
J H M Gosden	6-28	2-7	2-14	0-0	2-7	21.4	+ 19.08
P F I Cole	5-20	1-7	1-3	1-3	2-7	25.0	+ 45.91
M R Stoute	5-22	3-8	1-8	0-2	1-4	22.7	+ 15.25
R Charlton	5-22	1-9	3-5	0-4	1-4	22.7	+ 3.50
R Hannon	5-57	3-17	0-0	1-14	1-26	8.8	- 20.75

NEWCASTLE (Group 1)

Leading Trainers 1989-93

	Total W-R	Non-handicaps 2-y-o	3-y-o+	Handicaps 2-y-o	3-y-o+	Per cent	£1 Level Stake
J Berry	22-126	11-57	6-19	0-8	5-42	17.5	- 46.53
Mrs M Reveley	17-102	2-15	1-13	1-5	13-69	16.7	- 30.34
H R A Cecil	14-36	5-8	6-19	0-0	3-9	38.9	- 4.85
M R Stoute	14-47	5-11	7-21	0-1	2-14	29.8	- 23.80
B W Hills	12-43	3-9	6-21	0-1	3-12	27.9	+ 0.11
J W Watts	12-72	2-15	3-13	0-1	7-43	16.7	- 14.83
Sir M Prescott	10-34	2-8	1-6	1-2	6-18	29.4	+ 7.74
M H Easterby	10-131	0-28	1-16	0-5	9-82	7.6	- 86.69
J H M Gosden	9-21	0-3	6-14	0-0	3-4	42.9	+ 14.42
M J Camacho	9-35	1-9	4-7	0-0	4-19	25.7	+ 37.70
Mrs J Ramsden	9-81	1-21	1-7	0-6	7-47	11.1	- 31.71
J L Dunlop	8-19	2-6	1-3	0-0	5-10	42.1	+ 15.63
L M Cumani	8-21	2-4	4-11	0-1	2-5	38.1	- 0.01
B Hanbury	8-32	3-8	2-15	0-0	3-9	25.0	+ 24.63
M S Johnston	7-63	1-19	1-6	1-2	4-36	11.1	- 14.20
R Hannon	6-21	2-8	2-5	0-1	2-7	28.6	+ 17.67
D Morley	6-34	2-7	0-10	0-1	4-16	17.6	- 8.57
G M Moore	6-42	0-4	3-10	0-1	3-27	14.3	+ 23.00
M W Easterby	6-48	1-16	1-5	0-6	4-21	12.5	- 13.07
F H Lee	6-52	0-9	0-5	2-3	4-35	11.5	- 13.00
A A Scott	5-13	3-5	1-6	0-0	1-2	38.5	+ 5.77
B Beasley	5-14	2-4	0-2	0-1	3-7	35.7	+ 38.50

Leading Jockeys

	Total W-R	Per cent	£1 Level Stake	Best Trainer	W-R	Per cent	£1 Level Stake
J Carroll	22-130	16.9	- 15.86	J Berry	15-78	19.2	- 20.86
M Birch	22-148	14.9	- 21.77	M H Easterby	7-79	8.9	- 48.29
W Carson	21-55	38.2	+ 33.25	W R Hern	3-3	100.0	+ 8.07
K Darley	20-158	12.7	- 74.83	Mrs M Reveley	5-26	19.2	- 9.64
Pat Eddery	18-45	40.0	+ 0.20	M R Stoute	4-6	66.7	- 0.40
G Duffield	15-76	19.7	+ 5.15	Sir M Prescott	8-27	29.6	+ 4.98
N Connorton	12-69	17.4	+ 9.70	Miss S E Hall	5-16	31.3	+ 17.50
W Ryan	11-58	19.0	- 6.96	H R A Cecil	4-13	30.8	- 2.46
R Cochrane	10-45	22.2	+ 1.95	G Harwood	2-5	40.0	+ 1.30
J Lowe	10-139	7.2	- 83.87	Mrs M Reveley	4-27	14.8	- 12.25
L Dettori	7-34	20.6	- 8.49	L M Cumani	5-8	62.5	+ 8.01
B Raymond	7-40	17.5	+ 8.92	B Hanbury	4-6	66.7	+ 15.25

How the Favourites Fared

Non-handicaps	W-R	Per cent	£1 Level Stake	Handicaps	W-R	Per cent	£1 Level Stake
2-y-o	46-83	55.4	+ 13.45	2-y-o	5-13	38.5	+ 3.36
3-y-o	14-38	36.8	- 7.20	3-y-o	17-45	37.8	+ 3.21
Weight-for-age	28-54	51.9	- 4.81	All-aged	43-134	32.1	- 4.30
Totals	88-175	50.3	+ 1.44	Totals	65-192	33.9	+ 2.27
All favs	153-367	41.7	+ 3.71				

Leading Trainers by Month at Newcastle

March/April

	Total W-R	Non-handicaps 2-y-o	3-y-o+	Handicaps 2-y-o	3-y-o+	Per cent	£1 Level Stake
J W Watts	6-16	0-0	3-9	0-0	3-7	37.5	+ 7.80
M J Camacho	5-10	0-0	2-4	0-0	3-6	50.0	+ 41.00
J Berry	5-25	3-9	1-8	0-0	1-8	20.0	- 4.68
Mrs J Ramsden	4-19	0-1	1-5	0-0	3-13	21.1	+ 6.63
Sir M Prescott	3-10	0-0	1-5	0-0	2-5	30.0	+ 1.94

May

	Total W-R	Non-handicaps 2-y-o	3-y-o+	Handicaps 2-y-o	3-y-o+	Per cent	£1 Level Stake
J Berry	5-8	2-3	2-3	0-0	1-2	62.5	+ 7.78
Sir M Prescott	2-2	0-0	0-0	0-0	2-2	100.0	+ 3.33
Mrs M Reveley	2-10	1-1	0-5	0-0	1-4	20.0	- 4.05
M W Easterby	1-1	0-0	0-0	0-0	1-1	100.0	+ 3.50
W W Haigh	1-1	0-0	1-1	0-0	0-0	100.0	+ 3.50

June

	Total W-R	Non-handicaps 2-y-o	3-y-o+	Handicaps 2-y-o	3-y-o+	Per cent	£1 Level Stake
H R A Cecil	5-6	2-2	3-3	0-0	0-1	83.3	+ 1.75
J H M Gosden	4-7	0-0	1-4	0-0	3-3	57.1	+ 19.90
P T Walwyn	3-5	0-0	2-2	0-0	1-3	60.0	+ 4.50
M R Stoute	3-10	1-1	1-3	0-0	1-6	30.0	- 5.57
J W Watts	3-15	2-6	0-0	0-0	1-9	20.0	- 0.38

July

	Total W-R	Non-handicaps 2-y-o	3-y-o+	Handicaps 2-y-o	3-y-o+	Per cent	£1 Level Stake
Mrs M Reveley	7-19	1-4	0-0	0-0	6-15	36.8	+ 19.21
G Harwood	4-7	0-0	2-4	0-0	2-3	57.1	+ 6.80
M R Stoute	4-12	2-2	2-6	0-0	0-4	33.3	- 5.88
J Berry	4-19	3-10	1-1	0-1	0-7	21.1	- 11.08
H R A Cecil	3-5	0-1	1-1	0-0	2-3	60.0	+ 0.40

August

	Total W-R	Non-handicaps 2-y-o	3-y-o+	Handicaps 2-y-o	3-y-o+	Per cent	£1 Level Stake
B W Hills	5-14	1-4	2-5	0-0	2-5	35.7	+ 6.21
M R Stoute	3-11	2-3	1-4	0-1	0-3	27.3	- 5.30
F H Lee	3-12	0-0	0-1	2-3	1-8	25.0	+ 11.00
L M Cumani	2-2	0-0	2-2	0-0	0-0	100.0	+ 4.11
J L Dunlop	2-3	1-1	0-0	0-0	1-2	66.7	+ 7.50

September

	Total W-R	Non-handicaps 2-y-o	3-y-o+	Handicaps 2-y-o	3-y-o+	Per cent	£1 Level Stake
J L Dunlop	3-5	1-3	0-0	0-0	2-2	60.0	+ 3.13
A A Scott	2-2	2-2	0-0	0-0	0-0	100.0	+ 9.00
J Berry	2-5	0-2	1-2	0-0	1-1	40.0	+ 3.50
M Bell	1-1	1-1	0-0	0-0	0-0	100.0	+ 0.62
S G Norton	1-2	0-0	1-2	0-0	0-0	50.0	+ 9.00

Oct/Nov

	Total W-R	Non-handicaps 2-y-o	3-y-o+	Handicaps 2-y-o	3-y-o+	Per cent	£1 Level Stake
J H M Gosden	5-11	0-3	5-7	0-0	0-1	45.5	- 2.48
D Morley	4-12	2-5	0-3	0-0	2-4	33.3	+ 4.10
L M Cumani	3-10	2-4	1-3	0-1	0-2	30.0	- 1.98
M J Camacho	3-12	0-3	2-3	0-0	1-6	25.0	+ 0.70
Mrs M Reveley	3-16	0-2	0-1	1-1	2-12	18.8	- 7.25

NEWMARKET (Group 1)

Leading Trainers 1989-93

	Total W-R	Non-handicaps 2-y-o	3-y-o+	Handicaps 2-y-o	3-y-o+	Per cent	£1 Level Stake
H R A Cecil	71-346	23-96	42-194	0-0	6-56	20.5	- 48.06
M R Stoute	54-309	21-124	26-131	1-8	6-46	17.5	- 21.10
L M Cumani	53-355	12-99	30-168	1-5	10-83	14.9	- 90.07
R Hannon	53-487	24-172	14-106	7-55	8-154	10.9	- 95.70
J H M Gosden	45-266	6-57	28-129	0-5	11-75	16.9	- 0.45
B W Hills	44-337	15-101	11-125	1-5	17-106	13.1	- 72.54
C E Brittain	33-466	10-145	12-168	1-15	10-138	7.1	-168.77
J L Dunlop	29-232	5-66	14-71	0-7	10-88	12.5	- 71.04
P F I Cole	21-132	10-47	6-42	2-13	3-30	15.9	+ 25.13
G Wragg	21-167	8-44	8-75	1-4	4-44	12.6	- 44.06
W R Hern	20-99	8-33	10-44	0-0	2-22	20.2	- 11.68
A A Scott	19-162	7-66	9-55	0-10	3-31	11.7	- 42.93
J R Fanshawe	16-123	2-22	6-49	1-3	7-49	13.0	+ 6.98
M Bell	15-148	2-45	4-26	4-16	5-61	10.1	- 25.38
G Harwood	15-200	4-51	5-73	0-4	6-72	7.5	- 55.13
R Charlton	14-67	10-24	2-16	0-2	2-25	20.9	+ 25.06
P Chapple-Hyam	14-70	5-36	6-25	1-2	2-7	20.0	+ 8.80
M A Jarvis	14-157	1-49	7-39	0-9	6-60	8.9	- 49.70
J Berry	13-109	4-28	4-28	1-20	4-33	11.9	- 17.06
A C Stewart	12-116	2-14	5-52	0-0	5-50	10.3	+ 3.98
D R C Elsworth	12-159	2-46	6-61	1-4	3-48	7.5	- 29.50
B Hanbury	12-185	0-67	4-71	0-5	8-42	6.5	- 82.26

Leading Jockeys

	Total W-R	Per cent	£1 Level Stake	Best Trainer	W-R	Per cent	£1 Level Stake
Pat Eddery	99-534	18.5	- 95.12	H R A Cecil	21-59	35.6	+ 4.59
W Carson	87-580	15.0	- 71.43	J L Dunlop	21-94	22.3	+ 10.22
M Roberts	71-569	12.5	- 69.86	C E Brittain	23-184	12.5	+ 9.50
W R Swinburn	69-439	15.7	- 65.47	M R Stoute	26-129	20.2	- 20.57
L Dettori	59-474	12.4	-111.98	L M Cumani	30-173	17.3	- 36.77
R Cochrane	43-430	10.0	- 41.24	L M Cumani	11-75	14.7	- 0.61
M Hills	40-286	14.0	+ 71.01	B W Hills	16-87	18.4	+ 28.38
B Raymond	32-414	7.7	-197.13	R Hannon	6-55	10.9	- 32.26
J Reid	26-279	9.3	- 41.79	P Chapple-Hyam	4-31	12.9	+ 9.75
A Munro	25-269	9.3	-116.03	P F I Cole	6-34	17.6	- 12.49
L Piggott	21-178	11.8	- 42.38	R Hannon	7-24	29.2	+ 19.76
T Quinn	20-229	8.7	- 30.54	P F I Cole	9-56	16.1	+ 40.88

How the Favourites Fared

Non-handicaps	W-R	Per cent	£1 Level Stake	Handicaps	W-R	Per cent	£1 Level Stake
2-y-o	102-255	40.0	- 6.27	2-y-o	13-53	24.5	+ 1.59
3-y-o	91-209	43.5	+ 5.13	3-y-o	20-110	18.2	- 31.49
Weight-for-age	60-160	37.5	- 13.52	All-aged	49-228	21.5	- 58.07
Totals	253-624	40.5	- 14.66	Totals	82-391	21.0	- 87.97
All favs	335-101	33.0	-102.63				

500

Leading Trainers by Month at Newmarket

March/April

	Total W-R	Non-handicaps 2-y-o	Non-handicaps 3-y-o+	Handicaps 2-y-o	Handicaps 3-y-o+	Per cent	£1 Level Stake
H R A Cecil	15-63	0-0	14-55	0-0	1-8	23.8	- 2.47
J H M Gosden	8-39	0-0	5-28	0-0	3-11	20.5	+ 9.63
R Hannon	7-59	4-10	2-30	0-0	1-19	11.9	+ 14.13
C E Brittain	7-65	0-3	5-40	0-0	2-22	10.8	+ 3.75
B W Hills	7-68	0-4	1-50	0-0	6-14	10.3	- 12.25

May

	Total W-R	Non-handicaps 2-y-o	Non-handicaps 3-y-o+	Handicaps 2-y-o	Handicaps 3-y-o+	Per cent	£1 Level Stake
M R Stoute	9-37	1-3	7-30	0-0	1-4	24.3	- 11.93
L M Cumani	9-48	0-0	7-39	0-0	2-9	18.8	+ 15.79
H R A Cecil	9-58	0-2	8-50	0-0	1-6	15.5	- 36.42
R Hannon	8-58	2-14	5-27	0-0	1-17	13.8	- 20.71
C E Brittain	8-64	2-10	3-40	0-0	3-14	12.5	+ 10.75

June

	Total W-R	Non-handicaps 2-y-o	Non-handicaps 3-y-o+	Handicaps 2-y-o	Handicaps 3-y-o+	Per cent	£1 Level Stake
J H M Gosden	5-16	0-1	4-10	0-0	1-5	31.3	+ 10.11
J R Fanshawe	4-15	0-0	1-6	0-0	3-9	26.7	+ 23.00
H R A Cecil	4-18	1-2	3-13	0-0	0-3	22.2	- 8.27
J L Dunlop	3-8	1-3	2-3	0-0	0-2	37.5	+ 0.07
P F I Cole	3-9	1-2	1-4	0-0	1-3	33.3	+ 4.50

July

	Total W-R	Non-handicaps 2-y-o	Non-handicaps 3-y-o+	Handicaps 2-y-o	Handicaps 3-y-o+	Per cent	£1 Level Stake
H R A Cecil	20-69	9-22	9-33	0-0	2-14	29.0	- 3.01
R Hannon	19-103	11-44	4-16	1-4	3-39	18.4	+ 6.30
M R Stoute	8-44	3-20	3-17	0-0	2-7	18.2	- 9.01
L M Cumani	8-59	1-9	5-30	0-0	2-20	13.6	- 18.56
G Wragg	7-36	2-8	2-15	1-1	2-12	19.4	+ 10.70

August

	Total W-R	Non-handicaps 2-y-o	Non-handicaps 3-y-o+	Handicaps 2-y-o	Handicaps 3-y-o+	Per cent	£1 Level Stake
R Hannon	11-62	4-25	2-9	4-15	1-13	17.7	+ 32.58
M R Stoute	10-48	7-24	1-9	1-2	1-13	20.8	- 6.55
L M Cumani	8-39	3-13	3-14	0-1	2-11	20.5	- 11.50
P F I Cole	7-18	4-7	2-6	1-3	0-2	38.9	+ 10.25
J H M Gosden	6-25	1-5	3-13	0-0	2-7	24.0	+ 22.38

September

	Total W-R	Non-handicaps 2-y-o	Non-handicaps 3-y-o+	Handicaps 2-y-o	Handicaps 3-y-o+	Per cent	£1 Level Stake
J H M Gosden	2-8	2-5	0-0	0-0	0-3	25.0	+ 13.00
W A O'Gorman	1-1	0-0	0-0	0-0	1-1	100.0	+ 14.00
J W Watts	1-1	0-0	0-0	0-0	1-1	100.0	+ 5.00
J A Glover	1-1	0-0	0-0	0-0	1-1	100.0	+ 8.00
T Stack (Ire)	1-1	0-0	1-1	0-0	0-0	100.0	+ 11.00

Oct/Nov

	Total W-R	Non-handicaps 2-y-o	Non-handicaps 3-y-o+	Handicaps 2-y-o	Handicaps 3-y-o+	Per cent	£1 Level Stake
B W Hills	22-138	8-58	6-29	1-4	7-47	15.9	- 13.42
L M Cumani	20-132	7-71	8-27	1-4	4-30	15.2	- 23.52
M R Stoute	19-129	9-69	8-40	0-5	2-15	14.7	+ 27.48
H R A Cecil	18-107	11-61	6-30	0-0	1-16	16.8	+ 22.10
J H M Gosden	11-97	0-31	9-34	0-3	2-29	11.3	- 41.38

NOTTINGHAM (Group 3)

Leading Trainers 1989-93

	Total W-R	Non-handicaps 2-y-o	3-y-o+	Handicaps 2-y-o	3-y-o+	Per cent	£1 Level Stake
H R A Cecil	29-75	8-23	20-48	0-0	1-4	38.7	+ 10.74
J L Dunlop	22-120	6-39	6-36	2-7	8-38	18.3	- 31.13
P F I Cole	15-82	6-27	4-21	2-9	3-25	18.3	- 16.29
D Morley	15-86	3-20	2-17	1-2	9-47	17.4	+ 27.38
J Berry	14-98	8-57	3-23	2-14	1-4	14.3	- 34.53
J H M Gosden	13-40	2-6	10-27	0-1	1-6	32.5	+ 8.88
R Hannon	12-114	5-48	4-22	1-17	2-27	10.5	- 62.15
R Charlton	10-25	3-11	5-10	0-0	2-4	40.0	+ 20.19
L M Cumani	10-32	4-9	6-21	0-0	0-2	31.3	+ 4.64
M R Stoute	9-48	6-23	3-18	0-3	0-4	18.8	- 12.05
J Wharton	9-70	3-23	3-13	0-2	3-32	12.9	+ 27.00
R J Hodges	9-73	0-3	1-15	0-1	8-54	12.3	+ 33.00
P T Walwyn	8-40	4-11	4-13	0-3	0-13	20.0	- 5.83
M J Ryan	8-55	0-5	3-11	0-2	5-37	14.5	+ 7.88
C Tinkler	8-55	1-15	1-11	0-2	6-27	14.5	+ 6.08
G Lewis	8-56	1-11	3-11	0-6	4-28	14.3	+ 2.00
R M Whitaker	8-60	1-12	2-13	0-2	5-33	13.3	- 1.00
B W Hills	8-61	5-25	1-24	1-4	1-8	13.1	- 18.13
B A McMahon	8-103	2-21	2-26	0-2	4-54	7.8	- 26.00
N A Callaghan	7-33	1-10	4-10	1-4	1-9	21.2	+ 5.10
Sir M Prescott	7-43	2-14	0-5	0-0	5-24	16.3	+ 22.13
R Hollinshead	7-178	2-46	1-55	0-10	4-67	3.9	-106.00

Leading Jockeys

	Total W-R	Per cent	£1 Level Stake	Best Trainer	W-R	Per cent	£1 Level Stake
Pat Eddery	38-156	24.4	- 22.42	R Charlton	7-11	63.6	+ 11.70
W Carson	38-214	17.8	- 6.96	J L Dunlop	7-41	17.1	- 11.95
L Dettori	29-146	19.9	- 1.70	L M Cumani	4-14	28.6	- 0.33
W R Swinburn	19-116	16.4	+ 6.23	M R Stoute	6-25	24.0	- 5.78
W Ryan	18-154	11.7	- 60.86	H R A Cecil	10-32	31.3	- 6.11
R Cochrane	17-118	14.4	- 26.30	L M Cumani	3-9	33.3	+ 1.57
M Roberts	17-169	10.1	- 54.61	D Morley	2-10	20.0	+ 0.75
T Quinn	14-100	14.0	- 16.26	P F I Cole	7-37	18.9	- 9.49
Paul Eddery	14-121	11.6	- 35.56	Mrs J Cecil	3-8	37.5	- 0.97
G Duffield	11-138	8.0	- 49.68	Sir M Prescott	7-35	20.0	+ 30.13
J Carroll	9-73	12.3	- 22.73	J Berry	8-47	17.0	- 6.13
M Hills	9-104	8.7	- 68.24	B W Hills	3-23	13.0	- 13.62

How the Favourites Fared

Non-handicaps	W-R	Per cent	£1 Level Stake	Handicaps	W-R	Per cent	£1 Level Stake
2-y-o	61-144	42.4	- 5.50	2-y-o	5-23	21.7	- 11.51
3-y-o	61-123	49.6	+ 19.06	3-y-o	17-59	28.8	- 3.48
Weight-for-age	22-48	45.8	+ 8.28	All-aged	41-157	26.1	- 5.81
Totals	144-315	45.7	+ 21.84	Totals	63-239	26.4	- 20.80
All favs	207-554	37.4	+ 1.04				

Leading Trainers by Month at Nottingham

March/April	Total W-R	Non-handicaps 2-y-o	3-y-o+	Handicaps 2-y-o	3-y-o+	Per cent	£1 Level Stake
H R A Cecil	9-15	0-0	9-15	0-0	0-0	60.0	+ 6.79
J Berry	5-18	2-8	3-10	0-0	0-0	27.8	- 2.60
C Tinkler	4-16	0-2	1-7	0-0	3-7	25.0	+ 13.83
J L Dunlop	4-18	0-1	3-11	0-0	1-6	22.2	- 5.88
N A Callaghan	3-12	0-1	2-8	0-0	1-3	25.0	+ 6.10

May	Total W-R	Non-handicaps 2-y-o	3-y-o+	Handicaps 2-y-o	3-y-o+	Per cent	£1 Level Stake
H R A Cecil	4-7	1-1	3-6	0-0	0-0	57.1	+ 3.90
J H M Gosden	2-5	0-0	1-4	0-0	1-1	40.0	+ 2.50
G A P-Gordon	2-7	0-2	1-2	0-0	1-3	28.6	+ 10.50
M H Tompkins	2-9	1-4	1-4	0-0	0-1	22.2	+ 17.00
J L Dunlop	2-10	0-0	1-5	0-0	1-5	20.0	- 1.25

June	Total W-R	Non-handicaps 2-y-o	3-y-o+	Handicaps 2-y-o	3-y-o+	Per cent	£1 Level Stake
J H M Gosden	4-5	2-2	2-3	0-0	0-0	80.0	+ 3.00
H R A Cecil	4-11	1-3	2-7	0-0	1-1	36.4	+ 0.12
B A McMahon	4-23	1-6	0-5	0-0	3-12	17.4	+ 29.50
M A Jarvis	3-8	1-1	1-4	0-0	1-3	37.5	+ 6.00
M H Easterby	3-9	0-5	3-3	0-0	0-1	33.3	+ 7.50

July	Total W-R	Non-handicaps 2-y-o	3-y-o+	Handicaps 2-y-o	3-y-o+	Per cent	£1 Level Stake
J L Dunlop	4-11	2-4	1-2	0-0	1-5	36.4	- 0.67
Sir M Prescott	3-6	1-1	0-1	0-0	2-4	50.0	+ 12.13
H R A Cecil	3-7	1-1	2-6	0-0	0-0	42.9	- 2.21
R Charlton	2-2	1-1	1-1	0-0	0-0	100.0	+ 14.44
M W Easterby	2-3	1-2	0-0	0-0	1-1	66.7	+ 12.75

August	Total W-R	Non-handicaps 2-y-o	3-y-o+	Handicaps 2-y-o	3-y-o+	Per cent	£1 Level Stake
M J Ryan	3-7	0-0	0-1	0-0	3-6	42.9	+ 20.50
J Wharton	3-7	1-1	0-0	0-0	2-6	42.9	+ 31.50
D Morley	3-9	0-2	0-1	0-0	3-6	33.3	+ 13.00
H R A Cecil	2-3	1-1	1-1	0-0	0-1	66.7	+ 7.30
L M Cumani	2-3	1-1	1-2	0-0	0-0	66.7	+ 4.38

September	Total W-R	Non-handicaps 2-y-o	3-y-o+	Handicaps 2-y-o	3-y-o+	Per cent	£1 Level Stake
D Morley	6-24	1-7	1-3	1-2	3-12	25.0	+ 29.75
R Hannon	6-37	2-20	3-5	1-7	0-5	16.2	- 8.32
L M Cumani	4-7	3-4	1-2	0-0	0-1	57.1	+ 14.57
P A Kelleway	4-8	2-5	2-3	0-0	0-0	50.0	+ 62.75
J H M Gosden	4-9	0-1	4-7	0-0	0-1	44.4	+ 16.50

Oct/Nov	Total W-R	Non-handicaps 2-y-o	3-y-o+	Handicaps 2-y-o	3-y-o+	Per cent	£1 Level Stake
H R A Cecil	5-15	3-10	2-5	0-0	0-0	33.3	+ 4.68
P F I Cole	4-17	3-12	0-0	1-3	0-2	23.5	+ 8.85
A A Scott	3-6	1-2	0-1	1-1	1-2	50.0	+ 17.00
D Morley	3-11	1-6	1-2	0-0	1-3	27.3	+ 2.13
J L Dunlop	3-17	1-10	0-2	0-2	2-3	17.6	- 9.00

PONTEFRACT (Group 3)

Leading Trainers 1989-93

	Total W-R	Non-handicaps 2-y-o	3-y-o+	Handicaps 2-y-o	3-y-o+	Per cent	£1 Level Stake
R Hollinshead	26-200	8-45	6-48	0-8	12-99	13.0	- 79.58
J Berry	18-138	12-73	3-21	0-9	3-35	13.0	- 36.90
Mrs J Ramsden	18-145	1-17	0-16	0-8	17-104	12.4	- 64.33
Mrs M Reveley	17-81	1-17	3-17	2-7	11-40	21.0	+ 23.73
H R A Cecil	15-37	0-2	15-35	0-0	0-0	40.5	+ 10.48
M H Tompkins	15-100	5-27	6-30	1-7	3-36	15.0	- 16.41
B A McMahon	13-108	0-9	4-39	0-0	9-60	12.0	- 4.50
G Wragg	9-35	0-3	8-26	0-2	1-4	25.7	+ 18.64
M S Johnston	9-63	4-18	2-12	1-5	2-28	14.3	+ 15.25
G Harwood	8-25	1-5	3-12	2-2	2-6	32.0	+ 0.97
I A Balding	8-38	4-7	2-15	0-3	2-13	21.1	+ 1.42
T D Barron	8-75	2-10	0-2	1-7	5-56	10.7	- 3.50
M H Easterby	8-126	1-38	4-20	0-13	3-55	6.3	- 78.13
B Hanbury	7-30	1-5	3-13	0-2	3-10	23.3	- 10.88
J A Glover	7-65	2-7	1-11	0-3	4-44	10.8	- 10.00
J L Dunlop	6-16	1-3	2-6	1-2	2-5	37.5	+ 25.05
L M Cumani	6-21	1-3	5-15	0-1	0-2	28.6	- 4.85
W Jarvis	6-22	0-3	4-10	1-1	1-8	27.3	+ 15.25
H Thomson Jones	6-25	3-4	2-9	1-5	0-7	24.0	+ 0.79
M R Stoute	6-27	2-5	4-18	0-1	0-3	22.2	- 12.21
M J Camacho	6-41	0-11	1-10	0-1	5-19	14.6	+ 19.50
J W Watts	6-48	0-7	1-9	0-3	5-29	12.5	- 20.40

Leading Jockeys

	Total W-R	Per cent	£1 Level Stake	Best Trainer	W-R	Per cent	£1 Level Stake
K Darley	27-187	14.4	- 54.20	Mrs M Reveley	5-25	20.0	+ 2.88
M Roberts	20-87	23.0	+ 26.61	A C Stewart	3-11	27.3	- 4.48
W Ryan	16-92	17.4	- 44.88	H R A Cecil	7-22	31.8	- 1.62
K Fallon	16-134	11.9	+ 35.85	J J O'Neill	3-8	37.5	+ 2.75
L Dettori	15-80	18.8	- 1.28	L M Cumani	5-11	45.5	+ 2.95
J Carroll	15-131	11.5	- 49.40	J Berry	13-88	14.8	- 11.53
R Hills	13-65	20.0	+ 7.09	H Thomson Jones	6-18	33.3	+ 7.79
B Raymond	13-98	13.3	- 43.79	B Hanbury	5-17	29.4	- 3.51
A Munro	13-99	13.1	- 15.77	W A O'Gorman	3-7	42.9	+ 2.48
W R Swinburn	12-50	24.0	- 0.21	B Hanbury	2-2	100.0	+ 3.13
M Birch	12-171	7.0	-105.27	M H Tompkins	3-5	60.0	+ 4.35
R Cochrane	11-67	16.4	+ 0.43	J H M Gosden	2-6	33.3	+ 4.00

How the Favourites Fared

Non-handicaps	W-R	Per cent	£1 Level Stake	Handicaps	W-R	Per cent	£1 Level Stake
2-y-o	51-104	49.0	+ 15.16	2-y-o	6-20	30.0	+ 1.03
3-y-o	31-81	38.3	- 8.63	3-y-o	16-38	42.1	+ 5.56
Weight-for-age	26-59	44.1	+ 1.90	All-aged	57-187	30.5	- 7.79
Totals	108-244	44.3	+ 8.43	Totals	79-245	32.2	- 1.20
All favs	187-489	38.2	+ 7.23				

Leading Trainers by Month at Pontefract

March/April

	Total W-R	Non-handicaps 2-y-o	Non-handicaps 3-y-o+	Handicaps 2-y-o	Handicaps 3-y-o+	Per cent	£1 Level Stake
J Berry	7-29	4-12	2-6	0-0	1-11	24.1	+ 5.35
H R A Cecil	5-7	0-0	5-7	0-0	0-0	71.4	+ 7.55
Mrs J Ramsden	5-28	0-3	0-4	0-0	5-21	17.9	- 11.63
R Hollinshead	5-34	1-9	0-7	0-0	4-18	14.7	+ 3.54
G Wragg	4-15	0-0	4-14	0-0	0-1	26.7	+ 6.81

May

	Total W-R	Non-handicaps 2-y-o	Non-handicaps 3-y-o+	Handicaps 2-y-o	Handicaps 3-y-o+	Per cent	£1 Level Stake
B Hanbury	3-4	0-0	2-3	0-0	1-1	75.0	+ 6.75
Miss S E Hall	3-5	0-0	2-3	0-0	1-2	60.0	+ 25.00
J W Watts	3-7	0-0	0-2	0-0	3-5	42.9	+ 9.35
M H Tompkins	3-11	1-2	2-6	0-0	0-3	27.3	+ 15.44
C J Hill	2-2	0-0	0-0	0-0	2-2	100.0	+ 13.50

June

	Total W-R	Non-handicaps 2-y-o	Non-handicaps 3-y-o+	Handicaps 2-y-o	Handicaps 3-y-o+	Per cent	£1 Level Stake
J A Glover	4-14	2-3	1-2	0-0	1-9	28.6	+ 6.50
Mrs J Ramsden	4-18	1-3	0-1	0-0	3-14	22.2	- 0.29
R Hollinshead	4-31	2-12	0-3	0-0	2-16	12.9	- 21.34
T D Barron	3-10	2-3	0-1	0-0	1-6	30.0	+ 14.50
H R A Cecil	3-10	0-1	3-9	0-0	0-0	30.0	- 2.75

July

	Total W-R	Non-handicaps 2-y-o	Non-handicaps 3-y-o+	Handicaps 2-y-o	Handicaps 3-y-o+	Per cent	£1 Level Stake
R Hollinshead	7-30	3-5	0-8	0-0	4-17	23.3	+ 3.99
H R A Cecil	4-6	0-0	4-6	0-0	0-0	66.7	+ 11.52
F H Lee	3-10	0-0	0-2	0-0	3-8	30.0	+ 16.50
B A McMahon	3-23	0-2	0-8	0-0	3-13	13.0	- 9.00
Mrs J Ramsden	3-26	0-4	0-5	0-0	3-17	11.5	- 11.67

August

	Total W-R	Non-handicaps 2-y-o	Non-handicaps 3-y-o+	Handicaps 2-y-o	Handicaps 3-y-o+	Per cent	£1 Level Stake
Mrs M Reveley	7-15	0-0	3-6	1-2	3-7	46.7	+ 31.88
R Hollinshead	5-30	1-7	3-9	0-2	1-12	16.7	- 13.52
I A Balding	4-10	3-4	0-1	0-1	1-4	40.0	+ 8.67
M H Tompkins	4-20	2-7	0-2	1-3	1-8	20.0	- 4.40
S G Norton	3-11	2-4	0-1	1-2	0-4	27.3	- 4.06

September

	Total W-R	Non-handicaps 2-y-o	Non-handicaps 3-y-o+	Handicaps 2-y-o	Handicaps 3-y-o+	Per cent	£1 Level Stake
B A McMahon	4-12	0-1	1-2	0-0	3-9	33.3	+ 22.00
H Thomson Jones	3-5	2-2	0-1	1-1	0-1	60.0	+ 8.25
J D Bethell	3-9	0-1	0-0	0-0	3-8	33.3	+ 8.50
G A P-Gordon	2-3	0-0	0-0	0-0	2-3	66.7	+ 12.00
M R Stoute	2-6	0-1	2-5	0-0	0-0	33.3	+ 1.25

Oct/Nov

	Total W-R	Non-handicaps 2-y-o	Non-handicaps 3-y-o+	Handicaps 2-y-o	Handicaps 3-y-o+	Per cent	£1 Level Stake
M S Johnston	5-12	1-2	2-2	1-4	1-4	41.7	+ 47.25
J L Dunlop	4-9	1-3	0-0	1-2	2-4	44.4	+ 20.30
G Harwood	4-11	0-3	2-4	1-1	1-3	36.4	+ 3.50
Mrs M Reveley	3-15	0-2	0-2	0-4	3-7	20.0	+ 5.00
R Hollinshead	3-37	1-4	2-13	0-5	0-15	8.1	- 26.75

REDCAR (Group 2)

Leading Trainers 1989-93

	Total W-R	Non-handicaps 2-y-o	3-y-o+	Handicaps 2-y-o	3-y-o+	Per cent	£1 Level Stake
Mrs M Reveley	40-261	5-48	8-43	1-14	26-156	15.3	- 22.60
M H Easterby	30-205	13-89	3-17	8-23	6-76	14.6	- 48.68
H Thomson Jones	23-71	8-21	7-20	1-3	7-27	32.4	+ 28.15
J Berry	19-178	11-90	2-18	1-23	5-47	10.7	- 55.34
L M Cumani	17-69	1-17	13-30	0-1	3-21	24.6	- 15.22
W Carter	11-45	0-12	1-2	1-6	9-25	24.4	+ 67.00
J W Hills	11-49	1-8	3-12	0-0	7-29	22.4	+ 13.27
J H M Gosden	11-65	6-20	4-28	0-2	1-15	16.9	- 36.16
R Hollinshead	11-116	2-24	2-22	0-7	7-63	9.5	- 44.20
R M Whitaker	11-196	3-57	2-34	1-10	5-95	5.6	- 99.50
H R A Cecil	10-36	1-5	8-22	0-0	1-9	27.8	- 12.54
G Harwood	10-36	3-9	5-14	0-1	2-12	27.8	+ 6.71
J L Dunlop	9-40	2-7	1-10	1-2	5-21	22.5	- 12.20
Sir M Prescott	9-47	1-17	5-10	0-2	3-18	19.1	- 7.67
R Hannon	8-28	6-17	1-3	1-4	0-4	28.6	+ 10.69
M J Camacho	8-60	0-19	2-9	0-3	6-29	13.3	- 8.72
M S Johnston	8-112	4-42	1-16	0-11	3-43	7.1	- 48.38
M Bell	7-31	5-14	0-2	0-4	2-11	22.6	+ 2.93
B W Hills	7-37	1-9	4-15	0-0	2-13	18.9	- 16.33
J G FitzGerald	7-67	1-20	0-14	1-5	5-28	10.4	- 30.75
F H Lee	7-72	0-11	1-12	1-4	5-45	9.7	- 25.25
T D Barron	7-100	3-34	1-7	1-6	2-53	7.0	- 47.75

Leading Jockeys

	Total W-R	Per cent	£1 Level Stake	Best Trainer	W-R	Per cent	£1 Level Stake
K Darley	44-260	16.9	- 20.39	Mrs M Reveley	17-64	26.6	+ 24.92
R Hills	33-140	23.6	- 0.56	H Thomson Jones	21-59	35.6	+ 26.67
M Birch	30-223	13.5	- 67.03	M H Easterby	14-98	14.3	- 23.87
Paul Eddery	20-94	21.3	+ 29.83	P W Harris	2-3	66.7	+ 12.75
G Duffield	20-155	12.9	- 46.41	Sir M Prescott	7-38	18.4	- 15.66
K Fallon	19-175	10.9	- 46.43	Denys Smith	4-13	30.8	+ 0.92
W Ryan	18-98	18.4	+ 13.71	H R A Cecil	6-23	26.1	- 7.44
L Dettori	17-84	20.2	- 9.72	L M Cumani	8-30	26.7	+ 2.23
J Lowe	16-252	6.3	- 117.40	Mrs M Reveley	9-69	13.0	- 9.53
Pat Eddery	14-56	25.0	- 7.18	J L Dunlop	3-5	60.0	+ 5.75
M Hills	14-56	25.0	+ 2.50	J W Hills	6-12	50.0	+ 23.83
J Carroll	14-165	8.5	- 75.88	J Berry	8-93	8.6	- 57.62

How the Favourites Fared

	W-R	Per cent	£1 Level Stake		W-R	Per cent	£1 Level Stake
Non-handicaps				Handicaps			
2-y-o	64-148	43.2	- 11.51	2-y-o	11-30	36.7	+ 5.99
3-y-o	31-59	52.5	+ 4.93	3-y-o	22-63	34.9	+ 1.76
Weight-for-age	44-78	56.4	+ 11.45	All-aged	70-218	32.1	+ 14.39
Totals	139-285	48.8	+ 4.87	Totals	103-311	33.1	+ 22.14
All favs	242-596	40.6	+ 27.01				

Leading Trainers by Month at Redcar

March/April

	Total W-R	Non-handicaps 2-y-o	3-y-o+	Handicaps 2-y-o	3-y-o+	Per cent	£1 Level Stake
Mrs M Reveley	2-5	1-1	0-1	0-0	1-3	40.0	+ 1.38
L M Cumani	1-1	0-0	1-1	0-0	0-0	100.0	+ 4.50
M W Eckley	1-1	0-0	0-0	0-0	1-1	100.0	+ 10.00
J L Harris	1-1	0-0	0-0	0-0	1-1	100.0	+ 11.00
M Dods	1-2	0-0	0-0	0-0	1-2	50.0	+ 11.00

May

	Total W-R	Non-handicaps 2-y-o	3-y-o+	Handicaps 2-y-o	3-y-o+	Per cent	£1 Level Stake
Mrs M Reveley	6-27	0-3	0-6	0-0	6-18	22.2	- 3.00
M H Easterby	5-35	3-13	0-6	0-0	2-16	14.3	- 9.50
J Berry	4-28	2-13	1-6	0-0	1-9	14.3	+ 2.50
M R Stoute	3-5	0-0	3-3	0-0	0-2	60.0	+ 3.69
H R A Cecil	3-10	1-2	2-7	0-0	0-1	30.0	- 4.68

June

	Total W-R	Non-handicaps 2-y-o	3-y-o+	Handicaps 2-y-o	3-y-o+	Per cent	£1 Level Stake
L M Cumani	5-7	0-0	3-4	0-0	2-3	71.4	+ 6.93
J Berry	5-28	2-14	1-6	0-0	2-8	17.9	+ 16.40
J H M Gosden	4-8	0-0	3-6	0-0	1-2	50.0	- 0.13
C W C Elsey	3-5	0-0	1-3	0-0	2-2	60.0	+ 23.21
J W Hills	3-7	0-0	0-1	0-0	3-6	42.9	+ 12.33

July

	Total W-R	Non-handicaps 2-y-o	3-y-o+	Handicaps 2-y-o	3-y-o+	Per cent	£1 Level Stake
Mrs M Reveley	13-51	4-13	1-3	0-0	8-35	25.5	+ 37.95
J Berry	5-25	4-15	0-2	0-0	1-8	20.0	- 0.72
R M Whitaker	5-31	2-9	0-1	0-0	3-21	16.1	+ 6.55
L M Cumani	4-13	0-1	3-6	0-0	1-6	30.8	- 2.40
H Thomson Jones	3-7	1-1	1-3	0-0	1-3	42.9	+ 1.30

August

	Total W-R	Non-handicaps 2-y-o	3-y-o+	Handicaps 2-y-o	3-y-o+	Per cent	£1 Level Stake
M H Easterby	14-37	4-14	2-4	6-12	2-7	37.8	+ 23.89
Mrs M Reveley	7-57	0-11	4-17	0-2	3-27	12.3	- 13.75
H Thomson Jones	6-10	2-2	2-4	0-0	2-4	60.0	+ 8.89
R Hollinshead	5-26	1-4	1-7	0-1	3-14	19.2	- 5.70
W Jarvis	4-4	0-0	0-0	0-0	4-4	100.0	+ 11.88

September

	Total W-R	Non-handicaps 2-y-o	3-y-o+	Handicaps 2-y-o	3-y-o+	Per cent	£1 Level Stake
H Thomson Jones	5-11	2-3	1-1	1-3	1-4	45.5	+ 14.95
W Carter	4-14	0-5	0-0	0-2	4-7	28.6	+ 66.50
Mrs M Reveley	4-29	0-7	0-2	1-6	3-14	13.8	- 0.50
M H Easterby	3-29	1-14	1-1	0-7	1-7	10.3	- 8.50
R Charlton	2-2	1-1	1-1	0-0	0-0	100.0	+ 9.00

Oct/Nov

	Total W-R	Non-handicaps 2-y-o	3-y-o+	Handicaps 2-y-o	3-y-o+	Per cent	£1 Level Stake
G Harwood	7-21	3-7	2-6	0-1	2-7	33.3	+ 15.41
R Hannon	7-25	5-16	1-3	1-3	0-3	28.0	+ 8.69
J L Dunlop	5-22	2-7	0-5	0-1	3-9	22.7	- 7.45
H Thomson Jones	5-27	2-12	2-5	0-0	1-10	18.5	- 4.99
M H Easterby	5-43	2-18	0-1	2-4	1-20	11.6	- 3.25

RIPON (Group 2)

Leading Trainers 1989-93

	Total W-R	Non-handicaps 2-y-o	3-y-o+	Handicaps 2-y-o	3-y-o+	Per cent	£1 Level Stake
J Berry	24-130	15-73	3-17	2-10	4-30	18.5	- 16.50
H R A Cecil	22-44	2-3	19-35	0-0	1-6	50.0	+ 2.90
M H Easterby	16-222	6-64	3-25	0-8	7-125	7.2	-148.12
M R Stoute	13-46	1-4	7-21	0-0	5-21	28.3	+ 11.44
J L Dunlop	9-25	1-7	3-5	0-1	5-12	36.0	+ 11.05
L M Cumani	9-29	2-2	6-23	0-0	1-4	31.0	- 7.87
J H M Gosden	9-38	0-3	7-27	0-0	2-8	23.7	- 10.60
J W Watts	9-70	3-15	0-16	0-0	6-39	12.9	+ 8.00
B W Hills	8-38	1-5	4-17	0-0	3-16	21.1	- 8.37
P C Haslam	8-56	2-10	1-9	0-2	5-35	14.3	+ 25.50
J Etherington	8-59	3-20	3-13	0-1	2-25	13.6	- 4.29
Mrs M Reveley	8-71	0-4	2-17	0-2	6-48	11.3	- 26.67
R M Whitaker	8-116	2-24	3-30	0-3	3-59	6.9	- 49.95
M S Johnston	7-65	2-21	0-5	1-3	4-36	10.8	- 14.88
R Hollinshead	7-107	0-21	1-27	0-1	6-58	6.5	- 43.29
M Brittain	7-111	0-23	0-9	1-6	6-73	6.3	- 32.50
D Morley	6-26	0-1	1-8	0-0	5-17	23.1	+ 5.05
Miss S E Hall	6-75	1-19	4-23	0-1	1-32	8.0	- 45.68
D W Chapman	6-78	1-5	1-11	0-3	4-59	7.7	- 8.50
Sir M Prescott	5-22	1-1	1-7	0-0	3-14	22.7	+ 2.96
G Wragg	5-23	0-2	3-10	0-0	2-11	21.7	+ 11.20
A C Stewart	5-23	1-3	2-11	0-0	2-9	21.7	- 7.01

Leading Jockeys

	Total W-R	Per cent	£1 Level Stake	Best Trainer	W-R	Per cent	£1 Level Stake
K Darley	25-174	14.4	- 43.45	M H Easterby	5-26	19.2	- 3.38
M Birch	23-198	11.6	- 74.14	M H Easterby	10-103	9.7	- 58.74
J Carroll	15-113	13.3	- 27.59	J Berry	13-66	19.7	- 6.59
M Roberts	13-59	22.0	- 6.85	A C Stewart	5-10	50.0	+ 6.00
W Ryan	13-85	15.3	- 47.37	H R A Cecil	9-20	45.0	- 1.33
G Duffield	13-99	13.1	- 34.92	J H M Gosden	2-3	66.7	+ 2.38
J Lowe	13-170	7.6	- 68.92	Mrs M Reveley	5-29	17.2	+ 5.33
N Connorton	12-101	11.9	- 23.04	Miss S E Hall	5-23	21.7	+ 0.33
Pat Eddery	11-26	42.3	+ 9.69	R Charlton	2-2	100.0	+ 3.00
R Cochrane	11-57	19.3	+ 9.23	L M Cumani	2-4	50.0	- 0.40
Paul Eddery	11-61	18.0	+ 15.73	G Lewis	2-2	100.0	+ 8.23
A Culhane	9-104	8.7	- 35.20	R M Whitaker	6-59	10.2	- 8.95

How the Favourites Fared

Non-handicaps	W-R	Per cent	£1 Level Stake	Handicaps	W-R	Per cent	£1 Level Stake
2-y-o	34-90	37.8	- 25.85	2-y-o	1-8	12.5	- 4.87
3-y-o	35-63	55.6	+ 3.51	3-y-o	16-60	26.7	- 9.44
Weight-for-age	22-47	46.8	+ 6.96	All-aged	43-140	30.7	+ 7.25
Totals	91-200	45.5	- 15.38	Totals	60-208	28.8	- 7.06
All favs	151-408	37.0	- 22.44				

Leading Trainers by Month at Ripon

March/April	Total W-R	Non-handicaps 2-y-o	3-y-o+	Handicaps 2-y-o	3-y-o+	Per cent	£1 Level Stake
J Berry	8-33	5-19	0-7	0-0	3-7	24.2	+ 9.43
H R A Cecil	6-12	0-0	6-12	0-0	0-0	50.0	+ 1.94
J L Dunlop	4-7	0-0	2-4	0-0	2-3	57.1	+ 18.13
J H M Gosden	4-7	0-0	3-5	0-0	1-2	57.1	+ 0.02
J W Watts	4-22	0-2	0-7	0-0	4-13	18.2	+ 27.00

May	Total W-R	Non-handicaps 2-y-o	3-y-o+	Handicaps 2-y-o	3-y-o+	Per cent	£1 Level Stake
A C Stewart	3-3	0-0	2-2	0-0	1-1	100.0	+ 4.99
H R A Cecil	3-4	0-0	2-3	0-0	1-1	75.0	+ 4.24
Mrs L Piggott	2-2	0-0	0-0	0-0	2-2	100.0	+ 3.25
J Berry	2-5	1-3	1-2	0-0	0-0	40.0	- 0.75
J W Watts	2-6	0-0	0-2	0-0	2-4	33.3	+ 8.00

June	Total W-R	Non-handicaps 2-y-o	3-y-o+	Handicaps 2-y-o	3-y-o+	Per cent	£1 Level Stake
H R A Cecil	5-7	1-1	4-6	0-0	0-0	71.4	+ 5.25
J L Dunlop	4-8	0-2	1-1	0-0	3-5	50.0	+ 1.42
J Pearce	4-9	1-1	1-2	0-0	2-6	44.4	+ 10.88
M R Stoute	4-12	0-0	2-7	0-0	2-5	33.3	+ 14.33
M S Johnston	3-9	2-4	0-0	0-0	1-5	33.3	+ 16.00

July	Total W-R	Non-handicaps 2-y-o	3-y-o+	Handicaps 2-y-o	3-y-o+	Per cent	£1 Level Stake
L M Cumani	3-6	1-1	2-5	0-0	0-0	50.0	+ 0.72
J Berry	3-14	2-9	0-2	0-0	1-3	21.4	- 1.33
M H Easterby	3-28	1-6	1-2	0-0	1-20	10.7	- 11.88
C E Brittain	2-2	0-0	1-1	0-0	1-1	100.0	+ 7.25
G Wragg	2-3	0-0	1-1	0-0	1-2	66.7	+ 17.50

August	Total W-R	Non-handicaps 2-y-o	3-y-o+	Handicaps 2-y-o	3-y-o+	Per cent	£1 Level Stake
J Berry	7-48	4-24	1-3	2-10	0-11	14.6	- 12.93
B W Hills	6-18	1-3	4-8	0-0	1-7	33.3	+ 1.13
J Etherington	6-24	1-8	3-6	0-1	2-9	25.0	+ 17.21
M H Easterby	6-77	1-17	1-5	0-8	4-47	7.8	- 50.37
M R Stoute	5-16	1-4	2-4	0-0	2-8	31.3	+ 2.27

September	Total W-R	Non-handicaps 2-y-o	3-y-o+	Handicaps 2-y-o	3-y-o+	Per cent	£1 Level Stake
D W Chapman	3-5	1-1	0-0	0-0	2-4	60.0	+ 44.00
H R A Cecil	2-3	0-0	2-2	0-0	0-1	66.7	+ 0.20
W R Hern	1-1	0-0	1-1	0-0	0-0	100.0	+ 0.53
M R Channon	1-1	0-0	1-1	0-0	0-0	100.0	+ 8.00
P A Kelleway	1-2	0-1	1-1	0-0	0-0	50.0	+ 7.00

SALISBURY (Group 2)

Leading Trainers 1989-93

	Total W-R	Non-handicaps 2-y-o	3-y-o+	Handicaps 2-y-o	3-y-o+	Per cent	£1 Level Stake
R Hannon	42-320	21-135	10-56	0-5	11-124	13.1	- 65.27
G Harwood	27-93	10-29	6-24	2-2	9-38	29.0	+ 11.53
D R C Elsworth	21-164	7-42	3-43	0-0	11-79	12.8	- 39.00
I A Balding	17-132	5-45	6-37	0-0	6-50	12.9	- 33.09
P F I Cole	14-93	7-37	3-28	0-1	4-27	15.1	- 21.85
J L Dunlop	12-118	4-37	4-39	0-1	4-41	10.2	- 40.02
J H M Gosden	10-31	3-8	7-19	0-0	0-4	32.3	+ 20.50
L M Cumani	10-33	3-7	6-18	0-0	1-8	30.3	+ 16.46
R Charlton	8-52	2-18	3-25	0-0	3-9	15.4	- 24.92
R Akehurst	8-64	2-13	0-18	0-0	6-33	12.5	- 8.25
D A Wilson	7-52	0-4	0-1	0-0	7-47	13.5	- 1.00
K O C-Brown	7-57	1-13	4-9	0-0	2-35	12.3	+ 47.50
J R Fanshawe	6-19	1-2	3-12	0-1	2-4	31.6	+ 23.50
M R Stoute	6-24	1-11	2-9	0-0	3-4	25.0	- 2.27
Lord Huntingdon	6-51	0-13	5-22	0-0	1-16	11.8	- 29.43
C J Benstead	6-62	0-2	0-6	0-0	6-54	9.7	- 19.50
H Candy	6-73	2-16	1-21	0-0	3-36	8.2	+ 16.00
G B Balding	6-116	1-26	2-17	0-1	3-72	5.2	- 65.25
H R A Cecil	5-19	0-0	5-18	0-0	0-1	26.3	- 6.70
M Bell	5-33	1-6	1-5	0-1	3-21	15.2	+ 16.00
J W Hills	5-43	3-12	1-7	0-0	1-24	11.6	- 2.55
G Lewis	5-72	4-28	1-12	0-2	0-30	6.9	- 44.02

Leading Jockeys

	Total W-R	Per cent	£1 Level Stake	Best Trainer	W-R	Per cent	£1 Level Stake
Pat Eddery	26-123	21.1	- 19.58	K O C-Brown	3-3	100.0	+ 3.50
R Cochrane	24-159	15.1	- 40.60	G Harwood	10-31	32.3	- 5.06
J Williams	22-233	9.4	- 48.74	D R C Elsworth	8-57	14.0	- 7.74
J Reid	21-153	13.7	- 46.88	R Hannon	4-17	23.5	+ 2.28
W Carson	21-156	13.5	- 63.72	J L Dunlop	7-28	25.0	+ 1.48
B Rouse	18-185	9.7	- 74.50	R Hannon	12-67	17.9	+ 0.50
L Dettori	13-88	14.8	+ 9.41	L M Cumani	5-14	35.7	+ 11.13
W R Swinburn	12-55	21.8	+ 23.48	A A Scott	3-4	75.0	+ 6.00
M Roberts	12-68	17.6	- 7.34	G Harwood	2-3	66.7	+ 2.50
T Quinn	12-110	10.9	- 53.69	P F I Cole	6-41	14.6	- 19.77
A Munro	11-77	14.3	- 11.67	P F I Cole	2-5	40.0	+ 7.73
M Hills	10-60	16.7	- 4.27	J W Hills	4-12	33.3	+ 23.95

How the Favourites Fared

Non-handicaps	W-R	Per cent	£1 Level Stake	Handicaps	W-R	Per cent	£1 Level Stake
2-y-o	50-115	43.5	- 4.63	2-y-o	3-4	75.0	+ 2.02
3-y-o	32-80	40.0	- 8.47	3-y-o	12-41	29.3	+ 3.76
Weight-for-age	11-19	57.9	+ 3.23	All-aged	30-153	19.6	- 49.25
Totals	93-214	43.5	- 9.87	Totals	45-198	22.7	- 43.47
All favs	138-412	33.5	- 53.34				

Leading Trainers by Month at Salisbury

March/April

	Total W-R	Non-handicaps 2-y-o	3-y-o+	Handicaps 2-y-o	3-y-o+	Per cent	£1 Level Stake
L M Cumani	2-4	0-0	2-4	0-0	0-0	50.0	+ 13.38
I A Balding	2-5	0-0	1-4	0-0	1-1	40.0	+ 1.50
A C Stewart	1-1	0-0	0-0	0-0	1-1	100.0	+ 10.00
C James	1-2	0-0	0-0	0-0	1-2	50.0	+ 15.00
P D Cundell	1-3	0-0	0-0	0-0	1-3	33.3	+ 14.00

May

	Total W-R	Non-handicaps 2-y-o	3-y-o+	Handicaps 2-y-o	3-y-o+	Per cent	£1 Level Stake
R Hannon	12-73	4-17	4-20	0-0	4-36	16.4	+ 9.60
G Harwood	6-20	0-1	5-14	0-0	1-5	30.0	- 1.18
D R C Elsworth	5-31	2-3	1-14	0-0	2-14	16.1	- 9.13
M McCormack	4-15	3-5	0-4	0-0	1-6	26.7	- 0.01
J R Fanshawe	3-6	0-0	2-5	0-0	1-1	50.0	+ 15.50

June

	Total W-R	Non-handicaps 2-y-o	3-y-o+	Handicaps 2-y-o	3-y-o+	Per cent	£1 Level Stake
R Hannon	7-66	3-33	2-11	0-0	2-22	10.6	- 18.38
I A Balding	6-37	2-13	2-7	0-0	2-17	16.2	- 8.33
J L Dunlop	5-28	1-5	2-11	0-0	2-12	17.9	+ 1.23
G Harwood	4-11	1-4	0-1	0-0	3-6	36.4	+ 0.50
P F I Cole	4-19	2-8	0-3	0-0	2-8	21.1	- 4.05

July

	Total W-R	Non-handicaps 2-y-o	3-y-o+	Handicaps 2-y-o	3-y-o+	Per cent	£1 Level Stake
G Harwood	5-14	3-6	0-2	0-0	2-6	35.7	+ 11.10
R Hannon	5-35	3-15	1-4	0-0	1-16	14.3	- 17.70
I A Balding	2-9	1-3	0-1	0-0	1-5	22.2	+ 6.33
K O C-Brown	2-10	0-2	1-1	0-0	1-7	20.0	+ 41.00
P F I Cole	2-11	1-6	0-1	0-0	1-4	18.2	- 1.00

August

	Total W-R	Non-handicaps 2-y-o	3-y-o+	Handicaps 2-y-o	3-y-o+	Per cent	£1 Level Stake
R Hannon	10-72	7-33	2-11	0-5	1-23	13.9	- 29.80
D R C Elsworth	6-41	1-12	0-11	0-0	5-18	14.6	- 6.75
G Harwood	5-24	1-6	1-3	2-2	1-13	20.8	- 6.54
J H M Gosden	3-6	0-0	3-6	0-0	0-0	50.0	+ 12.20
R Akehurst	3-10	1-1	0-3	0-0	2-6	30.0	+ 9.25

September

	Total W-R	Non-handicaps 2-y-o	3-y-o+	Handicaps 2-y-o	3-y-o+	Per cent	£1 Level Stake
G Harwood	4-9	3-5	0-1	0-0	1-3	44.4	+ 7.75
R Hannon	4-32	3-22	0-1	0-0	1-9	12.5	- 4.50
P F I Cole	3-16	2-12	1-2	0-0	0-2	18.8	+ 5.25
J L Dunlop	3-25	2-16	0-2	0-0	1-7	12.0	- 8.25
J R Fanshawe	2-2	1-1	1-1	0-0	0-0	100.0	+ 12.00

Oct/Nov

	Total W-R	Non-handicaps 2-y-o	3-y-o+	Handicaps 2-y-o	3-y-o+	Per cent	£1 Level Stake
D R C Elsworth	4-15	2-7	0-2	0-0	2-6	26.7	+ 15.00
R Hannon	4-30	1-15	1-3	0-0	2-12	13.3	+ 7.50
J H M Gosden	3-6	2-5	1-1	0-0	0-0	50.0	+ 15.75
G Harwood	3-14	2-7	0-2	0-0	1-5	21.4	+ 0.90
L M Cumani	2-5	1-2	1-2	0-0	0-1	40.0	- 1.58

511

SANDOWN (Group 1)

Leading Trainers 1989-93

	Total W-R	Non-handicaps 2-y-o	3-y-o+	Handicaps 2-y-o	3-y-o+	Per cent	£1 Level Stake
R Hannon	35-264	12-94	6-47	1-14	16-109	13.3	- 54.05
M R Stoute	24-157	7-22	12-78	0-3	5-54	15.3	- 48.38
G Harwood	19-91	3-13	7-38	1-2	8-38	20.9	- 4.27
J H M Gosden	17-66	2-4	12-39	0-0	3-23	25.8	+ 12.21
H R A Cecil	17-82	6-12	11-57	0-0	0-13	20.7	- 32.27
I A Balding	17-99	5-21	4-29	1-2	7-47	17.2	+ 18.98
R Akehurst	16-125	0-4	1-22	0-4	15-95	12.8	- 24.79
J L Dunlop	13-101	4-30	4-27	0-1	5-43	12.9	- 10.13
P F I Cole	13-106	3-25	3-35	2-8	5-38	12.3	- 31.17
C E Brittain	13-158	1-34	7-49	0-4	5-71	8.2	- 15.18
B W Hills	12-86	5-22	5-42	1-2	1-20	14.0	+ 3.10
L M Cumani	10-61	0-4	9-43	0-0	1-14	16.4	- 6.31
Lord Huntingdon	10-76	2-15	2-18	0-2	6-41	13.2	- 19.38
P J Makin	8-39	0-6	3-13	0-0	5-20	20.5	+ 16.63
J R Fanshawe	8-44	1-4	5-20	0-1	2-19	18.2	+ 26.98
R W Armstrong	8-48	1-9	3-12	0-1	4-26	16.7	+ 32.70
W R Hern	8-48	3-8	5-29	0-0	0-11	16.7	- 17.62
J Berry	8-58	1-9	5-24	0-8	2-17	13.8	- 10.99
M R Channon	8-59	2-14	0-11	0-5	6-29	13.6	- 5.95
D R C Elsworth	8-121	1-17	4-52	0-3	3-49	6.6	- 78.03
Sir M Prescott	6-26	1-1	4-9	0-3	1-13	23.1	+ 15.50
W Jarvis	6-40	1-3	1-11	0-2	4-24	15.0	+ 39.50

Leading Jockeys

	Total W-R	Per cent	£1 Level Stake	Best Trainer	W-R	Per cent	£1 Level Stake
Pat Eddery	54-300	18.0	- 72.61	R Hannon	7-24	29.2	+ 1.55
M Roberts	42-254	16.5	+ 10.16	C E Brittain	8-68	11.8	- 0.75
W Carson	33-247	13.4	- 46.99	W R Hern	5-30	16.7	- 9.45
T Quinn	30-181	16.6	+ 30.36	P F I Cole	11-58	19.0	+ 4.83
W R Swinburn	30-189	15.9	- 35.30	M R Stoute	13-62	21.0	- 8.66
R Cochrane	23-164	14.0	- 8.90	I A Balding	4-15	26.7	+ 3.75
L Dettori	20-144	13.9	- 8.33	L M Cumani	4-35	11.4	- 9.75
J Reid	16-173	9.2	- 70.59	R Hannon	2-11	18.2	+ 1.50
A Munro	12-97	12.4	- 40.81	H Candy	2-2	100.0	+ 5.25
M Hills	11-94	11.7	- 18.87	B W Hills	3-21	14.3	+ 8.50
R Hills	10-75	13.3	+ 46.08	H Thomson Jones	4-19	21.1	+ 3.50
G Duffield	9-80	11.3	+ 43.50	Sir M Prescott	5-23	21.7	+ 15.50

How the Favourites Fared

Non-handicaps	W-R	Per cent	£1 Level Stake	Handicaps	W-R	Per cent	£1 Level Stake
2-y-o	49-101	48.5	+ 13.86	2-y-o	3-21	14.3	- 14.12
3-y-o	34-89	38.2	- 9.45	3-y-o	25-89	28.1	- 4.45
Weight-for-age	29-78	37.2	- 6.19	All-aged	46-148	31.1	+ 1.73
Totals	112-268	41.8	- 1.78	Totals	74-258	28.7	- 16.84
All favs	186-526	35.4	- 18.62				

Leading Trainers by Month at Sandown

March/April

	Total W–R	Non-handicaps 2-y-o	Non-handicaps 3-y-o+	Handicaps 2-y-o	Handicaps 3-y-o+	Per cent	£1 Level Stake
H R A Cecil	6-15	0-0	6-15	0-0	0-0	40.0	+ 2.84
J L Dunlop	5-15	0-0	3-9	0-0	2-6	33.3	+ 9.63
R Hannon	5-41	2-15	1-9	0-0	2-17	12.2	+ 5.00
C E Brittain	4-27	1-3	2-16	0-0	1-8	14.8	+ 15.00
B W Hills	3-18	1-5	2-12	0-0	0-1	16.7	+ 16.60

May

	Total W–R	Non-handicaps 2-y-o	Non-handicaps 3-y-o+	Handicaps 2-y-o	Handicaps 3-y-o+	Per cent	£1 Level Stake
M R Stoute	10-38	1-4	8-26	0-0	1-8	26.3	+ 10.69
R Hannon	8-37	3-10	1-8	0-0	4-19	21.6	+ 14.97
G Harwood	5-14	0-0	3-8	0-0	2-6	35.7	+ 5.33
Lord Huntingdon	4-7	1-1	2-5	0-0	1-1	57.1	+ 17.00
I A Balding	4-15	1-1	0-8	0-0	3-6	26.7	+ 16.00

June

	Total W–R	Non-handicaps 2-y-o	Non-handicaps 3-y-o+	Handicaps 2-y-o	Handicaps 3-y-o+	Per cent	£1 Level Stake
R Hannon	6-32	2-11	1-7	0-0	3-14	18.8	- 2.70
J H M Gosden	4-11	0-0	3-9	0-0	1-2	36.4	+ 0.83
R Akehurst	4-14	0-0	0-2	0-0	4-12	28.6	+ 2.83
B W Hills	3-9	1-2	2-6	0-0	0-1	33.3	+ 7.38
M R Stoute	3-14	2-2	0-5	0-0	1-7	21.4	- 5.22

July

	Total W–R	Non-handicaps 2-y-o	Non-handicaps 3-y-o+	Handicaps 2-y-o	Handicaps 3-y-o+	Per cent	£1 Level Stake
R Hannon	11-83	3-34	2-12	0-0	6-37	13.3	- 24.63
R Akehurst	8-45	0-4	1-7	0-0	7-34	17.8	+ 11.25
I A Balding	7-29	3-8	1-6	0-0	3-15	24.1	+ 2.75
G Harwood	7-35	3-9	1-12	0-0	3-14	20.0	+ 1.61
P F I Cole	5-23	1-5	1-7	0-0	3-11	21.7	+ 5.83

August

	Total W–R	Non-handicaps 2-y-o	Non-handicaps 3-y-o+	Handicaps 2-y-o	Handicaps 3-y-o+	Per cent	£1 Level Stake
J W Hills	3-10	1-1	1-4	1-1	0-4	30.0	+ 45.00
J R Fanshawe	3-10	1-1	1-4	0-1	1-4	30.0	+ 13.38
J Berry	3-11	0-0	2-4	0-4	1-3	27.3	+ 3.13
J L Dunlop	3-13	1-6	1-4	0-0	1-3	23.1	+ 12.50
G Harwood	3-15	0-2	1-7	1-2	1-4	20.0	- 1.83

September

	Total W–R	Non-handicaps 2-y-o	Non-handicaps 3-y-o+	Handicaps 2-y-o	Handicaps 3-y-o+	Per cent	£1 Level Stake
M H Easterby	3-8	0-0	2-3	0-3	1-2	37.5	+ 8.25
R W Armstrong	3-10	1-4	0-2	0-0	2-4	30.0	+ 46.00
C F Wall	3-10	1-2	0-1	1-2	1-5	30.0	+ 9.60
P F I Cole	3-21	1-7	0-3	1-2	1-9	14.3	- 9.00
R Hannon	3-34	1-15	1-4	0-3	1-12	8.8	- 16.42

SOUTHWELL (AW)

Leading Trainers 1989-93

	Total W-R	Non-handicaps 2-y-o	3-y-o+	Handicaps 2-y-o	3-y-o+	Per cent	£1 Level Stake
T D Barron	64-285	7-30	27-94	2-14	28-147	22.5	+ 17.01
D W Chapman	45-446	3-31	20-136	2-17	20-262	10.1	-163.71
W A O'Gorman	39-202	16-41	12-63	3-11	8-87	19.3	- 3.37
J Berry	33-209	19-97	3-37	1-9	10-66	15.8	- 34.58
R Hollinshead	28-340	3-53	11-127	2-15	12-145	8.2	-158.69
S G Norton	25-131	6-34	8-26	1-12	10-59	19.1	+ 29.38
C J Hill	25-152	2-11	7-60	2-4	14-77	16.4	- 36.43
Sir M Prescott	24-125	4-48	14-34	0-2	6-41	19.2	- 27.91
Mrs N Macauley	19-232	3-28	5-78	1-8	10-118	8.2	- 61.75
Lord Huntingdon	18-76	2-8	12-37	0-2	4-29	23.7	+ 6.59
J G FitzGerald	17-113	4-23	4-31	0-2	9-57	15.0	+ 12.93
M S Johnston	17-134	0-18	7-32	0-8	10-76	12.7	- 48.33
C N Allen	17-142	2-26	8-34	1-7	6-75	12.0	- 14.23
M Brittain	14-192	2-33	9-44	0-8	3-107	7.3	- 87.50
C R Nelson	13-39	2-7	8-19	0-0	3-13	33.3	+ 21.66
M Bell	13-76	6-21	3-24	0-2	4-29	17.1	+ 7.29
W W Haigh	13-86	1-5	6-37	0-2	6-42	15.1	+ 17.86
S R Bowring	13-152	0-8	3-25	0-6	10-113	8.6	- 3.00
R C Spicer	12-52	0-3	1-5	0-1	11-43	23.1	+ 51.00
P F I Cole	12-56	4-21	3-14	1-5	4-16	21.4	- 0.47
M J Ryan	12-71	0-4	4-16	0-3	8-48	16.9	+ 13.24
C Tinkler	12-101	2-8	1-26	1-4	8-63	11.9	+ 2.00

Leading Jockeys

	Total W-R	Per cent	£1 Level Stake	Best Trainer	W-R	Per cent	£1 Level Stake
Alex Greaves	59-257	23.0	+ 20.74	T D Barron	52-196	26.5	+ 4.76
G Duffield	43-282	15.2	- 71.20	Sir M Prescott	19-88	21.6	- 17.66
S Wood	39-414	9.4	-148.39	D W Chapman	31-273	11.4	- 91.52
Emma O'Gorman	32-206	15.5	- 49.40	W A O'Gorman	30-162	18.5	- 22.40
J Quinn	31-411	7.5	-162.42	C J Hill	8-31	25.8	- 11.17
G Bardwell	30-295	10.2	- 35.67	C J Hill	8-40	20.0	- 3.92
D Biggs	25-166	15.1	+ 12.21	T Thomson Jones	8-10	80.0	+ 22.97
J Fanning	23-253	9.1	- 49.71	T D Barron	3-11	27.3	+ 10.50
T Quinn	20-152	13.2	- 67.08	P F I Cole	8-34	23.5	- 3.21
D Holland	18-65	27.7	+ 25.16	B W Hills	4-12	33.3	- 3.14
M Hills	18-128	14.1	- 40.23	M Bell	3-15	20.0	- 9.96
N Day	17-118	14.4	+ 12.78	Lady Herries	4-6	66.7	+ 8.43

How the Favourites Fared

Non-handicaps	W-R	Per cent	£1 Level Stake	Handicaps	W-R	Per cent	£1 Level Stake
2-y-o	63-158	39.9	- 9.15	2-y-o	12-34	35.3	+ 10.01
3-y-o	63-145	43.4	- 10.67	3-y-o	31-94	33.0	- 13.86
Weight-for-age	86-216	39.8	- 23.82	All-aged	121-413	29.3	- 46.39
Totals	212-519	40.8	- 43.64	Totals	164-541	30.3	- 50.24
All favs	376-106	35.5	- 93.88				

Leading Trainers by Month at Southwell (AW)

January

	Total W-R	Non-handicaps 2-y-o	Non-handicaps 3-y-o+	Handicaps 2-y-o	Handicaps 3-y-o+	Per cent	£1 Level Stake
T D Barron	23-92	0-0	14-43	0-0	9-49	25.0	- 6.44
D W Chapman	16-104	0-0	8-39	0-0	8-65	15.4	- 10.17

February

	Total W-R	Non-handicaps 2-y-o	Non-handicaps 3-y-o+	Handicaps 2-y-o	Handicaps 3-y-o+	Per cent	£1 Level Stake
T D Barron	14-48	0-0	4-16	0-0	10-32	29.2	+ 4.65
T Thomson Jones	6-9	0-0	1-1	0-0	5-8	66.7	+ 10.58

March

	Total W-R	Non-handicaps 2-y-o	Non-handicaps 3-y-o+	Handicaps 2-y-o	Handicaps 3-y-o+	Per cent	£1 Level Stake
W A O'Gorman	6-21	0-0	5-10	0-0	1-11	28.6	+ 3.14
S G Norton	5-18	0-0	0-4	0-0	5-14	27.8	+ 13.00

April

	Total W-R	Non-handicaps 2-y-o	Non-handicaps 3-y-o+	Handicaps 2-y-o	Handicaps 3-y-o+	Per cent	£1 Level Stake
S G Norton	3-8	0-3	3-3	0-0	0-2	37.5	+ 15.00
C Tinkler	2-5	0-0	0-1	0-0	2-4	40.0	+ 4.63

May

	Total W-R	Non-handicaps 2-y-o	Non-handicaps 3-y-o+	Handicaps 2-y-o	Handicaps 3-y-o+	Per cent	£1 Level Stake
Sir M Prescott	5-10	1-1	3-5	0-0	1-4	50.0	+ 5.85
J Berry	4-23	3-8	0-9	0-0	1-6	17.4	- 0.77

June

	Total W-R	Non-handicaps 2-y-o	Non-handicaps 3-y-o+	Handicaps 2-y-o	Handicaps 3-y-o+	Per cent	£1 Level Stake
J Berry	10-32	6-21	0-2	0-0	4-9	31.3	+ 21.24
Sir M Prescott	4-22	0-7	4-8	0-0	0-7	18.2	- 10.27

July

	Total W-R	Non-handicaps 2-y-o	Non-handicaps 3-y-o+	Handicaps 2-y-o	Handicaps 3-y-o+	Per cent	£1 Level Stake
W A O'Gorman	6-16	6-10	0-1	0-0	0-5	37.5	+ 19.80
S G Norton	6-20	2-8	2-2	0-0	2-10	30.0	+ 13.63

August

	Total W-R	Non-handicaps 2-y-o	Non-handicaps 3-y-o+	Handicaps 2-y-o	Handicaps 3-y-o+	Per cent	£1 Level Stake
M W Easterby	6-35	3-19	1-1	2-3	0-12	17.1	+ 0.20
J Berry	5-26	3-13	0-0	0-3	2-10	19.2	- 4.25

September

	Total W-R	Non-handicaps 2-y-o	Non-handicaps 3-y-o+	Handicaps 2-y-o	Handicaps 3-y-o+	Per cent	£1 Level Stake
P J Makin	2-3	0-0	0-0	0-0	2-3	66.7	+ 10.50
M A Jarvis	2-4	1-3	1-1	0-0	0-0	50.0	+ 9.00

November

	Total W-R	Non-handicaps 2-y-o	Non-handicaps 3-y-o+	Handicaps 2-y-o	Handicaps 3-y-o+	Per cent	£1 Level Stake
W A O'Gorman	7-27	4-7	1-8	1-4	1-8	25.9	+ 18.25
T D Barron	7-35	1-3	4-10	0-5	2-17	20.0	+ 19.75

December

	Total W-R	Non-handicaps 2-y-o	Non-handicaps 3-y-o+	Handicaps 2-y-o	Handicaps 3-y-o+	Per cent	£1 Level Stake
T D Barron	15-48	5-13	3-12	2-8	5-15	31.3	+ 33.05
D W Chapman	9-64	3-8	4-18	1-10	1-28	14.1	- 6.93

SOUTHWELL (TURF)

Leading Trainers 1991-93

	Total W-R	Non-handicaps 2-y-o	3-y-o+	Handicaps 2-y-o	3-y-o+	Per cent	£1 Level Stake
M A Jarvis	4-5	2-2	0-0	0-0	2-3	80.0	+ 20.25
J Berry	4-23	0-12	3-5	0-1	1-5	17.4	- 9.38
P F I Cole	3-4	2-2	0-1	0-0	1-1	75.0	+ 7.23
M H Easterby	3-8	1-4	1-1	0-0	1-3	37.5	+ 25.25
J L Dunlop	3-12	1-5	0-2	0-1	2-4	25.0	+ 7.40
D R Loder	2-2	1-1	1-1	0-0	0-0	100.0	+ 4.88
M R Channon	2-3	1-1	1-1	0-0	0-1	66.7	+ 12.00
P S Felgate	2-4	0-0	1-2	0-0	1-2	50.0	+ 4.25
M C Pipe	2-5	2-2	0-1	0-0	0-2	40.0	+ 8.50
J G FitzGerald	2-7	0-2	1-1	0-0	1-4	28.6	+ 11.50
J Wharton	2-9	0-2	2-3	0-0	0-4	22.2	- 5.44
Mrs M Reveley	2-10	0-2	0-4	1-1	1-3	20.0	+ 6.73
T D Barron	2-11	0-1	1-4	0-0	1-6	18.2	+ 1.50
R Hollinshead	2-11	1-3	1-4	0-0	0-4	18.2	- 7.29
W A O'Gorman	2-18	0-6	0-3	0-0	2-9	11.1	+ 3.50
R W Armstrong	1-1	0-0	0-0	0-0	1-1	100.0	+ 11.00
I A Balding	1-1	1-1	0-0	0-0	0-0	100.0	+ 0.67
A Hide	1-1	0-0	0-0	0-0	1-1	100.0	+ 2.50
W Holden	1-1	0-0	0-0	0-0	1-1	100.0	+ 4.95
Lady Herries	1-1	0-0	0-0	0-0	1-1	100.0	+ 1.10
E A Wheeler	1-1	0-0	0-0	0-0	1-1	100.0	+ 10.00
P Chapple-Hyam	1-1	1-1	0-0	0-0	0-0	100.0	+ 0.67

Leading Jockeys

	Total W-R	Per cent	£1 Level Stake	Best Trainer	W-R	Per cent	£1 Level Stake
T Quinn	3-3	100.0	+ 10.73	P F I Cole	2-2	100.0	+ 4.73
L Dettori	3-6	50.0	+ 13.05	I A Balding	1-1	100.0	+ 0.67
J Lowe	3-11	27.3	+ 5.68	C A Smith	1-1	100.0	+ 8.00
S Maloney	3-15	20.0	+ 9.25	M H Easterby	1-3	33.3	+ 6.00
G Duffield	3-16	18.8	+ 0.88	W J Haggas	1-1	100.0	+ 1.38
W Ryan	3-17	17.6	- 5.58	M R Stoute	1-1	100.0	+ 2.75
K Rutter	2-6	33.3	+ 6.50	M A Jarvis	1-1	100.0	+ 5.00
K Fallon	2-9	22.2	- 0.87	Mrs J Ramsden	1-1	100.0	+ 1.63
A McGlone	2-10	20.0	+ 1.25	J S Moore	1-2	50.0	+ 1.25
B Raymond	2-10	20.0	+ 12.00	J L Dunlop	1-2	50.0	+ 5.00
G Hind	2-10	20.0	- 3.00	P S Felgate	1-1	100.0	+ 2.25
N Day	2-12	16.7	- 4.40	M A Jarvis	1-1	100.0	+ 4.50

How the Favourites Fared

Non-handicaps	W-R	Per cent	£1 Level Stake	Handicaps	W-R	Per cent	£1 Level Stake
2-y-o	10-19	52.6	+ 5.29	2-y-o	0-1	-	- 1.00
3-y-o	3-8	37.5	- 0.61	3-y-o	2-4	50.0	+ 2.50
Weight-for-age	7-11	63.6	+ 1.91	All-aged	6-27	22.2	- 6.92
Totals	20-38	52.6	+ 6.59	Totals	8-32	25.0	- 5.42
All favs	28-70	40.0	+ 1.17				

Leading Trainers by Month at Southwell (Turf)

June	Total W-R	Non-handicaps 2-y-o	3-y-o+	Handicaps 2-y-o	3-y-o+	Per cent	£1 Level Stake
P F I Cole	2-2	1-1	0-0	0-0	1-1	100.0	+ 4.73
M R Channon	1-1	0-0	1-1	0-0	0-0	100.0	+ 6.00
M H Easterby	1-2	0-1	1-1	0-0	0-0	50.0	+ 19.00
P S Felgate	1-2	0-0	0-0	0-0	1-2	50.0	+ 1.25
W A O'Gorman	1-2	0-0	0-0	0-0	1-2	50.0	+ 15.00

July	Total W-R	Non-handicaps 2-y-o	3-y-o+	Handicaps 2-y-o	3-y-o+	Per cent	£1 Level Stake
D R Loder	2-2	1-1	1-1	0-0	0-0	100.0	+ 4.88
M H Easterby	2-4	1-2	0-0	0-0	1-2	50.0	+ 8.25
R Hollinshead	2-4	1-1	1-1	0-0	0-2	50.0	- 0.29
J Berry	2-9	0-5	1-2	0-0	1-2	22.2	- 3.75
R Boss	1-1	0-0	0-0	0-0	1-1	100.0	+ 4.50

August	Total W-R	Non-handicaps 2-y-o	3-y-o+	Handicaps 2-y-o	3-y-o+	Per cent	£1 Level Stake
I A Balding	1-1	1-1	0-0	0-0	0-0	100.0	+ 0.67
A Hide	1-1	0-0	0-0	0-0	1-1	100.0	+ 2.50
W Holden	1-1	0-0	0-0	0-0	1-1	100.0	+ 4.95
M A Jarvis	1-1	0-0	0-0	0-0	1-1	100.0	+ 4.50
Mrs M Reveley	1-1	0-0	0-0	0-0	1-1	100.0	+ 0.73

September	Total W-R	Non-handicaps 2-y-o	3-y-o+	Handicaps 2-y-o	3-y-o+	Per cent	£1 Level Stake
M A Jarvis	2-3	2-2	0-0	0-0	0-1	66.7	+ 10.75
J L Dunlop	2-6	1-2	0-1	0-1	1-2	33.3	+ 6.40
J Berry	2-9	0-3	2-3	0-1	0-2	22.2	- 0.63
R W Armstrong	1-1	0-0	0-0	0-0	1-1	100.0	+ 11.00
H R A Cecil	1-1	1-1	0-0	0-0	0-0	100.0	+ 0.67

THIRSK (Group 2)

Leading Trainers 1989-93

	Total W-R	Non-handicaps 2-y-o	3-y-o+	Handicaps 2-y-o	3-y-o+	Per cent	£1 Level Stake
M H Easterby	29-189	11-67	4-37	1-12	13-73	15.3	+ 17.23
R M Whitaker	16-124	4-21	4-36	1-5	7-62	12.9	- 13.92
J Berry	16-143	7-69	6-28	0-9	3-37	11.2	- 84.14
H R A Cecil	11-32	2-5	8-22	0-1	1-4	34.4	- 8.23
T D Barron	11-138	2-25	0-12	2-5	7-96	8.0	- 54.17
J L Dunlop	10-22	1-4	3-8	1-1	5-9	45.5	+ 27.50
R Hollinshead	10-93	2-20	5-30	0-3	3-40	10.8	- 18.63
M S Johnston	9-58	2-12	3-11	0-3	4-32	15.5	+ 19.00
G Harwood	8-13	0-0	7-8	0-0	1-5	61.5	+ 2.79
F H Lee	8-61	1-11	0-9	1-5	6-36	13.1	- 0.50
D W Chapman	8-91	0-2	0-9	0-1	8-79	8.8	+ 28.50
Mrs J Ramsden	7-59	3-16	1-6	1-5	2-32	11.9	- 8.75
G Wragg	6-16	1-2	4-10	0-0	1-4	37.5	+ 11.51
J Wharton	6-17	2-2	1-4	0-1	3-10	35.3	+ 62.00
H Thomson Jones	6-26	3-8	2-11	0-0	1-7	23.1	- 7.66
A A Scott	6-29	1-4	5-12	0-2	0-11	20.7	- 6.93
Sir M Prescott	6-31	2-11	1-5	2-4	1-11	19.4	+ 5.75
W J Haggas	5-15	1-1	1-6	0-1	3-7	33.3	+ 10.10
P Calver	5-42	0-5	1-11	0-3	4-23	11.9	+ 6.00
C Tinkler	5-54	1-18	1-10	1-3	2-23	9.3	- 20.25
M P Naughton	5-74	0-0	2-20	0-0	3-54	6.8	- 16.63
M W Easterby	5-134	2-61	1-21	0-2	2-50	3.7	-112.38

Leading Jockeys

	Total W-R	Per cent	£1 Level Stake	Best Trainer	W-R	Per cent	£1 Level Stake
M Birch	29-190	15.3	- 16.24	M H Easterby	20-93	21.5	+ 30.33
G Duffield	24-123	19.5	- 3.46	Sir M Prescott	6-28	21.4	+ 8.75
R Hills	14-48	29.2	- 1.47	H Thomson Jones	6-16	37.5	+ 2.34
K Darley	13-166	7.8	-100.15	M H Easterby	3-23	13.0	- 7.35
K Fallon	12-106	11.3	+ 26.50	G M Moore	2-4	50.0	+ 17.00
A Culhane	11-96	11.5	+ 1.83	R M Whitaker	9-61	14.8	+ 5.83
J Carroll	11-106	10.4	- 48.58	J Berry	7-70	10.0	- 39.83
W Ryan	10-62	16.1	- 18.60	H R A Cecil	5-18	27.8	- 8.00
S Wood	10-75	13.3	+ 54.50	D W Chapman	7-40	17.5	+ 53.50
J Lowe	10-149	6.7	- 49.34	B R Cambidge	1-1	100.0	+ 5.00
W Newnes	9-38	23.7	- 0.31	M McCormack	2-3	66.7	+ 10.50
B Raymond	8-38	21.1	+ 3.65	B Hanbury	3-6	50.0	+ 5.00

How the Favourites Fared

Non-handicaps	W-R	Per cent	£1 Level Stake	Handicaps	W-R	Per cent	£1 Level Stake
2-y-o	35-92	38.0	- 7.80	2-y-o	8-19	42.1	+ 1.60
3-y-o	41-91	45.1	- 11.90	3-y-o	10-27	37.0	+ 9.53
Weight-for-age	22-41	53.7	+ 4.47	All-aged	28-137	20.4	- 47.50
Totals	98-224	43.8	- 15.23	Totals	46-183	25.1	- 36.37
All favs	144-407	35.4	- 51.60				

Leading Trainers by Month at Thirsk

March/April

	Total W-R	Non-handicaps 2-y-o	3-y-o+	Handicaps 2-y-o	3-y-o+	Per cent	£1 Level Stake
M H Easterby	8-44	3-7	2-17	0-0	3-20	18.2	+ 5.75
G Wragg	4-8	0-0	3-6	0-0	1-2	50.0	+ 13.38
J Berry	4-27	2-10	2-12	0-0	0-5	14.8	- 15.00
G Harwood	3-3	0-0	3-3	0-0	0-0	100.0	+ 5.00
M McCormack	3-6	0-0	2-4	0-0	1-2	50.0	+ 10.75

May

	Total W-R	Non-handicaps 2-y-o	3-y-o+	Handicaps 2-y-o	3-y-o+	Per cent	£1 Level Stake
M H Easterby	11-65	2-24	2-10	0-0	7-31	16.9	+ 34.00
J Berry	5-42	3-21	0-6	0-0	2-15	11.9	- 17.40
R M Whitaker	5-44	1-9	2-11	0-0	2-24	11.4	+ 6.50
W Jarvis	4-9	2-3	2-5	0-0	0-1	44.4	+ 9.30
J Wharton	3-8	1-1	0-0	0-0	2-7	37.5	+ 26.00

June

	Total W-R	Non-handicaps 2-y-o	3-y-o+	Handicaps 2-y-o	3-y-o+	Per cent	£1 Level Stake
J L Dunlop	4-5	1-1	0-1	0-0	3-3	80.0	+ 22.03
M H Easterby	3-14	2-8	0-0	0-0	1-6	21.4	+ 4.75
F H Lee	2-4	1-1	0-0	0-0	1-3	50.0	+ 2.50
J L Harris	1-1	1-1	0-0	0-0	0-0	100.0	+ 3.50
G Harwood	1-1	0-0	1-1	0-0	0-0	100.0	+ 0.03

July

	Total W-R	Non-handicaps 2-y-o	3-y-o+	Handicaps 2-y-o	3-y-o+	Per cent	£1 Level Stake
Mrs J Ramsden	4-13	1-4	1-1	1-4	1-4	30.8	+ 12.75
H R A Cecil	3-4	1-1	2-2	0-0	0-1	75.0	+ 4.00
M H Easterby	3-11	0-3	0-3	1-1	2-4	27.3	+ 4.13
W J Haggas	2-2	1-1	0-0	0-0	1-1	100.0	+ 2.88
S P C Woods	2-2	1-1	1-1	0-0	0-0	100.0	+ 7.25

August

	Total W-R	Non-handicaps 2-y-o	3-y-o+	Handicaps 2-y-o	3-y-o+	Per cent	£1 Level Stake
D W Chapman	5-25	0-1	0-1	0-0	5-23	20.0	+ 63.50
T D Barron	5-29	1-4	0-1	2-3	2-21	17.2	+ 1.50
J Berry	5-32	1-16	3-5	0-5	1-6	15.6	- 14.03
H R A Cecil	4-9	0-1	3-6	0-0	1-2	44.4	- 1.54
Sir M Prescott	4-12	2-5	0-0	2-3	0-4	33.3	+ 18.00

September

	Total W-R	Non-handicaps 2-y-o	3-y-o+	Handicaps 2-y-o	3-y-o+	Per cent	£1 Level Stake
R M Whitaker	3-18	1-4	1-7	0-2	1-5	16.7	- 4.42
H R A Cecil	2-3	1-1	1-1	0-1	0-0	66.7	+ 0.45
J G FitzGerald	2-4	0-1	0-0	0-0	2-3	50.0	+ 16.50
M R Stoute	2-5	1-3	1-2	0-0	0-0	40.0	- 0.96
Mrs M Reveley	2-6	0-0	0-1	0-1	2-4	33.3	+ 12.50

Oct/Nov

	Total W-R	Non-handicaps 2-y-o	3-y-o+	Handicaps 2-y-o	3-y-o+	Per cent	£1 Level Stake
B Hanbury	2-2	0-0	1-1	0-0	1-1	100.0	+ 5.00
J L Dunlop	1-1	0-0	0-0	1-1	0-0	100.0	+ 8.00
M P Naughton	1-1	0-0	0-0	0-0	1-1	100.0	+ 5.50
J Wharton	1-1	1-1	0-0	0-0	0-0	100.0	+ 33.00
R Hannon	1-2	1-1	0-1	0-0	0-0	50.0	+ 3.50

WARWICK (Group 4)

Leading Trainers 1989-93

	Total W-R	Non-handicaps 2-y-o	3-y-o+	Handicaps 2-y-o	3-y-o+	Per cent	£1 Level Stake
J Berry	20-118	6-57	4-19	3-17	7-25	16.9	+ 7.48
H R A Cecil	16-44	4-6	11-35	0-1	1-2	36.4	- 3.41
P Chapple-Hyam	9-35	3-11	3-13	1-2	2-9	25.7	+ 16.61
J L Dunlop	9-50	1-5	5-21	1-5	2-19	18.0	- 4.34
G Lewis	9-54	6-14	1-15	0-5	2-20	16.7	+ 32.98
B A McMahon	9-61	1-8	0-15	0-1	8-37	14.8	+ 14.71
P F I Cole	9-78	3-19	4-27	0-6	2-26	11.5	- 36.88
B W Hills	8-50	1-11	4-23	1-1	2-15	16.0	- 24.39
R Hollinshead	8-68	1-10	4-22	1-2	2-34	11.8	- 15.25
W R Hern	7-18	0-4	6-8	0-1	1-5	38.9	+ 5.23
R Charlton	7-24	0-1	4-15	1-1	2-7	29.2	+ 3.30
J W Hills	7-39	0-8	3-13	0-0	4-18	17.9	- 3.30
I A Balding	7-53	1-7	5-23	0-4	1-19	13.2	- 29.11
R Hannon	7-106	0-29	1-26	2-14	4-37	6.6	- 63.88
J H M Gosden	6-29	0-2	6-23	0-0	0-4	20.7	- 2.52
R Akehurst	6-31	0-3	0-3	0-0	6-25	19.4	+ 11.50
P T Walwyn	5-23	1-7	4-12	0-0	0-4	21.7	- 13.23
R F J Houghton	5-28	0-5	3-9	1-2	1-12	17.9	- 0.13
G Harwood	5-31	1-7	4-15	0-1	0-8	16.1	- 12.01
M R Stoute	5-32	3-10	2-15	0-0	0-7	15.6	- 19.37
G B Balding	5-33	1-3	0-5	0-2	4-23	15.2	+ 10.50
W Carter	5-37	2-9	0-6	0-1	3-21	13.5	+ 1.00

Leading Jockeys

	Total W-R	Per cent	£1 Level Stake	Best Trainer	W-R	Per cent	£1 Level Stake
W Carson	28-110	25.5	+ 2.91	P T Walwyn	3-4	75.0	+ 2.48
Pat Eddery	19-68	27.9	- 2.10	R Charlton	4-9	44.4	+ 6.01
Paul Eddery	16-92	17.4	+ 16.76	G Lewis	7-23	30.4	+ 45.48
T Quinn	15-110	13.6	+ 6.33	P F I Cole	5-37	13.5	- 7.00
J Williams	15-157	9.6	+ 9.00	G B Balding	5-15	33.3	+ 28.00
W Ryan	13-78	16.7	- 30.56	H R A Cecil	11-20	55.0	+ 8.94
R Cochrane	12-59	20.3	- 16.65	M H Tompkins	2-3	66.7	+ 3.75
W R Swinburn	12-67	17.9	- 1.39	M R Stoute	4-13	30.8	- 1.77
M Hills	11-65	16.9	+ 0.80	B W Hills	2-9	22.2	- 3.00
J Reid	10-69	14.5	- 9.83	R F J Houghton	2-5	40.0	+ 4.25
J Carroll	9-36	25.0	+ 23.60	J Berry	9-33	27.3	+ 26.60
M Roberts	9-38	23.7	+ 10.08	C E Brittain	3-13	23.1	+ 14.50

How the Favourites Fared

Non-handicaps	W-R	Per cent	£1 Level Stake	Handicaps	W-R	Per cent	£1 Level Stake
2-y-o	25-87	28.7	- 34.42	2-y-o	7-23	30.4	- 5.57
3-y-o	42-80	52.5	+ 7.23	3-y-o	14-43	32.6	- 0.53
Weight-for-age	22-51	43.1	+ 6.50	All-aged	25-133	18.8	- 58.48
Totals	89-218	40.8	- 20.69	Totals	46-199	23.1	- 64.58
All favs	135-417	32.4	- 85.27				

Leading Trainers by Month at Warwick

March/April

	Total W-R	Non-handicaps 2-y-o	3-y-o+	Handicaps 2-y-o	3-y-o+	Per cent	£1 Level Stake
J Berry	6-27	2-13	3-7	0-0	1-7	22.2	+ 11.50
B A McMahon	4-13	1-3	0-3	0-0	3-7	30.8	+ 23.00
M H Tompkins	3-10	0-2	3-5	0-0	0-3	30.0	+ 9.75
P Chapple-Hyam	3-11	0-0	3-9	0-0	0-2	27.3	+ 16.00
R Akehurst	3-12	0-0	0-2	0-0	3-10	25.0	+ 18.00

May

	Total W-R	Non-handicaps 2-y-o	3-y-o+	Handicaps 2-y-o	3-y-o+	Per cent	£1 Level Stake
J W Hills	3-9	0-0	2-5	0-0	1-4	33.3	+ 2.25
J Berry	3-15	3-11	0-2	0-0	0-2	20.0	- 0.75
W J Haggas	2-3	0-0	2-3	0-0	0-0	66.7	+ 9.00
C N Williams	2-5	1-1	0-0	0-0	1-4	40.0	+ 9.00
R Charlton	2-5	0-0	2-3	0-0	0-2	40.0	+ 1.80

June

	Total W-R	Non-handicaps 2-y-o	3-y-o+	Handicaps 2-y-o	3-y-o+	Per cent	£1 Level Stake
J L Dunlop	3-7	1-1	1-3	0-0	1-3	42.9	+ 0.93
H R A Cecil	3-10	1-2	2-8	0-0	0-0	30.0	- 5.99
R Charlton	2-3	0-0	1-1	0-0	1-2	66.7	+ 2.00
G B Balding	2-4	0-1	0-0	0-0	2-3	50.0	+ 3.50
I A Balding	2-4	0-0	1-3	0-0	1-1	50.0	+ 0.48

July

	Total W-R	Non-handicaps 2-y-o	3-y-o+	Handicaps 2-y-o	3-y-o+	Per cent	£1 Level Stake
J Berry	6-29	0-13	0-2	2-7	4-7	20.7	+ 3.23
H R A Cecil	5-9	0-0	5-9	0-0	0-0	55.6	- 0.39
B W Hills	5-12	1-1	3-5	1-1	0-5	41.7	+ 0.95
W R Hern	3-3	0-0	3-3	0-0	0-0	100.0	+ 2.98
G Lewis	3-6	3-4	0-0	0-1	0-1	50.0	+ 4.48

August

	Total W-R	Non-handicaps 2-y-o	3-y-o+	Handicaps 2-y-o	3-y-o+	Per cent	£1 Level Stake
P Chapple-Hyam	3-6	1-2	0-2	1-1	1-1	50.0	+ 5.54
H Candy	3-13	0-1	3-8	0-1	0-3	23.1	+ 4.00
R Hollinshead	2-4	0-0	2-4	0-0	0-0	50.0	+ 4.00
J Etherington	2-5	1-2	0-1	0-1	1-1	40.0	+ 7.63
K O C-Brown	1-1	0-0	0-0	0-0	1-1	100.0	+ 6.50

Oct/Nov

	Total W-R	Non-handicaps 2-y-o	3-y-o+	Handicaps 2-y-o	3-y-o+	Per cent	£1 Level Stake
H R A Cecil	4-10	3-4	1-5	0-1	0-0	40.0	+ 5.57
J Berry	3-19	1-7	0-1	1-7	1-4	15.8	+ 10.00
Mrs J Cecil	2-5	2-4	0-0	0-0	0-1	40.0	+ 4.00
J Wharton	2-6	1-3	0-0	0-1	1-2	33.3	+ 30.00
J H M Gosden	2-7	0-1	2-5	0-0	0-1	28.6	- 0.77

WINDSOR (Group 3)

Leading Trainers 1989-93

	Total W-R	Non-handicaps 2-y-o	3-y-o+	Handicaps 2-y-o	3-y-o+	Per cent	£1 Level Stake
R Hannon	36-223	17-92	5-38	4-23	10-70	16.1	- 17.46
L M Cumani	13-38	0-0	11-29	0-1	2-8	34.2	- 6.18
D R C Elsworth	12-77	2-17	9-35	0-1	1-24	15.6	+ 30.38
H R A Cecil	10-37	0-4	7-29	0-0	3-4	27.0	- 5.25
J Berry	10-52	6-29	1-4	3-10	0-9	19.2	- 10.90
G Harwood	9-37	1-1	3-20	1-1	4-15	24.3	+ 5.94
P F I Cole	9-77	4-24	1-25	0-3	4-25	11.7	- 8.08
R Akehurst	8-83	2-13	1-23	1-4	4-43	9.6	+ 26.88
M A Jarvis	7-34	0-3	2-14	0-1	5-16	20.6	- 6.85
P J Makin	7-38	1-7	6-18	0-0	0-13	18.4	- 12.85
J H M Gosden	7-42	2-2	4-31	0-2	1-7	16.7	- 0.84
W R Hern	7-49	1-3	3-32	0-0	3-14	14.3	- 27.96
M Bell	7-49	3-15	0-3	2-7	2-24	14.3	- 17.90
I A Balding	7-50	2-9	2-19	0-1	3-21	14.0	- 22.83
R Charlton	6-25	2-5	2-12	0-1	2-7	24.0	+ 5.83
A C Stewart	6-30	0-2	5-20	0-1	1-7	20.0	- 10.32
Lord Huntingdon	6-39	3-10	2-16	0-0	1-13	15.4	- 8.98
N A Callaghan	6-42	1-7	0-3	0-5	5-27	14.3	- 11.00
M R Stoute	6-42	2-10	1-16	0-0	3-16	14.3	- 19.60
P T Walwyn	6-44	1-9	2-16	0-0	3-19	13.6	- 7.00
B W Hills	6-48	0-13	3-28	2-2	1-5	12.5	- 18.01
C J Benstead	6-54	0-5	0-8	0-0	6-41	11.1	- 16.67

Leading Jockeys

	Total W-R	Per cent	£1 Level Stake	Best Trainer	W-R	Per cent	£1 Level Stake
Pat Eddery	52-217	24.0	- 47.08	R Hannon	10-34	29.4	- 0.76
M Roberts	22-124	17.7	- 34.41	A C Stewart	5-25	20.0	- 13.31
J Reid	19-149	12.8	- 35.50	C R Nelson	4-11	36.4	+ 2.50
R Cochrane	18-138	13.0	- 9.90	L M Cumani	3-12	25.0	- 3.65
L Dettori	17-108	15.7	- 38.40	L M Cumani	9-25	36.0	- 4.40
W Carson	17-162	10.5	- 90.74	W R Hern	6-33	18.2	- 15.95
T Quinn	16-139	11.5	+ 17.33	C J Benstead	4-13	30.8	+ 10.33
W R Swinburn	15-84	17.9	- 24.33	M R Stoute	4-21	19.0	- 5.23
A Munro	11-104	10.6	- 21.91	J D Bethell	2-4	50.0	+ 24.00
B Raymond	9-76	11.8	- 31.87	R Hannon	3-7	42.9	+ 4.13
M Hills	8-77	10.4	- 36.27	J W Hills	2-10	20.0	- 2.75
L Piggott	7-26	26.9	- 0.09	R Hannon	2-5	40.0	+ 5.00

How the Favourites Fared

Non-handicaps	W-R	Per cent	£1 Level Stake	Handicaps	W-R	Per cent	£1 Level Stake
2-y-o	42-99	42.4	- 1.59	2-y-o	8-26	30.8	- 0.77
3-y-o	29-52	55.8	+ 7.89	3-y-o	16-60	26.7	- 17.74
Weight-for-age	21-64	32.8	- 5.91	All-aged	30-95	31.6	- 2.36
Totals	92-215	42.8	+ 0.39	Totals	54-181	29.8	- 20.87
All favs	146-396	36.9	- 20.48				

Leading Trainers by Month at Windsor

March/April

	Total W–R	Non-handicaps 2-y-o	3-y-o+	Handicaps 2-y-o	3-y-o+	Per cent	£1 Level Stake
R Hannon	7-18	5-9	1-5	0-0	1-4	38.9	+ 22.75
H R A Cecil	2-2	0-0	2-2	0-0	0-0	100.0	+ 4.13
H Candy	2-3	0-0	0-1	0-0	2-2	66.7	+ 27.00
M J Ryan	1-1	0-0	0-0	0-0	1-1	100.0	+ 4.50
J D Bethell	1-2	0-0	0-1	0-0	1-1	50.0	+ 9.00

May

	Total W–R	Non-handicaps 2-y-o	3-y-o+	Handicaps 2-y-o	3-y-o+	Per cent	£1 Level Stake
R Hannon	6-25	2-10	0-4	0-0	4-11	24.0	+ 19.17
W J Musson	2-6	2-2	0-2	0-0	0-2	33.3	- 0.63
Miss B Sanders	2-6	0-0	0-2	0-0	2-4	33.3	+ 14.00
P F I Cole	2-7	2-2	0-2	0-0	0-3	28.6	+ 4.75
A C Stewart	2-7	0-0	1-5	0-0	1-2	28.6	- 1.38

June

	Total W–R	Non-handicaps 2-y-o	3-y-o+	Handicaps 2-y-o	3-y-o+	Per cent	£1 Level Stake
R Hannon	6-39	4-19	1-3	0-0	1-17	15.4	- 15.56
L M Cumani	5-7	0-0	3-5	0-0	2-2	71.4	+ 7.85
N A Callaghan	4-16	1-4	0-0	0-0	3-12	25.0	+ 8.00
Lord Huntingdon	3-7	2-3	1-3	0-0	0-1	42.9	+ 7.12
H R A Cecil	2-7	0-0	0-4	0-0	2-3	28.6	- 1.38

July

	Total W–R	Non-handicaps 2-y-o	3-y-o+	Handicaps 2-y-o	3-y-o+	Per cent	£1 Level Stake
R Hannon	10-79	3-34	2-13	2-8	3-24	12.7	- 29.33
D R C Elsworth	9-28	2-6	7-13	0-0	0-9	32.1	+ 67.50
R Akehurst	5-39	1-6	1-8	1-2	2-23	12.8	+ 23.50
G Harwood	4-10	0-0	2-3	0-0	2-7	40.0	+ 12.14
H R A Cecil	4-11	0-2	3-8	0-0	1-1	36.4	+ 1.42

August

	Total W–R	Non-handicaps 2-y-o	3-y-o+	Handicaps 2-y-o	3-y-o+	Per cent	£1 Level Stake
R Hannon	7-62	3-20	1-13	2-15	1-14	11.3	- 14.50
J Berry	6-17	2-4	1-3	3-9	0-1	35.3	+ 7.50
R Charlton	4-11	2-3	1-4	0-1	1-3	36.4	+ 12.45
A C Stewart	4-13	0-1	4-9	0-1	0-2	30.8	+ 1.06
B W Hills	4-14	0-5	2-6	2-2	0-1	28.6	+ 8.91

WOLVERHAMPTON (Group 4)

Leading Trainers 1989-93

	Total W-R	Non-handicaps 2-y-o	3-y-o+	Handicaps 2-y-o	3-y-o+	Per cent	£1 Level Stake
J L Dunlop	18-58	4-19	5-13	0-0	9-26	31.0	+ 10.37
J Berry	16-126	5-61	1-13	6-28	4-24	12.7	- 16.75
H R A Cecil	11-33	2-8	9-25	0-0	0-0	33.3	- 5.55
R Hollinshead	10-161	0-33	7-58	1-7	2-63	6.2	- 56.00
L M Cumani	9-21	3-6	5-13	0-0	1-2	42.9	+ 22.71
G Harwood	8-22	2-7	4-9	0-0	2-6	36.4	+ 7.58
B Hanbury	8-29	3-10	3-10	0-2	2-7	27.6	+ 21.88
J H M Gosden	7-14	3-4	3-8	0-0	1-2	50.0	+ 6.37
B W Hills	7-24	3-9	3-6	0-2	1-7	29.2	+ 10.86
R Boss	7-34	1-7	3-10	0-6	3-11	20.6	+ 6.83
J L Spearing	7-46	0-9	0-7	2-6	5-24	15.2	+ 20.50
G Wragg	6-11	2-2	4-6	0-0	0-3	54.5	+ 12.58
M A Jarvis	6-26	4-8	0-8	0-2	2-8	23.1	+ 27.63
M R Stoute	6-28	3-13	2-10	0-0	1-5	21.4	- 14.90
R Charlton	5-15	3-5	2-6	0-0	0-4	33.3	- 0.81
D Morley	5-22	1-4	1-9	1-1	2-8	22.7	+ 12.25
A C Stewart	5-27	1-5	2-14	0-1	2-7	18.5	- 12.63
Sir M Prescott	5-33	1-15	1-1	0-2	3-15	15.2	+ 5.75
C E Brittain	5-34	0-8	1-14	0-0	4-12	14.7	+ 39.00
P F I Cole	5-38	3-17	0-8	0-0	2-13	13.2	- 15.13
R J Hodges	5-55	2-9	1-17	0-2	2-27	9.1	- 30.18
Mrs N Macauley	5-61	2-13	1-14	1-7	1-27	8.2	- 5.00

Leading Jockeys

	Total W-R	Per cent	£1 Level Stake	Best Trainer	W-R	Per cent	£1 Level Stake
Pat Eddery	28-92	30.4	- 15.45	H R A Cecil	4-6	66.7	- 0.67
M Roberts	26-138	18.8	+ 19.19	A C Stewart	5-22	22.7	- 7.62
W Carson	18-80	22.5	- 13.71	J L Dunlop	5-12	41.7	+ 8.21
J Reid	13-78	16.7	- 22.12	M McCormack	3-9	33.3	+ 1.40
W Ryan	13-106	12.3	- 42.51	H R A Cecil	5-16	31.3	+ 1.49
R Cochrane	12-77	15.6	- 8.74	L M Cumani	5-6	83.3	+ 6.96
W R Swinburn	10-41	24.4	- 1.27	M R Stoute	4-10	40.0	- 0.27
G Duffield	10-79	12.7	+ 8.25	Sir M Prescott	4-22	18.2	+ 14.75
L Dettori	9-58	15.5	- 5.24	L M Cumani	2-8	25.0	+ 3.75
B Raymond	8-63	12.7	- 17.82	B Hanbury	4-10	40.0	+ 6.55
M Hills	7-42	16.7	+ 1.54	B W Hills	3-9	33.3	+ 9.79
T Quinn	7-53	13.2	- 20.13	P F I Cole	5-16	31.3	+ 6.87

How the Favourites Fared

Non-handicaps	W-R	Per cent	£1 Level Stake	Handicaps	W-R	Per cent	£1 Level Stake
2-y-o	41-98	41.8	- 18.96	2-y-o	2-23	8.7	- 17.25
3-y-o	34-66	51.5	- 4.19	3-y-o	15-52	28.8	- 4.74
Weight-for-age	16-44	36.4	+ 2.44	All-aged	26-86	30.2	- 4.41
Totals	91-208	43.8	- 20.71	Totals	43-161	26.7	- 26.40
All favs	134-369	36.3	- 47.11				

Leading Trainers by Month at Wolverhampton

March/April

	Total W-R	Non-handicaps 2-y-o	3-y-o+	Handicaps 2-y-o	3-y-o+	Per cent	£1 Level Stake
H R A Cecil	4-8	0-0	4-8	0-0	0-0	50.0	- 0.30
R J Hodges	3-16	1-1	0-5	0-0	2-10	18.8	- 6.38
R Hollinshead	3-23	0-3	2-11	0-0	1-9	13.0	+ 1.50
W A O'Gorman	2-2	2-2	0-0	0-0	0-0	100.0	+ 2.15
G Wragg	2-4	0-0	2-4	0-0	0-0	50.0	+ 1.70

May

	Total W-R	Non-handicaps 2-y-o	3-y-o+	Handicaps 2-y-o	3-y-o+	Per cent	£1 Level Stake
R Hollinshead	4-30	0-6	4-15	0-0	0-9	13.3	+ 23.00
L M Cumani	3-6	0-0	3-6	0-0	0-0	50.0	- 0.20
J L Dunlop	3-11	0-2	1-4	0-0	2-5	27.3	+ 1.63
J H M Gosden	2-4	0-0	2-4	0-0	0-0	50.0	- 1.46
H R A Cecil	2-5	0-0	2-5	0-0	0-0	40.0	+ 2.91

June

	Total W-R	Non-handicaps 2-y-o	3-y-o+	Handicaps 2-y-o	3-y-o+	Per cent	£1 Level Stake
J L Dunlop	3-4	0-0	1-1	0-0	2-3	75.0	+ 9.08
R Boss	3-6	1-3	1-1	0-0	1-2	50.0	+ 7.75
Lord Huntingdon	2-2	0-0	1-1	0-0	1-1	100.0	+ 21.50
J H M Gosden	2-2	2-2	0-0	0-0	0-0	100.0	+ 6.17
M A Jarvis	2-4	2-3	0-0	0-0	0-1	50.0	+ 11.00

July

	Total W-R	Non-handicaps 2-y-o	3-y-o+	Handicaps 2-y-o	3-y-o+	Per cent	£1 Level Stake
J Berry	8-26	4-19	1-1	1-1	2-5	30.8	+ 8.92
J L Dunlop	5-11	0-4	3-3	0-0	2-4	45.5	+ 4.54
D Haydn Jones	3-22	1-9	0-5	0-0	2-8	13.6	- 6.38
Sir M Prescott	2-2	0-0	1-1	0-0	1-1	100.0	+ 2.75
G Wragg	2-3	2-2	0-0	0-0	0-1	66.7	+ 6.75

August

	Total W-R	Non-handicaps 2-y-o	3-y-o+	Handicaps 2-y-o	3-y-o+	Per cent	£1 Level Stake
M J Ryan	3-4	0-0	1-1	0-0	2-3	75.0	+ 23.00
D Morley	3-5	1-1	1-2	1-1	0-1	60.0	+ 14.25
B W Hills	3-6	1-3	2-2	0-1	0-0	50.0	+ 8.50
I A Balding	3-8	2-3	0-2	0-0	1-3	37.5	+ 14.57
J L Spearing	3-12	0-2	0-2	2-5	1-3	25.0	+ 25.50

September

	Total W-R	Non-handicaps 2-y-o	3-y-o+	Handicaps 2-y-o	3-y-o+	Per cent	£1 Level Stake
J L Dunlop	4-10	3-5	0-0	0-0	1-5	40.0	+ 9.00
M C Pipe	3-5	0-0	2-4	0-0	1-1	60.0	+ 6.73
P F I Cole	3-8	3-5	0-0	0-0	0-3	37.5	- 0.63
J Berry	3-16	0-5	0-0	2-8	1-3	18.8	+ 25.00
Mrs J Cecil	2-2	1-1	0-0	0-0	1-1	100.0	+ 11.00

Oct/Nov

	Total W-R	Non-handicaps 2-y-o	3-y-o+	Handicaps 2-y-o	3-y-o+	Per cent	£1 Level Stake
G Harwood	4-9	1-3	3-4	0-0	0-2	44.4	- 3.17
L M Cumani	3-4	3-3	0-1	0-0	0-0	75.0	+ 17.00
H Thomson Jones	2-3	2-2	0-1	0-0	0-0	66.7	+ 5.25
C E Brittain	2-5	0-1	0-1	0-0	2-3	40.0	+ 27.00
M H Tompkins	2-5	0-1	1-1	0-0	1-3	40.0	+ 16.50

YARMOUTH (Group 3)

Leading Trainers 1989-93

	Total W-R	Non-handicaps 2-y-o	3-y-o+	Handicaps 2-y-o	3-y-o+	Per cent	£1 Level Stake
H R A Cecil	34-96	14-36	18-50	0-1	2-9	35.4	- 4.28
J H M Gosden	21-87	5-24	12-46	0-1	4-16	24.1	+ 8.68
M R Stoute	21-102	9-44	10-36	0-2	2-20	20.6	- 7.77
M H Tompkins	21-148	7-62	4-24	1-11	9-51	14.2	- 19.73
G Wragg	17-94	6-39	7-34	1-2	3-19	18.1	+ 21.52
A C Stewart	15-65	4-18	5-27	0-0	6-20	23.1	+ 16.27
L M Cumani	15-101	7-35	7-49	0-1	1-16	14.9	- 35.96
G A P-Gordon	14-98	3-33	2-24	1-2	8-39	14.3	+ 10.67
Mrs N Macauley	13-85	1-23	2-7	0-2	10-53	15.3	+ 32.78
C E Brittain	13-149	3-41	4-42	1-4	5-62	8.7	- 38.08
H Thomson Jones	11-67	5-24	3-21	0-1	3-21	16.4	- 0.43
B Hanbury	11-84	5-38	4-24	0-4	2-18	13.1	- 12.59
D Morley	11-90	6-26	2-14	0-1	3-49	12.2	- 13.58
M J Ryan	11-138	0-26	4-32	1-5	6-75	8.0	- 68.88
J Berry	9-37	7-28	2-4	0-1	0-4	24.3	+ 16.70
W J Haggas	9-53	2-16	1-10	2-7	4-20	17.0	+ 17.13
Sir M Prescott	9-60	2-27	1-6	0-1	6-26	15.0	+ 11.23
D T Thom	9-68	2-16	0-9	0-3	7-40	13.2	+ 68.50
W Jarvis	9-75	2-12	1-30	0-2	6-31	12.0	- 28.25
Mrs L Piggott	9-75	1-25	3-16	0-2	5-32	12.0	- 50.17
B W Hills	8-30	3-12	3-10	0-0	2-8	26.7	+ 5.91
N A Callaghan	8-45	2-18	2-3	1-5	3-19	17.8	- 8.67

Leading Jockeys

	Total W-R	Per cent	£1 Level Stake	Best Trainer	W-R	Per cent	£1 Level Stake
M Roberts	35-224	15.6	+ 0.51	A C Stewart	11-37	29.7	+ 9.68
W Ryan	27-132	20.5	+ 1.29	H R A Cecil	15-43	34.9	- 1.16
G Duffield	23-145	15.9	+ 16.84	Sir M Prescott	8-35	22.9	+ 34.61
L Dettori	22-136	16.2	- 27.13	L M Cumani	9-41	22.0	- 12.41
R Hills	20-125	16.0	- 7.80	H Thomson Jones	11-45	24.4	+ 21.57
R Cochrane	18-134	13.4	- 25.69	L M Cumani	4-12	33.3	+ 0.46
P Robinson	16-76	21.1	+ 0.38	M H Tompkins	9-39	23.1	+ 3.63
W R Swinburn	16-110	14.5	- 12.45	D Morley	3-12	25.0	+ 1.30
Pat Eddery	14-45	31.1	- 6.86	J Berry	2-2	100.0	+ 2.60
M Hills	14-92	15.2	- 5.00	J W Hills	3-10	30.0	+ 15.00
M Tebbutt	12-90	13.3	- 21.75	W Jarvis	6-34	17.6	+ 4.25
Paul Eddery	12-116	10.3	- 64.24	Mrs J Cecil	3-12	25.0	- 2.02

How the Favourites Fared

Non-handicaps	W-R	Per cent	£1 Level Stake	Handicaps	W-R	Per cent	£1 Level Stake
2-y-o	60-149	40.3	- 27.75	2-y-o	8-23	34.8	- 1.33
3-y-o	34-73	46.6	- 2.98	3-y-o	12-49	24.5	- 19.71
Weight-for-age	33-70	47.1	+ 5.41	All-aged	48-175	27.4	- 34.93
Totals	127-292	43.5	- 25.32	Totals	68-247	27.5	- 55.97
All favs	195-539	36.2	- 81.29				

Leading Trainers by Month at Yarmouth

June

	Total W-R	Non-handicaps 2-y-o	Non-handicaps 3-y-o+	Handicaps 2-y-o	Handicaps 3-y-o+	Per cent	£1 Level Stake
G Wragg	6-27	1-2	3-20	0-0	2-5	22.2	+ 6.49
M H Tompkins	6-38	4-16	0-4	0-0	2-18	15.8	+ 1.63
A C Stewart	5-11	0-0	2-7	0-0	3-4	45.5	+ 21.98
J H M Gosden	5-16	0-1	5-15	0-0	0-0	31.3	- 0.22
C E Brittain	5-36	1-5	2-14	0-0	2-17	13.9	- 1.75

July

	Total W-R	Non-handicaps 2-y-o	Non-handicaps 3-y-o+	Handicaps 2-y-o	Handicaps 3-y-o+	Per cent	£1 Level Stake
H R A Cecil	13-22	4-4	9-18	0-0	0-0	59.1	+ 8.69
M H Tompkins	10-56	3-25	1-11	1-1	5-19	17.9	- 6.60
D Morley	7-27	3-6	2-7	0-0	2-14	25.9	+ 31.93
M J Ryan	7-43	0-10	3-9	0-0	4-24	16.3	+ 2.63
M R Stoute	6-14	2-5	3-6	0-0	1-3	42.9	+ 12.00

August

	Total W-R	Non-handicaps 2-y-o	Non-handicaps 3-y-o+	Handicaps 2-y-o	Handicaps 3-y-o+	Per cent	£1 Level Stake
H R A Cecil	9-18	6-9	3-7	0-0	0-2	50.0	+ 1.47
W J Haggas	7-21	2-7	0-2	2-3	3-9	33.3	+ 41.79
M R Stoute	7-31	5-19	2-6	0-0	0-6	22.6	+ 2.84
Sir M Prescott	5-20	2-5	1-3	0-0	2-12	25.0	+ 11.73
J Pearce	4-16	0-0	2-5	0-0	2-11	25.0	+ 34.00

September

	Total W-R	Non-handicaps 2-y-o	Non-handicaps 3-y-o+	Handicaps 2-y-o	Handicaps 3-y-o+	Per cent	£1 Level Stake
H R A Cecil	8-28	3-12	3-9	0-1	2-6	28.6	- 0.88
J H M Gosden	5-19	2-5	1-9	0-0	2-5	26.3	+ 14.88
L M Cumani	5-35	2-18	3-12	0-1	0-4	14.3	- 7.84
P W Harris	4-7	0-1	0-0	0-0	4-6	57.1	+ 23.00
J Berry	4-11	3-7	1-2	0-0	0-2	36.4	+ 26.75

Oct/Nov

	Total W-R	Non-handicaps 2-y-o	Non-handicaps 3-y-o+	Handicaps 2-y-o	Handicaps 3-y-o+	Per cent	£1 Level Stake
J H M Gosden	5-12	3-8	2-4	0-0	0-0	41.7	+ 11.10
J W Hills	2-6	0-2	1-3	0-0	1-1	33.3	+ 11.00
R Hannon	2-7	1-4	0-0	1-2	0-1	28.6	+ 2.00
A C Stewart	2-7	2-5	0-1	0-0	0-1	28.6	+ 15.91
Mrs J Cecil	2-7	1-6	1-1	0-0	0-0	28.6	+ 1.25

YORK (Group 1)

Leading Trainers 1989-93

	Total W-R	Non-handicaps 2-y-o	3-y-o+	Handicaps 2-y-o	3-y-o+	Per cent	£1 Level Stake
J H M Gosden	30-107	6-16	15-50	0-2	9-39	28.0	+ 15.36
H R A Cecil	29-110	4-11	17-65	1-2	7-32	26.4	- 4.98
M R Stoute	27-140	2-15	19-63	0-3	6-59	19.3	- 3.65
R Hannon	21-162	13-63	3-20	3-15	2-64	13.0	- 27.29
M H Easterby	21-196	3-27	2-12	2-19	14-138	10.7	- 52.17
L M Cumani	17-85	2-8	12-45	0-2	3-30	20.0	- 0.72
J L Dunlop	16-72	7-19	4-22	0-3	5-28	22.2	- 7.58
C E Brittain	15-154	2-29	7-54	1-5	5-66	9.7	- 29.40
B W Hills	14-137	4-29	5-59	0-1	5-48	10.2	- 51.17
P F I Cole	13-49	11-26	1-15	0-1	1-7	26.5	+ 10.47
J Berry	11-102	6-34	0-10	2-11	3-47	10.8	- 52.61
D R C Elsworth	10-51	3-10	4-23	0-0	3-18	19.6	+ 18.75
P Chapple-Hyam	8-30	5-12	1-11	0-1	2-6	26.7	+ 12.49
R Charlton	8-35	4-8	1-7	0-2	3-18	22.9	+ 7.00
M S Johnston	8-55	3-10	0-6	0-2	5-37	14.5	+ 3.38
B Hanbury	8-78	5-15	1-26	0-3	2-34	10.3	- 37.33
M H Tompkins	8-80	1-17	1-6	0-6	6-51	10.0	- 10.75
R M Whitaker	8-124	1-21	2-12	0-9	5-82	6.5	- 61.50
G Harwood	7-35	1-4	4-20	0-0	2-11	20.0	+ 14.70
A A Scott	7-48	3-14	2-16	0-3	2-15	14.6	- 20.08
M Feth-Godley	6-17	0-1	0-0	0-0	6-16	35.3	+ 40.50
W Jarvis	6-45	1-13	3-15	2-3	0-14	13.3	- 16.27

Leading Jockeys

	Total W-R	Per cent	£1 Level Stake	Best Trainer	W-R	Per cent	£1 Level Stake
Pat Eddery	50-225	22.2	+ 16.16	H R A Cecil	7-21	33.3	- 2.01
W Carson	38-255	14.9	- 82.17	J L Dunlop	10-32	31.3	+ 2.21
M Roberts	36-251	14.3	- 1.34	C E Brittain	10-74	13.5	+ 16.38
L Dettori	27-160	16.9	- 6.69	L M Cumani	13-49	26.5	+ 10.90
W R Swinburn	23-191	12.0	- 59.21	M R Stoute	14-73	19.2	- 0.84
M Birch	20-175	11.4	- 32.92	M H Easterby	15-116	12.9	- 8.42
A Munro	17-158	10.8	- 45.15	P F I Cole	8-25	32.0	+ 14.35
R Cochrane	15-146	10.3	- 68.42	L M Cumani	4-23	17.4	+ 1.38
D Holland	12-68	17.6	+ 25.13	P Chapple-Hyam	3-3	100.0	+ 12.13
M Hills	12-116	10.3	- 44.42	B W Hills	8-50	16.0	+ 1.33
B Raymond	12-135	8.9	- 72.65	R Hannon	2-17	11.8	- 4.75
Paul Eddery	11-98	11.2	+ 5.83	H R A Cecil	2-3	66.7	+ 14.50

How the Favourites Fared

Non-handicaps	W-R	Per cent	£1 Level Stake	Handicaps	W-R	Per cent	£1 Level Stake
2-y-o	54-120	45.0	+ 3.93	2-y-o	5-27	18.5	- 10.41
3-y-o	32-80	40.0	- 15.43	3-y-o	18-61	29.5	+ 13.98
Weight-for-age	24-64	37.5	- 5.89	All-aged	45-145	31.0	+ 33.46
Totals	110-264	41.7	- 17.39	Totals	68-233	29.2	+ 37.03
All favs	178-497	35.8	+ 19.64				

Leading Trainers by Month at York

May	Total W-R	Non-handicaps 2-y-o	3-y-o+	Handicaps 2-y-o	3-y-o+	Per cent	£1 Level Stake
H R A Cecil	11-34	2-2	7-23	0-0	2-9	32.4	- 2.03
M R Stoute	10-38	1-2	8-23	0-0	1-13	26.3	- 3.02
M H Easterby	6-39	2-7	0-1	0-0	4-31	15.4	+ 6.75
D R C Elsworth	4-18	0-1	3-13	0-0	1-4	22.2	+ 14.00
R Hannon	4-29	1-8	2-4	0-0	1-17	13.8	- 0.77

June	Total W-R	Non-handicaps 2-y-o	3-y-o+	Handicaps 2-y-o	3-y-o+	Per cent	£1 Level Stake
H R A Cecil	5-8	1-1	3-4	0-0	1-3	62.5	+ 5.83
M R Stoute	4-19	0-0	4-12	0-0	0-7	21.1	- 8.46
A A Scott	3-5	2-2	0-1	0-0	1-2	60.0	+ 2.32
J L Dunlop	3-9	0-1	2-6	0-0	1-2	33.3	+ 0.65
B Hanbury	3-9	1-2	1-4	0-0	1-3	33.3	+ 6.90

July	Total W-R	Non-handicaps 2-y-o	3-y-o+	Handicaps 2-y-o	3-y-o+	Per cent	£1 Level Stake
J H M Gosden	4-6	0-0	3-3	0-0	1-3	66.7	+ 7.50
P F I Cole	4-9	3-6	1-2	0-0	0-1	44.4	- 0.01
R Hannon	4-16	4-10	0-1	0-0	0-5	25.0	- 1.70
H R A Cecil	3-9	0-0	2-5	0-0	1-4	33.3	+ 8.25
F H Lee	3-12	1-3	0-1	0-1	2-7	25.0	+ 4.80

August	Total W-R	Non-handicaps 2-y-o	3-y-o+	Handicaps 2-y-o	3-y-o+	Per cent	£1 Level Stake
R Hannon	9-64	7-28	1-10	1-6	0-20	14.1	+ 2.31
M R Stoute	7-50	1-8	4-20	0-2	2-20	14.0	+ 10.46
L M Cumani	6-28	0-1	6-15	0-0	0-12	21.4	+ 6.30
H R A Cecil	6-38	1-3	2-20	0-1	3-14	15.8	- 13.13
P F I Cole	5-19	5-10	0-7	0-0	0-2	26.3	+ 15.63

September	Total W-R	Non-handicaps 2-y-o	3-y-o+	Handicaps 2-y-o	3-y-o+	Per cent	£1 Level Stake
L M Cumani	6-18	1-3	3-10	0-0	2-5	33.3	+ 7.44
J H M Gosden	5-18	0-1	3-12	0-0	2-5	27.8	- 1.76
C E Brittain	5-20	1-3	2-7	0-2	2-8	25.0	+ 22.50
M Feth-Godley	3-6	0-0	0-0	0-0	3-6	50.0	+ 18.50
B W Hills	3-27	2-8	1-9	0-0	0-10	11.1	- 10.75

Oct/Nov	Total W-R	Non-handicaps 2-y-o	3-y-o+	Handicaps 2-y-o	3-y-o+	Per cent	£1 Level Stake
J H M Gosden	15-32	6-11	6-12	0-0	3-9	46.9	+ 21.12
J L Dunlop	5-21	3-8	0-4	0-2	2-7	23.8	- 2.21
M H Easterby	5-43	1-6	1-3	1-9	2-25	11.6	- 12.25
B Hanbury	4-20	3-4	0-2	0-2	1-12	20.0	- 7.23
C E Brittain	4-23	1-4	1-5	1-2	1-12	17.4	+ 5.38

TRAINERS' FAVOURITES AT ASCOT 1989-93

	Total W–R	Non-handicaps 2-y-o	3-y-o+	Handicaps 2-y-o	3-y-o+	Per cent	£1 Level Stake
J H M Gosden	11–34	3-6	4-10	0-0	4-18	32.4	+ 1.68
G Harwood	10–20	1-2	7-10	0-1	2-7	50.0	+ 10.46
L M Cumani	10–27	5-6	5-13	0-0	0-8	37.0	− 2.82
H R A Cecil	10–34	3-13	6-16	0-0	1-5	29.4	− 4.49
M R Stoute	10–37	1-8	9-21	0-1	0-7	27.0	− 12.12
P F I Cole	9–14	5-8	3-3	0-1	1-2	64.3	+ 9.38
G Wragg	8–17	4-6	3-6	0-0	1-5	47.1	+ 12.05
J L Dunlop	6–18	3-9	3-5	0-0	0-4	33.3	− 0.42
R Hannon	4–20	2-8	1-7	0-0	1-5	20.0	− 4.24
C A Cyzer	3–3	0-0	0-0	0-0	3-3	100.0	+ 12.75
R W Armstrong	3–4	1-1	1-1	0-0	1-2	75.0	+ 6.98
B Hanbury	3–4	0-0	2-3	0-0	1-1	75.0	+ 3.38
P Chapple-Hyam	3–5	2-3	1-1	0-0	0-1	60.0	− 0.13
P T Walwyn	3–6	0-1	0-0	0-0	3-5	50.0	+ 6.88
Lord Huntingdon	3–12	0-1	1-1	0-0	2-10	25.0	− 4.67
M H Tompkins	2–4	0-0	0-0	0-0	2-4	50.0	+ 7.00
W R Hern	2–6	0-1	1-2	0-0	1-3	33.3	− 1.78
A Fabre (Fra)	2–6	0-0	2-6	0-0	0-0	33.3	+ 2.50
H Thomson Jones	2–7	2-7	0-0	0-0	0-0	28.6	− 1.37
R Charlton	2–9	0-3	2-2	0-1	0-3	22.2	− 3.84
C E Brittain	2–10	0-2	2-2	0-0	0-6	20.0	− 4.00
R Boss	1–1	1-1	0-0	0-0	0-0	100.0	+ 1.10
D Morley	1–1	1-1	0-0	0-0	0-0	100.0	+ 1.25
M V O'Brien (Ire	1–1	0-0	1-1	0-0	0-0	100.0	+ 3.50

TRAINERS' FAVOURITES AT AYR 1989-93

	Total W–R	Non-handicaps 2-y-o	3-y-o+	Handicaps 2-y-o	3-y-o+	Per cent	£1 Level Stake
J Berry	15–33	7-14	7-9	1-3	0-7	45.5	− 0.23
B W Hills	11–22	2-5	6-12	0-0	3-5	50.0	+ 3.46
M H Easterby	10–23	3-7	2-4	1-3	4-9	43.5	− 1.11
J L Dunlop	8–15	4-6	2-4	0-0	2-5	53.3	+ 2.88
Mrs J Ramsden	8–29	2-2	0-2	1-3	5-22	27.6	+ 3.46
P Chapple-Hyam	6–13	4-8	2-4	0-0	0-1	46.2	− 4.61
T D Barron	4–7	0-1	0-0	1-2	3-4	57.1	+ 6.09
P C Haslam	4–7	0-0	0-2	0-0	4-5	57.1	+ 3.86
Sir M Prescott	4–7	2-4	1-1	0-0	1-2	57.1	+ 1.81
J W Watts	4–12	1-2	1-3	0-3	2-4	33.3	− 1.27
Mrs M Reveley	4–12	1-1	1-3	0-2	2-6	33.3	− 4.02
Lord Huntingdon	3–3	1-1	1-1	1-1	0-0	100.0	+ 3.41
M J Camacho	3–4	0-0	0-1	0-0	3-3	75.0	+ 8.38
J F Bottomley	3–4	1-1	0-0	0-0	2-3	75.0	+ 12.00
I A Balding	3–5	0-1	0-0	0-0	3-4	60.0	+ 5.50
D W Chapman	3–6	0-0	1-3	1-1	1-2	50.0	+ 1.48
M P Naughton	3–6	0-0	0-0	0-0	3-6	50.0	+ 5.25
C Tinkler	3–6	1-1	1-3	0-0	1-2	50.0	+ 2.13
G A Pritchard-Gordon	3–7	2-3	1-2	0-0	0-2	42.9	− 0.19
F H Lee	3–9	0-1	0-0	0-0	3-8	33.3	− 0.12
A Bailey	3–10	0-1	1-3	0-1	2-5	30.0	− 3.21
P F I Cole	2–2	0-0	1-1	0-0	1-1	100.0	+ 3.66
L M Cumani	2–2	0-0	2-2	0-0	0-0	100.0	+ 2.88
C B B Booth	2–3	2-2	0-1	0-0	0-0	66.7	+ 3.00

530

TRAINERS' FAVOURITES AT BATH 1989-93

	Total W-R	Non-handicaps 2-y-o	Non-handicaps 3-y-o+	Handicaps 2-y-o	Handicaps 3-y-o+	Per cent	£1 Level Stake
B W Hills	11-20	1-1	5-7	0-0	5-12	55.0	+ 8.21
G Harwood	9-14	0-2	7-7	0-0	2-5	64.3	+ 12.12
R Hannon	9-25	3-8	3-7	0-3	3-7	36.0	+ 2.51
R J Hodges	6-19	0-0	0-1	0-0	6-18	31.6	+ 1.01
P F I Cole	6-34	0-8	2-7	0-0	4-19	17.6	- 17.49
G Lewis	5-7	0-1	2-2	1-1	2-3	71.4	+ 8.13
C J Hill	5-9	0-0	0-0	1-1	4-8	55.6	+ 14.08
W R Hern	5-11	1-1	1-3	0-0	3-7	45.5	+ 3.50
J Berry	5-18	3-8	2-6	0-0	0-4	27.8	- 6.08
I A Balding	5-23	1-5	2-9	0-0	2-9	21.7	- 6.57
Sir M Prescott	4-7	2-2	2-3	0-0	0-2	57.1	+ 0.58
R Charlton	4-7	1-1	3-6	0-0	0-0	57.1	+ 2.05
R Akehurst	4-9	0-0	0-0	0-0	4-9	44.4	+ 6.58
J L Dunlop	4-16	1-5	1-3	0-0	2-8	25.0	- 6.25
H Candy	3-4	0-0	3-3	0-1	0-0	75.0	+ 6.07
M R Channon	3-6	1-2	1-1	0-0	1-3	50.0	+ 3.48
D R C Elsworth	3-9	1-2	1-4	0-0	1-3	33.3	+ 1.83
M J Ryan	2-3	1-1	0-1	1-1	0-0	66.7	+ 5.50
M R Stoute	2-4	0-0	2-4	0-0	0-0	50.0	+ 1.25
Lord Huntingdon	2-4	0-0	0-1	1-1	1-2	50.0	+ 0.91
L G Cottrell	2-5	1-1	0-2	0-0	1-2	40.0	+ 5.50
L M Cumani	2-5	0-0	2-3	0-0	0-2	40.0	- 0.95
R F J Houghton	2-5	0-1	2-2	0-0	0-2	40.0	- 1.80
J W Hills	2-5	1-1	0-0	0-0	1-4	40.0	0.00

TRAINERS' FAVOURITES AT BEVERLEY 1989-93

	Total W-R	Non-handicaps 2-y-o	Non-handicaps 3-y-o+	Handicaps 2-y-o	Handicaps 3-y-o+	Per cent	£1 Level Stake
H R A Cecil	13-25	1-3	10-18	0-0	2-4	52.0	+ 2.59
Mrs M Reveley	12-24	2-4	1-1	0-0	9-19	50.0	+ 5.91
J Berry	12-35	11-25	1-6	0-1	0-3	34.3	- 3.63
M R Stoute	10-17	1-1	9-14	0-0	0-2	58.8	+ 5.00
M H Easterby	10-31	6-13	3-5	1-2	0-11	32.3	- 5.63
I A Balding	8-14	2-2	2-5	0-0	4-7	57.1	+ 4.08
L M Cumani	7-13	1-1	5-10	0-0	1-2	53.8	+ 1.28
R Hollinshead	6-20	2-5	2-5	0-0	2-10	30.0	+ 0.10
T D Barron	6-22	0-1	0-1	1-3	5-17	27.3	- 1.77
J L Spearing	5-10	0-0	0-0	0-0	5-10	50.0	+ 6.76
J L Dunlop	5-12	1-3	1-3	0-1	3-5	41.7	+ 1.40
D Morley	5-14	0-0	1-3	0-0	4-11	35.7	+ 3.58
D R Loder	4-4	3-3	0-0	0-0	1-1	100.0	+ 5.88
P F I Cole	4-5	0-1	3-3	0-0	1-1	80.0	+ 4.07
G Harwood	3-5	1-1	2-4	0-0	0-0	60.0	- 0.90
A A Scott	3-5	2-2	0-0	0-0	1-3	60.0	+ 3.24
S G Norton	3-6	1-1	0-0	0-0	2-5	50.0	+ 1.73
M Brittain	3-6	0-0	1-1	1-1	1-4	50.0	+ 5.13
M H Tompkins	3-11	0-0	3-3	0-1	0-7	27.3	- 6.02
W Jarvis	3-11	2-5	1-3	0-0	0-3	27.3	- 4.92
B W Hills	3-12	1-3	2-3	0-0	0-6	25.0	- 4.00
P Calver	2-3	0-0	0-0	0-0	2-3	66.7	+ 6.50
H J Collingridge	2-3	1-1	0-0	0-0	1-2	66.7	+ 1.88
W W Haigh	2-3	0-0	1-1	0-0	1-2	66.7	+ 2.88

TRAINERS' FAVOURITES AT BRIGHTON 1989-93

	Total W-R	Non-handicaps 2-y-o	3-y-o+	Handicaps 2-y-o	3-y-o+	Per cent	£1 Level Stake
R Hannon	19-58	15-24	3-9	0-2	1-23	32.8	- 9.24
L M Cumani	18-29	6-8	8-14	1-2	3-5	62.1	+ 8.47
Sir M Prescott	13-32	1-4	5-6	0-1	7-21	40.6	+ 4.58
G Harwood	12-21	0-3	11-16	0-0	1-2	57.1	+ 2.34
P F I Cole	8-18	3-6	5-9	0-0	0-3	44.4	- 1.47
J H M Gosden	7-11	1-1	6-10	0-0	0-0	63.6	+ 1.31
R J Hodges	7-28	0-0	1-3	0-0	6-25	25.0	- 2.65
J L Dunlop	6-15	1-1	3-6	0-1	2-7	40.0	- 2.59
M J Ryan	4-10	1-1	0-0	0-0	3-9	40.0	+ 5.88
J Berry	4-11	1-2	0-1	2-3	1-5	36.4	0.00
B W Hills	4-12	0-1	2-8	1-1	1-2	33.3	- 0.27
I A Balding	4-13	0-3	3-4	0-0	1-6	30.8	- 4.11
M A Jarvis	3-4	0-0	1-1	0-0	2-3	75.0	+ 8.50
R J R Williams	3-4	0-0	1-1	0-0	2-3	75.0	+ 5.25
W R Hern	3-5	0-0	2-2	0-0	1-3	60.0	+ 3.13
H Thomson Jones	3-5	1-2	2-3	0-0	0-0	60.0	- 0.38
H R A Cecil	3-6	1-1	2-5	0-0	0-0	50.0	- 0.08
W Carter	3-6	1-1	0-0	0-0	2-5	50.0	+ 4.25
P J Makin	3-7	0-0	1-1	0-0	2-6	42.9	+ 2.13
Lord Huntingdon	3-7	1-2	0-2	0-0	2-3	42.9	+ 1.90
M Bell	3-8	2-3	0-1	0-3	1-1	37.5	- 0.75
R Boss	3-10	1-2	1-1	0-0	1-7	30.0	- 1.96
G Lewis	3-13	0-5	1-1	1-1	1-6	23.1	- 0.83
R Akehurst	3-18	0-0	1-5	0-0	2-13	16.7	- 5.75

TRAINERS' FAVOURITES AT CARLISLE 1989-93

	Total W-R	Non-handicaps 2-y-o	3-y-o+	Handicaps 2-y-o	3-y-o+	Per cent	£1 Level Stake
J Berry	8-27	3-13	3-9	0-0	2-5	29.6	- 4.02
Mrs M Reveley	6-13	0-0	2-3	0-0	4-10	46.2	+ 6.83
M H Easterby	6-17	3-7	1-3	0-0	2-7	35.3	- 0.80
M H Tompkins	5-12	2-3	1-3	0-1	2-5	41.7	+ 0.09
Sir M Prescott	5-13	0-0	2-4	0-0	3-9	38.5	+ 0.14
J L Dunlop	4-5	0-0	2-2	0-0	2-3	80.0	+ 13.87
N Tinkler	3-4	1-1	1-1	0-0	1-2	75.0	+ 3.95
A A Scott	3-4	0-1	3-3	0-0	0-0	75.0	+ 3.30
H Thomson Jones	3-5	1-2	1-1	0-0	1-2	60.0	+ 0.18
C R Nelson	2-2	0-0	2-2	0-0	0-0	100.0	+ 2.19
W J Haggas	2-2	0-0	2-2	0-0	0-0	100.0	+ 2.32
Miss S E Hall	2-4	0-0	1-3	0-0	1-1	50.0	+ 1.91
W Jarvis	2-4	1-1	1-3	0-0	0-0	50.0	+ 2.00
M R Stoute	2-5	0-0	2-5	0-0	0-0	40.0	- 1.80
R Hollinshead	2-6	1-3	0-1	0-0	1-2	33.3	- 1.62
M W Easterby	2-7	0-1	0-1	0-0	2-5	28.6	+ 0.63
F H Lee	2-7	0-2	0-0	0-0	2-5	28.6	- 0.62
M S Johnston	2-7	0-0	1-3	0-0	1-4	28.6	- 1.81
B R Cambidge	1-1	0-0	0-0	0-0	1-1	100.0	+ 3.50
C W C Elsey	1-1	0-0	1-1	0-0	0-0	100.0	+ 1.00
P S Felgate	1-1	0-0	0-0	0-0	1-1	100.0	+ 1.88
R E Peacock	1-1	0-0	0-0	0-0	1-1	100.0	+ 3.50
J A R Toller	1-1	0-0	1-1	0-0	0-0	100.0	+ 0.08
G Wragg	1-1	0-0	1-1	0-0	0-0	100.0	+ 0.29

TRAINERS' FAVOURITES AT CATTERICK 1989-93

	Total W-R	Non-handicaps 2-y-o	3-y-o+	Handicaps 2-y-o	3-y-o+	Per cent	£1 Level Stake
J Berry	14-31	8-16	5-9	1-3	0-3	45.2	- 1.01
T D Barron	10-25	3-4	0-5	1-1	6-15	40.0	+ 4.47
M H Easterby	9-31	3-13	3-6	1-2	2-10	29.0	- 11.56
Sir M Prescott	8-18	4-9	2-4	0-0	2-5	44.4	+ 1.81
B W Hills	8-23	0-3	8-18	0-1	0-1	34.8	- 6.20
J H M Gosden	6-9	1-1	5-7	0-1	0-0	66.7	+ 5.43
L M Cumani	6-11	0-1	6-9	0-0	0-1	54.5	- 1.86
Mrs M Reveley	5-8	0-0	3-3	0-0	2-5	62.5	+ 4.90
Miss S E Hall	4-6	1-2	2-3	0-0	1-1	66.7	+ 6.87
M Bell	4-6	1-2	2-3	0-0	1-1	66.7	+ 3.74
H R A Cecil	4-7	0-1	4-6	0-0	0-0	57.1	+ 0.09
A C Stewart	4-8	1-1	3-6	0-0	0-1	50.0	- 1.94
S G Norton	4-9	1-1	1-3	0-1	2-4	44.4	+ 0.86
P F I Cole	4-12	2-7	1-4	0-0	1-1	33.3	- 4.34
M R Stoute	4-12	1-3	3-8	0-0	0-1	33.3	- 3.59
Mrs J Ramsden	4-15	1-1	0-1	0-0	3-13	26.7	- 2.62
W A O'Gorman	3-3	3-3	0-0	0-0	0-0	100.0	+ 2.30
M J Camacho	3-4	1-1	1-1	1-1	0-1	75.0	+ 6.41
M P Naughton	3-5	0-0	0-0	0-0	3-5	60.0	+ 4.55
D W Chapman	3-7	0-0	0-0	0-0	3-7	42.9	+ 3.23
R M Whitaker	3-7	0-1	1-1	0-0	2-5	42.9	- 0.80
C E Brittain	2-2	1-1	1-1	0-0	0-0	100.0	+ 1.92
B A McMahon	2-3	0-0	1-1	0-0	1-2	66.7	+ 0.92
N Tinkler	2-4	0-0	1-2	0-0	1-2	50.0	- 1.02

TRAINERS' FAVOURITES AT CHEPSTOW 1989-93

	Total W-R	Non-handicaps 2-y-o	3-y-o+	Handicaps 2-y-o	3-y-o+	Per cent	£1 Level Stake
L M Cumani	10-13	0-0	9-10	1-1	0-2	76.9	+ 7.13
R Hannon	7-16	1-2	1-3	1-2	4-9	43.8	+ 8.51
H R A Cecil	6-10	0-0	4-7	0-0	2-3	60.0	+ 2.23
J Berry	5-6	2-3	3-3	0-0	0-0	83.3	+ 4.84
B W Hills	5-8	0-0	5-7	0-1	0-0	62.5	+ 4.55
G Harwood	4-9	1-4	2-3	0-0	1-2	44.4	+ 1.51
R J Hodges	4-9	0-0	0-0	0-0	4-9	44.4	+ 5.46
I A Balding	4-10	1-3	2-3	0-0	1-4	40.0	+ 1.98
J L Dunlop	4-13	0-2	3-4	0-0	1-7	30.8	- 2.57
G Lewis	3-7	0-0	2-4	1-2	0-1	42.9	- 0.63
M A Jarvis	2-2	1-1	1-1	0-0	0-0	100.0	+ 5.00
H Thomson Jones	2-3	0-0	2-3	0-0	0-0	66.7	+ 0.90
P T Walwyn	2-3	0-0	2-2	0-1	0-0	66.7	+ 0.23
M D I Usher	2-3	0-0	2-2	0-0	0-1	66.7	+ 1.29
Mrs L Piggott	2-3	1-1	1-1	0-0	0-1	66.7	+ 0.03
W R Hern	2-4	0-0	2-3	0-0	0-1	50.0	- 0.60
M H Tompkins	2-4	0-0	0-1	0-1	2-2	50.0	+ 2.38
J H M Gosden	2-4	0-1	2-2	0-0	0-1	50.0	- 0.36
R Hollinshead	2-5	0-0	0-1	0-1	2-3	40.0	+ 6.50
M C Pipe	2-5	0-0	0-1	0-0	2-4	40.0	+ 0.63
Sir M Prescott	2-6	0-1	2-5	0-0	0-0	33.3	- 3.03
D A Wilson	2-6	0-0	0-0	0-0	2-6	33.3	+ 5.50
R Akehurst	2-7	0-0	0-1	0-0	2-6	28.6	- 1.12
M R Stoute	2-8	1-1	1-6	0-0	0-1	25.0	- 4.94

TRAINERS' FAVOURITES AT CHESTER 1989-93

	Total W-R	Non-handicaps 2-y-o	3-y-o+	Handicaps 2-y-o	3-y-o+	Per cent	£1 Level Stake
B W Hills	11-26	2-4	6-12	0-0	3-10	42.3	+ 5.03
M R Stoute	9-16	4-4	4-8	0-0	1-4	56.3	+ 2.79
R Hannon	9-18	5-10	1-2	2-4	1-2	50.0	+ 3.66
H R A Cecil	9-20	3-5	6-14	0-0	0-1	45.0	- 1.67
J H M Gosden	7-17	3-4	2-6	0-0	2-7	41.2	+ 4.86
G Wragg	4-6	0-0	4-5	0-1	0-0	66.7	+ 5.38
P F I Cole	4-11	4-8	0-0	0-0	0-3	36.4	- 2.77
J Berry	4-19	2-6	0-2	0-0	2-11	21.1	- 3.25
C E Brittain	3-8	2-4	1-1	0-0	0-3	37.5	- 2.13
J D Bethell	2-3	0-0	0-0	0-0	2-3	66.7	+ 8.88
P Chapple-Hyam	2-3	1-1	1-1	0-0	0-1	66.7	+ 1.85
M J Camacho	2-4	0-0	0-1	0-0	2-3	50.0	+ 5.88
B Hanbury	2-5	0-1	2-2	0-1	0-1	40.0	- 1.67
W R Hern	2-5	0-1	1-3	1-1	0-0	40.0	- 0.15
J W Watts	2-5	1-2	0-0	0-0	1-3	40.0	+ 8.00
M H Easterby	2-6	1-3	1-1	0-1	0-1	33.3	+ 1.25
F H Lee	2-7	0-0	0-1	0-0	2-6	28.6	+ 2.00
A Bailey	2-8	0-0	1-1	0-2	1-5	25.0	- 2.33
L G Cottrell	1-1	0-0	0-0	0-0	1-1	100.0	+ 3.50
L M Cumani	1-1	0-0	1-1	0-0	0-0	100.0	+ 1.00
Mrs L Piggott	1-1	0-0	1-1	0-0	0-0	100.0	+ 2.75
B R Millman	1-1	0-0	0-0	0-0	1-1	100.0	+ 3.33
J R Fanshawe	1-1	0-0	0-0	0-0	1-1	100.0	+ 1.50
Mrs V Aconley	1-1	0-0	0-0	0-0	1-1	100.0	+ 3.00

TRAINERS' FAVOURITES AT DONCASTER 1989-93

	Total W-R	Non-handicaps 2-y-o	3-y-o+	Handicaps 2-y-o	3-y-o+	Per cent	£1 Level Stake
H R A Cecil	20-43	9-18	10-18	0-0	1-7	46.5	+ 2.44
J H M Gosden	15-36	4-10	7-13	0-0	4-13	41.7	+ 3.27
B W Hills	14-26	2-6	9-15	0-0	3-5	53.8	+ 12.95
R Hannon	11-29	6-13	2-5	0-2	3-9	37.9	+ 3.25
L M Cumani	10-24	0-3	7-17	0-0	3-4	41.7	+ 2.13
I A Balding	6-9	0-0	3-5	0-0	3-4	66.7	+ 9.29
M R Stoute	6-24	3-9	1-10	1-2	1-3	25.0	+ 0.73
Mrs J Ramsden	6-27	0-4	1-1	2-5	3-17	22.2	+ 0.13
J Berry	5-19	4-14	0-1	0-0	1-4	26.3	- 4.60
R W Armstrong	4-7	3-3	0-0	0-0	1-4	57.1	+ 2.11
M A Jarvis	4-7	2-2	1-1	0-1	1-3	57.1	+ 3.80
Mrs L Piggott	3-5	1-1	0-1	0-0	2-3	60.0	+ 6.11
W A O'Gorman	3-6	1-2	1-2	1-2	0-0	50.0	+ 6.00
M S Johnston	3-6	0-0	1-1	0-1	2-4	50.0	+ 8.50
D R C Elsworth	3-7	1-1	0-2	0-0	2-4	42.9	+ 9.50
P Chapple-Hyam	3-7	3-6	0-0	0-1	0-0	42.9	- 0.14
A A Scott	3-8	1-2	0-1	0-0	2-5	37.5	- 0.16
G Harwood	3-9	0-1	2-6	0-0	1-2	33.3	- 0.52
A C Stewart	3-11	0-1	1-4	0-1	2-5	27.3	- 1.50
J W Watts	3-13	1-3	0-0	0-2	2-8	23.1	- 3.75
Mrs M Reveley	3-13	0-1	1-2	0-2	2-8	23.1	- 3.00
J L Dunlop	3-14	1-5	0-2	0-0	2-7	21.4	- 5.82
M H Easterby	3-19	1-4	0-0	0-0	2-15	15.8	- 5.75
M W Easterby	2-3	2-3	0-0	0-0	0-0	66.7	+ 2.88

TRAINERS' FAVOURITES AT EDINBURGH 1989-93

	Total W-R	Non-handicaps 2-y-o	Non-handicaps 3-y-o+	Handicaps 2-y-o	Handicaps 3-y-o+	Per cent	£1 Level Stake
J Berry	18-38	13-26	4-5	1-1	0-6	47.4	+ 2.02
M H Easterby	8-14	3-5	1-1	0-1	4-7	57.1	+ 8.21
Sir M Prescott	7-21	1-4	2-9	0-0	4-8	33.3	+ 1.60
M H Tompkins	6-9	2-3	2-3	0-0	2-3	66.7	+ 6.15
J H M Gosden	6-10	1-3	4-5	0-0	1-2	60.0	+ 5.78
M S Johnston	5-10	1-3	2-2	1-1	1-4	50.0	+ 4.38
M J Camacho	4-4	0-0	2-2	0-0	2-2	100.0	+ 7.48
B W Hills	4-6	0-0	3-4	0-0	1-2	66.7	+ 3.61
N Tinkler	4-6	1-1	1-2	0-1	2-2	66.7	+ 9.20
M P Naughton	4-10	0-1	0-1	0-0	4-8	40.0	+ 1.88
J L Spearing	4-11	0-1	0-0	0-0	4-10	36.4	+ 4.88
F H Lee	3-4	1-2	0-0	0-0	2-2	75.0	+ 2.66
M Bell	3-5	1-2	0-1	0-0	2-2	60.0	+ 2.23
T D Barron	3-6	1-3	0-0	1-1	1-2	50.0	+ 4.06
J G FitzGerald	3-7	1-4	1-1	0-0	1-2	42.9	+ 0.38
R M Whitaker	3-9	1-2	0-3	1-1	1-3	33.3	- 0.83
Mrs M Reveley	3-17	2-2	0-2	0-0	1-13	17.6	- 11.74
R Hannon	2-2	2-2	0-0	0-0	0-0	100.0	+ 3.35
A N Lee	2-2	0-0	1-1	0-0	1-1	100.0	+ 3.13
J R Fanshawe	2-2	0-0	2-2	0-0	0-0	100.0	+ 2.63
P Calver	2-3	0-0	1-1	0-0	1-2	66.7	+ 4.75
J Etherington	2-3	0-0	2-3	0-0	0-0	66.7	0.00
W Jarvis	2-3	0-0	2-2	0-0	0-1	66.7	+ 1.20
L M Cumani	2-4	0-0	2-3	0-0	0-1	50.0	- 0.76

TRAINERS' FAVOURITES AT EPSOM 1989-93

	Total W-R	Non-handicaps 2-y-o	Non-handicaps 3-y-o+	Handicaps 2-y-o	Handicaps 3-y-o+	Per cent	£1 Level Stake
M R Stoute	7-12	1-2	4-5	0-0	2-5	58.3	+ 6.54
R Hannon	6-20	2-5	1-4	0-0	3-11	30.0	+ 5.12
J Berry	5-10	2-4	2-4	0-0	1-2	50.0	+ 0.45
J L Dunlop	4-8	0-1	3-4	1-1	0-2	50.0	+ 6.13
A C Stewart	3-6	0-0	3-4	0-0	0-2	50.0	- 1.04
L M Cumani	3-8	0-0	1-1	0-0	2-7	37.5	+ 3.25
H R A Cecil	3-10	0-2	2-7	0-0	1-1	30.0	- 1.17
R Akehurst	3-12	0-0	1-2	0-0	2-10	25.0	- 0.12
G Lewis	3-13	1-1	2-3	0-0	0-9	23.1	- 4.42
Lord Huntingdon	2-3	1-1	0-1	0-0	1-1	66.7	+ 3.38
Miss B Sanders	2-3	0-0	0-0	0-0	2-3	66.7	+ 7.00
J H M Gosden	2-3	0-0	2-3	0-0	0-0	66.7	+ 1.50
D R C Elsworth	2-8	0-1	2-4	0-0	0-3	25.0	- 3.02
D Morley	1-1	0-0	0-0	0-0	1-1	100.0	+ 3.00
Lady Herries	1-1	0-0	1-1	0-0	0-0	100.0	+ 2.75
F H Lee	1-1	0-0	0-0	0-0	1-1	100.0	+ 1.50
D Burchell	1-1	0-0	1-1	0-0	0-0	100.0	+ 0.80
R J O'Sullivan	1-1	0-0	0-0	0-0	1-1	100.0	+ 4.50
M Bell	1-1	1-1	0-0	0-0	0-0	100.0	+ 2.75
W R Hern	1-2	0-0	1-2	0-0	0-0	50.0	+ 0.25
P A Kelleway	1-2	1-1	0-0	0-1	0-0	50.0	+ 0.63
A Fabre (Fra)	1-2	0-0	1-2	0-0	0-0	50.0	+ 0.88
W Jarvis	1-2	0-1	1-1	0-0	0-0	50.0	+ 1.75
B R Millman	1-2	0-0	0-0	0-0	1-2	50.0	+ 3.00

TRAINERS' FAVOURITES AT FOLKESTONE 1989-93

	Total W-R	Non-handicaps 2-y-o	3-y-o+	Handicaps 2-y-o	3-y-o+	Per cent	£1 Level Stake
G Harwood	16-33	5-10	10-19	0-0	1-4	48.5	+ 0.30
R Hannon	11-36	5-15	4-12	0-1	2-8	30.6	- 10.40
N A Callaghan	7-14	2-4	2-6	1-1	2-3	50.0	+ 8.13
R Akehurst	7-20	0-1	3-4	0-0	4-15	35.0	+ 2.88
P F I Cole	6-13	1-1	2-2	1-1	2-9	46.2	+ 5.18
J Berry	6-14	3-9	3-3	0-2	0-0	42.9	+ 0.54
Mrs L Piggott	5-7	0-0	4-4	0-0	1-3	71.4	+ 10.80
J L Dunlop	5-12	1-2	3-3	1-1	0-6	41.7	- 0.96
D R C Elsworth	4-7	1-2	2-4	1-1	0-0	57.1	+ 4.43
G B Balding	4-9	1-2	1-2	0-0	2-5	44.4	+ 3.98
W Jarvis	3-4	0-0	1-2	0-0	2-2	75.0	+ 5.08
J H M Gosden	3-5	0-0	3-5	0-0	0-0	60.0	+ 0.61
W J Haggas	3-6	1-3	0-1	0-0	2-2	50.0	+ 2.53
L M Cumani	3-7	0-1	3-6	0-0	0-0	42.9	+ 2.35
D A Wilson	3-7	0-0	0-0	0-0	3-7	42.9	+ 3.83
B W Hills	3-8	1-2	2-2	0-0	0-4	37.5	- 2.83
M H Tompkins	3-8	1-2	0-3	1-1	1-2	37.5	+ 0.13
P T Walwyn	3-8	0-2	3-5	0-0	0-1	37.5	- 2.70
A Bailey	2-2	0-0	0-0	1-1	1-1	100.0	+ 5.25
J R Fanshawe	2-2	1-1	0-0	0-0	1-1	100.0	+ 4.91
H Candy	2-3	0-0	0-1	0-0	2-2	66.7	+ 4.25
K T Ivory	2-3	2-2	0-0	0-1	0-0	66.7	+ 3.13
Lord Huntingdon	2-3	0-0	2-3	0-0	0-0	66.7	+ 2.50
A A Scott	2-3	1-1	0-1	0-0	1-1	66.7	+ 3.00

TRAINERS' FAVOURITES AT GOODWOOD 1989-93

	Total W-R	Non-handicaps 2-y-o	3-y-o+	Handicaps 2-y-o	3-y-o+	Per cent	£1 Level Stake
H R A Cecil	16-31	9-10	6-15	0-1	1-5	51.6	+ 5.22
J H M Gosden	11-29	4-5	3-11	1-2	3-11	37.9	+ 2.75
J L Dunlop	11-34	5-10	4-7	1-3	1-14	32.4	- 8.05
I A Balding	10-25	4-8	4-9	0-2	2-6	40.0	+ 5.68
D R C Elsworth	9-21	4-6	1-4	0-0	4-11	42.9	+ 0.70
L M Cumani	9-24	2-3	5-16	0-0	2-5	37.5	+ 2.39
M R Stoute	8-21	3-6	4-10	0-0	1-5	38.1	- 4.16
R Hannon	8-34	3-11	4-10	0-1	1-12	23.5	- 15.74
J Berry	6-21	4-7	0-2	1-8	1-4	28.6	- 0.24
G Lewis	5-7	0-0	1-2	2-2	2-3	71.4	+ 11.01
P F I Cole	5-12	3-7	1-4	0-0	1-1	41.7	- 1.58
R Akehurst	5-15	0-0	1-1	0-0	4-14	33.3	+ 2.88
G Harwood	5-30	4-11	0-11	0-1	1-7	16.7	- 17.34
P J Makin	4-9	0-0	2-4	0-0	2-5	44.4	+ 2.68
D A Wilson	4-11	0-0	0-0	0-0	4-11	36.4	+ 1.46
R W Armstrong	3-4	2-2	1-1	0-0	0-1	75.0	+ 2.98
Lord Huntingdon	3-5	0-0	2-2	0-0	1-3	60.0	+ 4.88
L J Holt	3-8	0-1	1-1	0-0	2-6	37.5	+ 6.00
R Charlton	3-9	0-2	3-5	0-0	0-2	33.3	+ 0.38
W R Hern	3-11	3-4	0-4	0-1	0-2	27.3	- 4.88
W A O'Gorman	2-2	2-2	0-0	0-0	0-0	100.0	+ 2.44
M D I Usher	2-2	0-0	1-1	1-1	0-0	100.0	+ 4.75
J M P Eustace	2-2	1-1	0-0	0-0	1-1	100.0	+ 9.00
R F J Houghton	2-3	0-0	2-2	0-0	0-1	66.7	+ 0.83

TRAINERS' FAVOURITES AT HAMILTON 1989-93

	Total W-R	Non-handicaps 2-y-o	3-y-o+	Handicaps 2-y-o	3-y-o+	Per cent	£1 Level Stake
J Berry	33-72	13-32	11-17	2-5	7-18	45.8	+ 6.93
Mrs M Reveley	14-33	0-3	6-8	0-0	8-22	42.4	+ 2.70
Sir M Prescott	10-20	2-3	3-7	0-0	5-10	50.0	+ 6.15
M Bell	8-12	4-5	3-4	0-1	1-2	66.7	+ 5.46
Mrs J Ramsden	8-17	0-3	2-3	0-1	6-10	47.1	+ 5.29
M H Tompkins	5-18	2-3	3-6	0-1	0-8	27.8	- 7.74
C Tinkler	5-20	1-4	1-5	0-2	3-9	25.0	- 5.64
P C Haslam	4-5	0-0	1-2	0-0	3-3	80.0	+ 6.50
B Hanbury	4-6	0-0	2-3	1-1	1-2	66.7	+ 7.23
P J Makin	4-6	0-1	4-5	0-0	0-0	66.7	+ 5.08
S G Norton	4-8	0-0	2-4	0-0	2-4	50.0	+ 6.63
M H Easterby	4-16	3-7	0-3	0-0	1-6	25.0	- 8.66
M S Johnston	4-16	2-3	0-3	0-0	2-10	25.0	- 8.14
J Etherington	3-4	1-1	2-3	0-0	0-0	75.0	+ 3.65
J G FitzGerald	3-9	1-2	0-1	0-1	2-5	33.3	+ 4.75
I A Balding	2-2	0-0	1-1	0-0	1-1	100.0	+ 8.25
P Calver	2-2	0-0	1-1	0-0	1-1	100.0	+ 4.10
P S Felgate	2-2	2-2	0-0	0-0	0-0	100.0	+ 2.08
R Hannon	2-3	0-0	2-2	0-1	0-0	66.7	+ 1.68
C W Thornton	2-4	0-0	2-3	0-0	0-1	50.0	+ 0.50
R Akehurst	2-5	0-0	0-0	0-0	2-5	40.0	+ 4.75
R Boss	2-5	1-2	1-2	0-0	0-1	40.0	- 1.25
Denys Smith	2-5	0-0	1-3	0-0	1-2	40.0	+ 3.25
A C Stewart	2-5	0-0	2-3	0-0	0-2	40.0	- 0.75

TRAINERS' FAVOURITES AT HAYDOCK 1989-93

	Total W-R	Non-handicaps 2-y-o	3-y-o+	Handicaps 2-y-o	3-y-o+	Per cent	£1 Level Stake
H R A Cecil	12-29	4-8	6-15	0-0	2-6	41.4	- 2.82
J H M Gosden	10-19	2-3	5-7	0-0	3-9	52.6	+ 9.99
B W Hills	8-23	4-5	4-11	0-0	0-7	34.8	- 7.30
M R Stoute	8-28	2-8	5-12	0-2	1-6	28.6	- 10.89
M H Tompkins	6-14	1-1	2-5	0-0	3-8	42.9	+ 3.85
J L Dunlop	6-21	1-8	3-7	0-0	2-6	28.6	- 3.62
L M Cumani	6-24	1-4	3-11	0-0	2-9	25.0	- 9.04
R Boss	5-7	1-1	1-1	1-1	2-4	71.4	+ 13.25
J W Watts	5-11	0-2	1-2	0-1	4-6	45.5	+ 9.07
R Charlton	5-15	1-1	2-7	0-0	2-7	33.3	- 1.74
Mrs J Ramsden	5-27	1-2	1-2	0-2	3-21	18.5	- 12.75
G Harwood	4-13	0-1	1-6	0-0	3-6	30.8	+ 4.13
M H Easterby	4-21	4-7	0-1	0-1	0-12	19.0	- 11.25
R Hannon	4-21	3-6	0-7	0-0	1-8	19.0	- 9.32
J Berry	4-23	2-9	1-6	0-4	1-4	17.4	- 11.77
G Wragg	3-3	1-1	1-1	0-0	1-1	100.0	+ 4.55
P T Walwyn	3-5	1-1	1-2	0-0	1-2	60.0	+ 3.75
W R Hern	3-6	0-0	3-4	0-0	0-2	50.0	+ 0.16
H Thomson Jones	3-8	3-7	0-0	0-0	0-1	37.5	- 2.26
A C Stewart	3-8	0-0	3-5	0-0	0-3	37.5	- 0.40
F H Lee	3-13	0-0	0-0	1-1	2-12	23.1	- 1.50
T Thomson Jones	2-2	0-0	0-0	0-0	2-2	100.0	+ 6.00
Bob Jones	2-2	0-0	2-2	0-0	0-0	100.0	+ 1.53
M W Easterby	2-3	1-2	0-0	0-0	1-1	66.7	+ 2.10

TRAINERS' FAVOURITES AT KEMPTON 1989-93

	Total W-R	Non-handicaps 2-y-o	Non-handicaps 3-y-o+	Handicaps 2-y-o	Handicaps 3-y-o+	Per cent	£1 Level Stake
M R Stoute	10-24	4-5	3-12	1-1	2-6	41.7	+ 1.62
R Hannon	9-31	3-9	1-5	0-2	5-15	29.0	+ 1.08
J H M Gosden	8-23	0-1	7-17	0-1	1-4	34.8	+ 3.63
G Harwood	6-17	2-3	3-6	1-1	0-7	35.3	- 3.16
R Charlton	5-14	2-2	3-8	0-0	0-4	35.7	+ 0.65
L M Cumani	5-16	1-1	3-11	0-0	1-4	31.3	- 1.37
B Hanbury	4-9	1-1	3-4	0-0	0-4	44.4	+ 1.22
B W Hills	4-10	1-3	2-5	0-0	1-2	40.0	+ 4.00
P T Walwyn	4-10	1-3	3-4	0-0	0-3	40.0	+ 1.74
A A Scott	4-10	0-0	1-7	0-0	3-3	40.0	+ 4.75
P F I Cole	4-13	2-7	1-4	1-1	0-1	30.8	+ 0.20
H R A Cecil	4-14	0-1	4-11	0-0	0-2	28.6	- 3.87
G A Pritchard-Gordon	3-4	1-1	1-1	0-0	1-2	75.0	+ 2.80
Mrs J Cecil	3-4	0-0	2-2	0-0	1-2	75.0	+ 5.55
C E Brittain	3-8	0-1	2-4	0-0	1-3	37.5	+ 4.21
W R Hern	3-10	0-3	2-4	0-0	1-3	30.0	- 0.52
R Akehurst	3-11	0-0	0-1	0-1	3-9	27.3	+ 1.25
D R C Elsworth	3-13	1-3	2-8	0-0	0-2	23.1	- 3.26
Miss B Sanders	2-2	0-0	0-0	0-0	2-2	100.0	+ 3.80
L J Holt	2-3	0-0	1-1	0-0	1-2	66.7	+ 4.08
R F J Houghton	2-3	0-0	1-2	0-0	1-1	66.7	+ 1.00
H Thomson Jones	2-4	1-1	1-2	0-0	0-1	50.0	+ 1.13
Sir M Prescott	2-5	0-0	1-2	0-0	1-3	40.0	+ 1.60
J R Fanshawe	2-5	1-2	0-0	0-1	1-2	40.0	+ 1.83

TRAINERS' FAVOURITES AT LEICESTER 1989-93

	Total W-R	Non-handicaps 2-y-o	Non-handicaps 3-y-o+	Handicaps 2-y-o	Handicaps 3-y-o+	Per cent	£1 Level Stake
H R A Cecil	17-37	7-15	10-20	0-0	0-2	45.9	- 3.07
M R Stoute	15-37	7-17	7-16	0-0	1-4	40.5	- 10.10
J H M Gosden	11-22	6-10	3-9	0-0	2-3	50.0	+ 2.10
J L Dunlop	8-20	4-6	2-8	1-2	1-4	40.0	- 2.59
J Berry	7-15	4-9	2-2	1-1	0-3	46.7	+ 4.11
R Hannon	7-20	3-8	2-6	2-3	0-3	35.0	+ 5.75
N A Callaghan	5-6	2-3	2-2	0-0	1-1	83.3	+ 12.85
R F J Houghton	5-6	1-1	4-4	0-0	0-1	83.3	+ 6.55
H Thomson Jones	5-6	3-3	1-2	0-0	1-1	83.3	+ 4.76
L M Cumani	5-15	3-6	2-8	0-0	0-1	33.3	- 3.35
B Hanbury	4-8	1-2	2-4	0-0	1-2	50.0	+ 2.25
P F I Cole	4-13	1-4	2-6	1-2	0-1	30.8	- 3.12
G Harwood	4-15	1-3	3-11	0-0	0-1	26.7	- 4.02
W A O'Gorman	3-3	0-0	2-2	1-1	0-0	100.0	+ 7.08
R Charlton	3-5	0-0	2-3	0-0	1-2	60.0	+ 3.10
M C Pipe	3-7	0-0	1-1	0-0	2-6	42.9	+ 6.63
G Wragg	3-8	1-1	2-5	0-1	0-1	37.5	- 3.58
W R Hern	3-10	0-2	3-5	0-0	0-3	30.0	- 3.45
B W Hills	3-10	3-7	0-2	0-0	0-1	30.0	- 2.75
M A Jarvis	2-2	0-0	2-2	0-0	0-0	100.0	+ 4.63
M Williams	2-2	2-2	0-0	0-0	0-0	100.0	+ 3.40
Mrs J Cecil	2-3	2-2	0-0	0-0	0-1	66.7	+ 2.13
Sir M Prescott	2-4	1-1	1-3	0-0	0-0	50.0	+ 0.18
R J R Williams	2-4	1-1	0-1	1-1	0-1	50.0	+ 0.43

TRAINERS' FAVOURITES AT LINGFIELD 1989-93

	Total W-R	Non-handicaps 2-y-o	3-y-o+	Handicaps 2-y-o	3-y-o+	Per cent	£1 Level Stake
R Hannon	14-31	5-10	7-12	0-0	2-9	45.2	+ 8.38
H R A Cecil	11-24	3-7	7-14	0-0	1-3	45.8	- 5.49
G Harwood	10-27	3-8	3-9	0-1	4-9	37.0	+ 2.54
J H M Gosden	8-18	3-6	5-10	0-0	0-2	44.4	- 0.58
M R Stoute	8-23	3-7	5-10	0-0	0-6	34.8	- 7.40
J L Dunlop	7-19	1-4	2-5	0-0	4-10	36.8	- 3.53
B W Hills	6-8	1-2	2-2	1-1	2-3	75.0	+ 9.36
Sir M Prescott	6-12	0-2	4-6	0-0	2-4	50.0	+ 4.37
L M Cumani	6-16	1-2	5-14	0-0	0-0	37.5	- 2.45
P F I Cole	5-15	1-5	2-7	0-0	2-3	33.3	- 4.55
G Lewis	5-15	2-7	1-1	0-0	2-7	33.3	- 0.62
R Akehurst	5-26	0-1	0-2	0-0	5-23	19.2	- 7.92
I A Balding	4-12	0-1	3-5	0-0	1-6	33.3	- 0.97
J Berry	4-16	1-7	2-3	0-1	1-5	25.0	- 4.06
Pat Mitchell	3-5	0-0	0-0	0-0	3-5	60.0	+ 7.58
A C Stewart	3-5	0-1	1-2	0-0	2-2	60.0	+ 0.87
D R C Elsworth	3-7	1-2	1-1	0-0	1-4	42.9	+ 1.80
W Jarvis	3-7	0-1	1-3	0-0	2-3	42.9	+ 2.05
C E Brittain	3-8	0-3	2-3	0-0	1-2	37.5	+ 0.10
C R Nelson	2-4	1-2	1-2	0-0	0-0	50.0	- 0.69
J W Payne	2-4	1-2	0-0	0-0	1-2	50.0	+ 2.62
M R Channon	2-4	0-0	1-1	0-0	1-3	50.0	+ 7.25
R W Armstrong	2-5	0-1	0-1	0-0	2-3	40.0	+ 1.41
N A Callaghan	2-5	1-2	0-0	0-0	1-3	40.0	+ 1.38

TRAINERS' FAVOURITES AT LINGFIELD (AW) 1989-93

	Total W-R	Non-handicaps 2-y-o	3-y-o+	Handicaps 2-y-o	3-y-o+	Per cent	£1 Level Stake
B W Hills	17-34	1-5	9-15	0-0	7-14	50.0	- 0.57
P F I Cole	14-30	3-10	7-10	1-1	3-9	46.7	- 0.54
W A O'Gorman	13-47	0-2	9-24	1-2	3-19	27.7	- 14.14
J Berry	10-17	2-4	3-4	0-0	5-9	58.8	+ 11.91
Sir M Prescott	10-25	3-5	4-10	0-0	3-10	40.0	- 6.11
R J O'Sullivan	10-26	0-0	1-1	0-0	9-25	38.5	+ 6.88
M S Johnston	8-23	1-2	3-6	0-0	4-15	34.8	+ 0.79
Lord Huntingdon	7-21	0-2	3-10	0-1	4-8	33.3	- 2.12
R Hollinshead	5-9	0-0	5-8	0-0	0-1	55.6	- 1.32
J Pearce	5-9	0-0	4-5	0-0	1-4	55.6	+ 9.88
C A Cyzer	5-10	0-0	1-2	0-0	4-8	50.0	+ 5.73
J H M Gosden	5-10	2-2	0-2	1-2	2-4	50.0	+ 3.65
R Akehurst	5-15	0-0	2-7	0-0	3-8	33.3	- 1.27
C C Elsey	5-20	1-1	0-3	0-0	4-16	25.0	- 3.69
R Hannon	5-23	2-8	2-9	0-1	1-5	21.7	- 6.75
D R C Elsworth	4-4	2-2	1-1	0-0	1-1	100.0	+ 4.80
P J Makin	4-8	0-1	3-5	0-0	1-2	50.0	+ 2.70
M Fetherston-Godley	4-8	2-3	1-2	0-0	1-3	50.0	+ 4.58
Dr J D Scargill	4-8	0-0	0-2	0-0	4-6	50.0	+ 6.73
K O C-Brown	4-9	0-0	0-0	0-0	4-9	44.4	+ 10.75
A Bailey	4-11	0-0	1-1	0-0	3-10	36.4	+ 8.88
M J Ryan	4-11	0-0	1-3	0-0	3-8	36.4	+ 0.93
N A Callaghan	4-12	1-2	2-4	1-2	0-4	33.3	+ 0.62
D Murray Smith	4-13	1-1	1-5	0-0	2-7	30.8	+ 0.48

TRAINERS' FAVOURITES AT NEWBURY 1989-93

	Total W-R	Non-handicaps 2-y-o	3-y-o+	Handicaps 2-y-o	3-y-o+	Per cent	£1 Level Stake
H R A Cecil	17-45	4-11	13-28	0-0	0-6	37.8	- 6.59
R Hannon	15-37	6-13	4-6	3-7	2-11	40.5	+ 6.70
P Chapple-Hyam	14-18	11-13	2-4	1-1	0-0	77.8	+ 14.84
J H M Gosden	10-31	3-7	4-17	0-0	3-7	32.3	+ 0.96
M R Stoute	9-25	1-2	5-14	1-2	2-7	36.0	+ 7.92
L M Cumani	8-27	3-7	3-7	0-0	2-13	29.6	- 6.21
I A Balding	5-10	3-5	0-0	0-0	2-5	50.0	+ 9.82
Lord Huntingdon	5-13	0-0	0-3	1-1	4-9	38.5	+ 14.25
P T Walwyn	5-20	1-3	0-6	0-0	4-11	25.0	+ 2.50
R Charlton	5-20	0-2	3-10	0-0	2-8	25.0	- 5.25
B W Hills	5-23	3-9	1-6	0-0	1-8	21.7	- 6.52
J L Dunlop	4-10	0-1	2-3	1-1	1-5	40.0	+ 1.81
D R C Elsworth	4-15	1-5	0-4	0-0	3-6	26.7	+ 3.50
P F I Cole	4-17	3-10	1-4	0-0	0-3	23.5	- 4.61
R W Armstrong	3-6	1-3	2-2	0-0	0-1	50.0	+ 2.25
J Berry	3-6	3-6	0-0	0-0	0-0	50.0	+ 1.33
A A Scott	3-6	3-4	0-1	0-1	0-0	50.0	+ 6.50
A C Stewart	3-10	0-0	1-3	0-1	2-6	30.0	+ 3.45
W R Hern	3-12	2-5	1-6	0-0	0-1	25.0	- 7.53
M H Easterby	2-4	0-0	0-0	0-0	2-4	50.0	+ 4.83
B Hanbury	2-4	0-0	1-2	0-0	1-2	50.0	+ 1.16
R Akehurst	2-12	0-0	0-0	0-0	2-12	16.7	- 4.50
C W C Elsey	1-1	0-0	1-1	0-0	0-0	100.0	+ 4.00
H Thomson Jones	1-1	1-1	0-0	0-0	0-0	100.0	+ 1.75

TRAINERS' FAVOURITES AT NEWCASTLE 1989-93

	Total W-R	Non-handicaps 2-y-o	3-y-o+	Handicaps 2-y-o	3-y-o+	Per cent	£1 Level Stake
M R Stoute	12-22	5-7	5-10	0-0	2-5	54.5	- 3.93
Mrs M Reveley	12-23	1-3	1-1	1-1	9-18	52.2	+ 10.67
J Berry	12-29	8-14	3-6	0-1	1-8	41.4	+ 2.01
H R A Cecil	11-18	4-5	5-8	0-0	2-5	61.1	- 0.99
J W Watts	7-15	2-5	1-3	0-0	4-7	46.7	+ 2.81
L M Cumani	6-10	1-1	3-4	0-1	2-4	60.0	+ 0.98
M H Easterby	6-30	0-5	1-4	0-0	5-21	20.0	- 9.19
Sir M Prescott	5-10	0-1	1-3	0-1	4-5	50.0	+ 6.52
B W Hills	5-12	3-4	1-5	0-0	1-3	41.7	+ 0.44
A A Scott	4-5	2-2	1-2	0-0	1-1	80.0	+ 5.77
R Hannon	4-7	2-4	1-1	0-0	1-2	57.1	+ 5.17
J H M Gosden	4-9	0-1	3-7	0-0	1-1	44.4	- 2.08
J L Dunlop	4-10	1-2	0-1	0-0	3-7	40.0	+ 0.13
Mrs J Ramsden	4-14	1-2	0-1	0-1	3-10	28.6	- 2.54
M J Camacho	3-4	0-0	1-2	0-0	2-2	75.0	+ 5.20
C Tinkler	3-4	3-3	0-0	0-0	0-1	75.0	+ 10.91
M Bell	3-10	3-4	0-1	0-1	0-4	30.0	- 4.71
W R Hern	2-2	1-1	1-1	0-0	0-0	100.0	+ 1.57
P T Walwyn	2-2	0-0	2-2	0-0	0-0	100.0	+ 1.50
Miss S E Hall	2-3	1-2	0-0	1-1	0-0	66.7	+ 2.50
G Harwood	2-3	0-0	1-1	0-0	1-2	66.7	+ 3.80
R W Armstrong	2-4	1-2	1-1	0-0	0-1	50.0	+ 1.20
G Wragg	2-4	0-1	2-3	0-0	0-0	50.0	+ 0.75
D Morley	2-5	0-1	0-1	0-0	2-3	40.0	+ 1.43

TRAINERS' FAVOURITES AT NEWMARKET 1989-93

	Total W-R	Non-handicaps 2-y-o	3-y-o+	Handicaps 2-y-o	3-y-o+	Per cent	£1 Level Stake
H R A Cecil	47-121	14-35	29-69	0-0	4-17	38.8	- 16.79
L M Cumani	27-72	7-16	18-35	1-3	1-18	37.5	- 8.25
M R Stoute	26-63	10-26	14-30	0-2	2-5	41.3	- 1.54
R Hannon	19-56	10-22	5-13	3-6	1-15	33.9	+ 4.35
J H M Gosden	17-71	2-13	11-33	0-3	4-22	23.9	- 26.76
J L Dunlop	14-30	4-6	7-11	0-0	3-13	46.7	+ 9.72
B W Hills	14-38	3-7	6-10	0-0	5-21	36.8	+ 11.00
W R Hern	12-23	4-9	6-9	0-0	2-5	52.2	+ 7.07
P F I Cole	10-20	5-10	4-6	1-2	0-2	50.0	+ 10.76
A A Scott	7-20	3-6	4-8	0-1	0-5	35.0	- 2.97
M A Jarvis	6-16	0-3	4-5	0-0	2-8	37.5	+ 5.80
G Wragg	6-25	2-6	2-12	0-0	2-7	24.0	- 8.06
I A Balding	5-12	1-4	3-4	0-0	1-4	41.7	+ 2.96
J Berry	5-12	3-5	1-3	0-0	1-4	41.7	+ 4.20
P Chapple-Hyam	5-13	3-11	2-2	0-0	0-0	38.5	+ 0.06
C E Brittain	5-25	2-2	2-7	1-2	0-14	20.0	- 9.02
A Fabre (Fra)	4-7	3-3	1-3	0-0	0-1	57.1	+ 2.12
J R Fanshawe	4-12	1-2	2-5	0-1	1-4	33.3	+ 2.48
R Akehurst	4-13	0-0	1-1	0-0	3-12	30.8	+ 2.46
Mrs J Ramsden	4-14	1-1	0-0	1-5	2-8	28.6	- 0.37
R Charlton	4-14	3-6	1-5	0-0	0-3	28.6	- 5.43
W Jarvis	4-17	2-5	2-6	0-0	0-6	23.5	- 7.45
A C Stewart	4-18	1-2	2-6	0-0	1-10	22.2	- 4.27
N A Callaghan	4-20	1-6	3-4	0-5	0-5	20.0	- 4.49

TRAINERS' FAVOURITES AT NOTTINGHAM 1989-93

	Total W-R	Non-handicaps 2-y-o	3-y-o+	Handicaps 2-y-o	3-y-o+	Per cent	£1 Level Stake
H R A Cecil	21-43	4-9	17-34	0-0	0-0	48.8	- 3.23
J L Dunlop	12-33	4-12	3-6	0-0	5-15	36.4	- 1.25
J Berry	10-24	6-13	3-9	0-1	1-1	41.7	+ 5.47
J H M Gosden	9-14	2-4	6-9	0-0	1-1	64.3	+ 11.38
P F I Cole	9-18	5-10	2-2	0-0	2-6	50.0	+ 10.99
R Hannon	8-18	2-5	4-6	1-1	1-6	44.4	+ 6.10
M R Stoute	6-11	4-5	2-4	0-1	0-1	54.5	- 2.05
R Charlton	5-8	2-4	2-3	0-0	1-1	62.5	+ 2.20
L M Cumani	5-11	1-3	4-8	0-0	0-0	45.5	- 1.23
D Morley	5-11	3-4	0-1	0-0	2-6	45.5	+ 5.38
M J Camacho	3-3	0-0	1-1	0-0	2-2	100.0	+ 9.00
M W Easterby	3-3	2-2	0-0	0-0	1-1	100.0	+ 7.28
J R Fanshawe	3-3	1-1	1-1	1-1	0-0	100.0	+ 4.36
R M Whitaker	3-4	0-0	1-1	0-0	2-3	75.0	+ 16.50
A C Stewart	3-5	0-1	1-1	0-1	2-2	60.0	+ 0.86
W Jarvis	3-6	1-2	2-2	0-1	0-1	50.0	+ 0.40
J Wharton	3-6	1-1	2-2	0-0	0-3	50.0	+ 6.50
M S Johnston	3-7	0-2	2-3	1-1	0-1	42.9	- 0.90
Mrs J Cecil	3-7	2-5	0-1	0-0	1-1	42.9	+ 0.03
W R Hern	3-11	1-2	1-6	0-0	1-3	27.3	- 4.14
G Harwood	2-2	0-0	2-2	0-0	0-0	100.0	+ 0.78
W J Haggas	2-3	1-2	0-0	0-0	1-1	66.7	+ 3.38
C E Brittain	2-4	2-2	0-1	0-0	0-1	50.0	+ 0.36
N A Callaghan	2-4	0-1	1-2	1-1	0-0	50.0	+ 1.10

TRAINERS' FAVOURITES AT PONTEFRACT 1989-93

	Total W-R	Non-handicaps 2-y-o	3-y-o+	Handicaps 2-y-o	3-y-o+	Per cent	£1 Level Stake
R Hollinshead	13-20	5-8	2-3	0-0	6-9	65.0	+ 12.68
Mrs J Ramsden	13-38	0-2	0-3	0-2	13-31	34.2	+ 6.34
J Berry	9-23	7-9	2-9	0-0	0-5	39.1	+ 2.35
H R A Cecil	8-13	0-1	8-12	0-0	0-0	61.5	+ 6.74
M H Tompkins	6-11	2-4	3-4	0-0	1-3	54.5	+ 6.59
Mrs M Reveley	6-15	0-1	1-3	0-1	5-10	40.0	+ 2.73
M R Stoute	5-8	2-2	3-5	0-0	0-1	62.5	+ 2.29
G Harwood	5-9	1-1	2-6	2-2	0-0	55.6	+ 3.23
L M Cumani	5-11	1-3	4-7	0-0	0-1	45.5	- 0.85
B Hanbury	4-6	1-1	1-1	0-1	2-3	66.7	+ 2.62
I A Balding	4-7	3-3	1-3	0-0	0-1	57.1	+ 1.59
J W Watts	4-10	0-1	1-1	0-0	3-8	40.0	+ 0.60
J D Bethell	3-5	0-0	0-0	0-0	3-5	60.0	+ 12.50
M J Camacho	3-5	0-0	0-0	0-0	3-5	60.0	+ 8.50
H Thomson Jones	3-5	2-2	1-3	0-0	0-0	60.0	+ 1.79
J Etherington	3-6	3-3	0-0	0-1	0-2	50.0	+ 1.55
Lord Huntingdon	3-6	1-2	1-2	0-0	1-2	50.0	+ 3.18
M S Johnston	3-7	1-2	1-2	0-1	1-2	42.9	+ 3.00
G Wragg	3-8	0-0	3-7	0-0	0-1	37.5	- 1.19
T D Barron	3-10	1-3	0-0	1-2	1-5	30.0	+ 3.50
M H Easterby	3-10	0-3	1-1	0-0	2-6	30.0	- 0.12
J H M Gosden	3-10	1-1	1-5	0-0	1-4	30.0	- 1.62
P F I Cole	2-3	1-1	0-1	1-1	0-0	66.7	+ 0.80
M W Easterby	2-3	0-0	1-1	0-0	1-2	66.7	+ 2.42

TRAINERS' FAVOURITES AT REDCAR 1989-93

	Total W-R	Non-handicaps 2-y-o	3-y-o+	Handicaps 2-y-o	3-y-o+	Per cent	£1 Level Stake
Mrs M Reveley	17-39	3-3	4-5	0-1	10-30	43.6	+ 10.95
M H Easterby	16-37	7-14	2-3	3-7	4-13	43.2	+ 5.64
H Thomson Jones	11-20	5-7	4-6	0-0	2-7	55.0	+ 1.79
H R A Cecil	8-14	1-3	6-7	0-0	1-4	57.1	+ 0.46
J L Dunlop	8-14	2-2	1-3	1-1	4-8	57.1	+ 7.80
J H M Gosden	8-19	3-7	4-10	0-0	1-2	42.1	- 3.65
J Berry	8-29	3-14	1-6	1-3	3-6	27.6	- 6.33
L M Cumani	8-29	0-8	7-9	0-0	1-12	27.6	- 13.46
R Hannon	5-9	3-5	1-2	1-2	0-0	55.6	+ 4.69
F H Lee	5-10	0-1	0-0	1-1	4-8	50.0	+ 6.75
G Harwood	5-11	2-3	3-5	0-0	0-3	45.5	+ 1.86
M R Stoute	5-15	2-5	2-4	0-1	1-5	33.3	- 5.24
M Bell	4-4	3-3	0-0	0-0	1-1	100.0	+ 5.68
R Hollinshead	4-6	1-2	1-2	0-0	2-2	66.7	+ 5.80
M H Tompkins	4-7	2-4	0-0	1-1	1-2	57.1	+ 5.36
M J Camacho	4-8	0-1	2-2	0-0	2-5	50.0	+ 2.79
J W Hills	4-10	1-1	1-2	0-0	2-7	40.0	- 3.07
B W Hills	4-11	1-3	2-5	0-0	1-3	36.4	- 2.07
Sir M Prescott	4-12	1-3	2-3	0-0	1-6	33.3	- 3.37
R M Whitaker	4-16	1-5	1-3	0-0	2-8	25.0	- 5.50
J G FitzGerald	3-3	0-0	0-0	1-1	2-2	100.0	+ 12.50
M A Jarvis	3-3	1-1	1-1	0-0	1-1	100.0	+ 2.34
Lady Herries	3-3	0-0	0-0	0-0	3-3	100.0	+ 4.25
W Carter	3-4	0-0	0-0	1-2	2-2	75.0	+ 6.25

TRAINERS' FAVOURITES AT RIPON 1989-93

	Total W-R	Non-handicaps 2-y-o	Non-handicaps 3-y-o+	Handicaps 2-y-o	Handicaps 3-y-o+	Per cent	£1 Level Stake
H R A Cecil	20-30	1-2	18-26	0-0	1-2	66.7	+ 9.91
J Berry	11-27	8-18	2-6	0-2	1-1	40.7	+ 1.51
M H Easterby	9-28	3-9	2-4	0-0	4-15	32.1	- 5.12
L M Cumani	8-13	1-1	6-11	0-0	1-1	61.5	+ 5.38
J H M Gosden	6-12	0-0	4-8	0-0	2-4	50.0	+ 0.41
M R Stoute	6-14	1-2	2-2	0-0	3-10	42.9	+ 3.15
J L Dunlop	5-11	1-3	1-2	0-1	3-5	45.5	- 0.70
B W Hills	4-17	1-2	2-9	0-0	1-6	23.5	- 7.13
D Morley	3-4	0-0	1-1	0-0	2-3	75.0	+ 4.55
G Harwood	3-6	0-0	1-3	0-0	2-3	50.0	+ 5.75
Mrs M Reveley	3-13	0-0	1-3	0-0	2-10	23.1	- 3.17
R Akehurst	2-2	0-0	0-0	0-0	2-2	100.0	+ 6.50
G Lewis	2-2	1-1	0-0	0-0	1-1	100.0	+ 2.36
J L Spearing	2-2	0-0	0-0	0-0	2-2	100.0	+ 3.00
Capt J Wilson	2-2	0-0	0-0	0-0	2-2	100.0	+ 11.50
Mrs L Piggott	2-2	0-0	0-0	0-0	2-2	100.0	+ 3.25
J Pearce	2-3	0-0	1-1	0-0	1-2	66.7	+ 2.88
W J Haggas	2-3	2-2	0-0	0-0	0-1	66.7	+ 0.63
J Wharton	2-3	0-1	0-0	0-0	2-2	66.7	+ 6.00
R Charlton	2-3	0-0	1-1	0-0	1-2	66.7	+ 0.67
B Hanbury	2-4	0-1	1-1	0-0	1-2	50.0	- 0.66
W Jarvis	2-4	2-3	0-0	0-0	0-1	50.0	- 1.00
M J Camacho	2-5	0-1	1-1	0-0	1-3	40.0	+ 1.13
P C Haslam	2-5	0-0	0-1	0-0	2-4	40.0	+ 4.00

TRAINERS' FAVOURITES AT SALISBURY 1989-93

	Total W-R	Non-handicaps 2-y-o	Non-handicaps 3-y-o+	Handicaps 2-y-o	Handicaps 3-y-o+	Per cent	£1 Level Stake
G Harwood	17-32	6-14	3-7	2-2	6-9	53.1	+ 11.30
R Hannon	16-46	10-20	3-9	0-3	3-14	34.8	- 4.89
D R C Elsworth	9-31	4-10	1-6	0-0	4-15	29.0	- 1.99
P F I Cole	6-17	4-9	1-5	0-0	1-3	35.3	- 1.59
M R Stoute	5-10	1-4	2-4	0-0	2-2	50.0	+ 2.73
R Charlton	5-10	1-4	2-3	0-0	2-3	50.0	+ 2.09
I A Balding	5-21	3-7	0-4	0-0	2-10	23.8	- 5.59
A A Scott	4-5	1-1	3-3	0-0	0-1	80.0	+ 6.50
H R A Cecil	4-8	0-0	4-8	0-0	0-0	50.0	- 0.03
J H M Gosden	4-8	0-1	4-6	0-0	0-1	50.0	+ 2.00
Lord Huntingdon	4-10	0-0	3-5	0-0	1-5	40.0	+ 1.57
L M Cumani	4-11	1-2	3-7	0-0	0-2	36.4	- 3.37
J L Dunlop	4-14	1-3	2-6	0-0	1-5	28.6	- 1.52
K O C-Brown	3-5	1-1	2-2	0-0	0-2	60.0	+ 1.50
B W Hills	3-10	0-3	1-3	1-1	1-3	30.0	- 2.27
G Lewis	3-11	2-5	1-2	0-0	0-4	27.3	- 1.52
D R Laing	2-2	0-0	1-1	0-0	1-1	100.0	+ 6.25
M McCormack	2-2	2-2	0-0	0-0	0-0	100.0	+ 2.74
A C Stewart	2-3	0-0	1-2	0-0	1-1	66.7	+ 4.50
C J Hill	2-4	0-0	0-0	0-0	2-4	50.0	+ 7.00
M C Pipe	2-4	0-0	0-1	0-0	2-3	50.0	+ 4.75
Lady Herries	2-4	1-1	0-0	0-0	1-3	50.0	+ 6.00
P Chapple-Hyam	2-4	2-4	0-0	0-0	0-0	50.0	+ 0.25
J W Hills	2-5	2-4	0-0	0-0	0-1	40.0	- 1.05

TRAINERS' FAVOURITES AT SANDOWN 1989-93

	Total W-R	Non-handicaps 2-y-o	3-y-o+	Handicaps 2-y-o	3-y-o+	Per cent	£1 Level Stake
H R A Cecil	13-35	5-8	8-23	0-0	0-4	37.1	- 8.28
R Hannon	13-36	7-13	1-4	0-1	5-18	36.1	- 3.13
J H M Gosden	10-20	2-2	6-9	0-0	2-9	50.0	+ 6.47
G Harwood	10-22	1-4	5-11	0-1	4-6	45.5	+ 5.49
M R Stoute	9-32	5-7	4-12	0-1	0-12	28.1	- 10.95
R Akehurst	8-21	0-1	1-2	0-2	7-16	38.1	+ 8.96
J L Dunlop	5-14	1-6	1-1	0-0	3-7	35.7	+ 4.13
I A Balding	5-17	2-3	1-7	0-0	2-7	29.4	- 3.14
B W Hills	5-17	3-5	1-8	0-0	1-4	29.4	- 3.39
W R Hern	4-5	3-3	1-2	0-0	0-0	80.0	+ 1.63
M R Channon	4-7	2-3	0-1	0-0	2-3	57.1	+ 5.55
J Berry	4-15	0-1	3-9	0-2	1-3	26.7	- 2.86
J R Fanshawe	3-5	0-0	2-3	0-0	1-2	60.0	+ 4.48
A A Scott	3-8	1-2	0-2	0-1	2-3	37.5	+ 5.50
B Hanbury	3-9	0-2	0-2	0-0	3-5	33.3	- 0.66
P J Makin	3-9	0-1	1-3	0-0	2-5	33.3	+ 0.13
C R Nelson	3-10	1-4	1-3	0-0	1-3	30.0	- 0.84
Sir M Prescott	3-10	0-0	2-4	0-3	1-3	30.0	+ 1.50
Lord Huntingdon	3-10	0-0	1-4	0-0	2-6	30.0	- 0.87
C E Brittain	3-11	0-1	3-4	0-0	0-6	27.3	- 5.18
P F I Cole	3-13	1-5	1-4	1-2	0-2	23.1	- 3.00
L M Cumani	3-17	0-0	2-12	0-0	1-5	17.6	- 9.81
Mrs L Piggott	2-2	1-1	0-0	0-0	1-1	100.0	+ 3.38
Dr J D Scargill	2-2	1-1	1-1	0-0	0-0	100.0	+ 3.50

TRAINERS' FAVOURITES AT SOUTHWELL (AW) 1989-93

	Total W-R	Non-handicaps 2-y-o	3-y-o+	Handicaps 2-y-o	3-y-o+	Per cent	£1 Level Stake
T D Barron	34-78	5-5	17-36	2-4	10-33	43.6	+ 13.01
D W Chapman	24-49	0-0	15-26	1-3	8-20	49.0	+ 9.35
W A O'Gorman	20-63	8-14	6-24	1-3	5-22	31.7	- 10.65
Sir M Prescott	15-40	3-13	8-12	0-2	4-13	37.5	- 2.24
J Berry	14-37	11-25	0-3	1-2	2-7	37.8	+ 5.09
C J Hill	12-32	0-1	4-11	2-2	6-18	37.5	- 4.01
R Hollinshead	10-29	2-4	3-13	0-0	5-12	34.5	- 4.01
M S Johnston	9-27	0-2	3-6	0-0	6-19	33.3	+ 2.43
Lord Huntingdon	8-22	1-1	5-14	0-0	2-7	36.4	- 1.92
C R Nelson	6-9	1-2	4-5	0-0	1-2	66.7	+ 4.16
T Thomson Jones	6-10	0-0	1-1	0-0	5-9	60.0	+ 10.09
B W Hills	6-13	0-2	4-7	0-0	2-4	46.2	- 1.15
J G FitzGerald	6-15	2-3	2-3	0-0	2-9	40.0	+ 2.10
P F I Cole	6-19	2-6	2-9	0-1	2-3	31.6	- 2.71
Lady Herries	5-8	0-0	3-3	0-0	2-5	62.5	+ 4.23
C Tinkler	5-9	0-0	0-0	0-0	5-9	55.6	+ 3.51
P S Felgate	5-10	0-0	1-1	0-0	4-9	50.0	+ 6.95
M C Chapman	5-11	0-0	1-2	0-0	4-9	45.5	+ 6.75
C N Allen	5-11	0-2	2-2	1-1	2-6	45.5	+ 2.78
D R Loder	5-11	3-4	2-4	0-0	0-3	45.5	+ 0.56
J A Glover	5-14	0-1	0-0	0-0	5-13	35.7	+ 6.75
R W Armstrong	5-15	0-1	2-8	0-0	3-6	33.3	- 1.78
B A McMahon	5-16	0-0	3-8	0-0	2-8	31.3	- 2.45
M A Jarvis	4-6	0-0	0-1	1-1	3-4	66.7	+ 4.76

TRAINERS' FAVOURITES AT SOUTHWELL (TURF) 1991-93

	Total W-R	Non-handicaps 2-y-o	3-y-o+	Handicaps 2-y-o	3-y-o+	Per cent	£1 Level Stake
J Berry	3-5	0-0	2-2	0-0	1-3	60.0	+ 2.63
P F I Cole	2-2	2-2	0-0	0-0	0-0	100.0	+ 4.23
R Hollinshead	2-2	1-1	1-1	0-0	0-0	100.0	+ 1.71
J Wharton	2-3	0-0	2-2	0-0	0-1	66.7	+ 0.56
I A Balding	1-1	1-1	0-0	0-0	0-0	100.0	+ 0.67
H R A Cecil	1-1	1-1	0-0	0-0	0-0	100.0	+ 0.67
P S Felgate	1-1	0-0	0-0	0-0	1-1	100.0	+ 2.25
G Harwood	1-1	1-1	0-0	0-0	0-0	100.0	+ 3.50
A Hide	1-1	0-0	0-0	0-0	1-1	100.0	+ 2.50
M A Jarvis	1-1	1-1	0-0	0-0	0-0	100.0	+ 1.75
G Lewis	1-1	0-0	1-1	0-0	0-0	100.0	+ 0.62
M R Stoute	1-1	1-1	0-0	0-0	0-0	100.0	+ 2.75
Mrs J Ramsden	1-1	0-0	1-1	0-0	0-0	100.0	+ 1.63
Lady Herries	1-1	0-0	0-0	0-0	1-1	100.0	+ 1.10
B J McMath	1-1	0-0	0-0	0-0	1-1	100.0	+ 4.00
P Chapple-Hyam	1-1	1-1	0-0	0-0	0-0	100.0	+ 0.67
D R Loder	1-1	0-0	1-1	0-0	0-0	100.0	+ 1.38
S G Norton	1-2	0-0	1-1	0-0	0-1	50.0	+ 0.25
M H Tompkins	1-2	0-0	1-2	0-0	0-0	50.0	- 0.43
R J R Williams	1-2	0-0	0-0	0-0	1-2	50.0	+ 1.25
M H Easterby	1-3	1-2	0-0	0-0	0-1	33.3	+ 0.25
Mrs M Reveley	1-3	0-0	0-0	0-0	1-3	33.3	- 1.27
W A O'Gorman	1-4	0-1	0-0	0-0	1-3	25.0	+ 0.50

TRAINERS' FAVOURITES AT THIRSK 1989-93

	Total W-R	Non-handicaps 2-y-o	3-y-o+	Handicaps 2-y-o	3-y-o+	Per cent	£1 Level Stake
M H Easterby	13-35	6-14	1-4	1-4	5-13	37.1	+ 5.60
J Berry	9-33	5-18	4-7	0-2	0-6	27.3	- 12.38
H R A Cecil	8-17	2-3	5-11	0-0	1-3	47.1	- 1.22
G Harwood	7-8	0-0	6-7	0-0	1-1	87.5	+ 4.30
J L Dunlop	6-11	0-1	2-4	0-0	4-6	54.5	+ 3.00
B Hanbury	4-5	1-2	1-1	0-0	2-2	80.0	+ 7.40
A A Scott	4-6	1-2	3-3	0-0	0-1	66.7	+ 2.32
R Hannon	3-5	1-2	2-2	0-0	0-1	60.0	+ 5.75
B W Hills	3-6	0-1	2-3	0-0	1-2	50.0	+ 1.11
W J Haggas	3-6	1-1	1-2	0-0	1-3	50.0	+ 0.10
R Hollinshead	3-7	0-0	2-4	0-0	1-3	42.9	- 0.37
H Thomson Jones	3-7	2-2	1-5	0-0	0-0	42.9	- 2.66
N Tinkler	3-7	0-2	3-4	0-0	0-1	42.9	+ 0.74
P Chapple-Hyam	3-9	0-2	3-5	0-0	0-2	33.3	- 3.70
M R Stoute	3-14	1-3	2-8	0-0	0-3	21.4	- 7.20
M J Camacho	2-2	0-0	0-0	1-1	1-1	100.0	+ 4.50
H Candy	2-2	0-0	2-2	0-0	0-0	100.0	+ 0.86
J R Fanshawe	2-2	0-0	1-1	0-0	1-1	100.0	+ 5.64
P C Haslam	2-3	1-1	0-0	0-1	1-1	66.7	+ 3.07
J Etherington	2-4	0-1	1-2	0-0	1-1	50.0	+ 5.25
J Wharton	2-4	1-1	0-0	0-0	1-3	50.0	+ 6.00
J H M Gosden	2-4	0-0	2-4	0-0	0-0	50.0	+ 0.65
Mrs J Cecil	2-4	0-0	1-2	1-1	0-1	50.0	+ 1.50
L M Cumani	2-5	0-1	1-3	0-0	1-1	40.0	- 0.60

TRAINERS' FAVOURITES AT WARWICK 1989-93

	Total W-R	Non-handicaps 2-y-o	3-y-o+	Handicaps 2-y-o	3-y-o+	Per cent	£1 Level Stake
H R A Cecil	10-20	3-5	7-15	0-0	0-0	50.0	- 2.17
R Hollinshead	5-7	1-2	3-4	1-1	0-0	71.4	+ 8.25
I A Balding	5-13	1-1	3-6	0-2	1-4	38.5	- 0.94
J Berry	5-20	1-12	1-3	2-3	1-2	25.0	- 6.77
L M Cumani	4-4	0-0	4-4	0-0	0-0	100.0	+ 4.99
W R Hern	4-6	0-0	4-4	0-0	0-2	66.7	+ 2.85
P T Walwyn	4-6	1-1	3-5	0-0	0-0	66.7	+ 1.68
J W Hills	4-8	0-1	3-3	0-0	1-4	50.0	+ 4.61
M R Stoute	4-9	3-3	1-4	0-0	0-2	44.4	- 2.37
J L Dunlop	4-10	1-1	1-2	1-1	1-6	40.0	+ 1.81
G Harwood	4-12	1-2	3-6	0-0	0-4	33.3	- 5.01
J H M Gosden	4-13	0-1	4-10	0-0	0-2	30.8	- 0.52
B W Hills	4-14	0-4	3-5	1-1	0-4	28.6	- 7.48
G Lewis	3-4	2-3	0-0	0-0	1-1	75.0	+ 6.48
R Charlton	3-5	0-0	2-4	0-0	1-1	60.0	+ 2.18
P Chapple-Hyam	3-5	3-5	0-0	0-0	0-0	60.0	- 0.89
R Akehurst	3-8	0-1	0-0	0-0	3-7	37.5	+ 4.50
B A McMahon	3-8	0-0	0-0	0-0	3-8	37.5	+ 0.88
P F I Cole	3-11	1-4	2-5	0-0	0-2	27.3	- 5.38
R Hannon	3-16	0-6	0-2	1-4	2-4	18.8	- 4.37
R F J Houghton	2-3	0-0	2-3	0-0	0-0	66.7	+ 2.63
Mrs J Cecil	2-3	0-0	0-0	1-1	1-2	66.7	+ 1.58
Sir M Prescott	2-4	0-0	0-1	0-1	2-2	50.0	+ 2.63
J W Payne	2-4	2-3	0-0	0-1	0-0	50.0	- 0.33

TRAINERS' FAVOURITES AT WINDSOR 1989-93

	Total W-R	Non-handicaps 2-y-o	3-y-o+	Handicaps 2-y-o	3-y-o+	Per cent	£1 Level Stake
R Hannon	14-36	8-16	2-7	2-3	2-10	38.9	+ 1.29
L M Cumani	11-19	0-0	9-14	0-1	2-4	57.9	+ 5.83
M A Jarvis	5-9	0-0	1-2	0-0	4-7	55.6	+ 4.65
H R A Cecil	5-10	0-1	3-7	0-0	2-2	50.0	+ 0.04
P J Makin	5-10	0-0	5-8	0-0	0-2	50.0	+ 3.82
M R Stoute	5-10	2-4	0-0	0-0	3-6	50.0	+ 2.40
J Berry	5-20	1-8	1-1	3-6	0-5	25.0	- 2.00
C F Wall	4-5	3-3	1-1	0-0	0-1	80.0	+ 5.98
A C Stewart	4-6	0-0	3-4	0-0	1-2	66.7	+ 2.69
G Harwood	4-7	0-0	1-3	1-1	2-3	57.1	+ 3.19
A A Scott	4-7	2-4	1-1	0-0	1-2	57.1	+ 2.05
M Bell	4-9	2-6	0-0	0-0	2-3	44.4	+ 1.60
W R Hern	4-11	0-1	1-4	0-0	3-6	36.4	- 0.95
C R Nelson	3-4	2-2	0-0	0-0	1-2	75.0	+ 4.00
I A Balding	3-7	2-3	0-1	0-0	1-3	42.9	- 0.28
N A Callaghan	3-8	1-1	0-0	0-2	2-5	37.5	+ 2.50
W A O'Gorman	3-9	3-8	0-0	0-1	0-0	33.3	- 3.16
R Charlton	3-9	1-1	0-5	0-0	2-3	33.3	+ 1.58
B W Hills	3-10	0-2	1-4	1-1	1-3	30.0	+ 1.24
D R C Elsworth	3-14	0-4	2-5	0-1	1-4	21.4	- 1.50
N Tinkler	2-2	0-0	1-1	0-0	1-1	100.0	+ 5.23
Lord Huntingdon	2-2	2-2	0-0	0-0	0-0	100.0	+ 1.87
M S Johnston	2-2	0-0	1-1	0-0	1-1	100.0	+ 2.33
J R Fanshawe	2-2	0-0	2-2	0-0	0-0	100.0	+ 3.50

TRAINERS' FAVOURITES AT WOLVERHAMPTON 1989-93

	Total W-R	Non-handicaps 2-y-o	Non-handicaps 3-y-o+	Handicaps 2-y-o	Handicaps 3-y-o+	Per cent	£1 Level Stake
J L Dunlop	10-17	1-2	3-5	0-0	6-10	58.8	+ 9.55
H R A Cecil	8-16	2-4	6-12	0-0	0-0	50.0	- 2.31
J H M Gosden	5-6	2-2	3-4	0-0	0-0	83.3	+ 1.37
M R Stoute	5-9	3-5	2-3	0-0	0-1	55.6	- 1.40
L M Cumani	5-10	1-2	4-8	0-0	0-0	50.0	- 0.79
G Harwood	4-6	1-2	3-3	0-0	0-1	66.7	- 0.17
R Charlton	4-6	2-2	2-2	0-0	0-2	66.7	+ 1.19
R J Hodges	4-8	2-3	0-0	0-1	2-4	50.0	+ 3.83
M C Pipe	3-4	0-0	2-3	0-0	1-1	75.0	+ 7.73
R Boss	3-6	1-2	1-1	0-1	1-2	50.0	+ 4.00
R Hannon	3-6	1-3	2-2	0-1	0-0	50.0	+ 4.13
M A Jarvis	3-7	2-2	0-1	0-0	1-4	42.9	+ 3.63
P F I Cole	3-12	3-8	0-2	0-0	0-2	25.0	- 4.63
A C Stewart	3-13	1-3	1-6	0-0	1-4	23.1	- 6.25
J Berry	3-23	1-12	1-3	1-5	0-3	13.0	- 14.83
P Calver	2-2	0-0	2-2	0-0	0-0	100.0	+ 4.00
H Thomson Jones	2-2	2-2	0-0	0-0	0-0	100.0	+ 2.82
W A O'Gorman	2-2	2-2	0-0	0-0	0-0	100.0	+ 2.15
G Wragg	2-2	1-1	1-1	0-0	0-0	100.0	+ 1.95
W Jarvis	2-2	1-1	1-1	0-0	0-0	100.0	+ 1.98
Sir M Prescott	2-3	0-1	1-1	0-0	1-1	66.7	+ 1.75
J L Spearing	2-3	0-0	0-0	0-1	2-2	66.7	+ 6.00
I A Balding	2-4	1-1	1-2	0-0	0-1	50.0	- 1.07
B Hanbury	2-4	2-2	0-1	0-0	0-1	50.0	+ 0.30

TRAINERS' FAVOURITES AT YARMOUTH 1989-93

	Total W-R	Non-handicaps 2-y-o	Non-handicaps 3-y-o+	Handicaps 2-y-o	Handicaps 3-y-o+	Per cent	£1 Level Stake
H R A Cecil	26-54	13-27	11-23	0-0	2-4	48.1	- 2.86
A C Stewart	11-21	2-5	4-8	0-0	5-8	52.4	+ 6.78
J H M Gosden	9-21	1-4	6-11	0-0	2-6	42.9	- 0.31
Mrs L Piggott	8-14	1-3	3-3	0-0	4-8	57.1	+ 7.08
M H Tompkins	8-19	4-7	1-3	1-3	2-6	42.1	- 0.72
M R Stoute	8-21	3-9	4-7	0-0	1-5	38.1	- 3.76
C E Brittain	6-13	2-4	2-3	0-0	2-6	46.2	+ 6.82
J Berry	6-15	4-10	2-3	0-0	0-2	40.0	+ 3.71
G Wragg	6-19	3-10	3-6	0-0	0-3	31.6	- 5.98
W J Haggas	5-9	0-1	1-2	2-3	2-3	55.6	+ 4.13
D Morley	5-12	2-4	1-1	0-0	2-7	41.7	+ 2.93
L M Cumani	5-32	2-12	2-10	0-1	1-9	15.6	- 22.43
G A Pritchard-Gordon	4-9	0-2	2-2	0-0	2-5	44.4	+ 1.83
N A Callaghan	4-11	1-5	1-1	1-2	1-3	36.4	+ 0.50
B W Hills	4-11	2-4	1-5	0-0	1-2	36.4	- 1.09
J L Dunlop	3-5	0-0	1-2	0-0	2-3	60.0	+ 1.21
K T Ivory	3-6	0-2	0-0	0-0	3-4	50.0	+ 3.73
Sir M Prescott	3-8	1-1	1-3	0-0	1-4	37.5	- 1.27
W Jarvis	3-9	2-2	0-2	0-1	1-4	33.3	- 1.00
B Hanbury	3-11	2-4	1-3	0-1	0-3	27.3	- 2.09
H Thomson Jones	3-11	3-7	0-2	0-0	0-2	27.3	- 2.93
J Pearce	3-11	1-2	1-4	0-0	1-5	27.3	- 2.50
Mrs N Macauley	3-13	0-0	1-1	0-1	2-11	23.1	+ 0.50
P C Haslam	2-3	0-0	1-1	1-1	0-1	66.7	+ 3.75

TRAINERS' FAVOURITES AT YORK 1989-93

	Total W-R	Non-handicaps 2-y-o	3-y-o+	Handicaps 2-y-o	3-y-o+	Per cent	£1 Level Stake
J H M Gosden	15-28	2-3	6-12	0-1	7-12	53.6	+ 19.41
H R A Cecil	15-45	2-5	11-32	0-0	2-8	33.3	- 14.87
M R Stoute	14-43	2-8	10-23	0-0	2-12	32.6	- 5.34
J L Dunlop	10-23	5-11	2-4	0-1	3-7	43.5	+ 2.60
M H Easterby	9-41	1-4	1-2	1-4	6-31	22.0	- 1.17
P F I Cole	7-10	6-8	0-0	0-0	1-2	70.0	+ 8.98
R Hannon	7-15	5-9	1-1	1-2	0-3	46.7	+ 3.39
L M Cumani	7-23	1-3	5-11	0-1	1-8	30.4	- 7.97
B W Hills	5-21	2-8	1-7	0-0	2-6	23.8	- 1.92
J Berry	4-7	3-6	0-0	1-1	0-0	57.1	+ 0.89
D R C Elsworth	4-9	2-3	1-3	0-0	1-3	44.4	+ 10.25
M S Johnston	4-9	1-2	0-0	0-0	3-7	44.4	+ 8.88
A A Scott	4-10	2-4	1-3	0-0	1-3	40.0	- 0.58
G Wragg	4-11	2-5	2-4	0-0	0-2	36.4	- 0.79
B Hanbury	4-12	3-4	0-2	0-2	1-4	33.3	- 3.42
E Weymes	3-3	2-2	0-0	0-0	1-1	100.0	+ 5.75
P Chapple-Hyam	3-4	3-3	0-0	0-0	0-1	75.0	+ 3.50
R Charlton	3-10	1-3	0-1	0-1	2-5	30.0	+ 2.63
I A Balding	3-14	0-4	0-2	0-0	3-8	21.4	+ 0.50
M Fetherston-Godley	2-2	0-0	0-0	0-0	2-2	100.0	+ 10.00
F H Lee	2-3	2-2	0-0	0-0	0-1	66.7	+ 2.30
C E Brittain	2-4	0-0	2-3	0-0	0-1	50.0	+ 0.73
W Jarvis	2-4	0-2	1-1	1-1	0-0	50.0	+ 1.73
P J Makin	2-5	0-0	0-1	0-0	2-4	40.0	+ 3.83

TOP PERCENTAGE COURSES FOR FAVOURITES 1989-93

	W-R	Per cent	£1 Level Stake		W-R	Per cent	£1 Level Stake
Newcastle	153-367	41.7	+ 3.71	Brighton	198-555	35.7	- 82.06
Redcar	242-596	40.6	+ 27.01	Southwell (AW)	376-106	35.5	- 93.88
Southwell (Turf)*	28-70	40.0	+ 1.17	Lingfield (AW)	287-808	35.5	- 56.23
Edinburgh	151-379	39.8	- 0.78	Sandown	186-526	35.4	- 18.62
Chepstow	122-312	39.1	+ 5.98	Thirsk	144-407	35.4	- 51.60
Catterick	175-456	38.4	- 47.47	Doncaster	204-586	34.8	- 7.47
Ayr	167-436	38.3	- 3.23	Leicester	181-521	34.7	- 46.89
Pontefract	187-489	38.2	+ 7.23	Lingfield	180-527	34.2	- 66.50
Folkestone	172-453	38.0	- 3.46	Goodwood	194-573	33.9	- 36.94
Beverley	213-565	37.7	- 33.18	Newbury	162-479	33.8	- 11.23
Nottingham	207-554	37.4	+ 1.04	Salisbury	138-412	33.5	- 53.34
Ripon	152-408	37.3	- 19.44	Carlisle	96-289	33.2	- 38.14
Hamilton	197-530	37.2	- 29.55	Newmarket	335-101	33.0	-102.63
Windsor	146-396	36.9	- 20.48	Ascot	131-400	32.8	- 25.72
Bath	139-380	36.6	- 12.24	Warwick	135-417	32.4	- 85.27
Wolverhampton	134-369	36.3	- 47.11	Haydock	173-559	30.9	-111.75
Yarmouth	195-539	36.2	- 81.29	Kempton	133-446	29.8	- 49.21
Chester	105-291	36.1	- 23.90	Epsom	62-212	29.2	- 32.31
York	178-497	35.8	+ 19.64				

*Since 1991

FAVOURITES' PERFORMANCE BY TYPE OF RACE 1989-93

Non-h'caps	W-R	Per cent	£1 Level Stake	Handicaps	W-R	Per cent	£1 Level Stake
2-y-o	1640-3938	41.6	-270.95	2-y-o	204-681	30.0	- 5.98
3-y-o	1313-2956	44.4	- 93.05	3-y-o	558-1900	29.4	-187.30
Weight/age	1061-2483	42.7	- 51.71	All-aged	1604-5924	27.1	-616.32
Totals	4014-9377	42.8	-415.71	Totals	2366-8505	27.8	-809.60
All Favs	6380-17882	35.7	-1225.31				

When there is more than one favourite in a race then the £1 stake has been equally divided on each one. Only one favourite is counted for each race.

TRAINER SUMMARIES

WINNING FLAT TRAINERS 1993

	Total W-R	2-y-o	3-y-o	4-y-o+	Per cent	£1 Level Stake
R Hannon	182-1192	98-553	65-442	19-197	15.3	- 136.43
J Berry	132-806	48-353	54-279	30-174	16.4	- 80.19
J H M Gosden	110-453	18-62	62-292	30-99	24.3	+ 82.91
H R A Cecil	94-406	21-78	62-272	11-56	23.2	- 15.28
J L Dunlop	93-536	21-182	56-254	16-100	17.4	- 17.79
Mrs M Reveley	82-515	10-94	15-116	57-305	15.9	- 102.21
M S Johnston	73-506	21-119	36-222	16-165	14.4	- 106.17
M R Stoute	65-419	16-83	40-282	9-54	15.5	- 69.50
P F I Cole	62-468	33-181	24-238	5-49	13.2	- 137.95
Sir Mark Prescott	53-260	11-70	35-142	7-48	20.4	- 37.85
P Chapple-Hyam	52-238	28-84	23-134	1-20	21.8	- 49.52
I A Balding	50-339	12-93	20-155	18-91	14.7	- 59.80
R Charlton	47-185	16-62	24-101	7-22	25.4	+ 74.24
R Akehurst	46-288	0-16	7-78	39-194	16.0	+ 10.26
D R Loder	45-193	20-81	17-64	8-48	23.3	- 21.37
M Bell	42-364	18-132	24-199	0-33	11.5	- 83.14
R Hollinshead	42-580	11-166	9-203	22-211	7.2	- 310.35
S G Norton	41-293	7-76	17-117	17-100	14.0	- 56.44
M H Easterby	41-393	16-142	18-129	7-122	10.4	- 136.17
Lord Huntingdon	39-269	3-42	11-101	25-126	14.5	- 68.23
L M Cumani	39-277	12-48	24-197	3-32	14.1	- 95.64
B W Hills	39-353	13-98	20-203	6-52	11.0	- 148.21
M R Channon	39-406	17-178	14-127	8-101	9.6	- 66.74
G Wragg	35-201	13-45	16-110	6-46	17.4	- 24.64
B Hanbury	35-222	4-44	18-103	13-75	15.8	- 40.37
J R Fanshawe	34-268	4-33	25-188	5-47	12.7	- 56.17
C E Brittain	34-437	4-104	15-202	15-131	7.8	- 140.11
D R C Elsworth	32-271	10-56	14-119	8-96	11.8	- 56.79
G Lewis	30-247	19-125	7-77	4-45	12.1	- 52.69
Mrs J Ramsden	30-274	11-85	8-68	11-121	10.9	- 51.63
H Thomson Jones	28-181	10-53	18-121	0-7	15.5	- 30.39
Mrs J Cecil	28-205	12-56	8-89	8-60	13.7	- 79.06
C J Hill	27-164	0-5	13-50	14-109	16.5	+ 3.44
M H Tompkins	27-290	5-127	18-93	4-70	9.3	- 124.74
R W Armstrong	26-147	12-47	8-78	6-22	17.7	+ 49.00
T D Barron	26-249	1-33	13-95	12-121	10.4	- 90.92
J W Hills	24-239	5-54	9-87	10-98	10.0	- 65.80
M J Ryan	23-179	3-38	8-57	12-84	12.8	- 13.96
D A Wilson	23-197	0-3	2-33	21-161	11.7	- 31.75
W A O'Gorman	22-127	4-20	11-52	7-55	17.3	+ 6.77
D W Chapman	22-249	1-32	3-46	18-171	8.8	- 128.73
A Bailey	22-250	4-55	2-58	16-137	8.8	- 108.96
R M Whitaker	22-320	3-68	10-116	9-136	6.9	- 94.42
M A Jarvis	21-147	5-37	5-65	11-45	14.3	- 49.82
P W Harris	21-179	1-21	11-98	9-60	11.7	+ 42.25
G Harwood	21-214	2-33	13-115	6-66	9.8	- 74.01
S Dow	21-253	3-42	13-119	5-92	8.3	- 44.67
W Jarvis	20-183	4-45	11-111	5-27	10.9	- 51.36
E J Alston	20-187	2-20	4-45	14-122	10.7	- 0.57
A A Scott	20-197	4-50	9-109	7-38	10.2	- 52.88
C A Cyzer	20-220	3-22	9-151	8-47	9.1	- 61.74
B A McMahon	20-271	2-47	4-71	14-153	7.4	- 46.70
R J Hodges	20-315	0-17	1-57	19-241	6.3	- 115.75
M C Pipe	19-99	4-14	7-27	8-58	19.2	+ 37.88

	Total W–R	2-y-o	3-y-o	4-y-o+	Per cent	£1 Level Stake
T J Naughton	19-131	2-8	10-63	7-60	14.5	- 0.31
M J B Heaton-Ellis	19-216	6-43	4-102	9-71	8.8	- 18.10
Lady Herries	18-87	0-11	14-42	4-34	20.7	+ 8.93
D Morris	18-127	4-21	5-35	9-71	14.2	+ 37.05
R J O'Sullivan	18-131	0-0	1-21	17-110	13.7	- 27.75
D W P Arbuthnot	17-121	3-25	2-17	12-79	14.0	+ 26.75
J W Watts	17-161	3-30	9-81	5-50	10.6	- 29.51
J L Spearing	17-172	3-28	4-35	10-109	9.9	- 19.35
P T Walwyn	17-185	2-52	8-101	7-32	9.2	- 48.87
P C Haslam	17-219	7-81	1-58	9-80	7.8	- 55.68
D Morley	16-126	3-26	7-80	6-20	12.7	- 20.00
J G FitzGerald	16-164	4-41	9-84	3-39	9.8	- 61.24
M W Easterby	16-209	5-99	6-72	5-38	7.7	- 98.95
R J R Williams	16-215	5-53	6-93	5-69	7.4	-102.34
M McCormack	15-136	5-40	3-37	7-59	11.0	- 12.88
N Tinkler	15-142	0-15	10-62	5-65	10.6	- 47.40
Miss S E Hall	14-93	4-25	4-42	6-26	15.1	- 21.47
J Wharton	14-161	6-31	1-46	7-84	8.7	- 59.11
J Pearce	14-171	0-13	1-27	13-131	8.2	- 81.49
P D Evans	13-94	6-27	1-10	6-57	13.8	+ 15.18
C F Wall	13-107	3-24	7-40	3-43	12.1	- 17.62
W J Haggas	13-125	3-32	6-49	4-44	10.4	- 38.12
G A Pritchard-Gordon	13-130	6-54	4-53	3-23	10.0	- 13.75
P J Makin	13-139	3-28	5-54	5-57	9.4	- 29.72
W R Hern	13-157	0-22	7-115	6-20	8.3	- 92.16
G L Moore	13-176	0-48	7-64	6-64	7.4	- 73.77
B J Meehan	13-182	7-91	4-57	2-34	7.1	- 86.78
P Calver	12-99	0-8	3-21	9-70	12.1	+ 14.83
R C Spicer	12-113	0-13	0-23	12-77	10.6	- 4.75
Bob Jones	12-120	2-28	1-22	9-70	10.0	- 45.97
Denys Smith	12-158	4-34	1-22	7-102	7.6	- 62.50
P G Murphy	12-169	2-56	4-48	6-65	7.1	- 66.92
W R Muir	12-170	2-35	3-59	7-76	7.1	-105.72
T Thomson Jones	11-87	1-11	0-17	10-59	12.6	- 17.41
J W Payne	11-91	3-23	8-58	0-10	12.1	- 43.74
J White	11-99	0-13	3-27	8-59	11.1	- 19.38
M J Camacho	11-100	0-24	5-18	6-58	11.0	- 40.58
W W Haigh	11-100	0-23	4-22	7-55	11.0	- 30.00
A C Stewart	11-120	0-14	11-98	0-8	9.2	- 43.27
M D Hammond	11-155	3-16	3-40	5-99	7.1	- 46.00
W J Musson	11-172	1-23	4-59	6-90	6.4	- 51.00
M D I Usher	11-172	5-66	2-37	4-69	6.4	- 92.99
F H Lee	11-233	2-24	7-130	2-79	4.7	-150.50
D Burchell	10-62	0-1	4-27	6-34	16.1	+ 24.80
Mrs L Piggott	10-74	1-17	1-23	8-34	13.5	+ 1.61
L G Cottrell	10-87	1-8	2-19	7-60	11.5	+ 41.95
Miss Gay Kelleway	10-93	1-25	5-39	4-29	10.8	- 22.20
E Weymes	10-95	7-51	1-20	2-24	10.5	+ 16.25
R Boss	10-106	4-40	3-36	3-30	9.4	- 45.25
C C Elsey	10-117	0-15	2-22	8-80	8.5	- 30.17
Mrs N Macauley	10-122	1-21	2-25	7-76	8.2	- 56.00
W G M Turner	10-125	3-48	5-57	2-20	8.0	- 19.50
J Etherington	10-128	3-61	1-28	6-39	7.8	- 51.25
N A Callaghan	10-138	7-74	1-22	2-42	7.2	- 86.64
R Guest	9-72	3-21	3-25	3-26	12.5	- 20.92
C J Benstead	9-91	0-14	2-37	7-40	9.9	- 50.29

	Total W–R	2-y-o	3-y-o	4-y-o+	Per cent	£1 Level Stake
P Mitchell	9–92	0–14	2–40	7–38	9.8	− 27.25
Miss L C Siddall	9–109	2–18	0–14	7–77	8.3	+ 6.50
B Palling	9–111	3–51	3–33	3–27	8.1	− 11.17
Dr J D Scargill	9–113	2–30	3–31	4–52	8.0	− 25.87
A Moore	9–114	0–7	5–31	4–76	7.9	− 55.00
D R Laing	9–117	1–11	2–37	6–69	7.7	− 46.75
J A Glover	9–121	1–19	1–16	7–86	7.4	− 56.75
T G Mills	9–123	0–24	1–67	8–32	7.3	− 58.67
D Haydn Jones	9–135	0–27	2–46	7–62	6.7	− 60.25
T Fairhurst	9–138	2–35	6–77	1–26	6.5	− 33.45
J L Harris	9–147	0–18	0–8	9–121	6.1	− 67.37
L J Holt	9–152	0–15	5–65	4–72	5.9	− 67.17
M C Chapman	9–155	0–12	5–40	4–103	5.8	− 66.25
M Brittain	9–203	1–73	2–58	6–72	4.4	−123.00
P S Felgate	8–89	0–5	1–16	7–68	9.0	− 52.80
S R Bowring	8–91	0–1	2–35	6–55	8.8	− 40.50
R Bastiman	8–104	0–4	1–21	7–79	7.7	+ 20.50
P Howling	8–176	0–23	2–95	6–58	4.5	−115.42
J E Banks	7–45	2–8	2–3	3–34	15.6	+ 19.33
P D Cundell	7–60	0–8	0–3	7–49	11.7	+ 6.50
Miss B Sanders	7–64	0–4	3–31	4–29	10.9	+ 58.00
M J Fetherston-Godley	7–75	4–36	0–2	3–37	9.3	− 30.00
N A Graham	7–78	0–17	2–20	5–41	9.0	− 7.70
G B Balding	7–81	0–17	3–28	4–36	8.6	− 12.90
K R Burke	7–83	1–17	3–21	3–45	8.4	− 32.50
P A Kelleway	7–86	4–40	2–37	1–9	8.1	− 12.00
J D Bethell	7–122	0–29	4–52	3–41	5.7	− 48.00
Pat Mitchell	7–126	0–14	4–50	3–62	5.6	− 69.50
R F Johnson Houghton	7–127	1–41	5–63	1–23	5.5	− 68.18
S P C Woods	7–131	2–36	5–80	0–15	5.3	− 80.75
A P Jarvis	7–132	0–40	7–75	0–17	5.3	− 84.25
H J Collingridge	7–138	0–12	1–33	6–93	5.1	− 84.50
Miss L A Perratt	7–157	1–51	0–43	6–63	4.5	−115.00
M Williams	6–48	2–27	0–0	4–21	12.5	+ 11.25
A P Stringer	6–53	0–0	2–22	4–31	11.3	− 18.12
Mrs V Aconley	6–53	0–9	1–7	5–37	11.3	− 15.00
D J S Cosgrove	6–56	2–22	3–24	1–10	10.7	− 7.44
R Allan	6–57	0–0	0–11	6–46	10.5	− 1.12
J Balding	6–77	0–9	4–44	2–24	7.8	− 43.42
J M P Eustace	6–78	2–23	2–23	2–32	7.7	− 29.50
G M Moore	6–81	0–17	3–21	3–43	7.4	− 32.93
J M Bradley	6–83	0–7	0–2	6–74	7.2	− 33.25
Mrs A Knight	6–83	0–3	0–5	6–75	7.2	+ 0.33
A Hide	6–89	1–18	2–46	3–25	6.7	− 24.50
B Beasley	6–101	0–13	3–49	3–39	5.9	− 46.00
B R Millman	6–120	4–28	1–28	1–64	5.0	− 69.00
M Blanshard	6–122	0–28	1–39	5–55	4.9	− 69.00
H Candy	6–127	1–24	1–52	4–51	4.7	− 67.17
J M Carr	5–47	2–16	2–16	1–15	10.6	− 20.00
R F Fisher	5–49	1–14	2–16	2–19	10.2	− 12.50
R Ingram	5–49	0–6	2–22	3–21	10.2	− 0.50
M Dixon	5–49	0–6	0–15	5–28	10.2	− 2.00
J Parkes	5–57	0–0	0–21	5–36	8.8	− 17.67
Martyn Wane	5–66	0–0	0–0	5–66	7.6	+ 6.33
S E Kettlewell	5–68	0–0	0–11	5–57	7.4	− 27.25
R Simpson	5–82	0–12	4–33	1–37	6.1	− 35.00

	Total W-R	2-y-o	3-y-o	4-y-o+	Per cent	£1 Level Stake
J L Eyre	5-83	0-13	0-6	5-64	6.0	- 34.50
C A Horgan	5-87	0-9	3-30	2-48	5.7	- 45.87
M Dods	5-118	1-26	0-18	4-74	4.2	- 55.00
N Bycroft	5-133	0-52	4-47	1-34	3.8	- 90.17
D Shaw	4-43	0-0	0-13	4-30	9.3	- 15.00
W G R Wightman	4-51	0-0	2-28	2-23	7.8	- 24.00
S Mellor	4-55	0-0	0-19	4-36	7.3	- 7.37
J Mackie	4-55	0-9	0-11	4-35	7.3	- 13.00
P Monteith	4-61	0-5	4-26	0-30	6.6	- 33.09
M J Haynes	4-66	1-24	0-6	3-36	6.1	- 20.50
C James	4-66	0-26	2-14	2-26	6.1	+ 14.00
R Dickin	4-66	0-10	1-19	3-37	6.1	- 14.00
D T Thom	4-68	1-20	0-10	3-38	5.9	- 39.17
K W Hogg	4-69	2-26	0-28	2-15	5.8	- 41.62
G C Bravery	4-73	3-34	0-28	1-11	5.5	- 20.00
C N Allen	4-77	1-27	2-24	1-26	5.2	- 38.50
J Sutcliffe	4-82	1-24	0-15	3-43	4.9	- 49.50
C W C Elsey	4-92	0-18	0-39	4-35	4.3	- 22.00
Capt J Wilson	4-94	2-17	0-23	2-54	4.3	- 38.00
M P Naughton	4-117	0-0	0-0	4-117	3.4	- 71.00
B S Rothwell	4-123	3-62	1-54	0-7	3.3	- 59.00
J R Jenkins	4-140	0-29	1-39	3-72	2.9	-105.50
K O Cunningham-Brown	4-156	0-15	1-66	3-75	2.6	- 72.50
A Fabre (Fra)	3-15	0-0	3-10	0-5	20.0	- 3.17
P Leach	3-17	0-0	0-3	3-14	17.6	- 4.25
P J Bevan	3-21	0-2	1-3	2-16	14.3	+ 3.00
R M Flower	3-21	0-0	0-5	3-16	14.3	0.00
T M Jones	3-26	2-12	1-14	0-0	11.5	+ 26.00
A W Jones	3-32	0-0	0-0	3-32	9.4	- 6.50
J R Bosley	3-34	0-7	0-3	3-24	8.8	+ 1.00
A Smith	3-35	2-7	1-10	0-18	8.6	+ 39.50
C N Williams	3-40	2-6	0-17	1-17	7.5	- 26.75
C Weedon	3-41	0-0	1-24	2-17	7.3	- 23.50
D J G Murray Smith	3-42	1-22	2-19	0-1	7.1	+ 41.00
J A R Toller	3-44	1-4	1-18	1-22	6.8	- 20.56
A P Jones	3-46	0-0	1-30	2-16	6.5	- 7.00
B Richmond	3-48	0-0	0-10	3-38	6.3	+ 12.00
B Smart	3-49	1-17	2-22	0-10	6.1	- 1.00
P Butler	3-60	1-24	0-3	2-33	5.0	- 17.50
J Akehurst	3-73	2-18	0-10	1-45	4.1	- 58.12
D Moffatt	3-81	0-25	2-22	1-34	3.7	- 57.50
J A Bennett	3-83	0-4	0-20	3-59	3.6	- 49.25
J S Wainwright	3-89	1-43	0-8	2-38	3.4	- 61.50
C Tinkler	3-120	0-17	3-54	0-49	2.5	-106.04
Mrs C Head (Fra)	2-2	0-0	1-1	1-1	100.0	+ 5.83
E Lellouche (Fra)	2-2	0-0	2-2	0-0	100.0	+ 17.33
T Dyer	2-11	0-0	0-0	2-11	18.2	- 1.75
B J Curley	2-19	0-3	0-4	2-12	10.5	- 6.75
O O'Neill	2-24	0-0	0-6	2-18	8.3	+ 94.00
C D Broad	2-24	0-1	1-5	1-18	8.3	- 2.00
J S Bolger (Ire)	2-25	0-3	1-18	1-4	8.0	- 8.50
J O'Donoghue	2-28	1-9	0-5	1-14	7.1	- 6.00
J Hanson	2-29	2-14	0-15	0-0	6.9	- 5.75
R J Price	2-29	0-0	0-9	2-20	6.9	- 14.80
G R Oldroyd	2-31	0-2	1-12	1-17	6.5	- 18.50
Miss J S Doyle	2-31	1-10	1-10	0-11	6.5	- 19.50

	Total W-R	2-y-o	3-y-o	4-y-o+	Per cent	£1 Level Stake
W M Brisbourne	2-32	0-3	0-5	2-24	6.3	- 9.00
C Smith	2-33	1-12	1-13	0-8	6.1	- 25.50
J J O'Neill	2-34	2-17	0-12	0-5	5.9	- 18.50
C V Lines	2-34	0-0	1-10	1-24	5.9	- 18.50
C P Wildman	2-36	0-0	0-4	2-32	5.6	- 17.00
J S King	2-36	0-3	0-3	2-30	5.6	- 26.00
P R Hedger	2-37	0-5	0-7	2-25	5.4	- 27.75
I Campbell	2-38	0-8	0-4	2-26	5.3	- 34.12
T Craig	2-41	0-4	0-0	2-37	4.9	- 27.75
B R Cambidge	2-42	0-0	0-4	2-38	4.8	- 28.50
Mrs Barbara Waring	2-44	0-3	0-5	2-36	4.5	- 25.00
R Lee	2-49	0-8	0-0	2-41	4.1	- 20.00
J F Bottomley	2-50	1-12	1-19	0-19	4.0	- 31.00
D Marks	2-52	0-4	0-14	2-34	3.8	- 30.50
C B B Booth	2-58	0-8	1-46	1-4	3.4	- 41.00
J J Bridger	2-65	0-18	2-14	0-33	3.1	- 24.00
G H Eden	2-66	0-14	0-19	2-33	3.0	- 60.42
R J Baker	2-67	0-0	0-5	2-62	3.0	- 56.00
J Hetherton	2-78	0-23	1-44	1-11	2.6	- 29.00
J S Moore	2-78	1-49	0-6	1-23	2.6	- 57.75
K T Ivory	2-91	0-20	2-35	0-36	2.2	- 68.50
C W Thornton	2-97	0-24	1-52	1-21	2.1	- 69.00
T Stack (Ire)	1-1	0-0	1-1	0-0	100.0	+ 11.00
W Carter	1-2	0-0	1-2	0-0	50.0	+ 0.75
Seemar Satish (UAE)	1-2	0-0	1-2	0-0	50.0	0.00
N J Henderson	1-3	0-0	0-0	1-3	33.3	+ 6.00
M V O'Brien (Ire)	1-5	0-0	1-5	0-0	20.0	- 0.50
F Boutin (Fra)	1-5	0-1	1-3	0-1	20.0	- 3.60
S Sherwood	1-5	0-0	0-0	1-5	20.0	+ 46.00
A G Foster	1-5	1-3	0-0	0-2	20.0	+ 46.00
A Barrow	1-7	0-0	0-0	1-7	14.3	+ 27.00
C Parker	1-8	0-0	0-0	1-8	12.5	- 2.50
Mrs S Bramall	1-8	0-0	1-5	0-3	12.5	+ 18.00
P Cheesbrough	1-8	0-0	1-5	0-3	12.5	+ 18.00
D N Chappell	1-8	1-5	0-0	0-3	12.5	+ 26.00
R A Fahey	1-9	0-5	1-4	0-0	11.1	+ 4.00
N A Twiston-Davies	1-11	0-4	0-0	1-7	9.1	- 7.25
C R Egerton	1-12	1-11	0-1	0-0	8.3	- 8.50
P Wigham	1-13	0-0	0-0	1-13	7.7	- 8.50
A Smith (Bel)	1-13	1-7	0-6	0-0	7.7	+ 8.00
C R Barwell	1-14	0-7	0-2	1-5	7.1	+ 20.00
W Clay	1-15	0-3	0-2	1-10	6.7	- 6.00
T W Donnelly	1-15	0-0	1-9	0-6	6.7	0.00
F Jordan	1-16	0-0	0-0	1-16	6.3	- 7.00
R Thompson	1-16	0-0	0-0	1-16	6.3	- 3.00
C P E Brooks	1-17	0-0	0-2	1-15	5.9	- 6.00
N A Smith	1-17	0-0	0-2	1-15	5.9	- 11.50
D R Tucker	1-18	0-1	0-10	1-7	5.6	- 8.50
J P Smith	1-20	0-0	0-0	1-20	5.0	+ 1.00
J M Troy	1-21	1-16	0-5	0-0	4.8	- 15.00
P J McBride	1-21	0-5	1-10	0-6	4.8	- 15.00
Mark Campion	1-22	0-19	0-0	1-3	4.5	- 1.00
W Bentley	1-23	0-6	1-14	0-3	4.3	- 19.00
R A Bennett	1-25	0-0	0-0	1-25	4.0	- 17.00
M S Saunders	1-26	0-4	0-0	1-22	3.8	- 18.50
F O'Mahony	1-27	0-0	0-2	1-25	3.7	- 17.00

	Total W-R	2-y-o	3-y-o	4-y-o+	Per cent	£1 Level Stake
T P McGovern	1-28	0-0	0-11	1-17	3.6	- 19.00
B Gubby	1-29	1-5	0-6	0-18	3.4	- 25.25
T Kersey	1-29	0-2	0-0	1-27	3.4	- 22.50
R Harris	1-29	0-4	0-13	1-12	3.4	- 14.00
N Chamberlain	1-30	0-1	1-27	0-2	3.3	- 13.00
Ronald Thompson	1-30	0-7	1-22	0-1	3.3	- 20.00
Mrs P A Barker	1-30	0-1	0-7	1-22	3.3	- 22.50
M F Barraclough	1-30	0-2	0-0	1-28	3.3	- 17.00
Mrs A L M King	1-31	0-2	0-0	1-29	3.2	- 5.00
Mrs J C Dawe	1-31	0-3	0-4	1-24	3.2	+ 3.00
R Rowe	1-36	0-0	0-11	1-25	2.8	- 19.00
R T Phillips	1-36	1-14	0-6	0-16	2.8	- 29.60
P Burgoyne	1-38	0-5	0-13	1-20	2.6	- 32.00
J P Leigh	1-41	1-9	0-15	0-17	2.4	- 28.00
R Brotherton	1-41	0-12	0-10	1-19	2.4	- 7.00
B J McMath	1-42	0-7	1-14	0-21	2.4	- 37.00
B W Murray	1-44	0-14	0-15	1-15	2.3	- 34.00
A Harrison	1-47	0-15	0-8	1-24	2.1	- 38.00
W L Barker	1-47	0-9	0-11	1-27	2.1	- 34.00
T Casey	1-48	0-0	1-19	0-29	2.1	- 41.50
B Ellison	1-53	1-6	0-11	0-36	1.9	- 44.50
A A Hambly	1-55	0-18	1-19	0-18	1.8	- 42.00
P M McEntee	1-56	0-11	1-18	0-27	1.8	- 53.00
C A Smith	1-57	0-10	1-32	0-15	1.8	- 48.00
M P Muggeridge	1-71	0-36	1-18	0-17	1.4	- 56.00

WINNING FLAT JOCKEYS 1993

	1st	2nd	3rd	Unpl	Total Mts	Per cent	£1 Level Stake
Pat Eddery	169	131	83	430	813	20.8	- 59.57
K Darley	136	128	105	432	801	17.0	-139.16
L Dettori	136	115	116	488	855	15.9	- 59.38
T Quinn	121	114	99	533	867	14.0	-112.67
G Duffield	116	90	101	450	757	15.3	-139.95
W Carson	115	93	120	508	836	13.8	-216.68
M Roberts	114	96	109	395	714	16.0	-122.83
J Reid	108	108	70	478	764	14.1	-146.12
W Ryan	96	86	83	398	663	14.5	- 93.17
J Carroll	94	76	75	392	637	14.8	-111.85
W R Swinburn	93	77	77	319	566	16.4	+ 6.13
R Cochrane	83	103	82	454	722	11.5	-259.15
M Hills	82	91	75	367	615	13.3	-180.13
A Munro	73	80	70	448	671	10.9	-173.46
D McKeown	67	64	52	277	460	14.6	-112.38
D Holland	66	54	57	337	514	12.8	- 72.97
Paul Eddery	66	50	61	419	596	11.1	-185.59
J Quinn	63	85	67	556	771	8.2	-373.19
K Fallon	60	66	59	342	527	11.4	-104.41
J Williams	60	50	62	448	620	9.7	- 70.09
R Hills	57	59	53	271	440	13.0	- 77.33
P Robinson	52	46	61	302	461	11.3	-125.53
B Raymond	47	43	53	310	453	10.4	-139.46
G Carter	44	39	37	211	331	13.3	- 74.66
W Newnes	40	32	45	415	532	7.5	-171.70

	1st	2nd	3rd	Unpl	Total Mts	Per cent	£1 Level Stake
L Piggott	39	27	34	198	298	13.1	- 35.90
D Biggs	34	30	34	327	425	8.0	-189.12
G Hind	33	26	25	161	245	13.5	+ 9.64
B Rouse	33	27	31	305	396	8.3	- 76.11
A Mackay	32	32	29	344	437	7.3	-129.10
N Connorton	30	22	28	214	294	10.2	-109.49
M Birch	30	49	57	299	435	6.9	-223.38
J Lowe	28	48	33	416	525	5.3	-268.84
T Williams	27	38	30	264	359	7.5	-148.48
A McGlone	27	31	33	308	399	6.8	-177.33
J Fortune	25	27	27	237	316	7.9	- 15.51
G Bardwell	24	27	24	373	448	5.4	-212.92
W Woods	23	26	32	222	303	7.6	-119.75
L Charnock	23	24	26	329	402	5.7	-135.12
N Carlisle	22	17	21	275	335	6.6	- 20.50
S Wood	21	20	13	188	242	8.7	- 75.96
J Fanning	21	40	53	363	477	4.4	-270.95
S Whitworth	20	24	28	243	315	6.3	-156.25
N Adams	20	28	30	466	544	3.7	-308.24
S Perks	19	24	23	195	261	7.3	-148.63
T Sprake	17	10	22	138	187	9.1	- 10.23
M Tebbutt	17	30	17	158	222	7.7	- 80.25
A Culhane	17	20	19	191	247	6.9	- 80.17
A Clark	17	18	31	218	284	6.0	- 82.10
R Price	16	14	15	161	206	7.8	- 49.50
N Day	15	21	16	124	176	8.5	- 64.97
S Webster	14	15	27	168	224	6.3	-126.09
C Rutter	13	23	26	235	297	4.4	-131.87
S Raymont	11	13	4	81	109	10.1	- 33.22
Alex Greaves	10	11	18	99	138	7.2	- 62.63
M Wigham	10	21	19	206	256	3.9	-181.62
Dale Gibson	10	26	36	308	380	2.6	-301.17
T Lucas	9	13	10	99	131	6.9	- 64.20
S O'Gorman	8	3	6	88	105	7.6	- 53.25
R Perham	8	11	9	144	172	4.7	-107.62
J McLaughlin	7	6	3	20	36	19.4	+ 11.75
A Tucker	7	8	18	173	206	3.4	-126.17
M Perrett	6	5	8	77	96	6.3	- 65.65
P D'Arcy	5	7	0	19	31	16.1	+ 7.00
D Nicholls	5	8	8	87	108	4.6	- 70.25
Kim McDonnell	5	5	13	100	123	4.1	- 71.00
S D Williams	5	7	9	142	163	3.1	-132.34
Julie Bowker	4	1	1	10	16	25.0	+ 26.75
M J Kinane	4	1	2	25	32	12.5	+ 14.00
C Asmussen	4	5	5	29	43	9.3	- 20.10
W Hood	4	2	2	38	46	8.7	- 26.42
E Johnson	4	4	3	66	77	5.2	- 21.00
Kim Tinkler	4	7	7	96	114	3.5	- 88.00
R Street	3	0	0	20	23	13.0	+ 2.00
J Curant	2	0	1	6	9	22.2	- 2.75
B Crossley	2	1	0	24	27	7.4	- 12.00
B Marcus	2	1	0	28	31	6.5	- 11.50
S Morris	2	4	3	41	50	4.0	- 33.50
E Hide	1	0	0	0	1	100.0	+ 7.00
D Boeuf	1	0	0	0	1	100.0	+ 14.00
Bill Smith	1	0	0	0	1	100.0	+ 3.33

	1st	2nd	3rd	Unpl	Total Mts	Per cent	£1 Level Stake
G Mosse	1	0	0	0	1	100.0	+ 3.33
Peter Smith	1	0	0	1	2	50.0	+ 19.00
A Geran	1	0	0	6	7	14.3	- 1.00
T Lang	1	0	0	9	10	10.0	+ 24.00
J Comber	1	2	1	10	14	7.1	- 6.50
Lorna Vincent	1	4	3	7	15	6.7	- 8.00
C Roche	1	3	2	13	19	5.3	- 13.50
J Penza	1	1	3	14	19	5.3	- 11.00
C Nutter	1	3	3	16	23	4.3	- 20.75
J O'Reilly	1	0	0	25	26	3.8	- 13.00
C Dwyer	1	3	2	34	40	2.5	- 37.00
R P Elliott	1	5	12	44	62	1.6	- 57.00
C Avery	1	2	1	60	64	1.6	- 38.00
R Lappin	1	5	4	61	71	1.4	- 60.00
S Dawson	1	10	8	117	136	0.7	-121.00

WINNING APPRENTICES 1993

	1st	2nd	3rd	Unpl	Total Mts	Per cent	£1 Level Stake
J Weaver	60	36	35	234	365	16.4	+118.09
D Harrison	39	48	42	372	501	7.8	-208.61
B Doyle	33	26	29	250	338	9.8	+ 12.43
O Pears	32	30	35	197	294	10.9	- 81.42
S Maloney	27	22	29	208	286	9.4	- 61.92
D McCabe	25	19	36	174	254	9.8	+ 2.75
F Norton	24	18	27	252	321	7.5	-120.13
D Wright	23	28	29	349	429	5.4	-269.87
S Davies	21	20	33	176	250	8.4	- 92.96
D Moffatt	21	11	27	197	256	8.2	- 99.95
Emma O'Gorman	19	31	17	65	132	14.4	- 19.91
J Tate	18	15	18	117	168	10.7	- 96.87
K Rutter	16	14	7	88	125	12.8	+ 23.17
P McCabe	15	16	10	95	136	11.0	- 27.75
C Hodgson	15	15	9	101	140	10.7	- 23.95
M Fenton	14	17	16	132	179	7.8	- 57.05
R Painter	12	13	4	44	73	16.4	+ 16.13
Mark Denaro	11	17	8	90	126	8.7	- 20.50
B Russell	11	13	4	110	138	8.0	- 58.25
J Marshall	10	7	10	72	99	10.1	- 4.00
V Halliday	9	8	4	62	83	10.8	0.00
S Drowne	9	8	11	156	184	4.9	- 51.00
Claire Balding	8	5	12	100	125	6.4	- 70.92
S Mulvey	8	12	13	102	135	5.9	- 73.37
A Garth	8	15	19	152	194	4.1	-107.50
M Humphries	7	10	11	63	91	7.7	- 44.00
S Copp	6	5	1	18	30	20.0	+ 7.25
J D Smith	6	6	5	29	46	13.0	- 8.37
L Newton	6	6	5	37	54	11.1	+ 2.23
P Roberts	6	10	6	33	55	10.9	- 30.09
D Gibbs	6	3	5	42	56	10.7	- 20.87
T G McLaughlin	6	7	8	60	81	7.4	- 12.75
N Varley	6	10	5	84	105	5.7	- 45.50
S Knott	5	2	3	21	31	16.1	+ 7.33
H Bastiman	5	4	10	49	68	7.4	- 33.00

	1st	2nd	3rd	Unpl	Total Mts	Per cent	£1 Level Stake
C Hawksley	5	3	9	87	104	4.8	− 72.25
G Strange	4	8	8	29	49	8.2	− 14.00
A Procter	4	2	3	49	58	6.9	− 21.50
S Sanders	4	6	6	45	61	6.6	+ 3.00
D Carson	3	0	2	3	8	37.5	+ 7.75
Gaye Harwood	3	0	1	9	13	23.1	+ 39.25
E Husband	3	0	3	8	14	21.4	+ 22.50
D Meredith	3	1	2	10	16	18.8	+ 19.00
Sally Radford-Howes	3	1	0	14	18	16.7	+ 2.00
D Griffiths	3	5	0	18	26	11.5	− 0.50
Wendy Jones	3	0	4	19	26	11.5	+ 7.00
R Havlin	3	1	3	22	29	10.3	− 8.25
D Thomas	3	1	5	22	31	9.7	− 1.00
L Aspell	3	1	5	28	37	8.1	− 16.00
L Carter	3	3	3	32	41	7.3	− 24.12
G Forster	3	6	10	36	55	5.5	− 40.00
C Teague	3	3	6	44	56	5.4	− 22.00
N Kennedy	3	10	13	125	151	2.0	−119.50
G McGrath	2	0	1	3	6	33.3	+ 2.25
P Houghton	2	1	0	4	7	28.6	+ 1.20
Marie Plowright	2	0	0	9	11	18.2	+ 31.00
S Eiffert	2	1	1	16	20	10.0	− 11.00
D Toole	2	2	0	16	20	10.0	+ 40.00
D O'Neill	2	4	2	15	23	8.7	− 16.62
M Denaro	2	3	3	16	24	8.3	− 7.00
S Wynne	2	2	4	17	25	8.0	− 16.50
Sarah Thompson	2	2	6	19	29	6.9	− 17.00
A Whelan	2	5	3	20	30	6.7	+ 6.25
C N Adamson	2	1	2	27	32	6.3	+ 7.50
S McCarthy	2	3	2	27	34	5.9	+ 3.00
J Dennis	2	2	1	31	36	5.6	− 18.67
M Baird	2	2	1	44	49	4.1	− 37.12
Antoinette Armes	2	6	1	55	64	3.1	− 6.00
N Gwilliams	2	4	5	54	65	3.1	− 49.25
M Harris	1	0	0	1	2	50.0	+ 6.00
P Rose	1	0	0	1	2	50.0	+ 3.50
S James	1	0	1	1	3	33.3	+ 8.00
J Gotobed	1	0	0	2	3	33.3	− 1.43
S Drake	1	0	0	3	4	25.0	+ 5.00
C Scudder	1	0	0	4	5	20.0	+ 10.00
J Edmunds	1	0	0	6	7	14.3	− 2.00
Nicola Howarth	1	0	1	6	8	12.5	+ 5.00
Elizabeth Turner	1	0	1	6	8	12.5	+ 3.00
Martin Dwyer	1	0	0	7	8	12.5	− 3.67
Gina Faulkner	1	1	0	7	9	11.1	+ 4.00
J Wilkinson	1	1	0	8	10	10.0	− 6.25
Ruth Coulter	1	2	1	11	15	6.7	− 10.00
Michael Bradley	1	0	1	13	15	6.7	0.00
P Johnson	1	2	2	11	16	6.3	− 8.50
Iona Wands	1	5	1	12	19	5.3	− 6.00
J O'Dwyer	1	2	2	16	21	4.8	− 14.00
Sharon Millard	1	0	0	22	23	4.3	− 18.50
A Martinez	1	4	2	20	27	3.7	− 12.00

WINNING AMATEUR RIDERS 1993

	1st	2nd	3rd	Unpl	Total Mts	Per cent	£1 Level Stake
T Cuff	5	2	0	12	19	26.3	+ 38.50
Mrs L Pearce	5	4	4	25	38	13.2	- 7.70
Mrs M Cowdrey	4	3	6	12	25	16.0	- 8.24
Miss I D W Jones	4	7	6	17	34	11.8	- 10.12
M Buckley	3	2	2	5	12	25.0	+ 14.50
Mrs D Arbuthnot	3	0	0	11	14	21.4	+ 5.75
Mrs S Bosley	3	2	2	9	16	18.8	+ 19.00
L A Urbano	2	0	0	0	2	100.0	+ 12.50
Miss A Harwood	2	2	1	9	14	14.3	- 6.83
Mrs A Farrell	2	1	0	13	16	12.5	- 10.12
M Jenkins	1	0	0	0	1	100.0	+ 3.50
Mrs M Morris	1	0	0	0	1	100.0	+ 33.00
Renee Kierans	1	0	0	0	1	100.0	+ 5.50
N Moore	1	0	0	0	1	100.0	+ 8.00
Miss K Marks	1	0	0	2	3	33.3	+ 3.50
Miss L Perratt	1	0	0	3	4	25.0	+ 1.50
Mrs M Haggas	1	0	0	3	4	25.0	+ 7.00
G Lewis	1	0	0	3	4	25.0	0.00
Mrs D McHale	1	0	0	3	4	25.0	+ 3.00
Miss J Southcombe	1	1	1	2	5	20.0	+ 21.00
P P-Gordon	1	0	0	4	5	20.0	+ 2.00
Miss E Bronson	1	1	1	3	6	16.7	+ 1.50
S Swiers	1	2	1	2	6	16.7	- 4.33
Miss A Deniel	1	0	0	5	6	16.7	+ 4.00
Mrs D Kettlewell	1	0	0	5	6	16.7	- 2.25
Mrs J Naughton	1	1	1	3	6	16.7	+ 1.50
Miss A Elsey	1	3	0	2	6	16.7	- 1.67
Mrs J Musson	1	0	0	6	7	14.3	+ 4.00
R Teal	1	0	2	4	7	14.3	- 3.25
Miss L Eaton	1	0	0	6	7	14.3	+ 3.00
Mrs J Crossley	1	1	0	7	9	11.1	- 2.50
Miss L Hide	1	2	2	6	11	9.1	- 1.00
Miss A Purdy	1	1	0	11	13	7.7	+ 8.00

LEADING TRAINERS' AND OWNERS' PRIZE MONEY 1993

	Races Won	Value £		Races Won	Value £
H R A Cecil	94	1,248,388	Sheikh Mohammed	143	1,704,735
R Hannon	182	1,229,046	K Abdulla	66	1,218,578
M R Stoute	65	1,072,267	Hamdan Al-Maktoum	97	644,986
J H M Gosden	110	1,024,025	Maktoum Al Maktoum	38	638,486
J L Dunlop	93	700,801	R E Sangster	45	411,366
J Berry	132	553,814	Mrs G A E Smith	3	275,271
G Wragg	35	428,482	Daniel Wildenstein	2	273,980
P Chapple-Hyam	52	407,184	Roldvale Limited	20	262,896
C E Brittain	34	401,890	J C Smith	14	227,700
I A Balding	50	383,671	P D Savill	49	218,307
R Charlton	47	378,112	Fahd Salman	37	213,075
M S Johnston	73	351,678	Lord Howard De Walden	15	198,627

LEADING TRAINERS FIRST TIME OUT 1989-93*

	Total W-R	2-y-o	3-y-o	4-y-o+	Per cent	£1 Level Stake
H R A Cecil	168-596	59-203	97-344	12-49	28.2	+ 63.94
M R Stoute	123-678	51-287	59-339	13-52	18.1	-129.64
J H M Gosden	104-542	35-167	51-314	18-61	19.2	+ 32.78
J Berry	96-596	58-379	29-154	9-63	16.1	- 18.90
B W Hills	85-620	31-263	43-302	11-55	13.7	-129.60
P F I Cole	77-542	47-247	22-212	8-83	14.2	-151.15
L M Cumani	71-453	21-142	38-263	12-48	15.7	-121.50
R Hannon	71-827	35-439	30-294	6-94	8.6	-293.13
G Harwood	65-416	17-133	38-211	10-72	15.6	-136.88
J L Dunlop	49-570	22-248	19-241	8-81	8.6	-248.40
H Thomson Jones	47-250	28-99	18-124	1-27	18.8	- 43.11
Lord Huntingdon	44-316	9-100	25-135	10-81	13.9	+ 10.79
R Charlton	42-201	20-84	17-96	5-21	20.9	+ 73.82
Sir Mark Prescott	41-279	13-131	23-114	5-34	14.7	- 87.33
C E Brittain	40-558	10-212	16-224	14-122	7.2	-188.21
I A Balding	37-392	14-159	16-163	7-70	9.4	-118.51
G Wragg	35-240	13-80	17-126	5-34	14.6	- 31.46
W R Hern	34-241	15-86	15-131	4-24	14.1	- 86.85
D R C Elsworth	33-349	11-120	9-125	13-104	9.5	- 13.62
P Chapple-Hyam	31-167	18-96	11-62	2-9	18.6	- 10.73
A C Stewart	31-270	8-69	19-174	4-27	11.5	- 78.04
W A O'Gorman	30-156	10-75	12-54	8-27	19.2	+ 7.23
M S Johnston	28-220	8-91	13-79	7-50	12.7	+ 13.89
A A Scott	28-273	16-135	10-118	2-20	10.3	- 95.52
M H Easterby	28-406	14-175	7-120	7-111	6.9	-187.90
P T Walwyn	27-283	7-114	16-138	4-31	9.5	- 63.47
J W Watts	26-191	8-65	11-94	7-32	13.6	+ 11.77
B Hanbury	26-316	6-124	16-156	4-36	8.2	-134.15
M Bell	25-264	8-136	17-95	0-33	9.5	-127.68
M H Tompkins	24-367	4-147	10-113	10-107	6.5	-160.45
R Akehurst	23-263	0-44	5-67	18-152	8.7	- 64.44
Mrs J Ramsden	22-205	5-68	9-70	8-67	10.7	- 46.59
Mrs M Reveley	20-250	2-62	4-62	14-126	8.0	-132.75
R Hollinshead	20-422	2-151	9-142	9-129	4.7	-157.11
R W Armstrong	19-184	10-63	6-89	3-32	10.3	- 38.79
S G Norton	18-196	6-80	7-78	5-38	9.2	- 62.87
H Candy	18-222	5-67	9-100	4-55	8.1	+ 27.55
C R Nelson	17-114	3-32	10-59	4-23	14.9	+ 12.61
T D Barron	17-214	3-69	8-70	6-75	7.9	-106.59
W Jarvis	17-270	9-112	7-118	1-40	6.3	-125.85
R M Whitaker	17-274	6-85	5-94	6-95	6.2	- 73.50
W J Haggas	16-171	2-65	10-73	4-33	9.4	- 79.26
J R Fanshawe	16-182	3-65	11-98	2-19	8.8	- 17.40
M A Jarvis	16-243	5-97	9-110	2-36	6.6	-105.70
Mrs L Piggott	15-157	2-52	10-76	3-29	9.6	- 59.81
P J Makin	15-191	2-51	8-84	5-56	7.9	- 42.50
J Etherington	14-156	8-75	4-59	2-22	9.0	- 15.75
B A McMahon	14-230	2-60	2-60	10-110	6.1	+ 58.00
N A Callaghan	13-182	3-83	7-69	3-30	7.1	- 76.77
J W Hills	13-199	4-72	5-80	4-47	6.5	- 38.25
R J Hodges	13-212	2-28	1-46	10-138	6.1	- 62.87
Mrs J Cecil	12-127	5-58	6-51	1-18	9.4	- 62.07
D W P Arbuthnot	12-129	3-35	2-51	7-43	9.3	- 35.00
M McCormack	12-134	3-52	5-50	4-32	9.0	+ 4.37

	Total W-R	2-y-o	3-y-o	4-y-o+	Per cent	£1 Level Stake
M J Ryan	12-155	2-37	4-57	6-61	7.7	- 12.75
C Tinkler	12-171	6-80	2-46	4-45	7.0	- 88.12
R J R Williams	11-158	3-48	4-74	4-36	7.0	- 50.75
P A Kelleway	11-159	4-77	5-57	2-25	6.9	- 74.13
J Wharton	11-165	4-50	3-52	4-63	6.7	+ 28.50
T Thomson Jones	10-106	2-35	4-37	4-34	9.4	+ 5.50
M J Camacho	10-116	2-39	5-41	3-36	8.6	+ 4.25
M R Channon	10-172	6-77	3-55	1-40	5.8	- 65.67
D Morley	10-175	7-67	3-79	0-29	5.7	-105.50
F H Lee	10-179	2-48	3-67	5-64	5.6	- 49.50
J G FitzGerald	10-200	0-58	4-71	6-71	5.0	-114.18
G Lewis	10-244	4-116	4-84	2-44	4.1	-136.37
M Brittain	10-274	2-106	3-86	5-82	3.6	-154.00
D J G Murray Smith	9-83	2-28	5-32	2-23	10.8	- 14.27
M C Pipe	9-90	1-6	2-15	6-69	10.0	- 34.40
C W C Elsey	9-104	0-27	6-40	3-37	8.7	+ 4.75
R Guest	9-125	3-47	3-51	3-27	7.2	- 56.45
G B Balding	9-155	2-42	2-51	5-62	5.8	- 51.37
R Boss	9-155	6-71	3-60	0-24	5.8	-102.82
G A Pritchard-Gordon	9-222	5-92	4-88	0-42	4.1	-155.50
D R Loder	8-39	4-20	1-10	3-9	20.5	+ 17.13
D Burchell	8-87	0-6	1-14	7-67	9.2	+ 23.00
J Pearce	8-110	0-23	2-35	6-52	7.3	- 11.62
G M Moore	8-130	0-18	4-26	4-86	6.2	- 33.00
C A Cyzer	8-153	2-45	3-75	3-33	5.2	- 42.50
R F Johnson Houghton	8-164	2-62	4-74	2-28	4.9	- 94.37
D W Chapman	8-202	0-26	1-51	7-125	4.0	-101.70
D Morris	7-57	2-14	1-11	4-32	12.3	- 0.75
Miss B Sanders	7-88	0-15	2-24	5-49	8.0	- 29.00
Dr J D Scargill	7-153	1-62	4-53	2-38	4.6	- 86.00
Denys Smith	7-158	3-58	1-47	3-53	4.4	- 64.50
C F Wall	7-166	4-70	3-67	0-29	4.2	- 75.00
S Dow	7-169	5-55	0-55	2-59	4.1	- 77.50
N Tinkler	7-207	3-61	0-47	4-99	3.4	-142.00
D Moffatt	6-71	2-16	0-13	4-42	8.5	+ 1.50
J A R Toller	6-73	2-15	3-39	1-19	8.2	+ 16.75
Pat Mitchell	6-98	2-32	2-28	2-38	6.1	+ 31.00
J D Bethell	6-101	1-29	1-36	4-36	5.9	- 39.00
P C Haslam	6-102	2-39	3-34	1-29	5.9	- 33.92
L J Holt	6-120	1-42	5-46	0-32	5.0	- 45.00
A Bailey	6-122	3-38	2-43	1-41	4.9	- 86.12
C N Allen	6-127	1-47	4-42	1-38	4.7	- 61.83
Mrs N Macauley	6-148	2-40	4-48	0-60	4.1	-104.37
C J Hill	6-152	0-23	3-50	3-79	3.9	-120.37
M W Easterby	6-212	2-120	2-51	2-41	2.8	-141.50

*Six or more winners to qualify

LEADING TRAINERS SECOND TIME OUT 1989-93*

	Total W-R	2-y-o	3-y-o	4-y-o+	Per cent	£1 Level Stake
H R A Cecil	157-448	43-97	107-309	7-42	35.0	- 1.76
L M Cumani	115-382	32-97	77-241	6-44	30.1	- 49.10
M R Stoute	112-526	37-165	64-310	11-51	21.3	-190.48
J H M Gosden	108-423	28-98	68-270	12-55	25.5	- 60.76
R Hannon	96-771	63-407	28-279	5-85	12.5	-322.61
J L Dunlop	90-496	37-203	40-224	13-69	18.1	- 77.10
J Berry	88-568	59-358	22-152	7-58	15.5	-109.94
G Harwood	82-333	24-79	51-192	7-62	24.6	+ 15.78
B W Hills	81-513	35-178	43-281	3-54	15.8	-166.45
P F I Cole	68-450	37-191	25-189	6-70	15.1	-144.44
C E Brittain	48-477	16-156	20-208	12-113	10.1	-177.12
G Wragg	43-209	17-58	18-121	8-30	20.6	- 33.86
Lord Huntingdon	43-264	7-63	16-127	20-74	16.3	- 12.63
I A Balding	43-334	23-117	16-151	4-66	12.9	- 82.20
R Charlton	41-164	16-52	21-92	4-20	25.0	- 7.39
P T Walwyn	40-256	16-90	16-136	8-30	15.6	+ 31.31
Sir Mark Prescott	39-245	13-103	21-110	5-32	15.9	- 79.99
D R C Elsworth	39-296	18-91	10-118	11-87	13.2	- 32.76
M H Tompkins	37-326	16-131	11-102	10-93	11.3	- 85.51
A C Stewart	36-207	4-35	26-148	6-24	17.4	- 49.10
M Bell	35-232	27-117	8-87	0-28	15.1	- 31.61
P Chapple-Hyam	34-137	23-70	11-59	0-8	24.8	- 15.82
H Thomson Jones	32-210	21-77	9-109	2-24	15.2	- 89.92
M H Easterby	31-370	18-159	7-112	6-99	8.4	-188.53
A A Scott	30-216	13-90	14-108	3-18	13.9	- 72.58
Mrs M Reveley	28-229	6-59	6-57	16-113	12.2	- 68.01
B Hanbury	27-268	15-98	9-135	3-35	10.1	-133.42
T D Barron	26-197	5-63	8-65	13-69	13.2	- 37.76
R Akehurst	26-240	4-41	6-61	16-138	10.8	- 3.11
R Hollinshead	26-386	9-135	7-137	10-114	6.7	-160.05
J W Hills	24-181	6-59	13-78	5-44	13.3	- 19.22
M S Johnston	23-203	8-84	10-73	5-46	11.3	- 57.19
B A McMahon	23-204	2-51	4-58	17-95	11.3	- 17.13
W Jarvis	23-216	11-72	8-106	4-38	10.6	-114.29
Mrs J Cecil	22-99	11-38	8-45	3-16	22.2	+ 40.60
W J Haggas	22-137	11-49	10-61	1-27	16.1	+ 30.40
W A O'Gorman	21-125	9-58	6-42	6-25	16.8	- 54.68
R W Armstrong	21-146	14-47	5-74	2-25	14.4	+ 11.12
W R Hern	21-178	8-47	12-113	1-18	11.8	-108.04
J W Watts	20-172	6-53	10-87	4-32	11.6	- 22.13
M A Jarvis	20-217	6-77	11-107	3-33	9.2	-104.75
P J Makin	19-160	4-39	11-74	4-47	11.9	- 40.05
G Lewis	19-231	11-106	4-82	4-43	8.2	-123.77
S G Norton	18-175	6-71	7-75	5-29	10.3	- 66.52
Mrs J Ramsden	18-193	5-65	5-67	8-61	9.3	-102.82
J R Fanshawe	16-157	7-48	7-93	2-16	10.2	- 59.38
M R Channon	16-158	5-67	8-55	3-36	10.1	- 29.99
M J Camacho	15-105	1-33	6-39	8-33	14.3	- 13.61
R Boss	14-130	8-53	5-58	1-19	10.8	- 55.99
N A Callaghan	14-160	7-77	5-60	2-23	8.8	- 76.87
R M Whitaker	14-241	5-75	4-84	5-82	5.8	-150.75
M Brittain	14-243	5-90	6-79	3-74	5.8	- 95.42
R F Johnson Houghton	13-139	5-52	5-68	3-19	9.4	- 54.92
P A Kelleway	13-149	8-67	3-60	2-22	8.7	- 51.79

	Total W-R	2-y-o	3-y-o	4-y-o+	Per cent	£1 Level Stake
D Morley	13-155	6-54	4-74	3-27	8.4	- 53.17
H Candy	13-183	4-42	6-92	3-49	7.1	- 72.42
M C Pipe	12-72	0-4	2-13	10-55	16.7	- 10.87
J Wharton	12-138	5-43	4-46	3-49	8.7	- 24.00
R J R Williams	12-139	7-37	4-69	1-33	8.6	- 66.04
J G FitzGerald	12-163	3-52	4-59	5-52	7.4	- 69.17
Denys Smith	11-137	8-51	1-43	2-43	8.0	- 84.63
M J Ryan	11-142	2-33	4-54	5-55	7.7	- 36.96
F H Lee	11-168	6-46	1-65	4-57	6.5	-109.45
G A Pritchard-Gordon	11-194	6-80	4-82	1-32	5.7	- 58.70
Lady Herries	10-73	1-17	2-20	7-36	13.7	- 4.75
C R Nelson	10-103	6-30	1-53	3-20	9.7	- 17.93
Dr J D Scargill	10-133	5-52	4-47	1-34	7.5	- 90.32
W Carter	10-144	5-51	3-52	2-41	6.9	- 23.25
J Etherington	10-150	6-72	3-57	1-21	6.7	- 83.75
P Calver	9-78	1-22	3-31	5-25	11.5	+ 17.10
M O'Neill	9-83	2-17	4-29	3-37	10.8	+ 38.00
R Guest	9-102	3-39	3-43	3-20	8.8	- 51.25
C J Hill	9-126	0-18	3-42	6-66	7.1	- 44.26
M McCormack	9-126	3-48	4-48	2-30	7.1	- 79.98
Mrs N Macauley	9-128	2-35	3-45	4-48	7.0	- 62.25
C Tinkler	9-156	5-73	3-45	1-38	5.8	-118.30
M W Easterby	9-186	6-106	0-44	3-36	4.8	-136.20
D W Chapman	9-187	3-24	1-50	5-113	4.8	-107.71
D R Loder	8-34	5-16	2-10	1-8	23.5	- 10.47
J A R Toller	8-63	2-10	3-35	3-18	12.7	- 18.08
T Thomson Jones	8-86	2-23	1-34	5-29	9.3	- 45.88
C W C Elsey	8-89	2-21	4-37	2-31	9.0	- 27.17
G M Moore	8-115	2-17	1-24	5-74	7.0	- 36.42
Mrs L Piggott	8-131	3-38	3-69	2-24	6.1	- 89.20
C F Wall	8-135	4-49	4-61	0-25	5.9	- 96.98
R J Hodges	8-173	1-22	2-39	5-112	4.6	- 96.00
A Hide	7-91	3-25	2-38	2-28	7.7	- 23.67
M P Naughton	7-107	0-6	2-18	5-83	6.5	- 60.29
C N Allen	7-108	2-38	4-38	1-32	6.5	- 70.51
P W Harris	7-109	2-38	3-52	2-19	6.4	- 21.50
J L Spearing	7-114	1-23	2-24	4-67	6.1	- 79.79
D W P Arbuthnot	7-119	2-30	1-49	4-40	5.9	- 58.50
C A Cyzer	7-138	2-34	0-71	5-33	5.1	- 91.00
G B Balding	7-142	1-39	2-49	4-54	4.9	- 92.30
E J Alston	6-76	1-21	0-15	5-40	7.9	- 34.00
P S Felgate	6-83	0-26	2-26	4-31	7.2	- 25.12
M J Haynes	6-83	3-22	0-27	3-34	7.2	- 0.50
C J Benstead	6-85	1-17	0-36	5-32	7.1	- 45.25
J D Bethell	6-90	2-24	3-34	1-32	6.7	- 13.00
W J Musson	6-104	1-20	2-35	3-49	5.8	- 38.00

*Six or more winners to qualify

LEADING TRAINERS BY MONTH 1989-93

January

	Total W-R	2-y-o	3-y-o	4-y-o+	Per cent	£1 Level Stake
T D Barron	25-101	0-0	14-44	11-57	24.8	- 7.44
W A O'Gorman	17-62	0-0	6-30	11-32	27.4	+ 16.84
D W Chapman	17-116	0-0	4-29	13-87	14.7	- 19.16
R Hollinshead	15-81	0-0	4-27	11-54	18.5	- 10.94
M S Johnston	9-39	0-0	2-14	7-25	23.1	+ 7.50
C J Hill	8-50	0-0	4-12	4-38	16.0	- 26.16
C C Elsey	7-22	0-0	1-4	6-18	31.8	+ 44.83
J Berry	7-30	0-0	5-17	2-13	23.3	+ 14.00
Lord Huntingdon	6-17	0-0	5-10	1-7	35.3	+ 18.38
D J G Murray Smith	6-18	0-0	5-10	1-8	33.3	+ 28.31
M C Chapman	6-34	0-0	1-10	5-24	17.6	+ 15.50
R Akehurst	5-19	0-0	2-2	3-17	26.3	- 3.94
J L Harris	5-27	0-0	1-6	4-21	18.5	+ 8.75
P Mitchell	5-28	0-0	0-5	5-23	17.9	+ 2.50
D Burchell	5-29	0-0	0-1	5-28	17.2	+ 10.00
P A Kelleway	5-31	0-0	2-12	3-19	16.1	- 10.25
A Bailey	5-45	0-0	1-12	4-33	11.1	- 13.87
Mrs N Macauley	5-62	0-0	5-25	0-37	8.1	- 45.37
N A Callaghan	4-15	0-0	2-8	2-7	26.7	+ 13.88
D W P Arbuthnot	4-15	0-0	0-3	4-12	26.7	+ 8.00
T J Naughton	4-16	0-0	4-10	0-6	25.0	- 2.81
C Tinkler	4-24	0-0	0-0	4-24	16.7	- 14.12
J A Glover	4-26	0-0	0-2	4-24	15.4	+ 1.75
W J Musson	4-27	0-0	3-7	1-20	14.8	+ 7.75

February

	Total W-R	2-y-o	3-y-o	4-y-o+	Per cent	£1 Level Stake
T D Barron	18-63	0-0	8-26	10-37	28.6	+ 6.53
M S Johnston	12-40	0-0	9-17	3-23	30.0	+ 20.56
T Thomson Jones	8-15	0-0	0-2	8-13	53.3	+ 21.59
C N Allen	8-44	0-0	6-28	2-16	18.2	- 5.14
C J Hill	7-42	0-0	3-10	4-32	16.7	+ 11.35
W A O'Gorman	7-55	0-0	3-23	4-32	12.7	- 24.88
Lord Huntingdon	6-27	0-0	2-11	4-16	22.2	+ 0.25
Dr J D Scargill	6-28	0-0	1-6	5-22	21.4	+ 6.73
B W Hills	5-12	0-0	4-11	1-1	41.7	- 2.74
C C Elsey	5-25	0-0	1-8	4-17	20.0	+ 11.10
Mrs A Knight	5-33	0-0	0-0	5-33	15.2	+ 50.50
R Hollinshead	5-51	0-0	3-18	2-33	9.8	- 13.77
D W Chapman	5-91	0-0	2-19	3-72	5.5	- 67.27
C R Nelson	4-12	0-0	1-4	3-8	33.3	- 1.12
D Haydn Jones	4-13	0-0	0-1	4-12	30.8	+ 14.75
R C Spicer	4-13	0-0	0-1	4-12	30.8	+ 19.50
C P Wildman	4-19	0-0	0-3	4-16	21.1	+ 12.00
K O Cunningham-Brown	4-24	0-0	0-2	4-22	16.7	- 0.75
R J O'Sullivan	4-26	0-0	1-2	3-24	15.4	+ 4.00
A Moore	4-33	0-0	0-4	4-29	12.1	+ 37.50
M Brittain	4-33	0-0	3-16	1-17	12.1	+ 1.25
S Dow	4-33	0-0	1-12	3-21	12.1	+ 0.75

March

	Total W-R	2-y-o	3-y-o	4-y-o+	Per cent	£1 Level Stake
J Berry	34-123	13-52	13-47	8-24	27.6	+ 90.83
W A O'Gorman	17-59	2-5	9-24	6-30	28.8	+ 11.20
T D Barron	14-91	0-14	4-26	10-51	15.4	- 1.84
C E Brittain	13-92	0-0	4-48	9-44	14.1	- 9.59
B W Hills	11-34	1-3	8-24	2-7	32.4	+ 1.96
Sir Mark Prescott	10-35	0-0	9-29	1-6	28.6	+ 4.26
M R Channon	10-44	1-2	3-18	6-24	22.7	+ 41.00
S G Norton	10-52	0-2	7-35	3-15	19.2	+ 13.38
Mrs J Ramsden	10-70	0-2	4-33	6-35	14.3	- 6.92
M Brittain	9-114	1-22	3-40	5-52	7.9	- 33.25
Lord Huntingdon	8-47	0-0	3-23	5-24	17.0	+ 3.25
M Bell	8-59	2-12	6-33	0-14	13.6	- 18.71
R Hannon	8-94	2-17	6-44	0-33	8.5	- 52.12
R J O'Sullivan	7-37	0-0	0-1	7-36	18.9	+ 44.50
B A McMahon	6-37	1-3	1-13	4-21	16.2	+ 65.80
M J Ryan	6-42	0-0	4-17	2-25	14.3	+ 9.00
W W Haigh	5-17	0-0	0-2	5-15	29.4	+ 13.25
J H M Gosden	5-18	0-0	4-17	1-1	27.8	+ 11.80
R Boss	5-21	2-3	3-11	0-7	23.8	+ 12.25
Mrs M Reveley	5-29	1-6	0-6	4-17	17.2	- 1.50
P Mitchell	5-30	1-2	0-12	4-16	16.7	+ 5.50
R Akehurst	5-33	0-0	0-4	5-29	15.2	- 3.25
P A Kelleway	5-36	0-5	2-16	3-15	13.9	- 13.21
C Tinkler	5-44	2-9	1-12	2-23	11.4	- 13.75
Mrs N Macauley	5-53	0-1	3-29	2-23	9.4	- 1.00
M S Johnston	5-61	0-4	3-26	2-31	8.2	- 31.20
D W Chapman	5-94	0-3	0-18	5-73	5.3	- 78.37
R Hollinshead	5-134	1-16	4-52	0-66	3.7	- 75.00
C R Nelson	4-14	0-0	2-8	2-6	28.6	- 2.74
M C Pipe	4-14	0-0	1-2	3-12	28.6	- 2.97
J G FitzGerald	4-19	0-1	1-1	3-17	21.1	+ 34.25
D R C Elsworth	4-24	0-0	1-9	3-15	16.7	- 8.37
N A Callaghan	4-25	0-0	2-19	2-6	16.0	+ 8.20
G Wragg	4-27	0-0	4-20	0-7	14.8	- 18.68
Mrs A Knight	4-29	0-0	0-1	4-28	13.8	- 3.50
P F I Cole	4-30	0-1	3-21	1-8	13.3	- 14.75
M W Easterby	4-35	1-11	0-9	3-15	11.4	- 6.00
S Dow	4-56	1-3	1-20	2-33	7.1	- 9.00
J Etherington	3-6	0-1	1-2	2-3	50.0	+ 23.00
M R Stoute	3-10	0-0	3-8	0-2	30.0	+ 4.96
Miss B Sanders	3-11	0-0	1-5	2-6	27.3	+ 8.50
P T Walwyn	3-13	0-0	3-8	0-5	23.1	- 7.20
G Harwood	3-14	0-0	3-6	0-8	21.4	- 6.39
I Campbell	3-14	0-0	0-4	3-10	21.4	+ 1.88
D W P Arbuthnot	3-17	0-0	0-5	3-12	17.6	- 5.75
C C Elsey	3-19	0-1	0-5	3-13	15.8	- 8.00
Mrs L Piggott	3-21	0-0	2-13	1-8	14.3	+ 6.50
M H Tompkins	3-23	0-1	3-7	0-15	13.0	- 9.75
K O Cunningham-Brown	3-24	0-1	0-4	3-19	12.5	- 0.75
J Pearce	3-26	0-0	0-4	3-22	11.5	- 12.62
C J Hill	3-28	0-0	2-10	1-18	10.7	- 11.25
C A Cyzer	3-32	0-0	0-14	3-18	9.4	- 15.50
G Lewis	3-41	1-3	2-23	0-15	7.3	- 23.62
N Tinkler	3-55	2-13	0-13	1-29	5.5	- 41.50

April

	Total W-R	2-y-o	3-y-o	4-y-o+	Per cent	£1 Level Stake
J Berry	81-393	41-169	30-160	10-64	20.6	+ 12.94
H R A Cecil	77-212	0-0	64-178	13-34	36.3	+ 47.50
R Hannon	56-427	24-104	26-235	6-88	13.1	- 41.01
J L Dunlop	34-231	0-5	25-157	9-69	14.7	- 39.72
M R Stoute	31-179	0-1	25-150	6-28	17.3	- 52.23
C E Brittain	30-243	1-9	16-150	13-84	12.3	+ 28.22
J H M Gosden	28-142	0-0	21-102	7-40	19.7	- 8.24
P F I Cole	26-236	2-32	20-154	4-50	11.0	-112.02
M H Easterby	25-242	9-64	9-92	7-86	10.3	- 99.81
Sir Mark Prescott	24-111	0-0	17-85	7-26	21.6	- 13.48
Mrs J Ramsden	23-186	0-9	11-87	12-90	12.4	- 80.81
G Harwood	21-104	0-1	19-71	2-32	20.2	- 24.18
R Hollinshead	21-262	4-47	6-120	11-95	8.0	- 60.67
B W Hills	20-222	1-13	14-171	5-38	9.0	- 64.53
J W Watts	19-109	0-4	13-74	6-31	17.4	+ 39.72
P T Walwyn	19-121	0-0	11-89	8-32	15.7	+ 21.64
M Bell	19-149	4-36	14-84	1-29	12.8	- 40.37
R J Hodges	18-144	2-2	2-29	14-113	12.5	- 9.12
G Wragg	17-119	1-3	12-86	4-30	14.3	- 35.65
M Brittain	17-295	2-45	8-123	7-127	5.8	-118.00
P Chapple-Hyam	16-62	2-4	12-51	2-7	25.8	+ 28.64
M J Camacho	16-66	0-3	6-32	10-31	24.2	+ 60.26
I A Balding	16-146	1-3	10-89	5-54	11.0	- 50.12
L M Cumani	15-113	0-0	12-92	3-21	13.3	- 52.52
M S Johnston	14-119	0-17	11-59	3-43	11.8	- 22.30
B Hanbury	14-128	0-6	8-89	6-33	10.9	- 51.59
Lord Huntingdon	13-91	0-0	7-51	6-40	14.3	- 4.08
G Lewis	13-175	4-43	4-87	5-45	7.4	- 58.00
Mrs M Reveley	12-77	1-11	2-17	9-49	15.6	- 27.57
A A Scott	12-99	1-7	11-77	0-15	12.1	- 20.65
W A O'Gorman	11-65	6-19	5-27	0-19	16.9	- 24.12
M A Jarvis	11-97	0-5	9-70	2-22	11.3	+ 25.30
R Akehurst	11-116	0-1	1-13	10-102	9.5	- 27.00
M McCormack	10-70	0-9	6-36	4-25	14.3	+ 30.25
B A McMahon	10-100	0-19	4-34	6-47	10.0	- 9.00
S G Norton	10-106	0-12	6-69	4-25	9.4	- 27.00
T D Barron	10-125	0-17	5-46	5-62	8.0	- 41.50
Mrs J Cecil	9-36	1-1	4-23	4-12	25.0	+ 17.13
A C Stewart	9-66	0-1	6-54	3-11	13.6	- 4.86
J Wharton	9-73	4-23	1-20	4-30	12.3	+ 21.00
M R Channon	9-98	4-23	5-44	0-31	9.2	- 26.12
M J Ryan	9-101	0-5	5-40	4-56	8.9	- 6.62
N A Callaghan	9-104	2-23	6-56	1-25	8.7	- 44.75
D R C Elsworth	9-116	0-8	2-54	7-54	7.8	- 44.87
W Carter	9-118	6-25	2-55	1-38	7.6	- 3.50
M W Easterby	9-129	2-50	2-37	5-42	7.0	- 70.97
R Charlton	8-52	0-1	7-43	1-8	15.4	- 22.59
H Thomson Jones	8-63	0-0	7-53	1-10	12.7	- 28.78
C R Nelson	8-67	1-6	4-34	3-27	11.9	- 1.29
Dr J D Scargill	8-69	3-13	5-40	0-16	11.6	- 11.25
R Boss	8-95	3-16	3-58	2-21	8.4	- 50.04
C A Cyzer	8-97	0-7	3-58	5-32	8.2	+ 17.00
M H Tompkins	8-110	0-19	4-53	4-38	7.3	- 56.37
C Tinkler	8-114	2-33	4-49	2-32	7.0	- 63.80

May

	Total W-R	2-y-o	3-y-o	4-y-o+	Per cent	£1 Level Stake
M R Stoute	98-360	7-16	76-300	15-44	27.2	+ 9.85
J Berry	98-544	62-270	25-190	11-84	18.0	- 29.03
R Hannon	97-634	34-187	50-349	13-98	15.3	- 96.91
H R A Cecil	85-303	7-13	75-250	3-40	28.1	- 47.78
B W Hills	53-338	7-46	39-229	7-63	15.7	-101.79
J H M Gosden	44-205	0-7	36-160	8-38	21.5	- 16.38
G Harwood	44-215	3-10	34-148	7-57	20.5	- 17.56
J L Dunlop	42-307	1-22	34-219	7-66	13.7	-123.35
P F I Cole	40-322	16-49	16-198	8-75	12.4	-141.98
I A Balding	36-240	3-14	16-146	17-80	15.0	+ 28.55
M H Tompkins	36-241	6-50	20-111	10-80	14.9	+ 51.80
M H Easterby	36-368	14-115	9-127	13-126	9.8	-125.50
L M Cumani	35-189	1-5	28-155	6-29	18.5	- 42.82
Sir Mark Prescott	33-145	2-5	26-105	5-35	22.8	- 7.46
M S Johnston	29-194	6-37	14-87	9-70	14.9	+ 6.14
C E Brittain	28-352	3-38	13-198	12-116	8.0	- 92.11
Mrs M Reveley	26-168	5-27	5-43	16-98	15.5	- 17.42
B Hanbury	26-171	3-21	19-121	4-29	15.2	- 7.26
R M Whitaker	26-251	6-34	10-104	10-113	10.4	+ 5.93
A A Scott	25-157	7-21	15-119	3-17	15.9	- 38.10
G Wragg	24-143	5-10	12-103	7-30	16.8	- 24.71
M Bell	24-169	10-48	14-93	0-28	14.2	- 36.17
R Hollinshead	24-348	3-67	10-146	11-135	6.9	-117.87
R Akehurst	23-179	0-6	6-55	17-118	12.8	- 31.17
G Lewis	23-217	5-57	16-105	2-55	10.6	- 10.64
P T Walwyn	22-197	0-9	17-157	5-31	11.2	- 32.31
D R C Elsworth	22-209	3-15	8-113	11-81	10.5	- 36.85
W Jarvis	21-135	6-18	10-85	5-32	15.6	- 32.21
J W Hills	21-144	0-7	9-81	12-56	14.6	+ 1.58
J W Watts	21-167	2-19	9-97	10-51	12.6	- 6.92
J R Fanshawe	20-98	0-5	18-81	2-12	20.4	+ 51.03
S G Norton	20-147	2-20	10-90	8-37	13.6	- 32.76
R Charlton	19-90	1-2	13-69	5-19	21.1	+ 21.72
Mrs J Ramsden	19-182	3-17	8-84	8-81	10.4	- 51.67
P Chapple-Hyam	18-71	5-16	13-51	0-4	25.4	- 2.62
Lord Huntingdon	18-107	4-14	6-58	8-35	16.8	- 26.09
M McCormack	18-122	8-28	7-51	3-43	14.8	- 2.36
H Thomson Jones	18-141	6-12	11-108	1-21	12.8	- 63.70
N A Callaghan	18-148	4-41	11-76	3-31	12.2	- 14.40
M A Jarvis	17-147	1-15	13-100	3-32	11.6	- 54.24
M Brittain	17-305	5-92	3-106	9-107	5.6	- 90.42
A C Stewart	16-99	0-1	12-81	4-17	16.2	- 35.26
P J Makin	15-105	1-7	7-56	7-42	14.3	+ 18.89
M J Ryan	15-114	1-8	4-47	10-59	13.2	+ 8.76
T D Barron	15-176	4-41	2-57	9-78	8.5	- 64.70
R J R Williams	14-108	5-15	5-55	4-38	13.0	+ 97.06
R F Johnson Houghton	14-125	2-26	10-86	2-13	11.2	- 29.09
C Tinkler	14-164	7-59	3-61	4-44	8.5	- 47.37
W A O'Gorman	13-101	11-37	2-40	0-24	12.9	- 51.12
J Wharton	13-116	4-21	4-39	5-56	11.2	+ 55.95
F H Lee	13-178	2-22	4-77	7-79	7.3	- 73.12

June

	Total W-R	2-y-o	3-y-o	4-y-o+	Per cent	£1 Level Stake
J Berry	100-602	54-333	37-199	9-70	16.6	-141.51
H R A Cecil	86-279	13-33	69-210	4-36	30.8	+ 55.81
R Hannon	78-683	36-252	36-323	6-108	11.4	-133.49
J L Dunlop	73-327	10-56	52-210	11-61	22.3	+ 28.99
P F I Cole	72-338	30-99	33-179	9-60	21.3	- 21.09
J H M Gosden	61-243	7-20	45-181	9-42	25.1	- 0.13
L M Cumani	56-226	3-11	51-186	2-29	24.8	- 48.19
M R Stoute	56-313	9-29	40-242	7-42	17.9	-101.65
B W Hills	40-282	7-40	30-195	3-47	14.2	-125.52
B Hanbury	38-226	8-44	21-141	9-41	16.8	- 8.92
M H Easterby	38-383	17-137	11-121	10-125	9.9	-194.73
I A Balding	37-276	7-47	19-155	11-74	13.4	- 36.47
C E Brittain	37-355	8-75	22-173	7-107	10.4	- 90.74
G Harwood	34-229	5-23	21-152	8-54	14.8	- 46.79
Sir Mark Prescott	33-175	5-36	23-109	5-30	18.9	- 31.74
D R C Elsworth	32-243	4-32	12-120	16-91	13.2	+ 15.46
R Akehurst	31-214	1-21	9-62	21-131	14.5	+ 7.30
Lord Huntingdon	30-131	4-20	13-70	13-41	22.9	+119.25
P T Walwyn	30-182	3-17	20-127	7-38	16.5	+ 46.33
M S Johnston	30-194	10-44	13-80	7-70	15.5	+ 31.07
R Hollinshead	30-354	5-78	6-141	19-135	8.5	-106.46
R Charlton	28-87	3-14	21-53	4-20	32.2	+ 45.77
G Wragg	27-127	5-12	18-92	4-23	21.3	+ 17.97
A A Scott	27-170	12-42	12-111	3-17	15.9	- 58.84
S G Norton	27-183	5-43	14-92	8-48	14.8	- 48.56
M H Tompkins	27-302	9-88	10-131	8-83	8.9	-170.36
H Thomson Jones	25-153	7-29	17-107	1-17	16.3	+ 25.51
M A Jarvis	25-172	7-29	14-96	4-47	14.5	- 40.00
R M Whitaker	24-244	4-39	10-99	10-106	9.8	- 42.77
G Lewis	24-257	10-82	10-112	4-63	9.3	-113.95
F H Lee	22-176	4-31	8-74	10-71	12.5	+ 4.50
M Bell	22-192	11-64	10-105	1-23	11.5	- 29.97
B A McMahon	22-197	1-35	3-53	18-109	11.2	- 2.12
A C Stewart	21-119	0-1	16-99	5-19	17.6	- 31.54
Mrs M Reveley	21-196	2-27	2-50	17-119	10.7	-105.62
P J Makin	20-123	2-14	12-61	6-48	16.3	- 4.23
R J Hodges	20-211	0-9	1-36	19-166	9.5	- 56.27
D A Wilson	19-122	0-2	2-22	17-98	15.6	- 10.66
M P Naughton	19-147	0-2	4-26	15-119	12.9	- 3.25
N A Callaghan	19-151	6-47	9-69	4-35	12.6	- 47.88
D Morley	18-124	4-11	8-80	6-33	14.5	- 8.92
M R Channon	18-156	5-56	10-64	3-36	11.5	- 10.74
Denys Smith	18-182	5-41	5-69	8-72	9.9	- 75.00
Mrs J Ramsden	18-184	5-40	6-76	7-68	9.8	- 83.13
P Chapple-Hyam	17-78	8-23	9-51	0-4	21.8	+ 0.13
W R Hern	17-112	3-16	9-80	5-16	15.2	- 42.02
J W Hills	17-137	1-19	9-66	7-52	12.4	- 19.17
J W Watts	17-163	6-26	8-98	3-39	10.4	- 70.83
J R Fanshawe	16-120	2-13	10-94	4-13	13.3	- 30.50
J L Spearing	16-124	2-15	0-23	14-86	12.9	+ 6.50
W Jarvis	16-150	4-29	8-85	4-36	10.7	- 70.97
T D Barron	16-183	6-43	6-58	4-82	8.7	- 74.87

July

	Total W-R	2-y-o	3-y-o	4-y-o+	Per cent	£1 Level Stake
J Berry	120-695	75-415	27-185	18-95	17.3	-212.02
H R A Cecil	117-297	31-58	81-216	5-23	39.4	+ 66.68
R Hannon	104-713	53-333	37-285	14-95	14.6	-126.15
Mrs M Reveley	69-279	10-50	21-85	38-144	24.7	+ 78.97
L M Cumani	67-253	5-28	55-190	7-35	26.5	+ 7.65
B W Hills	64-301	15-74	43-189	6-38	21.3	- 16.01
P F I Cole	63-299	26-100	27-144	10-55	21.1	- 26.42
J H M Gosden	60-260	12-41	36-179	12-40	23.1	+ 4.21
M H Easterby	56-413	21-149	17-133	18-131	13.6	-183.50
M R Stoute	53-319	15-71	31-214	7-34	16.6	-113.21
G Harwood	52-228	10-34	32-136	10-58	22.8	+ 0.63
I A Balding	50-299	11-68	21-143	18-88	16.7	- 17.05
J L Dunlop	48-290	14-108	28-135	6-47	16.6	- 52.34
F H Lee	44-226	7-46	23-102	14-78	19.5	+ 87.04
G Lewis	43-246	19-91	12-109	12-46	17.5	- 19.78
R Hollinshead	39-390	12-85	12-157	15-148	10.0	-200.39
Sir Mark Prescott	38-191	7-54	26-108	5-29	19.9	- 43.24
M Bell	35-205	22-93	10-82	3-30	17.1	- 17.33
D R C Elsworth	35-213	7-38	23-98	5-77	16.4	+ 54.70
G Wragg	33-153	12-35	18-91	3-27	21.6	+ 35.72
M H Tompkins	33-278	15-113	6-82	12-83	11.9	-114.60
W R Hern	32-136	10-29	15-87	7-20	23.5	- 8.47
M S Johnston	32-220	12-57	16-92	4-71	14.5	- 55.82
R Akehurst	31-238	2-29	7-72	22-137	13.0	- 40.99
B Hanbury	28-166	12-53	12-84	4-29	16.9	- 28.18
Lord Huntingdon	27-140	5-28	10-67	12-45	19.3	- 5.32
M P Naughton	27-158	0-3	5-23	22-132	17.1	- 14.41
R Charlton	26-106	10-25	12-60	4-21	24.5	+ 16.56
A C Stewart	26-129	4-16	21-97	1-16	20.2	+ 10.35
W Jarvis	26-143	6-27	12-85	8-31	18.2	+ 57.63
Mrs J Ramsden	26-164	9-54	10-54	7-56	15.9	- 7.75
C E Brittain	26-394	9-112	12-178	5-104	6.6	-191.06
P T Walwyn	25-173	7-30	13-117	5-26	14.5	+ 28.43
R M Whitaker	25-265	6-48	5-87	14-130	9.4	- 91.15
M J Ryan	24-150	2-31	11-53	11-66	16.0	- 10.83
M A Jarvis	24-155	3-30	7-88	14-37	15.5	- 40.25
N A Callaghan	24-182	10-72	9-74	5-36	13.2	- 71.45
B A McMahon	23-197	4-32	5-58	14-107	11.7	- 61.98
P J Makin	22-115	3-21	13-66	6-28	19.1	- 1.63
R Boss	22-137	9-48	9-61	4-28	16.1	- 12.97
G A Pritchard-Gordon	22-161	8-53	12-83	2-25	13.7	- 33.66
T D Barron	22-222	8-62	5-65	9-95	9.9	- 98.94
R F Johnson Houghton	21-105	8-28	11-64	2-13	20.0	+ 13.40
H Thomson Jones	21-123	8-27	11-87	2-9	17.1	- 38.87
C A Cyzer	21-150	1-24	10-75	10-51	14.0	+ 12.66
C Tinkler	21-168	8-73	5-47	8-48	12.5	- 63.81
M W Easterby	21-230	10-116	3-59	8-55	9.1	- 85.17
W A O'Gorman	20-102	15-50	5-35	0-17	19.6	- 7.13
D Morley	20-123	4-21	6-70	10-32	16.3	+ 7.84
A Bailey	20-133	4-37	5-44	11-52	15.0	+ 10.70
A A Scott	20-160	5-56	12-84	3-20	12.5	- 77.72
R J Hodges	20-188	2-14	3-38	15-136	10.6	- 42.33
N Tinkler	19-173	4-56	11-58	4-59	11.0	- 86.23

August

	Total W-R	2-y-o	3-y-o	4-y-o+	Per cent	£1 Level Stake
R Hannon	87-646	56-349	23-227	8-70	13.5	-147.26
J Berry	82-561	46-348	28-137	8-76	14.6	-141.58
B W Hills	65-326	17-109	39-186	9-31	19.9	- 39.16
M R Stoute	60-328	29-116	30-184	1-28	18.3	- 45.23
L M Cumani	59-220	11-38	42-157	6-25	26.8	- 23.48
H R A Cecil	59-234	18-48	38-166	3-20	25.2	- 68.84
P F I Cole	50-269	26-125	13-104	11-40	18.6	- 22.21
G Harwood	49-239	13-51	30-153	6-35	20.5	+ 4.28
M H Easterby	49-354	23-158	16-108	10-88	13.8	- 88.00
Sir Mark Prescott	46-173	18-64	20-74	8-35	26.6	+ 66.60
J H M Gosden	45-219	8-41	31-149	6-29	20.5	+ 9.03
J L Dunlop	45-260	21-120	21-104	3-36	17.3	- 27.77
I A Balding	44-271	17-79	16-118	11-74	16.2	- 23.32
Mrs M Reveley	33-236	2-54	12-63	19-119	14.0	- 71.60
W R Hern	32-135	4-24	24-98	4-13	23.7	+ 11.93
R Hollinshead	31-338	9-95	9-120	13-123	9.2	-135.07
C E Brittain	30-312	8-91	15-139	7-82	9.6	- 64.88
M H Tompkins	28-218	10-92	10-63	8-63	12.8	- 73.32
G Lewis	27-224	13-109	3-68	11-47	12.1	- 61.16
W Jarvis	26-139	6-42	14-70	6-27	18.7	+ 0.47
R Akehurst	26-190	3-27	7-65	16-98	13.7	+ 18.75
P Chapple-Hyam	25-94	17-48	8-41	0-5	26.6	+ 10.33
H Thomson Jones	25-126	9-41	15-77	1-8	19.8	- 1.75
R Charlton	24-108	11-34	12-65	1-9	22.2	- 2.78
M Bell	24-192	15-90	7-77	2-25	12.5	- 2.29
A C Stewart	22-128	1-21	20-91	1-16	17.2	- 51.50
D R C Elsworth	22-203	8-60	7-79	7-64	10.8	- 84.49
B Hanbury	22-215	6-83	8-103	8-29	10.2	- 45.84
M S Johnston	21-194	6-60	8-71	7-63	10.8	- 48.62
G Wragg	20-128	9-40	10-72	1-16	15.6	- 46.75
H Candy	20-145	3-29	11-73	6-43	13.8	+ 28.96
Lord Huntingdon	20-169	5-35	8-87	7-47	11.8	- 53.45
F H Lee	20-187	6-42	5-70	9-75	10.7	- 31.75
R M Whitaker	20-254	4-71	6-83	10-100	7.9	- 89.90
A A Scott	19-158	9-60	9-86	1-12	12.0	- 76.71
T D Barron	19-173	8-56	5-48	6-69	11.0	- 31.05
W J Haggas	18-106	8-36	8-44	2-26	17.0	+ 21.28
D W Chapman	18-233	1-23	0-53	17-157	7.7	- 13.17
Mrs L Piggott	17-107	4-32	5-46	8-29	15.9	+ 11.70
M A Jarvis	17-149	3-36	9-77	5-36	11.4	- 53.32
J W Hills	17-150	6-38	5-61	6-51	11.3	- 13.49
C A Cyzer	17-152	1-26	8-78	8-48	11.2	- 4.24
Mrs J Ramsden	17-152	5-55	6-56	6-41	11.2	- 32.82
P T Walwyn	17-168	6-56	11-95	0-17	10.1	- 79.52
J Etherington	16-128	4-60	9-46	3-22	12.5	- 43.58
M J Ryan	15-96	1-15	7-42	7-39	15.6	+ 28.25
P J Makin	15-102	3-18	7-51	5-33	14.7	+ 8.39
N Tinkler	15-103	0-41	7-30	8-32	14.6	- 53.82
D Morley	15-114	4-31	9-56	2-27	13.2	- 32.20
M R Channon	15-167	10-83	5-56	0-28	9.0	- 45.44
Mrs N Macauley	15-171	4-52	2-50	9-69	8.8	- 66.60
R J Hodges	15-192	0-13	2-36	13-143	7.8	- 62.50

September

	Total W–R	2-y-o	3-y-o	4-y-o+	Per cent	£1 Level Stake
J H M Gosden	79-302	25-74	39-184	15-44	26.2	+101.07
R Hannon	71-635	36-345	21-212	14-78	11.2	-118.42
L M Cumani	64-304	24-93	36-184	4-27	21.1	- 31.41
J L Dunlop	60-403	34-199	21-151	5-53	14.9	-101.02
M R Stoute	57-331	29-156	23-149	5-26	17.2	- 86.16
B W Hills	56-351	25-155	27-161	4-35	16.0	- 64.29
H R A Cecil	53-219	24-81	28-122	1-16	24.2	- 36.98
J Berry	45-511	30-292	12-146	3-73	8.8	-178.59
I A Balding	33-297	11-129	14-98	8-70	11.1	- 23.25
G Wragg	32-146	8-46	21-89	3-11	21.9	+ 49.36
C E Brittain	31-373	12-141	15-163	4-69	8.3	-111.14
H Thomson Jones	30-149	17-60	12-73	1-16	20.1	+ 31.19
R Charlton	29-135	14-61	12-61	3-13	21.5	+ 28.01
G Harwood	28-199	10-63	15-107	3-29	14.1	- 55.24
M H Tompkins	28-274	6-114	15-80	7-80	10.2	-108.65
B Hanbury	27-205	12-94	12-94	3-17	13.2	- 9.74
P F I Cole	27-261	17-143	7-83	3-35	10.3	- 80.62
Mrs M Reveley	26-173	6-52	6-42	14-79	15.0	+ 0.96
Lord Huntingdon	26-189	5-61	12-87	9-41	13.8	+ 8.42
M H Easterby	26-288	9-125	8-82	9-81	9.0	-106.68
R W Armstrong	25-129	12-48	9-58	4-23	19.4	+128.98
R M Whitaker	23-250	6-88	7-88	10-74	9.2	- 76.17
R Akehurst	22-178	5-32	5-53	12-93	12.4	+ 24.50
A C Stewart	21-135	2-34	15-87	4-14	15.6	- 20.79
Mrs J Ramsden	21-174	10-64	7-59	4-51	12.1	- 52.75
Sir Mark Prescott	19-173	7-81	9-61	3-31	11.0	- 51.99
P Chapple-Hyam	18-101	16-62	2-31	0-8	17.8	- 29.01
W R Hern	18-137	6-42	10-83	2-12	13.1	- 65.89
D R C Elsworth	18-185	11-82	5-58	2-45	9.7	- 68.62
D Morley	17-131	4-44	11-65	2-22	13.0	+ 6.35
G Lewis	17-185	9-102	6-58	2-25	9.2	- 49.55
C A Cyzer	16-131	5-35	8-65	3-31	12.2	+ 16.50
J W Hills	16-144	3-44	8-59	5-41	11.1	+ 4.50
M Bell	16-162	12-92	3-50	1-20	9.9	- 59.63
M S Johnston	16-192	6-64	7-68	3-60	8.3	- 58.74
M A Jarvis	15-144	7-56	5-63	3-25	10.4	- 37.97
W Jarvis	15-153	5-51	8-72	2-30	9.8	- 56.75
A A Scott	15-154	8-71	3-70	4-13	9.7	- 36.93
W Carter	15-157	2-56	7-52	6-49	9.6	+ 82.73
W J Haggas	14-109	5-46	7-45	2-18	12.8	- 29.29
M J Camacho	13-86	4-26	5-28	4-32	15.1	+ 40.13
H Candy	13-162	2-49	8-73	3-40	8.0	- 72.40
Mrs J Cecil	12-70	10-34	1-26	1-10	17.1	+ 10.54
J G FitzGerald	12-119	4-47	5-44	3-28	10.1	- 24.43
J R Fanshawe	12-119	5-45	6-59	1-15	10.1	- 48.94
T D Barron	12-149	9-54	0-55	3-40	8.1	- 74.29
B A McMahon	12-172	3-41	1-38	8-93	7.0	- 43.62
R Boss	11-84	5-42	4-36	2-6	13.1	- 21.12
D W P Arbuthnot	11-110	4-28	4-41	3-41	10.0	- 1.40
G A Pritchard-Gordon	11-123	6-60	1-37	4-26	8.9	+ 16.50
D W Chapman	11-186	2-16	2-45	7-125	5.9	- 66.75
P T Walwyn	11-205	6-75	5-102	0-28	5.4	-130.25

October/November

	Total W-R	2-y-o	3-y-o	4-y-o+	Per cent	£1 Level Stake
J H M Gosden	96-447	40-169	42-223	14-55	21.5	- 27.21
R Hannon	81-773	60-459	17-231	4-83	10.5	-231.79
H R A Cecil	71-338	43-166	25-158	3-14	21.0	+ 10.75
B W Hills	70-430	32-195	31-202	7-33	16.3	- 30.00
L M Cumani	65-332	31-148	31-165	3-19	19.6	- 43.64
J L Dunlop	60-441	25-218	28-177	7-46	13.6	- 62.79
M R Stoute	59-365	38-236	20-104	1-25	16.2	- 49.17
G Harwood	48-340	21-150	22-151	5-39	14.1	- 98.31
P F I Cole	36-319	26-189	6-87	4-43	11.3	+ 17.27
D R C Elsworth	35-259	20-134	6-69	9-56	13.5	+ 27.61
H Thomson Jones	34-192	23-102	11-79	0-11	17.7	+ 2.16
M H Tompkins	34-365	12-166	8-85	14-114	9.3	- 84.25
M S Johnston	31-299	13-140	11-87	7-72	10.4	- 25.95
J Berry	31-415	22-257	6-107	3-51	7.5	-179.61
B Hanbury	29-191	9-84	16-88	4-19	15.2	- 27.41
C E Brittain	29-438	11-200	12-141	6-97	6.6	-146.94
Sir Mark Prescott	28-239	17-166	6-47	5-26	11.7	- 62.08
G Wragg	27-200	9-71	17-116	1-13	13.5	- 40.82
R Akehurst	25-260	0-61	10-89	15-110	9.6	- 81.00
G Lewis	24-201	13-105	8-51	3-45	11.9	+ 43.65
Mrs J Cecil	23-97	13-61	9-29	1-7	23.7	+ 79.48
M H Easterby	23-255	12-96	3-77	8-82	9.0	- 49.83
Lord Huntingdon	23-283	6-98	13-121	4-64	8.1	-119.75
Mrs M Reveley	22-178	3-48	5-38	14-92	12.4	- 47.72
T D Barron	22-203	9-72	6-67	7-64	10.8	- 21.87
J W Hills	22-218	3-90	10-77	9-51	10.1	- 62.91
R Hollinshead	22-477	12-218	4-146	6-113	4.6	-181.75
M J Camacho	21-124	2-43	6-37	13-44	16.9	- 2.50
R Charlton	19-111	8-56	10-47	1-8	17.1	+ 16.23
W A O'Gorman	19-136	13-69	4-45	2-22	14.0	- 18.41
N A Callaghan	19-162	12-110	7-48	0-4	11.7	- 9.25
M J Ryan	19-205	4-58	7-84	8-63	9.3	- 9.79
R W Armstrong	18-118	11-50	4-48	3-20	15.3	+ 13.71
R Boss	18-131	14-78	3-38	1-15	13.7	+ 12.38
D Morley	18-191	6-89	8-72	4-30	9.4	- 50.77
W Jarvis	18-199	7-99	9-76	2-24	9.0	- 94.01
S G Norton	18-234	6-116	8-96	4-22	7.7	- 74.22
A C Stewart	17-201	9-53	8-128	0-20	8.5	- 97.11
M A Jarvis	17-228	8-123	6-70	3-35	7.5	-112.45
A A Scott	16-160	13-118	2-36	1-6	10.0	- 54.94
P T Walwyn	16-233	8-109	7-104	1-20	6.9	-120.38
J R Fanshawe	15-140	9-59	6-61	0-20	10.7	+ 9.76
P J Makin	15-187	2-58	11-89	2-40	8.0	- 64.54
W R Hern	14-122	6-61	8-58	0-3	11.5	- 52.97
Mrs J Ramsden	14-181	5-77	5-54	4-50	7.7	-105.17
C J Hill	13-94	4-22	1-32	8-40	13.8	- 10.58
P Chapple-Hyam	13-99	12-73	1-24	0-2	13.1	- 53.21
J G FitzGerald	13-131	4-52	4-41	5-38	9.9	- 39.29
G B Balding	13-138	3-47	2-34	8-57	9.4	+ 1.13
H Candy	13-174	4-54	7-85	2-35	7.5	- 29.50
D W Chapman	13-233	2-45	1-57	10-131	5.6	-141.96

LEADING TRAINERS BY TYPE OF RACE 1989-93

2-y-o Non-Handicaps

	W-R	Per cent	£1 Level Stake		W-R	Per cent	£1 Level Stake
J Berry	238-1393	17.1	- 381.67	R Hannon	237-1603	14.8	- 384.63
H R A Cecil	136-395	34.4	+ 62.22	P F I Cole	126-632	19.9	- 28.35
M R Stoute	121-573	21.1	- 124.54	B W Hills	91-591	15.4	- 160.51
J H M Gosden	90-332	27.1	+ 10.42	J L Dunlop	88-641	13.7	- 253.59
L M Cumani	72-304	23.7	- 19.05	H Thomson Jones	66-248	26.6	+ 2.56
P Chapple-Hyam	66-248	26.6	- 28.64	M H Easterby	61-520	11.7	- 225.83
W A O'Gorman	58-239	24.3	- 26.67	M Bell	58-361	16.1	- 75.17
G Harwood	52-288	18.1	- 89.92	D R C Elsworth	51-341	15.0	- 41.39
A A Scott	50-315	15.9	- 105.74	I A Balding	49-386	12.7	- 91.23
G Wragg	48-204	23.5	+ 6.18	Sir M Prescott	47-317	14.8	- 81.67
G Lewis	47-395	11.9	- 57.75	R Charlton	44-174	25.3	+ 53.23
B Hanbury	44-326	13.5	- 76.11	C E Brittain	42-582	7.2	- 345.03
M S Johnston	40-288	13.9	- 14.87	R W Armstrong	39-161	24.2	+ 73.63
R Hollinshead	38-578	6.6	- 299.12	R Boss	37-235	15.7	- 18.61
M H Tompkins	36-375	9.6	- 164.67	W Jarvis	33-244	13.5	- 31.26
Mrs J Cecil	30-138	21.7	+ 23.99	P T Walwyn	30-279	10.8	- 95.73
W R Hern	27-164	16.5	- 65.00	N A Callaghan	27-246	11.0	- 61.44
J Etherington	26-245	10.6	- 52.52	M R Channon	26-276	9.4	- 70.07
T D Barron	25-193	13.0	- 58.59	M A Jarvis	24-243	9.9	- 115.62
S G Norton	23-250	9.2	- 130.07	R M Whitaker	22-241	9.1	- 90.72
G A P-Gordon	21-254	8.3	- 69.20	W J Haggas	20-151	13.2	- 38.66
Lord Huntingdon	20-203	9.9	- 126.70	C Tinkler	20-276	7.2	- 133.59
J W Watts	19-169	11.2	- 39.50	J R Fanshawe	18-150	12.0	- 25.42
D R Loder	17-70	24.3	- 9.70	C R Nelson	17-100	17.0	+ 11.73
A C Stewart	16-115	13.9	- 26.05	D Morley	16-151	10.6	- 32.75
Mrs J Ramsden	16-173	9.2	- 73.51	W Carter	16-179	8.9	+ 10.50
Denys Smith	16-207	7.7	- 98.90	M McCormack	15-183	8.2	- 88.26
P A Kelleway	15-230	6.5	- 113.66	M W Easterby	15-308	4.9	- 212.27
Mrs L Piggott	14-136	10.3	- 84.38	Mrs M Reveley	14-160	8.8	- 72.30
C F Wall	13-160	8.1	- 60.85	F H Lee	13-179	7.3	- 109.95
R F J Houghton	13-198	6.6	- 115.24	E Weymes	12-99	12.1	+ 11.00
J W Payne	12-121	9.9	- 77.90	S Dow	12-166	7.2	- 73.12
J W Hills	12-188	6.4	- 76.80	J Wharton	11-130	8.5	+ 2.13
H Candy	11-144	7.6	- 33.50	J G FitzGerald	11-162	6.8	- 107.30
N Tinkler	11-162	6.8	- 98.87	Dr J D Scargill	11-164	6.7	- 90.04

3-y-o Non-Handicaps

	W-R	Per cent	£1 Level Stake		W-R	Per cent	£1 Level Stake
H R A Cecil	324-1046	31.0	- 5.63	L M Cumani	198-755	26.2	- 79.98
J H M Gosden	187-823	22.7	- 55.54	M R Stoute	179-855	20.9	- 167.98
B W Hills	153-832	18.4	- 184.61	G Harwood	114-511	22.3	- 92.80
J L Dunlop	105-609	17.2	- 104.33	R Hannon	104-725	14.3	- 154.89
J Berry	90-437	20.6	- 40.65	G Wragg	86-446	19.3	- 23.57
P F I Cole	74-554	13.4	- 243.87	C E Brittain	70-678	10.3	- 162.95
W R Hern	62-386	16.1	- 158.43	R Charlton	59-243	24.3	+ 14.39
A C Stewart	59-396	14.9	- 122.33	B Hanbury	59-418	14.1	- 33.30
Sir M Prescott	54-209	25.8	+ 0.54	Lord Huntingdon	53-293	18.1	+ 51.91
H Thomson Jones	51-285	17.9	- 50.18	I A Balding	49-412	11.9	- 113.60
P T Walwyn	47-401	11.7	- 138.95	W Jarvis	40-316	12.7	- 135.83

	W-R	Per cent	£1 Level Stake		W-R	Per cent	£1 Level Stake
D R C Elsworth	40-388	10.3	- 137.00	J R Fanshawe	39-260	15.0	+ 17.14
A A Scott	37-312	11.9	- 149.23	P Chapple-Hyam	35-189	18.5	- 47.96
M A Jarvis	35-287	12.2	- 80.87	R F J Houghton	31-200	15.5	- 41.54
M H Tompkins	30-215	14.0	- 24.53	M S Johnston	28-178	15.7	- 57.47
P J Makin	28-186	15.1	+ 4.66	H Candy	28-267	10.5	- 6.94
S G Norton	27-182	14.8	- 3.57	R Hollinshead	27-473	5.7	- 244.62
N A Callaghan	26-149	17.4	- 3.39	W J Haggas	26-169	15.4	- 55.51
J W Hills	26-206	12.6	- 42.44	T D Barron	24-136	17.6	- 19.76
W A O'Gorman	23-122	18.9	- 32.23	C R Nelson	22-139	15.8	- 48.31
M Bell	22-161	13.7	- 56.44	M H Easterby	22-198	11.1	- 59.98
Mrs J Cecil	21-133	15.8	- 20.76	R Boss	20-156	12.8	- 34.66
G Lewis	20-210	9.5	- 127.05	P A Kelleway	20-217	9.2	- 93.51
Mrs L Piggott	18-194	9.3	- 98.50	R W Armstrong	18-197	9.1	- 72.40
Mrs M Reveley	17-101	16.8	- 21.37	M McCormack	15-143	10.5	- 25.47
R Akehurst	15-152	9.9	- 76.17	R M Whitaker	15-191	7.9	- 43.12
J A R Toller	14-111	12.6	- 21.31	C F Wall	14-146	9.6	- 64.85
D Morley	14-150	9.3	- 69.07	Mrs N Macauley	13-162	8.0	- 73.77
R J R Williams	13-194	6.7	- 25.00	D R Loder	12-37	32.4	+ 10.09
Miss S E Hall	12-76	15.8	- 12.68	M J Camacho	12-78	15.4	- 0.20
J Pearce	12-88	13.6	+ 52.25	C N Allen	12-104	11.5	- 23.23
J Etherington	12-125	9.6	- 45.60	M J Ryan	11-106	10.4	- 41.74
J G FitzGerald	11-122	9.0	- 15.07	J W Watts	11-148	7.4	- 75.62
M R Channon	11-154	7.1	- 96.49	P W Harris	11-156	7.1	+ 5.25

4-y-o+ Non-Handicaps

	W-R	Per cent	£1 Level Stake		W-R	Per cent	£1 Level Stake
J H M Gosden	41-140	29.3	+ 50.66	M R Stoute	35-141	24.8	+ 12.77
R Hannon	30-165	18.2	+ 35.84	H R A Cecil	24-116	20.7	- 25.36
D W Chapman	24-162	14.8	- 62.46	C E Brittain	23-236	9.7	- 32.28
J Berry	22-111	19.8	- 36.57	Sir M Prescott	20-50	40.0	+ 11.08
L M Cumani	19-96	19.8	- 22.87	R Hollinshead	19-170	11.2	- 84.74
J L Dunlop	18-99	18.2	- 0.57	I A Balding	18-101	17.8	- 42.61
B W Hills	18-104	17.3	- 18.19	Lord Huntingdon	17-70	24.3	+ 52.63
G Harwood	17-109	15.6	+ 8.46	B A McMahon	17-137	12.4	+ 21.88
T D Barron	16-65	24.6	+ 2.71	B Hanbury	15-63	23.8	- 11.04
W A O'Gorman	15-72	20.8	- 24.59	M C Pipe	15-76	19.7	- 7.14
R Akehurst	14-113	12.4	- 21.97	G Wragg	13-88	14.8	+ 4.25
Mrs M Reveley	13-90	14.4	- 50.29	M H Tompkins	13-96	13.5	+ 8.22
P J Makin	12-57	21.1	- 5.47	J Wharton	12-65	18.5	+ 6.84
D R C Elsworth	12-128	9.4	- 12.12	P F I Cole	11-89	12.4	- 39.98
M J Ryan	10-62	16.1	- 18.83	G Lewis	10-64	15.6	- 1.50
A Bailey	10-66	15.2	- 18.83	N Tinkler	10-116	8.6	- 70.79
M J Camacho	9-39	23.1	+ 6.95	M H Easterby	9-54	16.7	- 14.87
D Burchell	9-56	16.1	+ 55.50	P T Walwyn	9-72	12.5	+ 16.91
J Pearce	9-75	12.0	- 40.11	W R Hern	8-30	26.7	+ 1.25
W W Haigh	8-44	18.2	+ 40.50	W Jarvis	8-57	14.0	- 9.74
M R Channon	7-38	18.4	+ 21.50	A C Stewart	7-43	16.3	- 11.49
N A Callaghan	7-47	14.9	+ 20.23	G B Balding	7-48	14.6	- 15.87
J W Hills	7-54	13.0	- 18.49	G M Moore	7-58	12.1	+ 7.75
M S Johnston	7-65	10.8	- 31.84	C R Nelson	6-28	21.4	- 5.49
A A Scott	6-39	15.4	- 8.40	P A Kelleway	6-40	15.0	- 11.00
R M Whitaker	6-49	12.2	+ 67.80	M McCormack	6-74	8.1	- 28.87
M P Naughton	6-118	5.1	- 73.37				

Selling Non-Handicaps

	W-R	Per cent	£1 Level Stake		W-R	Per cent	£1 Level Stake
J Berry	83-517	16.1	- 122.48	M H Easterby	32-211	15.2	- 94.20
M H Tompkins	26-193	13.5	- 75.61	N Tinkler	20-178	11.2	- 94.38
R Hannon	19-144	13.2	- 18.25	C Tinkler	18-124	14.5	- 41.12
M W Easterby	18-206	8.7	- 103.86	Mrs M Reveley	17-85	20.0	- 0.99
R Hollinshead	16-132	12.1	- 22.71	G Lewis	15-97	15.5	- 5.09
R M Whitaker	15-145	10.3	- 54.59	Mrs J Ramsden	14-84	16.7	- 22.90
M S Johnston	13-94	13.8	- 27.24	N A Callaghan	12-81	14.8	- 13.19
J Wharton	12-90	13.3	+ 15.00	P F I Cole	11-57	19.3	+ 3.32
D Morley	11-72	15.3	- 9.12	W G M Turner	10-108	9.3	- 21.50
Sir M Prescott	9-74	12.2	- 29.34	M R Channon	9-103	8.7	- 38.90
M Brittain	9-172	5.2	- 83.67	M A Jarvis	8-25	32.0	+ 16.75
C N Allen	8-63	12.7	+ 11.50	J Pearce	8-69	11.6	- 28.00
D R Loder	7-9	77.8	+ 16.83	M Feth-Godley	7-43	16.3	+ 14.50
M Bell	7-54	13.0	- 7.50	S Dow	7-64	10.9	- 14.84
J L Harris	7-67	10.4	- 0.37	W Carter	7-67	10.4	- 20.37
T D Barron	7-92	7.6	- 29.87	Ronald Thompson	7-112	6.3	- 47.12

Apprentice Non-Handicaps

	W-R	Per cent	£1 Level Stake		W-R	Per cent	£1 Level Stake
L M Cumani	10-41	24.4	- 21.90	J H M Gosden	9-18	50.0	+ 30.99
B W Hills	9-20	45.0	+ 0.83	Sir M Prescott	6-10	60.0	+ 10.20
G Harwood	5-12	41.7	+ 11.53	H R A Cecil	5-19	26.3	- 7.42
P F I Cole	5-21	23.8	- 9.70	M R Stoute	4-9	44.4	+ 1.59
W J Haggas	3-4	75.0	+ 11.00	C E Brittain	3-7	42.9	+ 8.80
P T Walwyn	3-7	42.9	+ 1.05	G Wragg	3-8	37.5	+ 0.91
M H Tompkins	3-13	23.1	- 3.68	I A Balding	3-14	21.4	+ 0.83
R Hannon	3-16	18.8	- 4.25	B A McMahon	3-22	13.6	+ 8.50
J A R Toller	2-4	50.0	+ 29.00	M C Pipe	2-5	40.0	+ 4.00
M A Jarvis	2-6	33.3	- 1.00	J White	2-6	33.3	+ 3.67
Denys Smith	2-7	28.6	+ 17.00	Mrs M Reveley	2-7	28.6	- 1.43
B Hanbury	2-9	22.2	+ 9.00	J W Hills	2-9	22.2	- 3.20
H Candy	2-10	20.0	+ 8.00	M H Easterby	2-10	20.0	+ 2.50
R M Whitaker	2-12	16.7	- 6.65	A C Stewart	2-12	16.7	- 5.50
M Bell	2-12	16.7	- 6.17	D Morley	2-18	11.1	- 14.09
C A Cyzer	2-18	11.1	- 8.90	R Hollinshead	2-33	6.1	- 21.00

Amateur Non-Handicaps

	W-R	Per cent	£1 Level Stake		W-R	Per cent	£1 Level Stake
B W Hills	5-13	38.5	+ 0.12	G Harwood	5-24	20.8	- 11.28
H R A Cecil	4-9	44.4	+ 3.94	M R Stoute	4-11	36.4	+ 2.30
L M Cumani	3-4	75.0	+ 3.57	M C Pipe	3-5	60.0	+ 1.09
J W Hills	3-6	50.0	+ 6.75	R F J Houghton	3-9	33.3	+ 37.25
J H M Gosden	3-9	33.3	+ 1.63	R Charlton	2-3	66.7	+ 2.88
Lord Huntingdon	2-4	50.0	+ 3.38	J Berry	2-5	40.0	- 0.57
P T Walwyn	2-6	33.3	- 1.00	H Thomson Jones	2-7	28.6	+ 2.67
Sir M Prescott	2-12	16.7	- 8.61	I A Balding	2-13	15.4	+ 18.50
J Pearce	2-13	15.4	+ 2.00				

2-y-o Handicaps

	W–R	Per cent	£1 Level Stake		W–R	Per cent	£1 Level Stake
R Hannon	52-375	13.9	+ 5.06	J Berry	38-325	11.7	- 84.14
M H Easterby	21-156	13.5	+ 11.08	T D Barron	20-112	17.9	+ 19.09
G Lewis	17-120	14.2	+ 11.08	M Bell	17-128	13.3	+ 30.38
J L Dunlop	14-80	17.5	+ 39.58	P F I Cole	13-89	14.6	+ 3.13
N A Callaghan	13-90	14.4	- 21.20	Mrs J Ramsden	13-91	14.3	- 12.00
B W Hills	11-39	28.2	+ 31.48	W A O'Gorman	10-60	16.7	+ 5.00
M S Johnston	9-85	10.6	- 35.37	R Hollinshead	9-131	6.9	- 17.00
M H Tompkins	9-136	6.6	- 79.59	G Harwood	8-37	21.6	- 3.19
Lord Huntingdon	8-48	16.7	+ 0.33	A Bailey	8-64	12.5	+ 12.25
F H Lee	8-65	12.3	+ 1.00	C E Brittain	8-83	9.6	- 2.00
D R C Elsworth	7-24	29.2	+ 34.25	W J Haggas	7-42	16.7	- 6.33
Mrs M Reveley	7-65	10.8	- 3.62	M J Camacho	6-20	30.0	+ 57.50
R Boss	6-41	14.6	- 7.00	M R Stoute	6-50	12.0	- 4.50
G A P-Gordon	6-53	11.3	- 4.00	J R Fanshawe	5-23	21.7	+ 10.38
W R Muir	5-31	16.1	- 1.00	I A Balding	5-43	11.6	- 6.00
M D I Usher	5-54	9.3	- 14.75	Sir M Prescott	5-58	8.6	- 18.00
M W Easterby	5-83	6.0	- 47.00	M R Channon	5-87	5.7	- 28.75

3-y-o Handicaps

	W–R	Per cent	£1 Level Stake		W–R	Per cent	£1 Level Stake
J L Dunlop	106-558	19.0	- 30.40	R Hannon	99-1025	9.7	- 146.39
J Berry	67-541	12.4	- 38.69	B W Hills	66-487	13.6	- 102.06
Sir M Prescott	64-342	18.7	- 21.17	M R Stoute	64-469	13.6	- 98.48
J H M Gosden	60-345	17.4	- 2.60	M S Johnston	59-371	15.9	+ 65.85
H R A Cecil	49-229	21.4	+ 1.39	G Harwood	47-350	13.4	- 83.19
P F I Cole	45-360	12.5	- 59.79	L M Cumani	44-315	14.0	- 52.27
M Bell	42-362	11.6	- 27.02	J W Watts	41-351	11.7	- 77.76
I A Balding	41-365	11.2	- 99.76	M H Easterby	41-464	8.8	- 201.29
C E Brittain	41-500	8.2	- 55.00	A C Stewart	37-216	17.1	- 27.79
F H Lee	36-343	10.5	- 33.39	B Hanbury	35-280	12.5	- 50.84
Mrs J Ramsden	35-336	10.4	- 112.91	P T Walwyn	35-371	9.4	- 45.01
H Thomson Jones	32-287	11.1	+ 5.19	R Akehurst	31-246	12.6	- 38.27
G Lewis	31-332	9.3	- 40.00	M J Ryan	29-258	11.2	- 15.62
M H Tompkins	29-316	9.2	- 145.37	T D Barron	28-309	9.1	- 144.19
R Charlton	26-146	17.8	+ 0.11	D Morley	26-229	11.4	- 37.47
P J Makin	25-172	14.5	- 28.82	A A Scott	25-235	10.6	- 93.02
Mrs M Reveley	24-179	13.4	- 49.46	W Jarvis	24-193	12.4	- 46.12
G Wragg	24-213	11.3	- 43.75	J R Fanshawe	24-219	11.0	- 66.00
M A Jarvis	23-250	9.2	- 112.37	D R C Elsworth	21-201	10.4	- 30.26
Lord Huntingdon	21-247	8.5	- 79.34	R W Armstrong	20-163	12.3	+ 51.24
M R Channon	20-186	10.8	+ 6.66	N A Callaghan	20-228	8.8	- 92.50
S G Norton	20-276	7.2	- 142.15	R Hollinshead	19-410	4.6	- 244.42
W J Haggas	18-129	14.0	+ 14.83	J G FitzGerald	18-166	10.8	- 30.12
J W Hills	18-214	8.4	- 71.67	C J Hill	16-132	12.1	- 12.54
W R Hern	16-147	10.9	- 53.62	M Brittain	16-388	4.1	- 229.42
Mrs L Piggott	15-159	9.4	- 52.75	C A Cyzer	15-176	8.5	- 11.25
R Boss	15-195	7.7	- 97.00	D W P Arbuthnot	15-201	7.5	- 68.00
R F J Houghton	15-228	6.6	- 111.87	R M Whitaker	15-318	4.7	- 194.00
Lady Herries	14-72	19.4	+ 30.60	M J Camacho	14-104	13.5	+ 49.88
M W Easterby	14-163	8.6	- 41.54	S Dow	14-175	8.0	+ 0.83
W A O'Gorman	14-176	8.0	- 87.08	G A P-Gordon	14-183	7.7	- 85.84

	W-R	Per cent	£1 Level Stake		W-R	Per cent	£1 Level Stake
						3-y-o Handicaps	
W Carter	14-211	6.6	- 41.29	Mrs J Cecil	13-89	14.6	+ 38.00
D A Wilson	13-120	10.8	+ 17.00	P C Haslam	13-123	10.6	- 58.26
H J Collingridge	13-147	8.8	- 27.62	P Chapple-Hyam	12-98	12.2	- 4.60
J W Payne	12-118	10.2	- 51.87	L J Holt	12-135	8.9	- 6.00
N Tinkler	12-157	7.6	- 93.36	C F Wall	12-171	7.0	- 85.07
J Wharton	11-98	11.2	+ 11.50	C Tinkler	11-123	8.9	- 37.04
R J R Williams	11-152	7.2	- 62.97	C W C Elsey	11-156	7.1	- 65.04
G B Balding	11-161	6.8	- 39.00	H Candy	11-173	6.4	- 36.50
T J Naughton	10-53	18.9	+ 21.33	M P Naughton	10-78	12.8	- 27.67
E Weymes	10-82	12.2	- 26.71	M McCormack	10-104	9.6	- 28.25
Dr J D Scargill	10-122	8.2	- 47.37	C W Thornton	10-155	6.5	- 59.17

4-y-o+ Handicaps

	W-R	Per cent	£1 Level Stake		W-R	Per cent	£1 Level Stake
R Akehurst	100-668	15.0	+ 26.95	Mrs M Reveley	96-527	18.2	- 4.35
R J Hodges	69-712	9.7	- 164.93	T D Barron	61-522	11.7	- 101.69
R Hollinshead	59-669	8.8	- 149.81	M H Easterby	58-626	9.3	- 258.34
D W Chapman	54-880	6.1	- 373.27	B A McMahon	53-482	11.0	- 3.78
M P Naughton	53-591	9.0	- 149.74	Lord Huntingdon	46-256	18.0	+ 69.18
R M Whitaker	46-543	8.5	- 156.83	I A Balding	42-298	14.1	+ 48.25
M S Johnston	42-439	9.6	- 52.75	D R C Elsworth	41-327	12.5	+ 39.26
M H Tompkins	41-388	10.6	- 82.77	M J Ryan	40-340	11.8	+ 15.88
F H Lee	40-397	10.1	- 80.49	J L Spearing	39-412	9.5	- 126.34
R J O'Sullivan	38-298	12.8	+ 41.13	J Berry	38-380	10.0	- 85.65
Mrs J Ramsden	38-389	9.8	- 156.36	C E Brittain	37-447	8.3	- 78.34
R Hannon	37-447	8.3	- 142.52	J L Dunlop	35-291	12.0	- 43.24
J W Hills	32-256	12.5	+ 10.74	Mrs N Macauley	32-372	8.6	- 75.77
S G Norton	31-169	18.3	+ 37.37	D W P Arbuthnot	31-253	12.3	+ 44.58
C A Cyzer	30-211	14.2	+ 1.54	D A Wilson	30-421	7.1	- 210.99
P F I Cole	29-238	12.2	- 40.87	E J Alston	29-268	10.8	- 22.57
M Brittain	29-577	5.0	- 182.00	P S Felgate	28-248	11.3	- 47.92
C J Hill	28-289	9.7	- 82.08	L G Cottrell	28-341	8.2	- 101.67
J H M Gosden	27-142	19.0	+ 47.34	R Bastiman	27-215	12.6	+ 28.75
W Carter	27-270	10.0	- 80.00	A Bailey	27-280	9.6	- 76.09
J A Glover	26-232	11.2	+ 10.25	G B Balding	26-273	9.5	- 37.01
G Harwood	25-173	14.5	+ 31.01	R J R Williams	25-234	10.7	- 37.40
J D Bethell	25-252	9.9	- 31.12	M A Jarvis	24-171	14.0	- 3.37
Capt J Wilson	24-240	10.0	+ 10.71	B Hanbury	23-137	16.8	+ 38.38
D Morley	23-140	16.4	- 6.08	P Calver	23-170	13.5	+ 39.83
C C Elsey	23-184	12.5	- 16.32	J W Watts	23-218	10.6	- 28.92
M W Easterby	23-220	10.5	- 36.79	C Tinkler	23-226	10.2	- 77.43
G Lewis	23-240	9.6	- 61.37	C J Benstead	23-241	9.5	- 78.42
G M Moore	23-323	7.1	- 92.60	P W Harris	22-108	20.4	+ 80.25
Mrs L Piggott	22-146	15.1	- 9.29	B W Hills	22-163	13.5	- 29.57
M J Camacho	21-152	13.8	- 9.11	P Mitchell	21-213	9.9	- 36.67
W Jarvis	20-139	14.4	+ 10.45	Lady Herries	20-167	12.0	- 25.36
J G FitzGerald	20-189	10.6	- 28.12	M R Channon	20-192	10.4	- 3.50
Denys Smith	20-273	7.3	- 127.33	P Howling	20-415	4.8	- 226.87
M C Pipe	19-137	13.9	- 22.87	Sir M Prescott	19-156	12.2	- 44.88
A Hide	19-159	11.9	+ 52.50	S R Bowring	19-196	9.7	+ 18.00
Pat Mitchell	19-210	9.0	- 42.42	H Candy	19-225	8.4	- 53.87
P T Walwyn	17-120	14.2	+ 19.00	Mrs A Knight	17-146	11.6	+ 3.58
S Dow	17-232	7.3	- 80.62	W J Musson	17-263	6.5	- 138.75

4-y-o+ Handicaps

	W–R	Per cent	£1 Level Stake		W–R	Per cent	£1 Level Stake
R W Armstrong	16-124	12.9	- 11.52	T Thomson Jones	16-127	12.6	+ 1.97
D Morris	16-156	10.3	+ 0.75	E A Wheeler	16-158	10.1	- 8.00
W W Haigh	16-162	9.9	- 28.64	P J Makin	16-163	9.8	+ 5.75
K O C-Brown	16-165	9.7	+ 53.33	Miss L Siddall	16-204	7.8	- 47.17
M Blanshard	16-251	6.4	- 97.00	H J Collingridge	16-258	6.2	- 99.50
B R Millman	16-285	5.6	- 137.00	R Charlton	15-75	20.0	+ 51.13
P C Haslam	15-133	11.3	- 38.96	K T Ivory	15-162	9.3	+ 34.23
J Mackie	15-182	8.2	- 4.50	M O'Neill	15-188	8.0	+ 23.25
C A Horgan	15-191	7.9	- 32.42	J Wharton	15-239	6.3	- 58.80
R C Spicer	14-78	17.9	+ 52.75	N A Callaghan	14-109	12.8	- 25.40
R Boss	14-110	12.7	+ 1.50	M McCormack	14-117	12.0	- 0.75
G A P-Gordon	14-124	11.3	- 22.00	W A O'Gorman	14-140	10.0	- 28.75
Miss B Sanders	14-165	8.5	- 38.50	A P Stringer	13-141	9.2	- 12.00
M D Hammond	13-148	8.8	- 40.24	Dr J D Scargill	13-165	7.9	- 87.14
J Pearce	13-166	7.8	- 76.37	M Feth-Godley	13-169	7.7	- 72.12
W R Hern	12-61	19.7	+ 2.55	G Wragg	12-78	15.4	+ 3.30
J S King	12-94	12.8	- 8.75	M Dods	12-117	10.3	+ 11.60
Miss L A Perrat	12-117	10.3	- 11.00	J White	12-118	10.2	- 8.00
T Casey	12-124	9.7	- 32.67	D Haydn Jones	12-167	7.2	- 66.37
A C Stewart	11-65	16.9	- 7.55	Bob Jones	11-86	12.8	- 12.50
W R Muir	11-124	8.9	- 33.50	J L Harris	11-180	6.1	- 85.25
L J Holt	11-221	5.0	- 115.67	L M Cumani	10-85	11.8	- 22.92
Miss S E Hall	10-99	10.1	- 11.17	R Curtis	10-144	6.9	- 33.37
D T Thom	10-146	6.8	- 79.05	N Tinkler	10-261	3.8	- 167.17

Selling Handicaps

	W–R	Per cent	£1 Level Stake		W–R	Per cent	£1 Level Stake
R Bastiman	12-52	23.1	+ 44.83	J Berry	11-86	12.8	+ 22.50
Mrs J Ramsden	10-53	18.9	+ 5.25	Sir M Prescott	9-47	19.1	+ 17.55
C N Allen	7-44	15.9	+ 17.50	M H Tompkins	7-54	13.0	+ 12.00
D Morley	6-29	20.7	+ 10.71	M P Naughton	6-39	15.4	- 1.07
C A Cyzer	6-39	15.4	+ 15.63	R M Whitaker	6-68	8.8	- 17.00
R Hollinshead	6-69	8.7	- 15.00	R J Hodges	6-72	8.3	- 31.75
P J Feilden	5-35	14.3	+ 21.00	J White	5-38	13.2	- 1.50
D W Chapman	5-86	5.8	- 38.50	J W Hills	4-17	23.5	+ 18.25
R Akehurst	4-18	22.2	+ 12.00	M Blanshard	4-24	16.7	+ 34.00
J Parkes	4-24	16.7	+ 16.00	M O'Neill	4-25	16.0	+ 23.75
C J Hill	4-56	7.1	- 22.67	M H Easterby	4-57	7.0	- 19.87
M Brittain	4-81	4.9	- 38.25	G B Balding	3-11	27.3	+ 21.50
P F I Cole	3-11	27.3	+ 11.25	M A Jarvis	3-14	21.4	+ 7.50
D W P Arbuthnot	3-16	18.8	+ 31.75	J Balding	3-17	17.6	+ 10.25
M J Camacho	3-21	14.3	- 5.00	R J R Williams	3-23	13.0	+ 17.00
Capt J Wilson	3-27	11.1	+ 21.50	A Moore	3-28	10.7	+ 23.00
J Wharton	3-28	10.7	+ 5.00	D A Wilson	3-31	9.7	- 12.42
I Campbell	3-31	9.7	+ 10.00	J G FitzGerald	3-33	9.1	- 5.00
Mrs M Reveley	3-33	9.1	- 14.12	M J Ryan	3-36	8.3	- 6.00
N A Callaghan	3-38	7.9	- 26.50	M D I Usher	3-39	7.7	- 8.50
J L Spearing	3-40	7.5	- 19.50	G Lewis	3-41	7.3	- 19.87
T D Barron	3-45	6.7	- 17.00	M Dixon	2-6	33.3	+ 20.00

Apprentice Handicaps

	W-R	Per cent	£1 Level Stake		W-R	Per cent	£1 Level Stake
Mrs M Reveley	15-58	25.9	+ 20.76	Mrs J Ramsden	11-54	20.4	- 2.04
R J R Williams	10-59	16.9	+ 27.46	J Berry	10-65	15.4	+ 7.54
R Hollinshead	9-105	8.6	- 39.75	F H Lee	8-66	12.1	- 1.25
G Lewis	7-30	23.3	+ 19.50	C A Cyzer	7-39	17.9	+ 35.50
Lord Huntingdon	7-45	15.6	- 21.18	H Candy	7-54	13.0	+ 22.50
D A Wilson	7-63	11.1	- 12.17	R Hannon	7-109	6.4	- 64.62
D T Thom	6-22	27.3	+ 26.25	B W Hills	6-27	22.2	+ 4.48
M W Easterby	6-28	21.4	+ 3.50	D R C Elsworth	6-30	20.0	+ 9.00
A Bailey	6-52	11.5	- 11.67	C J Hill	6-54	11.1	- 14.00
M H Tompkins	6-59	10.2	- 14.00	M Brittain	6-73	8.2	+ 4.75
R J Hodges	6-85	7.1	- 41.42	P J Makin	5-32	15.6	+ 17.50
P C Haslam	5-33	15.2	+ 22.00	J L Spearing	5-38	13.2	- 3.25
J M Bradley	5-40	12.5	+ 12.00	B A McMahon	5-41	12.2	+ 39.00
I A Balding	5-56	8.9	- 17.50	M P Naughton	5-60	8.3	- 10.50
G B Balding	5-63	7.9	+ 1.00	M J Camacho	4-13	30.8	+ 14.25

Amateur Handicaps

	W-R	Per cent	£1 Level Stake		W-R	Per cent	£1 Level Stake
D A Wilson	24-121	19.8	+ 40.50	I A Balding	12-43	27.9	+ 14.34
J Pearce	11-62	17.7	+ 3.88	P F I Cole	7-24	29.2	+ 20.63
G A P-Gordon	5-24	20.8	+ 12.50	S Dow	5-24	20.8	+ 33.50
M J Haynes	5-27	18.5	+ 20.50	Mrs M Reveley	5-35	14.3	0.00
P J Feilden	5-53	9.4	- 8.00	G Harwood	4-42	9.5	- 15.75
J R Bosley	3-13	23.1	+ 22.00	P Mitchell	3-22	13.6	- 10.75
D T Thom	3-22	13.6	+ 12.50	A W Jones	3-26	11.5	+ 11.00
A Hide	3-32	9.4	- 2.00	P Calver	2-4	50.0	+ 8.50
F Jordan	2-4	50.0	+ 15.00	Sir M Prescott	2-5	40.0	+ 5.00
W J Haggas	2-6	33.3	+ 7.38	L G Cottrell	2-7	28.6	+ 13.50
D R C Elsworth	2-10	20.0	+ 0.33	S E Kettlewell	2-10	20.0	+ 14.75
D W P Arbuthnot	2-11	18.2	+ 13.00	Lady Herries	2-12	16.7	+ 2.00
J W Hills	2-12	16.7	+ 0.38	R M Whitaker	2-16	12.5	+ 2.50
F H Lee	2-16	12.5	+ 18.00	M Bell	2-18	11.1	+ 7.00
J Berry	2-19	10.5	+ 4.00	P T Walwyn	2-19	10.5	- 6.00
W J Musson	2-24	8.3	- 15.25	E J Alston	2-26	7.7	- 5.00
H J Collingridge	2-27	7.4	+ 41.00	M P Naughton	2-31	6.5	- 23.00
G B Balding	2-33	6.1	- 14.50	R J Hodges	2-33	6.1	+ 8.00
C Tinkler	2-35	5.7	- 16.50	J L Spearing	2-36	5.6	- 26.75

LEADING TRAINERS' FAVOURITES 1989-1993

	W-R	Per cent	£1 Level Stake	% of Runners that Started Favourite	% of Winners that Started Favourite
H R A Cecil	322-724	44.5	- 56.66	38.4	58.7
J Berry	267-712	37.5	- 9.43	18.3	44.4
M R Stoute	220-561	39.2	- 50.41	25.4	52.8
R Hannon	220-639	34.4	- 16.31	13.6	37.3
J H M Gosden	204-488	41.8	+ 35.13	26.3	48.1
L M Cumani	196-490	40.0	- 46.08	29.9	54.3
B W Hills	169-471	35.9	- 36.44	20.4	43.7
J L Dunlop	167-437	38.2	+ 11.69	18.9	45.1
G Harwood	150-355	42.3	+ 21.19	22.4	53.0
P F I Cole	127-355	35.8	- 37.08	16.8	39.0
Sir M Prescott	118-302	39.1	+ 14.14	23.4	49.4
M H Easterby	114-380	30.0	- 52.92	16.1	44.7
Mrs M Reveley	91-252	36.1	+ 1.28	18.8	42.5
I A Balding	81-246	32.9	- 8.18	14.1	35.5
A C Stewart	69-203	34.0	- 24.71	23.1	52.3
A A Scott	68-166	41.0	+ 27.36	15.5	50.7
M H Tompkins	68-220	30.9	- 32.29	11.7	33.8
T D Barron	67-215	31.2	- 16.28	14.0	35.6
R Charlton	66-174	37.9	+ 0.45	25.1	43.1
W R Hern	64-159	40.3	- 9.75	19.9	50.0
Lord Huntingdon	64-198	32.3	+ 2.20	16.2	35.4
M S Johnston	63-192	32.8	- 3.28	12.2	31.5
W A O'Gorman	62-180	34.4	- 31.25	21.4	44.6
R Akehurst	62-228	27.2	- 0.56	15.6	33.5
Mrs J Ramsden	62-239	25.9	- 36.33	18.3	41.6
R Hollinshead	60-170	35.3	- 6.46	6.1	29.4
H Thomson Jones	59-152	38.8	- 20.16	15.9	36.2
G Wragg	59-173	34.1	- 31.33	16.4	31.4
B Hanbury	59-178	33.1	- 18.90	13.4	31.4
P Chapple-Hyam	55-120	45.8	- 5.86	20.2	45.8
M Bell	53-174	30.5	- 37.75	13.3	32.5
D R C Elsworth	50-164	30.5	- 4.11	11.0	27.3
M A Jarvis	47-124	37.9	+ 11.79	11.1	36.4
G Lewis	47-174	27.0	- 32.26	11.3	27.0
W Jarvis	45-128	35.2	- 14.52	12.4	33.6
P T Walwyn	45-152	29.6	- 34.66	11.6	30.6
P J Makin	44-133	33.1	+ 0.73	16.0	42.3
C E Brittain	43-150	28.7	- 26.19	5.8	18.9
D W Chapman	41-124	33.1	- 10.07	6.9	36.6
N A Callaghan	40-131	30.5	- 3.97	12.9	32.3
J W Watts	38-124	30.6	- 1.82	12.9	38.0
Mrs L Piggott	37-107	34.6	- 2.18	13.8	45.1
J R Fanshawe	35-98	35.7	+ 18.48	12.5	34.3
R W Armstrong	34-92	37.0	+ 1.86	13.0	34.7
M J Camacho	33-64	51.6	+ 53.77	11.4	42.3
R J Hodges	33-130	25.4	- 2.47	9.7	31.4
W J Haggas	32-91	35.2	+ 3.62	13.2	35.6
F H Lee	31-105	29.5	+ 4.17	8.1	25.8
D Morley	31-113	27.4	- 12.67	12.7	29.5
J W Hills	30-120	25.0	- 35.97	11.5	26.5
C R Nelson	29-72	40.3	+ 6.34	13.5	43.3
Mrs J Cecil	28-84	33.3	- 4.76	18.2	36.4
N Tinkler	27-78	34.6	+ 1.10	7.2	34.6

	W-R	Per cent	£1 Level Stake	% of Runners that Started Favourite	% of Winners that Started Favourite
C Tinkler	27-98	27.6	- 7.80	9.3	31.4
M W Easterby	27-105	25.7	- 16.93	8.9	31.4
D R Loder	26-55	47.3	+ 13.35	26.7	55.3
S G Norton	26-82	31.7	- 7.10	7.5	22.0
G A P-Gordon	26-96	27.1	- 5.68	10.0	33.3
R M Whitaker	26-108	24.1	- 11.42	6.3	19.4
R Boss	25-92	27.2	- 13.72	11.4	26.0
J G FitzGerald	24-74	32.4	+ 6.76	8.6	30.4
M C Pipe	24-80	30.0	- 6.51	22.0	38.1
M J Ryan	24-92	26.1	- 7.02	8.9	21.2
M R Channon	24-95	25.3	- 8.05	8.6	23.1
R F J Houghton	23-75	30.7	- 21.46	9.0	29.1
C J Hill	23-81	28.4	- 3.01	9.8	30.3
R J R Williams	23-83	27.7	- 11.26	8.8	28.0
B A McMahon	23-96	24.0	- 19.97	7.2	21.3
P C Haslam	22-63	34.9	- 3.20	10.7	36.7
J Etherington	22-65	33.8	- 3.48	7.7	31.9
Lady Herries	20-53	37.7	+ 10.94	13.3	40.0
D A Wilson	20-77	26.0	+ 2.67	8.9	25.6
J Pearce	19-74	25.7	- 12.43	10.9	29.7
A Bailey	19-75	25.3	- 8.75	8.2	26.8
Miss S E Hall	18-41	43.9	+ 20.11	8.6	38.3
Dr J D Scargill	18-47	38.3	+ 4.40	6.8	35.3
M P Naughton	18-73	24.7	- 10.41	6.9	20.5
Denys Smith	17-42	40.5	+ 14.88	4.5	28.3
C A Cyzer	17-52	32.7	+ 13.43	5.5	18.9
J L Spearing	17-57	29.8	+ 8.64	6.5	26.2
H Candy	17-60	28.3	- 4.57	6.4	20.7
G B Balding	17-85	20.0	- 27.26	9.5	23.3
J Wharton	16-42	38.1	+ 16.64	5.2	22.5
M McCormack	16-57	28.1	+ 4.27	8.0	25.0
P Calver	15-40	37.5	+ 20.35	8.0	29.4
P A Kelleway	15-44	34.1	- 7.13	6.0	26.3
J A Glover	15-44	34.1	+ 14.00	7.3	32.6
C F Wall	14-48	29.2	- 10.02	7.2	27.5
W Carter	14-57	24.6	- 3.41	5.8	17.9
Mrs N Macauley	14-62	22.6	- 10.04	5.3	17.3
R Guest	13-41	31.7	+ 0.51	8.2	30.2
M Brittain	13-52	25.0	- 6.89	2.7	14.4
C N Allen	12-45	26.7	- 8.43	5.6	22.6
P S Felgate	12-47	25.5	- 8.46	8.1	26.1
L J Holt	12-59	20.3	- 7.42	7.6	27.9
E Weymes	11-29	37.9	+ 7.04	6.0	31.4
C J Benstead	11-37	29.7	+ 5.46	6.3	28.9
R J O'Sullivan	11-50	22.0	- 11.37	11.7	21.6
T Thomson Jones	10-31	32.3	+ 3.60	6.7	26.3
C A Horgan	10-34	29.4	+ 8.21	7.7	38.5
R Bastiman	10-36	27.8	+ 7.58	6.8	19.6
S Dow	10-49	20.4	- 15.04	5.0	14.9

TRAINER SECTION

(IRISH FLAT SEASON 1993)

P ASPELL

	No. of Horses	Races Run	1st	2nd	3rd	Unpl	Per cent	£1 Level Stake
2-y-o	3	4	0	0	0	4	-	- 4.00
3-y-o	14	46	4	3	0	39	8.7	- 2.00
4-y-o+	4	20	0	0	2	18	-	- 20.00
Totals	21	70	4	3	2	61	5.7	- 26.00

Mar/Apr	May	Jun	Jul	Aug	Sep	Oct/Nov
1-10	0-8	2-5	0-17	1-8	0-6	0-16

Winning Jockeys	W-R	£1 Level Stake			W-R	£1 Level Stake
W J O'Connor	3-12	+ 23.00	J J Behan		1-31	- 22.00

Winning Courses						
Clonmel	1-1	+ 5.00	Naas		1-5	+ 16.00
Roscommon	1-3	+ 6.00	The Curragh		1-14	- 6.00

Winning Horses	Age	Races Run	1st	2nd	3rd	Unpl	Win £
Weekend Madness	3	3	1	1	0	1	3,450
Limbo Lady	3	4	1	1	0	2	2,762
Overcast	3	8	1	0	0	7	2,417
Drift Apart	3	6	1	1	0	4	2,245

Favourites	0-0	Total winning prize-money	£10,874

1992 Form	0-10

J F BAILEY JNR

	No. of Horses	Races Run	1st	2nd	3rd	Unpl	Per cent	£1 Level Stake
2-y-o	1	4	0	0	0	4	-	- 4.00
3-y-o	2	34	2	0	7	25	5.9	- 13.50
4-y-o+	2	7	0	0	0	7	-	- 7.00
Totals	5	45	2	0	7	36	4.4	- 24.50

Mar/Apr	May	Jun	Jul	Aug	Sep	Oct/Nov
0-7	0-9	0-6	0-6	0-8	2-3	0-6

Winning Jockey	W-R	£1 Level Stake			W-R	£1 Level Stake
R V Skelly	2-13	+ 7.50				

Winning Courses						
Fairyhouse	1-2	+ 3.50	The Curragh		1-11	+ 4.00

Winning Horse	Age	Races Run	1st	2nd	3rd	Unpl	Win £
Bene Merenti	3	23	2	0	5	16	8,280

Favourites	0-1			Total winning prize-money			£8,280
1992 Form	1-20	5.0%	+ 1.00				

J R BANAHAN

	No. of Horses	Races Run	1st	2nd	3rd	Unpl	Per cent	£1 Level Stake
2-y-o	0	0	0	0	0	0	-	0.00
3-y-o	1	5	1	0	0	4	20.0	+ 2.00
4-y-o+	0	0	0	0	0	0	-	0.00
Totals	1	5	1	0	0	4	20.0	+ 2.00

Mar/Apr	May	Jun	Jul	Aug	Sep	Oct/Nov
0-0	0-0	1-1	0-0	0-3	0-1	0-0

Winning Jockey	W-R	£1 Level Stake	Winning Course	W-R	£1 Level Stake
C Roche	1-1	+ 6.00	Gowran Park	1-1	+ 6.00

Winning Horse	Age	Races Run	1st	2nd	3rd	Unpl	Win £
Center Moriches	3	5	1	0	0	4	2,762

Favourites	0-0		Total winning prize-money		£2,762
1992 Form	0-11		1991 Form	0-2	

P BEIRNE

	No. of Horses	Races Run	1st	2nd	3rd	Unpl	Per cent	£1 Level Stake
2-y-o	2	12	1	1	1	9	8.3	- 8.00
3-y-o	4	19	0	1	2	16	-	- 19.00
4-y-o+	0	0	0	0	0	0	-	0.00
Totals	6	31	1	2	3	25	3.2	- 27.00

Mar/Apr	May	Jun	Jul	Aug	Sep	Oct/Nov
0-3	0-9	0-3	1-8	0-4	0-2	0-2

Winning Jockey	W-R	£1 Level Stake	Winning Course	W-R	£1 Level Stake
Joanna Morgan	1-14	- 10.00	Bellewstown	1-2	+ 2.00

Winning Horse	Age	Races Run	1st	2nd	3rd	Unpl	Win £
Summerhill Special	2	8	1	1	1	5	2,935

Favourites	1-1	100.0%	+ 3.00	Total winning prize-money	£2,935

F BERRY

	No. of Horses	Races Run	1st	2nd	3rd	Unpl	Per cent	£1 Level Stake
2-y-o	1	2	0	1	1	0	-	- 2.00
3-y-o	0	0	0	0	0	0	-	0.00
4-y-o+	5	15	2	0	2	11	13.3	- 3.50
Totals	6	17	2	1	3	11	11.8	- 5.50

Mar/Apr	May	Jun	Jul	Aug	Sep	Oct/Nov
0-1	0-1	1-2	1-1	0-1	0-7	0-4

Winning Jockeys	W-R	£1 Level Stake		W-R	£1 Level Stake
Mr D J Kavanagh	1-2	+ 5.50	W J Supple	1-5	- 1.00

Winning Courses					
Clonmel	1-1	+ 3.00	Galway	1-2	+ 5.50

Winning Horse	Age	Races Run	1st	2nd	3rd	Unpl	Win £
Shankorak	6	5	2	0	0	3	13,677

Favourites	1-1	100.0%	+ 3.00	Total winning prize-money	£13,677

1992 Form	0-10		1991 Form	0-12

J S BOLGER

	No. of Horses	Races Run	1st	2nd	3rd	Unpl	Per cent	£1 Level Stake
2-y-o	42	153	27	28	22	76	17.6	- 15.25
3-y-o	48	231	22	33	33	143	9.5	-131.60
4-y-o+	39	136	8	17	8	103	5.9	- 85.34
Totals	129	520	57	78	63	322	11.0	-232.19

BY MONTH

2-y-o	W-R	Per cent	£1 Level Stake	3-y-o	W-R	Per cent	£1 Level Stake
Mar/Apr	2-5	40.0	+ 1.25	Mar/Apr	3-35	8.6	- 25.15
May	1-14	7.1	- 7.00	May	5-35	14.3	- 10.20
June	0-15	-	- 15.00	June	7-41	17.1	- 4.25
July	6-22	27.3	+ 4.75	July	3-29	10.3	- 18.00
August	8-36	22.2	+ 10.40	August	1-48	2.1	- 43.00
September	5-29	17.2	- 5.15	September	2-26	7.7	- 22.00
Oct/Nov	5-32	15.6	- 4.50	Oct/Nov	1-17	5.9	- 9.00

4-y-o+	W-R	Per cent	£1 Level Stake	Totals	W-R	Per cent	£1 Level Stake
Mar/Apr	2-18	11.1	+ 2.00	Mar/Apr	7-58	12.1	- 21.90
May	0-18	-	- 18.00	May	6-67	9.0	- 35.20
June	2-20	10.0	- 11.12	June	9-76	11.8	- 30.37
July	2-27	7.4	- 22.85	July	11-78	14.1	- 36.10
August	1-30	3.3	- 27.37	August	10-114	8.8	- 59.97
September	1-14	7.1	+ 1.00	September	8-69	11.6	- 26.15
Oct/Nov	0-9	-	- 9.00	Oct/Nov	6-58	10.3	- 22.50

DISTANCE

2-y-o	W-R	Per cent	£1 Level Stake	3-y-o	W-R	Per cent	£1 Level Stake
5f-6f	6-55	10.9	- 23.25	5f-6f	3-26	11.5	- 9.50
7f-8f	19-93	20.4	+ 6.25	7f-8f	4-65	6.2	- 46.90
9f-13f	2-5	40.0	+ 1.75	9f-13f	15-127	11.8	- 62.20
14f+	0-0	-	0.00	14f+	0-13	-	- 13.00

4-y-o+	W-R	Per cent	£1 Level Stake	Totals	W-R	Per cent	£1 Level Stake
5f-6f	0-19	-	- 19.00	5f-6f	9-100	9.0	- 51.75
7f-8f	0-35	-	- 35.00	7f-8f	23-193	11.9	- 75.65
9f-13f	5-58	8.6	- 26.12	9f-13f	22-190	11.6	- 86.57
14f+	3-24	12.5	- 5.22	14f+	3-37	8.1	- 18.22

TYPE OF RACE

Non-Handicaps	W-R	Per cent	£1 Level Stake	Handicaps	W-R	Per cent	£1 Level Stake
2-y-o	22-133	16.5	- 35.75	2-y-o	5-20	25.0	+ 20.50
3-y-o	15-160	9.4	- 95.60	3-y-o	7-62	11.3	- 27.00
4-y-o+	3-36	8.3	- 23.10	4-y-o+	3-83	3.6	- 50.25
Apprentice	0-0	-	0.00	Apprentice	0-9	-	- 9.00
Amat/Ladies	2-15	13.3	- 9.99	Amat/Ladies	0-2	-	- 2.00
Totals	42-344	12.2	-164.44	Totals	15-176	8.5	- 67.75

FIRST TIME OUT

	W-R	Per cent	£1 Level Stake
2-y-o	5-42	11.9	- 22.15
3-y-o	4-48	8.3	- 36.35
4-y-o+	2-39	5.1	- 34.97
Totals	11-129	8.5	- 93.47

JOCKEYS RIDING

	W-R	Per cent	£1 Level Stake		W-R	Per cent	£1 Level Stake
C Roche	31-198	15.7	- 72.50	Mr A P O'Brien	1-4	25.0	- 1.62
K J Manning	16-155	10.3	- 81.70	A P McCoy	1-8	12.5	- 4.00
J A Heffernan	6-74	8.1	- 2.00	T E Durcan	1-23	4.3	- 15.00
Mr P Fenton	1-2	50.0	+ 0.63				

M W Martin	0-7	R M Burke	0-3	C McCormack	0-1
B A Hunter	0-6	S Craine	0-3	J F Egan	0-1
Miss C Hutchinson	0-6	W J O'Connor	0-3	Mr F Cooper	0-1
Joanna Morgan	0-4	G M Moylan	0-2	P P Murphy	0-1
D Manning	0-3	Miss I Leahy	0-2	W Carson	0-1
D Quirke	0-3	P V Gilson	0-2	W J Supple	0-1
Mr J A Hayes	0-3	R Fitzpatrick	0-2	W R Swinburn	0-1

COURSE RECORD

	Total W-R	Non-Handicaps 2-y-o	Non-Handicaps 3-y-o+	Handicaps 2-y-o	Handicaps 3-y-o+	Per cent	£1 Level Stake
Leopardstown	12-102	3-22	5-47	1-4	3-29	11.8	- 30.02
The Curragh	11-136	4-38	2-46	1-2	4-50	8.1	- 75.50
Tipperary	6-33	3-9	2-19	0-0	1-5	18.2	- 9.95
Gowran Park	5-29	3-11	2-8	0-4	0-6	17.2	- 1.65
Fairyhouse	4-21	2-6	1-9	0-0	1-6	19.0	- 3.37
Navan	3-16	2-8	1-7	0-0	0-1	18.8	+ 0.25
Naas	3-25	2-5	0-9	1-4	0-7	12.0	- 8.50
Down Royal	2-6	1-4	0-1	0-0	1-1	33.3	- 0.75
Killarney	2-12	0-1	2-7	0-0	0-4	16.7	- 7.70
Galway	2-25	0-7	2-5	0-1	0-12	8.0	- 18.00
Thurles	1-3	0-0	1-2	0-0	0-1	33.3	+ 5.00
Wexford	1-7	0-0	1-5	0-0	0-2	14.3	- 5.60
Mallow	1-9	1-2	0-5	0-0	0-2	11.1	- 5.00
Dundalk	1-12	0-3	1-8	0-0	0-1	8.3	- 10.00
Listowel	1-14	0-4	0-4	1-2	0-4	7.1	- 8.50
Roscommon	1-19	1-6	0-7	0-1	0-5	5.3	- 16.90
Tralee	1-29	0-4	0-9	1-2	0-14	3.4	- 14.00

Clonmel	0-9	Sligo	0-4	Bellewstown	0-2
Limerick	0-4	Punchestown	0-3		

WINNING HORSES

	Age	Races Run	1st	2nd	3rd	Unpl	Win £
Cois Na Tine	2	4	4	0	0	0	33,005
Ivory Frontier	3	3	1	0	0	2	26,250
Zavaleta	2	6	3	1	1	1	24,599
Perfect Impostor	3	3	1	0	1	1	24,000
Kirov Premiere	3	5	3	1	1	0	22,090
Alouette	3	4	2	1	0	1	15,527
Pernilla	3	9	2	1	0	6	14,500
Nordic Fox	3	10	2	0	4	4	10,600

Swift Riposte	2	4	2	0	0	2	9,317
Malvernico	5	7	1	2	0	4	8,725
Shandon Lake	3	1	1	0	0	0	8,625
Clifdon Fog	2	7	2	1	1	3	8,625
Ballykett Lady	3	6	1	3	0	2	8,280
Via Condotti	2	3	2	0	1	0	7,937
Lackel	5	7	1	0	0	6	6,900
Riszard	4	6	2	2	1	1	6,557
Lyphard Abu	5	12	2	2	2	6	6,212
Don't Know	2	8	1	2	0	5	5,520
Specs Appeal	2	3	1	0	1	1	5,244
Cashel Market	2	2	1	0	1	0	5,244
Kly Green	2	4	1	2	0	1	4,830
Solas Abu	3	9	2	1	2	4	4,662
Jomacoon	2	6	1	0	0	5	4,142
Alyreina	3	5	1	1	0	3	4,142
Special Pageant	3	9	1	2	0	6	4,140
Jedwa	2	3	1	1	1	0	4,140
Back From Heaven	2	6	1	1	0	4	3,797
Razida	2	9	1	2	2	4	3,797
Miss Kristin	2	4	1	1	1	1	3,797
Ballykett Nancy	2	3	1	1	0	1	3,797
Tragic Point	2	6	1	3	0	2	3,795
Valona	3	8	1	0	3	4	3,452
Mia Georgina	4	2	1	0	0	1	3,452
Desert Wish	3	2	1	0	0	1	3,450
Albertazzi	3	5	1	2	0	2	3,450
Danita	2	5	1	0	2	2	3,105
Shelwa	2	2	1	0	1	0	3,105
Ferragosto	4	1	1	0	0	0	2,762
Gold Braisim	3	9	1	1	0	7	2,760
Giulio Romano	2	5	1	2	1	1	2,415
Nordic Thorn	3	6	1	1	3	1	2,243

WINNING OWNERS

	Races Won	Value £		Races Won	Value £
Mrs Catherine Shubotham	5	35,199	Mrs Una Manning	1	5,520
Niall Quinn	4	33,005	Des Vere Hunt	1	5,244
Peter J P Gleeson	1	26,250	Maktoum Al Maktoum	1	4,830
Michael W J Smurfit	1	24,000	E R Madden	2	4,662
John L Wood	3	22,090	J David Brillembourg	1	4,142
T F Brennan	4	21,057	Hamad Ali	1	4,140
D H W Dobson	6	20,879	Benners Hotel Syndicate	1	3,797
J P Hill	3	17,250	Exors Of The Late N Keating	1	3,797
Miss K Rausing	2	15,527	Mrs Kristin Cherry Renfroe	1	3,797
Mount Juliet Ltd	2	9,317	Mrs Patricia O'Rourke	1	3,795
Mrs D Mahony	1	8,725	William J Brennan	1	3,452
Mrs J S Bolger	2	8,694	Ms Patricia Reddy	1	3,452
Stephen Keating	1	8,280	Abdullah Ali	1	3,450
Mrs E Kube	1	6,900	Hilal Salem	1	3,105
Henryk De Kwiatkowski	2	6,557	John Hayes	1	3,105
D Bernie	2	6,212	Saeed Suhail	1	2,760

Favourites	27-78	34.6%	- 2.17	Total winning prize-money			£332,990

Longest winning sequence		2	Average SP of winner		4.0/1
Longest losing sequence		33	Return on stakes invested		-44.7%

1992 Form	119-671	17.7%	-160.84	1990 Form	125-562	22.2%	- 95.72
1991 Form	111-622	17.8%	-124.92	1989 Form	80-444	18.0%	- 51.68

LIAM BROWNE

	No. of Horses	Races Run	1st	2nd	3rd	Unpl	Per cent	£1 Level Stake
2-y-o	19	68	8	3	7	50	11.8	+ 1.50
3-y-o	5	23	1	4	0	18	4.3	- 21.20
4-y-o+	6	26	2	3	2	19	7.7	- 21.10
Totals	30	117	11	10	9	87	9.4	- 40.80

BY MONTH

2-y-o	W-R	Per cent	£1 Level Stake	3-y-o	W-R	Per cent	£1 Level Stake
Mar/Apr	0-3	-	- 3.00	Mar/Apr	1-5	20.0	- 3.20
May	2-6	33.3	+ 17.50	May	0-3	-	- 3.00
June	1-9	11.1	- 3.00	June	0-2	-	- 2.00
July	1-6	16.7	- 1.50	July	0-3	-	- 3.00
August	1-12	8.3	+ 1.00	August	0-5	-	- 5.00
September	1-11	9.1	- 6.50	September	0-1	-	- 1.00
Oct/Nov	2-21	9.5	- 3.00	Oct/Nov	0-4	-	- 4.00

4-y-o+	W-R	Per cent	£1 Level Stake	Totals	W-R	Per cent	£1 Level Stake
Mar/Apr	0-2	-	- 2.00	Mar/Apr	1-10	10.0	- 8.20
May	0-0	-	0.00	May	2-9	22.2	+ 14.50
June	0-2	-	- 2.00	June	1-13	7.7	- 7.00
July	0-5	-	- 5.00	July	1-14	7.1	- 9.50
August	1-7	14.3	- 4.00	August	2-24	8.3	- 8.00
September	1-5	20.0	- 3.10	September	2-17	11.8	- 10.60
Oct/Nov	0-5	-	- 5.00	Oct/Nov	2-30	6.7	- 12.00

DISTANCE

2-y-o	W-R	Per cent	£1 Level Stake	3-y-o	W-R	Per cent	£1 Level Stake
5f-6f	4-30	13.3	+ 7.00	5f-6f	0-3	-	- 3.00
7f-8f	4-34	11.8	- 1.50	7f-8f	0-8	-	- 8.00
9f-13f	0-4	-	- 4.00	9f-13f	1-12	8.3	- 10.20
14f+	0-0	-	0.00	14f+	0-0	-	0.00

592

4-y-o+	W-R	Per cent	£1 Level Stake	Totals	W-R	Per cent	£1 Level Stake
5f-6f	0-5	-	- 5.00	5f-6f	4-38	10.5	- 1.00
7f-8f	0-7	-	- 7.00	7f-8f	4-49	8.2	- 16.50
9f-13f	1-7	14.3	- 4.00	9f-13f	2-23	8.7	- 18.20
14f+	1-7	14.3	- 5.10	14f+	1-7	14.3	- 5.10

TYPE OF RACE

Non-Handicaps	W-R	Per cent	£1 Level Stake	Handicaps	W-R	Per cent	£1 Level Stake
2-y-o	7-64	10.9	+ 1.00	2-y-o	1-4	25.0	+ 0.50
3-y-o	1-20	5.0	- 18.20	3-y-o	0-2	-	- 2.00
4-y-o+	1-7	14.3	- 5.10	4-y-o+	1-16	6.3	- 13.00
Apprentice	0-0	-	0.00	Apprentice	0-1	-	- 1.00
Amat/Ladies	0-3	-	- 3.00	Amat/Ladies	0-0	-	0.00
Totals	9-94	9.6	- 25.30	Totals	2-23	8.7	- 15.50

FIRST TIME OUT

	W-R	Per cent	£1 Level Stake
2-y-o	0-19	-	- 19.00
3-y-o	0-5	-	- 5.00
4-y-o+	0-6	-	- 6.00
Totals	0-30	-	- 30.00

JOCKEYS RIDING

	W-R	Per cent	£1 Level Stake		W-R	Per cent	£1 Level Stake
J J Behan	6-37	16.2	+ 2.90	P V Gilson	1-3	33.3	+ 3.00
S Craine	2-23	8.7	- 1.00	R Hughes	1-13	7.7	- 6.50
C Roche	1-2	50.0	- 0.20				

J F Egan	0-7	D Hogan	0-1	P D Carey	0-1
J D Eddery	0-6	J Barcoe	0-1	P P Murphy	0-1
M J Kinane	0-3	K J Manning	0-1	Pat Eddery	0-1
A Ward	0-2	L O'Shea	0-1	R V Skelly	0-1
J Ely	0-2	M Hills	0-1	W J O'Connor	0-1
N G McCullagh	0-2	Miss A Sloane	0-1	W R Swinburn	0-1
W J Supple	0-2	Miss C Cashman	0-1		
B Carson	0-1	Mrs J M Mullins	0-1		

COURSE RECORD

	Total W-R	Non-Handicaps 2-y-o	3-y-o+	Handicaps 2-y-o	3-y-o+	Per cent	£1 Level Stake
Naas	2-8	1-3	0-2	1-3	0-0	25.0	+ 13.50
The Curragh	2-30	2-13	0-8	0-0	0-9	6.7	- 14.50
Clonmel	1-1	0-0	1-1	0-0	0-0	100.0	+ 0.90
Tramore	1-1	0-0	0-0	0-0	1-1	100.0	+ 2.00
Mallow	1-2	0-1	1-1	0-0	0-0	50.0	- 0.20
Dundalk	1-2	1-1	0-0	0-0	0-1	50.0	+ 4.00
Galway	1-3	1-1	0-1	0-0	0-1	33.3	+ 1.50
Punchestown	1-3	1-2	0-0	0-0	0-1	33.3	+ 6.00
Fairyhouse	1-8	1-7	0-1	0-0	0-0	12.5	+ 5.00

Leopardstown	0-19	Roscommon	0-3	Downpatrick	0-1
Gowran Park	0-8	Wexford	0-3	Killarney	0-1
Tipperary	0-7	Ballinrobe	0-2	Laytown	0-1
Tralee	0-6	Limerick	0-2	Sligo	0-1
Listowel	0-3	Navan	0-2		

WINNING HORSES

	Age	Races Run	1st	2nd	3rd	Unpl	Win £
Marvin's Faith	2	3	1	0	1	1	5,250
Sharp Try	2	3	1	0	0	2	5,244
Newport Madam	2	5	1	0	0	4	3,797
Dancing Success	2	4	1	1	1	1	3,797
Sharp Phase	2	3	1	0	0	2	3,795
Miss Provider	2	2	1	0	0	1	3,795
Valid Victress	2	3	1	0	0	2	3,107
Viva Victor	2	6	1	1	1	3	2,762
Simply Marilyn	4	7	1	2	0	4	2,762
Different Times	3	8	1	2	0	5	2,243
Strong Case	5	3	1	1	0	1	2,243

WINNING OWNERS

	Races Won	Value £		Races Won	Value £
Marvin Malmuth	5	20,158	Mrs St J O'Connell	1	2,762
Mrs Anna Doyle	1	3,797	Park Beech Racing Syndicate	1	2,243
Frederick J Ellis	1	3,797	J A Stewart	1	2,243
Park Racing Syndicate	1	3,795			

Favourites	3-10	30.0% - 3.30	Total winning prize-money	£38,795

Longest winning sequence	2	Average SP of winner	5.9/1
Longest losing sequence	24	Return on stakes invested	-34.9%

1992 Form	8-130	6.2%	- 83.04	1990 Form	13-202	6.4% - 121.25
1991 Form	9-128	7.0%	- 43.12	1989 Form	15-184	8.2% - 76.92

P BURKE

	No. of Horses	Races Run	1st	2nd	3rd	Unpl	Per cent	£1 Level Stake
2-y-o	2	10	0	0	0	10	-	- 10.00
3-y-o	2	11	2	0	0	9	18.2	+ 2.33
4-y-o+	1	3	1	0	1	1	33.3	+ 0.25
Totals	5	24	3	0	1	20	12.5	- 7.42

Mar/Apr	May	Jun	Jul	Aug	Sep	Oct/Nov
0-2	0-3	0-2	1-7	2-7	0-1	0-2

Winning Jockey	W-R	£1 Level Stake			W-R	£1 Level Stake
C Roche	3-6	+ 10.58				

Winning Courses						
Killarney	1-1	+ 2.25	Tralee		1-3	+ 1.33
Roscommon	1-2	+ 7.00				

Winning Horses	Age	Races Run	1st	2nd	3rd	Unpl	Win £
Penny A Day	3	7	2	0	0	5	7,102
Big Matt	5	3	1	0	1	1	3,450

Favourites	1-2	50.0%	+ 2.33	Total winning prize-money	£10,552

1992 Form	0-1

J BURNS

	No. of Horses	Races Run	1st	2nd	3rd	Unpl	Per cent	£1 Level Stake
2-y-o	15	33	1	2	5	25	3.0	- 22.00
3-y-o	13	41	0	2	6	33	-	- 41.00
4-y-o+	6	21	0	2	1	18	-	- 21.00
Totals	34	95	1	6	12	76	1.1	- 84.00

Mar/Apr	May	Jun	Jul	Aug	Sep	Oct/Nov
0-11	0-9	1-10	0-30	0-3	0-25	0-7

Winning Jockey	W-R	£1 Level Stake	Winning Course	W-R	£1 Level Stake
N G McCullagh	1-31	- 20.00	Gowran Park	1-5	+ 6.00

Winning Horse	Age	Races Run	1st	2nd	3rd	Unpl	Win £
Memories	2	2	1	0	0	1	3,795

Favourites	0-5		Total winning prize-money	£3,795

1992 Form	7-56	12.5%	- 4.25	1990 Form	0-0
1991 Form	0-0			1989 Form	0-2

A BUTLER

	No. of Horses	Races Run	1st	2nd	3rd	Unpl	Per cent	£1 Level Stake
2-y-o	1	2	1	0	0	1	50.0	+ 3.50
3-y-o	0	0	0	0	0	0	-	0.00
4-y-o+	1	1	0	0	0	1	-	- 1.00
Totals	2	3	1	0	0	2	33.3	+ 2.50

Mar/Apr	May	Jun	Jul	Aug	Sep	Oct/Nov
0-0	0-0	0-0	0-0	0-1	0-0	1-2

Winning Jockey	W-R	£1 Level Stake	Winning Course	W-R	£1 Level Stake
W J Supple	1-1	+ 4.50	The Curragh	1-2	+ 3.50

Winning Horse	Age	Races Run	1st	2nd	3rd	Unpl	Win £
Claradane	2	2	1	0	0	1	5,244

Favourites	0-1		Total winning prize-money		£5,244
1992 Form	0-0		1991 Form	0-9	

J M CANTY

	No. of Horses	Races Run	1st	2nd	3rd	Unpl	Per cent	£1 Level Stake
2-y-o	1	6	0	0	1	5	-	- 6.00
3-y-o	8	30	2	1	1	26	6.7	- 21.50
4-y-o+	7	44	4	2	2	36	9.1	- 20.00
Totals	16	80	6	3	4	67	7.5	- 47.50

Mar/Apr	May	Jun	Jul	Aug	Sep	Oct/Nov
0-6	0-8	0-8	2-15	3-13	1-17	0-13

Winning Jockeys	W-R	£1 Level Stake		W-R	£1 Level Stake
P V Gilson	3-15	+ 4.50	N G McCullagh	1-16	- 12.50
J Reid	1-1	+ 3.50	J P Murtagh	1-19	- 14.00

Winning Courses					
Roscommon	3-7	+ 10.50	Galway	1-5	+ 2.00
Mallow	1-1	+ 2.50	Leopardstown	1-14	- 9.50

Winning Horses	Age	Races Run	1st	2nd	3rd	Unpl	Win £
Sweet Nasha	4	11	3	1	1	6	11,044
Often Ahead	5	7	1	0	0	6	2,935
My Gossip	3	6	1	1	0	4	2,245
Particular	3	6	1	0	1	4	2,243

Favourites	2-3	66.7%	+ 5.00	Total winning prize-money			£18,467
1992 Form	1-58	1.7%	- 56.56	1990 Form	6-55	10.9%	- 28.62
1991 Form	3-72	4.2%	- 40.00	1989 Form	0-57		

MS E CASSIDY

	No. of Horses	Races Run	1st	2nd	3rd	Unpl	Per cent	£1 Level Stake
2-y-o	0	0	0	0	0	0	-	0.00
3-y-o	1	2	0	0	0	2	-	- 2.00
4-y-o+	2	18	1	0	0	17	5.6	- 5.00
Totals	3	20	1	0	0	19	5.0	- 7.00

Mar/Apr	May	Jun	Jul	Aug	Sep	Oct/Nov
0-0	0-0	0-1	0-2	1-5	0-3	0-9

Winning Jockey	W-R	£1 Level Stake	Winning Course	W-R	£1 Level Stake
C Everard	1-5	+ 8.00	Gowran Park	1-1	+ 12.00

Winning Horse	Age	Races Run	1st	2nd	3rd	Unpl	Win £
Brackloon Boy	4	10	1	0	0	9	3,797

Favourites	0-0		Total winning prize-money	£3,797

NOEL T CHANCE

	No. of Horses	Races Run	1st	2nd	3rd	Unpl	Per cent	£1 Level Stake
2-y-o	3	7	0	0	0	7	-	- 7.00
3-y-o	1	10	2	1	1	6	20.0	+ 14.00
4-y-o+	3	14	2	1	1	10	14.3	- 3.90
Totals	7	31	4	2	2	23	12.9	+ 3.10

Mar/Apr	May	Jun	Jul	Aug	Sep	Oct/Nov
0-0	1-2	0-5	2-7	1-6	0-5	0-6

Winning Jockeys	W-R	£1 Level Stake		W-R	£1 Level Stake
Mr J A Nash	1-1	+ 7.00	C Everard	1-3	- 0.90
P Carberry	1-2	+ 5.00	J J Behan	1-4	+ 13.00

Winning Courses					
Downpatrick	1-1	+ 1.10	Laytown	1-2	+ 5.00
Bellewstown	1-1	+ 7.00	Ballinrobe	1-3	+ 14.00

Winning Horses	Age	Races Run	1st	2nd	3rd	Unpl	Win £
Pearl Dawn	3	10	2	1	1	6	4,662
Hacketts Cross	5	10	2	1	1	6	4,142

Favourites	1-2	50.0%	+ 0.10	Total winning prize-money	£8,804

1992 Form	0-21		1990 Form	1-32	3.1%	- 21.00
1991 Form	0-38		1989 Form	4-30	13.3%	- 2.50

C COLLINS

	No. of Horses	Races Run	1st	2nd	3rd	Unpl	Per cent	£1 Level Stake
2-y-o	16	54	5	0	5	44	9.3	- 24.00
3-y-o	20	120	11	14	12	83	9.2	- 63.51
4-y-o+	6	42	6	3	3	30	14.3	+ 5.00
Totals	42	216	22	17	20	157	10.2	- 82.51

BY MONTH

2-y-o	W-R	Per cent	£1 Level Stake	3-y-o	W-R	Per cent	£1 Level Stake
Mar/Apr	0-4	-	- 4.00	Mar/Apr	1-27	3.7	- 12.00
May	2-5	40.0	+ 5.00	May	1-15	6.7	- 13.33
June	1-3	33.3	+ 3.50	June	1-14	7.1	- 11.75
July	1-10	10.0	- 7.50	July	2-20	10.0	- 11.50
August	1-10	10.0	+ 1.00	August	4-21	19.0	- 6.93
September	0-10	-	- 10.00	September	1-10	10.0	- 3.00
Oct/Nov	0-12	-	- 12.00	Oct/Nov	1-13	7.7	- 5.00

4-y-o+	W-R	Per cent	£1 Level Stake	Totals	W-R	Per cent	£1 Level Stake
Mar/Apr	0-11	-	- 11.00	Mar/Apr	1-42	2.4	- 27.00
May	0-10	-	- 10.00	May	3-30	10.0	- 18.33
June	0-4	-	- 4.00	June	2-21	9.5	- 12.25
July	3-4	75.0	+ 22.50	July	6-34	17.6	+ 3.50
August	1-7	14.3	- 2.50	August	6-38	15.8	- 8.43
September	1-2	50.0	+ 3.00	September	2-22	9.1	- 10.00
Oct/Nov	1-4	25.0	+ 7.00	Oct/Nov	2-29	6.9	- 10.00

DISTANCE

2-y-o	W-R	Per cent	£1 Level Stake	3-y-o	W-R	Per cent	£1 Level Stake
5f-6f	4-21	19.0	+ 6.50	5f-6f	1-20	5.0	- 14.00
7f-8f	1-32	3.1	- 29.50	7f-8f	6-56	10.7	- 37.08
9f-13f	0-1	-	- 1.00	9f-13f	4-44	9.1	- 12.43
14f+	0-0	-	0.00	14f+	0-0	-	0.00

4-y-o+	W-R	Per cent	£1 Level Stake	Totals	W-R	Per cent	£1 Level Stake
5f-6f	1-13	7.7	- 7.00	5f-6f	6-54	11.1	- 14.50
7f-8f	1-8	12.5	+ 7.00	7f-8f	8-96	8.3	- 59.58
9f-13f	4-16	25.0	+ 10.00	9f-13f	8-61	13.1	- 3.43
14f+	0-5	-	- 5.00	14f+	0-5	-	- 5.00

Collins C

TYPE OF RACE

Non-Handicaps	W-R	Per cent	£1 Level Stake	Handicaps	W-R	Per cent	£1 Level Stake
2-y-o	5-47	10.6	- 17.00	2-y-o	0-7	-	- 7.00
3-y-o	11-83	13.3	- 26.51	3-y-o	0-36	-	- 36.00
4-y-o+	0-4	-	- 4.00	4-y-o+	4-29	13.8	+ 1.50
Apprentice	0-0	-	0.00	Apprentice	2-10	20.0	+ 6.50
Amat/Ladies	0-0	-	0.00	Amat/Ladies	0-0	-	0.00
Totals	16-134	11.9	- 47.51	Totals	6-82	7.3	- 35.00

FIRST TIME OUT

	W-R	Per cent	£1 Level Stake
2-y-o	0-16	-	- 16.00
3-y-o	0-20	-	- 20.00
4-y-o+	0-6	-	- 6.00
Totals	0-42	-	- 42.00

JOCKEYS RIDING

	W-R	Per cent	£1 Level Stake		W-R	Per cent	£1 Level Stake
P V Gilson	16-140	11.4	- 52.51	R M Burke	2-10	20.0	+ 12.00
P M Donohue	3-21	14.3	+ 0.50	P Shanahan	1-4	25.0	- 1.50

J J Mullins	0-25	Joanna Morgan	0-2	J J Behan	0-1
D G O'Shea	0-3	K J Manning	0-2	P P Murphy	0-1
S Craine	0-3	Ann Corish	0-1		
A C O'Brien	0-2	E A Leonard	0-1		

COURSE RECORD

	Total W-R	Non-Handicaps 2-y-o	3-y-o+	Handicaps 2-y-o	3-y-o+	Per cent	£1 Level Stake
Leopardstown	6-25	2-7	4-12	0-2	0-4	24.0	- 4.43
Sligo	2-6	2-2	0-3	0-0	0-1	33.3	+ 11.50
Mallow	2-7	1-2	1-4	0-0	0-1	28.6	+ 15.00
Tralee	2-10	0-2	2-3	0-0	0-5	20.0	- 5.25
The Curragh	2-56	0-12	1-20	0-2	1-22	3.6	- 37.00
Bellewstown	1-2	0-0	0-0	0-0	1-2	50.0	+ 13.00
Listowel	1-2	0-1	1-1	0-0	0-0	50.0	+ 5.00
Limerick	1-3	0-0	1-2	0-0	0-1	33.3	- 1.33
Down Royal	1-4	0-1	0-1	0-0	1-2	25.0	+ 2.00
Tramore	1-5	0-0	0-1	0-0	1-4	20.0	- 0.50
Dundalk	1-8	0-1	0-4	0-0	1-3	12.5	- 3.00
Ballinrobe	1-8	0-0	0-3	0-0	1-5	12.5	- 2.50
Galway	1-8	0-3	1-3	0-2	0-0	12.5	- 3.00

Navan	0-13	Gowran Park	0-11	Punchestown	0-4
Naas	0-12	Tipperary	0-10	Thurles	0-1
Fairyhouse	0-11	Roscommon	0-8	Wexford	0-1

Collins C

WINNING HORSES

	Age	Races Run	1st	2nd	3rd	Unpl	Win £
The Bower	4	16	5	1	2	8	18,473
Eurostorm	3	8	2	1	0	5	17,250
Bartok	2	5	2	0	2	1	13,455
Bonnie Crathie	2	8	2	0	0	6	4,490
Mayasta	3	6	1	2	1	2	4,140
Monopoly Money	3	5	1	2	0	2	4,052
Ladies Gallery	3	6	1	1	0	4	3,797
Master Tribe	3	5	1	1	2	1	3,795
Kiltimony	3	9	1	2	1	5	3,450
General Chaos	3	8	1	1	0	6	3,450
Abel Tasman	3	5	1	0	2	2	3,450
Never Told	2	4	1	0	2	1	3,107
Teazel Boy	3	3	1	2	0	0	2,245
Touching Moment	3	6	1	0	0	5	2,243
Fantante	4	8	1	0	0	7	1,380

WINNING OWNERS

	Races Won	Value £		Races Won	Value £
Mrs G W Jennings	4	30,705	David F Howard	1	3,450
Mrs C Collins	9	27,793	J N Anthony	1	3,450
J H McLoughlin	1	4,140	Mrs Geraldine Ryan	1	3,107
A McLean	1	4,052	James McNeil	1	2,245
Donal O'Buachalla	1	3,797	Mrs H D McCalmont	1	2,243
Lord Harrington	1	3,795			

Favourites	4-17	23.5%	- 7.51	Total winning prize-money	£88,777
Longest winning sequence		3		Average SP of winner	5.1/1
Longest losing sequence		23		Return on stakes invested	-38.2%
1992 Form	16-167	9.6%	- 78.45	1990 Form 19-255 7.5%	-119.27
1991 Form	22-208	10.6%	- 73.25	1989 Form 32-287 11.1%	-100.64

J G COOGAN

	No. of Horses	Races Run	1st	2nd	3rd	Unpl	Per cent	£1 Level Stake
2-y-o	10	44	2	5	2	35	4.5	- 36.50
3-y-o	11	48	1	2	2	43	2.1	- 39.00
4-y-o+	2	9	0	1	0	8	-	- 9.00
Totals	23	101	3	8	4	86	3.0	- 84.50

Mar/Apr	May	Jun	Jul	Aug	Sep	Oct/Nov
0-8	1-18	1-10	0-18	1-19	0-17	0-11

Winning Jockeys	W-R	£1 Level Stake				W-R	£1 Level Stake
G Coogan	2-14	- 2.50		B Coogan		1-59	- 54.00

Winning Courses							
Mallow	2-7	+ 0.50		The Curragh		1-20	- 11.00

Winning Horses		Age	Races Run	1st	2nd	3rd	Unpl	Win £
Peace Token		2	9	2	2	0	5	5,352
Shoot The Dealer		3	9	1	0	1	7	3,105

Favourites	1-4	25.0%	- 1.50	Total winning prize-money			£8,457

1992 Form	7-75	9.3%	- 41.50	1990 Form	1-26	3.8%	- 18.00
1991 Form	5-67	7.5%	- 16.50	1989 Form	1-15	6.7%	- 5.00

M J CORBETT

	No. of Horses	Races Run	1st	2nd	3rd	Unpl	Per cent	£1 Level Stake
2-y-o	0	0	0	0	0	0	-	0.00
3-y-o	0	0	0	0	0	0	-	0.00
4-y-o+	4	8	1	0	0	7	12.5	+ 1.00
Totals	4	8	1	0	0	7	12.5	+ 1.00

Mar/Apr	May	Jun	Jul	Aug	Sep	Oct/Nov
0-0	0-1	0-2	1-2	0-2	0-1	0-0

Winning Jockey	W-R	£1 Level Stake	Winning Course	W-R	£1 Level Stake
P P Murphy	1-1	+ 8.00	Killarney	1-1	+ 8.00

Winning Horse	Age	Races Run	1st	2nd	3rd	Unpl	Win £
Native Portrait	6	5	1	0	0	4	6,902

Favourites	0-0	Total winning prize-money	£6,902

1992 Form	0-4	1990 Form	0-9		
1991 Form	0-2	1989 Form	1-32	3.1%	- 24.50

M CUNNINGHAM

	No. of Horses	Races Run	1st	2nd	3rd	Unpl	Per cent	£1 Level Stake
2-y-o	1	1	0	0	0	1	-	- 1.00
3-y-o	3	12	2	0	1	9	16.7	+ 3.50
4-y-o+	2	7	0	2	0	5	-	- 7.00
Totals	6	20	2	2	1	15	10.0	- 4.50

Mar/Apr	May	Jun	Jul	Aug	Sep	Oct/Nov
0-0	0-4	0-4	0-5	1-3	0-2	1-2

Winning Jockeys	W-R	£1 Level Stake			W-R	£1 Level Stake
Joanna Morgan	1-1	+ 12.00	B J Walsh		1-1	+ 1.50

Winning Courses						
Tralee	1-1	+ 12.00	Down Royal		1-2	+ 0.50

Winning Horse	Age	Races Run	1st	2nd	3rd	Unpl	Win £
Dairine's Delight	3	9	2	0	1	6	4,832

Favourites	1-2	50.0%	+ 0.50	Total winning prize-money	£4,832

1992 Form	0-54			1990 Form	7-84	8.3%	- 36.75
1991 Form	2-86	2.3%	- 67.00	1989 Form	3-79	3.8%	- 66.00

J P DALY

	No. of Horses	Races Run	1st	2nd	3rd	Unpl	Per cent	£1 Level Stake
2-y-o	1	1	0	0	0	1	-	- 1.00
3-y-o	2	11	1	1	0	9	9.1	- 7.75
4-y-o+	2	9	0	1	2	6	-	- 9.00
Totals	5	21	1	2	2	16	4.8	- 17.75

Mar/Apr	May	Jun	Jul	Aug	Sep	Oct/Nov
0-1	0-2	1-2	0-7	0-7	0-1	0-1

Winning Jockey	W-R	£1 Level Stake	Winning Course	W-R	£1 Level Stake
N G McCullagh	1-9	- 5.75	Ballinrobe	1-2	+ 1.25

Winning Horse	Age	Races Run	1st	2nd	3rd	Unpl	Win £
Goodies Two Step	3	10	1	1	0	8	2,245

Favourites	0-0	Total winning prize-money	£2,245

1992 Form	0-10	1990 Form	0-0
1991 Form	0-0	1989 Form	0-9

F DOYLE

	No. of Horses	Races Run	1st	2nd	3rd	Unpl	Per cent	£1 Level Stake
2-y-o	0	0	0	0	0	0	-	0.00
3-y-o	2	12	1	1	1	9	8.3	+ 14.00
4-y-o+	0	0	0	0	0	0	-	0.00
Totals	2	12	1	1	1	9	8.3	+ 14.00

Mar/Apr	May	Jun	Jul	Aug	Sep	Oct/Nov
0-0	0-1	0-4	0-2	1-4	0-1	0-0

Winning Jockey	W-R	£1 Level Stake	Winning Course	W-R	£1 Level Stake
Mrs C Doyle	1-2	+ 24.00	Leopardstown	1-1	+ 25.00

Winning Horse	Age	Races Run	1st	2nd	3rd	Unpl	Win £
Up She Flew	3	6	1	1	1	3	3,450

Favourites	0-0	Total winning prize-money	£3,450

1992 Form	0-1	1991 Form	0-4

P M DOYLE

	No. of Horses	Races Run	1st	2nd	3rd	Unpl	Per cent	£1 Level Stake
2-y-o	1	1	1	0	0	0	100.0	+ 7.00
3-y-o	0	0	0	0	0	0	-	0.00
4-y-o+	0	0	0	0	0	0	-	0.00
Totals	1	1	1	0	0	0	100.0	+ 7.00

Mar/Apr	May	Jun	Jul	Aug	Sep	Oct/Nov
0-0	1-1	0-0	0-0	0-0	0-0	0-0

Winning Jockey	W-R	£1 Level Stake	Winning Course	W-R	£1 Level Stake
S Craine	1-1	+ 7.00	Tipperary	1-1	+ 7.00

Winning Horse	Age	Races Run	1st	2nd	3rd	Unpl	Win £
Follow The Breeze	2	1	1	0	0	0	2,762

Favourites	0-0	Total winning prize-money	£2,762

F DUNNE

	No. of Horses	Races Run	1st	2nd	3rd	Unpl	Per cent	£1 Level Stake
2-y-o	6	27	2	3	2	20	7.4	+ 8.00
3-y-o	9	42	3	1	8	30	7.1	- 20.50
4-y-o+	3	18	4	2	2	10	22.2	+ 4.50
Totals	18	87	9	6	12	60	10.3	- 8.00

Mar/Apr	May	Jun	Jul	Aug	Sep	Oct/Nov
0-8	3-14	1-15	3-16	1-19	1-12	0-3

Winning Jockeys	W-R	£1 Level Stake		W-R	£1 Level Stake
J P Murtagh	7-46	+ 16.00	N G McCullagh	2-14	+ 3.00

Winning Courses					
Bellewstown	2-4	+ 6.50	Naas	1-8	+ 18.00
Down Royal	2-6	+ 11.00	Roscommon	1-11	- 7.00
Downpatrick	1-2	+ 2.50	The Curragh	1-12	- 3.00
Galway	1-3	+ 5.00			

Winning Horses	Age	Races Run	1st	2nd	3rd	Unpl	Win £
Sense Of Value	4	9	3	0	2	4	5,522
Common Rumpus	2	7	1	2	1	3	5,250
My Ragamuffin	2	10	1	0	1	8	3,797
Glowing Value	3	9	1	0	3	5	3,450
Happy Rover	8	4	1	1	0	2	2,935
Safe Conduct	3	6	1	1	1	3	2,762
Sportstyle	3	4	1	0	0	3	1,380

Favourites	0-3		Total winning prize-money		£25,096

1992 Form	10-138	7.2%	- 53.92	1990 Form	3-55	5.5%	- 39.25
1991 Form	10-139	7.2%	- 47.50	1989 Form	11-96	11.5%	+ 7.25

FRANCIS ENNIS

	No. of Horses	Races Run	1st	2nd	3rd	Unpl	Per cent	£1 Level Stake
2-y-o	0	0	0	0	0	0	-	0.00
3-y-o	1	1	0	0	0	1	-	- 1.00
4-y-o+	3	10	2	0	0	8	20.0	- 1.25
Totals	4	11	2	0	0	9	18.2	- 2.25

Mar/Apr	May	Jun	Jul	Aug	Sep	Oct/Nov
0-2	0-1	0-1	0-1	1-2	1-2	0-2

Winning Jockeys	W-R	£1 Level Stake			W-R	£1 Level Stake
Mr G J Harford	1-1	+ 2.25	C Everard		1-2	+ 3.50

Winning Courses						
Sligo	1-1	+ 2.25	Downpatrick		1-1	+ 4.50

Winning Horses	Age	Races Run	1st	2nd	3rd	Unpl	Win £
Shirwan	4	5	1	0	0	4	2,762
Nora Ann	4	3	1	0	0	2	1,380

Favourites	0-0		Total winning prize-money	£4,142

1992 Form	0-4		1990 Form	0-16
1991 Form	0-15		1989 Form	0-7

OLIVER FINNEGAN

	No. of Horses	Races Run	1st	2nd	3rd	Unpl	Per cent	£1 Level Stake
2-y-o	0	0	0	0	0	0	-	0.00
3-y-o	1	2	0	0	0	2	-	- 2.00
4-y-o+	3	15	1	0	0	14	6.7	- 8.00
Totals	4	17	1	0	0	16	5.9	- 10.00

Mar/Apr	May	Jun	Jul	Aug	Sep	Oct/Nov
0-1	1-6	0-3	0-2	0-1	0-2	0-2

Winning Jockey	W-R	£1 Level Stake	Winning Course	W-R	£1 Level Stake
J J Behan	1-4	+ 3.00	Dundalk	1-4	+ 3.00

Winning Horse	Age	Races Run	1st	2nd	3rd	Unpl	Win £
Ardlea House	4	9	1	0	0	8	2,245

Favourites	0-0			Total winning prize-money	£2,245

1992 Form	1-29	3.4%	- 8.00	1990 Form	0-8
1991 Form	0-11			1989 Form	0-19

F FLOOD

	No. of Horses	Races Run	1st	2nd	3rd	Unpl	Per cent	£1 Level Stake
2-y-o	0	0	0	0	0	0	-	0.00
3-y-o	2	7	1	0	0	6	14.3	+ 4.00
4-y-o+	1	1	0	0	0	1	-	- 1.00
Totals	3	8	1	0	0	7	12.5	+ 3.00

Mar/Apr	May	Jun	Jul	Aug	Sep	Oct/Nov
0-1	0-0	0-0	1-1	0-0	0-3	0-3

Winning Jockey	W-R	£1 Level Stake	Winning Course	W-R	£1 Level Stake
J P Murtagh	1-1	+ 10.00	Galway	1-1	+ 10.00

Winning Horse	Age	Races Run	1st	2nd	3rd	Unpl	Win £
Loughmogue	3	4	1	0	0	3	4,140

Favourites	0-0		Total winning prize-money	£4,140

1992 Form	1-12	8.3%	- 5.00	1990 Form	2-7	28.6%	+ 2.40
1991 Form	3-14	21.4%	+ 11.25	1989 Form	0-7		

P J FLYNN

	No. of Horses	Races Run	1st	2nd	3rd	Unpl	Per cent	£1 Level Stake
2-y-o	11	34	4	0	3	27	11.8	- 7.50
3-y-o	15	97	8	6	10	73	8.2	- 31.25
4-y-o+	13	64	5	8	3	48	7.8	- 34.25
Totals	39	195	17	14	16	148	8.7	- 73.00

BY MONTH

2-y-o	W-R	Per cent	£1 Level Stake	3-y-o	W-R	Per cent	£1 Level Stake
Mar/Apr	0-0	-	0.00	Mar/Apr	0-4	-	- 4.00
May	0-0	-	0.00	May	1-20	5.0	- 16.50
June	1-6	16.7	- 4.50	June	2-13	15.4	- 4.75
July	1-3	33.3	+ 8.00	July	1-15	6.7	- 11.00
August	0-3	-	- 3.00	August	0-13	-	- 13.00
September	1-6	16.7	0.00	September	3-21	14.3	+ 16.00
Oct/Nov	1-16	6.3	- 8.00	Oct/Nov	1-11	9.1	+ 2.00

4-y-o+	W-R	Per cent	£1 Level Stake	Totals	W-R	Per cent	£1 Level Stake
Mar/Apr	1-10	10.0	- 3.50	Mar/Apr	1-14	7.1	- 7.50
May	2-8	25.0	+ 5.75	May	3-28	10.7	- 10.75
June	0-10	-	- 10.00	June	3-29	10.3	- 19.25
July	0-9	-	- 9.00	July	2-27	7.4	- 12.00
August	0-7	-	- 7.00	August	0-23	-	- 23.00
September	0-5	-	- 5.00	September	4-32	12.5	+ 11.00
Oct/Nov	2-15	13.3	- 5.50	Oct/Nov	4-42	9.5	- 11.50

DISTANCE

2-y-o	W-R	Per cent	£1 Level Stake	3-y-o	W-R	Per cent	£1 Level Stake
5f-6f	3-15	20.0	+ 5.50	5f-6f	2-12	16.7	- 3.75
7f-8f	1-17	5.9	- 11.00	7f-8f	3-27	11.1	+ 16.00
9f-13f	0-2	-	- 2.00	9f-13f	3-49	6.1	- 34.50
14f+	0-0	-	0.00	14f+	0-9	-	- 9.00

4-y-o+	W-R	Per cent	£1 Level Stake	Totals	W-R	Per cent	£1 Level Stake
5f-6f	0-3	-	- 3.00	5f-6f	5-30	16.7	- 1.25
7f-8f	1-21	4.8	- 10.00	7f-8f	5-65	7.7	- 5.00
9f-13f	2-19	10.5	- 10.00	9f-13f	5-70	7.1	- 46.50
14f+	2-21	9.5	- 11.25	14f+	2-30	6.7	- 20.25

TYPE OF RACE

Non-Handicaps	W-R	Per cent	£1 Level Stake	Handicaps	W-R	Per cent	£1 Level Stake
2-y-o	4-32	12.5	- 5.50	2-y-o	0-2	-	- 2.00
3-y-o	3-25	12.0	- 13.25	3-y-o	5-66	7.6	- 12.00
4-y-o+	3-21	14.3	- 5.00	4-y-o+	2-32	6.3	- 18.25
Apprentice	0-0	-	0.00	Apprentice	0-10	-	- 10.00
Amat/Ladies	0-3	-	- 3.00	Amat/Ladies	0-4	-	- 4.00
Totals	10-81	12.3	- 26.75	Totals	7-114	6.1	- 46.25

FIRST TIME OUT

	W-R	Per cent	£1 Level Stake
2-y-o	1-11	9.1	- 5.00
3-y-o	0-15	-	- 15.00
4-y-o+	0-13	-	- 13.00
Totals	1-39	2.6	- 33.00

607

JOCKEYS RIDING

	W-R	Per cent	£1 Level Stake		W-R	Per cent	£1 Level Stake
J F Egan	8-93	8.6	- 31.75	J A Heffernan	1-2	50.0	+ 3.00
J R Barry	7-35	20.0	+ 14.25	J P Murtagh	1-6	16.7	+ 0.50

S P Cooke	0-10	P Shanahan	0-2	G M Moylan		0-1
Mr E Norris	0-7	P V Gilson	0-2	J J Stack		0-1
J J Behan	0-6	R Fitzpatrick	0-2	L Piggott		0-1
D G O'Shea	0-4	R V Skelly	0-2	M Duffy		0-1
J D Eddery	0-4	W J Walsh	0-2	M F Ryan		0-1
P P Murphy	0-3	C Roche	0-1	Mr P Fenton		0-1
S Craine	0-3	D Hogan	0-1	W J Supple		0-1
K J Manning	0-2	D J O'Donohoe	0-1			

COURSE RECORD

	Total W-R	Non-Handicaps 2-y-o	3-y-o+	Handicaps 2-y-o	3-y-o+	Per cent	£1 Level Stake
Gowran Park	2-13	1-2	1-5	0-0	0-6	15.4	- 6.00
Naas	2-17	1-7	0-3	0-1	1-6	11.8	+ 2.00
The Curragh	2-29	0-5	1-6	0-0	1-18	6.9	+ 3.50
Thurles	1-3	0-0	1-2	0-0	0-1	33.3	+ 4.00
Sligo	1-3	0-0	1-2	0-0	0-1	33.3	- 0.25
Limerick	1-5	0-0	0-1	0-0	1-4	20.0	- 2.25
Bellewstown	1-5	1-1	0-0	0-0	0-4	20.0	+ 6.00
Roscommon	1-6	1-2	0-1	0-0	0-3	16.7	0.00
Navan	1-7	0-2	0-1	0-0	1-4	14.3	+ 6.00
Fairyhouse	1-7	0-1	0-2	0-0	1-4	14.3	- 1.00
Killarney	1-7	0-1	0-1	0-0	1-5	14.3	- 3.00
Tramore	1-9	0-0	1-2	0-0	0-7	11.1	- 5.50
Leopardstown	1-17	0-3	1-10	0-0	0-4	5.9	- 14.50
Galway	1-17	0-0	0-4	0-0	1-13	5.9	- 12.00

Listowel	0-11	Tralee	0-7	Wexford	0-3
Mallow	0-9	Ballinrobe	0-5	Punchestown	0-2
Tipperary	0-7	Clonmel	0-5	Dundalk	0-1

WINNING HORSES

	Age	Races Run	1st	2nd	3rd	Unpl	Win £
Glenbrack	3	8	3	1	0	4	13,924
Cheviot Amble	5	12	2	2	0	8	12,420
Salmon Eile	5	9	1	0	1	7	8,625
Brazen Angel	3	10	2	0	1	7	6,565
Guided Tour	2	4	1	0	2	1	5,175
Alalja	3	6	1	0	0	5	4,982
Alzuma	2	3	1	0	0	2	3,797
Nurmi	2	4	1	0	1	2	3,107
Lady's Vision	2	3	1	0	0	2	3,105
For Reg	4	6	1	2	0	3	2,760
Mrs Barton	5	6	1	1	1	3	2,245
Blue Diana	3	9	1	0	1	7	2,245
Auld Stock	3	11	1	3	1	6	2,245

WINNING OWNERS

	Races Won	Value £		Races Won	Value £
John Bernard O'Connor	4	18,906	J A O'Gorman	1	5,175
Michael W J Smurfit	3	15,525	E Hannan	1	3,797
Mrs M C O'Connor	1	8,625	D H O'Reilly	1	2,760
Albany Syndicate	2	6,565	Mrs Patrick Flynn	1	2,245
Mrs Anna Doyle	2	5,352	Miss E Kiely	1	2,245

Favourites	4-16	25.0%	- 6.50	Total winning prize-money £71,195
Longest winning sequence			2	Average SP of winner 6.2/1
Longest losing sequence			42	Return on stakes invested -37.4%
1992 Form	22-181	12.2%	- 71.72	1990 Form 15-154 9.7% - 61.27
1991 Form	16-166	9.6%	- 49.37	1989 Form 11-92 12.0% - 19.87

D GILLESPIE

	No. of Horses	Races Run	1st	2nd	3rd	Unpl	Per cent	£1 Level Stake
2-y-o	14	53	3	4	7	39	5.7	- 33.17
3-y-o	16	85	7	4	4	70	8.2	- 23.25
4-y-o+	5	21	0	2	0	19	-	- 21.00
Totals	35	159	10	10	11	128	6.3	- 77.42

BY MONTH

2-y-o	W-R	Per cent	£1 Level Stake	3-y-o	W-R	Per cent	£1 Level Stake
Mar/Apr	0-3	-	- 3.00	Mar/Apr	0-9	-	- 9.00
May	1-7	14.3	- 2.50	May	0-17	-	- 17.00
June	1-5	20.0	- 0.67	June	0-10	-	- 10.00
July	0-12	-	- 12.00	July	3-22	13.6	+ 14.00
August	0-13	-	- 13.00	August	4-14	28.6	+ 11.75
September	1-6	16.7	+ 5.00	September	0-10	-	- 10.00
Oct/Nov	0-7	-	- 7.00	Oct/Nov	0-3	-	- 3.00

4-y-o+	W-R	Per cent	£1 Level Stake	Totals	W-R	Per cent	£1 Level Stake
Mar/Apr	0-5	-	- 5.00	Mar/Apr	0-17	-	- 17.00
May	0-5	-	- 5.00	May	1-29	3.4	- 24.50
June	0-3	-	- 3.00	June	1-18	5.6	- 13.67
July	0-2	-	- 2.00	July	3-36	8.3	0.00
August	0-2	-	- 2.00	August	4-29	13.8	- 3.25
September	0-1	-	- 1.00	September	1-17	5.9	- 6.00
Oct/Nov	0-3	-	- 3.00	Oct/Nov	0-13	-	- 13.00

Gillespie D

DISTANCE

2-y-o	W-R	Per cent	£1 Level Stake	3-y-o	W-R	Per cent	£1 Level Stake
5f-6f	1-23	4.3	- 18.50	5f-6f	2-21	9.5	- 3.50
7f-8f	2-27	7.4	- 11.67	7f-8f	4-28	14.3	+ 11.75
9f-13f	0-3	-	- 3.00	9f-13f	1-35	2.9	- 30.50
14f+	0-0	-	0.00	14f+	0-1	-	- 1.00

4-y-o+	W-R	Per cent	£1 Level Stake	Totals	W-R	Per cent	£1 Level Stake
5f-6f	0-1	-	- 1.00	5f-6f	3-45	6.7	- 23.00
7f-8f	0-6	-	- 6.00	7f-8f	6-61	9.8	- 5.92
9f-13f	0-10	-	- 10.00	9f-13f	1-48	2.1	- 43.50
14f+	0-4	-	- 4.00	14f+	0-5	-	- 5.00

TYPE OF RACE

Non-Handicaps	W-R	Per cent	£1 Level Stake	Handicaps	W-R	Per cent	£1 Level Stake
2-y-o	3-44	6.8	- 24.17	2-y-o	0-9	-	- 9.00
3-y-o	6-43	14.0	+ 5.75	3-y-o	1-40	2.5	- 27.00
4-y-o+	0-2	-	- 2.00	4-y-o+	0-12	-	- 12.00
Apprentice	0-0	-	0.00	Apprentice	0-7	-	- 7.00
Amat/Ladies	0-2	-	- 2.00	Amat/Ladies	0-0	-	0.00
Totals	9-91	9.9	- 22.42	Totals	1-68	1.5	- 55.00

FIRST TIME OUT

	W-R	Per cent	£1 Level Stake
2-y-o	0-14	-	- 14.00
3-y-o	0-16	-	- 16.00
4-y-o+	0-5	-	- 5.00
Totals	0-35	-	- 35.00

JOCKEYS RIDING

	W-R	Per cent	£1 Level Stake		W-R	Per cent	£1 Level Stake
J P Murtagh	3-15	20.0	+ 12.50	P V Gilson	1-7	14.3	+ 6.00
P Shanahan	2-28	7.1	- 12.67	R Hughes	1-8	12.5	+ 5.00
W J Supple	1-4	25.0	+ 0.50	P Carberry	1-9	11.1	- 4.50
S Craine	1-6	16.7	- 2.25				

D Manning	0-25	J J Behan	0-3	P P Murphy	0-2
D G O'Shea	0-10	J M Buckley	0-3	J C Deegan	0-1
G M Moylan	0-9	R V Skelly	0-3	J Cornally	0-1
J F Egan	0-4	B J Walsh	0-2	K J Manning	0-1
R Fitzpatrick	0-4	Joanna Morgan	0-2	Miss C Rogers	0-1
C Roche	0-3	Mr E Kelly	0-2	W J Smith	0-1
J A Heffernan	0-3	N G McCullagh	0-2		

COURSE RECORD

	Total W-R	Non-Handicaps 2-y-o	3-y-o+	Handicaps 2-y-o	3-y-o+	Per cent	£1 Level Stake
Tipperary	3-11	0-4	3-4	0-0	0-3	27.3	+ 16.50
Limerick	1-5	1-1	0-2	0-0	0-2	20.0	- 0.67
Tralee	1-5	0-2	1-1	0-1	0-1	20.0	+ 8.00
Navan	1-6	1-2	0-2	0-0	0-2	16.7	- 1.50
Sligo	1-6	0-2	1-2	0-0	0-2	16.7	- 1.50
Dundalk	1-7	1-2	0-1	0-0	0-4	14.3	+ 4.00
Gowran Park	1-9	0-3	1-4	0-0	0-2	11.1	- 5.25
Naas	1-11	0-3	0-5	0-1	1-2	9.1	+ 2.00

The Curragh	0-32	Fairyhouse	0-5	Listowel	0-1
Leopardstown	0-13	Killarney	0-5	Punchestown	0-1
Galway	0-9	Clonmel	0-4	Thurles	0-1
Mallow	0-8	Bellewstown	0-2	Wexford	0-1
Roscommon	0-7	Down Royal	0-2		
Ballinrobe	0-6	Tramore	0-2		

WINNING HORSES

	Age	Races Run	1st	2nd	3rd	Unpl	Win £
Doreg	3	6	3	1	0	2	14,149
Genuine Bid	2	6	1	1	1	3	4,487
Moonlight Partner	3	9	1	1	0	7	2,762
Alaskan Girl	3	5	1	0	0	4	2,762
Oiche Mhaith	3	10	1	1	1	7	2,760
Oranedin	2	6	1	2	1	2	2,245
Ocean Blue	3	7	1	0	0	6	2,243
Brief Respite	2	5	1	0	1	3	2,243

WINNING OWNERS

	Races Won	Value £		Races Won	Value £
Patrick F Headon	3	14,149	Mrs O O'Connor	1	2,245
Patrick H Burns	2	5,524	Michael H Keogh	1	2,243
M A Ryan	1	4,487	Mrs B Keogh	1	2,243
Mrs J Costelloe	1	2,760			

Favourites	0-5			Total winning prize-money		£33,651
Longest winning sequence		1		Average SP of winner		7.2/1
Longest losing sequence		35		Return on stakes invested		-48.7%
1992 Form	14-199	7.0%	-129.50	1991 Form	17-162	10.5%	- 62.49

J T GORMAN

	No. of Horses	Races Run	1st	2nd	3rd	Unpl	Per cent	£1 Level Stake
2-y-o	6	21	0	0	0	21	-	- 21.00
3-y-o	4	31	2	5	1	23	6.5	- 5.00
4-y-o+	2	22	2	4	0	16	9.1	+ 13.00
Totals	12	74	4	9	1	60	5.4	- 13.00

Mar/Apr	May	Jun	Jul	Aug	Sep	Oct/Nov
1-6	1-11	2-12	0-10	0-9	0-8	0-18

Winning Jockeys	W-R	£1 Level Stake		W-R	£1 Level Stake
R Fitzpatrick	3-44	+ 6.00	P Lowry	1-21	- 10.00

Winning Courses					
Sligo	1-1	+ 14.00	Mallow	1-4	+ 7.00
Naas	1-4	+ 5.00	Leopardstown	1-10	+ 16.00

Winning Horses	Age	Races Run	1st	2nd	3rd	Unpl	Win £
Magic Don	4	15	2	3	0	10	6,212
Slightly Scruffy	3	6	1	1	0	4	2,245
Rafferty's Inner	3	11	1	1	1	8	2,245

Favourites	0-0		Total winning prize-money	£10,702

1992 Form	1-72	1.4%	- 51.00	1990 Form	5-44	11.4%	+ 9.00
1991 Form	2-81	2.5%	- 65.00	1989 Form	0-26		

M J GRASSICK

	No. of Horses	Races Run	1st	2nd	3rd	Unpl	Per cent	£1 Level Stake
2-y-o	9	33	5	3	4	21	15.2	- 7.25
3-y-o	12	63	7	5	10	41	11.1	- 20.37
4-y-o+	7	23	4	1	3	15	17.4	- 6.50
Totals	28	119	16	9	17	77	13.4	- 34.12

BY MONTH

2-y-o	W-R	Per cent	£1 Level Stake	3-y-o	W-R	Per cent	£1 Level Stake
Mar/Apr	0-0	-	0.00	Mar/Apr	0-7	-	- 7.00
May	1-4	25.0	- 0.50	May	2-12	16.7	+ 13.00
June	0-4	-	- 4.00	June	1-9	11.1	- 5.00
July	2-7	28.6	+ 0.25	July	1-10	10.0	- 8.10
August	2-6	33.3	+ 9.00	August	1-12	8.3	- 8.00
September	0-1	-	- 1.00	September	0-6	-	- 6.00
Oct/Nov	0-11	-	- 11.00	Oct/Nov	2-7	28.6	+ 0.73

4-y-o+	W-R	Per cent	£1 Level Stake	Totals	W-R	Per cent	£1 Level Stake
Mar/Apr	0-5	-	- 5.00	Mar/Apr	0-12	-	- 12.00
May	2-10	20.0	- 3.25	May	5-26	19.2	+ 9.25
June	2-4	50.0	+ 5.75	June	3-17	17.6	- 3.25
July	0-2	-	- 2.00	July	3-19	15.8	- 9.85
August	0-2	-	- 2.00	August	3-20	15.0	- 1.00
September	0-0	-	0.00	September	0-7	-	- 7.00
Oct/Nov	0-0	-	0.00	Oct/Nov	2-18	11.1	- 10.27

DISTANCE

2-y-o	W-R	Per cent	£1 Level Stake	3-y-o	W-R	Per cent	£1 Level Stake
5f-6f	4-18	22.2	- 1.25	5f-6f	2-8	25.0	- 2.10
7f-8f	1-12	8.3	- 3.00	7f-8f	2-16	12.5	- 8.00
9f-13f	0-3	-	- 3.00	9f-13f	3-36	8.3	- 7.27
14f+	0-0	-	0.00	14f+	0-3	-	- 3.00

4-y-o+	W-R	Per cent	£1 Level Stake	Totals	W-R	Per cent	£1 Level Stake
5f-6f	0-3	-	- 3.00	5f-6f	6-29	20.7	- 6.35
7f-8f	0-2	-	- 2.00	7f-8f	3-30	10.0	- 13.00
9f-13f	4-15	26.7	+ 1.50	9f-13f	7-54	13.0	- 8.77
14f+	0-3	-	- 3.00	14f+	0-6	-	- 6.00

TYPE OF RACE

Non-Handicaps	W-R	Per cent	£1 Level Stake	Handicaps	W-R	Per cent	£1 Level Stake
2-y-o	5-28	17.9	- 2.25	2-y-o	0-5	-	- 5.00
3-y-o	6-42	14.3	- 3.37	3-y-o	1-19	5.3	- 15.00
4-y-o+	2-4	50.0	+ 2.75	4-y-o+	2-9	22.2	+ 0.75
Apprentice	0-1	-	- 1.00	Apprentice	0-8	-	- 8.00
Amat/Ladies	0-2	-	- 2.00	Amat/Ladies	0-1	-	- 1.00
Totals	13-77	16.9	- 5.87	Totals	3-42	7.1	- 28.25

FIRST TIME OUT

	W-R	Per cent	£1 Level Stake
2-y-o	1-9	11.1	- 5.50
3-y-o	3-12	25.0	+ 19.00
4-y-o+	2-7	28.6	- 0.25
Totals	6-28	21.4	+ 13.25

JOCKEYS RIDING

	W-R	Per cent	£1 Level Stake		W-R	Per cent	£1 Level Stake
R Hughes	7-26	26.9	+ 15.40	W J Supple	2-16	12.5	- 10.25
J F Egan	4-19	21.1	+ 7.00	D Hogan	1-5	20.0	- 3.27
G M Moylan	2-15	13.3	- 5.00				

D G O'Shea	0-7	L O'Shea	0-3	P V Gilson		0-2
T J Daly	0-7	M J Kinane	0-3	G Mylan		0-1
L Piggott	0-5	Mr R Neylon	0-3	S Craine		0-1
N G McCullagh	0-4	N Byrne	0-2			

COURSE RECORD

	Total W-R	Non-Handicaps 2-y-o	3-y-o+	Handicaps 2-y-o	3-y-o+	Per cent	£1 Level Stake
Leopardstown	3-13	0-2	2-6	0-1	1-4	23.1	+ 1.00
Ballinrobe	2-3	1-1	0-1	0-0	1-1	66.7	+ 8.00
Limerick	2-7	0-1	2-3	0-0	0-3	28.6	+ 16.25
Down Royal	2-8	1-2	1-4	0-0	0-2	25.0	- 2.77
Sligo	2-9	1-4	1-3	0-0	0-2	22.2	+ 1.00
Bellewstown	1-2	0-0	1-2	0-0	0-0	50.0	- 0.10
Downpatrick	1-3	0-0	1-3	0-0	0-0	33.3	+ 1.50
Dundalk	1-3	0-1	0-0	0-0	1-2	33.3	+ 0.75
Tralee	1-3	1-1	0-0	0-0	0-2	33.3	+ 6.00
Naas	1-9	1-3	0-4	0-1	0-1	11.1	- 6.75

The Curragh	0-21	Galway	0-2	Laytown	0-1
Mallow	0-9	Gowran Park	0-2	Listowel	0-1
Navan	0-5	Punchestown	0-2	Thurles	0-1
Fairyhouse	0-3	Roscommon	0-2	Tipperary	0-1
Killarney	0-3	Tramore	0-2		
Clonmel	0-2	Wexford	0-2		

WINNING HORSES

	Age	Races Run	1st	2nd	3rd	Unpl	Win £
Danse Royale	3	7	1	1	3	2	12,500
Legal Flair	3	5	1	0	0	4	5,620
Vanishing Prairie	3	2	2	0	0	0	5,175
Coronado	5	3	2	0	1	0	4,490
Ridge Pool	2	4	1	0	1	2	3,795
Mascot	2	5	1	0	1	3	3,452
Sophie's Pet	2	7	1	1	1	4	3,107
Killeen Star	3	8	1	2	0	5	2,762
Two Magpies	6	7	1	0	0	6	2,245
Sirsan	3	5	1	0	0	4	2,245
Markievicz	3	7	1	1	1	4	2,245
Winter's Over	2	4	1	0	0	3	2,243
Long Gallery	2	3	1	1	1	0	2,070
Pretty Nice	5	1	1	0	0	0	1,208

Grassick M J

WINNING OWNERS

	Races Won	Value £		Races Won	Value £
Miss P F O'Kelly	2	18,120	R Fabrizius	1	2,762
Mrs M J Grassick	3	7,245	J M Vander-Poel	1	2,245
Lord White Of Hull	3	6,733	E O'Riordan	1	2,245
H E The President Of Ireland	1	3,795	J Crowley	1	2,245
Rudy Weiss	1	3,452	K M Campbell	1	1,208
Mrs C Grassick	1	3,107			

Favourites	5-13	38.5%	- 0.87	Total winning prize-money		£53,157
Longest winning sequence			2	Average SP of winner		4.3/1
Longest losing sequence			19	Return on stakes invested		-28.7%
1992 Form	14-134	10.4%	- 31.20	1990 Form	16-185	8.6% - 81.70
1991 Form	8-119	6.7%	- 61.50	1989 Form	9-149	6.0% - 98.80

M HALFORD

	No. of Horses	Races Run	1st	2nd	3rd	Unpl	Per cent	£1 Level Stake
2-y-o	8	21	0	3	1	17	-	- 21.00
3-y-o	7	30	2	3	4	21	6.7	- 19.00
4-y-o+	6	17	3	1	3	10	17.6	- 0.50
Totals	21	68	5	7	8	48	7.4	- 40.50

Mar/Apr	May	Jun	Jul	Aug	Sep	Oct/Nov
0-2	0-11	0-4	3-14	0-10	2-18	0-9

Winning Jockeys	W-R	£1 Level Stake		W-R	£1 Level Stake
P V Gilson	3-25	- 8.50	W J Smith	1-4	+ 2.00
M J Kinane	1-1	+ 4.00			

Winning Courses	W-R	£1 Level Stake		W-R	£1 Level Stake
Killarney	2-5	+ 5.50	Downpatrick	1-4	+ 2.00
Bellewstown	1-3	0.00	Galway	1-7	+ 1.00

Winning Horses	Age	Races Run	1st	2nd	3rd	Unpl	Win £
Steel Mirror	4	3	1	0	0	2	3,452
Pulmicort	3	8	1	0	2	5	3,450
Fortune's Girl	5	2	1	0	1	0	3,450
Angareb	4	6	1	1	1	3	2,762
Sunset Cafe	3	6	1	2	2	1	1,380

Favourites	2-4	50.0%	+ 4.50	Total winning prize-money		£14,494
1992 Form	5-103	4.9%	- 79.17	1990 Form	3-87	3.4% - 64.00
1991 Form	6-79	7.6%	- 40.75	1989 Form	7-74	9.5% - 13.50

615

D HANLEY

	No. of Horses	Races Run	1st	2nd	3rd	Unpl	Per cent	£1 Level Stake
2-y-o	2	4	0	0	0	4	-	- 4.00
3-y-o	6	18	5	4	0	9	27.8	+ 8.25
4-y-o+	2	11	3	0	0	8	27.3	+ 40.00
Totals	10	33	8	4	0	21	24.2	+ 44.25

Mar/Apr	May	Jun	Jul	Aug	Sep	Oct/Nov
0-0	0-0	1-2	3-6	1-8	1-7	2-10

Winning Jockeys	W-R	£1 Level Stake		W-R	£1 Level Stake
N G McCullagh	5-19	+ 42.25	K J Manning	1-1	+ 8.00
R Hughes	2-5	+ 2.00			

Winning Courses					
The Curragh	2-12	+ 14.00	Navan	1-2	+ 1.25
Tipperary	1-1	+ 12.00	Listowel	1-2	+ 5.00
Dundalk	1-1	+ 8.00	Galway	1-3	+ 14.00
Roscommon	1-1	+ 1.00			

Winning Horses	Age	Races Run	1st	2nd	3rd	Unpl	Win £
Rosie's Mac	4	5	2	0	0	3	20,627
Be My Hope	4	6	1	0	0	5	16,752
Dinesen	3	3	2	1	0	0	6,040
Corporate Sport	3	2	1	0	0	1	4,685
Tales Of Hearsay	3	7	1	2	0	4	2,760
Trouble Shoot	3	2	1	0	0	1	2,245

Favourites	2-4	50.0%	+ 1.25	Total winning prize-money		£53,109

1992 Form	5-35	14.3%	- 7.90	1990 Form	0-6		
1991 Form	3-22	13.6%	+ 1.50	1989 Form	1-8	12.5%	- 1.00

J C HARLEY

	No. of Horses	Races Run	1st	2nd	3rd	Unpl	Per cent	£1 Level Stake
2-y-o	6	18	2	4	2	10	11.1	- 0.50
3-y-o	6	18	1	1	2	14	5.6	- 7.00
4-y-o+	5	37	3	8	4	22	8.1	- 19.50
Totals	17	73	6	13	8	46	8.2	- 27.00

Mar/Apr	May	Jun	Jul	Aug	Sep	Oct/Nov
0-10	1-13	1-5	1-13	1-16	1-11	1-5

Winning Jockey	W-R	£1 Level Stake		W-R	£1 Level Stake
R M Burke	6-61	- 15.00			

Winning Courses					
Roscommon	1-1	+ 3.50	Sligo	1-4	+ 9.00
Limerick	1-2	+ 9.00	Dundalk	1-4	+ 2.50
Wexford	1-2	+ 6.00	Galway	1-6	- 3.00

Winning Horses		Age	Races Run	1st	2nd	3rd	Unpl	Win £
Sensitive King		5	5	2	1	0	2	6,557
Share A Dream		2	3	1	0	0	2	2,935
My Trelawny		3	3	1	0	1	1	2,245
Tinco Paleno		9	11	1	2	1	7	2,245
Tongabezi		2	5	1	2	1	1	2,243

Favourites	1-3	33.3%	0.00	Total winning prize-money		£16,225

1992 Form	4-79	5.1%	- 48.75

E P HARTY

	No. of Horses	Races Run	1st	2nd	3rd	Unpl	Per cent	£1 Level Stake
2-y-o	3	5	0	0	0	5	-	- 5.00
3-y-o	1	10	2	1	2	5	20.0	- 4.20
4-y-o+	3	11	1	1	1	8	9.1	- 8.00
Totals	7	26	3	2	3	18	11.5	- 17.20

Mar/Apr	May	Jun	Jul	Aug	Sep	Oct/Nov
0-1	0-2	0-2	2-9	1-6	0-4	0-2

Winning Jockeys	W-R	£1 Level Stake		W-R	£1 Level Stake
M J Kinane	1-1	+ 3.00	C Everard	1-3	0.00
L Piggott	1-3	- 1.20			

Winning Courses					
Down Royal	1-1	+ 0.80	Tipperary	1-2	+ 2.00
Tramore	1-1	+ 2.00			

Winning Horses	Age	Races Run	1st	2nd	3rd	Unpl	Win £
Elizabeth's Pet	3	10	2	1	2	5	4,832
This Is My Life	4	6	1	1	0	4	2,245

Favourites	3-3	100.0%	+ 5.80	Total winning prize-money		£7,077

1992 Form	0-15			1990 Form	4-41	9.8%	- 21.00
1991 Form	4-61	6.6%	+ 2.50	1989 Form	2-48	4.2%	- 41.93

JOHN HOUGHTON

	No. of Horses	Races Run	1st	2nd	3rd	Unpl	Per cent	£1 Level Stake
2-y-o	1	5	0	0	0	5	-	- 5.00
3-y-o	1	5	0	0	1	4	-	- 5.00
4-y-o+	2	5	1	0	0	4	20.0	+ 2.00
Totals	4	15	1	0	1	13	6.7	- 8.00

Mar/Apr	May	Jun	Jul	Aug	Sep	Oct/Nov
0-0	0-0	1-2	0-3	0-1	0-4	0-5

Winning Jockey	W-R	£1 Level Stake	Winning Course	W-R	£1 Level Stake
Miss O Glennon	1-3	+ 4.00	Gowran Park	1-2	+ 5.00

Winning Horse	Age	Races Run	1st	2nd	3rd	Unpl	Win £
Keppols Prince	6	4	1	0	0	3	2,762

Favourites	0-0		Total winning prize-money	£2,762

1992 Form	0-9		1991 Form	0-13

G T HOURIGAN

	No. of Horses	Races Run	1st	2nd	3rd	Unpl	Per cent	£1 Level Stake
2-y-o	3	10	2	0	3	5	20.0	+ 1.00
3-y-o	0	0	0	0	0	0	-	0.00
4-y-o+	1	6	1	0	1	4	16.7	+ 2.00
Totals	4	16	3	0	4	9	18.8	+ 3.00

Mar/Apr	May	Jun	Jul	Aug	Sep	Oct/Nov
0-0	0-0	0-3	1-5	1-3	1-1	0-4

Winning Jockeys	W-R	£1 Level Stake		W-R	£1 Level Stake
P V Gilson	1-1	+ 4.00	S Craine	1-6	+ 2.00
R Hughes	1-3	+ 3.00			

Winning Courses					
Ballinrobe	2-2	+ 12.00	The Curragh	1-4	+ 1.00

Winning Horses	Age	Races Run	1st	2nd	3rd	Unpl	Win £
Slick Dealer	2	3	1	0	1	1	3,795
Mulmus	2	5	1	0	2	2	3,107
Junorius	4	6	1	0	1	4	2,245

Favourites	0-1			Total winning prize-money	£9,147

1992 Form	1-21	4.8%	- 6.00	1991 Form	0-5

M HOURIGAN

	No. of Horses	Races Run	1st	2nd	3rd	Unpl	Per cent	£1 Level Stake
2-y-o	0	0	0	0	0	0	-	0.00
3-y-o	2	3	1	0	1	1	33.3	+ 8.00
4-y-o+	2	3	0	0	1	2	-	- 3.00
Totals	4	6	1	0	2	3	16.7	+ 5.00

Mar/Apr	May	Jun	Jul	Aug	Sep	Oct/Nov
0-1	0-1	0-1	0-0	1-1	0-0	0-2

Winning Jockey	W-R	£1 Level Stake	Winning Course	W-R	£1 Level Stake
R M Burke	1-1	+ 10.00	Tralee	1-1	+ 10.00

Winning Horse	Age	Races Run	1st	2nd	3rd	Unpl	Win £
Tropical Lake	3	2	1	0	1	0	3,797

Favourites	0-0		Total winning prize-money	£3,797

1992 Form	0-10		1990 Form	0-3
1991 Form	0-0		1989 Form	0-6

D T HUGHES

	No. of Horses	Races Run	1st	2nd	3rd	Unpl	Per cent	£1 Level Stake
2-y-o	0	0	0	0	0	0	-	0.00
3-y-o	8	42	5	5	1	31	11.9	- 12.50
4-y-o+	12	29	2	1	6	20	6.9	- 15.00
Totals	20	71	7	6	7	51	9.9	- 27.50

Mar/Apr	May	Jun	Jul	Aug	Sep	Oct/Nov
0-4	1-8	1-8	0-10	3-12	2-14	0-15

Winning Jockeys	W-R	£1 Level Stake		W-R	£1 Level Stake
R Hughes	3-34	- 15.50			
Miss C E Hyde	1-1	+ 3.00	P Carberry	1-5	+ 1.00
G M Moylan	1-5	+ 4.00	P P Murphy	1-15	- 9.00

Winning Courses					
The Curragh	2-12	+ 4.50	Tramore	1-3	+ 3.00
Mallow	1-1	+ 4.00	Gowran Park	1-4	+ 2.00
Fairyhouse	1-3	+ 1.00	Dundalk	1-4	+ 2.00

Winning Horses	Age	Races Run	1st	2nd	3rd	Unpl	Win £
State Princess	3	10	3	2	0	5	8,110
Touchdown	6	13	2	1	3	7	4,662
Return Again	3	6	1	2	0	3	3,450
Cortija Park	3	7	1	1	0	5	2,245

Favourites	0-9			Total winning prize-money			£18,467

1992 Form	3-40	7.5%	- 11.00	1990 Form	2-65	3.1%	- 55.67
1991 Form	0-45			1989 Form	5-49	10.2%	- 9.75

M KAUNTZE

	No. of Horses	Races Run	1st	2nd	3rd	Unpl	Per cent	£1 Level Stake
2-y-o	12	37	5	6	6	20	13.5	+ 6.00
3-y-o	13	69	8	6	8	47	11.6	- 11.83
4-y-o+	4	21	0	4	1	16	-	- 21.00
Totals	29	127	13	16	15	83	10.2	- 26.83

BY MONTH

2-y-o	W-R	Per cent	£1 Level Stake	3-y-o	W-R	Per cent	£1 Level Stake
Mar/Apr	0-1	-	- 1.00	Mar/Apr	2-7	28.6	+ 8.00
May	2-5	40.0	+ 13.00	May	1-15	6.7	- 7.00
June	2-4	50.0	0.00	June	1-10	10.0	- 6.00
July	0-4	-	- 4.00	July	1-10	10.0	- 8.33
August	1-8	12.5	+ 13.00	August	0-7	-	- 7.00
September	0-7	-	- 7.00	September	2-7	28.6	+ 8.50
Oct/Nov	0-8	-	- 8.00	Oct/Nov	1-13	7.7	0.00

4-y-o+	W-R	Per cent	£1 Level Stake	Totals	W-R	Per cent	£1 Level Stake
Mar/Apr	0-4	-	- 4.00	Mar/Apr	2-12	16.7	+ 3.00
May	0-4	-	- 4.00	May	3-24	12.5	+ 2.00
June	0-3	-	- 3.00	June	3-17	17.6	- 9.00
July	0-4	-	- 4.00	July	1-18	5.6	- 16.33
August	0-4	-	- 4.00	August	1-19	5.3	+ 2.00
September	0-1	-	- 1.00	September	2-15	13.3	+ 0.50
Oct/Nov	0-1	-	- 1.00	Oct/Nov	1-22	4.5	- 9.00

DISTANCE

2-y-o	W-R	Per cent	£1 Level Stake	3-y-o	W-R	Per cent	£1 Level Stake
5f-6f	3-14	21.4	+ 5.50	5f-6f	0-6	-	- 6.00
7f-8f	2-23	8.7	+ 0.50	7f-8f	6-23	26.1	+ 21.50
9f-13f	0-0	-	0.00	9f-13f	2-39	5.1	- 26.33
14f+	0-0	-	0.00	14f+	0-1	-	- 1.00

4-y-o+	W-R	Per cent	£1 Level Stake	Totals	W-R	Per cent	£1 Level Stake
5f-6f	0-0	-	0.00	5f-6f	3-20	15.0	- 0.50
7f-8f	0-0	-	0.00	7f-8f	8-46	17.4	+ 22.00
9f-13f	0-18	-	- 18.00	9f-13f	2-57	3.5	- 44.33
14f+	0-3	-	- 3.00	14f+	0-4	-	- 4.00

TYPE OF RACE

Non-Handicaps	W-R	Per cent	£1 Level Stake	Handicaps	W-R	Per cent	£1 Level Stake
2-y-o	5-35	14.3	+ 8.00	2-y-o	0-2	-	- 2.00
3-y-o	4-35	11.4	- 1.00	3-y-o	4-33	12.1	- 9.83
4-y-o+	0-7	-	- 7.00	4-y-o+	0-9	-	- 9.00
Apprentice	0-0	-	0.00	Apprentice	0-4	-	- 4.00
Amat/Ladies	0-1	-	- 1.00	Amat/Ladies	0-1	-	- 1.00
Totals	9-78	11.5	- 1.00	Totals	4-49	8.2	- 25.83

FIRST TIME OUT

	W-R	Per cent	£1 Level Stake
2-y-o	2-12	16.7	+ 18.00
3-y-o	3-13	23.1	+ 10.00
4-y-o+	0-4	-	- 4.00
Totals	5-29	17.2	+ 24.00

JOCKEYS RIDING

	W-R	Per cent	£1 Level Stake		W-R	Per cent	£1 Level Stake
W J O'Connor	7-49	14.3	- 8.00	P Carberry	1-6	16.7	+ 2.00
P V Gilson	2-18	11.1	- 0.50	R M Burke	1-6	16.7	+ 15.00
R Hughes	2-20	10.0	- 7.33				

T G Hagger	0-7	Miss S Kauntze	0-2	J J Behan	0-1
W J Supple	0-5	W Carson	0-2	L Piggott	0-1
N G McCullagh	0-4	D G O'Shea	0-1	M Roberts	0-1
J P Murtagh	0-2	F Woods	0-1	Pat Eddery	0-1

COURSE RECORD

	Total W-R	Non-Handicaps 2-y-o	3-y-o+	Handicaps 2-y-o	3-y-o+	Per cent	£1 Level Stake
The Curragh	3-35	2-10	1-14	0-0	0-11	8.6	+ 6.00
Down Royal	2-7	0-1	1-2	0-0	1-4	28.6	- 1.33
Tipperary	2-12	1-4	0-4	0-0	1-4	16.7	- 6.50

Leopardstown	2-22	1-6	0-5	0-1	1-10	9.1		0.00
Galway	1-3	0-0	0-2	0-0	1-1	33.3	+	1.50
Naas	1-5	0-2	1-2	0-0	0-1	20.0	+	3.00
Dundalk	1-6	1-1	0-3	0-0	0-2	16.7	-	3.50
Fairyhouse	1-8	0-3	1-3	0-0	0-2	12.5	+	3.00

Navan	0-9	Wexford	0-2	Listowel	0-1
Gowran Park	0-6	Bellewstown	0-1	Punchestown	0-1
Tramore	0-3	Downpatrick	0-1	Roscommon	0-1
Tralee	0-2	Killarney	0-1	Sligo	0-1

WINNING HORSES

	Age	Races Run	1st	2nd	3rd	Unpl	Win £
Kurdistan	3	10	2	1	2	5	10,350
The Puzzler	2	5	1	1	2	1	8,725
Majestic Role	2	1	1	0	0	0	8,625
Flame Of Persia	3	13	2	0	1	10	6,900
Danish	2	4	1	1	0	2	5,522
Wave The Wand	2	4	1	1	0	2	3,797
Colour Party	3	5	1	0	0	4	3,450
Devil's Holiday	3	7	1	1	1	4	3,450
La Berta	2	5	1	1	1	2	3,107
Sans Ceriph	3	7	1	2	1	3	2,762
Miss Twin Peaks	3	5	1	0	1	3	1,380

WINNING OWNERS

	Races Won	Value £		Races Won	Value £
C S Gaisford-St Lawrence	3	13,800	Sheikh Mohammed	1	3,450
Major Victor McCalmont	2	9,319	Mrs M Cattaneo	1	3,107
Lady Richard Wellesley	1	8,725	Lady Clague	1	2,762
M Haga	1	8,625	Mrs H H Morriss	1	1,380
E Flynn	2	6,900			

Favourites	4-17	23.5%	- 7.33	Total winning prize-money			£58,068
Longest winning sequence			3	Average SP of winner			6.7/1
Longest losing sequence			19	Return on stakes invested			-21.1%
1992 Form	16-142	11.3%	- 55.33	1990 Form	29-226	12.8%	- 60.94
1991 Form	19-184	10.3%	- 86.80	1989 Form	19-193	9.8%	- 93.66

E J KEARNS

	No. of Horses	Races Run	1st	2nd	3rd	Unpl	Per cent	£1 Level Stake
2-y-o	0	0	0	0	0	0	-	0.00
3-y-o	0	0	0	0	0	0	-	0.00
4-y-o+	1	9	1	0	1	7	11.1	- 2.00
Totals	1	9	1	0	1	7	11.1	- 2.00

Mar/Apr	May	Jun	Jul	Aug	Sep	Oct/Nov
0-0	1-2	0-1	0-1	0-0	0-3	0-2

Winning Jockey	W-R	£1 Level Stake	Winning Course	W-R	£1 Level Stake
C Everard	1-2	+ 5.00	Tramore	1-1	+ 6.00

Winning Horse	Age	Races Run	1st	2nd	3rd	Unpl	Win £
Tranquil Beauty	4	9	1	0	1	7	2,245

Favourites	0-1		Total winning prize-money		£2,245
1992 Form	0-12		1990 Form	0-0	
1991 Form	0-3		1989 Form	1-2	50.0% + 32.00

B V KELLY

	No. of Horses	Races Run	1st	2nd	3rd	Unpl	Per cent	£1 Level Stake
2-y-o	4	13	0	0	0	13	-	- 13.00
3-y-o	5	20	0	1	1	18	-	- 20.00
4-y-o+	6	31	6	1	5	19	19.4	+ 36.50
Totals	15	64	6	2	6	50	9.4	+ 3.50

Mar/Apr	May	Jun	Jul	Aug	Sep	Oct/Nov
3-10	0-7	0-5	3-7	0-13	0-8	0-14

Winning Jockeys	W-R	£1 Level Stake		W-R	£1 Level Stake
S Craine	4-20	+ 13.50	P P Murphy	1-3	+ 5.00
P Carberry	1-2	+ 24.00			

Winning Courses	W-R	£1 Level Stake		W-R	£1 Level Stake
Ballinrobe	2-2	+ 29.00	Mallow	1-3	+ 5.00
Galway	2-4	+ 20.00	Bellewstown	1-3	+ 1.50

Winning Horses	Age	Races Run	1st	2nd	3rd	Unpl	Win £
Fontanays	5	11	3	1	2	5	8,283
Mejeve	5	9	2	0	2	5	7,075
The Main Choice	4	1	1	0	0	0	2,243

Favourites	2-6	33.3% + 3.50	Total winning prize-money		£17,601
1992 Form	4-98	4.1% - 73.67	1990 Form	4-76	5.3% - 54.75
1991 Form	9-107	8.4% - 27.00	1989 Form	8-62	12.9% - 13.00

D P KELLY

	No. of Horses	Races Run	1st	2nd	3rd	Unpl	Per cent	£1 Level Stake
2-y-o	2	3	0	0	0	3	-	- 3.00
3-y-o	2	9	1	0	1	7	11.1	- 1.00
4-y-o+	7	35	3	3	6	23	8.6	- 6.50
Totals	11	47	4	3	7	33	8.5	- 10.50

Mar/Apr	May	Jun	Jul	Aug	Sep	Oct/Nov
1-6	0-5	2-7	0-2	0-5	0-7	1-15

Winning Jockeys	W-R	£1 Level Stake		W-R	£1 Level Stake
N G McCullagh	1-1	+ 14.00	P Carberry	1-4	+ 5.00
Joanna Morgan	1-4	+ 4.00	W J Supple	1-8	- 3.50

Winning Courses					
The Curragh	3-21	+ 6.50	Gowran Park	1-2	+ 7.00

Winning Horses	Age	Races Run	1st	2nd	3rd	Unpl	Win £
Cons Prince	3	3	1	0	1	1	3,105
Three Musketeers	4	6	1	0	1	4	3,105
Lord Glenvara	5	6	1	0	2	3	2,762
Macquarie Ridge	5	8	1	1	2	4	2,417

Favourites	1-5	20.0%	- 0.50	Total winning prize-money	£11,389

1992 Form	3-35	8.6%	+ 10.00	1991 Form	0-14

T F LACY

	No. of Horses	Races Run	1st	2nd	3rd	Unpl	Per cent	£1 Level Stake
2-y-o	1	4	0	0	0	4	-	- 4.00
3-y-o	9	52	3	1	5	43	5.8	- 19.00
4-y-o+	8	30	4	1	4	21	13.3	+ 5.00
Totals	18	86	7	2	9	68	8.1	- 18.00

Mar/Apr	May	Jun	Jul	Aug	Sep	Oct/Nov
1-11	1-12	3-16	0-15	1-13	1-14	0-5

Winning Jockeys	W-R	£1 Level Stake		W-R	£1 Level Stake
P J Smullen	4-52	- 11.50	D G O'Shea	1-8	+ 5.00
J A Heffernan	2-4	+ 10.50			

Winning Courses					
Naas	2-9	+ 13.00	Tralee	1-8	+ 3.00
Navan	1-6	+ 3.00	Dundalk	1-9	- 3.50
Listowel	1-7	+ 8.00	Leopardstown	1-10	- 4.50

Winning Horses	Age	Races Run	1st	2nd	3rd	Unpl	Win £
Ferrycarrig Hotel	4	8	3	1	0	4	11,732
Fairydel	3	10	1	0	0	9	3,797
Bellissi	3	10	1	1	3	5	3,450
Bobadil	3	11	1	0	1	9	2,762
Vicosa	4	9	1	0	2	6	2,245

Favourites	0-1			Total winning prize-money			£23,986

1992 Form	3-87	3.4%	- 75.25	1990 Form	2-62	3.2%	- 51.00
1991 Form	0-89			1989 Form	1-73	1.4%	- 64.00

B LAWLOR

	No. of Horses	Races Run	1st	2nd	3rd	Unpl	Per cent	£1 Level Stake
2-y-o	2	4	1	2	0	1	25.0	+ 8.00
3-y-o	4	16	0	0	0	16	-	- 16.00
4-y-o+	2	7	0	0	0	7	-	- 7.00
Totals	8	27	1	2	0	24	3.7	- 15.00

Mar/Apr	May	Jun	Jul	Aug	Sep	Oct/Nov
0-8	0-4	1-4	0-2	0-3	0-4	0-2

Winning Jockey	W-R	£1 Level Stake	Winning Course	W-R	£1 Level Stake
D V Smith	1-6	+ 6.00	The Curragh	1-7	+ 5.00

Winning Horse	Age	Races Run	1st	2nd	3rd	Unpl	Win £
Tango Trio	2	2	1	1	0	0	5,244

Favourites	0-0		Total winning prize-money	£5,244

1992 Form	0-10			1990 Form	0-5
1991 Form	2-13	15.4%	+ 1.50	1989 Form	0-3

AUGUSTINE LEAHY

	No. of Horses	Races Run	1st	2nd	3rd	Unpl	Per cent	£1 Level Stake
2-y-o	4	18	0	1	1	16	-	- 18.00
3-y-o	6	27	0	1	4	22	-	- 27.00
4-y-o+	11	44	2	3	8	31	4.5	- 27.00
Totals	21	89	2	5	13	69	2.2	- 72.00

Mar/Apr	May	Jun	Jul	Aug	Sep	Oct/Nov
0-5	1-11	0-13	0-14	0-19	1-13	0-14

Leahy Augustine

Winning Jockeys	W-R	£1 Level Stake		W-R	£1 Level Stake
D G O'Shea	1-5	+ 2.00	B Fenton	1-40	- 30.00

Winning Courses	W-R	£1 Level Stake		W-R	£1 Level Stake
Clonmel	1-7	+ 3.00	Listowel	1-10	- 3.00

Winning Horses	Age	Races Run	1st	2nd	3rd	Unpl	Win £
Woodfield Rose	4	9	1	1	1	6	3,795
Solba	4	2	1	0	0	1	2,245

Favourites	0-4			Total winning prize-money			£6,040
1992 Form	8-91	8.8%	- 44.67	1990 Form	11-107	10.3%	- 31.50
1991 Form	1-106	0.9%	- 91.00	1989 Form	3-65	4.6%	- 49.50

EDWARD LYNAM

	No. of Horses	Races Run	1st	2nd	3rd	Unpl	Per cent	£1 Level Stake
2-y-o	6	16	0	3	1	12	-	- 16.00
3-y-o	14	87	6	8	8	65	6.9	- 26.50
4-y-o+	1	7	2	2	0	3	28.6	+ 14.00
Totals	21	110	8	13	9	80	7.3	- 28.50

Mar/Apr	May	Jun	Jul	Aug	Sep	Oct/Nov
0-15	2-11	0-16	3-18	0-19	1-18	2-13

Winning Jockeys	W-R	£1 Level Stake		W-R	£1 Level Stake
R Hughes	2-9	+ 6.00	J A Heffernan	1-6	+ 3.00
R M Burke	1-1	+ 14.00	N G McCullagh	1-16	+ 1.00
P Carberry	1-3	- 0.50	N Byrne	1-20	- 12.00
P V Gilson	1-4	+ 11.00			

Winning Courses	W-R	£1 Level Stake		W-R	£1 Level Stake
Naas	2-8	+ 18.00	Listowel	1-4	+ 11.00
Killarney	1-1	+ 16.00	Down Royal	1-5	- 1.00
Punchestown	1-1	+ 8.00	Dundalk	1-7	- 4.50
Tramore	1-3	+ 5.00			

Winning Horses	Age	Races Run	1st	2nd	3rd	Unpl	Win £
Kar Or	3	6	1	0	0	5	6,900
Rustic-Ort	5	7	2	2	0	3	4,830
Commodity Market	3	6	1	0	1	4	4,140
Miss Anita	3	2	1	0	0	1	3,452
Sara Maurette	3	9	1	0	1	7	2,895
Kentucky Baby	3	15	1	1	1	12	2,760
Relentless Boy	3	5	1	1	1	2	2,245

Favourites	1-9	11.1%	- 5.00	Total winning prize-money			£27,222
1992 Form	5-92	5.4%	- 35.50	1990 Form	4-144	2.8%	-127.67
1991 Form	1-93	1.1%	- 87.50	1989 Form	3-79	3.8%	- 56.00

NIALL MADDEN

	No. of Horses	Races Run	1st	2nd	3rd	Unpl	Per cent	£1 Level Stake
2-y-o	0	0	0	0	0	0	-	0.00
3-y-o	0	0	0	0	0	0	-	0.00
4-y-o+	2	14	1	0	1	12	7.1	- 3.00
Totals	2	14	1	0	1	12	7.1	- 3.00

Mar/Apr	May	Jun	Jul	Aug	Sep	Oct/Nov
0-0	0-1	0-1	0-3	1-4	0-4	0-1

Winning Jockey	W-R	£1 Level Stake	Winning Course	W-R	£1 Level Stake
P Carberry	1-3	+ 8.00	Tramore	1-3	+ 8.00

Winning Horse	Age	Races Run	1st	2nd	3rd	Unpl	Win £
Morning Nurse	4	8	1	0	1	6	2,836

Favourites	0-0		Total winning prize-money	£2,836

1992 Form	0-3	1991 Form	0-1

C P MAGNIER

	No. of Horses	Races Run	1st	2nd	3rd	Unpl	Per cent	£1 Level Stake
2-y-o	0	0	0	0	0	0	-	0.00
3-y-o	0	0	0	0	0	0	-	0.00
4-y-o+	5	25	1	2	1	21	4.0	- 8.00
Totals	5	25	1	2	1	21	4.0	- 8.00

Mar/Apr	May	Jun	Jul	Aug	Sep	Oct/Nov
0-2	0-5	0-5	1-6	0-3	0-1	0-3

Winning Jockey	W-R	£1 Level Stake	Winning Course	W-R	£1 Level Stake
L O'Shea	1-10	+ 7.00	Bellewstown	1-2	+ 15.00

Winning Horse	Age	Races Run	1st	2nd	3rd	Unpl	Win £
Afterglow	4	9	1	0	1	7	2,762

Favourites	0-1		Total winning prize-money	£2,762

1992 Form	2-17	11.8%	- 3.00	1990 Form	0-12
1991 Form	0-14			1989 Form	0-1

P MARTIN

	No. of Horses	Races Run	1st	2nd	3rd	Unpl	Per cent	£1 Level Stake
2-y-o	2	3	0	0	0	3	-	- 3.00
3-y-o	3	8	0	1	0	7	-	- 8.00
4-y-o+	5	19	1	1	1	16	5.3	- 6.00
Totals	10	30	1	2	1	26	3.3	- 17.00

Mar/Apr	May	Jun	Jul	Aug	Sep	Oct/Nov
0-3	0-4	0-6	0-3	1-4	0-4	0-6

Winning Jockey	W-R	£1 Level Stake	Winning Course	W-R	£1 Level Stake
C Everard	1-8	+ 5.00	Roscommon	1-2	+ 11.00

Winning Horse	Age	Races Run	1st	2nd	3rd	Unpl	Win £
Toast And Honey	4	5	1	0	0	4	2,245

Favourites	0-0			Total winning prize-money	£2,245

1992 Form	3-45	6.7%	- 12.50	1990 Form	0-14		
1991 Form	1-21	4.8%	- 4.00	1989 Form	1-40	2.5%	- 29.00

PEADAR MATTHEWS

	No. of Horses	Races Run	1st	2nd	3rd	Unpl	Per cent	£1 Level Stake
2-y-o	2	9	1	0	0	8	11.1	0.00
3-y-o	4	10	0	0	0	10	-	- 10.00
4-y-o+	0	0	0	0	0	0	-	0.00
Totals	6	19	1	0	0	18	5.3	- 10.00

Mar/Apr	May	Jun	Jul	Aug	Sep	Oct/Nov
0-3	0-3	0-2	0-1	0-3	0-1	1-6

Winning Jockey	W-R	£1 Level Stake	Winning Course	W-R	£1 Level Stake
J F Egan	1-6	+ 3.00	Naas	1-2	+ 7.00

Winning Horse	Age	Races Run	1st	2nd	3rd	Unpl	Win £
Quintiliani	2	4	1	0	0	3	3,795

Favourites	0-0			Total winning prize-money	£3,795

1992 Form	0-21			1990 Form	0-28		
1991 Form	1-3	33.3%	+ 18.00	1989 Form	1-27	3.7%	- 16.00

A J MAXWELL

	No. of Horses	Races Run	1st	2nd	3rd	Unpl	Per cent	£1 Level Stake
2-y-o	5	13	2	0	0	11	15.4	+ 2.50
3-y-o	1	5	0	0	0	5	-	- 5.00
4-y-o+	3	18	0	0	1	17	-	- 18.00
Totals	9	36	2	0	1	33	5.6	- 20.50

Mar/Apr	May	Jun	Jul	Aug	Sep	Oct/Nov
0-1	0-4	0-6	0-6	0-8	1-6	1-5

Winning Jockey	W-R	£1 Level Stake			W-R	£1 Level Stake
R Hughes	2-2	+ 13.50				

Winning Courses						
Gowran Park	1-1	+ 3.50	Leopardstown		1-7	+ 4.00

Winning Horse	Age	Races Run	1st	2nd	3rd	Unpl	Win £
Broadmara	2	2	2	0	0	0	18,170

Favourites	0-0		Total winning prize-money	£18,170

1992 Form	0-58		1991 Form	3-37	8.1%	- 10.00

D G MCARDLE

	No. of Horses	Races Run	1st	2nd	3rd	Unpl	Per cent	£1 Level Stake
2-y-o	0	0	0	0	0	0	-	0.00
3-y-o	1	2	0	0	0	2	-	- 2.00
4-y-o+	3	22	1	0	1	20	4.5	- 5.00
Totals	4	24	1	0	1	22	4.2	- 7.00

Mar/Apr	May	Jun	Jul	Aug	Sep	Oct/Nov
0-1	0-3	0-3	0-3	0-2	1-5	0-7

Winning Jockey	W-R	£1 Level Stake	Winning Course	W-R	£1 Level Stake
D A O'Sullivan	1-4	+ 13.00	Galway	1-1	+ 16.00

Winning Horse	Age	Races Run	1st	2nd	3rd	Unpl	Win £
Sutton Centenary	5	10	1	0	1	8	3,452

Favourites	0-0		Total winning prize-money	£3,452

1992 Form	0-5

PETER MCCREERY

	No. of Horses	Races Run	1st	2nd	3rd	Unpl	Per cent	£1 Level Stake
2-y-o	4	12	0	0	1	11	-	- 12.00
3-y-o	2	15	2	0	0	13	13.3	+ 15.00
4-y-o+	4	19	0	0	0	19	-	- 19.00
Totals	10	46	2	0	1	43	4.3	- 16.00

Mar/Apr	May	Jun	Jul	Aug	Sep	Oct/Nov
1-5	0-4	1-10	0-11	0-6	0-7	0-3

Winning Jockey	W-R	£1 Level Stake			W-R	£1 Level Stake
J A Heffernan	2-16	+ 14.00				

Winning Courses						
Dundalk	1-3	+ 12.00	Down Royal		1-6	+ 9.00

Winning Horse	Age	Races Run	1st	2nd	3rd	Unpl	Win £
Bobross	3	9	2	0	0	7	3,453

Favourites	0-0		Total winning prize-money		£3,453

1992 Form	0-16			1990 Form	2-27	7.4%	- 1.00
1991 Form	0-3			1989 Form	2-18	11.1%	+ 6.00

NEIL S MCGRATH

	No. of Horses	Races Run	1st	2nd	3rd	Unpl	Per cent	£1 Level Stake
2-y-o	5	24	0	2	3	19	-	- 24.00
3-y-o	3	16	1	0	1	14	6.3	- 10.00
4-y-o+	1	5	0	1	0	4	-	- 5.00
Totals	9	45	1	3	4	37	2.2	- 39.00

Mar/Apr	May	Jun	Jul	Aug	Sep	Oct/Nov
0-4	1-9	0-6	0-3	0-8	0-10	0-5

Winning Jockey	W-R	£1 Level Stake	Winning Course	W-R	£1 Level Stake
R Hughes	1-7	- 1.00	Tramore	1-2	+ 4.00

Winning Horse	Age	Races Run	1st	2nd	3rd	Unpl	Win £
Any Minute Now	3	6	1	0	0	5	2,245

Favourites	0-1		Total winning prize-money		£2,245

1992 Form	3-51	5.9%	- 14.00	1990 Form	3-43	7.0%	- 29.50
1991 Form	0-32			1989 Form	6-70	8.6%	- 15.75

MALACHY McKENNA

	No. of Horses	Races Run	1st	2nd	3rd	Unpl	Per cent	£1 Level Stake
2-y-o	0	0	0	0	0	0	-	0.00
3-y-o	0	0	0	0	0	0	-	0.00
4-y-o+	1	12	1	0	1	10	8.3	+ 3.00
Totals	1	12	1	0	1	10	8.3	+ 3.00

Mar/Apr	May	Jun	Jul	Aug	Sep	Oct/Nov
0-2	1-2	0-1	0-3	0-2	0-1	0-1

Winning Jockey	W-R	£1 Level Stake	Winning Course	W-R	£1 Level Stake
Joanna Morgan	1-5	+ 10.00	Navan	1-2	+ 13.00

Winning Horse	Age	Races Run	1st	2nd	3rd	Unpl	Win £
Southern Rule	6	12	1	0	1	10	2,762

Favourites	0-1		Total winning prize-money	£2,762

1992 Form	0-17	1990 Form	0-6
1991 Form	0-0	1989 Form	0-5

H McMAHON

	No. of Horses	Races Run	1st	2nd	3rd	Unpl	Per cent	£1 Level Stake
2-y-o	1	1	0	0	0	1	-	- 1.00
3-y-o	2	14	0	0	0	14	-	- 14.00
4-y-o+	3	16	3	2	0	11	18.8	+ 4.88
Totals	6	31	3	2	0	26	9.7	- 10.12

Mar/Apr	May	Jun	Jul	Aug	Sep	Oct/Nov
0-5	0-4	0-5	1-5	0-4	1-5	1-3

Winning Jockeys	W-R	£1 Level Stake		W-R	£1 Level Stake
J J Behan	2-8	+ 10.50	R V Skelly	1-1	+ 1.38

Winning Courses					
Listowel	1-1	+ 1.38	Naas	1-5	+ 8.00
Killarney	1-2	+ 3.50			

Winning Horse	Age	Races Run	1st	2nd	3rd	Unpl	Win £
Thatching Craft	4	14	3	2	0	9	16,217

Favourites	1-1	100.0%	+ 1.38	Total winning prize-money	£16,217

1992 Form	2-35	5.7%	- 23.50	1990 Form	0-8
1991 Form	0-20				

E MCNAMARA

	No. of Horses	Races Run	1st	2nd	3rd	Unpl	Per cent	£1 Level Stake
2-y-o	3	15	0	0	2	13	-	- 15.00
3-y-o	2	14	1	2	1	10	7.1	- 7.00
4-y-o+	2	2	0	0	0	2	-	- 2.00
Totals	7	31	1	2	3	25	3.2	- 24.00

Mar/Apr	May	Jun	Jul	Aug	Sep	Oct/Nov
0-0	0-2	0-4	0-9	0-9	1-6	0-1

Winning Jockey	W-R	£1 Level Stake	Winning Course	W-R	£1 Level Stake
R M Burke	1-2	+ 5.00	Clonmel	1-2	+ 5.00

Winning Horse	Age	Races Run	1st	2nd	3rd	Unpl	Win £
Millers Mill	3	11	1	1	1	8	2,243

Favourites	0-1	Total winning prize-money	£2,243

1992 Form	0-13	1990 Form	0-2
1991 Form	0-18	1989 Form	0-3

NOEL MEADE

	No. of Horses	Races Run	1st	2nd	3rd	Unpl	Per cent	£1 Level Stake
2-y-o	15	46	1	5	4	36	2.2	- 39.00
3-y-o	19	106	13	16	12	65	12.3	+ 7.00
4-y-o+	12	42	7	8	6	21	16.7	+ 16.00
Totals	46	194	21	29	22	122	10.8	- 16.00

BY MONTH

2-y-o	W-R	Per cent	£1 Level Stake	3-y-o	W-R	Per cent	£1 Level Stake
Mar/Apr	0-1	-	- 1.00	Mar/Apr	0-16	-	- 16.00
May	0-2	-	- 2.00	May	2-17	11.8	+ 1.00
June	0-4	-	- 4.00	June	1-16	6.3	- 1.00
July	0-7	-	- 7.00	July	5-23	21.7	+ 17.75
August	0-4	-	- 4.00	August	4-15	26.7	+ 16.25
September	1-12	8.3	- 5.00	September	1-8	12.5	0.00
Oct/Nov	0-16	-	- 16.00	Oct/Nov	0-11	-	- 11.00

4-y-o+	W-R	Per cent	£1 Level Stake	Totals	W-R	Per cent	£1 Level Stake
Mar/Apr	0-4	-	- 4.00	Mar/Apr	0-21	-	- 21.00
May	1-7	14.3	- 3.00	May	3-26	11.5	- 4.00
June	0-7	-	- 7.00	June	1-27	3.7	- 12.00
July	2-8	25.0	+ 16.00	July	7-38	18.4	+ 26.75
August	2-7	28.6	+ 5.50	August	6-26	23.1	+ 17.75
September	1-4	25.0	+ 11.00	September	3-24	12.5	+ 6.00
Oct/Nov	1-5	20.0	- 2.50	Oct/Nov	1-32	3.1	- 29.50

DISTANCE

2-y-o	W-R	Per cent	£1 Level Stake	3-y-o	W-R	Per cent	£1 Level Stake
5f-6f	0-20	-	- 20.00	5f-6f	0-8	-	- 8.00
7f-8f	1-26	3.8	- 19.00	7f-8f	3-38	7.9	- 9.00
9f-13f	0-0	-	0.00	9f-13f	9-53	17.0	+ 23.00
14f+	0-0	-	0.00	14f+	1-7	14.3	+ 1.00

4-y-o+	W-R	Per cent	£1 Level Stake	Totals	W-R	Per cent	£1 Level Stake
5f-6f	0-1	-	- 1.00	5f-6f	0-29	-	- 29.00
7f-8f	2-17	11.8	+ 9.00	7f-8f	6-81	7.4	- 19.00
9f-13f	4-15	26.7	+ 13.50	9f-13f	13-68	19.1	+ 36.50
14f+	1-9	11.1	- 5.50	14f+	2-16	12.5	- 4.50

TYPE OF RACE

Non-Handicaps	W-R	Per cent	£1 Level Stake	Handicaps	W-R	Per cent	£1 Level Stake
2-y-o	1-43	2.3	- 36.00	2-y-o	0-3	-	- 3.00
3-y-o	3-35	8.6	- 7.75	3-y-o	10-63	15.9	+ 22.75
4-y-o+	3-14	21.4	+ 19.00	4-y-o+	3-24	12.5	- 2.50
Apprentice	0-0	-	0.00	Apprentice	0-8	-	- 8.00
Amat/Ladies	1-2	50.0	+ 1.50	Amat/Ladies	0-2	-	- 2.00
Totals	8-94	8.5	- 23.25	Totals	13-100	13.0	+ 7.25

FIRST TIME OUT

	W-R	Per cent	£1 Level Stake
2-y-o	0-15	-	- 15.00
3-y-o	0-19	-	- 19.00
4-y-o+	0-12	-	- 12.00
Totals	0-46	-	- 46.00

JOCKEYS RIDING

	W-R	Per cent	£1 Level Stake		W-R	Per cent	£1 Level Stake
P Carberry	15-89	16.9	+ 40.50	Mr S R Murphy	1-3	33.3	+ 0.50
R Hughes	4-27	14.8	+ 10.00	Joanna Morgan	1-5	20.0	+ 3.00

S Craine	0-32	J J Behan	0-2	N Carlisle	0-1
N G McCullagh	0-8	C F Swan	0-1	P Shanahan	0-1
W J Supple	0-4	J Cornally	0-1	R M Burke	0-1
J A Heffernan	0-3	K J Manning	0-1	R V Skelly	0-1
J F Egan	0-3	L O'Shea	0-1	T P Treacy	0-1
P P Murphy	0-3	M Cornally	0-1	W Carson	0-1
R Fitzpatrick	0-3	Mrs A Ferris	0-1		

COURSE RECORD

	Total W-R	Non-Handicaps 2-y-o	Non-Handicaps 3-y-o+	Handicaps 2-y-o	Handicaps 3-y-o+	Per cent	£1 Level Stake
Leopardstown	4-32	0-5	2-11	0-0	2-16	12.5	+ 11.00
The Curragh	4-40	1-7	0-5	0-1	3-27	10.0	- 7.00
Fairyhouse	3-10	0-3	1-3	0-0	2-4	30.0	+ 22.00
Laytown	2-2	0-0	1-1	0-0	1-1	100.0	+ 18.00
Roscommon	2-5	0-1	2-3	0-0	0-1	40.0	+ 11.25
Galway	2-22	0-3	0-3	0-1	2-15	9.1	- 11.25
Clonmel	1-4	0-0	0-1	0-0	1-3	25.0	- 1.50
Tralee	1-5	0-0	1-1	0-0	0-4	20.0	- 1.50
Tipperary	1-11	0-5	0-3	0-0	1-3	9.1	- 5.00
Dundalk	1-12	0-3	0-4	0-0	1-5	8.3	- 1.00

Naas	0-13	Ballinrobe	0-2	Tramore	0-2
Gowran Park	0-8	Bellewstown	0-2	Wexford	0-2
Navan	0-8	Killarney	0-2	Down Royal	0-1
Mallow	0-3	Limerick	0-2	Sligo	0-1
Thurles	0-3	Punchestown	0-2		

WINNING HORSES

	Age	Races Run	1st	2nd	3rd	Unpl	Win £
Kayfa	4	9	3	1	1	4	22,772
Shirley's Delight	3	10	3	5	0	2	13,285
Mubadir	5	6	2	2	2	0	11,730
Bizana	3	7	2	0	0	5	6,902
Classic Match	5	7	1	1	0	5	6,900
La Cenerentola	3	8	2	0	0	6	6,385
Micks Delight	3	7	2	2	1	2	5,865
Regal Access	2	4	1	0	1	2	5,244
Rupert The Great	3	5	1	0	1	3	2,762
Life Saver	4	2	1	0	0	1	2,760
Bothsidesnow	3	9	1	3	3	2	2,245
Coral Sound	3	8	1	0	0	7	2,072
Aran Exile	3	5	1	0	0	4	2,072

WINNING OWNERS

	Races Won	Value £		Races Won	Value £
Vincent Loughnane	3	22,772	Mrs Rita Holly	1	5,244
Liam Doherty	3	13,285	H Cheung	1	2,762
Liam Keating	2	11,730	Mrs H A Hegarty	1	2,760
Breffni Syndicate	2	6,902	T J Duffy	1	2,245
Ms P Haselden	1	6,900	Mrs M Cahill	1	2,072
Mrs Maureen Hunt	2	6,385	Kerr Technology Ltd	1	2,072
M J McCarthy	2	5,865			

Favourites	2-19	10.5%	- 13.00	Total winning prize-money	£90,994
Longest winning sequence			4	Average SP of winner	7.5/1
Longest losing sequence			29	Return on stakes invested	-8.2%
1992 Form	18-170	10.6%	- 61.54	1990 Form	14-209	6.7%	-129.13
1991 Form	17-207	8.2%	-123.39	1989 Form	11-188	5.9%	-122.34

E P MITCHELL

	No. of Horses	Races Run	1st	2nd	3rd	Unpl	Per cent	£1 Level Stake
2-y-o	2	11	1	0	3	7	9.1	+ 2.00
3-y-o	0	0	0	0	0	0	-	0.00
4-y-o+	4	18	1	3	1	13	5.6	- 13.00
Totals	6	29	2	3	4	20	6.9	- 11.00

Mar/Apr	May	Jun	Jul	Aug	Sep	Oct/Nov
0-2	0-4	0-6	0-4	1-7	0-3	1-3

Winning Jockeys	W-R	£1 Level Stake		W-R	£1 Level Stake
B J Halligan	1-1	+ 4.00	J J Behan	1-6	+ 7.00

Winning Courses	W-R	£1 Level Stake		W-R	£1 Level Stake
Down Royal	1-2	+ 3.00	Roscommon	1-2	+ 11.00

Winning Horses	Age	Races Run	1st	2nd	3rd	Unpl	Win £
Ludden Lady	2	9	1	0	3	5	2,245
Hawaian Tasca	4	9	1	1	1	6	1,208

Favourites	0-0		Total winning prize-money	£3,453
1992 Form	1-12	8.3% + 14.00	1990 Form	0-8
1991 Form	0-27		1989 Form	0-1

J MORRISON

	No. of Horses	Races Run	1st	2nd	3rd	Unpl	Per cent	£1 Level Stake
2-y-o	0	0	0	0	0	0	-	0.00
3-y-o	1	5	0	0	0	5	-	- 5.00
4-y-o+	2	9	1	1	0	7	11.1	+ 4.00
Totals	3	14	1	1	0	12	7.1	- 1.00

Mar/Apr	May	Jun	Jul	Aug	Sep	Oct/Nov
0-4	0-1	0-0	0-3	0-2	1-2	0-2

Winning Jockey	W-R	£1 Level Stake	Winning Course	W-R	£1 Level Stake
R V Skelly	1-1	+ 12.00	Listowel	1-2	+ 11.00

Winning Horse	Age	Races Run	1st	2nd	3rd	Unpl	Win £
Alshou	4	6	1	1	0	4	3,795

Favourites	0-0			Total winning prize-money			£3,795
1992 Form	1-11	9.1%	- 2.00	1990 Form	1-11	9.1%	- 3.00
1991 Form	0-10			1989 Form	0-8		

J E MULHERN

	No. of Horses	Races Run	1st	2nd	3rd	Unpl	Per cent	£1 Level Stake
2-y-o	1	2	0	0	1	1	-	- 2.00
3-y-o	2	12	1	1	1	9	8.3	- 8.50
4-y-o+	10	42	2	4	4	32	4.8	- 16.67
Totals	13	56	3	5	6	42	5.4	- 27.17

Mar/Apr	May	Jun	Jul	Aug	Sep	Oct/Nov
0-6	0-5	0-7	0-11	3-17	0-6	0-4

Winning Jockeys	W-R	£1 Level Stake		W-R	£1 Level Stake
N G McCullagh	1-1	+ 2.50	G M Moylan	1-1	+ 20.00
J Reid	1-1	+ 3.33			

Winning Courses					
Tipperary	1-1	+ 2.50	Leopardstown	1-12	- 7.67
Tralee	1-6	+ 15.00			

Winning Horses	Age	Races Run	1st	2nd	3rd	Unpl	Win £
Command 'N Control	4	11	1	1	1	8	13,150
Approach The Bench	5	9	1	3	2	3	8,625
Asta Madera	3	9	1	1	1	6	2,760

Favourites	1-5	20.0%	- 1.50	Total winning prize-money			£24,535
1992 Form	4-76	5.3%	- 35.00	1990 Form	4-44	9.1%	- 22.25
1991 Form	2-50	4.0%	- 34.00	1989 Form	3-35	8.6%	- 7.00

P MULLINS

	No. of Horses	Races Run	1st	2nd	3rd	Unpl	Per cent	£1 Level Stake
2-y-o	3	11	0	0	0	11	-	- 11.00
3-y-o	6	41	4	7	2	28	9.8	- 7.33
4-y-o+	14	45	6	4	3	32	13.3	+ 3.25
Totals	23	97	10	11	5	71	10.3	- 15.08

BY MONTH

2-y-o	W-R	Per cent	£1 Level Stake	3-y-o	W-R	Per cent	£1 Level Stake
Mar/Apr	0-0	-	0.00	Mar/Apr	1-1	100.0	+ 16.00
May	0-0	-	0.00	May	0-3	-	- 3.00
June	0-0	-	0.00	June	0-8	-	- 8.00
July	0-2	-	- 2.00	July	0-9	-	- 9.00
August	0-5	-	- 5.00	August	1-7	14.3	- 5.33
September	0-4	-	- 4.00	September	0-7	-	- 7.00
Oct/Nov	0-0	-	0.00	Oct/Nov	2-6	33.3	+ 9.00

4-y-o+	W-R	Per cent	£1 Level Stake	Totals	W-R	Per cent	£1 Level Stake
Mar/Apr	0-4	-	- 4.00	Mar/Apr	1-5	20.0	+ 12.00
May	1-7	14.3	- 4.00	May	1-10	10.0	- 7.00
June	1-7	14.3	+ 6.00	June	1-15	6.7	- 2.00
July	0-7	-	- 7.00	July	0-18	-	- 18.00
August	2-6	33.3	+ 10.25	August	3-18	16.7	- 0.08
September	1-6	16.7	- 1.00	September	1-17	5.9	- 12.00
Oct/Nov	1-8	12.5	+ 3.00	Oct/Nov	3-14	21.4	+ 12.00

DISTANCE

2-y-o	W-R	Per cent	£1 Level Stake	3-y-o	W-R	Per cent	£1 Level Stake
5f-6f	0-2	-	- 2.00	5f-6f	0-5	-	- 5.00
7f-8f	0-9	-	- 9.00	7f-8f	1-9	11.1	+ 8.00
9f-13f	0-0	-	0.00	9f-13f	2-26	7.7	- 11.00
14f+	0-0	-	0.00	14f+	1-1	100.0	+ 0.67

4-y-o+	W-R	Per cent	£1 Level Stake	Totals	W-R	Per cent	£1 Level Stake
5f-6f	1-2	50.0	+ 11.00	5f-6f	1-9	11.1	+ 4.00
7f-8f	2-4	50.0	+ 14.00	7f-8f	3-22	13.6	+ 13.00
9f-13f	2-13	15.4	+ 1.00	9f-13f	4-39	10.3	- 10.00
14f+	1-26	3.8	- 22.75	14f+	2-27	7.4	- 22.08

TYPE OF RACE

Non-Handicaps	W-R	Per cent	£1 Level Stake	Handicaps	W-R	Per cent	£1 Level Stake
2-y-o	0-11	-	- 11.00	2-y-o	0-0	-	0.00
3-y-o	2-25	8.0	- 14.33	3-y-o	2-14	14.3	+ 9.00
4-y-o+	3-13	23.1	+ 4.25	4-y-o+	1-20	5.0	- 7.00
Apprentice	1-1	100.0	+ 12.00	Apprentice	1-3	33.3	+ 2.00
Amat/Ladies	0-6	-	- 6.00	Amat/Ladies	0-4	-	- 4.00
Totals	6-56	10.7	- 15.08	Totals	4-41	9.8	0.00

FIRST TIME OUT

	W-R	Per cent	£1 Level Stake
2-y-o	0-3	-	- 3.00
3-y-o	1-6	16.7	+ 11.00
4-y-o+	1-14	7.1	- 1.00
Totals	2-23	8.7	+ 7.00

JOCKEYS RIDING

	W-R	Per cent	£1 Level Stake		W-R	Per cent	£1 Level Stake
T P Treacy	5-12	41.7	+ 36.00	J P Murtagh	1-4	25.0	+ 13.00
P Shanahan	1-1	100.0	+ 8.00	Mrs S McCarthy	1-6	16.7	- 3.00
G M Moylan	1-3	33.3	+ 0.25	J J Behan	1-15	6.7	- 13.33

S Craine	0-12	P Carberry	0-2	J F Egan	0-1
K J Manning	0-7	P J Smullen	0-2	J R Barry	0-1
R V Skelly	0-6	P V Gilson	0-2	Mr P A Roche	0-1
Mr T Mullins	0-5	R Fitzpatrick	0-2	P P Murphy	0-1
R Hughes	0-5	C Everard	0-1	W J Supple	0-1
C F Swan	0-3	C Roche	0-1		
N G McCullagh	0-2	D V Smith	0-1		

COURSE RECORD

	Total W-R	Non-Handicaps 2-y-o	3-y-o+	Handicaps 2-y-o	3-y-o+	Per cent	£1 Level Stake
Tramore	2-7	0-0	2-2	0-0	0-5	28.6	- 2.08
Punchestown	1-1	0-0	1-1	0-0	0-0	100.0	+ 8.00
Naas	1-2	0-0	0-1	0-0	1-1	50.0	+ 4.00
Tralee	1-3	0-1	0-1	0-0	1-1	33.3	+ 10.00
Thurles	1-4	0-0	1-3	0-0	0-1	25.0	+ 9.00
Tipperary	1-4	0-1	1-2	0-0	0-1	25.0	+ 7.00
Killarney	1-5	0-0	1-4	0-0	0-1	20.0	- 2.00
Galway	1-8	0-2	0-3	0-0	1-3	12.5	- 3.00
Gowran Park	1-14	0-3	0-7	0-0	1-4	7.1	+ 3.00

Leopardstown	0-8	Wexford	0-4	Roscommon	0-2
The Curragh	0-8	Bellewstown	0-3	Ballinrobe	0-1
Fairyhouse	0-5	Dundalk	0-3	Down Royal	0-1
Clonmel	0-4	Downpatrick	0-2	Limerick	0-1
Listowel	0-4	Mallow	0-2	Sligo	0-1

WINNING HORSES

	Age	Races Run	1st	2nd	3rd	Unpl	Win £
Hang A Right	6	11	3	1	0	7	9,494
My Kerry Dancer	3	11	2	2	0	7	8,280
Force Seven	6	4	2	0	1	1	6,385
Wheatsheaf Lady	3	5	1	1	0	3	2,760
No Dunce	3	11	1	3	0	7	2,245
Simply Swift	6	5	1	0	0	4	2,243

WINNING OWNERS

	Races Won	Value £		Races Won	Value £
Thomas Mullins	4	12,254	Mrs P Mullins	1	2,245
Hudson Valley Equine Inc	2	8,280	J M Cusack	1	2,243
Mrs C A Moore	2	6,385			

Favourites	3-7	42.9%	+ 3.92	Total winning prize-money		£31,407
Longest winning sequence			2	Average SP of winner		7.2/1
Longest losing sequence			30	Return on stakes invested		-15.5%
1992 Form	3-56	5.4%	+ 6.00	1990 Form	10-147	6.8% - 65.30
1991 Form	1-48	2.1%	- 42.00	1989 Form	14-168	8.3% - 88.45

W P MULLINS

	No. of Horses	Races Run	1st	2nd	3rd	Unpl	Per cent	£1 Level Stake
2-y-o	3	11	0	0	0	11	-	- 11.00
3-y-o	2	21	4	1	4	12	19.0	0.00
4-y-o+	10	41	5	4	3	29	12.2	- 13.25
Totals	15	73	9	5	7	52	12.3	- 24.25

Mar/Apr	May	Jun	Jul	Aug	Sep	Oct/Nov
1-6	2-7	3-13	0-6	0-9	2-14	1-18

Winning Jockeys	W-R	£1 Level Stake		W-R	£1 Level Stake
J J Behan	2-15	− 7.75	B J Halligan	1-3	+ 5.00
John O'Connor	1-1	+ 7.00	W J Supple	1-5	+ 1.00
M J Kinane	1-1	+ 4.50	Mrs J M Mullins	1-10	− 3.00
P Carberry	1-2	+ 1.00	N G McCullagh	1-11	− 7.00

Winning Courses					
Naas	2-5	+ 6.00	Clonmel	1-3	+ 1.50
The Curragh	2-11	+ 3.00	Tramore	1-5	− 2.25
Ballinrobe	1-2	+ 2.00	Listowel	1-8	− 1.00
Fairyhouse	1-3	+ 2.50			

Winning Horses	Age	Races Run	1st	2nd	3rd	Unpl	Win £
Never Back Down	3	11	2	1	2	6	11,040
Padashpan	4	6	2	2	0	2	10,625
Shragraddy Lass	3	10	2	0	2	6	5,350
Gilt Dimension	6	7	1	0	1	5	2,760
Sharp Invite	6	4	1	1	1	1	2,245
Karabakh	4	7	1	0	0	6	240

Favourites	3-7	42.9%	+ 5.75	Total winning prize-money		£32,260

1992 Form	7-99	7.1%	− 56.75	1990 Form	4-27	14.8%	+ 2.00
1991 Form	4-59	6.8%	− 28.00	1989 Form	1-23	4.3%	− 14.00

DANIEL J MURPHY

	No. of Horses	Races Run	1st	2nd	3rd	Unpl	Per cent	£1 Level Stake
2-y-o	6	17	1	0	2	14	5.9	0.00
3-y-o	8	40	2	2	2	34	5.0	− 19.50
4-y-o+	6	34	1	3	7	23	2.9	− 26.00
Totals	20	91	4	5	11	71	4.4	− 45.50

Mar/Apr	May	Jun	Jul	Aug	Sep	Oct/Nov
0-7	1-17	0-14	1-13	1-18	0-11	1-11

Winning Jockeys	W-R	£1 Level Stake		W-R	£1 Level Stake
P V Gilson	2-17	− 3.50	R V Skelly	1-19	− 4.00
P J Smullen	1-3	+ 14.00			

Winning Courses					
Down Royal	1-3	+ 14.00	Mallow	1-5	+ 10.00
Tramore	1-4	+ 4.00	Ballinrobe	1-7	− 1.50

Winning Horses	Age	Races Run	1st	2nd	3rd	Unpl	Win £
Kilmood Lass	2	1	1	0	0	0	2,588
Yonoka	4	11	1	2	1	7	2,245
Topseys Tipple	3	4	1	0	0	3	2,245
Slightly Scruffy	3	5	1	1	1	2	2,245

Favourites	0-1			Total winning prize-money			£9,323

1992 Form	6-79	7.6%	- 14.50	1990 Form	8-55	14.5%	- 7.18
1991 Form	2-69	2.9%	- 58.00	1989 Form	0-48		

J G MURPHY

	No. of Horses	Races Run	1st	2nd	3rd	Unpl	Per cent	£1 Level Stake
2-y-o	1	3	1	2	0	0	33.3	+ 4.00
3-y-o	2	10	0	0	1	9	-	- 10.00
4-y-o+	0	0	0	0	0	0	-	0.00
Totals	3	13	1	2	1	9	7.7	- 6.00

Mar/Apr	May	Jun	Jul	Aug	Sep	Oct/Nov
0-3	0-1	0-2	1-3	0-2	0-2	0-0

Winning Jockey	W-R	£1 Level Stake	Winning Course	W-R	£1 Level Stake
P Shanahan	1-4	+ 3.00	Galway	1-1	+ 6.00

Winning Horse	Age	Races Run	1st	2nd	3rd	Unpl	Win £
Miss Nutwood	2	3	1	2	0	0	6,210

Favourites	0-0		Total winning prize-money	£6,210

1992 Form	0-6	1991 Form	0-10

MRS A M O'BRIEN

	No. of Horses	Races Run	1st	2nd	3rd	Unpl	Per cent	£1 Level Stake
2-y-o	2	3	0	0	1	2	-	- 3.00
3-y-o	9	27	1	4	4	18	3.7	- 22.00
4-y-o+	6	13	1	3	2	7	7.7	- 8.50
Totals	17	43	2	7	7	27	4.7	- 33.50

Mar/Apr	May	Jun	Jul	Aug	Sep	Oct/Nov
0-8	2-24	0-11	0-0	0-0	0-0	0-0

Winning Jockey	W-R	£1 Level Stake			W-R	£1 Level Stake
J P Murtagh	2-12	- 2.50				
Winning Courses						
Gowran Park	1-2	+ 2.50		Killarney	1-5	0.00

Winning Horses	Age	Races Run	1st	2nd	3rd	Unpl	Win £
Tryarra	3	2	1	0	1	0	3,452
Pharfetched	4	3	1	1	0	1	2,760

Favourites	0-3		Total winning prize-money	£6,212

A P O'BRIEN

	No. of Horses	Races Run	1st	2nd	3rd	Unpl	Per cent	£1 Level Stake
2-y-o	17	61	2	3	7	49	3.3	- 39.00
3-y-o	16	69	9	6	10	44	13.0	- 3.00
4-y-o+	15	45	9	5	4	27	20.0	- 4.62
Totals	48	175	20	14	21	120	11.4	- 46.62

BY MONTH

2-y-o	W-R	Per cent	£1 Level Stake	3-y-o	W-R	Per cent	£1 Level Stake
Mar/Apr	0-0	-	0.00	Mar/Apr	0-0	-	0.00
May	0-0	-	0.00	May	0-0	-	0.00
June	0-4	-	- 4.00	June	3-7	42.9	+ 30.00
July	0-8	-	- 8.00	July	2-20	10.0	- 10.75
August	0-7	-	- 7.00	August	3-21	14.3	- 5.75
September	1-17	5.9	- 8.00	September	0-10	-	- 10.00
Oct/Nov	1-25	4.0	- 12.00	Oct/Nov	1-11	9.1	- 6.50

4-y-o+	W-R	Per cent	£1 Level Stake	Totals	W-R	Per cent	£1 Level Stake
Mar/Apr	0-0	-	0.00	Mar/Apr	0-0	-	0.00
May	0-0	-	0.00	May	0-0	-	0.00
June	4-12	33.3	+ 3.50	June	7-23	30.4	+ 29.50
July	1-8	12.5	- 4.75	July	3-36	8.3	- 23.50
August	2-10	20.0	+ 0.63	August	5-38	13.2	- 12.12
September	1-7	14.3	0.00	September	2-34	5.9	- 18.00
Oct/Nov	1-8	12.5	- 4.00	Oct/Nov	3-44	6.8	- 22.50

DISTANCE

2-y-o	W-R	Per cent	£1 Level Stake	3-y-o	W-R	Per cent	£1 Level Stake
5f-6f	0-13	-	- 13.00	5f-6f	0-1	-	- 1.00
7f-8f	1-42	2.4	- 33.00	7f-8f	0-7	-	- 7.00
9f-13f	1-6	16.7	+ 7.00	9f-13f	9-51	17.6	+ 15.00
14f+	0-0	-	0.00	14f+	0-10	-	- 10.00

4-y-o+	W-R	Per cent	£1 Level Stake	Totals	W-R	Per cent	£1 Level Stake
5f-6f	0-0	-	0.00	5f-6f	0-14	-	- 14.00
7f-8f	5-11	45.5	+ 14.50	7f-8f	6-60	10.0	- 25.50
9f-13f	3-12	25.0	- 0.37	9f-13f	13-69	18.8	+ 21.63
14f+	1-22	4.5	- 18.75	14f+	1-32	3.1	- 28.75

TYPE OF RACE

Non-Handicaps	W-R	Per cent	£1 Level Stake	Handicaps	W-R	Per cent	£1 Level Stake
2-y-o	0-49	-	- 49.00	2-y-o	2-12	16.7	+ 10.00
3-y-o	3-28	10.7	- 6.25	3-y-o	6-39	15.4	+ 5.25
4-y-o+	1-12	8.3	- 10.00	4-y-o+	7-21	33.3	+ 14.75
Apprentice	0-0	-	0.00	Apprentice	1-3	33.3	- 0.37
Amat/Ladies	0-8	-	- 8.00	Amat/Ladies	0-3	-	- 3.00
Totals	4-97	4.1	- 73.25	Totals	16-78	20.5	+ 26.63

FIRST TIME OUT

	W-R	Per cent	£1 Level Stake
2-y-o	0-15	-	- 15.00
3-y-o	0-6	-	- 6.00
4-y-o+	1-10	10.0	- 6.75
Totals	1-31	3.2	- 27.75

JOCKEYS RIDING

	W-R	Per cent	£1 Level Stake		W-R	Per cent	£1 Level Stake
J P Murtagh	5-25	20.0	+ 0.50	J F Egan	1-4	25.0	- 1.75
J J Behan	3-11	27.3	+ 11.00	R V Skelly	1-5	20.0	+ 10.00
K Darley	1-1	100.0	+ 8.00	D G O'Shea	1-12	8.3	- 9.00
B J Walsh	1-2	50.0	+ 4.00	N G McCullagh	1-12	8.3	- 5.00
P Carberry	1-2	50.0	+ 2.50	W J Supple	1-12	8.3	- 4.00
P V Gilson	1-3	33.3	+ 0.50	C Roche	1-14	7.1	- 1.00
J R Barry	1-4	25.0	- 1.37	J A Heffernan	1-16	6.3	- 9.00

Mr A P O'Brien	0-6	M J Cullen	0-2	M J Kinane	0-1
R Hughes	0-6	P P Murphy	0-2	Mr G F Ryan	0-1
Miss F M Crowley	0-4	R McAuliffe	0-2	Mr G R Ryan	0-1
N Byrne	0-4	W J Smith	0-2	R Fitzpatrick	0-1
S P Kelly	0-4	B A Hunter	0-1	R M Burke	0-1
Joanna Morgan	0-3	B J Halligan	0-1	S Craine	0-1
L Piggott	0-3	G M Moylan	0-1	S M Kelly	0-1
L Dettori	0-2	K J Manning	0-1	T P Treacy	0-1

COURSE RECORD

	Total	Non-Handicaps		Handicaps		Per	£1 Level
	W-R	2-y-o	3-y-o+	2-y-o	3-y-o+	cent	Stake
The Curragh	4-22	0-8	0-3	0-0	4-11	18.2	+ 3.00
Gowran Park	3-15	0-7	0-2	1-1	2-5	20.0	+ 10.00
Clonmel	2-7	0-0	2-4	0-0	0-3	28.6	+ 10.00
Wexford	2-7	0-0	1-3	0-0	1-4	28.6	- 1.50
Tralee	2-8	0-0	0-4	0-0	2-4	25.0	+ 3.50
Ballinrobe	1-4	0-1	0-1	0-0	1-2	25.0	+ 2.00
Mallow	1-5	0-1	0-0	1-4	0-0	20.0	+ 8.00
Tramore	1-6	0-0	0-2	0-0	1-4	16.7	0.00
Navan	1-7	0-3	1-3	0-0	0-1	14.3	- 2.50
Fairyhouse	1-7	0-2	0-2	0-0	1-3	14.3	- 4.37
Galway	1-17	0-2	0-6	0-1	1-8	5.9	- 13.75
Leopardstown	1-19	0-6	0-3	0-2	1-8	5.3	- 10.00

Listowel	0-13	Punchestown	0-3	Sligo	0-2
Roscommon	0-10	Bellewstown	0-2	Thurles	0-2
Tipperary	0-8	Dundalk	0-2	Limerick	0-1
Naas	0-6	Killarney	0-2		

WINNING HORSES

		Races					Win
	Age	Run	1st	2nd	3rd	Unpl	£
Wandering Thoughts	4	13	7	2	2	2	36,664
Tryarra	3	11	3	2	2	4	17,492
Metroella	2	7	1	0	2	4	5,040
Loshian	4	3	1	0	0	2	4,140
Trillick	3	4	1	0	0	3	3,452
Assert Star	3	5	1	2	1	1	2,762
Alibar's Pet	3	5	1	1	0	3	2,762
Magic Feeling	3	4	1	0	2	1	2,760
Saint Hilda	3	5	1	0	1	3	2,245
Crazy Gail	6	5	1	0	0	4	2,245
Hopesville	3	7	1	0	2	4	2,245
Susie Sunshine	2	5	1	0	0	4	2,243

WINNING OWNERS

	Races Won	Value £		Races Won	Value £
W Mythen	7	36,664	Ms M Hogan	1	2,762
Mrs K Doyle	3	17,492	J F Grogan	1	2,762
M Hanrahan	1	5,040	Liam O'Maobhuidhe	1	2,245
Mrs J M Ryan	2	5,005	S Bolger	1	2,245
Mrs Anna Foxe	1	4,140	Woodgrove Syndicate	1	2,243
Fergus McGirr	1	3,452			

Favourites	7-23	30.4%	- 3.12	Total winning prize-money	£84,050
Longest winning sequence			2	Average SP of winner	5.4/1
Longest losing sequence			25	Return on stakes invested	-26.6%

CHARLES O'BRIEN

	No. of Horses	Races Run	1st	2nd	3rd	Unpl	Per cent	£1 Level Stake
2-y-o	10	23	2	2	1	18	8.7	- 8.50
3-y-o	10	40	7	5	9	19	17.5	- 12.15
4-y-o+	3	6	1	0	3	2	16.7	- 0.50
Totals	23	69	10	7	13	39	14.5	- 21.15

BY MONTH

2-y-o	W-R	Per cent	£1 Level Stake	3-y-o	W-R	Per cent	£1 Level Stake
Mar/Apr	0-0	-	0.00	Mar/Apr	0-3	-	- 3.00
May	0-0	-	0.00	May	1-3	33.3	+ 0.25
June	0-4	-	- 4.00	June	3-5	60.0	+ 10.50
July	0-0	-	0.00	July	1-7	14.3	- 4.90
August	0-2	-	- 2.00	August	1-6	16.7	- 3.00
September	1-5	20.0	- 1.50	September	1-8	12.5	- 4.00
Oct/Nov	1-12	8.3	- 1.00	Oct/Nov	0-8	-	- 8.00

4-y-o+	W-R	Per cent	£1 Level Stake	Totals	W-R	Per cent	£1 Level Stake
Mar/Apr	0-2	-	- 2.00	Mar/Apr	0-5	-	- 5.00
May	0-1	-	- 1.00	May	1-4	25.0	- 0.75
June	0-1	-	- 1.00	June	3-10	30.0	+ 5.50
July	0-0	-	0.00	July	1-7	14.3	- 4.90
August	0-0	-	0.00	August	1-8	12.5	- 5.00
September	0-0	-	0.00	September	2-13	15.4	- 5.50
Oct/Nov	1-2	50.0	+ 3.50	Oct/Nov	2-22	9.1	- 5.50

DISTANCE

2-y-o	W-R	Per cent	£1 Level Stake	3-y-o	W-R	Per cent	£1 Level Stake
5f-6f	0-4	-	- 4.00	5f-6f	0-0	-	0.00
7f-8f	2-17	11.8	- 2.50	7f-8f	2-14	14.3	- 4.50
9f-13f	0-2	-	- 2.00	9f-13f	4-24	16.7	- 9.65
14f+	0-0	-	0.00	14f+	1-2	50.0	+ 2.00

4-y-o+	W-R	Per cent	£1 Level Stake	Totals	W-R	Per cent	£1 Level Stake
5f-6f	0-0	-	0.00	5f-6f	0-4	-	- 4.00
7f-8f	0-0	-	0.00	7f-8f	4-31	12.9	- 7.00
9f-13f	0-4	-	- 4.00	9f-13f	4-30	13.3	- 15.65
14f+	1-2	50.0	+ 3.50	14f+	2-4	50.0	+ 5.50

TYPE OF RACE

Non-Handicaps	W-R	Per cent	£1 Level Stake	Handicaps	W-R	Per cent	£1 Level Stake
2-y-o	2-22	9.1	- 7.50	2-y-o	0-1	-	- 1.00
3-y-o	7-37	18.9	- 9.15	3-y-o	0-3	-	- 3.00
4-y-o+	0-4	-	- 4.00	4-y-o+	0-0	-	0.00
Apprentice	0-0	-	0.00	Apprentice	0-0	-	0.00
Amat/Ladies	1-2	50.0	+ 3.50	Amat/Ladies	0-0	-	0.00
Totals	10-65	15.4	- 17.15	Totals	0-4	-	- 4.00

FIRST TIME OUT

	W-R	Per cent	£1 Level Stake
2-y-o	0-10	-	- 10.00
3-y-o	2-9	22.2	+ 4.50
4-y-o+	1-3	33.3	+ 2.50
Totals	3-22	13.6	- 3.00

JOCKEYS RIDING

	W-R	Per cent	£1 Level Stake		W-R	Per cent	£1 Level Stake
P V Gilson	7-35	20.0	- 6.65	Mr A J Martin	1-2	50.0	+ 3.50
J A Heffernan	1-1	100.0	+ 10.00	L Piggott	1-7	14.3	- 4.00

J J Behan	0-4	J P Murtagh	0-2	K J Manning	0-1
C Roche	0-3	N Byrne	0-2	N G McCullagh	0-1
W J O'Connor	0-3	R Hughes	0-2	P Shanahan	0-1
W J Supple	0-3	A J Nolan	0-1	S Craine	0-1

COURSE RECORD

	Total W-R	Non-Handicaps 2-y-o	3-y-o+	Handicaps 2-y-o	3-y-o+	Per cent	£1 Level Stake
Leopardstown	3-14	1-2	2-11	0-0	0-1	21.4	+ 3.25
Gowran Park	2-4	1-3	1-1	0-0	0-0	50.0	+ 3.50
Limerick	1-1	0-0	1-1	0-0	0-0	100.0	+ 1.00
Dundalk	1-1	0-0	1-1	0-0	0-0	100.0	+ 1.10
Naas	1-4	0-0	1-4	0-0	0-0	25.0	+ 2.50
Navan	1-4	0-1	1-3	0-0	0-0	25.0	+ 1.50
The Curragh	1-26	0-13	1-10	0-1	0-2	3.8	- 19.00

Tipperary	0-6	Fairyhouse	0-1	Roscommon	0-1
Galway	0-3	Mallow	0-1	Tralee	0-1
Down Royal	0-1	Punchestown	0-1		

WINNING HORSES

	Age	Races Run	1st	2nd	3rd	Unpl	Win £
Family Fortune	3	2	2	0	0	0	5,695
Lake Kariba	2	3	1	0	0	2	5,244
Semple Stadium	3	6	1	1	1	3	4,487
Crystal Lake	2	2	1	0	1	0	4,485
Fairy Lore	3	4	1	0	0	3	3,452
Crystal Ship	3	6	1	0	2	3	3,450
Portrait Gallery	3	2	1	1	0	0	2,760
Nightman	4	2	1	0	1	0	2,760
Platinum Empire	3	4	1	0	1	2	2,245

WINNING OWNERS

	Races Won	Value £		Races Won	Value £
Mrs M V O'Brien	7	22,089	Mrs D V O'Brien	1	4,485
Mrs John Magnier	1	5,244	Mrs A Manning	1	2,760

Favourites	3-11	27.3% - 3.40	Total winning prize-money	£34,578
Longest winning sequence		2	Average SP of winner	3.8/1
Longest losing sequence		11	Return on stakes invested	-30.7%

M J P O'BRIEN

	No. of Horses	Races Run	1st	2nd	3rd	Unpl	Per cent	£1 Level Stake
2-y-o	1	4	0	0	0	4	-	- 4.00
3-y-o	1	1	1	0	0	0	100.0	+ 2.50
4-y-o+	4	10	0	1	1	8	-	- 10.00
Totals	6	15	1	1	1	12	6.7	- 11.50

Mar/Apr	May	Jun	Jul	Aug	Sep	Oct/Nov
0-1	0-0	0-2	1-3	0-4	0-2	0-3

Winning Jockey	W-R	£1 Level Stake	Winning Course	W-R	£1 Level Stake
D G O'Shea	1-1	+ 2.50	Wexford	1-1	+ 2.50

Winning Horse	Age	Races Run	1st	2nd	3rd	Unpl	Win £
Nurse Maid	3	1	1	0	0	0	2,762

Favourites	0-2		Total winning prize-money		£2,762

1992 Form	0-16		1990 Form	4-47	8.5%	+ 6.00
1991 Form	0-25		1989 Form	1-26	3.8%	- 5.00

M V O'BRIEN

	No. of Horses	Races Run	1st	2nd	3rd	Unpl	Per cent	£1 Level Stake
2-y-o	4	5	2	0	0	3	40.0	- 1.10
3-y-o	4	14	4	3	0	7	28.6	+ 5.50
4-y-o+	0	0	0	0	0	0	-	0.00
Totals	8	19	6	3	0	10	31.6	+ 4.40

Mar/Apr	May	Jun	Jul	Aug	Sep	Oct/Nov
1-3	1-5	1-3	0-2	1-2	1-2	1-2

Winning Jockeys	W-R	£1 Level Stake		W-R	£1 Level Stake
J P Murtagh	3-4	+ 2.40	W J Supple	1-1	+ 12.00
L Piggott	2-10	- 6.00			

Winning Courses					
The Curragh	4-13	+ 6.60	Leopardstown	2-5	- 1.20

Winning Horses	Age	Races Run	1st	2nd	3rd	Unpl	Win £
College Chapel	3	2	2	0	0	0	25,875
Mysterious Ways	3	8	2	1	0	5	7,935
Perugino	2	1	1	0	0	0	5,520
Lake Country	2	2	1	0	0	1	5,244

Favourites	5-10	50.0%	+ 0.40	Total winning prize-money		£44,574

1992 Form	19-53	35.8%	+ 1.32	1990 Form	37-119	31.1%	+ 0.64
1991 Form	36-105	34.3%	+ 9.79	1989 Form	27-100	27.0%	- 9.42

E J O'GRADY

	No. of Horses	Races Run	1st	2nd	3rd	Unpl	Per cent	£1 Level Stake
2-y-o	5	23	2	1	2	18	8.7	- 13.25
3-y-o	5	31	5	3	4	19	16.1	- 5.93
4-y-o+	10	29	5	0	2	22	17.2	+ 18.00
Totals	20	83	12	4	8	59	14.5	- 1.18

BY MONTH

2-y-o	W-R	Per cent	£1 Level Stake	3-y-o	W-R	Per cent	£1 Level Stake
Mar/Apr	0-0	-	0.00	Mar/Apr	0-0	-	0.00
May	0-1	-	- 1.00	May	1-6	16.7	- 4.33
June	1-2	50.0	+ 5.00	June	2-8	25.0	+ 8.00
July	1-3	33.3	- 0.25	July	1-5	20.0	+ 0.50
August	0-8	-	- 8.00	August	1-5	20.0	- 3.10
September	0-3	-	- 3.00	September	0-5	-	- 5.00
Oct/Nov	0-6	-	- 6.00	Oct/Nov	0-2	-	- 2.00

4-y-o+	W-R	Per cent	£1 Level Stake	Totals	W-R	Per cent	£1 Level Stake
Mar/Apr	1-7	14.3	+ 1.00	Mar/Apr	1-7	14.3	+ 1.00
May	0-5	-	- 5.00	May	1-12	8.3	- 10.33
June	2-6	33.3	+ 16.00	June	5-16	31.3	+ 29.00
July	2-4	50.0	+ 13.00	July	4-12	33.3	+ 13.25
August	0-3	-	- 3.00	August	1-16	6.3	- 14.10
September	0-0	-	0.00	September	0-8	-	- 8.00
Oct/Nov	0-4	-	- 4.00	Oct/Nov	0-12	-	- 12.00

DISTANCE

2-y-o	W-R	Per cent	£1 Level Stake	3-y-o	W-R	Per cent	£1 Level Stake
5f-6f	1-10	10.0	- 3.00	5f-6f	3-14	21.4	+ 7.50
7f-8f	0-10	-	- 10.00	7f-8f	1-6	16.7	- 4.33
9f-13f	1-3	33.3	- 0.25	9f-13f	1-11	9.1	- 9.10
14f+	0-0	-	0.00	14f+	0-0	-	0.00

4-y-o+	W-R	Per cent	£1 Level Stake	Totals	W-R	Per cent	£1 Level Stake
5f-6f	0-5	-	- 5.00	5f-6f	4-29	13.8	- 0.50
7f-8f	1-3	33.3	+ 5.00	7f-8f	2-19	10.5	- 9.33
9f-13f	1-10	10.0	+ 1.00	9f-13f	3-24	12.5	- 8.35
14f+	3-11	27.3	+ 17.00	14f+	3-11	27.3	+ 17.00

O'Grady E J

TYPE OF RACE

Non-Handicaps	W-R	Per cent	£1 Level Stake	Handicaps	W-R	Per cent	£1 Level Stake
2-y-o	2-16	12.5	- 6.25	2-y-o	0-7	-	- 7.00
3-y-o	0-4	-	- 4.00	3-y-o	4-26	15.4	- 11.93
4-y-o+	0-3	-	- 3.00	4-y-o+	4-20	20.0	+ 19.00
Apprentice	0-0	-	0.00	Apprentice	1-2	50.0	+ 9.00
Amat/Ladies	1-5	20.0	+ 3.00	Amat/Ladies	0-0	-	0.00
Totals	3-28	10.7	- 10.25	Totals	9-55	16.4	+ 9.07

FIRST TIME OUT

	W-R	Per cent	£1 Level Stake
2-y-o	0-5	-	- 5.00
3-y-o	0-5	-	- 5.00
4-y-o+	1-10	10.0	- 2.00
Totals	1-20	5.0	- 12.00

JOCKEYS RIDING

	W-R	Per cent	£1 Level Stake		W-R	Per cent	£1 Level Stake
M J Kinane	4-11	36.4	+ 2.32	C Roche	1-4	25.0	+ 4.00
D G O'Shea	2-10	20.0	+ 6.00	R M Burke	1-4	25.0	+ 1.50
Mr E Bolger	1-1	100.0	+ 7.00	J J Behan	1-5	20.0	+ 4.00
P Carberry	1-4	25.0	+ 7.00	C Everard	1-7	14.3	+ 4.00

J F Egan	0-7	A J Nolan	0-1	Mr T N Cloke	0-1
R Hughes	0-7	C F Swan	0-1	N G McCullagh	0-1
D Manning	0-3	D J O'Donohoe	0-1	P P Murphy	0-1
J P Murtagh	0-3	Mr A J Martin	0-1	T Horgan	0-1
L Piggott	0-3	Mr A K Wyse	0-1	W J Smith	0-1
P V Gilson	0-3	Mr P Fenton	0-1		

COURSE RECORD

	Total W-R	Non-Handicaps 2-y-o	3-y-o+	Handicaps 2-y-o	3-y-o+	Per cent	£1 Level Stake
Down Royal	2-3	1-1	0-0	0-0	1-2	66.7	+ 1.42
Killarney	2-3	0-0	0-0	0-0	2-3	66.7	+ 14.00
Leopardstown	2-7	0-0	0-1	0-1	2-5	28.6	+ 9.50
Tipperary	2-9	1-3	0-3	0-0	1-3	22.2	- 0.10
Wexford	1-1	0-0	0-0	0-0	1-1	100.0	+ 10.00
Thurles	1-2	0-0	0-1	0-0	1-1	50.0	+ 9.00
Sligo	1-3	0-2	0-0	0-0	1-1	33.3	+ 2.00
The Curragh	1-17	0-3	1-3	0-2	0-9	5.9	- 9.00

Gowran Park	0-7	Roscommon	0-3	Tramore	0-2
Listowel	0-4	Tralee	0-3	Bellewstown	0-1
Mallow	0-4	Ballinrobe	0-2	Limerick	0-1
Clonmel	0-3	Galway	0-2	Punchestown	0-1
Naas	0-3	Navan	0-2		

WINNING HORSES

	Age	Races Run	1st	2nd	3rd	Unpl	Win £
Pilgrim Bay	3	12	3	2	2	5	10,009
Let It Ride	4	5	2	0	0	3	8,282
Time For A Run	6	1	1	0	0	0	4,155
Tinerana	3	5	2	1	2	0	3,970
Catwalker	2	5	1	0	0	4	3,797
Anseo	4	3	1	0	1	1	3,450
The Man From Cooks	4	4	1	0	0	3	2,245
King Sancho	2	6	1	1	1	3	1,380

WINNING OWNERS

	Races Won	Value £		Races Won	Value £
Frank A McNulty	3	10,009	R Salter-Townshend	1	3,797
J S Gutkin	2	8,282	Lloyd Thompson	1	3,450
John P McManus	1	4,155	P Senezio	1	2,245
Dr Paschal Carmody	2	3,970	Dr Jerome Torsney	1	1,380

Favourites	3-7	42.9%	- 0.68	Total winning prize-money		£37,288
Longest winning sequence			4	Average SP of winner		5.8/1
Longest losing sequence			26	Return on stakes invested		-1.4%
1992 Form	5-108	4.6%	- 86.10	1990 Form	4-136	2.9%	-128.35
1991 Form	6-106	5.7%	- 16.00	1989 Form	5-112	4.5%	- 83.75

PAT O'LEARY

	No. of Horses	Races Run	1st	2nd	3rd	Unpl	Per cent	£1 Level Stake
2-y-o	1	1	0	0	0	1	-	- 1.00
3-y-o	6	23	2	0	2	19	8.7	+ 1.00
4-y-o+	5	25	0	4	4	17	-	- 25.00
Totals	12	49	2	4	6	37	4.1	- 25.00

Mar/Apr	May	Jun	Jul	Aug	Sep	Oct/Nov
1-9	0-15	0-8	0-6	0-3	0-1	1-7

Winning Jockeys	W-R	£1 Level Stake		W-R	£1 Level Stake
D G O'Shea	1-1	+ 8.00	R M Burke	1-14	+ 1.00

Winning Courses					
Thurles	1-2	+ 13.00	The Curragh	1-7	+ 2.00

Winning Horses	Age	Races Run	1st	2nd	3rd	Unpl	Win £
Andante	3	7	1	0	2	4	3,450
Man Of Arran	3	5	1	0	0	4	2,243

Favourites	0-1			Total winning prize-money			£5,693

1992 Form	3-26	11.5%	- 15.10	1990 Form	0-18
1991 Form	0-20			1989 Form	0-9

T J O'MARA

	No. of Horses	Races Run	1st	2nd	3rd	Unpl	Per cent	£1 Level Stake
2-y-o	1	3	0	0	0	3	-	- 3.00
3-y-o	2	15	1	0	0	14	6.7	+ 36.00
4-y-o+	2	8	1	0	1	6	12.5	+ 2.00
Totals	5	26	2	0	1	23	7.7	+ 35.00

Mar/Apr	May	Jun	Jul	Aug	Sep	Oct/Nov
0-2	2-7	0-5	0-3	0-5	0-2	0-2

Winning Jockeys	W-R	£1 Level Stake			W-R	£1 Level Stake
J A Heffernan	1-3	+ 7.00	D G O'Shea		1-8	+ 43.00

Winning Courses						
Roscommon	1-1	+ 9.00	Killarney		1-4	+ 47.00

Winning Horses	Age	Races Run	1st	2nd	3rd	Unpl	Win £
Dark Swan	3	9	1	0	0	8	3,452
Magic Arts	5	6	1	0	1	4	2,245

Favourites	0-1			Total winning prize-money			£5,697

T O'NEILL

	No. of Horses	Races Run	1st	2nd	3rd	Unpl	Per cent	£1 Level Stake
2-y-o	0	0	0	0	0	0	-	0.00
3-y-o	1	5	0	0	1	4	-	- 5.00
4-y-o+	1	12	1	0	2	9	8.3	- 1.00
Totals	2	17	1	0	3	13	5.9	- 6.00

Mar/Apr	May	Jun	Jul	Aug	Sep	Oct/Nov
0-0	0-2	0-0	0-4	1-5	0-3	0-3

Winning Jockey	W-R	£1 Level Stake	Winning Course	W-R	£1 Level Stake
R V Skelly	1-4	+ 7.00	Laytown	1-2	+ 9.00

Winning Horse	Age	Races Run	1st	2nd	3rd	Unpl	Win £
Bolero Dancer	5	12	1	0	2	9	1,727

Favourites	0-0			Total winning prize-money			£1,727
1992 Form	0-3			1990 Form	0-6		
1991 Form	1-19	5.3%	- 6.00	1989 Form	0-3		

K F O'SULLIVAN

	No. of Horses	Races Run	1st	2nd	3rd	Unpl	Per cent	£1 Level Stake
2-y-o	3	7	2	1	0	4	28.6	+ 11.00
3-y-o	2	7	0	0	1	6	-	- 7.00
4-y-o+	3	6	0	0	0	6	-	- 6.00
Totals	8	20	2	1	1	16	10.0	- 2.00

Mar/Apr	May	Jun	Jul	Aug	Sep	Oct/Nov
0-3	0-8	1-3	1-3	0-2	0-0	0-1

Winning Jockeys	W-R	£1 Level Stake		W-R	£1 Level Stake
P Shanahan	1-2	+ 1.00	J F Egan	1-6	+ 9.00

Winning Courses					
Tralee	1-2	+ 1.00	The Curragh	1-4	+ 11.00

Winning Horse	Age	Races Run	1st	2nd	3rd	Unpl	Win £
Eichtercua	2	4	2	1	0	1	18,170

Favourites	1-1	100.0%	+ 2.00	Total winning prize-money		£18,170
1992 Form	2-31	6.5%	- 20.67	1991 Form	0-8	

M A O'TOOLE

	No. of Horses	Races Run	1st	2nd	3rd	Unpl	Per cent	£1 Level Stake
2-y-o	5	20	2	0	0	18	10.0	+ 15.00
3-y-o	3	12	0	0	1	11	-	- 12.00
4-y-o+	11	35	1	2	5	27	2.9	- 28.00
Totals	19	67	3	2	6	56	4.5	- 25.00

Mar/Apr	May	Jun	Jul	Aug	Sep	Oct/Nov
0-6	0-9	1-11	0-12	0-11	0-2	2-16

O'Toole M A

Winning Jockeys	W-R	£1 Level Stake		W-R	£1 Level Stake
M J Kinane	1-1	+ 6.00	J F Egan	1-22	- 13.00
W J Smith	1-2	+ 24.00			

Winning Courses	W-R	£1 Level Stake		W-R	£1 Level Stake
Wexford	1-4	+ 3.00	The Curragh	1-8	+ 18.00
Naas	1-7	+ 2.00			

Winning Horses	Age	Races Run	1st	2nd	3rd	Unpl	Win £
Join Forces	2	8	2	0	0	6	6,555
Marilyn	4	4	1	0	0	3	2,762

Favourites	0-2		Total winning prize-money	£9,317

1992 Form	9-107	8.4%	- 63.93	1990 Form	12-126	9.5%	- 18.75
1991 Form	6-120	5.0%	- 82.50	1989 Form	19-151	12.6%	- 48.09

MISS I T OAKES

	No. of Horses	Races Run	1st	2nd	3rd	Unpl	Per cent	£1 Level Stake
2-y-o	2	10	0	1	2	7	-	- 10.00
3-y-o	4	26	2	2	0	22	7.7	- 1.00
4-y-o+	1	2	0	0	0	2	-	- 2.00
Totals	7	38	2	3	2	31	5.3	- 13.00

Mar/Apr	May	Jun	Jul	Aug	Sep	Oct/Nov
0-3	1-9	0-3	0-10	0-6	1-2	0-5

Winning Jockeys	W-R	£1 Level Stake		W-R	£1 Level Stake
F Woods	1-2	+ 6.00	P P Murphy	1-8	+ 9.00

Winning Courses	W-R	£1 Level Stake		W-R	£1 Level Stake
Downpatrick	1-2	+ 15.00	Down Royal	1-7	+ 1.00

Winning Horses	Age	Races Run	1st	2nd	3rd	Unpl	Win £
Mangans Hill	3	12	1	1	0	10	1,380
Lowlack	3	7	1	1	0	5	1,380

Favourites	0-0		Total winning prize-money	£2,760

JOHN M OXX

	No. of Horses	Races Run	1st	2nd	3rd	Unpl	Per cent	£1 Level Stake
2-y-o	33	81	20	13	9	39	24.7	- 12.84
3-y-o	63	239	58	30	34	117	24.3	- 17.36
4-y-o+	3	7	2	1	2	2	28.6	+ 12.50
Totals	99	327	80	44	45	158	24.5	- 17.70

BY MONTH

2-y-o	W-R	Per cent	£1 Level Stake	3-y-o	W-R	Per cent	£1 Level Stake
Mar/Apr	0-0	-	0.00	Mar/Apr	10-33	30.3	+ 17.82
May	0-0	-	0.00	May	9-41	22.0	- 9.10
June	1-2	50.0	+ 2.50	June	11-48	22.9	- 0.30
July	2-8	25.0	+ 4.25	July	12-37	32.4	- 5.51
August	5-19	26.3	- 3.87	August	11-33	33.3	+ 3.99
September	5-19	26.3	- 2.77	September	3-25	12.0	- 5.50
Oct/Nov	7-33	21.2	- 12.95	Oct/Nov	2-22	9.1	- 18.76

4-y-o+	W-R	Per cent	£1 Level Stake	Totals	W-R	Per cent	£1 Level Stake
Mar/Apr	0-0	-	0.00	Mar/Apr	10-33	30.3	+ 17.82
May	2-3	66.7	+ 16.50	May	11-44	25.0	+ 7.40
June	0-1	-	- 1.00	June	12-51	23.5	+ 1.20
July	0-1	-	- 1.00	July	14-46	30.4	- 2.26
August	0-1	-	- 1.00	August	16-53	30.2	- 0.88
September	0-1	-	- 1.00	September	8-45	17.8	- 9.27
Oct/Nov	0-0	-	0.00	Oct/Nov	9-55	16.4	- 31.71

DISTANCE

2-y-o	W-R	Per cent	£1 Level Stake	3-y-o	W-R	Per cent	£1 Level Stake
5f-6f	5-18	27.8	- 6.45	5f-6f	4-23	17.4	+ 3.50
7f-8f	15-62	24.2	- 5.39	7f-8f	17-81	21.0	+ 4.72
9f-13f	0-1	-	- 1.00	9f-13f	33-120	27.5	- 20.05
14f+	0-0	-	0.00	14f+	4-15	26.7	- 5.53

4-y-o+	W-R	Per cent	£1 Level Stake	Totals	W-R	Per cent	£1 Level Stake
5f-6f	0-0	-	0.00	5f-6f	9-41	22.0	- 2.95
7f-8f	0-1	-	- 1.00	7f-8f	32-144	22.2	- 1.67
9f-13f	1-3	33.3	+ 10.00	9f-13f	34-124	27.4	- 11.05
14f+	1-3	33.3	+ 3.50	14f+	5-18	27.8	- 2.03

TYPE OF RACE

Non-Handicaps	W-R	Per cent	£1 Level Stake	Handicaps	W-R	Per cent	£1 Level Stake
2-y-o	20-78	25.6	- 9.84	2-y-o	0-3	-	- 3.00
3-y-o	49-177	27.7	+ 5.64	3-y-o	7-55	12.7	- 24.25
4-y-o+	2-6	33.3	+ 13.50	4-y-o+	0-1	-	- 1.00
Apprentice	0-1	-	- 1.00	Apprentice	0-1	-	- 1.00
Amat/Ladies	2-5	40.0	+ 3.25	Amat/Ladies	0-0	-	0.00
Totals	73-267	27.3	+ 11.55	Totals	7-60	11.7	- 29.25

FIRST TIME OUT

	W-R	Per cent	£1 Level Stake
2-y-o	11-33	33.3	+ 7.30
3-y-o	20-63	31.7	+ 22.66
4-y-o+	1-3	33.3	+ 10.00
Totals	32-99	32.3	+ 39.96

JOCKEYS RIDING

	W-R	Per cent	£1 Level Stake		W-R	Per cent	£1 Level Stake
M J Kinane	28-55	50.9	+ 9.54	C Everard	3-6	50.0	+ 15.25
J P Murtagh	26-110	23.6	- 16.08	Miss L Robinson	3-6	50.0	+ 3.82
R Hughes	12-63	19.0	- 3.83	M Roberts	2-7	28.6	+ 21.00
D Hogan	5-43	11.6	- 12.20	L Piggott	1-1	100.0	+ 0.80

D G O'Shea	0-24	Jacqueline Freda	0-1	W Carson	0-1
L Dettori	0-2	P Carberry	0-1	W R Swinburn	0-1
W J O'Connor	0-2	P Shanahan	0-1		
W J Supple	0-2	P V Gilson	0-1		

COURSE RECORD

	Total W-R	Non-Handicaps 2-y-o	3-y-o+	Handicaps 2-y-o	3-y-o+	Per cent	£1 Level Stake
The Curragh	22-112	6-29	14-60	0-0	2-23	19.6	- 2.49
Leopardstown	13-68	3-13	9-41	0-1	1-13	19.1	- 12.50
Tipperary	11-24	3-6	7-17	0-0	1-1	45.8	+ 24.80
Killarney	5-6	0-0	5-6	0-0	0-0	83.3	+ 2.37
Wexford	4-5	0-0	3-4	0-0	1-1	80.0	+ 6.55
Gowran Park	4-19	1-8	3-8	0-2	0-1	21.1	- 7.40
Navan	3-8	2-4	1-3	0-0	0-1	37.5	+ 2.05
Tralee	3-10	0-2	2-5	0-0	1-3	30.0	+ 0.05
Dundalk	3-15	0-0	3-12	0-0	0-3	20.0	- 1.93
Naas	3-19	0-5	2-10	0-0	1-4	15.8	- 7.00
Fairyhouse	2-10	1-3	1-5	0-0	0-2	20.0	- 5.02
Clonmel	1-1	0-0	1-1	0-0	0-0	100.0	+ 0.50
Ballinrobe	1-1	0-0	1-1	0-0	0-0	100.0	+ 0.67

Punchestown	1-3	1-2	0-1	0-0	0-0	33.3	-	1.00
Roscommon	1-4	1-1	0-2	0-0	0-1	25.0	-	2.00
Mallow	1-5	0-0	1-5	0-0	0-0	20.0	-	3.33
Listowel	1-6	1-2	0-3	0-0	0-1	16.7	-	4.27
Galway	1-8	1-3	0-3	0-0	0-2	12.5	-	4.75

Down Royal	0-1	Limerick	0-1	Thurles	0-1

WINNING HORSES

		Races					Win
	Age	Run	1st	2nd	3rd	Unpl	£
Manntari	2	2	2	0	0	0	65,344
Massyar	3	5	2	0	2	1	31,625
Takarouna	3	5	2	0	0	3	30,400
George Augustus	5	1	1	0	0	0	28,750
Rayseka	3	3	3	0	0	0	23,575
Foresee	3	4	1	0	3	0	23,000
Morcote	2	2	2	0	0	0	23,000
Shaiybara	3	3	3	0	0	0	18,289
Keraka	2	4	2	0	0	2	18,170
Cajarian	2	2	2	0	0	0	18,170
Chanzi	3	6	1	0	0	5	14,375
Idris	3	5	2	1	1	1	12,765
Erzadjan	3	4	3	0	0	1	12,424
Hushang	3	4	2	1	0	1	12,065
Madaniyya	3	7	3	1	2	1	9,319
Garabagh	4	4	1	1	1	1	8,627
Dawnsio	3	6	1	0	1	4	8,627
Miami Sands	3	2	1	0	0	1	8,625
Mamoura	3	6	2	1	0	3	7,592
Khalyani	3	4	2	2	0	0	6,902
Advocat	3	4	2	1	0	1	6,557
Birthplace	3	5	2	0	0	3	6,462
Tawar	3	3	2	0	0	1	6,214
Sharkashka	3	7	2	0	0	5	6,212
Bawardi	2	3	1	0	1	1	5,865
Ansariya	2	4	1	0	0	3	5,865
Musical Insight	2	3	1	0	0	2	5,522
Sumy	3	6	1	0	0	5	5,520
Gothic Dream	2	3	1	1	0	1	5,244
Zorina	2	4	1	0	1	2	5,244
Akhiyar	2	1	1	0	0	0	5,244
Saffron Crocus	3	7	2	1	0	4	5,007
Lock's Heath	3	5	2	1	0	2	4,825
Icy Tundra	2	3	1	1	0	1	4,485
Tadjik	3	1	1	0	0	0	4,142
Farmaan	3	4	1	1	1	1	4,140
Shahzadi	3	5	1	1	2	1	4,140
Kindness Itself	3	8	1	2	2	3	4,140
Tanakara	2	1	1	0	0	0	4,140
Timiniya	2	3	1	0	1	1	3,797
Daftari	3	4	1	3	0	0	3,795
Flying Eagle	2	4	1	2	0	1	3,795
Ridgewood Ben	2	1	1	0	0	0	3,795

Caliandak	3	3	1	0	0	2	3,452
Suekar	3	5	1	0	1	3	3,452
Rajaura	3	6	1	2	0	3	3,450
Mande Merchant	3	1	1	0	0	0	3,450
Parnala	3	5	1	0	3	1	3,450
Krisdaline	3	4	1	1	0	2	3,450
Balawhar	3	3	1	0	2	0	3,450
Gainsborough's Boy	2	5	1	2	0	2	3,107
Dayadan	3	2	1	1	0	0	2,935
Kharasar	3	4	1	0	2	1	2,760
Manzala	3	5	1	0	0	4	2,245
Tarakana	3	8	1	1	2	4	2,243
Karar	3	3	1	0	0	2	2,243

WINNING OWNERS

	Races Won	Value £		Races Won	Value £
H H Aga Khan	50	346,592	Mrs Anne Coughlan	1	3,795
Sheikh Mohammed	16	111,470	T J Monaghan	1	3,452
Lady Clague	7	32,852	Miss E Oxx	1	3,450
Dieter H Hofemeier	3	31,625	Dundalk Racing Club	1	2,245

Favourites	45-100	45.0%	- 2.33	Total winning prize-money	£535,481
Longest winning sequence			3	Average SP of winner	2.9/1
Longest losing sequence			17	Return on stakes invested	-5.4%

1992 Form	85-356	23.9%	- 36.00	1990 Form	65-376	17.3%	- 95.59
1991 Form	93-403	23.1%	+ 7.22	1989 Form	47-296	15.9%	- 81.25

K PRENDERGAST

	No. of Horses	Races Run	1st	2nd	3rd	Unpl	Per cent	£1 Level Stake
2-y-o	28	111	8	14	14	75	7.2	- 64.25
3-y-o	26	223	18	30	29	146	8.1	- 90.53
4-y-o+	11	89	14	13	6	56	15.7	- 1.04
Totals	65	423	40	57	49	277	9.5	-155.82

BY MONTH

2-y-o	W-R	Per cent	£1 Level Stake	3-y-o	W-R	Per cent	£1 Level Stake
Mar/Apr	0-4	-	- 4.00	Mar/Apr	2-20	10.0	- 2.00
May	0-11	-	- 11.00	May	3-32	9.4	- 4.50
June	1-10	10.0	- 6.00	June	2-40	5.0	- 27.00
July	3-16	18.8	- 0.50	July	1-43	2.3	- 34.00
August	2-22	9.1	- 12.75	August	7-40	17.5	- 2.60
September	2-17	11.8	+ 1.00	September	0-18	-	- 18.00
Oct/Nov	0-31	-	- 31.00	Oct/Nov	3-30	10.0	- 2.43

4-y-o+	W-R	Per cent	£1 Level Stake	Totals	W-R	Per cent	£1 Level Stake
Mar/Apr	2-11	18.2	0.00	Mar/Apr	4-35	11.4	- 6.00
May	1-8	12.5	0.00	May	4-51	7.8	- 15.50
June	1-13	7.7	- 10.50	June	4-63	6.3	- 43.50
July	1-14	7.1	- 8.50	July	5-73	6.8	- 43.00
August	5-17	29.4	+ 12.63	August	14-79	17.7	- 2.72
September	2-11	18.2	+ 8.33	September	4-46	8.7	- 8.67
Oct/Nov	2-15	13.3	- 3.00	Oct/Nov	5-76	6.6	- 36.43

DISTANCE

2-y-o	W-R	Per cent	£1 Level Stake	3-y-o	W-R	Per cent	£1 Level Stake
5f-6f	3-54	5.6	- 36.00	5f-6f	3-27	11.1	+ 0.50
7f-8f	5-55	9.1	- 26.25	7f-8f	4-63	6.3	- 31.00
9f-13f	0-2	-	- 2.00	9f-13f	9-124	7.3	- 61.60
14f+	0-0	-	0.00	14f+	2-9	22.2	+ 1.57

4-y-o+	W-R	Per cent	£1 Level Stake	Totals	W-R	Per cent	£1 Level Stake
5f-6f	3-15	20.0	+ 17.00	5f-6f	9-96	9.4	- 18.50
7f-8f	7-29	24.1	+ 4.13	7f-8f	16-147	10.9	- 53.12
9f-13f	1-28	3.6	- 20.00	9f-13f	10-154	6.5	- 83.60
14f+	3-17	17.6	- 2.17	14f+	5-26	19.2	- 0.60

TYPE OF RACE

Non-Handicaps	W-R	Per cent	£1 Level Stake	Handicaps	W-R	Per cent	£1 Level Stake
2-y-o	6-94	6.4	- 56.25	2-y-o	2-17	11.8	- 8.00
3-y-o	7-109	6.4	- 68.03	3-y-o	10-105	9.5	- 30.50
4-y-o+	5-26	19.2	- 10.87	4-y-o+	7-46	15.2	+ 14.50
Apprentice	0-2	-	- 2.00	Apprentice	1-17	5.9	0.00
Amat/Ladies	0-3	-	- 3.00	Amat/Ladies	2-4	50.0	+ 8.33
Totals	18-234	7.7	-140.15	Totals	22-189	11.6	- 15.67

FIRST TIME OUT

	W-R	Per cent	£1 Level Stake
2-y-o	0-28	-	- 28.00
3-y-o	2-26	7.7	- 8.00
4-y-o+	1-11	9.1	- 5.00
Totals	3-65	4.6	- 41.00

JOCKEYS RIDING

	W-R	Per cent	£1 Level Stake		W-R	Per cent	£1 Level Stake
W J Supple	27-287	9.4	-101.12	Capt J Ledingham	1-1	100.0	+ 0.57
B J Walsh	9-76	11.8	- 25.60	I Browne	1-12	8.3	+ 5.00
Mr J K Connolly	2-3	66.7	+ 9.33				

R Fitzpatrick	0-14	D G O'Shea	0-1	Mr J A Nash		0-1
J Cornally	0-11	E A Leonard	0-1	Mrs M Mullins		0-1
S Craine	0-6	Joanna Morgan	0-1	W J Smith		0-1
J F Clarke	0-3	L Dettori	0-1			
Mr A K Wyse	0-2	L O'Shea	0-1			

COURSE RECORD

	Total W-R	Non-Handicaps 2-y-o	3-y-o+	Handicaps 2-y-o	3-y-o+	Per cent	£1 Level Stake
The Curragh	12-89	2-23	3-24	0-3	7-39	13.5	+ 14.90
Tramore	4-11	0-0	1-5	0-0	3-6	36.4	+ 10.40
Bellewstown	3-9	1-3	1-2	0-0	1-4	33.3	+ 7.00
Tipperary	3-26	1-6	2-13	0-0	0-7	11.5	- 3.20
Leopardstown	3-65	0-10	1-25	1-3	1-27	4.6	- 50.50
Downpatrick	2-4	0-0	2-3	0-0	0-1	50.0	+ 3.50
Clonmel	2-12	0-0	0-6	0-0	2-6	16.7	+ 6.00
Roscommon	2-19	2-5	0-6	0-1	0-7	10.5	- 9.75
Laytown	1-4	0-0	0-1	0-0	1-3	25.0	+ 0.33
Sligo	1-8	0-3	0-3	0-0	1-2	12.5	- 4.00
Tralee	1-8	0-1	0-1	0-1	1-5	12.5	+ 1.00
Punchestown	1-8	0-3	0-2	0-0	1-3	12.5	0.00
Galway	1-12	0-1	0-2	1-1	0-8	8.3	- 9.00
Dundalk	1-15	0-3	1-6	0-0	0-6	6.7	- 9.50
Navan	1-20	0-8	0-6	0-0	1-6	5.0	- 11.00
Gowran Park	1-21	0-7	0-4	0-3	1-7	4.8	- 15.00
Naas	1-32	0-9	1-11	0-2	0-10	3.1	- 27.00

Fairyhouse	0-14	Listowel	0-8	Thurles	0-5
Mallow	0-10	Ballinrobe	0-5	Wexford	0-4
Killarney	0-8	Down Royal	0-5	Limerick	0-1

WINNING HORSES

	Age	Races Run	1st	2nd	3rd	Unpl	Win £
Bradawn Breever	4	13	3	2	0	8	25,275
Tony's Fen	4	12	3	0	1	8	20,455
Ready	3	7	3	0	1	3	16,750
Millie's Choice	4	12	3	5	1	3	15,184
Nanarch	9	6	3	0	0	3	7,794
Manaafis	2	7	2	0	1	4	6,904
Diligent Dodger	2	9	2	1	2	4	6,902
Island Vision	3	13	2	3	2	6	5,697
What A Pleasure	3	12	2	0	2	8	5,524
Yahthab	2	6	1	0	1	4	5,244

Lake Of Loughrea	3	10	2	1	0	7	5,178
Call My Guest	3	10	2	2	0	6	5,005
Wicklow Way	3	14	2	1	3	8	5,003
Desert Calm	4	8	1	2	0	5	4,292
Mahaseal	2	5	1	1	0	3	3,797
Oliver Messel	2	5	1	2	1	1	3,107
Corleonie	2	6	1	2	3	0	3,107
Southern Review	3	7	1	1	0	5	3,105
Imad	3	11	2	0	2	7	2,760
Blues Composer	4	8	1	3	0	4	2,760
Flora Wood	3	14	1	3	3	7	2,245
Tebre	3	12	1	1	2	8	1,380

WINNING OWNERS

	Races Won	Value £		Races Won	Value £
M A Murray	3	25,275	Mrs D M Donohoe	2	6,902
Mrs C Harrington	3	20,455	Mrs M O'Connell	2	5,697
Hamdan Al-Maktoum	6	18,705	P Conlan	2	5,003
Mrs Anne Coughlan	3	16,750	Mrs Isobel Folly	1	3,107
Colm McEvoy	3	15,184	Noel Carter	1	3,105
Mrs Kevin Prendergast	5	13,318	Aidan Walsh	1	2,760
Bezwell Fixings Ltd	4	10,183	Steinbeck Syndicate	1	2,245
Mrs Catherine McNulty	2	7,399	Mrs H De Burgh	1	1,380

Favourites	14-54	25.9%	- 11.15	Total winning prize-money		£157,468
Longest winning sequence			3	Average SP of winner		5.7/1
Longest losing sequence			52	Return on stakes invested		-36.8%
1992 Form	30-373	8.0%	-196.85	1990 Form	59-533	11.1%	-159.45
1991 Form	36-467	7.7%	-214.25	1989 Form	52-435	12.0%	-169.60

P PRENDERGAST

	No. of Horses	Races Run	1st	2nd	3rd	Unpl	Per cent	£1 Level Stake
2-y-o	7	25	1	1	2	21	4.0	- 12.00
3-y-o	5	23	2	0	1	20	8.7	+ 6.00
4-y-o+	7	40	4	9	2	25	10.0	- 23.40
Totals	19	88	7	10	5	66	8.0	- 29.40

Mar/Apr	May	Jun	Jul	Aug	Sep	Oct/Nov
1-15	0-10	0-12	3-15	1-12	0-11	2-13

Prendergast P

Winning Jockeys	W-R	£1 Level Stake		W-R	£1 Level Stake
J J Behan	4-29	+ 7.60	R Fitzpatrick	1-4	+ 1.50
W J Supple	1-1	+ 12.00	R V Skelly	1-6	- 2.50

Winning Courses					
Leopardstown	2-6	+ 23.00	Tralee	1-5	+ 0.50
Mallow	1-3	+ 0.50	Galway	1-5	+ 8.00
Tipperary	1-3	+ 2.50	Ballinrobe	1-7	- 4.90

Winning Horses	Age	Races Run	1st	2nd	3rd	Unpl	Win £
Macgillycuddy	4	10	3	2	0	5	9,145
Soundproof	3	7	2	0	0	5	6,555
Spring Force	2	8	1	1	1	5	3,795
Lady President	4	12	1	4	2	5	3,452

Favourites	2-12	16.7%	- 6.40	Total winning prize-money		£22,947

1992 Form	11-82	13.4%	- 26.37	1990 Form	7-69	10.1%	- 33.95
1991 Form	5-69	7.2%	- 31.50	1989 Form	9-110	8.2%	- 50.50

A REDMOND

	No. of Horses	Races Run	1st	2nd	3rd	Unpl	Per cent	£1 Level Stake
2-y-o	1	2	0	0	0	2	-	- 2.00
3-y-o	2	18	0	2	2	14	-	- 18.00
4-y-o+	5	15	1	0	1	13	6.7	- 12.50
Totals	8	35	1	2	3	29	2.9	- 32.50

Mar/Apr	May	Jun	Jul	Aug	Sep	Oct/Nov
0-2	0-4	0-4	1-6	0-9	0-6	0-4

Winning Jockey	W-R	£1 Level Stake	Winning Course	W-R	£1 Level Stake
Mr A K Wyse	1-4	- 1.50	Wexford	1-2	+ 0.50

Winning Horse	Age	Races Run	1st	2nd	3rd	Unpl	Win £
Paget	6	3	1	0	0	2	2,245

Favourites	1-2	50.0%	+ 0.50	Total winning prize-money		£2,245

1992 Form	0-52			1990 Form	0-70		-
1991 Form	2-72	2.8%	- 65.12	1989 Form	4-139	2.9%	-111.40

L T REILLY

	No. of Horses	Races Run	1st	2nd	3rd	Unpl	Per cent	£1 Level Stake
2-y-o	0	0	0	0	0	0	-	0.00
3-y-o	0	0	0	0	0	0	-	0.00
4-y-o+	1	6	1	0	0	5	16.7	+ 15.00
Totals	1	6	1	0	0	5	16.7	+ 15.00

Mar/Apr	May	Jun	Jul	Aug	Sep	Oct/Nov
0-1	0-0	0-1	0-1	1-1	0-2	0-0

Winning Jockey	W-R	£1 Level Stake	Winning Course	W-R	£1 Level Stake
R M Burke	1-3	+ 18.00	Sligo	1-1	+ 20.00

Winning Horse	Age	Races Run	1st	2nd	3rd	Unpl	Win £
Sheslookinatme	4	6	1	0	0	5	2,762

Favourites	0-0		Total winning prize-money	£2,762

1992 Form	0-8		1990 Form	0-19		
1991 Form	0-4		1989 Form	2-43	4.7%	- 24.00

W M ROPER

	No. of Horses	Races Run	1st	2nd	3rd	Unpl	Per cent	£1 Level Stake
2-y-o	3	8	0	0	0	8	-	- 8.00
3-y-o	1	5	0	0	0	5	-	- 5.00
4-y-o+	4	9	1	0	0	8	11.1	+ 2.00
Totals	8	22	1	0	0	21	4.5	- 11.00

Mar/Apr	May	Jun	Jul	Aug	Sep	Oct/Nov
0-0	0-4	1-3	0-5	0-5	0-3	0-2

Winning Jockey	W-R	£1 Level Stake	Winning Course	W-R	£1 Level Stake
Mr A R Coonan	1-1	+ 10.00	Limerick	1-1	+ 10.00

Winning Horse	Age	Races Run	1st	2nd	3rd	Unpl	Win £
Buzz Along	7	3	1	0	0	2	2,245

Favourites	0-0		Total winning prize-money	£2,245

1992 Form	1-31	3.2%	- 26.00	1990 Form	0-17		
1991 Form	2-33	6.1%	- 11.00	1989 Form	1-20	5.0%	- 5.00

T STACK

	No. of Horses	Races Run	1st	2nd	3rd	Unpl	Per cent	£1 Level Stake
2-y-o	19	45	1	7	2	35	2.2	- 36.00
3-y-o	23	112	11	8	10	83	9.8	- 54.37
4-y-o+	6	15	0	1	0	14	-	- 15.00
Totals	48	172	12	16	12	132	7.0	-105.37

BY MONTH

2-y-o	W-R	Per cent	£1 Level Stake	3-y-o	W-R	Per cent	£1 Level Stake
Mar/Apr	0-2	-	- 2.00	Mar/Apr	3-18	16.7	- 2.50
May	0-1	-	- 1.00	May	2-20	10.0	- 15.37
June	1-3	33.3	+ 6.00	June	2-19	10.5	- 9.50
July	0-5	-	- 5.00	July	1-20	5.0	- 12.50
August	0-9	-	- 9.00	August	2-22	9.1	- 9.50
September	0-10	-	- 10.00	September	1-9	11.1	- 1.00
Oct/Nov	0-15	-	- 15.00	Oct/Nov	0-4	-	- 4.00

4-y-o+	W-R	Per cent	£1 Level Stake	Totals	W-R	Per cent	£1 Level Stake
Mar/Apr	0-6	-	- 6.00	Mar/Apr	3-26	11.5	- 10.50
May	0-5	-	- 5.00	May	2-26	7.7	- 21.37
June	0-2	-	- 2.00	June	3-24	12.5	- 5.50
July	0-1	-	- 1.00	July	1-26	3.8	- 18.50
August	0-1	-	- 1.00	August	2-32	6.3	- 19.50
September	0-0	-	0.00	September	1-19	5.3	- 11.00
Oct/Nov	0-0	-	0.00	Oct/Nov	0-19	-	- 19.00

DISTANCE

2-y-o	W-R	Per cent	£1 Level Stake	3-y-o	W-R	Per cent	£1 Level Stake
5f-6f	1-17	5.9	- 8.00	5f-6f	5-27	18.5	- 5.25
7f-8f	0-27	-	- 27.00	7f-8f	1-29	3.4	- 23.50
9f-13f	0-1	-	- 1.00	9f-13f	5-52	9.6	- 21.62
14f+	0-0	-	0.00	14f+	0-4	-	- 4.00

4-y-o+	W-R	Per cent	£1 Level Stake	Totals	W-R	Per cent	£1 Level Stake
5f-6f	0-3	-	- 3.00	5f-6f	6-47	12.8	- 16.25
7f-8f	0-2	-	- 2.00	7f-8f	1-58	1.7	- 52.50
9f-13f	0-9	-	- 9.00	9f-13f	5-62	8.1	- 31.62
14f+	0-1	-	- 1.00	14f+	0-5	-	- 5.00

TYPE OF RACE

Non-Handicaps	W-R	Per cent	£1 Level Stake	Handicaps	W-R	Per cent	£1 Level Stake
2-y-o	1-45	2.2	- 36.00	2-y-o	0-0	-	0.00
3-y-o	8-69	11.6	- 31.87	3-y-o	3-40	7.5	- 19.50
4-y-o+	0-6	-	- 6.00	4-y-o+	0-8	-	- 8.00
Apprentice	0-0	-	0.00	Apprentice	0-2	-	- 2.00
Amat/Ladies	0-2	-	- 2.00	Amat/Ladies	0-0	-	0.00
Totals	9-122	7.4	- 75.87	Totals	3-50	6.0	- 29.50

FIRST TIME OUT

	W-R	Per cent	£1 Level Stake
2-y-o	1-19	5.3	- 10.00
3-y-o	2-23	8.7	- 11.75
4-y-o+	0-6	-	- 6.00
Totals	3-48	6.3	- 27.75

JOCKEYS RIDING

	W-R	Per cent	£1 Level Stake		W-R	Per cent	£1 Level Stake
S Craine	11-140	7.9	- 80.87	P P Murphy	1-2	50.0	+ 5.50

J J Stack	0-13	G M Moylan	0-1	R Hughes	0-1
L Piggott	0-3	Mr K Whelan	0-1	W Carson	0-1
D G O'Shea	0-2	Mr S P Hennessy	0-1	W J Smith	0-1
D W O'Sullivan	0-2	P P O'Grady	0-1	
J J Behan	0-2	P Shanahan	0-1	

COURSE RECORD

	Total W-R	Non-Handicaps 2-y-o	Non-Handicaps 3-y-o+	Handicaps 2-y-o	Handicaps 3-y-o+	Per cent	£1 Level Stake
Roscommon	2-10	0-3	2-5	0-0	0-2	20.0	- 2.12
Mallow	2-12	0-0	2-9	0-0	0-3	16.7	- 6.25
Leopardstown	2-31	1-9	0-14	0-0	1-8	6.5	- 15.00
Ballinrobe	1-6	0-1	1-2	0-0	0-3	16.7	- 2.00
Gowran Park	1-7	0-2	0-1	0-0	1-4	14.3	- 1.50
Navan	1-8	0-5	1-2	0-0	0-1	12.5	- 5.00
Tipperary	1-11	0-2	1-7	0-0	0-2	9.1	- 2.00
Killarney	1-11	0-1	1-7	0-0	0-3	9.1	- 3.50
The Curragh	1-28	0-10	0-7	0-0	1-11	3.6	- 20.00

Tralee	0-10	Clonmel	0-4	Punchestown	0-1
Listowel	0-7	Sligo	0-3	Thurles	0-1
Naas	0-7	Fairyhouse	0-2	Wexford	0-1
Galway	0-5	Limerick	0-2	
Bellewstown	0-4	Downpatrick	0-1	

WINNING HORSES

	Age	Races Run	1st	2nd	3rd	Unpl	Win £
My-O-My	3	7	2	1	1	3	9,145
Las Meninas	2	2	1	1	0	0	8,627
Oenothera	3	11	2	1	1	7	6,385
Forest	3	8	2	1	0	5	5,697
Miss Mistletoes	3	10	2	1	2	5	5,522
Kerb Crawler	3	3	1	0	1	1	3,450
Tropical Lake	3	6	1	0	1	4	3,450
Tartan Lady	3	6	1	0	1	4	2,243

WINNING OWNERS

	Races Won	Value £		Races Won	Value £
R E Sangster	7	29,679	Mrs E Irwin	1	3,450
T Corden	3	9,147	John Thompson	1	2,243

Favourites	3-7	42.9%	+ 0.63	Total winning prize-money	£44,519
Longest winning sequence			1	Average SP of winner	4.6/1
Longest losing sequence			29	Return on stakes invested	-61.3%
1992 Form	20-199	10.1%	- 78.70	1990 Form	22-216	10.2%	-101.10
1991 Form	49-263	18.6%	+ 22.70	1989 Form	23-167	13.8%	- 54.60

ADRIAN TAYLOR

	No. of Horses	Races Run	1st	2nd	3rd	Unpl	Per cent	£1 Level Stake
2-y-o	0	0	0	0	0	0	-	0.00
3-y-o	1	5	0	0	0	5	-	- 5.00
4-y-o+	2	19	2	3	3	11	10.5	- 1.00
Totals	3	24	2	3	3	16	8.3	- 6.00

Mar/Apr	May	Jun	Jul	Aug	Sep	Oct/Nov
0-0	0-2	0-6	0-3	0-5	2-5	0-3

Winning Jockeys	W-R	£1 Level Stake		W-R	£1 Level Stake
W J Supple	1-1	+ 10.00	B Fenton	1-1	+ 6.00

Winning Courses	W-R	£1 Level Stake		W-R	£1 Level Stake
Roscommon	1-1	+ 6.00	Ballinrobe	1-2	+ 9.00

Winning Horses	Age	Races Run	1st	2nd	3rd	Unpl	Win £
Just One Canaletto	5	12	1	1	1	9	2,245
Zuhal	5	7	1	2	2	2	2,243

| Favourites | 0-1 | | | | Total winning prize-money | | £4,488 |

| 1992 Form | 2-22 | 9.1% | + 14.00 | 1990 Form | 1-28 | 3.6% | - 15.00 |
| 1991 Form | 1-22 | 4.5% | - 1.00 | 1989 Form | 0-26 | | |

S TREACY

	No. of Horses	Races Run	1st	2nd	3rd	Unpl	Per cent	£1 Level Stake
2-y-o	0	0	0	0	0	0	-	0.00
3-y-o	1	8	2	1	1	4	25.0	- 0.25
4-y-o+	2	3	0	1	0	2	-	- 3.00
Totals	3	11	2	2	1	6	18.2	- 3.25

Mar/Apr	May	Jun	Jul	Aug	Sep	Oct/Nov
1-2	1-2	0-3	0-4	0-0	0-0	0-0

Winning Jockeys	W-R	£1 Level Stake		W-R	£1 Level Stake
D J O'Donohoe	1-2	+ 1.25	P P Murphy	1-7	- 2.50

Winning Courses					
Limerick	1-1	+ 3.50	Mallow	1-2	+ 1.25

Winning Horse	Age	Races Run	1st	2nd	3rd	Unpl	Win £
The Beruki	3	8	2	1	1	4	4,488

| Favourites | 1-2 | 50.0% | + 1.25 | Total winning prize-money | | £4,488 |

| 1992 Form | 0-6 | 1990 Form | 0-0 |
| 1991 Form | 0-1 | 1989 Form | 0-5 |

T M WALSH

	No. of Horses	Races Run	1st	2nd	3rd	Unpl	Per cent	£1 Level Stake
2-y-o	3	18	1	2	1	14	5.6	- 16.10
3-y-o	1	10	0	1	3	6	-	- 10.00
4-y-o+	4	18	4	5	1	8	22.2	+ 29.00
Totals	8	46	5	8	5	28	10.9	+ 2.90

Mar/Apr	May	Jun	Jul	Aug	Sep	Oct/Nov
0-2	2-4	1-9	1-11	1-11	0-5	0-4

Walsh T M

Winning Jockeys	W-R	£1 Level Stake		W-R	£1 Level Stake
R V Skelly	3-13	+ 28.00	J J Behan	1-5	+ 1.00
M J Kinane	1-1	+ 0.90			

Winning Courses					
Leopardstown	2-7	+ 14.00	Galway	1-2	- 0.10
The Curragh	2-15	+ 11.00			

Winning Horses	Age	Races Run	1st	2nd	3rd	Unpl	Win £
Classical Affair	4	9	3	3	1	2	20,255
Doherty	2	3	1	0	1	1	4,142
Nunivak	5	6	1	2	0	3	3,795

Favourites	1-3	33.3%	- 1.10	Total winning prize-money		£28,192

1992 Form	3-45	6.7%	- 16.00	1991 Form	1-26	3.8%	- 18.50

D K WELD

	No. of Horses	Races Run	1st	2nd	3rd	Unpl	Per cent	£1 Level Stake
2-y-o	43	126	26	20	12	68	20.6	- 36.05
3-y-o	54	260	49	43	25	143	18.8	- 30.21
4-y-o+	36	166	34	24	19	89	20.5	- 6.08
Totals	133	552	109	87	56	300	19.7	- 72.34

BY MONTH

2-y-o	W-R	Per cent	£1 Level Stake	3-y-o	W-R	Per cent	£1 Level Stake
Mar/Apr	2-3	66.7	+ 4.00	Mar/Apr	4-39	10.3	- 22.02
May	1-9	11.1	- 7.75	May	7-32	21.9	+ 3.80
June	1-11	9.1	- 7.25	June	6-42	14.3	- 8.98
July	5-23	21.7	- 4.12	July	10-41	24.4	+ 3.22
August	5-23	21.7	- 5.58	August	12-49	24.5	- 10.98
September	6-21	28.6	- 7.23	September	7-29	24.1	+ 4.75
Oct/Nov	6-36	16.7	- 8.12	Oct/Nov	3-28	10.7	0.00

4-y-o+	W-R	Per cent	£1 Level Stake	Totals	W-R	Per cent	£1 Level Stake
Mar/Apr	3-19	15.8	- 5.25	Mar/Apr	9-61	14.8	- 23.27
May	3-21	14.3	- 11.25	May	11-62	17.7	- 15.20
June	5-24	20.8	- 6.40	June	12-77	15.6	- 22.63
July	9-29	31.0	+ 17.50	July	24-93	25.8	+ 16.60
August	5-31	16.1	- 11.93	August	22-103	21.4	- 28.49
September	3-18	16.7	- 5.75	September	16-68	23.5	- 8.23
Oct/Nov	6-24	25.0	+ 17.00	Oct/Nov	15-88	17.0	+ 8.88

DISTANCE

2-y-o	W-R	Per cent	£1 Level Stake	3-y-o	W-R	Per cent	£1 Level Stake
5f-6f	9-46	19.6	- 20.82	5f-6f	6-31	19.4	- 8.02
7f-8f	16-76	21.1	- 14.23	7f-8f	16-98	16.3	- 25.65
9f-13f	1-4	25.0	- 1.00	9f-13f	24-125	19.2	- 7.29
14f+	0-0	-	0.00	14f+	3-6	50.0	+ 10.75

4-y-o+	W-R	Per cent	£1 Level Stake	Totals	W-R	Per cent	£1 Level Stake
5f-6f	2-28	7.1	- 19.00	5f-6f	17-105	16.2	- 47.84
7f-8f	8-41	19.5	+ 6.50	7f-8f	40-215	18.6	- 33.38
9f-13f	15-60	25.0	+ 0.82	9f-13f	40-189	21.2	- 7.47
14f+	9-37	24.3	+ 5.60	14f+	12-43	27.9	+ 16.35

TYPE OF RACE

Non-Handicaps	W-R	Per cent	£1 Level Stake	Handicaps	W-R	Per cent	£1 Level Stake
2-y-o	24-113	21.2	- 31.80	2-y-o	2-13	15.4	- 4.25
3-y-o	34-167	20.4	- 27.91	3-y-o	13-81	16.0	- 3.80
4-y-o+	12-43	27.9	+ 22.10	4-y-o+	18-100	18.0	- 21.50
Apprentice	1-5	20.0	+ 3.00	Apprentice	0-14	-	- 14.00
Amat/Ladies	5-13	38.5	+ 8.82	Amat/Ladies	0-3	-	- 3.00
Totals	76-341	22.3	- 25.79	Totals	33-211	15.6	- 46.55

FIRST TIME OUT

	W-R	Per cent	£1 Level Stake
2-y-o	8-43	18.6	- 15.48
3-y-o	7-53	13.2	- 14.60
4-y-o+	5-36	13.9	- 15.00
Totals	20-132	15.2	- 45.08

JOCKEYS RIDING

	W-R	Per cent	£1 Level Stake		W-R	Per cent	£1 Level Stake
M J Kinane	78-283	27.6	+ 10.77	W J Smith	4-39	10.3	- 18.50
P Shanahan	13-137	9.5	- 52.37	Miss U Smyth	3-6	50.0	+ 6.01
D J O'Donohoe	8-43	18.6	+ 14.50	Mr J A Nash	3-9	33.3	+ 2.25

D V Smith	0-9	C Roche	0-1	Miss J McDowell	0-1
J J Byrne	0-5	D G O'Shea	0-1	Mr K Dempsey	0-1
W J Walsh	0-4	D O'Callaghan	0-1	P Lowry	0-1
R Dolan	0-3	J F Egan	0-1	R M Burke	0-1
T Quinn	0-2	K M Chin	0-1	W Carson	0-1
B Coogan	0-1	L Cummins	0-1		

COURSE RECORD

	Total W-R	Non-Handicaps 2-y-o	3-y-o+	Handicaps 2-y-o	3-y-o+	Per cent	£1 Level Stake
Leopardstown	23-105	4-18	11-45	1-3	7-39	21.9	+ 5.40
The Curragh	18-115	3-29	9-36	0-0	6-50	15.7	- 27.10
Galway	11-34	2-5	5-9	0-2	4-18	32.4	+ 0.10
Listowel	8-16	4-4	2-4	0-1	2-7	50.0	+ 16.95
Tipperary	7-33	1-8	3-18	0-0	3-7	21.2	- 5.50
Dundalk	6-17	1-4	3-9	0-0	2-4	35.3	+ 11.85
Tralee	5-23	3-3	1-9	0-1	1-10	21.7	- 10.00
Gowran Park	5-26	2-8	2-9	1-2	0-7	19.2	+ 1.90
Naas	5-40	1-8	3-18	0-2	1-12	12.5	- 0.62
Sligo	4-9	0-1	3-6	0-0	1-2	44.4	+ 6.73
Fairyhouse	4-19	1-6	2-8	0-0	1-5	21.1	- 0.43
Down Royal	3-10	1-2	2-6	0-0	0-2	30.0	- 3.31
Clonmel	2-7	0-0	1-3	0-0	1-4	28.6	+ 2.00
Mallow	2-14	0-1	2-11	0-1	0-1	14.3	- 7.50
Roscommon	2-21	0-5	1-6	0-1	1-9	9.5	- 10.43
Tramore	1-4	0-0	1-3	0-0	0-1	25.0	0.00
Thurles	1-5	0-0	0-4	0-0	1-1	20.0	- 2.25
Ballinrobe	1-5	0-1	1-2	0-0	0-2	20.0	- 2.75
Killarney	1-7	1-1	0-2	0-0	0-4	14.3	- 5.38

Navan	0-13	Punchestown	0-5	Downpatrick	0-3
Limerick	0-8	Laytown	0-4		
Bellewstown	0-5	Wexford	0-4		

WINNING HORSES

	Age	Races Run	1st	2nd	3rd	Unpl	Win £
Vintage Crop	6	5	3	1	1	0	107,590
Pre-Eminent	6	8	4	1	0	3	42,475
Tropical	3	6	3	0	1	2	37,375
Asema	3	5	3	1	0	1	28,750
Cliveden Gail	4	6	3	2	1	0	23,697
Phase In	3	7	3	1	0	3	14,665
Low Key Affair	2	3	2	0	1	0	13,869
City Nights	2	7	2	3	2	0	13,455
Skipo	3	5	2	0	0	3	12,420
Ciseaux	4	8	3	0	1	4	11,065
Aiybak	5	6	2	0	0	4	10,150
Il Caravaggio	2	3	2	0	0	1	10,007
Rienroe	4	8	3	3	0	2	8,804
Unusual Heat	3	4	1	0	0	3	8,625
Artema	2	3	2	0	0	1	8,625
Peace Role	2	7	2	2	0	3	7,937
Glacial Arctic	3	4	2	0	0	2	7,592
Blazing Spectacle	3	3	2	0	0	1	7,245
Saibot	4	8	2	5	0	1	7,075
Strategic Timing	3	5	2	2	0	1	6,902
Garboni	4	4	1	0	0	3	6,902
Nassau	6	3	1	1	0	1	6,900
Duharra	5	3	1	1	0	1	6,900

Topographe	3	4	2	0	0	2	6,210
Creative Bloom	2	1	1	0	0	0	5,865
Sylvia Fox	6	5	2	1	0	2	5,693
Aljawza	2	6	1	2	0	3	5,670
Astronave	2	4	1	0	1	2	5,522
Soviet Choice	3	5	1	3	0	1	5,520
Monte Mario	2	4	1	0	0	3	5,344
Elusive Domain	2	1	1	0	0	0	5,244
Suave Groom	3	5	2	1	0	2	5,005
Petofi	3	5	2	1	1	1	5,005
Porterstown Boy	3	5	2	0	0	3	4,490
Market Slide	2	4	1	1	1	1	4,485
Persian Tactics	4	1	1	0	0	0	4,142
Clear Ability	3	6	1	1	1	3	4,140
Lustrino	3	4	1	0	1	2	4,140
Tigersong	3	2	1	0	0	1	4,140
Missus Murhill	2	2	1	0	0	1	4,140
Paugim	2	6	1	1	0	4	3,797
Dancing Action	2	2	1	0	0	1	3,797
Profit Release	2	2	1	0	0	1	3,797
Treble Bob	3	7	1	0	0	6	3,795
Diamonds Galore	8	9	1	3	1	4	3,795
Uncertain Affair	3	5	1	0	1	3	3,795
Private Guy	4	5	1	0	1	3	3,795
Rahal	2	5	1	1	0	3	3,795
Velma	3	6	2	0	0	4	3,625
Political Surge	3	4	1	1	1	1	3,452
Ziravello	2	4	1	1	0	2	3,452
Principle Music	5	3	1	1	0	1	3,452
Push The Button	3	2	1	0	0	1	3,452
Radical Tactic	3	1	1	0	0	0	3,452
Arabic Treasure	3	8	1	1	2	4	3,450
Ormsby	4	5	1	0	1	3	3,450
Continuous	2	2	1	0	0	1	3,450
Ruvolina	2	1	1	0	0	0	3,450
Dobie	5	8	1	0	2	5	3,105
Millmount	3	6	1	1	1	3	2,962
Nordicolini	3	6	1	0	0	5	2,935
Reticent Bride	3	7	1	3	0	3	2,762
Sir Slaves	3	8	1	0	0	7	2,762
Safayn	3	9	1	4	0	4	2,762
Sleet Skier	6	4	1	0	1	2	2,762
Seek The Faith	4	8	1	1	1	5	2,762
Brave Raider	3	5	1	2	1	1	2,762
Brata	3	4	1	1	0	2	2,762
Alterezza	6	3	1	0	0	2	2,760
Speedwell Blue	2	2	1	0	0	1	2,245
Lucky Prince	3	11	1	1	2	7	2,243
Pennine Mist	3	4	1	1	0	2	2,243
Great Cabaret	3	6	1	3	1	1	2,243
Somerton Boy	3	9	1	0	1	7	1,208
Shiowen	2	6	1	0	1	4	1,208

Weld D K

WINNING OWNERS

	Races Won	Value £		Races Won	Value £
Michael W J Smurfit	16	189,029	R E Sangster	2	7,073
Moyglare Stud Farm	20	85,714	Mrs M Togher	1	6,900
Allen E Paulson	8	47,557	Philip Monahan	3	5,698
The Sussex Stud Ltd	3	37,375	Mrs C L Weld	2	5,693
Andrea Schiavi	9	36,580	M G Hynes	2	5,522
Int Th'Bred Breeders Inc	3	23,697	Miss K McGann	2	5,348
Michael Hilary Burke	3	14,665	Saleh Y Al-Homaisi	1	5,344
G Olivero	3	11,065	Dr Anne J F Gillespie	2	5,005
Raymond J Rooney	2	10,352	T J Monaghan	1	3,797
Mrs A J F O'Reilly	3	10,350	Frank Stronach	1	3,795
Michael Watt	3	10,007	Peter Wetzel	1	3,450
Ovidstown Investments Ltd	3	8,804	T F Gammell	1	2,962
Mrs S Khan	3	8,800	Ronald Arculli	1	2,935
Thomas T S Liang	1	8,625	A J O'Reilly	1	2,762
Saleh Y Al-Homaisi	2	8,625	M Benaceraf	1	2,245
Rachid Damania	1	8,625	Mrs Sean M Collins	1	2,243
Hamdan Al-Maktoum	2	8,432	Bezwell Fixings Ltd	1	2,243

Favourites	53-167	31.7%	- 28.35	Total winning prize-money	£601,316
Longest winning sequence			4	Average SP of winner	3.4/1
Longest losing sequence			27	Return on stakes invested	-13.1%

1992 Form	106-597	17.8%	-179.63	1990 Form	82-559	14.7%	-266.83
1991 Form	120-645	18.6%	-119.34	1989 Form	104-511	20.4%	-130.30

O WELDON

	No. of Horses	Races Run	1st	2nd	3rd	Unpl	Per cent	£1 Level Stake
2-y-o	1	6	1	0	0	5	16.7	- 0.50
3-y-o	4	22	0	1	0	21	-	- 22.00
4-y-o+	6	21	1	2	3	15	4.8	- 10.00
Totals	11	49	2	3	3	41	4.1	- 32.50

Mar/Apr	May	Jun	Jul	Aug	Sep	Oct/Nov
0-4	1-10	0-7	0-8	0-7	1-6	0-7

Winning Jockeys	W-R	£1 Level Stake		W-R	£1 Level Stake
P Shanahan	1-3	+ 2.50	P Carberry	1-6	+ 5.00

Winning Courses					
Down Royal	1-3	+ 2.50	Leopardstown	1-8	+ 3.00

Winning Horses	Age	Races Run	1st	2nd	3rd	Unpl	Win £
Clandolly	5	6	1	0	0	5	4,142
Smart Rosie	2	6	1	0	0	5	2,415

Favourites	0-0			Total winning prize-money		£6,557
1992 Form	1-47	2.1%	- 38.50	1990 Form	0-20	
1991 Form	3-14	21.4%	+ 15.00	1989 Form	1-26	3.8%	- 17.00

TRAINERS WITH NO WINNERS IN IRELAND 1993

	No. of Horses	Races Run	2nd	3rd	Unpl
D J Barry	2	3	0	0	3
N C Bell	5	23	1	0	22
Thomas Bergin	4	11	1	0	10
W T Bourke	2	7	0	0	7
V Bowens	14	37	3	0	34
W F Brannigan	1	1	0	0	1
J Brassil	2	3	0	0	3
M Brew	1	5	0	0	5
W P Browne	6	23	3	0	20
Arthur Bunyan	3	12	0	0	12
Mrs S Burke	1	6	0	0	6
J P Byrne	2	2	0	0	2
J Cahill	1	1	0	0	1
T Carberry	1	3	0	0	3
T Carmody	1	6	0	0	6
D Carroll	7	16	0	0	16
Peter Casey	4	12	0	1	11
P J Casserly	2	6	0	0	6
N Cassidy	2	2	0	0	2
Mrs P Collier	1	6	1	0	5
Luke Comer	2	4	0	1	3
R J Cotter	2	8	0	0	8
J Cox	2	8	0	0	8
Mrs Crowley-O'Brien	1	1	0	0	1
James William Cullen	3	10	0	1	9
M Cullinane	2	7	0	0	7
T G Curtin	4	20	1	2	17
R F Dalton	2	3	0	0	3
H De Bromhead	2	5	0	0	5
P J Deegan	4	16	0	0	16
P Delaney	2	4	0	0	4
C P Donoghue	1	1	0	0	1
R Donoghue	2	3	0	1	2
P J Doyle	1	1	1	0	0
T Duggan	3	12	1	0	11
M Dunne	2	2	0	1	1
H Eastwood	1	1	0	0	1
A D Evans	3	13	1	1	11
S Fahey	2	2	1	0	1
G Farrell	1	4	0	0	4
W Fennin	1	5	0	1	4
I Ferguson	1	1	0	0	1
T Foley	2	5	0	0	5
Mrs Ian Fox	2	15	1	0	14
Noel Furlong	3	3	0	0	3
P Griffin	1	2	0	0	2
W M Halley	1	1	0	0	1
Mrs John Harrington	1	1	0	0	1
J L Hassett	3	14	0	0	14
J C Hayden	8	19	0	1	18
Mrs Seamus Hayes	1	2	0	0	2
N Henley	1	1	0	0	1
P Henley	3	13	1	0	12

	No. of Horses	Races Run	2nd	3rd	Unpl
P Hughes	5	9	0	1	8
J P Kavanagh	5	24	0	2	22
T Keaney	1	1	1	0	0
P G Kelly	2	7	0	0	7
Paul Kelly	1	2	0	0	2
V Kennedy	7	26	1	3	22
J E Kiely	3	3	0	0	3
P Kiely	1	1	0	0	1
T Kinane	5	18	0	0	18
Basil King	1	2	0	0	2
F J Lacy	1	2	0	0	2
P J Lally	5	19	0	1	18
P R Lenihan	1	2	0	1	1
F Lennon	1	4	0	0	4
R Lister	3	14	1	1	12
P M Lynch	3	10	0	0	10
M V Manning	3	4	0	0	4
A J Martin	3	9	1	0	8
W J Martin	3	16	0	1	15
J F C Maxwell	3	8	0	1	7
T G McCourt	6	27	2	1	24
M A McCullagh	3	17	2	0	15
M McDonagh	1	4	0	0	4
D McDonogh	5	13	0	0	13
D J McGrath	1	1	0	0	1
L McHugh	1	3	0	0	3
J J McLoughlin	16	59	5	5	49
A J McNamara	7	13	1	0	12
P J Molloy	2	13	1	2	10
P Mooney	1	4	0	1	3
A L T Moore	5	12	0	2	10
R M Moore	1	4	0	0	4
Ms J Morgan	4	18	0	0	18
Anthony Mullins	9	28	2	0	26
W T Murphy	1	1	0	0	1
T B Naughton	1	3	0	0	3
J Nicholson	1	3	0	0	3
John W Nicholson	2	5	0	0	5
Robert Norris	1	3	0	0	3
P O'Brady	1	1	0	0	1
F M O'Brien	1	3	0	0	3
V T O'Brien	3	6	1	0	5
A F O'Callaghan	1	2	0	0	2
N O'Callaghan	5	19	1	1	17
D O'Connell	2	6	0	1	5
E O'Connell	3	4	0	0	4
J A O'Connell	3	11	0	0	11
P F O'Donnell	4	12	0	2	10
R O'Donovan	2	8	0	0	8
J O'Haire	2	4	0	1	3
R O'Neill	2	10	1	1	8
F Oakes	1	1	0	0	1
F W Pennicott	5	21	0	0	21
A Persse	2	6	0	1	5
P Phelan	2	2	0	0	2
M Purcell	2	9	3	0	6

	No. of Horses	Races Run	2nd	3rd	Unpl
M Quaid	5	13	0	0	13
E Quinn	1	1	0	0	1
T A Regan	4	11	3	0	8
M H B Robinson	2	4	0	2	2
W Rock	2	3	0	0	3
Ms Rosemary Rooney	1	5	0	1	4
P Rooney	1	1	0	0	1
B J Ryan	1	4	0	0	4
Countess Schulenburg	1	2	0	0	2
J H Scott	1	1	0	0	1
J Sheahan	2	10	2	0	8
J C Shearman	2	4	0	0	4
William Sheehy	1	2	0	0	2
D T Sheridan	1	2	0	0	2
S Spillane	1	6	1	0	5
G Stack	2	4	0	0	4
F Sutherland	1	2	0	0	2
Capt D G Swan	8	18	0	2	16
Wilbert Tolerton	6	15	1	1	13
Mrs S Treacy	1	1	0	0	1
Eamon Tyrrell	2	4	0	0	4
T Walker	2	12	0	0	12
John J Walsh	3	10	1	0	9
S Walsh	1	1	0	0	1
J Ward	1	3	0	0	3
J Weld	3	5	0	1	4
Miss A M Winters	1	2	0	0	2
Patrick Woods	6	31	2	2	27

OVERSEAS TRAINERS WITH WINNERS IN IRELAND 1993

T D BARRON (England)

	No. of Horses	Races Run	1st	2nd	3rd	Unpl	Per cent	£1 Level Stake
2-y-o	0	0	0	0	0	0	-	0.00
3-y-o	1	2	1	0	0	1	50.0	+ 6.00
4-y-o+	0	0	0	0	0	0	-	0.00
Totals	1	2	1	0	0	1	50.0	+ 6.00

Mar/Apr	May	Jun	Jul	Aug	Sep	Oct/Nov
0-0	0-0	1-1	0-0	0-0	0-1	0-0

Winning Jockey	W-R	£1 Level Stake	Winning Course	W-R	£1 Level Stake
K Darley	1-1	+ 7.00	Leopardstown	1-2	+ 6.00

Winning Horse	Age	Races Run	1st	2nd	3rd	Unpl	Win £
Sea Gazer	3	2	1	0	0	1	14,625

Favourites	0-0	Total winning prize-money	£14,625

J BERRY (England)

	No. of Horses	Races Run	1st	2nd	3rd	Unpl	Per cent	£1 Level Stake
2-y-o	2	2	1	0	0	1	50.0	+ 6.00
3-y-o	2	3	0	0	2	1	-	- 3.00
4-y-o+	0	0	0	0	0	0	-	0.00
Totals	4	5	1	0	2	2	20.0	+ 3.00

Mar/Apr	May	Jun	Jul	Aug	Sep	Oct/Nov
0-0	0-0	0-1	0-0	1-2	0-2	0-0

Winning Jockey	W-R	£1 Level Stake	Winning Course	W-R	£1 Level Stake
S Craine	1-1	+ 7.00	The Curragh	1-2	+ 6.00

Winning Horse	Age	Races Run	1st	2nd	3rd	Unpl	Win £
Palacegate Jack	2	1	1	0	0	0	73,750

Favourites	0-0	Total winning prize-money	£73,750

1992 Form	1-3	33.3%	- 1.47	1990 Form	2-9	22.2%	+ 3.00
1991 Form	0-7			1989 Form	0-2		

H R A CECIL (England)

	No. of Horses	Races Run	1st	2nd	3rd	Unpl	Per cent	£1 Level Stake
2-y-o	0	0	0	0	0	0	-	0.00
3-y-o	1	1	1	0	0	0	100.0	+ 0.57
4-y-o+	0	0	0	0	0	0	-	0.00
Totals	1	1	1	0	0	0	100.0	+ 0.57

Mar/Apr	May	Jun	Jul	Aug	Sep	Oct/Nov
0-0	0-0	1-1	0-0	0-0	0-0	0-0

Winning Jockey	W-R	£1 Level Stake	Winning Course	W-R	£1 Level Stake
Pat Eddery	1-1	+ 0.57	The Curragh	1-1	+ 0.57

Winning Horse	Age	Races Run	1st	2nd	3rd	Unpl	Win £
Commander In Chief	3	1	1	0	0	0	342,500

Favourites	1-1	100.0%	+ 0.57	Total winning prize-money	£342,500

1992 Form	0-1		1990 Form	1-5	20.0%	- 3.50
1991 Form	0-2		1989 Form	5-8	62.5%	+ 1.59

P CHAPPLE-HYAM (England)

	No. of Horses	Races Run	1st	2nd	3rd	Unpl	Per cent	£1 Level Stake
2-y-o	2	2	1	0	1	0	50.0	+ 0.75
3-y-o	1	1	0	0	1	0	-	- 1.00
4-y-o+	0	0	0	0	0	0	-	0.00
Totals	3	3	1	0	2	0	33.3	- 0.25

Mar/Apr	May	Jun	Jul	Aug	Sep	Oct/Nov
0-0	0-0	0-0	0-1	1-1	0-1	0-0

Winning Jockey	W-R	£1 Level Stake	Winning Course	W-R	£1 Level Stake
J Reid	1-3	- 0.25	Leopardstown	1-1	+ 1.75

Winning Horse	Age	Races Run	1st	2nd	3rd	Unpl	Win £
Turtle Island	2	1	1	0	0	0	85,500

Favourites	1-2	50.0%	+ 0.75	Total winning prize-money	£85,500

1992 Form	2-6	33.3%	+ 0.23	1991 Form	0-1

L CUMANI (England)

	No. of Horses	Races Run	1st	2nd	3rd	Unpl	Per cent	£1 Level Stake
2-y-o	0	0	0	0	0	0	-	0.00
3-y-o	2	2	1	0	0	1	50.0	- 0.43
4-y-o+	0	0	0	0	0	0	-	0.00
Totals	2	2	1	0	0	1	50.0	- 0.43

Mar/Apr	May	Jun	Jul	Aug	Sep	Oct/Nov
0-0	1-2	0-0	0-0	0-0	0-0	0-0

Winning Jockey	W-R	£1 Level Stake	Winning Course	W-R	£1 Level Stake
M Roberts	1-1	+ 0.57	The Curragh	1-2	- 0.43

Winning Horse	Age	Races Run	1st	2nd	3rd	Unpl	Win £
Barathea	3	1	1	0	0	0	149,649

Favourites	1-1	100.0%	+ 0.57	Total winning prize-money	£149,649

1992 Form	0-1		1990 Form	0-4		
1991 Form	0-0		1989 Form	2-5	40.0%	+ 2.63

J L DUNLOP (England)

	No. of Horses	Races Run	1st	2nd	3rd	Unpl	Per cent	£1 Level Stake
2-y-o	1	1	1	0	0	0	100.0	+ 3.33
3-y-o	5	5	0	1	1	3	-	- 5.00
4-y-o+	1	1	0	0	1	0	-	- 1.00
Totals	7	7	1	1	2	3	14.3	- 2.67

Mar/Apr	May	Jun	Jul	Aug	Sep	Oct/Nov
0-0	0-0	0-1	0-1	0-1	0-1	1-3

Winning Jockey	W-R	£1 Level Stake	Winning Course	W-R	£1 Level Stake
W Carson	1-3	+ 1.33	The Curragh	1-5	- 0.67

Winning Horse	Age	Races Run	1st	2nd	3rd	Unpl	Win £
Sheridan	2	1	1	0	0	0	17,250

Favourites	0-0	Total winning prize-money	£17,250

1992 Form	1-2	50.0%	+ 8.00	1990 Form	2-8	25.0%	- 2.63
1991 Form	0-2			1989 Form	1-9	11.1%	- 4.00

A FABRE (France)

	No. of Horses	Races Run	1st	2nd	3rd	Unpl	Per cent	£1 Level Stake
2-y-o	1	1	0	1	0	0	-	- 1.00
3-y-o	2	2	1	0	0	1	50.0	+ 3.50
4-y-o+	0	0	0	0	0	0	-	0.00
Totals	3	3	1	1	0	1	33.3	+ 2.50

Mar/Apr	May	Jun	Jul	Aug	Sep	Oct/Nov
0-0	0-0	0-0	1-2	0-0	0-1	0-0

Winning Jockey	W-R	£1 Level Stake	Winning Course	W-R	£1 Level Stake
Pat Eddery	1-1	+ 4.50	The Curragh	1-3	+ 2.50

Winning Horse	Age	Races Run	1st	2nd	3rd	Unpl	Win £
Wemyss Bight	3	1	1	0	0	0	113,000

Favourites	0-2	Total winning prize-money	£113,000

1992 Form	0-1	1991 Form	0-2

J H M GOSDEN (England)

	No. of Horses	Races Run	1st	2nd	3rd	Unpl	Per cent	£1 Level Stake
2-y-o	0	0	0	0	0	0	-	0.00
3-y-o	2	2	0	0	0	2	-	- 2.00
4-y-o+	2	2	1	0	0	1	50.0	+ 6.00
Totals	4	4	1	0	0	3	25.0	+ 4.00

Mar/Apr	May	Jun	Jul	Aug	Sep	Oct/Nov
0-0	0-1	0-1	0-0	0-0	1-2	0-0

Winning Jockey	W-R	£1 Level Stake	Winning Course	W-R	£1 Level Stake
W Carson	1-2	+ 6.00	Leopardstown	1-1	+ 7.00

Winning Horse	Age	Races Run	1st	2nd	3rd	Unpl	Win £
Muhtarram	4	1	1	0	0	0	84,300

Favourites	0-0	Total winning prize-money	£84,300

1992 Form	1-4	25.0%	- 0.25	1990 Form	0-2
1991 Form	0-2			1989 Form	0-1

B HANBURY (England)

	No. of Horses	Races Run	1st	2nd	3rd	Unpl	Per cent	£1 Level Stake
2-y-o	1	1	1	0	0	0	100.0	+ 1.50
3-y-o	1	1	0	0	1	0	-	- 1.00
4-y-o+	0	0	0	0	0	0	-	0.00
Totals	2	2	1	0	1	0	50.0	+ 0.50

Mar/Apr	May	Jun	Jul	Aug	Sep	Oct/Nov
0-0	0-0	1-1	0-0	0-1	0-0	0-0

Winning Jockey	W-R	£1 Level Stake	Winning Course	W-R	£1 Level Stake
W R Swinburn	1-2	+ 0.50	The Curragh	1-1	+ 1.50

Winning Horse	Age	Races Run	1st	2nd	3rd	Unpl	Win £
Polish Laughter	2	1	1	0	0	0	13,125

Favourites	1-1	100.0%	+ 1.50	Total winning prize-money	£13,125

1992 Form	0-1			1990 Form	1-3	33.3%	+ 0.50
1991 Form	1-4	25.0%	+ 0.50	1989 Form	0-4		

R HANNON (England)

	No. of Horses	Races Run	1st	2nd	3rd	Unpl	Per cent	£1 Level Stake
2-y-o	2	2	1	0	0	1	50.0	+ 2.33
3-y-o	1	1	0	0	0	1	-	- 1.00
4-y-o+	1	1	0	1	0	0	-	- 1.00
Totals	4	4	1	1	0	2	25.0	+ 0.33

Mar/Apr	May	Jun	Jul	Aug	Sep	Oct/Nov
0-0	0-0	0-0	0-0	0-1	1-3	0-0

Winning Jockey	W-R	£1 Level Stake	Winning Course	W-R	£1 Level Stake
L Piggott	1-1	+ 3.33	The Curragh	1-3	+ 1.33

Winning Horse	Age	Races Run	1st	2nd	3rd	Unpl	Win £
Lemon Souffle	2	1	1	0	0	0	56,100

Favourites	0-0	Total winning prize-money	£56,100

1992 Form	1-4	25.0%	+ 7.00	1990 Form	2-4	50.0%	+ 2.75
1991 Form	2-4	50.0%	+ 6.50	1989 Form	1-2	50.0%	+ 0.10

B W HILLS (England)

	No. of Horses	Races Run	1st	2nd	3rd	Unpl	Per cent	£1 Level Stake
2-y-o	0	0	0	0	0	0	-	0.00
3-y-o	2	2	1	0	0	1	50.0	+ 7.00
4-y-o+	0	0	0	0	0	0	-	0.00
Totals	2	2	1	0	0	1	50.0	+ 7.00

Mar/Apr	May	Jun	Jul	Aug	Sep	Oct/Nov
0-0	1-1	0-1	0-0	0-0	0-0	0-0

Winning Jockey	W-R	£1 Level Stake	Winning Course	W-R	£1 Level Stake
M Hills	1-1	+ 8.00	The Curragh	1-2	+ 7.00

Winning Horse	Age	Races Run	1st	2nd	3rd	Unpl	Win £
Nicer	3	1	1	0	0	0	113,000

Favourites	0-0		Total winning prize-money	£113,000

1992 Form	1-7	14.3%	- 3.00	1990 Form	4-15	26.7%	- 0.87
1991 Form	1-8	12.5%	- 1.00	1989 Form	5-12	41.7%	+ 10.00

J TOLLER (England)

	No. of Horses	Races Run	1st	2nd	3rd	Unpl	Per cent	£1 Level Stake
2-y-o	0	0	0	0	0	0	-	0.00
3-y-o	0	0	0	0	0	0	-	0.00
4-y-o+	1	2	1	0	1	0	50.0	+ 4.00
Totals	1	2	1	0	1	0	50.0	+ 4.00

Mar/Apr	May	Jun	Jul	Aug	Sep	Oct/Nov
0-0	0-0	0-0	0-0	1-1	0-1	0-0

Winning Jockey	W-R	£1 Level Stake	Winning Course	W-R	£1 Level Stake
W Newnes	1-2	+ 4.00	The Curragh	1-1	+ 5.00

Winning Horse	Age	Races Run	1st	2nd	3rd	Unpl	Win £
Lord Of The Field	6	2	1	0	1	0	11,500

Favourites	0-0		Total winning prize-money	£11,500

OVERSEAS TRAINERS WITH NO WINNERS IN IRELAND 1993

	No. of Horses	Races Run	2nd	3rd	Unpl
E J Alston (Eng)	1	1	1	0	0
F Boutin (Fra)	1	1	1	0	0
C E Brittain (Eng)	4	4	1	0	3
Mrs J Cecil (Eng)	1	1	0	0	1
R Charlton (Eng)	1	1	0	0	1
P F I Cole (Eng)	3	3	0	0	3
C W C Elsey (Eng)	1	1	0	0	1
J M P Eustace (Eng)	1	1	0	0	1
Mrs C Head (Fra)	1	1	0	0	1
R F J Houghton (Eng)	1	1	0	0	1
Lord Huntingdon (Eng)	2	3	0	0	3
M S Johnston (Eng)	1	1	0	0	1
H T Jones (Eng)	2	2	0	0	2
G Lewis (Eng)	1	1	0	0	1
D R Loder (Eng)	1	1	0	1	0
P J Makin (Eng)	1	1	0	0	1
M McCormack (Eng)	1	1	1	0	0
W R Muir (Eng)	1	1	0	1	0
Miss L Perratt (Eng)	1	1	0	0	1
Satish Seemar (UAE)	1	1	0	0	1
Miss L Siddall (Eng)	1	1	0	0	1
M R Stoute (Eng)	4	4	2	0	2
R J R Williams (Eng)	1	1	0	0	1
G Wragg (Eng)	1	1	0	0	1
N C Wright (Eng)	1	1	0	0	1

COURSE SECTION

(IRISH FLAT 1989-93)

BALLINROBE

Leading Trainers 1989-93

	Total W-R	Non-handicaps 2-y-o	Non-handicaps 3-y-o+	Handicaps 2-y-o	Handicaps 3-y-o+	Per cent	£1 Level Stake
D K Weld	8-37	1-9	4-14	0-0	3-14	21.6	- 14.80
J S Bolger	7-32	1-6	2-16	0-0	4-10	21.9	- 8.50
John M Oxx	6-8	0-1	5-6	0-0	1-1	75.0	+ 8.13
D Gillespie	5-23	0-3	2-9	0-0	3-11	21.7	- 2.48
Augustine Leahy	3-5	0-1	2-3	0-0	1-1	60.0	+ 7.75
B V Kelly	3-12	1-3	0-4	0-0	2-5	25.0	+ 26.00
P Prendergast	3-12	1-2	1-3	0-0	1-7	25.0	+ 3.10
C Collins	3-16	0-2	1-5	0-0	2-9	18.8	- 4.63
G T Hourigan	2-3	1-2	1-1	0-0	0-0	66.7	+ 11.00
Daniel J Murphy	2-11	0-3	0-4	0-0	2-4	18.2	+ 11.50
M J Grassick	2-16	1-4	0-3	0-0	1-9	12.5	- 5.00
T Stack	2-18	0-5	2-10	0-0	0-3	11.1	- 10.75
Edward Lynam	2-19	0-2	1-5	0-0	1-12	10.5	- 11.67
J Bryce Smith	1-1	0-0	0-0	0-0	1-1	100.0	+ 3.00
T G McCourt	1-1	0-0	0-0	0-0	1-1	100.0	+ 10.00
W M Roper	1-2	0-1	0-0	0-0	1-1	50.0	+ 3.00
W P Mullins	1-2	0-0	0-0	0-0	1-2	50.0	+ 2.00
D McDonogh	1-3	0-0	0-1	0-0	1-2	33.3	+ 3.00
Adrian Taylor	1-3	0-0	0-0	0-0	1-3	33.3	+ 8.00
Patrick Woods	1-4	0-0	0-2	0-0	1-2	25.0	+ 47.00
D Hanley	1-4	0-1	1-2	0-0	0-1	25.0	+ 6.00
A P O'Brien	1-4	0-1	0-1	0-0	1-2	25.0	+ 2.00

Leading Jockeys

	Total W-R	Per cent	£1 Level Stake	Best Trainer	W-R	Per cent	£1 Level Stake
M J Kinane	11-39	28.2	- 8.25	D K Weld	7-30	23.3	- 10.80
W J Supple	9-29	31.0	+ 24.40	J S Bolger	4-12	33.3	+ 2.50
J F Egan	4-26	15.4	- 10.25	M J Grassick	2-3	66.7	+ 8.00
N G McCullagh	4-26	15.4	- 10.75	W P Mullins	1-1	100.0	+ 3.00
S Craine	4-34	11.8	- 13.75	T Stack	2-18	11.1	- 10.75
C Roche	3-16	18.8	- 7.00	J S Bolger	3-15	20.0	- 6.00
J J Behan	3-16	18.8	+ 7.10	P Prendergast	2-6	33.3	+ 0.10
P Shanahan	3-21	14.3	- 13.87	C Collins	2-5	40.0	+ 0.88
R Hughes	3-36	8.3	- 21.67	G T Hourigan	1-1	100.0	+ 5.00
B J Walsh	2-5	40.0	+ 6.00	A P O'Brien	1-1	100.0	+ 5.00
M Fenton	2-14	14.3	- 3.75	Augustine Leahy	1-2	50.0	+ 1.25
P V Gilson	2-20	10.0	- 10.17	Daniel J Murphy	1-4	25.0	+ 1.50

How the Favourites Fared

Non-handicaps	W-R	Per cent	£1 Level Stake	Handicaps	W-R	Per cent	£1 Level Stake
2-y-o	3-10	30.0	- 1.25	2-y-o	0-0	-	0.00
3-y-o	1-2	50.0	+ 1.25	3-y-o	1-5	20.0	- 2.62
Weight-for-age	13-29	44.8	+ 8.70	All-aged	12-29	41.4	+ 3.98
Totals	17-41	41.5	+ 8.70	Totals	13-34	38.2	+ 1.36
All favs	30-75	40.0	+ 10.06				

BELLEWSTOWN

Leading Trainers 1989-93

	Total W-R	Non-handicaps 2-y-o	3-y-o+	Handicaps 2-y-o	3-y-o+	Per cent	£1 Level Stake
D K Weld	9-40	2-10	5-12	0-0	2-18	22.5	- 9.40
K Prendergast	7-40	3-11	2-11	0-0	2-18	17.5	- 9.33
John M Oxx	4-13	0-0	3-9	0-0	1-4	30.8	+ 6.00
J S Bolger	4-24	1-5	2-8	0-0	1-11	16.7	- 10.00
M Kauntze	4-28	1-9	1-8	0-0	2-11	14.3	- 13.55
F Dunne	3-10	0-3	1-4	0-0	2-3	30.0	+ 11.50
M A O'Toole	3-26	1-7	2-8	0-0	0-11	11.5	- 16.08
E J O'Grady	2-6	1-1	0-2	0-0	1-3	33.3	+ 29.00
B V Kelly	2-14	0-3	0-3	0-0	2-8	14.3	- 4.00
M J Grassick	2-18	0-2	2-12	0-0	0-4	11.1	- 14.10
Noel T Chance	1-2	0-0	1-2	0-0	0-0	50.0	+ 6.00
M V O'Brien	1-2	0-0	1-2	0-0	0-0	50.0	- 0.20
P Beirne	1-2	1-1	0-0	0-0	0-1	50.0	+ 2.00
Mrs P V Doyle	1-4	0-1	1-1	0-0	0-2	25.0	+ 17.00
P Prendergast	1-4	0-1	0-1	0-0	1-2	25.0	- 0.50
P Hughes	1-4	0-1	0-0	0-0	1-3	25.0	+ 11.00
C P Magnier	1-6	0-0	0-3	0-0	1-3	16.7	+ 11.00
T Keaney	1-6	0-0	0-1	0-0	1-5	16.7	- 0.50
V Kennedy	1-7	0-0	1-2	0-0	0-5	14.3	+ 10.00
A Redmond	1-7	0-1	0-3	0-0	1-3	14.3	- 2.50
M Halford	1-8	0-1	0-2	0-0	1-5	12.5	- 5.00
J T Gorman	1-8	0-1	0-0	0-0	1-7	12.5	+ 1.00

Leading Jockeys

	Total W-R	Per cent	£1 Level Stake	Best Trainer	W-R	Per cent	£1 Level Stake
M J Kinane	13-43	30.2	+ 2.47	D K Weld	9-32	28.1	- 1.40
P V Gilson	4-29	13.8	- 3.20	Daniel J Murphy	1-1	100.0	+ 3.00
R M Burke	3-26	11.5	+ 5.00	C Collins	1-1	100.0	+ 14.00
S Craine	3-35	8.6	- 16.00	B V Kelly	2-7	28.6	+ 3.00
Mr A P O'Brien	2-3	66.7	+ 4.25	J S Bolger	2-3	66.7	+ 4.25
B J Walsh	2-6	33.3	+ 8.50	K Prendergast	2-6	33.3	+ 8.50
R Griffiths	2-14	14.3	- 8.83	K Prendergast	2-14	14.3	- 8.83
M Fenton	2-17	11.8	+ 9.50	Edward Lynam	1-3	33.3	+ 2.50
C Roche	2-22	9.1	- 15.25	J S Bolger	2-12	16.7	- 5.25
R Hughes	2-32	6.3	- 24.10	M J Grassick	1-8	12.5	- 6.10
Mr D Marnane	1-1	100.0	+ 0.67	M A O'Toole	1-1	100.0	+ 0.67
Mr J A Nash	1-1	100.0	+ 7.00	Noel T Chance	1-1	100.0	+ 7.00

How the Favourites Fared

Non-handicaps	W-R	Per cent	£1 Level Stake	Handicaps	W-R	Per cent	£1 Level Stake
2-y-o	7-12	58.3	+ 3.04	2-y-o	0-0	-	0.00
3-y-o	0-0	-	0.00	3-y-o	0-0	-	0.00
Weight-for-age	9-23	39.1	- 3.78	All-aged	11-25	44.0	+ 7.35
Totals	16-35	45.7	- 0.74	Totals	11-25	44.0	+ 7.35
All favs	27-60	45.0	+ 6.61				

CLONMEL

Leading Trainers 1989–93

	Total W–R	Non-handicaps 2-y-o	Non-handicaps 3-y-o+	Handicaps 2-y-o	Handicaps 3-y-o+	Per cent	£1 Level Stake
J S Bolger	7–39	0-0	4-25	0-0	3-14	17.9	- 10.60
John M Oxx	6–15	0-0	6-13	0-0	0-2	40.0	- 3.06
D K Weld	6–22	0-0	4-13	0-0	2-9	27.3	+ 10.80
J J McLoughlin	5–11	0-0	1-4	0-0	4-7	45.5	+ 22.25
K Prendergast	4–33	0-0	2-19	0-0	2-14	12.1	- 1.00
P J Flynn	4–34	0-0	3-16	0-0	1-18	11.8	- 9.50
Capt D G Swan	3–9	0-0	1-7	0-0	2-2	33.3	+ 13.83
Noel Meade	3–15	0-0	2-10	0-0	1-5	20.0	+ 0.50
A P O'Brien	2–7	0-0	2-4	0-0	0-3	28.6	+ 10.00
C Collins	2–8	0-0	1-7	0-0	1-1	25.0	+ 10.00
Daniel J Murphy	2–9	0-0	1-5	0-0	1-4	22.2	- 1.25
Liam Browne	2–11	0-0	2-8	0-0	0-3	18.2	- 3.10
Augustine Leahy	2–27	0-0	1-22	0-0	1-5	7.4	- 6.00
F Berry	1–1	0-0	0-0	0-0	1-1	100.0	+ 3.00
P Aspell	1–1	0-0	1-1	0-0	0-0	100.0	+ 5.00
P Griffin	1–2	0-0	1-2	0-0	0-0	50.0	+ 2.00
P F O'Donnell	1–2	0-0	1-2	0-0	0-0	50.0	+ 4.00
J P Byrne	1–3	0-0	1-3	0-0	0-0	33.3	0.00
E McNamara	1–3	0-0	1-3	0-0	0-0	33.3	+ 4.00
J P Kavanagh	1–4	0-0	1-3	0-0	0-1	25.0	- 1.50
Mrs Crowley-O'Brien	1–4	0-0	1-3	0-0	0-1	25.0	- 1.75
T A Regan	1–5	0-0	0-3	0-0	1-2	20.0	- 2.75

Leading Jockeys

	Total W–R	Per cent	£1 Level Stake	Best Trainer	W–R	Per cent	£1 Level Stake
M J Kinane	7–21	33.3	+ 5.95	D K Weld	4-9	44.4	+ 11.80
C Roche	6–31	19.4	- 12.12	J S Bolger	3-21	14.3	- 10.60
W J Supple	6–33	18.2	0.00	J S Bolger	3-7	42.9	+ 4.00
J J Behan	3–10	30.0	+ 2.40	W P Mullins	1-1	100.0	+ 3.50
S Craine	3–29	10.3	- 10.00	Noel Meade	2-5	40.0	+ 8.00
N G McCullagh	3–31	9.7	- 14.75	J J McLoughlin	3-6	50.0	+ 10.25
J F Egan	3–33	9.1	- 13.00	P J Flynn	3-18	16.7	+ 2.00
P Shanahan	2–20	10.0	- 2.00	C Collins	2-5	40.0	+ 13.00
W J O'Connor	2–25	8.0	- 16.00	P Aspell	1-1	100.0	+ 5.00
R Hughes	2–29	6.9	- 10.00	Capt D G Swan	1-1	100.0	+ 14.00
P Carberry	1–1	100.0	+ 1.50	Noel Meade	1-1	100.0	+ 1.50
T P Treacy	1–2	50.0	+ 4.00	P F O'Donnell	1-1	100.0	+ 5.00

How the Favourites Fared

Non-handicaps	W–R	Per cent	£1 Level Stake	Handicaps	W–R	Per cent	£1 Level Stake
2-y-o	0-0	-	0.00	2-y-o	0-0		0.00
3-y-o	3-12	25.0	- 3.95	3-y-o	1-4	25.0	- 2.00
Weight-for-age	20-30	66.7	+ 12.42	All-aged	9-19	47.4	+ 8.15
Totals	23-42	54.8	+ 8.47	Totals	10-23	43.5	+ 6.15
All favs	33-65	50.8	+ 14.62				

THE CURRAGH

Leading Trainers 1989-93

	Total W-R	Non-handicaps 2-y-o	3-y-o+	Handicaps 2-y-o	3-y-o+	Per cent	£1 Level Stake
J S Bolger	106-688	45-204	34-261	3-18	24-205	15.4	-114.33
John M Oxx	83-523	23-147	42-248	0-3	18-125	15.9	- 52.55
D K Weld	65-589	15-156	32-216	2-9	16-208	11.0	-312.12
M V O'Brien	55-172	23-71	29-87	0-0	3-14	32.0	+ 10.66
K Prendergast	40-530	10-144	13-168	2-17	15-201	7.5	-240.47
T Stack	24-235	5-62	12-95	1-6	6-72	10.2	- 53.87
C Collins	24-284	6-63	6-94	2-8	10-119	8.5	- 95.90
M Kauntze	21-185	8-57	8-72	0-3	5-53	11.4	- 33.66
P J Flynn	9-118	1-14	3-30	0-3	5-71	7.6	- 25.00
Noel Meade	9-167	1-36	4-43	1-5	3-83	5.4	- 91.00
P Prendergast	8-108	2-30	3-30	1-6	2-42	7.4	- 39.60
M A O'Toole	8-112	1-27	1-37	1-5	5-43	7.1	- 21.50
F Dunne	7-66	1-11	2-23	0-1	4-31	10.6	+ 17.00
Liam Browne	6-176	4-68	1-51	0-10	1-47	3.4	-114.00
H R A Cecil (Eng)	5-12	1-1	4-11	0-0	0-0	41.7	- 2.09
P F I Cole (Eng)	5-16	0-2	5-13	0-0	0-1	31.3	+ 3.63
J L Dunlop (Eng)	5-20	2-5	3-15	0-0	0-0	25.0	+ 4.70
B W Hills (Eng)	5-30	1-7	3-22	0-0	1-1	16.7	- 4.50
D Hanley	5-32	0-10	4-15	0-0	1-7	15.6	+ 10.50
D P Kelly	5-33	0-4	0-3	1-3	4-23	15.2	+ 22.50
T M Walsh	5-39	0-3	1-13	0-1	4-22	12.8	+ 12.50
W P Mullins	5-52	0-2	0-10	0-4	5-36	9.6	- 19.00

Leading Jockeys

	Total W-R	Per cent	£1 Level Stake	Best Trainer	W-R	Per cent	£1 Level Stake
C Roche	87-456	19.1	- 51.83	J S Bolger	85-387	22.0	+ 5.17
M J Kinane	76-510	14.9	-205.92	D K Weld	57-406	14.0	-173.60
L Piggott	28-121	23.1	- 19.67	M V O'Brien	24-62	38.7	+ 10.27
J Reid	28-127	22.0	+ 15.85	M V O'Brien	17-49	34.7	+ 1.02
W J Supple	27-287	9.4	- 17.17	K Prendergast	10-62	16.1	+ 23.33
S Craine	25-378	6.6	-210.87	T Stack	21-190	11.1	- 53.87
R Hughes	24-290	8.3	-112.63	John M Oxx	8-47	17.0	- 9.03
P Shanahan	23-315	7.3	-180.65	C Collins	13-91	14.3	- 7.40
W J O'Connor	19-216	8.8	- 90.16	M Kauntze	14-99	14.1	- 13.16
P V Gilson	17-271	6.3	-138.75	C Collins	7-105	6.7	- 38.50
D G O'Shea	13-138	9.4	- 18.99	John M Oxx	7-35	20.0	+ 35.01
J F Egan	11-205	5.4	- 80.00	P J Flynn	5-44	11.4	+ 14.00

How the Favourites Fared

Non-handicaps	W-R	Per cent	£1 Level Stake	Handicaps	W-R	Per cent	£1 Level Stake
2-y-o	72-178	40.4	- 22.48	2-y-o	6-16	37.5	+ 6.35
3-y-o	42-93	45.2	+ 2.68	3-y-o	7-21	33.3	+ 4.13
Weight-for-age	52-164	31.7	- 32.74	All-aged	37-154	24.0	- 13.10
Totals	166-435	38.2	- 52.54	Totals	50-191	26.2	- 2.62
All favs	216-626	34.5	- 55.16				

DOWN ROYAL

Leading Trainers 1989-93

	Total W-R	Non-handicaps 2-y-o	3-y-o+	Handicaps 2-y-o	3-y-o+	Per cent	£1 Level Stake
D K Weld	12-46	1-8	9-28	0-1	2-9	26.1	- 8.54
J S Bolger	11-34	2-13	6-16	1-1	2-4	32.4	+ 8.56
M Kauntze	10-44	3-13	3-18	0-0	4-13	22.7	- 8.56
M J Grassick	7-31	2-6	3-14	0-0	2-11	22.6	- 5.52
J C Hayden	5-14	2-4	3-7	0-0	0-3	35.7	+ 13.80
B V Kelly	5-37	2-11	2-12	0-0	1-14	13.5	- 17.50
F Dunne	4-19	0-3	2-11	0-0	2-5	21.1	+ 6.25
C Collins	4-20	2-4	0-9	0-0	2-7	20.0	- 6.25
Liam Browne	3-12	2-4	1-7	0-0	0-1	25.0	+ 4.35
E J O'Grady	3-15	1-3	0-3	0-0	2-9	20.0	+ 10.42
John M Oxx	3-17	0-0	3-15	0-0	0-2	17.6	- 12.17
P Prendergast	2-5	0-0	1-2	0-0	1-3	40.0	+ 7.00
Daniel J Murphy	2-8	2-4	0-1	0-1	0-2	25.0	+ 13.50
J J McLoughlin	2-12	0-0	0-3	0-0	2-9	16.7	- 3.50
V Bowens	2-17	0-2	0-7	0-0	2-8	11.8	- 1.75
Noel Meade	2-22	1-5	1-12	0-0	0-5	9.1	- 6.50
G T Hourigan	1-1	0-0	0-0	0-0	1-1	100.0	+ 14.00
E P Mitchell	1-2	0-0	0-0	0-0	1-2	50.0	+ 3.00
T Stack	1-3	0-0	1-3	0-0	0-0	33.3	+ 2.00
E P Harty	1-4	0-2	1-2	0-0	0-0	25.0	- 2.20
D McDonogh	1-5	0-1	0-1	0-0	1-3	20.0	+ 0.50
J Burns	1-5	1-2	0-2	0-0	0-1	20.0	+ 1.50

Leading Jockeys

	Total W-R	Per cent	£1 Level Stake	Best Trainer	W-R	Per cent	£1 Level Stake
C Roche	8-12	66.7	+ 18.78	J S Bolger	7-10	70.0	+ 17.28
P V Gilson	8-22	36.4	+ 6.25	C Collins	4-9	44.4	+ 4.75
P Shanahan	8-33	24.2	- 6.77	M Kauntze	3-6	50.0	- 0.16
M J Kinane	6-21	28.6	- 2.83	D K Weld	4-12	33.3	+ 1.75
N G McCullagh	5-20	25.0	+ 5.80	F Dunne	2-3	66.7	+ 14.00
W J Supple	5-26	19.2	- 5.50	J S Bolger	3-12	25.0	+ 2.00
W J O'Connor	5-31	16.1	+ 11.44	M Kauntze	4-20	20.0	+ 1.44
M Fenton	4-16	25.0	+ 9.25	P Prendergast	1-1	100.0	+ 5.00
K J Manning	4-27	14.8	- 8.75	M J Grassick	3-8	37.5	+ 1.25
R Hughes	3-24	12.5	- 14.83	Edward Lynam	1-1	100.0	+ 3.00
D Duggan	3-27	11.1	- 7.50	Daniel J Murphy	1-1	100.0	+ 3.50
W Carson	2-2	100.0	+ 6.50	B V Kelly	2-2	100.0	+ 6.50

How the Favourites Fared

Non-handicaps	W-R	Per cent	£1 Level Stake	Handicaps	W-R	Per cent	£1 Level Stake
2-y-o	12-25	48.0	- 0.71	2-y-o	1-1	100.0	+ 0.50
3-y-o	3-15	20.0	- 7.90	3-y-o	1-3	33.3	- 0.50
Weight-for-age	13-31	41.9	- 7.37	All-aged	14-30	46.7	+ 7.52
Totals	28-71	39.4	- 15.98	Totals	16-34	47.1	+ 7.52
All favs	44-105	41.9	- 8.46				

DOWNPATRICK

Leading Trainers 1989-93

	Total W-R	Non-handicaps 2-y-o	3-y-o+	Handicaps 2-y-o	3-y-o+	Per cent	£1 Level Stake
K Prendergast	4-11	0-0	4-9	0-0	0-2	36.4	+ 4.00
Peter Casey	3-11	0-0	2-9	0-0	1-2	27.3	+ 7.50
M J Grassick	3-12	0-0	3-12	0-0	0-0	25.0	- 0.70
D K Weld	3-16	0-0	3-16	0-0	0-0	18.8	+ 1.00
F Dunne	2-4	0-0	1-3	0-0	1-1	50.0	+ 4.00
J F C Maxwell	2-7	0-0	2-6	0-0	0-1	28.6	+ 3.00
Francis Ennis	1-1	0-0	1-1	0-0	0-0	100.0	+ 4.50
J F Bailey Jnr	1-1	0-0	1-1	0-0	0-0	100.0	+ 20.00
T O'Neill	1-2	0-0	1-2	0-0	0-0	50.0	+ 11.00
J Burns	1-2	0-0	1-2	0-0	0-0	50.0	+ 13.00
P Hughes	1-2	0-0	1-2	0-0	0-0	50.0	- 0.33
E P Harty	1-2	0-0	1-2	0-0	0-0	50.0	- 0.43
F Flood	1-2	0-0	1-2	0-0	0-0	50.0	- 0.60
Miss I T Oakes	1-2	0-0	1-2	0-0	0-0	50.0	+ 15.00
Noel T Chance	1-3	0-0	1-2	0-0	0-1	33.3	- 0.90
T Stack	1-3	0-0	1-2	0-0	0-1	33.3	- 1.00
J S Bolger	1-4	0-0	1-4	0-0	0-0	25.0	+ 3.50
Noel Meade	1-4	0-0	1-3	0-0	0-1	25.0	- 0.50
M A O'Toole	1-5	0-0	0-3	0-0	1-2	20.0	+ 3.00
M Halford	1-6	0-0	1-4	0-0	0-2	16.7	0.00
Daniel J Murphy	1-6	0-0	1-5	0-0	0-1	16.7	- 1.00
M Cunningham	1-7	0-0	1-7	0-0	0-0	14.3	- 5.33

Leading Jockeys

	Total W-R	Per cent	£1 Level Stake	Best Trainer	W-R	Per cent	£1 Level Stake
W J Smith	4-13	30.8	+ 10.00	J P Byrne	1-1	100.0	+ 6.00
S Craine	3-7	42.9	+ 0.07	E P Harty	1-1	100.0	+ 0.57
C Everard	2-4	50.0	+ 3.60	Francis Ennis	1-1	100.0	+ 4.50
J A Heffernan	2-6	33.3	+ 22.50	J F Bailey Jnr	1-1	100.0	+ 20.00
B J Walsh	2-7	28.6	+ 0.50	K Prendergast	2-4	50.0	+ 3.50
D Duggan	2-9	22.2	+ 5.50	Peter Casey	1-3	33.3	+ 0.50
R Hughes	2-10	20.0	+ 2.50	M J Grassick	1-2	50.0	+ 2.50
D V Smith	2-14	14.3	+ 10.00	J Burns	1-1	100.0	+ 14.00
N Byrne	2-15	13.3	+ 3.00	T O'Neill	1-1	100.0	+ 12.00
F Berry	1-1	100.0	0.00	J F C Maxwell	1-1	100.0	+ 20.00
C O'Dwyer	1-1	100.0	+ 0.40	F Flood	1-1	100.0	+ 0.40
P P Murphy	1-1	100.0	+ 16.00	Miss I T Oakes	1-1	100.0	+ 16.00

How the Favourites Fared

Non-handicaps	W-R	Per cent	£1 Level Stake	Handicaps	W-R	Per cent	£1 Level Stake
2-y-o	0-0	-	0.00	2-y-o	0-0	-	0.00
3-y-o	2-6	33.3	- 2.18	3-y-o	0-0	-	0.00
Weight-for-age	9-27	33.3	- 7.36	All-aged	1-5	20.0	- 1.50
Totals	11-33	33.3	- 9.54	Totals	1-5	20.0	- 1.50
All favs	12-38	31.6	- 11.04				

DUNDALK

Leading Trainers 1989-93

	Total W-R	Non-handicaps 2-y-o	3-y-o+	Handicaps 2-y-o	3-y-o+	Per cent	£1 Level Stake
John M Oxx	20-67	6-16	12-38	0-0	2-13	29.9	- 3.27
J S Bolger	20-81	8-29	7-34	1-1	4-17	24.7	- 20.37
D K Weld	17-100	5-31	5-26	0-2	7-41	17.0	- 34.97
K Prendergast	8-80	1-16	2-24	0-1	5-39	10.0	- 36.73
F Dunne	7-33	0-7	4-13	0-0	3-13	21.2	+ 20.75
M J Grassick	5-32	0-7	1-6	0-0	4-19	15.6	- 9.58
Noel Meade	5-48	1-12	1-13	0-0	3-23	10.4	- 18.04
M Kauntze	5-48	1-13	3-14	0-0	1-21	10.4	- 12.20
J C Hayden	4-27	1-10	0-5	0-0	3-12	14.8	+ 4.25
C Collins	4-39	0-11	2-16	0-0	2-12	10.3	- 16.50
M V O'Brien	3-3	1-1	2-2	0-0	0-0	100.0	+ 2.90
Liam Browne	3-22	3-16	0-4	0-0	0-2	13.6	- 10.13
D Gillespie	3-26	1-7	0-5	0-1	2-13	11.5	- 9.10
Edward Lynam	3-29	1-8	1-2	0-0	1-19	10.3	- 3.50
J C Harley	2-10	0-1	0-1	0-0	2-8	20.0	+ 4.50
V Kennedy	2-14	0-1	0-3	0-0	2-10	14.3	+ 1.00
Oliver Finnegan	2-15	0-0	0-3	0-0	2-12	13.3	+ 13.00
Mrs Crowley-O'Brien	1-1	1-1	0-0	0-0	0-0	100.0	+ 1.75
Charles O'Brien	1-1	0-0	1-1	0-0	0-0	100.0	+ 1.10
A L T Moore	1-2	0-0	1-2	0-0	0-0	50.0	+ 7.00
Peter McCreery	1-4	0-3	0-0	0-0	1-1	25.0	+ 11.00
D Hanley	1-5	0-1	1-3	0-0	0-1	20.0	+ 4.00

Leading Jockeys

	Total W-R	Per cent	£1 Level Stake	Best Trainer	W-R	Per cent	£1 Level Stake
M J Kinane	19-80	23.8	- 16.93	D K Weld	13-59	22.0	- 18.00
C Roche	17-59	28.8	- 4.09	J S Bolger	16-48	33.3	- 1.09
P V Gilson	9-46	19.6	+ 2.25	M V O'Brien	3-3	100.0	+ 2.90
R Hughes	7-62	11.3	- 36.20	M J Grassick	4-10	40.0	+ 5.42
W J Supple	7-63	11.1	- 34.02	J S Bolger	4-17	23.5	+ 3.27
P Shanahan	6-56	10.7	- 8.58	D K Weld	2-14	14.3	- 1.33
D Hogan	5-24	20.8	+ 16.50	John M Oxx	3-13	23.1	+ 4.50
P Carberry	5-27	18.5	+ 7.50	Noel Meade	2-7	28.6	+ 10.00
W J O'Connor	5-61	8.2	- 37.20	M Kauntze	3-31	9.7	- 18.20
J J Behan	3-12	25.0	+ 18.63	Oliver Finnegan	2-3	66.7	+ 25.00
J A Heffernan	3-16	18.8	+ 5.25	Mrs C-O'Brien	1-1	100.0	+ 1.75
K J Manning	3-43	7.0	- 21.00	F Dunne	1-3	33.3	+ 6.00

How the Favourites Fared

Non-handicaps	W-R	Per cent	£1 Level Stake	Handicaps	W-R	Per cent	£1 Level Stake
2-y-o	16-34	47.1	+ 1.51	2-y-o	0-1	-	- 1.00
3-y-o	14-21	66.7	+ 7.56	3-y-o	3-8	37.5	- 1.44
Weight-for-age	14-27	51.9	+ 1.49	All-aged	13-44	29.5	- 7.85
Totals	44-82	53.7	+ 10.56	Totals	16-53	30.2	- 10.29
All favs	60-135	44.4	+ 0.27				

690

FAIRYHOUSE

Leading Trainers 1989-93

	Total W-R	Non-handicaps 2-y-o	3-y-o+	Handicaps 2-y-o	3-y-o+	Per cent	£1 Level Stake
John M Oxx	16-55	6-18	6-21	0-0	4-16	29.1	- 1.11
D K Weld	13-97	3-30	7-39	0-1	3-27	13.4	- 37.70
J S Bolger	11-84	6-28	4-31	0-1	1-24	13.1	- 49.23
Noel Meade	5-35	0-8	2-18	0-1	3-8	14.3	+ 11.50
M Kauntze	5-43	1-15	4-15	0-0	0-13	11.6	- 18.75
T Stack	4-14	1-6	3-4	0-1	0-3	28.6	- 3.58
D Hanley	3-9	3-3	0-4	0-0	0-2	33.3	+ 14.50
P J Flynn	3-15	1-2	0-4	0-1	2-8	20.0	+ 2.00
D Gillespie	3-18	0-7	1-6	0-0	2-5	16.7	- 4.25
K Prendergast	3-63	1-19	1-25	0-1	1-18	4.8	- 43.00
D T Hughes	2-9	0-1	2-6	0-0	0-2	22.2	+ 4.00
P Prendergast	2-10	1-5	0-2	1-1	0-2	20.0	+ 6.73
J C Hayden	2-10	1-4	0-2	0-1	1-3	20.0	+ 18.00
P Mullins	2-15	0-3	1-5	0-0	1-7	13.3	- 2.00
J J McLoughlin	2-17	0-2	0-5	0-0	2-10	11.8	- 5.25
Liam Browne	2-31	1-17	1-10	0-0	0-4	6.5	- 7.00
C Collins	2-35	0-12	1-14	0-0	1-9	5.7	- 20.00
B W Hills (Eng)	1-1	0-0	1-1	0-0	0-0	100.0	+ 6.00
Lord Huntingdon (Eng)	1-2	1-1	0-1	0-0	0-0	50.0	+ 7.00
J F Bailey Jnr	1-2	0-0	1-2	0-0	0-0	50.0	+ 3.50
Noel T Chance	1-3	0-2	0-0	0-0	1-1	33.3	+ 5.00
E J Kearns	1-3	0-0	1-3	0-0	0-0	33.3	+ 31.00

Leading Jockeys

	Total W-R	Per cent	£1 Level Stake	Best Trainer	W-R	Per cent	£1 Level Stake
M J Kinane	17-72	23.6	- 1.47	D K Weld	13-63	20.6	- 3.70
R Hughes	10-49	20.4	+ 9.73	D Hanley	3-4	75.0	+ 19.50
C Roche	8-47	17.0	- 15.95	J S Bolger	7-38	18.4	- 15.95
S Craine	6-52	11.5	- 23.83	T Stack	3-12	25.0	- 5.33
P Carberry	3-11	27.3	+ 21.00	Noel Meade	3-7	42.9	+ 25.00
D G O'Shea	3-26	11.5	- 11.25	John M Oxx	2-6	33.3	+ 5.50
K J Manning	3-30	10.0	+ 9.50	P Prendergast	1-2	50.0	+ 13.00
N G McCullagh	3-35	8.6	- 12.25	J J McLoughlin	2-8	25.0	+ 3.75
P V Gilson	3-49	6.1	- 23.00	C Collins	2-15	13.3	0.00
J R Barry	2-2	100.0	+ 6.63	P J Flynn	1-1	100.0	+ 5.00
Miss S Kauntze	2-3	66.7	+ 4.00	M Kauntze	2-3	66.7	+ 4.00
P Shanahan	2-48	4.2	- 32.00	M Kauntze	1-4	25.0	+ 1.00

How the Favourites Fared

Non-handicaps	W-R	Per cent	£1 Level Stake	Handicaps	W-R	Per cent	£1 Level Stake
2-y-o	14-27	51.9	+ 2.14	2-y-o	0-1	-	- 1.00
3-y-o	6-11	54.5	+ 3.34	3-y-o	2-7	28.6	+ 0.75
Weight-for-age	9-29	31.0	- 10.52	All-aged	5-17	29.4	- 0.62
Totals	29-67	43.3	- 5.04	Totals	7-25	28.0	- 0.87
All favs	36-92	39.1	- 5.91				

GALWAY

Leading Trainers 1989–93

	Total W–R	Non-handicaps 2-y-o	3-y-o+	Handicaps 2-y-o	3-y-o+	Per cent	£1 Level Stake
D K Weld	44-157	11-29	14-46	0-6	19-76	28.0	+ 6.58
J S Bolger	15-141	4-27	7-38	0-6	4-70	10.6	- 92.36
P J Flynn	12-69	0-5	7-21	0-0	5-43	17.4	- 21.00
John M Oxx	10-54	3-7	5-24	0-0	2-23	18.5	+ 12.00
T Stack	9-40	1-6	5-16	1-1	2-17	22.5	+ 15.05
C Collins	8-65	1-13	4-22	0-3	3-27	12.3	- 16.38
Noel Meade	7-84	0-15	1-15	0-3	6-51	8.3	- 52.67
M Kauntze	5-24	1-7	1-5	0-2	3-10	20.8	+ 17.00
K Prendergast	5-68	0-14	0-16	2-4	3-34	7.4	- 29.00
P Prendergast	4-21	1-4	1-8	1-2	1-7	19.0	+ 7.50
M J Grassick	3-27	0-3	1-9	0-1	2-14	11.1	+ 12.00
Augustine Leahy	3-30	0-7	1-8	0-2	2-13	10.0	- 10.50
M Cunningham	3-32	0-4	0-8	0-0	3-20	9.4	- 1.00
J J McLoughlin	3-37	0-1	0-5	1-2	2-29	8.1	- 2.00
D Hanley	2-8	0-0	1-5	0-0	1-3	25.0	+ 14.50
B V Kelly	2-21	0-3	0-6	0-2	2-10	9.5	+ 3.00
E J O'Grady	2-25	0-6	0-9	0-0	2-10	8.0	- 13.50
Liam Browne	2-27	1-11	0-6	0-2	1-8	7.4	- 7.50
M Halford	2-28	0-2	0-6	0-0	2-20	7.1	- 13.50
P Mullins	2-35	1-5	0-10	0-1	1-19	5.7	+ 21.00
J G Murphy	1-1	1-1	0-0	0-0	0-0	100.0	+ 6.00
J C Shearman	1-1	0-0	1-1	0-0	0-0	100.0	+ 1.25

Leading Jockeys

	Total W–R	Per cent	£1 Level Stake	Best Trainer	W–R	Per cent	£1 Level Stake
M J Kinane	42-139	30.2	+ 6.99	D K Weld	40-127	31.5	+ 12.09
S Craine	16-114	14.0	- 21.37	T Stack	7-31	22.6	+ 8.05
P Shanahan	12-88	13.6	- 11.12	C Collins	7-36	19.4	+ 7.63
P V Gilson	8-64	12.5	+ 2.00	M Halford	2-10	20.0	+ 4.50
C Roche	8-81	9.9	- 61.20	J S Bolger	9-68	13.2	- 47.20
M Fenton	5-40	12.5	- 3.00	Augustine Leahy	2-11	18.2	+ 4.00
K J Manning	5-63	7.9	- 30.15	J S Bolger	3-22	13.6	- 14.15
R M Burke	4-54	7.4	- 25.50	K Prendergast	2-14	14.3	+ 6.50
N G McCullagh	4-78	5.1	- 15.00	E J O'Grady	1-2	50.0	+ 6.00
J F Egan	4-84	4.8	- 56.00	P J Flynn	3-31	9.7	- 18.00
R Hughes	4-89	4.5	- 59.50	D Hanley	1-1	100.0	+ 4.50
Mr S R Murphy	3-5	60.0	+ 6.40	Noel Meade	2-3	66.7	+ 6.50

How the Favourites Fared

Non-handicaps	W–R	Per cent	£1 Level Stake	Handicaps	W–R	Per cent	£1 Level Stake
2-y-o	16-29	55.2	+ 0.66	2-y-o	3-6	50.0	+ 4.50
3-y-o	4-7	57.1	+ 3.37	3-y-o	5-8	62.5	+ 2.88
Weight-for-age	17-48	35.4	- 10.31	All-aged	18-75	24.0	- 15.79
Totals	37-84	44.0	- 6.28	Totals	26-89	29.2	- 8.41
All favs	63-173	36.4	- 14.69				

GOWRAN PARK

Leading Trainers 1989-93

	Total W-R	Non-handicaps 2-y-o	3-y-o+	Handicaps 2-y-o	3-y-o+	Per cent	£1 Level Stake
D K Weld	31-134	8-33	17-57	2-13	4-31	23.1	- 16.37
J S Bolger	26-141	12-44	7-50	3-15	4-32	18.4	- 17.27
John M Oxx	16-79	4-28	10-34	0-4	2-13	20.3	- 23.49
M Kauntze	7-51	5-18	1-13	1-6	0-14	13.7	- 17.45
K Prendergast	6-99	0-29	4-31	0-13	2-26	6.1	- 69.95
J J McLoughlin	4-30	0-7	1-9	1-3	2-11	13.3	+ 2.75
F Dunne	4-35	0-7	3-16	0-4	1-8	11.4	+ 6.00
P Mullins	4-46	0-10	1-17	1-4	2-15	8.7	- 17.75
Noel Meade	4-48	1-18	2-16	1-4	0-10	8.3	- 30.52
C Collins	4-49	1-15	3-21	0-3	0-10	8.2	- 26.00
P J Flynn	4-54	2-13	1-22	0-4	1-15	7.4	- 33.50
A P O'Brien	3-15	0-7	0-2	1-1	2-5	20.0	+ 10.00
D Gillespie	3-25	0-8	1-7	0-4	2-6	12.0	- 6.25
M A O'Toole	3-38	0-8	0-9	0-2	3-19	7.9	- 23.25
Charles O'Brien	2-4	1-3	1-1	0-0	0-0	50.0	+ 3.50
M V O'Brien	2-12	1-4	1-8	0-0	0-0	16.7	- 6.43
M Halford	2-17	0-3	1-8	0-1	1-5	11.8	- 4.00
W P Mullins	2-21	0-6	0-3	2-5	0-7	9.5	- 4.00
T Stack	2-26	0-6	0-10	1-2	1-8	7.7	- 15.50
Liam Browne	2-32	2-15	0-7	0-5	0-5	6.3	- 25.77
Ms E Cassidy	1-1	0-0	0-0	0-0	1-1	100.0	+ 12.00
B Lawlor	1-2	0-0	0-1	0-0	1-1	50.0	+ 7.00

Leading Jockeys

	Total W-R	Per cent	£1 Level Stake	Best Trainer	W-R	Per cent	£1 Level Stake
M J Kinane	32-118	27.1	- 7.14	D K Weld	26-92	28.3	+ 0.13
C Roche	18-91	19.8	- 17.49	J S Bolger	16-76	21.1	- 17.49
W J O'Connor	8-72	11.1	- 29.45	M Kauntze	7-29	24.1	+ 4.55
R Hughes	7-77	9.1	- 29.75	A J Maxwell	1-1	100.0	+ 3.50
N G McCullagh	6-69	8.7	- 12.25	J J McLoughlin	3-15	20.0	+ 2.75
K J Manning	5-69	7.2	- 44.40	J S Bolger	3-14	21.4	+ 0.10
P V Gilson	5-77	6.5	- 51.93	Charles O'Brien	2-3	66.7	+ 4.50
W J Supple	5-80	6.3	- 52.37	J S Bolger	4-21	19.0	+ 0.63
P Shanahan	5-86	5.8	- 64.50	C Collins	3-25	12.0	- 13.00
S Craine	5-91	5.5	- 70.52	T Stack	2-22	9.1	- 11.50
C Everard	3-13	23.1	+ 8.50	J S Bolger	2-6	33.3	+ 2.50
B J Walsh	2-8	25.0	+ 4.00	K Prendergast	2-6	33.3	+ 6.00

How the Favourites Fared

Non-handicaps	W-R	Per cent	£1 Level Stake	Handicaps	W-R	Per cent	£1 Level Stake
2-y-o	20-41	48.8	+ 0.37	2-y-o	4-13	30.8	+ 0.25
3-y-o	6-21	28.6	- 7.55	3-y-o	2-9	22.2	- 1.50
Weight-for-age	14-36	38.9	- 7.43	All-aged	10-32	31.3	- 2.45
Totals	40-98	40.8	- 14.61	Totals	16-54	29.6	- 3.70
All favs	56-152	36.8	- 18.31				

KILLARNEY

Leading Trainers 1989-93

	Total W-R	Non-handicaps 2-y-o	Non-handicaps 3-y-o+	Handicaps 2-y-o	Handicaps 3-y-o+	Per cent	£1 Level Stake
J S Bolger	16-64	1-6	7-27	0-0	8-31	25.0	- 22.57
T Stack	12-44	2-5	7-22	0-0	3-17	27.3	+ 1.23
D K Weld	11-40	2-3	8-20	0-0	1-17	27.5	- 14.15
John M Oxx	6-15	0-0	6-14	0-0	0-1	40.0	- 4.13
M V O'Brien	5-5	1-1	2-2	0-0	2-2	100.0	+ 5.25
P J Flynn	5-31	0-1	1-7	0-0	4-23	16.1	- 16.85
M Halford	3-18	0-0	0-4	0-0	3-14	16.7	- 3.50
T G Curtin	3-25	0-0	0-9	0-0	3-16	12.0	+ 3.00
K Prendergast	3-26	0-1	3-16	0-0	0-9	11.5	- 15.13
Neil S McGrath	2-8	0-0	0-1	0-0	2-7	25.0	+ 0.50
H McMahon	2-9	0-1	0-5	0-0	2-3	22.2	+ 3.50
Edward Lynam	2-10	0-0	0-6	0-0	2-4	20.0	+ 14.00
M Kauntze	2-10	0-1	2-3	0-0	0-6	20.0	- 6.28
M J Grassick	2-12	0-0	2-6	0-0	0-6	16.7	+ 2.80
J J McLoughlin	2-19	0-1	0-3	0-0	2-15	10.5	- 11.43
P Mullins	2-20	0-0	1-12	0-0	1-8	10.0	- 11.00
E J O'Grady	2-21	0-1	0-8	0-0	2-12	9.5	- 4.00
P Burke	1-1	0-0	1-1	0-0	0-0	100.0	+ 2.25
P F O'Donnell	1-2	0-0	0-0	0-0	1-2	50.0	+ 6.00
K F O'Sullivan	1-2	0-0	0-1	0-0	1-1	50.0	+ 2.33
Noel T Chance	1-3	0-0	0-1	0-0	1-2	33.3	+ 2.50
H De Bromhead	1-3	0-0	0-0	0-0	1-3	33.3	+ 14.00

Leading Jockeys

	Total W-R	Per cent	£1 Level Stake	Best Trainer	W-R	Per cent	£1 Level Stake
C Roche	17-54	31.5	+ 0.74	J S Bolger	11-36	30.6	- 11.09
M J Kinane	16-51	31.4	- 11.96	D K Weld	10-27	37.0	- 2.64
S Craine	13-67	19.4	- 15.92	T Stack	10-40	25.0	- 4.17
J F Egan	6-43	14.0	- 10.90	P J Flynn	2-15	13.3	- 9.65
P Shanahan	4-17	23.5	- 5.63	Liam Browne	1-1	100.0	+ 4.00
Miss C Hutchinson	3-4	75.0	+ 4.90	D K Weld	1-1	100.0	+ 0.50
L Piggott	3-5	60.0	+ 1.43	M V O'Brien	3-3	100.0	+ 3.43
D G O'Shea	3-26	11.5	+ 32.80	T J O'Mara	1-2	50.0	+ 49.00
N G McCullagh	3-38	7.9	- 13.43	J J McLoughlin	2-11	18.2	- 3.43
W J Supple	3-43	7.0	- 33.62	J S Bolger	1-7	14.3	- 2.00
D Duggan	2-6	33.3	+ 4.33	M Cunningham	1-1	100.0	+ 3.33
J R Barry	2-8	25.0	- 2.20	P J Flynn	2-5	40.0	+ 0.80

How the Favourites Fared

Non-handicaps	W-R	Per cent	£1 Level Stake	Handicaps	W-R	Per cent	£1 Level Stake
2-y-o	5-6	83.3	+ 2.95	2-y-o	0-0	-	0.00
3-y-o	12-15	80.0	+ 9.07	3-y-o	4-8	50.0	- 0.38
Weight-for-age	18-31	58.1	+ 1.73	All-aged	15-43	34.9	- 6.10
Totals	35-52	67.3	+ 13.75	Totals	19-51	37.3	- 6.48
All favs	54-103	52.4	+ 7.27				

694

LAYTOWN

Leading Trainers 1989-93

	Total W-R	Non-handicaps 2-y-o	3-y-o+	Handicaps 2-y-o	3-y-o+	Per cent	£1 Level Stake
D K Weld	4-15	0-0	2-6	0-0	2-9	26.7	- 0.75
M A O'Toole	4-22	0-0	1-9	0-0	3-13	18.2	- 9.02
K Prendergast	3-20	0-0	0-7	0-0	3-13	15.0	+ 1.13
P Martin	2-6	0-0	1-2	0-0	1-4	33.3	+ 15.50
Noel Meade	2-8	0-0	1-3	0-0	1-5	25.0	+ 12.00
T O'Neill	1-3	0-0	0-2	0-0	1-1	33.3	+ 8.00
B V Kelly	1-4	0-0	1-2	0-0	0-2	25.0	+ 0.33
Noel T Chance	1-4	0-0	1-3	0-0	0-1	25.0	+ 3.00
Daniel J Murphy	1-6	0-0	1-2	0-0	0-4	16.7	- 4.43
P Prendergast	1-7	0-0	1-2	0-0	0-5	14.3	- 1.00
D J Reddan	1-7	0-0	0-2	0-0	1-5	14.3	+ 0.50
M Halford	1-8	0-0	0-4	0-0	1-4	12.5	+ 3.00
J T Gorman	1-10	0-0	1-7	0-0	0-3	10.0	- 2.00
Peter Casey	1-12	0-0	0-4	0-0	1-8	8.3	+ 1.00

Leading Jockeys

	Total W-R	Per cent	£1 Level Stake	Best Trainer	W-R	Per cent	£1 Level Stake
P Carberry	3-5	60.0	+ 22.00	Noel Meade	2-3	66.7	+ 17.00
W J Smith	3-12	25.0	+ 6.50	D K Weld	2-6	33.3	- 0.50
P V Gilson	2-12	16.7	+ 3.50	M Halford	1-2	50.0	+ 9.00
R M Burke	2-14	14.3	+ 18.00	P Martin	1-1	100.0	+ 16.00
S Craine	2-16	12.5	- 3.67	B V Kelly	1-2	50.0	+ 2.33
Miss C Hutchinson	1-1	100.0	+ 5.00	P Prendergast	1-1	100.0	+ 5.00
D J Walsh	1-1	100.0	+ 0.80	K Prendergast	1-1	100.0	+ 0.80
Mr J K Connolly	1-1	100.0	+ 3.33	K Prendergast	1-1	100.0	+ 3.33
R Carroll	1-2	50.0	+ 0.75	D K Weld	1-2	50.0	+ 0.75
Mr D Marnane	1-2	50.0	+ 0.50	M A O'Toole	1-2	50.0	+ 0.50
D Duggan	1-3	33.3	- 1.43	Daniel J Murphy	1-2	50.0	- 0.43
B Bowens	1-3	33.3	+ 4.50	D J Reddan	1-1	100.0	+ 6.50

How the Favourites Fared

Non-handicaps	W-R	Per cent	£1 Level Stake	Handicaps	W-R	Per cent	£1 Level Stake
2-y-o	0-0	-	0.00	2-y-o	0-0	-	0.00
3-y-o	0-0	-	0.00	3-y-o	0-0	-	0.00
Weight-for-age	3-11	27.3	- 4.18	All-aged	5-14	35.7	- 2.72
Totals	3-11	27.3	- 4.18	Totals	5-14	35.7	- 2.72
All favs	8-25	32.0	- 6.90				

LEOPARDSTOWN

Leading Trainers 1989-93

	Total W-R	Non-handicaps 2-y-o	3-y-o+	Handicaps 2-y-o	3-y-o+	Per cent	£1 Level Stake
J S Bolger	92-494	31-120	30-206	4-13	27-155	18.6	- 72.65
D K Weld	91-476	14-97	54-199	3-9	20-171	19.1	-101.11
John M Oxx	58-322	12-65	32-160	1-4	13-93	18.0	- 45.14
K Prendergast	32-359	8-74	11-136	2-12	11-137	8.9	-160.36
M V O'Brien	23-72	8-21	13-47	0-0	2-4	31.9	- 11.41
T Stack	17-147	3-35	7-66	0-1	7-45	11.6	- 32.25
C Collins	16-144	7-39	7-67	0-3	2-35	11.1	- 51.18
M A O'Toole	8-91	0-18	3-25	1-2	4-46	8.8	- 25.00
M Kauntze	8-163	2-40	4-64	0-5	2-54	4.9	-100.75
J E Mulhern	7-76	0-8	2-24	0-1	5-43	9.2	- 19.17
Noel Meade	7-131	1-18	3-46	0-4	3-63	5.3	- 60.97
P Prendergast	5-30	0-9	0-9	0-1	5-11	16.7	+ 18.50
E J O'Grady	4-58	1-10	0-17	0-4	3-27	6.9	- 23.50
M J Grassick	4-58	0-9	2-25	0-2	2-22	6.9	- 37.50
J J McLoughlin	4-93	0-22	2-29	0-2	2-40	4.3	- 48.50
Charles O'Brien	3-14	1-2	2-11	0-0	0-1	21.4	+ 3.25
R Lister	3-18	0-4	1-11	0-0	2-3	16.7	+ 13.00
Neil S McGrath	3-23	1-9	0-7	0-0	2-7	13.0	+ 12.00
W P Mullins	3-26	0-1	0-9	0-1	3-15	11.5	- 4.00
T G Curtin	3-27	0-4	2-5	0-0	1-18	11.1	+ 22.00
Daniel J Murphy	3-28	1-5	1-14	0-1	1-8	10.7	+ 4.00
P Mullins	3-51	0-7	3-14	0-3	0-27	5.9	- 24.13

Leading Jockeys

	Total W-R	Per cent	£1 Level Stake	Best Trainer	W-R	Per cent	£1 Level Stake
M J Kinane	83-346	24.0	- 33.22	D K Weld	80-313	25.6	- 22.22
C Roche	68-335	20.3	- 49.53	J S Bolger	63-269	23.4	+ 0.17
S Craine	28-272	10.3	- 80.67	T Stack	16-123	13.0	- 13.75
P V Gilson	25-204	12.3	- 58.74	C Collins	10-63	15.9	- 2.43
R Hughes	20-170	11.8	- 34.85	John M Oxx	5-19	26.3	- 2.35
P Shanahan	16-214	7.5	-136.12	D K Weld	6-57	10.5	- 22.37
J Reid	14-74	18.9	- 11.57	M V O'Brien	6-19	31.6	- 3.65
W J Supple	12-175	6.9	- 99.75	J S Bolger	7-56	12.5	- 14.25
R Griffiths	10-102	9.8	- 29.19	K Prendergast	10-94	10.6	- 21.19
K J Manning	9-142	6.3	- 87.93	J S Bolger	7-61	11.5	- 29.93
D G O'Shea	8-97	8.2	- 54.83	John M Oxx	6-35	17.1	- 8.33
P Carberry	7-38	18.4	+ 39.50	Noel Meade	5-22	22.7	+ 42.00

How the Favourites Fared

Non-handicaps	W-R	Per cent	£1 Level Stake	Handicaps	W-R	Per cent	£1 Level Stake
2-y-o	46-103	44.7	- 5.06	2-y-o	6-12	50.0	+ 4.48
3-y-o	30-67	44.8	- 5.11	3-y-o	4-14	28.6	- 2.25
Weight-for-age	65-140	46.4	+ 2.51	All-aged	26-128	20.3	- 36.42
Totals	141-310	45.5	- 7.66	Totals	36-154	23.4	- 34.19
All favs	177-464	38.1	- 41.85				

LIMERICK

Leading Trainers 1989-93

	Total W-R	Non-handicaps 2-y-o	3-y-o+	Handicaps 2-y-o	3-y-o+	Per cent	£1 Level Stake
J S Bolger	10-41	2-4	4-25	0-0	4-12	24.4	+ 6.54
P J Flynn	9-38	0-3	2-14	0-1	7-20	23.7	+ 7.00
D K Weld	7-53	4-9	2-29	0-1	1-14	13.2	- 30.73
Liam Browne	4-17	1-4	3-11	0-0	0-2	23.5	- 4.38
Mrs Crowley-O'Brien	3-5	0-0	0-2	0-0	3-3	60.0	+ 14.00
J C Hayden	3-14	1-4	0-6	0-0	2-4	21.4	+ 9.00
C Collins	3-19	0-2	2-10	0-0	1-7	15.8	- 2.33
J J McLoughlin	2-12	0-0	0-4	0-0	2-8	16.7	0.00
M A O'Toole	2-13	0-1	2-7	0-0	0-5	15.4	- 9.10
D Gillespie	2-15	1-4	0-5	0-1	1-5	13.3	- 8.57
T Stack	2-25	0-7	1-11	0-1	1-6	8.0	- 19.25
M J Grassick	2-28	0-2	2-16	0-1	0-9	7.1	- 4.75
S Treacy	1-1	0-0	0-0	0-0	1-1	100.0	+ 3.50
Charles O'Brien	1-1	0-0	1-1	0-0	0-0	100.0	+ 1.00
D P Kelly	1-3	0-0	1-2	0-0	0-1	33.3	+ 14.00
M V O'Brien	1-4	0-0	1-3	0-0	0-1	25.0	- 1.00
W M Roper	1-4	0-0	0-2	0-0	1-2	25.0	+ 7.00
Neil S McGrath	1-5	1-2	0-3	0-0	0-0	20.0	+ 8.00
M Kauntze	1-5	0-0	1-3	0-0	0-2	20.0	- 2.25
J T Gorman	1-5	0-0	1-2	0-0	0-3	20.0	+ 16.00
J C Harley	1-5	0-0	1-3	0-0	0-2	20.0	+ 6.00
M Cunningham	1-9	1-1	0-5	0-0	0-3	11.1	+ 2.00

Leading Jockeys

	Total W-R	Per cent	£1 Level Stake	Best Trainer	W-R	Per cent	£1 Level Stake
M J Kinane	9-41	22.0	- 15.03	D K Weld	7-33	21.2	- 10.73
C Roche	7-29	24.1	+ 1.29	J S Bolger	6-21	28.6	+ 6.54
P V Gilson	5-32	15.6	- 15.83	Charles O'Brien	1-1	100.0	+ 1.00
J F Egan	4-22	18.2	- 2.75	P J Flynn	4-14	28.6	+ 5.25
W J Supple	4-27	14.8	- 5.25	J S Bolger	2-7	28.6	+ 3.50
S Craine	4-38	10.5	- 23.87	Liam Browne	2-6	33.3	+ 1.38
R M Burke	3-23	13.0	+ 2.00	Mrs C-O'Brien	1-1	100.0	+ 8.00
W J O'Connor	3-24	12.5	- 4.50	C Collins	1-1	100.0	+ 6.00
Mr A P O'Brien	2-3	66.7	+ 6.50	J S Bolger	2-3	66.7	+ 6.50
J R Barry	2-7	28.6	- 0.25	P J Flynn	2-3	66.7	+ 3.75
P Shanahan	2-19	10.5	- 6.67	D Gillespie	1-2	50.0	+ 2.33
N G McCullagh	2-25	8.0	- 7.00	M Cunningham	1-1	100.0	+ 10.00

How the Favourites Fared

Non-handicaps	W-R	Per cent	£1 Level Stake	Handicaps	W-R	Per cent	£1 Level Stake
2-y-o	6-12	50.0	- 1.73	2-y-o	0-1	–	- 1.00
3-y-o	3-14	21.4	- 7.80	3-y-o	0-2	–	- 2.00
Weight-for-age	10-18	55.6	+ 3.65	All-aged	5-24	20.8	- 11.65
Totals	19-44	43.2	- 5.88	Totals	5-27	18.5	- 14.65
All favs	24-71	33.8	- 20.53				

LISTOWEL

Leading Trainers 1989-93

	Total W-R	Non-handicaps 2-y-o	3-y-o+	Handicaps 2-y-o	3-y-o+	Per cent	£1 Level Stake
D K Weld	20-58	8-15	4-14	0-4	8-25	34.5	+ 21.61
J S Bolger	8-58	5-14	1-23	1-5	1-16	13.8	- 24.63
John M Oxx	6-30	2-6	2-13	0-0	2-11	20.0	- 11.27
M Kauntze	3-18	0-2	1-2	2-3	0-11	16.7	+ 4.00
T Stack	3-36	0-12	2-12	0-1	1-11	8.3	- 23.50
J Morrison	2-9	0-1	0-1	0-0	2-7	22.2	+ 12.00
T F Lacy	2-18	0-2	0-7	0-0	2-9	11.1	0.00
K Prendergast	2-19	1-5	0-5	0-4	1-5	10.5	- 2.00
W P Mullins	2-20	0-2	0-6	1-2	1-10	10.0	- 4.00
M Halford	2-23	0-6	0-3	0-1	2-13	8.7	- 9.50
Augustine Leahy	2-32	0-12	0-8	0-3	2-9	6.3	- 20.67
P J Flynn	2-47	1-14	0-13	0-0	1-20	4.3	- 22.00
Countess Schulenburg	1-1	0-0	1-1	0-0	0-0	100.0	+ 14.00
M V O'Brien	1-2	0-0	1-2	0-0	0-0	50.0	- 0.20
D Hanley	1-2	0-0	1-2	0-0	0-0	50.0	+ 5.00
J Queally	1-2	0-0	1-2	0-0	0-0	50.0	+ 5.00
H De Bromhead	1-3	0-1	0-0	0-0	1-2	33.3	+ 2.00
David A Kiely	1-3	0-0	0-1	0-0	1-2	33.3	+ 6.00
M Purcell	1-4	0-0	1-2	0-0	0-2	25.0	+ 1.50
F Flood	1-5	0-1	0-3	0-0	1-1	20.0	+ 3.00
Mrs Crowley-O'Brien	1-5	0-1	0-0	0-0	1-4	20.0	- 1.75
Neil S McGrath	1-7	0-2	1-1	0-2	0-2	14.3	+ 4.00

Leading Jockeys

	Total W-R	Per cent	£1 Level Stake	Best Trainer	W-R	Per cent	£1 Level Stake
M J Kinane	19-61	31.1	+ 14.64	D K Weld	17-47	36.2	+ 24.53
C Roche	7-39	17.9	- 10.13	J S Bolger	6-26	23.1	- 6.13
R M Burke	4-33	12.1	- 7.25	M Halford	2-2	100.0	+ 11.50
P V Gilson	4-34	11.8	- 3.20	Edward Lynam	1-1	100.0	+ 14.00
S Craine	4-50	8.0	- 27.50	T Stack	2-28	7.1	- 20.00
N G McCullagh	4-50	8.0	- 6.00	J M Canty	1-1	100.0	+ 20.00
R V Skelly	2-12	16.7	+ 3.38	J Morrison	1-1	100.0	+ 12.00
B Bowens	2-12	16.7	+ 6.00	J Morrison	1-3	33.3	+ 5.00
M Fenton	2-21	9.5	- 12.67	Liam Browne	1-2	50.0	+ 2.00
D G O'Shea	2-27	7.4	- 15.00	Augustine Leahy	1-2	50.0	+ 5.00
K J Manning	2-28	7.1	- 19.50	T F Lacy	1-1	100.0	+ 2.00
W J O'Connor	2-32	6.3	- 17.00	M Kauntze	2-14	14.3	+ 1.00

How the Favourites Fared

Non-handicaps	W-R	Per cent	£1 Level Stake	Handicaps	W-R	Per cent	£1 Level Stake
2-y-o	12-19	63.2	+ 8.38	2-y-o	2-5	40.0	+ 1.25
3-y-o	0-6	-	- 6.00	3-y-o	0-0	-	0.00
Weight-for-age	9-18	50.0	+ 3.44	All-aged	10-31	32.3	+ 5.91
Totals	21-43	48.8	+ 5.82	Totals	12-36	33.3	+ 7.16
All favs	33-79	41.8	+ 12.98				

MALLOW

Leading Trainers 1989-93

	Total W-R	Non-handicaps 2-y-o	3-y-o+	Handicaps 2-y-o	3-y-o+	Per cent	£1 Level Stake
John M Oxx	13-35	3-7	8-23	0-0	2-5	37.1	- 5.89
J S Bolger	9-52	5-16	3-21	0-1	1-14	17.3	- 13.15
D K Weld	9-57	3-12	6-34	0-2	0-9	15.8	- 22.84
J J McLoughlin	6-18	0-1	1-7	0-2	5-8	33.3	+ 7.00
Liam Browne	5-20	2-5	2-9	0-0	1-6	25.0	+ 11.30
T Stack	5-41	0-3	4-28	0-1	1-9	12.2	- 24.75
C Collins	4-20	1-5	3-11	0-0	0-4	20.0	+ 21.50
B V Kelly	3-7	0-0	2-3	0-1	1-3	42.9	+ 8.00
J G Coogan	3-12	1-5	1-4	1-2	0-1	25.0	+ 2.50
D Gillespie	3-21	1-3	0-7	1-4	1-7	14.3	- 3.90
P J Flynn	3-46	0-13	1-13	0-1	2-19	6.5	- 18.50
T G Curtin	2-4	0-0	0-2	0-0	2-2	50.0	+ 15.00
M V O'Brien	2-5	2-4	0-1	0-0	0-0	40.0	+ 6.38
J T Gorman	2-18	0-2	0-8	0-1	2-7	11.1	0.00
P Prendergast	2-22	1-2	1-18	0-0	0-2	9.1	- 16.70
E J O'Grady	2-27	0-4	1-11	1-2	0-10	7.4	- 20.10
K Prendergast	2-38	1-7	0-18	0-2	1-11	5.3	- 29.50
J M Canty	1-2	0-0	0-1	0-0	1-1	50.0	+ 1.50
S Treacy	1-2	0-0	0-0	0-0	1-2	50.0	+ 1.25
D T Hughes	1-3	0-1	1-1	0-0	0-1	33.3	+ 2.00
E O'Connell	1-4	0-0	0-1	0-0	1-3	25.0	- 1.00
A P O'Brien	1-5	0-1	0-0	1-4	0-0	20.0	+ 8.00

Leading Jockeys

	Total W-R	Per cent	£1 Level Stake	Best Trainer	W-R	Per cent	£1 Level Stake
C Roche	13-55	23.6	+ 9.55	J S Bolger	8-39	20.5	- 1.65
S Craine	10-64	15.6	- 25.25	T Stack	4-33	12.1	- 19.25
M J Kinane	8-46	17.4	- 9.84	D K Weld	7-31	22.6	- 5.84
N G McCullagh	6-35	17.1	- 5.50	J J McLoughlin	2-7	28.6	- 1.00
P Shanahan	5-43	11.6	- 24.25	J S Bolger	1-1	100.0	+ 0.50
E A Leonard	4-22	18.2	- 3.00	J J McLoughlin	4-8	50.0	+ 11.00
R Hughes	4-38	10.5	- 27.80	John M Oxx	2-2	100.0	+ 1.40
J F Egan	3-33	9.1	- 4.00	P J Flynn	2-23	8.7	- 2.00
D V Smith	2-10	20.0	- 2.00	D K Weld	1-3	33.3	0.00
B Coogan	2-11	18.2	+ 1.00	J G Coogan	2-8	25.0	+ 4.00
R V Skelly	2-16	12.5	+ 2.50	P Prendergast	1-2	50.0	+ 1.50
P V Gilson	2-24	8.3	+ 4.00	C Collins	2-6	33.3	+ 22.00

How the Favourites Fared

Non-handicaps	W-R	Per cent	£1 Level Stake	Handicaps	W-R	Per cent	£1 Level Stake
2-y-o	10-20	50.0	+ 1.26	2-y-o	2-4	50.0	+ 0.60
3-y-o	10-17	58.8	+ 5.57	3-y-o	3-7	42.9	+ 0.18
Weight-for-age	10-25	40.0	- 2.69	All-aged	6-17	35.3	- 2.08
Totals	30-62	48.4	+ 4.14	Totals	11-28	39.3	- 1.30
All favs	41-90	45.6	+ 2.84				

Leading Trainers 1989-93

	Total	Non-handicaps		Handicaps		Per	£1 Level
	W-R	2-y-o	3-y-o+	2-y-o	3-y-o+	cent	Stake
D K Weld	30-179	8-43	12-74	1-9	9-53	16.8	- 33.30
J S Bolger	25-150	11-41	5-46	4-23	5-40	16.7	- 40.91
John M Oxx	19-96	4-21	10-43	0-4	5-28	19.8	- 25.18
K Prendergast	10-152	3-43	5-52	0-14	2-43	6.6	-108.00
C Collins	8-74	4-21	1-27	0-6	3-20	10.8	- 42.08
Liam Browne	6-48	3-20	2-13	1-6	0-9	12.5	+ 11.00
M V O'Brien	5-14	1-4	3-8	0-1	1-1	35.7	+ 4.52
P J Flynn	5-36	1-9	0-6	0-1	4-20	13.9	+ 13.50
J J McLoughlin	5-42	2-7	0-12	0-2	3-21	11.9	- 6.38
M Kauntze	5-46	1-14	3-13	1-5	0-14	10.9	- 13.00
F Dunne	5-47	2-12	2-18	0-1	1-16	10.6	+ 12.83
Noel Meade	5-64	0-16	2-23	0-6	3-19	7.8	- 32.25
M J Grassick	4-35	2-7	1-15	0-5	1-8	11.4	- 13.25
W P Mullins	3-13	0-0	2-4	0-0	1-9	23.1	+ 0.25
T F Lacy	3-34	0-4	1-18	0-2	2-10	8.8	- 4.00
Edward Lynam	3-36	1-8	1-16	0-5	1-7	8.3	- 5.00
M A O'Toole	3-39	1-12	1-11	1-4	0-12	7.7	- 20.50
P Mullins	2-18	0-1	0-6	1-3	1-8	11.1	- 5.00
N O'Callaghan	2-19	1-8	1-13	0-0	0-8	10.5	- 7.00
J G Coogan	2-23	1-9	0-4	0-5	1-5	8.7	- 8.00
D Gillespie	2-28	0-7	0-9	0-2	2-10	7.1	- 8.50
E J O'Grady	2-37	0-9	1-14	1-3	0-11	5.4	- 15.00

Leading Jockeys

	Total	Per	£1 Level	Best Trainer		Per	£1 Level
	W-R	cent	Stake		W-R	cent	Stake
C Roche	22-91	24.2	- 5.90	J S Bolger	22-64	34.4	+ 21.10
M J Kinane	18-84	21.4	- 11.06	D K Weld	16-70	22.9	- 10.56
P Shanahan	14-102	13.7	- 15.70	C Collins	6-30	20.0	- 6.33
R Hughes	10-99	10.1	- 23.50	M J Grassick	3-13	23.1	+ 1.75
D G O'Shea	8-46	17.4	+ 0.37	John M Oxx	4-14	28.6	- 5.63
J F Egan	7-73	9.6	- 11.00	P J Flynn	3-22	13.6	+ 12.00
W J O'Connor	7-73	9.6	- 8.00	M Kauntze	3-28	10.7	- 10.50
P V Gilson	7-85	8.2	- 48.31	M V O'Brien	4-10	40.0	+ 6.94
J J Behan	4-27	14.8	+ 15.50	Liam Browne	3-6	50.0	+ 23.50
R M Burke	4-61	6.6	- 30.92	K Prendergast	2-23	8.7	- 12.25
N G McCullagh	4-88	4.5	- 50.37	J J McLoughlin	3-23	13.0	- 6.37
S Craine	4-104	3.8	- 77.75	N O'Callaghan	1-2	50.0	+ 4.00

How the Favourites Fared

Non-handicaps	W-R	Per cent	£1 Level Stake	Handicaps	W-R	Per cent	£1 Level Stake
2-y-o	23-49	46.9	+ 7.24	2-y-o	2-13	15.4	- 4.70
3-y-o	9-26	34.6	- 4.65	3-y-o	4-13	30.8	- 2.00
Weight-for-age	12-35	34.3	- 3.16	All-aged	13-39	33.3	+ 6.24
Totals	44-110	40.0	- 0.57	Totals	19-65	29.2	- 0.46
All favs	63-175	36.0	- 1.03				

NAVAN

Leading Trainers 1989-93

	Total W-R	Non-handicaps 2-y-o	3-y-o+	Handicaps 2-y-o	3-y-o+	Per cent	£1 Level Stake
J S Bolger	16-83	10-32	5-30	0-1	1-20	19.3	- 20.38
K Prendergast	10-97	5-33	2-27	0-1	3-36	10.3	- 41.50
John M Oxx	9-49	4-18	5-22	0-0	0-9	18.4	- 19.93
D K Weld	5-82	3-25	2-34	0-1	0-22	6.1	- 50.56
M Kauntze	4-38	1-15	2-11	0-0	1-12	10.5	- 22.25
C Collins	4-57	0-12	3-28	0-0	1-17	7.0	- 38.00
Liam Browne	3-16	3-8	0-4	0-1	0-3	18.8	+ 2.50
D T Hughes	3-20	1-6	0-5	0-0	2-9	15.0	+ 11.00
Noel Meade	3-58	1-16	1-21	0-0	1-21	5.2	- 40.00
M V O'Brien	2-6	2-5	0-1	0-0	0-0	33.3	- 0.13
V Kennedy	2-15	0-2	0-9	0-0	2-4	13.3	+ 10.00
M A O'Toole	2-18	0-4	2-7	0-2	0-5	11.1	- 10.90
T F Lacy	2-20	0-5	1-8	0-0	1-7	10.0	- 8.25
M Halford	2-20	1-5	1-7	0-0	0-8	10.0	- 4.00
J J McLoughlin	2-22	0-3	0-9	0-0	2-10	9.1	- 10.50
T Stack	2-35	0-11	2-16	0-0	0-8	5.7	- 28.50
M J Grassick	2-42	0-10	0-17	0-0	2-15	4.8	- 20.50
T G Curtin	1-3	0-1	1-1	0-0	0-1	33.3	+ 3.00
C P Magnier	1-3	0-0	0-0	0-0	1-3	33.3	+ 6.00
D Hanley	1-3	0-0	1-3	0-0	0-0	33.3	+ 0.25
Mrs Ian Fox	1-3	0-0	0-2	0-0	1-1	33.3	+ 12.00
Charles O'Brien	1-4	0-1	1-3	0-0	0-0	25.0	+ 1.50

Leading Jockeys

	Total W-R	Per cent	£1 Level Stake	Best Trainer	W-R	Per cent	£1 Level Stake
C Roche	16-67	23.9	+ 2.44	J S Bolger	13-47	27.7	- 6.89
P Shanahan	5-64	7.8	- 33.00	D K Weld	2-13	15.4	+ 3.00
S Craine	5-72	6.9	- 45.50	T Stack	2-24	8.3	- 17.50
M Fenton	4-20	20.0	+ 15.00	Liam Browne	2-4	50.0	+ 8.00
K J Manning	4-47	8.5	- 17.75	J S Bolger	2-9	22.2	+ 4.50
W J O'Connor	4-53	7.5	- 33.75	M Kauntze	3-17	17.6	- 4.75
P V Gilson	4-59	6.8	- 38.62	M V O'Brien	1-1	100.0	+ 1.38
M J Kinane	4-61	6.6	- 42.06	D K Weld	3-47	6.4	- 31.56
R Hughes	4-67	6.0	- 37.25	John M Oxx	2-5	40.0	+ 3.25
N G McCullagh	3-48	6.3	- 32.25	W P Mullins	1-1	100.0	+ 8.00
P P Murphy	2-10	20.0	+ 10.00	D T Hughes	2-5	40.0	+ 15.00
P Carberry	2-15	13.3	- 1.50	A P O'Brien	1-1	100.0	+ 3.50

How the Favourites Fared

Non-handicaps	W-R	Per cent	£1 Level Stake	Handicaps	W-R	Per cent	£1 Level Stake
2-y-o	17-32	53.1	+ 9.31	2-y-o	1-1	100.0	+ 1.75
3-y-o	8-24	33.3	- 5.58	3-y-o	1-7	14.3	- 3.00
Weight-for-age	9-14	64.3	+ 10.13	All-aged	1-21	4.8	- 19.20
Totals	34-70	48.6	+ 13.86	Totals	3-29	10.3	- 20.45
All favs	37-99	37.4	- 6.59				

PUNCHESTOWN

Leading Trainers 1989-93

	Total W-R	Non-handicaps 2-y-o	3-y-o+	Handicaps 2-y-o	3-y-o+	Per cent	£1 Level Stake
J S Bolger	4-14	2-5	0-6	0-0	2-3	28.6	− 5.29
John M Oxx	3-17	3-10	0-3	0-0	0-4	17.6	− 5.50
D K Weld	3-24	0-7	2-8	0-0	1-9	12.5	− 8.00
M Kauntze	2-9	1-3	0-3	0-0	1-3	22.2	+ 6.00
K Prendergast	2-23	0-8	0-5	0-0	2-10	8.7	− 8.50
Mrs Crowley-O'Brien	1-1	0-0	1-1	0-0	0-0	100.0	+ 2.00
J E Mulhern	1-2	0-0	1-2	0-0	0-0	50.0	+ 2.00
Edward Lynam	1-3	0-1	0-0	0-0	1-2	33.3	+ 6.00
Peadar Matthews	1-4	0-1	0-1	0-0	1-2	25.0	+ 7.00
Anthony Mullins	1-4	0-1	0-0	0-0	1-3	25.0	+ 6.00
P Prendergast	1-6	1-4	0-0	0-0	0-2	16.7	+ 1.00
Liam Browne	1-7	1-3	0-2	0-0	0-2	14.3	+ 2.00
J C Hayden	1-8	1-4	0-1	0-0	0-3	12.5	+ 7.00
P Mullins	1-9	0-2	1-3	0-0	0-4	11.1	0.00
M J Grassick	1-12	0-7	1-1	0-0	0-4	8.3	+ 1.00

Leading Jockeys

	Total W-R	Per cent	£1 Level Stake	Best Trainer	W-R	Per cent	£1 Level Stake
C Roche	3-14	21.4	− 2.12	J S Bolger	2-6	33.3	− 1.12
J A Heffernan	2-7	28.6	+ 12.00	Edward Lynam	1-1	100.0	+ 8.00
K J Manning	2-12	16.7	+ 16.00	M J Grassick	1-3	33.3	+ 10.00
W J O'Connor	2-12	16.7	+ 3.00	M Kauntze	2-8	25.0	+ 7.00
M J Kinane	2-16	12.5	− 2.00	D K Weld	2-14	14.3	0.00
W J Supple	2-17	11.8	− 7.67	J S Bolger	1-2	50.0	− 0.67
A J Beale	1-1	100.0	+ 3.00	J E Mulhern	1-1	100.0	+ 3.00
C Everard	1-3	33.3	− 0.50	J S Bolger	1-2	50.0	+ 0.50
S Craine	1-13	7.7	− 4.00	Liam Browne	1-1	100.0	+ 8.00
J F Egan	1-14	7.1	− 11.00	Mrs C-O'Brien	1-1	100.0	+ 2.00
P Shanahan	1-16	6.3	− 7.00	P Mullins	1-1	100.0	+ 8.00

How the Favourites Fared

Non-handicaps	W-R	Per cent	£1 Level Stake	Handicaps	W-R	Per cent	£1 Level Stake
2-y-o	4-9	44.4	+ 0.46	2-y-o	0-0	−	0.00
3-y-o	0-2	−	− 2.00	3-y-o	0-2	−	− 2.00
Weight-for-age	3-4	75.0	+ 5.00	All-aged	4-7	57.1	+ 9.25
Totals	7-15	46.7	+ 3.46	Totals	4-9	44.4	+ 7.25
All favs	11-24	45.8	+ 10.71				

ROSCOMMON

Leading Trainers 1989-93

	Total W-R	Non-handicaps 2-y-o	3-y-o+	Handicaps 2-y-o	3-y-o+	Per cent	£1 Level Stake
J S Bolger	17-86	9-27	3-38	0-1	5-20	19.8	- 16.96
K Prendergast	16-94	4-23	7-38	0-1	5-32	17.0	+ 20.83
John M Oxx	15-52	3-5	9-33	0-0	3-14	28.8	- 10.99
D K Weld	12-90	6-28	3-32	0-1	3-29	13.3	- 28.96
T Stack	9-37	1-9	7-20	0-0	1-8	24.3	+ 22.88
Noel Meade	4-37	1-9	3-15	0-0	0-13	10.8	- 9.75
J M Canty	3-16	0-7	1-5	0-0	2-4	18.8	+ 1.50
M Kauntze	3-18	0-3	2-10	0-0	1-5	16.7	- 2.17
D Gillespie	3-29	0-6	1-8	0-1	2-14	10.3	- 13.00
T G Curtin	2-9	0-0	1-4	0-0	1-5	22.2	- 1.00
M A O'Toole	2-17	0-5	0-2	0-0	2-10	11.8	+ 5.00
J J McLoughlin	2-25	0-7	0-6	0-0	2-12	8.0	- 15.75
M J Grassick	2-29	0-3	2-15	0-0	0-11	6.9	- 15.00
C Collins	2-31	1-4	1-16	0-0	0-11	6.5	- 23.27
F Dunne	2-34	0-11	0-12	0-1	2-10	5.9	- 24.50
R O'Donovan	1-1	0-0	1-1	0-0	0-0	100.0	+ 7.00
C P Donoghue	1-1	0-0	0-0	0-0	1-1	100.0	+ 4.00
D Hanley	1-1	0-0	1-1	0-0	0-0	100.0	+ 1.00
T J O'Mara	1-1	0-0	0-0	0-0	1-1	100.0	+ 9.00
P Burke	1-2	0-0	0-0	0-1	1-1	50.0	+ 7.00
E P Mitchell	1-2	0-0	0-0	1-1	0-1	50.0	+ 11.00
T Kinane	1-4	0-0	1-4	0-0	0-0	25.0	- 1.50

Leading Jockeys

	Total W-R	Per cent	£1 Level Stake	Best Trainer	W-R	Per cent	£1 Level Stake
C Roche	13-55	23.6	+ 6.86	J S Bolger	10-43	23.3	- 4.64
M J Kinane	12-79	15.2	- 33.78	D K Weld	7-59	11.9	- 27.53
S Craine	10-67	14.9	- 8.12	T Stack	7-30	23.3	+ 15.38
W J Supple	7-52	13.5	- 16.75	J S Bolger	5-19	26.3	+ 7.00
R Griffiths	5-27	18.5	+ 20.33	K Prendergast	5-26	19.2	+ 21.33
R Hughes	5-61	8.2	- 31.10	D Hanley	1-1	100.0	+ 1.00
R M Burke	4-30	13.3	- 2.50	K Prendergast	3-10	30.0	+ 13.00
P Shanahan	4-50	8.0	- 24.20	J S Bolger	1-1	100.0	+ 0.80
N G McCullagh	3-49	6.1	- 30.75	J J McLoughlin	2-13	15.4	- 3.75
P V Gilson	3-50	6.0	- 33.75	J M Canty	2-2	100.0	+ 10.50
W J O'Connor	3-51	5.9	- 34.00	M Kauntze	2-13	15.4	- 1.50
K J Manning	3-55	5.5	- 36.50	D Gillespie	1-5	20.0	+ 1.50

How the Favourites Fared

Non-handicaps	W-R	Per cent	£1 Level Stake	Handicaps	W-R	Per cent	£1 Level Stake
2-y-o	9-27	33.3	- 7.86	2-y-o	0-1	-	- 1.00
3-y-o	5-20	25.0	- 10.80	3-y-o	4-10	40.0	+ 3.58
Weight-for-age	13-30	43.3	- 2.11	All-aged	4-29	13.8	- 18.63
Totals	27-77	35.1	- 20.77	Totals	8-40	20.0	- 16.05
All favs	35-117	29.9	- 36.82				

SLIGO

Leading Trainers 1989-93

	Total W-R	Non-handicaps 2-y-o	3-y-o+	Handicaps 2-y-o	3-y-o+	Per cent	£1 Level Stake
D K Weld	14-56	5-11	5-27	0-0	4-18	25.0	+ 0.40
M J Grassick	8-42	1-8	4-21	0-0	3-13	19.0	+ 3.63
Noel Meade	7-24	1-5	2-9	0-0	4-10	29.2	- 1.15
John M Oxx	4-12	0-1	3-9	0-0	1-2	33.3	+ 8.50
P J Flynn	4-17	0-1	2-4	0-0	2-12	23.5	- 3.13
M Halford	3-9	1-1	1-4	0-0	1-4	33.3	+ 10.00
C Collins	3-18	2-4	1-10	0-0	0-4	16.7	+ 2.25
J S Bolger	3-37	0-10	2-16	0-0	1-11	8.1	- 10.00
T G Curtin	2-3	1-1	1-1	0-0	0-1	66.7	+ 13.50
J Burns	2-4	1-3	1-1	0-0	0-0	50.0	+ 10.00
Anthony Mullins	2-5	0-1	2-3	0-0	0-1	40.0	+ 1.25
Wilbert Tolerton	2-6	0-0	1-2	0-0	1-4	33.3	+ 23.00
O Weldon	2-6	0-0	0-2	0-0	2-4	33.3	+ 14.00
M McDonagh	2-8	0-0	0-5	0-0	2-3	25.0	+ 1.50
J T Gorman	2-8	1-1	0-2	0-0	1-5	25.0	+ 16.00
J C Hayden	2-10	1-3	1-5	0-0	0-2	20.0	+ 2.25
E J O'Grady	2-20	0-6	1-9	0-0	1-5	10.0	- 11.50
D Gillespie	2-23	0-4	2-12	0-0	0-7	8.7	- 15.00
K Prendergast	2-35	0-9	1-13	0-0	1-13	5.7	- 27.25
C P Magnier	1-2	0-0	0-1	0-0	1-1	50.0	+ 3.00
Francis Ennis	1-2	0-0	1-2	0-0	0-0	50.0	+ 1.25
Thomas Bergin	1-2	0-0	1-2	0-0	0-0	50.0	+ 7.00

Leading Jockeys

	Total W-R	Per cent	£1 Level Stake	Best Trainer	W-R	Per cent	£1 Level Stake
M J Kinane	13-41	31.7	+ 13.41	D K Weld	12-35	34.3	+ 15.91
R Hughes	7-37	18.9	- 2.40	Noel Meade	2-4	50.0	+ 1.60
S Craine	6-37	16.2	- 16.75	Anthony Mullins	2-3	66.7	+ 3.25
P Shanahan	5-28	17.9	- 5.25	J Burns	2-3	66.7	+ 11.00
J F Egan	5-36	13.9	- 13.12	P J Flynn	3-10	30.0	+ 1.63
D G O'Shea	3-17	17.6	+ 1.50	E J O'Grady	1-1	100.0	+ 4.00
J A Heffernan	3-17	17.6	+ 13.00	O Weldon	2-3	66.7	+ 17.00
W J Smith	3-23	13.0	+ 9.00	Wilbert Tolerton	2-5	40.0	+ 24.00
W J Supple	3-38	7.9	- 15.00	M Halford	1-2	50.0	+ 4.00
N G McCullagh	3-41	7.3	- 24.00	Noel Meade	1-1	100.0	+ 5.00
G M Moylan	2-2	100.0	+ 8.00	M J Grassick	2-2	100.0	+ 8.00
P Carberry	2-9	22.2	- 1.75	Noel Meade	1-1	100.0	+ 1.75

How the Favourites Fared

Non-handicaps	W-R	Per cent	£1 Level Stake	Handicaps	W-R	Per cent	£1 Level Stake
2-y-o	4-16	25.0	- 7.05	2-y-o	0-0	-	0.00
3-y-o	9-18	50.0	+ 4.59	3-y-o	0-1	-	- 1.00
Weight-for-age	8-22	36.4	+ 0.88	All-aged	8-30	26.7	- 9.24
Totals	21-56	37.5	- 1.58	Totals	8-31	25.8	- 10.24
All favs	29-87	33.3	- 11.82				

THURLES

Leading Trainers 1989-93

	Total	Non-handicaps		Handicaps		Per	£1 Level
	W-R	2-y-o	3-y-o+	2-y-o	3-y-o+	cent	Stake
D K Weld	3-16	0-0	2-14	0-0	1-2	18.8	+ 16.75
P J Flynn	3-16	0-0	3-12	0-0	0-4	18.8	- 5.55
J S Bolger	3-20	0-0	2-15	0-0	1-5	15.0	+ 18.00
E J O'Grady	2-7	0-0	1-4	0-0	1-3	28.6	+ 6.25
Noel Meade	2-7	0-0	2-6	0-0	0-1	28.6	+ 7.00
T G Curtin	1-1	0-0	0-0	0-0	1-1	100.0	+ 4.00
F Flood	1-2	0-0	0-0	0-0	1-2	50.0	+ 0.75
Mrs Crowley-O'Brien	1-2	0-0	1-2	0-0	0-0	50.0	+ 1.50
R Lister	1-3	0-0	1-3	0-0	0-0	33.3	+ 0.25
Edward Lynam	1-4	0-0	1-4	0-0	0-0	25.0	+ 3.00
B V Kelly	1-4	0-0	1-3	0-0	0-1	25.0	+ 1.00
John M Oxx	1-5	0-0	1-5	0-0	0-0	20.0	0.00
Pat O'Leary	1-7	0-0	1-3	0-0	0-4	14.3	+ 8.00
T Stack	1-7	0-0	1-6	0-0	0-1	14.3	- 5.27
K Prendergast	1-8	0-0	1-6	0-0	0-2	12.5	- 4.25
Capt D G Swan	1-10	0-0	0-7	0-0	1-3	10.0	- 7.00
P Mullins	1-12	0-0	1-6	0-0	0-6	8.3	+ 1.00

Leading Jockeys

	Total	Per	£1 Level			Per	£1 Level
	W-R	cent	Stake	Best Trainer	W-R	cent	Stake
P Shanahan	3-11	27.3	+ 19.75	D K Weld	2-5	40.0	+ 18.75
M J Kinane	3-12	25.0	+ 2.00	F Flood	1-1	100.0	+ 1.75
S Craine	2-14	14.3	- 7.27	B V Kelly	1-1	100.0	+ 4.00
C Roche	2-17	11.8	- 2.00	J S Bolger	1-10	10.0	- 1.00
T E Durcan	1-1	100.0	+ 7.00	J S Bolger	1-1	100.0	+ 7.00
A P McCoy	1-2	50.0	+ 19.00	J S Bolger	1-2	50.0	+ 19.00
M Duffy	1-3	33.3	- 1.27	P J Flynn	1-2	50.0	- 0.27
M F Ryan	1-3	33.3	+ 2.00	Noel Meade	1-1	100.0	+ 4.00
T P Treacy	1-4	25.0	+ 9.00	P Mullins	1-2	50.0	+ 11.00
D V Smith	1-5	20.0	+ 2.00	Edward Lynam	1-1	100.0	+ 6.00
R M Burke	1-5	20.0	+ 10.00	Pat O'Leary	1-1	100.0	+ 14.00
C Everard	1-5	20.0	+ 6.00	E J O'Grady	1-1	100.0	+ 10.00

How the Favourites Fared

		Per	£1 Level			Per	£1 Level
Non-handicaps	W-R	cent	Stake	Handicaps	W-R	cent	Stake
2-y-o	0-0	-	0.00	2-y-o	0-0	-	0.00
3-y-o	2-9	22.2	- 5.02	3-y-o	0-0	-	0.00
Weight-for-age	3-11	27.3	- 4.29	All-aged	3-8	37.5	+ 0.50
Totals	5-20	25.0	- 9.31	Totals	3-8	37.5	+ 0.50
All favs	8-28	28.6	- 8.81				

TIPPERARY

Leading Trainers 1989-93

	Total W-R	Non-handicaps 2-y-o	3-y-o+	Handicaps 2-y-o	3-y-o+	Per cent	£1 Level Stake
J S Bolger	38-169	14-48	17-88	0-2	7-31	22.5	- 47.26
D K Weld	34-158	4-37	23-84	1-1	6-36	21.5	- 30.38
John M Oxx	21-85	6-16	14-56	0-0	1-13	24.7	- 7.57
T Stack	16-92	4-18	10-56	1-3	1-15	17.4	- 0.94
K Prendergast	16-107	6-29	6-52	0-0	4-26	15.0	- 19.93
M V O'Brien	7-22	2-3	5-18	0-0	0-1	31.8	- 3.32
D Gillespie	6-31	2-10	3-9	0-1	1-11	19.4	+ 14.63
Noel Meade	6-41	2-12	2-16	0-0	2-13	14.6	- 15.38
M Kauntze	4-26	1-6	2-14	0-0	1-6	15.4	- 15.00
M J Grassick	4-30	2-4	2-23	0-0	0-3	13.3	- 3.60
B V Kelly	3-18	0-0	0-9	0-0	3-9	16.7	+ 12.00
J G Coogan	3-18	3-13	0-2	0-1	0-2	16.7	- 1.50
P Mullins	3-44	1-17	2-16	0-0	0-11	6.8	- 18.75
Liam Browne	3-50	1-17	1-26	0-0	1-7	6.0	- 24.00
Augustine Leahy	3-55	0-14	1-24	0-0	2-17	5.5	- 38.25
D Hanley	2-4	0-0	2-3	0-0	0-1	50.0	+ 11.10
Daniel J Murphy	2-12	0-3	1-7	0-0	1-2	16.7	+ 8.00
P Prendergast	2-14	0-5	1-6	0-0	1-3	14.3	- 6.40
J Burns	2-19	1-11	1-8	0-0	0-0	10.5	- 7.75
E J O'Grady	2-35	1-8	0-14	0-0	1-13	5.7	- 26.10
J J McLoughlin	2-38	0-9	0-11	0-0	2-18	5.3	- 18.00
Peter Casey	1-1	0-0	0-0	0-0	1-1	100.0	+ 5.50

Leading Jockeys

	Total W-R	Per cent	£1 Level Stake	Best Trainer	W-R	Per cent	£1 Level Stake
M J Kinane	34-127	26.8	+ 7.98	D K Weld	30-103	29.1	+ 17.28
C Roche	30-113	26.5	- 9.89	J S Bolger	28-91	30.8	- 6.89
S Craine	23-137	16.8	- 14.78	T Stack	15-71	21.1	+ 16.06
K J Manning	10-73	13.7	+ 2.74	J S Bolger	6-24	25.0	+ 1.24
P Shanahan	9-90	10.0	- 46.08	D K Weld	3-26	11.5	- 19.83
R Griffiths	8-29	27.6	+ 20.91	K Prendergast	8-27	29.6	+ 22.91
W J Supple	8-77	10.4	- 23.10	K Prendergast	3-17	17.6	+ 5.80
R Hughes	6-63	9.5	- 25.75	John M Oxx	4-9	44.4	+ 15.25
N G McCullagh	5-80	6.3	- 38.25	P Mullins	2-13	15.4	+ 1.25
W J O'Connor	4-59	6.8	- 41.50	M Kauntze	3-18	16.7	- 9.50
P V Gilson	4-82	4.9	- 57.00	M V O'Brien	2-9	22.2	- 0.25
E A Leonard	3-44	6.8	- 14.90	C Kinane	1-1	100.0	+ 1.50

How the Favourites Fared

Non-handicaps	W-R	Per cent	£1 Level Stake	Handicaps	W-R	Per cent	£1 Level Stake
2-y-o	23-53	43.4	- 9.11	2-y-o	2-2	100.0	+ 1.85
3-y-o	15-36	41.7	+ 0.79	3-y-o	3-8	37.5	+ 1.00
Weight-for-age	35-70	50.0	+ 6.85	All-aged	12-39	30.8	- 9.32
Totals	73-159	45.9	- 1.47	Totals	17-49	34.7	- 6.47
All favs	90-208	43.3	- 7.94				

TRALEE

Leading Trainers 1989-93

	Total W-R	Non-handicaps 2-y-o	3-y-o+	Handicaps 2-y-o	3-y-o+	Per cent	£1 Level Stake
D K Weld	28-97	6-16	11-33	1-5	10-43	28.9	+ 4.86
J S Bolger	15-108	9-22	2-40	1-4	3-42	13.9	- 45.26
John M Oxx	12-44	1-5	9-25	0-0	2-14	27.3	- 9.20
C Collins	6-55	0-11	3-19	0-1	3-24	10.9	- 31.25
T G Curtin	4-28	0-0	1-7	0-0	3-21	14.3	+ 21.00
Liam Browne	4-35	4-17	0-9	0-1	0-8	11.4	- 16.40
Augustine Leahy	4-44	0-11	0-12	0-3	4-18	9.1	- 24.50
T Stack	4-48	1-7	2-18	0-2	1-21	8.3	- 38.33
M Kauntze	3-16	1-2	2-5	0-1	0-8	18.8	- 1.20
D Gillespie	3-21	0-5	3-5	0-2	0-9	14.3	0.00
K Prendergast	3-28	0-3	0-8	1-3	2-14	10.7	+ 2.50
P Prendergast	3-28	1-8	0-5	0-1	2-14	10.7	- 14.25
M McDonagh	2-4	0-1	0-0	0-0	2-3	50.0	+ 9.75
A P O'Brien	2-8	0-0	0-4	0-0	2-4	25.0	+ 3.50
P Mullins	2-11	0-2	1-4	0-1	1-4	18.2	+ 5.00
J C Hayden	2-12	1-6	0-3	0-1	1-2	16.7	+ 5.50
M Cunningham	2-13	0-0	0-5	0-0	2-8	15.4	+ 7.00
Edward Lynam	2-16	0-2	1-6	1-1	0-7	12.5	+ 16.00
Noel Meade	2-21	0-2	1-5	0-1	1-13	9.5	- 13.00
T F Lacy	2-25	0-4	1-7	0-0	1-14	8.0	- 5.00
B Lawlor	1-1	0-0	1-1	0-0	0-0	100.0	+ 4.50
M Hourigan	1-2	0-0	0-0	0-0	1-2	50.0	+ 9.00

Leading Jockeys

	Total W-R	Per cent	£1 Level Stake	Best Trainer	W-R	Per cent	£1 Level Stake
M J Kinane	26-86	30.2	+ 11.09	D K Weld	22-69	31.9	+ 8.34
C Roche	11-63	17.5	- 23.03	J S Bolger	8-46	17.4	- 23.36
W J Supple	8-68	11.8	- 26.05	J S Bolger	3-18	16.7	- 8.90
S Craine	6-65	9.2	- 37.25	T Stack	2-30	6.7	- 24.75
R M Burke	5-37	13.5	+ 20.00	M Hourigan	1-1	100.0	+ 10.00
P V Gilson	5-39	12.8	- 10.75	C Collins	3-13	23.1	- 1.25
K J Manning	5-46	10.9	- 19.07	T Stack	2-2	100.0	+ 2.43
P Shanahan	5-56	8.9	- 40.60	D K Weld	2-8	25.0	- 0.60
W J O'Connor	4-36	11.1	- 20.90	M Kauntze	2-9	22.2	+ 0.30
J A Heffernan	3-20	15.0	+ 5.50	J S Bolger	3-11	27.3	+ 14.50
W J Smith	3-22	13.6	+ 20.50	Edward Lynam	1-2	50.0	+ 19.00
M Fenton	3-40	7.5	- 27.15	Augustine Leahy	2-16	12.5	- 5.25

How the Favourites Fared

Non-handicaps	W-R	Per cent	£1 Level Stake	Handicaps	W-R	Per cent	£1 Level Stake
2-y-o	15-26	57.7	+ 3.25	2-y-o	0-5	-	- 5.00
3-y-o	5-9	55.6	+ 2.10	3-y-o	1-2	50.0	+ 2.33
Weight-for-age	22-38	57.9	+ 13.57	All-aged	18-55	32.7	- 6.85
Totals	42-73	57.5	+ 18.92	Totals	19-62	30.6	- 9.52
All favs	61-135	45.2	+ 9.40				

TRAMORE

Leading Trainers 1989-93

	Total W-R	Non-handicaps 2-y-o	3-y-o+	Handicaps 2-y-o	3-y-o+	Per cent	£1 Level Stake
K Prendergast	9-35	0-0	3-16	0-0	6-19	25.7	+ 8.40
P Mullins	6-22	0-0	5-10	0-0	1-12	27.3	+ 2.70
C Collins	4-12	0-0	2-7	0-0	2-5	33.3	+ 1.13
W P Mullins	4-16	0-0	1-8	0-0	3-8	25.0	+ 1.75
T Stack	3-6	0-0	2-4	0-0	1-2	50.0	+ 5.50
M A McCullagh	2-2	0-0	0-0	0-0	2-2	100.0	+ 5.50
Liam Browne	2-4	0-0	1-1	0-0	1-3	50.0	+ 0.73
John M Oxx	2-4	0-0	2-3	0-0	0-1	50.0	+ 0.30
E P Harty	2-5	0-0	2-4	0-0	0-1	40.0	+ 32.00
Mrs Crowley-O'Brien	2-5	0-0	0-2	0-0	2-3	40.0	- 0.52
W P Browne	2-5	0-0	2-5	0-0	0-0	40.0	+ 4.67
Edward Lynam	2-13	0-0	1-7	0-0	1-6	15.4	- 1.00
Daniel J Murphy	2-15	0-0	2-11	0-0	0-4	13.3	+ 2.00
P J Flynn	2-17	0-0	1-5	0-0	1-12	11.8	- 11.25
Augustine Leahy	2-21	0-0	1-9	0-0	1-12	9.5	0.00
D K Weld	2-26	0-0	2-17	0-0	0-9	7.7	- 16.00
D McDonogh	1-1	0-0	0-0	0-0	1-1	100.0	+ 10.00
Mrs John Harrington	1-1	0-0	1-1	0-0	0-0	100.0	+ 8.00
E J Kearns	1-1	0-0	1-1	0-0	0-0	100.0	+ 6.00
R Donoghue	1-1	0-0	1-1	0-0	0-0	100.0	+ 3.50
J S Bolger	1-2	0-0	0-1	0-0	1-1	50.0	+ 0.10
A L T Moore	1-2	0-0	1-2	0-0	0-0	50.0	+ 0.25

Leading Jockeys

	Total W-R	Per cent	£1 Level Stake	Best Trainer	W-R	Per cent	£1 Level Stake
R Hughes	7-31	22.6	+ 7.15	W P Browne	2-2	100.0	+ 7.67
N G McCullagh	7-42	16.7	- 10.58	P Mullins	2-6	33.3	+ 1.17
J J Behan	6-17	35.3	+ 3.15	Liam Browne	2-2	100.0	+ 2.73
W J O'Connor	5-20	25.0	+ 6.50	C Collins	1-1	100.0	+ 3.00
B J Walsh	3-13	23.1	+ 0.40	K Prendergast	3-7	42.9	+ 6.40
P V Gilson	3-14	21.4	+ 2.50	Daniel J Murphy	1-2	50.0	+ 6.00
D G O'Shea	3-18	16.7	+ 7.00	W P Mullins	1-1	100.0	+ 4.00
T J O'Sullivan	3-22	13.6	+ 3.50	Augustine Leahy	1-3	33.3	+ 3.00
D Duggan	3-24	12.5	- 8.50	R Donoghue	1-1	100.0	+ 3.50
W J Smith	3-26	11.5	- 14.33	D K Weld	2-9	22.2	+ 1.00
R Griffiths	2-4	50.0	+ 1.00	K Prendergast	2-4	50.0	+ 1.00
P Shanahan	2-6	33.3	- 1.62	C Collins	1-2	50.0	0.00

How the Favourites Fared

Non-handicaps	W-R	Per cent	£1 Level Stake	Handicaps	W-R	Per cent	£1 Level Stake
2-y-o	0-0	-	0.00	2-y-o	0-0	-	0.00
3-y-o	1-7	14.3	- 4.50	3-y-o	2-2	100.0	+ 3.00
Weight-for-age	19-37	51.4	+ 2.58	All-aged	13-37	35.1	- 3.82
Totals	20-44	45.5	- 1.92	Totals	15-39	38.5	- 0.82
All favs	35-83	42.2	- 2.74				

WEXFORD

Leading Trainers 1989-93

	Total W-R	Non-handicaps 2-y-o	3-y-o+	Handicaps 2-y-o	3-y-o+	Per cent	£1 Level Stake
John M Oxx	16-30	0-0	13-24	0-0	3-6	53.3	+ 15.93
P Mullins	5-21	0-0	2-10	0-0	3-11	23.8	+ 7.08
K Prendergast	4-19	0-0	3-12	0-0	1-7	21.1	+ 1.67
P J Flynn	4-20	0-0	0-6	0-0	4-14	20.0	+ 7.03
J S Bolger	4-39	0-0	3-25	0-0	1-14	10.3	- 18.10
M J Grassick	3-11	0-0	2-7	0-0	1-4	27.3	+ 3.00
J J McLoughlin	2-7	0-0	0-3	0-0	2-4	28.6	+ 12.50
A P O'Brien	2-7	0-0	1-3	0-0	1-4	28.6	- 1.50
T G Curtin	2-8	0-0	1-2	0-0	1-6	25.0	+ 9.00
C Collins	2-10	0-0	2-5	0-0	0-5	20.0	+ 7.00
J C Shearman	1-1	0-0	1-1	0-0	0-0	100.0	+ 5.00
F Flood	1-2	0-0	1-2	0-0	0-0	50.0	+ 3.50
J E Kiely	1-2	0-0	0-0	0-0	1-2	50.0	+ 1.50
Mrs Crowley-O'Brien	1-2	0-0	1-1	0-0	0-1	50.0	+ 5.00
J Morrison	1-3	0-0	0-0	0-0	1-3	33.3	+ 6.00
M J P O'Brien	1-3	0-0	1-3	0-0	0-0	33.3	+ 0.50
M A O'Toole	1-4	0-0	0-0	0-0	1-4	25.0	+ 3.00
W M Roper	1-5	0-0	0-2	0-0	1-3	20.0	+ 10.00
J C Harley	1-5	0-0	0-2	0-0	1-3	20.0	+ 3.00
J C Hayden	1-6	0-0	1-3	0-0	0-3	16.7	+ 3.00
Noel Meade	1-7	0-0	0-4	0-0	1-3	14.3	- 2.67
R Lister	1-7	0-0	1-3	0-0	0-4	14.3	0.00

Leading Jockeys

	Total W-R	Per cent	£1 Level Stake	Best Trainer	W-R	Per cent	£1 Level Stake
J F Egan	5-25	20.0	+ 16.25	P J Flynn	2-10	20.0	+ 9.00
M J Kinane	4-18	22.2	+ 2.50	John M Oxx	2-2	100.0	+ 5.50
S Craine	4-21	19.0	- 6.53	P Mullins	2-4	50.0	+ 7.50
C Roche	4-26	15.4	- 17.33	J S Bolger	2-20	10.0	- 15.50
D G O'Shea	3-8	37.5	+ 3.75	John M Oxx	2-2	100.0	+ 6.25
P V Gilson	3-17	17.6	+ 15.00	C Collins	2-6	33.3	+ 11.00
K J Manning	3-20	15.0	- 8.10	M J Grassick	2-2	100.0	+ 8.50
B P Harding	2-3	66.7	+ 5.50	F Flood	1-1	100.0	+ 4.50
J R Barry	2-10	20.0	+ 3.33	P Mullins	2-6	33.3	+ 7.33
R Hughes	2-26	7.7	- 18.17	Noel Meade	1-2	50.0	+ 2.33
Mr K Whelan	1-1	100.0	+ 8.00	J Morrison	1-1	100.0	+ 8.00
E A Leonard	1-2	50.0	+ 7.00	K Prendergast	1-1	100.0	+ 8.00

How the Favourites Fared

Non-handicaps	W-R	Per cent	£1 Level Stake	Handicaps	W-R	Per cent	£1 Level Stake
2-y-o	0-0	-	0.00	2-y-o	0-0	-	0.00
3-y-o	4-13	30.8	- 3.71	3-y-o	3-3	100.0	+ 3.50
Weight-for-age	14-24	58.3	+ 3.32	All-aged	8-23	34.8	+ 1.61
Totals	18-37	48.6	- 0.39	Totals	11-26	42.3	+ 5.11
All favs	29-63	46.0	+ 4.72				

TRAINERS' FAVOURITES AT THE CURRAGH 1989-93

	Total W-R	Non-handicaps 2-y-o	Non-handicaps 3-y-o+	Handicaps 2-y-o	Handicaps 3-y-o+	Per cent	£1 Level Stake
J S Bolger	44-110	25-48	12-33	1-5	6-24	40.0	- 3.99
M V O'Brien	40-81	19-38	18-36	0-0	3-7	49.4	+ 16.84
D K Weld	36-125	10-29	16-48	1-2	9-46	28.8	- 18.60
John M Oxx	31-95	9-24	14-38	0-0	8-33	32.6	- 2.03
K Prendergast	14-31	2-8	6-12	2-3	4-8	45.2	+ 20.03
C Collins	6-20	1-1	1-5	1-2	3-12	30.0	+ 2.60
M Kauntze	4-16	1-3	3-10	0-1	0-2	25.0	- 8.66
T Stack	4-17	1-4	2-6	0-0	1-7	23.5	- 5.95
P J Flynn	3-6	0-0	0-1	0-0	3-5	50.0	+ 13.50
H R A Cecil (Eng)	3-8	0-0	3-8	0-0	0-0	37.5	- 3.34
P F I Cole (Eng)	3-10	0-1	3-9	0-0	0-0	30.0	- 2.37
P T Walwyn (Eng)	2-2	0-0	2-2	0-0	0-0	100.0	+ 2.67
C E Brittain (Eng)	2-4	1-2	1-2	0-0	0-0	50.0	- 0.17
L Cumani (Eng)	2-4	0-0	2-4	0-0	0-0	50.0	+ 0.20
P Prendergast	2-14	0-3	1-3	1-2	0-6	14.3	- 6.10
T G Curtin	1-1	0-0	1-1	0-0	0-0	100.0	+ 2.00
P J Deegan	1-1	0-0	0-0	0-0	1-1	100.0	+ 3.00
R Hannon (Eng)	1-1	0-0	1-1	0-0	0-0	100.0	+ 1.25
I A Balding (Eng)	1-1	1-1	0-0	0-0	0-0	100.0	+ 1.75
W R Hern (Eng)	1-1	0-0	1-1	0-0	0-0	100.0	+ 1.50
B Hanbury (Eng)	1-1	1-1	0-0	0-0	0-0	100.0	+ 1.50
H T Jones (Eng)	1-1	0-0	1-1	0-0	0-0	100.0	+ 1.10
G Wragg (Eng)	1-1	0-0	1-1	0-0	0-0	100.0	+ 0.80

TRAINERS' FAVOURITES AT LEOPARDSTOWN 1989-93

	Total W-R	Non-handicaps 2-y-o	Non-handicaps 3-y-o+	Handicaps 2-y-o	Handicaps 3-y-o+	Per cent	£1 Level Stake
D K Weld	48-128	7-20	32-65	0-1	9-42	37.5	- 6.97
J S Bolger	44-104	17-38	16-35	4-6	7-25	42.3	+ 5.62
John M Oxx	27-71	7-15	14-34	0-0	6-22	38.0	+ 5.24
M V O'Brien	16-34	7-9	8-24	0-0	1-1	47.1	- 1.32
K Prendergast	9-27	1-3	5-8	1-2	2-14	33.3	+ 1.23
C Collins	3-8	1-2	2-5	0-0	0-1	37.5	+ 0.07
M Kauntze	3-16	1-5	2-7	0-1	0-3	18.8	- 7.75
H R A Cecil (Eng)	2-2	0-0	2-2	0-0	0-0	100.0	+ 0.75
B W Hills (Eng)	2-3	0-0	2-3	0-0	0-0	66.7	+ 3.25
M A O'Toole	2-5	0-0	1-3	1-1	0-1	40.0	+ 0.50
P Mullins	2-6	0-0	2-3	0-0	0-3	33.3	+ 3.88
T Stack	2-8	0-0	1-4	0-1	1-3	25.0	+ 1.25
P F I Cole (Eng)	1-1	0-0	1-1	0-0	0-0	100.0	+ 3.00
Lord Huntingdon	1-1	0-0	1-1	0-0	0-0	100.0	+ 1.00
J Berry (Eng)	1-1	1-1	0-0	0-0	0-0	100.0	+ 0.53
P Chapple-Hyam (Eng)	1-1	1-1	0-0	0-0	0-0	100.0	+ 1.75
B V Kelly	1-2	0-0	1-1	0-0	0-1	50.0	+ 1.25
P Prendergast	1-2	0-0	0-0	0-0	1-2	50.0	+ 2.50
D T Hughes	1-2	0-0	0-0	0-0	1-2	50.0	+ 1.25
R Hannon (Eng)	1-2	1-2	0-0	0-0	0-0	50.0	+ 1.00
J E Hammond (Fra)	1-2	0-0	1-2	0-0	0-0	50.0	- 0.33
P J Flynn	1-4	0-1	1-1	0-0	0-2	25.0	- 1.50
M R Stoute (Eng)	1-4	1-2	0-2	0-0	0-0	25.0	- 1.75
Noel Meade	1-5	0-0	1-2	0-0	0-3	20.0	- 3.47

TOP PERCENTAGE COURSES FOR FAVOURITES 1989-93

	W-R	Per cent	£1 Level Stake		W-R	Per cent	£1 Level Stake
Killarney	54-103	52.4	+ 7.27	Fairyhouse	36-92	39.1	- 5.91
Clonmel	33-65	50.8	+ 14.62	Leopardstown	177-464	38.1	- 41.85
Wexford	29-63	46.0	+ 4.72	Navan	37-99	37.4	- 6.59
Punchestown	11-24	45.8	+ 10.71	Gowran	56-152	36.8	- 18.31
Mallow	41-90	45.6	+ 2.84	Galway	63-173	36.4	- 14.69
Tralee	61-135	45.2	+ 9.40	Naas	63-175	36.0	- 1.03
Bellewstown	27-60	45.0	+ 6.61	The Curragh	216-626	34.5	- 55.16
Dundalk	60-135	44.4	+ 0.27	Limerick	24-71	33.8	- 20.53
Tipperary	90-208	43.3	- 7.94	Sligo	29-87	33.3	- 11.82
Tramore	35-83	42.2	- 2.74	Laytown	8-25	32.0	- 6.90
Down Royal	44-105	41.9	- 8.46	Downpatrick	12-38	31.6	- 11.04
Listowel	33-79	41.8	+ 12.98	Roscommon	35-117	29.9	- 36.82
Ballinrobe	30-75	40.0	+ 10.06	Thurles	8-28	28.6	- 8.81

FAVOURITES' PERFORMANCE BY TYPE OF RACE 1989-93

Non-h'caps	W-R	Per cent	£1 Level Stake	Handicaps	W-R	Per cent	£1 Level Stake
2-y-o	359-785	45.7	- 13.57	2-y-o	31-86	36.0	+ 8.16
3-y-o	204-496	41.1	- 42.48	3-y-o	57-158	36.1	+ 10.01
Weight/age	452-1031	43.8	- 12.26	All-aged	295-1020	28.9	-116.57
Totals	1015-2312	43.9	- 68.31	Totals	383-1264	30.3	- 98.40
All Favs	1398-3576	39.1	- 166.71				

When there is more than one favourite in a race then the £1 stake has been equally divided on each one. Only one favourite is counted for each race.

IRISH TRAINER SUMMARIES

WINNING FLAT TRAINERS IN IRELAND 1993

	Total W–R	2-y-o	3-y-o	4-y-o+	Per cent	£1 Level Stake
D K Weld	109-552	26-126	49-260	34-166	19.7	- 72.34
John M Oxx	80-327	20-81	58-239	2-7	24.5	- 17.70
J S Bolger	57-520	27-153	22-231	8-136	11.0	-232.19
K Prendergast	40-423	8-111	18-223	14-89	9.5	-155.82
C Collins	22-216	5-54	11-120	6-42	10.2	- 82.51
Noel Meade	21-194	1-46	13-106	7-42	10.8	- 16.00
A P O'Brien	20-175	2-61	9-69	9-45	11.4	- 46.62
P J Flynn	17-195	4-34	8-97	5-64	8.7	- 73.00
M J Grassick	16-119	5-33	7-63	4-23	13.4	- 34.12
M Kauntze	13-127	5-37	8-69	0-21	10.2	- 26.83
E J O'Grady	12-83	2-23	5-31	5-29	14.5	- 1.18
T Stack	12-172	1-45	11-112	0-15	7.0	-105.37
Liam Browne	11-117	8-68	1-23	2-26	9.4	- 40.80
Charles O'Brien	10-69	2-23	7-40	1-6	14.5	- 21.15
P Mullins	10-97	0-11	4-41	6-45	10.3	- 15.08
D Gillespie	10-159	3-53	7-85	0-21	6.3	- 77.42
W P Mullins	9-73	0-11	4-21	5-41	12.3	- 24.25
F Dunne	9-87	2-27	3-42	4-18	10.3	- 8.00
D Hanley	8-33	0-4	5-18	3-11	24.2	+ 44.25
Edward Lynam	8-110	0-16	6-87	2-7	7.3	- 28.50
D T Hughes	7-71	0-0	5-42	2-29	9.9	- 27.50
T F Lacy	7-86	0-4	3-52	4-30	8.1	- 18.00
P Prendergast	7-88	1-25	2-23	4-40	8.0	- 29.40
M V O'Brien	6-19	2-5	4-14	0-0	31.6	+ 4.40
B V Kelly	6-64	0-13	0-20	6-31	9.4	+ 3.50
J C Harley	6-73	2-18	1-18	3-37	8.2	- 27.00
J M Canty	6-80	0-6	2-30	4-44	7.5	- 47.50
T M Walsh	5-46	1-18	0-10	4-18	10.9	+ 2.90
M Halford	5-68	0-21	2-30	3-17	7.4	- 40.50
Noel T Chance	4-31	0-7	2-10	2-14	12.9	+ 3.10
D P Kelly	4-47	0-3	1-9	3-35	8.5	- 10.50
P Aspell	4-70	0-4	4-46	0-20	5.7	- 26.00
J T Gorman	4-74	0-21	2-31	2-22	5.4	- 13.00
Daniel J Murphy	4-91	1-17	2-40	1-34	4.4	- 45.50
G T Hourigan	3-16	2-10	0-0	1-6	18.8	+ 3.00
P Burke	3-24	0-10	2-11	1-3	12.5	- 7.42
E P Harty	3-26	0-5	2-10	1-11	11.5	- 17.20
H McMahon	3-31	0-1	0-14	3-16	9.7	- 10.12
J E Mulhern	3-56	0-2	1-12	2-42	5.4	- 27.17
M A O'Toole	3-67	2-20	0-12	1-35	4.5	- 25.00
J G Coogan	3-101	2-44	1-48	0-9	3.0	- 84.50
Francis Ennis	2-11	0-0	0-1	2-10	18.2	- 2.25
S Treacy	2-11	0-0	2-8	0-3	18.2	- 3.25
F Berry	2-17	0-2	0-0	2-15	11.8	- 5.50
M Cunningham	2-20	0-1	2-12	0-7	10.0	- 4.50
K F O'Sullivan	2-20	2-7	0-7	0-6	10.0	- 2.00
Adrian Taylor	2-24	0-0	0-5	2-19	8.3	- 6.00
T J O'Mara	2-26	0-3	1-15	1-8	7.7	+ 35.00
E P Mitchell	2-29	1-11	0-0	1-18	6.9	- 11.00
A J Maxwell	2-36	2-13	0-5	0-18	5.6	- 20.50
Miss I T Oakes	2-38	0-10	2-26	0-2	5.3	- 13.00
Mrs A M O'Brien	2-43	0-3	1-27	1-13	4.7	- 33.50
J F Bailey Jnr	2-45	0-4	2-34	0-7	4.4	- 24.50

	Total				Per	£1 Level
	W-R	2-y-o	3-y-o	4-y-o+	cent	Stake
Peter McCreery	2-46	0-12	2-15	0-19	4.3	- 16.00
Pat O'Leary	2-49	0-1	2-23	0-25	4.1	- 25.00
O Weldon	2-49	1-6	0-22	1-21	4.1	- 32.50
Augustine Leahy	2-89	0-18	0-27	2-44	2.2	- 72.00
P M Doyle	1-1	1-1	0-0	0-0	100.0	+ 7.00
H R A Cecil (Eng)	1-1	0-0	1-1	0-0	100.0	+ 0.57
B W Hills (Eng)	1-2	0-0	1-2	0-0	50.0	+ 7.00
B Hanbury (Eng)	1-2	1-1	0-1	0-0	50.0	+ 0.50
L Cumani (Eng)	1-2	0-0	1-2	0-0	50.0	- 0.43
T D Barron (Eng)	1-2	0-0	1-2	0-0	50.0	+ 6.00
J Toller (Eng)	1-2	0-0	0-0	1-2	50.0	+ 4.00
A Fabre (Fra)	1-3	0-1	1-2	0-0	33.3	+ 2.50
A Butler	1-3	1-2	0-0	0-1	33.3	+ 2.50
P Chapple-Hyam (Eng)	1-3	1-2	0-1	0-0	33.3	- 0.25
R Hannon (Eng)	1-4	1-2	0-1	0-1	25.0	+ 0.33
J H M Gosden (Eng)	1-4	0-0	0-2	1-2	25.0	+ 4.00
J Berry (Eng)	1-5	1-2	0-3	0-0	20.0	+ 3.00
J R Banahan	1-5	0-0	1-5	0-0	20.0	+ 2.00
M Hourigan	1-6	0-0	1-3	0-3	16.7	+ 5.00
L T Reilly	1-6	0-0	0-0	1-6	16.7	+ 15.00
J L Dunlop (Eng)	1-7	1-1	0-5	0-1	14.3	- 2.67
F Flood	1-8	0-0	1-7	0-1	12.5	+ 3.00
M J Corbett	1-8	0-0	0-0	1-8	12.5	+ 1.00
E J Kearns	1-9	0-0	0-0	1-9	11.1	- 2.00
Malachy McKenna	1-12	0-0	0-0	1-12	8.3	+ 3.00
F Doyle	1-12	0-0	1-12	0-0	8.3	+ 14.00
J G Murphy	1-13	1-3	0-10	0-0	7.7	- 6.00
J Morrison	1-14	0-0	0-5	1-9	7.1	- 1.00
Niall Madden	1-14	0-0	0-0	1-14	7.1	- 3.00
M J P O'Brien	1-15	0-4	1-1	0-10	6.7	- 11.50
John Houghton	1-15	0-5	0-5	1-5	6.7	- 8.00
T O'Neill	1-17	0-0	0-5	1-12	5.9	- 6.00
Oliver Finnegan	1-17	0-0	0-2	1-15	5.9	- 10.00
Peadar Matthews	1-19	1-9	0-10	0-0	5.3	- 10.00
Ms E Cassidy	1-20	0-0	0-2	1-18	5.0	- 7.00
J P Daly	1-21	0-1	1-11	0-9	4.8	- 17.75
W M Roper	1-22	0-8	0-5	1-9	4.5	- 11.00
D G McArdle	1-24	0-0	0-2	1-22	4.2	- 7.00
C P Magnier	1-25	0-0	0-0	1-25	4.0	- 8.00
B Lawlor	1-27	1-4	0-16	0-7	3.7	- 15.00
P Martin	1-30	0-3	0-8	1-19	3.3	- 17.00
E McNamara	1-31	0-15	1-14	0-2	3.2	- 24.00
P Beirne	1-31	1-12	0-19	0-0	3.2	- 27.00
A Redmond	1-35	0-2	0-18	1-15	2.9	- 32.50
Neil S McGrath	1-45	0-24	1-16	0-5	2.2	- 39.00
J Burns	1-95	1-33	0-41	0-21	1.1	- 84.00

WINNING FLAT JOCKEYS IN IRELAND 1993

	1st	2nd	3rd	Unpl	Total Mts	Per cent	£1 Level Stake
M J Kinane	115	71	51	143	380	30.3	+ 15.03
J P Murtagh	50	45	49	161	305	16.4	- 40.68
C Roche	38	42	34	145	259	14.7	- 87.12
P V Gilson	38	33	39	207	317	12.0	- 91.66
R Hughes	38	20	36	205	299	12.7	- 61.26
W J Supple	38	66	52	284	440	8.6	-178.87
P Carberry	27	21	17	132	197	13.7	+ 36.00
J J Behan	24	17	26	210	277	8.7	- 90.08
S Craine	21	32	28	249	330	6.4	-187.62
P Shanahan	20	28	21	195	264	7.6	-137.04
K J Manning	17	26	30	178	251	6.8	-168.70
J F Egan	16	17	23	246	302	5.3	-179.50
R M Burke	15	18	16	144	193	7.8	- 29.50
J A Heffernan	15	14	13	155	197	7.6	- 38.50
N G McCullagh	15	11	28	217	271	5.5	-128.50
B J Walsh	11	11	9	72	103	10.7	- 44.10
R V Skelly	11	6	7	105	129	8.5	- 7.62
C Everard	10	9	10	59	88	11.4	- 12.15
W J O'Connor	10	12	9	88	119	8.4	- 43.00
D J O'Donohoe	9	4	2	42	57	15.8	+ 3.75
J R Barry	8	8	5	29	50	16.0	+ 1.88
D G O'Shea	8	9	16	189	222	3.6	-119.50
L Piggott	6	8	5	30	49	12.2	- 34.07
D Hogan	6	7	3	47	63	9.5	- 30.47
P P Murphy	6	7	12	91	116	5.2	- 64.00
W J Smith	6	13	8	145	172	3.5	-119.50
T P Treacy	5	2	3	13	23	21.7	+ 25.00
P J Smullen	5	0	3	67	75	6.7	- 17.50
G M Moylan	5	3	4	70	82	6.1	- 38.75
Joanna Morgan	5	5	6	108	124	4.0	- 76.00
R Fitzpatrick	4	14	6	114	138	2.9	- 82.50
J A Nash	4	4	0	5	13	30.8	+ 6.25
J Reid	3	1	3	0	7	42.9	+ 4.58
M Roberts	3	1	3	7	14	21.4	+ 15.57
P M Donohue	3	1	3	17	24	12.5	- 2.50
Miss U Smyth	3	0	1	2	6	50.0	+ 6.01
Miss L Robinson	3	0	0	5	8	37.5	+ 1.82
Pat Eddery	2	0	1	1	4	50.0	+ 3.07
K Darley	2	0	0	3	5	40.0	+ 12.00
W Carson	2	2	2	8	14	14.3	- 1.67
B J Halligan	2	1	0	22	25	8.0	- 12.00
G Coogan	2	1	0	27	30	6.7	- 18.50
B Fenton	2	2	5	49	58	3.4	- 41.00
J K Connolly	2	1	1	1	5	40.0	+ 7.33
M Hills	1	0	0	3	4	25.0	+ 5.00
F Woods	1	0	0	3	4	25.0	+ 4.00
W Newnes	1	0	2	1	4	25.0	+ 2.00
W R Swinburn	1	3	1	7	12	8.3	- 9.50
P Lowry	1	1	0	22	24	4.2	- 13.00
B Coogan	1	5	3	64	73	1.4	- 68.00
N Byrne	1	6	7	95	109	0.9	-101.00
D A O'Sullivan	1	0	1	8	10	10.0	+ 7.00
A P McCoy	1	0	1	9	11	9.1	- 7.00
I Browne	1	0	0	11	12	8.3	+ 5.00

	1st	2nd	3rd	Unpl	Total Mts	Per cent	£1 Level Stake
T E Durcan	1	1	2	24	28	3.6	- 20.00
L O'Shea	1	0	2	30	33	3.0	- 16.00
D V Smith	1	3	0	51	55	1.8	- 43.00
E Bolger	1	0	0	0	1	100.0	+ 7.00
John O'Connor	1	0	0	0	1	100.0	+ 7.00
Capt John Ledingham	1	0	0	0	1	100.0	+ 0.57
Miss C E Hyde	1	0	0	1	2	50.0	+ 2.00
Mrs C Doyle	1	1	0	0	2	50.0	+ 24.00
G J Harford	1	0	0	2	3	33.3	+ 0.25
Miss O Glennon	1	0	0	2	3	33.3	+ 4.00
A J Martin	1	0	1	2	4	25.0	+ 1.50
Mrs S McCarthy	1	1	1	3	6	16.7	- 3.00
D J Kavanagh	1	1	0	4	6	16.7	+ 1.50
P Fenton	1	1	0	5	7	14.3	- 4.37
A R Coonan	1	0	2	4	7	14.3	+ 4.00
S R Murphy	1	1	1	5	8	12.5	- 4.50
A K Wyse	1	0	1	6	8	12.5	- 5.50
A P O'Brien	1	1	1	7	10	10.0	- 7.62
Mrs J M Mullins	1	2	0	8	11	9.1	- 4.00

LEADING TRAINERS' AND OWNERS' PRIZE MONEY 1993

	Races Won	Value £		Races Won	Value £
D K Weld	109	601,316	K Abdulla	2	455,500
John M Oxx	80	535,481	H H Aga Khan	50	346,592
H R A Cecil (Eng)	1	342,500	Sheikh Mohammed	18	264,569
J S Bolger	57	332,990	Michael W J Smurfit	20	228,554
K Prendergast	40	157,468	R E Sangster	11	127,772
L Cumani (Eng)	1	149,649	Mrs J M Corbett	1	113,000
B W Hills (Eng)	1	113,000	Hamdan Al-Maktoum	9	111,437
A Fabre (Fra)	1	113,000	Moyglare Stud Farm	20	85,714
Noel Meade	21	90,994	Palacegate Corporation	1	73,750
C Collins	22	88,777	Lord Carnarvon	1	56,100
P Chapple-Hyam (Eng)	1	85,500	Mrs M V O'Brien	10	53,208
J H M Gosden (Eng)	1	84,300	Allen E Paulson	8	47,557

LEADING IRISH TRAINERS FIRST TIME OUT 1989-93

	Total W-R	2-y-o	3-y-o	4-y-o+	Per cent	£1 Level Stake
J S Bolger	120-663	60-252	34-258	26-153	18.1	-210.08
D K Weld	100-699	35-263	44-282	21-154	14.3	-294.66
John M Oxx	99-500	38-177	57-292	4-31	19.8	- 34.03
M V O'Brien	50-165	23-73	24-84	3-8	30.3	+ 7.51
T Stack	29-254	9-93	11-117	9-44	11.4	- 64.77
K Prendergast	21-361	8-158	9-155	4-48	5.8	-205.94
M Kauntze	20-192	12-85	7-85	1-22	10.4	- 74.90
C Collins	14-255	7-93	6-107	1-55	5.5	-143.00
M J Grassick	10-172	3-50	5-73	2-49	5.8	- 96.25
P J Flynn	8-165	1-36	2-54	5-75	4.8	-120.77
F Dunne	7-84	1-25	1-40	5-19	8.3	- 10.50
P Mullins	7-122	0-20	2-32	5-70	5.7	- 51.87
Liam Browne	7-177	3-86	3-64	1-27	4.0	-135.50
T G Curtin	6-54	1-3	2-14	3-37	11.1	- 10.00
B V Kelly	6-83	1-26	3-35	2-22	7.2	- 20.00

LEADING IRISH TRAINERS BY MONTH 1989-93

March/April

	Total W-R	2-y-o	3-y-o	4-y-o+	Per cent	£1 Level Stake
J S Bolger	75-308	18-34	38-190	19-84	24.4	+ 57.19
D K Weld	41-328	3-19	33-222	5-87	12.5	-190.26
John M Oxx	31-173	0-1	29-153	2-19	17.9	- 16.80
T Stack	21-151	0-5	12-101	9-45	13.9	- 19.79
K Prendergast	21-234	5-29	13-152	3-53	9.0	-102.19
M V O'Brien	14-37	0-0	13-34	1-3	37.8	+ 14.35
C Collins	12-197	2-22	8-128	2-47	6.1	- 90.00
M Kauntze	11-91	0-4	9-68	2-19	12.1	- 6.25
Noel Meade	9-152	1-16	8-101	0-35	5.9	- 97.00
B V Kelly	7-44	0-0	4-26	3-18	15.9	+ 25.50
E J O'Grady	6-87	0-2	5-54	1-31	6.9	- 66.60
P J Flynn	5-54	0-0	2-24	3-30	9.3	- 26.50
Liam Browne	5-94	2-12	3-65	0-17	5.3	- 60.20
M Halford	4-61	0-4	4-43	0-14	6.6	- 25.00
P Prendergast	4-75	0-9	2-48	2-18	5.3	- 40.50

May

	Total W-R	2-y-o	3-y-o	4-y-o+	Per cent	£1 Level Stake
D K Weld	72-353	7-52	47-202	18-99	20.4	- 63.09
J S Bolger	55-354	15-75	23-171	17-108	15.5	-115.89
John M Oxx	43-201	1-9	38-176	4-16	21.4	- 27.63
K Prendergast	20-268	5-54	12-173	3-41	7.5	-146.67
T Stack	19-155	1-13	12-104	6-38	12.3	- 63.77
C Collins	18-158	8-30	7-85	3-43	11.4	- 69.31
M V O'Brien	16-63	0-1	14-55	2-7	25.4	- 13.64
M J Grassick	15-105	1-8	8-65	6-32	14.3	- 6.95
M Kauntze	15-135	5-28	10-85	0-22	11.1	- 42.59
J J McLoughlin	12-81	4-13	6-41	2-27	14.8	+ 14.58
Liam Browne	12-93	4-21	7-58	1-14	12.9	- 16.25
M A O'Toole	11-78	0-15	6-35	5-28	14.1	+ 11.23
P J Flynn	11-119	0-1	4-53	7-65	9.2	- 47.15
Noel Meade	11-137	1-16	6-82	4-39	8.0	- 64.62
F Dunne	7-72	1-6	3-47	3-19	9.7	- 7.00
D T Hughes	5-47	1-4	0-15	4-28	10.6	- 8.67
D Gillespie	5-68	3-15	1-42	1-11	7.4	- 33.25

June

	Total W-R	2-y-o	3-y-o	4-y-o+	Per cent	£1 Level Stake
D K Weld	67-363	11-73	38-195	18-95	18.5	- 103.93
J S Bolger	60-378	20-83	30-196	10-99	15.9	- 100.81
John M Oxx	56-242	2-20	53-201	1-21	23.1	- 6.08
K Prendergast	38-312	9-62	27-193	2-57	12.2	- 106.12
C Collins	17-127	7-23	7-66	3-38	13.4	- 24.87
M V O'Brien	16-46	5-9	10-36	1-1	34.8	+ 6.92
T Stack	16-130	4-19	11-84	1-27	12.3	- 33.77
Noel Meade	13-132	1-23	8-72	4-37	9.8	- 55.90
J J McLoughlin	10-80	0-12	8-42	2-26	12.5	- 31.43
P J Flynn	10-93	1-13	3-38	6-42	10.8	- 55.07
M J Grassick	9-92	0-11	6-52	3-29	9.8	- 50.82
D Gillespie	8-70	1-15	4-42	3-13	11.4	- 26.77
P Mullins	8-79	0-9	0-24	8-46	10.1	- 2.87
Liam Browne	8-111	6-45	2-53	0-13	7.2	- 54.67
M Kauntze	8-118	3-25	5-70	0-23	6.8	- 91.33
A P O'Brien	7-23	0-4	3-7	4-12	30.4	+ 29.50
W P Mullins	6-43	0-8	2-12	4-23	14.0	- 10.25
E J O'Grady	6-72	1-15	3-41	2-16	8.3	- 23.50
F Dunne	6-79	1-20	2-38	3-21	7.6	- 0.50
P Prendergast	5-40	2-10	0-14	3-16	12.5	- 6.55
Edward Lynam	5-61	1-11	3-40	1-10	8.2	- 24.00
M A O'Toole	5-67	0-10	2-25	3-32	7.5	- 41.90

July

	Total W-R	2-y-o	3-y-o	4-y-o+	Per cent	£1 Level Stake
D K Weld	105-468	25-121	48-230	32-117	22.4	- 49.72
J S Bolger	104-463	34-118	40-217	30-128	22.5	- 54.20
John M Oxx	60-271	11-39	46-209	3-23	22.1	- 59.12
K Prendergast	35-381	10-99	18-214	7-68	9.2	- 161.32
Noel Meade	19-153	4-26	9-81	6-46	12.4	- 36.90
T Stack	16-143	4-32	8-83	4-28	11.2	- 74.57
C Collins	15-135	3-28	7-74	5-33	11.1	- 38.87
M Kauntze	15-144	5-42	7-76	3-26	10.4	- 81.86
M V O'Brien	13-44	4-9	9-31	0-4	29.5	- 15.59
M J Grassick	13-89	4-18	8-46	1-25	14.6	- 20.95
M A O'Toole	12-103	2-18	6-56	4-29	11.7	- 31.83
D Gillespie	11-97	1-27	10-55	0-15	11.3	- 22.37
P J Flynn	10-89	1-9	3-29	6-51	11.2	- 23.50
F Dunne	9-102	0-23	4-49	5-30	8.8	- 33.17
Liam Browne	9-113	7-53	2-47	0-13	8.0	- 64.52
P Prendergast	8-51	3-15	3-20	2-16	15.7	- 4.40
J J McLoughlin	8-108	1-24	7-53	0-31	7.4	- 27.00
E J O'Grady	7-76	2-17	3-49	2-10	9.2	- 7.75
B V Kelly	6-65	1-18	2-31	3-16	9.2	- 15.00
Augustine Leahy	6-81	0-17	3-37	3-27	7.4	- 52.50
Edward Lynam	5-87	0-18	3-55	2-14	5.7	- 61.00

August

	Total W-R	2-y-o	3-y-o	4-y-o+	Per cent	£1 Level Stake
D K Weld	115-541	31-149	58-270	26-122	21.3	-126.94
J S Bolger	84-534	54-179	22-233	8-122	15.7	-191.33
John M Oxx	71-279	15-67	54-195	2-17	25.4	+ 1.06
K Prendergast	49-385	9-113	29-219	11-53	12.7	-123.47
C Collins	25-178	4-52	14-91	7-35	14.0	- 59.07
T Stack	25-179	7-58	12-99	6-22	14.0	- 29.95
M V O'Brien	18-56	9-23	9-32	0-1	32.1	- 4.53
Noel Meade	16-144	3-34	9-85	4-25	11.1	- 59.51
M Kauntze	15-133	5-45	9-70	1-18	11.3	- 35.67
P J Flynn	13-106	2-18	4-37	7-51	12.3	- 36.22
M A O'Toole	13-121	3-33	6-60	4-28	10.7	- 36.52
M J Grassick	11-91	3-21	6-47	2-23	12.1	- 15.50
J J McLoughlin	11-116	1-25	7-55	3-36	9.5	- 35.75
T G Curtin	10-50	1-5	2-13	7-32	20.0	+ 54.00
P Mullins	10-83	0-21	4-31	6-31	12.0	- 31.96
F Dunne	10-114	0-28	6-54	4-32	8.8	- 50.75
W P Mullins	8-47	0-8	3-7	5-32	17.0	+ 4.00
D Gillespie	8-73	1-25	6-40	1-8	11.0	- 27.65
J C Hayden	8-94	3-31	5-49	0-14	8.5	- 35.50
P Prendergast	7-81	0-23	4-33	3-25	8.6	- 46.80
Augustine Leahy	7-85	0-22	6-33	1-30	8.2	- 40.00
Liam Browne	7-120	5-70	1-37	1-13	5.8	- 81.27
E P Harty	6-43	1-16	4-16	1-11	14.0	+ 14.57
J E Mulhern	6-59	1-11	2-22	3-26	10.2	- 1.17
B V Kelly	6-64	1-21	5-27	0-16	9.4	- 19.17
M Halford	6-71	0-12	2-33	4-26	8.5	- 38.17
E J O'Grady	6-93	2-29	2-56	2-8	6.5	- 63.60
A P O'Brien	5-38	0-7	3-21	2-10	13.2	- 12.12
Daniel J Murphy	5-51	1-10	3-29	1-12	9.8	- 8.43
J M Canty	5-53	0-12	1-22	4-19	9.4	- 25.00

September

	Total W-R	2-y-o	3-y-o	4-y-o+	Per cent	£1 Level Stake
D K Weld	70-394	33-140	27-169	10-85	17.8	-112.30
John M Oxx	54-280	20-107	34-158	0-15	19.3	- 5.62
J S Bolger	45-342	24-137	14-145	7-60	13.2	-127.94
K Prendergast	28-252	10-89	14-125	4-38	11.1	- 56.53
M Kauntze	21-111	9-43	11-55	1-13	18.9	+ 2.09
T Stack	20-150	8-68	11-68	1-14	13.3	- 49.95
M V O'Brien	16-65	8-38	7-26	1-1	24.6	- 22.76
P J Flynn	15-148	2-31	8-65	5-52	10.1	- 38.77
C Collins	14-154	3-51	8-76	3-27	9.1	- 71.50
Liam Browne	9-101	5-63	3-27	1-11	8.9	- 13.22
Noel Meade	8-104	2-45	4-42	2-17	7.7	- 37.97
F Dunne	7-49	0-11	4-23	3-15	14.3	+ 8.75
P Prendergast	6-52	1-20	4-20	1-12	11.5	- 16.20
D Gillespie	6-77	2-25	4-44	0-8	7.8	- 41.62
M J Grassick	6-96	1-27	3-50	2-19	6.3	- 42.33
W P Mullins	5-53	1-12	0-7	4-34	9.4	- 13.50
M Halford	5-64	0-20	4-23	1-21	7.8	- 30.00
J J McLoughlin	5-119	2-34	0-59	3-26	4.2	- 89.00

October/November

	Total W-R	2-y-o	3-y-o	4-y-o+	Per cent	£1 Level Stake
J S Bolger	69-440	40-216	25-171	4-53	15.7	-131.50
John M Oxx	55-312	37-174	18-129	0-9	17.6	-109.13
D K Weld	51-417	22-178	12-150	17-89	12.2	-122.20
M V O'Brien	32-85	20-57	11-26	1-2	37.6	+ 41.98
K Prendergast	26-399	9-168	11-170	6-61	6.5	-199.67
P J Flynn	17-179	2-56	6-60	9-63	9.5	- 48.02
M Kauntze	11-140	7-75	4-60	0-5	7.9	- 67.95
C Collins	10-184	2-76	7-79	1-29	5.4	-100.50
T Stack	9-109	2-60	7-39	0-10	8.3	- 45.27
M J Grassick	8-146	2-62	5-59	1-25	5.5	- 88.27
P Mullins	7-99	2-32	3-37	2-30	7.1	- 50.00
Liam Browne	6-129	5-88	1-28	0-13	4.7	- 75.00
D Hanley	5-30	1-10	4-17	0-3	16.7	- 10.65
Mrs Crowley-O'Brien	5-35	1-12	4-19	0-4	14.3	- 5.75
P Prendergast	5-64	3-39	2-16	0-9	7.8	- 17.00
J C Hayden	5-80	4-49	1-30	0-1	6.3	- 23.00
J J McLoughlin	5-107	1-37	3-41	1-29	4.7	- 66.87
Noel Meade	5-146	0-61	4-64	1-21	3.4	-100.50

LEADING IRISH TRAINERS BY TYPE OF RACE 1989-93

2-y-o Non-Handicaps

	W-R	Per cent	£1 Level Stake		W-R	Per cent	£1 Level Stake
J S Bolger	186-744	25.0	-149.32	D K Weld	122-665	18.3	-235.36
John M Oxx	85-400	21.3	- 72.98	K Prendergast	50-534	9.4	-222.95
M V O'Brien	46-136	33.8	- 5.80	Liam Browne	33-318	10.4	- 88.06
M Kauntze	30-235	12.8	- 96.48	C Collins	27-257	10.5	-105.43
T Stack	22-234	9.4	-106.29	M J Grassick	11-129	8.5	- 65.85
J C Hayden	10-118	8.5	- 35.45	Noel Meade	10-193	5.2	-134.50
P Prendergast	9-108	8.3	- 69.22	J G Coogan	9-133	6.8	- 76.25
P J Flynn	8-114	7.0	- 55.50	D Gillespie	7-124	5.6	- 74.29

3-y-o Non-Handicaps

	W-R	Per cent	£1 Level Stake		W-R	Per cent	£1 Level Stake
John M Oxx	199-836	23.8	- 66.60	D K Weld	199-888	22.4	-162.78
J S Bolger	122-849	14.4	-239.60	K Prendergast	67-698	9.6	-371.87
M V O'Brien	65-214	30.4	- 12.52	T Stack	54-386	14.0	-120.03
C Collins	39-417	9.4	-204.90	M Kauntze	31-250	12.4	- 79.58
Noel Meade	24-232	10.3	- 80.69	M J Grassick	21-240	8.8	-108.52
Liam Browne	16-204	7.8	- 96.47	F Dunne	15-141	10.6	- 27.50
M A O'Toole	12-130	9.2	- 64.42	D Gillespie	12-134	9.0	- 64.10
D Hanley	11-46	23.9	+ 14.35	P J Flynn	10-121	8.3	- 55.65
P Mullins	9-96	9.4	- 30.83	B V Kelly	9-105	8.6	- 54.92
Daniel J Murphy	8-81	9.9	- 18.93	P Prendergast	8-107	7.5	- 71.40
Charles O'Brien	7-37	18.9	- 9.15	T G Curtin	7-48	14.6	+ 4.50
M Halford	7-112	6.3	- 61.25	Edward Lynam	6-146	4.1	-111.67
Mrs Crowley-O'Brien	5-24	20.8	+ 2.00	E J O'Grady	5-138	3.6	-126.85

4-y-o+ Non-Handicaps

	W-R	Per cent	£1 Level Stake		W-R	Per cent	£1 Level Stake
D K Weld	48-207	23.2	- 16.17	J S Bolger	31-202	15.3	- 84.27
T Stack	11-66	16.7	- 15.65	P J Flynn	11-94	11.7	- 41.91
Noel Meade	8-66	12.1	- 6.97	K Prendergast	8-76	10.5	- 40.87
M J Grassick	7-57	12.3	- 12.20	P Mullins	6-52	11.5	- 11.63
John M Oxx	5-42	11.9	- 9.75	Augustine Leahy	5-49	10.2	- 6.50
M V O'Brien	4-14	28.6	+ 15.17	W P Browne	4-17	23.5	- 3.33
W P Mullins	4-39	10.3	- 18.75	R Lister	3-14	21.4	+ 5.25
P Prendergast	3-23	13.0	- 12.10	J M Canty	3-27	11.1	- 17.26
C Collins	3-32	9.4	- 22.87	D T Hughes	3-32	9.4	- 17.67

Apprentice Non-Handicaps

	W-R	Per cent	£1 Level Stake		W-R	Per cent	£1 Level Stake
John M Oxx	4-8	50.0	+ 3.95	D K Weld	3-27	11.1	- 12.00
M Kauntze	2-6	33.3	- 2.33	K Prendergast	2-19	10.5	- 6.00

Amateur Non-Handicaps

	W-R	Per cent	£1 Level Stake		W-R	Per cent	£1 Level Stake
J S Bolger	14-85	16.5	- 38.19	D K Weld	12-59	20.3	- 10.35
M Kauntze	6-15	40.0	+ 15.75	John M Oxx	5-20	25.0	+ 0.08
C Collins	5-23	21.7	+ 10.23	T Stack	5-24	20.8	- 1.60
F Dunne	5-27	18.5	+ 24.00	M A O'Toole	4-15	26.7	- 5.83
P J Flynn	4-21	19.0	- 11.25	P Mullins	4-35	11.4	- 10.87
Noel Meade	3-16	18.8	- 8.88				

2-y-o Handicaps

	W-R	Per cent	£1 Level Stake		W-R	Per cent	£1 Level Stake
J S Bolger	19-96	19.8	+ 2.05	D K Weld	10-67	14.9	- 13.69
K Prendergast	7-78	9.0	- 39.27	M A O'Toole	5-22	22.7	+ 25.25
T Stack	4-21	19.0	- 0.50	M Kauntze	4-27	14.8	- 1.25
W P Mullins	3-14	21.4	+ 12.00	J J McLoughlin	3-21	14.3	+ 4.00
P Prendergast	3-24	12.5	+ 10.00	E J O'Grady	3-28	10.7	+ 5.00
A P O'Brien	2-12	16.7	+ 10.00	P Mullins	2-20	10.0	- 8.50
B V Kelly	2-21	9.5	- 10.00	C Collins	2-25	8.0	- 9.90
Noel Meade	2-28	7.1	- 17.50				

3-y-o Handicaps

	W-R	Per cent	£1 Level Stake		W-R	Per cent	£1 Level Stake
John M Oxx	61-339	18.0	- 26.52	J S Bolger	60-410	14.6	- 64.23
D K Weld	57-455	12.5	-176.85	K Prendergast	49-479	10.2	-109.42
J J McLoughlin	26-199	13.1	- 19.93	Noel Meade	23-262	8.8	- 94.57
P J Flynn	20-167	12.0	- 15.50	C Collins	18-161	11.2	- 20.25
M Kauntze	16-207	7.7	- 78.50	T Stack	15-160	9.4	- 63.00
D Gillespie	13-132	9.8	- 54.62	Augustine Leahy	12-77	15.6	- 11.92
M J Grassick	11-114	9.6	- 36.00	B V Kelly	9-89	10.1	+ 1.00
E J O'Grady	9-157	5.7	- 97.68	M V O'Brien	8-26	30.8	+ 1.88
W P Mullins	7-43	16.3	- 4.00	M Halford	7-86	8.1	- 38.00
M A O'Toole	7-95	7.4	- 38.00	Edward Lynam	7-137	5.1	- 65.00
A P O'Brien	6-39	15.4	+ 5.25	P Prendergast	6-58	10.3	- 6.00
J C Hayden	6-103	5.8	- 53.25	E P Harty	5-28	17.9	- 4.00
J T Gorman	5-72	6.9	- 16.00	Daniel J Murphy	5-84	6.0	- 32.50

4-y-o+ Handicaps

	W-R	Per cent	£1 Level Stake		W-R	Per cent	£1 Level Stake
D K Weld	66-400	16.5	- 65.74	J S Bolger	48-354	13.6	- 74.64
P J Flynn	24-207	11.6	- 51.92	K Prendergast	24-244	9.8	- 61.10
F Dunne	15-101	14.9	+ 29.83	C Collins	14-172	8.1	- 80.50
M A O'Toole	12-115	10.4	- 3.00	T Stack	10-87	11.5	0.00
T G Curtin	10-103	9.7	- 1.00	P Mullins	9-130	6.9	- 75.25
P Prendergast	8-73	11.0	- 5.90	W P Mullins	8-89	9.0	- 37.25
A P O'Brien	7-21	33.3	+ 14.75	J M Canty	7-101	6.9	- 61.25
J J McLoughlin	7-138	5.1	- 69.50	E J O'Grady	6-50	12.0	+ 6.50
B V Kelly	6-85	7.1	- 22.00	M J Grassick	6-85	7.1	- 54.75
M Halford	6-87	6.9	- 40.50	Noel Meade	6-125	4.8	- 90.54
T M Walsh	5-27	18.5	+ 35.00	P Hughes	5-33	15.2	+ 14.25
V Kennedy	5-63	7.9	- 7.00	John M Oxx	5-70	7.1	- 38.75
T F Lacy	5-79	6.3	- 38.00	M Kauntze	5-80	6.3	- 41.17
J E Mulhern	5-82	6.1	- 25.50	M Cunningham	5-83	6.0	- 49.67

Apprentice Handicaps

	W-R	Per cent	£1 Level Stake		W-R	Per cent	£1 Level Stake
J S Bolger	7-49	14.3	- 7.75	John M Oxx	5-25	20.0	- 0.75
J J McLoughlin	5-31	16.1	+ 1.63	M J Grassick	5-44	11.4	+ 0.50
K Prendergast	5-78	6.4	- 41.42	D Gillespie	4-26	15.4	- 2.60
D T Hughes	3-22	13.6	+ 9.00	T Stack	3-27	11.1	- 13.00
T F Lacy	3-29	10.3	- 9.00	C Collins	3-38	7.9	- 12.50
D K Weld	3-86	3.5	- 69.50				

Amateur Handicaps

	W-R	Per cent	£1 Level Stake		W-R	Per cent	£1 Level Stake
J S Bolger	5-21	23.8	- 0.40	K Prendergast	3-10	30.0	+ 4.13
W Fennin	2-4	50.0	+ 6.00	F Flood	2-4	50.0	+ 11.00
M A O'Toole	2-8	25.0	- 3.77	Noel Meade	2-8	25.0	+ 3.50
M Cunningham	2-9	22.2	+ 1.25	D Gillespie	2-9	22.2	+ 6.10
P J Flynn	2-17	11.8	- 8.50				

LEADING IRISH TRAINERS' FAVOURITES 1989-1993

	W-R	Per cent	£1 Level Stake	% of Runners that Started Favourite	% of Winners that Started Favourite
D K Weld	284-774	36.7	- 76.22	27.0	54.5
J S Bolger	245-598	41.0	- 33.17	21.2	49.8
John M Oxx	211-462	45.7	+ 69.96	26.3	57.0
M V O'Brien	89-186	47.8	+ 18.61	47.0	71.2
K Prendergast	68-236	28.8	- 32.66	10.6	31.3
T Stack	41-99	41.4	+ 15.10	9.7	32.5
M Kauntze	39-107	36.4	- 13.89	12.3	40.6
C Collins	36-102	35.3	+ 4.88	9.0	32.4
P J Flynn	28-73	38.4	+ 12.52	9.3	34.6
Noel Meade	21-80	26.3	- 24.23	8.3	25.9
M J Grassick	18-47	38.3	+ 1.93	6.7	28.6
M A O'Toole	17-51	33.3	- 7.85	8.9	34.7
D Gillespie	14-43	32.6	- 5.37	8.3	34.1
P Prendergast	14-45	31.1	- 2.97	10.8	35.9
Liam Browne	14-48	29.2	- 13.01	6.3	25.0
J J McLoughlin	13-29	44.8	+ 9.20	4.2	24.5
P Mullins	12-39	30.8	+ 3.09	7.6	31.6
E J O'Grady	9-28	32.1	- 5.88	5.1	28.1
Mrs Crowley-O'Brien	7-13	53.8	+ 5.23	10.9	46.7
M Halford	7-22	31.8	+ 6.75	5.4	26.9
A P O'Brien	7-23	30.4	- 3.12	13.1	35.0
Augustine Leahy	7-27	25.9	- 2.67	5.9	28.0
E P Harty	6-11	54.5	+ 5.87	5.8	46.2
B V Kelly	6-25	24.0	- 3.25	6.1	19.4
J C Hayden	5-13	38.5	+ 0.80	3.0	20.0
J M Canty	5-18	27.8	- 3.01	5.6	31.3
A Redmond	5-22	22.7	- 9.02	6.0	71.4
D Hanley	4-7	57.1	+ 10.35	6.7	23.5
W P Mullins	4-9	44.4	+ 6.00	3.2	16.0
J G Coogan	4-12	33.3	- 1.00	4.2	23.5
F Dunne	4-16	25.0	- 3.00	3.1	9.3
Edward Lynam	4-24	16.7	- 5.50	4.6	19.0
M Cunningham	3-4	75.0	+ 2.17	1.2	21.4
J E Kiely	3-6	50.0	+ 1.28	14.3	75.0
Anthony Mullins	3-6	50.0	+ 2.75	4.5	60.0
W P Browne	3-9	33.3	- 3.33	18.8	75.0
T F Lacy	3-10	30.0	- 1.25	2.5	23.1
T G Curtin	3-10	30.0	+ 0.50	4.4	11.5
Capt D G Swan	3-11	27.3	- 1.62	7.7	60.0
Charles O'Brien	3-11	27.3	- 3.40	15.9	30.0
J E Mulhern	3-17	17.6	- 6.00	6.5	18.8
D T Hughes	3-26	11.5	- 12.75	9.6	17.6
K F O'Sullivan	2-2	100.0	+ 5.33	3.4	50.0
M A McCullagh	2-3	66.7	+ 4.50	8.1	66.7
F Flood	2-4	50.0	+ 0.15	8.3	28.6
N O'Callaghan	2-4	50.0	+ 5.75	1.9	22.2
P Hughes	2-7	28.6	- 2.08	6.6	28.6
J C Harley	2-7	28.6	- 1.25	4.6	20.0
T M Walsh	2-9	22.2	- 4.10	7.7	22.2
Daniel J Murphy	2-15	13.3	- 10.68	4.4	10.0

TRAINER TIPS FOR 1994

J Berry	-	Runners in March
H R A Cecil	-	Runners at Catterick, Chepstow and Royal Ascot
P Chapple-Hyam	-	Runners at Ayr
R Charlton	-	Runners at Nottingham Two-year-olds at Newmarket Three-year-olds in June
L M Cumani	-	Runners at Brighton in October
J L Dunlop	-	Runners at Thirsk
J H M Gosden	-	Runners at Haydock and Newcastle Runners at York in October
B Hanbury	-	Runners at Hamilton
H Thomson Jones	-	Runners at Redcar
D R Loder	-	Runners in selling non-handicaps

TRAINER INDEX

COURSE INDEX